If you want your students to **get better grades** and to **become better teachers**

adopt and assign
MyEducationLab today
www.myeducationlab.com

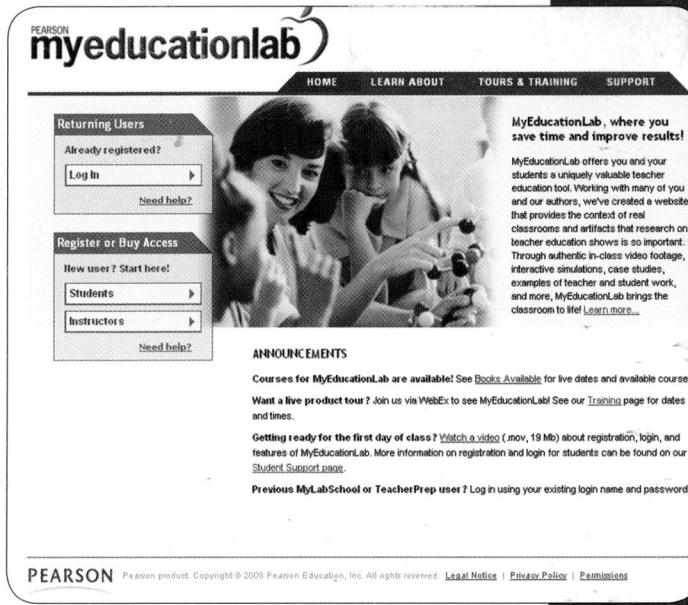

What is MyEducationLab?

MyEducationLab grounds teacher education in real classrooms—among real teachers and students and among actual examples of students' and teachers' work—to prepare your students for the complexities of teaching today's students in today's classrooms:

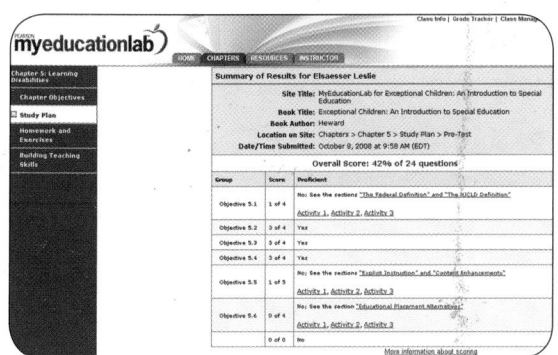

PRACTICE TESTS: These self-paced assessments give students an opportunity to test their knowledge of chapter content. Based on a student's performance on the test, MyEducationLab generates an individual study plan to help each student identify topics for which he or she needs additional study. MyEducationLab then provides the appropriate chapter excerpts and, in some instances, interactive, multimedia activities to help the student master that content.

ASSIGNMENTS AND IN-CLASS ACTIVITIES: Each chapter in MyEducationLab includes assignable Activities and Applications exercises that use authentic classroom video, teacher and student artifacts, or case studies to help students understand course content more deeply and to practice applying that content.

PRACTICE TEACHING: Building Teaching Skills and Dispositions exercises use video, artifacts, and/or case studies to help your students truly see and understand how specific teaching techniques and behaviors impact learners and learning environments. These exercises give your students practice in developing the skills and dispositions that are essential to quality teaching.

Does it work?

A survey of student users from across the country tells us that it does!

93% MyEducationLab was easy to use.

70% MyEducationLab's video clips helped me to get a better sense of real classrooms.

79% I would recommend my instructor continue using MyEducationLab.

Percentage of respondents who agree or strongly agree.

Where is it?

- Online at www.myeducationlab.com
- Integrated right into this text! Look for margin annotations and end-of-chapter activities throughout the book.

What do I have to do to use MyEducationLab in my course?

Just contact your Pearson sales representative and tell him/her that you'd like to use MyEducationLab with this text next semester. Your representative will work with your bookstore to ensure that your students receive access with their books.

What if I need help?

We've got you covered 24/7. Your Pearson sales representative offers training in using MyEducationLab for you and your students. There is also a wealth of helpful information on the site, under "Tours and Training" and "Support." And technical support is available 24 hours a day, seven days a week, at http://247pearsoned.custhelp.com.

Exceptional Lives

SPECIAL EDUCATION
IN TODAY'S SCHOOLS

SIXTH EDITION

Ann Turnbull
University of Kansas

Rud Turnbull
University of Kansas

Michael L. Wehmeyer
University of Kansas

Merrill
Upper Saddle River, New Jersey
Columbus, Ohio

Library of Congress Cataloging-in-Publication Data

Turnbull, Ann P.
  Exceptional lives : special education in today's schools / Ann Turnbull, Rud Turnbull, Michael L. Wehmeyer.—6th ed.
    p. cm.
  Includes bibliographical references and index.
  ISBN-13: 978-0-13-502696-0
  ISBN-10: 0-13-502696-2
  1. Children with disabilities—Education—United States—Case Studies. 2. Special education—United States—Case studies. 3. Inclusive education—United States—Case studies. I. Turnbull, Rud. II. Wehmeyer, Michael L. III. Title.
  LC4031.E87 2010
  371.90973—dc22

                                2008038567

Vice President and Editor in Chief: Jeffery W. Johnston
Executive Editor: Ann Castel Davis
Development Editor: Heather Doyle Fraser
Editorial Assistant: Penny Burleson
Senior Managing Editor: Pamela D. Bennett
Production Editor: Sheryl Glicker Langner
Art Director: Candace Rowley
Photo Coordinator: Lori Whitley
Cover Design: Christine Cantera
Operations Specialist: Laura Messerly
Vice President, Director of Sales and Marketing: Quinn Perkson
Marketing Manager: Quinn Perkson
Marketing Coordinator: Brian Mounts

This book was set in Garamond by S4Carlisle Publishing Services. It was printed and bound by Courier Kendallville, Inc. The cover was printed by Phoenix Color Corp.

Photo Credits: photo credits are on page xxvii.

Pearson® is a registered trademark of Pearson plc
Merrill® is a registered trademark of Pearson Education, Inc.

Pearson Education Ltd., London
Pearson Education Singapore Pte. Ltd.
Pearson Education Canada, Inc.
Pearson Education–Japan
Pearson Education Australia PTY, Limited

Pearson Education North Asia, Ltd., Hong Kong
Pearson Educación de Mexico, S.A. de C.V.
Pearson Education Malaysia Pte. Ltd.
Pearson Education Upper Saddle River, New Jersey

Merrill
is an imprint of

www.pearsonhighered.com

10 9 8 7 6 5 4 3 2 1
ISBN-13:   978-0-13-502696-0
ISBN-10:   0-13-502696-2

Ann and Rud dedicate this book to their family: Jay Turnbull, their son with a disability; Amy Turnbull Khare and Kate Turnbull, their two daughters; Rahul Khare, their son-in-law; and Dylan Kumar Khare, Cameron Turnbull Khare, and Maya Annika Khare, their grandchildren.

Michael dedicates this book to his family: Kathy, Geoff, and Graham.

Preface

It has been said of the city of Paris, "plus ca change, plus c'est la meme chose"—the more she changes, the more she remains the same thing. That is almost true of this sixth editon of *Exceptional Lives*.

What remains the same are the authors; each is a professor of special education at The Univeristy of Kansas.

What also remains the same is our emphasis on inclusion of students with disabilities into general education. We gave the first edition that emphasis; some thought we were too pro-inclusion, but the capacity of special educators, general educators, related service professionals, and families to collaborate with each other has demonstrated that inclusion is not only possible but desirable.

Moreover, there is an ever-increasing body of evidence that supports inclusion; we cite the most recent evidence about effective teaching, whether in general or special programs.

The two federal education laws we discuss—Individuals with Disabilities Education Act and No Child Left Behind Act—continue to provide the framework within which special and general educators work; as we point out, these laws presume that children with disabilities will be in classes with students who do not have disabilities and that accountability for their progress is the responsibility of both special and general educators. So, we continue to emphasize access to and progress in the general curriculum—that is, inclusion.

Inclusion, as we noted, results from collaborations, so the role of parent–professional and professional–professional partnerships remains a core theme of this edition, as it was in the previous one.

Technology, too, makes the general curriculum more accessible to students with disabilities, so it continues to merit our attention.

Universal design in learning also retains a prominent place in this edition, as it is another means for inclusion.

It does not do a student with a disability much good to "teach" him to depend on others; while we all depend on others, we also value our ability to choose whether, and then when, where, how, and why, to seek support from others. These ideas about independnece and dependence, and about choice, appear in the text when we discuss self-determination. In this edition, we give added attention to self-determination.

Paris changes, even as she remains the same, and so does our book. In this edition, we have given greater attention than in previous editions to accountability for results and assessment of student progress. After all, inclusion and its various strategies—collaboration, technology, and universal design—is a means for assuring that students do benefit from special education. The word "benefit" implicates measurement of benefit—call it accountability. And measurment implicates assessment.

We also have totally revised our chapter about cultural diversity. There, we "connect the dots" by linking the over-representation of minority students in special education with societal issues related to linguistic diversity, poverty, and family structure.

OUR VISION AND OUR VALUES

Our vision is that the two laws, NCLB and IDEA, will be more than the foundations on which educators, students, and families will rely. Our vision is also that a deep sense of values will permeate every action that every educator takes.

Envision great expectations for all students. Create an enviable life for all students.

Encourage students' positive contributions. Recognize that every student has gifts to bestow on other students and all communities.

Build on students' strengths. By all means acknowledge and address student needs, but abandon the "fix it" approach in education and adopt a strengths-based one instead.

Enable students to become self-determined and to make choices for themselves. Dare to let go of them and their lives, develop their abilities to know what they want and how to realize their dreams, and do so on the basis of a powerful curriculum taught universally in all aspects of the general curriculum.

Expand students' relationships with their peers without disabilities, as well as their peers with disabilities and with all educators and relevant community members.

Ensure students' full citizenship. Less able does not mean less worthy. Build your students' capacities to exercise their rights and responsibilities in this country.

At the end of each chapter we refer to these values in two features, **Values and Outcomes** and **Addressing the Standards: Values Connection**. These features reinforce our vision—to connect educational actions, outcomes, and the law to the values.

OUR BOOK'S ORGANIZATION

Chapters 1 through 4 lay the foundation for the rest of the book, including a newly revised chapter on diversity in today's schools. In addition, because of our commitment to families, we have a chapter fully devoted to the role of families and the strengths they bring to the education of their children.

Chapters 5 through 15 comprehensively describe the most research-based, state-of-the-art techniques for evaluating and teaching students with different types of disability, and for doing so in the context of the general curriculum. Chapter 16 devotes itself to the education of students with unusual gifts and talents. Each of these chapters encompasses a similar organization and focus.

Inclusion

Real Students, Real Issues

This is not a book of fiction. There are no imagined characters here. Every student, every teacher, every parent, every friend is real. To tell their stories serves a powerful didactic purpose: to describe, in their own words and through these snapshots of their lives, how special education benefits each and every one of them. These students, educators, family members, and friends show you what can happen—how exceptional lives can be made all the more exceptional—when you approach them on the basis of principles and state-of-the-art teaching techniques.

Chapter Vignettes. These opening narratives tell the stories of students and their families, friends, teachers, and other educators and service providers. These people represent a wide range of cultural and linguistic groups, and they live in a wide variety of geographic locations across the country. We refer to these vignettes throughout each chapter to exemplify our key points and content. We augment the vignettes and our summaries of research-based, state-of-the-art techniques by highlighting many strategies and tips for educators throughout the chapter. Many of the students featured in the vignettes are also featured on the MyEducationLab course that accompanies the text.

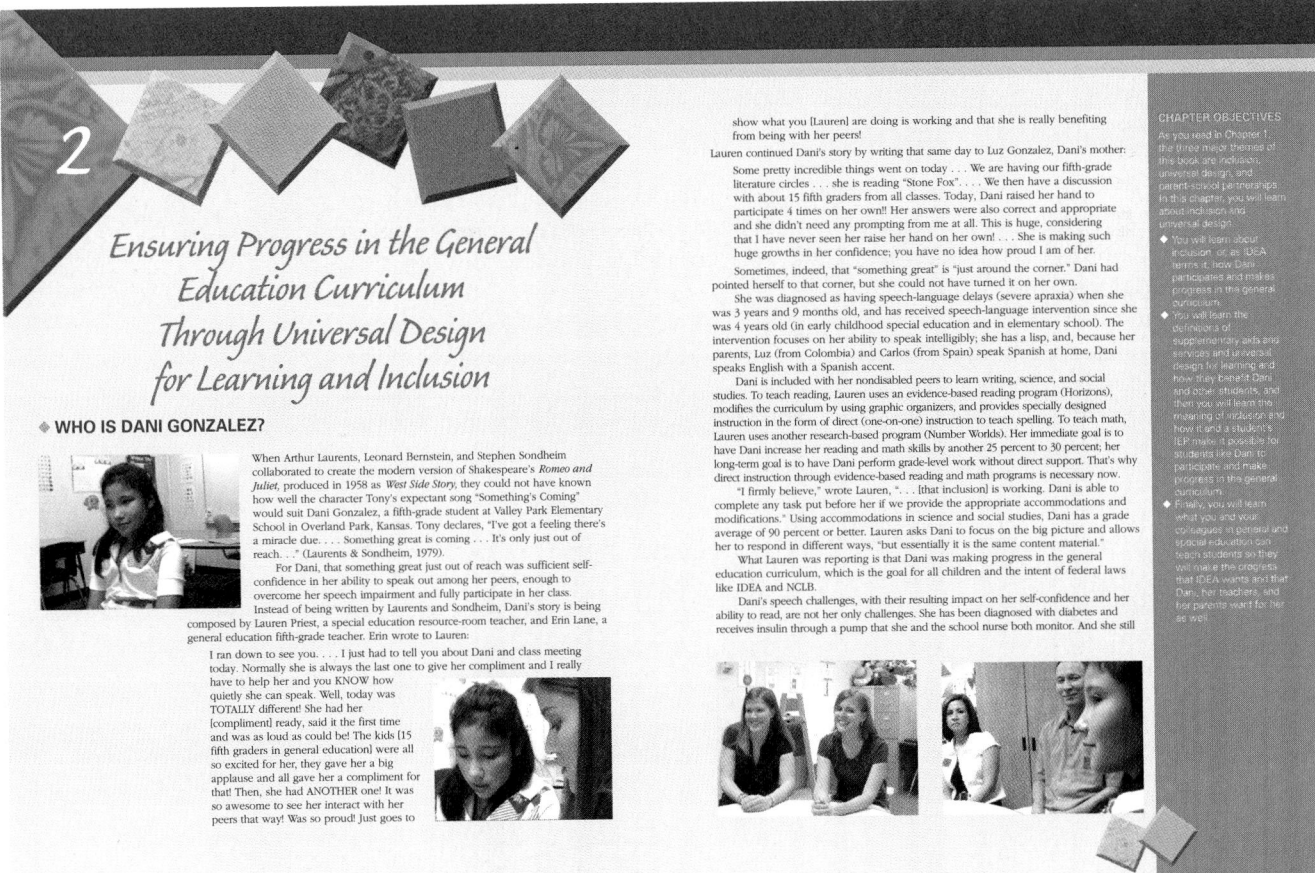

Box 3.2

	What You Might See	What You Might Be Tempted to Do	Alternate Responses	Ways to Include Peers in the Process
INCLUSION TIPS				
Behavior	A Latino student who is an English-language learner and has learning disabilities puts her head on her desk when she does not understand written instructions. She rarely completes assignments.	Tell her that she should go to bed at a reasonable hour so that she can stay awake and complete her classwork.	List steps of the instructions in sequence on the board. Use pictures whenever possible. Ask parents how help is requested and provided in their culture.	Model the skill of asking for help for all students and let them role-play. Provide reinforcement when they use the skill and encourage their classmates to use it.
Social interactions	She rarely initiates a greeting but usually responds to one appropriately.	Do not push her to initiate because you believe this skill will develop as her English improves.	Have students share greetings from the different languages represented in the classroom.	Have this student and others teach the different greetings and reinforce use of them in and outside the classroom.
Educational performance	The student has strong math skills but performs poorly on word problems when she has to read them.	Request that she have more time outside of the general education classroom for intensive English instruction.	Provide word problems in the student's native language and English.	Establish a peer tutoring system within the class: she can tutor students who have problems with computation. Students who share the same primary language can help her read the word problems.
Classroom attitudes	She complains of a head- or stomachache and asks to go to the clinic when assigned to read a children's novel and answer comprehension questions in written form.	Allow her to go to the clinic, hoping that she will grow out of this behavior as her English improves.	Try to obtain a copy of the book in her native language.	Have students work in cooperative groups to partner-read and answer questions.

VALUES AND OUTCOMES

It is not at all difficult to have great expectations for Briana: admission to a highly selective college or honors program in public university, probably with scholarship aid as an inducement, based on her academic or artistic talents; perhaps admission to a conservatory for dance training. She will have many choices.

Nor is it difficult to identify her positive contributions—academic excellence, performance in dance or even athletics will enhance any college or university that a[...]

Like many gifted students, Briana has more than one strength; as brig[ht] academic strengths shine, they do not overshadow her artistic and athletic [qu]alities. In addition, Briana's modesty is a strength—she is no braggard and i[...] to hide her talents, making it easier for her to have friendships with students [...] as talented as her.

Briana will have many choices about her future—whether to dig deeply int[o] ics or the performance arts, or to balance each against the other for some peri[od] not hurrying her adulthood.

The meaning of "full citizenship" for Briana depends in large part on her [...] academics, arts, or both in balance; it is certain that whatever she chooses, she w[ill] engaged in her school and community.

WHAT DO YOU THINK?

1. Have you regarded "giftedness" as an academic trait only? When you wer[e in] secondary school, were "gifted" students only those who were exceptiona[lly] academically superior? Did that seem right or not?

2. What talents do you bring to bear, or want to develop, to educate gifted a[nd] talented students? Are you willing to encounter the challenges they will p[ut...] you be willing to offer differentiated instruction and various opportunities [...] to face challenges peculiar to their special talents?

3. Recognizing that giftedness is a product of a student's natural talents and environment and remembering (from Chapters 1 and 3) that students from ethnic, cultural, and linguistic backgrounds often are disproportionately underrepresented in disability-based special education, what are educators' responsibilities to the families of apparently gifted students who are from [...] backgrounds?

Inclusion Tips. The information in the feature provides helpful advice and strategies for including students in the general curriculum. We address student behaviors, social interactions, educational performance, and classroom attitudes in relation to what teachers may see in the classroom, what they may be tempted to do, other responses, and best practices for including the student's peers in the process. Because IDEA commands that students be educated, to the maximum extent appropriate, in the general curriculum, we describe how the strategies lead to students' inclusion in the general curriculum. We supplement each highlighted *Inclusion Tips* with information about universally designed learning and self-determination.

Values and Outcomes and Addressing the Standards: The Values Connection. At the end of each chapter we return to the student we featured at the beginning of the chapter. We discuss the ideal educational outcomes for each student—outcomes that can occur if teachers put highly effective, research-based strategies into practice and uphold the values we have addressed throughout the book. Additionally, in the *Addressing the Standards: Values Connection* piece that follows our discussion on values and outcomes we connect the six values we discuss in the text to The Council for Exceptional Children (CEC) Common Core professional standards for special educators. This feature helps you see how the book's content and the values relate to your future professional educational behaviors and dispositions.

ADDRESSING THE STANDARDS: THE VALUES CONNECTION

The following CEC Knowledge and Skill Standards: Common Core and Values are addressed in this chapter through the content and concepts we discuss.

CEC Knowledge and Skill Standards: Common Core		Values/Standards Connection
CEC Knowledge and Skill Standard II. Development and Characteristics of Learners		When you learn about the characteristics of students who are gifted and address the similarities, differences, and varying needs of these students, you are applying CEC Standard 2, Development and Characteristics of Learners.
CC2K1	Typical and atypical human growth and development.	
CC2K2	Educational implications of characteristics of various exceptionalities.	
CC2K4	Family systems and the roles of families supporting development.	
CC2K5	Similarities and differences of individuals with and without exceptional learning needs.	
CC2K6	Similarities and differences of individuals with exceptional learning needs.	
CEC Knowledge and Skill Standard III. Individual Learning Differences		Standard 3 suggests differentiated instruction to develop a student's special gifts and *strengths* and create *great expectations*.
CC3K1	Effects that an exceptional condition(s) can have on an individual's life.	
CC3K2	Impact of learner's academic and social abilities, attitudes, interests, and values on instruction and career development.	
CEC Knowledge and Skill Standard IV. Instructional Strategies		Using differentiation strategies is one way to address CEC Standard 4, Instructional Strategies. By selecting and adapting strategies and materials, you are adapting for the individual and her *strengths*.
CC4S1	Use strategies to facilitate integration into various settings.	
CC4S2	Teach individuals to use self-assessment, problem-solving, and other cognitive strategies to meet their needs.	Because students who are gifted know what modifications work best for them, teachers should consider giving them a *choice* about how they would like to learn. When students choose how to learn, they often are more successful in their schoolwork.
CC4S3	Select, adapt, and use instructional strategies and materials according to characteristics of the individual with exceptional learning needs.	
CC4S5	Use procedures to increase the individual's self-awareness, self-management, self-control, self-reliance, and self-esteem.	Using the autonomous learning model discussed in this chapter—in regard to teaching self-assessment and problem-solving strategies—reflects CEC Standard 4, Instructional Strategies.

Partnerships
Real Educators, Real Families

Partnership Tips. To reflect the focus on families and partnerships that guides the book, this feature provides practical, workable ways to develop and maintain effective partnerships between professionals in and out of school, families, and educators. This critical collaboration process makes the difference between effective learning and progress toward goals and unsuccessful attempts.

IEP Margin Notes. For students who have disabilities, the IEP and the IEP process is the guiding force to their inclusion and progress in the general education curriculum. Throughout the chapters we include margin notes that help link content with this practical focus. These margin notes supplement the narrative that describes how professionals can be partners with other professionals, parents, and students to provide an appropriate education in the general curriculum. All of these additional references help inform teachers of their role in the IEP and the IEP process and integrate this content into meaningful, professional contexts.

IEP Tip

The IEP team must determine what constitutes the "maximum extent" to which the student will be involved with the general education curriculum, but team members must remember that the intent is to maximize, not minimize, the student's involvement and to set high expectations for student performance.

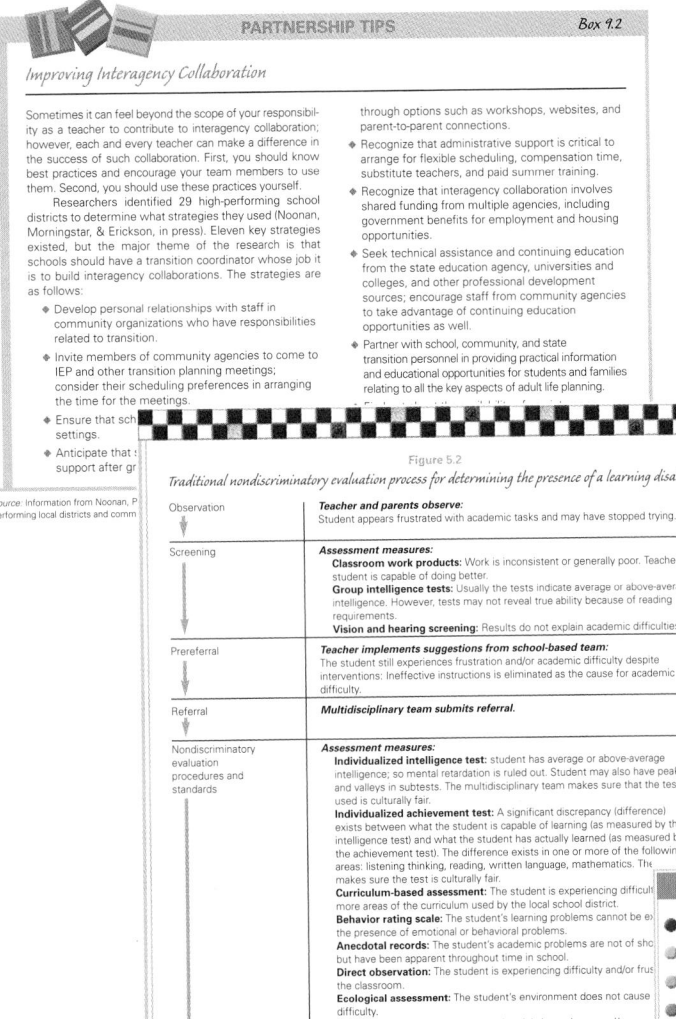

Box 4.2 — PARTNERSHIP TIPS

Improving Interagency Collaboration

Sometimes it can feel beyond the scope of your responsibility as a teacher to contribute to interagency collaboration; however, each and every teacher can make a difference in the success of such collaboration. First, you should know best practices and encourage your team members to use them. Second, you should use these practices yourself.

Researchers identified 29 high-performing school districts to determine what strategies they used (Noonan, Morningstar, & Erickson, in press). Eleven key strategies existed, but the major theme of the research is that schools should have a transition coordinator whose job it is to build interagency collaborations. The strategies are as follows:

♦ Develop personal relationships with staff in community organizations who have responsibilities related to transition.
♦ Invite members of community agencies to come to IEP and other transition planning meetings; consider their scheduling preferences in arranging the time for the meetings.
♦ Ensure that sch... settings.
♦ Anticipate that s... support after gr...

through options such as workshops, websites, and parent-to-parent connections.

♦ Recognize that administrative support is critical to arrange for flexible scheduling, compensation time, substitute teachers, and paid summer training.
♦ Recognize that interagency collaboration involves shared funding from multiple agencies, including government benefits for employment and housing opportunities.
♦ Seek technical assistance and continuing education from the state education agency, universities and colleges, and other professional development sources; encourage staff from community agencies to take advantage of continuing education opportunities as well.
♦ Partner with school, community, and state transition personnel in providing practical information and educational opportunities for students and families relating to all the key aspects of adult life planning.

Source: Information from Noonan, P... performing local districts and comm...

Figure 5.2
Traditional nondiscriminatory evaluation process for determining the presence of a learning disability

Observation	**Teacher and parents observe:** Student appears frustrated with academic tasks and may have stopped trying.
Screening	**Assessment measures:** **Classroom work products:** Work is inconsistent or generally poor. Teacher feels student is capable of doing better. **Group intelligence tests:** Usually the tests indicate average or above-average intelligence. However, tests may not reveal true ability because of reading requirements. **Vision and hearing screening:** Results do not explain academic difficulties.
Prereferral	**Teacher implements suggestions from school-based team:** The student still experiences frustration and/or academic difficulty despite interventions: Ineffective instructions is eliminated as the cause for academic difficulty.
Referral	**Multidisciplinary team submits referral.**
Nondiscriminatory evaluation procedures and standards	**Assessment measures:** **Individualized intelligence test:** student has average or above-average intelligence; so mental retardation is ruled out. Student may also have peaks and valleys in subtests. The multidisciplinary team makes sure that the test used is culturally fair. **Individualized achievement test:** A significant discrepancy (difference) exists between what the student is capable of learning (as measured by the intelligence test) and what the student has actually learned (as measured by the achievement test). The difference exists in one or more of the following areas: listening thinking, reading, written language, mathematics. The... makes sure the test is culturally fair. **Curriculum-based assessment:** The student is experiencing difficult... more areas of the curriculum used by the local school district. **Behavior rating scale:** The student's learning problems cannot be e... the presence of emotional or behavioral problems. **Anecdotal records:** The student's academic problems are not of sho... but have been apparent throughout time in school. **Direct observation:** The student is experiencing difficulty and/or frus... the classroom. **Ecological assessment:** The student's environment does not cause difficulty. **Portfolio assessment:** The student' work is inconsistent and/or poor... subjects.
Determination	The nondiscriminatory multidisciplinary evaluation team determines that... has a learning disability and needs special education and related service...

My Voice. This feature continues our focus on connecting in personal ways to the content of the book. My Voice is a reflection about living with exceptionalities and how education affects the person's life; it further connects you to real people and helps you understand the impact you and others can make.

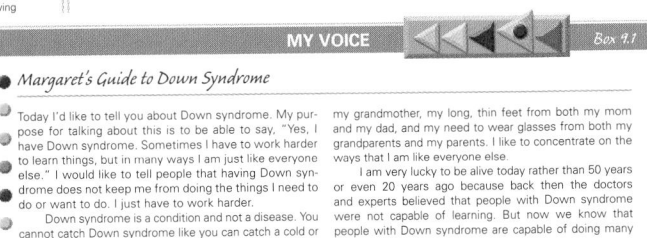

Box 4.1 — MY VOICE

Margaret's Guide to Down Syndrome

Today I'd like to tell you about Down syndrome. My purpose for talking about this is to be able to say, "Yes, I have Down syndrome. Sometimes I have to work harder to learn things, but in many ways I am just like everyone else." I would like to tell people that having Down syndrome does not keep me from doing the things I need to do or want to do. I just have to work harder.

Down syndrome is a condition and not a disease. You cannot catch Down syndrome like you can catch a cold or virus. It is something you are just born with—like blond hair and blue eyes. If you have Down syndrome when you are born, you will have it your whole life.

People without Down syndrome have 46 chromosomes, which carry all the genetic information about a person, in each of their cells. People with Down syndrome have one extra chromosome. So a person with Down syndrome has a total of 47 chromosomes in each cell. Doctors and experts are not really sure what causes it, but they say it occurs in about 1 of every 700 babies. This happens randomly, like flipping a coin or winning the lottery.

Everyone with Down syndrome is a totally unique person. The extra chromosome makes it harder for me to learn. Sometimes I need someone to say, "Settle down and get busy!" Also, it's really easy for me to be stubborn, so I don't mind if you say, "Hey, Margaret, please stop."

Even though I have one extra chromosome, the rest of my chromosomes carry information from generation to generation just like yours. Chromosomes control certain genetic characteristics, like eye color, skin color, height, and some abilities like music, art, or math.

For example, I get my blue eyes from my father, my fair skin and freckles from my mother, my blond hair from my grandmother, my long, thin feet from both my mom and my dad, and my need to wear glasses from both my grandparents and my parents. I like to concentrate on the ways that I am like everyone else.

I am very lucky to be alive today rather than 50 years or even 20 years ago because back then the doctors and experts believed that people with Down syndrome were not capable of learning. But now we know that people with Down syndrome are capable of doing many different things.

I personally am doing things that some people didn't think I could do. When I was born, somebody told my mom that it was too bad that I was named "Margaret" because I would never even be able to say my name. That person might never have expected that I could win four medals in Special Olympics swimming, be a green belt in karate, cook a pizza, read a novel, run half a mile, or get up in front of the class and give a speech! With a lot of hard work and encouragement, I have been able to do all these things.

I am not sad about the fact that I have Down syndrome. It is just part of me. I have a great brother (most of the time) and parents who love me a lot. I have wonderful friends who enjoy hanging out and having fun with me. I have teachers who help me keep on learning new things. I am glad to be a student at Lincoln Middle School because it is a great school and almost everyone is really nice. Down syndrome has not stopped me from having a worthwhile life.

—Margaret Muller
Cape Cod, Massachusetts

Source: By Margaret Muller, from www.patriciaebauer.com <http://www.patriciaebauer.com/>. Originally printed in The Washington Post, September 14, 1999.

The majority of students with disabilities can progress in the general education curriculum if educators will apply the techniques we have described and use the strategies and tips we highlight in each chapter.

Into Practice. In every chapter, this feature describes practical, step-by-step examples of how to use universal design, secure inclusion, respond to the multicultural nature of American schools, and practice collaboration and partnerships. Every categorical chapter presents strategies across grade-levels to give all prospective teachers real-life examples. These strategies represent the best of the best from teachers and programs across the country.

Technology Outcomes. This resourceful feature highlights a technology that teachers can use in the classroom (or one that supports classroom instruction) to help meet the educational needs of students with disabilities. The technology featured can be anything from a software program to an assistive or adaptive technology, or even specific educational websites.

MyEducationLab.

Throughout the chapters we include margin notes that help link content with a practical focus—MyEducationLab. This new online learning tool offers Self-Assessments to test mastery of chapter objectives; Review, Remediation and Enrichment Exercises to deepen understanding, Activities and Application exercises to foster comprehension of chapter concepts, and Building Teaching Skills activities to provide interactive practice applying the core principles and concepts of special education. The video clips of real children and classrooms featured in the text and formerly available on the DVD accompanying the textbook are now located on MyEducationLab.

myeducationlab

Go to the Activities and Application section in Chapter 2 of MyEducationLab and complete Activity 6. As you watch the video, compare and contrast this teacher's perspectives on inclusion with those presented in Figure 2.7.

This sixth edition of *Exceptional Lives: Special Education in Today's Schools* boasts the most comprehensive and integrated collection of supplements to date. A number of items assist students and professors alike in maximizing learning and instruction. This book has always tried to immerse the student in its content, and students and instructors who embrace this approach benefit from a deeper and more meaningful learning experience. All of the supplements were designed and updated to reflect first-hand experiences with the content and the individuals in the book and its supplements. The supplements also embrace universal design by using multiple ways of presenting material, multiple ways of engaging the students, and multiple ways of allowing students to respond.

PEARSON
myeducationlab
Where the Classroom Comes to Life

"Teacher educators who are developing pedagogies for the analysis of teaching and learning contend that analyzing teaching artifacts has three advantages: it enables new teachers time for reflection while still using the real materials of practice; it provides new teachers with experience thinking about and approaching the complexity of the classroom; and in some cases, it can help new teachers and teacher educators develop a shared understanding and common language about teaching. . . ."[1]

As Linda Darling-Hammond and her colleagues point out, grounding teacher education in real classrooms—among real teachers and students and among actual examples of students' and teachers' work—is an important, and perhaps even an essential, part of training teachers for the complexities of teaching today's students in today's classrooms. We have created a website that provides you with the context of real classrooms and artifacts that research on teacher education tells us is so important. Through authentic in-class video footage, interactive skill-building exercises and more, MyEducationLab offers you a uniquely valuable teacher education tool. MyEducationLab is easy to use!

In *Exceptional Lives: Special Education in Today's Schools*, Sixth Edition, look for the MyEducationLab logo and directive at the beginning and end of each chapter, in the margins, and at the end of each Into Practice feature. Follow the directive and the simple navigation instructions to access the multimedia ***Individualized Study Plan, Activities and Application*** exercises, and ***Building Teaching Skills and Dispositions*** assignments in MyEducationLab that correspond with the chapter content.

◆ *Individualized Study Plan:* Students have the opportunity to take self-assessment quizzes after reading each chapter of the text. Each self-assessment question is tied to a chapter objective, so the students are assessed on their knowledge and comprehension of all of the concepts presented in each chapter. The quiz results automatically generate a personalized study plan for each student, identifying areas of the chapter that still need some additional study time. In this study plan, students are presented with Review, Remediation, and Enrichment exercises to help ensure learning and to deepen understanding of chapter concepts—when just re-reading and studying chapter content is not enough. The study plan is designed to help each student perform well on exams and to promote deep understanding of chapter content.

[1] Darling-Hammond, l., & Bransford, J., Eds. (2005). *Preparing Teachers for a Changing World*. San Francisco: John Wiley & Sons

◆ *Activities and Application:* These exercises offer opportunities to understand content more deeply and are explicitly connected to chapter content. These exercises present thought-provoking questions that probe the students' understanding of the concept or strategy that is presented in the text through classroom video footage, simulations, or teacher and student artifacts.

◆ *Building Teaching Skills and Dispositions:* These application assignments help students practice and strengthen skills that are essential to quality teaching. Students watch authentic classroom video footage or interact with thought-provoking simulations and critically analyze how they can learn these skills and strategies and then hopefully incorporate them into their teaching repertoire or portfolio.

The rich, authentic, and interactive elements that support the Individualized Study Plan, the Activities and Applications and the Building Teaching Skills and Dispositions you will encounter throughout MyEducationLab include:

◆ *Video:* The authentic classroom videos in MyEducationLab show how real teachers handle actual classroom situations. Viewing videos and discussing and analyzing them not only deepens understanding of concepts presented in the book, but also builds skills in observing and analyzing children and classrooms.

◆ *Simulations:* Created by the IRIS Center at Vanderbilt University, these interactive simulations give you hands-on practice at adapting instruction for a full spectrum of learners.

◆ *Student & Teacher Artifacts:* Authentic preK–12 student and teacher classroom artifacts are tied to course topics and offer you practice in working with the different materials you will encounter daily as teachers.

◆ *Case Studies:* A diverse set of robust cases illustrate the realities of teaching and offer valuable perspectives on common issues and challenges in education.

◆ *Strategies:* These teacher-tested, research-based strategies span grade levels pre-K through 12 and all content areas.

◆ *Lesson & Portfolio Builders:* With this effective and easy-to-use tool, you can create, update, and share standards-based lesson plans and portfolios.

Visit www.myeducationlab.com for a demonstration of this exciting new online teaching resource.

FOR THE PROFESSOR

All of the instructor supplements are available at the Instructor Resource Center. To access the manual, the PowerPoint lecture presentation, and the test bank and TestGen software (see below) go to the Instructor Resource Center at www.pearsonhighered.com and click on the "Educators" link. Here you will be able to login or complete a one-time registration for a user name and password.

Online Instructor's Manual with Test Items. The Instructor's Manual helps to synthesize all of the resources available for each chapter, but also helps to sift through the materials to match the delivery method (e.g., semester, quarter) and areas of emphasis for the course. These materials can be used for traditional courses as well as online or online supported courses. The Instructor's Manual is fully integrated with the MyEducationLab that accompanies this text and includes the following resources for the professor:

◆ Chapter Objectives: Guiding Online Reading

◆ Chapter Outline: Presenting Chapter Content

◆ Activities: Applying Student Learning

◆ Classroom-Based Activities: Bringing the Content to Life

◆ Test Items with Answer Key: Multiple Choice, Short Answer, and Essay questions

Online Test Bank and TestGen Software. Students learn better when they are held accountable for what they have learned. That is why we have developed a bank of over 50 test questions per chapter in a variety of formats (including multiple choice, short answer, and essay) that match the issues, questions, and activities that we set out in each chapter. The Test Bank is available online at the Instructor Resource Center for ease of use. Questions have been updated and cross-referenced to match the content of this new edition.

Online PowerPoint Slides/Transparency Masters. These visual aids display, summarize, and help explain core information presented in each chapter. They can be downloaded from our Instructor's Resource Center. All PowerPoint slides have been updated for consistency and to reflect current content in this new edition.

Acknowledgments

Many people have contributed to this book. From the Turnbulls' perspective, their son, Jay, who is now 41 years old and was one of the students who first benefited from IDEA (when it was enacted in 1975 as Education of All Handicapped Children Act), has been their best professor, teaching them time and again how and why to respond to his very self-determined ways, his great expectations, and his insistence on living as a full citizen. He's their best professor, but he often gives them the final examination before giving them the class. That's not bad; it makes them better educators and advocates and (they hope) better authors of this book. Amy Turnbull Khare and Kate Turnbull, the Turnbulls' two daughters, Rahul Khare, their son-in-law, and Dylan Kumar Khare, Cameron Turnbull Khare, and Maya Annika Khare, their grandchildren, have taught us to preserve the enthusiasm of youth as we write the sixth edition of this book, and to bear in mind that every child is special.

Michael Wehmeyer would like to acknowledge the ongoing support of his wife Kathy and sons Geoff and Graham in all his professional activities, as well as his colleagues in the University of Kansas Department of Special Education, at the Beach Center on Disability, and in the Kansas University Center on Developmental Disabilities.

Of course, the families, students, and teachers featured in the vignettes are indispensable to this book. Unless they opened their lives to us, we could not have written about them. In every way, they are your professors, and ours, too. Our gratitude to them is unbounded.

This book is the product of a collaboration among many different talented professionals. At the Beach Center on Disability at the University of Kansas, where we work, we have had the immeasurable benefit of Lois Weldon's many skills. She never flinched when presented with yet another draft of a chapter, with still another request to create figures and boxes, and with unexpected deadlines. We could not do what we do daily without her calm, cool, and composed work ethic.

Jane Wegner, of the Schiefelbusch speech-language-hearing clinic at the University of Kansas, and Evette Edmister, a speech-language pathologist in Des Moines, Iowa (who trained with Jane at the University of Kansas), once again contributed a superb chapter on communication impairment.

Sally Roberts, associate professor in the Department of Special Education and associate dean at the School of Education at the University of Kansas, did likewise with respect to the chapter on hearing impairment. Sandy Lewis at Florida State University once again wrote the chapter on visual impairment and helped us all understand how to educate students with that disability.

Heather Doyle Fraser, our development editor, contributed greatly as we planned how to organize this new edition; she played a key role in the development of the ancillaries; and she added immensely to the content of each chapter by aligning the CEC standards with our six values, thereby helping our readers to put professional standards, our book's content, and our "preaching" alongside each other.

Ann Davis, the executive editor of our publisher's special education texts, returned as a key member of our planning team and reminded us how important it is to humanize our book by emphasizing those six values and recapturing the "voices" of the students, teachers, and family members. Having been our editor for the first through third editions, she was more than welcomed as a key visionary for this one.

Jeff Johnston, vice president and editor-in-chief, has supported us in numerous ways and shepherded us and safeguarded our book as through the ever-changing world of textbook publishers.

Sheryl Langner reprised her role as our production editor; no authors could have a more cheerful and eagle-eyed colleague than Sheryl. She and the copy editor, Laura Bidwa, caught our mistakes; if there are any left, they are attributable to us, not the publisher.

Our colleague at the University of Kansas, Sean Smith, had a hand in the fourth edition, and there are traces of his good work in this edition. We are grateful for his collegiality.

We also gratefully acknowledge the input and insight of several reviewers who helped us keep our book current and in step with their classrooms and students: Alice E. Christie, Malone College; Tammy A. Feil, Neumann College; Blanche J. Glimps, Tennessee State University; David Hamblin, Morehead State University; Juliet Hart, University of Kansas; Erica Ruegg, Oakland University; Shawnee Wakeman, University of North Carolina at Charlotte; and Donna Wandry, West Chester University.

Brief Contents

Contents

Chapter 15 ◆ Understanding Students with Visual Impairments 428

Note: Every effort has been made to provide accurate and current Internet information in this book. However, the Internet and information posted on it are constantly changing, so it is inevitable that some of the Internet addresses listed in this textbook will change.

Special Features

MY VOICE

INTO PRACTICE

TECHNOLOGY OUTCOMES

INCLUSION TIPS

PARTNERSHIP TIPS

Photo Credits

Chapter 1
Courtesy of the Ellenson family, pp. 2, 3, 9, 23, 27; Comstock Royalty Free Division, p. 7; Ellen Senisi/The Image Works, p. 17.

Chapter 2
Courtesy of the Gonzalez family, pp. 32, 33; Katelyn Metzger/Merrill, p. 35; Laima Druskis/PH College, p. 38; Anthony Magnacca/Merrill, p. 45; Lori Whitley/Merrill, p. 47; George Dodson/PH College, p. 55; courtesy of Fiskars Brands, Inc., p. 41.

Chapter 3
Courtesy of the Magee family, pp. 64, 65, 66; © Bettmann/Corbis, p. 70; Tom Watson/Merrill, p. 73; Laima Druskis/PH College, p. 86; © Ariel Skelley/Corbis, 90.

Chapter 4
Courtesy of the Holley family, pp. 98, 99, 100; Jonathan Nourok/PhotoEdit Inc., p. 101; Jose Carrillo/PhotoEdit Inc., p. 110; Paul J. Richards/Agence France Presse/Getty Images, p. 111; Robin L. Sachs/PhotoEdit Inc., p. 117.

Chapter 5
Courtesy of the Marsh family, pp. 124, 125, 129, 141, 147; Masterfile Royalty Free Division, p. 127.

Chapter 6
Courtesy of the Wedge family, pp. 152, 153; PH College, p. 154; Will & Deni McIntyre/Photo Researchers, Inc., p. 158; Lori Whitley/Merrill, p. 161; courtesy of Ann & Rud Turnbull, p. 164; David Roth/Getty Images, Inc.–Stone Allstock, p. 167; Anthony Magnacca/Merrill, p. 169.

Chapter 7
Courtesy of the Ackinclose family, pp. 182, 183; Barbara Schwartz/Merrill, p. 186; Richard Hutchings/Photo Researchers, Inc., p. 187; Tony Freeman/PhotoEdit Inc., p. 199; Mary Kate Denny/PhotoEdit Inc., p. 201.

Chapter 8
Courtesy of the Blankenship family, pp. 210, 211; Bill Aron/PhotoEdit Inc.; p. 214; courtesy of Chris Fraser, p. 215; Aaron Haupt/Photo Researchers, Inc., p. 225.

Chapter 9
Courtesy of the Sabia family, pp. 238, 239; Robin Nelson/PhotoEdit Inc., pp. 244, 252; Anthony Magnacca/Merrill, p. 251; Bob Daemmrich/PhotoEdit Inc., p. 255; courtesy of Judy O'Halloran, p. 256; courtesy of Project TASSEL, Shelby, NC, p. 259.

Chapter 10
Courtesy of the Smith family, pp. 270, 271; Scott Cunningham/Merrill, p. 273; courtesy of the Spoor family, p. 275; Michael Newman/PhotoEdit Inc., p. 279.

Chapter 11
Courtesy of the Conroy family, pp. 300, 301, 313, 319; Ellen Senisi/Ellen Senisi Photography, p. 304; courtesy of Western Psychological Services, p. 310; Lori Whitley/Merrill, p. 316.

Chapter 12
Courtesy of the Frisella family, pp. 332, 336, 352; courtesy of the Drayton family, pp. 333, 334, 341, 342, 346; courtesy of the Lorenzo family, p. 348.

Chapter 13
Courtesy of the Outlaw family, pp. 364, 365; © Tom Stewart/Corbis All Rights Reserved, p. 368; Anthony Magnacca/Merrill, p. 370; Victoria Arocho/AP Wide World Photos, p. 374; Carl D. Walsh/Aurora Photos, Inc., p. 381.

Chapter 14
Courtesy of the Thomas family, pp. 392, 393; David Young-Wolff/PhotoEdit Inc., p. 400; Mark Lewis/Getty Images Inc.–Stone Allstock, p. 401; CC Studio/Photo Researchers, Inc., p. 407; Michael Newman/PhotoEdit Inc., pp. 408, 421; © Gabe Palmer/Corbis, p. 412; courtesy of Dr. Barbara Leutke, p. 418.

Chapter 15
Courtesy of the Sumner family, pp. 428, 429; Lori Whitley/Merrill, p. 431 (a–d); Todd Yarrington/Merrill, p. 432; Scott Cunningham/Merrill, pp. 433, 448 (bottom), 451; David Young-Wolff/Getty Images Inc. – Stone Allstock, p. 448 (top); Bob Rowan/Corbis/Bettmann, p. 452.

Chapter 16
Courtesy of the Hoskins family, pp. 460, 461; Getty Images, Inc. – Photodisc, p. 465; Will Hart/PhotoEdit Inc., p. 473; Keith Weller/USDA Natural Resources Conservation Service, p. 476; courtesy of the Wehmeyer family, p. 482.

1

Overview of Today's Special Education

◆ WHO IS THOMAS ELLENSON?

"Easy magic."

"That's the key," says Richard Ellenson, the father of 7-year-old Thomas.

The key to what? To being with Thomas, to entering into his life, to educating him, and especially to including him in school and in life outside school.

And why does Thomas need a key? Because he has cerebral palsy. That condition makes it extremely difficult for him to move from place to place. It also greatly impedes his ability to speak.

So what is the way for a typical person to understand Thomas, to access his obviously good mind, to communicate with him, to hear what is in his head? Without mobility and reciprocity in communication, Thomas could be nearly entirely cut off from others, whether in school or elsewhere.

Richard looks at his son's life from a unique perspective: as a successful New York advertising executive. To be an effective ad man, he tries to understand how prospective buyers will quickly respond to his ads.

Richard asks us to look at Thomas in the same way. Look at him from an outsider's point of view, from the perspective of people who are not directly affected by a disability. See Thomas from society's point of view. But don't stop there. Try to see him as "just Thomas." Think about how you and he can communicate and relate to each other. In all of this, regard Thomas for who he is, but also regard him as a surrogate for others with a disability. From an ad man's perspective, that is an enormous load. So Richard looked for ways to communicate his son's easy magic.

Knowing that people are curious about disability, Richard headed up an advertising campaign for United Cerebral Palsy of New York City. It consisted of four simple words: "See me. Not CP."

Look at Thomas. What do you see? Richard does not hesitate to answer, "The killer smile." When people see it, "they get that moment of personality."

A killer smile. That's the easy magic. And it is invaluable. Richard believes that when people understand a killer smile, or any engaging characteristic, as an indicator of ability or personality, they don't simply feel sympathy or, at best, empathy for a person's disability. Instead, they see the light that shines from inside it.

"You can't expect the world to always work to find the less obvious magic," he says. "You need to find the easy magic that will open that door for people quickly. After that, people will do the work for themselves. Once people have taken an interest, building a relationship is much easier."

The Ellensons' world has hardly been easy. Richard and Lora (a physician and research scientist at New York–Presbyterian Hospital Weill Medical College of Cornell University) redesigned their city home so that it is accessible for Thomas. Richard left the advertising business to develop and market the assistive technology he developed for Thomas. (You will find it at www.blinktwice.com.) Those were deliberate steps. Richard, Lora, and Thomas also were prisoners to the luck of the day. Fortuitously, they encountered New York's mayor, Michael Bloomberg, at a restaurant. Richard approached him and persuaded him to connect them with the city school officials who would help build an innovative new program that did not exist within the current school system.

Their advocacy then took them to school administrators, teachers, therapists of all kinds, designers of assistive technologies, and, of course, the parents of children who have disabilities and the parents of children who do not. And their advocacy caused them to become experts about education in their own right, not just for Thomas but for all students.

"It's very fair to ask the questions that a typical parent is going to ask about including Thomas in the same school and same program as the typical child of a typical parent," Richard said. Parents of nondisabled students may well ask, "Will Thomas or other students with disabilities take valuable teacher time away from my child?"

When addressing that point, Richard begins to use lawyers' language. "You have to give all those kids [with disabilities] the benefit of the doubt. Frankly, when you do that, you will be developing techniques for better teaching for everyone. You will be gaining insights into delivering curriculum to an increasingly broad group of students. That's benefiting everyone. In short, the benefit of the doubt benefits everybody."

Now Richard's focus changes from law to philosophy, from benefit of the doubt to creating the greatest good for the greatest number. And then it shifts from enhancing

CHAPTER OBJECTIVES

◆ You will learn six values that should guide you as you teach. You will find each of these values in the "Values and Outcomes" section at the end of each chapter.

◆ You will learn about students, such as Thomas, who are in special education, and about the professionals who work with them.

◆ You will learn about the federal special education law and its principles and how the law benefits infants and toddlers (birth–3), young children (3–6), and school-aged students (6–21).

◆ You will learn about the federal general education law and its six principles and how the special education and general education laws are aligned with each other.

◆ You will learn about other federal laws that benefit students with disabilities.

◆ You will learn about the outcomes that these laws have helped achieve for students, and that much more remains to be achieved.

someone's cognitive and mobility capacities to something much more ephemeral. "The joy of all of this is that we don't have to convince people. Thomas convinces the kids and the kids convince everyone else."

Joy quotients enter the world of general and special education. Now they become an essential element of the profession and of the partnerships that the Ellensons have with Thomas's educators.

"The fact is, you always need to learn how to best communicate with a person," says Richard. "If you become sensitive to that, your life will open up and, you know, that's the joy."

Richard and Lora will be the first to admit that there are difficult aspects about Thomas's disability. Refusing to use some typical techniques to help Thomas communicate is hard. Knowing that Thomas will not be a ballplayer entails some sadness. Their compensation comes in knowing that Thomas is developing patience with himself and others and that he can still appreciate the times he must be a spectator in life, even as he is a player in many others. And having a goal in mind—teaching Thomas to become all he can be and wanting for him whatever he wants in life for himself—sustains them and, truth be told, Thomas's teachers.

Infusing joy into their lives, into Thomas's, and into the educators'—well, the killer smile is the easy magic. It is a small gesture. But it opens into an enormous and glittering world.

Special education involves advocacy, inclusion, universal design of places and curricula, self-determination, the law's presumptions against segregation and in favor of inclusion, and utilitarianism—finding the greatest good for the greatest number and then making sure that schools practice what is good.

As you listen to Richard and look at Thomas, you'll also find that there's an easy magic in it, too. As Richard puts it, "Find that one thing that is simple now and just build on it."

Building on a student's strengths. It makes sense. It's what education is all about.

PEARSON
myeducationlab

As you read this text, you will notice connections to MyEducationLab at www.myeducationlab.com. Each chapter in the course contains Chapter Objectives, a Study Plan (including a self-assessment and review, practice, and enrichment exercises), Activities and Application, and Building Teaching Skills and Dispositions exercises. These self-assessments and study aids will help you gauge your comprehension of chapter content and also help you build a deeper, more applied understanding of the concepts discussed in each chapter.

PROFILE OF SPECIAL EDUCATION STUDENTS AND PERSONNEL IN TODAY'S SCHOOLS

Perhaps you have heard these lines, which powerfully apply to all of us today but were written in 1624 by the poet John Donne: "Never send to know for whom the bell tolls; It tolls for thee" (from *Devotions upon Emergent Occasions*, Meditation 17).

Disability affects 9.1 percent of the school-aged population (U.S. Department of Education, 2007b); it eventually affects most of us as we age. For you, then, the disability bell could toll at least twice: once as you teach, and once as you age. For some of you, the bell peals more frequently because you have a family member or close friend with a disability or because you yourself have special needs.

When the bell tolls, it tolls not only for people with a disability but also for their families, friends, teachers, school administrators, and communities. That is why we recite stories about real families, real children and youth, and real educators at the beginning of each chapter. But stories alone are not enough to introduce you to the field of special education, so we also review the most recent research data, combining the real-life personal face of exceptionality with evidence-based practices in special education, public policy, and overarching values that we encourage you to adopt. In particular, we discuss three themes: inclusion, universal design for learning, and family-professional partnerships.

Remember Thomas? He is included in the general curriculum, and he benefits from teachers who adapt their teaching for him and others (universal design) and use assistive technology for him (we define assistive technology in Figure 1.3).

Figure 1.1 Values to guide you in your career

GREAT EXPECTATIONS   CHOICES
VALUES   POSITIVE CONTRIBUTIONS   STRENGTHS
RELATIONSHIPS   FULL CITIZENSHIP

Envisioning great expectations. Students have many capabilities that have not been tapped. We can develop new visions of what is possible. These visions can become realities. We need new perspectives of what life can be as well as support for fulfilling these dreams.

Enhancing positive contributions. Students contribute positively to their families, schools, friends, and communities. We need to develop greater opportunities for these contributions.

Building on strengths. Students and families have many natural capacities. They need opportunities for educational programs to identify, highlight, and build upon their strengths.

Becoming self-determined. Students and families can direct their own lives. Enabling them to act on their own preferences promotes their self-determination.

Expanding relationships. Connections are crucial to quality of life. Students and families need to connect with each other, educators, and friends in the community.

Ensuring full citizenship. Less able does not mean less worthy. All students, including those with exceptionalities, and their families are entitled to full participation in American life.

Exemplary special education occurs when values guide practices. And when values-guided practices are as state-of-the-art as the ones you will read about in this book, no challenge that students and their families, schools, and teaching staff face will be too daunting. Figure 1.1 identifies these values.

Who Are the Students?

To answer the question "Who are the students in special education?", we describe (1) the total number of students with disabilities, (2) the gender of those students, (3) the provision of gifted education, (4) the categories of disabilities, and (5) issues about labels and language.

Before we tell you about the students, let's define "special education." It is specially designed instruction, at no cost to a child's parents, that meets a child's unique needs in school. It consists of "related services" (Figure 1.3) and supplementary aids and services (which we describe later in this chapter).

Total Number of Students Served

In the 2003–2004 school year, 369,596 infants and toddlers (ages birth through 2), or 2.2 percent of U.S. infants and toddlers, received early intervention services; and 670,750 preschool children (ages 3 through 5), or 5.8 percent of the preschool-aged population, received early childhood services (U.S. Department of Education, 2007b). Approximately 6 million students ages 6 through 21 received some form of special education.

Gender of Students

In the general education school population males and females are enrolled in equal proportion, but in special education approximately two thirds of the students are male and one third are female (U.S. Department of Education, 2008).

Gifted Students

Special education also serves students who have unusual gifts and talents (see Chapter 16). The percentage of students identified as gifted ranges from a low of 1.8 percent to a high

IEP Tip

It is good practice to ask the family member who is most involved with each student whether there are other family members with whom you should enter into a partnership in educating the student.

of 18 percent in different states (National Association for Gifted Children, 2007). Overall, 6.4 percent of the school population is identified as gifted and talented (U.S. Department of Education, 2006a). Females slightly outnumber males.

Disability Categories

The U.S. Department of Education collects data from the states according to students' type or category of disability. Figure 1.2 sets out the numbers and percentages of students associated with the highest frequency categories. Slightly more than two thirds of all students with disabilities are classified into two categories: specific learning disabilities (47.4 percent) and speech or language impairments (18.7 percent). These two categories, when combined with the categories of mental retardation, now called intellectual disability (9.6 percent), and emotional disturbance, which we call emotional or behavioral disorders (8 percent), account for 84 percent of all students with disabilities. In each chapter, you will meet students who have disabilities, just as you have been introduced to Thomas. You will read about their characteristics, their families, and the education they receive. But before you read about educational characteristics, a word of caution is in order.

Labels and Language

How would you feel if you were Thomas, and other students or even teachers referred to you as the "CP kid"? Remember that Richard, Thomas's father, worked on an advertising campaign to get the message across: "See me. Not CP." Sometimes people might use outdated terms such as "crippled kid" or "handicap student" to refer to Thomas and other students who have disabilities. How would you feel if you were known only by your

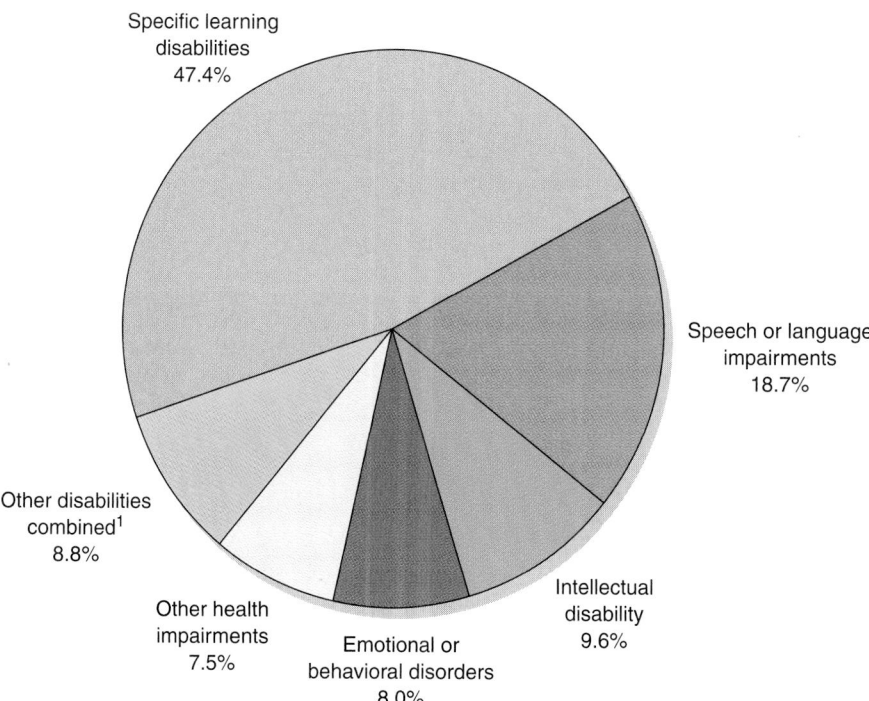

Figure 1.2   Disability distribution for students ages 6 through 21 receiving special education and related services under IDEA: Fall 2007

Specific learning disabilities
47.4%

Speech or language impairments
18.7%

Intellectual disability
9.6%

Emotional or behavioral disorders
8.0%

Other health impairments
7.5%

Other disabilities combined[1]
8.8%

Source: U.S. Department of Education (2007).

[1]Other disabilities include multiple disabilities (2.2 percent), hearing impairments (1.2 percent), orthopedic impairments (1.1 percent), visual impairments (0.4 percent), autism (2.3 percent), deaf-blindness (0.03 percent), traumatic brain injury (0.4 percent), and developmental delay (1.1 percent).

disability and not according to your abilities? Devalued? Probably. Indeed, that is precisely how many families and special educators respond when a child with disabilities is labeled as a "disabled person" first and foremost.

There is controversy about labeling and its consequences, which include classification in schools—specifically, classification into special education. Some students may benefit if a label qualifies them to receive services because the benefit of the services can outweigh the stigma that accompanies some labels. Indeed, some people, including those with hearing and visual impairments (see Chapters 14 and 15), accept and celebrate the labels because the labels create a cultural solidarity among those so labeled.

On the other hand, labeling can lead educators to regard a student as a broken person whom they must "fix." It can segregate students with disabilities from their classmates without disabilities. Finally, it can contribute to biases against students based on their ethnic, cultural, and linguistic backgrounds.

So we ask you to be cautious about using labels. Let Thomas be Thomas, not a youngster with a label. If you or other educators must use labels, avoid those that demean and stigmatize, for they always separate and devalue people, in and outside school (Goffman, 1963; Smith, 1999), and they impair students' self-esteem (Lapadat, 1998). In Chapter 2 you will learn about a relatively new approach in special education, responsiveness to intervention (RTI). RTI directs teachers to intensify their instruction for students who experience learning challenges before referring them for special education testing and ultimately for a formal label. This approach—respond and intensify—can help to avoid the labeling process because RTI applies to all students (Chapters 2, 3, and 5) (Moore-Brown, Montgomery, Bielinski, & Shubin, 2005).

We want to point out two major changes in terminology over the last three decades. The first change abandons the term *handicap* and favors the term *disability*. The second change—called "people-first" language—puts the person before the disability. For example, instead of using phrases such as "physically disabled children," teachers say "students with physical disabilities." Even better, they and you might consider not labeling at all. Why not just say "students"? Best of all, just "Thomas."

Who Are Special Education Personnel?

If you are considering a career in special education, your job prospects are good. According to the U.S. Department of Education (2007b), 421,333 special education teachers were employed in fall 2005 to teach students ages 6 through 21. To completely understand your opportunities, you should know that a study of the national shortage of fully certified special education teachers, in contrast to fully certified general education teachers, reported the following (Boe & Cook, 2006):

◆ An increase of almost 5 percentage points from 1993–2002 in the shortage of fully certified special education teachers. This increase reflected a 2 percent to 4 percent increase in the shortage of certified special educators compared to the shortage of fully certified general education teachers.

◆ From the 1993–1994 to the 2001–2002 school year, the need for fully certified special education teachers almost doubled.

◆ Almost half (44 percent) of first-year special education teachers are not fully certified.

◆ Approximately 5 percent to 15 percent of the school social workers, occupational therapists, physical therapists, speech pathologists, and audiologists who provide special education and related services are not fully certified.

The profession of special education offers you many career paths.

Another national study of special education teachers reported that (Carlson, Brauen, Klein, Schroll, & Willig, 2002):

◆ Females constitute 85 percent of the workforce.

◆ White teachers represent 86 percent of the workforce.

◆ Based on self-report, 14 percent of teachers have a disability.

◆ Teachers' average age is 43 years.

◆ Fifty-nine percent of special education teachers have a master's degree.

◆ Teachers have an average of about 14 years of teaching experience.

Not all special education professionals are teachers. Other educational personnel include school social workers, occupational therapists, physical therapists, recreation and therapeutic specialists, paraprofessionals, physical education teachers, supervisors/administrators (local and state levels), psychologists, diagnostic/evaluation staff, audiologists, work-study coordinators, vocational education teachers, counselors, rehabilitation counselors, interpreters, and speech pathologists. The number of certified nonteaching personnel in these roles during the fall 2005 school year totaled 194,217. Across all of these roles, the percentage of non-certified staff was 3 percent.

Additionally, 389,824 paraprofessionals served special education students during fall 2005. The typical paraprofessional working in special education is a white female who is 44 years old (Carlson et al., 2002) and serves 21 students, 15 of whom have disabilities. Approximately one third of paraprofessionals are fluent or almost fluent in languages other than English.

You know now that there is a broad range of roles in the special education field, many of them filled by personnel who are not fully certified. What you may not know is how rewarding it can be to be a special educator and how federal law provides a structure for that rewarding career.

OVERVIEW OF THE LAW AND SPECIAL EDUCATION

For more than 30 years now, the education of students with disabilities has been governed by a law that Congress enacted in 1975 called the Individuals with Disabilities Education Act (IDEA). Whatever role you play in American schools, you almost certainly will have to know about this law, the rights it gives to students, and the duties it imposes on schools. Let's begin with a bit of its history.

Two Types of Discrimination

During the early and middle decades of the 20th century, schools discriminated against students with disabilities in two significant ways (Turnbull, Stowe, & Huerta, 2007). First, they completely excluded many students with disabilities, or if they did admit them, they did not always provide them with an effective or appropriate education. Second, schools often classified students as having disabilities who in fact did not have disabilities. This practice is known as misclassification. Frequently, these students were members of culturally or linguistically diverse groups. In addition, schools sometimes labeled students with one kind of disability when the students really had other kinds of disabilities.

Beginning in the early 1970s, advocates for students with disabilities—primarily their families, parent advocacy organizations, and civil rights lawyers—began to sue state and local school officials, claiming that exclusion and misclassification violated the students' rights to an equal education opportunity under the U.S. Constitution (Turnbull et al., 2007). Relying on the Supreme Court's decision in the school race-desegregation case *Brown v. Board of Education* (1954), they argued that because the Court held that schools may not segregate by race, schools also may not segregate or otherwise discriminate by ability and disability. Students are students, regardless of their race or disability. You will learn more about *Brown*'s impact in Chapter 3 when we describe the deplorable history of discrimination against students from culturally diverse backgrounds, especially in special education.

PEARSON
myeducationlab

Go to the Activities and Application section in Chapter 1 of MyEducationLab and complete Activity 1. As you read the Overview information regarding the IDEA Improvement Act of 2004 and answer the accompanying questions, think about how this legislation is implemented every day in the classroom.

Judicial Decisions and Legislation

The advocates for students with disabilities were successful. In 1972, federal courts ordered the Commonwealth of Pennsylvania and the District of Columbia to (1) provide a free appropriate public education to all students with disabilities, (2) educate students with disabilities in the same schools and basically the same programs as students without disabilities, and (3) put into place certain procedural safeguards so that parents of students with disabilities could challenge schools that did not live up to the courts' orders (*Mills v. Washington, DC, Board of Education*, 1972; *Pennsylvania Association for Retarded Citizens [PARC] v. Commonwealth of Pennsylvania*, 1972).

These two cases prompted Congress to act. In 1975, it enacted IDEA (then called the Education of All Handicapped Students Act, or Public Law [P.L.] 94–142). At that time Congress intended to open up the schools to all students with disabilities and make sure that those students had the chance to benefit from special education. Nowadays the challenge is to provide access and assure that the students really do benefit. Special education is explicitly outcome-driven. There are four outcomes: equality of opportunity, full participation, independent living, and economic self-sufficiency. Later in this chapter you will read about these outcomes, but now you need to know about IDEA's basic components.

When Congress reauthorized IDEA in 2004, it enacted the "Individuals with Disabilities Education Improvement Act." Sometimes you will hear people refer to the law by that name or its abbreviation, IDEIA. But Congress recognized that people are familiar with the law's former name (before the 2004 reauthorization), so it provided that the "short title" of the reauthorized law is "Individuals with Disabilities Education Act" (abbreviated as IDEA). Therefore, in every place where we refer to the 2004 law, we call it "Individuals with Disabilities Education Act" or IDEA.

The Span of Special Education: Birth Through Age 21

Having enacted IDEA in 1975 to benefit students ages 6 to 18, Congress has expanded the group of students who have a right to special education. The law now applies to infants and toddlers from birth through age 2, young children (ages 3 through 5), and older students (through age 21). Infants and toddlers have needs unlike those of older children (ages 3 through 21); accordingly, IDEA consists of two parts, each of which is age-specific—Part B and Part C. (Part A sets out Congress's intent and national policy to provide a free appropriate public education to all students with disabilities, from birth to age 21.)

The purpose of IDEA is to ensure that all students with disabilities have a free appropriate public education in the least restrictive setting.

Part B

Part B benefits students (such as Thomas Ellenson) who are ages 3 through 21, each inclusive. To define the eligible students, IDEA combines a categorical approach (that is, it describes the categories of disabilities—Thomas's is "other health impairments," a term that includes cerebral palsy) with a functional approach (that is, it provides that the student must be unable to function successfully in the general curriculum without special education—Thomas needs mobility and communication help). The IDEA categories for students ages 3 through 21, in order from the most frequent to the least frequent are: specific learning disabilities, speech or language impairments, intellectual disability (IDEA uses the term "mental retardation"), emotional disorders, multiple disabilities, hearing impairments, other health impairments, autism, visual impairments, and traumatic brain injury. We provide a chapter about each disability (including physical disabilities). We also cover attention deficit/hyperactivity disorder (AD/HD), which is a component of other health impairments, and students who are gifted. You will learn about communication and mobility challenges in Chapters 6 and 12, respectively, so you will know better how to teach Thomas.

IEP Tip

With student and parental permission, peers who participate in the student's circle of friends might be very appropriate members of the IEP team to help develop a plan to facilitate more friendships.

These same categories apply to children ages 3 to 6 (those in early childhood special education), but each state may also provide special education to children who meet only the functional approach to disability—namely, those who

◆ Are experiencing developmental delays in one or more of the following areas—physical development, cognitive development, communication development, social or emotional development, or adaptive behavior and development—and

◆ Because of these delays, need special education and related services

IDEA gives the states discretion whether to serve children ages 3 through 5 (early education). As of early 2002, all states do so.

Part C

IDEA also gives the states discretion whether to serve infants and toddlers (ages birth through 2, also known as 0 to 3). As of early 2002, all states do. **Part C** benefits any child under age 3 who (1) needs early intervention services because of developmental delays in one or more of the areas of cognitive development, physical development, communication development, social or emotional development, and adaptive development; or (2) has a diagnosed physical or mental condition that has a high probability of resulting in a developmental delay.

Part C does more than benefit the children who have identified delays. It also gives each state the option of serving at-risk infants and toddlers (children under age 3). These are children who would be at risk of experiencing a substantial developmental delay if they did not receive early intervention services. Note the difference: A child with a diagnosed condition that has a "high probability" of resulting in a developmental delay is not the same as a child who is "at risk" of having a delay.

Special Education and Students' Eligibility

Eligibility Based on Need

As you read earlier, IDEA (Part B, ages 3 through 5 optional, ages 6 through 21 not) defines special education as specially designed instruction, at no cost to the child's parents, to meet the unique needs of a student with a disability. A student with a disability is one who has the disabilities identified above (the categorical definition) and who, because of the disability, needs special education and related services (the functional definition). Special education is reserved for students who need it because of their disabilities and because their needs cannot be satisfied in general education without special education.

Where Special Education Is Provided

Special education occurs in classrooms (where Thomas receives his), students' homes, hospitals and institutions, and other settings. Under IDEA, special education must be available wherever there are students who qualify for its benefits.

Components of Special Education

Special education is individualized to the student; that is the meaning of "to meet the unique needs" of a student. To meet a student's needs, it is usually necessary to provide more than individualized instruction. Educators and other professionals in special education do this by supplementing their instruction with "related services." These are services that are necessary to assist the student in benefiting from special education. Figure 1.3 identifies and defines related services.

Figure 1.3 ▶ **Definitions of related services in IDEA**

The related services apply to Part B and students ages 3 through 21 unless we note that they belong to Part C only and thus only to children ages birth through 2.

- *Assistive technology and services:* acquiring and using devices and services to restore lost capacities or improve impaired capacities (Part C, but also a "special consideration" for Part B students' IEPs).
- *Audiology:* determining the range, nature, and degree of hearing loss and operating programs for treatment and prevention of hearing loss.
- *Counseling services:* counseling by social workers, psychologists, guidance counselors, or other qualified professionals.
- *Early identification:* identifying a disability as early as possible in a child's life.
- *Interpreting services:* various means for communicating with children who have hearing impairments or who are deaf-blind.
- *Family training, counseling, and home visits:* assisting families to enhance their child's development (Part C only).
- *Health services:* enabling a child to benefit from other early intervention services (Part C only).
- *Medical services:* determining a child's medically related disability that results in the child's need for special education and related services.
- *Occupational therapy:* improving, developing, or restoring functions impaired or lost through illness, injury, or deprivation.
- *Orientation and mobility services:* assisting a visually impaired or blind student to get around within various environments.
- *Parent counseling and training:* providing parents with information about child development.
- *Physical therapy:* services by a physical therapist.
- *Psychological services:* administering and interpreting psychological and educational tests and other assessment procedures and managing a program of psychological services, including psychological counseling for children and parents.
- *Recreation and therapeutic recreation:* assessing leisure function, recreation programs in schools and community agencies, and leisure education.
- *Rehabilitative counseling services:* planning for career development, employment preparation, achieving independence, and integration in the workplace and community.
- *School health services:* attending to educationally related health needs through services provided by a school nurse or other qualified professional.
- *Service coordination services:* assistance and services by a service coordinator to a child and family (Part C only).
- *Social work services in schools:* preparing a social or developmental history on a child, counseling groups and individuals, and mobilizing school and community resources.
- *Speech pathology and speech-language pathology:* diagnosing specific speech or language impairments and giving guidance regarding those impairments.
- *Transportation and related costs:* providing travel to and from services and schools, travel in and around school buildings, and specialized equipment (e.g., special or adapted buses, lifts, and ramps).
- *Vision services:* assessing vision in an infant/toddler (Part C only).

IDEA: SIX PRINCIPLES

It is not enough for IDEA simply to identify the eligible students and to specify the services they have a right to receive. Because of schools' past discrimination through exclusion and misclassification, IDEA also establishes six principles that govern students' education (Turnbull et al., 2007). Figure 1.4 describes those six principles. Because IDEA is complex and contains general rules, exceptions to the general rules, and even exceptions to the exceptions, we will describe only the general rules. Sometimes we will give you some detail about a rule, the exceptions, or both.

- *Zero reject:* a rule against excluding any student.
- *Nondiscriminatory evaluation:* a rule requiring schools to evaluate students fairly to determine if they have a disability and, if so, what kind and how extensive.
- *Appropriate education:* a rule requiring schools to provide individually tailored education for each student based on evaluation and augmented by related services and supplementary aids and services.
- *Least restrictive environment:* a rule requiring schools to educate students with disabilities alongside students without disabilities to the maximum extent appropriate for the students with disabilities
- *Procedural due process:* a rule providing safeguards for students against schools' actions, including a right to sue schools in court.
- *Parental and student participation:* a rule requiring schools to collaborate with parents and adolescent students in designing and carrying out special education programs.

Zero Reject

The **zero-reject** principle prohibits schools from excluding any student with a disability (as defined by IDEA) from a free appropriate public education. The purpose of the zero-reject principle is to ensure that all children and youth (ages 3 through 21), no matter how severe their disabilities, will have an appropriate education provided at public expense. To carry out this purpose, the zero-reject rule applies to the state and all of its school districts and private schools (if the public system places a student into a private school), state-operated programs such as schools for students with visual or hearing impairments, psychiatric hospitals, and institutions for people with other disabilities.

Educability

To carry out the zero-reject rule, courts have ordered state and local education agencies to provide services to children who traditionally have been regarded as ineducable (not able to learn) because of the profound extent of their disabilities. The courts are saying that "all" means "all"—Congress was very clear that it intends IDEA to benefit *all* children with disabilities, no matter how disabled they are.

Discipline

To assure that all students with a disability receive an appropriate education and that the schools are safe places for teaching and learning, IDEA regulates how schools may discipline students who qualify for IDEA's protection. The principles of the IDEA discipline amendments are simple, but their details are complex. The general principles are as follows:

- ◆ *Equal treatment.* The school may discipline a student with a disability in the same way and to the same extent as it may discipline a student without a disability, for the same offense, subject to the special provisions described below.

- ◆ *No cessation.* No matter what the student does to violate a school code, the school may not expel or suspend the student for more than 10 school days in any one school year.

> **IEP Tip**
>
> When you have siblings of children with disabilities as students in your class, you might encourage them to share any ideas that they have for fostering their brother's or sister's successful education with their parents so that these ideas could be incorporated into the development of their sibling's IEP.

- *Unique circumstances.* The school may take into account any unique circumstances related to the student and the student's behavior in violating a school code of behavior when the school is deciding whether to change the student's placement in order to discipline the student.

- *Short-term removals.* The school may suspend the student for not more than 10 school days in any one school year. It has no duty to offer any services to the suspended student.

- *Manifestation determinations.* When the school proposes to change the student's placement for more than 10 days, it must determine whether the student's behavior is a manifestation of the student's disability. A manifestation exists when the student's behavior was caused by the disability or had a direct and substantial relationship to the disability; or when the student's conduct was the direct failure of the school to implement the student's IEP.

- *Response to no manifestation.* If the school determines that the student's behavior is not a manifestation of the disability, it may discipline the student in the same way as it disciplines students without disabilities except that it may not terminate the student's education (the "no cessation" rule). It may, however, place the student in an interim alternative educational setting.

- *Response to manifestation.* When a school determines that the student's behavior is a manifestation of the disability, the school must take immediate steps to remedy any deficiencies contributing to the school's failure to implement the student's IEP. The school also must conduct a functional behavioral assessment and develop a behavioral intervention plan to address the student's behavior (whether or not the manifestation is IEP-deficiency based). Unless the school and parents agree to place the student in an interim alternative setting, the student then returns to the student's previous school placement.

- *Services in interim alternative educational settings.* When it places a student in this setting, the school must still offer an education that assures that the student will make progress according to the student's IEP.

- *Weapons, drugs, and injury.* When a student has weapons or knowingly has or uses illegal drugs in school, or when a student seriously injures another person at school, the school may place the student in an interim alternative educational setting, without first making any manifestation determination, for up to 45 days.

Nondiscriminatory Evaluation

The effect of the zero-reject rule is to guarantee all students with a disability access to school. Once in school, they are entitled to a **nondiscriminatory evaluation.**

Two Purposes

The nondiscriminatory evaluation has two purposes. The first is to determine whether a student has a disability. If the student does not have a disability, then she has no right to receive special education under IDEA or any further evaluation related to special education under IDEA.

If the evaluation reveals that the student has a disability, the evaluation process must then accomplish its second purpose: to identify special education and related services the student will receive. This information is necessary to plan an appropriate education for the student and determine where the student will be educated.

Nondiscriminatory Evaluation Requirements

Because evaluation has such a significant impact on students and their families, IDEA surrounds the evaluation process with procedural safeguards. Figure 1.5 highlights IDEA's procedural safeguards and its provisions related to parents' notice and consent.

To determine whether a student has a disability and then decide the nature of the special education and related services the student needs, educators typically follow a four-step process: screening, prereferral, referral, and nondiscriminatory evaluation. The first three steps are not required by IDEA but are put into place by educators as a matter of good practice or state or local policy. Picture these five steps as a funnel (see Figure 1.6).

- ◆ *Screening:* administering tests to all students to identify which students seem to need further testing to determine whether they qualify for special education.
- ◆ *Prereferral (including response to intervention):* providing more intensive instruction for students who are not making expected progress in order to prevent

---

Figure 1.5 ▶ **Nondiscriminatory evaluation safeguards**

Assessment Procedures
- They use a variety of assessment tools and strategies to gather relevant functional, developmental, and academic information, including information provided by the student's parent that may enable the team to determine if the student has a disability and the nature of specially designed instruction needed.
- They should include more than one assessment because no single procedure may be used as the sole basis of evaluation.
- They may be requested by a parent, the state education agency, another state agency, or the local education agency (initial evaluations).
- They are selected and administered so as to not be discriminatory on a racial or cultural basis.
- They are administered in the language and form most likely to produce accurate information about the student's current levels of academic, development, and functional performance.
- They must be used for the purposes for which the assessments are valid and reliable.
- They are administered by trained and knowledgeable personnel and in conformance with instructions by the producer of the tests or material.

Parental Notice and Consent
- Inform the parents fully and secure their written consent before the initial evaluation and each reevaluation.
- If the parents do not consent to the initial evaluation, the school may use dispute resolution (due process) procedures to secure approval to proceed with the evaluation or reevaluation.
- Obtain parents' consent before any reevaluation unless the school can demonstrate that it has taken reasonable measures to obtain their consent and parents have failed to respond.
- Provide to the parents a full explanation of all due process rights, a description of what the school proposes or refuses to do, a description of each evaluation procedure that was used, a statement of how the parents may obtain a copy of their procedural safeguards and sources that they can contact to obtain assistance in understanding the provisions of the notice, a description of any other options considered, and an explanation of any other factors that influenced the educators' decisions.
- Do not treat the parents' consent for evaluation as their consent for placement into or withdrawal from a special education program; secure separate parental consent for these changes.
- If the parents do not consent to placement, the school has no duty to provide special education and is not liable to the parents or child if it does not use dispute resolution (due process) to get authority to provide services.

Figure 1.6 Nondiscriminatory evaluation: A funneling process

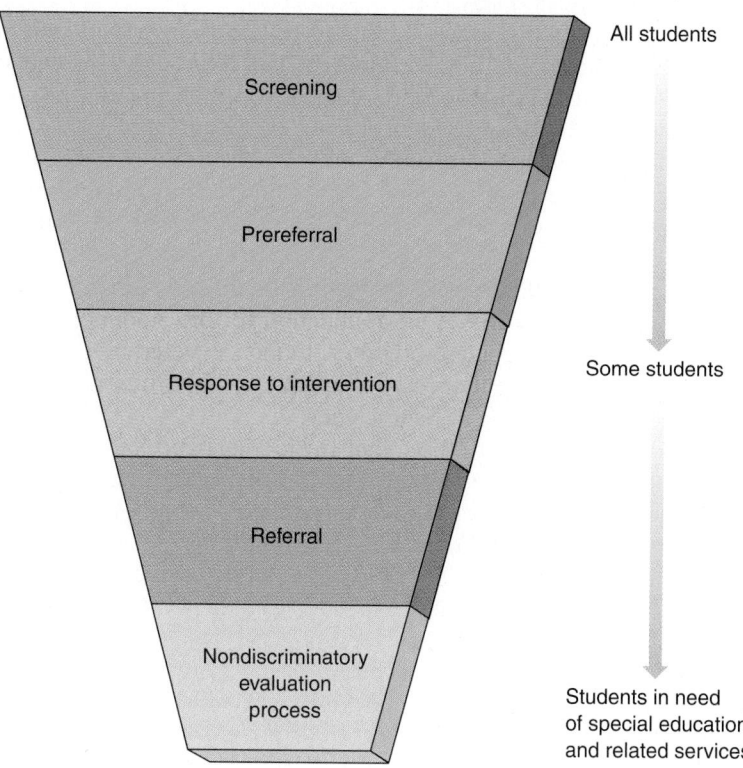

the need for a referral, a full nondiscriminatory evaluation, and possible placement in special education (Bahr, Fuchs, & Fuchs, 1999; Bahr, Whitten, Dieker, Kocarek, & Manson, 1999).

◆ *Response to intervention:* offering beefed-up general education services and then determining whether the student responds to them (see Chapters 2, 3, and 5).

◆ *Referral:* submitting a formal written request for a student to receive a full nondiscriminatory evaluation.

◆ *Nondiscriminatory evaluation:* adhering to the safeguards of the full evaluation process in Figure 1.4.

Once the evaluation team has determined that a student has a disability (or, in some states, is gifted) and has identified the special education and related services the student needs, then educators must provide the student with that kind of education and those services, describing them in the student's IEP. In short, the nondiscriminatory evaluation leads to, and is the very foundation of, the student's appropriate education.

IDEA does not specify who the members of the evaluation team must be. It simply says that a local educational agency must ensure that qualified personnel and the student's parents are part of the evaluation team. But because one of the members of the student's IEP team must be a person qualified to interpret the evaluation results, it usually is the case that at least one member of the evaluation team will be a member of the IEP team. To the greatest extent possible, it is helpful to have overlap between the members of the multidisciplinary evaluation team and the members of the IEP team. Regardless of the precise team membership, the result is the same: the evaluation leads to IEP decisions about program (appropriate education) and placement (least restrictive environment).

Appropriate Education

By enrolling students (zero reject) and evaluating their strengths and needs (nondiscriminatory evaluation), schools still do not ensure that students' education will be appropriate and beneficial. That is why Congress has given each student in special education the right to an **appropriate education** and related services.

As we noted earlier, the key to an appropriate special education is *individualization*. Educators individualize by developing a plan for each student ages 3 through 21 called an **Individualized Education Program (IEP).** The plan for each student from birth through age 2 is the student's and family's **Individualized Family Services Plan (IFSP).** To guide you through IDEA's appropriate education requirements, we will discuss (1) the basic contents of IEPs/IFSPs; (2) age-specific provisions, including early intervention and transitions to adulthood; (3) the participants who develop the IEP/IFSP; and (4) timelines. You will learn more about the IEP in Chapter 2.

As you just read, each student's IEP is based on the student's evaluation and is outcome-oriented. Taken as a whole, the IEP is the foundation for the student's appropriate education; it is the assurance that Thomas and other students covered by IDEA will benefit from special education and have real access to equality of opportunity, full participation, independent living, and economic self-sufficiency.

The IFSP describes the services that both the infant (or toddler) and the family will receive. Like the IEP, the IFSP is based on the child's development and needs; it specifies outcomes for the child. Unlike the IEP, however, the IFSP also provides the option for families to identify their resources, priorities, and concerns related to enhancing their child's development. Furthermore, the IFSP must include outcomes and services for the child's family if the family wants to achieve specific outcomes related to the child's development.

Participants Who Develop the IEP/IFSP

At the beginning of our discussion about appropriate education, we wrote that the nondiscriminatory evaluation lays the foundation for the student's individualized plan (IEP or IFSP). We also wrote that the IEP team therefore must include at least one person who can link the evaluation to the IEP. But the team must include others as well:

- The student's parents
- At least one general education teacher with expertise related to the student's educational level
- At least one special education teacher
- A representative of the school system who is qualified to provide or supervise special education and is also knowledgeable about the general education curriculum and the availability of school resources
- An individual who can interpret the evaluation results
- At the discretion of the parent or agency, other individuals with expertise regarding the student's educational needs, including related-service personnel (for Thomas, those who know about mobility, communication, and assistive technology)
- The student, when appropriate

Other people may be included in the IEP or IFSP conference. For example, a parent might wish to bring a friend who knows about the special education process.

Timelines

IDEA requires an IEP to be developed for all students ages 3 through 21 and to be in effect at the beginning of each school year. Educators and parents may make changes in the IEP either through a team meeting or by developing a written document that amends or changes the current IEP. Also, the team must review and, if appropriate, revise the student's IEP at least once a year.

IDEA requires an IFSP to be developed within "a reasonable time" after the child has been assessed for early intervention services. The IFSP must be evaluated at least annually, and families have the right to a semi-annual review or a more frequent review based on the needs of the family, infant, and/or toddler.

IDEA does not have detailed requirements about the process that must be followed at IEP/IFSP conferences. Ideally, however, those conferences reflect partnerships among educators and parents. Sadly, research on the IEP/IFSP has generally reported that the traditional process tends to involve legal compliance—a paperwork process—rather than problem-solving, dynamic teamwork (Turnbull, Turnbull, Erwin, & Soodak, 2006). That fact is regrettable because the United States Supreme Court, in interpreting IDEA, has said that the "core" of IDEA is the "cooperative process" that occurs among the IEP team members, especially the student's parents (*Schaffer v. Weast*, 2005).

To ensure that the conference is indeed a meeting of partners, including the parents, IEP conferences should incorporate 10 activities (Turnbull et al., 2006):

1. Prepare in advance.
2. Connect and get started.
3. Review formal evaluation and current levels of performance.
4. Share resources, priorities, and concerns.
5. Share visions and great expectations.
6. Consider interaction of proposed student goals, placement, and services.
7. Translate student priorities into written goals (or outcomes).
8. Determine placement, supplementary aids/services, and related services.
9. Address assessment modifications and special factors.
10. Conclude the conference.

The purpose of the required IEP review is to determine whether the student is making progress toward achieving annual goals (IEP) or outcomes (IFSP). Accordingly, IDEA requires the IEP team to review the student's IEP and revise it as appropriate to secure that kind of progress. A review may cause a reevaluation and even change of placement.

Least Restrictive Environment

Once the schools have enrolled a student (the zero-reject principle), fairly evaluated the student (the nondiscriminatory evaluation principle), and provided an IEP/IFSP (the appropriate education principle), they must contribute one more element to the student's education— namely, education alongside students who do not have disabilities. This is the principle of the **least restrictive environment (LRE),** formerly known as the mainstreaming or integration rule and now known as the inclusion principle. Thomas benefits from the LRE presumption, as you see from this photo.

In early intervention (ages 0 through 2), IDEA favors education in the student's "natural environment," which could be home or an out-of-home center. In all other education (ages 3 through 21), IDEA favors placement in general education. The term *general education* has three dimensions: the academic curriculum, extracurricular activities, and other nonacademic activities (for example, recess, transportation, mealtimes, dances, and sports).

The Rule: A Presumption in Favor of Inclusion

IDEA creates a presumption in favor of educating students with disabilities alongside those who do not have disabilities. It does this by requiring that

IDEA favors education in general education classrooms. Educators use the term *inclusion*, while IDEA uses the term *least restrictive environment*.

(1) a school must educate a student with a disability with students who do not have disabilities to the maximum extent appropriate for the student; and (2) a school may not remove the student from the regular education environment unless, because of the nature or severity of the student's disability, he or she cannot be educated there successfully (appropriately, in the sense that the student will benefit), even after the school provides supplementary aids and support services for the student.

PEARSON
myeducationlab

Go to the Activities and Application section in Chapter 1 of MyEducationLab and complete Activity 3. As you interact with this simulation, think about how the principles described here in the text apply to this situation.

Access to General Education Curriculum

IDEA specifically states that the education of children with disabilities can be made more effective by having "high expectations" for them and ensuring their maximum access to the general education curriculum in the regular classroom, to meet their developmental goals and, to the greatest extent possible, the challenging academic expectations established for all children.

Setting Aside the Presumption

The school may set aside this presumption of inclusion only if the student cannot benefit from being educated with students who do not have disabilities and only after the school has provided the student with supplementary aids and services. In that event, the school may place the student in a less typical, more specialized, less inclusive program.

The Continuum of Services

Schools must offer a continuum, or range, of services from more to less typical and inclusive—that is, from less to more restrictive or separate. The most typical and inclusive setting is general education, followed by resource rooms, special classes, special schools, homebound services, and hospitals and institutions (also called residential or long-term care facilities). You will learn more about these different settings in Chapter 2.

Extracurricular and Nonacademic Inclusion

Schools also have to ensure that students with disabilities may participate in extracurricular and other nonacademic activities and services such as meals, recess periods, counseling, athletics, transportation, health services, recreational activities, special interest groups or clubs, and referrals to agencies that assist in employment and other aspects of life outside school.

In short, when providing academic, extracurricular, and other nonacademic activities and services to students who do not have disabilities, schools must include students with disabilities in all those activities and services, to the maximum extent appropriate for each child with a disability. That is because, as Congress said in 1997 and repeated in 2004, special education is a service for children rather than a place where they are sent.

Procedural Due Process

Schools do not always carry out IDEA's first four principles: zero reject, nondiscriminatory evaluation, appropriate education, and least restrictive environment. What's a parent to do? Or what if a school believes that one type of special education is appropriate, but a parent disagrees and believes that the proposed placement will not benefit the student? The answer lies in the **procedural due process** principle, which basically seeks to make schools and parents accountable to each other for carrying out the student's IDEA rights.

When parents and educators disagree, IDEA provides each with three different ways to resolve their disagreements. First, they may meet face to face in a "resolution" session. Second, they may resort to mediation. IDEA does not require mediation, and mediation may not be used to deny or delay the right to a due process hearing. But IDEA strongly encourages mediation. Third, if they still cannot resolve their disagreements, each has a right to a due process hearing (a mini-trial) before an impartial hearing officer. The due process hearing is similar to a regular courtroom trial. At the hearing, the parents and schools are entitled to be represented by lawyers, present evidence, and cross-examine each other's witnesses. If the local education agency or the parent is dissatisfied with the decision of the hearing officer, either may appeal to state or federal courts.

Parent and Student Participation

Although due process hearings and other procedural safeguards provide a system of checks and balances for schools and parents, IDEA also offers another, less adversarial accountability technique: the parent-student participation principle. You have already read that parents have many rights. They have the right to be members of the IEP team, to receive notice before the school does anything about the student's right to a free appropriate public education, and to use three dispute-resolution techniques (procedural due process).

In addition, parents have the right to have access to school records concerning their child and to control who has access to those records. Further, the state education agency must include parents on state and local special education advisory committees, thereby ensuring that their perspectives are incorporated into policy and program decisions.

Finally, one year before a student reaches the age of majority (usually age 18), the school must advise her that all of the IDEA rights that belonged to the parent will transfer to her when she attains the age of majority. The only exception to this transfer-of-rights rule is that the parents' rights will not transfer to the student if the student has been determined, under state law, to be incompetent. In that event, the rights transfer to the student's legally appointed guardian.

Bringing the Six Principles Together

How do the six principles ensure an appropriate education for students with disabilities? Figure 1.7 highlights the fact that the first four principles—zero reject, nondiscriminatory evaluation, appropriate education, and least restrictive environment—are the *inputs* into a student's education. The other two principles—procedural due process and parent-student participation—are *accountability techniques*, ways to make sure that the other four principles are implemented correctly. The figure identifies the principles and their purposes and shows their relationships.

Federal Funding of IDEA

Rights run with revenues. Accordingly, Congress grants federal money to state and local educational agencies (school districts) to assist them in educating students ages birth to 21. The state and local agencies, however, must agree to comply with IDEA's principles, or else they will not receive the federal money.

The state and local agencies may not simply substitute the federal money for the funds that they themselves raise and spend on special education; they may not supplant state and local money with federal money. The federal money supplements state and local contributions.

There is no doubt about this fact: special education is expensive, as the following facts reveal (Chambers, Shkolnik, & Pérez, 2003; Parrish et al., 2004):

◆ The federal investment in special education was $7.5 billion in the 2002–2003 school year. By contrast, the federal investment in the first year of IDEA's implementation (1977–1978) was $252 million. Although IDEA authorizes the federal government to cover the excess cost of special education up to 40 percent, federal aid in 2002–2003 was only 15.5 percent of the excess cost.

Figure 1.7 The relationships among the six principles of IDEA

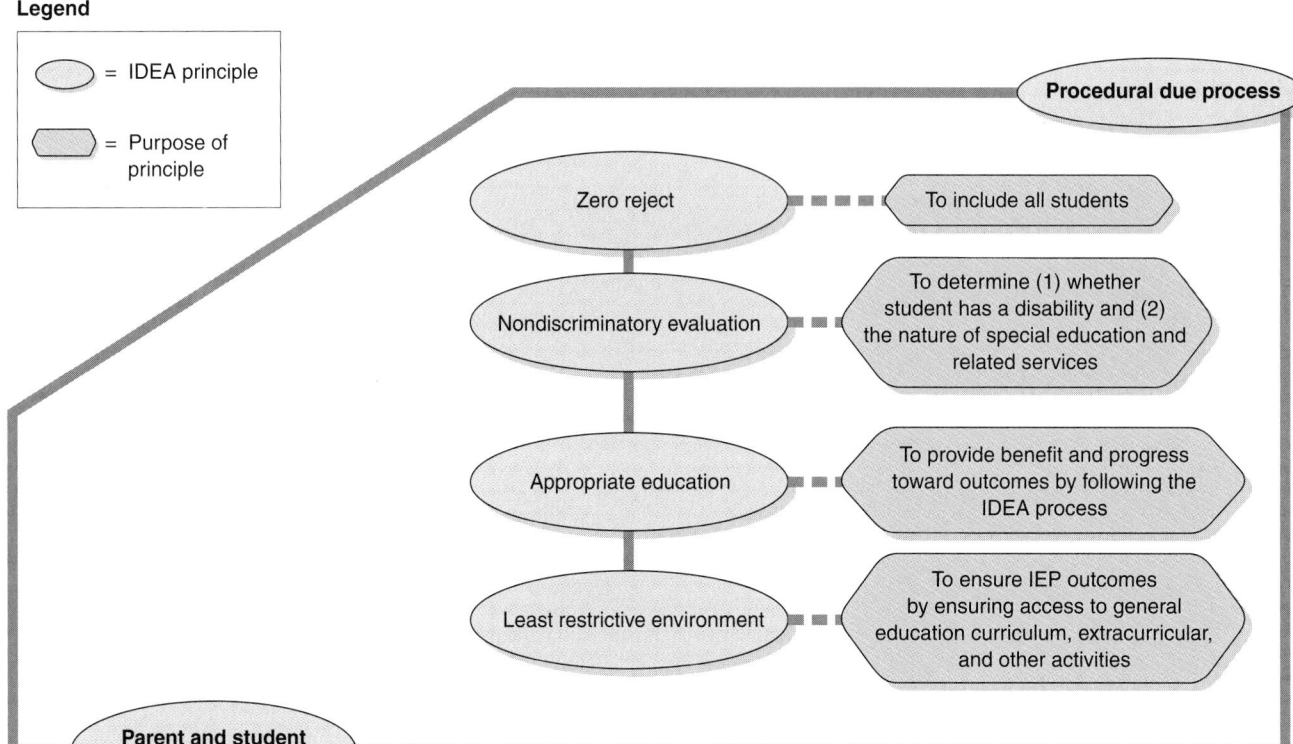

Legend

= IDEA principle

= Purpose of principle

Procedural due process

Zero reject
- - - To include all students

Nondiscriminatory evaluation
- - - To determine (1) whether student has a disability and (2) the nature of special education and related services

Appropriate education
- - - To provide benefit and progress toward outcomes by following the IDEA process

Least restrictive environment
- - - To ensure IEP outcomes by ensuring access to general education curriculum, extracurricular, and other activities

Parent and student participation

◆ It costs approximately $6.7 billion annually for all students with disabilites to go through the processes of referral, nondiscriminatory evaluation, and IEP development. That is a cost of $1,086 for each special education student, just to get to the point of delivering services.

◆ The average annual expenditure for a student with a disability ($12,525) (excluding students who are homebound) is 1.91 times greater than for a student in general education ($6,556).

◆ Two types of students with disabilities are the least expensive to educate: students with a specific learning disability and those with a communication disorder have per-student costs of approximately $10,750. By contrast, students with multiple disabilities are the most expensive and have an annual average cost of about $20,000 each.

As states seek to make education more cost-efficient, will they sacrifice effectiveness? Will cost cutting be undertaken at the expense of appropriate services? And how can schools be made more accountable for producing the results that Congress wants—equality of opportunity, full participation, independent living, and economic self-sufficiency—in light of the fact that the demand for services may be larger than the resources available to meet the demand?

Those are good questions. But consider them in this light: Each state has taken upon itself, usually in its constitution, the obligation to educate all children, including those with disabilities. Thus, IDEA assists the states to do what they would have to do in any event—educate all children with disabilities. IDEA supplements state and local school budgets.

The real question is this: Do the expenditures result in good outcomes for the students? Before we get to that question and its answers, let's consider a few other laws that apply to students with disabilities.

NCLB AND OTHER FEDERAL LAWS

Other federal laws affect special education and students in those programs. There are two types of laws: Some create an entitlement for students or authorize services for them. Others prohibit students from discrimination based on their disabilities.

No Child Left Behind Act

The No Child Left Behind Act (NCLB) of 2001 authorizes services. It seeks to improve educational outcomes for all students—those with and those without disabilities. President Bush justified NCLB in these words: "Too many children in America are segregated by low expectations, illiteracy, and self-doubt. In a consistently changing world that is demanding increasingly complex skills from its workforce, children are literally being left behind" (Bush, 2001a). He also observed that there are uneven educational outcomes for students, declaring: "We have a genuine national crisis. More and more, we are divided into two nations. One that reads, and one that doesn't. One that dreams, and one that doesn't" (Bush, 2001b).

Figure 1.8 identifies NCLB's six principles and highlights two requirements associated with each. We want to highlight findings related to NCLB's principle focusing on issues important to you, namely, teacher quality. Although most teachers are highly qualified (as defined by NCLB), there are shortages of special educators. Indeed, only 15 percent of special education teachers, 9 percent of middle school teachers, and 6 percent of teachers of students with limited English proficiency meet the NCLB standards of highly qualified (U.S. Department of Education, 2007a). Fifty-seven percent of all school districts face challenges in recruiting highly qualified special education teachers. The only teaching areas with greater recruitment challenges are science and math.

IDEA is aligned with NCLB because each seeks improved outcomes for students with disabilities (Turnbull et al., 2007; Yell, Shriner, & Katsiyannis, 2006). Has each, especially NCLB, been successful with respect to the principle of accountability for results by students with disabilities? Undoubtedly, NCLB holds schools accountable for the learning of students with disabilities. But it is not yet obvious that NCLB helps students with disabilities close the achievement gap between themselves and their classmates without disabilities (Perner, 2007; Wakeman, Browder, Meir, & McColl, 2007; Yell, Drasgow, & Lowrey, 2005).

Rehabilitation Act

The most important of several federal employment-related laws for students with disabilities is the Rehabilitation Act. Like NCLB, it authorizes services. If a person has a severe disability but, with rehabilitation, is able to work despite the disability, the person is entitled to two types of vocational rehabilitation services under the Rehabilitation Act. First, when the person is 16 years old, he may receive work evaluations, financial aid to pursue job training, and job locator services, all from the state rehabilitation agency.

Second, a person with severe disabilities, including a student, may enroll in a supported employment program. There, the student will work with the assistance of a job coach whose duties are to teach the person how to do a job and then help her to do it independently. The supported worker must be paid at least the minimum wage, work at least 20 hours a week in a typical work setting, and be able, after 18 months of supported employment, to do the job alone without support.

1. *Accountability for results.* Schools should sufficiently educate all students so that they demonstrate proficiency in certain core academic subjects (English, mathematics, and others). School districts that achieve student outcomes will be rewarded, and those that do not will be reformed.
   - By the 2005–2006 school year, each state must test students annually in grades 3 through 8 in reading and math and students in grades 10–12 at least once in reading and math.
   - Every student will be assessed accordng to each states' standard for proficiency in reading/language arts, math, and science by the end of the 2013–2014 school year.
2. *School safety.* Because all students need a safe environment in which to learn and achieve outcomes, schools are required to establish a plan for keeping schools safe and drug-free.
   - States must establish a uniform procedure for reporting data to parents and other citizens regarding school safety and drug-free schools.
   - When a state identifies a school as being persistently dangerous, the state must notify parents of every student and offer them opportunities to transfer to a safe school.
3. *Parental choice.* Parents of all students should have the opportunity to stay informed, in a full and accurate manner about achievement and safety so that they will be in a position to be full partners in their child's education.
   - Parents must receive a report about the overall achievement of students and the particular school their child attends, the qualifications of their child's teacher, and school safety.
   - Parents must be notified if their child is eligible to move to another school or district when their child's school is not making adequate progress in student outcomes, the school is considered to be "persistently dangerous," or the student has been a victim of a violent crime while on school grounds.
4. *Teacher quality.* Teachers should be proficient to teach and thus must meet certain federal and states' standards before they are certified to teach. States' receipt of federal funds will depend on their record in hiring "highly qualified" teachers.
   - Each state must develop a plan to ensure that all teachers of core academic subjects will be highly qualified by the end of the 2005–2006 school year. ("Highly qualified" means that each teacher has full certification and a bachelor's degree and has passed a state-administered test on core academic subject knowledge.)
   - Paraprofessionals hired after January 2002 must have an associate's degree or higher, or they must have completed two years of postsecondary study at an institution of higher education.
5. *Scientifically based methods of teaching.* Highly qualified teachers must use research-based curricula and instructional methods in order to ensure students' academic success.
   - Each state is responsible for establishing a Reading Leadership Team to ensure that schools that need to improve their reading achievement scores are using scientifically based instructional methods.
   - Schools that fail to meet adequate student achievement goals are required to use scientifically based instructional methods in order to remain open.
6. *Local flexibility.* State and local educational agencies have some discretion in using federal and state matching funds in order to respond to local problems in particularly local ways.
   - Education funding programs are consolidated so they will be easier to administer at the local level.
   - Money may be transferred from many federal programs to another federal program in order to address local needs (but no transfers of IDEA money are allowed).

Tech Act

The Technology-Related Assistance to Individuals with Disabilities Act of 1988 (as amended), often called the Tech Act, grants federal funds to the states so that they can help create statewide systems for delivering assistive technology devices and services to people with disabilities, including students with disabilities (Kemp, Hourcade, & Parette, 2000; Lahm, Bausch, Hasselbring, & Blackhurst, 2001). In Chapters 5 through 16, we describe how technology benefits students. You may remember that Thomas benefits from his assistive technology device, the "blinktwice" one his father helped design (www.blinktwice.com).

Assistive technology substantially increases opportunities for students with disabilities to make progress in the general curriculum.

Antidiscrimination Laws

IDEA and the Rehabilitation Act create personal entitlements; they provide direct services to eligible people. By contrast, the Tech Act creates a statewide capacity to serve people with disabilities. Instead of directly benefiting the people themselves, it helps the states meet the people's needs.

Education and rehabilitation are, of course, necessary to ameliorate the effects of a student's disability. But they are not sufficient by themselves to overcome the effects of the disability. IDEA, for example, does not prohibit public or private agencies from discriminating against the student on the basis of the student's disability. Yes, a student may receive special education, but that service might not create opportunities for the student to use the skills she has acquired through special education. Prejudice against people with disabilities may still foreclose opportunities for the student to show that, although she has a disability, the student is nonetheless still able.

How can society attack the prejudice? One answer is to use antidiscrimination laws like those that prohibit discrimination based on race or gender. The first such law, enacted in 1975 as an amendment to the Rehabilitation Act, is known as Section 504 (29 U.S.C. Sec. 794). The second, enacted in 1990, is the Americans with Disabilities Act (ADA) (42 U.S.C. Sections 12101–12213) (Huber & Jones, 2003; Rea & Davis-Dorsey, 2004; Wall & Sarver, 2003). These are fundamentally similar laws; they provide that no otherwise qualified individual with a disability shall, solely by reason of the disability, be discriminated against in certain realms of American life. Figure 1.9 sets out the meaning of "person with a disability" under Section 504 and ADA. The two laws use basically the same definition.

Section 504 applies to any program or activity receiving federal financial assistance. Because state and local education agencies receive federal funds, they may not discriminate against students or other persons with disabilities on account of their disabilities. As you will learn in Chapters 8 and 13, not all students with disabilities are entitled to IDEA benefits. But they are entitled to be free from disability discrimination. That's the effect of Section 504.

Clearly, Section 504 is limited in scope. What if an individual seeks employment from a company that does not receive any federal funds, wants to participate in state and local government programs that are not federally aided, or wants to have access to telecommunications systems such as closed captioning for people with hearing impairments? In none of those domains of life will the person receive any protection from Section 504. Instead, ADA comes to the rescue.

ADA extends its civil rights/nondiscrimination protection to the following sectors of American life: private-sector employment, transportation, state and local government activities and programs, privately operated businesses that are open to the public ("public accommodations"), and telecommunications.

Basically, IDEA and the Rehabilitation Act authorize federal, state, and local educational agencies to undertake programs in education and employment, respectively. Both laws

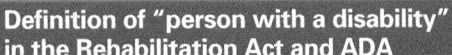

| Figure 1.9 | Definition of "person with a disability" in the Rehabilitation Act and ADA |

Section 504 of the Rehabilitation Act and ADA define a person with a disability as one who

- Has a physical or mental impairment that substantially limits one or more major life activities (e.g., traumatic brain injury)
- Has a record of such an impairment (e.g., history of cancer that is now in remission)
- Is regarded as having such an impairment (e.g., a person who is especially creative but simultaneously is chronically "wired" or "high" may be regarded as having some emotional disturbances or attention-deficit/hyperactivity disorders)

Note: A student who has HIV but is not so impaired that he or she needs special education is protected under Section 504 and ADA because the person meets the last two criteria: the person has a history of a disability, and others regard that person as having a disability. The same is true of a person who has attention-deficit/hyperactivity disorder (AD/HD). See Chapters 12 and 8, respectively, for other health impairments and AD/HD students' rights under IDEA, Section 504, and ADA.

provide funds for the state and local agencies to pay for those programs. By contrast, Section 504 and ADA prohibit discrimination solely on the basis of disability in education, employment, and other sectors of American life. But these two laws do not provide federal aid.

Together, these four laws support students' transition from school to postschool activities, including work. That is why the transition components of a student's IEP anticipate outcomes that are largely consistent with those that any student—whether one with a disability or not—typically will want: work, education, and opportunities to participate in the community. Those results cannot be achieved as long as discrimination exists.

SPECIAL EDUCATION RESULTS

After the schools started to implement IDEA in 1977, the federal criteria for evaluating special education results were primarily numerical. The questions were "How many more students are being served annually, and in what types of placements are they served?" Numbers, however, do not tell the full story.

That is why Congress amended IDEA in 1997 to require state and local education agencies to report outcomes. State and local education agencies still count and report to the U.S. Department of Education the number of students being served and tally their placements. But they now must report data that show that students are making progress toward their individual goals and toward other goals, too.

The reasoning behind this outcome-based accountability is that Congress has declared (in the 1997 and 2004 versions of IDEA) that improving education results for students with disabilities is an "essential element" of the nation's policy of ensuring equal opportunity, full participation, independent living, and economic self-sufficiency. Results count. They count for Congress. They count for your students. They certainly count for Stelios Gragoudas, who, like Thomas, has cerebral palsy. Read about Stel in Box 1.1 and consider his outcome.

The same task exists for general education under NCLB: to improve the educational results for all students. Each state and each of its school districts must set 5-year goals for improving the academic scores of all students, whether in general or special education, on standardized tests. If the students do not meet these goals by obtaining higher scores, NCLB provides several ways of improving the schools.

Like IDEA, NCLB emphasizes that outcomes—measured by academic achievement— count for all students. For that reason, each student with a disability must take the state and district assessments, the tests of student achievement. If a student's IEP team excuses the student because of the extent of the student's disability, the student takes an alternative assessment (see Chapter 2).

Stel Goes to Graduate School

Education has always been an important part of my life. My parents always stressed the importance of having the best education you possibly could obtain. It wasn't only learning that excited me; it was also being with other students, playing kickball, and making friends that enriched my educational experience.

I began my school career at the same time that P.L. 94-142 (better known today as IDEA) was passed. Therefore, educating students with disabilities was a new experience for my school district. The faculty did not know how to include students with disabilities into a program for students without disabilities. My teachers did the best they could by including me in all the instances they thought were appropriate. For the subjects that I needed extra help in, I went to a resource room where I could receive the extra assistance I needed. Thinking back, I liked that system. Even though I was out of my homeroom for a couple of hours a week, I still felt as if that room was my base. It was where all my friends were and where I could do exactly what all the other students were doing.

All that changed when I went to middle school and high school. It was as if my education took a 360-degree turn. When a student moves up to middle school, academics are the focal point of the educational experience. Therefore, my educational team had to answer a very important question: Could I keep up with the academic program that was offered at the middle school? My teachers were not too optimistic. They believed that even though I had fared well in elementary school, middle school was going to be too challenging for me. My parents, however, insisted that I be included in the general curriculum as much as possible. So my IEP called for me to be placed in the general curriculum for some of my subjects and in a resource room for the others.

This program was similar to my elementary school experience with one great distinction. In middle school, my base was not the place where I felt included. It was the place where I felt excluded. That base was my resource room, where I was excluded from most of the students who were in my academic classes. This did not allow me to form the kinds of friendships that I did in elementary school. I do not have many fond memories of that period of my educational career.

High school was a similar situation. Even though I had good grades in all of my academic classes, my teachers still recommended that academics should not be the focal point of my education and that I should focus on vocational goals. My parents did not agree with this plan. They always believed that I should be pushed to my limit.

The school agreed with hesitation and opted to place me in a collaborative program within the high school. I would be able to participate in the high school classes, and the collaborative program would provide me with a tutor and other supports that I needed to succeed in high school. As I look back, the program was not all that bad. It provided me with additional services that I needed to succeed in my high school, such as speech therapy and adapted gym.

However, the same thing that had happened in middle school was happening all over again. Instead of feeling like a student at my high school, I felt like a guest. Even though I had my classes with students in the high school, when class was over, they would go in one direction and I would go back to the collaborative program. Even though I was free to eat lunch with them, I chose not to because I felt like an outsider who was only a guest in the high school and I felt at home eating lunch with my fellow classmates in the collaborative program.

I always knew that I wanted to go to college. It was what everyone else in my class was thinking about, so I caught the bug as well. Once again, however, I met opposition from my special education teachers. The teachers from my high school classes were more supportive because they knew the work I had done in their classes and felt that I was ready for college-level academics.

The process of applying to school was very exciting. The experience of going to visit schools, meeting students with disabilities who were already in college, writing essays, and finding out how colleges supported people with disabilities was extremely informative.

It also provided me with a new idea of what it meant to be independent. To that point, independence to me meant going to the mall by myself or going on a trip with my friend instead of my family. In college, independence meant making sure I had all of the supports that I needed to live independently or talking with professors about accommodations that I needed in class. College gave me two things. It gave me the academic background that I needed to begin the career that I am still in today. Equally important, it gave me the skills I needed to live independently and to direct my own future.

I have earned my Ph.D. and am working in higher education in Massachusetts. Sometimes I think it would be amusing to go back to my high school and show some of my old teachers what I have accomplished since I started postsecondary education, but then I think it would be a better idea to focus my attention on improving special education and education as a whole so that every student with a disability can receive the most appropriate education alongside classmates without disabilities.

Having described the policy, let's return to IDEA and its results. What did Congress mean when it spoke about equality of opportunity, full participation, independent living, and economic self-sufficiency as the national goals and thus the appropriate outcomes for students with disabilities? Here are the four terms and general definitions for each:

- *Equality of opportunity.* People with disabilities will have the same chances and opportunities in life as people without disabilities. Without equal opportunity, they cannot achieve the other three outcomes.
- *Full participation.* People with disabilities will have opportunities to be included in all aspects of their community and will be protected from any attempts by people to segregate them solely on the basis of their disability.
- *Independent living.* People with disabilities will have the opportunity to fully participate in decision making and to experience autonomy in making choices about how to live their lives.
- *Economic self-sufficiency.* People with disabilities will be provided with opportunities to engage fully in income-producing work or unpaid work that contributes to a household or community.

What is the evidence related to these results? Unfortunately, research on results for students with disabilities does not provide definitive answers. Three indicators, however, show that substantial tasks lie ahead.

The first indicator is the extent to which students with disabilities are completing their high school education. People with disabilities are twice as likely not to complete high school or college as people without disabilities (21 percent versus 10 percent) (National Organization on Disability, 2004). Students with visual impairments, hearing impairments, and traumatic brain injury are more likely than other IDEA students to earn diplomas. Those with emotional or behavioral disorders, intellectual disability, and multiple disabilities are least likely to earn their diplomas (U.S. Department of Education, 2007b). From 1993–1994 through 2002–2003, students in almost all disability categories had an improved graduation rate; the largest gains were made by students with deaf-blindness and autism. Students who are American Indian/Alaskan Native and African American are more likely to drop out of school than other racial/ethnic groups (see Chapter 3).

The second indicator relates to the area of postschool employment. Clearly, adults who are employed increase their chances for full participation, independent living, and especially economic self-sufficiency. Although the rate of full- or part-time employment for people without disabilities is 78 percent, the rate for individuals with disabilities is only 35 percent—a gap of 43 percentage points (National Organization on Disability, 2004). The employment rate for individuals with more severe disabilities is even lower: Only 19 percent of individuals with severe disabilities work either full or part time. Further, Latino and African American individuals with severe disabilities are much less likely to be employed than are European American individuals with severe disabilities (National Council on Disability, 2000).

The third indicator relates to overall satisfaction with life. Approximately two thirds of individuals without disabilities report that they are very satisfied with life in general; by contrast, approximately one third of individuals with disabilities report the same satisfaction. People with very severe disabilities are much less satisfied with life in general than are people with somewhat severe, slight, or moderate disabilities. The following trends contribute to general life satisfaction (National Organization on Disability, 2004):

- Three times as many individuals with disabilities live in households whose annual income is below $15,000, compared to individuals without disabilities (26 percent versus 9 percent).
- Individuals with disabilities are twice as likely to have inadequate transportation.
- Individuals with disabilities are less likely to attend religious services, socialize, and eat out in restaurants.
- People with disabilities are more than twice as likely to go without needed health care.

Here's the question you have to answer for yourself: Given that there is a great deal of room for improvement in achieving results for students with disabilities, what role will you play in making it possible for students with disabilities to make progress in the special and general curriculum so that their long-term results are as positive as possible? We hope our book helps you answer the question.

VALUES AND OUTCOMES

No one is more qualified to write about Thomas Ellenson's future and about the values that drive them and his special educators than his father and mother, Richard and Lora. This is their view of their son's future. Truth be told, it is a vision that we, the authors of this book and the parents of children with exceptional traits, share wholeheartedly. Please note that, in the remaining chapters, we, the authors, write the "values and outcomes statement." For this chapter, however, the Ellensons speak for themselves.

For us, Tom is best understood through a story that's a bit hard to tell.

When he was 5, Tom went in for a double osteotomy, a surgery needed by many kids with CP. When children don't walk, their hipbones often don't settle in the hip sockets quite right. To fix the problem before it gets worse, the children have an operation during which both femurs are sawed in half, hip sockets are filled out with bone chip, and the bones are bolted back together at a new angle.

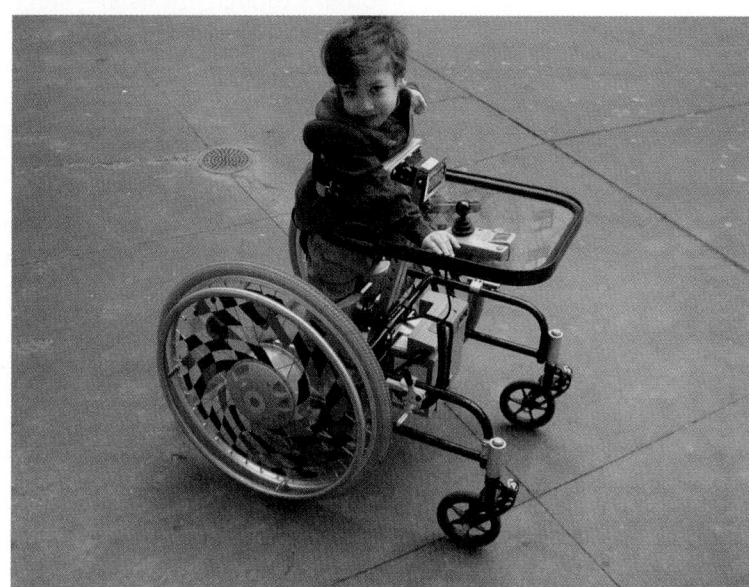

Tom's parents look toward his future and envision him embracing his potential and striving to reach it.

Tom came home from the hospital after five days. His entire body was in a cast. It went from the middle of his chest down to his ankles. His legs were spread out in a large "v": a steel bar went from one calf to the other so there could be absolutely no movement.

Tom lay on his side for nearly four weeks, held up by plaster, steel, and a half-dozen pillows. But he never showed sadness. He never showed frustration or anger. He watched *Blue's Clues* and *Monty Python*, and every night, as a family, we watched *Emeril Live*. A friend of ours got Tom a Spongebob Squarepants karaoke machine and Tom gurgled and wailed to the CDs we played on it: Beatles and Kidz Bop and Avril Lavigne. Think of that: our friend knew Tom couldn't verbalize, but she also understood that, in Tom's head, that didn't mean he wasn't singing.

During this time, Tom's 13-month-old sister, Taite, would lie and crawl on the floor in front of the TV. And one day as we were all watching, Taite got up and took her first steps. She wobbled from the TV over to where Tom lay, his body held rigid by the steel and cobalt blue gauze, and she plopped forward onto the couch. "Taite!" she warbled. And Tom just giggled and giggled, his face alight with love.

That is our son.

What do we expect for his future? Well, having now met many people in the disabled community, we realize they are filled with many feelings. But among them are so often patience, focus, realism, and optimism. This is not simply the reality we choose to see. It is the way things are. Amid the struggles and the difficulties and, certainly, the moments of sadness and depression we have shared with many people—disabled children, disabled adults, their parents and friends—the overriding emotion in this world is one of happiness. We live within a community that embraces the gift of life.

From a practical perspective, we expect Tom to continue his education and eventually attend college. We expect he will find a job that satisfies him. Like many parents, we do not want to force the specifics of our expectations nor our own backgrounds and interests on him.

Certainly there are many challenges ahead: Tom will need to develop physical access methods so he can work more effectively on the computers with which he already has reasonable proficiency. As he gets older, he will need to develop more consistent and deeper methods of communication. On a very fundamental level, he will need to learn to eat a wider variety of foods.

But although these are certainly significant issues, they are secondary to the broader foundation behind a meaningful life. And as such, what we wish primarily for Tom is that he embraces his potential and then always strives to reach it. We know he will do his share to make that happen. Yet to some degree, it is up to those of us who surround and support the disabilities community to make sure others understand that this is possible.

It must be difficult for people if they cannot verbalize. But it is only tragic if they are not heard. It must be hard to be unable to walk. But it is tragic to be left behind. Our dream for Tom is that he find those individuals who understand these distinctions and who see not the limitations but the person who lives among them, for these will be the people who share Tom's infinite capacity to appreciate life.

WHAT DO YOU THINK?

1. Do you agree with Richard Ellenson that it is important to teach Thomas to be all he can be? If so, you value great expectations.

2. Do you agree with Richard Ellenson that teaching techniques that work for Thomas help all students, not just those with disabilities? If you do, you have just subscribed to universally designed learning (UDL), a technique that highlights Thomas's positive contributions to others.

3. Is Thomas's "killer smile"—that "easy magic"—his only positive attribute? If not, what are his others? His willingness to work at being "just Thomas" and part of his school? Aren't those his strengths?

4. Do you agree that Thomas's teachers should help him achieve "whatever he wants in life for himself?" If so, you believe in choices.

5. Does it make sense for Richard and Lora, and Thomas's teachers, to adapt their home and schools for him? If so, you subscribe to inclusion and relationships.

6. Would you deny Thomas an effective, outcome-driven education? If not, you believe in his full citizenship and its hallmarks—equal opportunity, economic self-sufficiency, independent living, and full participation.

ADDRESSING THE STANDARDS: THE VALUES CONNECTION

The following CEC Knowledge and Skill Standards: Common Core and Values are addressed in this chapter through the content and concepts we discuss.

CEC Knowledge and Skill Standards: Common Core	Values/Standards Connection
CEC Knowledge and Skill Standard I. Foundations CC1K1 Models, theories, and philosophies that form the basis for special education practice. CC1K2 Laws, policies, and ethical principles regarding behavior management, planning, and implementation. CC1K3 Relationship of special education to the organization and function of educational agencies. CC1K4 Rights and responsibilities of students, parents, teachers, and other professionals, and schools related to exceptional learning needs. CC1K5 Issues in definition and identification of individuals with exceptional learning needs, including those from culturally and linguistically diverse backgrounds. CC1K6 Issues, assurances, and due process rights related to assessment, eligibility, and placement within a continuum of services. CC1K7 Family systems and the role of families in the educational process. CC1S1 Articulate personal philosophy of special education.	CEC Standard 1 incorporates knowledge and skills related to IDEA and its requirements. IDEA implements the U.S. Constitution's guarantee that everyone will be treated equally under the law. Equal opportunity is a national policy goal and a pathway to *full citizenship* in America. By knowing how special education has developed in this country and the rights of the students and their families, you will be more effective in teaching and learning from students. Negative labeling can inhibit students', families', and teachers' *great expectations*.
CEC Knowledge and Skill Standard V. Learning Environments and Social Interactions CC5S2 Identify realistic expectations for personal and social behavior in various settings. CC5S3 Identify supports needed for integration into various program placements. CC5S4 Design learning environments that encourage active participation in individual and group settings. CC5S6 Use performance data and information from all stakeholders to make or suggest modifications in learning environments.	Developing knowledge and skills related to the continuum of services ties to CEC Standard 5. Expect Thomas and other students with a disability to develop (with the assistance of general and special educators, their peers, and their families) their inherent *strengths* and to make *positive contributions* to their peers, their schools, and their communities.
CEC Knowledge and Skill Standard VII. Instructional Planning CC7S1 Identify and prioritize areas of the general curriculum and accommodations for individuals with exceptional learning needs. CC7S2 Develop and implement comprehensive, longitudinal individualized programs in collaboration with team members. CC7S3 Involve the individual and family in setting instructional goals and monitoring progress.	Developing knowledge and skills related to the IEP/IFSP reflects an application of CEC Standard 7, Instructional Planning. A student with a disability can make *positive contributions* to other IEP team members by identifying what the student needs to make progress in the general curriculum.

Source: From CEC Knowledge and Skill Standards: Common Core and Values. Copyright by The Council for Exceptional Children. Reprinted with permission.

SUMMARY

Profile of Special Education Students and Personnel in Today's Schools

◆ Over 6 million infants, young children, and students ages 6 through 21 have disabilities and benefit from special education.

◆ Approximately two thirds of special education students are male.

◆ Students who are gifted and talented represent 6.4 percent of the schools' enrolled students.

◆ Slightly more than two thirds of all students with disabilities are classified into the categories of specific learning disabilities and speech or language impairments.

◆ Language sensitivity is important; along with nearly all professionals, we recommend the use of people-first language.

◆ There are shortages of teachers and related-service personnel.

◆ The teacher shortage in special education is greater than the teacher shortage in general education.

Overview of the Law and Special Education

◆ The preludes to today's federal special education law were the school desegregation case (*Brown*) and two cases requiring schools to educate students with disabilities.

◆ The federal law, enacted in 1975 and reauthorized in 2004, is the Individuals with Disabilities Education Act.

◆ There are 12 categories of disabilities for children ages 6 through 21.

◆ The law benefits infants and toddlers (Part C) and students ages 6 through 21 (Part B).

IDEA: Six Principles

◆ IDEA has six principles:
  • Zero reject, a rule against exclusion
  • Nondiscriminatory evaluation, a rule of fair assessments
  • Appropriate education, a rule of individualized benefit
  • Least restrictive placement, a presumption in favor of placement in general education programs
  • Procedural due process, a rule of fair dealing and accountability
  • Parent and student participation, a rule of shared decision making

◆ The first four principles are inputs into a student's education. The last two are accountability techniques.

◆ Federal funding of special education supplements state and local funding.

No Child Left Behind Act and Other Federal Laws

◆ NCLB has six principles:
  • Accountability for results, a rule for enhanced student academic outcomes
  • Teacher quality, a rule to improve teacher credentials
  • Scientifically based methods of teaching, a rule to increase the delivery of research-based instruction
  • School safety, a rule to keep schools safe and drug-free
  • Local flexibility, a rule to increase local decision making
  • Parental choice, a rule to provide options to parents to transfer their child

◆ The Rehabilitation Act provides for work training, especially supported employment.

◆ The Tech Act makes assistive technology available statewide in each state.

◆ The Americans with Disabilities Act and Section 504 of the Rehabilitation Act prohibit discrimination solely on the basis of disability in a wide range of services, both in and outside school.

Special Education Results

◆ Students with disabilities are twice as likely not to complete high school or college as students without disabilities.

◆ From 1993–1994 through 2002–2003, students in almost all disability categories had an improved graduation rate. But the employment rate for individuals with disabilities is only about 35 percent—

a gap of 43 percentage points below individuals without disabilities.

◆ Across both graduation rates and employment, individuals from culturally diverse backgrounds are less likely to have favorable outcomes.

◆ Individuals without disabilities are twice as satisfied with life as are individuals with disabilities.

Now go to MyEducationLab at www.myeducationlab.com and take the Self-Assessment to gauge your initial comprehension of chapter content. Once you have taken the Self-Assessment, use your individualized Study Plan for Chapter 1 to enhance your understanding of the concepts discussed in the chapter.

2

Ensuring Progress in the General Education Curriculum Through Universal Design for Learning and Inclusion

◆ WHO IS DANI GONZALEZ?

When Arthur Laurents, Leonard Bernstein, and Stephen Sondheim collaborated to create the modern version of Shakespeare's *Romeo and Juliet,* produced in 1958 as *West Side Story,* they could not have known how well the character Tony's expectant song "Something's Coming" would suit Dani Gonzalez, a fifth-grade student at Valley Park Elementary School in Overland Park, Kansas. Tony declares, "I've got a feeling there's a miracle due. . . . Something great is coming . . . It's only just out of reach. . ." (Laurents & Sondheim, 1979).

For Dani, that something great just out of reach was sufficient self-confidence in her ability to speak out among her peers, enough to overcome her speech impairment and fully participate in her class. Instead of being written by Laurents and Sondheim, Dani's story is being composed by Lauren Priest, a special education resource-room teacher, and Erin Lane, a general education fifth-grade teacher. Erin wrote to Lauren:

I ran down to see you. . . . I just had to tell you about Dani and class meeting today. Normally she is always the last one to give her compliment and I really

have to help her and you KNOW how quietly she can speak. Well, today was TOTALLY different! She had her [compliment] ready, said it the first time and was as loud as could be! The kids [15 fifth graders in general education] were all so excited for her, they gave her a big applause and all gave her a compliment for that! Then, she had ANOTHER one! It was so awesome to see her interact with her peers that way! Was so proud! Just goes to

show what you [Lauren] are doing is working and that she is really benefiting from being with her peers!

Lauren continued Dani's story by writing that same day to Luz Gonzalez, Dani's mother:

> Some pretty incredible things went on today . . . We are having our fifth-grade literature circles . . . she is reading "Stone Fox". . . . We then have a discussion with about 15 fifth graders from all classes. Today, Dani raised her hand to participate 4 times on her own!! Her answers were also correct and appropriate and she didn't need any prompting from me at all. This is huge, considering that I have never seen her raise her hand on her own! . . . She is making such huge growths in her confidence; you have no idea how proud I am of her.

Sometimes, indeed, that "something great" is "just around the corner." Dani had pointed herself to that corner, but she could not have turned it on her own.

She was diagnosed as having speech-language delays (severe apraxia) when she was 3 years and 9 months old, and has received speech-language intervention since she was 4 years old (in early childhood special education and in elementary school). The intervention focuses on her ability to speak intelligibly; she has a lisp, and, because her parents, Luz (from Colombia) and Carlos (from Spain) speak Spanish at home, Dani speaks English with a Spanish accent.

Dani is included with her nondisabled peers to learn writing, science, and social studies. To teach reading, Lauren uses an evidence-based reading program (Horizons), modifies the curriculum by using graphic organizers, and provides specially designed instruction in the form of direct (one-on-one) instruction to teach spelling. To teach math, Lauren uses another research-based program (Number Worlds). Her immediate goal is to have Dani increase her reading and math skills by another 25 percent to 30 percent; her long-term goal is to have Dani perform grade-level work without direct support. That's why direct instruction through evidence-based reading and math programs is necessary now.

"I firmly believe," wrote Lauren, ". . . [that inclusion] is working. Dani is able to complete any task put before her if we provide the appropriate accommodations and modifications." Using accommodations in science and social studies, Dani has a grade average of 90 percent or better. Lauren asks Dani to focus on the big picture and allows her to respond in different ways, "but essentially it is the same content material."

What Lauren was reporting is that Dani was making progress in the general education curriculum, which is the goal for all children and the intent of federal laws like IDEA and NCLB.

Dani's speech challenges, with their resulting impact on her self-confidence and her ability to read, are not her only challenges. She has been diagnosed with diabetes and receives insulin through a pump that she and the school nurse both monitor. And she still

CHAPTER OBJECTIVES

As you read in Chapter 1, the three major themes of this book are inclusion, universal design, and parent-school partnerships. In this chapter, you will learn about inclusion and universal design.

◆ You will learn about inclusion, or, as IDEA terms it, how Dani participates and makes progress in the general curriculum.
◆ You will learn the definitions of supplementary aids and services and universal design for learning and how they benefit Dani and other students, and then you will learn the meaning of inclusion and how it and a student's IEP make it possible for students like Dani to participate and make progress in the general curriculum.
◆ Finally, you will learn what you and your colleagues in general and special education can teach students so they will make the progress that IDEA wants and that Dani, her teachers, and her parents want for her as well.

needs instruction in some functional academic skills (stating and writing completely her name, birthday, address, and important telephone numbers) and self-help skills (knowing how many carbohydrates she is ingesting and then giving herself appropriate amounts of insulin).

Her teachers describe Dani as "extremely happy . . . social . . . gets along wonderfully with her peers and adults . . . very responsible, always completing her homework and able to independently follow a schedule and make changes/judgments as needed . . . extremely hard worker who is eager to learn . . . always puts forth her best effort . . . beginning to demonstrate more self-confidence than in past years."

What explains how Dani found "just around the corner" that "something great," her self-confidence among her peers? Was it her well (and recently) trained teachers? Their use of evidence-based practices? The support she receives at home from Luz, Carlos, and her brother Juan? The fact that she has been included in the general education classroom during her fifth-grade year (in contrast to her fourth-grade year)? Her personality? Will her social self-confidence become academic self-confidence, too?

There is no single, right answer; indeed, all of the questions should be answered "yes."

Still just around the corner lie two challenges. First, to sustain Dani's progress in all aspects of fifth grade. Second, to continue planning her transition from the substantially separate curriculum that comprised her work in fourth grade into the general education curriculum, extracurricular, and other school activities of middle school in fall 2008. A multidisciplinary team of general and special educators from Dani's current school and the middle school started the planning in August of her last year in elementary school. The planning will continue throughout the school year, with Luz and Carlos fully participating in it.

Is it unrealistic for Dani's teacher-parent team to expect something great, just around the school-year corner? No. Indeed, it would violate IDEA's theme of high expectations achieved through qualified teachers using evidence-based interventions for them to expect anything but "something great" from Dani.

If you were in Valley Park Elementary School, you would hear a song as you enter the fourth- and fifth-grade pod where Dani and her peers attend classes. A chorus consisting of Dani, her teachers, and her family is singing. You know the song already: "Could be! Who knows? . . . I've got a feeling there's a miracle due. . . . Come on, deliver to me!"

IEP Tip

The IEP team must design an IEP that ensures student involvement with and progress in the general education curriculum as well as addressing the student's other educational needs.

WHAT IS "PROGRESS IN THE GENERAL EDUCATION CURRICULUM"?

In this chapter, we address universal design and inclusion as foundations for high quality special education services. In Chapter 3 we discuss multiculturalism, and in Chapter 4 we discuss partnerships. Inclusion and universal design are means to an end. That end is that students like Dani Gonzalez will make progress in the general education curriculum. Before we talk about the means, then, we should think more about the end. What does "progress in the general education curriculum" mean?

First, progress is what federal law promotes and requires. As you learned from reading Chapter 1, IDEA requires each student's IEP to state how the student will be involved with and progress in the general education curriculum, how the student's progress will be assessed, and how state- and district-wide assessments will be modified (as appropriate) for the student. The No Child Left Behind Act (NCLB) requires assessment of students' proficiency and exempts no students from assessment. NCLB covers students with disabilities but, like IDEA, it allows for appropriate individualized modifications as set out in a student's IEP.

Second, progress in the general education curriculum is achieved by **standards-based reform:** a process that identifies the academic content (reading, mathematics, sci-

lists the department's categories of educational placement and defines each placement (also called "environment").

Figure 2.5 shows the percentage of students with disabilities who are educated in each category and changes in placement in each category. The figure underscores the steady increase in the number of students being included in the general education curriculum.

For example, in 1984–1985 about one quarter of students with disabilities received their education outside the regular class for less than 21 percent of the school day, but by 2003–2004 this percentage had increased to 50 percent (U.S. Department of Education, 2005a).

Clearly, fewer students with disabilities are being served outside the general education classroom than in years past, and the amount of time they spend outside the classroom has decreased. In addition, the number of students in self-contained and separate facilities is gradually decreasing. The number of students in residential facilities and in homebound or hospital placements has remained at a low level over this entire time period.

Not surprisingly, the percentage of students with disabilities in the different placement categories varies according to the age of students and their type of disability. More elementary students than secondary students are served in typical schools with peers who do not have disabilities. Students with less intensive support needs (e.g., speech or language impairments and learning disabilities) are more likely to be in general education classrooms for the largest percentage of time compared with students with more intensive support needs (e.g., students with intellectual disability or multiple disabilities). In Chapters 5 through 16 you will learn what percentage of students, by disability category, are in general education. In Chapter 4, you will learn that students from racially or ethnically diverse backgrounds are disproportionately represented in special education, and you will revisit that challenge throughout the book.

Issues in Residential, Home, and Hospital Placements

Settings that have a residential component—special boarding schools and hospitals and students' homes—are generally regarded as the most restrictive placements. Students who attend residential schools sometimes do so because their local schools have not developed

Figure 2.5 Percentage of students (rounded upward) ages 6–21 in different education environments during the 2006–2007 school year

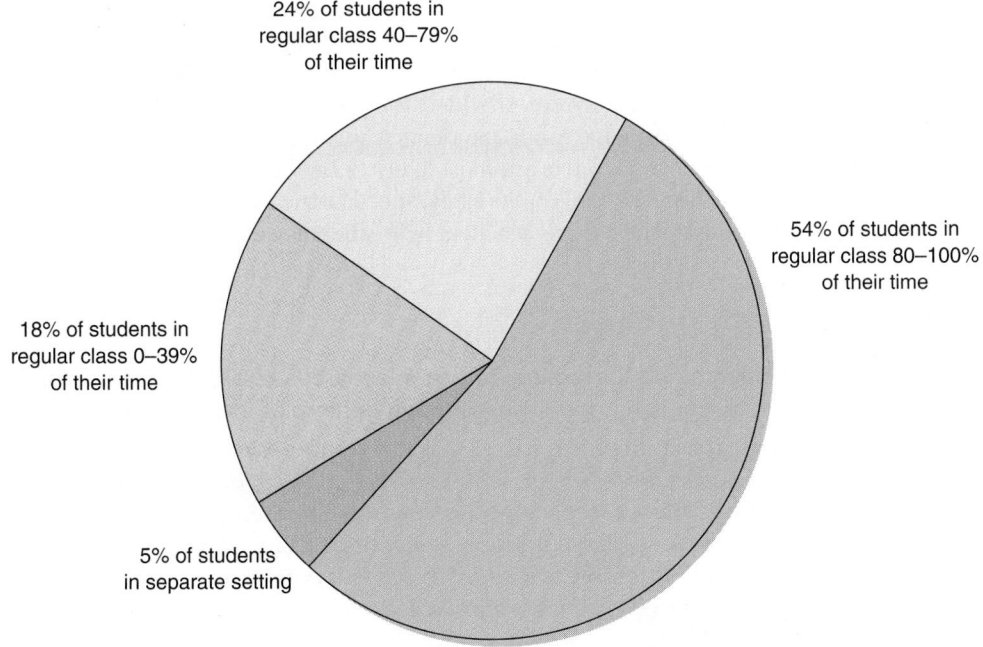

24% of students in regular class 40–79% of their time

54% of students in regular class 80–100% of their time

18% of students in regular class 0–39% of their time

5% of students in separate setting

the capacity to provide special education services for them. Sometimes, however, they attend special schools to acquire capacity to learn in more typical settings, as, for example, when they are relearning after a traumatic brain injury (Chapter 13). Thus, it is important to distinguish situations in which a student needs a more restrictive environment from those in which schools need to expand their capacity to serve all students.

Yet residential settings can also provide a concentrated group of talented educators and can benefit students, some of whom may prefer to be with other students with the same disability. As compared with other students with disabilties, students with hearing impairments, visual impairments, and deaf-blindness are most likely to attend residential schools (U.S. Department of Education, 2005a). Similarly, students with physical disabilities, emotional disorders, and traumatic brain injury are most likely to be educated in a hospital or their home (U.S. Department of Education, 2005a). As illustrated in Figure 2.4, however, a low percentage of students are in these settings; this percentage has remained relatively stable over time.

PEARSON myeducationlab

Go to the Activities and Application section in Chapter 2 of MyEducationLab and complete Activity 4. As you watch the videos and answer the accompanying questions, consider the benefits of this placement setting for students with visual impairments.

Issues in Special-School Placements

Separate schools typically congregate students from a specific disability category and provide services specifically related to the characteristics of that disability. As compared with other students with disabilties, students with emotional or behavioral disorders are those most likely to be educated in special schools; the next most likely are students with deaf-blindness and autism (U.S. Department of Education, 2005a). Students, particularly those with emotional disorders and autism, are frequently placed in special schools because of problem behavior that many teachers do not know how to address.

Issues in Specialized-Settings Placements Within Typical Schools

Specialized settings in many schools include resource rooms and self-contained classes. As reflected in Figure 2.4, students who receive 21 percent to 60 percent of their education outside the regular classroom typically are served in resource rooms. Resource rooms are staffed by special education teachers who work with students with disabilities for as little as one period or as many as several periods during the school day, depending upon students' needs for specially designed instruction. Students with learning disabilities and other health impairments are most likely to be served in resource rooms (U.S. Department of Education, 2005a). But students with other disabilities also benefit from resource rooms. Dani is one of them. She has special reading and math instruction from Lauren Priest in a resource room, but she also participates in Erin Lane's fifth-grade general education class for writing, science, and social studies (with support by a paraprofessional).

The second type of specialized setting within typical schools is the special education classroom. Special classrooms usually are provided for students with more intense needs than those students served in resource rooms. Students with mental retardation, autism, multiple disabilities, and emotional disorders are most likely to be served in special classrooms (U.S. Department of Education, 2005a). Traditionally, special education classrooms serve students with more severe disabilities; there, teachers help students acquire functional skills.

◆ **IEP Tip**

The IEP team is responsible for making placement decisions, and while IDEA allows placement across several settings, IDEA's presumption is for students with disabilities to be educated in the general education classroom with their nondisabled peers.

What Is Inclusion?

As we said at the beginning of this section, inclusion is based on IDEA's principle of the least restrictive environment. IDEA has a presumption in favor of inclusion. It states that

> each state must establish procedures to assure that, to the *maximum extent appropriate, children with disabilities . . . are educated with children who are not disabled*, and special classes, separate schooling, or other removal of children with disabilities from the regular educational environment occurs *only when the nature or severity of the disability of a child is such that education in regular education with the use of supplementary aids and services cannot be achieved satisfactorily.*" [italics added].

Inclusion, then, refers to the participation of students with disabilities alongside their nondisabled peers in academic, extracurricular, and other school activities. Inclusive practices have a long history in the field of special education. Figure 2.6 summarizes that history.

Supplementary aids and services are "aids, services, and other supports that are provided in general education classes, other education-related settings, and in extracurricular and nonacademic settings, *to enable children with disabilities to be educated with nondisabled children to the maximum extent appropriate* [italics added]." These aids and services facilitate placement in and compliance with the regulations for the least restrictive environment: "*To the maximum extent appropriate, children with disabilities . . . are educated with children who are nondisabled* [italics added]." IDEA allows placements other than the general education classroom, but it presumes that the setting of choice for students is the general education classroom and that students must not be removed from that setting unless inclusion in the general education classroom cannot be achieved satisfactorily with the use of supplementary aids and services and specially designed instruction. Consistent with IDEA and with Luz and Carlos Gonzalez's expectations for their daughter, Dani has a placement (general education classroom with support for writing, science, and social studies, plus resource room for highly individualized reading instruction) and supplementary aids and services (the school nurse's assistance with her diabetes pump) that exemplify the inclusion principle.

Inclusion is mandatory for all school activities.

Characteristics of Inclusion

Inclusion has four key characteristics: home-school placement, the principle of natural proportions, restructuring teaching and learning, and age- and grade-appropriate placements.

Home-school placement. Within an inclusive model, students attend the same school they would have attended if they did not have an exceptionality. This is the same school other children in the student's neighborhood attend. Dani lives in the Valley Park elementary school neighborhood and attends her neighborhood school; by attending Valley Park, Dani,

Figure 2.6 ▶	**Four consecutive phases of inclusion**

1. *Mainstreaming:* an educational arrangement of returning students from special education classrooms to general education classrooms, typically for nonacademic portions of the school day, such as art, music, and physical education (Grosenick & Reynolds, 1978; Turnbull & Schulz, 1979)

2. *Regular Education Initiative:* an attempt to reform general and special education by creating a unified system capable of meeting individual needs in general education classrooms (Gartner & Lipsky, 1987; Reynolds, Wang, & Walberg, 1987; Will, 1986)

3. *Inclusion through accommodations (instructional adaptations):* an additive approach to inclusion that assumes the only viable approach to including students with disabilities in general education classrooms is to add instructional adaptions to the predefined general education teaching and learning approaches (Pugach, 1995)

4. *Inclusion through restructuring:* a design to inclusion that re-creates general and special education by merging resources to develop more flexible learning environments for all students and educators (McGregor & Vogelsberg, 1998; Pugach & Johnson, 2002; Sailor, 2002; Thousand, Villa, & Nevin, 2002)

like other students with a disability, contributes to a sense of a learning community (Hunt, Hirose-Hatae, Doering, Karasoff, & Goetz, 2000; Ryndak & Fisher, 2003).

Principle of natural proportions. The principle of natural proportions holds that students with exceptionalities should be placed in schools and classrooms in natural proportion to the occurrence of exceptionality within the general population (Brown et al., 1991). If, for example, 10 percent of students in a school district receive special education services, the principle of natural proportions holds that, if a classroom has 30 students, not more than 3 should have a disability. In a modification of this principle, Walther-Thomas, Korinek, and McLaughlin (1999) suggest that not more than 20 percent of the total classroom should have disabilities. For a classroom of 30 students, this means 6 students. They also suggest that if some of the students have more severe disabilities and need extensive support, the overall number of students with disabilities in the class should be reduced.

Restructuring teaching and learning. Inclusion through restructuring requires general and special education educators to work in partnership with related service providers, families, and students to provide supplementary aids and services and special education and related services. You will recall from "Who is Dani Gonzalez?" how closely Lauren Priest (special educator) and Erin Lane (general educator) work together. Tremendous variability exists in how teachers provide special education services within general education classrooms. Just consider the descriptions in Figure 2.6 of inclusion through add-on services and inclusion through restructured services. State-of-the-art schools, such as Dani's, that implement inclusion through restructuring pool the strengths and talents of educators who have different types of training and capacities to provide individualized instruction within the general education classroom.

Age- and grade-appropriate placements. Finally, inclusion favors educating all students in age- and grade-appropriate placements, just as Dani spends most of her school days at Valley Park Elementary School with other fifth-graders.

These four principles are not without controversy. Two major issues are at the heart of the inclusion debate: (1) eliminating the continuum of placements and (2) increasing the amount of time students spend in the general education classroom.

Eliminating the continuum of placements. The concept of a continuum of services has been part of special education ever since Congress enacted IDEA in 1975. The continuum refers to services that range from the most typical and most inclusive settings to the most atypical and most segregated settings.

There was a time when accommodating students with disabilities in general education classrooms through supplementary aids and services was not considered an option. That limited perspective caused Taylor (1988) to observe that students with disabilities were caught in the continuum of services. Unfortunately, once students were placed in more-restrictive settings, few ever left them for general education classrooms.

The inclusion movement has tried to limit the need for more restrictive settings by creating a new partnership between special and general educators. This partnership seeks to provide individualized instruction to students in general education classrooms through a universally designed general education curriculum (King-Sears, 2001). Inclusion now rests on the premise that it is not often appropriate or even necessary to remove some students from the general education classroom and place them in a more specialized and restrictive setting to provide individualized and appropriate education.

To advance this belief, general and special educators partner with each other and with students' parents to promote students' academic success, participation in extracurricular and other school activities, and sense of belonging (Voltz, Brazil, & Ford, 2001). They also create separate spaces in schools that are used by many students for various purposes: resource centers or rooms (such as Lauren Priest's, where Dani works some of the school day), study labs, and breakout rooms to enable students to meet together for cooperative learning groups, peer tutoring, and group activities (Voltz et al., 2001). The approach of having separate spaces used by many students contrasts with the approach of having spe-

PEARSON
myeducationlab

Go to the Activities and Application section in Chapter 2 of MyEducationLab and complete Activity 5. As you watch the video and answer the accompanying questions, reflect on the effort and time Dani's teachers have put toward ensuring her progress in the general education curriculum.

cialized placements used exclusively by students with disabilities.

Increasing the amount of time in general education classrooms. Should educators increase the amount of time a student spends in an age- and grade-appropriate general classroom? If so, how? Inclusion proponents generally agree that placement in general education classrooms does not mean that the student never leaves those classrooms for special services. If that were the case, Dani would never leave Erin Lane's classroom to go to Lauren Priest's. When supplementary aids and services are readily available within general education classrooms and instructional materials are universally designed, students with disabilities will be more likely to perceive themselves as valued classroom members and will not need to leave the classroom as often to receive an appropriate education.

The four characteristics of inclusion guide Prairie Valley Elementary School faculty when educating Dani Gonzalez.

Educator, parent, and student perspectives on inclusion. The research on inclusion has some limitations. For example, most research studies do not describe the quality of inclusive practices or allow for the amount of time spent in inclusive settings, the impact of universal design, and the extent to which students from culturally and linguistically diverse backgrounds have appropriate respect, support, and accommodations. Bear those limitations in mind as you consider Figure 2.7, which identifies the perspectives of educators, parents, and students on inclusive practices. As you read Figure 2.7, remember that Luz and Carlos Gonzalez exemplify the "pro-inclusion" parents—perhaps because they know Dani's own preferences and strengths and because they have great expectations for her.

As you can see, there is a wide range of perspectives on the benefits of and barriers to inclusion. Still, over time, those perceptions have improved across all stakeholder groups, consistent with IDEA's presumption in favor of inclusion. Increasingly, parents and family members expect their child to be included (Erwin, Soodak, Winton, & Turnbull, 2001; Turnbull, Turnbull, Erwin, & Soodak, 2007). Certainly many of the perceptions set out in Figure 2.7 were formed without taking into account the availability of universally designed materials. How might the introduction of such materials change perspectives? As we show in Chapters 5 through 16, the answer is that universal design for learning can enhance the education of all students in inclusive settings and thus can blunt some of the negative perceptions about inclusion.

PEARSON
myeducationlab

Go to the Activities and Application section in Chapter 2 of MyEducationLab and complete Activity 6. As you watch the video, compare and contrast this teacher's perspectives on inclusion with those presented in Figure 2.7.

What Student Outcomes Are Associated with Inclusion?

We have just described various perspectives about inclusion. As you know, however, perception is not always reality. In fact, research has shown that many of the perceived concerns or barriers identified in Figure 2.7 are, in fact, not accurate. For example, there is almost universal agreement that students with disabilities gain social and communication benefits from their involvement in inclusive settings (McGregor & Vogelsberg, 1998). Dani's increased self-confidence and ability to read underscore the data. Indeed, research shows that students with disabilities can and do benefit academically from involvement in the general education classroom. Cole, Waldron, and Majd (2004) found that students without disabilities educated in inclusive classrooms made significantly greater academic progress in mathematics and reading than did students without disabilities who did not have students with disabilities in their classroom. Cole and colleagues offer an explanation: The additional supports provided in the general education classroom that are intended to support the students with disabilities benefit all students. Now that's universal design for learning!

Figure 2.7

Perspectives of educators, parents, and students on inclusive practices

Perspective	Perceived Benefits	Studies	Perceived Concerns	Studies
Educators	Students with disabilities, including early childhood students, can be successfully educated in the general education classroom if given adequate supplementary aids and services and specially designed instruction.	Andrews et al. (2000); Bruns & Mogharreban (2007); Thousand, Villa, & Nevin (2002).	Students with disabilities need specialized settings outside the general education classroom to receive the benefit of intensive and individualized instruction.	Kauffman (1995); Kavele & Forness (2000); MacMillan, Gresham, & Forness (1996); Zigmond et al. (1995).
			Not all students with disabilities should always be held to the same academic content standards as nondisabled students.	Agran, Alper, & Wehmeyer (2002)
	When given support, most general education teachers feel successful at teaching students with disabilities and believe that those students gain social benefits and that the experience promotes acceptance.	Frederickson, Dunsmuir, Lang, & Monsen (2004); Idol (2006); Lohrmann & Bambara (2006); Praisner (2003); Study of Personnel Needs in Special Education (2002)	Special education resources have not been sufficiently infused into general education to ensure effective teaching, and class size is a major obstacle to inclusive practices.	Study of Personnel Needs in Special Education (2002)
	The better trained and experienced a teacher is, the more the teacher will know how to practice inclusion and favor it.	McLesky, Waldron, So, Swanson, & Loveland (2001); Soodak et al. (2002).	Special and general education teachers do not receive adequate time or training to implement inclusive practices.	Agran et al. (2002); Van Reusen, Shoho, & Barker (2000).
Parents	General classrooms do a better job of (1) improving self-concept, (2) promoting friendships, (3) teaching academics, and (4) preparing for the real world.	Duhaney & Salend (2000); Frederickson et al. (2004); Leyser & Kirk (2004); Palmer, Fuller, Arora, & Nelson (2001)	Availability of qualified educators and individualized services are concerns, as are frustrations in getting schools to provide inclusive supports.	Duhaney & Salend (2000); Leyser & Kirk (2004)
			Parents of children with disabilities, particularly more severe disabilities, are concerned that the general education classroom will not be appropriate for their child's educational needs and will not be welcoming.	Leyser & Kirk (2004); Palmer et al. (2001)
	Parents of children without disabilities identified benefits (sensitivity to the needs of others, greater acceptance of diversity, educational benefit) for their children.	Cole, Waldron, & Majd (2004); Duhaney & Salend (2000); Peck, Staub, Gallucci, & Schwartz (2004)	Parents of children without disabilities are concerned that the inclusion of students with disabilities, particularly students with behavior problems, will negatively impact their son's or daughter's academic performance.	Cole et al. (2004); Kniveton (2004); Peck et al. (2004)

Figure 2.7 (continued)

Perspectives of educators, parents, and students on inclusive practices

Perspective	Perceived Benefits	Studies	Perceived Concerns	Studies
Students	Students with disabilities believe inclusive settings provide more opportunities for making friends and favor having special educators provide assistance to all students in general education classrooms rather than to only students with exceptionalities.	Wiener & Tardif (2004)	Students with disabilities believe resource rooms provide useful help, a quiet place to work, and less difficult and more enjoyable instructional activities.	Vaughn & Klingner (1998)
	Generally, students without disabilities favor inclusion.	Siperstein, Parker, Bardon, & Widaman (2007); Wiener & Tardif (2004)	Students without disabilities express concern about students being teased and about the participation of some students with more severe disabilities in academic content classes.	Klingner, Vaughn, Schumm, Cohen, & Forgan (1998); Siperstein et al. (2007)

A second concern is that inclusion will adversely affect the academic performance of students without disabilities. A research synthesis (McGregor & Vogelsberg, 1998) focusing mostly on severe disabilities reported that the academic performance of students without disabilities was not detrimentally impacted by the inclusion of students with disabilities. Idol (2006) evaluated the impact of inclusion on a number of factors for eight elementary and secondary schools and found that students in inclusive settings were not negatively impacted in their statewide testing performance and, in fact, showed incremental improvement year-by-year on state testing. This is not to imply that the inclusion itself was a causal factor in improved statewide testing performance, but simply to note that inclusion had, at the least, no negative effects on overall testing scores.

Although teachers and others believe that, with adequate suppports, they can successfully educate students with disabilities, it is often hard to ensure and maintain those supports, especially the availability of paraprofessionals (see Chapter 11) (Ghere & York-Barr, 2007).

Clearly, inclusion with support (through individually designed instruction, related services, supplementary aids and services, and universal design in learning) is feasible. Box 2.2 illustrates some effective practices to promote inclusion. The Inclusion Tips boxes in Chapters 5 through 16 will provide similar information for students covered in each of those chapters.

How Does Inclusion Facilitate Progress?

In their discussion of the findings from their comprehensive analysis and synthesis of research on the efficacy of special education, Kavale and Forness (1999) concluded that "features of instruction are probably the major influence on outcomes, but these are not unique to setting. Setting is thus a macrovariable; the real question becomes one of examining what happens in that setting" (p. 70). Research is increasingly showing that what happens in inclusive settings differs from what happens in segregated settings. Soukup,

Box 2.2

INCLUSION TIPS

	What You Might See	What You Might Be Tempted to Do	Alternate Responses	Ways to Include Peers in the Process
Behavior	The student shows an apparently poor attitude toward other students and does not easily cooperate with them during instructional activities.	Discipline him for his poor behavior and separate him from the rest of the class.	Identify his strengths and work together on a list of positive things he can say when responding to other students during instructional activities.	Ask him to identify peers he would like to work with. Then work with this small group to practice verbal responses that would be helpful.
Social interactions	He has few friends and doesn't appear to want any.	Encourage him to take the initiative toward others but also allow him to be by himself whenever he chooses.	Collaborate with the school counselor to plan ways to teach him specific social skills.	Work with identified peers to practice the specific social skills with him in and out of the classroom.
Educational performance	His work is acceptable, but he needs constant supervision.	Assign an aide to work with him and allow him to complete unfinished work at home.	Collaborate with the special education teacher to create step-by-step assignments that he can do on his own. Set up a reward system for each step successfully completed without supervision.	Encourage him to work with his peers to monitor the assignments. Ask peers to work with him to construct a tracking system for class assignments.
Classroom attitudes	He never volunteers answers and is reluctant to participate in class activities.	Carefully choose activities that allow him to work alone.	Together with the special education teacher, work with him ahead of time on content to be covered and plan specific things for him to contribute.	Plan with peers positive contributions that each can make to upcoming class activities.

Wehmeyer, Bashinski, & Bovaird (2007) and Wehmeyer, Lattin, Lapp-Rincker, and Agran (2003) found that the percentage of time intervals students with disabilities spent engaged in tasks linked to a grade-level general education curriculum standard was significantly higher in the general education classroom than in any other educational setting. In short, inclusion advances academic progress. That's so for Dani: Her self-confidence contributes to her desire and thus her ability to read.

Until now, the inclusion movement has consisted of two generations of different practices. The first generation focused on moving students with disabilities from segregated settings into the general education classroom. The second focused on developing and evaluating practices to support the presence of students with disabilities in the general classroom. Both of these phases focused primarily on the place in which students were educated.

Now, however, NCLB's standards-based reforms and IDEA's command for access to the general education curriculum have created conditions for a third generation of inclusive practices. Today, the focus is no longer exclusively on where a student is taught; it also includes (1) "what"—curriculum mastery, or what a student is taught and learns and (2) "how"—the methods and pedagogy that teachers use. Nothing about the first two generations of inclusive practices is obsolete or unimportant. In fact, as we describe in Chapters 5 through 16, efforts to achieve outcomes associated with first- and second-generation inclusive practices (inclusion in the general education classroom and implementation of high-quality instructional strategies to support students in the general education classroom) continue, but with new emphasis on "what" and "how." You will learn more about third generation inclusive practices later in this chapter as well as in each of Chapters 5 through 16.

HOW DOES A STUDENT'S IEP SUPPORT PROGRESS?

You have learned about two initiatives, universal design for learning (a supplementary aid and service) and inclusion (a principle that IDEA calls "least restrictive education") that promote students' progress in the general education curriculum. We discuss other practices in future chapters.

To lay the foundation for those chapters, however, we turn your attention to other important practices, beginning with students' Individualized Education Programs (IEPs). We discussed the IEP in Chapter 1, but we add to that discussion below. In developing a student's IEP, you should remember two basic propositions of special education practices. First, individualization is a hallmark of special education practices (Turnbull, Turnbull, Wehmeyer, & Park, 2003), and nothing about standards-based reform changes that basic fact. Second, IDEA requires a student's IEP to ensure involvement with and progress in the general education curriculum and also to address his unique learning needs.

Who Designs an IEP and What Are Their Duties?

In Chapter 1, you learned that the Individualized Education Program (IEP) is the plan for an education program for each student aged 3 through 21. For children birth through age 2, that plan is called the Individualized Family Services Plan (IFSP). You also learned who participates in an IEP meeting and how the IEP process aligns with the priorities of the six principles of IDEA. To refresh your memory, we'll restate who must be involved in writing an IEP: the student's parents, a general educator, a special educator, a school representative who supervises or provides special education and knows about general education and school resources, a person who interprets the results of the student's non-discriminatory evaluation, any other person with expertise about the student's educational needs (at the parent's discretion), and, when appropriate, the student.

The members of Dani's IEP team were Luz Gonzalez (her mother), Erin Lane (general education teacher), Deb Murray (school psychologist), Karen Hathaway (speech-language pathologist), Lauren Priest (special educator), Chris LaBouty (paraprofessional), Chery Mundweiler (general educator), and Susan Flanagan (school nurse). Because a special educator and general educator were on the team, Dani's special education under IDEA is aligned with NCLB. As you learned in Chapter 1, IDEA and NCLB align with each other; so does Dani's IEP.

You should also know that Dani participated in and signed off on her IEP. There is an expression in the disability world, "Nothing About Me Without Me." It means that the person with a disability is the focus of the action and has the right and should be supported to participate in decisions about himself. Dani's participation reflects that saying.

Now, let's consider these participants' duties when writing the IEP. They must:

◆ Ensure that all of the individuals identified by IDEA as mandatory members of the team participate.

◆ Follow IDEA's process for developing an IEP by considering the student's strengths; the parents' concerns about how to enhance their child's education; the results of the nondiscriminatory evaluations; the student's academic, developmental, and functional needs; and five "special factors." (We describe those below under "Components of the IEP.") In Chapters 5 to 16, you'll learn how to conduct a nondiscriminatory evaluation for a student with a particular categorical disability and how to assess the student's progress in the general education curriculum and other educational needs.

◆ Include all of the required components of an IEP (we describe them below under "Components of the IEP").

◆ Specify the student's educational placement, consistent with the principle of the least restrictive environment (which you read about in Chapter 1 and will learn more about in this chapter).

What Are the Components of the IEP?

PEARSON
myeducationlab

Go to the Building Teaching Skills and Dispositions section in Chapter 2 of MyEducationLab. As you watch the videos and complete the activities, consider first the components of the IEP and then how this relates to Dani's teachers, her IEP history, and how she is meeting her current IEP goals.

IDEA requires the IEP to include eight components. Figure 2.8 sets out the required components of each student's IEP. It is absolutely necessary, to comply with IDEA and to ensure that the student will benefit from special education, for a student's IEP team to include every component in each IEP.

In addition to addressing each of these eight IEP components, each IEP team must also carefully consider five "special factors" when developing a student's IEP. If any factors apply to the student, the IEP team must address them through the student's IEP as part of the student's special education, related services, or supplementary aids and services. The five special factors are:

◆ If the child's behavior impedes his or other students' learning, the IEP team must consider whether to use positive behavioral interventions and supports, or other strategies, to address the child's behavior. This consideration does not apply to Dani; she's an eager and well-behaved student.

◆ If the child has limited English proficiency, the IEP team must consider his language needs in IEP. This does not apply to Dani.

◆ If the child is blind or visually impaired, the IEP team must provide (not merely consider providing) instruction in Braille and the use of Braille. The team may determine that instruction in Braille and the use of Braille are not appropriate for the child, but only after it evaluates the child's reading and writing skills, needs, and appropriate reading and writing media, including an evaluation of his future needs for instruction in Braille or the use of Braille. Dani is not visually impaired, so this consideration does not apply to her.

◆ For every child, the IEP must consider the child's communication needs. If the child is deaf or hard of hearing, the team must consider his language and communication needs, opportunities for direct communication with peers and professional personnel in his language and communication mode, academic level, and full range of needs, including opportunities for direct instruction in his language and communication mode. Dani has no hearing impairment, so this consideration does not apply to her.

◆ Also for every child, the IEP team must consider whether the child needs assistive technology devices and services. Dani does use a device (a pump) that administers insulin, but her device is implanted. That makes a difference because IDEA does not regard an implanted device as a related service. Still, IDEA does not relieve the school from monitoring the pump to make sure it works and assisting Dani to use it.

You learned in Chapter 1 that IDEA defines special education as specially designed instruction, and you have just learned about the required eight components of an IEP and the five special factors the IEP must consider. Now, let's consider the IDEA definition of special education and the component requirements as they apply to Dani. Dani's IEP has a "long-range vision" section ("expressing and communicating her thoughts and opinions with confidence in herself"), a statement of her academic and functional achievement, and

Figure 2.8 ▶ **Required components of every IEP**

The IEP is a written statement for each student aged 3 through 21. Whenever it is developed or revised, it must contain the following statements:

1. The student's present levels of academic achievement and functional performance, including

   - How the student's disability affects the student's involvement and progress in the general curriculum (for students aged 6 through 21)
   - How a preschooler's disability affects the child's participation in appropriate activities (for children aged 3 through 5)
   - A description of the benchmarks or short-term objectives for students who take alternate assessments that are aligned to alternate achievement standards

2. Measurable annual goals, including academic and functional goals, designed to

   - Meet each of the student's needs resulting from the disability in order to enable the student to be involved in and make progress in the general curriculum
   - Meet each of the student's other educational needs that result from the disability

3. How the student's progress toward annual goals will be measured and when periodic reports on the student's progress and meeting annual goals will be provided

4. The special education and related services and supplementary aids and services, based on peer-reviewed research to the extent practicable, that will be provided to the student or on the student's behalf and the program modifications or supports for school personnel that will be provided for the student to

   - Advance appropriately toward attaining the annual goals
   - Be involved in and make progress in the general curriculum and participate in extracurricular and other nonacademic activities
   - Be educated and participate in those three types of activities with other students with disabilities and with students who do not have disabilities

5. An explanation of the extent, if any, to which the student will not participate with students who do not have disabilities in the regular classroom and in extracurricular and other nonacademic activities

6. Any individual appropriate accommodations that are necessary to measure the student's academic and functional performance on state- and district-wide assessments; if the IEP team determines that the student will not participate in a regular state- or district-wide assessment or any part of an assessment, an explanation of why the student cannot participate and the particular alternate assessment that the team selects as appropriate for the student

7. The projected date for beginning the special education, related services, supplemental aids and services, and modifications, as well as the anticipated frequency, location, and duration of each

8. Beginning no later than the first IEP that will be in effect after the student turns 16, and then updated annually, a transition plan that must include

   - Measurable postsecondary goals based on transition assessments related to training, education, employment, and, where appropriate, independent living skills
   - A statement of transition services, including courses of study, needed to assist the student to reach those postsecondary goals
   - Beginning no later than one year before the student reaches the age of majority under state law (usually age 18), a statement that the student has been informed of those rights under IDEA that will transfer to the student from the parents when the student comes of age

a specification of the types of education she will have in reading, math, life skills, writing, science, and social studies. It also identifies her speech-language challenges but does not provide the related service of speech-language therapy. If that were all Dani's IEP team were to consider and all her teachers would address, Dani might be shortchanged.

That is because IDEA requires each IEP team not only to address the eight components and consider the five factors, but also to consider

◆ the child's strengths

◆ the child's parents' concerns for enhancing their child's education

◆ the results of initial or subsequent nondiscriminatory evaluations

◆ the child's academic, developmental, and functional needs

Dani, her parents, and her teachers have taken into account her strengths (determination to learn), the concerns that Luz and Carlos have (integrated education that leads to a life more like that of people who do not have disabilities), Dani's evaluations, and Dani's various needs. It is especially important for the IEP team to consider a student's strengths, as Dani's team has done, because it is too easy for educators to focus primarily on a student's needs. A student's present strengths, especially as educators build on them and address the student's needs, often shape the expectations that educators, parents, and even the students have. In Box 2.3, My Voice, you will read about a student who knew her strengths and had great expectations for herself and her future.

Knowlton (2007) recommends that well-written annual goals should be clear and concise; expressed in terms of observable behavior and the conditions under which it will occur; logically derived from one or more present levels of educational performance; related to relevant academic, social, vocational, and or community-referenced skills appropriate

---

MY VOICE  Box 2.3

● **The Power of Great Expectations and Visions**

I had a learning disability throughout grades K–12, but in May 2002 I graduated with my first bachelor of science degree (in geography) from Western Kentucky University in Bowling Green. I am going for two more degrees at WKU. One is the bachelor of fine arts in graphic design and the other a bachelor of arts in broadcasting. I received both degrees in May 2004. I never imagined so much success as I am now having in my life.

My teachers in high school believed it was impossible for me to attend a major university and graduate due to my severe learning disability. I was determined to succeed in life, though, and get a good college education despite what the test scores said, the Board of Education said to me, and my teachers said to me. It took a while for them to accept my goals in life and to support me. My high school teachers wanted me to just graduate with an associate's degree and never attend a university. I just wish they had pushed me more to my full potential in high school and had me reach for my dreams.

One of my goals had been to work for the Weather Channel as an on-camera meteorologist. I have had to abandon that goal because the math and physics required to be a meteorologist are just too hard for me and too challenging. But I am looking into attending the University of Hawaii—Manoa to get a bachelor of science degree in global environmental science and to take other courses in geography and oceanography.

I am getting a lot of support from my professors, but accomplishing these degrees at Western Kentucky University has been extremely challenging. Still, I am getting through them all right with hard work and persistence. My learning disability was in math, which is a weak subject for me; so you can understand why being a meteorologist was beyond my reach, even with all the work I put in and all the support I received. But I can pursue other work in the area of the natural sciences, and that is what I will do at the University of Hawaii.

I also am getting support from the president of my university, the dean, the professors, and the advisors and alumni association. However, they don't know the entire story and all that I had to go through to get to this point in my life. I really can't believe my dreams of working in the natural sciences are coming true. That is why I would also like to help out in some way with kids who have learning disabilities.

—Chandra Beyerck,
Western Kentucky
University, Bowling Green

to the age of and expectations for the student; and readily accomplished in one year's time. Heinich, Molenda, Russel, and Smaldino (1999) recommended that well-written goals address the ABCDs of goal writing:

(A)udience—Who is the target of the goal?

(B)ehavior—What do you expect the target for the goal to be able to do? This should be an overt, observable behavior, even if the actual behavior is covert or mental in nature, otherwise it is not measurable.

(C)ondition—Under what conditions or circumstances do you expect the student to perform the behavior?

(D)egree of proficiency—What are the criteria that you will use to determine if the student has met the goal?

Addressing Progress Through the IEP

It is worthwhile to repeat that one of IDEA's purposes is to ensure that the student has equal opportunities in education and that those opportunities will lead to his economic self-sufficiency, independent living, and full participation. To secure these outcomes, educators must address the student's progress in school. Because the IEP is the linchpin to the student's education and progress, they have to take into account the supplementary aids and services the student will need and how special education, related services, and supplementary aids and services shape annual goals and progress toward those goals.

Determining Supplementary Aids and Services

Relying on the student's nondiscriminatory evaluation and IEP, the IEP team should ask what supplementary aids and services the student needs to be educated with his non-disabled peers and to progress in the general education curriculum. There is a connection between supplementary aids and services and the five special considerations that a student's IEP team must take into account. To repeat, those five considerations are (1) strategies to address a student's behavior that impedes his or other students' learning; (2) language needs of students with limited English proficiency; (3) instruction in Braille for students who are blind; (4) communication needs, especially when the student is deaf or hard of hearing; and (5) use of assistive technology devices and services.

Each factor can guide the IEP team as it considers what supplementary aids and services a student needs. Does the student need to be seated near the teacher to see or hear the lesson? Does the student work best when seated individually or with other students around a table? What is the role of the paraprofessional in providing supports? What assistive technologies might promote access? Does the student need certain assessment or task modifications to succeed? These are all part of determining needed supplementary aids and supports.

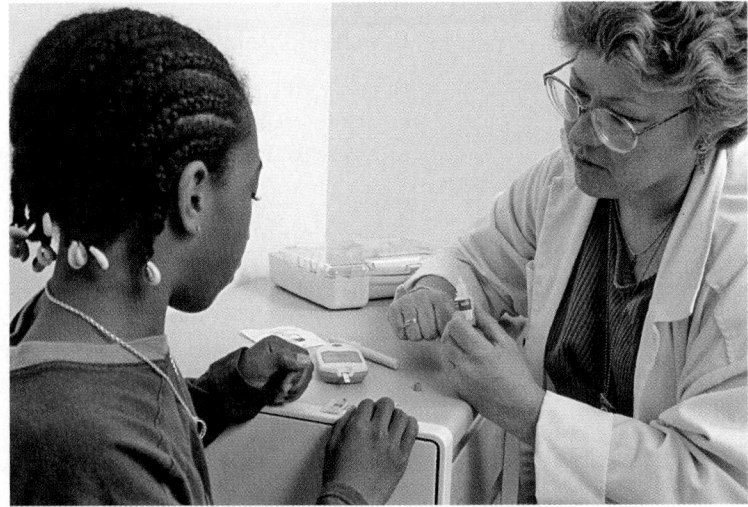

Determining Annual Goals

As you know, the IEP must state the student's annual goals and how educators will measure the student's progress toward those goals, especially as the student participates in the general curriculum. The goals must relate to both the student's educational goals and the student's other educational needs.

With regard to goals addressing the student's other educational needs, students with severe disabilities need functional or life-skills content that other students acquire outside school or at a

School nurses are members of some IEP teams.

younger age and that may not be part of the general education curriculum, particularly for older students. Most students, whether receiving special education services or not, need instruction related to making the transition from school to the adult world, including instruction in employment and community living; yet this is often lacking in general curriculum standards. Further, some students with disabilities (especially those who have visual impairments) need specialized instruction in areas such as orientation and mobility—namely, how to get from place to place—that other students do not need.

The IEP team should take into account the content of the general education curriculum and how it will fail to provide the student with the skills and knowledge he needs to be a productive, independent adult. Then the team should develop goals and objectives to address those areas. Historically, the IEPs of students with disabilities began with these alternative or functional curricular content areas. That practice, however, limited students to instruction in only those areas that the IEP team believed were important or possible. In the end, those IEPs failed to hold students to the high expectations of the general education curriculum.

Remember that IDEA does not limit a student's educational program to content in the general education curriculum. IDEA allows educators to address students' other educational needs, but it requires them to begin by considering how a student can participate and make progress in the general education curriculum. Thus, the team will consider the other educational needs of a student with disabilities (such as how Dani can learn to calculate the proper dosages of her insulin), but it will start by asking how the student can participate and make progress in the general education curriculum.

Determining Specially Designed Instruction

Having considered supplementary aids and services and written goals, the IEP team should identify the **specially designed instruction** the student needs to ensure participation and progress in the general education curriculum. Ordinarily, the IEP team does not have to identify all possible instructional techniques and strategies a student might need; that is the role of the student's teachers for each course. Dani's IEP specifies the reading program she will have (Horizons), her math program (Number Worlds), and her life skills program (using a calculator, reading nutritional labels, writing her name, address, telephone number, etc.). Consistent with IDEA's requirement that the IEP must identify a student's strengths, Dani's IEP begins by acknowledging that she is "an extremely happy and social child . . . gets along wonderfully with her peers and adults . . . is very responsible . . . is an extremely hard worker . . . is proud of herself when she succeeds and is beginning to demonstrate more self-confidence than in past years." In Chapters 5 through 16, you will learn about an array of specially designed instruction across all age and grade levels and about how students' IEPs, like Dani's, can reflect their strengths as well as their educational needs.

Specifying Related Services

Next, the IEP team should consider related services (identified in Chapter 1) that are necessary to enable a student to benefit from special education and to participate and make progress in the general education curriculum.

Determining Test Accommodations or Alterations

Finally, the IEP team should consider whether the student can take the state or district assessments without modification, needs a modified test or other accommodations, or needs to take an alternate assessment. The IEP team may not completely exempt the student from assessments. That is not an option.

WHAT SHOULD EDUCATORS DO TO SUPPORT PROGRESS?

Promoting access begins with inclusive practices, UDL, and effective planning, but the heavy lifting occurs day in and day out in the classroom. Three campus- and classroom-level actions promote student progress in the general curriculum: creating learning communities, designing unit and lesson plans, and implementing schoolwide quality instruction.

Creating Learning Communities

Effective instruction begins when educators intentionally create learning environments in which students learn to respect and value each other and everyone's individual differences, understand their roles and responsibilities, work in a self-directed manner, and participate in setting classroom rules. You can create an effective learning community by discovering the abilities of all your students, developing systematic ways to collect information on student progress for use in planning future lessons, and using collaborative teaching, grouping, and differentiated instructional strategies to individualize student educational experiences. In Chapters 3 and 4 you will learn more about the community, about respecting and valuing diversity, and about creating partnerships with families.

Designing Units and Lessons

Units of study are the "maps" teachers create to organize and plan content and to support student learning and achievement in the general education curriculum. Units of study identify end-of-school-year goals, standards for determining whether the goals are met, and knowledge that students will acquire. Once you as a teacher understand the big picture for the school year, you must "backwards-map" to determine what your students will need to know and do at the middle of the school year and then plan for manageable instructional units. When you have an overall idea of what you need to accomplish by the end of the school year and have "chunked" the content, skills, and knowledge into midyear and quarterly components, you are ready to plan specific units of instruction (Wehmeyer, Sands, Knowlton, & Kozleski, 2002).

Having identified the learning targets, you can plan day-to-day activities to support students in achieving the outcomes of each unit of instruction. Generally, lesson plans identify the theme of a lesson, the purpose of the lesson, how the lesson will be conducted, what students are expected to accomplish, and how those accomplishments will be measured. Dani's teachers use evidence-based reading and math curricula that are highly specific on what to teach (curriculum), how to teach (methodology), and how to measure progress.

At both the unit- and lesson-planning level, you should identify the skills, processes, or knowledge that *all* students, including students with disabilities, should master and how the teacher and other educators will support all students in doing so. Spooner, Baker, Harris, Ahlgrim-Delzell, and Browder (2007) found that as little as one hour of training on UDL enabled teachers to implement lesson plans that were accessible for all students, so it is important for school administrators to ensure that teachers have those opportunities to learn about how to write lesson plans and units that incorporate UDL features. You will learn about more of these practices in Chapters 5 through 16.

One such strategy is to identify the big ideas that all students should learn from the lesson or unit. Once you know what you want all students to know, you can develop lesson objectives that allow students to demonstrate, through different means, that they grasp the big ideas (Grossen et al., 2002). Dani's IEP calls for her to "focus on the basic concepts being taught."

One way to create those objectives is to use **cognitive taxonomies.** Cognitive taxonomies classify the cognitive demands of learning targets. Perhaps the most familiar cognitive taxonomy is that developed by Bloom and associates. Bloom's taxonomy is a means of categorizing the cognitive skills students use when achieving learning targets. As one ascends Bloom's taxonomy, the cognitive demands from students are more complex. By developing lesson objectives that range from less to more complex cognitive demands, you can ensure that all of your students acquire knowledge about the content and have flexible options for providing evidence of that knowledge.

Implementing Schoolwide Instructional Strategies

In subsequent chapters you will learn more about high-quality, schoolwide instructional strategies that promote students' progress in the general education curriculum. Pay careful attention to the word *schoolwide*. These strategies are effective not in just one classroom but in all school environments. Indeed, their payoff comes in every classroom. Further, like UDL, these strategies benefit not just the students who have qualified for special education under IDEA or reasonable accommodations under Section 504, but all students. They include learning communities, differentiated instruction, positive behavior support, cooperative learning, collaborative teaming, peer-mediated learning, and many more. You will learn about them in future chapters.

Introducing Two Approaches in Assessing Progress and Modifying Instruction

As you just learned, the IEP team must decide how to assess the student's progress and modify instruction so the student does make progress. IEP teams can do so by considering two strategies for designing educational supports, "response to intervention" and "positive behavior support." We will explain each briefly below and then in detail throughout the rest of the book.

Go to the Activities and Application section in Chapter 2 of MyEducationLab and complete Activity 7. As you interact with the simulation, think about how RTI could be implemented in your future classroom.

What is response to intervention? Response to intervention (RTI) is a means to determine whether any student, regardless of type of disability, needs more intensive instruction. It was developed for determining whether a student has a specific learning disability and is eligible for special education. But it has been broadened to refer to "individual, comprehensive student-centered assessment models that apply a problem-solving framework to identify and address a student's learning difficulties" (Deshler, Mellard, Tollefson, & Byrd, 2005), basically asking whether any student responds to interventions. Klotz and Canter (2007) identified the following as some of the key components of RTI:

- ◆ The implementation of high-quality, research-based instruction and behavioral supports in general education settings.
- ◆ Universal (schoolwide or districtwide) screening of academics and behavior to determine which students need closer monitoring or additional interventions.
- ◆ Multiple tiers of increasingly intense, research-based interventions matched to student needs.
- ◆ Continuous monitoring of student progress to determine if students are meeting their goals.

RTI is a component of the third generation of inclusive practices because it emphasizes universal practices. That is, RTI does not focus on singling out students who are "different" because they have certain characteristics. Instead, RTI asks teachers to implement high-quality, research-based interventions for all students. Having done that and having used systematic and ongoing measurement of student progress and universal screening procedures, teachers then can determine which students are not responding to an intervention—that is, which students are not learning. Only at that point should teachers implement increasingly intense, individualized, and specialized instruction until, quite simply, the student receives the instruction he or she needs to succeed. The National Association of State Directors of Special Education (2005) emphasized the problem-solving nature of RTI, as shown in Figure 2.9.

What is positive behavior support? Klotz and Canter (2005) refer to high-quality, reserach-based instruction *and* behavioral support. In Chapter 11, you will learn more about **positive behavior support** (PBS). At this point, however, you need to know only that positive behavior support is a systems-level, problem-solving-oriented, and data-based approach to reducing problem behavior, improving appropriate behavior, and achieving important academic, social, and communication outcomes for a particular student and for all students throughout the school building (Bambera & Kern, 2005). Teachers instruct students to replace their problem behavior with appropriate behavior, enabling

Figure 2.9 Responsiveness to intervention as a problem-solving approach

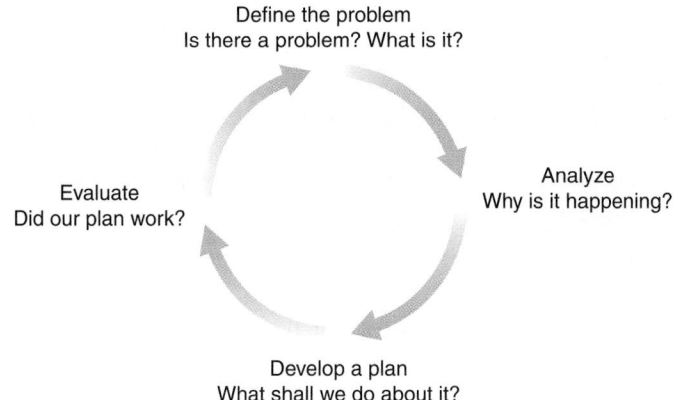

Problem-solving method

Define the problem
Is there a problem? What is it?

Analyze
Why is it happening?

Evaluate
Did our plan work?

Develop a plan
What shall we do about it?

Source: National Association of State Directors of Special Education (NASDSE). 2005. *Response to Intervention: Policy Considerations and Implementation.* Available at www.nasdse.org.

them to benefit much more effectively from the general curriculum. In addition, PBS seeks to rearrange school environments and change school systems to eliminate the value for students of engaging in problem behaviors in the first place. Because a student's problem behavior often results from someone else's failure to provide individualized and comprehensive support (Janney & Snell, 2008), positive behavior support involves tailoring students' environments to their preferences, strengths, and needs.

School reform models have adopted RTI and PBS, with some researchers applying RTI to students' social domains as well as academic domains (Fairbanks, Sugai, Guardino, & Lathrop, 2007). More than just applying RTI to different domains and populations, however, the principles underlying such practices as RTI, PBS, and UDL, which you learned about previously, are requiring educators to rethink inclusion and to generate new models for school reform.

For example, Sailor, Stowe, Turnbull, and Kleinhammer-Tramill (2007) have argued that schoolwide PBS is especially desirable today, when standards-based reforms (under the No Child Left Behind Act) are so important. They regard schoolwide PBS as an inclusive and preventive approach and contend it is fundamentally different from previous educational models. Earlier models, even when directed at students with and without disabilities, were still reactive—they responded to a student's failure, did not seek to prevent the failure, and did not increase the intensity of interventions to head off potential failure experiences.

Sailor and Roger (2005) suggest that the new conceptualization of inclusion should take into account the entire school, not merely the classrooms where students with disabilities learn. They advocate using RTI, PBS, and UDL together and on a schoolwide basis. Indeed, they have developed the Schooldwide Applications Model (SAM), incorporating six guiding principles:

1. General education guides all student learning.
2. All school resources are configured to benefit all students.
3. Schools address social development and citizenship forthrightly.
4. Schools are democratically organized, data-driven, problem-solving systems.
5. Schools have open boundaries in relation to their families and communities.
6. Schools enjoy district support for undertaking an extensive systems-change effort (pp. 506–508).

Approaches such as SAM incorporate aspects of RTI, RBS, and UDL. In doing so, they create new and universal approaches to education: They benefit all students, not just those with disabilities. That is why they are particularly important to members of a student's IEP team. If the team calls for and the student's teachers use RTI, PBS and UDL, the student has a greater chance of being included alongside students who do not have disabilities, just as the legal principle of least restrictive environment wants and just as the theory of inclusion envisions.

VALUES AND OUTCOMES

VALUES	GREAT EXPECTATIONS	CHOICES
	POSITIVE CONTRIBUTIONS	STRENGTHS
	RELATIONSHIPS	FULL CITIZENSHIP

Dani's mother and father, Luz and Carlos; her brother Juan; and her special education teacher, Lauren Priest, deliberately advance the values we want you to incorporate into your work as a teacher.

- ◆ They expect her to be in the general curriculum, progress through it, and, upon graduation, to go to work or continue her education.
- ◆ They believe she will be productive; teaching her life skills, math, reading, and writing lays a foundation for her to be employed.
- ◆ They celebrate her social skills and her contributions to students with greater disabilities (she reads to them daily) and to those who have no disabilities.
- ◆ They secure her full participation at Valley Park School, in both the general and special education programs and in all other school activities.
- ◆ They honor her choices, especially her choice to be a member of her IEP team, even while they hold her responsible, like any other full citizen, for completing her assignments and meeting their (and her) expectations.

WHAT DO YOU THINK?

1. From what you know about the research on inclusion and universal design, and from what you know about Dani, what's your opinion about inclusion?
2. Do you agree with Congress when, in IDEA, it declares that inclusion is the presumably correct placement for students with disabilities? Do you believe that the general education classroom should be the placement of first resort and that special education is a service, not a place, that assists students like Dani?
3. What experiences have you had with people who have disabilities? Were those experiences in inclusive or separate places? How did those experiences shape your response to this chapter and your long-distance view of Dani, her parents, and her teachers?

ADDRESSING THE STANDARDS: THE VALUES CONNECTION

The following CEC Knowledge and Skill Standards: Common Core and Values are addressed in this chapter through the content and concepts we discuss.

CEC Knowledge and Skill Standards: Common Core	Values/Standards Connection
CEC Knowledge and Skill Standard I. Foundations	Understanding how special education fits into today's schools—their organization and their classrooms—exemplifies CEC Standard 1, Foundations, and will help you be a more effective teacher of the general education curriculum to students with disabilities.
CC1K2 — Laws, policies, and ethical principles regarding behavior management, planning, and implementation.	
CC1K4 — Rights and responsibilities of students, parents, teachers, and other professionals, and schools related to exceptional learning needs.	For too long, people with disabilities have been denied the opportunity to be *full citizens*. General educational reform efforts properly include students with disabilities.
CC1K5 — Issues in definition and identification of individuals with exceptional learning needs, including those from culturally and linguistically diverse backgrounds.	
CCIK6 — Issues, assurances, and due process rights related to assessment, eligibility and placement within a continuum of services.	
CC1K7 — Family systems and the role of families in the educational process.	
CEC Knowledge and Skill Standard V. Learning Environments and Social Interactions	As you learn about teachers' attitudes and behaviors and how they influence students' behavior, you employ CEC Standard 5, Learning Environments and Social Interactions.
CC5S2 — Identify realistic expectations for personal and social behavior in various settings.	
CC5S3 — Identify supports needed for integration into various program placements.	When educators form meaningful partnerships and *relationships* with students, families, and other professionals, they advance students' progress in the general education curriculum.
CC5S4 — Design learning evnironments that encourage active participation in individual and group settings.	As a rule, students achieve at the level their teachers expect. Historically, many teachers have not had high expectations for students with disabilities. IDEA challenges teachers to have *high expectations* for these students.
CC5S6 — Use performance data and information from all stakeholders to make or suggest modifications in learning environments.	
CEC Knowledge and Skill Standard VII. Instructional Planning	Developing knowledge and skills related to the IEP reflects an application of CEC Standard 7, Instructional Planning.
CC7S1 — Identify and prioritize areas of the general curriculum and accommodations for individuals with exceptional learning needs.	Meeting students' needs through individualized programming and placement decisions is one way to ensure that students with disabilities have opportunities to develop the skills that lead to *full citizenship*. By focusing on the general education curriculum, students are challenged to "be the best they can be," and teachers are challenged to build on their *students' strengths*.
CC7S2 — Develop and implement comprehensive, longitudinal individualized programs in collaboration with team members.	
CC7S3 — Involve the individual and family in setting instructional goals and monitoring progress.	
CC7S6 — Sequence, implement, and evaluate individualized learning objectives.	
CC7S7 — Integrate affective, social, and life skills with academic curricula.	
CC7S9 — Incorporate and implement instructional and assistive technology into the educational program.	

continued

CEC Knowledge and Skill Standards: Common Core	Values/Standards Connection
CEC Knowledge and Skill Standard VIII. Assessment CC8K2 Legal provisions and ethical principles regarding assessment of individuals. CC8K3 Screening, prereferral, referral, and classification procedures. CC8K5 National, state or provincial, and local accommodations and modifications. CC8S2 Administer nonbiased formal and informal assessments. CC8S6 Use assessment information in making eligibility, program, and placement decisions for individuals with exceptional learning needs, including those from culturally and/or linguistically diverse backgrounds.	All students contribute positively to their families, schools, friends, and communities. We need to develop greater opportunities for these *contributions* by providing accomodations and modifications to the general education curriculum as warranted by formal and informal assessments.

Source: From CEC Knowledge and Skill Standards: Common Core and Values. Copyright by The Council for Exceptional Children. Reprinted with permission.

SUMMARY

What Is Progress in the General Education Curriculum?

◆ IDEA requires each student's IEP to state how the student will be involved and progress in the general education curriculum, how the student's progress will be assessed, and how state- and district-wide assessments will be modified (as appropriate) for the student.

◆ NCLB requires states to establish challenging academic content and student achievement standards that apply to all students, including those with disabilities.

◆ The general education curriculum refers to the same curriculum taught to nondisabled students, and IDEA requires that students with disabilities be involved in the general education curriculum to the maximum extent appropriate (beneficial) for the particular student.

How Do Supplementary Aids and Services and Universal Design for Learning Support Progress?

◆ Supplementary aids and services are noninstructional aids, services, and other supports that are provided in

general education classes or other education-related settings to enable children with disabilities to be educated alongside nondisabled children to the maximum extent appropriate.

◆ Supplementary aids and services include modifications to ensure physical and cognitive access to the environment, classroom ecological variables such as seating arrangements or classroom acoustics, educational or assistive technology, assessment or task modifications, and support from other persons.

◆ Universal design for learning refers to the design of instructional materials and activities to make the content information accessible to all children.

◆ The three elements of UDL are multiple means of representing the curriculum, multiple means of using materials, and multiple means of engaging students in learning.

How Does Inclusion Support Progress?

◆ Inclusion refers to students with disabilities learning in general education classes and, it is hoped, having a sense of belonging in these classes. There has been a steady increase in the number of students with disabilities placed in general education.

- Inclusion has four key characteristics: home-school placement, the principle of natural proportions, restructuring teaching and learning, and age- and grade-appropriate placements.

- When supplementary aids and services are readily available within general education classrooms and universal design for learning has been fully implemented, students with disabilities will be more likely to perceive themselves as valued classroom members and will not need to leave the classroom as often to receive an appropriate education.

- The general education classroom is the place in which the general education curriculum is most likely to be taught to students with disabilities, and inclusion ensures that students will have access to the general education curriculum.

How Does a Student's IEP Support Progress?

- A student's IEP must be based on both the general education curriculum and the student's unique learning needs.

- There are required members for every IEP team.

- The team must develop the IEP based on the student's strengths, the parents' concerns, the nondiscriminatory evaluation, the student's needs, and five "special factors."

- There are eight required components of an IEP; the team must address each component.

What Should Educators Do to Support Progress?

- Educators should create learning communities that enable students with disabilities to become integrated into their classrooms.

- Educators should create unit and lesson plans that incorporate universal design features and include goals and objectives that vary in complexity, thereby ensuring that all students can show progress.

- Educators should use schoolwide strategies such as response to intervention and positive behavior support because these approaches promote students' progress in the general education curriculum.

PEARSON
myeducationlab

Now go to MyEducationLab at www.myeducationlab.com and take the Self-Assessment to gauge your initial comprehension of chapter content. Once you have taken the Self-Assesment, use your individualized Study Plan for Chapter 2 to enhance your understanding of the concepts discussed in the chapter.

3

Issues and Responses in Today's Culturally Diverse Schools

◆ WHO IS DE'JA MCGEE?

You are about to meet De'ja and Sharilyn McGee. De'ja is in the 6th grade at Broken Arrow Elementary School in Lawrence, Kansas, where she has been classified as having a specific learning disability. That fact alone does not mean much, for it does not tell you much at all about her. All it really says is that she has a certain type of disability. It does not tell you any of the other information that you, as her prospective teacher, most likely want and certainly need to know: De'ja has scored at 97% on her standardized reading test; she struggles with mathematics; she receives both special and general education, with support in general education; and she participates in after-school tutoring. Classification, a label, simply does not reveal the entire person. A person is far more than her label or test scores.

So you naturally look at De'ja's photograph. Here, too, you find some clues to her. Perhaps you can see what her teachers and friends see in her: a cheerfulness that might seem unjustified if you knew more about her life.

As we just said, appearances and labels are just that—appearances and labels. Although De'ja has a learning disability and smiles in her photograph, these two facts still do not fully describe her reality. There is another layer below the label and the smiling young woman in the photograph.

At the age of only 11, De'ja is actually a young woman, not a girl. That is so because she is indispensable to her mother, Sharilyn, and she and her mother constitute the McGee family. Sharilyn is divorced from De'ja's father. Well, you may say, a lot of children have divorced parents.

True, but not many children have a single parent who herself has such significant disabilities that she is unable to work, and fewer still have the ability to provide home health care to their parents. De'ja is one of those very few.

As a consequence of various work-related injuries, Sharilyn is unable to work; her knees and wrists simply don't do what they used to do. Moreover, Sharilyn has had to have surgeries on her knees and needs home health care. That's where De'ja comes in: changing the dressings on Sharilyn's wounds, injecting pain-killing medicines, and assisting her mother with simple but essential matters of daily living such as getting dressed.

Sharilyn has another child, a son who lives about 40 miles away; he is an adult and has his own family responsibilities. So for De'ja and Sharilyn, "family" means the two of them and no one else. As a result, De'ja has a maturity—born of necessity and experience—beyond her years.

Together, then, De'ja and Sharilyn exemplify certain aspects of the culture of American families: single-parent family, disability within the family (here, both De'ja's and Sharilyn's), and, because De'ja's father rarely provides child support and Sharilyn is unable to work, life on the economic edge. They are typical of many families who live on the economic edge because disability and single-parent status often go hand-in-hand.

These traits sometimes coincide with another aspect of De'ja's and Sharilyn's life, which is intra-district migrancy. De'ja and Sharilyn move from apartment to apartment, nearly once every year. The reasons are complex. One is that De'ja's father does not provide child support and Sharilyn cannot work, so the family's income depends on public support and private charity. Another is that some landlords do not want to rent to people who receive public support for housing (assistance in paying their rent), and yet another is that rents increase faster than public support. So to find acceptable housing, moving has become part of their life. For educators such as De'ja's teacher John Koester, that means De'ja may attend several different schools during her middle-school years. The consistency in teaching and parent-teacher/student-teacher relationships that is so important to teaching and learning are hard to achieve.

As we discuss parent-teacher relationships, it is worth noting that Sharilyn herself was a student in special education, also classified as having a specific learning disability. She dropped out of high school to give birth to her son, but she later earned her GED. From time to time, her own experiences as a student shape her relationships with De'ja's teachers; skepticism about their commitment to De'ja creeps into her attitudes about De'ja's school experiences.

Finally, you will note that De'ja and Sharilyn are African American. That singular fact should not lead you to make any assumptions about them. Parents from all ethnic, cultural, and linguistic backgrounds have children with disabilities, including specific learning disabilities. Similarly, parents from all backgrounds have disabilities, are or will become poor, and are or will become skeptical about schools and teachers. What race does mean, for De'ja and Sharilyn, is this: it is an aspect, but only one, of their culture.

Their membership and active participation in their church is another. De'ja's sought-after talents as an actress in

CHAPTER OBJECTIVES

◆ You will learn that there are challenges in providing effective special education to students from different cultural, ethnic, and linguistic backgrounds. But you also will learn how to respond to the challenges.

◆ You will learn about the history of discrimination in education and the beliefs that supported discrimination against students from various cultural, ethnic, and linguistic backgrounds. You will learn that schools still disproportionately place into special education students who are not European American, do not speak English as their first language, and come from families who meet the federal definition of "poor."

◆ You will learn that family structure and parents' education also correlate with placement into special education.

◆ You will learn how to become a culturally responsive educator by being introspective about yourself. Then you will learn how to take into account your students' cultures, broaden your education about people who do not share your culture, and teach in culturally responsive ways.

◆ You will be challenged to be not just a teacher but also an advocate for your students from diverse backgrounds.

school and community theatre are still another aspect of their culture. Their multigenerational experiences in special education are also parts of their culture that have shaped their ways of experiencing education—deeply valuing it for its own sake and as an avenue away from living on the economic edge.

People are like puzzles, and no puzzle is complete without all of its parts. Teachers who work for De'ja understand that. After reading this vignette and certainly after reading this chapter, you too will understand it. "Seeing" De'ja as a student with a label tells you something but not everything; it is just one piece of the puzzle.

It is far more accurate to regard her and Sharilyn as people who have disabilities, face economic uncertainty, are intra-district migrants, have had their own experiences with teachers and peers, and are optimistic about their future and determined to benefit from school.

By understanding each of them as a whole person and both as a whole family—a completed puzzle—you will begin to understand that, when educators use the term *culturally diverse* to refer to students, families, and schools, you can interpret it as we present it in this chapter. Culture refers to customary beliefs, forms of a person's life, and material traits. You have your own culture—customary beliefs, forms of life, and material traits. We all do. Seeing De'ja and Sharilyn—indeed, seeing yourself—in only one way is deceptive. Worse, it impedes your ability to be an effective teacher. You can do something about that: Keep reading and consider your attitudes.

It is natural for some people to think that "my way" is "the right way"—that how we ourselves teach, learn, and live is how others should, too. Of course, that's not true: There is no single "right" way, no culture that is more "right" or less "right" than any other. Diversity is a fact in American life, it always has been, and it is increasingly a fact of life in all schools. An effective teacher will see through De'ja's classification and understand and respond nonjudgmentally to the beliefs, forms, and material traits that characterize De'ja's and Sharilyn's lives.

DEFINING CULTURE AND ITS IMPLICATIONS FOR SPECIAL EDUCATION

The dictionary definition of *culture* is the "customary beliefs, social forms, and material traits of a racial, religious, or social group; also: the characteristic features of everyday existence (as diversions or a way of life) shared by people in a place and time" (*Merriam-Webster's Collegiate Dictionary,* 2003, p. 304). Using this definition, you would understand that culture reflects the basic values of a particular group of people. When the members of a particular group perceive themselves, others, and their communities and nation in a particular way, they are reflecting their culture. Culture is the lens through which we "see" the world. When we act in a particular way, we are mirroring our culture. Culture interprets even as it drives behavior (Chamberlain, 2005; Turnbull, Turnbull, Erwin, & Soodak, 2006). As an educator, you should be acutely conscious of your own culture—how you interpret your school and how you act. But you also should understand and respect the cultures of your students, their families, other educators, your school, your community, and society at large.

Culture is by definition not monolithic; there is no single culture in the United States or in its schools. Indeed, our country and schools consist of many microcultures. People who are Scots-Irish in origin have certain traditions and cultures; their own native lan-

Figure 3.1 Cultural identity and microcultures

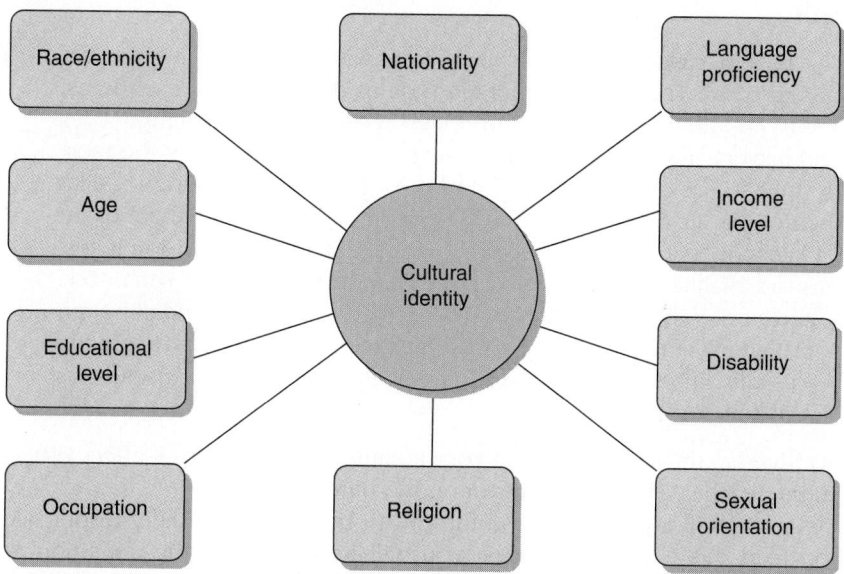

Source: Reprinted with the permission of James A. Banks from James A. Banks, "Multicultural Education: Characteristics and Goals," in James A. Banks & Cherry A. McGee Banks (Eds.), MULTICULTURAL EDUCATION: ISSUES AND PERSPECTIVES, 6th Edition. Hoboken, NJ: Wiley, page 16.

guage (Celtic or English) and music; common religions (Protestant or Roman Catholic); and common geographic origins (England, Scotland, Ireland, and Wales). Similar common identities—race/ethnicity, religion, language, and geographic origin—apply to other Americans, whether they are from Scandinavia, middle Europe, Southeast Asia, Central and South America, Africa, or the Middle East. Groups from each of these places have distinct traditions and cultures; each is a "micro" (smaller) group within the "macro" (larger) group known as Americans.

But these common traits are not the only ones that characterize a "micro" group or culture. Figure 3.1 identifies the principal microcultures that you will encounter in your schools, according to race/ethnicity, language, income, religion, disability, gender, sexual orientation, age, and geography. Throughout this chapter we use the term *diverse backgrounds,* or terms like it, to refer to students or others who are traditionally regarded as being from nonmajority ethnic, cultural, and linguistic backgrounds. We base our decision on IDEA, which refers to individuals who are from "minority" backgrounds, meaning that they, as a group, do not constitute the majority of people in America. Indeed, IDEA specifically refers to students who are not proficient in English and African American students when it describes its purposes of assisting schools to respond to "the growing needs of an increasingly diverse society." Simply put by Congress, "America's ethnic profile is rapidly changing".

Reflect on Figure 3.1. What microcultures comprise your own culture? With whom do you experience a sense of "we-ness"—a sense of identity with others' behaviors, communication styles, interests, and traditions? At Broken Arrow Middle School, De'ja's team of educators consists entirely of European American individuals: the school's principal, four sixth-grade general education teachers, a special education teacher, and a school social worker. Their culture differs from De'ja's and Sharilyn's in significant ways: by race, income, and level of education (remember, Sharilyn was in special education and earned her GED after leaving school to deliver her son). Let's consider what these facts mean as we begin to explore the IDEA language about a diverse society and rapidly changing ethnic profile, and let's do so by returning to that term *culture.*

Banks and Banks (2001) emphasize the "everyday existence" feature of culture: "Culture is in us and all around us, just as is the air we breathe. It is personal, familial, communal, institutional, societal, and global in its scope and distribution" (p. 31). Janet Vohs, the mother of a daughter who has cerebral palsy as well as special artistic talents, is a professional in the field of disabilities and memorably describes how pervasive, yet invisible, culture is:

> In Europe, years ago, castles and homes were built with a small, enclosed room used for making bread. Today, after generations of making bread in these rooms, it is unnecessary to add yeast to the bread dough. The yeast culture simply lives in the air and leavens any dough that happens to be placed there. For the most part, I have come to see our assumptions and presuppositions as invisible—like the yeast, part of the air we breathe. We do not consciously choose them or invent them: Philosophers have described them as "inherited." As I envision it, our "culture," instead of little yeast bacteria, is made up of millions of sentences, metaphors, and stories about life that we have learned to call true. And although the conditions that make the sentences and stories seem like the truth frequently change, they usually linger in the cultural atmosphere long after their usefulness has been exhausted. (Vohs, 1993, pp. 56–57)

What culture has "lived in the air" throughout your lifetime, and how does it affect you as a student and future teacher? How will you respond to different cultures?

In this chapter, we will lay a foundation for you to become a culturally responsive educator. As you read this chapter, we hope you will keep in mind the definition of *cultural responsiveness.*

> Cultural responsiveness is the extent to which research and practice in instruction and assessment take into consideration the cognitive, linguistic, and social assets of an individual (such as epistemologies, world views, and learning, teaching, and communication styles) that are culturally determined and shape the ways in which that individual learns and makes sense of his or her experiences. Cultural responsiveness refers to the fact that, in order to be fair and effective, education should be compatible with those assets and build on them, rather than disparage or ignore them. (Klingner & Solano-Flores, 2007, p. 231)

With the goal of helping you become more culturally responsive, we start with a history lesson.

THE SOCIAL CONTEXT OF SPECIAL EDUCATION

You cannot fully understand the social and cultural context of special education (or for that matter, general education) without knowing something about the history of special education in America's schools. That history is problematic. Educators who worked diligently to create effective and equal educational opportunities for *all* students often met resistance. The questions today are whether resistance still exists, and, if so, how does it affect the school systems, teachers and other professionals, and students and their families?

History Justifying IDEA

The history underlying IDEA's statements about diversity is reflected in theories about diversity, school systems' responses to those theories, and court cases related to nondiscriminatory evaluation.

Theories About Diversity

Three main theories of diversity exist—genetic deficit, cultural deficit, and cultural difference. Beginning in the 1700s, pseudo-scientists have developed **genetic deficit theories.** These theories held that white people are genetically superior to nonwhite people. For instance, craniologists—professionals who measured people's head size and classified their head shape—disagreed whether whites and nonwhites evolved from the same species. For the most part, however, they agreed that the supposedly larger brains of whites rendered them superior to nonwhites. Their theories contributed to justifying a two-track system of education, one for the "superior" whites and another for other people (McCray, Webb-Johnson, & Neal, 2003).

Other professionals have resorted to a **cultural deficit theory.** It blames the academic failure of students from diverse backgrounds on the inherent disadvantages that exist within the students' cultures. These professionals argue that the students' cultural deprivation (e.g., the lack of books in their schools or homes) explain why there are significantly disparate academic and behavioral outcomes between students from racially/ethnically diverse backgrounds and poverty backgrounds, on one hand, and their European American, middle-class counterparts, on the other (Harry & Klingner, 2007; McCray et al., 2003).

Genetic and cultural deficit theories reemerged in the early 1990s with the publication of *The Bell Curve* (Herrstein & Murray, 1994). In that book, the authors discussed the role that IQ (genetic deficit theory) plays in the social and economic differences among racial groups (cultural deficit theory). The book spurred intense controversy over its assertions that African Americans and other people of color are biologically less intelligent than European Americans. In an effort to bring evidence into the debates, the American Psychological Association issued a report stating that research does not support a genetic interpretation of IQ test-score differences between African Americans and European Americans. Nor does it support segregation and even racial **eugenics.** (The term *eugenics* refers to procedures to improve the human race by encouraging birth of children with allegedly "good" hereditary qualities and discouraging or preventing the birth of those with allegedly "undesirable" hereditary qualities.)

Still other professionals have advanced a theory of **cultural difference.** That theory is not identical with the cultural deficit theory, which we have just discussed, because cultural difference adherents argue that the academic failures of students from diverse backgrounds cannot be attributed to perceived disadvantages existing within their own cultures. Instead, school failure results principally because there is a mismatch (difference) between students' cultures and the cultures of the schools themselves (Harry & Klingner, 2006; Losen & Orfield, 2002).

Within the broad cultural difference theory there is a subtheory called the **cultural reproduction theory** (Bowles & Gintas, 1976; Skiba et al., 2006). It holds that ". . . racial and class inequity are reproduced over time through institutional and individual actions and decisions that maintain the status quo at the expense of less privileged groups (Mehan, 1993; Oakes, 1982; Skiba, Bush, & Knesting, 2002)" (Skiba et al., 2006, p. 1426).

How might these theories be educationally useful for De'ja's teachers? Certainly the genetic deficit theories are unhelpful. What about the cultural deficit theory? Undoubtedly, Sharilyn has lived on the economic edge; poverty is a fact of her everyday existence. But her ambition for De'ja—"De'ja, you have to go to school and work hard every day. A young black girl has to get her education or else end up like me"—belies any surrender to that harsh reality and in fact uses it as a motivator for her daughter.

What about the cultural difference theory? Although De'ja's teachers do not use the theory of cultural difference to explain how they relate to De'ja and Sharilyn, they might well do so. Just consider what you learned about Sharilyn in the vignette that opened this chapter and then take into account that all of De'ja's teachers and school administrators are fully certified, highly qualified professionals. We will return to the cultural difference theory throughout this chapter because it has so many implications for what you do and how you do it when working with students and families from diverse backgrounds.

School Systems' Responses to Theories

Genetic deficit, cultural deficit, and cultural difference theories have all played important roles in American education. During the early to mid-19th century, for example, advocates of the common school focused on developing educational programs that would provide all children with equal educational opportunities in integrated settings. They believed that an education that focused on basic skills, morality, and citizenship would put students

Inequities in education have existed for centuries in the United States.

from immigrant backgrounds (those from culturally and linguistically diverse backgrounds) on par with even the most privileged European American students who were born in the United States.

Nonetheless, students whose families immigrated to America still experienced school failure in large numbers and were often blamed for those failures, as though the fault were inherent in them and not in a school system that did not take their cultural differences into account but remained rigidly Eurocentric. Interestingly, at this same time, some states enacted antiliteracy laws that prohibited educators from teaching free or enslaved African Americans how to read (Span, 2003).

During the last half of the 19th century, school systems retained in grade second- and third-generation students from immigrant backgrounds and African American students at alarmingly high rates. Only rarely, however, did these same educators entertain the notion that students' poor performance might be linked to a combination of factors such as inappropriate instruction and racial discrimination (Deschenes, Cuban, & Tyack, 2001).

The progressive movement of the first half of the 20th century produced educational reforms designed to promote educational equity for all students, this time through differentiated instruction. Many educators believed that the new technology of standardized testing, when combined with differentiated instruction, would result in school placements that were more aligned with students' abilities and that differentiated placements—tracking—would provide the differently placed students with the skills they needed to be successful in life (Safford & Safford, 1998).

However well-intentioned, the consequence of differentiated instruction and standardized testing (administered in English) was that many children from immigrant backgrounds were retained in grade or assigned to schools' remedial and vocational tracks.

In turn, many students from racially/ethnically diverse backgrounds were segregated from their more "typical" European American peers largely because of their race, socioeconomic status, immigrant status, and language (Safford & Safford, 1998). School segregation was emblematic of segregation in nearly every other part of life (Mickelson, 2003).

Brown v. Board of Education. In the middle of the 20th century, segregation itself, in all of its forms, received frontal challenges from civil rights activists and their allies. These reformers attacked the most American of American institutions: schools and school racial segregation. They argued that the 14th Amendment to the U.S. Constitution, prohibiting a state from denying equal protection of the laws to anyone in its jurisdiction, required the schools to desegregate by race. In what many regard as one of its most far-reaching decisions, the U.S. Supreme Court, in *Brown v. Board of Education* (1954), agreed and ordered the defendants in the case (school boards in Topeka, Kansas, and state education agencies in Delaware, South Carolina, and Virginia) to desegregate by race with all due deliberate speed (Blanchett, Mumford, & Beachum, 2005; Ferri & Connor, 2005; Skiba et al., 2008).

One early consequence of the efforts at school racial desegregation was that, as enrollment of culturally and linguistically diverse children in previously all-white schools increased, so did their enrollment in self-contained programs for students who allegedly were "mildly mentally retarded" (Dunn, 1968; Mercer, 1973; National Research Council, 2002). History was repeating itself. Educators were tracking both African American and Latino students into programs for students with intellectual disability (at that time, the term used was *mental retardation*) and justifying their decisions with students' scores on standardized tests, which were usually administered in English and not students' native languages (Mercer & Richardson, 1975).

Just as African American students used the theory of equal opportunity and the facts of racial segregation to defeat school segregation, advocates for both Latino and African American students subsequently used the same theory and the same kind of data—the demographics of segregated placement—to successfully attack special education classification based on standardized tests administered in English to students who were not English-speaking (*Diana v. State Board of Education*, 1970; *Larry P. v. Riles*, 1972/1974/1979/1984).

Inarguably, *Brown* and other school-classification/segregation cases were the legal foundation that made it possible for advocates for students with disabilities to challenge classification procedures and seek the remedy of a free appropriate public education in the least restrictive environment (Turnbull, Stowe, & Huerta, 2007). As we pointed out in Chapter 1, these advocates were successful: Congress enacted P.L. 94–142, the Education for All Handicapped Children Act, in 1975 (later renamed the Individuals with Education Disabilities Act, or IDEA).

Court Cases Related to Nondiscriminatory Evaluation

The basis for IDEA's nondiscriminatory evaluation principle was a lawsuit brought by advocates for students with disabilities against the state of California. In that suit, the advocates alleged that the state and its schools classified students by relying on tests that were inherently biased against students from racially and linguistically diverse backgrounds. They even sought to prevent the state's school system from using standardized tests for evaluating students and classifying them into special education. They were resoundingly successful. In *Larry P. v. Riles* (1972/1974/1979/1984), a federal court held that the tests were inherently discriminatory and ordered the state and its schools to abandon the tests, use tests that were not discriminatory, and use other means for evaluating students for school placement. Each of those three remedies found its way into IDEA's principle of nondiscriminatory evaluation (Chapter 1). You will find them in the evaluation processes we describe in each of the chapters about categorical disability.

DISPROPORTIONATE REPRESENTATION

Let's return to De'ja, Sharilyn, and Broken Arrow Elementary School. After all, De'ja exemplifies the data about disproportionate representation. It is not too early to conclude that De'ja's placement in special education benefits her. She makes progress on academic subjects from one year to the next, as measured by her scores on assessments her teachers administer. She receives tutoring after school, and she and Sharilyn have captured the close attention of the school social worker, who serves as the channel for much of the communication among De'ja, her friends and supporters, and the school faculty.

In this section we will identify three data sources related to disproportionality: (a) the proportion of students served in special education by disability and race/ethnicity; (b) the percentage of students in special education in different educational environments by race/ethnicity; and (c) the percentage of students in racial/ethnic groups participating in education for students who are classified as gifted.

Risk Ratios

Risk ratio is the first aspect of disproportionality. Figure 3.2 identifies the **risk ratios** for students aged 6 through 21 receiving special education and related services by race/ethnicity and disability category (U.S. Department of Education, 2007). Risk ratios compare the proportion of a specific racial/ethnic group receiving special education services to the proportion among the total combined other racial/ethnic groups receiving special education.

The risk ratio of 1.0 represents expected representation. Risk ratios over 1.0 reflect overrepresentation for a particular racial/ethnic group as compared to the combination of all other groups; likewise, a risk ratio below 1.0 indicates underrepresentation of a particular group as compared to the combination of others. Figure 3.2 reveals that African American students are three times more likely to receive special education and related services for students with intellectual disabilities and 2.3 times more likely to receive these services for emotional disturbance than all other racial/ethnic groups combined.

◆ American Indian/Alaska Native students are 1.8 times more likely to receive special education and related services for students with specific learning disabilities,

Figure 3.2

Risk ratios for students ages 6 through 21 receiving special education and related services by race/ethnicity and disability category: Fall 2003

DISABILITY	AMERICAN INDIAN/ ALASKA NATIVE	ASIAN/ PACIFIC ISLANDER	BLACK (NOT HISPANIC)	HISPANIC	WHITE (NOT HISPANIC)
Specific learning disabilities	1.8	0.4	1.4	1.1	0.8
Speech/language impairments	1.3	0.7	1.1	0.9	1.1
Mental retardation	1.2	0.5	3.0	0.7	0.6
Emotional disturbance	1.5	0.3	2.3	0.5	0.8
Multiple disabilities	1.4	0.6	1.4	0.7	1.0
Hearing impairments	1.3	1.2	1.1	1.2	0.8
Orthopedic impairments	0.9	0.8	1.0	1.0	1.1
Other health impairments	1.2	0.4	1.1	0.4	1.6
Visual impairments	1.3	1.0	1.2	0.9	0.9
Autism	0.7	1.2	1.1	0.5	1.3
Deaf-blindness	2.5	1.2	0.9	1.0	0.9
Traumatic brain injury	1.4	0.6	1.2	0.6	1.2
Developmental delay	3.6	0.6	1.6	0.5	1.0
All disabilities	1.5	0.5	1.5	0.9	0.9

Note: The Department of Education still uses the term "mental retardation" rather than "intellectual disability" (see Chapter 9) and the term "emotional disturbance" rather than "emotional or behavioral disorders" (see Chapter 7). The Department uses the terms "Black" and "White," so we do, too.

Source: U.S. Department of Education (2007). 27th annual report to Congress on the implementation of the Individuals with Disabilities Education Act, 2005 (Vol. 1). Washington, DC: Author.

2.5 times as likely for those with deaf-blindness, and 3.6 times as likely for those with developmental delay than all other racial/ethnic groups combined.

- ◆ Across all disability categories, American Indian/Alaska Native and African American students are 1.5 times as likely to receive special education and related services, and Asian/Pacific Islander, Hispanic, and White students are slightly underrepresented in special education.

These are national figures. Variations exist at state and local levels, as we will discuss later in the chapter.

Percentage of Students in Special Education in Different Environments by Race/Ethnicity

The second aspect of disproportionality is the extent to which students are included in general education classrooms rather than more restrictive settings. Figure 3.3 highlights the percentage of students aged 6 through 21 who receive special education and related services in different educational environments, according to race/ethnicity (U.S. Department of Education, 2007).

Black students with disabilities are least likely to spend the greatest amount of time in the general education classroom and are most likely to spend the greatest time in special settings. Alternatively, White students with disabilities are most likely to experience inclusiveness rather than restrictiveness. These findings on restrictive placements also ex-

Figure 3.3 Percentage of students ages 6 through 21 with disabilities receiving special education and related services in different environments, by race/ethnicity: Fall, 2003

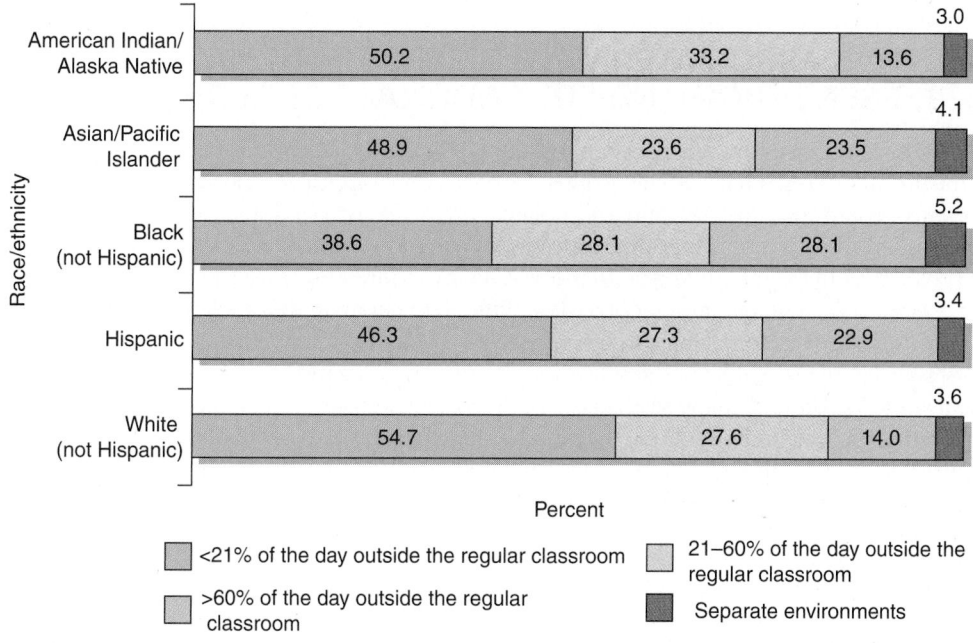

American Indian/Alaska Native: 50.2 | 33.2 | 13.6 | 3.0
Asian/Pacific Islander: 48.9 | 23.6 | 23.5 | 4.1
Black (not Hispanic): 38.6 | 28.1 | 28.1 | 5.2
Hispanic: 46.3 | 27.3 | 22.9 | 3.4
White (not Hispanic): 54.7 | 27.6 | 14.0 | 3.6

Race/ethnicity

Percent

☐ <21% of the day outside the regular classroom   ☐ 21–60% of the day outside the regular classroom
☐ >60% of the day outside the regular classroom   ■ Separate environments

Source: U.S. Department of Education (2007). 27th annual report to Congress on the implementation of the Individuals with Disabilities Education Act, 2005 (Vol. 1). Washington, DC: Author.

ist in studies from the Office for Civil Rights (Fierros & Conroy, 2002); in statewide data from Indiana (Skiba, Poloni-Staudinger, Gallini, Simmons, & Feggins-Azziz, 2006); and in district-level data in a southwestern state (de Valenzuela, Copeland, Qi, & Park, 2006). De'ja, however, participates in the general education courses in reading, writing, science, math, and social studies with support in reading, math, and study hall from a special educator, Mr. Koester.

Obviously, educational placements at the elementary and secondary level impact post-secondary educational opportunities. What trends do you predict from Figure 3.2 regarding differential rates of dropout and post-secondary educational attainment?

Gifted Education Placement

If you predicted an increase in dropout and post-secondary educational attainment, you would have been correct. What about the representation of students across racial/ethnic groups in programs for students regarded as gifted? The answer comes from data about the percentage of gifted and talented students in public elementary and secondary schools by race/ethnicity in 2002 (U.S. Department of Education, 2008). Each percentage reported below is the percentage of the total population of each racial/ethnic group within the gifted and talented public school programs.

- ◆ American Indian/Alaska Native—4.9 percent
- ◆ Asian/Pacific Islander—11.1 percent
- ◆ Black—3.1 percent
- ◆ Hispanic—3.7 percent
- ◆ White—7.8 percent
- ◆ Average Total—6.4 percent

Overrepresentation of culturally and linguistically diverse students in special education placements remains a problem today.

Clearly, Asian/Pacific Islander and White students are overrepresented in gifted programs, and American Indian/Alaska Native, Black, and Hispanic students are underrepresented.

FACTORS ASSOCIATED WITH DISPROPORTIONATE REPRESENTATION AND EDUCATIONAL EQUALITY

Go to the Activities and Application section in Chapter 3 of MyEducationLab and complete Activity 2. As you read the case and answer the accompanying questions, reflect on how the teacher's perception may or may not have been a factor in recommending this student for special education services.

Let's consider these findings and explore the factors associated with the outcomes for students from different racial/ethnic groups. Figure 3.4 provides a composite of numerous factors that contribute, individually and collectively, to disproportionate representation and disproportionate opportunities for educational equality.

We will help you understand these data by addressing three key microcultures—race/ethnicity, language, and income. It is difficult to separate these microcultures because they often overlap. To distinguish them, it helps to take two steps: first, understand the factors associated with each microculture and, second, understand how these factors affect the educational success of many students from diverse backgrounds. It cannot be said that De'ja is not making progress in school; the data her teachers have accumulated show she is making progress (with greater progress in some courses than others). Yet it is undeniable that race and poverty strongly influence her educational experiences and progress.

Racial/Ethnic Considerations

The national data on placement in special education programs make it clear that African American and American Indian/Alaska Native students are at special risk of being identified as having a disability. They are also at risk for not being identified as eligible for gifted education. Most research on racial disproportionality has focused on African American students; there is scant research about American Indian/Alaska Native students. Overall, the research reveals that African American students are disproportionately placed into programs for students with intellectual disabilities or emotional-behavioral disorders. (We will discuss language considerations separately, in the next section.)

Three special education categories where educators have the greatest leeway for exercising their judgments about students' abilities and needs are learning disabilities, intellectual disabilities, and emotional-behavioral disorders (O'Connor & Fernandez, 2006; National Research Council, 2002). These categories are called "high judgment categories" because they collect students with milder disabilities who are usually identified after starting school, and they rely on educational and psychological assessments that entail professional judgment. Two of these categories—intellectual disabilities and emotional-behavioral disorders—are especially problematic for disproportionality. In comparison, students in so-called nonjudgment categories, such as visual impairments, hearing impairments, and orthopedic impairments, often are identified early; their assessments tend to focus on biological, objectively determined traits.

Professional judgment is not the only factor related to the disproportionate placement of African American students in the categories of intellectual disabilities and emotional-behavioral disorders. As you will recall, the National Research Council (2002) identified poverty as the major contributing factor. Researchers in special education have questioned that finding. They have tried to disentangle race and poverty and determine how each factor contributes to disproportionality (Skiba, Poloni-Staudinger, Simmons, Feggins-Azziz, & Chung, 2005). By studying placement trends in Indiana, they concluded that poverty either had no effect on the extent of placement disparities; conversely, it magnified the effect of race. Given these seemingly conflicting conclusions, the researchers tried to identify other factors. They concluded that the strongest predictor of disproportionate special education placement is the rate of school suspensions and expulsions.

In light of that finding, we encourage you to study Figure 3.3 and its data on the percentage of students suspended or expelled by race/ethnicity. You will find that Black students

Figure 3.4

Factors differentially associated with students from diverse racial/ethnic backgrounds

INDICATOR	TOTAL	WHITE	BLACK	HISPANIC	ASIAN/PACIFIC ISLANDER	AMERICAN INDIAN/ ALASKAN NATIVE
A. Child/Youth Factors						
a.1 Percentage of babies with low birth weight	8	7	13	7	8	7
a.2 Child mortality rates (deaths per 100,000 population), 1–4 years	68	28	47	30	23	45
a.3 Percentage of children aged 12–17 who used alcohol during past month	18	20	11	16	69	20
a.4 Number of live births per 1,000 females 15–19 years old	41	38	63	83	17	53
B. Family Factors						
b.1 Percentage distribution of family households, by female householder, no husband present	19	4	47	24	13	29
b.2 Percentage of children under 5	21	16	39	31	11	43
b.3 Percentage of children aged 6–18 whose mother had completed high school	85	93	84	57	87	84
b.4 Percentage distribution of 8th-grade public school students who report that people in their home speak a language other than English all or most of time	13	4	7	47	49	11
b.5 Percentage of 8th-grade students in public schools with more than 25 books at home	70	80	58	46	69	62
b.6 Percentage of 8th-grade students in public schools who use a computer at home	88	93	80	75	94	78
b.7 Percentage of 8th-grade students in public schools who watch 6 hours or more of television daily outside of school hours	15	11	32	17	11	11
C. School Factors						
c.1 Percentage of public school students in kindergarten through 12th grade who had ever been suspended	11	9	20	10	6	11
c.2 Percentage of public school students in kindergarten through 12th grade who had ever been expelled	10	6	11	24	4	15

continued

Figure 3.4 (continued)

INDICATOR	TOTAL	WHITE	BLACK	HISPANIC	ASIAN/PACIFIC ISLANDER	AMERICAN INDIAN/ ALASKAN NATIVE
c.3 Percentage of public school students in kindergarten through 12th grade who repeated a grade	2	1	5	1	.5	3
c.4 Percentage of 16- to 24-year-olds who were high school dropouts in 2003	10	8	17	11	5	10
c.5 Percentage distribution of students below basic reading achievement levels in 8th grade	26	17	46	44	21	43
c.6 Percentage distribution of students below basic math achievement levels in 8th grade	32	20	61	52	22	48
c.7 Percentage of high school graduates who completed advanced academic coursework in mathematics	44	47	32	31	69	29
c.8 Percentage of high school students who reported that they engaged in a physical fight on school property	12	10	17	17	13	24

All percentages are rounded off to the nearest percentage point.

Source: Kewal Ramani, A., Gilbertson, L., Fox, M. A., & Provasnik, S. (2007). *Status and trends in the education of racial and ethnic minorities.* Washington, DC: U.S. Department of Education; U.S. Department of Education Office of Special Programs. (2005). *Status and trends in the education of American Indians and Alaska Natives.* Washington, DC: Author.

are approximately two times more likely than White, Hispanic, and American Indian/Alaska Native students to be suspended or expelled and four times more likely than Asian/Pacific Islander students tend to experience the same discipline (U.S. Department of Education Office of Special Programs, 2005). These data do not reveal how many instructional hours these students lost, but the lost learning opportunities were certainly substantial and damaging. Culturally responsive discipline is especially important as an effective way to reduce suspensions and expulsions and increase opportunities to learn (Cartledge & Kourea, 2008; Skiba et al., 2008).

Uppermost in any discipline plan is to encourage the student to want to engage in the socially appropriate behavior. The definition of a culturally responsive disciplined classroom may vary; but at the very least, key features need to include cultures of fairness, attitudes of caring and commitment to teaching [diverse] students with disabilities, and teachers skilled in implementing culturally responsive behavioral interventions. (Cartledge & Kourea, 2008, p. 362)

Discipline is not a problem for the educators who work with De'ja. They note (in her IEP) that she sometimes is "easily upset and pulled off task by others" and can become "very frustrated with the other students" because she "has some difficulty distinguishing between a person doing something by accident and a person doing something on purpose." But they also speak about her personality as a "plus" for her, and they praise her resiliency in dealing with the challenges she faces.

IEP Tip

It is especially helpful when IEP teams include a person knowledgeable about the student's cultural background who can help interpret behaviors and make recommendations about appropriate classroom strategies.

When a male classmate began to bully her verbally (with sexual and racial innuendos constituting the majority of his taunts), De'ja responded by not going to school. Her truancy impeded her progress; her IEP addressed that and her academic scores. Nothing that Sharilyn did—no degree of complaining to the school staff—seemed to blunt the bullying. Nothing, that is, until she told one of De'ja's teachers that, the year before, she was so angry that she had thought about giving De'ja a gun to bring to school.

Upon hearing that, the teacher immediately contacted the school security officer, who was duty-bound to investigate. He went to Sharilyn's home, confronted her, determined she had no intention to give a gun or other weapon to De'ja, and then filed a report with the local police department.

Incensed that the school staff would cause a police officer to investigate a conversation that related to the year before, Sharilyn has cut off almost all contact with De'ja's teachers. Now the school social worker communicates with one of Sharilyn's friends, who in turn communicates with Sharilyn.

The school is watching the bully "like a hawk" and has developed a plan to shape the boy's behavior. The plan is working: De'ja is back in school.

Box 3.1 adds a valuable perspective about mediating cultural differences. Its author, Michael Lamb, graduated from an elite private school in Chicago and from an equally selective university. Turning his back on law school and an unquestionably bright financial future, he chose to return to Chicago and teach in the general education program in its public schools. His story is worth your careful attention; notice how he converts the traditional "three R's" (reading, writing, and arithmetic) into "four R's"—respect, relationships, rigor, and resilience. Just consider how supported De'ja and Sharilyn would feel if they had the benefits of the "Four R's" approach.

Language Considerations

It is difficult to teach you about language as an element of culture unless we lay a foundation that consists of several points. The first point has to do with terminology. Formerly, teachers described students who need special language instruction because of their cultural background as being limited English proficient (LEP). More often nowadays, they refer to them as English language learners. They may even use the shorthand term "ELLs." In the spirit of using person-first language, as we recommend in Chapter 1, we use the phrase "students who are learning English." That phrase—not LEP or ELL—is consistent with Barrera's (2006) recommendation to use a "more respectful manner of reference to these students" (p. 142).

The second point relates to students' English proficiency. Quite naturally, students vary in their English proficiency. Their proficiency can be represented by a continuum of five stages (Hoover, Klingner, Baca, & Patton, 2008):

◆ Stage 1: Silence/Receptive or Preproduction Stage—Students understand approximately 500 English words but cannot use them. For 1 to 6 months, students tend to rely on gestures, body language, or yes/no responses.

◆ Stage 2: Early Production Stage—Students expand their receptive vocabulary to about 1,000 words and begin to use short phrases to respond to simple questions. This stage lasts about 6 months.

◆ Stage 3: Speech Emergence Stage—Students' receptive vocabulary expands to about 3,000 words. They begin to use simple sentences. This stage often lasts 1 year.

◆ Stage 4: Intermediate Language Proficiency Stage—For another year or so, students expand their understanding and use about 6,000 words. They move from simple to complex statements, provide opinions, and are able to write essays.

◆ Stage 5: Advanced Language Proficiency Stage—During the final stage, students have a vocabulary and grammar comparable to same-age native speakers. They can participate in content discussions at grade level and can succeed in complicated writing tasks. Reaching Stage 5 may take 5 to 7 years.

The Four-R Approach

"Mr. Lamb, why do I gotta raise my hand?"

"I ain't no little kid!"

"You not my daddy!"

I often heard these comments as a first-year reading teacher on Chicago's South Side. On good days, I faced skepticism; on bad, defiance.

To my students, I had no depth. Why, I asked myself, can't they detect my good intentions? Why don't they give me the benefit of the doubt? How can I reach and convince them?

I was shocked when my assistant principal told me in my second month there, "I think you've lost them for the year, you'll just have to try to find some way to make the best of it." Was this how my teaching career would go: a white liberal with good intentions who ultimately failed? I intended the opposite result.

Critical self-reflection forced me to realize that I had no context to my students. Particularly after half of the staff left each year, they had no idea why I would stay at the school, let alone genuinely care about them. I had been operating on assumptions about myself and my students, but to communicate with my students, I had to ask myself: Why am I here? Is it about me or about them? Who am I and where did I come from? What do I bring to them? What strengths do they bring to the table? I found that the most important tools were concepts any teacher can use.

I needed to make my respect for my students, families, and their lives clear. No matter who I was, what decisions I had made in my own life, or what my values were, I had to show them that I respected their essential humanity, their innate goodness.

Nor could I let their misbehavior cause me to think that they were flawed. Equally, I could not judge them by their test scores alone. I had to affirm that each could become a better reader, regardless of their scores.

Now, I started to connect with my students. However, it was not until I brought my mother to school for Thanksgiving that relationships began to form. I knew about the importance of relationships, but I was not sure exactly how to build them.

I had determined that my students' parents were essential for both me and their children's education. I called all of them the first day of school, seeking their trust. At the first parent-teacher conference, I said I was all about power and opportunity for our students. From then on, they were major resources for me. I do not remember one interaction that ended negatively that year. But I couldn't get my students to buy in.

I thought about relationships and differences and realized I needed to find roots with my students. Could they and I transcend the power-over relationship where I was dominant and they were acquiescent? I believed so; now, my duty would be to reach out and learn about my students.

To reach out meant giving them the benefit of the doubt and teaching them to give the same to me. We had to find ways to create relationships. With a relationship, we could understand; with understanding, we could give each the benefit of any doubts. We could begin to trust, to solve our problems together.

When I brought my mother to class before Thanksgiving, my students saw me as not just their teacher, but as a man with a visible origin and palpable values. They asked her, "What was he like as a kid?" They asked me, "What was your most embarrassing moment?" We began to see each other as a person; the common humanity became manifest. Now, my students saw me as a more whole person; they also could get some dirt on me. My mother was now "Grandma," making me "school Daddy." They were still skeptical, but less so; still angry, but less so.

Late in fall term, I asked my assistant principal for guidance. She turned the question back on me, asking what I learned at my high school and what I thought my students deserved to know. That was a turning point: thereafter, I built rigor into my curriculum. We would become critical thinkers together, whether reading Shakespeare's *Much Ado About Nothing* or *Fahrenheit 451*.

I knew I could not control whether my students liked me or thought I was cool. But I could control my academic expectations of them. I knew hard work in school gave me power to make my own decisions about the opportunities that came to me because of that work.

I was determined to give my students this same sense of control over their own futures by insisting on hard work and academic rigor. At the start of the school year, only 12 percent of my eighth-grade students met standards on the ITBS reading test; at the end, 71 percent met national standards on the state test. The next year I began a two-year loop with my new homeroom; after the seventh- and eighth-grade years, these students had the same success: from only 12 percent achieving standards, 67 percent did Three of them started below the 36th percentile and ended up scoring in the 94th their eighth-grade year.

Expecting hard work also caused the students to feel more respected. When low expectations exist, students feel unchallenged; they believe their teachers are condescending.

When challenges arise, resilience is essential. My students usually would get in trouble or fail academically because they let little issues spiral out of control; they were uncertain of forgiveness and lacked strategies to resolve routine problems. When called to account for minor matters, they would escalate their reactions; they did not expect understanding and forgiveness.

Challenged by test questions or difficult reading passages, they would make the problem appear to be a question of their behavior instead of their intelligence.

Obviously, it takes a student who does not use English a long time to master it for school purposes. While the student is learning English, she also must master the content of a curriculum offered in English. The lack of useful English undoubtedly impedes that mastery and may suggest to some teachers that the student has a disability. Be cautious of reaching that conclusion; the student may not have one and may simply need to learn the majority language.

It is a simple fact that language issues are tied to racial/ethnic issues, especially for Hispanic, American Indian/Alaska Native, and Asian/Pacific Islander students. During the 2003–04 school year, 3.8 million students (11 percent of the student population) received services to learn English. California and Texas have the greatest number of students receiving instruction in English; the New York City public schools, Los Angeles Unified schools, and Dade County (Miami) schools are the cities with the greatest density of non-English-speaking students (U.S. Department of Education, 2006). Of the 3.8 million students who are receiving English instruction, 466,122 are also served in special education (12 percent of the population of students receiving English language instruction) (U.S. Department of Education, 2008). Remarkably, students speak over 400 different languages, with Spanish by far the most prevalent (U.S. Department of Education, 2001).

Should you, as a future educator and perhaps special educator, be concerned that students who are learning English are disproportionately identified as having disabilities (Klingner, Artiles, & Méndez Barletta, 2006; Rueda & Windmueller, 2006; Wilkinson, Ortiz, Robertson, & Kushner, 2006)? Undoubtedly, the answer is "yes." Racial disproportionality is not the only cultural challenge in special education; disproportionality is also associated with language proficiency.

Look at the data in Figure 3.2 and especially the data related to the risk ratio for different racial/ethnic groups and different disability categories. You will note that the risk ratio for Hispanic students for the category of learning disabilities is 1.1; that fact does not indicate a national problem with overrepresentation (U.S. Department of Education, 2007). But, national data can mask differences at state and local levels.

An in-depth analysis of placement trends of students learning English (with over 90 percent being of Hispanic heritage) found that in California the proportion of students receiving special education services across the state was proportional; however, within this overall statewide proportionality, there were pockets of disproportionality.

◆ Students learning English were disproportionately identified as having a disability in the three largest urban districts.

◆ Elementary-level placement patterns were proportional; however, at the end of elementary school and throughout high school, placement patterns were disproportional.

◆ Students with limitations in both their native language and in English had the highest rate of being identified as having a disability.

◆ Students learning English from low-income backgrounds had larger representation in special education programs as contrasted to their counterparts with middle and higher incomes (Artiles, Rueda, & Salazar, 2005).

Similarly, analysis of district placement trends in a school district comprised of 12.1 percent students who are learning English indicated that they were more likely to be identified as having learning disabilities and to be placed in more segregated educational settings as contrasted to students with English proficiency (de Valenzuela, Copeland, Qi, & Park, 2006).

How can you as a teacher be culturally responsive, ensuring that students who are learning English receive the language instruction that they need and not unjustifiably identifying them as having a learning disability? Some answers come from research about the correctness of decisions that educators made to classify students who are learning English into special education (Wilkinson et al., 2006). After examining the decisions of multidisciplinary evaluation teams, researchers developed questions intended to guide future evaluation team members as they collect data and decide whether to make a student eligible for special education. These questions focus on what has been done in the past to modify instruction and engage in systematic problem-solving; alternative explanations for students' academic and behavioral challenges as contrasted to suspecting a disability; ensuring that procedures for evaluation are nondiscriminatory; and taking precautions to increase the likelihood that the multidisciplinary team addresses key questions through appropriate procedures and includes people with the necessary expertise to make sound instructional decisions. The tips provided in Box 3.2 can be helpful in considering how you can be culturally responsive in including students who are learning English in the general curriculum.

A greatly overlooked issue is language diversity as it relates to Native American students. Almost all research on language diversity and English instruction for students receiving special education has focused on students whose families have immigrated to the U.S. and their process in learning English. However, Native American students and families have experienced language loss, perhaps more than any other racial/ethnic group. For example, more than 300 Native American languages were used in the United States in the 19th century, but only approximately half of those exist today (Aguilera & LeCompte, 2007). As of about 10 years ago, only about 50 of these languages were being taught to children and about 20 were used widely by children. Many Native American families desperately want their children to learn their native language and even to use it rather than English. As stated by a professor at the University of Hawaii:

> To learn your language is to learn the soul of your culture, and when the language is gone you are forever disconnected from the wisdom of ancestors; the loss of language inevitably results in losing the gods you pray to, the land you live on, and your own government and sovereignty. (Kameyeleihiwa, cited in Aguilera & LeCompte, 2007, p. 11)

A number of language immersion programs have been developed to promote the maintenance of the language of Native American students while simultaneously teaching them English (Hermes, 2007; Yazzie-Mintz, 2007). When you have a student whose native language is not English, you may want to consider referring the student to an English-as-second-language program or a comparable English immersion program.

Poverty Considerations

As compared to approximately one fourth of students in the general population, over one third of students with disabilities live in households with incomes of $25,000 or less (Wagner, Marder, Blackorby, & Cardeso, 2002). De'ja is one of those students. Furthermore, almost twice as many students in the general population, as compared to students with disabilities, live in households with incomes of more than $75,000. A national study of el-

Box 3.2

INCLUSION TIPS

	What You Might See	What You Might Be Tempted to Do	Alternate Responses	Ways to Include Peers in the Process
Behavior	A Latino student who is an English-language learner and has learning disabilities puts her head on her desk when she does not understand written instructions. She rarely completes assignments.	Tell her that she should go to bed at a reasonable hour so that she can stay awake and complete her classwork.	List steps of the instructions in sequence on the board. Use pictures whenever possible. Ask parents how help is requested and provided in their culture.	Model the skill of asking for help for all students and let them role-play. Provide reinforcement when they use the skill and encourage their classmates to use it.
Social interactions	She rarely initiates a greeting but usually responds to one appropriately.	Do not push her to initiate because you believe this skill will develop as her English improves.	Have students share greetings from the different languages represented in the classroom.	Have this student and others teach the different greetings and reinforce use of them in and outside the classroom.
Educational performance	The student has strong math skills but performs poorly on word problems when she has to read them.	Request that she have more time outside of the general education classroom for intensive English instruction.	Provide word problems in the student's native language and English.	Establish a peer tutoring system within the class: she can tutor students who have problems with computation. Students who share the same primary language can help her read the word problems.
Classroom attitudes	She complains of a head- or stomachache and asks to go to the clinic when assigned to read a children's novel and answer comprehension questions in written form.	Allow her to go to the clinic, hoping that she will grow out of this behavior as her English improves.	Try to obtain a copy of the book in her native language.	Have students work in cooperative groups to partner-read and answer questions.

ementary and middle school students with disabilities revealed that students classified into the categories of intellectual disabilities and emotional-behavioral disorders are significantly more likely to have a single parent with a lower educational level than students in any other disability category. Both single-parent status and low parental education are associated with greater levels of poverty (Fujiura & Yamaki, 2000). That is the case for Sharilyn, who is a single parent and has earned her GED but not attended college. Additionally, parents who are less educated and who have lower incomes have a lower perception of their child's needs for specialized health care services and less access to the special therapies their children need (Porterfield & McBride, 2007).

The normal curve of intelligence, as we will describe in Chapter 5, assumes a bell-shaped curve with an average IQ of 100. One of the criteria for identifying a student with intellectual disabilities is that the student has an IQ two standard deviations below the mean (100)—that is, an IQ of 70 or below. The effect of poverty seems to be to enlarge the number of students classified as having an intellectual disability (National Research Council, 2002; O'Connor & Fernandez, 2006).

IDEA pays special attention to homeless students. It requires state and local educational agencies to cooperate with social service agencies in reaching out to and enrolling these students and then assuring that they have all of IDEA's benefits if they qualify. A child who is homeless is defined as one who does not have a regular and adequate night-time residence (Gargiulo, 2006). In part because Sharilyn cannot always pay rent, she and De'ja have lived in different places, sometimes several different ones each school year, in their hometown. They are not exactly homeless. But their residences are not particularly stable. Moving from one place to another, De'ja misses school more than many other students do, and her academic progress suffers.

Many risk factors contribute to homelessness, including poverty, domestic violence, alcohol/drug addiction, and low levels of parental education, as evidenced by a study of approximately 44,500 urban women. Among them, 11 percent reported at least one experience with homelessness in a 7-year period (Webb, Culhane, Metraux, Robbins, & Culhane, 2003). These researchers reported that the most vulnerable group of women were African American mothers with low levels of education who had four or more children during the 7-year period.

Children and youth who are homeless also are more frequently identified as having emotional or behavioral disorders (Jozefowicz-Simbeni & Israel, 2006). These students are embarrassed that they do not have a home (DeForge & Zehnder, 2001). When asked about how her classmates might respond if they knew she lived in a shelter, one student answered, rather typically: "They all have houses or apartments. And if I told one person they would tell everyone. Then I would get teased, 'nah nah, you live in a shelter'" (p. 4). When Congress enacted the No Child Left Behind Act, it also reauthorized the McKinney-Vento Homeless Assistance Act, which authorizes services to assist schools to educate students who are homeless. Similarly, when Congress reauthorized IDEA in 2004, it blended the McKinney-Vento act into special education (Jozefowicz-Simbeni & Israel, 2006).

Earlier in the chapter, we said it is important to "unpack" the various factors related to students and their cultural and other backgrounds. We have been doing that by showing you the connections between racial/ethnic factors, language, poverty, and homelessness. As you will recall, the National Research Council (2002) concluded that poverty was the major contributor to over-representation in disability categories and under-representation in gifted education for racial/ethnic groups. Further, as you have already learned, factors of disproportionality are not only related to poverty in and of itself but also to a range of racial/ethnic and language considerations.

Let's return to an analysis of Figure 3.4, particularly focusing on the data about the percentages of individuals under 5 years of age and between the ages of 5 and 11 years living in poverty by race/ethnicity. Black students under the age of 5 experience the highest rate of poverty—approximately 2.5 times the poverty rate for White and 3.5 times the poverty rate for Asian/Pacific Islander students (U.S. Department of Education, Office of Special Programs, 2005). Problematically, there are a number of other risk factors associated with poverty, also reflected in Figure 3.4, that put students at educational risk; these are the demographic factors of family structure and low birth weight and the social/educational environmental factors of parental education, access to books at home, and access to computers.

Research reveals that teachers readily comment on their students' poverty (Skiba, Simmons, et al., 2006), as a teacher participating in the study did:

> I don't really get to teach as much as I want to teach because I'm dealing with social problems, discipline problems, the welfare of the students, do they have

IEP Tip

When school social workers and school counselors are members of the IEP team, you can partner with them to identify how schools can reduce the educational challenges facing students from poverty backgrounds.

clothes, do they have shoes, do they have socks? Just basic survival things that I deal with before they can even do academics. (p. 1433)

That one teacher's comments reflected many colleagues' perspectives about the challenges of appropriately educating students from poverty-affected backgrounds (Skiba, Simmons, et al., 2006):

Respondents . . . appeared to resonate with the perspective that a "culture of poverty" creates disjuncture between what schools expect of students and families, and what students and families from poverty backgrounds bring with them (Payne, 2001). Further, our respondents made it clear that the needs of students from poverty backgrounds vastly outpace the resources available for meeting those needs, and were in substantial agreement with research (e.g., National Research Council) suggesting that a strong commitment to early intervention could significantly offset socioeconomic risk factors. (Skiba, Simmons, et al., 2006, p. 1446)

The educators who participated in the interviews in this research study strongly emphasized the role of poverty in creating disproportionate placement; however, the researchers detected a trend among respondents of being exceedingly hesitant to talk about race as a factor. They provided the following example:

Teacher: When you say minorities, are you, what are you speaking of?

Interviewer: Ethnic and racial minorities.

Teacher: Oh . . . OK . . . Alright. We have like . . . I guess we have about half and half. I don't know that, I've never really paid attention to it. (Skiba, Simmons, et al., 2006, pp. 1444–1445)

These same researchers, in a study published a year earlier, found that poverty made an inconsistent and weak contribution to the prediction of disproportional placement across different disability categories; when it did make a contribution, it typically magnified already existing racial disparities (Skiba et al., 2005). The researchers concluded that educators might be overlooking the contribution of race and instead attributing what are really racial disparities to poverty. Further, the researchers highlighted how hard it is for educators to discuss racial issues comfortably and candidly. The researchers, like the educators they interviewed, detected the tension—the cultural concerns—that affect professionals as they try to understand or discuss the relative contributions that race and poverty make to disproportionate representation in special education.

As an effective teacher, you can act on a daily basis to make a positive difference for students who experience poverty. Some of these include (Turnbull, Turnbull, Summers, & Poston, 2008):

◆ Partnering with the school social worker and/or school counselor to provide information to families on government benefits that are designed to assist families who experience poverty and have children with disabilities, such as Supplemental Security Income and Medicaid.

◆ Partnering with other educators in referring families to community agencies that provide economic resources related to food banks, job training, and affordable housing.

◆ Connecting students with organizations interested in providing direct support to students who have economic needs, such as Big Sister/Big Brother programs, community service programs, and religious programs.

◆ "Standing in the shoes" of students who experience poverty and seeking to understand the increased difficulties of concentrating on academic work given challenges associated with hunger, health care, cleanliness, and stress that results from environmental factors such as unsafe neighborhoods.

◆ Providing clear and understandable information to parents who have low levels of education to ensure that they are comfortable in partnering to support their child's educational success.

Relationships Among Race/Ethnicity, Language, and Poverty

As the evidence indicates, race, language, and poverty affect the classification of students into a disability category or into programs for students who have unusual gifts and talents. Figure 3.5 depicts the many factors that ultimately influence classification and student outcomes. It consists of six levels, starting from the macro (largest) perspective of values and then reflecting increasingly smaller (macro to micro) factors (Bronfenbrenner, 1979).

Figure 3.5 shows you the big picture, the multiple influences that affect children, families, and schools and how those influences align with race, language, and poverty. It suggests that it is wrong to conclude that all of the problems you may face in educating students reside in and originate from the students and their families. Let's examine Figure 3.5 in depth.

Majority Values (Layer 1)

As a rule, Americans value independence, personal control, achievement, competition, directness, future orientation, etc. (Hanson, 2004). These values are culturally rooted in our nation's history, but that does not mean they are the only acceptable ones. These values are the "yeast in the air" that you read about earlier in the chapter: ". . . our 'culture,' instead of little yeast bacteria, is made up of millions of sentences, metaphors, and stories about life that we have learned to call true" (Vohs, 1993, p. 57).

Figure 3.5 Ecological layers influencing the provision of appropriate education to students from diverse backgrounds

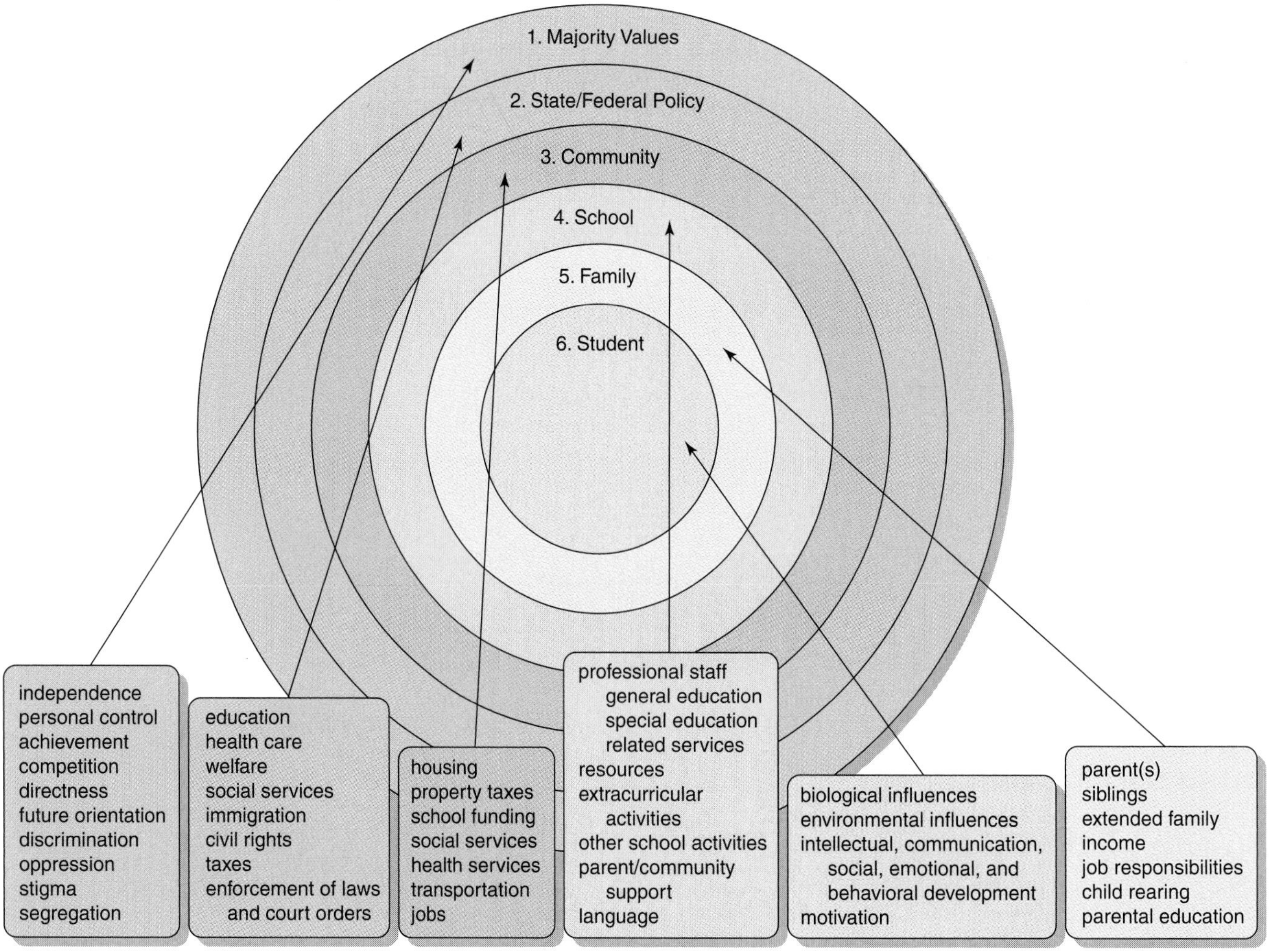

Many American families, however, have different cultural values. They believe in interdependence rather than independence, elder control rather than personal control, contentment rather than achievement, cooperation rather than competition, indirectness rather than directness, and present orientation rather than future orientation (Lynch & Hanson, 2004). Nevertheless, the standard expectation is that students will adhere to majority values and use English at school (Goff, Martin, & Thomas, 2007; Rueda, Klingner, Sager, & Velasco, 2008).

State/Federal Policy Factors (Layer 2)

The second ecological layer, state/federal policy, includes legislation and court decisions, especially those dealing with education, health care, welfare, immigration, and civil rights. But tax laws and the distribution of the income they raise are also important. It has been estimated that New York City alone requires more than $9 billion to improve its school facilities and $5 billion annually in operating funds (Evans, 2005). Thus, if communities (layer 3) and schools (layer 4) are going to be able to make those improvements, state and federal policy, including tax policy, must be taken into account.

Community Factors (Layer 3)

The interaction of race, language, and poverty is especially acute in urban communities and affects their efforts to deliver special education (Voltz & Fore, 2006). The 100 largest school districts in the United States provide education to approximately 68% of students of color (National Center for Educational Statistics, 2001). These urban communities, as well as communities around the country that are not in urban settings, must deal with issues of housing, property taxes, school funding, social services, health services, transportation, and jobs in order to provide a community context that advances the education of students from diverse backgrounds. Schools (layer 4), families (layer 5), and students (layer 6) are rarely able to improve unless their communities do, too.

> Current school funding formulas based on property taxes have been a corrupting influence on the road to equality, leading to a qualitatively different level of education for students based on their race, socioeconomic status, and community backgrounds. A system that bases equity in education on property taxes is inherently flawed, because property taxes reflect inequity. The current system of funding education functions much like a societal sorting mechanism for class, race, and privilege and creates a separate and unequal system of "haves" and "have-nots" with regard to education access. (Blanchett et al., 2005, p. 79)

School Factors (Layer 4)

At layer 4, school factors include the professional staff's qualifications, cultural responsiveness, and ongoing professional development. They also include resources in general education, special education, related services, and other special supports. Other factors come into play, too: parental support of schools; community support of schools; extracurricular opportunities; and transportation. Unfortunately, schools that have the highest number of students from diverse backgrounds also tend to have the greatest number of noncertified teachers, the highest teacher turnover, the most inadequate resources for providing differentiated instruction, the lowest overall funding, the most distrusting relationships with families, and the greatest deficit of support from the community (Berliner & Biddle, 1995; Blanchett et al., 2005; Kozol, 1991; Voltz & Fore, 2006). "Most achievement critics I meet believe that schools can be instruments of social change. They discount decades of evidence that schools reflect society much more than they shape it" (Evans, 2005, p. 586).

Family Factors (Layer 5)

You have already learned about a number of family factors that are more associated with different racial/ethnic, language, and poverty trends—number of parents in the home,

Rarely do highly qualified teachers (such as the one pictured here) find their way to the classrooms where students from diverse backgrounds constitute the majority of all students.

parental education, family income, family partnerships with educators, and reading materials in the home (see Figure 3.4).

> Research has shown that low maternal education is associated with the following increased risks: 9.9 times for having a mild intellectual disability, 5.3 times for having an emotional or behavioral disorder, and 2.1 times for having a specific learning disability. (Delgado & Scott, 2006)

Unfortunately, some educators blame parents for their children's problems when these educators should recognize that many parents from diverse backgrounds have been marginalized or oppressed.

All too often, parents of the students are themselves victims of unequal opportunities and are so encased within the ecological layers of Figure 3.5 that they are not as free to change as some people who have not experienced oppression might believe. That is not to say that they do not have strengths related to their survival skills, religious faith, access to extended family support, diligence in spite of adversity, and strong desire for their children to have opportunities that they did not have as a child (Harry & Klingner, 2006; Harry, Klingner, & Hart, 2005).

How does Sharilyn prevail? She and De'ja both receive Social Security benefits—Sharilyn because she has a disability and De'ja because she has one and is in a family the federal government classifies as "poor." Sharilyn is active in a small church; some of its members have created a circle of support for her, substituting for her mother who lives an hour's drive away and is raising some of her other grandchildren. As you read before, Sharilyn is adamant that De'ja should go to school, telling her that an education is the key for De'ja to achieve her goal of being a chef. De'ja herself is resilient; she still attends school, is making progress there, and has endeared herself to her teachers.

Student Factors (Layer 6)

At last, we come to the students. It may be easy for some educators to criticize the students who do not achieve academically, whose behavior leads to classroom disruption, or who have excessive absenteeism. Using the ecological framework shown in Figure 3.5, however, they might easily understand that biological and environmental factors shape students' achievement, behavior, school attendance, and other characteristics.

What's the "take away" message? It is that disproportionality in special education placement needs to be understood within the context of disproportionality in society across all six ecological layers of Figure 3.5. To ensure equal opportunities for students from culturally diverse backgrounds, it is necessary to provide not only culturally responsive instruction of students, but also culturally responsive support of families, culturally responsive support of schools, culturally responsive community living, culturally responsive state/federal policy, and culturally diverse societal values (Blanchett et al., 2005; Reid & Knight, 2006). Being a culturally responsive educator means being not only an effective teacher of students but also being an advocate at all six ecological layers.

BECOMING A CULTURALLY RESPONSIVE TEACHER AND ADVOCATE

In this section, we offer four strategies that will assist you to be a culturally responsive teacher in rapidly changing American schools. They are: enhancing your self-awareness, increasing your knowledge and experiences concerning other cultures, implementing culturally responsive instruction, and advocating for systems change across layers.

Enhancing Your Self-Awareness

To become more self-aware culturally, we all should examine our own cultural values; realize that they are cultural values rather than the ultimate truth about what is "right" and "wrong;" and become aware of our stereotypes, biases, and prejudices. Change may follow awareness; certainly change requires awareness (Chamberlain, 2005; Sparks, 2008).

To examine your own culture, study Figure 3.6. You will see that it incorporates the picture of microcultures from Figure 3.1 and adds questions for you to consider in light of each

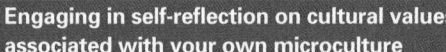

Figure 3.6 | Engaging in self-reflection on cultural values associated with your own microculture

1. As you reflect on Figure 3.1 in terms of your own overall cultural identity and the microcultures that shape your cultural identity, which microcultures are most influential in how you characterize your culture and which are least influential?
2. In light of your overall cultural identity and the contributing factors associated with each microculture, what do you consider to be your core cultural values?
3. In light of your own experiences and cultural values, what are your preferences and biases regarding the microcultures that are different from your own? (Go through each microculture and think carefully about what it is that draws you to other people and what it is that makes you uncomfortable or tends to make you feel judgmental about other people.)
4. How might your cultural values influence your preferences to work with students with particular characteristics and your biases against working with students with other characteristics?
5. How do your cultural values influence your views of standards and expectations associated with:
   • Academic achievement
   • Classroom behavior
   • Participation in extracurricular activities
   • Developing trusting partnerships with families
   • Likelihood of becoming a culturally responsive teacher
   • Likelihood of becoming a culturally responsive systems advocate
6. How do your own microcultures influence your reaction to the information in this chapter? Were there any times in reading this chapter that you felt "your buttons being pushed"? If so, how does your own cultural identity contribute to that? If not, why not?

microculture. As you use Figure 3.6 to reflect on your culture, keep a journal of your reflections, have conversations with friends and acquaintances within your own culture and across cultures, be perceptive to the social and political media, examine your own values, and ask whether your culture is really the one and only right way or just another way to follow.

Increasing Your Knowledge and Experiences of Other Cultures

It can be fascinating to learn about other cultures. As students, you can join community and campus organizations with a diversity focus, have extended conversations with people from diverse backgrounds, and develop friendships with people from diverse backgrounds. In time, you may be invited to partake in their cultural traditions, holiday celebrations, and routines. You can follow international and national news stories about people from other cultures, read books about them, go to movies produced in other countries, take courses in cultural sociology or anthropology, and, if time and money permit, travel to other countries and try, while there, to "get into spiritual community" with the places you visit. Your studies about, say, the Navajo culture should identify the similarities and dissimilarities of that culture and your own. Consider the issues of independence and interdependence; determine which values the two cultures have in common and which they do not.

As you learn about other cultures, you will begin to understand how cultural values influence how families interpret the kind of instruction that feels right to them. It can be easy for European American educators not to realize how many educational approaches rely on European American values. For example, researchers describe the implementation of positive behavior support (you will learn about this approach in Chapter 10—it is a proactive, problem-solving approach for improving appropriate behavior and school outcomes) with Chinese American families (Wang, McCart, & Turnbull, 2007). They provide a case study showing how educators who wanted to offer positive behavior support for Meng, a 14-year-old middle school student identified as having AD/HD and problem behavior, needed to take into account the fact that Meng's grandmother was the family's decision maker. Meng's father and mother were not, and certainly Meng was not.

The researchers had to acknowledge that it was consistent with the family's culture for Meng's parents to give him a "cold face" (stern, reprimanding look) and not allow him to eat dinner if he had not finished his homework; these were punishing, not positive, responses. They had to understand that Meng's grandmother believed that Meng's problem behaviors resulted from something she had done wrong in her previous life and were influenced by bad spirits. In short, they had to understand Meng's culture and then adapt a culturally different intervention to suit him and his family.

Implementing Culturally Responsive Instruction

You can use four different strategies to implement culturally appropriate instruction. We describe each below.

Use the Adapted Posture of Cultural Reciprocity

IEP Tip

The IEP conference is an excellent time to use the adapted posture of cultural reciprocity as you learn from culturally diverse parents about their priorities and how they relate to their child's education.

Let's return to Meng. Having expanded your knowledge and experience about different cultures, you should be able to enter into a partnership with Meng's family and then use an educational practice that is acceptable to them. That's easier said than done. Under this approach, you and Meng's family share your respective views about how to teach Meng; you listen carefully (Harry, Kalyanpur, & Day, 1999; Kalyanpur & Harry, 1999). Box 3.3, Partnership Tips, describes the adapted posture of cultural reciprocity and decisions that were made by Meng's positive behavior support team based on their responsiveness to Meng's family's Chinese American values. Kalyanpur and Harry (1999) describe this strategy's purpose as follows:

> Awareness of cultural differences provides merely the scaffolding for building collaborative relationships. Knowledge of the underlying belief and value that brings about the difference in perspective provides the reinforcing strength to the relationship. . . . We suggest that professionals . . . engage in explicit discussions

Implementing Adapted Posture of Cultural Reciprocity

Steps in Adapted Posture of Cultural Reciprocity

1. Learn about the family's strengths, needs, preferences, and priorities by having informal conversations with them and by welcoming them and their child into your classroom. Identify their priorities and preferences for their child's educational program—IEP, placement, related services, extracurricular activities, and other school activities. Try to understand and honor their cultural values and priorities in order to establish a trusting partnership with them.

2. Invite the family to describe their cultural values and how they relate to their strengths, needs, preferences, and priorities. Ask why they have those values.

3. Identify any disagreements or alternative perspectives that you or other professionals have about providing educational supports and services to the student and/or family. Identify the cultural values embedded in *your* interpretation or in that of the other professionals. Identify how the family's views differ from your own.

4. Acknowledge and explicitly show respect for any cultural differences. Fully explain the cultural basis of your and your colleagues' professional assumptions or the assumptions of the student and family.

5. Through discussion and collaboration, determine the most effective way of adapting your and your colleagues' professional interpretations to the family's value system.

Decisions Made for Meng's Positive Behavior Support Plan

1. The behavior support team decided to use informal contacts (phone calls and home visits) rather than formal planning meetings at the beginning.

2. After Meng's family became more comfortable with his teachers, the behavior team asked a Chinese American teacher in his school to facilitate the behavior team.

3. The team recognized that Meng's family did not feel comfortable being an equal partner and accommodated to their choice.

4. The team respected Meng's family priority about addressing learning issues before behavior issues.

5. The team demonstrated respect for Meng's grandmother and listened to and accepted her suggestions about herbal treatments.

6. The team did not criticize Meng's family or make judgments about their practices.

7. The team had many conversations about punishment and did not ask the family to give up their current discipline practices, but did share information with them about alternative strategies.

8. The team supported the family's goal of Meng's academic expectations and encouraged his family to recognize the importance of Meng having some after-school time without stress.

Readers interested in a much more detailed description of the partnership between the behavior team and Meng's family can read about it in: Wang, M., McCart, A., & Turnbull, A. (2007). Implementing positive behavior support with Chinese American families: Enhancing cultural competence. *Journal of Positive Behavior Interventions, 9*(1), 38–51.

---

with families regarding different cultural values and practices, bringing to the interactions an openness of mind, the ability to be reflective in their practice, and the ability to listen to the other perspectives. Furthermore, they must respect the new body of knowledge that emerges from these discussions and make allowances for differences in perspectives when responding to the family's need. (Kalyanpur & Harry, 1999, p. 118)

Incorporate Five Components for Delivering Culturally Responsive Instruction

Having reached agreements with your students' families about their culturally driven priorities, you will need to instruct in ways that honor those understandings and the student's culture. Your instruction should "take into consideration the cognitive, linguistic, and social assets of an individual . . . that are culturally determined and shape the ways in which individuals learn and make sense of his or her experiences" (Klingner & Solano-Flores, 2007, p. 231). Box 3.4, Into Practice, depicts a useful framework for tailoring your instruction to the following five components of culturally responsive instruction: integrate content into your curriculum; help students understand cultural assumptions and biases; create a curriculum that facilitates the

PEARSON
myeducationlab

Go to the Building Teaching Skills and Dispositions section in Chapter 3 of MyEducationLab and complete the activities. As you interact with the simulation, consider how you could incorporate some of these strategies into your classroom.

Establishing a classroom conducive to learning for culturally and linguistically diverse students is important for the success of all children.

academic growth of students from diverse backgrounds; use your curriculum and teaching methods to modify your students' unacceptable racial attitudes; and include your students in various decisions about their education (Banks, 2002; van Garderen & Whittaker, 2006).

Capitalize Upon Instructional Consultation Teams

The good news is that you are not alone in your efforts to seek cultural responsiveness. A standard practice in schools is to have a referral process for special education. It is at the point of referral to special education that many problems associated with disproportionate placement begin. Thus, it has become increasingly prevalent for schools to develop a broad range of prereferral supports for students and for teachers in order to prevent inappropriate special education referrals.

There are different methods for implementing prereferral strategies that are often described by different names—instructional consultation teams (Gravois & Rosenfield, 2006), child study teams (Klingner & Harry, 2006), intervention assistance teams (Ortiz, Wilkinson, Robertson-Courtney, & Kushner, 2006), and teacher assistance teams (Chalfant & Pysh, 1989). These teams usually consist of general and special educators, bilingual specialists, school psychologists, and other specialists. Together, these professionals observe the student, brainstorm about the challenges and solutions, and create action plans to address the student's learning and behavioral challenges and ensure participation and progress in the general education curriculum.

These teams have been able to influence the disproportionate referral and placement of students from diverse backgrounds into special education (Gravois & Rosenfield, 2006).

INTO PRACTICE

Box 3.4

Components and Action Steps for Culturally Responsive Instruction

Offering a culturally responsive curriculum can involve five different components. This box identifies each component, defines it, and describes the relevant action steps.

Components	Definition	Action Steps
Content Integration	Content integration involves teachers using examples and content from a variety of cultures and groups to illustrate key concepts, principles, generalizations, and theories in their subject area or discipline.	• Reading biographies of women and people of color who are scientists and mathematicians • Learning about demographics of diverse groups • Using primary documents about the history of non-Anglo-European peoples • Reading multicultural literature • Including images of many kinds of families in the curriculum

The Knowledge Construction Process	The knowledge construction process includes teachers helping students to understand, investigate, and determine how the implicit cultural assumptions, frames of references, perspectives, and biases within a discipline influence the ways in which knowledge is constructed within it.	• Examining the degree to which authors in the curriculum are female and/or people of color • Including the perspectives of both the dominant and nondominant cultures in any description of historical conflict • Examining labels applied to people with disabilities from the perspective of the person • Validating the importance of languages other than English • Discussing the difference between Western and non-Western views on science • Interviewing community elders about their immigration experiences
An Equity Pedagogy	An equity pedagogy exists when teachers modify their teaching in ways that will facilitate the academic achievement of students from diverse racial, cultural, and social-class groups. This includes using a variety of teaching styles consistent with the wide range of learning styles within various cultural and ethnic groups.	• Knowing the cultural background of students and incorporating them into classroom instruction and procedures • Using cooperative learning or group experiences with students who learn best collaboratively • Placing students in pairs to encourage question-and-answer exchanges
Prejudice Reduction	This dimension focuses on the characteristics of students' racial attitudes and how they can be modified by teaching methods and materials.	• Making cooperative learning groups heterogeneous by gender, race, and language • Developing racial identity (e.g., through a family tree) • Teaching the concept of race as a social, not biological, construct • Studying various religions in the context of a winter holiday season or historical event
An Empowering School Culture and Social Structure	Grouping and labeling practices, sports participation, disproportionality in achievement, and the interaction of staff and students across ethnic and racial lines are among the components of the school culture that must be examined to create a school culture that empowers students from diverse racial, ethnic, and cultural groups.	• Including students in determining classroom rules or allowing them choices of assignments • Including students with disabilities or all students who try out for a performance • Actively recruiting and hiring teachers of color • Reducing the numbers of African Americans and Hispanics who are inappropriately placed in special education programs • Working with community groups to provide mentoring and tutoring programs • Involving families in school decision-making bodies

Source: TEACHING EXCEPTIONAL CHILDREN by Delinda van Garderen and Catharine Whittaker. Copyright 2006 by Council for Exceptional Children (VA). Reproduced with permission of Council for Exceptional Children (VA) in the format Textbook and Other book via Copyright Clearance Center.

Researchers found major differences between 13 schools that used instructional consultation teams and 9 schools that did not. After using instructional consultation teams for 2 years, schools had lower rates of students from diverse backgrounds being placed in special education than schools that did not use the teams. The consultation-team schools offered training, online coaching, and follow-up support related to collaborative and reflective communication skills, problem-solving skills, curriculum-based assessment, and collection and analysis of classroom data. Here's what the research tells you: Wherever you work in schools, inquire from the outset whether prereferral assistance is available and especially whether it is culturally responsive. If it is, take advantage of it.

Implement Response to Intervention

In Chapter 2 you learned about response to intervention (RTI). Just as RTI is effective for students with disabilities, so it seems to be effective at blunting diversity-based discrimination and unjustified placement into special education (Harris-Murri, King, & Rostenberg, 2006; Klingner & Edwards, 2006; Linan-Thompson, Cirino, & Vaughn, 2007). Using RTI, educators ask whether the student is receiving adequate instruction; they do not presume that the student's educational needs arise from disabilities or other limitations that lie within the student (Harry & Klingner, 2006). Alternatively, they inquire into issues surrounding the student's language and the cultural roots of the student's behavior. They do all these things before referring the student for special education evaluation or placement (Linan-Thompson et al., 2007).

Encouragingly, an RTI program in kindergarten helped students who were learning English to perform significantly better than their counterparts who were not part of the RTI program; further, the RTI program was just as effective for students who were learning English as it was for those already proficient in English. This program involved providing 20–30 minutes of reading instruction per session for each of 4 days per week. Finally, it appeared that the students who were learning English were more responsive to this program than they were to traditional instruction (McMaster, Kung, Han, & Cao, 2008). Because language is only one aspect of culture, it may be that for students who already speak English but whose behavior reflects their cultural background rather than their school's, RTI may be effective to prevent those students from being unjustifiably referred for special education evaluation and placement.

Advocating for Systems Change

Providing quality instruction in a culturally responsive way is a big enough challenge in and of itself, but it is not your only challenge. As you know from Figure 3.5 (depicting the six ecological levels that contribute to cultural barriers), culturally responsive schools depend on culturally responsive societies. As a teacher and citizen, you will want to ask yourself: What can I do to contribute to a culturally responsive society? You can begin by reflecting on the barriers associated with each of the six layers; what can you do within each? For starters, we suggest in Box 3.5 two actions that you might take at each of the six levels.

As you reflect on your own commitments to being a systems advocate, we encourage you to remember the Japanese proverb: "When I want to think, I sit. When I want to change, I act." Your actions at each of the six ecological layers, in combination with the actions of others, can indeed create a more just society.

VALUES AND OUTCOMES

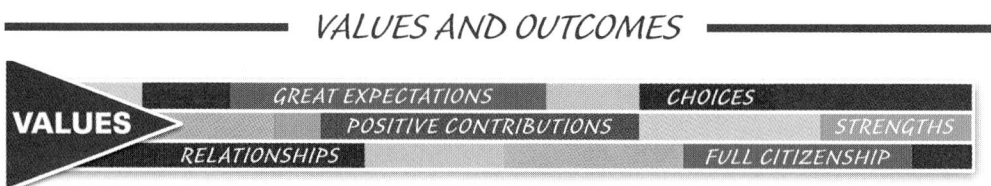

Just as no parent is fully independent of her culture, nor is any child. That is true, too, of the child's teachers, who create a culture within the school even as they respond to the culture of their communities and its diverse members. Does that mean that Sharilyn, De'ja,

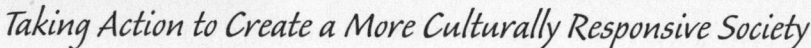

Taking Action to Create a More Culturally Responsive Society

Unlike Box 3.4, which suggested action you can take as you teach, this box suggests what you might do if you want to extend your culturally responsive teaching.

Layer 1: Majority Values

◆ In all of your words and actions, demonstrate and model for others respect for people whose cultural values are different from your own.

◆ Hold your family, friends, fellow educators, and community citizens accountable for being respectful in their comments about interactions with others from diverse backgrounds. For example, if your fellow teachers make critical comments in the teacher's lounge about the culture of students or families, let them know that their comments make you uncomfortable and highlight a cultural strength of the student or family as an example of how cultural differences might be viewed more positively.

Layer 2: Federal/State Policy

◆ Participate actively in elections by learning the positions of candidates, volunteering for candidates who demonstrate cultural respect, and voting for them.

◆ Advocate actively with state and federal policy leaders in support of legislation that will provide equal opportunities for all citizens and will improve the capacity of the educational system, as well as other human service systems, to be responsive.

Layer 3: Community Factors

◆ Serve as a volunteer in your community with agencies and nonprofit organizations whose mission is to respond to the needs of citizens who experience oppression.

◆ Vote in local elections for candidates who demonstrate cultural responsiveness and a track record of supporting policies that will make a positive difference in the lives of citizens from diverse backgrounds.

Layer 4: School Factors

◆ Volunteer to serve on committees for the school district that particularly focus on developing and implementing programs related to cultural responsiveness.

◆ Provide information to decision-makers in your community about the importance of increasing educational resources that can equalize educational opportunities for students from diverse backgrounds.

Layer 5: Family Factors

◆ "Go the second mile" in providing information and responsive support to families who face challenges associated with ethnicity/race, language diversity, and poverty.

◆ Be a partner in your school in creating school policies that value family partnerships and encourage families from diverse backgrounds to share their experiences, traditions, and culturally related hobbies with the school community.

Layer 6: Student Factors

◆ Seek to "walk in the shoes" of students from culturally diverse backgrounds in your class and suspend your own perceptions in order to see the world from their point of view.

◆ Explore every opportunity to highlight the strengths and value the contributions of all students, particularly those from culturally diverse backgrounds who feel marginalized.

---

and her dedicated teachers at Broken Arrow School have different values and seek different outcomes? No.

◆ All of them, De'ja included, want her to have an appropriate education so she can be economically self-sufficient, live independently, and fully participate in her community. They share the same great expectations for the outcomes of her education.

◆ All of them support De'ja's goals to be productive as a chef and, in that way, make a positive contribution to her community, even as she now contributes so much to taking care of her mother when necessary.

◆ To a person, they build on her strengths—her personality, her perseverance in taking after-school tutoring, and her determination to return to school despite the bullying and other impediments to her learning that other students erect.

◆ They explain that every choice she makes—whether to skip school or simply be tardy—incurs consequences, and they counsel her to come to school regularly.

- They celebrate De'ja's friendship with a "big sister" who takes her to community arts programs, and they commend her for avoiding discipline by respecting her classmates and establishing good relationships with them.
- By teaching appropriate behavior to the boy who bullied her so much that she was often truant, they acknowledge that she is a full citizen within her school.

WHAT DO YOU THINK?

1. Is your culture likely to impede or facilitate you as an effective teacher?
2. If there is any degree of mismatch between your culture and your duty to educate students appropriately, what is that mismatch and how do you explain it?
3. To what degree do the examples of De'ja, Sharilyn, and the faculty at Broken Arrow Middle School exemplify the "layers" that you should "unpack" as you plan to work in culturally diverse schools? How might they help you understand and respond to students or even schools themselves that do not derive from your culture?

ADDRESSING THE STANDARDS: THE VALUES CONNECTION

The following CEC Knowledge and Skill Standards: Common Core and Values are addressed in this chapter through the content and concepts we discuss.

CEC Knowledge and Skill Standards: Common Core		Values/Standards Connection
CEC Knowledge and Skills Standard I. Foundations		When you learn about the history of special education and about diversity in special education, you are applying CEC Standard 1, Foundations.
CC1K1	Models, theories, and philosophies that form the basis for special education practice.	
CC1K4	Rights and responsibilities of students, parents, teachers and other professionals, and schools related to exceptional learning needs.	Unfortunately, the theories we discussed do not take into account the entire scope of knowledge about cultural diversity in American schools. By failing to assess teaching and learning from a broad sociocultural perspective, theorists have squelched the opportunity of students from diverse backgrounds to attain *full citizenship* in this country. Now, IDEA and NCLB advance students' claims to an equal educational opportunity and, through education, to status as *full citizens*.
CC1K5	Issues in definition and identification of individuals with exceptional learning needs, including those from culturally and linguistically diverse backgrounds.	
CC1K6	Issues, assurances, and due process rights related to assessment, eligibility, and placement within a continuum of services.	
CC1K7	Family systems and the role of families in the educational process.	
CC1K8	Historical points of view and contributions of culturally diverse groups.	
CC1K9	Impact of the dominant culture on shaping schools and the individuals who study and work in them.	
CC1K10	Potential impact of differences in values, languages, and customs that can exist between the home and school.	

CEC Knowledge and Skill Standards: Common Core	Values/Standards Connection
CEC Knowledge and Skill Standard III. Individual Learning Differences	Connections with others are a critical component to ensuring quality of life. Students and families need to build and expand their relationships with others while also celebrating their individual differences.
CC3K3 Variations in beliefs, traditions, and values across and within cultures and their effects on relationships among individuals with exceptional learning needs, family, and schooling.	
CC3K4 Cultural perspectives influencing the relationships among families, schools, and communities as related to instruction.	
CC3K5 Differing ways of learning of individuals with exceptional learning needs, including those from culturally diverse backgrounds, and strategies for addressing these differences.	
CEC Knowledge and Skill Standard V. Learning Environments and Social Interactions	In creating safe and equitable environments and monitoring social interactions, teachers can develop new visions of what is possible for students. Young people like De'ja have many capabilities and dreams that have not yet been tapped. As teachers support those dreams and capabilities, they can become realities.
CC5K4 Teacher attitudes and behaviors that influence behavior of individuals with exceptional learning needs.	
CC5K7 Strategies for preparing individuals to live harmoniously and productively in a culturally diverse world.	
CC5K8 Ways to create learning environments that allow individuals to retain and appreciate their own and each other's respective language and cultural heritage.	
CC5S1 Create a safe, equitable, positive, and supporting learning environment in which diversities are valued.	
CC5S13 Organize, develop, and sustain learning environments that support positive intracultural and intercultural experiences.	
CEC Knowledge and Skills Standard VI. Language	Students and families have many natural capacities. They need opportunities for educational programs to identify, highlight, and build upon their strengths—cultural, linguistic, academic, or social.
CC6K1 Effects of cultural and linguistic differences on growth and development.	
CC6K2 Characteristics of one's own culture and use of language and the ways in which these can differ from other cultures and uses of languages.	
CC6K3 Ways of behaving and communicating among cultures that can lead to misinterpretation and misunderstanding.	
CC6S2 Use communication strategies and resources to facilitate understanding of subject matter for students whose primary language is not the dominant language.	

continued

CEC Knowledge and Skill Standards: Common Core	Values/Standards Connection
CEC Knowledge and Skill Standard VIII. Assessment CC8K2 — Legal provisions and ethical principles regarding assessment of individuals. CC8K3 — Screening, prereferral, referral, and classification procedures. CC8S2 — Administer nonbiased formal and informal assessments. CC8S6 — Use assessments information in making eligibility, program, and placement decisions for individuals with exceptional learning needs, including those from culturally and/or linguistically diverse backgrounds.	Culturally responsive assessment highlights student's *strengths*, not just their needs, and leads to curricular and instructional methods that foster *self-determination*, especially in students whose cultures may not value self-determination and independence.
CEC Knowledge and Skill Standard IX. Professional and Ethical Practice CC9K1 — Personal cultural biases and differences that affect one's teaching. CC9S6 — Demonstrate sensitivity for the culture, language, religion, gender, disability, socioeconomic status, and sexual orientation of individuals.	Cultural bias, whether against or for a particular student or group of students, profoundly affects teachers' *great expecations* of students and the students' own opportunities to capitalize on their *strengths*, expand their *relationships* with others, be self-determined and *make choices*, make *positive contributions* to their schools and communities, and become *full citizens*.
CEC Knowledge and Skill Standard X. Collaboration CC10K4 — Culturally responsive factors that promote effective communication and collaboration with individuals with exceptional learning needs, families, school personnel, and community members. CC10S10 — Communicate effectively with families of individuals with exceptional learning needs from diverse backgrounds.	As you learn about strategies for working with colleagues, parents, and students, you are addressing CEC Standard 10, Collaboration. There is power in numbers. When a school-based team grapples with the issues of culture and discrimination, it becomes more powerful than any one of its members to assure that students from diverse backgrounds have equal opportunity and *full citizenship* within their schools, especially within the inclusive general curriculum.

Source: From CEC Knowledge and Skill Standards: Common Core and Values. Copyright by The Council for Exceptional Children. Reprinted with permission.

SUMMARY

Defining Culture and Its Implications for Special Education

◆ Culture is the "customary beliefs, social forms, and material traits of a racial, religious, or social group; also: the characteristic features of everyday existence (as diversions or a way of life) shared by people in a place and time" (*Merriam-Webster's Collegiate Dictionary*, 2003, p. 304).

◆ "Cultural responsiveness is the extent to which research and practice in instruction and assessment take into consideration the cognitive, linguistic, and social assets of an individual (such as epistemologies, world views, and learning, teaching, and communication styles) that are culturally determined and shape the ways in which that individual learns and makes sense of his or her experiences. Cultural responsiveness refers to the fact that, in order to be fair and effective, education should be compatible with those assets and build on them, rather than disparage or ignore them." (Klingner & Solano-Flores, 2007, p. 231)

The Social Context of Special Education

◆ Three theories about diversity have influenced the history that justified IDEA—genetic deficit theory, cultural deficit theory, and cultural difference theory.

◆ Early in the 20th century, tracking led to segregation by race and disability.

◆ Court cases, including *Brown v. Board of Education* (1954), *Diana v. Board of Education* (1973), and *Larry P. v. Riles* (1972/1974/1979/1984), were instrumental in systematically addressing problems related to segregation.

Disproportionate Representation

◆ Two reports from the National Research Council documented the problem of disproportionate representation of students from diverse racial/ethnic backgrounds in special education and in gifted education.

◆ National data on disproportionality indicate that African American and Native American students are much more likely to receive special education for a disability.

◆ African American students are least likely to spend the greatest amount of time in the general education classroom and are the most likely to spend the greatest amount of time in special settings.

◆ American Indian/Alaskan Native, Black, and Hispanic students are underrepresented in gifted education.

Factors Associated with Disproportionate Representation and Educational Equality

◆ Racial/ethnic considerations are major factors in disproportionate placement. The strongest predictor of disproportionate placement is the rate of school suspensions and expulsions. Culturally responsive discipline is especially important in reducing suspensions and expulsions and increasing opportunities to learn.

◆ Language considerations are also a major contributor to disproportionate placement. Developing English proficiency for students who do not speak English involves five stages of development and usually takes 5 to 7 years.

◆ Hispanic students are not overrepresented in the category of learning disabilities according to national data; however, they are overrepresented in some school districts with high proportions of Spanish-speaking students.

◆ Language loss is a major concern for many Native American families, and language immersion schools seek to ensure that Native American students learn to speak their indigenous languages.

◆ Poverty substantially contributes to disproportionate placement and is identified by teachers as a major factor limiting their ability to focus on academics.

◆ IDEA particularly addresses the need to provide appropriate instruction to children and youth who are homeless.

◆ Strong relationships exist among ethnic/race, language, and poverty considerations in creating educational disadvantages for students who face these challenges.

◆ An ecological perspective requires educators to understand the powerful influences of factors at the following six layers—majority values, state/federal policy, community, school, family, and student. Being a culturally responsive educator carries responsibilities to address barriers at each of these levels.

Becoming a Culturally Responsive Teacher and Advocate

◆ Enhancing self-awareness involves analyzing one's own cultural values, as well as stereotypes, biases, and prejudices.

◆ It is essential to increase your knowledge and experiences concerning other cultures as a context for culturally responsive instruction.

◆ Four strategies for delivering culturally responsive instruction are using the adapted posture of cultural reciprocity; incorporating five areas of focus for delivering culturally responsive instruction; capitalizing upon support from instructional consultation teams; and implementing RTI in the delivery of systematic instruction.

◆ Advocating for systems change across ecological layers is a responsibility of all educators, as well as all citizens.

PEARSON
myeducationlab

Now go to MyEducationLab at www.myeducationlab.com and take the Self-Assessment to gauge your initial comprehension of chapter content. Once you have taken the Self-Assessment, use your individualized Study Plan for Chapter 3 to enhance your understanding of the concepts discussed in the chapter.

4

Today's Families and Their Partnerships with Professionals

◆ WHO IS THE HOLLEY FAMILY?

It's Homecoming Day at Bonner Springs High School in suburban Kansas City, Kansas. Football players have donned their jerseys (the pads come later); cheerleaders are wearing their uniforms. The school band marches up and down the halls, playing the school's fight song. In every classroom and every hallway, students sport the school's orange and black. So, too, does Sean Holley, a freshman who has autism, epilepsy, and significant intellectual disability.

At the school assembly, candidates for Homecoming King and Homecoming Queen lobby for votes before the balloting begins. All students vote. Repeat: All students vote—emphasis on "all." Every vote is important, yet Sean's is different; he receives assistance from his teacher, Jim Mitchell, in casting it. Just as each student's vote is emblematic of the democratic process in miniature, Sean's vote symbolizes his inclusion in the school in which he had just been enrolled a few weeks before.

More than that, Sean's vote pays tribute to the undaunted efforts of his mother, Leia, to secure his inclusion and participation in his school. She exercised all of her IDEA rights under the principle of parent participation. But she did more: She created a partnership by being clear about what she wanted, respecting Sean's new teachers, earning their respect for her knowledge about Sean and his education, making herself their equal when it comes to his education, advocating for him and for his teachers, being as fully committed to him as to his school, and, in the end, earning the teachers' trust. They know she is in Sean's corner; they also know she is in theirs, but with an eagle eye for how they could educate Sean as effectively as possible.

Just as Sean's father, Jamie, is on a mission for his country, serving as a senior military officer in the command headquarters in Baghdad, Iraq, so Leia is on her own mission. It is to include Sean in school in such a way that he learns, participates, and contributes. It's a life-long mission because Sean's disabilities—autism, challenging behaviors, epilepsy, and language delays—have been part of him since he was a preschooler.

Leia and Sean's teachers would be the first to say that the mission has been difficult. During Sean's years at Bonner Springs Elementary School, Leia lived a night-and-day existence. The "night" part of it occurred during the long, oft-repeated, and always emotionally charged confrontations she had with the school board, the school's principals

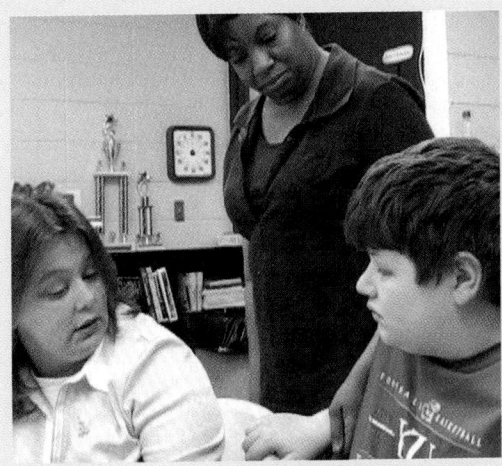

and assistant principals, and Sean's teacher, Tierney Thompson. The "day" part of it occurred as she and especially Tierney and the school's vice principal decided to stop being adversaries and start being partners on Sean's behalf.

It wasn't easy then, and it isn't easy now for Leia to decide which strategies to use as she pursues Sean's rights. It's no longer a matter of his diagnosis and evaluation; the former is clear and the data on the latter are extensive. Rather, it's a matter of asking herself and his teachers the "so what" question: So, now that Sean is in school, what will he get out of it?

That's an "in your face" question and can be off-putting. It need not be so. Leia knew it was confrontational, so she also used other ways to become a partner with Sean's teachers. She resorted to confrontation only when necessary. Relying on IDEA, she sometimes had to threaten to send letters to the school board and school administrators, reminding them of their duties under IDEA and citing federal laws and regulations and state regulations. Sometimes she had to write those letters, showing school staff that she would indeed powerfully advocate for Sean.

Both in writing and in face-to-face meetings with administrators and teachers, she asked for and Sean received training that enabled him to move easily from middle school to high school. At her suggestion, Sean received the opportunity while at high school to continue his vocational training at the middle school as well as to practice work skills at high school. She respected the training he had received, and the high school staff in turn respected her judgment.

She insisted that staff at the high school be prepared to respond to Sean's life-threatening seizures. After inquiring into general educators' experiences in teaching students with disabilities, she got Sean included in some of the general curriculum classes (physical science and geography), with modifications. Sean's safety and education depended on his teachers' capacity to meet his unique educational needs.

When Sean could not open his gym locker because it had not been retrofitted with a lock he could use, Leia went to the principal and asked him to remember how frustrating it is to be needlessly inconvenienced. (She knew he had recently locked himself out of his own car.) His response: "Point taken." Sean's locker was fixed the next day.

She sits in on Sean's class with his special educator, Jim Mitchell, offering tips on how to teach Sean and keep him from becoming agitated. Because swimming allows Sean to reduce his weight, she has arranged for Karen Parsons, his paraeducator, to take him swimming daily. She has even persuaded the swim coach to let Sean join the

team. He practices with the other students and competes in both home and away meets. His coach and teammates cheer him on as he finishes his first lap, and often even the opposing team and their parents join in to encourage him to finish his second lap. He is teaching his classmates, especially those on the swim team, a lesson about his ability to contribute to their education. Partnerships involve not just teachers and parents, but students and their teachers and coaches as well.

Mindful of Sean's father's duty in Iraq and determined that her son would learn skills he could transfer to a job after he leaves school, Leia arranged for Sean to be the designated chairman of the school project "Operation Braves." Operating out of Sean's and Jim Mitchell's special education classroom, the project allows students to earn the service-learning credits they need for graduation. General and special education students collect, catalogue, box, and ship supplies to Jamie's comrades in arms. Not by coincidence, the project title "Operation Braves" uses a military term (*operation*) because the school is so close to Fort Leavenworth. It also contains a word (*brave*) that signifies the way Leia, Sean, his circle of support, and his teachers have to be when educating a young man with autism and health-related disabilities. In addition, it capitalizes on the nickname ("Braves") of the Bonner Springs High School athletic teams.

Like the smaller circles of support Leia has helped Sean develop, "Operation Brave" creates other partnerships around Sean. His general and special education schoolmates become his partners; Leia and Jim Mitchell become each other's partners, as well as partners to general educators and school administrators. Leia has found ways to spread partnership around the school. She has taken it from a 1:1 to a 1:many relationship.

Leia Holley knows the path she wants Sean to follow and the outcomes his education should promote: inclusion and contribution. Her strategies vary. Her persistence does not. By being both civil and candid and by remembering that anger begets resistance but that taking the easy way out shortchanges Sean and his classmates, Leia has improved her family's quality of life and the likelihood that Sean will be a job-holding member of his community after he graduates.

PEARSON
myeducationlab

Go to the Activities and Application section in Chapter 4 of MyEducationLab and complete Activity 1. The video you will watch depicts the beginning of Sean Holley's IEP meeting. Think about how these goals for Sean's future could become a reality with successful partnerships between school professionals and his family.

PEARSON
myeducationlab

After reading this chapter, complete the Self-Assessment for Chapter 4 on MyEducationLab to gauge your initial understanding of chapter content.

WHO ARE TODAY'S FAMILIES?

Defining Family

Who is in your family? Before answering, try to define the word *family* as it applies to you. Does it include only your blood relatives? What about in-laws? Or others, such as uncles, aunts, and grandparents? Does it also include close friends? Even some teachers? In a word, just how nuclear or extended is your family? How much has your family changed in the past 10 years? What changes can you now project for the next 5 years? Answering these questions may prompt you to learn more about how others define family.

The U.S. Census Bureau defines family as a group of two or more people related by birth, marriage, or adoption who reside together (Iceland, 2000). Does this definition fit your own family? Do all of the members of your family reside together? If "reside together" is a controlling element of the definition, how do we account for the fact that Major Holley has not resided with his family during some of his international tours of duty? Does "marriage" override "reside" when it comes to the Holleys? Of course.

We define **family** as two or more people who regard themselves to be a family and who carry out the functions that families typically perform (Poston et al., 2003). This means that people who do not reside together and who may not even be related by birth, marriage, or adoption qualify as family if each regards the others as family members and if, together, they carry out some of the various family functions that we will describe later in this chapter. It may be stretching the point a bit, but Sean's family includes two friends, Tanner and Devin, who have been hanging out with Sean and his brother JP, usually in Leia's home, for nearly a decade.

As an educator, you will find that some of your students have families whose composition is very different from your own. Researchers who focused on 12 African American families described the composition of the family as follows:

Who in this family photograph is the person you would exclude from an IEP meeting, and why?

> It turned out that only 1 of the 12 families fit the model of the nuclear family headed by two biological parents that is assumed to be the ideal in American society. This one family was Haitian, with both parents in the home and the father working two full-time jobs. The range of configurations among the other 11 families defied any traditional classification of "single-parent" or "intact" families. As far as we could discern, there was more than one adult in all the homes. Three families were headed by fathers only, 1 by a grandmother, 5 by mothers, 2 by a mother and stepfather, and 1 by an uncle. In 2 cases, there was a parent with mental illness. In 2 families, an absent parent was living abroad. In the case of the uncle who cared for his young nephew, several deaths in the family and the uncle's own terminal illness made this a very sad family situation (Harry, Klingner, & Hart, 2005, p. 106).

Traditionally, educators have communicated primarily with mothers of children with and without disabilities, having parent-teacher conferences, reporting progress, and being involved in school activities. But there may be other family members—even *many* other family members—who are willing and able to be involved in educating your students.

Demographics of Today's Families

In many ways, families of children with exceptionalities are not all that different from families whose children do not have special needs. A mother of two children, one with multiple disabilities and the other without any disability, described her family as the universal family:

> I am the universal parent. . . . [A]s such I have many joys, sorrows, fears, and questions. Deep inside I feel that I am normal. I look around my home, and I observe my family, and I see us to be very normal. We wake up in the morning, and we rush to get teeth brushed and hair combed in time to inhale Cream of Wheat before the bus arrives. I go about my routine as parent and provider and often momentarily forget that I am a parent of a child . . . [with a disability]. I love to party on Friday night, feel proud when the teacher says my child did well, get angry when the lawn mower won't start, and worry when I realize that my not-so-long-ago high school days happened 20 years ago (how could time pass so quickly). I have dreams of making a lot of money, fears of having more month than paycheck, and hopes of a brighter tomorrow. (Gerdel, 1986, p. 1)

Like the parents of children who are developing typically, parents of children who have various exceptionalities face challenges of family life: job changes and loss, the deaths of family members, financial problems, physical or mental illnesses, substance abuse, child abuse or community violence, and uncertainty about the future. They also experience many of the joys of life: graduations, job promotions, vacations, birthday parties, weddings, and births.

IEP Tip

It is good practice to ask the family member who is most involved with each student whether there are other family members with whom you should enter into a partnership in educating the student.

Figure 4.1

Household composition of youth with disabilities and youth in the general population

INDIVIDUAL CHARACTERISTICS	YOUTH WITH DISABILITIES	YOUTH IN THE GENERAL POPULATION
Percentage of household with		
No biological parents present	19	3
Biological father present	4	3
Biological mother present	35	21
Both biological parents present	42	73
Percentage living in a single-parent household	36	26
Average number of children in the household	3	2

Source: U.S. Department of Education (2002). *To assure the free appropriate public education of all children with disabilities: Twenty-fourth annual report to Congress on the implementation of the Individuals with Disabilities Act.* Washington, DC: Author.

Do not, however, think that families of children with exceptionalities are identical to other families; in fact, they differ in a number of ways. As you learned in Chapter 3, these families, as a group, are disproportionately from culturally and linguistically diverse populations and have fewer socioeconomic resources.

Indeed, approximately 36 percent of students with disabilities come from a family where the annual income is less than $25,000. By contrast, 24 percent of students without disabilities come from families earning less than $25,000 annually (U.S. Department of Education, 2003). In addition, approximately 22 percent of youth with disabilities come from a family where the head of the family household has less than a high school education (U.S. Department of Education, 2002). This number drops to approximately 13 percent for youth without disabilities.

Families of children with exceptionalities also differ from other families in terms of household composition. Figure 4.1 compares youth with and without disabilities in terms of parents living within the household, single-parent status, and the average number of children per family.

It reveals that the percentage of youth with disabilities living in a single-parent household is substantially higher than the percentage of youth without disabilities. Approximately one third of youth with disabilities live in a single-parent household where the parent is a biological mother. Families headed by single female parents have a particularly high poverty rate—almost 40 percent when a child in the family has a disability (Fujiura & Yamaki, 2000). As you learned in Chapter 3, two characteristics contribute greatly to the likelihood that families will experience poverty: the presence of children (particularly more than one child) who have a disability and a single female parent as the head of the household. How can you be a partner to these families, remembering that many of them, like the Holleys, have high expectations for their children and their children's teachers?

WHAT ARE PARTNERSHIPS AND WHY ARE THEY IMPORTANT?

Defining Partnerships

The term *partnership* refers to a relationship involving joint responsibilities (*Merriam-Webster,* 2003). In the Holley family, Jamie's responsibilities were clear to him: Do as the

Army tells you to do. "Duty, Honor, Country"—the three words that constitute the motto of the U.S. Military Academy at West Point—were Jamie's guideposts in his career. But in order to keep a good soldier, the Army's responsibilities to him also were clear: accommodate Jamie's family's exceptional needs and keep him permanently posted at Fort Leavenworth so Sean could go to school in nearby Bonner Springs. Together, Jamie and the Army created a partnership.

In Chapter 1, you learned that both IDEA and NCLB set out the rights and responsibilities of educators with respect to other professionals, families, and students. Taken as a whole, these reciprocal rights and responsibilities mean that families and professionals should become partners in making decisions about a student's education. That's the IDEA principle of parent participation.

What do we mean by **family-professional partnerships?** These are relationships in which families and professionals collaborate, capitalizing on each other's judgments and expertise in order to increase the benefits of education for students, families, and professionals (Turnbull, Turnbull, Erwin, & Soodak, 2006).

When Congress enacted the federal special education law in 1975, it conferred rights on students with disabilities and their parents, expecting parents to hold schools accountable for satisfying the students' rights (Turnbull, Turnbull, & Wheat, 1982). (We reviewed those rights in Chapter 1.) There is, however, no federal law granting parents of children who are gifted the right to make decisions in partnership with teachers. Approximately 40 percent of states do not have state requirements related to the involvement of parents of children who are gifted in educational decision-making (National Association for Gifted Children, 2007). Whether required by federal or state policy or not, it is sound educational practice to form partnerships with the families of all of your students.

PEARSON myeducationlab

Go to the Activities and Application section in Chapter 4 of MyEducationLab and complete Activity 2. As you watch the video and answer the accompanying questions, think about how this partnership has made a difference in Sean's life.

Importance of Partnerships

There are several reasons why partnerships are important. First, schools that foster partnerships among administrators, faculty, families, and students are more likely to have high levels of trust than are schools where partnerships are fragile or nonexistent (Hoy, 2002; Sweetland & Hoy, 2000). When trust exists, morale is better, the school climate is more positive, and problems with teaching, learning, and behavior are easier to solve. Second, student achievement in the elementary grades (Goddard, Tschannen-Moran, & Hoy, 2001), middle school grades (Sweetland & Hoy, 2000), and high school grades (Hoy & Tarter, 1997) is likely to be higher than it is in schools where partnerships and trust do not abound.

Three decades of research in general education have documented many positive student outcomes associated with family participation in a child's education, including at each of the following levels (Harvard Family Research Project, 2006, 2006/2007, 2007):

◆ Early childhood—Associated gains in child skills (language, self-help, social, motor, pre-academic skills); more positive engagement with peers and adults; higher promotion rate from kindergarten into first grade; and fewer referrals to special education (Barnard, 2004; Mantizicopoulos, 2003; Marcon, 1999; McWayne, Hampton, Fantuzzo, Cohen, & Sekino, 2004).

◆ Elementary school—Increased academic achievement; reduction of gap between White and non-White students; and increased literacy performance (Barnard, 2004; Dearing, Kreider, Simpkins, & Weiss, 2006; Jeynes, 2005b; McBride, Schoppe-Sullivan, & Moon-Ho, 2005).

◆ Middle/high school—Improved academic achievement; improved compliance with academic standards; successful transitions from middle to secondary school; and a greater likelihood of attending post-secondary education (Anguiano, 2003; Auerbach, 2004; Jeynes, 2005a; Marshall, 2006).

Go to the Activities and Application
section in Chapter 4 of
MyEducationLab and complete
Activity 3. As you watch this
portion of Sean's IEP meeting and
answer the accompanying
questions, consider the importance
of the relationship between family-
professional partnerships and
Sean's academic achievement.

A national longitudinal study of family involvement in the education of secondary students with disabilities also reported a strong relationship between family-professional partnerships and student achievement (Newman, 2005). This study found that:

◆ Youth whose families are more involved in their schools are less far behind grade level in reading, tend to receive better grades, and have higher rates of involvement in organized groups (many of which are school based) and with individual friendships than youth with less family involvement at school.

◆ In the independence domain, youth whose families are more involved in their schools are more likely than youth from less-involved families to have had regular paid jobs in the preceding year.

In addition to contributing to school achievement, family-professional partnerships enhance families' quality of life. That certainly has been the case for the Holleys. The more they are able to trust Sean's teachers, the less emotional and physical stress they experience and the more their parenting and disability-related support increases. Research bears out the relationship between (on the one hand) early childhood services for children with disabilities that are delivered through quality family-professional partnerships and (on the other hand) enhanced family quality of life (Summers et al., 2007). Think about that finding in these terms: You can very likely boost families' quality of life by partnering with them in educating their children. For an example of how partnerships are needed and what a family endures when they do not exist, read Box 4.1, My Voice.

Before you learn how you can form partnerships with families, you should learn how children with exceptionalities affect their families. Learning how disability-related needs affect families can help you "walk in their shoes." And the more you walk in their shoes, the greater the chances are that you will understand their perspectives and become partners with them. Just imagine being Leia, even if for only one day, as she advocates for Sean.

HOW DO CHILDREN WITH EXCEPTIONALITIES AFFECT THEIR FAMILIES' QUALITY OF LIFE, AND WHAT IS YOUR ROLE AS AN EDUCATOR?

Researchers have been documenting the impact of children with disabilities on their families for nearly 50 years. Most of the research has measured mothers' stress and depression (Singer, 2006; Turnbull, Summers, Lee, & Kyzar, 2007). The findings have been mixed. A recent comprehensive analysis of many research studies related to maternal depression concluded that approximately one third of mothers of children with disabilities experienced depression; by contrast, approximately 18 percent of mothers who have children without disabilities experience depression (Singer, 2006). Alternately stated, approximately two thirds of the mothers of children with disabilities do not experience depression.

More recently, we and our colleagues at the Beach Center on Disability at the University of Kansas investigated what "quality of life" means to families who have children with and without disabilities (Hoffman, Marquis, Poston, Summers, & Turnbull, 2006; Summers et al., 2005). Using the families' descriptions, we concluded that **family quality of life** refers to the extent to which (1) the family's needs are met, (2) family members enjoy their life together, and (3) family members have a chance to do the things that are important to them.

Let's apply that definition to the Holley family. Their needs are met by the schools and the Army. They enjoy their time together, however interrupted it may be by tours of duty overseas. They have the chance to do the activities that are important to them—Leia to remain in Kansas as an advocate in the Kansas Parent Training and Information Center,

It's the Best I Can Do

I feel honored to be our daughter's mother and will continue to do the best I can to provide an environment that will allow her to unfold into a loving, happy adult. I am, however, battle weary from urging her schools to do the same.

When our daughter was in first grade I requested an educational evaluation. The teacher smiled and said, "You are just trying to get services." We home-schooled to ensure she would.

Six years later she enrolled in seventh grade equipped with medications and lifestyle changes to mitigate her pre-diabetes and mental health issues. We gave the school nurse a doctor's letter, and I asked about a 504 plan. We were encouraged to work informally with them. They were wonderful!

Prior to her first day in high school, we took a letter from her doctor to the school and introduced our freshman to her teachers.

During the first semester she had to transfer out of a class because of a rigid teacher, was given a detention because of a cell phone alert to renew her meds, and endured another teacher who used sarcasm as a tool. Our daughter cried regularly after school. It was evident we needed a formal document to ensure an appropriate environment.

In January I mailed a written request to the district for a 504 plan.

Four months later a meeting was held. We were told our daughter was ineligible because her grades and behavior were good.

Not receiving a written document, I filed a complaint with the U.S. Office of Civil Rights (OCR).

I received a letter from the school stating they had NOT made a 504 determination but would if I filled out the *paper form*.

The school requested a meeting in regard only to our daughter's endocrine issues. I reminded them that we wanted to also consider mental health issues. I enclosed letters from her G.P., endocrinologist, psychiatrist, and therapist.

I copied the OCR.

No replies.

At the meeting our daughter was again determined ineligible. In order to consider her mental health issues, they would need to have all of her medical [psychiatric] records.

I forwarded this information to the OCR.

The OCR phoned and I was told the school had "just checked the wrong box."

The principal phoned.

At the meeting he had a paper with the "right" box checked. I asked if I could take it home. I gave him a list of accommodations suggested by the doctors. He didn't have this authority. He took the documents.

I received an invitation to meet with the district's attorney, deputy superintendent, school principal, and vice-principal to discuss "matters of mutual interest."

I declined. It's now April of the year after I started the legal process. Fifteen months have passed just in trying to get to the table with OCR and the school. Finally, we have begun a discussion about when to meet and what the agenda is; process over substance, again.

I began trying to get accommodations for my daughter ten years ago. She's failing Spanish; she has diabetic lapses in class; the teacher says she is sleeping and won't allow her to take make-up examinations except after school, when she is already exhausted from just being in school and needing to come home for rest. She is not allowed to take her cell phone into school, even though it alerts her when she needs to take meds or get stuck (to give blood) to check her blood levels. She is not allowed to bring the diabetic stick into school; the school regards it as a weapon. Whatever she needs, the school says "no." And so the legal process is all I have left for her, and it grinds slowly and ever so finely. I think the idea is to wear me down or have me pull my daughter out of school again.

I don't know yet what "the best I can do is" . . . I'm still working on it. I hope it's better than I've done so far.

—April Bruce-Stewart
Suburban Kansas City,
Kansas

Sean and JP to remain in effective schools, and Jamie to pursue his career and answer his call to duty.

Through both open-ended interviews with families and national surveys, we identified five **domains of family life** (Poston et al., 2003; Hoffman et al., 2006):

- ◆ Emotional well-being
- ◆ Parenting
- ◆ Family interaction
- ◆ Physical/material well-being
- ◆ Disability-related support

We will briefly describe each of these domains, then suggest what you can do to support families through your partnerships with them. We will highlight only one family need in each domain.

Emotional Well-Being

Emotional well-being refers to the feelings or affective considerations within the family. Families experience better emotional well-being when they have:

◆ Friends or others who provide support

◆ The support they need to relieve stress

◆ Some time to pursue their own interests

◆ Outside help available to take care of the special needs of all family members

Families of children with disabilities tend to report lower satisfaction on the domain of emotional well-being than on any of the other four domains (Jackson & Turnbull, 2004; Mannan, 2005). Consider, for example, the element of having "friends or others who provide support." Many families of children with exceptionalities worry because their children are lonely and generally lack friends (Turnbull & Ruef, 1997). That has been one of Leia's major concerns about Sean; it's also a concern she has for herself, for she has described her relationships with schools as a "night and day" one in which "night" distressed her and "day" delighted her (Turnbull, Turnbull, & Wehmeyer, 2007; Turnbull et al., 2006). In one research study, 40 percent of the mothers were worried that their preschool children would be rejected by peers and that this rejection would cause their children to have problems with self-esteem (Guralnick, Conner, & Hammond, 1995).

Many teachers want to know how to foster positive interactions among children with and without disabilities. One effective approach is through the technique called **circle of friends,** an approach that worked wonders for Sean at his elementary school and that is still in effect in his middle school (Turnbull et al., 2006). Box 4.2 provides guidance from Leia's experience in implementing a circle of friends for Sean. Professionals or parents invite peers to form a support network for a student with a disability so the student will have friends (Falvey, Forest, Pearpoint, & Rosenberg, 2002). Elementary school students with emotional and behavior disorders who have circles of friends are more socially accepted than those who do not (Frederickson & Turner, 2003).

In addition to families wanting their child with an exceptionality to have more friends, parents themselves may feel isolated and stigmatized by their child's disability. Parents of preschool children with disabilities tend to interact with equal frequency with parents of children with and without disabilities; however, parents of children without disabilities in the same classroom are less likely to interact with parents of children with disabilities than with parents of children without disabilities (Bailey & Winton, 1989). Moreover, parents of children without disabilities are more satisfied than parents of children with disabilities with their awareness about other families of children in the classroom.

Children with problem behavior sometimes cause family members to feel embarrassed or isolated in public. One parent described the situation:

> One time I took George to the supermarket, and he kind of jumped up and down and rocked and hummed. He was laughing a lot, and a woman gave me a look. She wouldn't dare say anything, but she gave me a look almost to say, "Why would you bring a boy like that in here?" She didn't have to say anything. Her look told it all. (Turnbull & Ruef, 1996, p. 283)

You can be helpful to parents of children with disabilities by introducing them to the parents of other students; use open houses or group parent meetings for that purpose. Also, remember to not only teach appropriate behavior in school settings but to support the student in how to use appropriate behavior outside school.

Tips for Implementing a Circle of Friends

When Sean was in first grade we knew very little about how to help peers get to know "the real Sean." His outbursts, head banging, biting, and other self-injurious behaviors reinforced the wall autism was building around him. He couldn't talk. His receptive language skills were very poor. He didn't play like or with other kids. His actions screamed, "Let me be by myself," while his eyes said, "I need you to need me."

We needed to create a circle that would include Sean and other students. But we knew the key was to build on Sean and other students' strengths and interests. It would not be "Sean's Circle!" It would be and is "The Students' Circle." Here's what we did and what we recommend:

Recruit students. Send a letter to all age-appropriate peers' parents: "Participation in this group would allow your child the opportunity to model appropriate social skills like compassion, empathy, and understanding. Our objective is to ensure that children at our school are included in social activities and feel peer acceptance." Do not address a specific child who needs help. Do emphasize the importance of social and communication skills for all students. All of the parents sent back an "agreed" permission slip.

Identify a facilitator. Select a general or special education teacher, social worker, related service provider, paraprofessional or a peer. No one person should be solely responsible. Find some professionals or parents who can resonate with the student's likes, dislikes, interests, cultural needs, environmental needs. The student's age and gender is important. The facilitators for Sean's circle are the school social worker and special education teacher, with great support from the general educators. The social worker is a woman; the special education teacher is a man. The circle has boys and girls in it.

Determine the size of the group based on the student's needs. It wasn't good for the entire class to be in the circle at the same time. Sean was distracted. So the students divided themselves into groups that met on rotating weeks. Sean's core group took hold when he was in elementary school and continues to provide support throughout high school. In fifth grade, students desperately wanted to be a part of the Students' Circle.

Decide where and when to meet. During lunch, recess, and clubs at school? Sean's friends meet in the school counselor's office weekly. During these times activities focus on similarities and the gifts of each child. The key is to set up a safe environment for all members. Build in success.

Identify the activities the group will do. Will the activities be based on the general education curriculum or special interests of the group? In the beginning (first grade) Sean's group watched "Winnie the Pooh" and "The Right Thing to Do," read and acted out the Three Bears story, and sang Happy Birthday. In sixth grade, as the group transitioned into middle school, the focus turned to the needs of the group more. Topics included transitioning to the new school, new teachers, new friends, and bullying.

Also in middle school the group became a *Lunch Bunch vs. Circle.* The Circle met during lunch and ate in a classroom or meeting room. Because so many students were involved, they divided themselves into two smaller circles, sometimes going to KFC for lunch, sometimes having a pizza I bought for them, and always enjoying a special treat from the school principal. Starting in sixth grade the group facilitated Autism Awareness Week. They made posters and pins, and provided information during morning announcements. Each class had activities to do weekly, thanks to the group. Members went to other classes answering peers' questions regarding autism. Prior to sixth grade the subject of autism was not a primary topic. Questions about why Sean hit himself or couldn't talk were answered when asked. Books on various disabilities were read, yet the focus remained on the strengths of each student. Everything should be fun and functional.

Take care of "housekeeping" matters, especially establishing three ground rules: (1) Everyone has access to all of the materials used during meeting. (2) All activities must be age appropriate. (3) Everyone participates in all activities.

Give students ownership of their Circle. Once the routine and "rules" for meetings are established, let students determine/suggest activities. Stay away from formal learning. Circle of friends should be a fun social time for all students. Make sure there are planned activities or discussions for each meeting.

Peers have come and gone since first grade, yet eight core students still remain connected. All students in the Students' Circle have benefited over the years. Through the Circle, Sean's peers saw him as another student who liked to have fun and had some unique ways of doing things. They became Sean's natural teachers and began to teach the adults how to best support Sean. They instinctively know when to push Sean and when to back off. They know how to communicate with him and get frustrated when adults "talk down" to him. They look at Sean as a peer/friend. They are his voice when he can't find his, but they make him use his voice when they know he can.

A Circle of Friends/Lunch Bunch is a safe place for all students to be themselves. Everyone in the Circle is accepted and cared for and about. All students learn to grow together without worrying about cliques, peer pressure, or bullying.

Leia Holley, *Bonner Springs, Kansas*

PEARSON
myeducationlab

Go to the Building and Teaching Skills and Dispositions section in Chapter 4 of MyEducationLab. As you watch some of the videos from Sean's IEP meeting and complete the accompanying activities, think about the dispositions you would need as a teacher to facilitate a Circle of Friends program. Additionally, consider how this type of peer interaction can benefit all students — not just those with disabilities.

Parenting

The second domain of family quality of life is parenting—namely, those activities that adult family members do to help children grow and develop. This domain is strong when families do the following:

- Know how to help their child learn to be independent
- Know how to help their child with schoolwork and activities
- Know how to teach their child to get along with others
- Know how to have time to take care of the individual needs of every child

Let's think about parents who help their child with schoolwork and activities. Do you remember when you were in elementary and secondary school and your parents helped you with your homework? Were those experiences generally positive, negative, or mixed? On the whole, it can be challenging for parents and children to work together to complete the child's homework. Students with disabilities receive more assistance from their families with homework than do their classmates without disabilities (Newman, 2005). Approximately 20 percent of secondary students with disabilities receive homework assistance five or more times a week, and students with disabilities are five times as likely as their classmates without disabilities to get frequent homework assistance. This is especially hard for families whose child struggles with schoolwork. Many children with disabilities need to rely on their parents to help with homework.

Box 4.3 provides tips for how you can best support students and families in completing homework. In order to promote positive family quality of life, you can be sensitive to this situation and provide support to both the student and the parents to make homework as do-able as possible. Significantly, students in general education programs whose parents help them with homework usually take more responsibility for completing their work, experience more self-confidence, and have a more positive attitude about homework (Hoover-Dempsey et al., 2001). Furthermore, students who receive special education services who complete homework typically show greater improvement in academic achievement (Epstein, Polloway, Foley, & Patton, 1993).

Family Interaction

The quality-of-life domain called family interaction focuses on the relationships among family members. Children with exceptionalities affect every other member of their family—with the emphasis on "every." Their effect on the entire family is interactive, just as a mobile is:

> In a mobile all the pieces, no matter what size or shape, can be grouped together and balanced by shortening or lengthening the strings attached or rearranging the distance between the pieces. So it is with the family. None of the family members is identical to any others; they are all different and at different levels of growth. As in a mobile, you can't arrange one without thinking of the other. (Satir, 1972, pp. 119–120)

Think of the Holleys as a mobile: Jamie's duty to the Army and his family, Leia's duty as an advocate for her children with disabilities, and Sean's right to an appropriate education. Each factor interacts with the others; each affects each member of the Holley family. Families who have high levels of family interaction

- Enjoy spending time together
- Talk openly with each other
- Solve problems together
- Show they love and care for each other

Tips for Improving Homework Completion

Research has documented a number of strategies that you can implement to help ensure that students complete homework and that they become as independent as possible in doing so (Bryan & Burstein, 2004):

◆ Set firm guidelines and teach students that they do not have a "hedge factor" in turning in homework.

◆ Ensure that homework is the appropriate length, especially for students who require more time for completion or who have lower levels of energy. Seek feedback from students after each assignment, such as through circling a face that matches their feeling about the assignment, in order to make continual adjustments.

◆ Ask students to evaluate the time required and accuracy of their homework which is completed while watching television, listening to the radio, and working in a quiet setting. Encourage them to reflect on the most effective setting as well as on their personal preferences.

◆ Provide reinforcement such as extra resource time or special treats for homework completion.

◆ Teach students to graph homework completion and then explain the graphs to their parents in parent-student-teacher conferences.

◆ Provide homework that links the classroom with "real life," such as learning to tell time by developing a schedule of favorite television shows.

◆ Teach students to use homework planners and have them write down all of their homework assignments.

◆ Use cooperative homework teams in which three or four students work together to submit assignments to one team member who is assigned to be the checker, who then grades the papers and gives them to the teacher. Students then work together on corrections.

◆ Teach students self-management strategies for homework, including how to listen to and correctly write down the assignment, estimate the time it will require for completion, identify materials needed in order to take them home, recruit assistance when needed, monitor progress, and self-reward homework completion.

You also can inform parents how to assist with homework. Some of these strategies include (Jayanthi, Sawyer, Nelson, Bursuck, & Epstein, 1995; Salend, Duhaney, Anderson, & Gottschalk, 2004; Turnbull et al., 2008):

◆ Provide them with teachers' names and preferred times and methods for being contacted with questions about homework.

◆ Discuss homework expectations with them during conferences and seek to identify strategies that will work best for each family.

◆ Use regular communication (notes, progress reports, phone calls, email messages) to communicate with them, especially when challenges exist.

◆ Use the Internet to provide guidance to them on homework, including directions, an exemplary model, an evaluation rubric, and the linkage between homework and general curriculum standards.

PEARSON
myeducationlab

Go to the Activities and Application section in Chapter 4 of MyEducationLab and complete Activity 4. As you watch this video and answer the accompanying questions, think about how you could incorporate some of this special education teacher's ideas for communicating with parents with the homework completion tips described here.

A question we posed at the beginning of this chapter bears repeating: Who are the members of your students' families? As you answer that question for each family, pay special attention to the effect of giftedness and disability on the siblings of the child with the exceptionality. In families who have one or more children who are gifted, siblings who do not have special gifts and talents may feel incapable of earning their parents' pride and approval for their own accomplishments and may feel neglected as the family responds to the special needs of the gifted member (Keirouz, 1990). Research has documented both negative and positive effects (Dykens, 2005; Orsmond & Seltzer, 2007; Stoneman, 2005). Some studies have found that brothers and sisters experience embarrassment, guilt, isolation, resentment, increased responsibility, and increased pressure to achieve. When Kate Turnbull, the younger daughter of two of this book's authors, was

When families incorporate their child into family activities, they often promote family interaction and family quality of life.

in second grade, she shared the following feelings concerning her older brother, Jay, who has an intellectual disability, autism, and a bipolar disorder:

> Jay embarrasses me sometimes like when he has such a loud voice in movie theatres. He says loudly, "Don't talk, Jay." His voice is so loud that lots of people stare at us. I kinda bend down . . . because I'm really embarrassed that everyone is looking at me. They're probably saying, "What, who said that? Maybe some 'wacko' or something." And it really makes me feel mad when they think my brother is a 'wacko.' I try to teach Jay not to do that. Every time he does, I say, "Jay, be quiet." I kinda elbow him softly and go, "Now, Jay, quiet down, please," and then I feel better. (K. Turnbull, personal communication, 1985)

But brothers and sisters also often develop problem-solving skills, empathy, the ability to advocate, a capacity for understanding and seeking social justice, and a greater sense of self-directedness. Kate also characterized one of her brother's positive contributions, writing in the 11th grade as follows:

> Jay's many accomplishments and my parents' struggle have taught me to have great expectations for *myself.* If Jay, with his problems, can face his challenges with courage and a sense of optimism, then so can I. Jay's lesson is a universal one: We all have the capacity for human greatness. (Turnbull, 1997, pp. 91–92)

Kate's perspectives are typical: The child with a disability offers both challenges and benefits to all family members (Turnbull et al., 2006). That is one reason why it is helpful for family members, including siblings, to have opportunities to reflect on their conflicting feelings and to know how to respond to them in the most constructive way. "Sibshops" are helpful resources for brothers and sisters. Sibshops are workshop-based support programs for brothers and sisters of children and youth with exceptionalities (Meyer & Vadasy, 2008), offering them the chance to share their feelings and gather information about the special needs of their brother or sister.

Physical/Material Well-Being

The fourth domain of family quality of life involves physical and material well-being—namely, the resources available to the family to meet its members' needs. Family quality of life rises when families

- ◆ Have transportation to get to the places they need to be
- ◆ Have a way to take care of expenses
- ◆ Feel safe at home, work, school and in their neighborhood
- ◆ Get medical and dental help when needed

Family resources often largely depend upon family income; yet as you learned in Chapter 3 and previously in this chapter, families of children with disabilities are more likely than families of children without disabilities to experience poverty. What does a family's poverty status have to do with you as a teacher? Consider only one: the capacity of families from poverty backgrounds to attend school activities and teacher-parent conferences. A parent described her financial situation as follows:

> If you have no money, it's very difficult to be—to do—to be together, to do fun things, to be at peace, to come home to a haven. . . . Because if you have no

IEP Tip

When you have siblings of children with disabilities as students in your class, you might encourage them to share their ideas on how to foster their brother or sister's education. You could then incorporate these ideas into the IEP of the sibling with a disability.

money, the bills not paid, you're not gonna rest when you get home. You might have a good family, you know, a good husband, whatever, whatever. But, you don't have money, all that can go down the drain, so. . . . Money provides a way of release. You can go on a vacation, maybe, once a year, whereas if you don't have the money, you won't be able to do that. And when you can't do those things, you have this feeling of insecurity which floods over into other problems, emotionally. Anger, bitterness, and then it jumps off on the other family members and you got chaos. (Beach Center, 1999)

How might this mother attend school activities and teacher-parent conferences? How might her lack of financial resources affect her opportunity to be at evaluation and IEP meetings, other teacher-parent conferences, and various school events? What about transportation, clothing, child care for their other children at home, self-confidence to interact with educators and other parents, and the ability to get time off from a job that pays by the hour? When parents do not attend school meetings or events, some educators think the parents lack interest and concern for the child, but the truth is that lack of financial resources is a major barrier. You can help minimize parents' barriers by working with other educators in your school, student service clubs, or other community resources to arrange child care during school activities and transportation assistance.

Unfortunately, stereotypes exist regarding families from poverty backgrounds. Because wealthy people are distanced from the poor geographically and psychologically, their impressions are likely to have little connection to the actuality of what living in poverty means. Regardless of myths and stereotypes, poor people share the reverence of the middle class for education, as well as the perception that mobility depends on school achievement and attainment (Brantlinger, 1985; MacLeod, 1987). Yet, in spite of the shared perceptions of the good life, there are low expectations regarding educational and occupational attainment for low-income students and parents (Ryan, Sheldon, Kasser, & Deci, 1996; Brantlinger, 2001).

When families who experience poverty attend school events, let them know how much you value their presence. Show your respect for them and connect them to school or other staff who in turn can link them to community resources and sources of economic support related to their children's disabilities, including benefits under the Social Security Act such as Supplemental Security Income, Medicaid, and food stamps (Turnbull et al., 2006).

> **IEP Tip**
>
> You might also meet with the family in their home or in a setting in their neighborhood such as the parents' place of worship, a recreational center, or a library. Parents may be able to walk to these places. They also may feel less intimidated there than at your school.

Exceptionality-Related Support

The fifth and final domain of family quality of life is exceptionality-related support—namely, support from family members and others to benefit the child with exceptional needs. Among the aspects of exceptionality-related support are those targeted toward the individual with an exceptionality:

- Achieve goals at school or work
- Make progress at home
- Make friends
- Have a good relationship between the family and service providers

What does it mean to have support to "achieve goals at school and work"? A survey of 100 Latino parents whose children were receiving services to improve their English proficiency revealed that approximately three fourths of the parents wanted their children to be assessed in Spanish and wanted to have a Spanish translator for educational meetings (Lian & Fontanez-Phelan, 2001). Slightly less than half of the parents who were not English proficient

School social workers can assist teachers as they help families address their material needs.

indicated that they were less confident in pursuing their parental rights related to special education because of their educational level.

Two national studies, one focusing on the elementary/middle school level and one focusing on the high school level, reported the following about parents' satisfaction with the special education program of their child with a disability (U.S. Office of Special Education Programs, 2005):

◆ Parents of elementary/middle school students are 12–19 percentage points more likely than parents of secondary students to be satisfied with their child's education.

◆ Approximately 1 in 5 parents of 13–17-year-olds reports dissatisfaction with their children's school in general.

◆ Parents of students with disabilities tend to be less satisfied with their child's education as contrasted to peers in general education.

◆ Across all disability categories, parents of students with emotional and behavioral disorders have the lowest levels of satisfaction.

◆ Parents of younger African-American students with disabilities are less likely to be satisfied with their children's schools, overall education, and teachers as contrasted to parents of White or Hispanic students.

◆ Parents' satisfaction tends not to differ in light of household income.

◆ Eleven percent of families of 13–17-year-olds have been through mediation and 5 percent have been through a due process hearing.

A different national survey of parents of children in special education found that approximately 16 percent of parents reported that they had considered legal action because of the lack of quality in their child's special education program (Johnson, Duffett, Farkas, & Wilson, 2002). Thirty-one percent of parents of children with severe disabilities indicated that they had considered suing, as contrasted with 13 percent of parents of students with mild disabilities. There is no question about the fact that Leia Holley considered suing the Bonner Springs schools when Sean was in elementary school and that her threats caused Sean's teachers to react negatively. But suing is costly, and many parents cannot afford to hire a lawyer. As one parent noted:

> You have no rights actually unless you're wealthy enough to defend yourself in court. That's what it boils down to. If you don't have the money to challenge the system, they don't care about your complaining; they don't care that you're unhappy. You can sit in the IEP meeting, fine, so what are you gonna do about it? Like, "We're not doing what you want, Ms. C, what ARE you gonna do about it? Unless you take us to court, we're finished talking to you." So, now the laws are only in place to defend the people who are wealthy enough to hire an attorney and take them to court over that. (Beach Center, 1999)

IEP Tip

The IEP team should describe to the parent why its members are "highly qualified" and what evidence-based curriculum and instructional techniques it will use.

Having financial resources to pursue legal remedies is especially important given the recent Supreme Court case *Schaffer v. Weast* (2005). In it, the Court held that parents must bear the burden of proof when pursing litigation against a school district. This means that parents have to demonstrate why their child's education is not appropriate. This decision has tremendous implications for families, especially for those from low-income and low-education backgrounds. As you can imagine, it is exceedingly difficult for parents, especially parents from culturally diverse backgrounds, to go up against a very large school district and prove why the school district is not providing an appropriate education.

The good news (from the data we cited) is that a substantial number of parents of children with disabilities are satisfied. That is often so because teachers and school administrators become their partners, as one parent observed:

> The last two years have been like in a dream world. It is like I want to call them up and say, "You do not have nothing negative to say?" This educational system—this school itself has worked wonders with my son. It has taken a lot of stress off ME, so that when I go home, I do not have to get into it with him and say, "Oh,

you know, the school called me today about this and that." They will call me, but they have already worked it out. Or they will call me to praise him and tell me how wonderful and how positive a role model he is now, and it's because they have worked with us. It is like I said, it has been a dream world to me. (Beach Center, 2000)

When parents are dissatisfied with their child's education, they, like Leia Holley, often become advocates for their children and for others, too. Indeed, they are more likely to be advocates than are parents of children and youth with typically developing children (Fiedler, 2000; Turnbull, Zuna, Turnbull, Poston, & Summers, 2007). Additionally, parents of children who are gifted also often take on advocacy roles, especially because there is not a federal mandate for gifted education and many states do not have a state policy requiring specially designed instruction for students who are gifted (Stephens, 1999). Many families, however, would prefer to be partners with educators, not advocates; like Leia, they would prefer to not have to reform school systems. A recent study of parental perspectives on advocacy revealed the underlying hostility that comes from dashed expectations and broken partnerships; parents often used words and phrases such as *fighting, ammunition, being armed,* or *gun.* For example, one parent commented:

> Ninety-five percent of the time was a fight. . . . [I]t's the parents who have to, the parents have to prove why they think their child needs the service, and I don't think that's the way it should be. (Wang, Mannan, Poston, Turnbull, & Summers, 2004, p. 148)

Another parent commented, "But, you know, it is really unfortunate that you have to pull out those kinds of guns" (Wang et al., p. 148).

Parents sometimes complain that educators are not adequately trained to deal with the challenges associated with some exceptionalities. Sadly, approximately one half of parents of children with autism, Down syndrome, and learning disabilities have reported that educators need more training in order to teach their children effectively (Starr, Foy, Cramer, & Singh, 2006). This parent comment is typical:

> Because K's teacher was late or she was coming a half-day, the school is calling me to see if I could pick K up because the "aide is nervous" . . . that's exactly what they said—"the aide is nervous," and [K] wants to do a lot of work. You know, and I couldn't believe that the school was calling me. And I told them no—first of all I asked them, "Is she okay? Is she ill?" "She's not ill." "Did she hit anybody?" "She didn't hit anybody." "Well, what are you telling me?" "She wanted to do a lot of work that the aide could not do." . . . I said, "No, she needs to stay in school." (Wang et al., 2004, p. 150)

To make a positive contribution to a family's quality of life, you can provide such excellent services that parents do not need to become advocates against you or your colleagues. In short, you can become a trusted partner.

HOW CAN YOU FORM PARTNERSHIPS WITH FAMILIES?

We have defined a **partnership** as a relationship in which families and professionals collaborate with each other by capitalizing on each other's judgment and expertise in order to increase benefits for students, families, and professionals alike (Turnbull et al., 2006). We also identified several positive outcomes of partnerships, including a trusting school climate, improved student achievement, and positive influences on family quality-of-life outcomes. And we discussed the challenges facing families in terms of their quality of life and how you can make a difference, minimizing problems and maximizing positive outcomes. So how can you develop and carry out your partnerships with families?

Partnerships build on the strengths, talents, resources, and expertise of educators, families, and others who are committed to making a positive difference in the lives of children

Figure 4.2 The arch and its seven partnership principles

and youth with exceptionalities. Figure 4.2 illustrates the seven principles of partnerships, using the structure of an arch (Turnbull et al., 2006). On each side of the arch, there are three partnership principles; trust, the final partnership principle, is the arch's keystone. A keystone is the wedge-shaped piece in the arch's crown that secures the other pieces in place (*Merriam-Webster,* 1996). Trust is the partnership principle that holds all of the other principles together.

In the best of worlds, educators, parents, and students are partners with each other; in time, they come to trust each other. Without trust, the partnership is weak or may not even exist. With trust, the partnership remains strong and can sustain all partners. They can move together to secure good outcomes for the student. But they cannot do it well and joyously without trusting each other (Turnbull et al., 2006).

Each of the seven principles has three to five key practices associated with it. We will highlight only one practice for each principle.

Communication

The first partnership principle is communication—the verbal, nonverbal, or written messages that partners exchange among themselves. Following are five practices for effective communication (Blue-Banning, Summers, Frankland, Nelson, & Beegle, 2004):

- Be friendly
- Listen

- Be clear
- Be honest
- Provide and coordinate information

In terms of providing and coordinating information, families appreciate it when professionals provide information to them about current services, possible future services, the nature of their child's exceptionality, community resources, and their legal rights (Ruef & Turnbull, 2001; Shapiro, Monzo, Rueda, Gomez, & Blacher, 2004; Turnbull et al., 2008). Consistent with the cultural challenges that you learned about in Chapter 3, families who speak English receive more communication from educators than families who speak Spanish (U.S. Department of Education, 2006). Furthermore, families with higher incomes receive more communication than families who experience poverty. There are resources that provide information directly to families and to professionals as well. We will highlight two national networks—Parent Training and Information Centers and Parent to Parent USA.

The first resource is a Parent Training and Information Center. There are approximately 107 Parent Training and Information Centers (PTIs) funded by the U.S. Department of Education. These centers support parents to be effective educational decision makers. Leia Holley works for the Kansas Parent Training and Information Center and is responsible for its work in eastern Kansas. Box 4.4 describes the Kansas PTI. We encourage you to sign up for the mailings of your state's PTI and participate in its training activities (see www.taalliance.org for contact information).

The second resource is Parent to Parent programs. In more than two thirds of the states, Parent to Parent provides a one-to-one match between a veteran parent who has had experience with a challenging issue associated with disability and a parent who is just

PARTNERSHIP TIPS — Box 4.4

Partnering with Parent Training and Information Center Staff

When you are a teacher in special or general education, you have some "string" to guide you through the maze of school programs for students, whether they have any exceptional needs or not. That string is your training and your colleagues' assistance.

But if you are a parent of a child with a disability, especially if you are coming into special education for the first time, you have to find your "string" because you almost never have any training or much assistance from other people.

Guiding parents through the maze is exactly what the Kansas Parent Training and Information Center, Families Together, does, says its director, Connie Zienkewicz. In that respect, it is nearly identical to the Parent Training and Information Centers that exist in every other state. (Some states have more than one.) "We have families standing by who have the experience and expertise to help other families," Connie proclaims, citing Leia Holley as an example of the PTI staff available to families in eastern Kansas.

Families Together provides statewide coverage, family experience, training by experts (families and professionals alike), and knowledge of local situations. Like

other PTI centers, Families Together supports parents to understand their children's disabilities and related needs, communicate more effectively with school and other professionals, participate in evaluation and IEP meetings, and connect with advocacy and professional associations related to their child's disability.

Putting These Strategies to Work for Progress in the General Curriculum

1. Locate the name, address, telephone, fax, website, and email address for your state's Parent Training and Information (PTI) center, for any Community Parent Resource Centers (CPRCs) in your state, and for your state's Protection and Advocacy (P&A) agency.

2. Develop a one-page handout that lists that information. Distribute the handout to your students' families. Keep extra copies for yourself, the school secretary, and other special education staff to distribute.

3. Send an email to your state's PTI and ask them to put your name on their mailing list. When the material comes in the mail, pay special attention to it.

beginning to experience the challenge. The veteran parent offers emotional support and information, so the new one learns from an experienced person.

> When our son with Down syndrome was born three years ago, my husband and I were shocked and devastated. We called our Parent to Parent program, which supplied us with invaluable information, as well as sending us a "support couple" to talk with. It was important to us to meet with the couple—not just the mother—since my husband takes as much responsibility for caring for our children as I do. Also important was that we were matched with a couple whose child had also been through open heart surgery (our son had major defects). The couple that our Parent to Parent program sent us were such warm, optimistic, "normal" people, they gave us hope. About a year later, my husband and I were trained by our program to be support parents. The Parent to Parent office has many requests for visits from both father and mother. My husband was one of very few men willing to go through formal training. I have also found that support for non-English speaking families is hard to come by. It has been satisfying to me to be able to serve the Spanish-speaking community. (Beach Center, 1999)

We encourage you to find out about state and local Parent to Parent programs near you, refer parents to them, and even attend their conferences and workshops (see www. p2pusa.org for contact information). Indeed, we encourage you to acknowledge that one of your key roles is to be knowledgeable about all sorts of resources so that you can recommend them to families and benefit from them yourself.

Professional Competence

The second partnership principle is professional competence—being highly qualified for one's professional role. Remember how concerned Leia has been that Sean's teachers may not know how to respond to his seizures? There are three practices associated with professional competence within family-professional partnerships (Blue-Banning et al., 2004):

- Providing a quality education
- Continuing to learn
- Setting high expectations

As you learned in Chapter 1, both IDEA and NCLB declare that educators should have high expectations for all students and should hold all students to high standards for their educational, developmental, and functional outcomes. In Chapter 2, you learned about standards-based assessment and the importance of determining just how much progress students with disabilities are making in the general curriculum. It is never too early to set high expectations for students and convey those expectations to the students themselves and to their families. The sooner you do, the sooner you will help the families develop a vision for the future and plans to make that vision come true.

Respect

The third partnership principle is respect—namely, that each partner regards all others with esteem and communicates that esteem through actions and words (Blue-Banning et al., 2004). Professionals who demonstrate respect

- Honor cultural diversity
- Affirm strengths
- Treat students and families with dignity

In Chapter 3, you learned key practices for honoring cultural diversity. Can you recognize the strong link between the material in Chapter 3 and this partnership principle of respect?

To respect and esteem others is to recognize, value, and affirm their strengths. Recognizing and valuing strengths is critically important in forming partnerships with all parents. It is especially important in partnerships with families from culturally diverse backgrounds (Harry et al., 2005). Consider the perspective of the following adolescent mother in terms of the disrespect that she felt from her young child's early interventionists:

Meeting with parents should focus on the student's strengths, not just weaknesses, and support the student's parents.

> Sometimes she act all nervous or scared around me like I'm gonna bite her. She so phony. I know what she think of me, you know, just another young black girl who had a baby and not married. I know she look down on me but I just play the game. They don't know me. They don't know nothin' about me. Just like they believe Ariel's father is dead but like I told you, he just dead to us and s#@* 'cause he in prison. They don't know I got Arrie private speech therapy neither cause they not helpin' her talk . . . (Beach Center, 2000)

If you were the early interventionists working with this mother, how might you use the adapted posture of cultural reciprocity (see Box 3.3) to find your common ground with her and, ultimately, demonstrate the respect that would lead to a trusting partnership?

In addition to respecting parents, you should respect students with special needs. A parent describes how painful it is when educators do not affirm her daughter's strengths:

> I often think if [school staff] could do one-on-one instead of [coming] with five people, telling me Susie can't do this, and Susie can't do that, and Susie can't this, and Susie can't that. And I am thinking, What about "Susie *can* do this and Susie *can* do that"? (Lake & Billingsley, 2000, p. 245)

Take the "shoes test"—imagine standing in the shoes of this parent. Or picture yourself in a meeting with five of your current or past teachers; each is highlighting what you are not able to do. How would you feel, and what impact would such a meeting have on your own self-esteem? Although Susie obviously has many needs, certainly she has strengths as well. The more you communicate about the student's strengths, the more you will encourage the parents to talk about their children's needs.

Commitment

The fourth partnership principle is commitment—feeling loyalty to each other. Commitment is hard to achieve when parents and educators believe that the only reason they are working together is because the law compels them to do so. Leia is persistent; she spent a whole semester persuading the school swim coach to let Sean practice with the team. Now Sean swims in meets; his coach has become committed to him. A committed professional will

◆ Be available and accessible
◆ Go above and beyond
◆ Be sensitive to emotional needs

Professionals who are available and accessible seek to arrange their schedule so that students and families can communicate with them. Although it can be a challenge to schedule parent-teacher conferences and IEP meetings at times when all parties can be available, it can be especially frustrating for families when professionals walk in and out of a meeting (Salembier & Furney, 1997):

> I had to leave my job to go to the [IEP] conference. . . . Do you want to know how many educators came in and had me sign something and walked out? And I just, I thought that was so rude. . . . They do not give me or my daughter the respect that we need. . . . It's like you're just being brushed through like an assembly line. Or they were like scanning you through the grocery line. And then, they leave. (Beach Center, 2000)

Obviously, professionals have busy schedules and personal lives outside their workday. Sometimes it takes a great deal of creativity to find times to connect with parents who also have work responsibilities and limited time available. Options include using a dialogue journal, telephone contacts with voice mail, and technology such as e-mail and school websites.

Many parents want educators to carry out their jobs with the attitude that it means more to them than "just a paycheck." Some parents even talk about wanting to have a family-like relationship or friendship with professionals working with their children. That occurs when educators participate in family events such as birthday parties, weddings, and funerals. An early childhood service provider commented:

> A lot of them [parents] do not have other supports. Their own family members, for whatever reasons, are absent, and they don't have neighbors that they feel like they can call on. So, I mean, if they see that for six hours a day that their child is with us, and that yes, we love them and we're going to care for them . . . it's just a bond that we seem to make, not that we really set out to do that, but it just happens. It's just like we're an extension of their family. (Lord-Nelson, Summers, & Turnbull, 2004, p. 160)

As a teacher, you will need to consider your own values and availability in the extent to which you are able to be available and accessible to families.

Equality

The fifth partnership principle is equality—each partner has roughly equal opportunity and talent to influence the decisions that the partners make. Professionals who seek equality in their partnerships

- ◆ Share power
- ◆ Foster empowerment
- ◆ Provide options

The human service professions traditionally have been characterized by hierarchies, not partnerships. In these hierarchies, professionals have the greatest amount of power, and parents have the least, receiving direction from the professionals. Increasingly, however, and especially within special education, policies and practices attempt to avoid hierarchies and instead establish partnerships in which people have equal power. Each partner agrees to defer to the others' judgment and expertise. Sometimes professionals defer to parents' expertise; sometimes parents defer to professionals'. Professional dominance, or having power over others, can be particularly prevalent in situations in which there are many more professionals than parents. Previously you read a quotation from a parent who felt outnumbered when there were five professionals and only one parent (herself) in a meeting. The same perspective is expressed by another parent, but it is complicated by professionals who are emphasizing their professional degrees:

> I was told that this is a room full of professionals. All the people have college degrees. She told me, there's an MSW, and there's a Ph.D., and I mean she was naming off more initials than I even know what they mean. . . . And I'm just sitting here, nobody looked at me as the professional of knowing how these boys live. (Wang et al., 2004, p. 15)

Power-sharing partnerships are an alternative to power-over hierarchies. In power-sharing partnerships, everyone shares their strengths, talents, resources, and time so that the best possible decisions can be made. A parent describes a power-sharing process as follows:

> It has been WONDERFUL. It has absolutely been the best thing. Not only have there been benefits and services that have come, but all of the people that we deal with have got to where there's relationships there with everybody and there's this bonding and we're getting to where we're on the same page and . . . nobody gets 100% of their way. It's everybody there, you put it in a pile, and it's give and take. (Wang et al., 2004, p. 151)

As you work with families in making decisions, we encourage you to recognize that, ultimately, families must be comfortable with decisions in order to implement them. So professionals should be humble; after all, their roles usually are short term, but the family's role is for a lifetime, as this parent said:

> I said, you intend to do this regardless of what I say. I said, if you made the wrong mistake, what will happen to you? Nothing, I said. I have to live with the outcome of any erroneous decision for the rest of my life because I will be caring for my child until I'm gone from this planet and I have to reap the consequences. . . . I said, I want to make the decisions about my child, and I'll live with the consequences if I happen to make the wrong one. But it's difficult to live with the consequence for the decision you made that I was against. (Beach Center, 2000)

Advocacy

The sixth partnership principle is advocacy—speaking out and taking action to pursue a cause on a personal, organizational, or societal level or on any two or more of those levels. In Chapter 3, you learned about the importance of being an advocate at each of many "layers" in a child's life. To advocate effectively, professionals should (Blue-Banning et al., 2004; Turnbull et al., 2006):

◆ Seek win-win solutions

◆ Prevent problems

◆ Keep your conscience primed

◆ Pinpoint and document problems

◆ Form alliances

We want to emphasize the importance of creating win-win solutions. When a solution is win-win, it satisfies all of the partners; each understands that everyone's perspective was considered by everyone else, even if it was not adopted. A win-win solution differs from a win-lose situation. In the former, all perspectives are valued, and each partner's desired result is maximized to the greatest extent possible. In the latter, not all perspectives are valued, and some perspectives prevail completely over others; there is *my* right way, and it's better than *your* wrong way. Win-win solutions are more likely to occur when the other partnership principles are put into place. For example, good communication, respect, and equality all contribute to win-win solutions.

One strategy for reaching win-win solutions is called **skilled dialogue.** This strategy involves two elements: **anchored understanding** and **third space** (Barrera & Corso, 2002). Anchored understanding occurs when there is a "compassionate understanding of differences" that comes from truly getting to know individual families (Barrera & Corso, 2002, p. 108). You have achieved an anchored understanding when you respect and appreciate the actions, intentions, and beliefs of a particular family, even in situations where you might have acted or thought differently.

Third space refers to a situation in which people creatively reframe each other's diverse perspectives and contradictions so that the perspectives merge to address challenging issues. A third-space perspective is achieved when family members and professionals each reach a new perspective without abandoning their individual points of view. Implementing skilled

PEARSON
myeducationlab

Go to the Activities and Application section in Chapter 4 of MyEducationLab and complete Activity 7. As you watch this video, think about how Leia Holley and Sean's special education teacher advocate for each other and for Sean in their professional partnership.

IEP Tip

The IEP team should consider describing which member of the team will take various advocacy roles in the school, with the school board, or at other decision-making venues through which the student's appropriate education may be affected.

dialogue during interpersonal interactions encourages you to generate questions such as the following (Turnbull et al., 2006, p. 193):

- What is the meaning of this person's actions?
- How does my behavior influence this interaction?
- What can I learn from this person?

We encourage you to think of your partnerships with families as opportunities to advocate for both their interest and systems change. Families can also be some of your most reliable allies in advocating for your and your colleagues' needs.

Trust

The final partnership principle is trust—having confidence in another person's word, judgment, and action and believing that the trusted person will act in the best interest of the person who trusts him or her (Baier, 1986; Tschannen-Moran, & Hoy, 2000; Turnbull et al., 2006). Four practices are associated with being a trusted partner:

- Being reliable
- Using sound judgment
- Maintaining confidentiality
- Trusting yourself

We will emphasize maintaining confidentiality because there often is a great deal of personal information in students' school records. As you learned in Chapter 1, students must have nondiscriminatory evaluations in order to be identified as having a disability. Those evaluations reveal psychometric and other scores and assessments that characterize a student's performance and provide a portrait of the student's family. In multidisciplinary team meetings related to the evaluation or the IFSP or IEP, often a great deal of personal information is revealed. The Family Educational Rights and Privacy Act (FERPA) and IDEA require that teachers keep all information confidential, disclosing it only when the student's parents consent to the disclosure or when the law compels disclosure (National Forum on Education Statistics, 2004). An educator's perspective is revealing:

> It's purely a matter of trust, that they can trust that person so that they can tell them whatever. I have heard all kinds of things, ya know, from families and from the children that I work with, and I consider that pretty sacred, actually. It's kind of a compliment, as far as I can see, that they're willing to trust me with those kinds of things. (Blue-Banning et al., 2004, p. 179)

Typically, educators share confidential information about a student in multidisciplinary team meetings in order to make decisions that will enhance the quality of that student's education. This information should not be discussed outside the meeting, such as within the school building, teachers' lounge, or anywhere else. Keeping information confidential will encourage parents and other professionals to trust you.

VALUES AND OUTCOMES

It's easy, isn't it, to identify the values and outcomes that Leia Holley and Sean's teachers want for him.

- They expect him to learn how to work and then to find work in Bonner Springs. That's Leia's great expectation. Sean's teachers share it.

- They make it possible for him to make positive contributions to his school and others. "Operation Braves" does just that.

- They build on his strengths and his determination to learn to swim.

- They enable him to make choices, especially about using headphones when he experiences sensory overload.

- They use his core circle of support, his brother JP and his buddies Tanner and Devin, to expand his relationships at school and in his community.

- They honor his full citizenship by helping him understand about balloting for Homecoming King and Queen and then by helping him cast his vote.

WHAT DO YOU THINK?

1. Is it appropriate for Leia to be so regularly involved in Sean's school days, such as by sitting in on his class and coaching his teacher Jim Mitchell and his paraeducator Karen Parsons on how to involve him in learning? What's the alternative for him and them?

2. Is it useful for her to play "good mom" and "bad mom," reinforcing his teachers even as she calls them to account by threats or recourse to the state department of education?

3. What would the Holley family's quality of life be if Sean were not effectively educated?

4. What partnership strategies would you most want to develop if you were working with a skilled mother on a mission? Communication? Competence? Respect? Commitment? Equality? Advocacy? How do you build trust with the professionals on whom you rely?

ADDRESSING THE STANDARDS: THE VALUES CONNECTION

The following CEC Knowledge and Skill Standards: Common Core and Values are addressed in this chapter through the content and concepts we discuss.

CEC Knowledge and Skill Standards: Common Core		Values/Standards Connection
CEC Knowledge and Skill Standard I. Foundations		When you comply with the IDEA's requirements for a free appropriate education, you offer your students an opportunity to be *full citizens*—you create equal opportunities for them to have an education that can support them to be economically self-sufficient, live independently, *make choices*, and fully participate and have *relationships* in their communities.
CC1K4	Rights and responsibilities of students, parents, teachers and other professionals, and schools related to exceptional learning needs.	
CC1K7	Family systems and the role of families in the educational process.	
CEC Knowledge and Skill Standard II. Development of Characteristics and Learners		Family members can make *positive contributions* to students with disabilities. These contributions prepare the students to make their own positive contributions to others and to *make choices* about how they want to live, independently or with support.
CC2K3	Characteristics and effects of the cultural and environmental milieu of the individual with exceptional learning needs and the family.	
CC2K4	Family systems and the role of families in supporting development.	

continued

CEC Knowledge and Skill Standards: Common Core	Values/Standards Connection
CEC Knowledge and Skill Standard V. Learning Environments and Social Interactions	When you teach your students to be more self-directed, you are applying CEC Standard 5, Learning Environments and Social Interactions, and you are developing their *strengths* and their ability to *make choices*.
CC5S2 — Identify realistic expectations for personal and social behavior in various settings.	
CC5S3 — Identify supports needed for integration into various program placements.	Assisting students with disabilities to expand their *relationships* with their peers without disabilities can advance their *full citizenship* in their schools and communities.
CC5S6 — Use performance data and information from all stakeholders to make or suggest modifications in learning environments.	
CEC Knowledge and Skill Standard VII. Instructional Planning	Students and families can direct their own lives and make their own choices. Fostering an environment that enables students and families to act on their preferences and needs promotes self-determination.
CC7S3 — Involve the individual and family in setting instructional goals and monitoring progress.	
CC7S7 — Integrate affective, social, and life skills with academic curricula.	
CEC Knowledge and Skill Standard IX. Professional and Ethical Practice	When you build on a student's *strengths,* you enable the student and family to begin to envision *great expectations*.
CC9S2 — Uphold high standards of competence and integrity and exercise sound judgment in the practice of the professional.	
CC9S3 — Act ethically in advocating for appropriate services.	
CC9S5 — Demonstrate commitment to developing the highest education and quality-of-life potential of individuals with exceptional learning needs.	
CEC Knowledge and Skill Standard X. Collaboration	As you see with Leia and Sean Holley, collaboration between and among students, their families, and the professionals who work with them is paramount. These relationships can create beneficial, lasting academic and social success for students.
CC10K2 — Roles of individuals with exceptional learning needs, families, and school and community personnel in planning of an individualized program.	
CC10K3 — Concerns of families of individuals with exceptional learning needs and strategies to help address these concerns.	
CC10S3 — Foster respectful and beneficial relationships between families and professionals.	

SUMMARY

Who Are Today's Families?

◆ Families consist of two or more people who regard themselves to be a family and carry out the functions that families typically perform.

◆ As contrasted with the families of children without exceptionalities, a greater proportion of families of children with exceptionalities have a higher rate of poverty and lower educational levels.

What Are Partnerships and Why Are They Important?

◆ Family-professional partnerships are relationships in which families and professionals collaborate with each other, capitalizing on each other's judgment and expertise in order to increase benefits for students, families, and professionals alike.

◆ Three reasons why family-professional partnerships are important are that (a) schools with strong partnerships are more likely to have high levels of trust, (b) partnerships result in more positive student outcomes, and (c) positive family quality of life is more likely when families experience positive partnerships with professionals.

How Do Children with Exceptionalities Affect Their Families' Quality of Life, and What Is Your Role as an Educator?

◆ The five domains of family quality of life are emotional well-being, parenting, family interaction, physical/material well-being, and disability-related support.

◆ Regarding emotional well-being, students often do not have friendships, and their families sometimes feel isolated. Teachers can be helpful friendship facilitators.

◆ Regarding parenting, teachers can support parents by teaching children to be more independent with their homework and supporting parents to provide helpful homework assistance.

◆ Regarding family interaction, siblings of children and youth with exceptionalities typically experience both positive and negative impacts from their experiences. Siblings can benefit from information that will help them understand their brother or sister's special needs, and they can also provide good ideas for the IEP.

◆ Regarding physical/material well-being, families who experience poverty often need additional supports in order to be able to attend school conferences and school activities.

◆ Regarding disability-related supports, professionals can positively contribute to families by ensuring that the services that they offer are high quality.

How Can You Form Partnerships with Families?

◆ The seven partnership principles are communication, professional competence, respect, commitment, equality, advocacy, and trust.

◆ National resources that provide relevant information for families and professionals include Parent Training and Information Centers and Parent to Parent programs.

◆ Setting high expectations for students and implementing the educational support to achieve those high expectations is a way to demonstrate professional competence.

◆ Respect, characterized by regarding others with esteem through actions and words, is important in all partnerships, especially in partnerships with families from culturally diverse backgrounds.

◆ Professionals who demonstrate commitment by being available and accessible, as well as by going "above and beyond," are more likely to form trusting partnerships with families.

◆ Equality involves power-sharing in which professionals avoid establishing power-over hierarchies.

◆ Advocacy entails speaking out and taking action to pursue a cause on a personal, organizational, or societal level, with an emphasis on creating win-win solutions.

◆ Trust is the key element of partnerships and is characterized and occurs when families and professionals have confidence in each other's word, judgment, and action and believe that the other party will act in the best interest of the person who trusts him or her.

Now go to MyEducationLab at www.myeducationlab.com and take the Self-Assessment to gauge your initial comprehension of chapter content. Once you have taken the Self-Assessment, use your individualized Study Plan for Chapter 4 to enhance your understanding of the concepts discussed in the chapter.

5

Understanding Students with Learning Disabilities

◆ WHO IS LAUREN MARSH?

There is a special place in this world for the peacemakers. However much we might worship the victorious warrior, we value still more the person who offers the olive branch and induces opposing parties to accept it. That is one reason why at Bohemia Manor Middle School in Elkton, Maryland, Lauren Marsh is so well respected. She's the one who (in her words) tells her classmates to "calm down, sit down, chill out, and leave it alone" when they get "really hyper" or start crying or fighting. She's the one who (in the words of one of her teachers, Sherry Eichinger) is a candidate for the school-designated role of peer mediator.

There is a special place, too, for the problem solvers. However much we admire a person who acts passionately about issues, we look to the analyst to figure out what the problem is, why something is a problem at all, what the possible solutions are, and how to evaluate whether the

solutions are working once they are applied. That is one reason why Lauren is so important in school. She brings her analytical ability to bear as a member of a clique of white and African American girls who are the school's leaders. And it is also one of the reasons why Sherry Eichinger is so important at Bohemia Manor Middle School. As a special educator, she teaches Lauren and other students to use various strategies for learning how to calculate and how to learn to read and read to learn; she also teaches other teachers how to be as effective as possible in educating students who, like Lauren, have a specific learning disability in math or, unlike Lauren, find math or other subjects to be relatively easy. It's all about **differentiated instruction—**

teaching strategies, altering some students' tasks, and modifying how they perform those tasks.

As an eighth grader, Lauren takes courses in math, English, science, social studies, fine arts, gym, music, and technology (using computers). If you were to go to Lauren and Sherry's school, you would find Lauren in class with students who have no disabilities and with those who do. You might find her working in a small group with other students, receiving special help from Sherry, or serving in another small group of students as a tutor for her peers. But you would find her using the same strategies that all eighth graders use to understand the books, even though at times she, like other students, might read somewhat below that grade level. Differentiated instruction promotes Lauren's inclusion in the general curriculum.

If you explored Bohemia Manor Middle School further, you would find Sherry being a "Jill of All Trades." Sometimes she collaborates with a general educator to teach math, language arts, and reading, and sometimes she provides consultation for the general educators who teach science or social studies. In these roles, she focuses on differentiated instruction and collaborative teaching. You will learn more about differentiated instruction later in this chapter.

You would not find Sherry, however, in Lauren's art, computer, or physical education classes. Always, you would find her among the educators who convene as a student's individualized education team; always you would find her advocating for Lauren to have some extra time to take the math section of the Maryland statewide assessments of student proficiency; and always you would find her following up on what Lauren is learning, how she is learning, and how her teachers are instructing her. Sherry's a collaborator, a specialist, an advocate, and an accountability-for-progress monitor on behalf of Lauren and the school as a whole. She's also a person who encourages Lauren to advocate for herself; a self-determined student ultimately becomes a more effective adult.

Lauren has two other important allies in her education. Her father, Jeff Moore, is an interstate truck driver who owns his own 18-wheeler and covers the east coast from New Jersey to the South Carolina–Georgia border. Her mother, Florence Moore, has her own job: making sure the Moore household, consisting of Lauren and her five brothers, runs as smoothly as Jeff's tractor-trailer. Whenever Jeff is not on the road, he and Florence both attend regular teacher-parent meetings and IEP meetings with Lauren's teachers. When he is on the road, Florence represents both of them.

Lauren's reliable allies—Sherry and her parents—concur that Lauren brings something extra to her education and her

CHAPTER OBJECTIVES

◆ You will learn what a specific learning disability is and is not and how to identify a student by using procedures and standards that apply especially to specific learning disabilities, including response to intervention and inclusionary and exclusionary criteria for concluding a student has a specific learning disability.

◆ You will learn strategies for teaching students with learning disabilities in the general curriculum, especially the strategies known as embedded learning, self-determination, and differentiated instruction.

◆ You will learn how to determine how well a student is progressing by using curriculum-based measurements.

school. It underlies her peacemaking and her happy personality, and perhaps explains both. It's a sense that Lauren can do whatever she chooses to do if she puts her mind to it, learns the strategies for doing it, and applies her problem-solving skills to make her choices come true, whether on her own or with help. Lauren puts it this way: What she most likes about school is "learning new things." Florence describes that sense of great expectations somewhat differently: "I tell Lauren that there is nothing she can't accomplish." And Sherry explains why Lauren's future seems bright. It's because there are "so many positives" in Lauren's life—her leadership capacities; her ability to advocate for herself and others; her willingness to work; her diligent use of the strategies she is learning for mastering her coursework; her circle of friends; and her family's support.

PEARSON
myeducationlab

After reading this chapter, complete the Self-Assessment for Chapter 5 on MyEducationLab to gauge your initial understanding of chapter content.

IDENTIFYING STUDENTS WITH LEARNING DISABILITIES

Defining Learning Disabilities

Ever since Sam Kirk first coined the term *learning disabilities* in 1963, legislators, parents, and professionals have debated about how to define the condition (Kavale & Forness, 2000; Lyon et al., 2001). IDEA provides one definition, but even that one is controversial. Let's consider the IDEA definition first and an alternative one later.

IDEA defines the term **specific learning disability** as a "disorder in 1 or more of the basic psychological processes involved in understanding or in using language, spoken or written" (Individuals with Disabilities Education Act, 2004). IDEA adds that the "disorder may manifest itself in an imperfect ability to listen, think, speak, read, write, spell, or do mathematical calculations."

IDEA also sets the criteria for determining whether a student has a specific learning disability. Under IDEA, the evaluation team may determine that a student has a specific learning disability under two circumstances, and both must exist. First, the student must have "a disorder in one or more of the basic psychological processes involved in understanding or using written or spoken language." The "disorder may manifest itself in an imperfect ability to listen, think, speak, read, write, spell, or do mathematical calculations." The disorder includes "perceptual disabilities, brain injury, minimal brain dysfunction, dyslexia, and developmental aphasia." This is the **inclusionary standard;** it identifies what conditions are included.

Second, the definition stipulates that the learning disabilities category does not include "a learning problem that is primarily the result of visual, hearing, or motor disabilities of mental retardation, of emotional disturbance, or of environment, cultural, or economic disadvantage." This is the **exclusionary standard;** it says that these causal conditions are excluded.

Note that the definition has two special components: the inclusionary standard and the exclusionary standard. These standards both enlarge and constrict students' eligibility to be classified as having a specific learning disability. The inclusionary standard encompasses listening, thinking, speaking, reading, writing, spelling, and calculating. The exclusionary standard addresses impairments arising from other disabilities or from socioeconomic conditions. Lauren's specific learning disability relates to "calculating"—her math skills.

Learning disabilities continue to be the most prevalent of all disabilities. Slightly less than half (47.4 percent) of all students with disabilities served under IDEA have specific learning disabilities (U.S. Department of Education, 2007). In the 1979–1980 school year, there were 1,281,379 students with learning disabilities between the ages of 3 and 21 receiving services. By contrast, there were 2,669,257 in the 2006–2007 school year (U.S. Department of Education, 2008), a 48 percent increase. Learning disabilities were first recognized as a category of disability in the mid-1960s, as contrasted to other categories such as intellectual disability, visual impairments, and hearing impairments, all of which were recognized much earlier. That fact partially explains the huge increase.

Unlike some of the other categories of disability, there have not been particular concerns about the disproportionate representation of African American or Latino students in the category of learning disabilities (National Research Council, 2002). Apparently, that is so because the dramatic increase in learning disabilities has occurred across all racial/ethnic groups, with the exception of Asian/Pacific Islander students. There is a higher-than-expected placement rate for children from low socioeconomic backgrounds in this category (Blair & Scott, 2002). Boys are four to five times more likely than girls to be identified as having a learning disability (Shapiro, Church, & Lewis, 2002).

Describing the Characteristics

Go to the Activities and Application section in Chapter 5 of MyEducationLab and complete Activity 1. As you watch the video and answer the accompanying questions, think about how this student's situation and educational circumstances might have been different if she didn't have a supportive family and teachers.

In this section we will review the characteristics related to students' academic achievement, memory, executive functioning, and behavior and social/emotional adjustment. Individuals with learning disabilities commonly have average or above-average intelligence. Nevertheless, they almost always demonstrate low academic achievement in one or more areas. There is no such thing as a typical student with learning disabilities. One student may exhibit strengths in math and nonverbal reasoning but weaknesses in receptive and expressive language skills. Another student may be strong in motor skills, reading, and receptive language but weak in math and expressive language. Lauren, for example, has powerful social skills, quite satisfactory language skills, and average reading skills; math, however, challenges her greatly.

Academic Achievement

Reading. One of the most significant challenges facing students with learning disabilities relates to reading (Lyon, Fletcher, & Barnes, 2003; Young & Beitchman, 2007). That fact is especially troublesome because reading is so important to performance in most academic domains and to adjustment to most school activities.

The term *reading disorder* is often used in the educational literature, whereas **dyslexia** is used in the medical literature (McNamara, 2007; Sawyer, 2006). Sometimes these terms are used interchangeably; however, dyslexia indicates a more severe reading disorder than is associated with a neurological impairment. Throughout this chapter, we will use the term *reading disorder* to refer to reading difficulties associated with decoding words, comprehending text, and having appropriate speed and fluency (Young & Beitchman, 2007).

IEP Tip

IEPs should not only address reading instruction but also how to support students' reading in other courses.

Students with reading disabilities may exhibit word recognition errors. When asked to read orally, they may omit, insert, substitute, and/or reverse words (Johnston & Morrison, 2007; Mody, 2003). Students who lack skills in phonological awareness cannot recognize sound segments in spoken words (e.g., "push" has three sound segments, or phonemes: /p/ /u/ /sh/). They also may have difficulty comprehending what they have read because they have limited ability to recall or discern basic facts, sequences, and/or themes. Likewise, they may lose their place while reading; read in a choppy, halting manner; or struggle to comprehend the text they are reading (National Reading Panel, 2000).

Written language. Children and youth with reading disorders frequently also experience problems with written expression (Berninger & Amtmann,

Computers can help students with learning disabilities write more easily.

2003). Even students with learning disabilities who read well often have problems with written language (Young & Beitchman, 2007). Their difficulties usually occur in the areas of handwriting, spelling, productivity, text structure, sentence structure, word usage, and composition. They may:

- Feel overwhelmed by the idea of getting started.
- Struggle to organize and use the mechanics of writing.
- Struggle to develop their ideas fluently.
- Have frequent difficulties spelling and constructing written products legibly.
- Submit written work that is too brief.

Students' handwriting problems can arise from a lack of fine-motor coordination, failure to attend to task, inability to perceive and/or remember visual images accurately, or inadequate handwriting instruction in the classroom. Students with handwriting challenges may learn much less from an assignment because they must focus on the mechanics of writing instead of the content of their assignment.

Students may also have difficulty with spelling. Common spelling errors include addition of unneeded letters, omission of needed letters, reversal of vowels, reversal of syllables, and phonemic spelling of nonphonemic words.

Mathematics. Students' mathematical difficulties can range from mild to severe; it is likely that Lauren's are mild to moderate. Students' difficulties with math may include the following (Geary, 2006):

- **Procedural problems:** frequent errors in understanding math concepts and difficulty sequencing the steps of complex problems.
- **Semantic memory problems:** difficulty remembering math facts.
- **Visual-spatial problems:** difficulty reproducing numerals.

Math disability can occur in isolation or in combination with reading and written expression disorders. One half to slightly more than two thirds of children with math disabilities have been found to experience a reading disability as well (Barbaresi, Katusic, Colligan, Weaver, & Jacobsen, 2005). Students who experience both reading and math disorders often experience greater challenges in math (Jordan, Hanich, & Kaplan, 2003). It stands to reason that these students would have difficulty with word problems because of the language-processing requirements. A major contributor to math disability is working memory, as you will learn in the next section (Swanson & Jerman, 2006).

Memory

Many students with learning disabilities have difficulty with short-term, long-term, and working memory (Pickering, 2006; Swanson & Jerman, 2006, 2007). **Short-term memory** challenges cause difficulty in recalling information shortly after it is presented. **Long-term memory** challenges involve difficulty in storing information permanently for later recall. **Working memory** refers to how students process information in order to remember it.

> Our conclusions from approximately two decades of research are that WM [working memory] deficits are fundamental problems of children and adults with LD. Further, these WM problems are related to difficulties in reading, mathematics, and perhaps writing. Students with LD in reading and/or math demonstrate WM deficits related to the phonological loop, a component of WM that specializes in the retention of speech-based information. This system is of service in complex cognition, such as reading comprehension, problem solving, and writing. (Swanson & Sáez, 2006, p. 196)

Executive Functioning

When you study for a test on this chapter, how will you do it? You might review chapter headings, definitions, summaries, or class notes. Or you might use flashcards or memory devices, called mnemonics, such as acronyms for lists. (You will learn more about mnemonics in Chapter 11.) You probably have found an approach to studying that works best for you. If so, you likely have good skills in the area of **metacognition.** That term refers to focusing attention, being organized, engaging in future planning, and solving problems (Meltzer, 2007). Efficient learners take control and direct their own thinking process, but students with learning disabilities tend to lack these skills and have deficits in the following areas of executive function (Garrett, Mazzocco, & Baker, 2006; Meltzer & Krishnan, 2007):

- Acquiring, organizing, and prioritizing key informational themes without getting overloaded by details.
- Checking and revising performance during learning tasks.
- Initiating new strategies or tasks.
- Shifting to different approaches when a given approach is not working.
- Evaluating correct and incorrect solutions.
- Predicting which problems they could and could not solve correctly.

Due to her well-honed social skills, Lauren and her teachers feel confident about her inclusion in the general education program.

Social Characteristics

Approximately three fourths of students with learning disabilities experience challenges in the social arena (Kavale & Forness, 1996). Areas of concern include (Bryan, Burstein, & Ergul, 2004):

- Having more negative academic self-concepts as related to social self-concepts.
- Experiencing negative emotions more frequently, including feelings of loneliness.
- Perceiving the nonverbal feelings and emotions of others.
- Finding appropriate solutions to social dilemmas.
- Carrying on conversations with others.
- Initiating and sustaining friendships and social relationships.

IEP Tip

The IEP should address a student's social, emotional, and behavioral needs, not just the student's academic needs.

Processing problems can also cause difficulty understanding social cues and behaving in socially acceptable ways. (Note that we said "can," not "will." Lauren, for instance, clearly does not have any such problems; indeed, she is highly skilled in social, emotional, and behavioral dimensions.) If you add the frustration that these learning problems cause and the difficulty that can arise when dealing with people who do not understand why a student does not pick up on social cues, you have some students at risk for social, emotional, and behavioral problems.

Determining the Causes

Neurological Mechanisms

Learning disabilities result from a central nervous system dysfunction—that is, from underlying neurological problems (Lyon et al., 2001). New neuroimaging technologies have enhanced scientists' ability to assess brain activity accurately. These technologies have enabled researchers to pinpoint brain activity associated with reading (Shapiro, Church, & Lewis, 2007).

Figure 5.1 Overview of major reading circuits defined by functional neuroimaging studies

Temporo-parietal (dorsal) region
Facts
- Pseudoword reading > word reading
- Increased activation during phonological analysis
- Relatively late response
- Decreased activity with faster presentation rates

RD vs. NI
- NI > RD in word and pseudoword reading

Hypothesized Function
- Rule based analysis functions— integration of orthographic, phonological, lexical-semantic dimentions

Frontal (anterior) region
Facts
- Pseudoword reading > word reading
- Sensitive to consistency of orthographic to phonological mapping (regularity)

RD vs. NI
- RD > NI in word and pseudoword reading

Hypothesized Function
- Fine-grained articulatory recoding (i.e., output phonology)

Occipito-temporal (ventral) region
Facts
- Word reading > pseudoword reading
- Consistent activation across tasks
- Early repsonse (150–180 msec)
- Increased activity with faster presentation rates
- Activation increases with age and predicts reading skill

RD vs. NI
- NI > RD in word and pseudoword reading

Hypothesized Function
- Linquistically structured memory-based word identification system (word-form area)

(a)

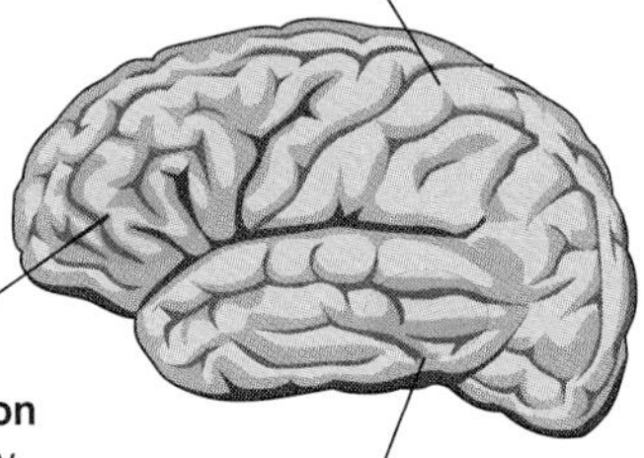

Temporo-parietal (dorsal) region
Rule-based analysis function— integration of orthographic, phonological, and lexical-semantic dimensions

Frontal (anterior) region
Fine-grained articulatory recoding (i.e., output phonotogy)

Occipito-temporal (ventral) region
Linguistically structured, memory-based word identification system (word-form area)

(b)

(a) *Source:* Adapted from p. 209 of Functional Neuroimaging Studies of Reading and Reading Disability (Developmental Dyslexia) by Pugh, K. R., Mencl, W. E., Jenner, A. R., et al. (2000). *Mental Retardation and Developmental Disabilities Research Reviews,* 6(3). Copyright © 2000 Wiley-Liss, Inc.
(b) *Source:* Shapiro, B, Church, R. P., Lewis, M. E. B. (2002). Specific learning disabilities. In M. L. Batshaw (Ed.), *Children with disabilities* (5th ed., pp. 417–442). Baltimore: Paul H. Brookes.

Figure 5.1 illustrates three areas of the brain that are key to the development of successful reading skills. Neuroimaging research has documented increased activation of the dorsal and anterior systems (see Figure 5.1) after intensive reading remediation (Shaywitz et al., 2004).

Genetics

Evidence continues to accumulate that there is a strong genetic contribution to different learning disabilities (Isles & Humby, 2006; Robertshaw & MacPherson, 2006; Shapiro et al., 2007). A research study conducted in Australia, Scandinavia, and the United States with preschoolers and kindergartners who were same-sex twins reported strong genetic influences at the preschool level on phonological awareness and verbal memory (Byrne et al., 2006). Environment was identified as being more important for letter awareness, vocabulary, and grammar/vocabulary.

Environmental Causes

There are connections between genetic and environmental causes because parents who experience problems with reading are likely to read less to their children during their children's early years (Lyon et al., 2001; Petrill, Deater-Deckard, Schatschneider, & Davis, 2005). A study of adopted children and their adopting families ruled out genetics and found small but statistically significant relationships between the home literacy environment and children's reading outcomes (Petrill et al., 2005). The environmental influences were powerful when children were younger as well as older. The effect of the home environment on reading outcomes was stable over time.

EVALUATING STUDENTS WITH LEARNING DISABILITIES

As we pointed out when defining a learning disability, a student must have a disorder that manifests itself in an imperfect ability to listen, think, speak, read, write, spell, or do mathematical calculations. The question facing state and local education agencies is how to operationalize that definition. Just how much of an impairment must a student demonstrate?

To answer that question, previous IDEA regulations authorized the agencies to apply a discrepancy standard—"severe discrepancy" between the student's ability and performance. A severe discrepancy is one that is statistically significant. During the 1970s and 1980s, 98 percent of the states used the discrepancy standard for identifying students as having a learning disability (Frankenberger & Fronzaglio, 1991).

The current IDEA, however, adopts a different, two-part approach. First, it provides that a state or local educational agency may take into consideration whether a student has a severe discrepancy between achievement and intellectual ability in oral expression, listening comprehension, written expression, basic reading skill, reading comprehension, mathematical calculation, or mathematical reasoning. An agency *may* use the discrepancy standard; it is simply not required to do so under federal law.

Second, an agency now may use a process that determines if the student responds to scientific, research-based intervention. This is the responsiveness to intervention approach we first discussed in Chapter 2. We discuss it again on page 135.

It is far too early to detect how state and local agencies will use these options. Some may continue to use the discrepancy standard; some may not. Some may use the responsiveness-to-intervention approach; others may not. Some may use both.

Accordingly, we will explain how agencies have been evaluating students, discussing both standards. We will then explain some of the controversy surrounding that standard, clarifying why the 2004 reauthorization made these two changes.

Determining the Presence of a Learning Disability

Figure 5.2 shows the traditional nondiscriminatory evaluation procedure for identifying learning disabilities (Speece & Hines, 2007). Generally, students are referred for evaluation because, even after prereferral, they seem to have more ability than their academic performance in one or more subject areas indicates.

The Discrepancy Model

A nondiscriminatory evaluation traditionally has established a discrepancy between the student's intellectual ability, as measured by an IQ test, and the student's achievement, as measured by a standardized achievement test. Educators use "the discrepancy model" as the shorthand term for the difference between a student's intellectual ability and her achievement.

In the field of learning disabilities, educators usually use an intelligence test, such as the Wechsler Intelligence Scale for Children—IV Integrated (WISC-IV). This and other intelligence tests measure a sample of a student's performance on tasks related to reasoning, memory,

Figure 5.2

Traditional nondiscriminatory evaluation process for determining the presence of a learning disability

Observation	**Teacher and parents observe:**
	Student appears frustrated with academic tasks and may have stopped trying.
Screening	**Assessment measures:**
	Classroom work products: Work is inconsistent or generally poor. Teacher feels student is capable of doing better.
	Group intelligence tests: Usually the tests indicate average or above-average intelligence. However, tests may not reveal true ability because of reading requirements.
	Vision and hearing screening: Results do not explain academic difficulties.
Prereferral	**Teacher implements suggestions from school-based team:**
	The student still experiences frustration and/or academic difficulty despite interventions. Ineffective instruction is eliminated as the cause for academic difficulty.
Referral	**Multidisciplinary team submits referral.**
Nondiscriminatory evaluation procedures and standards	**Assessment measures:**
	Individualized intelligence test: Student has average or above-average intelligence, so intellectual disability is ruled out. Student may also have peaks and valleys in subtests. The multidisciplinary team makes sure that the test is culturally fair.
	Individualized achievement test: A significant discrepancy (difference) exists between what the student is capable of learning (as measured by the intelligence test) and what the student has actually learned (as measured by the achievement test). The difference exists in one or more of the following areas: listening, thinking, reading, written language, mathematics. The team makes sure the test is culturally fair.
	Curriculum-based assessment: The student is experiencing difficulty in one or more areas of the curriculum used by the local school district.
	Behavior rating scale: The student's learning problems cannot be explained by the presence of emotional or behavioral problems.
	Anecdotal records: The student's academic problems are not of short duration but have been apparent throughout time in school.
	Direct observation: The student is experiencing difficulty and/or frustration in the classroom.
	Ecological assessment: The student's environment does not cause the learning difficulty.
	Portfolio assessment: The student'work is inconsistent and/or poor in specific subjects.
Determination	The nondiscriminatory multidisciplinary evaluation team determines that the student has a learning disability and needs special education and related services.

learning comprehension, and ability to learn academic skills; based on the student's performance, educators infer the student's intellectual capacity. IQ tests yield an intelligence quotient (IQ) that is a ratio of the student's mental age (MA) to his or her chronological age (CA): $IQ = MA \div CA \times 100$. So if a student has a mental age of 12 and a chronological age of 10, the student's IQ would compute at 12 divided by 10 times 100, which equals 120.

Figure 5.3 Ranges of Intelligence

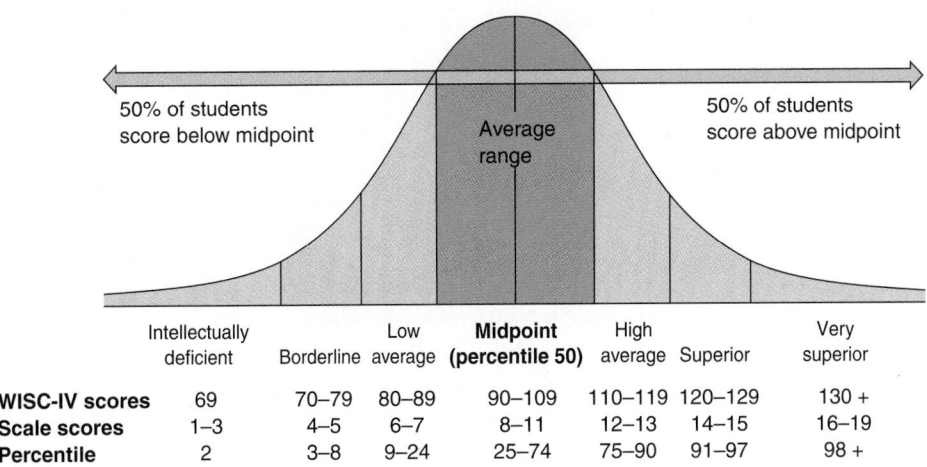

	Intellectually deficient	Borderline	Low average	**Midpoint (percentile 50)**	High average	Superior	Very superior
WISC-IV scores	69	70–79	80–89	90–109	110–119	120–129	130 +
Scale scores	1–3	4–5	6–7	8–11	12–13	14–15	16–19
Percentile	2	3–8	9–24	25–74	75–90	91–97	98 +

Source: Adapted from *The WISC-IV Companion: A Guide to Interpretation and Educational Intervention* (p. 47), by S. Truch, 2006, Austin, TX: PRO-ED. Copyright 2006 by PRO-ED, Inc. Adapted with permission.

The bell-shaped curve in Figure 5.3 shows below-average, average, and above-average ranges of intelligence on the WISC-IV. Note that 50 percent of the students at any particular age average an IQ below 100, and 50 percent average an IQ above 100. Most states identify students with IQs at or above 130 as gifted (Chapter 16) and students with IQs at or below 70 as having an intellectual disability if they also meet other criteria (Chapters 9 and 10).

The WISC-IV is appropriate for use with students aged 6 years to 16 years, 11 months. It provides scores related to the following four indexes: Verbal Comprehension, Perceptual Reasoning, Processing Speed, and Working Memory (Prifitera, Weiss, Saklofske, & Rolfhus, 2005). Diagnosticians compare and contrast index scores in discerning patterns of relative strengths and weaknesses. Sixteen subtests measure the four index areas. Caution exists about whether it is appropriate to use the profile analysis to map students' strengths and weaknesses (Maller, 2005).

In addition to using intelligence tests, educators typically also administer a **norm-referenced** achievement test. The Wechsler Individualized Achievement Test—Second Edition (WIAT-II) is one of the tests often used. This test reveals the student's academic skills in reading, written language, and mathematics.

One benefit of using IQ and norm-referenced tests concurrently is that the same group of students (called a **norm group**) took the tests initially to develop standard scores. Both tests have a **mean** (or average) score of 100 and a **standard deviation** (a way to determine how much a particular score differs from the mean) of 15 points. Therefore, with two different scores, evaluators can compare a student's IQ and achievement scores.

Woodcock (1990) has described three types of discrepancies:

◆ **Aptitude-achievement** (also called ability-achievement): the discrepancy between an ability and a related area of achievement (e.g., IQ and reading score).

◆ **Intracognitive:** the discrepancy between different abilities (e.g., performance and verbal scores).

◆ **Intra-achievement:** the discrepancy between different areas of academic achievement.

When educators determine that a student has a severe discrepancy, they nearly always look at the first type: aptitude-achievement. States have different criteria for defining a severe discrepancy. Your state might use 1 standard deviation (15 points, as in the hypothetical case), 1.5 standard deviations (22 or 23 points), or 2 standard deviations (30 points). Regardless of the extent of discrepancy that a particular state specifies, the discrepancy model rests on the premise that students do not achieve at their expected level

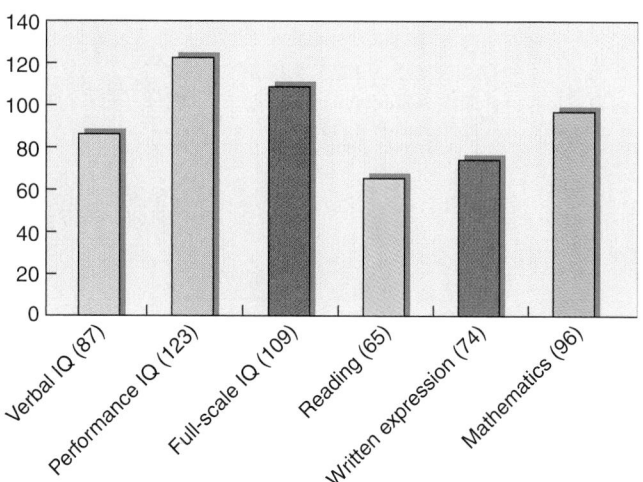

Figure 5.4 Joseph's nondiscriminatory evaluation scores

of ability. Thus, measurement compares and contrasts what a student is expected to achieve based on IQ and what a student actually achieves based on achievement test scores. Some states change the discrepancy requirement based on age, and others use complicated statistical formulas to determine discrepancy (Mercer & Pullen, 2005).

Let's consider "Joseph" and whether he has a severe discrepancy (see Figure 5.4). Notice that he has peaks and valleys in his scores, suggesting the possibility of a severe discrepancy. (By comparison, students with intellectual disability typically have flat profiles.) The first obvious discrepancy is intracognitive. There is a difference of 36 points (more than 2 standard deviations) between his verbal and performance IQs. There is also an intra-achievement discrepancy of 2 standard deviations between his reading and mathematics scores. Some states would allow him to qualify for services based on this criterion alone.

In addition, Joseph has an IQ achievement discrepancy between his full-scale IQ and his reading and written expression. So he does not qualify for special education services in mathematics based on his full-scale IQ. But if the state in which he lives allows educators to compare his verbal with his reading and written expression, he could qualify for services in reading but not written expression because of the discrepancy. And he could even qualify for services in mathematics when his math score is compared to his performance IQ, also because of the discrepancy.

One criticism of the **discrepancy model** is that it is biased against students from diverse racial/ethnic backgrounds who score lower on IQ tests (Fuchs & Young, 2006; Warner, Dede, Garvan, & Conway, 2002). When students have a lower IQ, it is more difficult to establish a discrepancy between their IQ and their achievement and thereby to qualify as having a specific learning disability. In Maryland, where Lauren lives, the state and her own school district use the discrepancy standard, so Lauren qualified for the specific learning disability category and, by definition, has only that academic disability and no other.

A second criticism of the discrepancy model is that a discrepancy between achievement and IQ frequently cannot be reliably assessed until a student is nearly 9 years old (Shaywitz, Escobar, Shaywitz, Fletcher, & Makuch, 1992; Stuebing et al., 2002). This is so because it takes a while for a student's achievement to become delayed enough to show up as a severe discrepancy. Educators must wait for the student to fail before detecting a specific learning disability. This means that early identification of learning disabilities is not possible and valuable learning opportunities for more intensive instruction do not occur (Bradley, Danielson, & Doolittle, 2007).

Other criticisms are that discrepancy formulas often vary from state to state; the psychometric accuracy of the discrepancy formula is doubtful and has been called into question; and there is not much information generated by the evaluation to help teachers plan effective instruction for the student (Lyon et al., 2001). These criticisms may explain why the reauthorized IDEA allows states to use both the discrepancy standard and the responsiveness-to-intervention standard.

The debate on the appropriateness of using the IQ-achievement discrepancy has been an intense one. When more than 200 editorial board members of scholarly journals related to reading disability were surveyed, almost three fourths reported believing that the IQ-achievement discrepancy should not be used to operationalize reading disability (Speece & Shekitka, 2002). Alternatively, there are also strong advocates in support of the IQ-achievement discrepancy (Holdnack & Weiss, 2006; Mayes & Calhoun, 2005).

The Response to Intervention Model

As we have noted, IDEA now takes into account criticisms of the IQ-achievement discrepancy approach by specifying that schools are not required to document a severe discrepancy between intellectual disability and achievement and that they may use alternative processes. Accordingly, it provides that a local educational agency may use a process that determines if the child responds to scientific, research-based intervention.

This language about a "scientific, research-based intervention" has become known within the field of special education as response to intervention (RTI). In Chapter 2, you learned about RTI as a problem-solving approach that involves multiple tiers of increasingly intense, research-based interventions matched to each student's needs. The Into Practice box (see Box 5.1) provides the steps schools should follow in using RTI to evaluate whether a student has a learning disability. Each of the tiers within the RTI model (there are typically three) involves increasing degrees of *systematic instruction* so that a student who does not respond to typical instruction in general education classes has the opportunity to receive more explicit, intensive, and/or supportive instruction (Torgesen, 2002).

IEP Tip

An RTI approach guides the IEP team concerning the nature of explicit, intensive, and supportive instruction for a student.

- ◆ More *explicit* instruction involves the systematic teaching of critical skills that enable the student to be more successful in mastering a subject.

- ◆ More *intensive* instruction involves a higher frequency of instructional opportunities than is typically provided in general education classrooms.

- ◆ More *supportive* instruction involves more precise scaffolding in order to (1) sequence skills and (2) provide more precise prompts to use necessary learning strategies.

RTI involves partnerships across general and special education, as well as partnerships with related service providers. These partnerships are necessary to provide systematic instruction at increasingly more explicit, intensive, and/or supportive tiers of instruction. Box 5.2, Partnership Tips, sets out the reading instruction tasks that must be addressed by different members of the multidisciplinary team in order to provide a full array of RTI options.

Current research is focusing on the nature of instruction at each tier and refinement of processes for implementing RTI (Bender & Shores, 2007; Fuchs, Fuchs, & Hollenbeck, 2007; Jimerson, Burns, & VanDerHeyden, 2007; Stecker, 2007; Vaughn & Roberts, 2007).

RTI is not without its critics. Some special education researchers worry that many aspects of RTI ". . . are best viewed as 'experimental' because their technical adequacy has not yet been established" (Kavale, Holdnack, & Mostert, 2006, p. 125). Experts in school psychology seek to integrate RTI with traditional methods for documenting IQ-achievement discrepancy; they favor assessing a student's psychological or cognitive processing, and they point out that neither RTI nor IQ testing accomplishes that goal adequately at the present time (Flanagan, Ortiz, Alfonso, & Dynda, 2006; Hale, Kaufman, Naglieri, & Kavale, 2006; Ofiesh, 2006).

myeducationlab
PEARSON

Go to the Activities and Application section in Chapter 5 of MyEducationLab and complete Activity 2. As you interact with the simulation and answer the accompanying questions, think about how you could adapt this intervention to another subject at the same grade level such as mathematics or science.

Determining the Nature of Specifically Designed Instruction and Services

For instruction to be more explicit, intensive, and supportive, it must be based on evaluation data (as we point out in this and all subsequent chapters). Educators have relied on general achievement tests, such as the Wechsler Individualized Achievement Test, for evaluating a student. Although the test scores help educators to compute a discrepancy, they

Responsiveness to Intervention as a Method for Determining the Presence of a Learning Disability

In order to use RTI as an evaluation method to determine the presence of a learning disability, schools must make sound decisions addressing the following six components:

1. Specify the number of prevention tiers.
   - Three key tiers in RTI programs include primary prevention, secondary prevention, and tertiary prevention.
   - Primary prevention is generally considered to be the general education program with the core curriculum and instruction associated with grade-level norms.
   - Secondary prevention consists of small-group tutoring in core academic subjects, especially reading and math.
   - Tertiary prevention consists of an individualized program characterized by systematic instruction and ongoing progress monitoring.

2. Identify students for prevention.
   - Provide quality instruction in the general curriculum (Tier 1).
   - Conduct universal screening of all students in the school at the beginning of the school year in order to identify students who are not successful with core instruction.

3. Provide intervention.
   - Implement two intervention models including problem solving and standard protocols (Tier 2).
     ✓ Problem solving involves defining the problem related to learning, analyzing the factors contributing to the problem, developing and implementing a plan to address the problem, and evaluating the effectiveness of systematic instruction.
     ✓ Standard protocols involve implementing instructional programs whose effectiveness has been verified through experimental research.
   - Implement intervention for a period of time, approximately 10–20 weeks for 3–4 times per week.

4. Classify response.
   - Identify criteria for determining when a student's response is adequate and when the student needs to receive more systematic instruction.
   - Consider student's rate of improvement and actual achievement as it compares to classmates whose learning is progressing at the Tier 1 level.

5. Conduct multidisciplinary evaluation.
   - For students unable to respond adequately to Tier 2 prevention, design a multidisciplinary evaluation to address the questions and issues that are problematic for the student (Tier 3).
   - Implement the multidisciplinary evaluation in order to pinpoint learning challenges around which Tier 3 intervention should be designed.
   - Rule out the presence of other disabilities, especially an intellectual disability.

6. Provide special education.
   - Implement intervention characterized by instruction that is highly explicit, intensive, and supportive (Tier 3).
   - Ensure lower student-teacher ratios and extended instructional time.

Go to the Building Teaching Skills and Dispositions section in Chapter 5 of MyEducationLab and complete the activities. As you interact with the simulations and answer the accompanying questions, think about how the RTI model is different from the traditional discrepancy model in successfully determining eligibility for special education services.

Source: Based on infomation from Fuchs & Fuchs (2007). A model for implementing responsiveness to intervention. *TEACHING Exceptional Children, 38*(5), 14–20.

do not provide explicit guidance for intervention and instruction. That is so, for example, with respect to reading.

Often students cannot read as young children because they have limitations in **phonological processing,** the capacity to use the sound system of language to process oral and written information (Johnston & Morrison, 2007; McBride-Chang et al., 2005; Schatschneider & Torgensen, 2004). Using this sound system involves skills related to phonological awareness, phonological memory, rapid naming of letters, and oral vocabulary.

The Comprehensive Test of Phonological Processing is a standardized way to evaluate a student's current level of performance related to the first three skills—awareness, memory, and rapid naming (Haight, 2006). The test identifies students whose achievement is significantly below their peers. It also identifies a student's strengths and weaknesses

Implementing Tiers 1, 2, and 3 for Reading Instruction

	Tier 1	**Tier 2**	**Tier 3**
Definitions	Implement reading instruction and programs and administer benchmark assessments (3 times per year)	Use instructional intervention in small groups to supplement, enhance, and support Tier 1	Extend individualized reading instruction in groups of 1–3 students beyond the time allocated for Tier 1
Focus	Include all students	Identify students with reading difficulties who have not responded to Tier 1 efforts	Identify students with marked difficulties in reading or reading difficulties who have not responded adequately to Tier 1 and Tier 2 efforts
Program	Provide scientifically based reading instruction and curriculum emphasizing the critical elements	Provide specialized, scientifically based reading instruction and curriculum emphasizing the critical elements	Provide sustained, intensive, scientifically based reading instruction and curriculum highly responsive to students' needs
Instruction	Provide sufficient opportunities to practice throughout the school day	Provide additional attention, focus, and support	Provide carefully designed and implemented, explicit, systematic instruction
Interventionist	Provide instruction through general education teacher	Provide instruction through personnel determined by the school (e.g., classroom teacher, specialized reading teacher, other trained personnel)	Provide instruction through personnel determined by the school (e.g., specialized reading teacher, special education teacher)
Setting	Provide instruction in a general education classroom	Provide instruction in an appropriate setting designated by the school	Provide instruction in an appropriate setting designated by the school
Grouping	Provide instruction through flexible grouping	Provide instruction through homogeneous small group instruction (e.g., 1:4, 1:5)	Provide instruction through homogeneous instruction in smaller groups (e.g., 1:2, 1:3)
Time	Provide instruction for minimum of 90 min per day	Provide instruction for 20–30 min per day in addition to Tier 1	Provide instruction for 50-min sessions (or longer) per day depending upon appropriateness of Tier 1
Assessment	Administer benchmark assessments at beginning, middle, and end of academic year	Administer progress monitoring twice a month on target skill to ensure adequate progress and learning	Administer progress monitoring at least twice a month on target skill to ensure adequate progress and learning

Source: Adapted from Vaughn Gross Center for Reading and Language Arts at The University of Texas at Austin, (2005). *Implementing the 3-tier reading model: Reducing reading difficulties for kindergarten through third grade students,* (2nd ed). Austin, TX, in Vaughn, S. & Roberts, G. (2007). Secondary interventions in reading: Providing additional instruction for students at risk. *TEACHING Exceptional Children, 39*(5), 40–46. Reprinted with permission from The Council for Exceptional Children.

and is useful to monitor progress based on interventions. One version of the test is appropriate for children ages 5 and 6, who are at the very beginning stage of reading. Another is appropriate for students aged 7 through 24. The test requires about 30 minutes for administration. Scores are stated according to percentiles, standard scores, and grade-equivalent scores. Separate scores also are given for each of the three major skills areas—awareness, memory, and rapid letter naming.

DESIGNING AN APPROPRIATE IEP

Partnering for Special Education and Related Services

As you read this and other chapters, you will learn how to become a partner with others who design and implement a student's IEP. Some of these strategies are specific to a student's unique disability-related needs. You may work with physicians, school nurses, rehabilitation specialists, and physical or occupational therapists to develop an appropriate education for a student with other health impairments (Chapter 12). Remember, however, that the student is the ultimate beneficiary of your work, so you also will want to know how to involve the student in developing and implementing the IEP.

Often, students become involved in developing their IEPs when they are transitioning out of secondary school. IDEA requires them to be notified the year before they attain the age of majority (usually 18) that they will become adults and have rights to make decisions for themselves when they are 18. IDEA also requires the transition planning to begin when they are 16 and to take into account their preferences for post-secondary activities. Why wait until they are 16? Some teachers believe that earlier is better. Mason, Field, and Sawilowsky (2004) surveyed more than 500 educators and found that 95 percent of them believed that active student involvement in educational planning was important, but only 10% reported that their students had been actively involved in the process the previous year. Indeed, Mason and other researchers found that almost half (46 percent) of all students were not involved in a meaningful manner. Martin, Marshall, and Sale (2004) studied the involvement and contributions of 1,638 IEP participants across 393 IEP meetings for middle/junior and senior high students held over 3 consecutive years.

Martin and colleagues found that simply the presence of students at their IEP meeting had multiple benefits: Parents were more positive about the IEP meeting, and participants in it focused more on the student's strengths, interests, and abilities. In addition, student involvement in IEP meetings tends to enhance a student's self-determination. Williams-Diehl, Wehmeyer, Palmer, Soukup, and Garner (in press) examined differences in level of self-determination between groups of students who differed in the level of their involvement in their IEP meetings. They found that students who were more involved were also more self-determined.

Despite the potential benefits of student participation, students generally are not involved in their IEP meetings. Of the more than 500 teachers in the Mason et al. (2004) study, only 10 percent reported that their students had been actively involved in the process the previous year. Similarly, Martin et al. (2004) found that students participated in their IEP at a level lower than all other participants across every indicator of participation. In a follow-up study, Martin et al. (2006) observed 109 middle and high school IEP meetings. They found that students only spoke during 3 percent of the IEP meeting intervals recorded, while special education teachers spoke in 51 percent of the intervals. Students' involvement, as measured by percentage of intervals in which the student spoke, was the lowest among all IEP team participants. Martin and colleagues concluded that instruction to promote student involvement would be central to improving these findings.

Student involvement in developing an IEP can take many forms, depending on the student's interest and capacity. All involvement begins with an invitation to participate. For many students with disabilities, the IEP process has not been a pleasant one because the focus, in many cases, has been on students' failures and deficits (Van Dycke, Martin, & Lovett, 2006). Given past experiences, it should not be surprising that many students opt

PEARSON
myeducationlab

Go to the Activities and Application section in Chapter 5 of MyEducationLab and complete Activity 3. As you watch this video, think back to some of the videos you watched in Chapter 4 on Sean Holley's IEP meeting.

IEP Tip

During the transition years, it is critical that IEP teams consider needed self-advocacy skills and actively involve students with learning disabilities in their planning meetings, starting no later than age 16.

out of the meetings or, when they do attend, choose to remain silent. It may not be sufficient to simply send the student a letter of invitation; a better approach may be a face-to-face, genuine offer of inclusion.

Once students are invited, however, what next? Three well-documented strategies are role-playing, prompting (verbal, visual, and physical), and designating a facilitator to direct questions to the student, clarify educators' jargon, and make sure the student comprehends what people are saying (Test et al. 2004). These strategies help students to be active decision makers while they are in secondary school and especially during their transition from high school to adulthood.

Instructional processes also promote student involvement. Martin, Marshall, Maxson, and Jerman (1997) developed a process called the Self-Directed IEP, which teaches students the skills they need to run their IEP meeting. Martin et al. (2006) conducted a randomized trial study of the effects of the Self-Directed IEP process with 130 high school students and found that students in the Self-Directed IEP intervention group increased the percentage of time they spoke at their meeting, started their meeting, and led their meeting when compared with students who did not receive the intervention.

Another approach is the Self-Advocacy Strategy (Schumaker & Deshler, 2003), which includes a step-by-step process for adolescents with learning disabilities to lead their IEP. Test and Neale (2004) showed that the Self-Advocacy Strategy was an effective instructional tool to promote student involvement in IEP meetings and enhance self-determination. Teachers can use technology—a hypermediated version—to advance the Self-Advocacy Strategy process, as Box 5.3 describes. Even without these and similar instructional packages, however, students with learning disabilities can be involved in setting goals and solving problems related to their education through instructional strategies such as the Self-Determined Learning Model of Instruction (Wehmeyer, Palmer, Agran, Mithaug, & Martin, 2000), which we discuss in detail in Chapter 9.

Determining Supplementary Aids and Services

In Chapter 2, you learned about the types of supplementary aids and services that enable students with disabilities to gain access to the general education curriculum and the benefit of universal design for learning. For most of these aids and services to be effective, however, it is often necessary for teachers, schools, and IEP teams to know the scope and sequence of content being delivered at a given school. They can learn this information by engaging in a curriculum mapping process. While not necessarily a supplementary aid and service in and of itself, the curriculum mapping process helps educators implement those supports and ensures high-quality planning (Udelhofen, 2005).

When members of a student's IEP team engage in curriculum mapping, they use the school calendar as an organizer—it is the rather inflexible statement of what must occur and when. The IEP team members then collect information about each teacher's curriculum. The information includes descriptions of the content to be taught during the year, the processes and skills emphasized, and the student assessments used. Often after discussing the curriculum with each of the student's teachers, they develop a curriculum map for the school, identifying gaps or repetitions in the curriculum content. At that point, they can determine whether they are teaching all parts of the curriculum framework, performance objectives, and other standards at the appropriate grade/course (Jacob, 2004).

The curriculum mapping process can identify where in the curriculum students with disabilities can receive instruction on content from the general curriculum that is based on the students' unique learning needs. So, for example, Lauren's teacher, Sherry, may be looking for opportunities across the school day to provide Lauren with additional opportunities to learn and practice math skills. If Bohemia Manor Middle School had conducted a curriculum map, she could turn to that document and explore where these additional math opportunities exist—maybe in the math-rich musical notations

Lauren's mother, Florence, and teacher, Sherry, have formed a successful partnership that contributes to the quality of Lauren's education.

Box 5.3

Using Hypermedia to Promote Self-Advocacy

The Self-Advocacy Strategy is one of the instructional strategies developed by researchers at the University of Kansas Center for Research on Learning. You learned about several such strategies in this chapter. The intent of the Self-Advocacy Strategy is to enable students with learning disabilities to participate more fully and meaningfully in educational planning and decision making. One important component of the strategy is the implementation of the I PLAN process. I PLAN is an acronym to assist students to remember the steps in setting goals. To set their own goals, students follow the five steps:

- **I**nventory your strengths, areas of needed improvement, and learning needs.
- **P**rovide your inventory information.
- **L**isten and respond.
- **A**sk questions.
- **N**ame your goals.

Lancaster, Schumaker, and Deshler (2002) developed an interactive, hypermedia version of the Self-Advocacy Strategy. Interactive hypermedia formats allow the use of video and audio segments, text, and graphics and provide multiple paths for students to follow in a nonlinear fashion as they interact with the material. The most common form of interactive hypermedia format is HTML (hypertext markup language), which is used to design web pages. The hypermedia version of the Self-Advocacy Strategy allowed students to navigate through the process at their own pace and with minimal teacher supervision. Students can begin and end lessons at any time. The hypermedia version includes video clips of instructors modeling each step in the strategy, including each of the I PLAN steps. At the end of the lesson, students model what they've learned to the teacher.

As with the I PLAN process itself, the goal of instruction using the hypermedia version is to assist students with learning disabilities to set academic and extracurricular goals. Using the hypermedia version of the strategy is straightforward, and students go through the process as follows:

i. The hypermedia version of the Self-Advocacy Strategy is provided on a compact disk (CD), so students simply begin by inserting the CD into a CD-ROM player in a personal computer.

ii. Students are presented content in the Self-Advocacy Strategy in a nonlinear fashion. That is, like navigating a web page, students can click between links leading to different activities and different components.

iii. Once they are familiar with the CD program, students begin to work at their own pace through each of six lessons. The first screen of each lesson reviews the content in that lesson. Each lesson includes video files that students can watch. The six lessons are:
1. *Introduction,* which provides an overview of the Self-Advocacy Strategy.
2. *SHARE,* which teaches students an acronym related to how they should present themselves during the IEP meeting (**S**it up straight; **H**ave a pleasant tone of voice; **A**ctivate your thinking; **R**elax; **E**ngage in eye contact).
3. *Inventory,* which lists three strengths, three areas to improve, and three learning or testing preferences.
4. *I PLAN,* which presents the steps of the I PLAN process discussed previously.
5. *Model Conference,* which provides a video of an IEP using the Self-Advocacy Strategy process.
6. *Review,* which, predictably, reviews the SHARE and I PLAN processes and their use in the IEP meeting.

The hypermedia version of the Self-Advocacy Strategy is available from the Center for Research on Learning (http://www.ku-crl.org/iei/index.html), but creating your own hypermedia materials is relatively simple. There are authoring software packages available that allow you to develop HTML-based materials, such as Microsoft DreamWorks. Even easier, most word processors have the capacity to save any text document as an HTML file, which then can be viewed with a web browser. Moreover, using a Macintosh platform, it is relatively simple to create hypermedia materials that incorporate video and audio clips that can be burned to a CD.

Is it worth the additional effort? Lancaster and colleagues (2002) found that students with learning disabilities, other health impairments, and behavioral disorders who learned the Self-Advocacy Strategy through the hypermedia program were able to run their own IEP conferences!

■ ■ ■

Source: Based on information from Lancaster, P. E., Schumaker, J. B., & Deshler, D. D. (2002). The development and validation of an interactive hypermedia program teaching a self-advocacy strategy to students with disabilities. *Learning Disability Quarterly, 25*(4), 277–302.

in band class or through history-related activities that deal with numbers. More important, perhaps, if Sherry were an active participant in the school curriculum mapping team, she could make sure that the type of information that would benefit the educational planning for students like Lauren was, in fact, available. Because administrators are part of the IEP team, the team can make sure that special educators like Sherry are represented on school mapping teams and that data from the curriculum mapping process are available to the team making educational planning decisions for students with learning disabilities.

Planning for Universal Design for Learning

As you also learned in Chapter 2, teachers can apply principles of universal design for learning to their instruction using both technology (such as the use of digital or electronic text, about which you will learn more in Chapter 12) and pedagogical methods.

Advance organizers design the curriculum universally—that is, so all students can benefit. They present information before students begin to learn it (Lenz, Deshler, & Kissam, 2004). Think of advance organizers as cognitive road maps. Maps tell us where we are and help us determine how to arrive at our destination. Similarly, advance organizers help students anticipate the relationships between their prior knowledge and the new curriculum they must master (Wehmeyer, Sands, Knowlton, & Kozleski, 2002). Advance organizers help students organize and process new material and become more active learners in traditionally passive instructional activities such as lectures and reading (Ausubel, 1963). There also are other ways to organize information. They include lesson organizers, chapter survey routines, unit organizers, and course organizers, some of which you will learn about later in this chapter.

Advance organizers are useful for students with learning disabilities. A meta-analysis of intervention studies that were designed to promote higher-order cognitive processes among adolescents with learning disabilities concluded that use of advance organizers was one of several factors that significantly increased the effect of the intervention (Swanson, 2001). Nearly 35 percent of studies in the Swanson meta-analysis involved an advance organizer component, which included "statements in the treatment description directing adolescents to look over material before instruction, directing adolescents to focus on particular information, providing prior information about the task, or directing the teacher to state the objectives of instruction" (Swanson & Deshler, 2003, p. 127). So powerful was the implementation of advance organizers in this study that Swanson and Deshler concluded organizers should be components of most interventions for students with learning disabilities.

Planning for Other Educational Needs

A critical area of concern for many students with learning disabilities is their transition from high school to postsecondary education. Despite the fact that during the past decade colleges and universities have increased their support services for individuals with disabilities to assist them in their transition to and through two- or four-year institutions, students with learning disabilities struggle in postsecondary programs.

One solution to this problem is to ensure that students with learning disabilities acquire the skills they need to advocate on their own behalf in college. They also must possess knowledge about how their disability impacts learning. A recent survey by researchers at the Virginia Commonwealth University Rehabilitation Research and Training Center on Workplace Supports asked college students with disabilities to identify the skills they believed were necessary for success in postsecondary education. The students identified these skills in priority order (Thoma & Wehmeyer, 2005):

1. Understanding their disability
2. Understanding their strengths and limitations
3. Learning to succeed despite their disability and learning what accommodations facilitate learning
4. Setting goals and learning how to access resources needed to attain those goals
5. Acquiring problem-solving skills
6. Acquiring self-management skills
7. Forming relationships with instructors, university or college disability support staff, friends, and mentors

The educational programs of students with learning disabilities should include instruction to learn these types of skills. Materials such as the Self-Advocacy Strategy (discussed

IEP Tip

Curriculum adaptations such as advance organizers are critical to success in the general education classroom for students with learning disabilities and have strong evidence as scientifically based practices. A student's IEP should include some form of curriculum adaptation, including advance organizers or the learning strategies discussed subsequently.

above) provide a systematic way to do this. Self-advocacy and self-determination–related skills were among those that successful college students with learning disabilities employed (Reis, McGuire, & Neu, 2000). A different study involving college students with disabilities and faculty members found that self-advocacy skills were critical to success in college (Izzo, Hertzfeld, & Aaron, 2001).

USING EFFECTIVE INSTRUCTIONAL STRATEGIES

Early Childhood Students: Embedded Learning Opportunities

IEP Tip

A student's IEP team should recommend embedded learning opportunities with other activity interventions.

PEARSON
myeducationlab

Go to the Activities and Application section in Chapter 5 of MyEducationLab and complete Activity 4. As you watch the video and answer the accompanying questions, compare and contrast the embedded learning activity in the video with the discussion in the text.

There is no substitute for early intervention for children from birth to age 3 who have or are at risk of having a learning disability or other disabilities. Numerous early childhood special educators have recommended incorporating instruction into these children's daily activities by using a strategy called embedded learning opportunities (Pretti-Frontczak, Barr, Macy, & Carter, 2003; Sandall, Schwartz, & Joseph, 2001). The embedded learning opportunities approach is one of several strategies classified under the broader category of activity-based interventions that includes routines-based instruction, activity-based instruction, and integrated therapy (Pretti-Frontczak et al., 2003).

The embedded learning opportunities strategy calls on teachers to "identify the opportunities that are most salient to the individualized learning objectives for each child and embed short, systematic instructional interactions that support the child's goals into existing routines and activities" (Horn, Leiber, & Li, 2000, p. 210). The embedded learning opportunities strategy is often useful for teaching language skills (Daugherty, Grisham-Brown, & Hemmeter, 2001; Wolery, Anthony, Caldwell, Snyder, & Morgante, 2002), though of course any skill can be taught using this approach, including reading and math skills during "circle time" for early childhood students (Wolery et al., 2002). Some teachers combine embedded learning opportunities strategies with a strategy called "constant time delay" (Daugherty et al., 2001; Wolery et al., 2002; see also Chapter 8). Constant time delay simply involves delaying the time between the teacher's instruction to a student to perform a task and the teacher's prompt that elicits the student's correct response. In constant time delay, the time delay between the instruction and the prompt remains the same. In progressive time delay, the time between instruction and prompt becomes progressively shorter.

The embedded learning approach is a promising intervention strategy because it (Pretti-Frontczak & Bricker, 2001):

♦ Provides children with lots of practice within the context of their daily activities and events.

♦ Can be used in inclusive environments.

♦ Capitalizes on a child's interest and motivation.

♦ Is available to parents, teachers, therapists, and peers.

♦ Is compatible with a wide range of curricular models.

A Nashville, Tennessee, child-care program exemplifies effective embedded learning opportunities. The program enrolls 12 3- to 4-year-old children and provides them with a single lead teacher. Among the children are several who have learning disabilities, including Alex. Alex is 4 years old and has moderate delays in the areas of expressive language and speech; because he also has cerebral palsy, he has delays in his gross- and fine-motor and cognitive and social development. In his classroom, the children's daily activities include a large-group circle as an opening activity for the day and as a transition between outdoor play and lunch; time focused on dramatic play, preliteracy, and hands-on science and computer; outdoor play; lunch; and self-care and cleanup.

Using this model, Alex's teacher created opportunities for him to place materials in centers (for example, he placed a pitcher in the snack center). Then she added a task as a requirement for his center participation (he had to pour paints from one container to another in the art corner) and provided verbal prompts, models, and physical guidance during play (guided his pouring between containers during water-table play).

In and of themselves, these activities do not guarantee that Alex or other children will make progress on their learning objectives, even when the activities are fun and engaging. Instead, teachers need to pair these learning opportunities with instruction that lets the children know what they need to do, how a correct response looks and feels to them, what the correct response is, and reassures them that a response will result in a positive outcome.

Elementary and Middle School Students: Differentiated Instruction

Differentiated instruction is perhaps the most prevalent strategy to promote participation in and progress through the general curriculum. To differentiate means to make something different by altering or modifying it. Differentiated instruction modifies traditional instruction.

In differentiated instruction, a teacher uses more than one instructional methodology, increasing students' access to instructional materials in a variety of formats, expanding test-taking and data collection options, and varying the complexity and nature of content presented during the course of a unit of study (Tomlinson, 2001, 2003).

Differentiated instruction is a logical companion to universal design for learning. Both attempt to ensure that content or instruction reaches all students, independent of student abilities, disabilities, language, or preparation for school. When working with Lauren, Sherry uses the same curriculum with Lauren as with all students in Lauren's class, but she and Lauren work in a special reading program for about 30 minutes each week so that Sherry can teach Lauren how to anticipate what she will read, how to review and recall what she has already read or will read in class that week, and how to implement other advance-organizer techniques. In addition, Sherry, Jean Clark (an instructional coach at Lauren's school), and Lauren's general education mathematics teacher also make special efforts to break down the word-math problems for Lauren because she not only has to read the problem but also has to solve it. Differentiated reading and math instruction go hand in hand.

Teachers can effectively differentiate curricular content, instructional process, product requirements, and/or assessment practices to facilitate students' access to and success within the general curriculum (Tomlinson, 2003). Examples of curricular content differentiation include reducing the number of math problems assigned to certain students and giving students the option of taking a weekly spelling pretest to opt out of spelling for that week.

Teachers can differentiate their instruction through techniques that should be implemented schoolwide for the benefit of all students. Each of the following techniques is effective for Lauren when applied by Sherry and Lauren's general education teachers (Janney & Snell, 2004), as well as for students without disabilities:

- Providing visual or graphic organizers to accompany oral presentations
- Incorporating models, demonstrations, or role play
- Using teacher presentation cues (e.g., gestural, visual, or verbal) to emphasize key points
- Scaffolding key concepts that students must learn
- Involving students by implementing every-pupil response techniques (e.g., lecture response cards) or incorporating manipulatives for students to use

Secondary and Transition Students: Learning Strategies

Don Deshler and his team of researchers at the University of Kansas Center for Research on Learning have developed a host of strategies for use with students with learning disabilities (Deshler & Schumaker, 2006; Lenz et al., 2004). These strategies, called **learning strategies,** help students with learning disabilities to learn independently and to generalize, or transfer, their skills and behaviors to new situations (Lenz et al., 2004).

Learning strategies work especially well for students who have learning disabilities in basic skill areas such as reading, language arts, writing, spelling, and math. They also are effective for specialized school tasks such as test taking, paragraph writing, and lecture comprehension (Lenz et al., 2004). And they are effective in assisting students to comprehend content-oriented classes such as science and social studies. Box 5.4 provides an example of one learning strategy, the sentence writing strategy.

IEP Tip

Differentiating instruction is good practice for all learners, not just students with learning disabilities, and should be among the most frequent classroom-wide interventions that IEP teams consider.

myeducationlab

Go to the Activities and Application section in Chapter 5 of MyEducationLab and complete Activity 5. As you watch these videos and answer the accompanying questions, focus on how the teacher in these videos uses differentiated instruction to help her students progress in the general education curriculum.

Sentence Writing Strategy

As with all the learning strategies developed by the Center for Research on Learning, students need to learn the sentence writing strategy so that they will use it automatically. Just as teachers use repetition to teach beginning readers to master basic sound-symbol relationships, so they instruct older students to master task-specific learning strategies through highly structured practice. Practice, practice, and practice again: That is how teachers help students to use the sentence writing strategy automatically.

Instruct students in how to use the strategy by pretesting them to measure each student's sentence writing skills. Then deliver the strategy in four parts, over and over again. The key is repetition and practice.

Part 1. Teach the skills involved in writing simple sentences, which contain at least a subject and a verb, and which express a complete thought ("The dog barked.") Skills for writing simple sentences include:
a. Thinking about the purpose of the sentence. What needs to be communicated?
b. Identifying subject (noun; dog) and verb (barked) needed to communicate that purpose.
c. Identify articles needed (the).
d. Identifying punctuation and capitalization.
e. Adding adjectives and adverbs ("The angry dog barked loudly.")

Part 2. Teach the skills involved in writing compound sentences, which contain two independent clauses ("The dog barked loudly, so the squirrel ran up the tree.") Compound sentences require students to integrate new skills with the previously taught skills for writing simple sentences. Skills for writing compound sentences include:
a. Thinking about the purpose of the sentence.
b. Writing and forming simple sentences.
c. Learning how to join simple sentences using a conjunction (e.g., and, or, so)
d. Using punctuation and capitalization, including using commas with conjunctions.

Part 3. Teach students how to write complex sentences, which have an independent clause joined by one or more dependent clauses ("After he was let off his leash, the dog barked loudly, so the squirrel ran up the tree.") and how to integrate those skills with the previously taught skills for writing simple and compound sentences. Such skills include:

a. Considering sentence structure.
b. Identifying independent ("After he was let off his leash") and dependent clauses.
c. Identifying subordinators (when, after, because).

Part 4. Teach students how to write compound-complex sentences, which contain at least two independent clauses and one or more dependent clauses ("After he was let off his leash, the dog, who rarely went out of the back yard, barked loudly, so the squirrel ran up the tree.") and how to integrate those skills with the three previously taught skills.

Students must reach mastery in each part of the sequence before moving to the next. Thus, the instruction is a building process whereby students are required to integrate new skills with previously learned skills.

This four-part instruction can be adapted to a variety of needs. For example, a student can receive instruction in all four parts in a large block of time (e.g., 30 minutes per day for 9 or 10 weeks). Alternatively, you can provide instruction in a single part and then shift to other strategies as students master that single part.

At some later time, the student may return to instruction in the sentence writing strategy to learn additional sentence types. For example, some teachers prefer to teach Parts 1 and 2 in the seventh grade, Part 3 in the eighth grade, and Part 4 in the ninth grade.

The strategy will not work unless the four parts are used in sequence. Although students can write simple sentences, they must go through the simple-sentence instruction because it provides them with the vocabulary and knowledge base upon which subsequent parts build. The foundation provided in the simple-sentence instruction is critical for success in the other parts, and each subsequent part logically builds on previous instruction.

myeducationlab

Go to the Activities and Application section in Chapter 5 of MyEducationLab and complete Activity 6. As you watch this video and answer the accompanying questions, think about how you could use the strategy shown in the video in conjunction with the sentence writing strategy discussed here.

The first step in using a learning strategy in any instructional area is to assess how well a student can perform a skill. The second step is to point out the benefit of using learning strategies—namely, the student will ultimately discover how to learn on her own and succeed in and out of school. And the third step is to explain specifically what a student will be able to accomplish when she has learned the skill. Although it is not possible in this chapter to introduce you to all of the learning strategies, we can give you some examples.

Acquiring Information

As we have noted, students with learning disabilities have difficulty acquiring information; they do not have particularly strong meta-cognition skills. The self-questioning strategy is one of six strategies for acquiring information. It requires students to create questions, predict answers to those questions, and search for the answers while they read a passage. Self-questioning is advantageous because

◆ It requires students to actively interact with the material.

◆ It helps divide the passage into small, manageable units so students can more easily acquire the information.

◆ It helps to promote intrinsic motivation for learning by having students identify their own reasons for reading a passage.

◆ It requires students to verbalize the information that they are learning, thereby enhancing their understanding and later recall of the information.

Storing Information and Remembering

Students with learning disabilities also have difficulty recalling what they have read or mastered earlier. To help them, teachers instruct them to use organizational strategies. The purpose of these strategies is to help students understand the direction they are taking when they are trying to learn and later recall information. Advance organizers, as you have learned, are especially helpful (Swanson & Deshler, 2003).

One type of advance organizer is called a graphic organizer. Sometimes referred to as webs, maps, or concept diagrams, graphic organizers assist students to (1) identify key concepts and subconcepts, (2) compare and contrast information, and (3) relate cause to effect (Friend & Bursuck, 2002). By enabling students to visualize information in an organized fashion, graphic organizers help them grasp key information. The styles of graphic organizers vary depending on concepts being taught and the maturity of the students. Generally, teachers and students brainstorm together to identify one or more effective models.

INCLUDING STUDENTS WITH LEARNING DISABILITIES

Figure 5.5 provides a breakdown of the extent to which students with learning disabilities are in various placements. Students with learning disabilities have the highest rates of inclusion in general education classes when compared to students with other disabilities. Nevertheless, their inclusion cannot be effective unless educators use evidence-based strategies for instructing them. Box 5.5 provides tips for increasing success for students with learning disabilities in the general education classroom.

ASSESSING STUDENTS' PROGRESS

Measuring Students' Progress

Progress in the General Curriculum

Curriculum-based measurement (CBM) is a useful method for tracking a student's progress in reading, writing, spelling, and math. It involves directly assessing a student's skills in the content of the curriculum being taught (Fuchs & Fuchs, 2002; Stecker, Fuchs, & Fuchs, 2005). Under standardized conditions, the teacher gives the student brief, timed samples or probes based on the student's course content. The teacher then scores the student's performance for speed, fluency, and accuracy. Because curriculum-based measurement probes are quick to administer and simple to score, they can be given repeatedly.

CBM tracks students' progress in various content areas, including math (Calhoon & Fuchs, 2003; Eckert, Dunn, Codding, Begeny, & Kleinmann, 2006), reading (Compton, Appleton, & Hosp, 2004), and social studies (Espin, Busch, Shin, & Kruschwitz, 2001; Espin, Shin, & Busch, 2005). A review of the CBM research literature showed that teachers who adjust their instruction as a function of data generated through CBM can significantly improve student performance across content areas, that the use of CBM enables teachers to be more

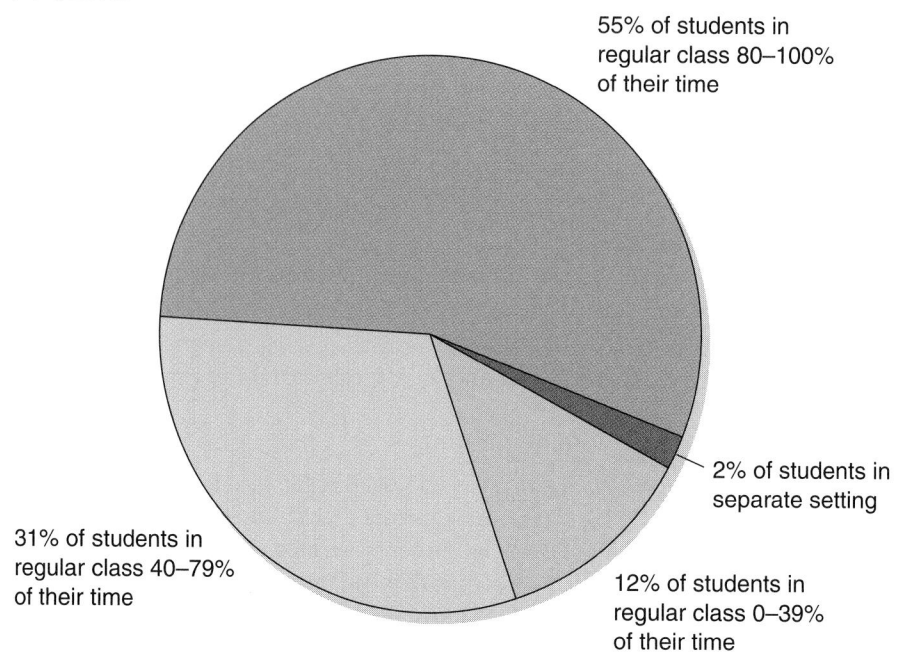

Figure 5.5 Educational placement of students with specific learning disabilities (Fall, 2006)

55% of students in regular class 80–100% of their time

2% of students in separate setting

31% of students in regular class 40–79% of their time

12% of students in regular class 0–39% of their time

Box 5.5	INCLUSION TIPS			
	What You Might See	*What You Might Be Tempted to Do*	*Alternate Responses*	*Ways to Include Peers in the Process*
Behavior	She continually disrupts other students when she needs to be working independently on assignments.	Move her away from peers or send her to the principal's office.	Use advance organizers to guide her learning on independent assignments.	Match her with a peer tutor of whom she can ask questions when she is not sure what she is supposed to be doing.
Social interactions	She misinterprets social cues. She misinterprets facial gestures and/or verbal inflections.	Point out the misinterpretation and tell her how to do it "right."	Include her in the IEP conference to plan collaboratively a social skills curriculum.	Establish a peer partnership where the peer can practice specific social cues with her.
Educational performance	Her work is inconsistent or generally poor.	Grade her down for poor or incomplete work.	Use differentiated instruction to ensure that her learning strengths and needs are addressed.	Use differentiated instruction with all students.
Classroom attitudes	She easily gives up in areas of weakness to get out of work.	Excuse her from some assignments or reprimand her for her unwillingness to try.	Use curriculum-based measurement to enhance her awareness about the progress she is making.	Give her opportunities to tutor others (peers or younger students) in areas of her success.

responsive to student needs, and that students of teachers who used classwide CBM showed more growth across content areas than did students whose teachers used other strategies (Stecker et al., 2005).

The types of probes vary according to content. Reading probes typically involve two measures: a maze task, in which a student reads a passage (aloud or silently) with words deleted and then selects words to replace the missing words; and reading aloud for a specified duration while a teacher counts the correct number of words read (oral reading fluency). CBM of spelling requires students to write words dictated to them for a specified time; the teacher counts the correct letter sequences. When CBM is applied to math, students answer computational questions for a set time period; the teacher then counts the number of correct answers (Hosp & Hosp, 2003).

Progress in Addressing Other Educational Needs

Although not the case for Lauren, the biggest barrier to successful inclusion and positive postsecondary outcomes for many students with disabilities may be their limited social skills (Bryan, 2005; Bryan, Burstein, & Ergul, 2004). That is why the strategies for tracking student progress that we will discuss in Chapter 7, including using rating scales and sociometric ratings, will be equally important for students with learning disabilities. There are few checklists to track progress in the types of self-advocacy skills discussed previously in this chapter, although there are some standardized measures of self-determination that have been used with students with learning disabilities (Wehmeyer, 2002). The Arc's Self-Determination Scale, available from *http://www.beachcenter.org/,* is a student self-report measure of self-determination for students with cognitive disabilities, including students with learning disabilities.

Sherry (left) and Jean (right) team with each other and with other faculty to include Lauren in the general education curriculum and to ensure that she makes progress in it.

PEARSON
myeducationlab

Go to the Activities and Application section in Chapter 5 of MyEducationLab and complete Activity 7. As you watch this video and answer the accompanying questions, reflect on how technology is improving this method of CBM.

Making Accommodations for Assessment

Perhaps in no other category of disability is the issue of test accommodations as controversial as it is in the area of specific learning disabilities. This is so because many test givers (teachers, local educational agencies, and state educational agencies) are concerned that students who do not require accommodations (so that they will have an authentic opportunity, equal to that of students without disabilities) will seek and obtain the accommodations and be placed at a competitive advantage relative to other students.

The fact remains, however, that students with learning disabilities may need a wide array of accommodations to be able to perform according to their highest level on standardized tests. For example, a research team found that providing a reader (either a person or a computer) on a standardized math test improved student outcomes (Calhoon, Fuchs, & Hamlett, 2000). Weaver (2000) found that extended time for taking an examination enabled students with learning disabilities to perform more effectively. Other effective test accommodations include the administration of a test via a computer or the use of a calculator (Fuchs, Fuchs, Eaton, Hamlett, & Karns, 2000).

--- *VALUES AND OUTCOMES* ---

VALUES > GREAT EXPECTATIONS | CHOICES | POSITIVE CONTRIBUTIONS | STRENGTHS | RELATIONSHIPS | FULL CITIZENSHIP

What values and outcomes apply to Lauren Marsh?

◆ Given her inclusion in general education classes with support, it is reasonable to expect her to graduate and go to college, especially one where there are strong supports for students with disabilities.

- Because both of her parents work, it seems likely Lauren is learning the value of being economically self-sufficient and, because of Sherry Eichinger's support, it is likely Lauren will indeed know how to do a variety of jobs.

- Lauren's most obvious positive contribution is her peace-making skills.

- Lauren has no problem with relationships; we might well assume she is popular among her peers, in large part, because she knows when and how to "cool it" when adolescent energies may become a bit "hot."

- Technology assists Lauren to be included in school; it seems predictable that she will use it throughout her lifetime to secure her inclusion in higher education and the workforce.

- Lauren already knows about making choices—social and academic ones alike. Self-determination is not a challenge for her.

WHAT DO YOU THINK?

1. Is it accurate to say that Lauren depends too much on accommodations from Sherry and through technology?

2. If so, what might Sherry do to mitigate Lauren's dependency? Or is it simply the case that Lauren, like many other students with and without disabilities, uses technology as a regular part of her life, not solely for "special" purposes?

3. Which accommodations, if any, seem a bit too "special" and perhaps "nice but not necessary" for Lauren? The learning strategies? The differentiated instruction? The pull-out into a group to learn reading strategies? The computer?

ADDRESSING THE STANDARDS: THE VALUES CONNECTION

The following CEC Knowledge and Skill Standards: Common Core and Values are addressed in this chapter through the content and concepts we discuss.

CEC Knowledge and Skill Standards: Common Core		Values/Standards Connection
CEC Knowledge and Skill Standard II. **Development and Characteristics of Learners**		Enhancing a student's self-concept and mitigating the effect of a label can help the student have *great expectations* for making progress in the general curriculum and developing *relationships* in school and in the community.
CC2K1	Typical and atypical human growth and development.	
CC2K2	Educational implications of characteristics of various exceptionalities.	
CC2K4	Family systems and the roles of families supporting development.	
CC2K5	Similarities and differences of individuals with and without exceptional learning needs.	
CC2K6	Similarities and differences of individuals with exceptional learning needs.	

CEC Knowledge and Skill Standards: Common Core	Values/Standards Connection
CEC Knowledge and Skill Standard IV. Instructional Strategies CC4S2 — Teach individuals to use self-assessment, problem-solving, and other cognitive strategies to meet their needs. CC4S3 — Select, adapt, and use instructional strategies and materials according to characteristics of the individual with exceptional learning needs. CC4S4 — Use strategies to facilitate maintenance and generalization of skills across environments. CC4S5 — Use procedures to increase the individual's self-awareness, self-management, self-control, self-reliance, and self-esteem.	Learning how to differentiate instruction and selecting and adapting instructional strategies are all ways to apply CEC Standard 4, Instructional Strategies. By differentiating instruction, you are building on your students' *strengths* and raising their *great expectations*.
CEC Knowledge and Skill Standard V. Learning Environments and Social Interactions CC5S2 — Identify realistic expectations for personal and social behavior in various settings. CC5S3 — Identify supports needed for integration into various program placements. CC5S4 — Design learning environments that encourage active participation in individual and group settings. CC5S9 — Create an environment that encourages self-advocacy and increased independence.	Involving all educators, especially special educators, in the curriculum-mapping process enhances school-wide collaboration, creates the potential for inclusive practices to emerge, and then increases the potential for *relationships* such as Lauren has with many of her peers with and without disabilities. By providing students with learning disabilities instruction in self-advocacy, you enhance their *self-determination* and ability to *make choices*—two skills they will need during and after school.
CEC Knowledge and Skill Standard VII. Instructional Planning CC7S1 — Identify and prioritize areas of the general curriculum and accommodations for individuals with exceptional learning needs. CC7S3 — Involve the individual and family in setting instructional goals and monitoring progress. CC7S6 — Sequence, implement, and evaluate individualized learning objectives. CC7S9 — Incorporate and implement instructional and assistive technology into the educational program.	Using curriculum mapping to identify appropriate instructional support is an application of CEC Standard 7, Instructional Planning.

continued

CEC Knowledge and Skill Standards: Common Core	Values/Standards Connection
CEC Knowledge and Skill Standard VIII. Assessment	As you learn strategies for evaluating students to determine if they have a learning disability, you are addressing CEC Standard 8, Assessment.
CC8K3 — Screening, prereferral, referral, and classification procedures.	
CC8S2 — Administer nonbiased formal and informal assessments.	
CC8S6 — Use assessment information in making eligibility, program, and placement decisions for individuals with exceptional learning needs, including those from culturally and/or linguistically diverse backgrounds.	
CC8S8 — Evaluate instruction and monitor progress of individuals with exceptional learning needs.	
CEC Knowledge and Skill Standard X. Collaboration	Involving a student with a disability in educational planning and decision making tells the student you have *great expectations* and enhances the student's self-determination and ability to *make choices*.
CC10S2 — Collaborate with families and others in assessment of individuals with exceptional learning needs.	
CC10S3 — Foster respectful and beneficial relationships between families and professionals.	A student's education and progress in the general education curriculum is a team effort. Involving a student with a disability in educational planning and decision making tells the student you have *great expectations* and enhances the student's self-determination and ability to *make choices*.
CC10S4 — Assist individuals with exceptional learning needs and their families in becoming active participants in the educational team.	
CC10S5 — Plan and conduct collaborative conferences with individuals with exceptional learning needs and their families.	

Source: From CEC Knowledge and Skill Standards: Common Core and Values. Copyright by The Council for Exceptional Children. Reprinted with permission.

SUMMARY

Identifying Students with Learning Disabilities

- IDEA has inclusionary (severe discrepancy between achievement and intellectual ability in math and reading) and exclusionary (not due to an intellectual disability or environmental/economic disadvantages) criteria for determining whether a student has a learning disability.

- Learning disabilities is the most prevalent disability category, comprising 47.4 percent of all students with disabilities.

- Students with learning disabilities typically have average or above-average intelligence.

- Students with learning disabilities are a heterogeneous population with varied academic problems related to reading, written language, and math.

- Students with learning disabilities often have difficulty with short-term, long-term, and working memory.

- Challenges associated with meta-cognition include focusing attention, being organized, engaging in future planning, and solving problems.

- Approximately three fourths of students with disabilities experience challenges related to social adjustment.

- Students with learning disabilities often have difficulties with social skills; they sometimes have poor self-concepts.
- Research suggests that different neurological regions of the brain are associated with particular learning problems and that learning disabilities have a strong genetic basis.
- Environmental causes can also contribute to the presence of learning disabilities.

Evaluating Students with Learning Disabilities

- The traditional nondiscriminatory evaluation practice in the field of learning disabilities has been to use standardized intelligence and achievement tests to pinpoint a severe discrepancy.
- IDEA 2004 allows states to use intervention in terms of identifying the presence of a learning disability as contrasted to using the severe discrepancy approach.
- An intense debate has occurred over the pros and cons of the severe discrepancy and RTI approach.
- The RTI approach involves implementing, as needed, three tiers of instruction for students and conducting an evaluation at each tier to document the extent to which students are making adequate progress in their learning.

Designing an Appropriate IEP

- Students with learning disabilities can be taught to successfully self-direct their IEP meeting.
- Curriculum mapping involves a determination of the scope and sequence of the delivery of content in a school and can be a critical source of data for IEP teams when making decisions about a student's educational program.
- Advance organizers, which present information to be learned in advance of a student's engagement in the learning activity, have been shown to be very powerful pedagogical tools that enable learners with learning disabilities to perform more effectively.
- Promoting student self-advocacy skills can enable students with learning disabilities to make the transition from high school to college.

Using Effective Instructional Strategies

- Embedded learning opportunities involve key-skills instruction that is embedded in other routines or tasks. These strategies have been shown to be very useful with young children with learning disabilities.
- Differentiated instruction involves the differentiation of content and instructional strategies to ensure that all students in a classroom have the opportunity to learn. This is among the most important strategy to ensure effective inclusive practices.
- Learning strategies instruction provides the opportunity for students with learning disabilities to acquire "learning-to-learn" strategies that impact knowledge acquisition, information storage and retrieval, and other higher-order cognitive functions.

Including Students with Learning Disabilities

- Students with learning disabilities have the highest rate of inclusion in general education classes.

Assessing Students' Progress

- Curriculum-based measurement involves the use of multiple, frequent probes that collect samples of student progress in content areas, including math, reading, science, and social studies.
- There are a number of test accommodations, including extended time, oral presentation, computer administration, and calculator use, that are effective with students with learning disabilities.

PEARSON
myeducationlab

Now go to MyEducationLab at www.myeducationlab.com and take the Self-Assessment to gauge your initial comprehension of chapter content. Once you have taken the Self-Assessment, use your individualized Study Plan for Chapter 5 to enhance your understanding of the concepts discussed in the chapter.

6

Understanding Students with Communication Disorders

Contributing authors: Jane Wegner, Ph.D., University of Kansas, and Evette Edmister, Ph.D., Des Moines, Iowa

◆ WHO IS GEORGE WEDGE?

You know that words have many meanings. Take the word *telegraph*. It is a noun (a sent message), an adjective (as in "telegraph mach'ine"), and a verb (to give advance warning). In the lives of George Wedge, age 12, and his parents, Linda and Phil, telegraphing has been a way of life, one that they experienced even before George was born.

Like many women, Linda underwent an ultrasound examination when she was pregnant. The results were alarming: Her unborn baby had a congenital malformation of his brain and surely would have a disability upon birth. What a telegraph! And what to do about it?

Step 1: Get help. Where? At the Douglas County, Kansas, Inter-Agency Coordinating Council for Infants and Toddlers (ICC). What kind of help? Information about their baby's speech-limiting condition, called Dandy Walker syndrome, and its likely effects. One potential effect was infant mortality. But even if the baby were to live, he might not walk, talk, or learn to read, and he might have a low IQ.

Step 2: Plan for early intervention. How? Don't give in and don't give up. As soon as George was born, Linda and Phil enrolled him in the county's early intervention program through the ICC. Enrollment led him into the University of Kansas's Sunnyside program for infants and toddlers (in a building on Sunnyside Avenue, of course). He began attending at the age of 3 months and graduated at the age of 3 years. Upon his graduation, George continued his education at the university's Hilltop Child Development Center, from which he graduated at the age of 6. George is now in the eighth grade in the Lawrence, Kansas public schools.

Step 3: Provide intensive intervention, not just one intervention but many: finger spelling and American Sign Language instruction, surgery to repair a cleft palate and insert a feeding tube because George has difficulty swallowing, instruction on how to swallow and shape words, a hearing aid for his right ear, and an assistive technology device for

augmentative communication (the Tablet Portable IMPACT from Enkidu Research).

Step 4: Assemble a team. Who? Start with the ICC staff; add the Sunnyside and Hilltop staff. Augment with physicians. Corral George's brother, Roy, and other school-age boys and girls. Get instruction on helpful devices from the Capper Foundation in nearby Topeka. Include the teachers and related service professionals. Give extended family and friends a role. Be sure Linda and Phil are the head coaches. And give the ball to George as often as he can carry it.

Step 5: Expect great results and celebrate them. When? Always, and be grateful—more, be joyful—that George is alive. Applaud him and everyone on his team for the outcomes: his ability to form words and talk to those who know him well or pay close attention to him; his ability to use sign language and finger-spell; his mastery of his assistive technology device; his progress through two early intervention settings that include children with and without disabilities in the same classrooms; his progress through fifth grade; his ability to walk, ride a horse, play on the school chess team, take classes at the local art center and museums; his participation on soccer and basketball teams; his developing talent as a chess player and his love of reading and drama; his ability to make friends; and the composure and wherewithal to summon help by calling 911 during two separate emergencies.

Step 6: Prepare for and face the challenges of today and tomorrow. Acknowledge that George still needs help learning to swallow; that after more palatal and ear surgery, he still needs to learn how to shape words; that his teacher is learning about communication disabilities but still wants to learn more; that George needs extra help in math; that his speech pathologist, Laura Teenor, has to teach not only George but also his teacher and other school staff so they can help George with

speech and swallowing at lunchtime; and that the best way for this team to communicate and work together is to have a "playbook" that travels daily between home and school.

Last Step: Take a good, hard look at George, Linda, Phil, and Roy Wedge. Why? Reread the first telegraph that Linda and Phil received, the bad-news one. Now let's send a different one, the good-news one. Let it read as follows: "Past is prologue. Hard work ahead. Nothing that you can't do. See you when George graduates from elementary, middle, and high school. Banking on him moving away for college or on to a satisfying job." Sign it "Special Educators and Related Service Providers." P. S.: "Speech pathology always available."

IDENTIFYING STUDENTS WITH COMMUNICATION DISORDERS

Defining Communication Disorders

Communication entails receiving, understanding, and expressing information, feelings, and ideas. It is such a natural part of our daily lives that most of us take our ability to communicate for granted. Most of us participate in many communicative interactions each day. For example, we talk with others face to face or on the phone; we e-mail a colleague or friend; we demonstrate social awareness by lowering our voices when we see a raised eyebrow or a frown; we wink at friends over private jokes.

Although we usually communicate through speech, we also communicate in many other ways. Some people communicate manually, using sign language and/or gestures. Others add nonlinguistic cues while speaking, such as body posture, facial and vocal expression, gestures, eye contact, and head and body movements. Many speakers vary their voices by changing their pitch or rate of speaking. All of these skills make our communication more effective.

Communication involves speaking as well as a multitude of nonverbal behaviors such as facial expression, gestures, and head and body movements.

Communication is the cornerstone of the teaching and learning process. Teaching and learning are typically carried out via spoken and written language. Although most children come to school able to understand others and express themselves and thus participate in school more easily, many children do not. Imagine the difficulties a student with a communication disorder might encounter with classroom activities, social interactions, instructional discourse exchanges, acquisition of knowledge and language, and the development of literacy skills. Effective communication in school is a complicated and vital process.

Speech and Language Disorders

Communication disorders relate to the components of the process affected: speech, language, or both (American Speech-Language-Hearing Association [ASHA], 2008a; Stuart, 2002; Hulit & Howard, 2002). A **speech disorder** refers to difficulty producing sounds as well as disorders of voice quality (for example, a hoarse voice) or fluency of speech, often referred to as stuttering. A **language disorder** entails difficulty receiving, understanding, or formulating ideas and information. A **receptive language disorder** is characterized by difficulty receiving or understanding information. An **expressive language disorder** is characterized by difficulty formulating ideas and information. IDEA recognizes that both speech disorders and language disorders can adversely affect a student's educational performance.

Speech and language disorders are often associated with other disorders. Specifically, speech disorders are sometimes associated with a **cleft palate or lip,** a condition in which a person has a split in the upper part of the oral cavity or the upper lip. George's speech difficulties are a result of his cleft palate, so he uses an augmentative and alternative communication (AAC) device called the Tablet to express himself more clearly as he works to improve his speech. Language disorders are sometimes the primary feature through which other disorders are identified. For example, a child with a hearing disorder may initially be referred for evaluation because he is not talking as well as other children his age.

Cultural Diversity in Communication

Students from different cultural backgrounds may have speech or language differences that affect their participation in the classroom. Although many individuals have a speech or language *difference,* they do not necessarily have a language or speech *disorder.* Difference does not always mean disorder (Battle, 1998).

Some students are bilingual, while others have dialectical differences or accents. An accent is a phonetic trait carried from a first language to the second (ASHA, 2007a). Every language contains a variety of forms, called dialects. A **dialect** is a language variation that a group of individuals uses and that reflects shared regional, social, or cultural/ethnic factors. Examples of culturally and linguistically diverse populations that may use an accent or a social dialect include African Americans, Latinos, Asian/Pacific Islanders, and Native Americans. Accents and dialects are not communication disorders; rather, they are differences (ASHA, 2007a). In Box 6.1, you will find tips for teaching students from culturally or linguistically diverse backgrounds.

| INTO PRACTICE | Box 6.1 |

Communicative Interactions

Instructors need to remember that students come from varied cultural and linguistic backgrounds. Their interactions at school may be very different from those at home (Allington & Cunningham, 2002; Bunce, 2003; Giangreco, 2000). "Teachers need to be aware of possible causes of communication failure in the school environment in order to circumvent misunderstandings and to facilitate academic achievement and acceptance of the bilingual/bicultural child in the school system" (Bunce, 2003, p. 370). Try some of these strategies to improve interactions:

◆ Use cooperative group activities to foster multicultural relationships.

◆ Highlight the value of diversity by including cultural influence and the contributions of events, celebrations, and people in curricular content.

◆ Incorporate community activities and speakers who reflect differing cultures.

◆ Invite parents to visit classes and share information about their cultures.

Students in the classroom need information about different cultural practices and reassurance that one cultural communicative practice is not better than another. They are simply different, and these differences need to be respected, understood, and considered when people communicate (Bunce, 2003).

Some children may have a cultural difference combined with a speech and/or language disorder. Others may not have a speech and/or language impairment and do not need support services. However, in all cases teachers need to consider how instruction and assessments may need to be adapted and/or augmented in order to assist students' learning and participation.

PEARSON
myeducationlab

Go to the Activities and Application section in Chapter 6 of MyEducationLab and complete Activity 2. As you study this case and answer the accompanying questions, consider how this teacher could incorporate the strategies discussed here with her students who have learning disabilities.

Incidence

In fall 2006, approximately 1.7 percent (1,144,277) of all students ages 6 through 21 in special education nationally were classified as having a speech-language disability. The percentage rises when preschoolers are included in the headcount: Of all the students from 3 to 21 years old receiving special education, 24.1 percent have received speech and language services (U.S. Department of Education, 2005). These figures do not include children who have communication disorders secondary to other conditions. Most students with communication disorders spend the majority of their day in the general education classroom.

Describing the Characteristics

For most children, the development of communication is uneventful and follows a typical, predictable pattern and timetable. For others, it does not; these children may have a communication disorder. It is helpful to understand the typical pattern of acquiring speech and language skills so you can recognize instances when communication disorders are present.

Typical Development

Speech is the oral expression of language. This expression occurs when a person produces sounds and syllables. (Figure 6.1 illustrates the speech mechanism that, through a coordinated effort, allows for sound production.) As a person pushes air from the lungs, the muscles in the larynx move the vocal folds, producing sounds. The larynx sits on top of the trachea and contains the vocal folds (ligaments of the larynx); voice is produced

Figure 6.1 Speech mechanism

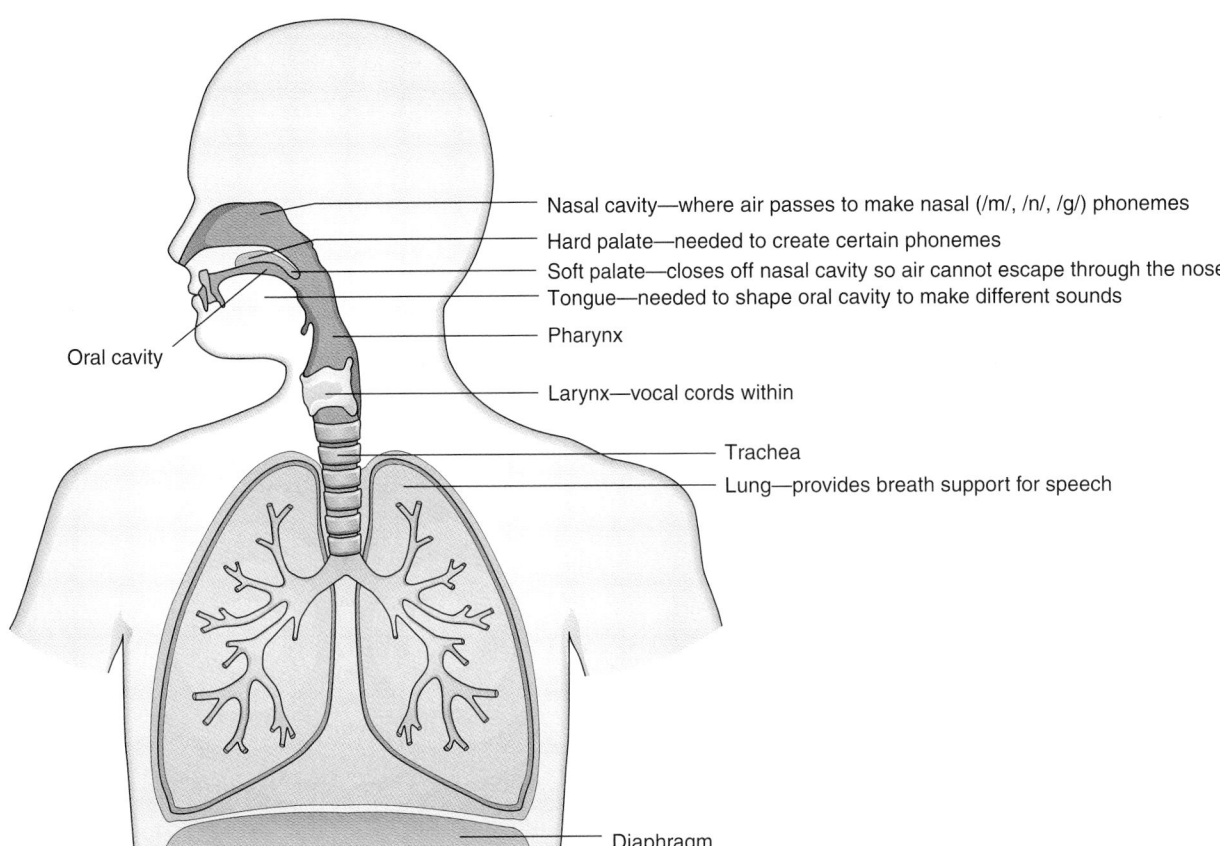

Nasal cavity—where air passes to make nasal (/m/, /n/, /g/) phonemes
Hard palate—needed to create certain phonemes
Soft palate—closes off nasal cavity so air cannot escape through the nose
Tongue—needed to shape oral cavity to make different sounds
Pharynx
Oral cavity
Larynx—vocal cords within
Trachea
Lung—provides breath support for speech
Diaphragm

here. A person forms sounds by varying the position of the lips, tongue, and lower jaw as air passes through the larynx (voice box), pharynx (a space extending from the nasal cavities to the esophagus), mouth, and nose.

Language is a structured, shared, rule-governed, symbolic system for communicating. The five components of our language system are phonology (sound system), morphology (word forms), syntax (word order and sentence structure), semantics (word and sentence meanings), and pragmatics (social use of language). Each dimension works together with the others to create a robust language system.

Phonology is the use of sounds to make meaningful syllables and words. Phonology encompasses the rules and sequencing of individual speech sounds (called **phonemes**) and how they are produced, depending on their placement in a syllable or word. For example, consonants at the beginning of syllables or words (e.g., "*t*ap") are produced slightly differently from those in the middle (e.g., "ca*tt*le") or at the end of syllables or words (e.g., "pa*t*"). Phonological use requires correct pronunciation as well as awareness of sound differences as they signal change in meaning. In English, for instance, the word "bill" is different from "pill" by only one phoneme: /b/. By changing one phoneme, a speaker can produce a totally different word. Although English spelling has 26 letters, English speakers use them to produce 45 different sounds. For example, /th/, /sh/, /oy/, and /ou/ are four completely different sounds that are represented in spelling as different combinations of 2 of the 26 letters (Owens, 2001).

Morphology is the system that governs the structure of words (Owens, 2005). Phonemes or single sounds have little meaning on their own, but some can be grouped into syllables or words that have meaning. The smallest meaningful unit of speech is called a morpheme. For instance, when -*s* is added to "bill," the word becomes plural. Formerly having had one **morpheme,** the word now has two: "bill" (a mouth structure on a bird, a written document) and -*s* (denoting plurality). Morphological rules allow speakers to add plurals, inflection, affixes, and past-tense markers to verbs. For example, correct use of morphological rules allows a child to change "swim" to "swimmed" and then, as the child matures, to "swam," an irregular past-tense verb. Understanding of morphological rules allows us to recognize meaning just by hearing it.

Syntax provides rules for putting together a series of words to form sentences (Owens, 2005). Receptively, a child must be able to note the significance in the order of others' words. For example, "I want that cookie" means that the speaker desires a cookie, whereas "Do I want that cookie?" indicates a question in which the speaker is determining if he wants a cookie. Expressively, a child must be able to use word order to generate new sentences and to know when sentences are not grammatically correct. Just as phonology provides the rules for putting together strings of phonemes to form words, syntax provides rules for putting together a series of words to construct sentences.

The first three dimensions of language—phonology, morphology, and syntax—combine to determine the form of language, that is, what the language looks like. The next two dimensions of language—semantics and pragmatics—determine the content and social use of language (Bloom & Lahey, 1978).

Semantics refers to the meaning of what is expressed. Semantic development has both receptive and expressive components. Children first learn to understand the meaning of words and then to verbally or manually use the words and sentences meaningfully. Children start out with a small number of words that represent a large number of objects in their environments; for example, to young children, all men may be "daddy." This is called an overextension and is typical in semantic development (Owens, 2005).

Pragmatics refers to the use of communication in contexts. Pragmatics is the overall organizer for language (Owens, 2005). Caregivers and infants use the rules of pragmatics in their interactions, and children learn to use social communication very early (Kuder, 2008). After using smiles and simple verbalizations, children request objects, actions, or information; protest actions; comment on objects or actions; greet; and acknowledge comments. These skills allow children to use language socially to interact within their environments and with people in those environments more efficiently.

It is important that young children learn and practice pragmatics in and outside school.

No one knows for sure just how the five dimensions of language come to work together so that children acquire useful language. Theories explaining how children acquire language abound (Hoff, in press). In the 1950s, Chomsky (1957) proposed that children are born ready to develop language skills because of an inborn language acquisition device. Later behaviorists proposed that the ability to learn and use language is not inborn but happens as children imitate and practice. Today researchers investigate the effects of a child's imitation, practice, and other social interactions on language development. Their research has been compiled into social interaction theories.

Social interaction theories emphasize that communication skills are learned through social interactions (Hoff, in press). Parents and caregivers teach language during their interactions. These theories hold that language development is the outcome of a child's drive for attachment with his or her world; communication develops in order for the child to convey information about the environment to others and is learned through interactions with others.

The belief that social context and interaction within that context influence communicative choice is supported by philosopher Lev Vygotsky (1978, 1987). He suggests that children develop by supplementing their independent problem-solving abilities with adult guidance or peer collaboration. Children learn by doing, from interacting with their more experienced partners. Social interactionists agree with Vygotsky's premise that children learn language by interacting either with adults, who naturally have more experiences, or with peers, who may have more or different experiences.

Children quickly learn to produce speech sounds during their early years. By the age of 8, they have learned to produce nearly all the consonants and vowels that make up the words of the family's native language. Learning these sounds usually proceeds in a fairly consistent sequence, but there may be variation among children in the time of acquisition. Figure 6.2 illustrates the times at which 90 percent of English-speaking children have mastered the consonant sounds needed for speech.

Children's language development is complex. It begins early and depends on biological preparation, successful nurturance, sensorimotor experiences, and linguistic experiences (McCormick, 2003). Within the first month, babies begin to respond to human voices and by 3 months, they turn, smile, and coo when spoken to (ASHA, 2008b). By their first birthdays, babies make sounds when spoken to, vary vocal pitch and intensity, and experiment with rhythm; they may even say their first words. Within the next year, their spoken vocabularies increase to 200 to 300 words, and the 2-year-old's "no shoe" may become the 3-year-old's "I don't want shoes." Three-year-old toddlers understand simple questions and prepositions such as "in," "on," "under," and "up" and are able to follow two-step directions. They have a vocabulary of 900 to 1,000 words and use 3- to 4-word sentences. Their rapid development continues, and by age 4, preschoolers ask questions using "who," "what," "when," "where," "why," and "how" and have vocabularies of 1,500 to 1,600 words. By age 6, they use irregular verbs such as "be," "go," "run," and "swim" and can verbally share their feelings and thoughts with an expressive vocabulary of 2,600 words (Owens, 2005).

Although most language development takes place in the preschool years, it continues throughout the school years. This later development occurs in the areas of language structure, vocabulary, and language use. During the school years the language skills of reading and writing are also learned (Hulit & Howard, 2002). Though not as rapid as earlier language development, this later progression is equally important.

Figure 6.2

Typical ages for mastery of consonant sounds

By age 3:	/p/, /m/, /h/, /n/, /w/
By age 4	/b/, /k/, /g/, /d/, /f/, /y/
By age 6:	/t/, /ng/, /r/, /l/, /s/
By age 7:	/ch/, /sh/, /j/, /th/ as in "think"
By age 8:	/s/, /z/, /v/, /th/ as in "that"
Even later:	/zh/ as in "measure"

Source: From "When Are Speech Sounds Learned?" by B. Sander, 1972, *Journal of Speech and Hearing Disorders, 37,* pp. 55–63. Copyright 1972 by the American Speech-Language-Hearing Association. Adapted with permission.

Speech Disorders

Speech disorders include disorders of articulation, voice, and fluency (rate and rhythm of speech). These disorders can occur alone, in combination, or in conjunction with other disorders. For example, students who have hearing losses (Chapter 14) or cerebral palsy (Chapter 12) often have articulation or voice disorders as well as language disorders. Similarly, a few students with intellectual disabilities (Chapter 9) may demonstrate slight communication delays, while others demonstrate speech delays, language delays, or both speech and language delays. Figure 6.2 describes the ages at which students typically master consonants' sounds.

Articulation disorders. Articulation disorders are one of the most frequent communication disorders in preschool and school-age children. **Articulation** is a speaker's production of individual or sequenced sounds. An articulation disorder occurs when the child cannot correctly produce the various sounds and sound combinations of speech.

Articulation errors may be in the form of substitutions, omissions, additions, and distortions. **Substitutions** are common, as when a child substitutes /d/ for the voiced /th/ ("doze" for "those"), /t/ for /k/ ("tat" for "cat"), or /w/ for /r/ ("wabbit" for "rabbit"). It is common for young children to make sound substitutions that disappear with maturation. It is pervasive and ongoing substitutions that are of concern.

Omissions occur when a child leaves a phoneme out of a word. Children often omit sounds from consonant pairs ("boo" for "blue," "cool" for "school") and from the ends of words ("ap" for "apple"). **Additions** occur when students place a vowel between two consonants, converting "tree" into "tahree."

Distortions are modifications of the production of a phoneme in a word; a listener gets the sense that the sound is being produced, but it seems distorted. Common distortions, called lisps, occur when /s/, /z/, /sh/, and /ch/ are mispronounced.

George substitutes, omits, and distorts speech sounds. His cleft palate has prevented him from moving his tongue against his palate, so he is learning where to place his tongue to make particular speech sounds.

Articulation problems, like all communication disorders, vary. Often children are identified in early childhood settings through school-based speech-language screenings. Many identified children have mild or moderate articulation disorders; their speech is understood by others yet contains sound-production errors. Other children have articulation disorders that have more significant impact on their interactions, making it nearly impossible for others to understand them. When individuals have serious articulation disorders, they usually benefit from evaluation for an augmentative and alternative communication (AAC) device.

There are many reasons for teachers to refer a student with articulation problems to a speech-language pathologist. If a student's articulation problem negatively affects his interactions in your class or his educational performance, referral is in order. Likewise, if a child's sound-production errors make his speech difficult or impossible to understand, referral is warranted. Furthermore, articulation problems resulting from neurological injuries (e.g., cerebral palsy and stroke) typically require therapy. Therapy is also needed to assist students with clefts of the palate or lip if they cannot produce speech sounds or sound combinations correctly. Therapy may also be needed to help a student with a hearing loss who is experiencing difficulty in correctly producing speech sounds because he cannot hear the sounds clearly.

Apraxia of speech. **Apraxia** is a motor speech disorder that affects the way in which a student plans to produce speech. The preferred term for children is childhood apraxia of speech (CAS) (ASHA, 2007b). Apraxia can be acquired as the result of a trauma such as a stroke, a tumor, or a head injury, or with other disorders. Apraxia can also occur early in life in isolation without trauma or other disorders. Students with apraxia have difficulty with the voluntary, purposeful movements of speech even though they have no paralysis or weakness of the muscles involved in speech. They have difficulty positioning the articulators and sequencing the sounds. Students with apraxia may be able to say the individual sounds required for speech in isolation or syllables, but they cannot produce them in longer words and sentences. They may be able to say sounds and words correctly when there is no pressure or request to do so but not when there is.

Some characteristics of apraxia are errors in production of vowels, inconsistent speech errors, more errors as words or sentences get longer, voicing errors (for example, /b/ for /p/ or /g/ for /k/), and stress on the wrong syllables, also referred to as prosody. These types of errors are not usually present in students who have traditional articulation disorders. Students with apraxia need frequent therapy that focuses on repetition, sound sequencing, and movement patterns (ASHA, 2007b; Caruso & Strand, 1999).

Voice disorders. Each person has a unique voice. This voice reflects the interactive relationship of pitch, duration, intensity, resonance, and vocal quality. Pitch is determined by the rate of vibration in the vocal folds; men tend to have lower-pitched voices than women. **Pitch** is affected by the tension and size of the vocal folds, the health of the larynx, and the location of the larynx. **Duration** is the length of time any speech sound requires.

Intensity (loudness or softness) is based on the perception of the listener and is determined by the air pressure coming from the lungs through the vocal folds. Rarely do individuals believe that their voices are too loud. Rather, they may seek professional voice therapy because their voices are too soft.

Resonance, the perceived quality of someone's voice, is determined by the way in which the tone coming from the vocal folds is modified by the spaces of the throat, mouth, and nose. Individuals with an unrepaired cleft palate may experience resonance problems because the opening from the mouth to the nasal cavity may be too large or inappropriately shaped. This type of resonance trait is an example of **hypernasality,** in which air is allowed to pass through the nasal cavity on sounds other than /m/, /n/, and /ng/. George's cleft palate causes his voice to be hypernasal. Sometimes students have another type of resonance problem; they may sound as if they have a cold or are holding their noses when speaking. This is referred to as **hyponasality** because air cannot pass through the nose and comes through the mouth instead. Speech therapy may be needed to teach these students appropriate ways to produce non-nasal sounds.

The quality of the voice is affected by problems of breath support or vocal-fold functioning as well as resonance. You might have experienced short-term vocal-quality problems after cheering at a football game. Repeated abuse of the vocal folds may cause vocal nodules, growths that result from the rubbing together of the vocal-fold edges. When the folds cannot vibrate properly or come together completely, the sound of your voice will change temporarily until the vocal nodules heal. This short-term problem usually heals because the vocal-fold abuse is not constant. If, however, nodules develop and persist, therapy may be needed to help a student learn to talk in a way that is less abusive to the vocal mechanisms. In most cases, nodules disappear after vocal rest and/or voice therapy. If vocal nodules are the result of an organic problem, therapy alone may not resolve them, and surgery may be required (Pannbacker, 1999).

IEP Tip

Unless everyone on a student's IEP team has heard the student try to communicate, it would be wise for them to observe the student before drafting the IEP.

Fluency disorders. Normal speech requires correct articulation, vocal quality, and **fluency** (rate and rhythm of speaking). Fluent speech is smooth, flows well, and appears to be effortless. Fluency problems are characterized by interruptions in the flow of speaking, such as atypical rate or rhythm, as well as repetitions of sounds, syllables, words, and phrases.

All children and adults have difficulties with fluency on occasion. They hesitate, repeat themselves, or use fillers such as "umm" at one time or another. In other instances, dysfluency is considered stuttering, which is frequent repetition and/or prolongation of words or sounds. More males than females stutter (ASHA, 2008c).

Language Impairments

Students may have language disorders that are receptive, expressive, or both. Their language impairment may be associated with another disability, such as autism or intellectual disability, or it may be **specific language impairment**—not related to any physical or intellectual disability. Despite the cause, language impairments have a substantial effect on classroom participation and learning.

Phonology. Students with phonological disorders may be unable to discriminate differences in speech sounds or sound segments that signify differences in words. For example, to them the word "pen" may sound no different from "pin." Their inability to differentiate sounds, as well as similar, rhyming syllables, may cause them to experience reading and/or spelling difficulties (Apel & Swank, 1999; Lombardino, Riccio, Hynd, & Pinheiro, 1997). Phonological difficulties are common in children with language impairments and may affect reading (McCormick & Loeb, 2003). Teachers should be sensitive to these phonological disorders as young children develop early literacy skills (Gillon, 2007).

Morphology. Children with morphological difficulties have problems using the structure of words to get or give information. They may make a variety of errors. For example, they may not use -*ed* to signal past tense, as in "walked," or -*s* to signal plurality. When a child is unable to use morphological rules appropriately, the average length of his utterances is sometimes shorter than that expected for the child's age because plurals, verb markers, and affixes may be missing from his statements (McCormick & Loeb, 2003). Students with morphological difficulties are unable to be as specific in their communication as others. For example, if they do not use verb markers such as -*ed,* it is difficult to know if they are referring to past or present tense.

Morphology errors can be associated with differences in dialects as well as with a variety of other conditions, including intellectual disabilities (Chapter 9), autism (Chapter 11), hearing loss or deafness (Chapter 14), and expressive language delay. Incorrect use of morphology is also associated with specific language impairment.

Syntax. Syntactical errors are those involving word order, such as ordering words in a manner that does not convey meaning to the listeners (e.g., "Where one them park at?"), using immature structures for a given age or developmental level (e.g., a 4-year-old child using two-word utterances, such as "Him sick"), misusing negatives (e.g., a 4-year-old child saying, "Him no go"), or omitting structures (e.g., "He go now"). As with phonology and morphology, differences in syntax sometimes can be associated with dialects and other conditions.

Semantics. Children who experience difficulty using words singly or together in sentences may have semantic disorders. They may have difficulty with multiple-meaning words and have restricted meanings for words (McCormick & Loeb, 2003). Some students with semantic disorders may have problems

Students can learn pragmatics by working together; each can become a coach for the others to communicate in a particular environment.

with words that express time and space (e.g., "night," "tiny"), cause and effect (e.g., "Push button, ball goes"), and inclusion versus exclusion (e.g., "all," "none"). Sometimes students with semantic language disorders rely on words with fairly nonspecific meanings (e.g., "thing," "one," "that") because of their limited knowledge of vocabulary. Difficulty with semantics can impact both understanding and expressing concepts in the classroom.

Pragmatics. Pragmatics focuses on the social use of language—the communication between a speaker and a listener within a shared social environment. Pragmatic skills include adapting communication to varied situations, obtaining and maintaining eye contact, using appropriate body language, maintaining a topic, and taking turns in conversations.

Pragmatic disorders are reflected in many different ways. A student who talks for long periods of time and does not allow anyone else an opportunity to converse may be displaying signs of a pragmatic disorder. Similarly, a student whose comments during class are unrelated to the subject at hand or who asks questions at an inappropriate time may be exhibiting a pragmatic disorder. Students who have difficulty with pragmatics include those with autism (Chapter 10) and traumatic brain injury (Chapter 13).

Determining the Causes

There are two types of speech and language disorders, each classified according to its cause: (1) **organic disorders,** those caused by an identifiable problem in the neuromuscular mechanism of the person; and (2) **functional disorders,** those with no identifiable organic or neurological cause.

The causes of organic disorders are numerous; they may originate in the nervous system, the muscular system, the chromosomes, or the formation of the speech mechanism. They may include hereditary malformations, prenatal injuries, toxic disturbances, tumors, traumas, seizures, infectious diseases, muscular diseases, and vascular impairments (Wang & Baron, 1997). Neuromuscular disabilities may result in difficulties with clear speech-sound production. The speech disorder would then have an organic origin and be classified as an organic speech disorder.

A functional speech and/or language disorder is present when the cause of the impairment is unknown. An articulation disorder with no known physical cause would be considered functional in nature.

Communication disorders can be classified further according to when the problem began. A disorder that occurs at or before birth is referred to as a **congenital disorder.** For instance, George, who was born with Dandy Walker syndrome, has a congenital organic speech disorder. A disorder that occurs well after birth is an **acquired disorder.** For example, a communication disorder may be present after a severe head injury (Chapter 13), which may then be described as an acquired organic speech and/or language disorder. A functional disorder may also be congenital or acquired. Some causes have both organic and functional origins. In addition, portions of the communication disorder may have been present at birth, and other parts may have been acquired later in life.

EVALUATING STUDENTS WITH COMMUNICATION DISORDERS

Determining the Presence of Communication Disorders

According to IDEA's current regulations, a speech or language impairment is a "communication disorder, such as stuttering, impaired articulation, a language impairment, or a voice impairment, that adversely affects a child's educational performance". Educators, early intervention specialists, and speech-language therapists try to meet the physical, cognitive, communication, social, or emotional and adaptive needs of infants and toddlers ages birth through 2 and young children ages 3 through 5 who have communication disorders.

They start by conducting a screening (an intervention also called problem solving and prereferral), a referral for evaluation, or both. Many school districts use interventions as the first step to determining if a referral is needed (ASHA, 2000). The emphasis of the intervention or prereferral "is on classroom modifications and supports that, when success-

Figure 6.3
Nondiscriminatory evaluation process for determining the presence of communication disorders

Observation	***Medical personnel observe:*** The child is not achieving developmental milestones related to communication skills or there is a change in a child's communication skills. ***Teacher and parents observe:*** The child has difficulty understanding or using language. The child may also have difficulty speaking clearly.
Screening	***Assessment measures:*** **Classroom work products:** The child may be hesitant to participate in verbal classroom work. Written classroom projects may reflect errors of verbal communication or, in some instances, be a preferred avenue of expression for the student. **Vision and hearing screening:** The child may have a history of otitis media (middle-ear infection). Hearing may be normal, or the student may have hearing loss. Limited vision may impact language skills.
Prereferral	***Implementation of suggestions from a school-based team:*** The teacher models speech sounds, expands language, asks open-ended questions, etc. If the child has been identified before entering school, the parents may implement suggestions from the school-based team.
Referral	If, in spite of interventions, the child still performs poorly in academics or continues to manifest communication impairments, the child is referred to a multidisciplinary team. The team may continue with more in-depth interventions.
Nondiscriminatory evaluation procedures and standards	***Assessment measures:*** **Speech and language tests (articulation, phonology, language sample, speech sample, oral motor functioning, receptive language, and expressive language):** The student performs significantly below average in one or more areas. **Anecdotal records:** The student may have genetic or medical factors that contribute to speech or language difficulties. Some students with other disabilities are at risk for having speech and language disorders. **Curriculum-based assessment:** A speech and/or language difficulty may affect progress in the curriculum. **Direct observation:** The student experiences difficulty communicating.
Determination	The nondiscriminatory evaluation team determines that the student has a communication disorder and needs special education and related services. The student's IEP team proceeds to develop appropriate education options for the child.

ful, actually prevent the need for special education intervention" (ASHA, 2000, p.15). Figure 6.3 describes the evaluation process.

During interventions, after a referral for an assessment, or both, the speech-language pathologist gathers information from sources such as school records, parent and teacher interviews, hearing and vision screenings, observations, speech samples, language samples, classwork samples/portfolios, checklists, standardized tests, nonstandardized tests, and curriculum-based assessments. Having completed the assessment, the speech-language pathologist will determine if a communication impairment/disorder is present and if it affects the child's learning.

Depending on the area of speech and/or language being assessed, the speech-language pathologist may obtain certain types of information using the assessment tools described in Figure 6.3, and described in more detail here.

Speech Assessments

Speech assessments determine the presence of articulation, voice, or fluency problems.

Articulation. Specifically, articulation assessments evaluate a student's abilities to produce speech sounds in single words, sentences, and conversation. Speech-language pathologists listen, noting the phonemes in error, the pattern of the error, and the frequency of the error. Test items include use of consonants in the initial, middle, and final positions of words (e.g., for /p/, students might name a "pig," a "zipper," and a "cup"). An **oral motor exam,** which is the examination of the appearance, strength, and range of motion of the lips, tongue, palate, teeth, and jaw, is also typically conducted.

Voice. Voice evaluations include information about the onset and course of the voice problem, environmental factors that might affect vocal quality, and typical voice use (Verdolini, 2000), including pitch, intensity, and nasality.

Fluency. When completing a fluency assessment, the speech-language pathologist measures the amount of dysfluency as well as the type and duration of dysfluencies while the student is speaking. The pathologist also notes associated speech and nonspeech behaviors such as eye blinking or head movements (Zebrowski, 2000).

Language Assessments

Language assessments focus on specific components of language such as phonology, semantics, morphology, syntax, pragmatics, and overall expressive and/or receptive language. Students who are nonverbal or use nonconventional means of communication require more descriptive than standardized assessment measures (Downing, 2005). The communicative forms (conventional and nonconventional) and the functions these forms serve are documented during observations across environments and communication partners (Downing, 2005). For example, a speech-language pathologist might observe this interaction: John looks at a friend's snack and then at his friend. He repeats this several times. When the friend gives John some of his snack, John smiles. The pathologist then notes the communication functions observed and the form the student used. In this example the student exhibited the following communication functions: initiated a communication interaction, requested an item, and expressed a social interaction (e.g., thank you or please). The following forms of communication were observed: eye contact (to gain attention to initiate communication), eye gaze (to request), and facial expression (a smile as thanks). Then the speech-language pathologist would determine what next steps could shape and expand on the communication forms (e.g., speech, pointing to pictures, voice output, etc.).

Multicultural Considerations

Sometimes a student will need specialized speech or language assessment, as when the student is bilingual or multilingual. The speech-language pathologist must be particularly skilled when assessing the communicative capabilities of students for whom English is not the primary language. Fair, unbiased evaluation is difficult for a student who is **bilingual** (uses two languages equally well) or **bidialectal** (uses two variations of a language) or for whom language dominance (the primary language of the student) is difficult to determine.

Bilingual and bidialectical skills make this speech-language pathologist especially effective, but note that she and her student also communicate by a semi-universal sign.

To assess such a student, it is not sufficient to simply translate test items into the child's primary language. The speech-language pathologist must determine whether a bilingual student should be tested in the student's first language or in English (ASHA, 1984). Then the speech-language pathologist tests the student in the dominant language with appropriate diagnostic tools to determine whether a language difference or a disability exists. The pathologist determines a student's language strengths and preferences using appropriate assessment tools and learns about the student's communicative abilities and needs. If the pathologist observes a communication disorder or disability, he then can plan appropriate therapies, using culturally sensitive standardized measures whenever possible.

Determining the Nature of Specifically Designed Instruction and Services

Curriculum-based assessment can allow an educational team to determine the student's entry point within the areas of the educational program and provide information to develop strategies helpful for a student to progress within the curriculum (Losardo & Notari-Syverson, 2001). Language occurs throughout the school day and is the vehicle for teaching the curriculum (Howell & Nolet, 2000; Losardo & Notari-Syverson, 2001). Whether the student is asked to discuss a topic verbally, answer questions, read language, write language, or work with others cooperatively, he is practicing language through the entire curriculum. Because communication is necessary for the student to participate in any aspect of the curriculum, a team approach is almost always necessary.

Within curriculum-based assessment, the team determines the nature of specifically designed instruction by data-based performance modifications and assisted assessment portions of the assessment model (Howard & Nolet, 2000). This portion of the assessment usually begins after the team identifies the student's problem and his degree of discrepancy from peers. The speech-language pathologist then develops theories aimed at decreasing the discrepancy, tests the theories systematically, and monitors the student's performance by collecting data.

Because speech and language occur throughout the day and data collection may need to be taken in multiple settings, the pathologist may need other members of the educational team to assist in data collection; usually this is the classroom teacher because that teacher is generally with the student for more of the day than other educational staff are. The pathologist then analyzes the data and makes decisions about instruction based on the data that reveal the student's best improvement in performance (Howard & Nolet, 2000). This procedure is called data-based performance modification (Howard & Nolet, 2000). Assisted assessment is the process of determining what strategy or supports the student may need to accomplish the task being monitored (Howard & Nolet, 2000). Both of these procedures help define the instruction that best suits a student and the supports he may need to be successful in communicating in school.

IEP Tip

As helpful as school-based assessment is, the IEP team should also consider conducting home- and community-based assessments to gain a thorough understanding of how the student communicates.

DESIGNING AN APPROPRIATE IEP

Partnering for Special Education and Related Services

Collaboration is critical when planning and providing services for students with communication disorders. Communication occurs throughout the day, so it is important that everyone who works with the student has a good understanding of how he best understands and/or expresses information. For instance, the lunchroom and recess staff may need to understand strategies to help a student initiate requests from others and take turns. Those staff members also could be an excellent resource for anecdotal information regarding progress toward the student's goals in a natural context with peers. Furthermore, collaboration may help lighten everyone's workload (Giangreco, 2000; Sandall & Schwartz, 2002).

ASHA (2003) has identified four different types of activities (called activity clusters) that speech-language pathologists engage in while working in schools: direct services to students, indirect services to implement students' education programs, indirect services to support students in the general education curriculum, and activities as members of the community of educators. Each requires a high level of collaboration with teachers and families.

Direct service involves services during which the student has direct contact with the speech-language pathologist. Historically, direct services have constituted the majority of the speech-language pathologist's workload. By contrast, indirect services consist, for example, of designing and programming a student's augmentative communication device and training paraeducators in how to use it. Indirect activities also include meeting and planning with teachers and paraprofessionals to align the student's IEP goals with the standards for the general curriculum and designing instructional strategies so the student can make progress in the general curriculum. Activities that speech-language pathologists engage in as members of a community of educators include staff meetings, school committees, and other duties expected of all educators. Partnerships between teachers and speech-language pathologists are critical to student success.

Teachers can expect speech-language pathologists to move away from the more traditional model of individual and group pullout services and instead participate in more collaborative consultation, curriculum-based intervention programs, and classroom-based services (ASHA, 2003). A few ways for speech-language pathologists to collaborate with teachers include supportive teaching, complementary teaching, consultation, and team teaching. Each requires a high level of collaboration with teachers and families, as exemplified in Box 6.2.

Determining Supplementary Aids and Services

An augmentative and alternative communication (AAC) system is an example of, in IDEA's terms, an assistive technology and supplementary aid. AAC systems are integrated

---

MY VOICE  *Box 6.2*

Elizabeth Smith

Fred Smith "amazes everybody," according to his mother, Elizabeth. "He's learning to read and likes being read to. Fred reading—that is a big step."

Why is learning to read a big step for Fred?

Fred, age 8, has both expressive and receptive language delays, attention-deficit/hyperactivity disorder (AD/HD), and a seizure disorder. He takes medication for his seizures and AD/HD. Elizabeth explains, "He has trouble expressing his thoughts and his feelings. This year, for the first time since he was three, he is not receiving speech therapy. He comprehends what others say more quickly than before. We also agreed at his IEP meeting that he learns useful language when talking with his friends in his classes."

Her positive tone fades: "Still, though, Fred doesn't talk a lot. I have to ask him questions like 'Did you color at school today?' or 'Did you go to music?' to get him to start talking, and then he will usually tell me more about that particular activity. Also, I ask him what he is feeling or thinking and usually give him a word to use, like, 'Fred, are you feeling angry or are you tired?' Then, he can usually tell me, using one of those words, how he is feeling."

At school, Fred receives his education in a special education classroom half of the day and in a general education second-grade classroom the other half of the day. Mary (Bo) McElmurray, his special education teacher, maintains close contact with his general education teacher, Marilyn Ammons, so that they can both be actively involved in making sure Fred does his best.

Bo notes, "His general education classroom teacher has worked very hard to provide modifications for him. For instance, she went over information from a social studies unit on symbols with Fred. However, even with the practice, he had a great deal of difficulty comprehending the information, so he couldn't tell me and his classmates in special education much about it. Even with repeated review he repeated words or phrases his teacher had said, rather than sharing about it."

Although he is performing better than "even 6 months ago," Elizabeth continues to have concerns about Fred's social development. Fred does not have neighbors to play with "out in the country. But he has several kids he gets in trouble with at school," she adds, laughing.

Elizabeth concludes, "All of us have worked together to help Fred, and we all have benefited. That's what is special about special education — taking care to meet the needs of individual children."

groups of components that supplement the communication abilities of individuals who cannot meet their communication needs through gesturing, speaking, and/or writing (Beukelman & Mirenda, 2005). An AAC system may include an AAC device, a physical object that transmits or receives messages. Such devices include communication books, communication/language boards, communication charts, mechanical or electronic voice output equipment, and computers.

An AAC device has two components: a symbol set and a means for selecting the symbols. A symbol is a visual, auditory, gestural, and/or tactile representation of a concept (ASHA, 2004). A symbol set includes gestures, photographs, manual sign sets/systems, pictographs (symbols that look like what they represent), ideographs (more abstract symbols), printed words, objects, partial objects, miniature objects, spoken words, braille, textures, or any combination of these symbols.

If educators are concerned about a student's ability to express and/or understand information in the classroom, they should contact the school's speech-language pathologist. A team approach is helpful when determining what assistive technology may be needed because so many areas need to be considered. Input from the parents as well as information regarding the student's vision skills, fine-motor skills, gross-motor skills, hearing, and curriculum requirements all help educators and pathologists determine what features the AAC system should have.

Assistive technology can be as simple and universal as a handheld personal assistant, and even that device can be specially tailored for a designated user.

Devices can range from low tech, such as line-drawn pictures in a notebook or a wallet, to high tech, such as a computer with a dynamic touch screen that stores pictures and photos and produces a voice output for items selected by the student. Some students may use a device for their primary communication but supplement it with speech, line drawings, voice-output switches, and gestures. The device, speech, and gestures all comprise the student's AAC system. Chapter 10 provides more information about AAC devices.

Once the student is trying out or using an AAC device, the educational team working with the student will want to develop a plan to provide the appropriate vocabulary. The speech-language pathologist is a key member of this team to help advise on selection and organization of vocabulary. Box 6.3 gives you partnership tips.

If the student is using a voice-output device, needed vocabulary will have to be programmed into the device so the student can press a button and hear the voice-output expression of the vocabulary. Many of the devices now come with software, so the programming can be completed on a separate computer and transferred to the student's device. It is possible on most devices to assign a single word, a phrase, or a sentence to a button.

Students, especially those who are still acquiring literacy skills, depend on others to make vocabulary available for them to communicate. It is critical that careful thought be given to making vocabulary available to participate throughout the school day. It may be helpful to consider vocabulary that occurs frequently across the day instead of vocabulary used only once or twice. Without vocabulary, students cannot express their thoughts or discuss topics being shared in their environments. The selection of a device, its features, and the degree of a student's needs and capacities all figure into establishing an AAC system.

 IEP Tip

The IEP team will want the student to learn a vocabulary that allows him to communicate with teachers, family, and peers at school.

Planning for Universal Design for Learning

When planning universal design for learning for students with communication disorders, a teacher must answer two questions: How can I assure that my student understands what I am teaching? and How can I assure that my student can express what he knows? Remember that universal design for learning includes modifications to how content is

Three Partnership Options

There are many ways for teachers and speech-language pathologists to work with each other and other professionals to support access to the curriculum for students receiving special education services. Consultation, supportive teaching, and complementary teaching are a few of these possible options (ASHA, 2003). Consultation involves activities such as meeting with the classroom teacher to discuss lessons and to develop adaptations and accommodations for the student in the classroom. For supportive teaching, the teacher and the pathologist plan lessons together, the pathologist completes some pre- and post-activities related to the lesson with the student, and the teacher and pathologist co-teach the lesson. In complementary teaching, the pathologist and the teacher co-teach material for the lesson related to their level of expertise. Examples of each are presented here.

Consultation. Cristen is a ninth grader with autism. She loves science, music, and drama. The science curriculum presents many challenges for Cristen, so the speech-language pathologist works with the classroom teacher to adapt text materials, handouts, and tests so that they match Cristen's language abilities. The adapted science handouts are used by many of the students in the class who need more visual presentations of the content.

Supportive teaching. Andrew is a second grader with Down syndrome. His class is studying the life cycle of the frog. The speech-language pathologist and teacher meet to plan for the unit and determine what extra supports Andrew will need to participate. They also discuss what responsibilities each will take during class. The pathologist works with Andrew individually to preteach vocabulary and then teaches part of the unit to the whole class. She may meet individually with Andrew again to clarify any information he did not understand.

Complementary teaching. Beth is in the fifth grade. She has language learning difficulties that include auditory processing weaknesses. For Beth, taking notes during social studies is hard. The speech-language pathologist takes notes while the teacher teaches. He also prepares study guides, teaches small groups that need more adaptation, and on occasions teaches organizational skills to the whole class.

Tips for Partnership with Speech-Language Pathologists

Remember that speech-language pathologists have a role in helping students succeed in the general education curriculum. There are many ways they can be involved to help support students. In order for the speech-language pathologist to optimally assist, he or she needs to be aware of curriculum plans and upcoming instructional opportunities the student may be involved in. Meeting on a regular basis can be beneficial. It may also be helpful to remember to define roles and responsibilities of each team member when collaborating to avoid confusion and misunderstanding, leaving more time to focus on the student's outcomes.

Putting Partnership Tips to Work for Progress in the General Curriculum

1. As Cristen's classroom teacher, how might you work to promote her self-determination in her own mastery of the science curriculum as she works with you and the speech-language pathologist?

2. Identify three ways that the speech-language pathologist's work with Andrew would benefit other students in the class.

3. Develop a plan for how the speech-language pathologist might involve Beth's classmates in a cooperative learning activity.

---

presented. When teachers use only one or two methods to teach, especially if they only use verbal methods, some students with communication disorders as well as some students without disabilities are not able to access the material. So teachers can vary the way in which they communicate, such as by using audio *and* text formats, visual representations with verbal information, graphics, graphic organizers, and controlled vocabulary. Similarly, teachers can vary the ways that students demonstrate their knowledge, such as by asking a student to convert a written report to a PowerPoint presentation, supplement a demonstration with visual supports, use a taped oral report, or perform a skit solo or with others. These and the facilitative language strategies set out in Box 6.4 provide access to the general curriculum.

Planning for Other Educational Needs

Students with communication disorders may need support in building social relationships because they are at greater risk for difficulties in social communication (Rice, 1993). Social interactions are important; they increase classroom participation and build social relationships. Most children learn social skills with no instruction or support. But some students with communication disorders, such as those with autism, will need to be taught specific social skills, while others, such as those with specific language impairments or those using communication devices, will need support to initiate and sustain interactions because of their limited expressive language.

One such support is a *social story*. Social stories (Gray, 2004) help children with autism spectrum disorders carry out various social interactions. A social story describes social concepts, skills, or situations by providing information about the situation and people involved. Social stories have been effective in increasing prosocial behaviors and decreasing inappropriate behaviors (Barry & Burley, 2004; Ivey, Heflin, & Alberto, 2004; Kuoch & Mirenda, 2003). You will learn more about social stories as an instructional strategy in Chapter 10.

USING EFFECTIVE INSTRUCTIONAL STRATEGIES

Early Childhood Students: Facilitative Language Strategies

Facilitating language development is a primary component of most early education programs. Because communication is social in nature and is learned across all parts of a child's day, the child's communication partners should use strategies to promote his speech and language development. A set of such strategies, described in Box 6.3, has been developed, researched, and refined in the Language Acquisition Preschool at the University of Kansas (Bunce & Watkins, 1995; Rice & Wilcox, 1995). In the preschool classroom, the adults' interactions provide the intervention with no additional pullout therapy, so children do not receive individual therapy. These strategies rest on several foundations: Language intervention is best when provided in a meaningful social context; language facilitation occurs across the preschool curriculum; language begins with the child; language is learned through interaction; valuable teaching occasions can arise in child-to-child interactions; and parents are valuable partners in language intervention programming. Box 6.4 teaches you about facilitation language strategies.

Elementary and Middle School Students: Graphic Organizer Modifications

When children leave early childhood programs, their curriculum begins to focus on learning to read and write in the early elementary grades and then on reading and writing to learn in the later elementary and middle school years. For students with communication disorders, these transitions are difficult. Graphic organizers are a form of advance organizer that you first learned about in Chapter 5. They can help students with communication disorders develop their literacy skills (Sturm & Rankin-Erickson, 2002).

Graphic organizers are tools that assist students to comprehend and write more effectively (Cunningham & Allington, 2007). They provide a visual representation in an organized framework. Graphic organizers have been especially useful for

Graphic organizers are simple yet effective methods for helping students with receptive language disorders remember information.

Facilitative Language Strategies

The facilitative language strategies described here have been validated in a variety of preschool settings with children with communication disorders (Bunce, 2008, Bunce & Watkins, 1995; Rice & Wilcox, 1995). They can be implemented in any adult-child interaction in any context and provide many natural teaching and learning opportunities. Examples of facilitative language strategies are:

Focused contrast. This is a production by an adult that highlights the difference between the child's speech or language and the adult's. This can occur as feedback or a model. During a feedback instance, when the child says, "Otey," for "Okay," the adult could say, "Oh, you said 'Otey,' and I said, 'Okay.'" During a modeled focused contrast, the adult provides many examples for the child. For example, if the focus is on the past-tense marker -ed, the adult, while playing house, may say, "She is walking," while moving the doll and then stop the movement and say, "She walked to the door." This can be repeated with numerous actions during play.

Modeling. Modeling is often used to help a child learn a language or speech structure he doesn't yet use. If the structure is the plural marker -s, the adult may use it to describe the plurals in the ongoing activity, highlighting them with extra emphasis or stress.

Event casts. Event casts provide an ongoing description of an activity, just like a sports broadcaster might. The events described can be what the child or adult is doing. For example, during dress-up play, the adult may say, "You are putting on the hat. Now you are putting on blue shoes."

Open questions. Questions that have a variety of possible answers are open questions. Examples include "What should we do next?" and "What do you think happens next?"

Expansions. The adult repeats the child's utterance, filling in the missing components. For example, if the child says, "Two horse," the adult expands with "Two brown horses."

Recasts. When recasting, the adult keeps the child's basic meaning but changes the structure or grammar of the child's utterance. For example, if the child says, "He has juice," the adult can say, "Yes, he is drinking juice now."

Redirects and prompted initiations. These strategies encourage children to interact with each other. When a child approaches an adult and makes a request that could be made to another child, the adult redirects him to ask a classmate: "You could tell Tom, 'I need a blue crayon.'" When a child does not make a request to an adult but has the opportunity to interact with another child, he might be prompted to ask another child to play or request some item.

To be able to use the facilitative language strategies described, it is important to follow these steps:

◆ Know the child's goals and objectives.
◆ View every interaction as an opportunity to use the strategies.
◆ Identify the goals and objectives that relate to specific activities of the day.
◆ Identify teaching strategies to be used during specific activities.
◆ Decide when to use strategies to emphasize targets within the activity.
◆ Use the strategies identified during the activity.
◆ Document the child's response.

PEARSON
myeducationlab

Go to the Building Teaching Skills and Dispositions section in Chapter 6 of MyEducationLab and complete the activities. As you watch the video and answer the accompanying questions, reflect on how the teacher is using facilitative language strategies in what appears to be play.

students with Down syndrome, autism spectrum disorders, and language-learning disabilities (Kumin, 2001; Myles & Simpson, 2003; Nelson & Van Meter, 2004). Graphic organizers can be hand-drawn or computer-generated. When using graphic organizers, it is important to first determine which organizer will best meet the desired curriculum outcome (Cunningham & Allington, 2007). A teacher might choose a web design, a story map, a feature matrix, or data charts, to name a few. It is also important to consider how students will participate when completing and utilizing a graphic organizer, and what adaptations a student may need.

For example, if a student with a receptive language delay or disorder needs to learn and remember information for a science unit on insects, the teacher may provide a web design using pictures to organize the insects' anatomical makeup, what the insects eat,

Figure 6.4 Graphic organizer generated by Kidspiration for a second-grade unit on frogs

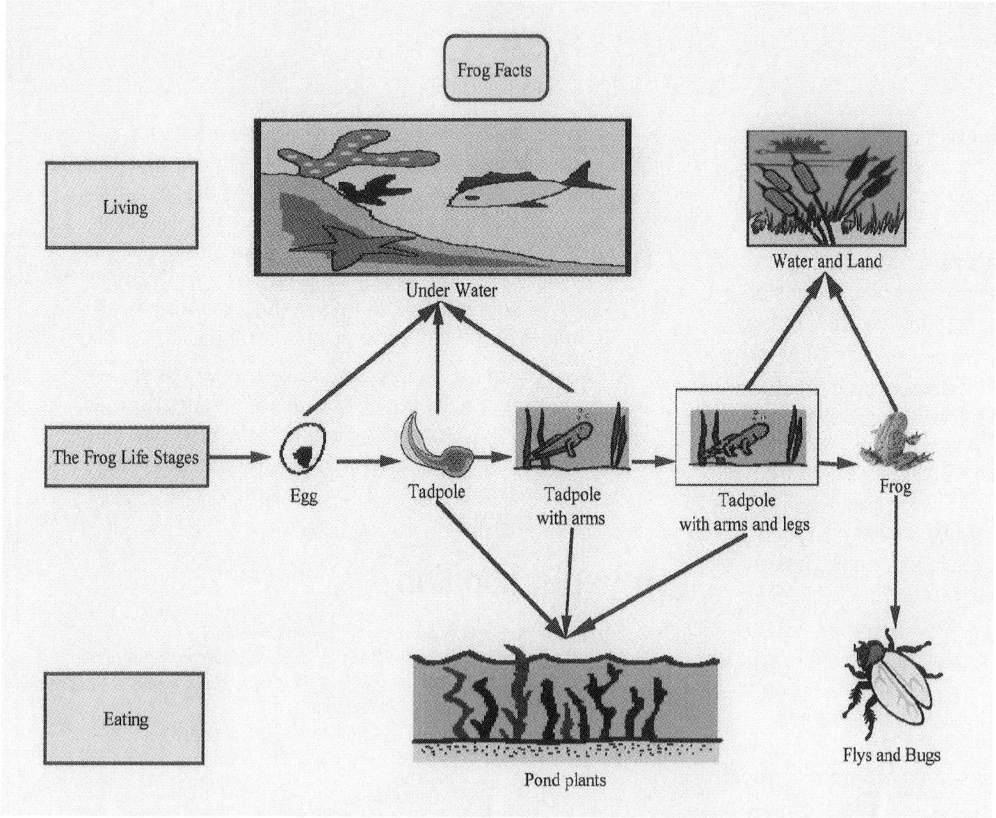

This sample graphic organizer was created by chapter co-author Evette Edmister, when she was a speech-language pathology doctoral student at the University of Kansas, using a graphic organizing software program entitled Kidspiration. The pictures within the graphic organizer were generated with Kidspiration and Meyer-Johnson's Boardmaker software.

what animals eat the insects, habitats the insects live in, and so on. The information in a graphic organizer visually links groups of important information together for the student. Box 6.5 provides more specific details about graphic organizers, and Figure 6.4 shows an example created for a second-grade classroom.

How Are Organizers Created?

A graphic organizer frame can be made on most classroom computers using standard drawing tools found in word processing software or in the computer's accessory tools. They can also easily be drawn by hand. Premade organizers can be located by searching the Web for graphic organizers or obtaining books with premade organizers. Some textbooks come with online companions that have graphic organizer ideas. There are also commercial programs that can be purchased that create graphic organizers on the computer.

What to Consider When Using Graphic Organizers?

The student's past experience with graphic organizers needs to be considered. Students may not necessarily know how to fill out a graphic organizer or how to utilize the information within a graphic organizer to answer questions. Teachers may need to provide examples of graphic organizers, model completing graphic organizers, and model finding information using a graphic organizer (Cunningham & Allington, 2007).

How the student feels about writing may also need to be considered. If the student were concerned about making mistakes, reluctant to rewrite information, or hesitant to

Graphic Organizers

When might graphic organizers be helpful?

◆ *During lecture.* A graphic organizer can help students learn information and understand how parts of a lesson are related (Boon, Burke, Fore, & Spencer, 2006). It can also serve as a reference during discussion, assist with answering comprehension questions after discussion, and be used as a study guide for later testing.

◆ *During reading.* A graphic organizer can help students organize information they have learned during reading (Cunningham & Allington, 2007). For example, if the purpose for a reading was to compare and contrast two characters within a story, all members of the class could use a Venn diagram while reading. Students could write the described qualities of each character within the organizer as they read.

◆ *During the development of reference material.* An organizer can be used to display data and information collected by a student (Cunningham & Allington, 2007). The student could then use the graphic organizer later as a reference tool. For example, in a math lesson students may survey others on a topic

and graph the responses. In another instance, students may be directed to try to use more describing words in their writing. To complete this task, perhaps they need to brainstorm a variety of describing words. Because the words may be less familiar to the students, synonyms and/or pictures may also be needed. All the information can be placed within a graphic organizer for reference.

◆ *During writing.* Graphic organizers can help students with writing activities (Sturm & Rankin-Erickson, 2002). The graphic display can assist them to sequence their thoughts. It can also be a visual to highlight where additional information may be needed. See Figure 6.4 for an example.

myeducationlab

Go to the Activities and Application section in Chapter 6 of MyEducationLab and complete Activity 3. As you watch the video and answer the accompanying questions, consider how using graphic organizers can help all students in the classroom, not just those with disabilities.

correct information, he could write ideas on repositionable sticky notes instead of directly onto the organizer. The student then could easily change the information or its placement (Foley & Staples, 2000). For some students, teachers provide concepts, facts, ideas, and/or events. Then the student chooses the information and places it in the organizer (Foley & Staples, 2000). Photos, drawings, and/or symbol sets from computer programs can also be used within graphic organizers to help increase understanding.

Secondary and Transitional Students: Augmented Input

AAC systems enable many students to participate in the curriculum. But learning to use these systems takes a team effort, and the student's familiar and frequent communication partners play an important role. AAC instructional strategies should focus on teaching communication rather than teaching the student to use AAC. AAC is simply a means to an end, the end being communication and participation.

As students transition to more community-based instruction, they need to learn new vocabulary and new ways to interact. This is a challenge even for students who have successfully used AAC in the classroom. Participating in social exchanges in the break room with less familiar partners is quite different from participating in more structured interactions with familiar partners in school. Transitioning students will need instruction and support to meaningfully integrate their AAC communication systems into this new communication environment. Box 6.6 describes how to model the use of an AAC system.

One instructional strategy that has been effective is the **System for Augmenting Language (SAL)** (Romski & Sevcik, 1988). SAL focuses on augmented input of language. Using SAL, communication partners augment their speech by activating the student's communication device in naturally occurring communication interactions at home and school

Aided Input

Some students who have difficulty communicating verbally use augmented and alternative communication (AAC). Many AAC systems include visual supports such as pictures and/or words. The pictures may be printed on paper or contained in a portable voice output device. Students learning language and beginning to use AAC systems need the opportunity to learn to use visual supports within natural contexts (Romski & Sevcik, 2003). Modeling the use of the symbols within the AAC system is a helpful strategy. Terms used to name the modeling procedures and descriptions of the précis procedure for modeling the use of visual supports vary from one research study to another (Blackstone, 2006).

Tips for modeling the use of an AAC system are as follows:

◆ Become familiar with the student's system. Determine what vocabulary is available and what additional supports may be needed to model the use of the device. Many of the computer voice output devices also have software that will allow the student's vocabulary to be viewed on the teacher's computer so the student's use will not be disrupted.

◆ It may be helpful to begin with a focus on one or two activities or settings and then expand to additional settings (Goossens, Crain, and Elder, 1992). For example, you might decide to start with an art activity and, once comfortable, add another activity like discussing a favorite book.

◆ Determine what will be modeled for the student (Goossens, Crain, and Elder, 1992).
  • For example, if a student was generally using one-word utterances consisting of primarily nouns, you might decide to target more two-word sequences with the device emphasizing the use of verbs.
  • In another example, if a student was having difficulty understanding directions, you might choose to target using the device to model directions.
  • The targets for modeling will vary over time for each student and from student to student.

◆ You can model language describing what you are doing or what the student is doing.
  • For instance, if the class activity is creating a card for a family member, and the goal is to target two-word utterances and emphasize the use of verbs, you can use the device to talk about what you did to create the card. The words in parentheses in the list below represent the words that might be selected on the AAC system. The teacher might voice the words not in parentheses.
    • I'm going to pick the red paper (pick red).
    • I'm cutting the paper (cut paper).
    • Oh, I need glue (need glue).

◆ Or model what the student is doing.
    • You cut the paper (cut paper).
    • Wow, you picked the sparkly red heart (pick heart).
    • Oh, glue, you need the glue (need glue).

◆ Remember to encourage, not demand, use of the device for modeling (Romski & Sevcik, 2003).

A helpful resource of research, terms, and focuses for modeling input can be found in Sarah Blackstone's article "The Effects of Modeling Aided AAC" in the September 2006 issue of *Augmentative Communication News*. ■ ■ ■

and in the community, encouraging but not requiring the student to use the device (Romski & Sevcik, 2003). For example, a student enters the bakery with his job coach. The job coach greets the cashier by saying, "Hello, how are you?" while activating the buttons for "hello" and "you" on the student's device. The student not only has a model of what vocabulary to use in that situation but also a model of how to use the vocabulary.

Although the SAL strategy was developed for use with electronic communication devices, augmented input can also be used if students have communication books or boards or sign language. It is sometimes then called *aided language stimulation* (Elder & Goossens, 1994; Goossens, Crain, & Elder, 1992) or, when sign language is used, *total communication*. The SAL strategy is effective with toddlers as well as students between the ages of 6 and 20 (Romski & Sevcik, 1992; Romski & Sevcik, 1996; Romski, Sevcik, & Forrest, 2001).

The SAL instructional strategy depends on the training of frequent and signficant communication partners. Blackstone, Hunt-Berg, Nygard, and Schultz (2004) have developed

IEP Tip

The IEP team should designate who should learn how to operate any technology devices.

a tool called Social Networks to identify these important partners. Special educators and speech-language pathologists can use this tool to determine who should receive training. Romski and Sevcik (2003) suggest that a student's communication partners should receive instruction about the importance of input with respect to understanding and the physical operation of the device, as well as practice in providing input, feedback, and coaching in natural settings.

INCLUDING STUDENTS WITH COMMUNICATION DISORDERS

Most students with speech and language impairments spend the majority of their day in the general education classroom (see Figure 6.5). According to the U.S. Department of Education, 88 percent of the children who receive speech and language services spend 80 to 100 percent of their time in the general education classroom for these services. The trend toward receiving services in the general educational classroom and spending more of the school day there has been increasing since 1984 (U.S. Department of Education, 2001). That is so, in part, because effective teachers use some of the tips that you will find in Box 6.7.

It is important for teachers to observe students' speech and language skills and contact the building speech-language pathologist if they have concerns. Students who do not develop speech and language skills early in life will have a difficult time acquiring these skills later (Downing, 2005). In addition, students who do not have a conventional communication system may look for unconventional means to meet their needs. These means may be inappropriate, aggressive, or ineffective (Downing, 2005). Some students may become passive when they feel their communication will not be understood. Language is also the basis for reading and writing skills; indeed, 50 percent or more of children with a language impairment in preschool or kindergarten have reading disabilities in primary or secondary grades (Catts & Kamhi, 1999). The communication skills that students learn in school are needed long after they graduate to "assume life in their community as contributing adults" (Downing, 2005). Figure 6.5 displays the students' education placement for school year 2006.

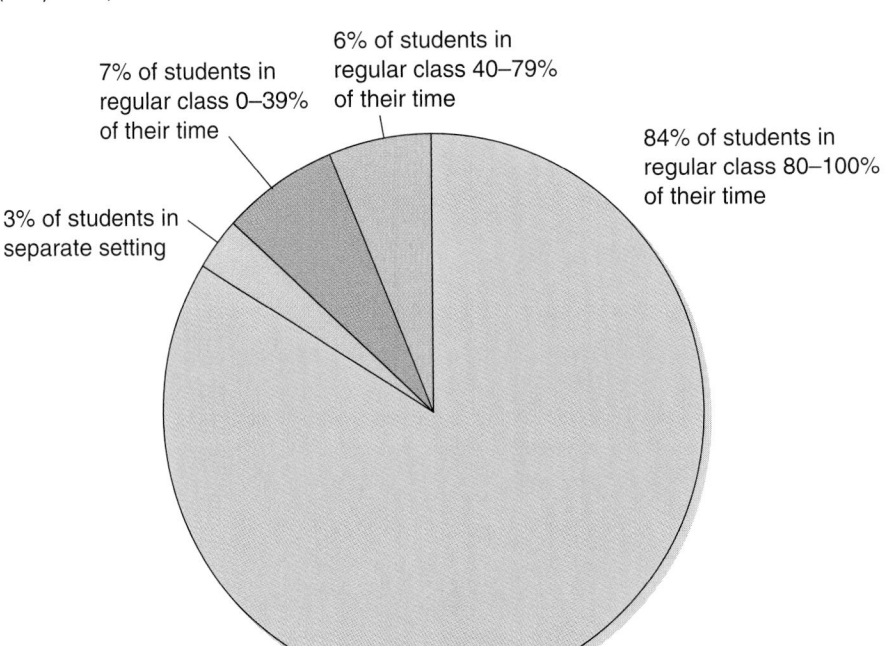

Figure 6.5 Educational placement of students with specific learning disabilities (Fall, 2006)

7% of students in regular class 0–39% of their time

6% of students in regular class 40–79% of their time

84% of students in regular class 80–100% of their time

3% of students in separate setting

Box 6.7	INCLUSION TIPS			
	What You Might See	*What You Might Be Tempted to Do*	*Alternative Responses*	*Ways to Include Peers in the Process*
Behavior	The student appears shy and reserved. He may not participate in large-group settings. It may take him time to compose a response when speaking in front of the class.	Encourage him to hurry or avoid calling on him in large groups.	Provide a multiple-choice response option. Write the questions on the board, giving time to compose before calling on specific children. Allow for small-group discussion and reporting.	Provide multiple-choice response options or alternate response options for all students, along with other types of question formats.
Social interactions	He is alone during unstructured times. He does not ask friends to play. He does not join in with other peer interactions.	Assume he is happy alone and let him be.	Demonstrate that you value his contributions. Provide a model to help him learn to interact with the other students.	Encourage a peer buddy to help model and encourage interactions with other children.
Educational performance	He produces syntactically incomplete sentences verbally and in writing. He avoids writing tasks.	Constantly correct him. Decrease the occurrence of writing assignments.	Provide visual and verbal models of complete sentences. Continue to provide lots of opportunities for writing. Provide positive feedback.	Allow small-group interactions with assigned roles that rotate to every student. The students can then provide models for each other.
Classroom attitudes	He expects the teacher to intercede when he has difficulty with other students. He might rely on the teacher to initiate interactions with other students.	Tell him to go play with others. Assume the children will work it out on their own.	Teach all the students ways to interact and solve problems.	Provide opportunities for the students to practice independent interactions with one another, providing assistance where needed.

ASSESSING STUDENTS' PROGRESS

Measuring Students' Progress

Progress in the General Curriculum

The reauthorization of IDEA in 2004 (see Chapters 1 and 2) emphasized that educators must measure a student's progress within the general education curriculum. There are many different tools for measuring a student's progress, but curriculum-based assessment, which you learned about in the previous chapter, is a favorite because it focuses on how a student's skills are progressing in the curriculum (Howell & Nolet, 2000; Losardo & Notari-Syverson, 2001). Educators working with students with communication disorders may use the data-based performance modification procedure of curriculum-based assessment that we discussed previously to monitor a student's progress and make decisions about instructional strategies.

With input from the educational team, the speech-language pathologist will work with the student's teachers to try to reduce the discrepancy between the student's current communication skill level and the curriculum standard against which the student's progress is assessed. For example, if a student exhibits atypical dysfluencies (or stuttering) and if the dysfluencies negatively affect participation in class, interaction with other students, or both, the pathologist should set a goal of monitoring the amount of class participation that occurs as a result of the student's improved fluency, give the teacher and the parents suggestions that may be helpful when speaking with someone who stutters, work with the student to teach different fluency strategies, observe in class to monitor the use of the strategies in the classroom and the student's class participation, and ask the teacher to rate the student's fluency during the day and tally class participation at agreed-upon times.

Progress in Addressing Other Educational Needs

Ecological inventories are another helpful tool for monitoring communication progress. You will learn more about the ecological inventory process in Chapter 9, but those inventories can also assist in determining the communication expectations that exist in natural environments (Downing, 2005). The first step in using an ecological inventory is for the speech-language pathologist and others to determine what interactions occur within the natural environment. For example, assume that the student is completing a vocational training for waiting on customers. The pathologist and others analyze the steps or components of the job, such as greeting the customer, asking how to help the customer, answering the customer's questions, recording the customer's order, clarifying any information not understood, and ending the conversation. The team then observes one of the student's peers completing the task and monitors the degree to which the peer is independent. Was the peer completely independent; did equipment need to be set up first; were verbal cues needed? Now the student completes the task, and the speech-language pathologist and others record the steps that the student needed assistance with or was not yet able to complete. The team then compares those data with the peer's data to determine the student's degree of discrepancy and target the areas of discrepancy for instruction, strategies, and possibly supplementary aids. With future reassessment of the student's performance in the environment using the ecological inventory, the pathologist and others can determine whether the instruction, strategies, and/or supplementary aids are helping the student decrease the discrepancy in the performance observed. For instance, the student may need additional vocabulary added to an AAC device, picture cues for the steps, pages of pictures of line drawings (called topic boards), or role playing and practice with others.

Making Accommodations for Assessment

Many students with communication disorders do not need accommodations for assessment. Other students may need additional time for tests or access to a word processor and computer software when writing. When assessing a student with more significant speech and language impairments, educators should ask, "What is being assessed, how does the student best receive information, and how does the student best express himself?" They should consider the focus of the assessment in order to reduce the chances that the student will be assessed in more than one area at one time. For instance, if the student's augmentative voice-output communication system is new or unfamiliar and he uses it during a science test, then teachers can assess the student's understanding of the communication system as well as his understanding of science. They may find it difficult, however, to determine whether the student did not answer a question correctly because he did not know how to find the answer with the new system or because he did not know that particular science concept. Similarly, if a student who exhibits difficulty understanding written complex language structures takes a science test but the test format is not adapted for him, then professionals may be assessing the student's ability to read complex sentence structures as well as his knowledge about science. If they want to assess the student's understanding of complex language structures, then they should make sure that the test consists of complex structures. If, however, they are assessing science, they may need to take into account the student's preferred manner of receiving information. When the assessment is isolated, the student may concentrate solely on what he knows about science.

It is important to present information in a manner that assists the student's comprehension of the assessment directions and questions. For instance, if a student finds it difficult to receive written information, he may benefit from having the assessment explained verbally or from having visual supports. If a student has difficulty understanding complex sentence structures, he may benefit from having the language adjusted or from being given visual supports to assist his comprehension.

If a student has difficulty expressing himself verbally or in written form, he may benefit from an assessment format that does not require long verbal or written output. For example, a multiple-choice or true-false format may be helpful. He may then only need to respond with a one-word answer, a switch activation, or a gesture indicating the correct answer. This change in format may decrease the probability that the student will not provide the answer because of the length of the response needed, his inability to clearly express an answer, or both.

The format should complement the student's most common means of expression. For instance, if the student has begun to explore a new communication system, such as a device using a computer screen, it may be advisable to use the more familiar system for assessment until he has had time to learn the new system.

VALUES AND OUTCOMES

VALUES — GREAT EXPECTATIONS — CHOICES — POSITIVE CONTRIBUTIONS — STRENGTHS — RELATIONSHIPS — FULL CITIZENSHIP

Despite a tenuous beginning, George's future looks positive. George, his family, and all the collaborating professionals are working together.

- They have their own dreams for him—their own great expectations. His parents would like George to be in college. His teachers see no reason why he cannot attend college.

- George is a bright boy and is likely to make one of his many positive contributions by participating as a member of his school's chess team.

- Professionals collaborating with George and his family expect him to progress through the general education curriculum. He's got the talent to do so; that, plus his own charm and determination, are his strengths.

- They want George to set his own goals and to achieve them. They want George to be self-determined. Perhaps he will pursue his interests in horses, computers, or the dramatic arts. It's his choice—on that they are clear.

- Given his outgoing nature and good pragmatic skills, they expect him to have good friends and a wide social network. As George masters the elements of speech, his parents, teachers and he himself expect that he will expand his relationships, which are already impressively broad.

- Full citizenship often comes when people can communicate about themselves and establish their place in their schools and communities. That is why George's parents and teachers expect to continue to collaborate to assist George with his communication and technology needs, especially as the complexities of his curriculum increase.

1. Might you or your colleagues, or even some students, regard George's use of augmentative and alternative communication (AAC) devices as "separating" him from his peers who do not have disabilities? When, if ever, do technological aides diminish a student's inclusion?

2. Is communication one of a student's most essential skills, whether in or out of school? How might students behave if they did not have the ability to communicate? Would their behavior be challenging?

3. Knowing that there is a difference between speech and language disorders (collectively called communication disorders), which one seems most important for a student to have? Or is each equally important?

ADDRESSING THE STANDARDS: THE VALUES CONNECTION

The following CEC Knowledge and Skill Standards: Common Core and Values are addressed in this chapter through the content and concepts we discuss.

CEC Knowledge and Skill Standards: Common Core	Values/Standards Connection
CEC Knowledge and Skill Standard II. Development and Characteristics of Learners CC2K1 Typical and atypical human growth and development. CC2K2 Educational implications of characteristics of various exceptionalities. CC2K4 Family systems and the roles of families supporting development. CC2K5 Similarities and differences of individuals with and without exceptional learning needs. CC2K6 Similarities and differences of individuals with exceptional learning needs.	CEC Standard 2, Development and Characteristics of Learners, involves learning about typical speech and language development and impairments and how to observe and distinguish typical and atypical articulation.
CEC Knowledge and Skill Standard IV. Instructional Strategies CC4S3 Select, adapt, and use instructional strategies and materials according to characteristics of the individual with exceptional learning needs. CC4S4 Use strategies to facilitate maintenance and generalization of skills across environments. CC4S5 Use procedures to increase the individual's self-awareness, self-management, self-control, self-reliance, and self-esteem.	All students have many natural strengths. However, like George, they need opportunities for educational programs to identify, highlight, and build upon these innate and acquired strengths.

CEC Knowledge and Skill Standards: Common Core	Values/Standards Connection
CEC Knowledge and Skill Standard V. Learning Environments and Social Interactions	It is important for students to be able to freely express themselves in order to *make choices* and become *self-advocates*.
CC5S3 Identify supports needed for integration into various program placements.	
CC5S4 Design learning environments that encourage active participation in individual and group settings.	Helping students succeed within the work environment will increase their later job opportunities and assist them to be more economically self-sufficient and make *positive contributions* to their communities.
CC5S9 Create an environment that encourages self-advocacy and increased independence.	
CEC Knowledge and Skill Standard VI. Language	As you develop an awareness of how to meet the needs of bilingual students, you are using CEC Standard 6, Language.
CC6K4 Augmentative and assistive communication strategies.	
CC6S1 Use strategies to support and enhance communication skills of individuals with exceptional learning needs.	Communication displays students' strengths and helps them be *self-determined*, build *relationships*, and be *full citizens* of their schools and communities.
CC6S2 Use communication strategies and resources to facilitate understanding of subject matter for students whose primary language is not the dominant language.	
CEC Knowledge and Skill Standard VII. Instructional Planning	When you support students through effective instructional planning, you increase the likelihood that they will have equal opportunities in the classroom and the community – a way to achieve full citizenship.
CC7S1 Identify and prioritize areas of the general curriculum and accommodations for individuals with exceptional learning needs.	
CC7S3 Involve the individual and family in setting instructional goals and monitoring progress.	
CC7S6 Sequence, implement, and evaluate individualized learning objectives.	
CC7S9 Incorporate and implement instructional and assistive technology into the educational program.	
CEC Knowledge and Skill Standard VIII. Assessment	In conducting assessments be sure to focus not only on the student's needs, but also his strengths in order to develop new visions of what is possible and achieve great expectations.
CC8K3 Screening, prereferral, referral, and classification procedures.	
CC8S2 Administer nonbiased formal and informal assessments.	
CC8S6 Use assessment information in making eligibility, program, and placement decisions for individuals with exceptional learning needs, including those from culturally and/or linguistically diverse backgrounds.	
CC8S8 Evaluate instruction and monitor progress of individuals with exceptional learning needs.	

continued

CEC Knowledge and Skill Standards: Common Core	Values/Standards Connection
CEC Knowledge and Skill Standard X. Collaboration	The collaboration and consultation of teachers and speech-language pathologists allow both the opportunity to learn from one another and share their respective expertise, building on each others' *strengths*.
CC10S2 Collaborate with families and others in assessment of individuals with exceptional learning needs.	
CC10S4 Assist individuals with exceptional learning needs and their families in becoming active participants in the educational team.	
CC10S5 Plan and conduct collaborative conferences with individuals with exceptional learning needs and their families.	

Source: From CEC Knowledge and Skill Standards: Common Core and Values. Copyright by The Council for Exceptional Children. Reprinted with permission.

SUMMARY

Identifying Students with Communication Disorders

◆ Communication disorders include both speech and language impairments.

◆ A speech disorder is an impairment of one's articulation of speech sounds, fluency, or voice.

◆ A language disorder reflects problems in receiving information; understanding it; and formulating a spoken, written, or symbolic response.

◆ Communication differences that are related to the culture of the individual are not considered impairments.

◆ Language is a shared system of rules and symbols for the exchange of information. It includes rules of phonology, morphology, syntax, semantics, and pragmatics.

◆ Five to 10 percent of the population has a communication disorder.

◆ Communication impairments can affect a student's academic, social, and emotional development.

Evaluating Students with Communication Disorders

◆ The speech-language pathologist is the professional most likely to determine the presence and extent of a speech and/or language impairment.

◆ Assessments include the use of informal and formal measures. They should occur in settings comfortable and natural for the student.

Designing an Appropriate IEP

◆ The collaborative participation of students, their teachers, speech-language pathologists, and parents to enhance communicative development results in students' language objectives being targeted in many settings and situations.

◆ When planning universal design for learning for students with communication disorders, a teacher must answer two questions: How can I assure that my student understands what I am teaching? and How can I assure that my student can express what he knows?

Using Effective Instructional Strategies

◆ Early childhood students with communication disorders benefit from language facilitation strategies.

- Graphic organizers and story webs can be helpful for elementary and secondary students with communication disorders.

- Students transitioning to community-based instruction will need instruction and support to meaningfully integrate their AAC communication systems into this new environment.

- One instructional strategy that has been effective is the System for Augmenting Language (SAL).

Including Students with Communication Disorders

- According to the U.S. Department of Education, 88 percent of the children who receive speech and language services spend 21 percent or less of their time outside the general education classroom.

Assessing Students' Progress with Communication Disorders

- Curriculum-based assessment can help monitor students' progress in the general education curriculum.

- Ecological inventories can be helpful for assessing and monitoring progress in and outside the classroom.

Now go to MyEducationLab at www.myeducationlab.com and take the Self-Assessment to gauge your initial comprehension of chapter content. Once you have taken the Self-Assessment, use your individualized Study Plan for Chapter 6 to enhance your understanding of the concepts discussed in the chapter.

Understanding Students with Emotional or Behavioral Disorders

◆ WHO IS MATTHEW ACKINCLOSE?

Matthew Ackinclose has been through some remarkable changes in the past few years. At one time, this 14-year-old eighth grader needed 22 prescriptions to manage his behavior, attended school for only one hour a day, and had conflicts with nearly everyone in school. Now he attends all of his classes, most of which focus on content in the general education curriculum. He also takes only two medications, and one is for occasional migraines. He has good relationships with his school's administrators and faculty and with his peers. He is earning As and Bs in school and has a 99.5-percent average in his general education math class!

Matt's resiliency—his ability to overcome emotional or behavioral challenges—is a result of his determination and the supportive relationships he has with his mother, his therapist/social worker, and a special education teacher, among others. Those relationships and outcomes were hard to come by.

During Matt's early years, professionals routinely told his mother, Laura, to place him in a residential setting, but she refused. She knew in her heart that being separated from Matt was not the answer.

Matt's behavioral challenges began when he was just an infant. One day, when he was 7 months old, his face was bloody when his mother picked him up from daycare. Matt had repeatedly banged his head on the crib and the wall before a teacher could stop him. That was when Laura knew Matt needed help. She began a long search for someone— a psychologist, a physician, a teacher— anyone who could meet her son's needs.

In the meantime, Laura contrived new ways to keep Matt safe at home. Unfortunately, on one Halloween all of her precautionary measures failed. Matt got out of the house when some trick-or-treaters came to the door. When Laura finally found him, he was standing in a nearby creek. She still remembers fearing that if she tried to get close to him, he would run, slip under the water, and drown or badly injure himself. At about this time he also threatened to kill Laura and himself; he was only 5 years old. Clearly, Matt was a boy in pain.

Instead of recognizing that Matt and Laura were struggling to overcome a serious disability, professionals criticized Laura's parenting. "They can make you feel like a war criminal!" Laura says of the treatment she received from teachers and other professionals who wanted to blame her for Matt's disability.

Laura saw the strengths in Matt that others were unwilling to see: his intelligence, persistence, and sensitivity. She was alone in her point of view until she made a fortuitous phone call 6 years ago to social worker Rebecca Hall.

Rebecca sensed that what Matt needed most was a caring relationship with someone he could trust who would connect with him and believe in his potential, not be intimidated by his words or behaviors, give him a sense of personal power by offering him choices, and work with him, not fight against him. She was determined to be that person.

Rather than focusing on Matt's deficits, Rebecca looked for his strengths. To Matt, she asked, "What do you do well? When do you feel successful?" She asked Laura about the times when Matt behaved in a way she liked. Then she worked with Matt and Laura to increase those positive behaviors. Rebecca taught Matt how much he had to offer others and also worked with him on problem-solving skills. She would ask, "What's the problem? What can be done to fix it? What would you be willing to do instead?"

Despite the fact that Matt's behaviors improved, Laura and Rebecca searched in vain for a teacher who was willing to work with him until they found special educator Charlotte Hott. Charlotte's history with Matt began on a positive note when Rebecca placed a call to her and asked if Matt could enroll in her class. Charlotte replied without hesitation over the speakerphone, "I would love to have him!" Matt heard her response and realized that this teacher would care about him.

Charlotte welcomed Matt into her classroom. She built on the foundations of trust and strength-based interventions that were already in place and encouraged Matt and Laura through consistent, positive communication. Charlotte tailored her teaching approach to Matt's individual needs and realized, as did Rebecca, that a cooperative relationship with Matt was the key. "It's about respect," Charlotte says. "To get respect you must give respect."

CHAPTER OBJECTIVES

◆ You will learn about the broad characteristics that define what IDEA refers to as emotional disturbance—the traits that once made Matthew Ackinclose dangerous to himself but that now have receded.

◆ You will learn the emotional characteristics of students and about various types of specific emotional or behavioral disorders, including anxiety disorders, mood disorders, oppositional defiant disorder, conduct disorder, and schizophrenia.

◆ You will learn about these students' behavioral characteristics, such as their externalizing and internalizing behaviors.

◆ You will learn that students with emotional or behavioral disorders are often quite intelligent and that, with support such as Matt has had, can progress through the general curriculum.

◆ You will learn the biological and environmental causes of emotional or behavioral disorders.

◆ You will learn how to evaluate students and how to connect evaluation data to the student's IEP using various rating scales and then to provide wrap-around supports, class-wide self-management skills, and classroom-centered interventions such as conflict-resolution training.

When confronted by a tough lesson or a challenging social task, Matt frequently asked Charlotte, "Why are you doing this?"

"I always explained my reasons," Charlotte says. "I never said, 'Because I'm the teacher.'" She realized Matt was really asking if he could trust her.

Charlotte is the hub of a team that includes Laura and Matt's general education teachers. Her role varies. For instance, Charlotte talked to Matt's physical education teacher and asked that he be allowed to participate in his school clothes rather than shorts and a T-shirt. This simple accommodation has made it easier for him to participate fully. Although he does not require any accommodations in his math, science, and social studies classes, he sometimes has difficulty expressing himself in papers and reports in his language arts class, so Charlotte spends extra time with him to help him with these assignments.

"You can be trained to do this job," Charlotte says, "but you have to want to do this job. It has to be genuine with Matt." The results of this mutual respect are clear: Matt can regulate his behavior, he takes fewer medications, he is making academic and social progress, he has better self-esteem, and he and others know about his strengths.

Matt is ultimately responsible for the positive changes in his life, but he acknowledges that because people care about him and teach him effectively, he wants to change and has learned how. These changes aren't going unnoticed. When Rebecca told Matt how excited she was that he was going to be featured in this textbook, Matt said, "Well, it's not like I won the principal's Pride Award or anything." What Matt didn't know at the time was that he would receive that award a few weeks later, an acknowledgment and a celebration of all of his hard work.

PEARSON
myeducationlab

After reading this chapter, complete the Self-Assessment for Chapter 7 on MyEducationLab to gauge your initial understanding of chapter content.

IDENTIFYING STUDENTS WITH EMOTIONAL OR BEHAVIORAL DISORDERS

Defining Emotional or Behavioral Disorders

IDEA uses the term *emotional disturbance* to refer to a condition that is accompanied by one or more of the following characteristics over a long time and to a marked degree and that adversely affect a child's educational performance:

- An inability to learn that cannot be explained by intellectual, sensory, or health factors
- An inability to build or maintain satisfactory interpersonal relationships with peers and teachers
- Inappropriate types of behavior or feelings under normal circumstances
- A general, pervasive mood of unhappiness or depression
- A tendency to develop physical symptoms or fears associated with personal or school problems

Emotional disturbance includes schizophrenia but does not apply to children who are socially maladjusted unless they also meet the other criteria for having an emotional or behavioral disorder.

Gender and ethnicity influence the prevalence of emotional or behavioral disorders (ED). The interaction of gender and ethnicity is clear:

White males were 3.8 times as likely as White females to be identified as ED while Black females were 1.4 times as likely as White females to be so identified. . . . Black males displayed the largest disproportionality, with an odds ratio of 5.5. These data starkly represent the extent of the problem of disproportionality in ED identification across gender and ethnic groups. (Coutinho, Oswald, Best, & Forness, 2002, p. 116)

In fall 2006, approximately 0.7 percent (457,731) of all students ages 6 through 21 in special education nationally were classified as having an emotional or behavioral disorder (U.S. Department of Education, 2008). Experts disagree about whether the official figure accurately reflects the number of students with this disability. A national study of special education services reported that 14 percent to 22 percent of students in the school population were identified as having an emotional or behavioral disorder (Wagner et al., 2006).

Describing the Characteristics

Not all students who have emotional or behavioral disorders receive services under IDEA; that is because their disorders do not interfere with their educational progress. A student with phobia of heights, for instance, may not need special education services or specially designed instruction. But a student who has phobia of school will likely need special education services under IDEA. We will highlight these stutents' principal characteristics: emotional, behavioral, and cognitive/academic.

Emotional Characteristics

The *Diagnostic and Statistical Manual of Mental Disorders* (DSM-IV-TR) (American Psychiatric Association, 2000) describes the standard classification system for mental illness and emotional or behavioral disorders. It identifies five causes for children and adolescents being classified as having emotional or behavioral disorders: (1) anxiety disorder, (2) mood disorder, (3) oppositional defiant disorder, (4) conduct disorder, and (5) schizophrenia.

Anxiety disorder. **Anxiety disorder** is the most common childhood disorder (Robb & Reber, 2007; Robin et al., 2006; Southam-Gerow & Chorpita, 2007). It is characterized by excessive fear, worry, or uneasiness. Students who have anxiety disorder experience these conditions:

- **Separation anxiety disorder:** excessive and intense fear associated with separating from home, family, and others with whom a child has a close attachment
- **Generalized anxiety disorder:** excessive, overwhelming worry not caused by any recent experience
- **Phobia:** unrealistic, overwhelming fear of an object or situation
- **Panic disorder:** overwhelming panic attacks resulting in rapid heartbeat, dizziness, and/or other physical symptoms
- **Obsessive-compulsive disorder:** obsessions manifesting as repetitive, persistent, and intrusive impulses, images, or thoughts (e.g., repetitive thoughts about death or illness) and/or compulsions manifesting as repetitive, stereotypical behaviors (e.g., handwashing or counting)
- **Post-traumatic stress disorder:** flashbacks and other recurrent symptoms following exposure to an extremely distressing or dangerous event such as witnessing violence or a hurricane

Students with anxiety disorders often are extremely conscientious with their school assignments and may have a tendency to avoid mistakes; perfectionism affects them (Robin et al., 2006). Their worry about school and pressure to be perfect can result in physical symptoms such as tension, headaches, and stomachaches. Socially, these students are often isolated from peers and tend to avoid threatening social situations.

Medication to treat anxiety disorders shows promising but preliminary results (Research Units on Pediatric Psychopharmacology Anxiety Study Group, 2001). Another intervention is known as **cognitive behavioral therapy (CBT).** CBT teaches a student how his thoughts influence his feelings and behaviors. CBT helps a student recognize her bodily anxiety symptoms, identify her thoughts in stressful situations, develop an array of coping strategies and recognize their results, and experience rewards (Cobb, Sample, Alwell, & Johns, 2006;

IEP Tip

When students are taking medication, it is important to identify the medication on the student's IEP medication schedule and the names and roles of the school staff responsible for administering the medication.

Kendall et al., 2005). By using CBT along with instructional approaches such as role playing, modeling, and relaxation training, Kendall and colleagues were successful in reducing students' anxiety.

Mood disorder. A **mood disorder** involves an extreme deviation in either a depressed or an elevated direction or sometimes in both directions at different times (Rudolph & Lambert, 2007; Youngstrom, 2007). Depression can occur at any age, including childhood. Students having a major depression may experience these changes:

◆ *Emotion:* feeling sad and worthless, crying often, or appearing tearful

◆ *Motivation:* losing interest in play, friends, and schoolwork, with a resulting decline in grades

◆ *Physical well-being:* eating or sleeping too much or too little, disregarding hygiene, or making vague physical complaints

◆ *Thoughts:* perhaps believing he or she is ugly and unable to do anything right and that life is hopeless

Each student with emotional or behavioral disorders has a unique combination of strengths and needs, and each teacher should seek out and build on those strengths.

The prevalence of depression has increased over the past several decades; the highest rate occurs in adolescent females (Garber & Carter, 2006). Major depressive episodes typically last 7 to 9 months for individuals who receive clinical treatment (Rudolph & Lambert, 2007), and depression frequently recurs.

Suicide is the third leading cause of mortality among adolescents (Knopf, Park, & Mulye, 2008). Indeed, suicide rates have declined by more than 28 percent over a 14-year period (from 1990–2003), but an 8 percent increase in suicides took place from 2003–2004 (Centers for Disease Control, 2007). It is unclear whether this is the beginning of a new upward trend.

The most common method of suicide during 2003–2004 for males was firearms. During this time there was a 119 percent increase among young adolescent girls in terms of committing suicide by hanging/suffocation. Four factors are strongly associated with an increased suicide risk: hopelessness, hostility, negative self-concept, and isolation (Rutter & Behrendt, 2004). If any student tells you she is having suicidal thoughts, take her seriously by referring her to a mental health center for treatment (APA & AACP, 2007). You also should seek advice from the school principal or district special education director about other procedures you should follow. School districts often have written guidelines and you should learn what they are and be sure to follow them. In addition, be alert to students who are significantly depressed; they may not talk about suicide, but you should not assume that not talking about it means that they are not thinking about it.

A **bipolar disorder** is characterized by exaggerated mood swings (Youngstrom, 2007). At times, the student experiences depression; at other times, she experiences euphoria, increased activity, self-confidence, racing thoughts, decreased need for sleep, and an exaggerated sense of strength. Experiencing this elevated state has been described as living on fast-forward speed (Miklowitz & Goldstein, 1997). Researchers who followed students with a bipolar disorder over four years reported that the children were having either a depressive or manic episode for two-thirds of the time during the 4-year study (Geller, Tillmann, Craney, & Bolhofner, 2004). Manic episodes were slightly more frequent that depressive ones. Many children and youth who experience a bipolar disorder also have been identified as having attention-deficit/hyperactivity disorder (AD/HD) (Consoli, Deniau, Huynh, Purper, & Cohen, 2007).

Both depression and bipolar disorders have a major impact on students' school success and their interactions with their peers. Depressed students have lower academic achievement and also lower scores on intelligence tests during their depressive episodes (Garber & Carter, 2006). They experience challenges in learning in both their depressed state, when they have fatigue and decreased interest, and in their manic state, when they have racing thoughts and hard-to-contain energy (Kowatch & Fristad, 2006). Both medication and cognitive-behavioral therapy have been successful in treating these students.

Oppositional defiant disorder. **Oppositional defiant disorder** causes a pattern of negativistic, hostile, disobedient, and defiant behaviors (American Psychiatric Association, 2000). According to the DSM-IV-TR, students must have some of the following: loss of temper, arguments with adults, refusal to cooperate with adult requests, frequent rule-breaking, deliberate annoyance of others, blaming others for mistakes, misbehavior, low self-esteem, easily annoyed, expressed resentfulness and anger, and tendency for vindictiveness. These behaviors must have occurred for a period of at least six months (American Psychiatric Association, 2000). Oppositional defiant disorder typically is diagnosed during the elementary school years and is often a precursor of conduct disorders (Whittinger, Langley, Fowler, Thomas, & Thapar, 2007).

Appropriate interventions may prevent a student's oppositional defiant disorder from escalating to the more serious level known as conduct disorder (Nelson-Gray et al., 2006; Skoulos & Tryon, 2007). To avoid arguments and power struggles with students, a teacher should use problem-solving approaches, provide choices, encourage physical activity, anticipate and prevent problems, and refer students for counseling or therapy.

Not surprisingly, students with oppositional defiant disorder often have poor relationships with their peers and challenge teachers' best efforts to help them learn (Greene, 2006). Successful intervention with these students has involved **cognitive-behavioral intervention**. That intervention focuses on problem-solving and learning to resolve challenges in nonconflictual ways (Greene & Ablon, 2005).

Conduct disorder. **Conduct disorder** consists of a persistent pattern of antisocial behavior that significantly interferes with others' rights or with schools' and communities' behavioral expectations (American Psychiatric Association, 2000). The DSM-IV-TR has identified four categories of conduct disorders: (1) aggressive conduct, resulting in physical harm to people or animals; (2) property destruction; (3) deceitfulness or theft; and (4) serious rule violations, such as truancy and running away (American Psychiatric Association, 2000).

Unlike students with oppositional defiant disorder, students with conduct disorders have severe aggressive and antisocial behavior; they often infringe on other students' rights (McMahon & Frick, 2007). Although anger and aggression can emerge in infancy and throughout the early childhood years, it is typically during elementary school years that students, especially boys, are identified as having conduct problems.

Often, students with conduct disorders also have attention deficit/hyperactivity disorder (see Chapter 8). Slightly over one third of boys and slightly over one half of girls with conduct disorders also have AD/HD (Waschbush, 2002). The most promising treatments are medication, coping skills training for students, and training and discipline for parents, each used in combination with the other (Hinshaw et al., 2000; Lochman & Wells, 2004).

Students who have conduct disorders often are placed into juvenile correction programs. A national survey of juvenile correction programs reported that 134,000 youths are incarcerated and that almost half of them have been identified as having an emotional or behavioral disorder—probably conduct disorders, although the study did not specify this (Quinn, Rutherford, Leone, Osher, & Poirier, 2005). African American students are about four times as likely to be incarcerated as their European American peers (Children's Defense Fund, 2007). Students who are participating in either work or school and who receive mental health and other services within 6 months of their incarceration are more

Intensive and early intervention can keep many students out of the rarely helpful criminal justice system.

likely to have long-term success (Bullis, Yovanoff, & Havel, 2004). Clearly, intervention must start at the time of birth and address the multiple risk factors that can lead to conduct problems and incarceration.

Schizophrenia. The DSM-IV-TR permits people to be classified as having **schizophrenia** if they have three attributes. A person must experience

- One of the following: highly unusual delusions; an auditory hallucination of one voice that provides commentary on the individual's characteristics, behavior, and/or feelings; auditory hallucinations with multiple voices conversing.
- At least two of the following: delusions, hallucinations, disorganized expressive language, disorganized or **catatonic behavior** (behavior that lacks typical movement, activity, and/or expression).
- Other negative symptoms characterized by a loss of contact with reality. (American Psychiatric Association, 2000)

The symptoms associated with schizophrenia must result in challenges associated with interpersonal and academic success and must be present for a period of at least 6 months. Schizophrenia occurs in phases: There are precursors associated with atypical behavior, followed by an acute phase in which symptoms are most pronounced. The person than enters a recovery phase, and, finally, a residual phase during which there are no symptoms. Most individuals with schizophrenia have multiple cycles, but some may have only one cycle (McDonell & McClellan, 2007). Schizophrenia is often treated with a combination of medication and social-skills interventions (Lehman et al., 2004).

Go to the Activities and Application section in Chapter 7 of MyEducationLab and complete Activity 1. As you watch the video and answer the accompanying questions think about what externalizing behaviors this boy has exhibited and how his teachers addressed those behaviors.

IEP Tip

Students with externalizing behaviors are subject to zero tolerance policies that allow educators to expel a student who exhibits violent behavior. However, IDEA protects them against total cessation of their education if they receive special education services under IDEA (see Chapter 1.)

Behavioral Characteristics

Students with emotional or behavioral disorders have one or both of two easily identifiable behavioral patterns: externalizing or internalizing.

Externalizing behavior. **Externalizing behaviors**—those that are persistently aggressive or involve acting-out and noncompliant behaviors—often are characteristics of conduct and oppositional defiant disorders. Students with externalizing behaviors are more likely than their peers to exhibit high-intensity but low-frequency behavioral events such as setting fires, assaulting someone, or exhibiting cruelty (Gresham, Lane, MacMillan, & Bocian, 1999). A comparison of students with emotional or behavioral disorders, learning disabilities, and intellectual disabilities concluded that students with emotional or behavioral disorders have significantly more behavioral problems than the other students, including aggression, acting out, and self-destructive behaviors (Sabornie, Cullinan, Osborne, & Brock, 2005; Sabornie, Evans, & Cullinan, 2006). Teachers have reported that students with emotional or behavioral disorders were twice as likely to fight with other students than were students with other disabilities (Wagner et al., 2006). In fact, one of the early risk factors associated with later problem behavior is property destruction (e.g., the child destroys his toys)—a type of externalizing behavior (Nelson, Stage, Duppong-Hurley, Synhorst, & Epstein, 2007).

Internalizing behavior. **Internalizing behavior** includes withdrawal, depression, anxiety, obsessions, and compulsions. Students with internalizing behavior have poorer social skills and are less socially accepted than their typical peers (Gresham et al., 1999). Students with emotional or behavioral disorders have been reported by teachers to display sadness or depression—key indicators of internalizing behavior—approximately three times more frequently than students with other types of disabilities across the school years (Wagner et al., 2006). These students often tend to blend into the background to the point that teachers forget they are in the classroom.

Because their behaviors are not as disruptive as externalizing behaviors, these students are less likely to be identified for special education services. Educators sometimes assume that internalizing problems do not pose the same or similar long-term risks as those associated with externalizing problems. However, the level of social withdrawal of second-grade students predicted their low self-regard and loneliness when they were in ninth grade (Rubin, Chen, McDougall, Bowker, & McKinnon, 1995).

Cognitive and Academic Characteristics

Students with emotional or behavioral disorders may be gifted or have an intellectual disability, but most have IQs in the low average range (Wagner, Kutash, Duchnowski, Epstein, & Sumi, 2005). In a national study of elementary/middle school students, parents reported that about 1 percent of their children with an emotional or behavioral disorder also have an intellectual disability and approximately 2.5 percent are gifted. Almost two thirds of parents indicated that their child also experienced AD/HD. A national profile of cognitive and academic characteristics of students with emotional or behavioral disorders revealed that (Wagner et al., 2005):

◆ Twenty-nine percent of the students were rated low on a self-control social skills measure, whereas only 11 percent of students with other disabilities were rated low.

◆ Slightly less than two thirds of the students had reading scores in the lowest 25 percent of all students in the school population. Forty-three percent were reported to be in the bottom 25 percent of scores in mathematics. This finding is consistent with other research documenting the presence of language disorders in a substantial number of students with emotional or behavioral disorders (Nelson, Benner, & Cheney, 2005).

◆ Twenty-two percent of elementary/middle and 38 percent of secondary students were reported to have been held back in a grade at least once, which is over twice the rate of the general population.

◆ Almost two thirds of students with emotional or behavioral disorders have expressive and/or receptive language disorders, and these disorders have been found to be stable across the full span of school years.

Language disorders pose special challenges because language is pivotal to students' academic and social success. Language ability has a significant influence on students' ability to process academic information and develop academic skills (Nelson, Benner, Neill, & Stage, 2006). Students with externalizing behavior may be more apt than other students to engage in aggressive behavior and less apt to use verbal communication to address their interpersonal problems. Students who do not comply with teachers' or others' directions after repeated requests may have receptive language impairments that interfere with their ability to conform to the behavioral expectations of their classrooms (Fujiki, Brinton, Morgan, & Hart, 1999). Clearly, students with emotional or behavioral disorders who experience language disorders benefit when they have opportunities to develop their language competence.

Determining the Causes

Although it is difficult to determine with confidence the precise causes of students' emotional or behavioral disorders, it is clear that the major general causes are biological and environmental (Gray & Hannan, 2007). One of the reasons that it is especially difficult to describe these causes is the tremendous breadth of different conditions in this category, as you learned in the previous section.

Biological Causes

Biological causes of emotional or behavioral disorders relate primarily to brain functioning and heredity (Rozenzweig, Breedlove, & Watson, 2005). For example, the brains of people with schizophrenia have some distinctive characteristics, including a lower volume of gray matter (Boos, Aleman, Cahn, Pol, & Kahn, 2007; Borgwardt et al., 2007). Additionally, the brain chemistry of children with schizophrenia appears to have a chemical imbalance in the activity of **neurotransmitters**, the chemicals that influence how the brain's neurons communicate with each other.

There are also hereditary influences, given that schizophrenia runs in families. For example, about 10 percent of people in the general population with a parent or sibling who has schizophrenia will, themselves, have that condition; by contrast, only about 1 percent of the general population who do not have a close relative with schizophrenia will have that condition (Cardno & Gottesman, 2000). An identical twin of a person with schizophrenia has a 40 percent to 65 percent chance of having the disorder. Overall, however, genetic influences appear to be at a small to moderate level for most types of emotional or behavioral disorders (Cullinan, 2007).

Genes also affect a person's temperament. **Temperament** refers to behavioral tendencies that are biologically based (Rothbart & Bates, 2006). For example, a child's temperamental tendency might be to be impulsive and to resist guidance or supervision from others. Because temperament is biologically based, it interacts with numerous environmental factors within the family, neighborhood, school, and community to produce more positive or more negative outcomes. When problems with temperament interact with environmental challenges, it becomes more likely that behaviors will become extreme and, in turn, become a trigger for an emotional or behavioral disorder. A child who is impulsive and resists others' guidance and supervision may establish behavioral patterns that in time lead to oppositional defiant behavior or even conduct disorder. The child's temperament—even if biologically based—can be negatively affected by her environment; family, neighborhood, school and community can shape her to be more or less attuned to environmental expectations.

Environmental Considerations

School factors and family factors can contribute to emotional or behavioral disorders.

School factors. Unquestionably, teachers have been effective in educating students with emotional or behavioral disabilities. That is not to say, however, that teachers are not challenged or that they always have sufficient resources to do their important work (Wagner et al., 2006):

- Although about one half to three fourths of students had a behavioral plan, no more than 40 percent received behavioral intervention or any mental health services.

- Students with emotional or behavioral disorders are twice as likely to be excluded from school as students with other disabilities (Zhang, Katsiyannis, & Herbst, 2004).

- Despite the extent of their cognitive, academic, language, and behavioral challenges, these students received nearly the same amount of whole-class and small-group instruction, peer tutoring, and presenting in front of the class as did classmates without disabilities.

- Although schools identified 14 percent to 22 percent of students as having an emotional or behavior disorder, only 9 percent of those students received an IEP.

- Only one fourth to one third of teachers believed that they possessed adequate training for teaching students with emotional or behavioral disorders or had received at least 8 hours of related in-service training.

A national study of 850 teachers of students with emotional or behavioral disorders compared their characteristics with a national sample of special education teachers (Billingsley, Fall, Williams, & Tech, 2006). Results indicated that teachers of students with emotional or behavioral disorders were the least qualified special educators. Compared to other special education teachers, they were less likely to be certified to teach in their specialty (emotional or behavioral disorders), they more frequently needed to take certification tests more than once, and they were less certified in the core academic areas in which they were teaching.

Family factors. Families of students with emotional or behavioral disorders, as well as the students themselves, experience special challenges, inlcuding the following (Wagner et al., 2005):

◆ Slightly more than one third of elementary students with emotional or behavioral disorders live in a single-parent household, compared to about one fourth of students in the general population.

◆ Approximately one fourth live in households where the head of the family is unemployed; the head of household in these families is twice as likely to not be a high school graduate than heads of households of students in the general population.

◆ Students are more likely to have an additional family member with a disability than their peers with other disabilities.

◆ Approximately twice as many elementary/middle school students with emotional or behavioral disorders live in poverty as do students in the general population.

Family considerations. Many parents of children with emotional or behavioral disorders believe that other people blame them for their child's problem. In the vignette you learned that Laura, who worked so hard to help her son, felt she was being treated like a war criminal. As you discovered in the section on causes, researchers are beginning to discover genetic and other biomedical bases for emotional or behavioral disorders. Blaming parents may give teachers an excuse to give up on a child, but placing blame does nothing to solve problems. "One of the most important things I learned going through school," Charlotte says, "is 'always remember that parents believe that their child is a direct reflection of them.' So when you say, 'That kid's a bad kid,' they're thinking, 'I'm a bad parent.' That's why I always try to be upbeat. Communication comes down to this: It's daily; it's immediate; it's positive." A strength-based perspective carries over to the family, building on what members do right and responding to their needs as well as the student's.

Within the field of mental health broadly and in special education of students with emotional or behavioral disorders specifically, experts emphasize how important it is for teachers to develop partnerships with the student's family and use a strengths-based approach to working with the student and family (Huang et al., 2005). Nevertheless, parents of students with emotional or behavioral disorders are significantly more likely to be dissatisfied with schools, teachers, and special education services than are the parents of students with other disabilities (Wagner et al., 2005). Their rates of dissatisfaction are triple that of parents of students in the general population. They also are more likely to spend time helping their child with homework five or more days a week and attending parent-teacher conferences than are parents of students with other disabilities or students in the general population. They are less likely to volunteer at school and to attend school or class events.

Although you should avoid blaming parents for their children's emotional or behavioral disorder, you also should recognize that family factors clearly play a role.

◆ Maternal depression and marital problems are associated with an increase in child adjustment problems (Nelson, Stage, Duppong-Hurley, Synhorst, & Epstein, 2007; Silk, Shaw, Skuban, Oland, & Kovacs, 2006).

◆ Parents' own family history and their emotional expression and regulation affect how children learn to express and regulate their own emotions (Morris, Silk, Steinberg, Myers, & Robinson, 2007; Saarni, Campos, Camras, & Witherington, 2006).

◆ Conflict between child's temperament and parent's temperament are related to each other (Morris et al., 2007; Nelson et al., 2007).

Interestingly, when parents rated what they perceived to be the cause of their child's emotional or behavioral disorder, African American families were less likely to see causes related to the family and to the child's relationship with others and more likely to see that the cause was related to prejudice (Yeh, Forness, Ho, McCabe, & Hough, 2004). Latino parents also tended to have this view, although the perception was not reported as strongly.

PEARSON
myeducationlab

Go to the Activities and Application section in Chapter 7 of MyEducationLab and complete Activity 2. As you read the case and answer the accompanying questions reflect on how this child's family situation has affected his behavior.

EVALUATING STUDENTS WITH EMOTIONAL OR BEHAVIORAL DISORDERS

Determining the Presence of Emotional or Behavioral Disorders

Figure 7.1 describes the standard nondiscriminatory evaluation process for students with emotional or behavioral disorders. Although various evaluation measures help teachers and other professionals identify students with emotional or behavioral disorders (Cullinan, 2007; Severson, Walker, Hope-Doolittle, Kratochwill, & Gresham, 2007), few align with or take into account IDEA's description of the five characteristics of emotional or behavioral disorders, namely, inability to learn, inability to build or maintain satisfactory relationships, inappropriate behavior, unhappiness or depression, and physical symptoms or fears.

Some researchers, however, have developed and proven the reliability and validity of a scale that specifically measures these five elements—the Scale for Assessing Emotional Disturbance (Cullinan, 2007; Epstein, Cullinan, Ryser, & Pearson, 2002). This norm-referenced scale contains five subscales, each of which corresponds directly to one of the five elements in the IDEA definition; additionally, it includes a sixth scale that focuses on social maladjustment with a particular emphasis on the student's involvement in antisocial behaviors in environments outside the school. This scale includes 45 items, each of which is a 4-point scale ranging from 3 to 0 (3 equals a severe problem; 0 equals no problem). For example, three of the items on the relationship subscale ask the evaluator (who should know the student well and can be a teacher, parent, or other adult) whether any of the following applies to the student:

◆ Does not work well in group activities

◆ Feels picked on or persecuted

◆ Avoids interacting with people

After completing the scale, the evaluator sums the subscale scores and converts them to percentiles, thereby attaining an overall indication of the student's emotional or behavioral functioning. The scale takes only about 10 minutes to complete and includes items to help identify a student's resources, competencies, and other assets (for example, family support).

Determining the Nature of Specially Designed Instruction and Services

It usually is the case that educators determine whether a student qualifies for IDEA services before they identify his areas of strengths and needs and build an IEP around strengths and needs. Although many educators tend to focus on the student's needs and be deficit-oriented, they can and should avail themselves of a tool developed specifically for identifying a student's strengths.

The Behavioral and Emotional Rating Scale–Second Edition (BERS-2) (Epstein, 1999; Epstein & Sharma, 1998; Epstein, 2004) is a companion to the Scale for Assessing Emotional Disturbance and assesses strengths within the five dimensions of interpersonal capacity, family involvement, intrapersonal competence, school functioning, and affective ability (Buckley, Ryser, Reid, & Epstein, 2006). There is a total of 52 items across these five scales. Each item is scored on a 4-point scale ranging from "not at all like the child" to "very much like the child." Teachers, parents, or other adults who know the student well can complete the Behavioral and Emotional Rating Scale in approximately 10 minutes. Research on the scale's reliability and validity shows that it has strong psychometric properties for measuring students' emotional or behavioral strengths (Epstein, Hertzog, & Reid, 2001; Epstein, Nordness, Nelson, & Hertzog, 2002; Epstein, 2004; Uhing, Mooney, & Ryser, 2005). The scale covers children ages 5 to 18 and enables the collection of assessment information from three perspectives—child (Youth Rating Scale), teacher (Teacher Rating Scale), and parent (Parent Rating Scale).

You might be wondering if a strengths-based assessment makes a real difference in terms of outcomes for students. A research study answered your question by investigating the impact of using the strengths-oriented Behavioral and Emotional Rating Scale with

Figure 7.1

Nondiscriminatory evaluation procedures for students with emotional or behavioral disabilities

Observation	**Teacher and parents observe:** **Predominantly inattentive type:** The student makes careless mistakes, has difficulty sustaining attention, doesn't seem to be listening, fails to follow through on tasks, has difficulty organizing, often loses things, is easily distracted, or is forgetful. **Predominantly hyperactive-impulsive type:** The student is fidgety, leaves his seat when expected to be seated, runs or climbs excessively or inappropriately, has difficulty playing quietly, talks excessively, blurts out answers or comments, has difficulty taking turns, or acts as if always on the go. **Combined type:** Characteristics of both are observed.
Screening	**Assessment measures:** **Classroom work products:** Work is consistently or generally poor. The student has difficulty staying on task, so his work may be incomplete or completed haphazardly. **Group Intelligence tests:** Tests may not reveal true ability because student has difficulty staying on task. **Group achievement tests:** Performance may not be a true reflection of achievement because the student has difficulty staying on task. **Medical screening:** The physician does not find a physical condition that could cause inattention or hyperactivity-impulsivity. Medication may be prescribed. **Vision and hearing screening:** Results do not explain academic difficulties.
Prereferral	**Teacher implements suggestions from school-based team:** The student still experiences frustration, inattention, or hyperactivity despite reasonable curricular and behavioral accommodations.
Referral	The child should be referred to a multidisciplinary team for a complete evaluation if prereferral intervention is not successful.
Nondiscriminatory evaluation procedures and standards	**Assessment measures:** **Psychological evaluation:** A psychiatrist or psychologist determines that the student meets DSM-IV-R criteria for AD/HD. **Individualized Intelligence tests:** The student's intelligence may range from below-average to gifted. **Individualized achievement tests:** The student's performance on achievement tests may suggest that his educational performance has been adversely affected by the condition. **Behavior rating scales:** The student scores in the significant range on measures of inattention or hyperactivity-impulsivity. **Teacher observation:** The student's educational performance has been adversely affected by the condition. The behaviors have been present in more than one setting, were first observed before age 7, and have lasted for more than 6 months. **Curriculum-based assessment:** The student may be experiencing difficulty in one or more areas of the curriculum used by the local school district because the behaviors have caused the student to miss important skills. **Direct observation:** The student exhibits inattention or hyperactivity-impulsivity during the observation.
Determination	The nondiscriminatory evaluation team determines that the student has AD/HD and needs special education and related services. The student's IEP team develops appropriate education options for the student.

youth ages 5 to 18 receiving psychotherapy services from a mental health agency (Cox, 2006). Overall, the findings suggested that in contrast to youth assessed by the traditional deficit-focused approach, youth receiving strengths-based assessment did not make significant gains in their functioning. The researchers, however, did find that youth receiving strengths-based assessment who also received services from a highly strengths-oriented therapist showed significant gains. Clearly, you should couple a strengths-based assessment with strengths-based services.

Another way to evaluate students' strengths is to talk with them about their interests, their preferences, and the experiences that give them a sense of excitement about their life. Imagine having a conversation with Matt Ackinclose, the student in the opening vignette. What questions would you ask to learn about his strengths, and how do you think he would react to a teacher who was genuinely interested in learning about what is working well for him in his life? Prominent Harvard psychiatrist Robert Coles (1989) describes the advice that one of his mentors gave to him: "Why don't you chuck the word 'interview,' call yourself a friend, call your exchanges 'conversations!'" (p. 32). Having conversations with students and listening carefully to their life stories can open the door to learning about their strengths. "Their personal narratives help us detect exceptions to their problems . . . because it is often in these exceptions that possibilities for solution construction lie and the leverage to bounce back from life's hardships can be found" (Laursen, 2000, p. 70).

IEP Tip

The IEP conference provides an excellent opportunity to make sure that students' strengths, identified through assessment, permeate the educational plan.

DESIGNING AN APPROPRIATE IEP

Partnering for Special Education and Related Services

Because students have educational *and* mental health needs, the best practice is to provide services that address all of those needs. The name of that practice is **wraparound.** Wraparound is family-driven, collaborative, individualized, culturally competent, and community- and strengths-based (Walker & Schutte, 2004). Just as the word itself suggests, school, community, mental health, and other services are "wrapped around" the student instead of being compartmentalized by field or agency.

According to the National Wraparound Initiative Advisory Group, there are 10 key principles for implementing the wraparound approach: voice and choice, team-based, natural supports, collaboration, community-based, culturally competent, individualized, strengths-based, persistence, and outcome-based (Bruns Suter, Force, & Burchard, 2004). Box 7.1, Partnership Tips, highlights the four phases of wraparound and the tasks within each phase (Quinn & Lee, 2007; Walker & Schutte, 2004).

Although a process as dynamic and individualized as the wraparound approach is extremely difficult to research, evidence does suggest that the implementation of wraparound leads to improved child and family outcomes (Burchard, Bruns, & Burchard, 2002; Bruns et al., 2005).

As effective as the wraparound approach is, some students may not remain with their families, and, instead, enter a state's foster-care system, either permanently or temporarily. In Box 7.2, you will read how the two systems—special education and foster care—often cause problems for the student and the student's family.

PEARSON
myeducationlab

Go to the Activities and Application section in Chapter 7 of MyEducationLab and complete Activity 3. As you watch the video and answer the accompanying questions consider how the teacher in this clip is engendering self-management strategies in her students.

Determining Supplementary Aids and Services

One of the supplementary aids and services that helps students have fewer negative interactions with their peers and thereby greater inclusion in school is classwide, peer-assisted self-management (Mitchem, 2001). This practice combines peer-mediated learning with self-management strategies to help students learn to manage their own behavior.

Classwide, peer-assisted self-management consists of several steps. First, students learn how to define self-management and why it is effective generally, and then explore how it might benefit them. Next, they learn the relationship among antecedents (the triggers of their behaviors), their specific behaviors, and the consequences of those behaviors.

Implementing the Four Phases of Wraparound

The wraparound process involves the individual with a mental health disorder, family members, representatives of agencies providing services, and other key people who are part of the support team coming together to engage in collaborative planning. The four major phases of wraparound and the tasks associated with each phase must be carried out in partnership in order to achieve success.

◆ Phase 1: Engagement and Team Preparation
  ✓ Orient family.
  ✓ Plan crises response.
  ✓ Identify long-term goal.
  ✓ Assemble team.
  ✓ Schedule meeting.

◆ Phase 2: Initial Plan Development
  ✓ Develop wraparound plan.
  ✓ Develop crises plan.
  ✓ Plan logistics and information dissemination.

◆ Phase 3: Implementation
  ✓ Implement plan.
  ✓ Update plan.
  ✓ Build cohesiveness and trust.
  ✓ Organize logistics.

◆ Phase 4: Transition
  ✓ Terminate services when appropriate.
  ✓ Plan and implement closure activities.
  ✓ Remain available.

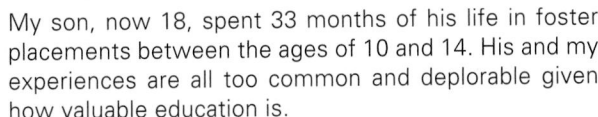

Caught 'Twixt and 'Tween

My son, now 18, spent 33 months of his life in foster placements between the ages of 10 and 14. His and my experiences are all too common and deplorable given how valuable education is.

Child welfare involvement is based on whether agencies believe a risk of abuse or neglect exists—and children with "special needs" are considered to be at higher risk than other children. Many disabilities, including emotional disturbances and learning disabilities, have biological components, so a parent of a child with a disability may also be struggling with the impact of the parent's own disability on her or his life.

For special education to work well, it must rely on the values of the disability rights movement—participation in society and participation in individual planning. Systems may not always live those values, but at least they are written into special education law. They are not written into child welfare laws, where "the best interest of the child" may disregard parent or child preferences, and "safety is paramount." Additionally, the judicial systems that oversee child welfare decisions are separate from the special education system.

Special ed parents may feel outnumbered by school personnel on IEP teams, but they still know they are the child's parents. When a child with a disability is in foster care, figuring out who the parent is gets murky. Parents, foster parents, caseworkers, and the courts all have some degree of "parental authority"—whether to share or fight over.

"Parental rights" also get shared—and possibly fought over—in the education of a foster child. My son entered foster care in the middle of an ongoing dispute with the school about whether he needed special education services. First he was moved to a different school farther away. While in foster care he attended four different schools in two states. When we could get evaluation started, he would be moved before it was completed. When eligibility was refused and we attempted due process, the school disputed my parental rights—but by then he was in yet another school system and we started over. There were so many school and foster-care records but so little education. Our lives were documented, not lived.

Now, at 18, my son has 4 of 22 credits required by his high school for a diploma. Many young adults who spent time in foster care, but especially those who needed special education, face the same future. But my son has his own kind of persistence. He has continued to show up at the schoolhouse door. Finally, too, he has found an academic subject (algebra) about which he can say, "I found out I like it and I'm good at it." Any student who can say that has found value beyond measure no matter what price has been paid. There has been educational benefit.

I've seen another kind of education benefit. In his IEP meetings, he's the decision maker. My son's school, like many schools, values student compliance over student self-advocacy. Many times students with disabilities can claim their independence only by rejecting what the school has to offer. But as the person who needs the services, my son is in a good position to focus on what he believes he needs and wants the most. He's not just a self-advocate, he's his own lobbyist.

Imagine what a young adult like that could do with a better education.

—*Sheri McMahon*
North Dakota

They also discuss how to respond appropriately and inappropriately to the triggers, and they identify positive consequences for appropriate behaviors.

Their teacher then reviews the school and classroom rules and tells the students about two important social skills: how to follow instructions and how to get the teacher's attention. Using an instruction given by the teacher as an antecedent, the students identify appropriate and inappropriate responses and consequences for those responses.

The teacher then instructs the students on how to use a rating scale of "honors, satisfactory, needs improvement, and unsatisfactory" to grade each other with respect to meeting or not meeting the classroom expectations (e.g., following the teacher's directions). After asking students each to list several students they would like to work with, the teacher pairs them and groups the pairs into two teams. Students then practice rating their partner's behavior according to a scale on a card. When cued, the students mark their own and their partner's behavior and reflect on how their ratings compare with their partner's. Perfect matches earn bonus points. At the end of class, students report their partner's totals and then tally those with the totals of other members of their team. Both teams receive praise for their efforts, and the team with the highest points for the week becomes the winning team.

The success of classwide, peer-assisted treatment demonstrates how important it is for teachers to plan carefully how they will address their students' problem behavior. These behaviors usually require interventions that have multiple components. In this case those components were peer tutoring and self-management strategies. Tournaki and Criscitiello (2003) found that **reverse-role tutoring**—that is, using students with emotional or behavioral disorders as tutors for nondisabled peers—not only resulted in benefits for the nondisabled peers but also improved the behavior and writing skills of the tutors. Similarly, Kamps, Kravits, Rauch, Kamps, and Chung (2000) combined social-skills training, peer tutoring, and classroom-management techniques to improve outcomes for youth with emotional or behavioral disorders. Whatever the actual intervention, it is critical that planning teams, such as those involved in wraparound, consider a wide array of supplementary aids and services and instructional strategies.

Planning for Universal Design for Learning

Modifications are almost always necessary to make it possible for students with emotional or behavioral disorders to demonstrate mastery (Gunter, Denny, & Venn, 2000). Allowing your students to use a computer with word processing software is one such modification; it can minimize their frustration by making it easier for them to revise their work and produce clean, legible products (Hasselbring & Glaser, 2000). Indeed, students who use standard word processing software programs may be more willing to edit and correct their work than if they have to hand-write original and revised products. Moreover, many affordable word processing programs include features such as word prediction and spelling correction that enable students who are struggling writers to identify the areas they need to improve. Box 7.3 provides information about word processing programs that might benefit not only your students with emotional or behavioral disabilities but also students with other disabilities.

Planning for Other Educational Needs

Dropping out of school will almost always create, not solve, students' problems. A 2002 report from the U.S. Department of Education determined that more than half of students served under the category of emotional disturbance dropped out of school before graduating, and only 41.9 percent graduated. Some students aged out of school; that is, they did not drop out, but neither did they earn enough credits to graduate with a diploma.

What are the consequences of dropping out? Two years after they dropped out, only 36 percent to 42 percent of all dropout students were employed, compared to 53 percent to 63 percent of their peers with emotional or behavioral disorders who graduated (Sitling-

Talking Word Processors: Using Technology to Improve Writing Performance

Schools rely heavily on written student products as a way to evaluate student progress. However, many students with disabilities, including those with emotional or behavioral disabilities, have barely legible handwriting or cannot write at all. In addition, students often have difficulty with spelling and sentence structure. There are a number of software and assistive technology products that enable students with disabilities to use a computer to improve their writing performance.

The simplest such modifications involve changes to how students input information on a computer. Students with emotional or behavioral disorders may benefit from a keyboard on which the letters are arranged alphabetically. The typical keyboard is called a QWERTY layout (those are the first six letters on the top row from the left). The alphabetically arranged keyboard is called, logically, the ABCDEF layout!

Of more potential benefit to students with emotional or behavioral disorders may be word processing software programs that make writing easier or more efficient. Perhaps the most common modified word processing program is the "talk-ing word processor. " These software programs are similar to typical word processing packages, except that as students type in words, the words are "read" back to them. In addition to this feature, various software programs incorporate other features that make writing more effective for students with disabilities. Like common word processing packages, most of the available programs include a spell-checking capacity. Some link the synthesized voice capacity to spell checking and can read out suggestions for spelling or sentence structure from which students can choose. Some packages have word prediction capacity. When a student types in the start of a word but can't remember the rest, the word prediction capacity makes suggestions for finishing the word.

Commercially available talking word processors include Write:Outloud, available from Don Johnstone, Inc. (http://www.donjohnstone.com/products/write_outloud/index.html.); and Aspire READER from CAST (http://cast.org/products/ereader/index.html).

■ ■ ■

ton & Neubert, 2004). These data give teachers a strong message: Try to prevent your students from dropping out.

Students with emotional or behavioral disorders leave school for many reasons, generally because they are not interested in what is being taught and feel negative about school in general (Scanlon & Mellard, 2002). According to a study by the Oregon Department of Education (Martin, Tobin, & Sugai, 2002, p. 11), there are 10 specific reasons why students drop out:

1. Insufficient credits to graduate
2. Lack of parental support for education
3. Problematic home lives
4. Student work schedule (greater than 15 hours per week)
5. Substance abuse
6. Frequent discipline problems and referrals
7. Student perceptions that he or she does not "fit in"
8. Student pregnancy or care for a small child
9. Peer pressure to leave school
10. Frequent moves between schools (attending three or more high schools)

Several studies have linked poverty to school failure (Christle, Jolivette, & Nelson, 2007). Reschly and Christenson (2006) identified student engagement—defined as a student's involvement in curricular and extracurricular activities in the school and feelings of belonging within the school—as a significant predictor of whether students with learning and emotional or behavioral disabilities would drop out of or remain in school.

Several universal and student-based interventions can reduce dropout rates (Martin et al., 2002). Universal interventions involve district- or campuswide interventions, the wraparound process, and schoolwide positive behavior support (discussed in Chapter 11). They also include the following interventions (Martin et al., 2002):

◆ *Establish a student advisory program* linking students to an adult mentor in the school.

◆ *Establish and involve students in extracurricular activities,* including sports, music, vocational activities, and other extracurriculars.

◆ *Systematically monitor risk factors associated with dropout,* tracking student attendance, tardiness, grades, and referrals for discipline.

◆ *Develop "schools within schools"* or smaller units.

◆ *Establish school-to-work programs,* demonstrating how school relates to work.

◆ *Engage in community-based learning,* making school more relevant and learning more practical.

◆ *Use the "check and connect" strategy,* linking an adult monitor with a student to track risk factors and work with the student and family to reduce them.

◆ *Provide vocational education,* attempting to forestall poor employment outcomes.

Combining the "check and connect" strategy with self-management and problem-solving skills engages students in school and reduces the chance that they will drop out (Sinclair, Christenson, & Thurlow, 2005). So do vocational education (Corbett, Sanders, Clark, & Blank, 2002), involvement in extracurricular activities (Mahoney, 2000), and instruction in conflict-resolution skills (Hunt et al., 2002).

As we have pointed out, a student's ethnicity and family make a difference in whether she is classified as having an emotional or behavioral disorder and how you work with the student's family as a partner. Being an effective partner with families from diverse backgrounds requires you to be culturally competent, as you learned in Chapter 3.

USING EFFECTIVE INSTRUCTIONAL STRATEGIES

Early Childhood Students: Multicomponent Interventions to Prevent Conduct Disorders

As early as first grade, a student's learning problems often predict depression; likewise, aggression predicts "antisocial behavior, criminality, and early substance abuse" (Ialongo, Poduska, Werthamer, & Sheppard, 2001, p. 147). That is why early intervention to prevent or counteract these challenges is essential. Complex behavioral problems require complex solutions. Two rules of thumb are particularly important: Begin early, and use all the tools available in your toolbox. Two models of early intervention illustrate this approach.

Researchers at Johns Hopkins University have created strategies to intervene against poor academic achievement and aggressive and shy behavior (Ialongo et al., 2001). Referred to as the **classroom-centered intervention,** the first intervention combined mastery learning and a good-behavior game (which we describe later in this section). The second strategy involved a family-school partnership intervention to improve parent-teacher communication and parents' behavior management strategies. Three first-grade classes in each of nine schools participated. One class received classroom-centered intervention, the second received the family-school partnership intervention, and the third received no special intervention.

The classroom-centered, mastery-learning intervention program enhanced the curriculum, applied specific behavior management strategies, and provided additional supports for students who were not performing adequately. The enhanced curriculum consisted of critical thinking, composition, listening, and comprehension skills. The behavior management strategies included once-weekly class meetings to develop social problem-solving skills and opportunities to play the good-behavior game. The class was divided into three groups, points were given to each group for precisely defined appropriate behavior, and points were taken away when a member of the group was shy or aggressive. Students could exchange points for tangible rewards that gradually were replaced by social reinforcers.

In the family-school partnership intervention, teachers and other school staff received training on communicating with parents. The parents themselves received weekly home-learning and communication activities from teachers and behavior management training from a school psychologist or social worker who was teamed with the first-grade teacher. Each school also provided a voicemail system to allow parents to communicate easily with school personnel.

The Johns Hopkins researchers learned that by the end of sixth grade, students in the classroom-centered intervention, when compared to students who received no intervention, were significantly less likely to receive a diagnosis of conduct disorder, to have been suspended, or to need or appear to need mental health intervention.

Many classroom-based interventions occur within the context of broader, campuswide interventions. Among them is schoolwide positive behavior support (McIntosh, Chard, Boland, & Horner, 2006), an approach that applies the principles of positive behavior support to all students, not just those with disabilities.

Another example of an effective multicomponent intervention to increase a young child's coping skills combined student-directed learning strategies (about which you will learn more in Chapter 10), social stories (discussed in Chapter 11), and an "apron storyboard" (an apron the student could wear with large pockets full of large cutouts that could be used to tell the story in the social story) (Haggerty, Black, & Smith, 2005). The student involved in this intervention showed reduced levels of frustration after the intervention.

IEP Tip

Complex behaviors and problems often require complex solutions. It's likely no single intervention will be sufficient for students with emotional or behavioral disorders, so a student's IEP team always should consider multi-component interventions.

Elementary and Middle School Students: Service Learning

Increasingly, students in public schools are engaging in service learning activities. **Service learning** refers to instructional activities that integrate teaching activities with community service. Service learning is usually designed to teach civic responsibility, to reinforce lessons learned in the classroom in the context of real life, and to improve communities. Students who participate in service learning show improved school attendance, greater self-esteem, enhanced leadership and communication skills, and increased awareness of community and governmental issues. They also report having greater social responsibility, career awareness, and acceptance of cultural diversity (Dymond, Renzablia, & Chun, 2007). For example, students can engage in service learning by participating in a community cleanup. That activity teaches them about individual responsibility for other members of their community; it also teaches other community members that students with emotional or behavioral disorders can contribute to the community and may well be able to do so at any number of jobs within the community.

Community clean-up events may be few and far between. There are, however, rather stable opportunities for community service learning. For example, Frey (2003) documented middle school students with emotional or behavioral disorders doing service activities at a senior citizens' apartment complex near their school. The service-learning activities required the students to beautify the complex's grounds. Students met with residents to identify their preferences,

Service learning helps students with emotional or behavioral disorders develop positive character traits.

measured the area for landscaping needs, developed architectural and landscaping plans, met with a local nursery owner to discuss cost and delivery issues, made decisions about types of shrubs and bushes based on cost and need, developed a budget, purchased the materials, and landscaped the grounds.

Did you notice a lot of measuring, calculating, developing, and deciding going on there? That's part of the point of service learning: Students learn skills they need! The students who participated in the project had increased attendance at school and were more positive about school as a result of being involved in the project.

Matt Ackinclose is fortunate to participate in a Work to Life program developed by the Pickaway-Ross Career and Technology Center. Among other things, the service learning incorporated into this program helps prepare students for good citizenship. Currently, Matt is writing to a soldier to thank him for serving our country. Charlotte and Matt are baking cookies to send with the letter. In Box 7.4, we describe how a program

---

INTO PRACTICE   Box 7.4

Service Learning for Students with Emotional and Behavioral Disorders

How can students with emotional or behavioral disorders develop friendships with peers; learn important character, academic, and prevocational skills; establish resilience-building relationships with older teens and adults in their communities; and develop a sense of significance, purpose, and accomplishment?

In Nashua, New Hampshire, a partnership among faculty and students at Riviera College and local elementary and secondary schools found the answer through the college's Service-Learning Opportunities (SO) Prepared for Citizenship program. Together, they:

- Identified their students' citizenship needs, such as reducing the incidents of cursing, bullying, and fighting; increasing understanding and compassion; and offering leadership training, team building, tolerance, and civic responsibility opportunities.

- Created a planning, implementation, and assessment team consisting of students and faculty from the college and the elementary and secondary schools.

- Awarded curriculum credits to the college students who helped coordinate the curriculum at the college and in the schools.

- Developed a curriculum that taught the traits of respect and appreciation for diversity, caring and compassion, trustworthiness, and fairness and justice.

- Implemented the curriculum by having a college student, a high school student, and an elementary school student become co-teachers at the college and in the schools.

- Participated in community activities, such as food drives, that put into practice the classroom-based curriculum.

- Regularly assessed what students were learning and doing in response to the curriculum.

- Held an awards ceremony that featured all of the participating students, their faculty, and community members.

The strategies that SO Prepared for Citizenship used apply to nearly every other kind of partnership activity that educators may want to undertake:

- Identify a common interest (in SO's case, student citizenship training).

- Identify others with the same interest, and recruit those stakeholders into partnership.

- Identify the goals and strategies to respond to the interest.

- Develop a plan for carrying out the goals and strategies.

- Implement the plan.

- Assess its effectiveness and incorporate the feedback into the action plans.

- Celebrate its success.

myeducationlab

Go to the Activities and Application section in Chapter 7 of MyEducationLab and complete Activity 5. As you examine the cases, think about how you might incorporate a service learning project on a school level that would be beneficial for multiple-age students with multiple issues.

Source: Based on information from Muscott, H. (2001). Fostering learning, fun, and friendship among students with emotional and behavioral disorders and their peers: The SO Prepared for Citizenship program. *Beyond Behavior, 10*(3) 36–47.

called SO Prepared for Citizenship benefits students with emotional or behavioral disorders.

Secondary and Transition Students: Conflict Resolution

Unfortunately, conflict between youth with emotional or behavioral disorders and peers, family members, educators, and other authority figures is all too common. In Chapter 11, you will learn more about using positive behavior support (PBS) by changing the environmental circumstances that contribute to problem behavior. PBS is not the only effective approach for students in secondary programs. When teachers instruct their students how to resolve conflicts, they reduce their students' inappropriate behaviors. The teachers will train their students to use three skills for resolving conflicts in a positive way: effective communication, anger management, and taking another's perspective (Johns, Crowley, & Guetzloe, 2005). The benefits of that instruction include "(a) providing students with a framework for resolving conflicts, (b) giving students an opportunity to assume responsibility for their behavior, (c) lowering teacher stress by reducing the number of student conflicts they have to handle, (d) increasing instructional time, and (e) helping students understand how cultural diversity can affect interpersonal communication and human interactions" (Daunic Smith, Robinson, Miller, & Landry, 2000, p. 95).

Conflict resolution skills can help students resolve problems with their peers.

Problem solving and successful decision making are important conflict-resolution skills (Bullock & Foegen, 2002), especially because these strategies can help students avoid backing down or acting out when confronting problems. Teachers should help their students identify the nature of the problem they face, brainstorm and evaluate the pros and cons of various solutions, determine which of several solutions seems likely to be most effective to resolve the problem, and make a plan to carry out that solution. In addition, a teacher should instruct students in negotiation skills that help them find solutions benefiting everyone and allowing others to save face so that they will not oppose the solution.

There are several ways for teachers to use conflict-resolution training to reduce conflicts on a schoolwide level (Nelson, Martella, & Marchand-Martella, 2002). For example, they can offer high school students who previously would have been suspended for violent behavior the option to enroll in a conflict-resolution program that teaches social problem-solving skills, negotiation skills, and anger-management skills. Students who were involved with one particular conflict-resolution training program were four times less likely to receive another suspension for violent behavior than were students who were not involved in the training (Breunlin, Cimmarusti, Bryant-Edwards, & Hetherington, 2002). Box 7.5 provides tips about how to teach conflict-resolution skills.

IEP Tip

If a student is prone to conflict, the IEP team should be sure to teach the student social problem-solving skills, negotiation skills, and anger-management skills.

INCLUDING STUDENTS WITH EMOTIONAL OR BEHAVIORAL DISORDERS

Figure 7.2 sets out the percentage of students with emotional or behavioral disorders in each of several educational placements. Note especially that, compared to all other students with disabilities, students with emotional or behavioral disorders are three times more likely to be educated in residential settings, hospitals, or homes (U.S. Department

Strategies for Teaching Conflict Resolution

Several strategies are helpful in resolving conflicts. After reviewing the research literature to identify strategies educators often use to teach conflict resolution, Bullock and Feogen (2002) found these strategies to be effective:

Cooperative Learning. Cooperative learning involves teaching students in small groups in which they focus, together, on a common learning task or activity (see Chapter 13). The benefits with regard to teaching conflict resolution are obvious: Students must learn how to communicate with one another, negotiate, and work collaboratively. You can teach conflict resolution by using cooperative learning strategies as you teach any content area.

Structured Controversy. The Structured (or Cooperative) Controversy strategy is a small-group, debate-like process in which students learn to explore and present positions on both sides of a controversial topic or issue (D'Eon, Proctor, & Reeder, 2007). Teachers assign a topic that has clear opposing views and, unlike in typical debate formats, where students are assigned (or choose) one side of that topic, within the Structured Controversy process, students study and present information on all the opposing views. Students learn that there are, as the old saying goes, two sides to every story; they learn perspective-taking skills as well as skills related to persuasion.

Mediation. Mediation strategies teach students conflict resolution through the use of a neutral party. Johns and colleagues (2005) suggest nine steps to implement a mediation session:

1. Bring together the two students who have a conflict. Have them sit at a table facing one another, with you or another mediator at the head of the table. It can often be useful to have another adult or, even better, a student serve as a mediator.
2. Open the session by introducing yourself (or having the mediator introduce herself) and having the participating students similarly introduce themselves.
3. Emphasize the confidentiality of the session and ensure that participants understand that outcomes must be discussed.
4. Emphasize active listening and turn taking.
5. Characterize the process as a fact-finding process, getting information from both sides.
6. Assist students to state issues in neutral terms by providing summaries and clarifications.
7. Once both sides have been stated and summarized, identify and emphasize common interests that will benefit from a solution to the conflict and ask participants to generate potential solutions.
8. Help students expand, clarify, and decide upon an agreeable resolution.
9. Write up the agreed-upon resolution and ask each student to sign it.

Negotiation. Negotiation is an integral part of virtually any conflict resolution process. It can be taught as a primary strategy, using these approaches:

1. *It's about being prepared.* To negotiate successfully, both students have to know what they want out of a negotiation and also what others might want, so they have to think through not only their interests, but the interests of others.
2. *It's about timing.* Students need to understand that there are good times to bring up a topic and bad times to do so. Negotiations occur in the context of conversations, so learning and applying some basic conversational skills—such as not interrupting someone else, staying on topic, and listening—are important to the negotiation process.
3. *It's about persuasion, not aggression.* Students should learn that to achieve their goal, they'll need, in part, to convince someone else to change their mind and give up some of their own goal. Bullying and aggressive behaviors simply never achieve that outcome. Instead, students should learn the skills of persuasion. First, teach students how to let people know they understand what the other person is saying, often by restating what that person has said. Second, teach students to emphasize how the other person could achieve the same goal in a different way, one that is of course more closely aligned with their own goal! Third, teach students to calmly and systematically tell others of the advantages to their plan or idea.
4. *It's about compromise.* Finally, students should learn that they may be more successful achieving their ultimate goal if they settle for incremental steps toward that goal instead of expecting it to be fully achieved all at once.

Group Problem Solving. Problem-solving is a critical strategy for resolving conflicts. There are three steps for teaching problem-solving:

1. Teach students to identify and communicate the problem to be solved.
2. Teach students to generate potential solutions to the problem.
3. Teach students to select one solution that best fits the problem.

Problem-solving instruction can and should occur in the context of real world problems that students might face.

myeducationlab

Go to the Building Teaching Skills and Dispositions section in Chapter 7 of MyEducationLab and complete the activities. As you watch the video, think about how you could incorporate social skills instruction into these conflict resolution strategies.

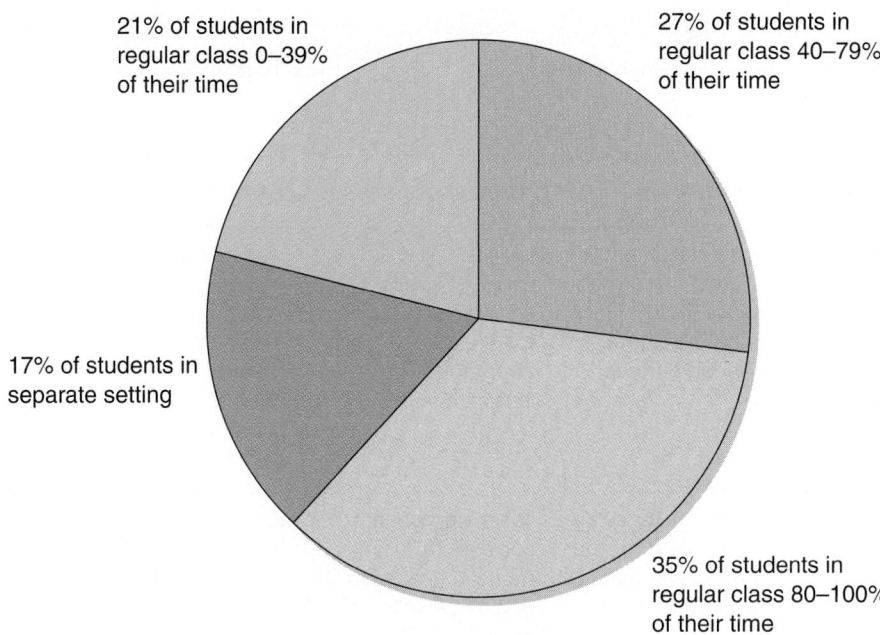

21% of students in regular class 0–39% of their time

27% of students in regular class 40–79% of their time

17% of students in separate setting

35% of students in regular class 80–100% of their time

Figure 7.2 Percentage of students with emotional or behavioral disorders in educational placement

of Education, 1998). Nevertheless, inclusion is entirely feasible, consistent with IDEA, as Box 7.6 shows.

More than 134,000 teenagers are in juvenile correctional facilities (Sickmund, 2002). It is estimated that 30 percent to 70 percent of those youth have disabilities (Leone, Meisel, & Drakeford, 2002). Typically, these teenagers are boys from a culturally and linguistically diverse background, are members of families who are poor, and have substantial learning and/or behavior problems (Leone et al., 2002). Although incarcerated youth have been reported to have academic achievement one to several years below grade level, the extent of their special education services in correctional facilities tends to be about two thirds less than that offered in public schools (Foley, 2001).

ASSESSING STUDENTS' PROGRESS

Measuring Students' Progress

Progress in the General Curriculum

In "mastery learning" or "mastery training" instruction, teachers frequently assess their students' mastery of content, determining whether it is timely to move to the next concept or activity. They offer more instruction to those students who do not show mastery, and then they assess these students again. In all of this, teachers intend to make it possible for all of their students to master the content, even if they do so at different rates. Mastery training has been used with students with disabilities, including those with emotional or behavioral disabilities (Lee, Belfiore, & Toro-Zambrana, 2001) and is a useful means of ensuring student progress in the general curriculum. To monitor students' progress toward mastery, you will (King-Sears & Mooney, 2004):

◆ *Ask questions of the whole class.* Ask all of the students in the class to indicate what they think the correct answer is. Ask them to raise their hands to answer a question. Some students will feel intimidated and will not participate. But technology-based response systems allow greater anonymity. There, students have remote-control devices and respond by pressing a button to represent a particular

| Box 7.6 | INCLUSION TIPS |

	What You Might See	*What You Might Be Tempted to Do*	*Alternate Responses*	*Ways to Include Peers in the Process*
Behavior	The student refuses to follow directions and uses inappropriate language.	Respond in anger and send her out of the classroom. Place her in time-out for extended periods.	Include her in conflict-resolution instruction and seek to capitalize on her strengths in this instruction.	Involve classmates in the conflict-resolution instruction so that all students have an opportunity to work closely and constructively with each other.
Social interactions	She fights with other students and is always on the defensive.	Seat her as far away as possible from the students with whom she is fighting.	Teach appropriate social skills, using modeling, videos, and social skills programs.	Pair her with different students who can model and help her practice social skills and responses.
Educational performance	She is rarely on task and appears to have an inability to learn.	Give poor grades and require her to remain after school until all her work is done.	Based on her interests, create the opportunity to engage in service learning that will enable her to make contributions to others.	Develop a buddy system in implementing service learning so that students work together collaboratively.
Classroom attitudes	She is sad all the time and does not speak or interact with others.	Discipline her for nonparticipation and instruct her to cheer up.	Recognize the warning signs of depression. Partner with the school counselor to get professional help.	Encourage all students to affirm each others' strengths by giving positive feedback to each other.

Go to the Activities and Application section in Chapter 7 of MyEducationLab and complete Activity 6. As you watch the video reflect on how the think-pair-share strategy is beneficial for all students in this classroom.

answer. The responses, when presented on the screen through the software that accompanies the program, are anonymous so far as all other students are concerned, but the teacher obtains data on the response from each student.

◆ *Use a cooperative learning strategy such as "think-pair-share"* (King-Sears & Mooney, 2004, p. 249). Create small groups of students, ask each group to *think* about a question, *pair* the student with a disability with a peer in the group, and ask each of them to *share* their responses to your question. Be sure that at least one student has the correct responses. You will learn more about how students can teach each other—cooperative learning—in Chapter 13.

Progress in Addressing Other Educational Needs

Students with emotional or behavioral disorders usually need to learn social skills, and teachers need to know how to chart their students' progress in learning those skills. A commonly used social skills rating scale, validated for use by students with emotional or behavioral disorders, is the Social Skills Rating System (Gresham & Elliott, 1990; Wright & Torrey, 2001). It has three rating forms (teacher, parent, and student) and two scales (the Social Skills Scale and the Problem Behaviors Scale) that allow students to report both the frequency and importance of the skill and how well they are learning it.

In addition to this commercially available measure, Algozzine, Serna, and Patton (2001) identified three strategies for tracking students' progress in which teachers can use sociometric ratings for rankings. They can ask their students to identify classmates with whom they play and would like to play; tally the number of times any particular student is identified; and then determine who is popular and who is not, based on frequency counts of peer nominations. This is a measure of student acceptance by class members, so if students with emotional or behavioral disorders are not frequently identified by peers, the teacher can infer that those students may need instruction in social skills. By extension, a teacher can also use the entire process to track, over time, how social skills instruction affects students' acceptance by their peers.

Making Accommodations for Assessment

As you have read, students with emotional or behavioral disorders are more likely than other students with disabilities to be served in alternative schools. Does this mean that those schools are no longer accountable for these students' performance? Certainly not.

Gagnon and McLaughlin (2004) conducted a survey of private and public day treatment and residential schools for elementary school students with emotional or behavioral disorders to evaluate whether the students were being given the opportunity to progress in the general curriculum and to participate in district accountability systems. The researchers also investigated whether these alternative schools offered accommodations in the state and district assessments. Nearly 20 percent of the schools had no accommodation policy. Of the 80 percent that did have such a policy, most simply adopted the school district's policy. The results of this research are disappointing. Students need those opportunities because when they return to their neighborhood schools, they will be behind other students if they have not been provided with instruction in the same curriculum.

State education agencies increasingly take into account students' "emotional anxiety" when determining whether to provide accommodations in statewide assessments (Thurlow, Lazarus, Thompson, & Robey, 2002). Students with emotional or behavioral disorders may have more difficulties completing tests than do other students because of their heightened anxiety problems. Accommodations to address this difference include extended time to take the tests, individual administration of the tests, and testing with breaks.

VALUES AND OUTCOMES

Let's revisit Matthew Ackinclose and determine what values and outcomes are part of his education.

◆ It is not unreasonable to have great expectations for Matt. He is participating in the general curriculum even as he also receives special support outside that environment.

◆ It is one thing to be the boy who never won a prize for contributing to his school, but it is quite another to be the boy who won the principal's Pride Award for his positive contributions to his school.

- Matt defies a stereotype that people with emotional or behavioral disorders cannot "recover"—Matt himself is resilient and determined, and those traits are great strengths for him now and later.
- By asking Matt why he acts in certain ways, his teacher Rebecca has taught him to consider his strengths and to make choices based on them.
- Matt's use of medication and his teachers' focus on his strengths help Matt have good relationships with his peers; the principal's Pride Award certainly testifies to his good relations with his peers and teachers.
- It seems clear that Matt is smart enough to get and hold a job; he will be regarded as, and will regard himself as, a full citizen when his education leads to his economic self-sufficiency.

WHAT DO YOU THINK?

1. Remembering the three women in Matt's life (his mother Laura, his social worker Rebecca, and his special education teacher Charlotte), to what degree has Matt's recovery depended on Laura's determination to avoid a residential treatment center for him, on Rebecca's strengths-based approach, or on Charlotte's diligent use of positive communication to build trust with Matt?

2. Recall that Charlotte has said "you can be trained" to work with students with emotional or behavioral disorders, but that she added, "You have to want to do this job." Do you believe that the training is more, less, or equally important as the desire to be an effective special educator?

3. Does it seem to you that Matt has fully recovered—after all, he now attends and is successful in school and takes far fewer medicines than he used to—or do you sense that Matt will almost always need some kind of support to be successful as a student and then as an adult?

ADDRESSING THE STANDARDS: THE VALUES CONNECTION

The following CEC Knowledge and Skill Standards: Common Core and Values are addressed in this chapter through the content and concepts we discuss.

CEC Knowledge and Skill Standards: Common Core	Values/Standards Connection
CEC Knowledge and Skill Standard II. Development of Characteristics and Learners	When you learn the characteristics of students with emotional or behavioral disorders, you are applying CEC Standard 2 Development and Characteristics of Learners.
CC2K1 Typical and atypical human growth and development.	
CC2K2 Educational implications of characteristics of various exceptionalities.	When you focus on students' strengths and positive contributions you enable them to have great expectations for themselves—with their families, in school, and in the community.
CC2K3 Characteristics and effects of the cultural and environmental milieu of the individual with exceptional learning needs and the family.	
CC2K4 Family systems and the role of families in supporting development.	
CC2K5 Similarities and differences of individuals with and without exceptional learning needs.	
CC2K7 Effects of various medications on individuals with exceptional learning needs.	

CEC Knowledge and Skill Standards: Common Core		Values/Standards Connection
CEC Knowledge and Skill Standard III. **Individual Learning Differences**		Understanding the various influences that affect students with emotional or behavioral disorders applies to CEC Standard 3, Individual Learning Differences.
CC3K1	Effects an exceptional condition(s) can have on an individual's life.	
CC3K2	Impact of learner's academic and social abilities, attitudes, interests, and values on instruction and career development.	
CEC Knowledge and Skill Standard V. **Learning Environments and Social Interactions**		You can support students by helping them to develop *relationships*, make friends, and minimize the stigma they might experience from peers without disabilities.
CC5K5	Social skills needed for educational and other environments.	
CC5K6	Strategies for crisis prevention and intervention.	
CC5S2	Identify realistic expectations for personal and social behavior in various settings.	
CC5S3	Identify supports needed for integration into various program placements.	
CC5S4	Design learning environments that encourage active participation in individual and group settings.	
CC5S5	Modify the learning environment to manage behaviors.	
CC5S6	Use performance data and information from all stakeholders to make or suggest modifications in learning environments.	
CC5S10	Use effective and varied behavior management strategies.	
CC5S11	Use the least intensive behavior management strategy consistent with the needs of the individual with exceptional learning needs.	
CEC Knowledge and Skill Standard VII. **Instructional Planning**		The wraparound process focuses on your students' *strengths* and abilities. It also ensures that the students and their family members have an opportunity to *make choices* about their education and related services.
CC7S3	Involve the individual and family in setting instructional goals and monitoring progress.	
CC7S7	Integrate affective, social, and life skills with academic curricula.	

continued

CEC Knowledge and Skill Standards: Common Core	Values/Standards Connection
CEC Knowledge and Skill Standard VIII. Assessment CC8K3 — Screening, prereferral, referral, and classification procedures. CC8S2 — Administer nonbiased formal and informal assessments. CC8S6 — Use assessment information in making eligibility, program, and placement decisions for individuals with exceptional learning needs, including those from culturally and/or linguistically diverse backgrounds. CC8S8 — Evaluate instruction and monitor progress of individuals with exceptional learning needs.	Strengths-based assessment ensures that you will build on your student's *strengths* in evaluating them and then providing an appropriate education.
CEC Knowledge and Skill Standard IX. Professional and Ethical Practice CC9S2 — Uphold high standards of competence and integrity and exercise sound judgment in the practice of the professional. CC9S3 — Act ethically in advocating for appropriate services. CC9S5 — Demonstrate commitment to developing the highest education and quality-of-life potential of individuals with exceptional learning needs.	Using research-validated teaching methods with children with emotional or behavior disorders is an application of CEC Standard 9, Professional and Ethical Practice. If your students are to achieve *full citizenship*, they must stay in school. Do all you can to prevent them from dropping out. Service learning allows your students to contribute to others in their community and, at the same time, lets community members see that students with disabilities make *positive contributions* to that community.
CEC Knowledge and Skill Standard X. Collaboration CC10K3 — Concerns of families of individuals with exceptional learning needs and strategies to help address these concerns. CC10S3 — Foster respectful and beneficial relationships between families and professionals.	Participating in the wraparound process is an example of applying CEC Standard 10, Collaboration. The wraparound process focuses on your students' *strengths* and abilities. It also ensures that the students and their family members have an opportunity to *make choices* about their education and related services.

Source: From CEC Knowledge and Skill Standards: Common Core and Values. Copyright by The Council for Exceptional Children. Reprinted with permission.

SUMMARY

Identifying Students with Emotional or Behavioral Disorders

◆ Students with emotional or behavioral disorders manifest emotional, behavioral, social, and/or academic characteristics that are chronic and severe and adversely affect their educational performance.

◆ Students may exhibit emotional characteristics related to anxiety disorder, mood disorder, oppositional defiant disorder, conduct disorder, and/or schizophrenia.

◆ Two broad categories of behavioral characteristics include externalizing (aggressive, acting-out, noncompliant) behaviors and internalizing (withdrawn, depressed, anxious, obsessive, compulsive) behaviors.

◆ Students with emotional or behavioral disorders typically have IQs in the normal range, but they have significant challenges related to academic achievement and social skills.

- Approximately 7 percent of all students with disabilities have emotional or behavioral disabilities, although there are estimates that the percentage is much larger than that.
- Emotional or behavioral disorders are caused by interactions between biological (for example, brain disorders and genetics) and environmental factors (for example, stressful living conditions and child maltreatment).

Evaluating Students with Emotional or Behavioral Disorders

- The Scale for Assessing Emotional Disturbance is a norm-referenced scale tied directly to the five elements of the IDEA definition; it adds the element of social maladjustment.
- The Behavioral and Emotional Rating Scale–Second Edition, a norm-referenced tool with strong psychometric properties, is designed to identify students' strengths and needs as the basis for educational planning.

Designing an Appropriate IEP

- The wraparound planning model is a process linking school, community, and mental health services to provide a family-driven, collaborative, individualized, culturally competent, and strengths-based planning approach.
- Complex problems require thoughtful planning and multicomponent interventions, such as the classwide, peer-assisted, self-management approach described in the chapter.
- An important universal design feature for all students, including those with emotional or behavioral disorders, involves modifications to the ways in which students respond to the curriculum content and provide evidence of their knowledge, either orally or through multimedia presentations.
- It is important to implement multiple dropout prevention strategies, such as linking youth with a mentor or involving them in extracurricular activities.

Using Effective Instructional Strategies

- Two rules of thumb need to be in place for preventing conduct disorders: Begin early, and use all the tools available.
- Service-learning strategies provide a means for students with emotional or behavioral disorders both to learn important skills and to contribute to their communities.
- Students with emotional or behavioral disorders need to acquire conflict-resolution skills, including negotiation skills, compromising, problem solving, and decision making, if they are to succeed as adults.

Including Students with Emotional or Behavioral Disorders

- Students with emotional or behavioral disorders have one of the lowest rates of inclusion in general education classrooms.
- Approximately three times as many students with emotional or behavioral disorders as all other students with disabilities are served in residential settings, hospitals, or homes.

Assessing Students' Progress

- Mastery evaluation takes a different approach to evaluation and is intended to provide information on student progress that teachers can use to modify instruction.
- Interventions to promote social skills are important for students with emotional or behavioral disorders. Teachers can use a commercially available scale to measure progress or can use sociometric ratings techniques.
- Students with emotional or behavioral disorders need access to the general curriculum. A critical component of that is the provision of accommodations, such as extended time, individual administration, and testing with breaks.

PEARSON
myeducationlab

Now go to MyEducationLab at www.myeducationlab.com and take the Self-Assessment to gauge your initial comprehension of chapter content. Once you have taken the Self-Assessment, use your individualized Study Plan for Chapter 7 to enhance your understanding of the concepts dicussed in the chapter.

8

Understanding Students with Attention-Deficit/ Hyperactivity Disorder

◆ WHO IS KELSEY BLANKENSHIP?

Imagine being 9 years old and acting in front of thousands of people. Kelsey Blankenship, a fourth grader from rural Ohio, performed twice to an audience of 6,000 in a Cincinnati competition and received a superior rating for both performances.

Superior acting abilities are remarkable for any child, but they are even more so for Kelsey. These performances represent a dramatic change in her because she has attention-deficit/hyperactivity disorder (AD/HD). According to her grandmother, Yvonne, a few years ago Kelsey would have "been all over the church" instead of learning her lines. Kelsey's second-grade teacher, Barb Tootle, remembers those days well:

> You would always know where Kelsey was: There would always be
> some commotion. I would
> have students saying, "Kelsey
> did this to me; Kelsey did
> that to me." Kelsey never
> walked slowly through the
> classroom. It was more like
> pushing her way through.
> She would raise her hand,
> but she wouldn't have
> anything to say or would
> make something up.

But these days, Kelsey is a different child. Barb describes the change that occurred during second grade:

> Kelsey always came in with a smile.
> She would sharpen her pencil, hand in
> her homework, and do an activity that
> was on the board. She kept her hands
> to herself, not hitting people or taking

their things, and she would pay attention. We would have good discussions, and Kelsey would be a part of them. She stayed on task. And her grades improved! She was happier.

Yvonne is also quick to comment on Kelsey's strengths:

One thing I like about her is her homework schedule. She does it immediately when she gets home. There's no fighting or fussing or anything. You wouldn't want a better kid. She'll do anything for you she can. She's a people person.

Kelsey still struggles with being patient and attentive. Now, however, she has friends and recently made the honor roll for the first time. She is focused enough to enjoy dramatics, art, music, cheerleading, and animals.

As her therapist, Chris Fraser, points out, the difference in Kelsey occurred primarily because Kelsey wanted to change and worked hard enough to make change happen. She was open to a treatment plan developed by her teacher, her therapist, and her psychiatrist, as well as the two most important people on her team: Yvonne and Bill, the grandparents who adopted her. Kelsey calls them Mom and Dad.

Kelsey's journey toward change began when Barb Tootle contacted Yvonne. Yvonne remembers, "Kelsey was having problems in Mrs. Tootle's class, and I would always stop by and ask her how she was doing. Mrs. Tootle started talking about this AD/HD problem she thought Kelsey might have. So I talked to a couple of her other teachers, and they agreed we should check it out."

The evaluation confirmed that Kelsey has AD/HD. She and her grandparents began seeing Chris regularly. Chris helped the family interact in new ways. One difficult issue the family faced was homework, so Chris brought Kelsey's teacher, Barb, into one of the sessions. He recalls:

Kelsey's grandparents were getting frustrated because every night they were fighting her about sitting still and doing her homework. So Barb told them, "This is Kelsey's homework. She has to do it. And if she doesn't do it, she has to be accountable to me. Don't fight the war with her at home." Then we had Kelsey come in, and we explained, "Kelsey, this is your responsibility. If you don't get it done, that's okay. But you will face the consequences at school." That allowed her grandparents to back off. She started doing better because there was less parent-child conflict.

CHAPTER OBJECTIVES

◆ You will learn there are three types of AD/HD: the predominantly inattentive type, the predominantly hyperactive-impulsive type, and the combined type. Kelsey has the second type.

◆ You will learn how to evaluate a student to determine if the student has AD/HD by using the Conners' Rating Scales—Revised, and how to determine the nature and extent of special education services by using the Attention Deficit Disorders Evaluation Scale—Third Edition.

◆ You will learn how to accommodate students with AD/HD by taking such relatively simple steps as rearranging a classroom, posting daily schedules, helping them organize their work, and partnering with their families or school nurses with respect to medication.

◆ You will learn that multiple interventions often are necessary to develop effective instructional strategies and include students in the general curriculum, and that assessment of their progress is based on in-class approaches as well as statewide assessments in which the student may need accommodations such as extra breaks, multiple sessions, or distraction-free testing environments.

Chris also worked with Kelsey on problem solving. When some of the other students teased her about living with her grandparents, Chris encouraged Kelsey to think of ways to respond appropriately. Her creative, three-page list included "So?" "Whatever," and "I already knew that."

Yvonne and Bill work hard as a team to help Kelsey. Yvonne says, "Bill has been a big help. Sometimes I have a little temper, and he reminds me that she's just a little girl. We both help her with her homework. If there's something I don't understand, and Bill understands it, he'll help her."

Another important factor in Kelsey's change is medication. Her psychiatrist prescribed the stimulant Adderall. Yvonne says:

> I was scared about the medication. I had heard all these things about what it causes you to do. Then I heard that when they get older, they turn into addicts because they've been on all this medicine. I was scared to death to even put her on it. It was a hard decision to make.

Despite Yvonne's concerns, the change resulting from the medication was positive and dramatic. Barb remembers, "I can't tell you the total difference in the way she related to the other students in the classroom, on the playground, walking in the hallway, and to the principal and the other teachers. Everyone noticed a difference."

Chris explains the key to making a multimodal treatment plan such as Kelsey's work: "Everybody needs to be pulled in. I think continuity is the most important part."

After reading this chapter, complete the Self-Assessment for Chapter 8 on MyEducationLab to gauge your initial understanding of chapter content.

IDENTIFYING STUDENTS WITH AD/HD

Defining Attention-Deficit/Hyperactivity Disorder

Instead of listing AD/HD as a separate disability category, IDEA includes it as a subcategory under the general category "other health impairments" (see Chapter 12). Under the IDEA definition, a student with other health impairments has limited strength, vitality, or alertness, including a heightened alertness with respect to the educational environment, that

◆ is due to chronic or acute health problems such as asthma, attention deficit disorder or attention deficit hyperactivity disorder, diabetes, epilepsy, a heart condition, hemophilia, lead poisoning, leukemia, nephritis, rheumatic fever, sickle cell anemia, and Tourette's syndrome; and

◆ adversely affects a child's educational performance. (IDEA regulations, 2006)

AD/HD accounts for slightly over two thirds of students identified in recent years in the category of other health impairments (Schnoes, Reid, Wagner, & Marder, 2006). Because of coexisting disabilities, students with AD/HD often are also served through IDEA in the categories of learning disability, emotional or behavioral disorders, and intellectual disabilities. You will learn more about coexistence with these other disabilities later in the chapter.

Because IDEA does not specifically define AD/HD, most professionals adhere to the definition offered by the American Psychiatric Association (APA) (2000) as set out in the *Diagnostic and Statistical Manual of Mental Disorders* (DSM-IV-TR):

> The essential feature of Attention-Deficit/Hyperactivity Disorder is a persistent pattern of inattention and/or hyperactivity-impulsivity that is more frequently displayed and severe than is typically observed in individuals at a comparable level of development. (p. 85)

The limiting criteria of persistence, frequency, and severity are important. Everyone is forgetful and absentminded at times, especially during periods of stress. Also, some people are simply more or less active or energetic than others. But unless those characteristics are persistent, frequent, and severe, the person does not meet the APA criteria. A student whose educational performance is not adversely affected will not qualify for IDEA services. The APA criteria also require that the symptoms must persist for at least 6 months, be present in at least two settings, and not be attributable to another disability. Finally the criteria for AD/HD require that symptoms occur before the age of seven, but studies show that approximately one third of children and one half of adults with AD/HD have an onset after the age of seven (Barkley, Fischer, Smallish, & Fletcher, 2006). Approximately 40 percent to 80 percent of children identified as having AD/HD persist in displaying the disorder into their secondary years (Smith, Barkley, & Shapiro 2007).

Approximately 3 percent to 8 percent of the general population is identified as having AD/HD (Biederman, 2005; Smith et al., 2007). The prevalence rate for preschoolers is 4.2 percent (Egger, Kondo, & Angold, 2006). Based on a recent national study of elementary-aged students, students with AD/HD were found to be disproportionately male—approximately four times as many males as females. African American students are not overrepresented (as they are in several other categories, such as emotional or behavioral disorders and intellectual disability), and Hispanic students are underrepresented (Schnoes et al., 2006). AD/HD has received increased attention in the last decade, and estimates suggest that rates have doubled or tripled since 1990 (Stevens & Ward-Estes, 2006).

Describing the Characteristics

Diagnostic Criteria for AD/HD

Under the DSM-IV-TR diagnostic criteria (APA, 2000), there are three subtypes of AD/HD: predominately inattentive type, predominately hyperactive-impulsive type, and combined type. Accordingly, the acronym AD/HD features a slash, indicating inclusion of all three subtypes: attention-deficit disorder, hyperactivity disorder, and a combination.

Predominately inattentive type. A student must exhibit six or more of the following characteristics to be classified as having the predominately inattentive type:

- Often fails to give close attention to details or makes mistakes in schoolwork, work, or other activities
- Often has difficulty sustaining attention in tasks or play activities
- Often does not seem to listen when spoken to directly
- Often does not follow through on instructions and fails to finish schoolwork, chores, or duties in the workplace (not due to oppositional behavior or failure to understand instructions)
- Often has difficulty organizing tasks and activities
- Often avoids, dislikes, or is reluctant to engage in tasks that require sustained mental effort (such as schoolwork or homework)
- Often loses things necessary for tasks or activities (e.g., toys, school assignments, pencils, books, or tools)
- Is often easily distracted by extraneous stimuli
- Is often forgetful in daily activities (APA, 2000, p. 92)

Because students with the inattentive type of AD/HD usually are not as disruptive as those with hyperactivity-impulsivity, their needs may be overlooked. These students often display a slow tempo in terms of their approach to academic tasks, and the inattentive type of AD/HD has a higher ratio of girls to boys than the other two types (Glanzman & Blum, 2007). Students with the inattentive diagnosis typically are identified later than students with **hyperactivity**. Without a specific diagnosis and appropriate interventions, these students are at risk for long-term academic, social, and emotional difficulties. They usually have difficulty working in a distracting environment,

IEP Tip

The IEP conference provides an excellent opportunity for you to work with other team members in planning for and implementing supplementary aids to support your students' organizational skills in order to help them be successful in school.

absorbing large amounts of new information, shifting flexibly from one task to another, or linearly linking a series of cognitive operations. That is why you should (1) make sure that your students with inattentive-type AD/HD have enough time to shift from one activity to another, (2) teach them techniques for organizing their thoughts and materials, (3) offer them flexible time limits for finishing their assignments or examinations, and (4) simplify tasks that have multiple steps.

Predominately hyperactive-impulsive type. A student must have six or more of the following characteristics to be classified as having the predominately hyperactive-impulsive type of AD/HD. You will recall that Kelsey Blankenship was the "commotion-making" student because of her hyperactivity. The six characteristics must have been present for at least 6 months and be present to the extent that the student is recognized as falling outside the range of adaptive behavior.

Hyperactivity

- ◆ Often fidgets with hands or feet or squirms in seat
- ◆ Often leaves seat in classroom or in other situations in which remaining seated is expected
- ◆ Often runs about or climbs excessively in situations in which it is inappropriate (in adolescents or adults, may be limited to subjective feelings of restlessness)
- ◆ Often has difficulty playing or engaging in leisure activities quietly
- ◆ Is often "on the go" or often acts as if "driven by a motor"
- ◆ Often talks excessively

Impulsivity

- ◆ Often blurts out answers before questions have been completed
- ◆ Often has difficulty waiting to take turns
- ◆ Often interrupts or intrudes on others (e.g., butts into conversations or games) (APA, 2000, p. 92)

Problems associated with hyperactivity and **impulsivity** typically start when a child is young—several years before problems with the inattentive type of AD/HD emerge (Glanzman & Blum, 2007). These students are often described as displaying fidgetiness and being in constant motion. In Chapter 7 you learned about **temperament** and how this early individual difference in children can affect their emotional development. Temperament domains connected to activity level relate to characteristics associated with hyperactivity (Bussing, Lehninger, & Eyberg, 2006). It is especially important for students with hyperactivity or impulsivity to have opportunities to take breaks, have extended time for assignments, and participate in instructional strategies that enable them to move around the classroom. Although hyperactivity tends to decrease with advancing age, impulsivity typically persists across the secondary school and adult years.

Many children with AD/HD have difficulty learning from their experiences and cannot remember routines and procedures so they often are corrected.

Combined type. The third classification describes students who have features of both inattention and hyperactivity-impulsivity; the literature refers to the combined type as ADHD (without the slash). Most students with AD/HD have combined ADHD, and the majority of research is done on this group of students (Glanzman & Blum, 2007).

Intellectual Functioning and Academic Achievement

Experts disagree concerning the extent to which students with AD/HD have typical or reduced levels of intelligence. One research team gave IQ tests to a group of children with AD/HD, another group with reading difficulties, and a third group with AD/HD plus reading difficulties. The researchers found that the IQ scores of all three groups were normally distributed, with a majority of them being in the average range (Kaplan, Crawford, Dewey, & Fisher, 2000). It seems clear that Kelsey is one of the students in the "average" range of intelligence. Barkley (2003), however, reported that IQ ranges of students with AD/HD tend to be 7 to 10 points below the norm (IQ 100). Approximately 21 percent of elementary students with AD/HD have also been identified as having an intellectual disability, which, as you will learn in Chapter 9, means that they have an IQ score of approximately 70 or below (Schnoes et al., 2006).

Although the majority of students with AD/HD have typical intelligence, they frequently have problems achieving academically. That certainly was true for Kelsey before she received special education. Research related to the academic achievement of students with AD/HD reveals the following:

- Over 50 percent of students with AD/HD receive modified tests, have tests read to them, and have more time for test taking; additionally, over half have extended time for assignments and shorter or different assignments. (Schnoes et al., 2006)

- Students with AD/HD typically attain low scores on standardized academic achievement tests. (Tannock, 2001)

- Approximately 20 percent of students with AD/HD are also identified as having a learning disability, and 5 percent also have a speech/language disorder. (Schnoes et al., 2006)

- Students with AD/HD often have impairments associated with motivation, memory, and goal-directed behavior. (Smith et al., 2007; Weyandt, 2005)

As in Chris Fraser's family, AD/HD is often multigenerational, suggesting a genetic link. Enjoying a family ski trip, Chris Fraser, a master's level licensed independent social worker, is pictured here with his father, J. Scott Fraser, a full professor at Wright State University.

Despite their academic challenges, students with AD/HD also have a variety of strengths. In Box 8.1, Chris Fraser, an adult who has experienced both personal and professional success and who also has grown up with AD/HD, shares his perspectives on ways to capitalize on strengths.

Behavioral, Social, and Emotional Characteristics

Many students with AD/HD face behavioral, social, and emotional challenges. Kelsey's grandmother, Yvonne, describes her as having been "all over the church" and her teacher, Barb Tootle, recalls that wherever Kelsey was, there too was "some commotion." In fact, a high overlap exists between the categories of AD/HD and emotional or behavioral disorders. For example, approximately 40 percent to 90 percent of students identified as having AD/HD also have been identified as having oppositional defiant disorder and/or conduct disorder (Pfiffner et al., 1999); additionally, approximately one third have been identified as having an anxiety disorder (Reddy & De Thomas, 2007). Kelsey has not been identified as having any emotional or behavioral disorder. Sleep problems are also more frequent within this group of students, which can have ripple effects in terms of behavioral manifestation throughout the day due to fatigue (Cortese, Lecendreux, Mouren, & Konofal, 2006). Frequently occuring behavioral, social, and emotional challenges consist of the following:

- Conflicts with parents, teachers, and peers (DuPaul, McGoey, Eckert, & VanBrakle, 2001; Smith et al., 2007; Stevens & Ward-Estes, 2006)

- Low self-esteem (Klassen, Miller, & Fine, 2004)

PEARSON myeducationlab

Go to the Activities and Application section in Chapter 8 of MyEducationLab and complete Activity 1. As you watch this video, reflect on the other issues that a child with AD/HD may face.

IEP Tip

IEP goals can be included on fostering friendships with students and increasing participation in extracurricular school activities. Friends and activity participation can provide alternatives to behavioral and social challenges.

● *Chris Fraser*

I've been waiting to have my voice heard for many years. I feel so happy and fortunate to be able to share what has been in my mind and heart regarding AD/HD. I have found that one of my life's greatest assets and greatest teachers has been growing up and living with attention-deficit disorder paired with a learning disability. Don't get me wrong: As you can imagine, I obviously haven't felt this way for the majority of my life. Rather, this has been a gradual realization that I have felt growing in my heart ever since I was a young child. Therefore, my personal perception of AD/HD is that describing it as a disorder is a matter of perspective.

As an adult, I work as a therapist in a community mental health center and share with children and their families an empowering and hopeful perspective about AD/HD: that it is a collection of adaptive mechanisms and temperament traits that are more suited to some societies and tasks than to others.

I share this information because I wish I had been told this as a young child and because I came up with the concept on my own in high school. I can remember specifically a conversation with my friend Jawn, who was also struggling through the academic confines of traditional academia, in which we agreed that if we lived in a different time in the past, we would survive while most National Merit Scholars would perish. Since then, many publications and articles have been written about this very topic. As I began to discover these articles and research my findings in graduate school, I saw confirmation of a concept that I had already come up with and had used as a source of energy. I enjoy looking at AD/HD as an inherited set of skills, abilities, and personality tendencies that I can use to my benefit to be successful. For me, this has been a very healing and empowering way of looking at things.

I have a number of tips about how people with AD/HD can survive in a world that doesn't automatically accommodate some of our personality characteristics. I have developed these tips on my journey through academia and life as a person with AD/HD.

Tip 1: *Use your resources and advocate for your needs.* I was very sensitive about other people thinking I was not intelligent, and I didn't want to be seen as different in any way. Therefore, I was embarrassed to go to the resource room each day in elementary school, and in high school I didn't even use available resources. I didn't learn that it was okay and smart to use those resources until after I suffered my way through high school.

Tip 2: *Find your joy or bliss and follow it.* In college I found that, like other students with AD/HD, I have the ability to hyperfocus and excel in subjects I have a passion for. This acknowledgment of my strengths and interests gave meaning to the frustrations I endured in academia and gave me a sense of hope for the future.

Tip 3: *Work on acknowledging your growth areas and develop your own special ways of dealing with them.* In college I also found out that the real world was not going to accommodate to me, so I needed my own bag of tricks to survive in it. This was a difficult realization: I figured out how to deal with my growth areas through trial and error. I confess that I still am disorganized occasionally and that I still have difficulty managing time. But I deal with this growth area by making lists. I write things down before I forget them. I find that even if I don't refer back to the list, the process of writing things down helps me remember them better.

Tip 4: *Never give up on your dreams, and view your mistakes as learning opportunities rather than personal failures.* To this day, I am still developing my own tips for learning how to compensate for my growth areas and to use my capabilities as a person with AD/HD.

Overall, my family has made all the difference in the way I have learned to view my challenges. My father also grew up with AD/HD traits and at the end of high school was told that he was not college material. But he went on to get a bachelor's degree, a master's degree, and a doctorate in psychology. Hence, I grew up knowing that my father had experienced the same struggles I had. He ingrained in me the idea that I was capable of doing whatever I put my mind to. My mother was always a strong student and now works as a remedial reading and gifted teacher. Therefore, I was doubly fortunate because my parents had both personal experience and professional knowledge about AD/HD. I am also fortunate to have a wife who has special traits that compensate for my growth areas, with the result that I become more functional each year we spend together.

My journey as a person with AD/HD has involved continuous learning, struggle, toil, frustration, realization, and finally peace. Along the way I obtained a bachelor's degree in social work and sociology with a psychology minor and a master's degree in social work. But most important, by learning about how to help myself, I am now in a position to pass on this information and help others who live with AD/HD.

◆ Higher rates of using alcohol and tobacco (Barkley, Fischer, Smallish, & Fletcher, 2004)

◆ Increased risk-taking behavior (Flory, Molina, Pelham, Gnagy, & Smith, 2006)

◆ Significantly higher likelihood of receiving behavior management programs, mental health services, social work services, and family counseling within school than other students receiving special education services (Schnoes et al., 2006)

Determining the Causes

Do you agree or disagree with each of these statements?

◆ AD/HD stems from a lack of will or effort at self-control.

◆ AD/HD is caused by parents who don't discipline their children.

◆ AD/HD results from children watching too much television or playing too many video games.

◆ Dietary issues such as too much sugar cause AD/HD.

◆ AD/HD results from living in a fast-paced, stressful culture. (Harman & Barkley, 2000)

If you did agree, you would have been wrong on all counts. There are three causes of AD/HD: heredity, structural differences in the brain, and other biological causes. It is not clear which cause affected Kelsey.

Heredity

Genetic factors cause AD/HD in about 80 percent of the children and youth who experience it (Cook, 1999). Children who have a parent with AD/HD have a 40 percent to 57 percent risk of having AD/HD, and siblings of children with AD/HD are five to seven times more likely to have AD/HD than children whose siblings do not have AD/HD (Barkley, Murphy, & Fischer, 2007; Wilens et al., 2005). Research on genetic factors in twins found that identical twins have AD/HD in 55 percent to 92 percent of cases (Faraone et al., 2005). Twins have highly stable AD/HD symptoms during elementary and secondary years, and the stability and similarity of their characteristics is mainly genetically based (Larsson, Larsson, & Lichtenstein, 2004). Current research is focusing on genes related to **dopamine,** which is one of the brain's **neurotransmitters,** carrying signals between neurons (Accardo, 2008).

Structural Differences in the Brain

Researchers have identified structural and functional differences in the brains of people who have AD/HD, particularly the frontal lobes, cerebellum, and basal ganglia (Accardo, 2008). The frontal lobes serve a key role in controlling cognitive, emotional, and motor responses, whereas the cerebellum and basal ganglia are central to motor planning, motivation, and behavioral inhabition. Structural brain differences in children with AD/HD appear to relate to their reduced brain volume as compared to children without AD/HD (Castellanos et al., 2002).

Other Causes

Prenatal factors (e.g., prenatal exposure to cigarette smoking, lead, and alcohol), perinatal factors (e.g., complications with labor and delivery), and postnatal causes (e.g., environmental toxins) also can cause AD/HD (Glanzman & Blum, 2007; Smith, Barkley, & Shapiro, 2007).

EVALUATING STUDENTS WITH AD/HD

Determining the Presence of AD/HD

Children can be accurately diagnosed with AD/HD starting at around 2 years of age but 4- and 5-year-old preschoolers are more likely to meet the criteria of AD/HD than are toddlers (Egger, Kondo, & Angold, 2006). It seems that Kelsey was formally diagnosed when she was about 6 years old. Although early diagnosis is possible, other students with AD/HD may not be identified until they enroll in school or even until they are in their adolescence. Often children with AD/HD encounter challenges in general education classrooms, and general education teachers are the first ones who develop concerns and initiate the process to receive expert assistance from others. That assistance usually comes from school-based special education teams, pediatricians, family doctors, psychiatrists, clinical psychologists, and neurologists. The purpose of these referrals is to receive expert assistance in performing IDEA's mandatory nondiscriminatory evaluation (see Figure 8.1).

The process described in Figure 8.1 begins after the student's parent(s) agrees to the nondiscriminatory evaluation (AACAP, 2007; Frazier & Youngstrom, 2006). When a medical evaluation is warranted as part of the AD/HD evaluation, the school district is responsible for paying the physician. If you suspect that a student has AD/HD, you will want to make a record of the student's behavior, referring (in your record) to the characteristics that we discussed when we defined AD/HD. You may recall that Kelsey takes medicine to treat her hyperactivity and that the effect of the medicine has been positive and dramatic. But medicine alone did not do the trick; as Chris Fraser, Kelsey's social worker, noted, teaching Kelsey's family to assist her as she does her homework and teaching Kelsey herself some problem-solving techniques also have made it possible for Kelsey to be an effective student. No single "silver bullet" exists; that's why the nondiscriminatory evaluation must be based on a variety of assessments.

The nondiscriminatory evaluation seeks to answer three questions: (1) does the student have AD/HD and can the evaluators rule out other disabilities, (2) what should the student's IEP contain, and (3) do other disabilities exist simultaneously with AD/HD (Smith et al., 2007)? Typically, evaluations involve rating scales, interviews, observations, and psychological and educational testing. Approximately 84 percent of school psychologists conduct classroom observations, 90 percent use rating scales with parents and teachers, and 80 percent interview parents and teachers (Demaray, Schaefer, & DeLong, 2003).

Because rating scales are easy and efficient to administer, they are an assessment of choice. For an initial evaluation of whether a student has AD/HD, many psychologists use the Conners' Rating Scales—Revised (Conners, 1997). The Conners' Rating Scales include tools for responses from teachers, parents, and adolescents. These tools are available in long and short versions. The long version for teachers contains 13 subscales (for example, Oppositional, Hyperactivity, Social Problems) and takes 15 to 20 minutes to complete. The short version for teachers contains only four subscales and requires 5 to 10 minutes to complete. Both the long and short versions are completed by parents (for students ages 3 to 17), teachers (for students ages 3 to 17), and the students themselves (for ages 12 to 17).

The technical manual describes the Conners' standardization, which involved developing norms for the scales. Based on a thorough review of this and four other frequently used rating scales, researchers describe the psychometric properties as strong and recommend the use of the Conners' Rating Scales for AD/HD assessment (Demaray, Schaefer, & DeLong, 2003).

In comparing five frequently used rating scales, researchers indicated that the Conners' is substantially more comprehensive than the other four. A national survey of school psychologists reported that the Conners' is the most frequently used rating scale that particularly focuses on AD/HD. Approximately 80 percent of school psychologists use it (Demaray, Schaefer, & DeLong, 2003).

Figure 8.1

Process for the nondiscriminatory evaluation of students with AD/HD

Observation	**Teacher and parents observe:**
	Predominantly inattentive type: The student makes careless mistakes, has difficulty sustaining attention, doesn't seem to be listening, fails to follow through on tasks, has difficulty organizing, often loses things, is easily distracted, or is forgetful.
	Predominantly hyperactive-impulsive type: The student is fidgety, leaves his seat when expected to be seated, runs or climbs excessively or inappropriately, has difficulty playing quietly, talks excessively, blurts out answers or comments, has difficulty taking turns, or acts as if always on the go.
	Combined type: Characteristics of both are observed.
Screening	**Assessment measures:**
	Classroom work products: Work is consistently or generally poor. The student has difficulty staying on task, so his work may be incomplete or completed haphazardly.
	Group Intelligence tests: Tests may not reveal true ability because student has difficulty staying on task.
	Group achievement tests: Performance may not be a true reflection of achievement because the student has difficulty staying on task.
	Medical screening: The physician does not find a physical condition that could cause inattention or hyperactivity-impulsivity. Medication may be prescribed.
	Vision and hearing screening: Results do not explain academic difficulties.
Prereferral	**Teacher implements suggestions from school-based team:**
	The student still experiences frustration, inattention, or hyperactivity despite reasonable curricular and behavioral accommodations.
Referral	The child should be referred to a multidisciplinary team for a complete evaluation if prereferral intervention is not successful.
Nondiscriminatory evaluation procedures and standards	**Assessment measures:**
	Psychological evaluation: A psychiatrist or psychologist determines that the student meets DSM-IV-R criteria for AD/HD.
	Individualized Intelligence tests: The student's intelligence may range from below-average to gifted.
	Individualized achievement tests: The student's performance on achievement tests may suggest that his educational performance has been adversely affected by the condition.
	Behavior rating scales: The student scores in the significant range on measures of inattention or hyperactivity-impulsivity.
	Teacher observation: The student's educational performance has been adversely affected by the condition. The behaviors have been present in more than one setting, were first observed before age 7, and have lasted for more than 6 months.
	Curriculum-based assessment: The student may be experiencing difficulty in one or more areas of the curriculum used by the local school district because the behaviors have caused the student to miss important skills.
	Direct observation: The student exhibits inattention or hyperactivity-impulsivity during the observation.
Determination	The nondiscriminatory evaluation team determines that the student has AD/HD and needs special education and related services. The student's IEP team develops appropriate education options for the student.

Determining the Nature of Specially Designed Instruction and Services

After determining that a student has AD/HD, the evaluation team must decide whether the student needs special education and related services. Many teams use the Attention Deficit Disorders Evaluation Scale—Third Edition (ADDES-3) because it prescribes interventions more often than any other available rating scales do (Demaray, Elting, & Schaefer, 2003). The ADDES-3 has three main scales:

- ◆ Attention Deficit Disorders Evaluation Scale—Third Edition (ADDES-3)
- ◆ Early Childhood Attention Deficit Disorders Evaluation Scale
- ◆ Attention Deficit Disorders Evaluation Scale—Secondary-Age Student

The ADDES-3 is based on the American Psychiatric Association definition of AD/HD in that it addresses both the inattentive type of AD/HD and the hyperactive-impulsive type. The ADDES-3 is suitable for evaluating students who are between 4 and 18 years old. It has both a home and a school version for parents and teachers, respectively. The ADDES-3 is supplemented by the following:

- ◆ Technical manual
- ◆ Prereferral checklist
- ◆ Intervention manual with IEP goals, objectives, and interventions
- ◆ Parent guide (includes practical strategies for helping child at home)
- ◆ Computer program for quick scoring
- ◆ Spanish language version
- ◆ A diagnostic tool for comparing the student's ADDES-3 score with DSM-IV-R eligibility criteria

IEP Tip

The supplemental information from the ADDES-3 can be helpful to the IEP team in aligning evaluation data with appropriate goals and objectives related to instructional accommodations.

Researchers who evaluated the ADDES-2 (note ADDES-2, not ADDES-3) and compared it to four other rating scales described the intervention manual (Demaray, Schaefer, & Delong, 2003):

> Each manual is outlined in a clear, comprehensive manner and provides helpful goal, objective, and intervention information, relevant to each of the specific behaviors described on its corresponding rating form. These manuals were defined to assist educators and parents in the development of programs to assist children and youth identified as ADHD. Although the addition of these intervention tools is an advantage for the ADDES, it should be noted that the intervention manuals are presented in a "cookbook" approach to intervention.

DESIGNING AN APPROPRIATE IEP

Partnering for Special Education and Related Services

Not every student with AD/HD qualifies for IDEA services. That is so because, as we explained at the beginning of this chapter, AD/HD must adversely affect a student's educational performance in order for the student to qualify for services. Many students with AD/HD, especially when they begin a treatment regimen that includes medication, can function well in a general classroom with modifications and accommodations that do not require specially designed instruction.

If a student does not qualify for special education and related services under IDEA, does that mean he cannot get the types of modifications and accommodations that are effective? No; in fact, another option is to develop what educators call a "504 plan." As you learned in Chapter 1, the Americans with Disabilities Act (ADA) and Section 504 of the Rehabilitation Act Amendments of 1973 both prohibit discrimination against students with AD/HD or other disabilities if their disabilities substantially limit one or more major life activities. To comply with these laws, states offer 504 plans (named after the anti-discrimination section of the Rehabilitation Act) to students who are not classified into the IDEA "other health impairments" category and provided with IDEA benefits. As you will recall from Chapter 1, the Rehabilitation Act of 1973 is a broad civil rights law that identifies individuals with a disability as those who have substantial limitations in one or more major life activities, have or have had a disability, or are regarded by others as having a disability. This is a functional definition of disability, as contrasted to IDEA's categorical definitions.

To assist students with AD/HD who do not meet the requirements of the IDEA category of "other health impairments," educators usually include in the student's 504 plan a list of reasonable accommodations (Section 504 requires reasonable accommodations). The accommodations typically include monitoring medication and using technological learning aids (Zentall, 2006). Box 8.2, Partnership Tips, outlines a three-step process for creating a 504 accommodation plan.

PARTNERSHIP TIPS · Box 8.2

Creating a 504 Accommodation Plan

Bonita Blazer has provided numerous workshops for teachers on classroom accommodations for students with AD/HD. She advocates a three-step process for creating 504 accommodation plans.

Step 1—Engage in collaborative problem-solving to identify preferred classroom accommodations and formalize a Certificate of Accommodations.

- Initiate conversations with parents and students (starting as young as five years of age) about the types of accommodations that would make school easier.
  - ✓ You can hold a first meeting with the parents and then a follow-up meeting with the student.
  - ✓ Share a list of instructional strategies and invite their input on what they think would work best.
  - ✓ Explain the relationship between accommodations and academic and social success.
  - ✓ Students unable to communicate verbally about accommodations can draw pictures or use computer-assisted means of communication.
- The student can list preferred classroom accommodations on a first draft of a Certificate of Accommodations.
  - ✓ A formal Certificate can enable the parent and student to recognize their entitlement or right to meaningful instructional accommodations.
  - ✓ It is helpful to have ongoing conversations with students and parents about the Certificate.
- Once agreement is reached, the student, parents, teachers, and principal can sign the Certificate to formalize it.
  - ✓ The student can keep the Certificate in a notebook as a constant reminder.
  - ✓ It is helpful to encourage students to use a plastic sheet protector, color folder, or other aid to protect the certificate and make it easy to locate.

Step 2—Reach team agreement on a more formal written 504 accommodation plan.

- Meet with the school-based team to describe the Certificate and to gain their input into accommodations that will be implemented for the student.
- Based on team input, develop a more comprehensive written list of 504 accommodations.
- Add a rating scale to the accommodation plan as a way to access the ongoing implementation of each accommodation.
- Include space in the plan for teacher reflections on the quality of implementing the plan.
- Engage in ongoing communication with the student, parent, and team about the implementation of the accommodations.
- As more information is available on accommodations that do and do not work successfully, develop an annual classroom accommodation review based on the data from the rating form.

Step 3—Implement the 504 plan.

- You and/or the team chairperson send a copy of the Annual 504 Classroom Accommodation Form to the person within the school district who is responsible for 504 implementation.
- You and the educational team, working collaboratively with the student and parent, are responsible for completing rating scales on a periodic basis to ensure that the instructional accommodations are being implemented.
- Teach the student self-determination skills focusing on communicating with teachers in a constructive way if required accommodations are withheld.
- Ensure that the 504 plan is placed in the student's permanent confidential file.

Source: Based on information from Blazer, B. (1999). Developing 504 classroom accommodation plans: A collaborative, systematic parent-student-teacher approach. *Teaching Exceptional Children, 32*(2), 28–33.

One of the roles of either the 504 or IEP team is to plan educational supports that can accompany the use of medication for students with AD/HD. You will learn later in the chapter about the effectiveness of medication with students who have AD/HD. Educators and other members of 504 or IEP teams should never suggest to parents that their child needs to be on or off medication. Only a physician can make that determination. Educators may suggest to parents that they may want to secure a medical evaluation because, as you have learned, AD/HD is linked to physiological conditions. That certainly seems to be the case for Kelsey. However, IDEA prohibits educators from requiring a student to take medication as a condition of attending school.

Determining Supplementary Aids and Services

You will want to take into account a variety of classroom factors when designing students' IEPs or reasonable accommodations. You will recall from Chapter 2 that supplementary aids and services involve modifications to aspects of the classroom environment. These include student seating arrangements, classroom furniture arrangement, and lighting and auditory features. For example, a student who is deaf and reads lips will need to be seated where he has a clear view of the teacher's face. A student with a physical disability who uses a wheelchair will need to have the classroom furniture arranged to allow physical access, and so on.

Box 8.3 sets out various classroom and educational program modifications that might benefit students with AD/HD. If a student has the predominately hyperactive-impulsive type, for example, he will have difficulty sitting for long periods of time and may need some classroom modifications to address these issues. Those modifications may be as simple as allowing the student to stand during work periods (rather than sit) or to get up from the chair every 5 or 10 minutes. Classroom arrangements that minimize the distraction associated with student movement and support more frequent instructional activities involving movement, like role plays and strategies derived from multiple intelligences theory (see Chapter 16), accommodate students with AD/HD. Carbone (2001) has suggested several classroom arrangement features that minimize disruption related to hyperactivity-impulsivity:

◆ Arrange the classroom in a consistent manner to maximize predictability.

◆ Although all students benefit from collaborative learning techniques (discussed in Chapter 13), it is not always best to seat students with hyperactivity-impulsivity with peers because they can be distracted and become a distraction.

◆ Seat the student in close proximity to the teacher, possibly the front row of a row of desks.

◆ Do not seat students with hyperactivity-impulsivity too near highly distracting areas, such as windows, open doors looking into a hallway or another room, or any area with movement or potential distractions.

◆ To address issues of impulsivity, clearly post the daily and weekly schedules where students can see and consult them, and provide prompts to students to engage in scheduled activities.

◆ Keep the schedule consistent to provide greater predictability and reduce impulsive behavior; reduce unstructured time for the same reasons.

◆ Minimize potentially distracting classroom decorations that are superfluous to learning.

◆ Arrange the classroom to facilitate smooth transitions between classroom activities.

Another characteristic of many learners with AD/HD, including Kelsey, is their lack of organization skills. In the next section you'll learn about curriculum augmentations related to goal setting and organizational skills that can enable students with AD/HD to be more organized and engage with the general curriculum more effectively.

There are also classroom ecological features that can assist in this. Teachers can establish clearly marked locations for students to store materials. Sometimes color-coding

PEARSON
myeducationlab

Go to the Activities and Application section in Chapter 8 of MyEducationLab and complete Activity 2. As you read this case consider how effective room arrangement can help students with disabilities.

Accommodations for AD/HD

Because students with AD/HD have various traits, you will need to make a variety of accommodations for them.

For students who display inattention, consider:

◆ Seating them in quiet areas, at desks that are unusually far apart, or near students who pay close attention in class, or near peers who study with them.

◆ Giving them more time to complete their work, reducing the amount of work you ask them to do (focus on the essentials), dividing long assignments into component parts and asking for completion of each part and then of the whole, requiring fewer correct answers to receive a passing grade, using cues (such as private signals to stay on task) and oral and written instructions simultaneously.

For students who are impulsive, consider:

◆ Ignoring their somewhat inappropriate behaviors, rewarding them promptly when they behave correctly, acknowledging the correct behavior of other students so that the impulsive students understand and model that behavior, correcting them gently, supervising them closely when they transition from one activity to another, and entering into a behavior contract with them.

For students with excessive motor activity, consider:

◆ Letting them stand while in class, asking them to run errands or otherwise use their energy physically, and breaking for a short while between assignments and asking them and the other students to do something physical ("stretch break").

For students who have mood characteristics, consider:

◆ Reassuring and encouraging them, speaking gently, and reviewing your assignments.

◆ Meeting with their parents and asking how they want to communicate.

◆ Being on the alert for unusual moods, especially frustration or anger, so you can modify your expectations at those times, provide support, and contact the student's parents.

◆ Helping the student learn anger-control strategies, or referring the student to professionals who can teach those strategies.

For students who have academic challenges, consider:

◆ In reading, offering more time for the student to complete reading assignments, reducing the amount of reading, using texts that are less "dense" (number of words on a page), and not having the student read aloud in front of peers.

◆ In speaking, accepting nearly every spoken response so as to encourage the student to speak out, allowing the student to develop a display of what the student has read and learned, and asking the student to speak about topics that interest the student.

◆ In writing, accepting displays or oral projects as substitutes for some written work, allowing the student to use a tape recorder or a computer, reducing the student's written workload, and using multiple-choice or similarly formatted questions.

◆ In mathematics, allowing the student to use a calculator or graph paper to space numbers, giving more time to complete an assignment, and frequently modeling the proper process to do a calculation.

For students who have problems organizing and planning, consider:

◆ Asking the student to use notebooks, dividers, palm pilots, computer programs, or other tools that help the student to remember what to do and when and how to do it.

◆ Providing daily or weekly reports to the student and the student's parents regarding organizational tools and devices and the work you require.

For students who have difficulty complying, consider:

◆ Praising the student's appropriate behavior, providing immediate feedback, ignoring minor misbehaviors (pick your issues), using a behavior contract for the student and for the entire class, and helping the student learn how to monitor his or her own behavior.

For students who have socialization challenges, consider:

◆ Praising their appropriate behavior, monitoring their social interactions, using behavior contracts, providing small-group study and cooperative learning and social skills opportunities, and publicly rewarding the student's leadership or participation.

PEARSON
myeducationlab

Go to the Building Teaching Skills and Dispositions section in Chapter 8 of MyEducationLab. As you complete the activities, think about how you as a teacher could help the child portrayed in this case.

Source: Based on information from Parker, H. C. (1992). ADAPT accommodation plan form. *ADD Warehouse* (http://www.addwarehouse.com).

IEP Tip

Sometimes the most important learning support involves the environment in which students with AD/HD learn; IEP teams need to consider classroom modifications and arrangements as a form of supplementary aid and services.

those areas can help students remember where materials belong. Similarly, teachers can provide clearly marked locations for students to store personal items, such as coats, backpacks, lunchboxes, and athletic gear. Minimizing the amount of clutter in a classroom can reduce student confusion about where materials and personal effects belong. Carbone (2001) suggests setting up student mailboxes in which students can turn in and retrieve handouts and homework papers.

Planning for Universal Design for Learning

Classroom modifications such as student mailboxes and storage bins are only the first steps to enabling students with AD/HD to succeed in the general education classroom. Teaching students organizational and goal-setting skills augments the curriculum and can help students engage effectively with the general curriculum. As you learned in Chapter 2, curriculum augmentations involve expanding or adding to the general curriculum to teach students learning-to-learn or self-regulation strategies that, in turn, enable them to learn more effectively.

Students who are more organized are more likely to know what tasks they need to accomplish and what homework needs to be completed or has been submitted. Often, parents need to help the student follow through at home; that's what Yvonne and Bill do for Kelsey, with Chris Fraser's assistance. Moreover, students can apply those organizational skills to improve their study habits. One component of effective study and academic skills involves setting goals related to the completion of academic work. Whether it is setting a goal to study for a set amount of time each night or to get a certain percentage of problems right on a quiz, students who set goals perform more effectively. By explaining to Kelsey that there would be consequences if she did not do her homework or otherwise accept responsibility for her actions, Chris helped her as a student and also de-escalated some of the conflict Kelsey, Yvonne, and Bill were having at home about homework.

Classroom modifications such as those listed in the previous section help students learn organizing skills. Teaching students to think about their own environmental modifications can be helpful—for example, organizing their notebooks by folders marked by different colors, with each color indicating a different course or topic.

Because they are easily distracted, students with AD/HD may also have difficulty with neatness. This is a common problem for students, certainly, but it can be particularly problematic for students with AD/HD. Students can be taught effective work skills (for example, making sure numbers in a math equation are lined up appropriately) and note-taking skills. Using strategies like self-instruction and self-monitoring (described in Chapter 11), they can develop the habit of checking their work to make sure it has been completed and meets the standard set by the teacher.

Goal-setting and organization skills go hand in hand to promote better outcomes. Goals specify what a person wishes to achieve and, as such, act as regulators of human action (Locke & Latham, 2002). Simply put, if a student sets a goal, it increases the likelihood that he will perform behaviors related to that goal. The value of teaching goal-setting skills cannot always be measured only in terms of goal achievement. People do not reach every goal they set. The process of setting and working toward that goal, however, improves the person's goal-setting and attainment skills and increases the probability of reaching subsequent goals.

Within educational settings, the process of promoting goal-setting skills involves helping students learn to do the following:

1. Identify and define a goal clearly and concretely.
2. Develop a series of objectives or tasks to achieve the goal.
3. Specify the actions necessary to achieve the desired outcome.

At each step, students must make choices and decisions about the goals they wish to pursue and the actions they wish to take to achieve their goals. The goal-setting process can be easily incorporated into a variety of educational activities and instructional areas, as well as into educational planning. Involving a student in his IEP or transition-planning meetings or simply in planning for educational activities can provide multiple opportunities to practice setting goals and also give the student a sense of involvement in and control over his educational experiences.

Research has suggested some general strategies to make goals both meaningful and attainable for students with disabilities. Goals should be challenging for the student. They should not be so challenging that the student cannot attain them, as this will lead to frustration, but they must provide enough motivation for the student to work to attain them. If goals are too easy, there is no motivation to engage in the work necessary to attain them, nor is there a feeling of accomplishment after achieving them. Finally, while it is preferable for students to participate in setting their own goals at whatever level is appropriate given the nature of their disability, if this is not possible and goals need to be set by teachers, then the student's preferences and interests should be incorporated into the goal to increase his motivation to pursue the goal. Goals that have personal meaning are more likely to be attained (Sands & Doll, 2005).

Students with AD/HD may have a difficult time attending to multiple goals. Several strategies are available to address this challenge. For example, complex goals should be broken down into smaller subgoals that the student can complete in a shorter amount of time with fewer steps. Students should make a list of their goals so they have a concrete, easy-to-find visual reminder of them. And the strategies to promote student-directed learning that we discuss in Chapter 11 can enable students with AD/HD to self-monitor their progress toward their goals.

Planning for Other Educational Needs

As is true for Kelsey, so it is for other students with AD/HD: Medication is often an important component of a student's multimodal educational program. (You'll learn more about multimodal treatments in the next section.) In addition, medication becomes an area of educational need for students with AD/HD.

Teachers working with students who are taking medicine to treat AD/HD should be familiar with the types, effects, and side effects of medications frequently used to treat AD/HD, such as Ritalin, Dexedrine, and Adderall. Side effects of these medications include sleep and appetite disruption, stomachaches, headaches, dizziness, irritability, anxiety, and sadness/unhappiness (Snider, Busch, & Arrowood, 2003). The American Academy of Child and Adolescent Psychiatry recommends that students treated with any type of medication have their height and weight monitored, as weight loss and growth reduction can be side effects of some medication regimens (AACAP, 2007).

Obviously, it is important for teachers to contribute to efforts to monitor the impact of medications on a child. Students who are drowsy may present less of a problem in the classroom, but trading hyperactivity or impulsivity for drowsiness does not ensure the student's educational progress. The student's IEP should stipulate what teacher training needs to occur to ensure an appropriate education program. It would be difficult for a teacher to be effective for a student with AD/HD unless the teacher knew about the student's medication—the name of the drug, its purposes, its effects (positive and other), and when the student must take it (at home or at school, and, if at school, when).

It is also important to assess systematically the effects of medication for students with AD/HD. Simple checklists of student behavior patterns and behavior states through the day can provide useful information. Indeed, pediatricians indicate that they prefer to have this type of information when

IEP Tip

The IEP team should consider how teachers and students can contribute to any assessment regarding medication use and recognize that parents' observations and a physician's assessment yield information about the student's functioning.

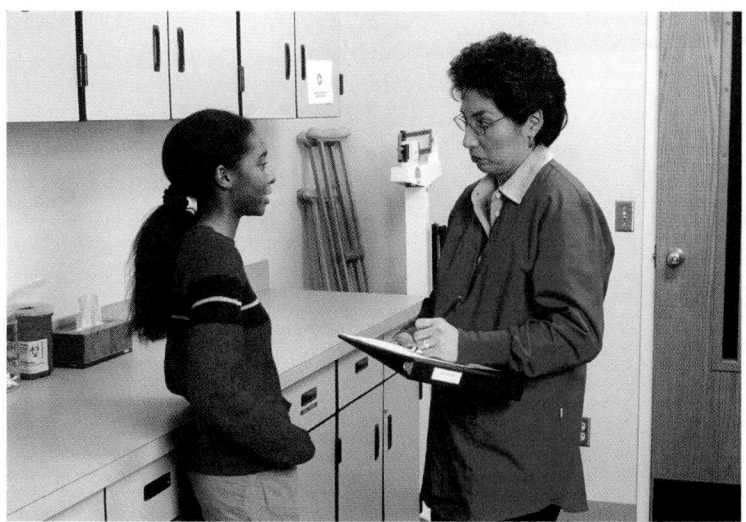
Consistent administration of medication, even at school, helps some children manage the symptoms of AD/HD.

they make prescription and medication decisions (HaileMariam, Bradley-Johnson, & Johnson, 2002). Furthermore, students can learn to self-monitor and self-evaluate their behaviors and feelings by using student-directed learning strategies such as those we discuss in Chapter 11. Finally, the IEP teams should consider teaching students to self-manage their medication process, increasing the likelihood that medicine will be taken as prescribed.

USING EFFECTIVE INSTRUCTIONAL STRATEGIES

Early Childhood Students: Multidisciplinary Diagnostic and Training Program

The strategies most effective for young children with AD/HD, and indeed for students with AD/HD throughout their life spans, involve the use of multimodal treatments. The term *multimodal treatments* does not simply mean using multiple intervention components, such as the multicomponent interventions you learned about in Chapter 5. **Multimodal treatments** involve multiple interventions or treatments across modes or types of therapies. Multimodal treatments for young children with AD/HD (such as Kelsey) typically involve medication and other behaviorally oriented treatments (dosReis, Owens, Puccia, & Leaf, 2004). Having conducted a review of early interventions for preschool students with AD/HD, researchers concluded that three primary treatment approaches were most effective: medication, parent training, and classroom behavior management interventions (McGoey, Eckert, and DuPaul, 2002).

Similarly, Kern and colleagues (2007) evaluated a multicomponent intervention that combined parent education and an individualized, assessment-based intervention program conducted in both home and day care settings. The multicomponent intervention involved student-focused behavioral interventions to address behavior problems, pre-academic readiness skills, and child safety skills. These student interventions included functional behavioral assessments, a focus on early literacy, and a token reinforcement system. The parent education content paralleled these areas, teaching parenting skills and strategies pertaining to behavior management, pre-academics, and child safety. Students in this treatment group made significant improvement in behavior and pre-academic skills compared with baseline data collected prior to the intervention. You may recall that Chris Fraser involved Kelsey's grandparents when developing an intervention for her; rather than targeting Kelsey only, he addressed her grandparents' needs as well.

Elementary and Middle School Students: Errorless Learning

Errorless learning is a procedure that presents the discriminative stimuli to the student and arranges the delivery of prompts for the student in such a way that the student gives only correct responses (or only a few incorrect responses) (Alberto & Troutman, 2003). The discriminative stimulus, called the S^D, is a specific event or environmental condition that elicits a desired response. This stimulus acquires control over the desired response when the response is paired with a reinforcer. Prompts are any additional stimuli that increase the chances that the S^D will elicit the desired response.

These are technical terms for some fairly simple concepts that provide powerful teaching strategies. When a teacher asks a student to perform a task, the teacher is providing an S^D. The instruction itself is intended to elicit a particular response from the student. For example, a teacher might ask a third-grade student, "Tell me what time it is." That S^D ("Tell me what time it is.") should result in the student's telling the time (the response). Let's say, though, that the student does not provide the correct response, no matter how many times the teacher repeats the instruction. Once the teacher knows this, she might again ask the student, "Tell me what time it is," and then point to the clock on the wall. The pointing gesture is a prompt; it is an additional stimulus intended to increase the chance that the S^D will elicit the desired response.

There are several kinds of prompts, including physical, verbal, and visual prompts. Taking a student's hand to help him shape a piece of clay is a physical prompt. Verbal prompts can be questions ("Does this have four sides?" in response to the S^D, "Find the

Video Self-Modeling

Video self-modeling (VSM) is an instructional strategy effective in teaching a wide array of students, including students with AD/HD, skills that enhance self-regulation (Mechling, 2005). Hitchcock, Dowrick, and Prater (2003) defined self-modeling as the "observation of images of oneself engaged in adaptive behavior" (p. 37). Video self-modeling is simply the use of video to project those images. Not only does VSM have proven effectiveness, but it is also a strategy that any teacher with access to some basic technology can implement, using these simple steps:

1. Select a recording technology.

   Creating a self-modeling image begins with the creation of the image to be viewed by the student. Up until recently, the simplest way to do that was to use a video camera to record the image onto a videotape that could be played on a VCR. This may still be the easiest route for many teachers, but the use of personal computers allows for the development of images that can be both student-directed and of better quality.

2. Create a self-modeling image.

   This step sounds obvious; after you figure out how you will record the student performing the desired behavior, you just film it, right? Ask yourself this, though: If the purpose of VSM is to have students view images of themselves engaged in a behavior you wish them to master, how can you film them performing the behavior at that mastery level before they actually achieve it?

There are two primary means to meet that challenge (Buggey, 2007). The first is to have students role-play or imitate the desired behavior. In this case, you must script out the role-play situation and provide support to have the student perform the behavior to the level desired. Another option is that if the desired behavior is performed occasionally, but not consistently, you can film the appropriate behavior when it does occur. Most self-modeling videos are no more than two to three minutes long.

3. Have students view the video image and imitate or repeat the desired behavior.

   Students should view their positive self-image 6 to 10 times during a 2- to 3-week period, either at home or school or both. You (or the student's parent if the student is watching the video at home) should view the video with the student and, for the first few viewings, point out some of the features of the behavior you want the student to particularly attend to.

4. Record student progress in mastering the behavior.

   As when teaching any behavior, you must assess student progress. How you do this is a function of the type of behavior you are trying to teach through VSM.

5. Use the video for occasional "booster sessions."

   The video can be used to remind students how to perform the behavior you are targeting after more intensive intervention has been completed.

   ■ ■ ■

Cognitive behavioral treatments are one form of "brain-based" instructional strategies. Prigge (2002) identified a host of ways to promote brain-based learning for students with AD/HD, as depicted in Box 8.4. In addition to these strategies, students across the age range with AD/HD may acquire enhanced self-regulatory skills by using technology, particularly computer-based technologies. Box 8.5 discusses the use of video self-modeling strategies to promote self-regulation and self-monitoring.

INCLUDING STUDENTS WITH AD/HD

Because AD/HD is not a separately identified category under IDEA, the U.S. Department of Education does not provide data on the extent to which students with AD/HD participate in general education classrooms. Box 8.6 provides some inclusion tips useful for students with AD/HD.

Although Kelsey has friends and many opportunities to enjoy her friendships through dramatics, art, music, and cheerleading, many students with AD/HD face particular challenges in making friends. An especially helpful guide in supporting girls with AD/HD to make friends is *The Girls' Guide to AD/HD* (Walker, 2004). Even though this book is written especially for girls, many of the helpful suggestions apply to boys as well. Figure 8.2 is an excerpt from that book, a conversation among three girls with AD/HD about how they deal with their disorder within the context of friendships. As you will see, they have their individual preferences about what works best.

Box 8.6   INCLUSION TIPS

	What You Might See	What You Might Be Tempted to Do	Alternate Responses	Ways to Include Peers in the Process
Behavior	*Inattentive type*: The student is inattentive, withdrawn, forgetful, a daydreamer, and/or lethargic. *Hyperactive-impulsive type*: He is restless, talkative, impulsive, and/or easily distracted. *Combined type:* The student has features of both.	*Inattentive type*: Overlook him. *Hyperactive-impulsive type*: Be critical and punitive.	*Inattentive type:* Consider changing the student's seating arrangement and providing daily schedules of activities. *Hyperactive-impulsive and combined types*: Teach the student organization and goal-setting skills.	Model acceptance and appreciation for him. Then peers are more likely to do the same.
Social interactions	*Inattentive type:* He withdraws from social situations. *Hyperactive-impulsive type*: He bursts into social situations and may be gregarious or inappropriate and annoying.	*Inattentive type*: Call attention to his isolation in front of other students; try to force him to play. *Hyperactive-impulsive type:* Pull him out of social situations for inappropriate behavior.	Role-play friendship skills. Help the student discover his strengths and encourage group participation in those activities. Start with small groups. Encourage membership in a support group for students with AD/HD.	For projects, pair him with another student who has similar interests and tends to be accepting. The initial goal is achieving one close friend.
Educational performance	His work is incomplete, full of errors, and sloppy.	Assign failing grades to the student.	Use errorless learning procedures to present discriminative stimuli and arrange prompts that will enable him to be successful.	Model for peers good prompting strategies that they can also use in peer-tutoring interactions.
Classroom attitudes	His motivation is inconsistent or lacking.	Send frequent notes to parents about your disappointment in their son's motivation.	Use goal attainment scaling (discussed in this chapter) as a way for the student to see his progress. Provide rewards on a periodic basis when he accomplishes his goals.	Enable the student to teach another member of the class how to document his progress through goal attainment scaling.

Maddy: I used to not want to talk about having AD/HD, but after a while, I realized it was hopeless to try to explain myself any other way, so I've become AD/HD Girl. I need a cape and a few superpowers, and I'll be ready to go. Maybe I'll get a tattoo that says AD/HD Girl!

Or not.

Anyway, if I find myself in a situation where I just know AD/HD is going to make for trouble (like working with other kids on a big project), I just tell the other kids that I have AD/HD. And mostly that works okay. It's amazing how people open up when you tell them something like that about yourself. I've learned that lots of people have lots of stuff going on. One of my best friends, Karla, and I together agree that Karla has AD/HD, even though she hasn't been diagnosed. We think Karla also has obsessive compulsive disorder (OCD). Then I tell her I wish I had some of her OCD, and she says fine, you can have it, but she won't take any of my depression, sheesh. Because I am willing to talk about having AD/HD, I've found out a lot about other kids in my classes. One of my friends is a superb artist and she has bipolar disorder. And a lot of the girls I know have either taken antidepressants or talked to a counselor at some time or other.

Sometimes, it is clear that the person I'm talking to thinks I'm faking it or that AD/HD isn't real or something equally supportive (NOT). So I just change the subject. If the person keeps bugging me about it, I tell the truth—that it doesn't do any good to talk to somebody about something when they won't listen. Because usually they just want to argue and say it isn't real or that I'm just lazy or whatever.

Eventually, I shrug my shoulders and walk away. I've learned that I don't have to take any abuse from anybody about it.

Like I said, most people start talking to you about their lives if you start talking openly about yours. It helps if you are matter-of-fact, I think, because it makes it easy for the other person to be nonjudgmental and matter-of-fact. People are sometimes afraid of emotions, even though I think that is silly. Anyway, I have found that if I stay calm and just bring AD/HD up without making a big deal, people seem okay with it most of the time. I also make jokes—most people appreciate a sense of humor especially when you gently poke fun at yourself. They see that you aren't taking yourself that seriously, even if you have brought up a serious topic like AD/HD.

My favorite AD/HD joke is this one that I made up:
Question: How many AD/HDers does it take to change a light bulb?
Answer: Want to go for a bike ride?
Get it? Zero attention span.

Bo: I don't talk about AD/HD. It's nobody's business. Once I get to know someone and trust them, I might talk about it. Until then, forget it. I don't say anything.

I'm not matter-of-fact, though I go home and sweat and worry about what I said. Sometimes the person I'm talking to acts like she doesn't want to hear it. Even worse, she might act like AD/HD is fake. So I clam up. Which is easy.

Helen: Me? I don't care. I'll talk about it. Or not. Depends on if it comes up. I talk a lot, so it just dribbles out of my mouth.

Bo: I wish, I think it's plain hard. Sometimes I feel like I walk around labeled. Other times I forget that I have AD/HD. Then it feels like it's my fault that I mess up. I feel like a failure. Then I might remember I have AD/HD. Even so, it feels like a lame excuse.

Helen: You should hang around me, then! I'll remind you, at least when I remember, and I'll talk about it so you don't have to.

Bo: Actually, that sounds great.

———
Source: From: *The girls' guide to AD/HD* by Beth Walker, pp. 127–128. Copyright 2004 by Woodbine House. Reprinted with permission.

ASSESSING STUDENTS' PROGRESS

Measuring Students' Progress

Progress in the General Curriculum

In Chapter 5 you learned about curriculum-based measurement as a means of tracking progress in the general curriculum. One of the advantages of CBM over standard pencil-paper measurements is that the assessing teachers collect data on an ongoing basis and use the information from CBM to modify their instruction.

Another potentially beneficial means of determining student progress within the general curriculum involves a process called "goal attainment scaling." Most students with AD/HD and other disabilities have educational goals pertaining to all aspects of their educational program, including general curriculum content areas. Unfortunately, comparing goals among students or even comparing among goals for an individual student is not very helpful. Some goals are simpler to reach than others, and some goals address areas that are very different from other educational areas.

The **goal attainment scaling** process allows teachers to compare goals and to quantify student goal attainment. This process begins by identifying a goal (Roach & Elliott, 2005). Having set a goal, the teacher must identify five potential outcomes of instruction to address it. These five outcomes range from a least-effective outcome to a highly effective outcome. Thus, the first outcome would quantify what the least-positive outcome would be, usually indicating no progress toward the goal. The second outcome would be better but still less than expected. The third outcome reflects what the teacher would consider an acceptable outcome, one that he would be satisfied to have the student achieve. The fourth outcome stipulates an outcome that is better than expected, and the fifth outcome identifies an outcome that far exceeds expectations.

Having identified the outcomes, the teacher then instructs the student through a curriculum or methodology that allows the student to attain the outcomes. When the student has completed the educational program, the teacher then returns to the rubric of outcomes created at the start and circles the outcome closest to the one the student achieved. From least to most effective, outcomes are awarded scores ranging from −2 to +2, with 0 being the middle outcome (the one that was viewed as an acceptable outcome).

Teachers can graph these scores across multiple goals to determine student progress or can transform the raw scores into a standardized t-score (which ranges from 0 to 100, with 50 as the middle or acceptable point), using tables published by Kiersuk, Smith, and Cardillo (1994). In most cases, however, simply graphing the goal attainment will suffice. Graphing allows a teacher to compare a student's progress on widely varying goals and to compare goals across multiple students so as to determine the effectiveness of an intervention. Palmer, Wehmeyer, Gibson, and Agran (2004) have used the goal attainment scaling process to evaluate the impact of teaching students with disabilities a wide array of skills, including goals linked to the general curriculum.

Progress in Addressing Other Educational Needs

Sometimes tracking progress in areas like social skills, self-control, and medication management (areas important to students with AD/HD) can be best accomplished by using T-Charts or checklists. A **T-Chart** is a chart that is laid out in the form of a capital letter T. The chart allows teachers to track two aspects of a behavior together. Stanford and Reeves (2005) created a T-Chart to help students figure out what appropriate behavior "looks like and sounds like" (p. 20), listing visual cues that reflect appropriate behavior on the left side and the auditory sounds on the right (e.g., sounds like using "please" and "thank you").

Checklists are even easier to design and simply involve breaking down the task into discrete steps, listing them, and then identifying ways of marking or quantifying progress, often using check boxes. While T-Charts and checklists cannot be quantified easily, they can be an important tool in collecting a wide array of data pertaining to student progress in areas of other educational needs.

Making Accommodations for Assessment

The most common areas of accommodations for students with AD/HD pertain to attention and concentration problems. Students with AD/HD who have a difficult time

IEP Tip

Goal attainment scaling goes hand-in-hand with teaching students goal-oriented behavior, as you learned earlier, and IEP teams should consider a program in which the student learns the goal attainment scaling process and evaluates her own progress toward her IEP goals.

sitting still and concentrating for longer periods of time may qualify for an accommodation to take extra breaks, which allow them to stretch. Students for whom such extra break times are not sufficient may request multiple testing sessions instead of a single session. Another possibility would be for students to request a reduced-distraction testing environment.

VALUES AND OUTCOMES

- ◆ Is it unreasonable for Kelsey to want to be a veterinarian? Not at all. She volunteers at a local animal shelter and is making progress in her general education curriculum.

- ◆ Does she make positive contributions in school or in the community? Yes. She participates in extracurricular activities and volunteers in a local business.

- ◆ Does she have strengths? Undoubtedly. With the benefit of her medication, she is learning how to behave and apply herself to her schoolwork.

- ◆ Does Kelsey make choices? Yes. She chooses how to respond to other students when they tease her, and (better yet) how to moderate her behavior so she is less hyperactive.

- ◆ Does she have solid relationships? Here, too, the answer is in the affirmative. She is now much more compatible with her grandparents, she has a trust-based relationship with Chris, and her behavior is such that she can have better relationships with her peers.

- ◆ Is she a full citizen in her school and community? Yes. She participates, carries her own weight, and makes progress through her studies.

WHAT DO YOU THINK?

1. What has made the greatest difference for Kelsey? The medication? The counseling with Chris? The talents of Barb Tootle, her second-grade teacher, in detecting Kelsey's AD/HD, or the methods her teachers use? Or is it the combination of these approaches—the multimodal aspects of her education?

2. What might happen to Kelsey if she did not take the medication, receive counseling from Chris, or have a qualified teacher?

ADDRESSING THE STANDARDS: THE VALUES CONNECTION

The following CEC Knowledge and Skill Standards: Common Core and Values are addressed in this chapter through the content and concepts we discuss.

CEC Knowledge and Skill Standards: Common Core	Values/Standards Connection
CEC Knowledge and Skill Standard II. **Development of Characteristics and Learners** CC2K1 — Typical and atypical human growth and development. CC2K2 — Educational implications of characteristics of various exceptionalities. CC2K3 — Characteristics and effects of the cultural and environmental milieu of the individual with exceptional learning needs and the family. CC2K4 — Family systems and the role of families in supporting development. CC2K5 — Similarities and differences of individuals with and without exceptional learning needs. CC2K7 — Effects of various medications on individuals with exceptional learning needs.	When you learn the characteristics of students with AD/HD, you are addressing CEC Standard 2, Development of Characteristics and Learners. Not every student with a disability is eligible for IDEA benefits; many may be eligible for Section 504 services that increase their opportunities to succeed in school and in life as *full citizens*.
CEC Knowledge and Skill Standard IV. **Instructional Strategies** CC4S2 — Teach individuals to use self-assessment, problem-solving, and other cognitive strategies to meet their needs. CC4S3 — Select, adapt, and use instructional strategies and materials according to characteristics of the individual with exceptional learning needs. CC4S4 — Use strategies to facilitate maintenance and generalization of skills across environments. CC4S5 — Use procedures to increase the individual's self-awareness, self-management, self-control, self-reliance, and self-esteem.	CEC Standard 4, Instructional Strategies, is reflected in developing your competency related to the delivery of instructional strategies such as errorless learning. Teaching students goal setting, attainment skills, and self-regulation skills decreases their dependency on others and enhances their capacity to be more *self-determined*.
CEC Knowledge and Skill Standard V. **Learning Environments and Social Interactions** CC5K5 — Social skills needed for educational and other environments. CC5S4 — Design learning environments that encourage active participation in individual and group settings. CC5S5 — Modify the learning environment to manage behaviors. CC5S6 — Use performance data and information from all stakeholders to make or suggest modifications in learning environments.	By arranging the learning environment to ensure that students with AD/HD can succeed, teachers build on their *strengths*.

CEC Knowledge and Skill Standards: Common Core	Values/Standards Connection
CEC Knowledge and Skill Standard VII. Instructional Planning CC7S1 Identify and prioritize areas of the general curriculum and accommodations for individuals with exceptional learning needs. CC7S3 Involve the individual and family in setting instructional goals and monitoring progress. CC7S6 Sequence, implement, and evaluate individualized learning objectives. CC7S9 Incorporate and implement instructional and assistive technology into the educational program.	When planning for instruction, keep in mind that all students, including those with exceptionalitites, are entitled to full participation in the classroom and the community.
CEC Knowledge and Skill Standard VIII. Assessment CC8K3 Screening, prereferral, referral, and classification procedures. CC8S6 Use assessment information in making eligibility, program, and placement decisions for individuals with exceptional learning needs, including those from culturally and/or linguistically diverse backgrounds. CC8S8 Evaluate instruction and monitor progress of individuals with exceptional learning needs.	As you evaluate students and monitor their progress in the general education curriculum, be sure to recognize their positive contributions and strengths rather than just their needs.
CEC Knowledge and Skill Standard X. Collaboration CC10S2 Collaborate with families and others in assessment of individuals with exceptional learning needs. CC10S3 Foster respectful and beneficial relationships between families and professionals. CC10S4 Assist individuals with exceptional learning needs and their families in becoming active participants in the educational team. CC10S5 Plan and conduct collaborative conferences with individuals with exceptional learning needs and their families.	Partnerships based on multimodal treatments build students' capacity for *relationships*.

Source: From CEC Knowledge and Skill Standards: Common Core and Values. Copyright by The Council for Exceptional Children. Reprinted with permission.

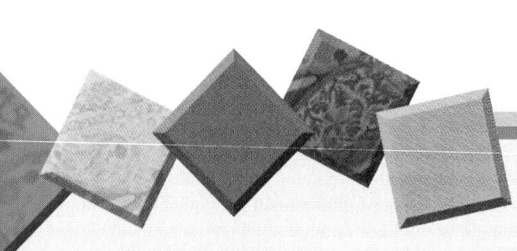

S U M M A R Y

Identifying Students with AD/HD

♦ As defined by criteria in the DSM-IV-TR (American Psychiatric Association, 2000), the three types of AD/HD include: (1) predominately inattentive type, (2) predominately hyperactive-impulsive type, and (3) combined type.

♦ Under IDEA, students with AD/HD are served under the "other health impairments" category.

♦ Although prevalence of AD/HD varies according to gender, age, and ethnicity, approximately 3 percent to 8 percent of the general population are identified as having AD/HD.

♦ In addition to the characteristics of AD/HD associated with the three types, other characteristics include intellectual functioning typically in the average range; impaired academic achievement; and challenges associated with behavioral, social, and emotional functioning.

♦ AD/HD has multiple causes associated with heredity, structural differences in the brain, and other causes.

Evaluating Students with AD/HD

♦ Diagnosis of AD/HD by a psychologist, a psychiatrist, or a physician often occurs outside the school system. The person who makes the diagnosis becomes part of the evaluation team.

♦ A frequently used evaluation tool to identify AD/HD is the Conners' Rating Scales—Revised, which come in teacher, parent, and adolescent versions.

♦ A particularly helpful evaluation tool for determining the nature and extent of specially designed instruction is the Attention Deficit Disorders Evaluation Scale—Third Edition (ADDES-3) because it prescribes interventions more often than any other available rating scale does.

Designing an Appropriate Individualized Education Program

♦ Students with AD/HD who do not qualify for special education services might still benefit from a Section 504 accommodation plan that enables them to receive some of the instructional supports they need to succeed in school.

♦ There are a number of classroom ecological variables that can benefit students with AD/HD, including arranging student seats to take distractability into account, posting daily schedules, and arranging the classroom to facilitate smooth transitions.

♦ Teaching students with AD/HD organization and goal-setting and attainment skills gives them strategies to better interact with the general curriculum.

♦ Many students with AD/HD take medicines, so it is important for the IEP team to address additional programmatic areas, including teacher knowledge about medicine use and potential side effects as well as student self-medication strategies.

Using Effective Instructional Strategies

♦ Young children with AD/HD can benefit from multimodal treatments—namely, multiple treatments across multiple fields or disciplines (e.g., medicine and behavioral programming).

♦ Errorless learning involves arranging the presentation of stimuli and the provision of prompts to ensure that students acquire new skills without the traditional errors associated with trial-and-error learning.

♦ Cognitive behavioral strategies can enable students with AD/HD to learn self-control strategies and to compensate for impairments in self-regulation.

♦ Video self-modeling is an effective tool to teach self-regulation and other skills.

Including Students with AD/HD

◆ The U.S. Department of Education does not provide data on the extent to which students with AD/HD participate in general education classrooms.

◆ A particular challenge associated with inclusive placements for many students with AD/HD is making friends.

Assessing Students' Progress

◆ Goal attainment scaling allows teachers to compare student progress in the general curriculum by tracking goal attainment and can be used to compare among students and, for a particular student, among goals.

◆ Simple T-Charts or checklists can be excellent ways to supplement more standardized data collection and to document progress in areas of other educational needs.

◆ To address problems with attention and concentration, students with AD/HD may need test accommodations that include extra breaks, multiple sessions, and distraction-free testing environments.

Now go to MyEducationLab at www.myeducationlab.com and take the Self-Assessment to gauge your initial comprehension of chapter content. Once you have taken the Self-Assessment, use your individualized Study Plan for Chapter 8 to enhance your understanding of the concepts discussed in the chapter.

Understanding Students with Intellectual Disability

◆ WHO IS STEPHEN SABIA?

Ownership.

It's as simple as that.

Just as he had for two years, Stephen Sabia arrived one winter morning at Paint Branch Middle School in Montgomery County, Maryland, ready to attend class.

Instead, he found himself in the middle of a fire emergency: Something was burning in the school. In the dim light of early morning, students were exiting buses and buildings and reforming into cliques on the football field, far away from the buildings. Fire engines were arriving. Controlled chaos was the order of the morning.

Caught up by the crowd, Stephen made his way to the football field. Amid the noise caused by nearly 1,700 excited and anxious students, he heard his classmates shouting his name as they searched for him. "Stephen, Stephen Sabia, where are you?" Having found him, they huddled together, Stephen clearly belonging to this particular group of students.

Who were they? They were the members of the JV football team. Why did they seek him out? Because he was the team's manager. Because he had some responsibility for them. Because he was meaningful to them. Because they, along with his parents Ricki and Peter, recognized that Stephen's team management was functional: It provided him with skills he could use after he graduated. And because from the very beginning of Stephen's association with the team, the team's coach, Bryan Walker, set the tone for Stephen to be a valued member of that team.

These students owned Stephen, not in the sense of commanding his obedience or having a person whom they possessed, but in the sense of being responsible for him. Just as he is responsible for them in football.

Ownership is evident in still other ways. Stephen attends Andrew White's ninth-grade honors-level American history class, sitting in the front row. There Andrew can easily supervise Stephen's work, making sure that Stephen identifies, on the map in his

textbook and on the larger map hanging in front of the class, the islands of the Philippines and Japan as Andrew explains why the Japanese invaded Pearl Harbor in Hawaii and not the American bases in the Philippines. Including Stephen in the class discussion, Andrew asks, "Stephen, what day did the Japanese invade Pearl Harbor?" Stephen's answer is correct: "Sunday, December 7, 1941."

Shifting from the start of World War II, Mr. White asks the class to consider President Franklin D. Roosevelt's Arsenal of Democracy speech, an articulation of why, other than in self-defense, America was fighting.

"Class, go to page 312 of your textbook. Tell me what President Roosevelt's Four Freedoms are."

With his paraeducator, Nate Wiles, beside him for this lesson, Stephen turns to that page, listens to his classmates respond to their teacher, and answers, in his turn, "Speech." Other students have given other correct answers: freedom of worship, freedom from fear, and freedom from want.

Military strategy, self-defense, and the fundamentals of democracy are not challenging concepts for the students in an honors course. Nor are they for Stephen, at least not if the essence of each is what he needs to learn. The essence constitutes Stephen's appropriate education.

Essence—an appropriate education—is accessible when Andrew applies the principles of universal design for learning and special educators adapt materials for him to use while teaching Stephen. It is accessible when Stephen's mother, Ricki, boils down his homework and rehearses the objectives of tomorrow's lessons with him. It is accessible when Ricki uses the summer recess to help Stephen read the books he will read again when school resumes. Or when she takes him to a museum to see artifacts of World War II. Or when she and his father, Peter, take him to the theater to view dramatic portrayals of the lessons he must master in school, or watch a DVD at home with him.

Stephen's appropriate education, his preparation for the jobs he wants when he graduates or for the junior college he may attend, is accessible when a common vision and commitment rest on universally designed learning—adapted curricula and individualized methodologies.

Appropriateness also occurs when Stephen, along with his teachers and his mother, holds himself accountable for coming to class prepared to participate. It bears repeating: IDEA favors Stephen's participation in the general curriculum, and the No Child Left Behind Act holds educators accountable for their students' learning.

Accessible education and appropriate education are linear; the zero reject rule (access to school) leads to an evaluation that underlies the appropriate education in the general curriculum and in extracurricular activities.

CHAPTER OBJECTIVES

◆ You will learn about students' intellectual characteristics, their limitations in three areas (memory, generalization, and motivation) and the degrees of their impairments, and you will recognize their strengths, such as Stephen Sabia's high motivation. You also will learn about their behavioral characteristics.

◆ You will learn about the causes of intellectual disability, especially the biological causes that affected Stephen, who has Down syndrome.

◆ You will learn how to evaluate students by assessing their intellectual and behavioral capacities and needs, especially through the Adaptive Behavior Scale developed by the nation's leading professional association in the field of intellectual disability.

◆ You will learn how to develop an appropriate IEP and how general educators adapt their curricula and methods to include students such as Stephen, even in honors courses.

◆ You will learn about "prelinguistic milieu teaching" for preschool and early education students, about self-determination for students in elementary schools, and about transition and community-based instruction that is similar to Stephen's.

◆ You will learn the value of including students in the general curriculum (as Stephen is included in it and in extracurricular activities) and how to assess their progress in that curriculum.

But how do they relate to "ownership"? The answer lies in understanding what "ownership" means in Stephen's life.

Ownership is not merely the result—a by-product, an artifact—of an accessible and appropriate general and special education. It is, indeed, the goal, not just for teachers and students in general and special education but also for the nation as well. It's what the Paint Branch High School history teacher, Andrew White, special education director, Christine Genua, paraeducator, Nate Wiles, and JV football coach, Bryan Walker have all adopted. It's what Stephen's previous teachers also adopted—both those at his elementary school (Maria Dummann, Dianne Chupka, and John Vigna) and those at his middle school (Kristen Andre, Kimberly Johnson, and Diane Filmore). At their best, inclusion, great expectations, and ownership begin early; that way, they endure.

The JV football players sensed that when they sought out Stephen that morning. In a very real sense, they, together with Stephen's teachers and Ricki, proclaimed that we are all responsible for each other, even as Stephen is responsible for learning. Ricki and Peter have said that their goal for Stephen is the same as their goal for his older brother: to maximize his potential so that he can maximize his opportunities in all aspects of life.

That's where ownership enters the picture. Unless everyone involved with Stephen understands, as the JV football players did, that they own some responsibility for him, that goal—maximized potential and opportunities—will be elusive.

IDENTIFYING STUDENTS WITH INTELLECTUAL DISABILITY

Defining Intellectual Disability

After reading this chapter, complete the Self-Assessment for Chapter 9 on MyEducationLab to gauge your initial understanding of chapter content.

How familiar is the term *intellectual disability* to you? You likely are much more familiar with the term *mental retardation*. What connotations do you associate with the term *mental retardation*, and what do you associate with the term *intellectual disability*? Perhaps your answer acknowledges the stigma that attaches to the term *mental retardation*. If so, you may easily understand why a major shift in terminology is occurring for the students whose education is the focus of this chapter.

Over approximately the last 50 years, the term used most often to describe this disability has been *mental retardation*. In fact, IDEA still uses the term *mental retardation*, defining it as "significantly subaverage general intellectual functioning, existing concurrently with deficits in adaptive behavior and manifested during the developmental period, that adversely affects a child's educational performance". But national organizations that advocate for these students and their parents have abandoned that term in favor of the term *intellectual disability*. For example, the American Association on Intellectual and Developmental Disabilities (AAIDD), the nation's oldest and largest professional association concerned with individuals who have intellectual disability, adopted that name in 2006 and is no longer the American Association on Mental Retardation. Likewise, the President's Committee on Mental Retardation is now called the President's Committee for People with Intellectual Disabilities. Indeed, professionals and families worldwide now prefer the term *intellectual disability*. Further, the AAIDD Terminology and Classification Committee will use the term *intellectual disability* in the next AAIDD Manual for Definition, Classification, and Systems of Support (Schalock et al., 2007). The term *intellectual disability* "covers the same population of individuals who were diagnosed previously with mental retardation in number, kind, level, type and duration of the disability and the need of people with this disability for individualized services and supports" (Schalock et al., 2007, p. 116). Intellectual disability is:

> . . . characterized by significant limitations both in intellectual functioning and in adaptive behavior as expressed in conceptual, social, and practical adaptive skills. This disability originates before age 18. (Schalock et al., 2007, p. 118)

This shift in terminology occurred primarily because the term *mental retardation* has stigmatized many people with this disability, their families, friends, and the professionals who work with them. Further, disability is now regarded less as an inherent limitation *within* an individual than as an outcome of the interaction between a person's capacities and the context in which the person wants to function (Luckasson et al., 2002; World Health Organization, 2001). Students who have been classified with an intellectual disability can function more effectively and independently when professionals, including teachers, incorporate appropriate supports into their school, home, and community environments.

You will understand that point by studying Figure 9.1. It lists the five assumptions of the AAIDD definition and shows how they apply to Stephen. Note that assumptions 4 and

---

Figure 9.1

Assumptions regarding the definition of intellectual disability and their application to Stephen Sabia

FIVE ASSUMPTIONS	APPLICATIONS TO STEPHEN
1. Limitations in present functioning must be considered within the context of community environments typical of the individual's age, peers, and culture.	Stephen's limitations are intellectual (although he prospers with support), but not behavioral, because he has sufficient social skills to be included in school and community activities with his peers and family.
2. Valid assessment considers cultural and linguistic diversity as well as differences in communication, sensory, motor, and behavioral factors.	Stephen has good skills in understanding what people say (receptive communication), but he struggles in using written and oral expressive language.
3. Within an individual, limitations often coexist with strengths.	Stephen's assessments reveal his limitations, such as in mathematics, as well as his strengths, such as self-direction, a sense of responsibility, self-esteem, and following rules.
4. An important purpose of describing limitations is to develop a profile of needed supports.	Stephen's supports are academic (he has a paraeducator and his general and special educators adapt curriculum for him) and social (from his peers on the football team; his paraprofessional, Nate; and, at home, his brother, David, and David's friends); the degree of those supports varies according to his environments (he is fairly independent in daily living skills but not as self-directed as usual if he is in a new situation that does not generalize to ones he already has mastered).
5. With appropriate personalized supports over a sustained period, the life functioning of the person generally will improve.	Stephen has benefited from inclusive education and extensive community experiences and, with the supports his teachers and family provide, has gained and is continuing to gain skills to work, use public transportation independently, and walk about in his neighborhood (although his parents worry about this and provide privately paid training for him to become more conscious that he must look both ways when crossing a street and not wander off from his friends or family while he is in the community.)

Figure 9.2

Definitions of intensities of support

Intermittent

Supports on an "as-needed" basis. Characterized by episodic nature, person not always needing the support(s), or short-term supports needed during life-span transitions (e.g., job loss, an acute medical crisis). Intermittent supports may be high- or low-intensity when provided.

Limited

An intensity of supports characterized by consistency over time, time-limited but not of an intermittent nature, may require fewer staff members and less cost than more intensive levels of support (e.g., time-limited employment training, transitional supports during the school-to-adult period).

Extensive

Supports characterized by regular involvement (e.g., daily) in at least some environments (such as work or home) and not time-limited (e.g., long-term vocational support, long-term home living support).

Pervasive

Supports characterized by their constancy, high intensity; provided across environments; potential life-sustaining nature. Pervasive supports typically involve more staff members and intrusiveness than do extensive or time-limited supports.

Source: From *Mental Retardation: Definition, Classification, and Systems of Supports*, by R. Luckasson, D. L. Coulter, E. A. Polloway, S. Relss, R. L. Schalock, M. E. Snell, D. M. Spitalnik, and J. A. Stark, 1992, Washington, DC: American Association on Mental Retardation. Copyright 1992 by the American Association on Mental Retardation. Reprinted with permission.

5 call for professionals, teachers, and family and community members to support people with an intellectual disability to function more competently in everyday environments. **Supports** are the services, resources, and personal assistance that enable a person to develop, learn, and live effectively (Luckasson et al., 2002). They can be intermittent (provided from time to time) or pervasive (constant), as Figure 9.2 describes.

At Paint Branch School, Stephen Sabia receives various kinds of support with various intensity. In his honors and other general education classes, the special education director, Christine Genua, has selected general education teachers who have the skills best suited for teaching Stephen, and, using Stephen's IEP, she helps them modify and adapt their curriculum and methods of teaching. Some of Stephen's teachers also have adapted some homework from texts other than the one they use in class; some offer DVDs about the class textbook, developed by the book's publisher; all play to his strength, namely, his ability to learn by studying graphics (maps, tables, figures, and illustrations with captions). Stephen's only separate special education class is mathematics; there his support is different than but no less intense than in his honors and general education classes. He also receives 90 minutes of speech therapy each week in school and an hour of extra help in study hall. In short, Stephen benefits from pervasive (constant) support in his academic program.

He is, however, completely independent in other aspects of his education. He takes the regular school bus to and from school. On his own, he negotiates his way around a large school (1700 students) that has many wings and annexes. He attends school dances. In many respects, he is no different than his age-peers who do not have disabilities.

Note especially that AAIDD does not define intellectual disability as a trait inherent in a person but as a state of functioning that describes the fit between an individual's capabilities and the structure and expectations of the individual's personal and social environment (Luckasson et al., 2002). Whether a person has an intellectual disability, then, depends in part on how she functions in the environments that are typical for people without disabilities.

IEP Tip

Students can improve their functioning in many environments through instruction and technology-based supports such as the computer-based literacy program you'll learn about later in this chapter. IEP teams must consider assistive technology for all students receiving special education services.

It is difficult to obtain an accurate prevalence rate for intellectual disability. Factors that influence prevalence include age (intellectual disability is diagnosed most frequently during school years), gender (more males than females are diagnosed), and socioeconomic level (poverty is strongly related to intellectual disability) (Emerson, 2007; Harris, 2006). The Centers for Disease Control have concluded that the prevalence of intellectual disability is 12 per 1,000 children (Avchen, Bhasin, Braun, & Yeargin-Allsopp, 2007). The CDC study found that the prevalence rate for European American students was 7.4 per 1,000, and it was 19.7 per 1,000 for African American students. In fall 2006, approximately 0.08 percent (511,041) of all students ages 6 through 21 in special education nationally were classified as having intellectual disabilities (U.S. Department of Education, Office of Special Education Programs, 2008).

Describing the Characteristics

The two major characteristics of intellectual disability are limitations in intellectual functioning and limitations in adaptive behavior.

Limitations in Intellectual Functioning

Intelligence refers to a student's general mental capability for solving problems, paying attention to relevant information, thinking abstractly, remembering important information and skills, learning from everyday experiences, and generalizing knowledge from one setting to another. Educators measure a student's intelligence by administering tests such as the Wechsler Intelligence Scale for Children—IV (see Chapter 5). Students with intellectual disability have an IQ score approximately two standard deviations below the mean—namely, an IQ of 70 or below on the Wechsler scale. Ninety-five percent of the population's intellectual functioning falls between two standard deviations below and above the mean. Approximately 85% of the students with intellectual disability have an IQ ranging from 50–55 to 70. The DSM-IV-TR (APA, 2000) classifies mental retardation according to IQ levels (the next version of the DSM will use the term *intellectual disability* instead of *mental retardation*):

◆ Mild mental retardation—IQ 50–55 to approximately 70

◆ Moderate mental retardation—IQ 35–40 to 50–55

◆ Severe mental retardation—IQ 20–25 to 30–40

◆ Profound mental retardation—IQ below 20–25

Stephen has had only one IQ test, when he was 5 years old. His parents and teachers doubt the test was helpful. He was asked to repeat words, testing his memory. Because of his language difficulties, he could not express clearly enough what he learned; the resulting IQ score showed little about his intellectual abilities. Assuming that he has moderate mental retardation seems defensible. What is significant, however, is that with the help of the Maryland Coalition for Inclusive Education, Stephen was the first student with intellectual disability in each of his schools to be fully included in the school's academic program, beginning with preschool and continuing through high school. As his teachers learned what he was able to accomplish, they became more invested in his academic performance. Simultaneously, Stephen developed the self-confidence and then the ability to work alongside nondisabled peers, to be independent, and to solve problems. These are highly functional skills for him in school, and they will serve him well after he leaves school.

The AAIDD classification system has moved away from the IQ-levels approach and instead recommends that professionals should identify the levels of support their students need. Nevertheless, you may find that some educators still use the IQ-levels approach. When you do, you should emphasize that supports, not levels, are what special educators are most concerned with. Regardless of their IQ score, however, students with intellectual disability typically have impaired intellectual functioning that impacts three areas for educators to address: memory, generalization, and motivation.

PEARSON
myeducationlab

Go to the Activities and Application section in Chapter 9 of MyEducationLab and complete Activity 1. As you watch the video and answer the accompanying questions, think about the outcomes that could be possible for this child with the early intervention she is receiving.

Memory. For many years, researchers documented that individuals with intellectual disability had impairments in memory, especially short-term memory (Ellis, 1970). **Short-term memory** refers to the ability to recall information that has been stored for a few seconds to a few hours, such as the step-by-step instructions teachers give their students. Although individuals with intellectual disability also often have impairments in speech and language, short-term memory impairments are associated with overall memory capacity and not with other contributing factors (Jarrold, Purser, & Brock, 2006). Many students can use strategies to improve their memory (Bray, Fletcher, & Turner, 1997; Taylor, Richards, & Brady, 2005). Indeed, when provided with verbal and physical prompts, 17-year-old students with an intellectual disability have used memory strategies at a rate comparable to 17-year-olds without intellectual disability, and younger students with intellectual disability also have improved their memory through verbal prompts (Fletcher, Huffman, & Bray, 2003). Effective strategies for you to use include teaching your students to repeat silent instructions to themselves, listen to tape-recorded instructions, and move objects in a particular order to remember a sequence of activities they need to perform.

Stephen has very good short-term memory, as evidenced by the 15–20 concepts he often learns for each unit in math, English and history. Even when school administers all tests in a single week ("finals week"), he does well. His memory has been greatly enhanced by higher academic expectations over the last few years. When he started middle school and needed to learn only a few subjects at one time, he struggled much more than he does now.

Generalization. **Generalization** refers to the ability to transfer knowledge or behavior learned for doing one task to another task and to make that transfer across different settings or environments (Horner, Dunlap, & Koegel, 1988; Stokes & Baer, 1977). Individuals with intellectual disability typically have difficulty generalizing the skills they have learned in school to their home and community settings; that is so because the cues, expectations, people, and environmental arrangements of one setting usually do not exist in other settings (Bebko & McPherson, 1997; Mechling, Gast, & Langone, 2002).

Home and community settings often have greater complexity, more distractions, and more irrelevant stimuli than classrooms. Outside the classroom, the cognitive demands on students increase greatly, yet they receive most of their instruction in classrooms, not community settings. As you will learn later in this chapter, one way to increase students' ability to generalize is to teach functional curricular content in the settings where these skills are typically used (Kaiser & Grim, 2006; Mechling & Ortega-Hurndon, 2007).

Ricki and Peter provide their own community instruction to Stephen, taking him shopping at grocery or department stores and going with him to restaurants, museums, baseball games, and hotels—sometimes on a plane, sometimes on a cruise ship, and sometimes in their van in and around Maryland and Washington, D.C. In the community, he applies what he has learned at school and home: how to read a menu (whether at McDonald's or a five-star restaurant), how to behave in public places (quiet talk and good manners), and how to "put a lid on" his enthusiastic approach to everyone, particularly strangers.

Motivation. No single profile of motivation applies to all people with intellectual disability, any more than any single profile applies to all people without intellectual disability (Switzky, 2006). But as a general rule, students with intellectual disability are often externally oriented (Tasse & Havercamp, 2006). Many tend to wait for other people to prompt them before acting and believe that they have little control over outcomes in their day-to-day lives (Wehmeyer & Mithaug, 2006). Most are not highly motivated because they too often experience failure when they choose to act. That helps

Community-based instruction teaches students to generalize skills to these everyday settings.

explain why they can be less hopeful about the future than their peers with learning disabilities or without disabilities (Palmer & Wehmeyer, 1998; Shogren, Lopez, Wehmeyer, Little, & Pressgrove, 2006). By contrast, Stephen's parents and teachers challenge him to be independent. The school's special education director, Christine Genua, allows him to choose his elective classes. Ricki and Peter expect him to choose what to pack for lunch and to go to bed himself at the agreed-upon hour. It helps that Stephen is motivated to please others, but the "others" also have to teach, expect, and respond to his choices.

Students' low motivation leads them to use a problem-solving style called **outer-directedness**—distrusting their own solutions and depending on others to guide them. This fact is troublesome (Zigler, 2001) because outer-directedness can make them especially vulnerable to control by others.

IEP Tip

You should advocate for training in self-determination, which we describe later in this chapter, when you help develop a student's IEP.

Limitations in Adaptive Behavior

Adaptive behavior refers to the "collection of conceptual, social, and practical skills that have been learned by people in order to function in their everyday lives" (Luckasson et al., 2002, p. 73). There are three domains of adaptive behavior (Luckasson et al., 2002):

◆ Conceptual skills include language (receptive and expressive), reading and writing, money concepts, and self-direction.

◆ Social skills include responsibility, self-esteem, gullibility, and rule-following.

◆ Practical skills include activities of daily living, occupational skills, and maintenance of safe environments.

By definition, people with intellectual disability have significant limitations in adaptive behavior. A significant limitation occurs when a student scores at least two standard deviations below the mean on (a) one or more scores on measures of conceptual, social, and practical skills or (b) an overall score on a standardized measure that includes conceptual, social, and practical skills (Luckasson et al., 2002).

Students' adaptive behavior relates to contextual considerations such as their culture, environment, and age (Borthwick-Duffy, 2007). Students with intellectual disability will almost always fall below the norm of their typically developing peers. The causes of their significant limitations may include not knowing how to perform a skill, not knowing when to perform a skill that has already been learned, and motivational factors that influence whether or not skills are performed. For example, Stephen has to learn many skills that other kids just absorb from being part of an environment. He needs a lot more repetition than his typical peers to master certain skills and sometimes has trouble knowing when to use a skill in a new situation. An example of a skill he has yet to fully master is tying his shoes. He knows the steps but can't seem to get his hands to perform the steps with enough finesse to tie the shoe tightly enough to last more than a few minutes.

Determining the Causes

There are two categories of causes of intellectual disability: timing and type (Luckasson et al., 2002).

Causes by Timing

Timing refers to the time of onset of the disability and has implications for causes (Glynn & Sandman, 2006; Percy, 2007).

◆ Prenatal (before birth, such as chromosomal disorders and disorders of brain formation)

◆ Perinatal (during the birth process, such as prematurity and birth injury)

◆ Postnatal (after birth, such as traumatic brain injury and infections)

The best evidence is that 12 percent of all students with intellectual disability had a prenatal cause, 6 percent had a perinatal cause, and 4 percent had a postnatal cause. A probable cause could not be determined for 78 percent of the children (Yeargin-Allsopp, Murphy, Cordero, Decouflé, & Hollowell, 1997). Intellectual disability that is identified early typically will be severe and require significant supports (Batshaw, Shapiro, & Farber, 2007).

Causes by Type

There are four categories of causes by type (Luckasson et al., 2002, p. 126):

◆ Biomedical factors relate to biologic processes, such as genetic disorders and nutrition.

◆ Social factors relate to social and family interaction, such as stimulation and adult responsiveness.

◆ Behavioral factors relate to potentially causal behaviors, such as dangerous activities and maternal substance abuse.

◆ Educational factors relate to the availability of educational supports that promote mental development of adaptive skills.

Biomedical causes. Biomedical causes develop within the individual. Typically, they originate early in a child's development. A biomedical cause can be identified in about two thirds of the children with intellectual disability who have more severe intellectual impairments and therefore require extensive and pervasive supports (Batshaw et al., 2007).

Chromosomal disorders occur at or soon after conception. When the egg and sperm unite during conception, they bring together genes from the mother and the father. These genes determine the personal characteristics of the developing embryo and are found on threadlike structures called **chromosomes.** Chromosomes direct each cell's activity. Humans have 23 pairs of chromosomes in each cell, with one chromosome in each pair coming from the mother and one from the father. A chromosomal disorder occurs when a parent contributes either too much (an extra chromosome is added) or too little (all or part of a chromosome is missing) genetic material. Chromosomal disorders cause intellectual disability for approximately 30 percent of individuals who require extensive and pervasive support and for 4 to 8 percent of individuals who need less intensive support (Murphy, Boyle, Schendel, Decouflé, & Yeargin-Allsopp, 1998).

There are two general types of chromosomal disorders—autosomal disorders and heterosomal disorders, typically referred to as sex chromosome disorders. **Autosomal chromosomes** are all chromosomes other than the X and Y chromosomes that determine gender. The most common autosomal chromosomal disorder is Down syndrome, which occurs when there is an extra 21st chromosome. Thus, an individual with Down syndrome has 47 individual chromosomes rather than 46. Stephen has Down syndrome; the cause of his disability is biological and prenatal.

The older a woman is when she is pregnant, the more likely it is that she will have a child with Down syndrome. Further, people with Down syndrome display characteristics of aging earlier than people who do not have the syndrome (Lovering & Percy, 2007). In Box 9.1, My Voice, Margaret Muller shares her perspectives about experiencing Down syndrome. Margaret wrote this essay with assistance and conducted some of her own research, including interviews with her pediatrician.

The most common sex-linked chromosomal disorder is Fragile X syndrome, which is the result of an unstable region of genetic material (a gene called FMR1) on the long arm of the X chromosome (Hessl, Rivera, & Reiss, 2004). Some studies suggest that Fragile X affects 1 in 2,000 males and 1 in 4,000 females of all races and ethnic groups and is the most common sex-linked chromosomal disorder resulting in intellectual disability; it is also the most common known cause of autism (Batshaw, Shapiro, & Farber, 2007).

Social, behavioral, and educational causes. We consider these three causes together because their boundaries often overlap, making it difficult to distinguish among them. Poverty is an element in each of these causes. Poverty is much more associated with in-

Margaret's Guide to Down Syndrome

Today I'd like to tell you about Down syndrome. My purpose for talking about this is to be able to say, "Yes, I have Down syndrome. Sometimes I have to work harder to learn things, but in many ways I am just like everyone else." I would like to tell people that having Down syndrome does not keep me from doing the things I need to do or want to do. I just have to work harder.

Down syndrome is a condition and not a disease. You cannot catch Down syndrome like you can catch a cold or virus. It is something you are just born with—like blond hair and blue eyes. If you have Down syndrome when you are born, you will have it your whole life.

People without Down syndrome have 46 chromosomes, which carry all the genetic information about a person, in each of their cells. People with Down syndrome have one extra chromosome. So a person with Down syndrome has a total of 47 chromosomes in each cell. Doctors and experts are not really sure what causes it, but they say it occurs in about 1 of every 700 babies. This happens randomly, like flipping a coin or winning the lottery.

Everyone with Down syndrome is a totally unique person. The extra chromosome makes it harder for me to learn. Sometimes I need someone to say, "Settle down and get busy!" Also, it's really easy for me to be stubborn, so I don't mind if you say, "Hey, Margaret, please stop."

Even though I have one extra chromosome, the rest of my chromosomes carry information from generation to generation just like yours. Chromosomes control certain genetic characteristics, like eye color, skin color, height, and some abilities like music, art, or math.

For example, I get my blue eyes from my father, my fair skin and freckles from my mother, my blond hair from my grandmother, my long, thin feet from both my mom and my dad, and my need to wear glasses from both my grandparents and my parents. I like to concentrate on the ways that I am like everyone else.

I am very lucky to be alive today rather than 50 years or even 20 years ago because back then the doctors and experts believed that people with Down syndrome were not capable of learning. But now we know that people with Down syndrome are capable of doing many different things.

I personally am doing things that some people didn't think I could do. When I was born, somebody told my mom that it was too bad that I was named "Margaret" because I would never even be able to say my name. That person might never have expected that I could win four medals in Special Olympics swimming, be a green belt in karate, cook a pizza, read a novel, run half a mile, or get up in front of the class and give a speech! With a lot of hard work and encouragement, I have been able to do all these things.

I am not sad about the fact that I have Down syndrome. It is just part of me. I have a great brother (most of the time) and parents who love me a lot. I have wonderful friends who enjoy hanging out and having fun with me. I have teachers who help me keep on learning new things. I am glad to be a student at Lincoln Middle School because it is a great school and almost everyone is really nice. Down syndrome has not stopped me from having a worthwhile life.

—Margaret Muller
Cape Cod, Massachusetts

Source: By Margaret Muller, from www.patriciaebauer.com <http://www.patriciaebauer.com/>. Originally printed in The *Washington Post,* September 14, 1999.

tellectual disability than with any other disability (National Research Council, 2002). Poverty during childhood creates risks for higher incidence of intellectual disability, lower educational attainment, poorer physical and mental health, and increased mortality (Emerson, 2007; Fujiura & Parish, 2007). Elementary and secondary school students who live in families who are at the bottom 20% of socioeconomic status are four times more likely to have intellectual disability than those in the top 20% of socioeconomic status (Emerson, Graham, & Hatton, 2006). Moreover, African American students are more than twice as likely to be identified as having intellectual disability than are European American students (National Research Council, 2002), and poverty among African Americans is three times as high as poverty among European Americans (Blank, 2001). Clearly, one of the greatest challenges in the field of intellectual disability is to respond more effectively and sensitively to the multiple educational challenges facing students who experience poverty, and to support their families (see Chapter 3).

There are other factors associated with social, behavioral, and educational causes.

◆ Low maternal education is the strongest predictor for having a child with an intellectual disability when the child does not have a serious neurological condition (Avchen, Bhasin, Braun, & Yeargin-Allsopp, 2007).

 IEP Tip

The IEP team should identify and develop supports to overcome poverty-related factors that influence a student's school performance, including inadequate nutrition, health care, and rest. School social workers on the IEP team should connect the student's family to appropriate school and community resources.

- By 3 to 4 years of age, children raised by adolescent mothers have been found to have difficulties with self-regulation, poor academic achievement, and lower language development (Borkowski et al., 2004).
- The more a pregnant woman consumes alcohol, the greater likelihood that her child's development will be impacted, with the most serious outcome being fetal alcohol syndrome (Burbacher & Grant, 2006).

EVALUATING STUDENTS WITH INTELLECTUAL DISABILITY

Determining the Presence of Intellectual Disability

To determine whether a student has intellectual disability, teachers and other professionals evaluate the student's intellectual functioning and adaptive behavior; you will recall that these are the two major characteristics of intellectual disability (Dixon, 2007; Tylenda, Beckett, & Barrett, 2007). The evaluation process includes observation, screening, and the IDEA nondiscriminatory evaluation process (see Figure 9.3). Stephen was born prematurely. For that reason, his diagnosis as having Down syndrome took two days; such a diagnosis of a trait with obvious physical manifestations is usually made almost immediately after a baby is born.

As you read earlier, educators should not identify a student as having intellectual disability unless the student has significant limitations in both intellectual functioning and adaptive behavior. You also read that evaluators frequently use the tests we described in Chapter 5 (learning disabilities), particularly the Wechsler Intelligence Scale for Children—IV, to determine whether a student's intellectual functioning is two standard deviations below the mean (that is, the student meets the cutoff point for "significant limitation" in intellectual functioning).

Evaluators must also assess a student's adaptive behavior. They need to know whether a student has conceptual, social, and practical adaptive skills appropriate to her age and the environments typical of her community. Accordingly, they rely on adaptive behavior scales that have been normed on individuals with and without disabilities.

Unlike intelligence tests, which are given directly to the student who is being evaluated, most adaptive behavior scales require the evaluator to rely on information provided by an individual who is familiar with the student's daily activities, such as one of the student's teachers or one or both of the student's parents. As we pointed out earlier, it is always necessary to take into account factors such as the student's culture, environment, and motivation (Borthwick-Duffy, 2007).

The AAIDD is developing the Diagnostic Adaptive Behavior Scale (DABS), a new standardized measure of adaptive behavior. DABS is based on the three components of conceptual, social, and practical skills that you learned about earlier in the chapter. It will assess significant limitations in adaptive behavior by determining a cut-off point that is approximately two standard deviations below the mean of individuals without intellectual disabilities within the age ranges of 4 through 21 years.

Significantly, the DABS is being normed (the range of scores across the population is being identified) with the general population. Past adaptive behavior measures were normed only with people with impaired adaptive skills performance. However, because adaptive behavior is normal with the general population, DABS will evaluate adaptive skills performance against a typical population average. DABS should be available for use in 2009.

Until the DABS is available, an alternative is the AAMR Adaptive Behavior Scale—School. This scale is appropriate for evaluating students ranging in age from 3 to 21 (Dixon, 2007; Lambert, Nihira, & Leland, 1993) and has scientifically adequate reliability and validity (Stinnett, Fuqua, & Coombs, 1999). Part 1 of the scale assesses personal independence in daily living and includes nine behavior domains: physical development, economic activity, language development, numbers and time, independent functioning, prevocational/vocational activity, self-direction, responsibility, and socialization. Part 2 concentrates on social behaviors in seven domains: social behavior, conformity, trustworthiness, stereotyped and hyperactive behavior, self-abusive behavior, social engagement, and disturbing

Figure 9.3

Nondiscriminatory evaluation process for determining the presence of intellectual disability

Observation	***Medical personnel observe:*** The student does not attain appropriate development milestones or has characteristics of a particular syndrome associated with intellectual disability.
	Teacher and parents observe: The student (1) does not learn as quickly as peers, (2) has difficulty retaining and generalizing learned skills, (3) has low motivation, and (4) has more limitations in adaptive behaviors than peers in the general education classroom.
Screening	***Assessment measures:***
	Medical screening: The student may be identified through a physician's use of various tests before the child enters school.
	Classroom work products: The student has difficulty in academic areas in the general education classroom; reading comprehension and mathematical reasoning/application are limited.
Prereferral	***Teacher implements suggestions from school-based team:*** The student still performs poorly in academics or continues to manifest impairments in adaptive behavior despite interventions. (If the student has been identified before entering school, this step is omitted.)
Referral	If, in spite of interventions, the student still performs poorly in academics or continues to manifest impairments in adaptive behaviors, the child is referred to a multidisciplinary team.
Nondiscriminatory evaluation procedures and standards	***Assessment measures:***
	Individualized intelligence test: The student has significantly subaverage intellectual functioning (bottom 2% to 3% of population) with IQ standard score of 70 to 75 or below. The nondiscriminatory evaluation team makes sure the test is not culturally biased.
	Adaptive behavior scales: The student scores significantly below average in two or more adaptive skill domains, indicating deficits in skill areas such as communication, home living, self-direction, and leisure.
	Anecdotal records: The student's learning problems cannot be explained by cultural or linguistic differences.
	Curriculum-based assessment: The student experiences difficulty in making progress in the general curriculum used by the local school district.
	Direct observation: The student experiences difficulty or frustration in the general classroom.
Determination	The nondiscriminatory evaluation team determines that the student has mental retardation and needs special education and related services. The student's IEP team proceeds to develop appropriate education options for the child.

interpersonal behavior. The domains of the Adaptive Behavior Scale—School were developed before AAMR categorized adaptive behavior into the three domains of conceptual, social, and practical; while it is useful, it is not sufficiently current.

The score for each domain is norm-referenced, enabling the evaluator to compare the student's performance with the performance of other students of the same age and thus to determine whether the student has intellectual disabilities because of low adaptive behavior. Although the majority of the items on the scale are not racially biased, approximately one third of the items in the scale's section on community do allegedly reflect racial bias. Ten of the items are biased in favor of European Americans, and four are biased in favor of races other than European American (Bryant, Bryant, & Chamberlain, 1999). The bias is problematic given the data about poverty and race that we noted earlier.

Although Stephen has not been formally evaluated for his adaptive behavior, he has both strengths and needs. His physical development seems normal; his economic activity and ability to use numbers leave much to be desired, as Stephen is not strong at math (which he learns in a separate special education class); his language development is delayed (hence, the speech therapy he gets at school and home); his prevocational activity is good, as evidenced by his being the JV football team manager; his self-direction is solid, in large part because his teachers and parents give him choices and teach how to make a choice; he has a sense of responsibility (the "ownership" factor); and he is highly social (a nearly nonstop dancer at school homecoming). His social behavior is good, in part because he regularly takes medication that levels out his sometimes excited behaviors; he generally conforms to rules (except those that prohibit snacks—he's clever and hides candy wrappers behind furniture instead of putting them into the trash, an obvious place to look for evidence of rule-breaking); he has no stereotyped or hyperactive behavior and no self-injurious behavior (though he needs to learn to cross the street only with a green light and only after looking both ways), nor does he have any disturbing interpersonal behavior.

Determining the Nature of Specially Designed Instruction and Services

Many other procedures help members of a student's nondiscriminatory evaluation team to identify the special education services that can meet the student's educational and other needs and the related services the student requires to benefit from general and special education. The team will emphasize a student's strengths as well as the student's education and other educationally related needs. Not every student learns the same way. Stephen, for example, learned how to distinguish his right side from his left by learning the phases of the moon in his sixth grade science class: The moon rises on your right and sets on your left. He learned how to follow a kitchen recipe during his chemistry class.

When a student is in secondary school, the student's IEP will concentrate on the skills needed to be successful at work and in the community as an adult. (You will learn more about transition services later in this chapter.) A useful procedure for determining the strengths and needs of older students and planning services and supports for them, especially for adult life, is the Transition Planning Inventory (Clark & Patton, 2006; Clark, 2007). The Inventory is appropriate for students aged 14 to 25. It focuses on nine areas of adulthood: Employment, Further Education/Training, Daily Living, Living Arrangements, Leisure Activities, Community Participation, Health, Self-Determination, Communication, and Personal Relationships. Within each area, the Inventory identifies the knowledge, skills, or behaviors that are associated with successful postsecondary outcomes.

The Inventory consists of four forms: student, home, and school forms and a form for profiles and further assessment recommendations. Students, parents (or other family members or guardians), and a school representative independently complete a five-point rating scale (strong disagreement to strong agreement) for each item.

The Inventory's senior author created a practical guide, *Assessment for Transitions Planning,* that instructs educators how to use the Inventory in assessing individuals with disabilities across all age levels (Clark, 2007). A Spanish version of the home form of the Inventory also has appropriate validity and reliability (Stevens, 2006).

DESIGNING AN APPROPRIATE IEP

Partnering for Special Education and Related Services

Despite the availability of tools such as the Transition Planning Inventory and the importance of a curriculum that takes into account a student's age and transition needs, students with intellectual disability typically experience some of the lowest postschool outcomes in terms of graduating with a regular diploma, receiving postsecondary education, and being employed after high school (Wagner, Newman, Cameto, Levine, & Garza, 2006). In 2003, The Arc of the U.S., with 40 other national or regional organizations in developmental disabilities, and several federal agencies, sponsored a National Goals Conference

IEP Tip

The Transition Planning Inventory enables the IEP committee to comply with IDEA's requirement that transition planning should be based on the student's needs, strengths, preferences, and interests.

to review the "policy promises" that the federal government has made to its citizens with developmental disabilities. Attending the conference were self-advocates, family members, researchers, policy leaders, and service administrators/providers. They set three key goals around transition (Hasazi et al., 2005):

> "To improve collaboration and links between systems to support student achievement of meaningful school and post-school outcomes."

> "To promote the student's self-determination and self-advocacy."

> "To increase parent participation and involvement."

Let's consider the first goal—to improve collaboration and links. Although IDEA requires IEP teams to collaborate with agencies and community resources serving both high school students and adults in ensuring a smooth transition, the current level of interagency communication is not sufficient (Bambara, Wilson, & McKenzie, 2007). Because interagency collaboration can be a daunting task given all of the different missions, challenges, and shortages facing various agencies, multilevel interagency transition teams are desirable (Blaylock, 1996; Stodden, Brown, Galloway, Mrazek, & Noy, 2005). There are four levels of teams:

Students with intellectual disability often can achieve positive outcomes, such as competitive employment, after they graduate if their educational program is based on their strengths and preferences.

◆ A statewide transition team that includes secondary educators, adult service providers, adults with disabilities, and family members

◆ A communitywide team representing all of the key agencies involved

◆ A schoolwide team consisting of key professionals and family members

◆ An IEP team for each student

When each team assesses the challenges and opportunities and links with the others, the resulting collaboration can eliminate barriers and create opportunities leading to the IDEA outcomes. Debbie Wilks, the special education supervisor in Richardson, Texas, does an excellent job of fostering partnerships within both the school and the community. With the support of the district's administrators, she attends regular weekly or monthly meetings of eight community and state organizations during her work days. Especially when working with local business leaders, Debbie gives a single, consistent message: The schools are producing students who are ready to work; some do not have disabilities, and some do. At these meetings, she learns about market demand, including how many employees the businesses need, what skills employees need, and so on. Debbie takes that information back to the schools so the faculty can teach those skills and bring that information to the transition-planning process. She sums up her partnership for successful transition in a few well-chosen sentences: "It's all about connecting; it's all about community. If we want our students to be full citizens and participating and contributing members of their communities, we educators have to connect with our communities. If we don't, our students won't" (personal communication, Summer 2005).

Debbie is "singing the same song" that Ricki Sabia sings. To quote Ricki, "Stephen was born when society's vision for individuals with Down syndrome was still limited to the acquisition of basic functional life skills and a part-time job usually unrelated to their interests and abilities. We were determined to provide Stephen with a more meaningful future and realized that an academic education with his nondisabled peers was the key to him having as many opportunities in his life as possible. Our goal for him is the same as for his older brother (a sophomore at Boston University), to maximize his potential so that he can maximize his opportunities in all aspects of life." With these goals in mind, Ricki and Peter expect that Stephen will begin to work in the community when he is in the 11th grade. But his job should be tied to his interests; he should not be pigeon-holed. Given that Stephen wants to be either

Improving Interagency Collaboration

Sometimes it can feel beyond the scope of your responsibility as a teacher to contribute to interagency collaboration; however, each and every teacher can make a difference in the success of such collaboration. First, you should know best practices and encourage your team members to use them. Second, you should use these practices yourself.

Researchers identified 29 high-performing school districts to determine what strategies they used (Noonan, Morningstar, & Erickson, in press). Eleven key strategies existed, but the major theme of the research is that schools should have a transition coordinator whose job it is to build interagency collaborations. The strategies are as follows:

- ◆ Develop personal relationships with staff in community organizations who have responsibilities related to transition.

- ◆ Invite members of community agencies to come to IEP and other transition planning meetings; consider their scheduling preferences in arranging the time for the meetings.

- ◆ Ensure that school staff network within community settings.

- ◆ Anticipate that students and families will need support after graduation and follow up with them

through options such as workshops, websites, and parent-to-parent connections.

- ◆ Recognize that administrative support is critical to arrange for flexible scheduling, compensation time, substitute teachers, and paid summer training.

- ◆ Recognize that interagency collaboration involves shared funding from multiple agencies, including government benefits for employment and housing opportunities.

- ◆ Seek technical assistance and continuing education from the state education agency, universities and colleges, and other professional development sources; encourage staff from community agencies to take advantage of continuing education opportunities as well.

- ◆ Partner with school, community, and state transition personnel in providing practical information and educational opportunities for students and families relating to all the key aspects of adult life planning.

- ◆ Find out about the availability of any interagency groups such as a community-wide transition council, learn who from your district is attending those meetings, and ask if that person will keep you informed about the decisions that are made.

Source: Information from Noonan, P. M., Morningstar, M. E., & Erikson, A. G. (in press). Improving inter-agency collaboration: Effective strategies used by high performing local districts and communities. *Career Development for Exceptional Individuals.*

a rock-music star or (like his father) a physician, work in a music store, concert venue, radio station, recording studio, or hospital seems to be in order. An alternative would be enrolling at Montgomery County Community College for higher education. Box 9.2 provides partnership tips based on a national study of exemplary school districts.

When students learn to take an active role in their IEP conferences, they can practice the self-determination skills that you will learn about later in this chapter. They also can express their preferences, consistent with IDEA's transition-planning provisions.

Determining Supplementary Aids and Services

You know that special education is a team enterprise and that many different professionals are involved in it (Chapter 1). Among them are paraprofessionals, sometimes called paraeducators. Paraprofessionals are school staff who are included under the IDEA term "supplementary aids and services." They often are IEP team members. Stephen Sabia has always had a paraeducator. Like his current one, Nate Wiles, their role is to adapt materials and assessments and provide direct support in the general education classroom. In areas where Stephen is independent, such as transition between classes; specialty classes such as art, physical education, and keyboarding; lunchtime; and riding the bus, Stephen needs no assistance—independence is his norm.

As you learned in Chapter 2, paraprofessionals enable students to be educated with their nondisabled peers, progressing in the general education curriculum. Paraprofessionals can play an important role in instruction pertaining to literacy (Causton-Theoharis, Giangreco, Doyle, & Vadasy, 2007), physical education (Lytle, Lieberman, & Aiello, 2007), learning strategies (which you learned about in Chapter 5) (Keller, Bucholz, & Brady, 2007), social stories (which you will read about in Chapter 9) (Quilty, 2007), and reading skills including phonological awareness (Lane, Fletcher, Carter, Dejud, & Delorenzo, 2007), alphabetic skills (Vadasy, Sanders, & Peyton, 2006a), and structural analysis (Vadasy, Sanders, & Payton, 2006b). The Department of Education estimated in 1999 that there were approximately 280,000 paraprofessionals providing special education supports and services to students with exceptionalities ages 3 through 21 who were being served in general and special education classrooms (U.S. Department of Education, 1999), and that number has almost certainly increased.

Appropriate roles for paraprofessionals include providing individualized instruction to groups of students with and without disabilities, facilitating friendships among students with and without disabilities, supporting peer tutors, using state-of-the-art technology, teaching in community settings, and assisting students with personal care (e.g., bathroom care and feeding). Significantly, most paraprofessionals provide direct instruction to students for at least three quarters of the time they are on the job (Riggs & Mueller, 2001). That role certainly assists students to progress in the general curriculum. It also enables general educators and special educators to concentrate on other students—those with and without disabilities—and on their progress in the general curriculum.

Some educators and researchers have expressed concerns about how paraprofessionals support students in general education classrooms (Giangreco & Broer, 2007). Although paraprofessionals can add appropriate and meaningful support for students with disabilities as well as their classmates, paraprofessionals may actually isolate students with disabilities. Ferguson (1995) referred to this as the "Velcroed effect" (p. 284). Here is how a student without a disability described the "Velcroed" situation of one of her classmates:

> Whenever you try to talk to her you can't because her aides are there and they just help her say what she's trying to say and you want to hear it from her. They do it for her, and then they say, "Is that right?" It's like you're having a three-way conversation and [the aide] is the interpreter and it is not right that way. . . . It just doesn't work. (Martin, Jorgensen, & Klein, 1998, p. 157)

Giangreco and Broer (2007) developed a 16-item screening tool that IEP teams can use to determine the extent to which the student's educational program may rely too much on paraprofessionals. The tool examines whether students spend an excessive or unnecessary amount of time in close proximity to a paraprofessional, if students receive their primary instruction from paraprofessionals, if classroom teachers are minimally involved in instruction with students who are in their class as a result of the presence of a paraprofessional, and so forth.

Planning for Universal Design for Learning

Other supplementary aids and services include various technologies. One such technology is the universally designed literacy software discussed in Box 9.3. The software embodies many of the principles of universal design because it presents an audio- and video-based curriculum and includes an audio-based glossary that defines words and gives examples of how to use them, as well as videos illustrating those uses. Teachers can tailor content to students' capacities (flexible use, cognitive taxonomies), and attention-grabbing cartoons help deliver that curriculum content. As you may remember, Stephen Sabia relies a great deal on graphics—illustrations of the concepts and content he needs to learn. He also uses a software program that helps him write DVDs and book summaries for some of his courses, and his special education director, Christine Genua, and the school district's UDL specialist, Denise DeCoste, have collaborated with his teachers to adapt his curriculum and make sure

IEP Tip

A student's IEP team should advocate for paraprofessionals when considering supplementary aids and services to ensure that students are educated with their nondisabled peers to the maximum extent possible and progress in the general education curriculum.

PEARSON
myeducationlab

Go the Building Teaching Skills and Dispositions section in Chapter 9 of MyEducationLab and complete the activities. As you watch these videos reflect on the collaborative role of the paraprofessional in a general education classroom or a special education classroom.

PEARSON
myeducationlab

Go to the Activities and Application section in Chapter 9 of MyEducationLab and complete Activity 2. As you watch the video clip, consider whether or not the guided notes study cards would be a good strategy for Stephen Sabia's teachers to implement.

Literacy by Design: Teaching Students with Intellectual Disability to Read

Researchers at CAST, Inc., are developing universally designed instructional materials. Their project, Learning by Design, led by researchers David Rose, Bridget Dalton, and Margaret Coyne from CAST and Lucille Zeph at the University of Maine, investigates the effects of the universally designed approach to literacy on the reading achievement of students with mental retardation. The project rests on research in literacy that suggests that, like all students, students with intellectual disability benefit from literacy instruction that focuses on reading for meaning and that also provides direct instruction in the skills and strategies needed to decode and understand print in meaningful contexts. To provide those learning opportunities, the researchers developed software that incorporates universal design features to enable young children with intellectual disability to learn to read.

Students begin by selecting the kind of interaction they want with the material (reading for understanding or reading aloud). They also select the book they want to read from a menu of several options. Students then use simple arrow icons to navigate the book, using button-driven options to access features such as having the text read to them. If they get stuck on a particular word, they can select a vocabulary button that takes them to a video- and audio-based menu that allows them to play a clip of the word in action.

Project director Bridget Dalton, chief education officer at CAST, says, "This project demonstrates that when we integrate research based literacy instruction, the principles of universal design for learning, and technology, it is possible to create learning environments that unlock the potential for students with significant cognitive disabilities." Researcher and project director Peggy Coyne notes, "Teachers view CAST's Universally Designed Picture Book as a powerful tool because it supports the challenging task of customizing curriculum materials for their students. After using it, one teacher said to me, 'I like Picture Book better because it has everything right in it.'"

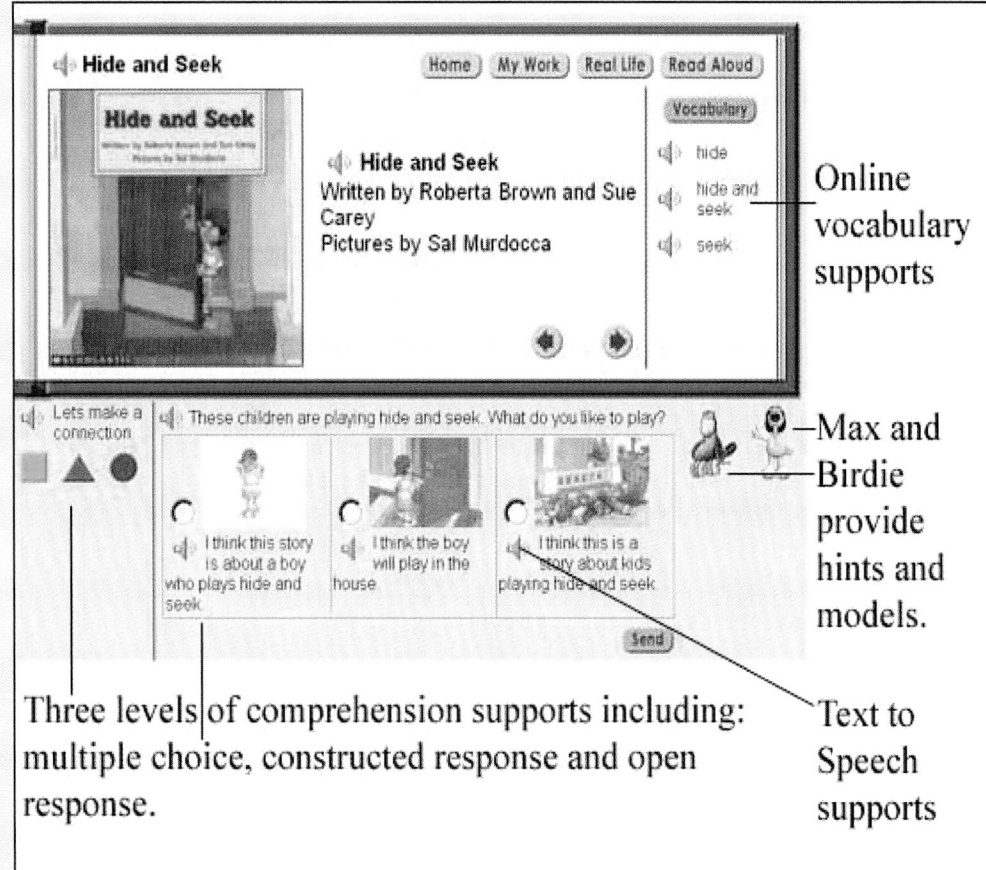

This screen shot from CAST's Universally Designed Picture Book illustrates scaffolded vocabulary, word recognition, and comprehension supports (Dalton & Coyne, 2003).

■ ■ ■

there are plenty of graphics for him (remember, he mapped the Philippines and Pearl Harbor as a way to learn about World War II).

Planning for Other Educational Needs

To address students' limitations in intellectual functioning and challenges associated with memory, generalization, and motivation; to develop their behavior in conceptual, social, and practical adaptive-skill areas; and to teach them to function successfully in their community, teachers need to support students to master skills that are sometimes more functional than the content of the general education curriculum. These skills include applied money concepts, applied time concepts, community mobility and access, grooming and self-care, leisure activities, health and safety, and career education (Wehmeyer, Sands, Knowlton, & Kozleski, 2002). Educators who use best-practice approaches provide their students with functional content and apply the concept of general-

Community-based instruction allows students to learn where they will have to use their skills; it promotes durable and generalizable skills.

ization and memory development by teaching in the settings in which their students will have to use the skills they are learning (Kluth, 2000; Langone, Langone, & McLaughlin, 2000).

To what extent should a functional curriculum be taught to students with intellectual disability in typical community environments rather than classroom settings? The answer is that when students with intellectual disability are unable to generalize skills to typical community settings such as home, places of worship and recreation, and work sites, their instruction should occur in some or all of those settings (Bates, Quvo, Miner, & Korabek, 2001; Test & Spooner, 2005). Further, students improve in their intellectual and adaptive behaviors when they learn in community settings (Agran, Snow, & Swaner, 1999; Langone et al., 2000). You will read about the results of effective community-based special education in Box 9.4, "My Voice: The O'Halloran Outcome."

USING EFFECTIVE INSTRUCTIONAL STRATEGIES

Early Childhood Students: Prelinguistic Milieu Teaching

All preschool-age children need to acquire language, but children with intellectual disability obviously are limited in doing so (Abbeduto, 2003). Prelinguistic milieu teaching (PMT) is an effective language-acquisition instructional strategy for these children (Brady & Warren, 2003; Fey, Warren, Brady, Finestack, Bredin-Oja, Fairchild, et al., 2006; Yoder & Warren, 2001).

Prelinguistic milieu teaching teaches children with intellectual disability who do not speak to make frequent, clear requests or comments with gestures or sounds while looking at the person with whom they are communicating. The steps in prelinguistic milieu teaching are simple and straightforward, as Box 9.5 shows. While following these steps, teachers should keep in mind a few basic principles. First, follow the child's lead. Children focus best on things in which they are interested. The teacher observes the child and begins a session only when she sees what the child is interacting or playing with. Face to face, at eye level with the child, she talks about that object.

Second, set the stage for communication. By putting a favorite toy in the room but out of reach, the teacher encourages the child to ask for it. By putting objects out of order in a room, the teacher may elicit a comment from the child.

Third, be strategic when using games like Pat-a-Cake and Peek-a-Boo. Children learn the game ritual; when the teacher interrupts or changes the ritual, the child will communicate in order to keep playing. Pat-a-Cake and Peek-a-Boo also reinforce face-to-face contact and entail give and take, like a conversation. As the developer of prelinguistic milieu teaching, Steve Warren, notes, "A substantial body of research has shown prelinguistic milieu

The O'Halloran Outcome

He's nineteen years old, a senior at North Ft. Myers High School in Florida. But he's a whole lot more than just a senior.

He's a member of the student council, having earned the requisite grade-point average and secured the required number of signatures to run for senior class representative. He's served as the manager of the varsity wrestling team for three straight years and is a "big-ticket" fund raiser at school. He's the greeter-employee of the local Gap store, and he's also a bus-boy, dishwasher, and counter man at Daddy Dee's Ice Cream Parlor. He's a Boy Scout who is working on the "Life" badge (the next-to-highest rank possible) and has been admitted to the exclusive Order of the Arrow at Troop 82 in Cape Coral. He's a member of the youth group at the local Methodist church and serves as an altar boy and volunteer at the children's liturgy for his church, St. Cecilia's Catholic Community.

He's Casey O'Halloran, the all-American kid. The youngster most apt to flirt with all the girls but who singled out one for the Junior-Senior Prom. The buddy of a hometown hero who represented the United States as a pentathlete in the summer 2000 Olympics and who inspires him to stay fit. The "knows no strangers" guy.

His course work consists of English and math, with a one-on-one tutor so he will learn real applications of the course content; the special education developmental speech class, where he focuses on articulation in his expressive speech; the leadership development class (for elected class officers and other student leaders), where he refines his social and self-determination skills; and the advanced weight-lifting class. He's headed toward graduation in the spring of 2001 and then to Edison Community College in Ft. Myers to sample some community development courses. In addition, he will continue his tutoring in academic subjects and work with a job coach.

What's Casey's secret? There is none. Combine home-based instruction with inclusion-plus education in subjects that will make a difference in his life. Add the types of community-based activities that other young men

undertake. Throw in two jobs. Set high expectations—better yet, let Casey set them for himself. And, then, just "watch it happen."

But remember this. The "O'Halloran Outcome"—the one that IDEA envisions—would not have occurred but for the conjunction of two factors. The first is family: a mother, father, and older brothers who would not take no for an answer when it came to inclusion and who knew their way around their community. The second is a school system that has responded in creative, flexible, and individualized ways to meet Casey's unique needs as well as IDEA's implied promise. Remember the promise? It is that the outcomes of education will be equal opportunity, full participation, independent living, and economic self-sufficiency. In North Fort Myers, let's call it the "O'Halloran Outcome."

teaching to be the most effective approach to enhancing the communication development of young children with developmental delays and disorders" (personal communication, October 2004). Further, PMT is consistent with the concept of self-determination, which you'll read about next, because its philosophy is that children will learn if their instruction matches their interests and abilities.

Elementary and Middle School Students: The Self-Determined Learning Model of Instruction

As you have learned, students with intellectual disability face challenges related to motivation; they tend to be outer-directed, not inner-directed. Happily, instructional strategies help teachers overcome this challenge. One of those strategies is the Self-Determined Learning

Steps to Prelinguistic Milieu Teaching

Prelinguistic milieu teaching is a research-validated, early intervention strategy for teaching young children with intellectual disability and other disabilities important prelinguistic skills, such as gesturing, vocalizing, and making eye contact, that serve as the foundation for language development. PMT has several advantages. It is implemented in children's natural environments; involves activities and routines that are based on the child's preferences and interests; enlists the child's natural communication partners, including parents and teachers; and creates opportunities for teachers and speech-language pathologists to be partners.

Prelinguistic milieu teaching improves language acquisition outcomes for children with intellectual disability, but it requires educators to follow these steps in carrying it out (Yoder & Warren, 2001):

Step 1: *Prompt the child to communicate.* To begin the training session, the trainer, whether a teacher or the child's parent, conveys through words or gestures an expectation that the child should communicate or use a particular communicative behavior to obtain a preferred object or engage in a preferred activity. The trainer might ask, for example, "What do you want?" or say, "Look at me," or provide a gesture, such as upturned or extended palms, to indicate a question and request. These prompts are contextually specific to the child's preferred object or activity.

Step 2: *Prompt the child to initiate.* Next, the trainer provides a verbal prompt to the child to imitate a sign or a word, such as "Say, 'Ball,'" with reference to a preferred activity (playing with a ball) or "Do this," while modeling the sign for "more" (obtaining more of something the child likes).

Step 3: *Vocally imitate the child's resultant vocalizations.* When the child responds to the prompt, the trainer provides an exact, reduced, or expanded imitation immediately following the child's vocalization. So, for example, if the child responds to the "Say, 'Ball,'" prompt in Step 2 with the vocalization "Aba," the trainer immediately imitates the vocalization, saying, "Aba." When the child repeats the "Aba" vocalization, the trainer expands that, saying, "Abada."

Step 4: *Comply with the child's request.* The child's vocalizations in Step 3 were the result of prompts in Steps 1 and 2 related to a preferred object or activity. In Step 4, the trainer complies with the intended or apparent request by the child ("Aba" to play with the ball, imitating the "more" sign to get more of an item). So when the child says, "Aba," the trainer repeats the vocalization and gives the child the ball.

Step 5: *Recode the child's communication act.* In the context of complying with the child's apparent request, the trainer recodes or interprets the child's communication in the form of a question or statement. Thus, as the child is reaching for the ball and looking at the trainer, the trainer says, "Ball," or "Do you want the ball?"

Step 6: *Acknowledge the child's communicative act.* In a reinforcing manner, the trainer tells the child he or she did what was required. So when the child obtains the ball, the trainer should say, "You asked for the ball!"

Step 7: *Talk to the child.* To continue the interaction and further reinforce the child, the trainer should continue to talk to the child, saying "Good, you are playing with the ball," or "You asked for the ball!"

Putting These Strategies to Work for Progress in the General Curriculum

1. Conduct an online search of prelinguistic milieu teaching and summarize five tips that you learn from this search.

2. Imagine that you have a child in your classroom who could benefit from prelinguistic milieu teaching. How might you and a speech-language pathologist partner in order to provide instruction?

3. What do you see as the advantages of teaching communication within natural environments and typical routines as contrasted to having language instruction in specialized therapy sessions?

PEARSON
myeducationlab

Go to the Activities and Application section in Chapter 9 of MyEducationLab. As you complete Activity 3, think about how you would implement some of these strategies in your teaching.

Source: Based on information from Yoder, P. J., and Warren, S. F (2001).

Model of Instruction (SDLMI). That model builds on the principles of self-determination (Wehmeyer, Abery, Mithaug, & Stancliffe, 2003; Wehmeyer, Agran, Hughes, Martin, Mithaug, & Palmer, 2007) and promotes middle school students' progress in achieving the goals of the general curriculum (Palmer, Wehmeyer, Gibson, & Agran, 2004) and other goals as well (Agran, Blanchard, & Wehmeyer, 2000; Wehmeyer et al., 2003; Wehmeyer et al., 2007).

The model involves three phases. In each phase, the teacher presents the student with a problem that the student must solve. In Phase 1, the problem is "What is my goal?" In Phase 2, it is "What is my plan?" In Phase 3, it is "What have I learned?" The student learns to solve the problem in each phase by answering a series of four questions. Although the questions vary in each phase, each question represents one of four steps in a typical problem-solving process: (1) identify the problem, (2) identify potential solutions to the problem, (3) identify barriers to solving the problem, and (4) identify consequences of each solution. Figure 9.4 shows each of the 12 questions.

These questions in turn connect to a set of teacher objectives. In each phase, the student is the person who makes the choices and takes various actions, even as the teacher remains in charge of the teaching. Each phase in the objectives includes a list of educational supports that teachers can use to enable students to direct their own learning.

Some students will learn and use all 12 questions exactly as they are written. Other students will need to have the teacher reword the questions. And still other students will need to have the teacher explain what the questions mean and give examples of each question.

The outcome of Phase 1 is that students set an instructional goal based on their preferences, interests, abilities, and learning needs. The outcome of Phase 2 is that they design a plan for achieving their goal and self-monitor to track their progress toward the goal. The outcome of Phase 3 is that they evaluate data from their self-monitoring process and, if necessary, alter their action plans or change their goal.

Figure 9.4	Student questions in the self-determination learning model of instruction

Phase 1 Problem: What Is My Goal?

Student question 1	What do I want to learn?
Student question 2	What do I know about it now?
Student question 3	What must change for me to learn what I don't know?
Student question 4	What can I do to make this happen?

Phase 2 Problem: What Is My Plan?

Student question 5	What can I do to learn what I don't know?
Student question 6	What could keep me from taking action?
Student question 7	What can I do to remove these barriers?
Student question 8	When will I take action?

Phase 3 Problem: What Have I Learned?

Student question 9	What actions have I taken?
Student question 10	What barriers have been removed?
Student question 11	What has changed about what I don't know?
Student question 12	Do I know what I want to know?

Source: Wehmeyer, M. L., Agran, M., Palmer, S. B., & Mithaug, D. (1999). *A teacher's guide to implementing the self-determined learning model of instruction (adolescent version).* Lawrence: University of Kansas, Beach Center.

Are students successful in setting and attaining their goals? Yes. Palmer and colleagues (2004) examined the effect of the model on the progress of 22 middle school students with intellectual disability on goals linked to the general curriculum (e.g., science, social studies, and language arts). The students received support to implement the model by addressing a goal based on a standard that had a self-determination focus (e.g., learn to solve a problem, set a goal, and create a study plan). Students who received intervention on self-determination skills (problem solving and study planning) significantly improved their knowledge and skills in these areas, achieving educationally relevant goals tied to district-level standards at expected or greater-than-expected levels and thereby showing that instruction in self-determination can serve as an entry point to the general curriculum.

Stephen Sabia participated in a transition interview (from middle to secondary school) and picked many of his elective courses. He has attended his IEP meetings and has self-determination advocacy goals. He has testified before the county board of education, advocating for the board to fund all teachers—general and special alike—to be trained to use UDL. When he told Ricki, his mother, "You are not my teacher," she responded, "No, so talk to someone who will help you at school so I don't have to do that at home." Stephen's response was to go to the school board hearing.

Secondary and Transition Students: Community-Based Instruction

"Learn it where you'll need to do it." That's good advice for any student who has intellectual disability and for that reason is challenged to remember and generalize her education to the community and to adapt to community expectations.

"Teach it where you want your students to practice it." That, on the other hand, is good advice for teachers, especially those whose students have intellectual disability and thus memory and generalization challenges.

Shelby, North Carolina, is the seat of a largely rural county. Its school system consists of approximately 3,000 students in grades K through 12, of whom approximately 250 are receiving special education services. In Shelby, students with intellectual disability graduate from high school with a regular diploma. They take local jobs for good pay and benefits, and they receive positive work evaluations. At the heart of their success is the practice of providing effective community-based instruction when teaching a functional curriculum related to employment and independent living. Community-based instruction involves teaching students transition-related skills in the actual community settings in which they will be used.

One hundred and twenty students ages 14 to 18, more than half of whom have intellectual disability, are involved in the district's Project TASSEL and are provided individualized, functional, community-based instruction. Project TASSEL is a good example of how school districts can provide community-based instruction. As with all instruction, community-based instruction begins with effective planning and assessment. Consistent with IDEA's requirements, educators in the Shelby schools create a school-level, community-referenced, interagency transition team by the time each student reaches transition age (which is now age 16). The teams consist of students, parents, teachers, vocational rehabilitation specialists, technical college administrators, and residential service providers. Each team focuses on a student's strengths and needs, particularly in the adaptive skill areas of work, community use, and self-direction/self-determination.

The "self-determination" motto is simple and clear, one the students learn and practice with the help of school and community teams: "Nothing about me without me." With support from their teams, the students identify their own future quality-of-life goals, especially those related to work. The curriculum for the community-based instruction is tied to everyday life experiences.

Jerry Moss and other students who choose Project TASSEL's occupational curriculum have schools-without-walls experiences. At this industrial site, Jerry receives on-the-job training that supplements his classroom instruction.

To begin, students simulate the challenges that they are likely to encounter in the community (you are sick and can't go to work, or you can't use your usual method of transportation this morning) and then apply the problem-solving skills that they would use in the community (what do you do, and whom do you call?). Over the course of their high school career, students increasingly move off campus for their instruction. In this way, they learn skills that will generalize to the world of work, and they increase their adaptive skills, learning what it takes to adapt to and have a good quality of life in Shelby. By the end of their senior year, they must also have 360 class hours of competitive employment (work in an inclusive setting for at least the minimum wage, with or without a job coach—a person who shares the job with them and teaches them how to do it on their own or with only a little help).

The students benefit from the cooperation of 50 local businesses that provide job-shadowing sites, paid community-based contracts, and individual job placements. This kind of school-industry collaboration means that when a student graduates with a diploma in the occupational curriculum, local employers know the student is well prepared. You should recall that one aspect of intellectual disability is the need for supports; now you see how schools and community businesses can collaborate to provide employment supports.

The challenge comes in aligning these community-based instructional approaches with the goals of inclusion. If students with disabilities are in the community but not at school, how can they also be included in the general curriculum with students who do not have disabilities? In response, some schools are demonstrating how to make community-based learning an important part of the curriculum for all students (Wehmeyer & Sailor, 2004). Like universally designed learning, community-based instruction is good for all students, not just students with intellectual disability. Consistent with that finding, and because teaching self-determination when a student is 18 through 21 years old is critical, Wehmeyer, Garner, Lawrence, Yeager, and Davis (2006) developed and evaluated a model infusing self-determination into programs for students ages 18 through 21. Box 9.6 provides tips on how to merge community-based education with self-direction training.

INCLUDING STUDENTS WITH INTELLECTUAL DISABILITY

To what extent are students with intellectual disability included in general education classes? Figure 9.5 illustrates the percentage who were educated in the entire continuum of educational environments during the 2003–2004 school year. You will observe that students with intellectual disability are more than twice as likely to spend the majority of their school time outside the general education classroom than are all other students with disabilities combined. Nevertheless, progress toward inclusion is happening.

Students with intellectual disability now spend more time in general education classes and less time in special education classes than they did a decade ago (Katsiyannis, Zhang, & Archwamety, 2002). That is certainly true with respect to Stephen. He is enrolled in two honors courses, four general education courses, and one special education course (math). But because he would have to pass a "high-stakes" assessment in order to earn a high school diploma, Stephen (who takes the unmodified alternate statewide assessment) will not earn a high school diploma. When Ricki was told that his teachers could not modify his curriculum unless she removed him from the diploma track, she opted to have Stephen participate in the curriculum and receive, instead of a diploma, a certificate of completion of high school. Ricki, like many parents, regards these artifacts as meaningless and believes that all students should receive an exit document that celebrates their academic achievements.

Despite the fact that IDEA has been outcome driven since Congress reauthorized it in 1997 and again in 2004, the percentage of students with intellectual disability who have earned a diploma and/or certificate has decreased over the past decade; this is true even as their inclusive placements have increased (Katsiyannis et al., 2002). It is likely that state assessments of students' academic proficiency have negatively affected the graduation rates for students with intellectual disabilities. To counteract the "no diploma" trend and ensure that schools will still practice inclusion, you can use some of the strategies that Stephen's teachers use (graphics, UDL, DVDs, book summaries), as well as those we explain in Box 9.7.

Merging Community-Based Instruction with Self-Determination Training for Students Ages 18 Through 21

Two approaches to teaching students with intellectual disability are community-based education and self-determination training. Community-based instruction originated in work by Dr. Lou Brown and his colleagues at the University of Wisconsin in the 1980s (Brown et al., 1979; Brown et al., 1983). They identified students who would benefit from a community-based focus as the lowest intellectually functioning 1% of the school population of a particular age. These students had difficulty generalizing learning from one environment to another; their learning needed to occur in ecologically valid settings where the student might eventually use the particular skill independently. Similarly, students with intellectual disability, by definition, learned fewer skills over the same time period than their nondisabled peers, making it more important for those skills to be functional and for students to learn them in environments in which they will be able to successfully use them.

Students ages 18 through 21 who are still receiving special education services should receive community-based instruction, which becomes the general curriculum for them. High-quality educational services and supports for these students have characteristics similar to those of community-based learning.

High-quality educational services are provided in an age-appropriate environment that allows for social interaction and promotes community inclusion. Because the typical high school may no longer be an age-appropriate environment for students 18 through 21, educational supports should be provided in environments that are age-appropriate and promote interaction with same-age peers, such as a community or junior college setting. This setting is normative for students in this age range, and community colleges frequently offer courses appropriate for these students. Indeed, students increasingly enroll in community colleges (Getzel & Wehman, 2005), as well as university and four-year college campuses, just as they are increasingly working in community-based business or agency settings.

High-quality educational services are ecologically valid and community based. As students grow into adulthood, they receive more of their instruction in community-based settings that approximate the environment in which they might live, work, learn, or play as adults. Accordingly, students ages 18 through 21 should spend most if not all of their time learning employment-related skills in work settings, living skills in homes, and recreation and leisure skills in the community.

High-quality transition services are results-oriented. The IDEA requires transition services to be results-oriented, especially with respect to employment, independent living, postsecondary education, and leisure outcomes. Transition programs are effective when students obtain competitive work; are integrated into and participate in their community; live where they prefer with needed supports; and engage in a full array of nonvocational leisure and recreation activities.

Academic instruction in quality programs is functional and focused on outcomes. Students continue to need academic instruction, so educators teach functional skills in inclusive settings, such as community and junior colleges.

Quality services emphasize person-centered planning and active family involvement. As illustrated by the Project TASSEL Process in Shelby, education leads to employment when community leaders, not just the school team, are involved.

Adult service providers actively participate in planning and implementing quality services. IDEA requires interagency collaboration in transition planning, especially by agencies that serve adults with and without disabilities and by community businesses where students may someday work or become customers.

Quality transition services implement best practices. Among the best practices are job shadowing, job sampling, and leisure training.

Implementing Community-Based Instruction

Community-referenced planning and community-based instruction are effective when based on an ecological inventory. To conduct an inventory:

1. Select the instructional domain (e.g., vocation, recreation-leisure, independent living, etc.).

2. Identify current and future environments in this domain in which the student needs to learn skills and knowledge to better enable her to succeed.

3. Prioritize the need for instruction in specific subenvironments in each environment.

4. Identify activities within each subenvironment.

5. Task-analyze the priority activities into their component skills.

For example, if a student wants to work with animals, the ecological inventory should identify a specific environment (e.g., pet store) and subenvironments within that environment (e.g., stock room, checkout counter, animal cages); prioritize the subenvironments in which the student will most likely function; identify tasks within prioritized subenvironments (e.g., cleaning cages, feeding animals, cleaning windows); and provide a task analysis for use in teaching each task.

continued

Box 9.6 continued

Community-referenced planning is locally referenced. By using an ecological inventory, teachers link the student's learning tasks to settings in the student's environment and local standards and performance demands. Consider, for example, McDonald's restaurants. They are, of course, present across the United States, but it is incorrect to assume that there is a standardized curriculum to teach all students how to develop skills to use in all McDonald's restaurants. Not every McDonald's restaurant is architecturally the same; the location of restrooms and counters, for example, is not uniform. Some stores fill a customer's drink behind the counter, while others give customers empty cups to fill with ice and drinks at a separate location. Some stores use wrapped straws available with other condiments, some use straw dispensers, and others have straws distributed by personnel. Some use prepackaged salt or ketchup; others use ketchup dispensers and have salt and pepper on the tables. Therefore, just because a student receives instruction in one McDonald's restaurant, there is no guarantee the student will be able to function as independently in another McDonald's. Instruction must be locally referenced.

After completing an ecological inventory, ask yourself the following questions when picking appropriate instructional strategies to teach the identified skills (Test & Spooner, 2005):

1. Will you train in a natural or simulated setting?
2. How can you plan for generalization?
3. What chaining procedure will you use?
4. What prompting procedure will you use?
5. Will you train individually or in a group? (p. 84)

To ensure generalization of skills through community-based instruction, teachers should expand their students' performance across stimuli, time, and responses.

Extending across stimuli. Students perform the skill with new or different prompts, materials, and people or in new settings.

Extending across time. Students perform the skill well after the training is completed.

Extending across responses. Students perform the skill learned to achieve one outcome to achieve another, similar outcome (Test & Spooner, 2005, p. 85).

Infusing Self-Determination into Transition Programs
Like any other type of instruction, community-based instruction can be heavily teacher-directed, or it can become heavily student-directed. Given the importance of self-determination training, especially during a student's transition years, follow these guidelines:

Goal setting and instructional planning should be student-directed. In their Beyond High School model to infuse self-determination into transition programs, Wehmeyer and colleagues (2006) emphasized the role of active student involvement in goal setting and planning. The Self-Determined Learning Model of Instruction also can ensure that students have a meaningful voice in planning for their future.

Instructional goals should be based upon student preferences, interests, and strengths. The rule of thumb is that students should not see any difference between their final day of school and the first day of the rest of their lives. That outcome can be achieved when students learn skills in environments in which they will work or live. Obviously, if the student's preferences, interests, and strengths do not significantly influence teachers' decisions, students are unlikely to use the skills they have learned.

Job development should begin with the student. Although high-quality transition programs focus on more than employment, employment affects the student's life in a great many ways. Under a self-determination approach, job development begins with student preferences and talents, and potential jobs are identified from that starting point.

Students should be taught to self-direct their learning. An effective generalization strategy is to teach students to do for themselves what someone else currently may be doing for them. Agran, King-Sears, Wehmeyer, and Copeland (2003) identified a host of student-directed learning strategies, such as self-monitoring and self-instruction, that are important to teach in community-based instruction. You'll learn more about these strategies in Chapter 10.

myeducationlab

Go to the Activities and Application section in Chapter 9 of MyEducationLab and complete Activity 4. As you watch the video and answer the accompanying questions, think about how these two women have benefited from the strategies discussed here.

Figure 9.5 Educational placement of students with intellectual disability (2006–2007)

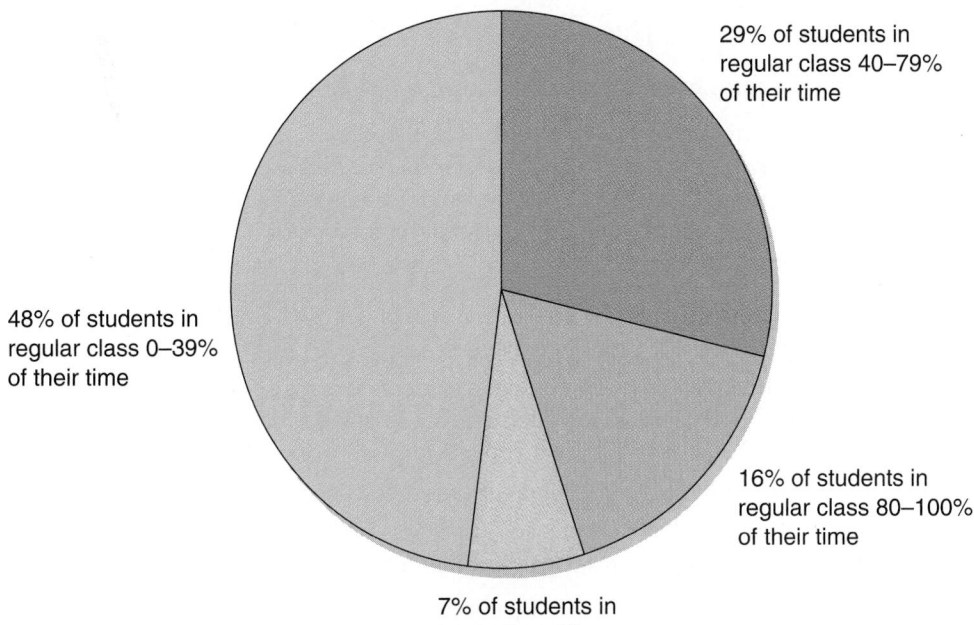

29% of students in regular class 40–79% of their time

48% of students in regular class 0–39% of their time

16% of students in regular class 80–100% of their time

7% of students in separate setting

Box 9.7	**INCLUSION TIPS**			
	What You Might See	*What You Might Be Tempted to Do*	*Alternate Responses*	*Ways to Include Peers in the Process*
Behavior	The student demonstrates potentially distracting behavior such as loud laughter.	Tell her to stop the behavior (laughter) and be quiet or leave the room.	Teach skills to enable students to self-regulate their behavior. For example, you could teach her to self-monitor loud laughter.	Encourage peers to ignore inappropriate behavior and praise classmates when they regulate their own behavior.
Social interactions	On her job-training sites, she feels very shy around co-workers.	Tell her she will never get a job unless she learns to interact with others on the job.	Include social skills as an important component of transition instruction.	Gather information from co-workers about preferences for social interactions at work.
Educational performance	She shows an apparent lack of interest and boredom with class activities.	Discipline her for lack of cooperation.	Create opportunities for community-based instruction of relevant skills.	Include other class members as part of the community-based instruction.
Classroom attitudes	She demonstrates learned helplessness with new activities.	Let her be excused from the activity.	Encourage her to identify motivational strategies that have worked in the past and incorporate them into the class.	Pair her with a partner who needs help in an area of her strength (e.g., music).

ASSESSING STUDENTS' PROGRESS

Measuring Students' Progress

Progress in the General Education Curriculum

An important and time-tested means for monitoring a student's progress is to observe how well the student has mastered certain skills and then to record those observations (Browder & Spooner, 2005; Farlow & Snell, 2005). Figure 9.6 illustrates the steps in this type of data-based decision making. Teachers regularly collect different types of data, including the following (Farlow & Snell, 2005):

1. *Response-by-response data.* How well has a student learned a task that has been broken down into discrete steps or subtasks?
2. *Instructional and test data.* How well does a student perform under teaching and nonteaching conditions? Instead of collecting data strictly on each step in a task, teachers collect data on the student's independent performance on the task as a whole.
3. *Error data.* How many and what kinds of errors does a student make, and how often, in performing a task?
4. *Anecdotal data.* What other student performance information has the teacher acquired?

As Figure 9.6 points out, teachers must collect data continuously and systematically; otherwise, the data will not yield particularly helpful information about the student's progress.

Progress in Addressing Other Educational Needs

Teachers can assess a student's progress in community-based instruction by using a process known as an ecological inventory (Snell & Brown, 2001; Test & Spooner, 2005). This process begins before teachers design and implement community-based instruction. Teachers collect two kinds of data: first, baseline data about how well a student functions in certain community settings; and second, data about the student's current environments and prospective environments for community-based instruction. This whole process is called the **life space analysis.** Figure 9.7 describes the steps in life space analysis.

Figure 9.6 ▶ **Guidelines for making data-based instructional decisions**

1. Collect response-by-response data.
2. Collect instructional and test data.
3. Collect error data and anecdotal data.
4. When a program is new, collect data daily. If instruction does not take place at least daily, collect data at each session.
5. When the student is making progress, collect data at least once a week.
6. Collect data more often and in more detail—at least twice a week—when the student is not making progress.
7. Draw a red line on graph paper showing the progress you want the student to make across time. This is called an aim line.
8. Plot student data points on the graph paper and connect those points with black lines. This is the student progress line.
9. Review the data at least once a week, comparing the progress line with the aim line, and decide whether to continue the program or to make a change.

Source: Farlow, L., & Snell, M. (2005). Making the most of student performance data. In M. Wehmeyer & M. Agran (Eds.), *Mental retardation and intellectual disabilities: Teaching students using innovative and research-based strategies.* Upper Saddle River, NJ: Merrill/Pearson.

Figure 9.7 ▷ **Steps in life space analysis**

Gather information. The first step in a life space analysis is to gather information about the student's daily environments, such as home and living, employment, school and education, recreation and leisure, and community integration. Who is present with the student, what activities are involved in those environments, and what skills does the student need to be successful in them? Teachers, family members, and others use the answers to these questions to determine how many subenvironments a student is involved in, the choices the student is making or can make to be involved in various activities common to all of the environments, the skills the student needs to succeed in these environments, and whom the student interacts with. They then use this information to determine what other environments the student might access and what unaccessed environments might be appropriate for community-based instruction.

Conduct ecological inventories. The second step in life space analysis involves conducting **ecological inventories** in each of the environments where teaching will occur and comparing those inventories with ecological inventories for peers who are the same age as the student but do not have a disability. These ecological inventories identify the subenvironments in which students function, the activities involved in them, and the skills needed in them. For example, a student may have a preferred fast-food restaurant (environment) in which community-based instruction might occur. Within that restaurant, there are several subenvironments (for example, the counter where food is ordered, the dining area, and the restrooms) in which different sets of skills are needed.

Conduct discrepancy analysis. Having completed ecological inventories for the student and for nondisabled peers, the evaluation team members then conduct a **discrepancy analysis,** examining where and how the two ecological inventories differ and whether the points of difference can be the basis for instruction or can be addressed through other means, such as assistive technology.

Analyze tasks. Once they have identified the specific activities and skills the student needs to function in each of the natural environments, team members perform an **activity task analysis,** identifying each step the student needs to master and the goals for community-based instruction.

Measure progress. At this point, the activity task analysis ceases to be a planning tool and becomes a means for measuring the student's progress. The team members use data-based decision-making procedures to measure the frequency of the student's behavior, percentage correct, level of prompts necessary, duration information, and error data. Then the team determines just how effective it has been in teaching the student to master the skills needed in those environments.

Making Accommodations for Assessment

To demonstrate their competencies through statewide or district-wide assessments, most students will require one or more accommodations when participating in assessments. IDEA requires a student's IEP team to set out in the student's IEP the accommodations the student will receive. The accommodations for students with intellectual disability typically include the following (Thurlow & Bolt, 2001):

◆ Dictating responses to a scribe

◆ Having extended time to complete an assessment

◆ Having test items read to them

◆ Securing clarification of test items

Up until his eighth-grade year, Stephen took the regular grade-level statewide assessments with some accommodations, using a calculator for math and having the benefit of a person who read directions to him. In Maryland, if he took the alternate mathematics test, he also would have had to take the alternate reading test, to which Ricki never agreed. Now that he is off diploma track, he has been put into alternate assessments for both subjects. He always was fairly close to proficiency in reading (320 out of 385), but usually was not in math.

VALUES AND OUTCOMES

- From the moment Stephen was born, Ricki and Peter Sabia had great expectations for him; not unexpectedly, Stephen has bought into the great expectations approach. While he will not be a heart specialist, as his father is, or a lawyer and advocate, as his mother is, he expects—and rightly expects, given his education—to work in the musical arts or health care fields.

- Stephen's positive contributions are easy to identify, even if we think only about his role with the JV football team. Truth be told, however, he is the poster boy for inclusion in the general curriculum, probably not just at Paint Branch School but also throughout Montgomery County, Maryland.

- Stephen's strengths are his social skills—he is a gregarious young man—and his determination—he takes to learning as the proverbial duck to water. This is undoubtedly a result of how his teachers, Andrew White and Christine Genua, have adapted his curriculum and his parents, Ricki and Peter, enrich his curriculum in their community.

- Stephen's choices are important, and he is quite a self-determined student, expressing his preferences for academic core courses and specific electives such as music instead of art.

- Relationships come easily for Stephen; just think of the "ownership" that the JV football team feels about him. They would not "own" him if he were not sociable, responsible, and willing to abide by the rules that govern him in the classroom and in extracurricular activities.

- Full citizenship results from equal opportunities; Stephen has had those when it comes to academics and extracurricular activities. It also comes from having the sense, as Stephen has, that while he has rights, he also has responsibilities toward others. Like Ricki, a policy advocate for the National Down Syndrome Society, Peter, the cardiologist, and his older brother David, who has always included Stephen in his own circle of friends, Stephen understands that to get, one must also give. Citizenship entails responsibilities, a lesson Stephen has been learning from his earliest years in school.

WHAT DO YOU THINK?

1. Did you ever hear the word "retard" used as a put-down? Did it offend you? What would you do if one of your friends used it, even in jest?

2. Given what you know about Stephen and what you have learned about the characteristics of other students with intellectual disability and the programs that benefit them, what is your view about teaching them as a general educator? As a special educator?

3. Do the concepts of "generalization" and "community-based instruction" seem useful for students with other disabilities? Would they have been useful for you before you started your postsecondary education?

ADDRESSING THE STANDARDS: THE VALUES CONNECTION

The following CEC Knowledge and Skill Standards: Common Core and Values are addressed in this chapter through the content and concepts we discuss.

CEC Knowledge and Skill Standards: Common Core	Values/Standards Connection
CEC Knowledge and Skill Standard II. Development and Characteristics of Learners	When you learn about the characteristics of students with intellectual disabilities, you are applying CEC Standard 2, Development and Characteristics of Learners.
CC2K1 Typical and atypical human growth and development.	
CC2K2 Educational implications of characteristics of various exceptionalities.	When you enhance your students' *self-determination*, you increase the likelihood that they will be able to make and act on their *choices*.
CC2K4 Family systems and the roles of families supporting development.	When you evaluate and remediate your students' adaptive behavior, you can help them be more successful in their *relationships* with peers.
CC2K5 Similarities and differences of individuals with and without exceptional learning needs.	
CC2K6 Similarities and differences of individuals with exceptional learning needs.	
CEC Knowledge and Skill Standard IV. Instructional Strategies	As you learn about successful strategies used with students with intellectual disabilities, you are addressing CEC Standard 4, Instructional Strategies.
CC4S1 Use strategies to facilitate integration into various settings.	
CC4S2 Teach individuals to use self-assessment, problem-solving, and other cognitive strategies to meet their needs.	The 12 guided *self-determination* questions discussed in the chapter can enable your students to identify their *strengths* and build on them.
CC4S3 Select, adapt, and use instructional strategies and materials according to characteristics of the individual with exceptional learning needs.	
CC4S4 Use strategies to facilitate maintenance and generalization of skills across environments.	
CC4S5 Use procedures to increase the individual's self-awareness, self-management, self-control, self-reliance, and self-esteem.	
CC4S6 Use strategies that promote successful transitions for individuals with exceptional learning needs.	
CEC Knowledge and Skill Standard V. Learning Environments and Social Interactions	When you support your students, you increase the likelihood that they will have equal opportunities—a way to achieve *full citizenship*.
CC5S2 Identify realistic expectations for personal and social behavior in various settings.	
CC5S3 Identify supports needed for integration into various program placements.	When your students have opportunities for competitive employment during high school, they begin to have *great expectations* for successful employment after they graduate.
CC5S4 Design learning environments that encourage active participation in individual and group settings.	
CC5S9 Create an environment that encourages self-advocacy and increased independence.	

continued

CEC Knowledge and Skill Standards: Common Core		Values/Standards Connection
CEC Knowledge and Skill Standard VII. Instructional Planning		These standards lead to your students' productivity and contribution and their *relationships* in their schools.
CC7S1	Identify and prioritize areas of the general curriculum and accommodations for individuals with exceptional learning needs.	
CC7S3	Involve the individual and family in setting instructional goals and monitoring progress.	
CC7S6	Sequence, implement, and evaluate individualized learning objectives.	
CC7S9	Incorporate and implement instructional and assistive technology into the educational program.	
CEC Knowledge and Skill Standard VIII. Assessment		Monitoring students' progress assures you are building on their innate and acquired *strengths*.
CC8K3	Screening, prereferral, referral, and classification procedures.	
CC8S2	Administer nonbiased formal and informal assessments.	
CC8S6	Use assessment information in making eligibility, program, and placement decisions for individuals with exceptional learning needs, including those from culturally and/or linguistically diverse backgrounds.	
CC8S8	Evaluate instruction and monitor progress of individuals with exceptional learning needs.	
CEC Knowledge and Skill Standard X. Collaboration		Collaboration, especially with the students themselves, fosters their *self-determination*.
CC10S2	Collaborate with families and others in assessment of individuals with exceptional learning needs.	
CC10S3	Foster respectful and beneficial relationships between families and professionals.	
CC10S4	Assist individuals with exceptional learning needs and their families in becoming active participants in the educational team.	
CC10S5	Plan and conduct collaborative conferences with individuals with exceptional learning needs and their families.	

Source: From CEC Knowledge and Skill Standards: Common Core and Values. Copyright by The Council for Exceptional Children. Reprinted with permission.

SUMMARY

Identifying Students with Intellectual Disability

- Intellectual disability consists of significant limitations in both intellectual functioning and adaptive behavior. It originates before age 18.
- In the 2006–2007 school year, 511,041 students aged 6–21 were identified with intellectual disabilities.
- The two major characteristics of intellectual disability are limitations in intellectual functioning (memory, generalization, and motivation) and limitations in adaptive behavior (conceptual, social, and practical skills).
- The causes of intellectual disability are classified according to timing and type. Timing classifications include prenatal, perinatal, and postnatal. Type classifications include biomedical, social, behavioral, and educational.

Evaluating Students with Intellectual Disability

- AAIDD proposes a comprehensive assessment that involves diagnosing intellectual disability, classifying and describing the student's strengths, weaknesses, and need for supports, and developing a profile that includes intensities of needed supports.
- The AAIDD Adaptive Behavior Scale—School assesses school-age children's adaptive behavior. A soon-to-be-published new adaptive behavior tool is the Diagnostic Adaptive Behavior Scale.
- The Transition Planning Inventory assesses nine knowledge, skill, and behavior areas to provide level-of-performance information related to transition needs.

Designing an Appropriate IEP

- It is especially important to form partnerships among students, parents, educators, and adult support providers in planning for the transition needs of students with disabilities.
- Paraprofessionals can be a valuable resource in enabling students with intellectual disability to make progress in the general curriculum.

- Assistive technologies include software that provides audio and video resources to improve students' literacy skills.
- A functional curriculum is important for teaching skills for independent living.

Using Effective Instructional Strategies

- Preschool and early-education students benefit from prelinguistic milieu teaching to elicit communication and language from them.
- Elementary and secondary students develop their abilities to function effectively in school and postschool environments by using the self-determined learning model.
- Students in transition programs benefit from community-based instruction.

Including Students with an Intellectual Disability

- Students are not often included in general education programs.
- But students achieve higher academic and social gains when they are included in general education classes.

Assessing Students' Progress

- Data-based decision-making strategies document students' progress in the general curriculum.
- The ecological inventory process is useful for both planning community-based instruction and assessing students' attainment of community-based instructional goals.
- Students' IEPs must describe the accommodations to which they are entitled, such as dictating responses, having questions read to them, having more time, and having items clarified for them.

Now go to MyEducationLab at www.myeducationlab.com and take the Self-Assessment to gauge your initial comprehension of chapter content. Once you have taken the Self-Assessment, use your individualized Study Plan for Chapter 9 to enhance your understanding of the concepts discussed in the chapter.

10

Understanding Students with Multiple Disabilities

◆ WHO IS SIERRA SMITH?

Sierra Smith, age 6, is a rarity and a paradox. Why a rarity? The incidence of Smith-Magenis syndrome (SMS), with which Sierra was born, is estimated at 1 in 25,000 children.

Why a paradox? Because she has seemingly contradictory qualities. Let's begin with her mental abilities. Her parents, Denise and David, describe her as a bookworm, always absorbing information from the printed page or her computer-assisted toys. Her teachers, Maureen Torres and Kreg McCune from the Albuquerque, New Mexico, Public Schools, say that she is on grade level with her kindergarten peers without disabilities, has made progress in the general education curriculum, and should be included with her nondisabled peers for first grade rather than placed in a self-contained classroom.

The paradox is created by some of Sierra's other traits, which are characteristic of children with SMS. She engages in self-injurious behaviors that include head banging, hand biting, and picking at her skin and sores. She experiences emotional meltdowns and has temper tantrums. She constantly has something in her mouth that doesn't belong there, including her hands, clothing, toys, and small objects. She has not yet learned to use the toilet independently; that's because her bladder and bowels do not send signals to her brain that she needs to do so. She frequently demands the attention of adults (often to the exclusion of peers in her kindergarten class or her brother and two sisters at home). At school, she experiences daytime sleepiness and requires frequent short naps and a few longer ones because, like other children with SMS, she does not have a great deal of stamina and her sleep cycle is opposite that of children without SMS. Sierra has an inverted circadian rhythm caused by inverted secretion of melatonin, a hormone that regulates the sleep/wake cycle. She awakens frequently during the night, usually four to five times, and she almost always is awake by 5:00 A.M. She is physically small for her age, yet strong enough to hurt herself. Her gross- and fine-motor challenges require several accommodations from her teachers, her one-to-one educational aide, and physical, occupational, and speech therapists at school.

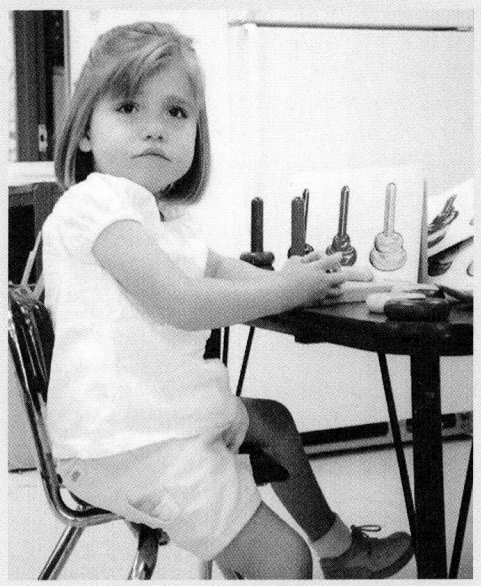

A rarity? Yes. Who would have expected Sierra to have SMS, given how unusual the condition is? Like other people with SMS, her genes were the cause of the syndrome, as you will learn more about in this chapter.

A paradox? Yes. Who would have expected her to have made such progress in school, to have earned the pro-inclusion support of her general education teacher, special education teacher, and principal, Bea Harris, and to have won the affection of her peers? All this despite her many challenges.

There's another aspect to Sierra that commands attention. It is her appearance—not her size, but her cherubic face, also typical of children with SMS. She is, beyond argument, an appealing-looking child.

Given Sierra's abilities and her angelic appearance, it is understandable why Maureen, Kreg, and Bea are committed to her. The paradox is that their commitment simply reinforces her behaviors—those that demand adults' attention and result in meltdowns when she does not get her way. They are drawn to her, and she in turn absorbs them, gaining even more attention from them.

This circular, symbiotic, paradoxical relationship itself is challenging. Sierra needs to learn to be more independent, not just for her own sake, looking ahead to her future in school and then as an adult, but also for her teachers' sake, so that they can attend to other students.

To teach Sierra how to become more independent, Kreg and Maureen had to learn how to depend on each other, for both of them have responsibilities in Sierra's classroom of 17 students without disabilities and 2 (including Sierra) who have disabilities. Here, too, is another paradox: two highly qualified teachers, expert in general early childhood education (Maureen) and early childhood special education (Kreg) must learn to be partners and depend on one another to teach a student to depend less on them.

Given her disabilities, Sierra's inclusion in a general education classroom is itself a rarity in many school districts across the country. Yet she has made so much progress in her kindergarten year that Maureen, Kreg, and Bea, together with Sierra's parents, Denise and David, have successfully advocated for her to be included in the typical first-grade classroom with her nondisabled peers. The partnership among Sierra's teachers and the principal on the one hand and her parents on the other may not be rare, but it is essential to her education.

Besides a commitment to inclusion and partnership, one other facet of Sierra's education is worth mentioning: Sierra's success in the general education setting is a function of the collaboration between her special and general educators to

CHAPTER OBJECTIVES

◆ You will learn the meaning of the term *multiple disabilities* and that, as much as children with these disabilities vary in their abilities and limitations and even as Sierra differs so much from other students in this category, they share common characteristics related to their intellectual, adaptive, motor, sensory, and communication needs.

◆ You will learn about the bi-ological and especially the genetic causes of these disabilities, and how to evaluate these students, including how physicians use the Apgar test at a child's birth to evaluate the baby's abilities.

◆ As you learn how to plan for these students' edu-cation and develop an IEP for each, you will learn about assistive technology, including augmentative and alter-native communication, person-centered planning (called "MAPs"), peer tu-toring, and handheld computers (an example of universally designed learning).

◆ You will learn about effective instructional strategies, including the Children's School Success program for preschoolers, the principle of partial participation, basic methods of task analysis, and student-directed learning strategies.

◆ You will learn about as-sessing students by using portfolio-based assess-ment, field observations, time sampling, and event recording.

provide specially designed instruction and curriculum modifications that enable Sierra to succeed. For example, Kreg McCune's long-term task of teaching Sierra to become a more independent person, less clinging to adults and less prone to self-injury and behavioral meltdowns, began with a simple, immediate curriculum adaptation strategy, the picture book, that was designed based upon an analysis of why Sierra behaves as she does.

Sierra needs consistency and predictability in her life, and she has difficulty communicating, which is part of why she acts out. She can acquire consistency and predictability each day at school and home by using her picture book to see what she will be doing that day; she can understand both the pictures and her teachers' and parents' directions and supports. There was a time when Sierra would engage in tantrum-like behavior whenever an adult asked her to do something she did not want to do. Yet it is in the nature of education itself that adults do and should direct students. So the challenge was to provide Sierra with consistency and predictability, direct her without causing her to experience an emotional crisis, and teach her how to secure additional consistency and predictability on her own.

The picture book does all that, but it is no substitute for consistent behavior from Kreg, Maureen, Denise, and David. Sierra's education is a 24-hour enterprise. She needs to practice at home what she learns at school. And that, in turn, requires her teachers and parents to follow through on each other's instruction and to communicate regularly via a communication log.

Sierra's picture book illustrates the activities of her school day. Because she is, as Denise says, a bookworm, always absorbing information through the printed page, a book is an ideal mode of communication. A simple response to a complex challenge, based on Sierra's own strengths and preferences and on adults' analysis of why she behaves as she does, has become a powerful and effective form of intervention. Here, too, a paradox arises, at least for Sierra: simple can often be better in situations fraught with complexity.

Let's return to the question "Who is Sierra Smith?" She is a rarity, in larger part because she has a rare syndrome and in lesser part because she is among the smallest population of students receiving special education services. She is a paradox because her gifts and challenges are so seemingly contradictory and because the ways in which Kreg, Maureen, Bea, Denise, and David respond—including her in the general education classroom, partnering to capitalize on talents and resources of each team member, and using simple methods to address complex needs—seem to be contra-indicated.

Yet in Albuquerque, these educators' response to rarity and paradox has produced a result that IDEA seeks—education that benefits, is inclusive, and leads to the outcome of independence.

PEARSON
myeducationlab

After reading this chapter, complete the Self-Assessment for Chapter 10 on MyEducationLab to gauge your initial understanding of chapter content.

IDENTIFYING STUDENTS WITH MULTIPLE DISABILITIES

Defining Multiple Disabilities

No single definition covers all the conditions associated with multiple disabilities. Schools sometimes use a compound of two terms, *severe disabilities and multiple disabilities,* as a single category for students who need unusually intensive support to mitigate their impairments. These students' impairments often occur in combination with each other. However, some of these students have average or above-average intelligence, although their physical and communication limitations may mask it. This is the case for Sierra, who reads at grade level but has physical, communicative, and behavioral challenges. Her coexisting abilities and disabilities present another challenge: How should educators classify her? What "type" of disability does she have? The answer is found in the federal regulations implementing IDEA:

> Multiple disabilities means concomitant impairments (such as mental retardation–blindness or mental retardation–orthopedic impairment), the combination of which

causes such severe educational needs that they cannot be accommodated in special education programs solely for one of the impairments. Multiple disabilities does not include deaf-blindness.

Sierra exemplifies the definition; she has more than one disability and severe educational needs, but (as you know) she also has intellectual strengths.

Some educators and researchers use the term *severe and multiple* disabilities. We include "severe" under "multiple" because the definition of "multiple" includes severity.

In fall 2006, approximately 0.2 percent (132,846) of all students aged 6–21 in special education nationally were classified as having multiple disabilities (U.S. Department of Education, Office of Special Education Programs, 2008).

Students with severe and multiple disabilities have complex needs that frequently involve cognitive, motor, and sensory functions.

Describing the Characteristics

Just as it is difficult to find a single definition of multiple disabilities, so it is also difficult to describe accurately all characteristics of all students classified as having multiple disabilities. Collectively, these students are a widely heterogeneous group in terms of their characteristics, capabilities, and educational needs. They are as diverse as people who do not have disabilities—with interests, preferences, personalities, socioeconomic levels, and cultural heritages as varied as those of any of their peers with and without disabilities (Giangreco, 2006). Nevertheless, students with multiple disabilities share five characteristics related to their intellectual functioning, adaptive skills, motor development, sensory functioning, and communication skills.

Intellectual Functioning

Most of students with multiple disabilities have significant impairments in intellectual functioning; their IQ scores are approximately 35 points or more below the norm—that is, IQ 65 or lower (Handen, 2007). However, students with a higher IQ still can be classified as having multiple disabilities because of their adaptive, motor, sensory, or communication impairments. No one yet knows exactly what Sierra's intellectual capacity is; she reads and is progressing in kindergarten, yet a nondiscriminatory evaluation has revealed she has an intellectual disability.

It is not easy to determine the capabilities of students like Sierra. As you read in Chapter 5, schools typically measure a student's intellectual functioning by administering an intelligence test. Yet these traditional methods are inappropriate for many students with multiple disabilities (Brown, Snell, & Lehr, 2006). This is so for three reasons. First, students with multiple disabilities usually are not included in the normative samples of standardized intelligence tests; accordingly, the information generated from these tests has limited utility when designing appropriate educational programs. Second, these students have not been exposed to some of the academic content on tests that are used to measure basic cognitive abilities. Third, most intelligence tests rely primarily on verbal abilities, and many students with multiple disabilities have language and communication impairments that limit their capacity to respond verbally, as Sierra does.

Students with multiple disabilities vary widely in their academic abilities. Some students develop functional academic skills such as how to count money, find items in a grocery store, and read basic vocabulary (Browder, Ahlgrim-Delzell, Courtade-Little, & Snell, 2006). Sierra's academic prospects are bright for learning functional academic skills and also for having strong literacy skills. By contrast, some students with the most severe intellectual impairments will learn only how to make eye contact, track objects with their eyes, and respond to stimuli around them (Lancioni et al., 2006).

IEP Tip

Students with the most profound intellectual impairments can still learn. Their IEP team should focus on what they can do and not just on their limitations.

Adaptive Skills

As you learned in Chapter 9, adaptive skills include conceptual, social, and practical competencies for functioning in typical community settings in an age-consistent way. Sierra's social competencies are amusing but counterproductive. Sierra sometimes gives the "Bronx cheer" (also known as a "raspberry cheer") to her classmates. They laugh, thereby reinforcing a behavior that Sierra should not practice. So who needs to be taught? All of these students, not just Sierra.

Self-care skills are especially important for students with multiple disabilities because these students are increasingly included in schools and community activities (Mandal, Smiroldo, & Haynes-Powell, 2007). Denise and David, together with Kreg and Maureen, want Sierra to understand when she should go to the bathroom and how to take care of herself there. Most students and adults with multiple disabilities can attain some level of independence in caring for their own needs (Farlow & Snell, 2006). School programs typically include instruction in self-care skills such as dressing, personal hygiene, toileting, feeding, and simple household chores as part of the focus on students' other educational needs. It is especially important to make sure that these skills generalize to home and community settings. That is why the student's parents and other caregivers should be highly involved in developing the student's IEP. In addition, teachers should be sure that they tell parents and caregivers about the school-based training, including how to carry it out at home and where to get support to do so (such as from nonschool professionals, family friends, members of the family's spiritual community, and parent associations such as the parent training and information centers you read about in Chapter 4).

Motor Development

Students with multiple disabilities usually have significant motor and physical challenges (Campbell, 2006; Frey, 2007). Again, Sierra is typical; her petite size and low stamina impede her ability to get around in school as quickly as other students or to use a pencil without tiring. Students with multiple disabilities usually have sensorimotor impairments that produce abnormal muscle tone. Some have underdeveloped muscle tone; they often have difficulty sitting and moving from a sitting to a standing position. Others have increased muscle tension and extremely tight muscles, causing spasticity. Any abnormal muscle tone can interfere with a student's ability to perform functional tasks such as eating, dressing, using the bathroom, and playing with toys (Szczepanski, 2004). Nevertheless, many of these students learn to walk, often with the use of some mobility device (such as a cane, crutch, or roller).

Sensory Functioning

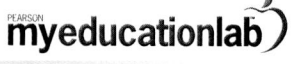

Go to the Activities and Application section in Chapter 10 of MyEducationLab and complete Activity 1. As you watch the videos reflect on the teaching strategies being used here for students with deaf-blindness.

Hearing and vision impairments are common among individuals with multiple disabilities (Silberman, Bruce, & Nelson, 2004). Although for our purposes we include deaf-blindness in the category of multiple disabilities, IDEA regulations currently regard it as a separate category of disability and defines it as follows:

> Deaf-blindness means concomitant hearing and visual impairments, the combination of which causes such severe communication and other developmental and educational needs that they cannot be accommodated in special education programs solely for children with deafness or children with blindness.

It is wrong to assume that students classified as deaf-blind are completely unable to hear or see. They have various combinations of vision and hearing impairments. Their impairments in each of these senses, however, are so severe that they need specially designed instruction, especially in developing meaningful communication, including how to recognize and respond to tactile and gestural cues (Rowland & Schweighert, 2003). For example, a student might learn a simple touch cue, such as a classmate waving good-bye right in front of the student's face so that the hand movement and the air movement it generates signal the student and elicit a response (Engleman, Griffin, Griffin, & Maddox, 1999).

Communication Skills

Almost all students with multiple disabilities, not just those who are deaf-blind, have communication impairments (Kaiser & Grim, 2006). Typically, these students have limited or no functional speech. Their teachers will instruct the student to use expressions, informal gestures, and rudimentary vocalizations to communicate (Schlosser, Sigafoos, Rothschild, Burke, & Palace, 2007). Many students with multiple disabilities use augmentative and alternative communication (AAC) systems, which you learned about in Chapter 6. AAC enlarges their communication abilities (Fossett & Mirenda, 2007). Kreg, Maureen, Denise, and David believe that many of Sierra's behavior problems occur because she can speak only a few words and cannot sufficiently express herself; they regard her disruptive or inappropriate behaviors as communication.

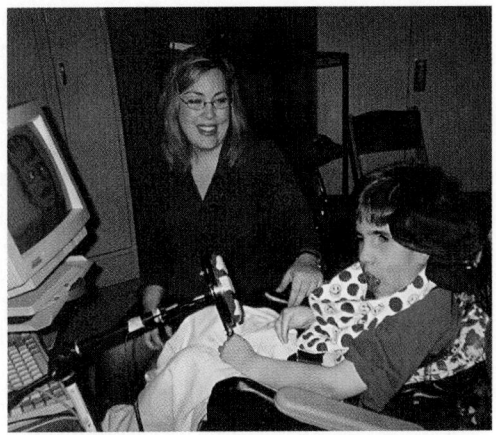

Joshua Spoor, from upstate New York, uses a computer and its "steering wheel" to help him communicate; he also uses a customized wheelchair. Both of these assistive technologies minimize the effects of his physical limitations.

Determining the Causes

Sometimes the cause of a student's disability is simply unknown; often, however, the cause is easy to pinpoint. In approximately three quarters of all children who have severe levels of intellectual disability, there is a biological cause—typically, a prenatal biomedical factor (Batshaw, Shapiro, & Farber, 2007). Complications during birth (perinatal causes) and after birth (postnatal causes) also account for some severe disabilities (Percy, 2007).

We will focus here on genetic causes and will distinguish between general and specific genetic factors. General genetic factors predispose an individual to a multiple disability, whereas a specific genetic factor actually causes the impairment resulting in the disability (Percy, 2007). An example of a general genetic factor that influences the prevalence of multiple disabilities is gender. Two X chromosomes determine the female gender; one X and one Y determine the male gender. Males have a higher prevalence of severe multiple disabilities. A geneticist explains this phenomenon as follows:

> One probable reason for this observation is the X chromosome carries a peculiarly large number of genes concerned with mental functions (Skuse, 2005) . . . [I]f genes on one X chromosome harbor mutations, then these mutations will affect males more than females, because males have only one X chromosome whereas females have two. (Percy, 2007, p. 130)

Specific genetic factors, in contrast to general genetic factors, cause particular types of impairments because of gene or chromosome abnormalities. These genetic factors may occur spontaneously through basic alterations in genes, or they may be inherited. Over 7,000 genetic disorders have been identified; slightly over one third of those are associated with an intellectual disability (Moser, 2004).

Fragile X syndrome, an example of a specific genetic factor, is caused by a single gene mutation on the X chromosome that is associated with the absence of a protein (**syndrome** refers to a group of concurrent signs or symptoms that are related to a particular condition). Fragile X syndrome typically manifests itself as intellectual disability, a severe multiple disability, and/or autism. As the most commonly known inherited cause of intellectual disability, Fragile X prevalence is approximately 1 in 4,000 males and 1 in 9,000 females (Mazzocco & Holden, 2007; Tartaglia, Hansen, & Hagerman, 2007).

Smith-Magennis syndrome (SMS) is the genetic disorder that Sierra experiences. It is caused by a deletion of genetic material on chromosome 17 (Tartaglia et al., 2007). Children with SMS typically experience an intellectual disability, behavior challenges, vocal chord impairments, speech and communication delays, sleep disruption, and hearing loss. Like Sierra, their height is usually below the typical range for their age. Individuals with more significant deletions have been found to have more severe impairments (Percy et al., 2007; Tartaglia et al., 2007).

In 1990, the International Human Genome Sequencing Consortium, led in the United States by the National Human Genome Research Institute and the Department of Energy, committed to a collaborative partnership to sequence all three billion base pairs in the human **genome** that constitutes the human body's DNA (National Institutes of Health, n.d.). The 23 pairs of chromosomes within the human body contain the three billion base pairs. The Human Genome Project (HGP) spurred a comprehensive international research effort that resulted, in 2000, with the production of a rough draft of the human genome sequence. The completion of the HGP provided information about the order of the genes and their general location in the DNA of all 46 human chromosomes. By mapping the location of human genes, the HGP provided a foundation for determining the function of each gene and its role in causing or influencing human characteristics, including disability.

That research in turn enabled scientists to create, in 2005, a catalog of the common genetic variations. The catalogue, named HapMap, enables scientists to find the causes of many disorders and diseases that arise from a genetic base. The discovery of causes now spurs research to prevent a wide range of genetic disorders, including those that cause multiple disabilities. Genetic research has the potential to enhance treatment, medication, prevention, and wellness; but it also has the potential to create new forms of discrimination, such as required disclosures to insurance companies, employers, and others about genetic conditions (Stowe, Turnbull, Schrandt, & Rack, 2007).

EVALUATING STUDENTS WITH MULTIPLE DISABILITIES

As you know, IDEA's nondiscriminatory evaluation process determines whether the student has a disability and requires specially designed instruction and, if necessary, the student's special education and related-service needs. Figure 10.1 describes this process for students with multiple disabilities.

Determining the Presence of Multiple Disabilities

The **Apgar test** is a traditional way to screen the health of a newborn (Ward & McCune, 2002) and can be the first indicator of an impairment leading to disability. When using this test, a physician ranks the child on five physical traits (heart rate, respiratory effort, muscle tone, gag reflex, and skin color) at 1 minute and 5 minutes after birth. The newborn receives a score of 0, 1, or 2 for each trait. A low Apgar score (less than 5 on a scale of 10) provides evidence that the infant has or is at risk of having a disability (Ward & McCune, 2002, p. 72).

Following an Apgar screening and assuming that the infant's Apgar score reveals present or potential disability-related complications, professionals conduct more precise and thorough tests to identify the nature of the disability, its possible causes, and the extent of the disabling conditions. They often use neuro-imaging to create anatomical pictures of the brain. Three techniques include:

> . . . computed tomography (CT) scans, magnetic resonance imaging (MRI), and magnetic resonance spectroscopy (MRS). A CT scan uses X rays and a computer to create a sophisticated picture of the brain's tissues and structures. MRI uses a combination of magnetic fields and radio waves, instead of radiation, to create a picture of the brain. MRS is a type of imaging that reveals levels of particular substances. (Percy et al., 2007, p. 230).

Unlike the process of identifying students as having a disability within educational settings, students with multiple disabilities are typically identified at birth or during their early years; physicians, not educators or psychologists, have the primary role in making the initial diagnosis.

Figure 10.1

Nondiscriminatory evaluation process for determining the presence of multiple disabilities

Observation	**Physician/medical professionals observe:** The newborn may have noticeable disabilities associated with a syndrome or may have medical complications that are often associated with severe disabilities. **Parents observe:** The child has difficulties nursing, sleeping, or attaining developmental milestones.
Screening	**Screening measures:** Apgar scores are below 4, indicating the possibility of severe disabilities.
Prereferral	Prereferral is typically not used for these children because the severity of the disability indicates a need for special education and related services.
Referral	Children with severe and multiple disabilities should be referred by medical personnel or parents for early intervention during the infancy/preschool years. Many states have Child Find organizations to make sure these children receive services. The child is referred upon reaching school age.
Nondiscriminatory evaluation procedures and standards	**Assessment measures:** **Genetic evaluations:** Evaluation leads to identification of a genetic cause. **Physical examinations:** Medical procedures, including vision and hearing tests, blood work, metabolic tests, spinal tests, etc., reveal the presence of a disabling condition. **Individualized intelligence test:** The student scores at least two standard deviations below the mean (i.e., 70 to 75 or lower), indicating that intellectual disability exists. Most students with severe and multiple disabilities have IQ scores that are significantly below 70, indicating severe cognitive impairment. **Adaptive behavior scales:** The student scores significantly below average in two or more areas of adaptive behavior, indicating severe deficits in skills such as communication, daily living, socialization, gross- and fine-motor coordination, and behavior. **Assistive technology assessment:** The student receives a comprehensive assessment for assistive technology needs in all of the environments in which the student participates. This evaluation should be consistent with IDEA's definition of assistive technology device and assistive technology service. The student's IEP team develops an IEP for the student.

Determining the Nature of Specially Designed Instruction and Services

Students with multiple disabilities are prime candidates for assistive technology—the use of existing, modified, or specially created technology to improve how a student functions. That is because assistive technologies can help students overcome any functional limitations they may have. Sierra uses a laptop computer and its software toys and games to supplement her classroom instruction. To determine whether a student needs assistive technologies, the student's evaluation team should ensure that assistive technology devices

◆ Are necessary for the student to make progress in the general education curriculum.

◆ Meet the IDEA definition—any commercial or noncommercial item, piece of equipment, or product system used to increase, maintain, or improve the student's functional capabilities.

◆ Are considered appropriate for the environments in which the student participates.

◆ Are examined through procedures that lead to potentially effective interventions.

Assistive technology evaluations typically are multidisciplinary; assistive technology specialists, speech-language pathologists, orientation and mobility specialists, and occupational and physical therapists usually are involved. Although experts must be involved in the assistive technology evaluation process, the student's family members and the student should participate to the maximum extent possible. Together, these individuals should consider the student's educational, medical, and behavioral records and provide the following assessments, each of which constitutes part of an overall assistive technology evaluation:

- A speech, language, and communication assessment
- A seating and positioning assessment
- A mobility assessment
- A switch use and input/output device assessment
- A writing evaluation, including hand and grip strength and fine-motor skills
- A visual and hearing assessment
- An assessment of home, school (classroom and campus), and community environmental factors

These assessments should be conducted in the child's naturally occurring environments, including the school building and home.

Zabala (2002) updated an outline of questions to help IEP teams make decisions about student assistive technology needs. Called the SETT framework, the process considers the Student's needs, interests, and abilities; the Environment in which the technology will be used; the Tasks for which the technology will be needed; and then the Tools that might be needed to meet the student's needs. Figure 10.2 illustrates the SETT framework.

Figure 10.2 ▶ **SETT (Student, Environment, Tasks, Tools) Framework for Making Evaluation Decisions**

The Student
- What does the student need to do?
- What are the student's special needs and current abilities?

The Environments
- What are the instructional and physical arrangements? Are there special concerns?
- What materials and equipment are currently available in the environments?
- What supports are available to the student and the people working with the student on a daily basis?
- How are the attitudes and expectations of the people in the environment likely to affect the student's performance?

The Tasks (Be as specific as possible.)
- What activities occur in the student's natural environments which enable progress toward mastery of identified goals?
- What is everyone else doing?
- What are the critical elements of the activities?
- How might the activities be modified to accommodate the student's special needs?

The Tools
- What no-tech, low-tech, and high-tech options should be considered for inclusion in an assistive technology system for a student with these needs and abilities doing these tasks in these environments?
- What strategies might be used to invite increased student performance?
- How might the student try out the proposed system of tools in the customary environments in which it will be used?

Source: Zabala (2002). Update of the SETT Framework. Retrieved October 18, 2007, from http://www.joyzabala.com.

DESIGNING AN APPROPRIATE IEP

Partnering for Special Education and Related Services

It is increasingly common for teachers to design IEPs for students with multiple disabilities by using person-centered planning (Chambers & Childres, 2005; Kim & Turnbull, 2004). That term emphasizes the active participation of everyone involved in the student's life (family, teachers, administrators, and, of course, the student), focuses on the student's and family's dreams and visions, and seeks school and community inclusion (Brown, Galambos, Poston, & Turnbull, 2007; Holburn, Gordon, & Vietze, 2007). It is especially important to consider the family's cultural values and to find ways to implement person-centered planning so that it responds to these values (Bui & Turnbull, 2003; Trainor, 2007; Turnbull, Turnbull, Erwin, & Soodak, 2006).

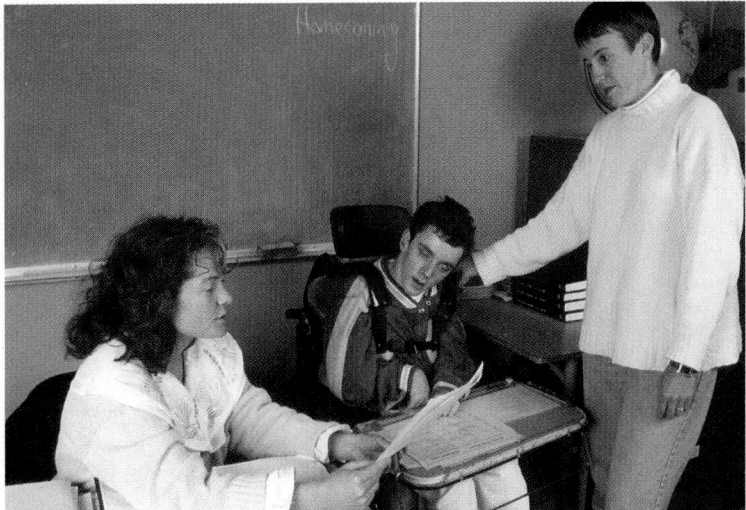

During the MAPs planning process, parents, family, friends, and teachers discuss the individual's strengths and challenges. What is unique to this process is that the student, himself, is also involved and offers a vital perspective.

One of the most popular person-centered planning approaches is called making action plans (MAPs). The **MAPs** process customizes students' educational programs to their specific visions, strengths, and needs (Downing, 2002; Falvey, Forest, Pearpoint, & Rosenberg, 2002). It is especially effective in planning transitions from school to postschool activities (Mount & O'Brien, 2002). Box 10.1 provides tips for how to implement the MAPs process.

Determining Supplementary Aids and Services

Supplementary aids and services can consist of support from teachers, paraprofessionals, and peers. **Peer tutoring** involves pairing students one on one, so students who have already developed certain skills can help teach those and other skills to less advanced students and also help those students practice skills they have already mastered. Can peer tutoring, which has worked so effectively for students without disabilities and for students with mild disabilities (Calhoon, 2005; Keller, 2002), also be successful for students with multiple disabilities? The answer is "yes."

- Peer tutors have successfully worked with middle school students in general education classrooms to teach them to record their own performance of skills (Gilberts, Agran, Hughes, & Wehmeyer, 2001).

- A classwide peer-tutoring program involving middle school students with severe disabilities in inclusive classrooms increased the rates of academic responding and reduced the rates of problem behavior among the students with disabilities (McDonnell, Mathot-Buckner, Thorson, & Fister, 2001).

- Peer tutoring for students with moderate and severe disabilities in inclusive classrooms helped them to understand the tasks their teachers asked them to perform (Collins, Hendricks, Fetko, & Land, 2002).

- The use of peer tutors has increased the social interactions among adolescents with and without severe disabilities (Carter & Hughes, 2005).

- Peer tutoring and peer-mediated learning has promoted the self-determination of students with severe disabilities (Wood, Fowler, Uphold, & Test, 2005).

IEP Tip

Peer tutoring is an evidence-based practice that promotes academic achievement and social/communication gains, and has benefits for students without disabilities. IEP teams should consider implementing peer-mediated learning strategies for all students with disabilities.

PEARSON
myeducationlab

Go to the Building Teaching Skills and Dispositions section in Chapter 10 of MyEducationLab and complete the activities. As you watch the videos, consider how these three models of peer tutoring could work with students who have multiple disabilities.

Implementing the MAPs Process

You may incorporate the MAPs process into a student's IEP meeting, or you may develop it independently of the IEP. If you incorporate it into the IEP meeting, you will need to make sure that everyone sets aside sufficient time to complete the MAPs process and incorporate its contents into the IEP.

Whether you do the MAPs process while developing a student's IEP or not, you will follow the same general process. You, or perhaps a facilitator who has done MAPs planning before, should guide the discussion, infuse the discussion with positive energy, and encourage brainstorming to generate as many creative ideas as possible. You and the other people involved in the MAPs process will want to think outside the box, asking yourselves what makes the student tick, identifying how you can build on the student's strengths to facilitate his well-being in school and community, recognizing what stands in the way, and deciding how to overcome those barriers.

You will need to have just the right people attend. They include the student, his family members, and friends who have formed an emotional bond with the student and who have taken the time to know what is most important in his life.

The facilitator should lead the meeting participants through the following questions (Turnbull, Turnbull, Erwin, & Soodak, 2006):

◆ *What is MAPs?* At the beginning of the meeting, the facilitator explains the purpose of the process, the type of questions that will be asked, and the general ground rules for open-ended and creative problem solving. The facilitator especially tries to create an upbeat, energized, and relational ambience.

◆ *What is your history or story?* Typically, the student and the student's family talk about what they regard

as their successes and triumphs, as well as the challenges still facing them, especially those impeding the student's visions, expectations, strengths, and preferences.

◆ *What are your dreams?* The student and family members share their great expectations for the future. The MAPs team members use these expectations to customize academic and extracurricular activities.

◆ *What are your nightmares?* Because students with exceptionalities and their families often have major fears that may cloud their great expectations, identifying their fears—their nightmares—lets everyone know them and plan to respond to them. Some fears are realistic, such as those about the progressive course of AIDS in a young child, but others can be addressed through support for the student and family.

◆ *Who are you?* The MAPs team members use as many adjectives as it takes to avoid the student's exceptionality label. Instead, they describe the student's noncategorical traits. For example, instead of identifying the student as having severe, multiple disabilities, they say she is curious, misbehaving at times, eager to please, or hard to understand.

◆ *What are your strengths, gifts, and talents?* Often teachers, friends, family members, and others can lose sight of the fact that the student has strengths on which to build. So the MAPs team members identify them.

◆ *What do you need?* What will it take to make the student's and family's great expectations come true? What barriers stand in the way? Identifying these needs and barriers lays the foundation for planning for the student to participate in academic, extracurricular, and other school activities.

◆ *What is the plan of action?* A plan of action includes the specific steps required to accomplish the great expectations. The plan of action should identify the people, tasks, timelines, and resources that will help the student and family realize their expectations.

 **IEP Tip**

Answers to the eight MAPs questions can provide highly relevant information for IEP teams making decisions about priority goals for the academic curriculum as well as for extracurricular activities.

Box 10.2 identifies the steps you should follow to implement peer tutoring with students with multiple disabilities.

Models of peer tutoring involve service learning (Scott, 2006) and course credits for peer tutors (Copeland et al., 2002). Although social interactions between disabled and nondisabled students increase with peer tutoring (Carter & Hughes, 2005), the nature of those social interactions may change as well. Peers involved in tutoring activities with stu-

Peer Buddies

Suppose you could accomplish several goals with a single effort? For example, you could effectively integrate the educational programs of students with severe and multiple disabilities into the general curriculum, remove them from their separate and self-contained classrooms for at least one class period a day, help them learn functional academic and employment skills, and increase the number of genuine friendships they have with students who do not have disabilities. Would you be interested in adopting that program in your school? Probably.

What if that same strategy could simultaneously benefit students without disabilities in three or four different ways? Give them academic credit? Teach them how to be good citizens? Still interested? Definitely. After all, this is a win-win proposition for everyone.

The strategy we are talking about is called peer buddies, and it was designed by researchers at Vanderbilt University to promote social relationships among students with severe disabilities and their same-age peers without disabilities. In the large urban school district of Nashville, Tennessee, 9 of 11 comprehensive high schools paired 200 students with severe disabilities with 115 students who had no disabilities. The program was a great success (Hughes et al., 2001).

How does the peer buddies strategy work? Pretty simply, really, as these steps show.

Step 1: *Introduce a 1-credit course.* Many high schools already require their students to engage in some sort of service learning. The peer buddies model fulfills the requirements for service learning.

Step 2: *Recruit peer buddies.* Recruit students who hold high-status roles to serve as peer buddies—student government leaders, sports and cheerleading standouts, and high academic performers. These high-status students add credibility to the program process.

Step 3: *Establish a screening process.* Peer buddies must be responsible and reliable students, such as those who have a good attendance record and have shown they can juggle extracurricular activities and academic demands. Once an initial screening has been completed,

allow a potential peer buddy to observe existing peer buddy activities and allow him or her to ask questions to get a better idea about the purpose of the activities.

Step 4: *Train the students.* Topics include people-first language and disability, awareness effective communication strategies, sample activities in which to engage with students with severe disabilities, and how to deal with inappropriate behavior in an effective but respectful way.

Step 5: *Establish expectations and evaluate progress.* Observe peer buddies, provide feedback and reinforcement on their interactions, and answer questions. Establish regularly scheduled times for the peer buddies to meet and to discuss what worked for them and what did not. This is also a good venue to teach peer buddies skills related to time management and organizational and scheduling strategies.

Putting These Ideas to Work for Progress in the General Curriculum

1. What do you see as the benefits of participating in a peer buddies program for students with and without disabilities?

2. Peer buddies was set up at the high school level. Do you think the program could be adapted to the elementary level? If so, what changes would you recommend for using this program with younger children?

3. What might be some comfort and knowledge concerns of students without disabilities when interacting with the student and teachers you met in the vignette?

PEARSON myeducationlab

Go to the Activities and Application section in Chapter 10 of MyEducationLab and complete Activity 2. As you watch the videos and answer the accompanying questions, reflect on how George's peer buddies help him achieve both academic and social goals.

---

dents with severe disabilities report that they see benefits to the tutored student as well as to themselves (Copeland et al., 2004).

But relying too much on students without disabilities to support their classmates who do have disabilities might lead to relationships that tend to be one-way rather than reciprocal. For example, researchers have found that peers without disabilities interacted in more socially relevant ways with students with severe disabilities when they were in a noninstructional role than they did when they were in an instructional (e.g., peer tutor) role (Hughes, Carter, Hughes, Bradford, & Copeland, 2002). Clearly, there is nothing wrong with help; friends often help each other. Help, however, is not and should never be the only basis for friendship. You should be careful not to overemphasize the helper-helpee aspect of a relationship. So you will want to find ways for all your students to do something for each other, such as giving a compliment or nominating another student for a class honor.

Planning for Universal Design for Learning

Many new advances in technology make it possible to include students with multiple disabilities in the general education curriculum. One of these exciting technologies is the handheld personal computer.

Assume you are teaching three high school students with severe disabilities to get jobs in their communities. One student needs to learn how to set the tables in a restaurant or in a senior citizens' home; another to wash, dry, and fold laundry in a fitness club near his home; the third to deliver the mail from a central mailroom to the offices of the judges and clerks of court in a county courthouse. Assume you have only one paraprofessional to assist you. How do you teach all three students, especially if they go off campus daily, to learn how to perform their duties?

One way to respond to that challenge is to use a software program called the Visual Assistant. The program operates on handheld computers running the Windows CE operating system. This innovative software, developed by AbleLink, Inc., of Colorado Springs, Colorado, is a "see it, hear it, do it" example of universal design for learning. As you can see in Box 10.3, the Visual Assistant uses the capacity of handheld computers to import and display digital pictures and to record and play audio messages, all in order to present information about tasks a student might be learning. In Chapter 2 we pointed out that UDL modifies how teachers present and represent the curriculum that a student must learn. Using handheld computer technology and software programs like Visual Assistant, teachers can import and display digital pictures that are individualized, like pictures of the student performing each step in a learning task, and play digital video clips.

Handheld computers are ideal for introducing universally designed learning features into instruction. They are unobtrusive; fit into a purse, a backpack, a waist pack, or the pockets of cargo pants; and unlike desktop computers, are very portable. Instead of using less-accessible input modes, such as a keyboard, handheld computers operate by a touch screen. Moreover, other devices, including digital cameras and global positioning satellite devices, can be inserted into the handheld computer. Some researchers are even developing handheld computer programs that use global positioning systems data to help people with cognitive disabilities use public buses equipped with transmitters.

Research with the Visual Assistant has shown that students with severe disabilities can learn to do their jobs faster and with fewer errors and prompts from teachers or coaches than if they were doing the same work under the same conditions without a teacher or coach (Davies, Stock, & Wehmeyer, 2002a, 2002b; Riffel et al., 2005). Now consider the possibilities for promoting a student's access to the general curriculum by using the Visual Assistant. In essence, the Visual Assistant is a multimedia version of a well-researched curriculum modification strategy—picture prompts—that uses pictures, graphics, or symbols to prompt students to complete a multistep task. Those strategies help teach students to direct their own learning and are as appropriate for teaching math or reading as for teaching functional content.

Planning for Other Educational Needs

You have already learned that students with multiple disabilities have limitations in communication. People rely on communication skills for many important things, from learning to making friends. Fortunately, one form of assistive technology, **augmentative and alternative communication (AAC),** enables students who cannot communicate verbally or through other formats, such as sign language, to do so through the use of technology. You learned a little about AAC in Chapter 6, but because those devices are so important for students with multiple disabilities, it's worth learning more about them here.

IEP Tip

Electronic and information technologies, such as the Visual Assistant shown in Box 10.3, are becoming less expensive and more powerful. IEP teams should consider what off-the-shelf technologies can be modified to meet students' unique needs rather than looking only at expensive disability-specific assistive devices.

Visual Assistant: The See-It, Hear-It, Do-It Handheld Portable Prompter

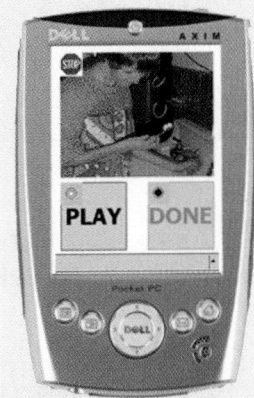

Pocket Compass—an instructional media task-prompting system from AbleLink Technologies.

The Visual Assistant provides powerful task-prompting support by including digital pictures along with custom-recorded audio messages to provide step-by-step instructional support for students with intellectual and other disabilities. This allows educators to set up instructional tasks by recording instructions and incorporating pictures of each step—preferably of the student performing the step in the real-world environment—to provide multimodal cues for task completion. The Visual Assistant is ideal for more complex or detailed tasks where the addition of a picture can increase student accuracy. Its setup and use are simple and take into account principles of universal design and cognitive accessibility.

When the student initiates the Visual Assistant program by double-clicking (tapping twice using a stylus pen) on the Visual Assistant icon on the screen, the software opens to a screen showing all the tasks set up for the person. Each task is depicted using an icon or a picture that represents the task.

So, for example, if Dan, a student with severe disabilities, wants to use the Visual Assistant to make coffee, he taps on the icon of the coffee maker. That action, in turn, opens a screen with a larger picture of the coffee maker and initiates an audio message saying. "Dan, if you want to make a pot of coffee, tap on the *Next* button."

When Dan taps on the *Next* button, it opens another screen, which has a picture of the first step in the coffee-making process and two buttons, one that reads *Play* and one that reads *Done*. Dan's teacher has already taught Dan to tap the *Play* button when he sees it, and when Dan does so, an audio message in the teacher's own voice says, "First, fill the glass coffee pitcher with water up to the 10-cup line."

Dan can play that message as often as he needs. If Dan needs more assistance, the picture of the pitcher can be zoomed in or there can be more steps depicted, such as a picture of Dan himself filling the coffee pitcher at the sink.

When Dan completes the task depicted in the picture and described in the audio message, he taps the *Done* button. Tapping on that button takes him to the next screen, with a picture of the next step in the process and the *Play* and *Done* buttons.

The Visual Assistant is a "see it" (the visual image), "hear it" (the spoken voice), "do it" (the job being done and then finished), universally designed device!

Visual Assistant—an instructional media task-prompting system from AbleLink Technologies, Inc.

IEP Tip

IEP teams should remember that among the "special factors" they are required to consider for every student receiving special education services are communication needs and the need for assistive technology. Alternative and augmentative communication devices cross both of these areas.

AAC refers to the devices, techniques, and strategies used by students who are unable to communicate fully through natural speech and/or writing (Schlosser, 2003). AAC frequently uses technology in the form of voice-output communication aids and synthesized speech, but it may also involve a wide array of other options for communication, from low-tech message boards, symbols, pictures, and visual prompts to very complex technology (Kaiser & Grim, 2006). The goal of AAC is to enable students to experience all the social, emotional, academic, recreational, and employment benefits that accrue from communication. Blackstone, Williams, and Wilkins (2007) identified basic principles underlying research and practice in AAC.

- ◆ AAC fosters the abilities, preferences, and priorities of individuals with complex communication needs, taking into account motor, sensory, cognitive, psychological, linguistic, and behavioral skills, strengths, and challenges.
- ◆ AAC recognizes the unique roles communication partners play during interactions.
- ◆ AAC enables individuals with complex communication needs to maintain, expand, and strengthen existing social networks and relationships and to fulfill societal roles. (p. 192)

Like other forms of assistive and educational technology, AAC devices are supplementary aids and services. When making decisions about appropriate AAC devices, IEP teams need to identify features that best meet the student's needs; these features relate to the symbols the device uses, the way the device displays information, the device's selection options, and its method for outputting information.

Symbols

Symbols represent meanings. Three forms of assistive technology use symbolic communication (Bigge, Best, & Heller, 2001; Heller, 2000):

- ◆ Non-electronic devices, such as communication boards and communication notebooks (see Figure 10.3)
- ◆ Dedicated communication devices specifically designed for communication
- ◆ Computer systems (not special devices)

Each form enables students to communicate through symbols such as drawings, photographs, letters, words, or a combination of them.

Displays

AAC devices have either fixed or dynamic displays. A fixed display offers an unchanging symbol arrangement. The pictures on the communication board in Figure 10.3 are in a fixed display; all of the pictures remain the same. By contrast, dynamic displays enable students to make choices that change the display on the device screen. More and more, AAC devices resemble computers, and the various dynamic displays are similar to displays presented on a computer screen, which users can modify or customize to their preferences.

Selection Options

AAC devices typically offer two major types of selection options: scanning or direct selection. Scanning is suitable for the student who has extensive motor loss; it involves pointing or using a cursor to scan an item at a time, a row of items, or a block of items. Many different options are available for scanning, and each can be tailored to the needs and preferences of a student. The options allow the student to point to a symbol or word without having any physical contact, such as by looking at the symbol, using light pointers, or using head- or mouth-controlled pointers; to touch or press the symbol or word; or to use speech recognition, which is a computer program that converts user vocalizations into keyboard input.

Figure 10.3 A communication board: Example of a fixed display

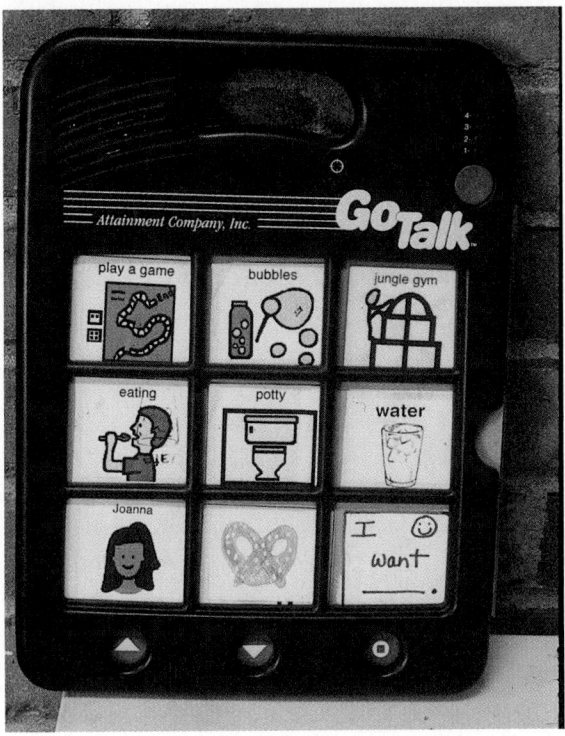

Source: Photo reprinted with permission of DynaVox Technologies, Pittsburgh, PA (telephone toll-free to 800-344-1778).

Output

Output options include low-tech and high-tech solutions, ranging from pointing to symbols pasted on a communication board to navigating multiple levels of options on a computer-type screen.

The student's IEP team needs to include and work closely with speech-language pathologists in the design of AAC and instructional areas pertaining to AAC. As you have learned, instruction related to AAC is complex. Students will need to learn how to use the device in different communicative situations and with different partners, as well as how to care for the equipment. They also must learn some of the basics of communication, whether you are using a device or communicating verbally. Those include how to maintain and sustain conversations (e.g., taking turns and showing interest in others) and when to use different kinds of messages (e.g., keeping secrets or telling jokes). Designing AAC to promote progress in the general curriculum is more than just buying a device; it involves thoughtful planning and effective instruction.

IEP Tip

IEP teams must have representation and active involvement from professionals from different disciplines, including speech-language therapy, assistive technology, and, possibly, physical or occupational therapy, to identify an AAC device that meets a student's communication and quality of life needs.

USING EFFECTIVE INSTRUCTIONAL STRATEGIES

Early Childhood Students: Children's School Success

By now you may have wondered how the IDEA general education curriculum mandates apply to early childhood education. What exactly, you may ask yourself, is the "general education curriculum" for preschoolers? That's an excellent question. Researchers at Indiana University, the University of North Carolina, Purdue University, the University of Maryland, the University of Kansas, and San Francisco State University are collaborating to answer that question and develop strategies for educators to use to include preschoolers with severe, multiple disabilities in the general curriculum. They have named their collaboration the Children's School Success (CSS) curriculum (Lieber, Horn, Palmer, & Fleming, 2008).

As we have stressed throughout this book, access to the general education curriculum occurs when students with disabilities are educated with their nondisabled peers in the general education classroom. The same is true for preschool children, and the CSS model presumes that preschool children are attending preschools with their nondisabled peers (Horn, Thompson, Palmer, Jensen, & Turbiville, 2004). The CSS model seeks to reduce the educational gap for students who are at risk for poor school performance, prepare children for school entry, support individualization, and provide evidence-based practices that lead to these outcomes. It addresses content areas such as math, literacy, and science by using developmentally age-appropriate activities. The model rests on five key assumptions, namely, that children

1. Are active, self-motivated learners who learn best from personal experience.
2. Learn best when they have opportunities to practice skills in the context of meaningful activities.
3. Construct knowledge by participating with others using problem-solving and self-evaluation skills.
4. Should be allowed to exercise choice in their learning environments.
5. Learn best through a curriculum that presents information in an integrated fashion.

The CSS model emphasizes an integrated general education curriculum. At some times in the school day, students may work on only one content area, such as reading or math, from a curriculum, but most of the time, instruction on these core content areas is integrated across activities. The focus on active learning and constructing knowledge through problem-solving and self-evaluation skills teaches young children critical self-regulation skills they will need to learn more effectively once they enter elementary school. The CSS model emphasizes four steps in the problem-solving process:

1. Reflect and act: Preschoolers learn to reflect on what they know about the problem and what they need to find out to know more.
2. Plan and predict: Based upon information from the first phase, children make predictions about what they think will happen next and use those to create a plan.
3. Act and observe: Children implement their plan and test out their predictions.
4. Report and reflect: Based upon the previous steps, children report the solution they have identified via multiple means, such as drawing a picture. (Odom et al., 2007)

Students receiving instruction with the CSS model make academic and social gains (Leiber et al., 2008). Of course, none of this should be particularly new to you. Look at the key assumptions and the problem-solving process again; notice anything familiar? Universal design for learning (multiple means of providing content and of students responding to the content); self-determination and student involvement (student-directed learning strategies, choice opportunities, problem solving); inclusion and integration with nondisabled peers; high expectations (emphasis on core academic content for all students); and scientifically based strategies. Good instructional practices are good for every student, no matter how young the students are.

Elementary and Middle School Students: The Partial Participation Principle

Several important principles govern the education of students with multiple disabilities. The first is the principle of maximal participation (Baumgart et al., 1982), which asserts the right of students with multiple disabilities to participate to the maximum degree possible in activities that contribute to the quality of their lives. The goal of the principle of maximal participation is, quite simply, to maximize participation in one's life.

A related principle is that of **partial participation** (Baumgart et al., 1982; Ferguson & Baumgart, 1991), which holds that students with multiple disabilities should not be denied all access to general education and other inclusive activities solely because of their intellectual, adaptive, skill, motor, sensory, and/or communication impairments (Snell & Brown, 2006). The principle rejects an all-or-none approach under which students either function independently in a given environment or not at all. Instead, it asserts that students with multiple disabilities can participate, even if only partially, and indeed can often learn and complete a task if it is adapted to their strengths. Under the partial participation principle, students are not kept out of the activities that benefit them simply because they cannot perform all of the activities without support (Bambara, Browder, & Koger, 2006), so teachers should ask themselves three questions to implement partial participation:

◆ What noninstructional supports does the student need for meaningful participation?

◆ How much does the student wish to participate?

◆ How can teachers enhance the student's independence, especially partial independence?

Once teachers have answered these questions, they need to observe the student performing a task and use well-developed observational methods (such as the ones we discuss below) to determine what parts of the task the student can do or can learn to do.

The principle of partial participation enables students with multiple disabilities to learn and participate in self-care and other functional skills (Farlow & Snell, 2006), but it also applies to instruction in literacy (Copeland & Keefe, 2007; Downing, 2005), math, and science (Browder & Spooner, 2006). To determine what a student can do or needs to learn to do, teachers usually conduct a task analysis. A task analysis identifies the individual steps that, in combination, are required to perform a skill or activity. According to Snell and Brown (2006), a task analysis follows these steps:

1. Define the target skill or task.
2. Perform the task yourself and observe the student's peers performing the task, noting the steps involved.
3. Identify the component or constituent parts or steps in the activity.
4. Write these parts or steps on a data collection form so that each is
   • Stated in terms of observable behavior.
   • Ordered in a logical sequence.
   • Written in second-person singular so it can serve as a verbal prompt (if used).
5. Observe the student performing the task and identify steps that he or she can or will be able to
   • Perform independently.
   • Learn to perform.
   • Use technology or other supports to perform if needed.

IEP Tip

In designing an educational program for students with multiple disabilities, and particularly in determining annual goals, IEP teams must keep the principle of partial participation in mind and ensure they are making decisions that will involve students in all aspects of learning.

Secondary and Transition Students: Student-Directed Learning Strategies

Consider this question: "If students were floated in life jackets for 12 years, would they be expected to swim if the jackets were suddenly jerked away?" (Martin, Marshall, Maxon, & Jerman, 1993, p. 4). The obvious answer is "of course not." Students would sink without specific instruction on how to swim. Depending on a life jacket does not ensure success once the life jacket is removed. Unfortunately, "the situation is similar for students receiving special education services. All too often these students are not taught how to self-manage their own lives before they are thrust into the cold water of post-school reality" (Martin et al., 1993, p. 4). In Box 10.4, you will read what self-management means in a global sense and you will find that being "his own man" is Madeleine Will's great expectation for her son Jon.

To avoid the life-jacket situation, you can use **student-directed learning strategies.** These strategies teach students with and without disabilities to modify and regulate their own learning (Agran, King-Sears, Wehmeyer, & Copeland, 2003). The educational supports

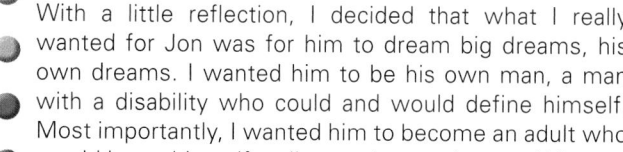

Madeleine Will

With a little reflection, I decided that what I really wanted for Jon was for him to dream big dreams, his own dreams. I wanted him to be his own man, a man with a disability who could and would define himself. Most importantly, I wanted him to become an adult who would know himself well enough to understand his own needs and assume responsibility to the greatest extent possible for his own happiness.

In my imaginary world of care and education for people with disabilities, the emphasis on making and maintaining friends would grow more pronounced in the adolescent years, especially as nondisabled friends went off to college or became preoccupied with job responsibilities. A job, an apartment or a house, and various material goods do not constitute a fulfilled existence for any of us. What matters most to people are their families and loved ones and the quality of those relationships. This fundamental human need should be reflected throughout every phase of education.

Source: Reprinted from *Journal of Vocational Rehabilitation, 3*(2), M. C. Will, "The Question of Personal Autonomy," pp. 9–10, 1993, with kind permission from Elsevier Science Ireland Ltd., Bay 15K, Shannon Industrial Estate, Co. Clare, Ireland.

that teachers use to implement the Self-Determined Learning Model of Instruction (Chapter 9) include many student-directed learning strategies, but three are particularly important for students with severe disabilities: picture prompts or antecedent cue regulation, self-instruction, and self-monitoring.

Picture Prompts or Antecedent Cue Regulation Strategies

You learned a little about these strategies when you read about the Visual Assistant software program earlier in this chapter. This software provides visual and audio prompts for students to successfully complete multistep tasks. The antecedent cue regulation strategy involves a similar approach: providing visual and/or audio cues to support students to regulate their own behavior and to complete assigned tasks. The visual cues include photographs, drawings and illustrations, video clips, and even actual items involved in the task. Audio cues are instructions or directions recorded on a tape, CD-ROM, or MP3 player. Technology platforms such as desktop or handheld computers provide both video and audio cues, just as the Visual Assistant software does.

Given the potential for multimedia devices to present cues in multiple formats, the term *antecedent cue regulation* is preferable to *picture prompts* because many cues are not visually oriented. *Antecedent* means "occuring before," so antecedent cue regulation simply means giving visual or auditory cues before a task to help students regulate their own behavior.

Antecedent cue regulation has three benefits. First, it reduces your students' reliance on others to complete a task. Second, it supports those who cannot remember the steps or sequence in a multistep task. Third, antecedent cue regulation can also be a temporary support, not a permanent one. As a temporary strategy, it promotes learning.

The strategy is effective for students with multiple disabilities. For example, Hughes and colleagues (2000) combined a peer-tutoring strategy with antecedent cue regulation and augmentative communication to improve social interactions among high school students with multiple disabilities and their nondisabled peers. Peer tutors learned how to support students with multiple disabilities to use a picture communication book (an augmentative strategy) to initiate conversations with peers without disabilities. The strategy improved the number and quality of social interactions for students with disabilities.

Self-Instruction Strategies

Self-instruction strategies involve teaching students to use their verbal or other communication skills to direct their learning. Like the antecedent cue regulation strategies, students use self-instructions as cues to what they need to do next to perform the task. Self-instruction strategies are often even more flexible than antecedent cue regulation strategies because students use something they have with them at all times—their means of communication (Agran et al., 2003). Several research-based templates for self-instruction exist, including the following (Agran et al., 2003):

◆ The traditional problem-solving self-instruction, in which students learn to verbally instruct themselves to identify the problem (What do I do next in this task?), identify a solution to the problem (I place the silverware in the napkin.), evaluate the effectiveness of the solution (Does this look right?), and reinforce themselves (Yes, that looks good!)

◆ The task sequencing or "did-next-now" strategy, in which students learn self-instruction statements related to the step they just completed (I placed the silverware in the napkin.), the next step (I need to roll the silverware in the napkin.), and when they will perform the next step (I'll do the next step now.)

◆ The "what-where" strategy, in which students learn statements about what they need to do (I need to roll the silverware in the napkin) and where they will do it (I roll the silverware in the napkin at my workstation in the restaurant.), which helps them remember the context in which they engage in certain activities

◆ The interactive or "did-next-ask" strategy, in which students learn self-instruction statements similar to the task-sequencing strategy but complete the statement by instructing themselves to ask someone about the next step or about some aspect of the task. It is helpful to teach this in conjunction with the task-sequencing strategy in case students forget the next step.

Self-Monitoring Strategies

One of the most widely evaluated and effective student-directed learning strategies involves teaching students to monitor their own behavior or actions. Essentially, when using **self-monitoring strategies,** students learn to collect data on their progress toward educational goals. They can do this through traditional formats, such as charting their progress on a sheet of graph paper or completing a checklist. For students with multiple disabilities, however, there are simpler ways to monitor themselves. They can place a marble in a jar each time they complete a task successfully or move a poker chip from one container to another. Once they fill the jar or move all of the chips from the original box, they learn that they have completed their specific goals. Agran and colleagues (2003) have provided these suggestions for implementing self-monitoring strategies:

◆ Implement self-monitoring strategies after the student has already learned to do the task that is being monitored.
◆ Teach the self-monitoring strategy to the student before implementing the strategy.
◆ Build in checks to determine the accuracy of the student's self-monitoring.

However, even when students are not entirely accurate, there are benefits to the use of self-monitoring.

IEP Tip

Student-directed learning strategies have proven educational efficacy with students with multiple disabilities and, indeed, all students. There probably should be few if any IEPs that don't include some student-directed learning.

INCLUDING STUDENTS WITH MULTIPLE DISABILITIES

Leaders in the field of multiple disabilities have almost always advocated for inclusive education (Downing, 2008; Snell & Brown, 2006; Orelove, Sobsey, & Silberman, 2004; Thousand, Villa, & Nevin, 2002). Indeed, the major professional organization in the field of multiple disabilities, TASH (formerly The Association for Persons with Severe Handicaps), has had a long-term commitment to inclusive education. Nevertheless, Figure 10.4 shows that most students with multiple disabilities still spend most of their time outside the regular classroom.

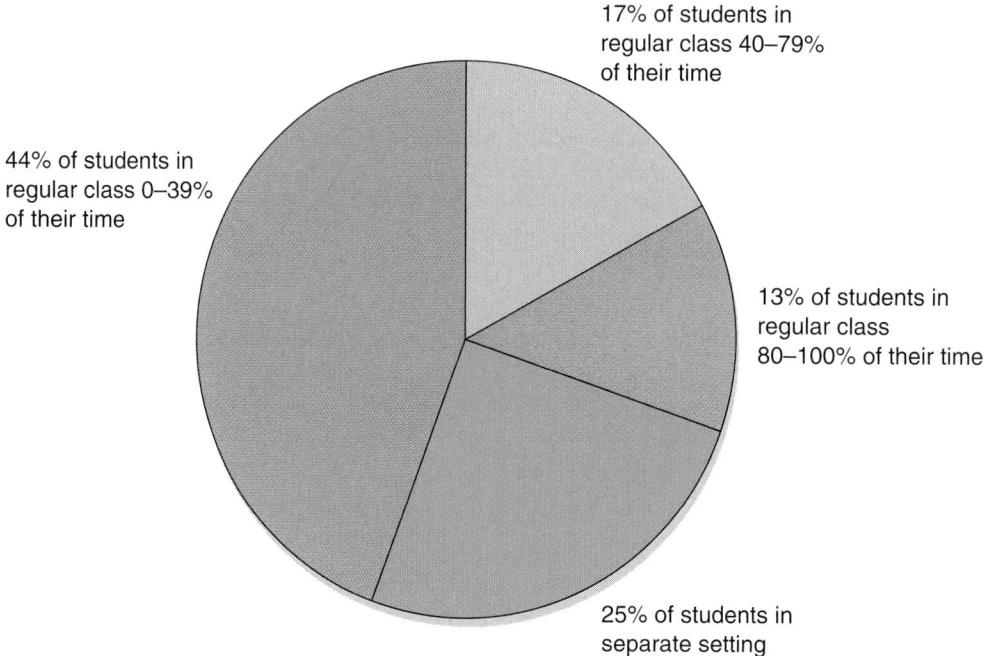

Figure 10.4 Educational placement of students with multiple disabilities (2006–2007)

17% of students in regular class 40–79% of their time

44% of students in regular class 0–39% of their time

13% of students in regular class 80–100% of their time

25% of students in separate setting

Advocacy alone does not ensure inclusion. Research into and application of evidence-based practices are also necessary. There is now convincing evidence that students with multiple disabilities can be successfully included in the general education classroom as well as extracurricular and other school activities (Ryndak & Fisher, 2003). As Sailor (2002) noted with regard to the "impressive amounts of published research" that has demonstrated that inclusion is feasible and beneficial, "after nearly two decades of special education efforts at policy reform in the direction of inclusive education, the corner has finally been turned and the question has shifted from 'should we do it?' to 'how do we do it?' " (p. 8). This research has shown several consistent characteristics of successful inclusion for students with multiple disabilities:

◆ Collaboration among teachers and parents at classroom, building, and systems levels, as Sierra's teachers and parents do

◆ Teaching of new skills in general education classrooms, as Kreg and Maureen do to Sierra

◆ Promotion of friendships in inclusive settings, as Sierra is finding them in her classroom

◆ Facilitation of positive outcomes for classmates without disabilities

◆ Adaptation of the students' curriculum (Wolfe & Hall, 2003), as Kreg and Maureen adapt Sierra's to her need for sleep, her difficulty in holding a pencil, and her behavioral challenges (through the picture book)

Box 10.5 offers tips for promoting inclusion.

Given that educators know how to include students with severe disabilities, why do more than half of all students with multiple disabilities spend most or all of their time outside the general education classroom? There are many reasons. Particularly at the high school level, many teachers still believe that students with those disabilities cannot be appropriately served in general education classes or even in their neighborhood schools (Smith, 2000). Other teachers believe they are not prepared to teach those students (Smith, 2000). As you learned in Chapter 2, the better trained a teacher is, the more likely it is that the teacher will support inclusion (Soodak et al., 2002). By contrast, the less well prepared teachers are, the less likely they are to support inclusion.

	What You Might See	*What You Might Be Tempted to Do*	*Alternate Responses*	*Ways to Include Peers in the Process*
Behavior	He has temper tantrums and hits himself or others.	Discipline and isolate him from the rest of the class.	Learn to identify cues that trigger positive behavior. Reward appropriate behavior.	Support the peers closest to him and teach them to recognize and give cues that encourage positive behavior in a way that is respectful of him.
Social interactions	He is unable to communicate needs or wants using words.	Allow him to remain a class observer rather than a participant.	Use assistive technology to enable him to communicate his needs and wants.	Teach peers to communicate with him using his assistive technology.
Educational performance	He is not able to read or write, and his functional skills are extremely limited.	Give up and let him color or do something quiet.	Create opportunities for him to benefit from peer tutoring.	Arrange for peers to assist him with follow-through on task completion. Support them to be friends as well as peer tutors.
Classroom attitudes	He appears bored or unresponsive and often sleeps during class instruction.	Ignore him and focus on other, more attentive students.	Use times of alertness to teach self-instruction strategies to enable him to engage in more proactive learning.	Encourage peers to prompt him to use his preferred self-instruction strategies.

Unfortunately, many parents also believe that general educators are not well prepared for inclusion (Palmer, Fuller, Arora, & Nelson, 2001). A survey of approximately 500 parents revealed that most of them believe that the nature of their child's disability is too severe and would overwhelm general education teachers; they are concerned about the mismatch among their child's needs in the general education curriculum, the lack of appropriate services, and peers' acceptance of their child (Palmer et al., 2001)

Yet there are effective practices that support students with multiple disabilities in the general education classroom. (We highlight several of them in this chapter.) Furthermore, the emphasis that IDEA and NCLB place on all students and their progress in the general curriculum may encourage schools to change (Browder et al., 2006). And parents have reported that the primary benefit of inclusion is that their child has a greater chance to learn more academic and functional skills in general education classes because there are higher expectations in those classes than in special education classrooms (Palmer et al., 2001).

The key to successful inclusion for all students, especially students with multiple disabilities, is partnerships among educators, families, and students. Box 10.6 describes how partnerships created inclusive supports and services at Whittier High School in Los Angeles County, California.

Inclusive Supports at Whittier High School

A good example of how inclusion for students with multiple disabilities can work exists at Whittier High School in southeastern Los Angeles County, California. This high school serves more than 2,000 students in grades 9 through 12, 84 percent of whom are Latino, 36 percent of whom participate in the free or reduced lunch program, and 19 percent of whom have limited ability to speak English.

In the mid-1990s, approximately 30 percent of Whittier's students were dropping out before graduating and only 10 percent to 15 percent of its graduates went to 4-year colleges. Conscious of these facts and intent on implementing state-of-the-art inclusive practices, faculty members, staff, administration, parents, and community leaders adopted a mission statement that promotes academic excellence, respect for self and others, acceptance of the diversity of students' abilities and culture, involvement of all students in all aspects of the school, and a commitment that all students will reach their full potential. "All means all" at Whittier, including students with multiple disabilities.

To improve the performance of students with disabilities as well as those not performing at grade level but not classified as having disabilities, students and faculty are divided into three teams at each grade level. Students remain in their team during their 9th- and 10th-grade years. Each team consists of the following:

◆ Eight to 10 core curriculum/general education teachers certified in math, science, social studies, and English

◆ Two support teachers certified in special education

◆ An administrator

◆ A school counselor

The teams share a common preparation period, their classes are located near each other, all teachers are responsible for teaching all students, and the teams provide seven different levels of support for the students in each team. These levels of support enable the teams to individualize their instruction without having to pull out students from the classroom. The levels begin with total staff support (nearly a one-to-one approach), range through daily in-class staff support and team teaching, and end in consultation (the least amount of support).

This tiered approach relies on the talents of each teacher and on the talents of the team as a whole. It also benefits students who receive special education services (including students with multiple disabilities), students who have not qualified for special education services but are at risk of school failure, and students who have succeeded in traditional school systems. Whittier students do not carry special education labels; the support teachers are not called special education teachers; and the staff, by adopting this noncategorical approach, has discarded the idea that only specialists can work with students with disabilities. The result of these many changes is that Whittier High School has developed a community of learners that supports all students. Does it actually work? Yes. José, a student with multiple disabilities, uses a wheelchair; his friends make sure he is wheeled from class to class each day. José works on recognizing numbers while most of his classmates study algebra. When it comes time for his math team to present its answer to an algebra problem, he writes the numbers (with help from his peers) on a poster using the lap tray attached to the front of his wheelchair as a desk (Eshilian et al., 2000; Falvey, Eshilian, & Hibbard, 2000). So including students with multiple disabilities is possible; the data and the Whittier example show that to be the case.

myeducationlab

Go to the Activities and Application section in Chapter 10 of MyEducationLab and complete Activity 3. Compare and contrast the model presented here with the model Star's team is using to include her in the general education curriculum.

ASSESSING STUDENTS' PROGRESS

Measuring Students' Progress

Progress in the General Education Curriculum

Many students with multiple disabilities are unable to take typical paper-pencil assessments that measure their progress in core curriculum areas. Others cannot perform the tests even with accommodations. Furthermore, the curriculum-based measurement techniques that we discussed in Chapter 5 have not been validated with students with multiple disabilities. So how can educators track those students' progress in the general curriculum? They can do so by using two strategies that resemble curriculum-based measurement techniques and that have been well developed for students with multiple disabilities. We discussed one of them, data-based decision making, in Chapter 9. The second strategy is portfolio-based assessment (Kleinert & Kearns, 2001).

Portfolio-based assessment requires teachers to accumulate permanent products that exemplify the student's work. These products are indicators—evidence—of student performance, do not require continuous observation (as do the observational methodologies we discuss later), and allow for ongoing analysis (**formative analysis**) and comparisons between less and more mature products (**summative evaluation**) (Brown & Snell, 2006).

Portfolios should include a range of products that reflect a student's progress, including the data-based and performance data discussed in Chapter 9; graphs of student progress; student, peer, and parent reflections; student products; and video or audiotapes of a student's work (Kearns, Burdge, & Kleinert, 2005). Portfolio approaches typically include observation records, records reviews, anecdotal notes, and permanent products or student work samples, including videos of the performance of students with more severe disabilities who cannot produce written products (Browder et al., 2003).

Progress in Addressing Other Educational Needs

While student work in academic content areas often results in products and thus lends itself to portfolio assessment procedures, many areas of instruction, particularly those that fall outside the realm of core content areas, do not yield permanent products. For example, many students with multiple disabilities engage in repetitive, stereotyped motor behaviors. Reducing or eliminating those behaviors is an important goal in the students' individualized educational programs. The only way to measure progress toward this goal is to observe a student's behavior and record data about it. In this way, teachers can compile evidence of the student's involvement and progress in the general curriculum and in other school settings as well.

Observational methodologies are just what their names imply: ways of collecting data by watching or observing student behavior. Teachers can carry out these observations by watching the student (live observation) or by coding videotapes made of the student. Live observational methods include field observations, time sampling, and event recording. **Field observations** involve simply observing and recording, in a longhand, anecdotal format, what the student is doing. Those anecdotal records are often the first step in collecting observational data because they identify the specific behaviors or events that warrant more systematic observation.

Time sampling and event recording enable teachers to collect samples of a student's behavior. It is almost impossible to observe across the entire school day, so these two strategies are especially useful.

When **time sampling,** an observer records the occurrence or nonoccurrence of specific behaviors during short, predetermined intervals. For example, a teacher who wants to know whether a particular intervention reduces a student's stereotyped behavior may set up three 10-minute observation times daily. Those times can be selected randomly or according to the periods when the behavior is most likely to occur. During the observation, the teacher has a list of behaviors in which the student might be engaged, including the stereotyped behavior. During each 10-minute observation period, she observes for 20 seconds and then spends 10 seconds checking off on the list the behaviors that occurred at any time during the 20-second period. The entire 10-minute session yields data for 20 unique 20-second observation intervals. The teacher counts the number of intervals in which the stereotyped behavior occurred and then tallies those frequencies across time as more 10-minute observations occur. By contrast, when an observer is using **event recording,** every occurrence of a behavior during an observation period is recorded, instead of using the yes/no recording per interval that is characteristic of time sampling.

Both methods are useful, and the one you use depends upon the behavior that you are counting. For example, some students with multiple disabilities have small, hardly noticeable seizures, called **absence seizures,** which may occur every 2 to 5 seconds. Obviously, it would be difficult to observe for 10 minutes and reliably count every such seizure. Similarly, some behavior episodes, such as temper tantrums, may last 5 to 10 minutes. Recording the frequency of one tantrum during a 10-minute observation is not very helpful because one tantrum is just that—a single tantrum.

Now consider the types of data collected through observational methods. Frequency counts involve literal counts of the number of times a behavior occurred or the number of intervals in which a behavior occurred. Frequency counts of intervals can be converted to percentage data by dividing the number of intervals in which a behavior occurred by the total number of intervals observed. With event recording, frequency counts cannot be converted to percentage data, but they can be converted to rate data—namely, an average of the frequency over a specific period of time.

Another measure involves collecting duration data. This method requires a teacher to use a stopwatch or timer to record the length of a behavioral event. Still another measure involves collecting latency data, the time that lapses from one point to another—typically, the lapsed time between a direction or instruction and the student's response.

Most teachers who rely on observational methods collect data using all or most of these methods and collect all or most of these types of data. They do so because collecting observational data is inexpensive and provides detailed information about students' performance.

IEP Tip

Data-based decision making is essential to determine the degree to which students are making progress and what modifications are necessary.

Making Accommodations for Assessment

Many students with disabilities receive accommodations in assessments and testing. Many students with multiple disabilities, however, will not be able to take state accountability assessments, even with accommodations. In Chapter 2, you learned that IDEA allows states to create alternate assessments for use with students with the most significant cognitive disabilities or other students who are identified by IEP teams as unable to take the regular assessment, even with accommodations.

Alternate assessments must be aligned with the state's academic content standards. They serve the same purpose as the typical accountability assessment—namely, to determine how well a student has mastered content that is aligned with standards. Increasingly, alternate assessments are being aligned with alternate achievement standards. Researchers at the National Center on Educational Outcomes (Quenemoen, Thompson, & Thurlow, 2003) have identified several formats for alternative assessments:

- *IEP-linked body of evidence.* Teachers collect student products, similar to portfolio assessment, but link them to IEP goals and objectives.

- *Performance assessment.* Teachers use the data-based measurement techniques described in Chapter 9.

- *Checklist.* Teachers identify a student's skills and abilities on a checklist.

- *Portfolio-based alternate assessment.* Teachers rely on samples of student products that are related to a state's standards. Educators score these portfolios by relying on rubrics that "identify the quality and quantify a student's performance and their level of independence in demonstrating the academic skills linked to the state's standards." (Snell & Brown, 2006, p. 83)

Alternate assessment also relies on scoring criteria. Scoring criteria "are specific definitions of what a score means and how specific student responses are to be evaluated" (Quenemoen et al., 2003). Educators who are scoring a portfolio must have examples of high-quality work so that they will be able to distinguish high-quality from poor-quality portfolios. Many states are still struggling with developing alternate assessments that are genuinely comparable with other state accountability procedures, but it is clear that this is the goal under federal law.

VALUES AND OUTCOMES

♦ Sierra's father, David, when asked what he wants for his daughter, answered, "To keep up with her peers." Recognizing it is a buzz word for what he really wants for her, he says, "Independence." His great expectation has become part of his daughter's curriculum of self-help skills and appropriate behavior.

♦ Because she is included in the Corrales School's programs and benefits from peer-to-peer contacts, Sierra becomes a teacher herself, making her positive contribution to others by simply being with them and even more by displaying her strengths.

♦ Sierra's strengths include computer skills and perceptual skills.

♦ Sierra knows her own mind and through her behavior communicates what she wants. She makes choices; the challenge for her teachers is to help her behavior be more appropriate and less injurious to herself and challenging for others.

♦ Concerned that Sierra might not have relationships with her peers, Kreg, Maureen, and Bea, her teachers, have resisted some educators who wanted to remove her from Corrales School and put her into a separate special education school. Instead, they rely on peer modeling and peer-to-peer learning.

♦ Sierra is, as we have written, a rarity, a paradox—the student who has significant disabilities but also remarkable strengths that, when developed throughout her school years, most likely will lead to a good measure of full citizenship for her.

WHAT DO YOU THINK?

1. If you were Sierra's teacher, which of her skills would you want to develop, and which of her needs would you address first?

2. What characteristic of students with multiple disabilities most distinguishes them from students with other disabilities—their intellectual, adaptive, motor, sensory, or communicative abilities? Or is it the combination of these disabilities that is their most distinguishing trait?

3. What is it about students with multiple disabilities that attracts you to teaching them? The challenges they present or their underlying strengths?

ADDRESSING THE STANDARDS: THE VALUES CONNECTION

The following CEC Knowledge and Skill Standards: Common Core and Values are addressed in this chapter through the content and concepts we discuss.

CEC Knowledge and Skill Standards: Common Core	Values/Standards Connection
CEC Knowledge and Skill Standard II. **Development and Characteristics of Learners** CC2K1 Typical and atypical human growth and development. CC2K2 Educational implications of characteristics of various exceptionalities. CC2K4 Family systems and the roles of families supporting development. CC2K5 Similarities and differences of individuals with and without exceptional learning needs. CC2K6 Similarities and differences of individuals with exceptional learning needs.	When you learn about the characteristics of students with severe and multiple disabilities, you are addressing CEC Standard 2, Development and Characteristics of Learners.
CEC Knowledge and Skill Standard IV. **Instructional Strategies** CC4S1 Use strategies to facilitate integration into various settings. CC4S2 Teach individuals to use self-assessment, problem-solving, and other cognitive strategies to meet their needs. CC4S3 Select, adapt, and use instructional strategies and materials according to characteristics of the individual with exceptional learning needs. CC4S4 Use strategies to facilitate maintenance and generalization of skills across environments. CC4S5 Use procedures to increase the individual's self-awareness, self-management, self-control, self-reliance, and self-esteem. CC4S6 Use strategies that promote successful transitions for individuals with exceptional learning needs.	By following Standard 4, you contribute to your students' inclusion in the general curriculum and thereby to their *relationships* with nondisabled peers.

CEC Knowledge and Skill Standards: Common Core	Values/Standards Connection
CEC Knowledge and Skill Standard V. Learning Environments and Social Interactions	Here, as is the case for Standards 4 and 6, you enhance your students' *relationships*.
CC5S2 Identify realistic expectations for personal and social behavior in various settings.	
CC5S3 Identify supports needed for integration into various program placements.	
CC5S4 Design learning environments that encourage active participation in individual and group settings.	
CC5S9 Create an environment that encourages self-advocacy and increased independence.	
CC5S12 Design and manage daily routines.	
CC5S15 Structure, direct, and support the activities of paraeducators, volunteers, and tutors.	
CEC Knowledge and Skill Standard VI. Language	Highly competent teachers, such as you can be, can provide their students with opportunities to be included in the general curriculum and to be *full citizens* in their schools and communities. You can foster these opportunities by using strategies that support students' communication skills thereby giving them a voice in the classroom and the community.
CC6K4 Augmentative and assistive communication strategies.	
CC6S1 Use strategies to support and enhance communication skills of individuals with exceptional learning needs.	
CEC Knowledge and Skill Standard VII. Instructional Planning	If you teach your students to master self-care skills such as dressing and personal hygiene, you can make it easier for them to have *relationships* that can bloom into friendships in school and the community.
CC7K5 Roles and responsibilities of the paraeducator related to instruction, intervention, and direct service.	Person-centered planning emphasizes a student's *strengths,* interests, preferences, and dreams, thereby promoting self-determination and *making choices*.
CC7S1 Identify and prioritize areas of the general curriculum and accommodations for individuals with exceptional learning needs.	
CC7S3 Involve the individual and family in setting instructional goals and monitoring progress.	
CC7S6 Sequence, implement, and evaluate individualized learning objectives.	
CC7S7 Integrate affective, social, and life skills with academic curricula.	
CC7S9 Incorporate and implement instructional and assistive technology into the educational program.	

continued

CEC Knowledge and Skill Standards: Common Core	Values/Standards Connection
CEC Knowledge and Skill Standard VIII. Assessment CC8K3 Screening, prereferral, referral, and classification procedures. CC8S2 Administer nonbiased formal and informal assessments. CC8S6 Use assessment information in making eligibility, program, and placement decisions for individuals with exceptional learning needs, including those from culturally and/or linguistically diverse backgrounds. CC8S8 Evaluate instruction and monitor progress of individuals with exceptional learning needs.	You address CEC Standard 8, Assessment, when you are able to determine the nature of specially designed instruction and services for students with severe and multiple disabilities. By involving students with disabilities in identifying products for a portfolio and evaluating the portfolio, teachers can promote skills that lead to greater *choice* and *self-determination*.
CEC Knowledge and Skill Standard X. Collaboration CC10S2 Collaborate with families and others in assessment of individuals with exceptional learning needs. CC10S3 Foster respectful and beneficial relationships between families and professionals. CC10S4 Assist individuals with exceptional learning needs and their families in becoming active participants in the educational team. CC10S5 Plan and conduct collaborative conferences with individuals with exceptional learning needs and their families.	Collaboration, Standard 10, advances your students' *self-determination/choices* and their relationships.

Source: From CEC Knowledge and Skill Standards: Common Core and Values. Copyright by The Council for Exceptional Children. Reprinted with permission.

SUMMARY

Identifying Students with Multiple Disabilities

◆ The term *multiple disabilities* defines a diverse group of people whose common characteristic is the severity of their educational needs.

◆ Students with multiple disabilities have impairments in intellectual functioning, adaptive skills, motor development, sensory functioning, and communication skills.

◆ The primary causes are tied to biological considerations, particularly genetic ones occurring during prenatal development.

◆ Approximately 0.2 percent of all students aged 6 through 21 with disabilities have multiple disabilities.

Evaluating Students with Multiple Disabilities

◆ Physicians use screening tests such as the Apgar to determine whether a newborn might have or definitely does have a disability.

◆ The evaluation process usually begins right after birth and may continue throughout a student's school career.

- The SETT framework provides an outline of questions helpful in conducting evaluations for appropriate assistive technology.

Designing an Appropriate IEP

- Person-centered planning procedures, such as the MAPs process, are effective tools for planning services and supports for students with multiple disabilities.
- Peer tutoring has been used successfully one-to-one and classwide to improve students' achievement.
- Technological devices such as the Visual Assistant, which apply new and emerging technologies, offer greater access to universally designed learning materials and practices.
- Many students require AAC systems. The IEP team must identify the device and establish instructional goals related to language use and communication skills.

Using Effective Instructional Strategies

- Access to the general education curriculum for preschool students with multiple disabilities is possible when teachers ensure inclusion and infuse content information into the typical preschool social context.
- Partial participation enables students with multiple disabilities to participate to the maximum extent possible for each of them in school, home, and community environments.
- Student-directed learning strategies such as antecedent cue regulation, self-instruction, and self-monitoring are empirically validated ways to teach students to self-regulate learning; they contribute to enhanced inclusion, generalization, and student empowerment.

Including Students with Multiple Disabilities

- Almost half of all students with multiple disabilities are educated in separate classes.
- Students with multiple disabilities can learn new skills, be involved and make progress in general education classrooms, and experience successful friendships.
- Preparing general educators to work with all students is a critical step in promoting inclusive practices.

Assessing Students' Progress

- Using portfolios to assess the progress of students with multiple disabilities involves collecting examples of permanent products for students.
- Observational methodologies such as field observations, time sampling, and event recording enable teachers to collect data on behavioral frequency, percentage, rate, duration, and latency.
- Students who cannot take the state's general assessment even with modifications can still be involved in accountability decisions through alternate assessment procedures such as portfolios, performance assessments, IEP-linked content data, and checklist data.

PEARSON
myeducationlab

Now go to MyEducationLab at www.myeducationlab.com and take the Self-Assessment to gauge your initial comprehension of chapter content. Once you have taken the Self-Assessment, use your individualized Study Plan for Chapter 10 to enhance your understanding of the concepts discussed in the chapter.

11

Understanding Students with Autism

◆ WHO IS SHAWN JACKSON?

There have been two kinds of hurricanes in nine-year-old Shawn Jackson's life. One has always been part of his life. It is called autism. The other came and went, but its effects, both immediate and longer-term, were devastating to Shawn. It was called Katrina.

Shawn's mother, Donnica, first suspected Shawn was different than other young boys when he was three. At home, Shawn would try to hide in the refrigerator or use bookcases, tables, or beds as platforms for his leaps into space. Flour and sugar fascinated him; opening a bag and playing with its ingredients pleased him to no end. Gadgets of all kinds—computers, TV sets, Nintendo controls—fascinated him. He was more than a mischievous boy.

He would not speak words; gibberish and babble were his means of communication. Trips to Target or Wal-Mart triggered his tantrums, screaming, and global meltdowns. Donnica's family was puzzled; was she not raising him properly? To which she had to respond, politely: You can't discipline autism out of a boy.

When Shawn was four, Donnica—a single parent trying to break into journalism after having graduated from Southern University in New Orleans—took Shawn to Charity Hospital, seeking answers to her question: Why is my son the way he is? The evaluation results were conclusive. Shawn acquired a label—autism. And Donnica acquired a mission—to make sure Shawn would have an effective education so that he would one day be a productive adult.

When Shawn entered school at age 6, Donnica expected results. "I didn't send him

to school to be baby-sat." Results, however, were not forthcoming, at least not in Shawn's first several years. Shawn's language did not improve, and, indeed, his behaviors deteriorated. Shawn would hit himself and other students to get attention or to express his frustration that he could not communicate what he wanted.

And then came Katrina in September 2006. Like thousands of others, Donnica and Shawn escaped to Houston. He went to school there for a year, but without benefit. Indeed, Shawn's ability to read, which had first become evident in the year before Katrina, vanished. His placement in the Houston schools was comparable to his placement in the New Orleans schools: a segregated classroom for students with autism and other disabilities. Bleak hardly describes Shawn's future when he returned to New Orleans and the state-operated school system.

However, after a year in fourth grade at John Dibert School, Shawn began to prosper. Under the guidance of skilled educators, bright replaced bleak. Richard Hubbard, a special educator, and Edna Crawford, a paraeducator, collaborated with two general educators, Geraldine Myers (reading and social studies) and Rochella Mitchell (math and science). They were aided by related service providers, Kirk Ealing, a speech-language trainer, and Miss Maxwell, an occupational therapist.

Could this team of six experts have converted Shawn's dismal prospects into optimistic ones alone? Possibly, but the decision of the leaders of the John Dibert School to use schoolwide positive behavior support and the omnipresence of Shawn's mother in all decision making contributed greatly to Shawn's progress. And so too did his classmates, those with and those without disabilities.

CHAPTER OBJECTIVES

◆ You will learn that autism affects a student's verbal and nonverbal communication and social interaction, and that there is a "theory of mind" explanation for their social impairments.

◆ You will learn about the characteristics of students with autism— their repetitive activities, stereotyped movements, behavioral challenges, need for predictability, unusual responses to sensory stimuli, and below-average intellectual functioning.

◆ You will learn that the precise causes of autism are unknown but that abnormalities in brain development, neurochemistry, and genetic factors are contributing factors.

◆ You will learn about two methods of evaluating a student with autism, the Autism Diagnostic Interview and the functional behavioral assessment.

◆ You will learn about effective interventions, including positive behavior supports (as applied to a particular student and as schoolwide support for all students), mnemonic strategies, social stories, and discrete trial teaching.

◆ You will learn about applied behavior analysis, discrete trial training, and the relationship of these to positive behavior support.

◆ You will become familiar with the Autism Screening Instrument for Educational Planning and its role in assessing students' progress.

IDENTIFYING STUDENTS WITH AUTISM

Defining Autism

Autism is a developmental disability that significantly affects a student's verbal and non-verbal communication, social interaction, and educational performance. It generally occurs before a child reaches age 3; typically the child engages in repetitive activities and stereotyped movements, resists environmental change or changes in daily routines, and displays unusual responses to sensory experiences. A student may not be classified as having autism if the student's educational performance is adversely affected primarily by a serious emotional disturbance.

Autism is a severe form of a broader group of disorders referred to as **pervasive developmental disorders** (Hyman & Towbin, 2007; Thompson, 2007). The DSM-IV-TR includes, as part of pervasive development disorders, five discrete conditions that have their onset in childhood (American Psychiatric Association, 2000): autistic disorder, Rett's disorder, childhood disintegrative disorder, Asperger's disorder, and pervasive developmental disorder not otherwise specified. Educators often use the term **autism spectrum disorder** when referring to some or all of these disorders.

In this chapter we will concentrate on the condition known as autistic disorder, or simply autism, because it has the highest prevalence of the five discrete conditions. Shawn is typical of students with autistic disorder. In fall 2006, approximately 0.073% (223,395) of all students aged 6 through 21 in special education nationally were classified as having autism (U.S. Department of Education Office of Special Education Programs, 2008).

As you just read, there is a spectrum of autism disorders. One of the disorders is Asperger syndrome. The term **Asperger syndrome** describes individuals who have significant challenges in social functioning but do not have significant delays in language development or intellectual functioning (Hyman & Towbin, 2007). The prevalence rate for Asperger syndrome is far less than for autism. Studies project the incidence rate to be as low as 2.5 per 1,000 (Mattila et al., 2007) or as high as 2.5 per 10,000 (Fombonne, 2003).

Caution is in order when discussing prevalence. Fombonne (2003) reviewed 32 prevalence surveys published between 1966 and 2001 and reported that the prevalence of autism is 10 per 10,000. Other studies have found a much higher rate, around 57–60 individuals with autism per 10,000 (Kadesjo, Gillberg, & Nagberg, 1999; Scott, Baron-Cohen, Bolton, & Brayne, 2002). The prevalence of autism has increased over the past decade (Shattuck & Grosse, 2007).

Professionals and families believe the reasons include greater public awareness concerning the condition and its manifestation in young children, more refined diagnostic procedures, especially of genetic origins of autism, and the alleged negative effect of vaccines (especially mercury) on young children's brain development. Recent research shows there is no known causative link between the vaccines and autism (Parker, Schwartz, Todd, & Pickering, 2005). Rates of autism tend to be higher among students during elementary and secondary school years than in preschool years, probably because of more precise identification. Males outnumber females by approximately four to one, and it appears that there are no variations in the prevalence of autism according to race or ethnicity (Fombonne, 2003).

Describing the Characteristics

Autism has six distinct characteristics: (1) atypical language development, (2) atypical social development, (3) repetitive behavior, (4) problem behavior, (5) sensory and movement disorders, and (6) differences in intellectual functioning.

Atypical Language Development

Students with autism have a broad range of language abilities, ranging from no verbal communication to quite complex communication (Myles et al., 2003; National Research Council, 2001). They usually have a number of language impairments.

More than two decades ago, experts assumed that only about 50 percent of individuals with autism would eventually develop useful speech (Prizant, 1983). They now predict that as many as 85 percent to 90 percent of children with autism can learn to speak effectively if they receive state-of-the-art teaching and motivational approaches and begin their education before age 5 (Koegel, 2000). Children with autism who develop speech before the age of five have more favorable long-term communication outcomes (Ballaban-Gill, Rapin, Tuchman, & Shinnar, 1996). Nevertheless, they often have limited communication skills. Two types of language disorders exist in young children with autism. One is characterized by disorders related to the sounds of speech and grammar. The other is characterized by disorders associated with the communication and meaning aspects of language (Rapin & Dunn, 2003). Communication of children with autism involves (Landa, 2007):

◆ Focusing attention on one topic only

◆ Limiting a communication topic to fewer than a couple of interactions

◆ Using limited gestures to supplement verbal skills

◆ Reversing pronouns (For example, the student may look at his teacher and say, "You want have a snack now," meaning that he, not the teacher, wants a snack.)

◆ Looking away from the speaker rather than maintaining eye contact

◆ Repeating or echoing other people's language (**echolalia**)

◆ Experiencing difficulty with receptive and expressive language

Shawn's language development is typical of many young students with autism. He can form sentences to make himself understood; "Momma, I want more chicken wings" or "Get dressed to go to the store" are examples of Shawn's ability to use words and grammar correctly to express what he wants. But Shawn is "lazy," says Donnica, and will resort to gestures, babble, and gibberish to communicate. His speech-language interventionist, Kirk Ealing, takes him aside for individual therapy and advises his teachers how to challenge him to speak in full sentences.

Of course, Donnica won't put up with gibberish; she commands, "Speak in words, Shawn." Together, Shawn's teachers, related service provider, and mother are helping Shawn generalize his ability to speak. The problem comes, says Donnica, with Shawn's peers. "They like him so much they let him get away with being lazy. I've got to work on them and so do his teachers." Generalizing skills means getting everyone—even a student's peers—to use the same approach all the time and in all places.

Atypical Social Development

Another hallmark of autism is atypical social development—delays in social interaction and social skills (McConnell, 2002; National Research Council, 2001; Thompson, 2007, 2008). The American Psychiatric Association (2000) has four criteria for diagnosing atypical social development in individuals with autism:

◆ Impaired use of nonverbal behavior

◆ Lack of peer relationships

◆ Failure to spontaneously share enjoyment, interests, and achievements with others

◆ Lack of reciprocity

One explanation for delayed social development is the **theory of mind.** Individuals with autism do not understand that their own beliefs, desires, and intentions may differ from those of others (Baron-Cohen, 2001; Baron-Cohen, Wheelwright, Lawson, Griffin, & Hill, 2002). They have difficulty comprehending others' feelings, preferences, and emotions even when other people directly say what their feelings are, and they often do not infer and intuit others' social cues and nonverbal signals. Students with autism also have difficulty in empathizing with others' feelings and emotions (Baron-Cohen & Wheelwright, 2004).

Impairments in students' theory of mind often make it difficult for them to develop relationships with others. You can help your students improve their social interactions such as by using technology to promote their social interactions and skills (Blacher, 2007; Thompson, 2007, 2008) (see the Technology Outcomes box in this chapter).

Students with Asperger syndrome often have difficulty making friends, interpreting social signals, understanding unwritten rules, and not being anxious in social situations (Farrugia & Hudson, 2006; Lee & Park, 2007; Winter-Messiers, 2007). A strengths-based approach builds on students' special interests to motivate them to make social connections and converse with their peers (Winter-Messiers, 2007).

Shawn has been slow to develop socially. As a younger child, he was aggressive to other students. Donnica thinks he was that way because he wanted attention, not because he was angry at the other students. Because he has acquired language, and because he is (in his mother's words) "a ladies' man," a charmer, he has learned not to be aggressive but to be affectionate—sometimes, however, giving too many hugs to those who may want simply a "high five."

He also has learned about himself. Because he cannot communicate as well as his classmates, he senses, Donnica says, that he is different. Yet, with her and his teachers' support, he is learning how to make friends, to "read" them. The proof of that is his circle of support from his classmates, which includes boys and girls alike, with and without disabilities. This year, he received his very first invitation to another student's birthday party.

It is hard to attribute that invitation—and its symbolic significance—entirely to Donnica and to Shawn's teachers. There is another factor. It is Yohance, who is Donnica's second husband and is not Shawn's biological father. He, more than anyone else, has taught Shawn to be "just a boy." Being that—being like other boys—has become another key to Shawn's social development and school inclusion.

Because Katrina wiped out Donnica's former home and because New Orleans has not been fully rebuilt or repopulated, all of Shawn's friends are at school; there are none in his neighborhood. For him, inclusion, coupled with consistent intervention, has created friendships and compensated for his early and natural (for children with autism) social delays. What he learns at school will generalize to his life in the community, particularly if other youngsters move into his neighborhood.

Despite their usually slow social development, students with autism frequently are highly social under one particular circumstance. When students with Asperger syndrome had conversations about their special interests, their "global organization abilities—physical, intellectual, oral, and social—came almost immediately into sharper focus and showed improvement for the duration of the . . . discussions" (Winter-Messiers et al., 2007, p. 73).

Isolation—even voluntary time-out—removes a student from a learning environment, but it also lets the student compose himself so he can return to that environment. It is a controversial method and can be overused.

Repetitive Behavior

Repetitive behavior involves repeated movements and verbalizations. These include motor movements (e.g., hand flapping), persistent attention to parts of objects (e.g., the moveable bolt in a door's deadbolt lock), and strict adherence to routines. These behaviors also include an insistence on sameness (Richler, Bishop, Kleinke, & Lord, 2007). Students use their repetitive behaviors as ways to communicate boredom and agitation or to regulate their levels of awareness (Carr et al., 1994). Obviously, these behaviors can interfere with their ability to learn and be included in typical work, school, and community settings. Simply decreasing students' repetitive behaviors, however, is not sufficient; increasing their appropriate communication and social skills and leisure activities is the state-of-the-art approach (Bellini, Peters, Benner, & Hopf, 2007).

Predictability and structure provide security to many individuals with autism (Green et al., 2006; Thompson, in press). When their predictability and structure are interrupted by events such as school vacations, overnight stays with friends or extended family, celebration of holidays, change in television schedules, or movement from one classroom to another, students can become highly anxious. In addition, having things in their usual place means a great deal to some students. Most of us do not think much about whether the telephone is straight on the desk, whether the cosmetics are always in the same place on the bathroom counter, or whether a door is open or closed. However, disruptions in these seemingly insignificant environmental patterns disturb many students and impede their ability to learn.

You can help your students predict what will happen to them by adhering to previously set schedules and routines and by teaching them strategies to accept changes (Thompson, 2008). For example, you might offer picture schedules to students who do not read, outlining the schedule of the different activities or classroom periods they will have each day. Your students with higher cognitive abilities may find that both daily and weekly work schedules are helpful.

Routines also enable students to understand when things will occur. For example, some students need to have activities that are almost always associated with the same time of day or the same day of the week. Because routines do change, students require instruction and support in learning to accept schedule changes. Later in this chapter, you will learn about **social stories**, an evidence-based approach for instructing students to anticipate changes and know how to respond to them.

Shawn prizes his routines, and Donnica has learned to accommodate them. Upon arriving home from school, Shawn changes his clothes; shorts and tee-shirts replace the school garb. He turns on nearly every electronic device in the house: TV, Nintendo, computer, and radio; all must be on, at high volume, all the time. Eschewing his former favorite channel, the Spanish-language one, Shawn locks onto the Shopping Channel. Using his computer, he downloads and watches the same three movies, over and over again.

Sensory overload is not a problem for him as long as it is part of his routine. But it remains a problem if there are too many people around him. "Please get out" is his command when Donnica, Yohance, and other family crowd him.

When bedtime comes, he puts everything in order throughout the rest of the house but leaves his school clothes scattered around his bedroom and insists on having a bottle of water near his bed. Having established some dominion over his environment and expressed his preferences, Shawn is ready to sleep.

Problem Behavior

IDEA requires educators to consider using positive behavior support (which we discuss later in this chapter) when students engage in behavior that impedes their or other students' learning. Four categories of problem behavior of students with autism are self-injurious behavior, aggression, tantrums, and property destruction. We will focus on the first two.

Self-injurious behavior. Some individuals have self-injurious behavior, such as head banging, biting, or scratching (Hyman & Towbin, 2007; Mace & Mauk, 1999). These behaviors often persist into adulthood. Individuals with severe self-injurious behaviors may permanently injure themselves; sometimes and usually for only a few people, self-injurious behaviors are life-threatening. One of those life-threatening behaviors is called pica—eating inedible items.

Aggression. Aggressive behaviors are similar to self-injurious behaviors, but the behavior is directed toward others. Aggressive behaviors can be problematic in all settings. By using positive behavior support, teachers enable students to learn a wider repertoire of appropriate behaviors. Once students learn appropriate alternative behaviors, they often stop using aggressive behaviors.

IEP Tip

Under IDEA, a student's IEP team must consider using positive behavior intervention and support if the student's behavior impedes her or others' learning.

Problem behavior can serve a communicative function, enabling the student to obtain something positive, avoid or escape something unpleasant, increase or decrease sensory stimulation, or achieve two or more of these results (Carr et al., 2002; Horner, Carr, Strain, Todd, & Reed, 2002; Reese, Richman, Belmont, & Morse, 2005). Given the functions that problem behavior serves, you will want to teach your students other ways to communicate these and other intentions (Carr, 2007; Hastings & Noone, 2005; Horner, Albin, Todd, & Sprague, 2006).

As you read earlier, Shawn has had serious problem behavior: aggression toward other students and some self-injurious behavior, primarily hitting his sides with his hands and elbows. But as you also know, those behaviors have dissipated as a result of speech-language training and positive behavioral supports at school and at home.

Sensory and Movement Disorders

Children and youth with autism and Asperger syndrome frequently experience sensory and movement disorders related to taste/smell, tactile sensitivity, visual/auditory sensitivity, and energy levels (O'Riordan & Passetti, 2006; Rogers, Hepburn, & Wehner, 2003). Some have under- or overresponsiveness to sensory stimuli, although more have overresponsiveness. Temple Grandin, who was identified as having autism as a child and then Asperger syndrome as an adult, is now one of the most successful designers of livestock equipment in the world. In Figure 11.1, she describes some typical problems with overresponsiveness to sensory stimuli as well as some practical solutions.

Movement disorders also are an element of autism (Dawson & Watling, 2000; Donnellan, 1999; National Research Council, 2001). Examples include abnormal posture; abnormal movements of the face, head, trunk, and limbs; abnormal eye movements; repeated gestures and mannerisms; and awkward gait (Kemner & van Engeland, 2005; Leary & Hill, 1996). Motor clumsiness and disorders are present in the majority of individuals who have Asperger syndrome (Lee & Park, 2007).

Differences in Intellectual Functioning

Autism occurs in children with all levels of intelligence, ranging from students who are gifted to students classified as having mental retardation. Approximately 64 percent to 70 percent of children and youth with autism have an intellectual disability (Fombonne, 2003; Yeargin-Allsopp et al., 2003). Although Shawn's primary diagnosis is autism, he, like many students with that classification, has an intellectual disability. As much as he loves to read, he is two years below grade level. Poor education before Katrina and then the enforced removal to Houston explain why he is at that level when, earlier, he had been only one grade level below. That is about the right level, Donnica and his teachers think, and that's their goal: to improve Shawn's reading and thereby his intellectual capacities to levels closer to his age-peers.

Individuals with Asperger syndrome, however, tend to have higher intellectual functioning than do individuals with other types of autism. Their IQ scores tend to fall in the average range and to reveal a frequency distribution similar to that of the general population.

Some people with autism also display the unusual **savant syndrome,** which consists of extraordinary talents in areas such as calendar calculating, musical ability, mathematical skills, memorization, and mechanical abilities (Miller, 2005; Mottron, Lemmens, Gragnon, & Seron, 2006). For example, a student with savant syndrome may be able to recite the baseball game scores and the batting averages of all players who ever participated in the major leagues. But a student's unusual ability in these areas occurs in conjunction with low ability in most other areas (Cheatham, Smith, Rucker, Polloway, & Lewis, 1995; Nettelbeck & Young, 1996).

Figure 11.1

Temple Grandin: Insights on how she experiences autism

- As an adult I find it difficult to determine exactly when I should break into a conversation. I cannot follow the rhythmic give and take of conversation. People have told me that I often interrupt, and I still have difficulty determining where the pauses are.

- Noise was a major problem for me. When I was confronted with loud or confusing noise, I could not modulate it. I either had to shut it all out and withdraw or let it all in like a freight train.

- I think a classroom should be quiet and free from distracting noises, such as a high pitched vent fan. Some teachers have found that disturbing noises can be blocked out with headphones and music. When a child has to make a trip to a busy shopping center, a headset with a favorite tape can help make the trip more peaceful.

- I often misbehaved in church and screamed because my Sunday clothes felt different—scratchy petticoats drove me crazy; a feeling that would be insignificant to most people may feel like sandpaper rubbing the skin raw to an autistic child. Most people habituate to different types of clothes, but I keep feeling them for hours.

- Calming sensory activities immediately prior to school lessons or speech therapy may help to improve learning. These activities should be conducted as fun games.

- Abstract concepts such as getting along with people have to have a visual image. For example, my visual image for relationships with people was a sliding glass door. If you push it too hard it will break. To make the abstract concept more real, I would some times act it out—for example, by walking through a real sliding door.

- At puberty I was desperate for relief from the "nerves." . . . At my aunt's ranch, I observed that the cattle sometimes appeared to relax when they were held in the squeeze chute, a device for holding cattle for veterinary procedures. The animal is held tightly between two sides, which squeeze the body. After a horrible bout of the "nerves" I got in the squeeze chute. For about 45 minutes I was much calmer. I then built a squeeze-chute-like device which I could use to apply pressure (which I controlled). . . . I have made a successful career based on my fixation with cattle squeeze chutes. I have designed livestock handling systems for major ranches and meet companies all over the world. When I was in high school, many of my teachers and psychologists wanted to get rid of my fixation on cattle chutes. I am indebted to Mr. Carlock, my high school science teacher. He suggested that I read psychology journals and study so I could learn why the cattle chute had a relaxing effect. If my fixation had been taken away, I could have ended up in an institution. Do not confuse fixations with stereotyped behavior, such as hand flapping or rocking. A fixation is an interest in something external that should be diverted and used to motivate.

Determining the Causes

Historical Perspective on Causes

When autism was first diagnosed and described in the early 1940s, parents of children with autism were often regarded as intelligent people of high socioeconomic status who were also "cold." At that time, incredibly, some professionals referred to mothers of children with autism as "refrigerator mothers."

IEP Tip

At IEP conferences, you should not suggest that the students' parents are the cause of their child's autism; you may not know the cause, so silence is your best practice.

By the 1970s, however, researchers had established that autism is caused by brain or biochemical dysfunction that occurs before, during, or after birth and that it is totally unwarranted to blame parents. In 1977 the National Society for Autistic Children (now known as the Autism Society of America) asserted, "No known factors in the psychological environment of a child have been shown to cause autism." Today parents are not seen as the cause of problems; they are seen as partners with educators, contributing to solving their children's problems. No one knows why Shawn has autism.

Biomedical Causes

The National Institutes of Health is sponsoring an international network of research to find the causes of autism and the most effective treatments (Kau, 2006). Yet much is already known. Studies of twins reveal a strong genetic etiology for autism (Hyman & Towbin, 2007; Pickles et al., 2000). Indeed, siblings of a child with autism are 10 times more likely to have autism than children who do not have such a sibling (Chakrabarti & Fombonne, 2001). There also appears to be a linkage between environmental factors and genes. Although there are controversies associated with the role that the vaccine against measles, mumps, and rubella may play, current research has not documented causation (Afzal et al., 2006; Archen, Bhasin, Braun, & Yeargin-Allsopp, 2007; Demicheli, Jefferson, Rivetti, & Price, 2005). Researchers now also investigate brain structure and function in individuals with autism. Some theorize that deviations in brain size are caused by an early brain overgrowth followed by slower growth so that the head size is in the normal range by middle childhood (Redcay & Courchesne, 2005). Other researchers focus on how the neurons communicate with each other (neurotransmitter functioning) (Scott & Deneris, 2005; Williams et al., 2005). The only environmental substances that have been documented to result in a higher prevalence of autism are some medications that pregnant women might take early in their pregnancy (Hyman & Towbin, 2007). Although there has been speculation that exposure to various chemicals might cause autism, research has not yet shown that to be the case (Hyman & Towbin, 2007).

EVALUATING STUDENTS WITH AUTISM

Determining the Presence of Autism

Many children receive the initial diagnosis of autism from an interdisciplinary evaluation team, typically during their early childhood years (Lord & Luyster, 2006; Rutter, 2005). Shawn was evaluated when he was 4 years old. Evaluators usually administer some of the same tests given to students with intellectual disability and students with severe and multiple disabilities (Mayes & Calhoun, 2003). Figure 11.2 highlights the standard techniques used for observations, screening, and nondiscriminatory evaluation.

Various diagnostic tools can detect the presence of autism (Risi et al., 2006). A medical diagnosis of autism requires that a physician or psychologist administer the evaluation according to the criteria of the DSM-IV-TR. One of the common tests is the Autism Diagnostic Interview—Revised. Only specially trained professionals administer and score the interview because scoring is based on clinical judgment regarding the caregiver's description of the child's development and behavior. The interview takes about $1^{1}/_{2}$ hours and focuses on the child's social interaction, communication and language, and repetitive and stereotyped behaviors. These three areas represent the six factors—spoken language, social intent, compulsions, developmental milestones, savant skills, and sensory aversion—that you read about earlier (Tadevosyan-Leyfer et al., 2003).

Children must meet the criteria for autism in each of the three content areas, and a child's atypical development in at least one content area must be manifest by 36 months of age. This test helps differentiate between children and youth who have autism and those who have intellectual disability. It also is the most frequently used instrument in autism research (Mazefsky & Oswald, 2006).

Figure 11.2

Nondiscriminatory evaluation process for determining the presence of autism

Observation ↓	**Medical or psychological professionals and parents observe:** The child is challenged by social conversations, does not play with others, is frequently unresponsive to voices, may exhibit echolalia or other unusual speech patterns, has language development delays, has problem behavior, is disrupted by changes in daily routine, engages in stereotypical behaviors, and has sensory and movement disorders.
Screening ↓	**Assessment measures:** **Physical examinations:** A physician notes that the child is not reaching developmental milestones, especially in areas of social and language development. The child's physical health is usually normal. The physician may refer the child to a psychiatrist or psychologist for further evaluation. **Psychological evaluations:** The child meets the *Diagnostic Standards Manual—IV* criteria for autism, including (1) qualitative impairment in social interaction, (2) qualitative impairment in communication, and (3) restricted, repetitive, and stereotyped patterns of behavior.
Prereferral ↓	The student is usually identified before starting school. In rare circumstances in which the student is not identified before starting school, the severity of the disability may make prereferral unnecessary.
Referral ↓	Children with autism should be referred by medical personnel or parents for early intervention during infancy or the preschool years. The child is referred to special education on reaching school age.
Nondiscriminatory evaluation procedures and standards	**Findings that suggest autism:** **Individualized intelligence test:** About 70 percent of students with autism perform two or more standard deviations below the mean, indicating intellectual disability. Others have average or even gifted intelligence. Evaluating intelligence is generally difficult because of challenging social and language behaviors. **Individualized achievement tests:** Students with autism who have average or above-average intelligence may perform at an average or above-average level in one or more areas of achievement. Some individuals with autism have unusual giftedness in one or more areas. Students with autism typically have below-average achievement. **Adaptive behavior scales:** The student usually scores significantly below average in areas of adaptive behavior, indicating severe deficits in skills such as communication, daily living, socialization, gross- and fine-motor coordination, and socially appropriate behavior. **Autism-specific scales:** The student's scores meet the criteria for identifying him or her as having autism. **Direct observation:** The student's self-initiated interactions with teacher and peers are limited. The student exhibits language delays and may use unusual speech patterns such as echolalia. The observer may notice that the student has difficulty with changes in routines and manifests stereotypical behaviors. **Anecdotal records:** Records suggest that performance varies according to moods, energy level, extent and pile-up of environmental changes, and whether or not individual preferences are incorporated.

Determining the Nature of Specially Designed Instruction and Services

As you read earlier, some students with autism have problem behaviors. To reduce or eliminate those behaviors, teachers and other professionals often use positive behavior support. Before offering that support, they conduct a functional behavioral assessment (FBA) of the student. A **functional behavioral assessment** identifies specific relationships between a student's behaviors and the circumstances that trigger those behaviors, especially those that impede the student's or others' ability to learn (Crone, Hawken, & Bergstrom, 2007; Lane, Barton-Arwood, Spencer, & Kalberg, 2007; Thompson, 2007). Although a functional behavioral assessment is helpful for many students who do not have autism, it is particularly apt for students with autism (Horner et al., 2002). Shawn's school-based team conducted a functional behavioral assessment, which is reproduced in Box 11.1. Note that his FBA includes baseline data about targeted behaviors, namely, doing in-class work, coming to school on time, returning documents that Donnica signed at the school's request, staying on task and not acting out, and surrendering his computer at home when Donnica needs it.

You will use these basic steps when you conduct a functional behavioral assessment:

1. Describe as precisely as you can the nature of the behaviors that are impeding the student's or others' ability to learn.

2. Gather information from teachers, related service providers, family members, the student, and any other individuals who have firsthand knowledge about the circumstances regularly associated with the student's problem behavior. Determine as specifically as you can the events that occur before, during, and after the student's appropriate and inappropriate behavior.

The Autism Diagnostic Interview—Revised is a semistructured interview consisting of 93 items. It is administered by a professional to caregivers of children and adults who might have autism.

IEP Tip

A student's IEP team should rely on the results of the functional behavioral assessment to create the student's positive behavior support plan (minimizing or eliminating problem behavior and teaching appropriate behavior).

3. Determine why the student engages in the problem behavior. What is the student trying to accomplish or communicate? Does the student want to obtain something positive, avoid or escape something unpleasant, or increase or decrease certain sensory stimulation?

4. Hypothesize the relationship between the problem behavior and the events occurring before, during, and after the behavior.

5. Incorporate the functional assessment information into the student's IEP. Focus on changing the environmental events and circumstances so that the student does not need to use problem behavior to accomplish an outcome.

6. Help the student develop alternative behaviors and new skills to accomplish the same outcome in more socially acceptable ways.

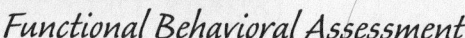

Functional Behavioral Assessment

A functional behavioral assessment (FBA) is a systematic process for gathering information that helps teachers and related service providers determine why a student engages in problem behaviors and how teachers can influence events and circumstances to change these behaviors. As discussed on page 310, there are a few basic steps teachers can use to conduct an FBA. Shawn's school-based team used these steps to create this functional behavioral assessment and the behavior intervention plan that follows the assessment. This plan is incorporated into his IEP and will allow him to interact with his peers and teachers in the general education classroom in more socially acceptable ways.

FUNCTIONAL BEHAVIORAL ASSESSMENT (FBA)

Student: *Shawn Jackson* **Grade:** *4* **School:** *John Dibert* **Date:** *November 19, 2001*
FBA/BIP developed for: Programming purposes **IEP requirement** **Participants:** _____

	ANTECEDENTS	CONSEQUENCES
In your own words, describe the behavior that prompted this FBA	Ask yourself: What is likely to "set off" (precede) the problem behavior? *Directions to academic work.*	Ask yourself: What "payoff" does the student obtain when she/he demonstrates the problem behavior?

In your own words, describe the behavior that prompted this FBA

Issues with off-task behavior; e.g.

PROBLEM BEHAVIOR

If the above explanation addresses multiple behaviors, identify the ONE BEHAVIOR to be targeted for intervention.

Avoiding an unpreferred activity by resting head on desk and covering ears.

The behavior I have targeted for intervention is:
✓   ✓
OBSERVABLE   MEASURABLE

ANTECEDENTS

Ask yourself: What is likely to "set off" (precede) the problem behavior? *Directions to academic work.*
WHEN is the problem behavior most likely to occur?

Morning   Approximate time(s) ✓
Afternoon   Approximate time(s) ✓
Before/after   Lunch/recess
school

WHERE
✓ Reg. Ed Classroom   Hallway
   Spec. Ed Classroom   Cafeteria

During what SUBJECT/ACTIVITY is the problem behavior most likely to occur?

Subject(s) *R/ LA, Soc, Stud. & Science*
✓ Seatwork   Classmates
  Group Activities   Other
  Lesson Presentation   peers

Are there OTHER EVENTS or CONDITIONS that immediately precede the problem behavior:

✓ A demand or request Unexpected changes in schedule or routine Consequences imposed for behavior Comments/teasing from other students

When is the student most successful? When DOESN'T the problem behavior occur? *When performing an academic task he enjoys.*

CONSEQUENCES

Ask yourself: What "payoff" does the student obtain when she/he demonstrates the problem behavior?

The student GAINS:
✓ Teacher/adult attention
  Peer attention
  Desired item or activity
✓ Control over others or the situation

What student AVOIDS or ESCAPES:
  Teacher/adult interaction
  Peer interaction
✓ Nonpreferred activity, task, or setting
  A difficult task or frustrating situation

What has been tried thus far to change the problem behavior?
  Implemented rules and consequences for behavior as posted
  Implemented behavior or academic contract
  Implemented home/school communication system
  Adapted curriculum. How? *Picture symbols, one on one.*

Modified instruction. How? *Smaller lessons*

Adjusted schedule. How?

Conferenced with parents: Dates:
Sent to office: Dates:

continued

FUNCTION OF PROBLEM BEHAVIOR	**REPLACEMENT BEHAVIOR**
Ask yourself: Why is the student behaving this way? What function/need is being met by the student's behavior?	Ask yourself: What alternative behavior would meet the same function/need for the student?
Complete the following preliminary analysis by summarizing information from the three columns on part one of the **FUNCTIONAL BEHAVIORAL ASSESSMENT.**	Complete the following:
When: _Teacher has asked Shawn to perform academic work he cannot do._ (summarize antecedents)	Rather than: _Tuning out, lowering head, covering ears._ (identify the problem behavior)
	I want this student to:
This student _will at times lower head onto desk & cover ears._ (identify the problem behavior)	_Attempt to perform his academics or explain to teacher that work is too difficult for Shawn._ (Note: This replacement behavior should represent an IEP goal)
In order to _avoid doing work he cannot perform (temporarily)._ (summarize payoff)	This definition is: (OBSERVABLE) (MEASURABLE)
EXAMPLES:	**EXAMPLES:**
1. When in the halls before school, after school, and during transitions, this student pushes other students and verbally threatens to beat them up in order to gain status and attention from peers.	1. Rather than pushing students and threatening to beat them up, I want this student to walk in the halls with his hands to his side and say "hello" to those with whom he wishes to interact.
2. When working on independent seatwork during his regular education math class, this student puts his head on his desk in order to escape work that is too difficult/frustrating.	2. Rather than putting his head on his desk because he doesn't know how to do the problem, I want this student to raise his hand for help and move onto the next problem while waiting for my assistance.

Behavior Intervention Plan
Name: *Shawn Jackson*
Date of Implementation: *11/19/07*

Behavior:
Avoidance of work
Challenging academics

Preventative Measures:
Determine Shawn's correct academic levels at all times!
Quietly redirect Shawn to complete his work.

Hypothesis:
From observation of antecedents, Shawn appears to display this behavior to avoid academic work which he cannot (or will not) do.

Reinforcement Schedule:
Computer time, 10 minutes per "successful" day. For a successful week, 20 minutes at the end of the week, Friday afternoon.

PEARSON
myeducationlab

Go to the Activities and Application section in Chapter 11 of MyEducationLab and complete Activity 2. As you read the case and answer the accompanying questions, reflect on how a functional behavioral assessment and a behavior intervention plan could help the student featured in the case.

DESIGNING AN APPROPRIATE IEP

Partnering for Special Education and Related Services

Partnerships among educators, related service providers, and family members are essential to assure that the student will benefit from special education. As members of the IEP team, these individuals must develop and use a common curriculum, instructional strategies, and positive behavior supports in school, home, and community settings. It is especially important to have a person on the evaluation and IEP team who has conducted or can interpret the functional behavioral assessment and can guide the team in developing a positive behavior supports plan.

Shawn's team consists of a special educator (Richard Hubbard), a paraeducator (Edna Crawford), two general educators (Geraldine Meyers and Rochella Mitchell), a speech-language specialist (Kirk Ealing), and an occupational therapist (Miss Maxwell).

Crone, Hawken, and Bergstrom (2007) have developed a model for teams to use as they conduct functional behavioral assessments and develop positive behavior support plans. Teams usually have six members. The model has six features:

Shawn's positive behavior support plan targets his communication and behaviors alike because the former affects the latter.

- ◆ Procedures defined—have a strong team leader and a handbook that outlines school discipline procedures and expectations.
- ◆ Procedures taught—train how to conduct a functional behavioral assessment and develop strategies for implementing a behavior plan.
- ◆ Procedures actively used—conduct a functional behavioral assessment and faithfully implement the strategies.
- ◆ Budget and resources applied—determine the extent to which the school has adequate personnel and financial support to do positive behavior support.
- ◆ Records kept—gather data before and after the training on students' needs and the impact of training.
- ◆ Leadership secured—determine whether the school principal and district administrators value positive behavior support.

In Box 11.2, you will read about Rosie Mack, a young child with autism, and how educators at the University of New Hampshire and Rosie's family adapted the Individual Support Program to implement positive behavior support. Rosie experienced dramatic improvement in a very short time.

 IEP Tip

The team that conducts the student's functional behavioral assessment should be the same as the team that develops the student's IEP; if that is not practicable, then there should be overlap between the two teams.

Determining Supplementary Aids and Services

In implementing positive behavior support, a student's IEP team should consider supplementary aids and services that address access, classroom ecology, and task modifications. These aids and services improve the student's access to an effective learning environment by modifying the community, campus, building, or classroom. They also provide "behavioral access"—by promoting positive behavior and minimizing disruptive behavior. Horner and colleagues (2002) have determined that "strategies for changing the physical characteristics of a setting, altering schedules, modifying curricula, and redesigning social groupings have all been demonstrated to alter the future likelihood of problem behaviors" (p. 425). Shawn benefits from two kinds of positive behavior interventions, or PBS. His school, John Dibert, uses schoolwide PBS, and Shawn has his own PBS plan. Equally important, Shawn has a paraeducator (Edna Crawford) and an occupational therapist (Miss Maxwell). Edna helps him with his reading and behaviors; Miss Maxwell shows him how to use simple technologies, such as raised paper to write on, a pencil with a rubberized grip, and, for those times when sensory overload threatens to invoke tantrums, vibrating tools that establish predictability, mimic his use of many electronic devices at home, and are not so obvious as to call great attention to his needs.

Implementing Positive Behavior Supports

It took only 6 months, an amazingly short period, for 3-year-old Rosie Mack to change dramatically—so dramatically that "progress in the general curriculum" was not just a phrase but a reality. The challenge was to help Rosie behave in such a way that she could be included in a preschool with students who do not have disabilities. What stood in the way was Rosie's erratic behavior: she was alternatively hyperactive and withdrawn and sobbing. Rosie's behaviors were typical for a preschooler with autism. She needed to learn appropriate behavior, such as how to calm down, how to comply with safety instructions and other directions ("Don't touch the hot stove"), and how to express her needs and choices other than by acting out ("Tell me what you want, Rosie"). By approaching the challenge step by step, Rosie and her team had remarkable success, but only because they acted as a team.

Step 1—*Create a team.* The partners consisted of Rosie's mother, Kathy; Kathy's parents, Lorraine and John Mack; Ann Dillon of the University of New Hampshire's Jump Start program (where positive behavior support is linked to family support and person-centered planning); Ann's graduate students; and the teachers and therapists in Rosie's early intervention program and elementary school.

Step 2—*Conduct an FBA and develop a PBS plan.* Under Ann's direction but with Kathy's diligent participation, the team began by conducting a functional assessment of Rosie's behavior; then they developed and carried out a plan for positive behavior support for Rosie. The plan included social stories (with graphic design by Kathy and photographs by Rosie's grandmother, Lorraine). At Ann's suggestion, Kathy or Ann's students read the stories to Rosie before she went to different places (e.g., the preschool or elementary school, the swimming pool, and the theater) or engaged in various activities (e.g., being a patient at a dentist's or physician's office). The stories prepped her for what lay ahead, gave her a sense of predictability, and helped her be calm when places changed and people entered her life.

Step 3—*Support the family.* Again under Ann's guidance, the team engaged in family support. Following the guidance of Kathy, Lorraine, and John, they developed a shared vision for Rosie, which was for her to be included in general education and to have friends—including both those who do and those who do not have disabilities. They also helped Kathy find child care, learn how to advocate for Rosie's inclusion in school and the community, and meet some of Rosie's needs for strenuous physical activity. Grandfather John himself built Rosie's swing-set.

Step 4—*Embed the plan.* Finally, the team worked with Rosie's teachers in the preschool and the elementary school to help them learn how to deliver positive behavior support to Rosie.

The results were remarkable. Rosie's problem behavior is a thing of the past. She progressed through the preschool and is now fully included, with support, in a typical first-grade classroom. She uses words and phrases to express her choices. If she doesn't know a word, she tells herself, "I will be okay," and uses hand signals, not acting-out behaviors, to communicate. She is fully included in her elementary school (with an aide), has friends who have and don't have disabilities, and has progressed from no literacy skills to knowing how to read and being a regular visitor to the community library. Rosie's favorite book is her well-worn copy of *The Tale of Peter Rabbit.*

Even though Ann pointed her team members in the right direction, everyone participated equally in leading and following. As in all the best partnerships, a teacher can jump-start the process, but everyone has to be a leader. Their comments recognize this shared leadership. As Kathy said, "We wouldn't be so much in control of our lives without Jump Start." Ann replied, "It's about the family and in turn about Rosie."

The key in partnerships, as Rosie's story illustrates, is to:

◆ Involve family members other than just the student's parents (remember how we defined "family" in Chapter 4?).

◆ Involve all school-based personnel and other professionals who work for the student.

◆ Seek and apply what researchers and their students know about interventions.

◆ Carry out a functional behavioral assessment, make it the basis for a positive behavior intervention plan, and implement the plan diligently and across all settings and times.

◆ Support each other, not just the student but also the student's family and teachers.

Putting These Tips to Work for Progress in the General Curriculum

1. Provide a rationale of why it is important to conduct a functional assessment and implement positive behavior support in multiple settings.

2. Identify related service providers who might be available to assist you as a teacher in providing family support. What types of assistance would you expect from each related service provider that you identify?

3. How can you involve family members to address problem behavior and enhance student outcomes?

The student's IEP team should also consider other campus or building modifications. The lunchroom is a place where problem behaviors occur frequently. It's noisy, there is not as much direct supervision, and there is constant movement. Modifications to the lunchroom environment can decrease problem behavior; consider replacing long rows of tables that accommodate many students with round tables around which fewer students congregate or rotating lunch periods to reduce the number of students in the cafeteria at any one time. Modifications before and after school and in the hallways between classes also can decrease problem behaviors.

Some students have behavioral problems because they can't see or hear well. Simply modifying the classroom arrangement can ensure better visual and acoustic access and help decrease problem behaviors. By contrast, some seating arrangements can precipitate problem behavior, so teachers should consider changing where they seat a student or limiting how many students interact with each other at any given time. Teachers also can create visual schedules for students to follow, thereby reducing off-task time and curtailing the times when problems may occur. Finally, problem behavior may arise because students become frustrated at being unable to complete required tasks. IEP teams should consider modifications, such as extended time, to address this situation.

Planning for Universal Design for Learning

Up to this point we have discussed the characteristics of autism that contribute to students' problems in learning and development. Paradoxically, some characteristics associated with autism spectrum disorders, particularly Asperger syndrome, are strengths and can be foundations for adaptations and augmentations to a student's curriculum. Some students may be able to focus their attention on detailed information for a long period of time, while others may excel in areas of the curriculum that are not language-based, such as math or science. As we noted in Chapter 2, curriculum adaptations modify either the way in which teachers present or represent curriculum content or the way in which students respond to the curriculum, while curriculum augmentations expand the general curriculum to teach students "learning-to-learn" strategies that will enable them to succeed in the general curriculum. Simpson (2005) identified cognitive learning strategies and social decision-making strategies, both forms of curriculum augmentation, as having "efficacy and utility for students with ASD" (p. 145). Similarly, Griffin, Griffin, Fitch, Albera, and Gingras (2006) identified similar learning-to-learn strategies as effective for students with Asperger syndrome.

Mnemonic Strategies

Some students with Asperger syndrome are skilled in memory tasks (Ozonoff, Dawson, & McPartland, 2002) that can form the basis for curriculum adaptations and augmentations; you should take these students' memory strengths into account when planning for universally designed instruction. One such curriculum modification involves mnemonic strategies (Lee et al., 2004; Marks et al., 2003). **Mnemonic,** or memory, strategies help students learn and retain information.

Keyword. **Keyword strategies** teach students to link a keyword to a new word or concept to help them remember the new material. The keyword is a word that sounds like the word or concept in question and can be easily pictured (Uberti, Scruggs, & Mastropieri, 2003). For example, to remember the three bones in the inner ear, you might use the following keyword strategies:

◆ *Malleus* sounds like mallets, and you can picture an image of hitting a bell with a mallet and causing it to ring (i.e., make sound).

◆ *Incus* sounds like ink, and you can picture an image of a large ear holding an ink pen and writing the word "incus."

◆ *Stapes* sounds like staple, and you can picture an image of a stapler with ears.

Pegword. The **pegword strategy** helps students remember numbered or ordered information by linking words that rhyme with numbers. The visual images help students remember a number or number sequence. There are standard pegwords that have come to represent numbers, such as the pegword "bun" representing the number one, the pegword "shoe" representing the number two, and so forth.

Letter. **Letter strategies** employ acronyms or a string of letters to help students remember a list of words or concepts. Recalling the acronym helps them recall the list or sequence. The fact that IDEA stands for Individuals with Disabilities Education Act helps you remember the law's name. Another common letter strategy uses the acronym HOMES to help people remember the list of the Great Lakes (Huron, Ontario, Michigan, Erie, Superior). Another letter strategy involves acronyms that do not form recognizable words. The letter mnemonic for the notes that fall on the lines of the musical staff of the treble clef is EGBDF, which is not a useful mnemonic in and of itself. However, forming an acrostic (that is, using each letter to identify a word in a sentence) helps: the acrostic letter strategy for remembering the notes on the treble clef is "*E*very *G*ood *B*oy *D*eserves a *F*avor."

Planning for Other Educational Needs

myeducationlab

Go to the Activities and Application section in Chapter 11 of MyEducationLab and complete Activity 3. As you watch the video and answer the accompanying questions, reflect on the benefits of promoting peer interaction among all students.

The most common characteristics of autism are impairments in language development and social development. We discussed language development in Chapter 6, so we will focus here on social development for children with autism.

Impairments in social skills and social interactions can result in problems in many areas, but for students with autism, none may be more of a problem than the impact of poor social skills on developing friendships. Sadly, teachers ranked student friendships as only 11th in importance among 20 potential outcomes for students with autism; they rated the likelihood of that outcome even lower (Ivey, 2007).

Promoting Friendships

We all know what friends are—people we like to be around and who like to be with us. Having friends is important at all points in life, perhaps especially during the school years. But difficulties with communication, poor social skills, and problem behavior too often cause students with autism to be isolated from their peers with and without disabilities. Orsmond, Krauss, and Seltzer (2004) studied peer relationships of more than 200 adolescents and adults with autism and found that only 8 percent of them had at least one "friend," that is, a person of the same age with whom the individual with autism engaged in activities outside the home. Twenty-one percent of those individuals had a peer relationship that fell short of the standard of a friend but involved some activities out of the home, while 24 percent were involved in peer relationships only in prearranged settings, such as school. Finally, almost half had no peer relationships whatsoever that met the criteria of same-age peer within or outside prearranged settings. Despite these data, there is good news: teaching students to acquire social skills can help them have friends (Koegel, 2007).

When a student participates in solving problems facing her, she is more likely to own the solution and overcome the problem itself.

While you probably knew immediately what we were talking about when we mentioned the word *friend*, you may not know quite as intuitively how one goes about planning for and teaching friendship skills. These are skills that most children—but not students with autism—learn through typical play activities and, of course, with the guidance of their parents or brothers and sisters.

The first step toward promoting friendships involves including students with autism in general education classrooms and in extracurricular and nonacademic activities such as school clubs, plays, sporting events, dances, and field trips (Boutot, 2007). The peer buddy program you learned about in Chapter 10 links same-age peers with and without intellectual disability in a wide array of activities, including those outside the classroom, and can be equally useful for students with autism. In fact, peer tutoring on social communication has helped students improve their communication skills (Theimann & Goldstein, 2004).

As we discussed in Chapter 10, however, you have to support students without disabilities to interact with and respond appropriately to students with disabilities. Simply placing students in proximity of their peers without disabilities will not be sufficient (Janney & Snell, 2006). You will need to do more than ensure that your students with autism interact with their classmates in general education settings. Perhaps because Shawn is such an outgoing boy (remember, Donnica described him as a "ladies' man") and perhaps because he is now included in general education classes his peers who do not have disabilities have taken a shine to him. His teachers have had no occasions to build friendships deliberately. If anything, Shawn's friendships may be a bit too patronizing; Donnica is concerned, as are his teachers, that his peers should not baby him and let him get away with using gibberish when he could use sentences.

Using person-centered planning models (described in Chapter 10) that involve peers is a good first step. A second step is considering the environment itself: a lack of friends may reflect a general lack of peer acceptance in the environment, so you should make sure that a student's peers learn about the goals of inclusion. An "environmental support plan" should identify the support peers will need to interact more appropriately, the role of supplementary aids and services in supporting those interactions, and the types of extracurricular activities that can lead to positive interactions (Janney & Snell, 2006). This plan can contribute to planning for positive behavior support as well. A third step is to identify the interests and abilities of your students with autism and then to connect those students with others who share their interests and abilities.

Obviously, planning for promoting friendship involves setting goals for instructional activities. Your students' IEPs should address the following instructional areas (Kluth, 2003; McConnell, 2002):

- *Trustworthiness and loyalty:* teaching your students how important it is to be a loyal friend by keeping secrets and promises, standing up for one's friends, and supporting friends' rights

- *Conflict resolution:* teaching your students how to resolve conflicts between and among friends and acquaintances, and how to help their peers to do so

- *General friendship skills:* teaching your students how to act around a friend, such as by taking turns speaking, asking about the well-being or feelings of a friend, and asking questions about hobbies and areas of shared interest

- *Positive interaction style:* teaching your students to be active listeners, give positive feedback, ask questions, and respond to the needs of others

- *Taking the perspective of others:* teaching your students to consider others' needs, feelings, and interests, compromise on activity choices, and listen to others' ideas

Because students with autism have difficulty recognizing emotions from others' facial or vocal patterns, they sometimes have problematic social interactions (LaCava, Golan, Baron-Cohen, & Myles, 2007). Using principles of UDL to design software to remedy this problem, Baron-Cohen, Golan, Wheelwright, and Hill (2004) developed a computer-based intervention to improve students' ability to recognize others' emotions. Box 11.3 provides information about this use of universally designed technology.

IEP Tip

A student's IEP team should address the student's social skills by prescribing peer tutoring, social skills groups, student-directed learning strategies, person-centered planning, and social stories.

Go to the Activities and Application section in Chapter 11 of MyEducationLab and complete Activity 4. As you watch these videos and answer the accompanying questions, reflect on the various ways in which strategies that include technology can be beneficial for students with autism.

Teaching Emotion Recognition to Students with Autism and Asperger Syndrome

One reason that students with autism have problems with social interactions is that they sometimes have difficulty comprehending others' feelings, preferences, and emotions. Think about it. If you deduce that someone is angry by noticing that the person's face is red from emotion and they're frowning, you can modify how you approach and communicate with the person based upon this knowledge. If you do not notice, it might lead to an uncomfortable exchange. This is the dilemma faced by many people with autism, and it certainly contributes to difficulty in making friends and maintaining friendships.

Simon Baron-Cohen and his colleagues have developed a multimedia software program called *Mind Reading: The Interactive Guide to Emotions* (Baron-Cohen, Golan, Wheelwright, & Hill, 2004) designed specifically to address these difficulties in determining emotion. This software program has three main sections: an Emotions Library, a Learning Center, and a Games Zone. The Emotions Library presents photographs, video clips, and audio of people who are expressing any one of 412 different emotions, grouped into 26 overarching groups. For example, the emotions depicted in the "excited emotions" group are: adventurous, alert, ardor, aroused, enthusiastic, excited, exhilarated, hysterical, inspired, invigorated, keen, lively, refreshed, spirited, titillated, and vibrant. For each of these emotions, there are six images of people ranging across ages and ethnic groups, stories showing how the emotion is used in a social situation, voices of people whose voice patterns depict the emotion, and additional information about the emotion. The Emotions Library is a good example of Universal Design for Learning using technology because it uses both video and audio output to represent content information (e.g., what a person looks and sounds like when expressing an emotion).

The Learning Center was designed specifically for use by people with autism spectrum disorders and provides lessons on emotions, followed by a quiz. Again conforming with UDL principles, the difficulty of lessons can be adjusted to ensure that students with varying cognitive abilities and ages can progress in the lessons, and the lessons are presented using both audio and video content.

The Games Zone provides a chance for students to play video games that incorporate emotion recognition features. For example, in the Hidden Face game, students are presented with a grid of nine squares. As they select each square, it reveals a portion of a photograph of a person's face. As more and more of the face is revealed, students can choose from among a selection of 10 possible emotions what emotion they believe the person is showing. Points are awarded for correct answers and deducted for incorrect answers. An audio feature provides audio instructions for playing the game.

Golan and Baron-Cohen (2006) found that British children with autism using the Mind Reading software for up to 15 weeks in a home-based intervention improved their emotion recognition capacity and were able to generalize these gains to new audio and video representations of emotion. LaCava, Golan, Baron-Cohen, and Myles (2007) used the Mind Reading program with 8 students from the United States with Asperger syndrome in both home and school settings and, like the British sample, found that after 10 weeks of use students improved their face and voice emotion recognition, including recognition of more complex emotions.

You can learn more about the Mind Reading software by going to the product's web page at http://www.jkp.com/mindreading/.

■ ■ ■

USING EFFECTIVE INSTRUCTIONAL STRATEGIES

Early Childhood Students: Social Stories

Early intervention and education, with special attention to your students' communication and social competence, are important for launching your students toward IDEA's four outcomes and for supporting their families (Cardon, 2007; Koegel & Koegel, 2006; Simpson & Myles, 2008). Early intervention and preschool programs use different approaches, including the following:

◆ Applied behavior analytic techniques, such as discrete trial training (which we discuss later in this chapter), that emphasize assessment, programming, systematic reinforcement of appropriate behavior, and generalization of skills and behavior across settings (places) and people (Koegel & Koegel, 2006; Simpson & Myles, 2008)

◆ Incidental teaching in natural environments, such as the child's home, a child-care center, and the community (McGee, Morrier, & Daley, 1999)

◆ Communication, sensory processing, motor planning, and shared affect with caregivers and peers (Cardon, 2007; Koegel, 2007)

Social stories are useful for preschool and older children with autism. That is so because students with autism and Asperger syndrome often need to learn how to interact appropriately with others in social situations: knowing what is cool and uncool behavior, understanding others' perspectives, and knowing the unwritten codes of conduct—what educators call the "hidden curriculum" (Simpson & Myles, 2008). **Social stories** are written by educators, parents, or students and describe social situations, social cues, and appropriate responses to those cues. These stories usually consist of four different types of sentences (Gray, 1998):

◆ Descriptive sentences define where a situation occurs, who is involved, what they are doing, and why.

◆ Perspective sentences describe a person's internal physical state or desire. They also describe another person's thoughts, feelings, beliefs, and motivations.

◆ Directive sentences define what is expected as a response to a cue or in a particular situation.

◆ Control sentences identify strategies students may use to recall the information in a social story, reassure themselves, or define their responses. (pp. 178–179)

The positive effects of social stories occur across different settings (Gray & White, 2002). For example, social stories enabled a 5-year-old boy with autism to decrease the number of tantrums he had at home (Lorimer, Simpson, Myles, & Ganz, 2002), a finding replicated in a study by Agosta, Graetz, Mastropieri, and Scruggs (2004). Social stories improve the social behavior of young children with Asperger syndrome (Sansosti & Powell-Smith, 2006). Similar results occurred with young children with autism (Delano & Snell, 2006). Indeed, a synthesis of research on the efficacy of social stories concluded that they yielded positive effects for students with autism, although the authors also called for more research on the strategy (Sansosti, Powell-Smith, & Kincaid, 2004).

Elementary and Middle School Students: Schoolwide Positive Behavior Support

Schoolwide positive behavior support (SWPBS) is a systems-level and evidence-based method for improving valued social and learning outcomes for all students, not just those with autism (Crone & Horner, 2003; Freeman et al., 2006; Janney & Snell, 2008). It is proactive, problem-solving-oriented, and data-based; it elicits appropriate behavior and contributes to academic, social, and communication outcomes throughout a school building (Bambera & Kern, 2005).

Because students' problem behavior often results from someone else's failure to provide individualized and comprehensive support (Janney & Snell, 2008), positive behavior support seeks to tailor students' environments to their preferences, strengths, and needs. It rearranges school environments and changes school systems to discourage students from engaging in problem behaviors in the first place.

In their review of more than 100 research articles published between 1985 and 1996 on behavioral outcomes for individuals with problem behavior (primarily individuals with intellectual disability, autism, or both), Carr et al. (1999) found:

◆ Positive behavior support was successful in achieving at least an 80 percent reduction in problem behavior for approximately two thirds of the behavioral outcomes studied.

◆ A functional assessment substantially increased the likelihood that positive behavior support would be effective.

◆ Positive behavior support was more effective when the focus was not just on the individual with problem behavior but also on other significant people, helping teachers and families change their behavior to support the individual more effectively.

At Shawn's school, teachers develop positive behavior support plans for him by also developing a positive plan for his peers.

◆ Positive behavior support was more effective when teachers and families reorganized environments to support the student's success.

◆ Positive behavior support was just as effective with individuals who have pervasive needs for support as it was with individuals who have only intermittent needs.

Schoolwide positive behavior support includes three components: (1) universal support, (2) group support, and (3) individual support. Box 11.4 describes how teachers put these components into practice.

Shawn's school (John Dibert) uses SWPBS. Its system is community-referenced, seeking to teach students behaviors they will need in their schools and communities by using reinforcements that are quintessentially American. The school has printed counterfeit money—John Dibert Dollars. Each student receives a fixed allowance of dollars. Students earn more of these faux dollars when they behave well and lose some when they do not.

INTO PRACTICE
Box 11.4

Implementing Schoolwide Positive Behavior Supports

Implementing Schoolwide Positive Behavior Supports (SPBS) involves interventions at three levels: universal support, group support, and individualized support, as needed.

The primary goal of universal support is to create a positive learning context for all students. You can carry out this goal by setting clear expectations for student behavior in all places and activities in a school (cafeteria, hallways, bathrooms, library, and playgrounds), making sure the students agree to those expectations, giving them many opportunities to meet these expectations, and rewarding them when they do. You will succeed in implementing universal support when you do the following:

◆ *Clearly define behavioral expectations.* These expectations are defined simply, positively, and succinctly.

◆ *Teach behavioral expectations.* Each expectation should be explicitly taught so that students know exactly what is expected of them.

◆ *Frequently acknowledge appropriate behaviors.* A rule of thumb is to have at least four times as many positive affirmations as negative sanctions.

◆ *Evaluate problems and make adaptations on an ongoing basis through a team approach.* A student's IEP team should review data on behavioral incidences, attendance rates, detentions, and suspension rates and then implement proactive strategies to discourage negative behavior and reward positive behavior.

◆ *Target support to address students who need more intense skill development and practice than is offered through universal support.* The targeted support might relate to particular behavior in the hallways or cafeteria, social skills, conflict resolution, and/or communication training.

Group support is the second component of positive behavior support (Janney & Snell, 2008). Group support addresses problem behavior that is occurring with at least 10 to

15 students, each of whom has received universal support but has not yet learned appropriate behavior. To provide group support, you typically will need to:

◆ Observe students individually and as a group.

◆ Interview those who are having problem behaviors.

◆ Develop hypotheses that deal with the behaviors of all of the members of the group.

◆ Teach the specific skills that all of the students need to eliminate their problem behaviors.

Group support often occurs where students have higher rates of problem behaviors, such as hallways, lunchrooms, and playgrounds.

The most intense level of positive behavior support is individual support. Individual support is for students who are not able to sufficiently eliminate their problem behavior through universal and group support; it often includes students with autism and other significant disabilities (Freeman et al., 2006). To provide individual support, begin with a functional behavioral assessment of the student; the functional behavioral assessment becomes part of the student's nondiscriminatory evaluation and is the basis on which you then develop the student's IEP. If a student has a behavior that impedes his or other students' learning, IDEA requires the student's IEP team to consider the use of positive behavior interventions and supports as well as other strategies to address the behavior. The functional behavioral assessment becomes the foundation for IEP goals that target reducing problem behavior, teaching appropriate behavior, and maximizing positive outcomes through communication and social skills.

PEARSON
myeducationlab

Go to the Activities and Application section in Chapter 11 of MyEducationLab and complete Activity 5. As you watch these videos and answer the accompanying questions, compare and contrast the different models of schoolwide positive behavior support.

Figure 11.3 Percentages of students with, at risk for, and without serious problem behavior

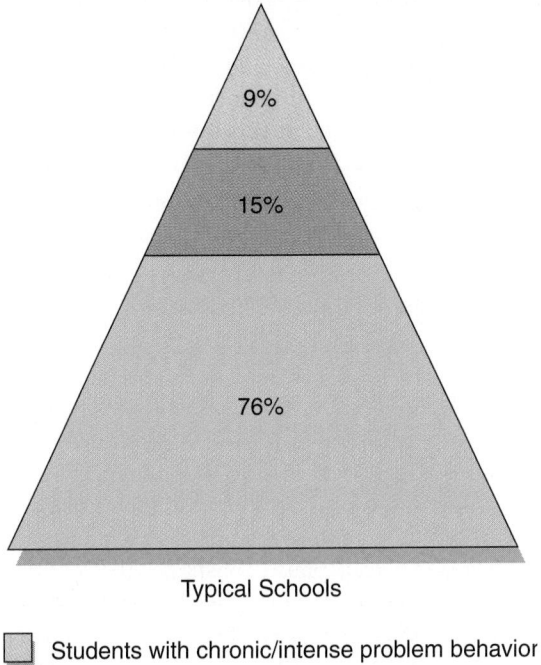

9%

15%

76%

Typical Schools

☐ Students with chronic/intense problem behavior
☐ Students at risk for problem behavior
☐ Students without serious problem behavior

Simply having "cash" to spend at the school store teaches a lesson about earning and productivity: the more you do to behave, the more you will earn, and vice versa.

There's a powerful element of peer reinforcement, too. The students who earn more receive their peers' approval; those who are penalized may lose their peers' approval but more often receive their support to redeem their losses. Finally, getting and losing money teaches the math skills of adding and subtracting. SWPBS at John Dibert combines economics, peer interaction, math skills, and community-referenced behaviors. It exemplifies the comprehensive approach that research supports: generalize across settings and make behaviors durable across time.

Why should teachers use these three components? The answer comes from research data. Approximately 76 percent of students receive no more than one office discipline referral during a school year; these students do not have serious problem behavior and can benefit from universal support. Another 15 percent of students receive two to five office referrals; these students are at risk for having problem behavior and can benefit from group support. Finally, about 9 percent receive six or more office referrals; these students have intense problem behavior (Sugai et al., 2000). Figure 11.3 illustrates the proportions of students whose behaviors vary from not problematic at all to intensely problematic. Typically, students with autism require individual support to learn appropriate behavior.

Secondary and Transition Students: Discrete Trial Teaching

You have learned that positive behavior support is important for many students with autism. The techniques underlying positive behavior support emerged from strategies and techniques referred to as applied behavior analysis. **Applied behavior analysis (ABA)** uses the principles of operant psychology to reduce problem behavior or increase positive behavior. ABA is the "process of applying sometimes tentative principles of behavior to the improvement of specific behaviors and simultaneously evaluating whether or not any changes noted are indeed attributable to the process of application" (Baer, Wolf, & Risley, 1968, p. 91).

ABA principles undergird instructional techniques and strategies that are essential to students' success. One of those strategies is discrete trial teaching. **Discrete trial teaching** uses three elements: the discriminative stimulus, the response, and the reinforcing stimulus or consequence.

◆ *Discriminative stimulus.* The discriminative stimulus is a specific event or environmental condition that elicits the response you want your student to give. The stimulus, such as an instruction or command to perform a task, controls the desired response when your student's response is paired with a reinforcer that you provide.

◆ *Response.* The response is the behavior your student performs when you present the discriminative stimulus. The response is the behavior you are trying to teach the child.

◆ *Reinforcing stimulus.* The reinforcing stimulus, or reinforcer, is an event or action that follows your student's response and increases the possibility that your student will exhibit that same response again.

Let's consider a simple example of these principles. You want to teach an adolescent with autism ("Jane") the steps in a vocational task, such as sorting silverware into bins. To do that job, Jane must distinguish each type of utensil (spoon, fork, knife). So you lay a spoon, a fork, and a knife in front of her and provide a discriminative stimulus by saying, "Jane, show me the spoon." Most likely, Jane will point to or touch one of the utensils or, if she is not certain, not respond at all. If she points to the spoon, you immediately praise her, saying, "Great job, Jane! That's right, that's the spoon." Your praise constitutes the reinforcing stimulus. If she points to a different utensil or to none of them, she does not get your reinforcer (verbal praise); instead, you prompt her again to identify the spoon. Eventually, if you reinforce ("Great job!") her correct response (pointing to the spoon) to your discriminative stimulus ("Show me the spoon"), while ignoring or not reinforcing Jane's other responses, she will respond more consistently to the stimulus with the appropriate response.

Discrete trial training is, then, a single instructional trial consisting of the following elements:

◆ Presentation of a discriminative stimulus, sometimes called a cue
◆ Presentation of a prompting stimulus, if needed
◆ The response
◆ Presentation of a reinforcing stimulus, if appropriate

In discrete trial teaching, this trial is followed by a brief interval, called the intertrial interval, before the sequence is repeated. You will notice that we have added a step to the original three steps—a prompting stimulus. If your student is learning a brand-new concept, she may need a variety of levels of prompts to be able to exhibit the correct response. A prompting stimulus is any stimulus that, when paired with the discriminative stimulus, increases the probability that the student will exhibit the correct response.

Let's go back to our example of sorting utensils. If Jane does not know what a spoon is, the probability is one in four that she will choose the right utensil. That means there is a three in four probability that she will not select the right utensil and will instead point to the fork or knife or simply not respond. If, however, when you present the discriminative stimulus ("Show me the spoon") you also provide a prompt (pointing to the spoon yourself, taking her hand and placing it on the spoon, looking at the spoon), you increase the probability that Jane will give the appropriate response.

Discrete trial teaching is particularly useful for teaching students with autism new forms of behavior (behaviors not previously in the child's repertoire) and how to discriminate among events and activities (DeBoer, 2007). It has been used to improve communication outcomes for students with autism (Goldstein, 2003) and has reduced their stereotyped behaviors (Dib & Sturmey, 2007).

INCLUDING STUDENTS WITH AUTISM

Although research demonstrates the success of teaching behavior change techniques to students with autism, these students have one of the lowest rates of inclusion in general

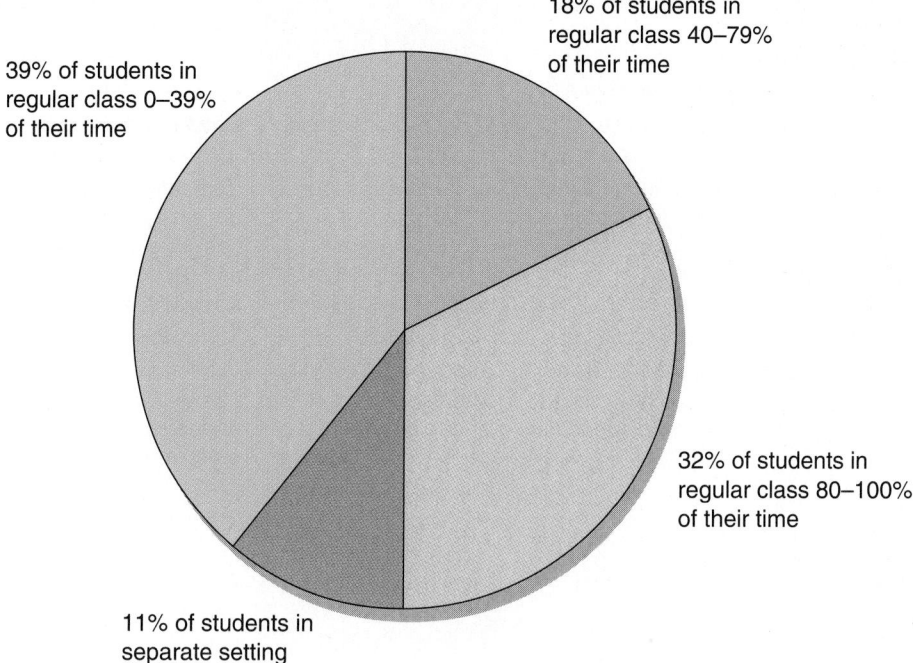

Figure 11.4 Educational placement of students with autism (2006–2007)

18% of students in regular class 40–79% of their time

39% of students in regular class 0–39% of their time

32% of students in regular class 80–100% of their time

11% of students in separate setting

education classes. As illustrated in Figure 11.4, fewer than one third of students with autism spend the majority of their time in general education classes (U.S. Department of Education, 2008). Yet effective educators can assure their students' progress in the general curriculum. Researchers examined the relationship that general education teachers had with second and third graders with autism who were in an inclusive classroom (Robertson, Chamberlain, & Kasari, 2003). Their findings were encouraging:

1. General education teachers reported that they have positive relationships with students with autism in their classes. Students with higher rates of problem behavior had less favorable relationships with their teachers.

2. There is a relationship between the quality of the teacher-student relationship and the peer status of the child with autism. Children with autism who had more positive relationships with their teachers also were included more by their peers.

3. Half of the children with autism have paraprofessionals; the presence of a paraprofessional did not interfere with the child's relationship with the teacher.

Donnica is candid about Shawn's inclusion. It was nil or non-effective during first through third grades. Either Shawn was in a class designed solely for students with autism, or he was simply taking up a seat in a general education class, not benefiting at all.

Just as she criticizes what the schools did in the past—"I didn't send Shawn to be babysat at school"—so she praises the staff at John Dibert School for what it does now. Shawn participates in classes in math and science (Rochella Mitchell) and reading and social studies (Geraldine Meyers), with support from his general educator (Richard Hubbard) and paraeducator (Edna Crawford). He does so because IDEA prefers inclusion to separation.

But he also is included because Donnica prepared a storyboard about Shawn before enrolling him at Dibert, met with his IEP team, and demonstrated, using the storyboard, how Shawn learns—principally by using symbols or pictures to understand the text he has to read and by using a computer program that combines text with pictures. She persuaded his team that, because he had been reading only one grade level below his peers before Katrina and the move to Houston, he would be capable of making progress, moving from being two grade levels behind his peers to one grade level behind them. His team agreed with her, and his goals now are both academic and behavioral.

Box 11.5 INCLUSION TIPS

	What You Might See	What You Might Be Tempted to Do	Alternate Responses	Ways to Include Peers in the Process
Behavior	She often rocks back and forth over and over during class activities she's not interested in.	Ignore her behavior or tell her to stop.	Conduct a functional behavioral assessment to understand why rocking is occurring.	Help peers to understand her behavior. Encourage and support their acceptance of her.
Social interactions	On the playground she is almost always left out of group interactions.	Assume that being alone is how she prefers to spend her time.	Teach her to ask if she can be included and to develop the skills to participate in play with one or two peers.	Pair her with students who understand her preferred communication method.
Educational performance	She learns very slowly and needs a great deal of extra help to learn simple concepts.	Expect less and make the requirements less structured.	Use visual images and music to teach abstract concepts.	Provide opportunities for peer tutoring with visual images and music.
Classroom attitudes	She becomes antagonistic during activities in which there is noise or confusion.	Remove her from class activities to work alone in the library.	Use social stories to help her learn ways to concentrate in noisy environments.	Teach peers to write social stories that include all students. Have small groups, including the student, revise and work out different scenarios.

Shawn benefits from other supports, principally a Dynavox that assists him as he spells out words and makes sentences that he cannot vocalize. (You learned about assistive technology, such as the Dynavox, that helps students communicate when you read Chapter 6.) Box 11.5 offers suggestions for promoting successful inclusion for students with autism.

ASSESSING STUDENTS' PROGRESS

Measuring Students' Progress

Progress in the General Curriculum

Most of the procedures for measuring a student's progress in the general curriculum are assessment strategies. Educators often combine them with other strategies to get a more robust understanding of a student's progress. When they bundle assessment strategies with other strategies, they create a holistic assessment or evaluation system. There are several such systems in use in the field of autism.

The Autism Screening Instrument for Educational Planning (ASIEP-2) (Krug, Arick, & Almond, 1993) has five components or subtests that enable educators to evaluate a student's capacity across communication, social interactions, behavior, academic content, and other domains. The most frequently used subtest of the ASIEP-2 is the Autism Behavior Checklist, which is a screening tool to identify the need for further assessment to determine whether the student has autism (Volkmar et al., 1988; Wadden, Bryson, & Rodger, 1991). The Sample of Vocal Behavior subscale and the Social Interaction Assessment help teachers track their students' progress in areas of other educational needs.

Of particular relevance to tracking students' progress in the general curriculum is the Educational Assessment subscale of the ASIEP-2. Although designed for screening and planning activities, the Educational Assessment subscale also has been administered to determine students' progress in school and at home (Arick et al., 2003).

Progress in Addressing Other Educational Needs

Just as teachers measure their students' academic outcomes, so they also measure the outcomes of schoolwide positive behavior interventions and supports. Measurement strategies such as the data-based measurement techniques you read about in Chapter 9 are effective for measuring each student's behavioral changes. Because positive behavior support involves multiple levels, however, it is necessary to measure all students' behavioral change at the school and district level.

What types of data do educators need to determine the effectiveness of schoolwide positive behavior interventions? Some data are direct counts of problem behavior, including the number of office referrals for the school or district on a weekly or monthly basis or the types of problem behavior reflected in those office referrals. Other data involve problem behavior reported by environment or time of day. Some data are indirect indicators of success, including student absences or attendance rates, both as a function of student enrollment. All of these data can be collected by hand or can be collected and analyzed using an online data collection system called the School-Wide Information System (May et al., 2003).

Another data collection tool is the School-Wide Evaluation Tool (SET) (Horner et al., 2006). It assists educators in assessing and evaluating the features of schoolwide behavior support across the academic year and from year to year. Finally, the Self-Assessment of Contextual Fit in Schools (Horner, Salentine, & Albin, 2003) enables educators to assess the need for and impact of the types of supplementary aids and services we have already discussed, such as access and classroom ecological modifications.

Recently, researchers at the University of South Florida have introduced an instrument, the School-wide Benchmarks of Quality (BoQ) (Kincaid, Childs, & George, 2005), to measure the implementation of SWPBS. The BoQ is a 53-item rating scale yielding data in 10 areas of interest in implementing SWPBS: PBS team, faculty commitment, effective discipline procedures, data entry, expectations and rules, reward system, lesson plans, implementation plans, crisis plans, and evaluation. Cohen, Kincaid, and Childs (2007) validated the use of the BoQ in a study in 105 schools in two states.

Making Accommodations for Assessment

Accommodations improve students' outcomes on standardized assessments. One particular accommodation differs from typical test modifications because it considers not the test itself but the examiner giving the test and his or her interactions with the student. Koegel, Koegel, and Smith (1997) found that students with autism performed better on standardized assessments when they were provided with more frequent positive reinforcement, and Szarko (2000) found the same result when the tests were administered by a familiar person. These findings are not specific to students with autism. In a meta-analysis of the impact of examiner familiarity, Fuchs and Fuchs (1986) found that students with a wide array of disabilities performed better with a familiar examiner.

Part of the benefit of a familiar examiner for students with autism comes from the fact that the presence of the examiner minimizes the students' anxiety and stress associated with testing. Students with autism frequently have difficulty during times of transition or stress. Typically, on days during which students complete standardized testing, the normal schedule is not followed. Between the disruption to the schedule and the stress associated with testing, particularly high-stakes testing, teachers and school administrators must do whatever they can to reduce the anxiety that students normally will experience, including providing a familiar examiner.

Like every other student in Louisiana, Shawn must take the state assessment of academic progress, LEAP (Louisiana Education Assessment Program). He is scheduled to receive an important accommodation: The questions will be read to him. He also is scheduled to make progress toward a certificate of attendance, not a diploma. That goal disquiets Donnica. Her goal, and that of Shawn's present IEP team, is to assure that he passes his academic assessment, moves forward with his peers to the next grade, and then shifts from the "certificate track" to the "diploma track."

They believe that it would not be good for Shawn to have to repeat a grade and be in "LEAP remediation" (as Louisiana requires) if he does not pass his assessment. They also believe that the diploma, more than the certificate, will signify to others—future employers especially—that Shawn can be the man Donnica and his teachers want him to be: a productive citizen of a recovered city.

VALUES AND OUTCOMES

VALUES	GREAT EXPECTATIONS		CHOICES	
	POSITIVE CONTRIBUTIONS			STRENGTHS
	RELATIONSHIPS		FULL CITIZENSHIP	

What values do Donnica and Shawn's school team endorse?

◆ They have great expectations for him: performing just slightly below grade level and earning a diploma, not a certificate. As you recall, IDEA proclaims that one of the obstacles facing students with disabilities is others' low expectations for them.

◆ They regard his social skills—once a barrier to his inclusion in the general curriculum—as positives because they bring people into Shawn's life and create social-support networks for him.

◆ They understand that Shawn's strengths include his ability to use computers, a communication board, and now the more sophisticated Dynavox for communicating, and they regard his fascination with gadgets—TV, DVD player, and Nintendo—as a foundation teaching him work skills, not just academic skills.

◆ They accede to his choices—his strict adherence to routines—so long as his choices do no harm, but they do not allow him to choose to injure himself, and they use positive behavior supports to control that behavior and to teach him more socially appropriate behavior.

◆ They value the relationships he is able to develop with his peers, but they worry whether he might be "babied" too much and learn to depend too much on others.

◆ They expect Shawn to be able to work, perhaps in a music or computer store, but they do not yet know whether he will be able to live independently. Full citizenship for Shawn may mean simply working; the rest will depend as much on public resources and policy as on Shawn and Donnica.

Are they deluding themselves by expecting so much? It is understandable if you answer "Yes," and then qualify your answer by adding, "But not if his future educators, like his present ones, use evidence-based approaches and hold true to the six core values." However, rethink your answer in light of the following questions.

WHAT DO YOU THINK?

1. Would more or less speech-language therapy be useful for Shawn? If it's a pull-out program? If it is part of Shawn's participation in general education classes?

2. Should his educators teach his peers how to do less for him and help them show him how to do more for himself? Is Donnica right to worry that they will "cripple" him?

3. Should they let Shawn use his Dynavox most of the time or insist that he use it only when he cannot form the words and sentences he needs to use?

4. Could peer interaction and assistive technology be counterproductive and make Shawn less independent?

5. How much more individualized positive behavior support should Shawn receive, given that he still melts down from time to time?

6. Bottom line: What more, if anything, should his educators do to assure that he achieves his and Donnica's goals and those that IDEA has set for him?

ADDRESSING THE STANDARDS: THE VALUES CONNECTION

The following CEC Knowledge and Skill Standards: Common Core and Values are addressed in this chapter through the content and concepts we discuss.

CEC Knowledge and Skill Standards: Common Core		Values/Standards Connection
CEC Knowledge and Skill Standard II. Development and Characteristics of Learners		Standard 2 asks you to consider your students' *strengths*.
CC2K1	Typical and atypical human growth and development.	
CC2K2	Educational implications of characteristics of various exceptionalities.	
CC2K4	Family systems and the roles of families supporting development.	
CC2K5	Similarities and differences of individuals with and without exceptional learning needs.	
CC2K6	Similarities and differences of individuals with exceptional learning needs.	

continued

CEC Knowledge and Skill Standards: Common Core	Values/Standards Connection
CEC Knowledge and Skill Standard IV. **Instructional Strategies**	It is important to build on the strengths of students with autism who have extraordinary abilities to increase the likelihood that they will make *positive contributions* to others.
CC4S1 Use strategies to facilitate integration into various settings.	
CC4S2 Teach individuals to use self-assessment, problem-solving, and other cognitive strategies to meet their needs.	Student-directed strategies, such as those discussed in Chapter 9, should also be included to promote student *choices* and self-direction.
CC4S3 Select, adapt, and use instructional strategies and materials according to characteristics of the individual with exceptional learning needs.	
CC4S4 Use strategies to facilitate maintenance and generalization of skills across environments.	
CC4S5 Use procedures to increase the individual's self-awareness, self-management, self-control, self-reliance, and self-esteem.	
CC4S6 Use strategies that promote successful transitions for individuals with exceptional learning needs.	
CEC Knowledge and Skill Standard V. **Learning Environments and Social Interactions**	Promoting friendships is one way to apply CEC Standard 5, Learning Environments and Social Interactions. Positive social interactions help prepare learners with realistic and even *high expectations* for social behaviors. *Relationships* don't just happen for many students with autism, and that is why educators should create opportunities for their students to interact with peers with and without disabilities.
CC5S2 Identify realistic expectations for personal and social behavior in various settings.	
CC5S3 Identify supports needed for integration into various program placements.	
CC5S4 Design learning environments that encourage active participation in individual and group settings.	By teaching your students how to be socially appropriate, you expand their opportunities to develop *relationships* that can bloom into genuine friendships.
CC5S9 Create an environment that encourages self-advocacy and increased independence.	
CC5S12 Design and manage daily routines.	
CC5S15 Structure, direct, and support the activities of paraeducators, volunteers, and tutors.	

CEC Knowledge and Skill Standards: Common Core	Values/Standards Connection
CEC Knowledge and Skill Standard VII. Instructional Planning CC7K5 Roles and responsibilities of the paraeducator related to instruction, intervention, and direct service. CC7S1 Identify and prioritize areas of the general curriculum and accommodations for individuals with exceptional learning needs. CC7S3 Involve the individual and family in setting instructional goals and monitoring progress. CC7S6 Sequence, implement, and evaluate individualized learning objectives. CC7S7 Integrate affective, social, and life skills with academic curricula. CC7S9 Incorporate and implement instructional and assistive technology into the educational program.	All students with disabilities have *strengths* as well as limitations. Too often, teachers emphasize only the limitations. To promote your students' access to the general curriculum, however, you will want to build on their *strengths*.
CEC Knowledge and Skill Standard VIII. Assessment CC8K3 Screening, prereferral, referral, and classification procedures. CC8S2 Administer nonbiased formal and informal assessments. CC8S6 Use assessment information in making eligibility, program, and placement decisions for individuals with exceptional learning needs, including those from culturally and/or linguistically diverse backgrounds. CC8S8 Evaluate instruction and monitor progress of individuals with exceptional learning needs.	Using a variety of diagnostic tools to identify the exceptional learning needs of students is an application of CEC Standard 8, Assessment. Assessment lets you build on your students' *strengths*.
CEC Knowledge and Skill Standard X. Collaboration CC10S2 Collaborate with families and others in assessment of individuals with exceptional learning needs. CC10S3 Foster respectful and beneficial relationships between families and professionals. CC10S4 Assist individuals with exceptional learning needs and their families in becoming active participants in the educational team. CC10S5 Plan and conduct collaborative conferences with individuals with exceptional learning needs and their families.	Being a part of collaborations and partnerships reflects CEC Standard 10, Collaboration. Collaboration fosters *relationships*.

SUMMARY

Identifying Students with Autism

◆ Autism is a developmental disability significantly affecting verbal and nonverbal communication and social interaction. It is generally evident before age 3 and adversely affects educational performance. Other characteristics include repetitive activities, stereotyped movements, behavioral challenges, need for environmental predictability, unusual responsiveness to sensory stimulation, and below-average intellectual functioning.

◆ Autism is part of a broader group of disorders called pervasive developmental disorders. Also in that group is the disorder known as Asperger syndrome.

◆ The majority of people with autism function intellectually as though they have an intellectual disability. Some have the savant syndrome.

◆ Autism is caused by abnormalities in brain development, neurochemistry, and genetic factors, but the specific biological trigger is unknown at this time.

◆ Conflicting data on the prevalence of autism suggests a range from 10 to 60 per 10,000 children.

Evaluating Students with Autism

◆ The Autism Diagnostic Interview—Revised is an assessment tool that frequently is used to determine whether children have autism.

◆ A functional behavioral assessment identifies specific relationships between environmental events and a student's problem behavior. It is used to tailor an intervention plan aimed at helping students to function as successfully as possible.

Designing an Appropriate IEP

◆ Planning to implement positive behavior support requires a team effort, with particular emphasis on creating an effective partnership among families, general and special educators, administrators, and behavior specialists.

◆ Implementing positive behavior support involves ensuring that issues pertaining to behavioral accessibility are addressed, including building and classroom ecological supplementary aids and supports that promote positive behavior.

◆ Mnemonic strategies are effective curriculum adaptations and augmentations that enable students with autism to succeed in the general curriculum.

Using Effective Instructional Strategies

◆ Social stories are effective ways to teach young children with autism a number of skills, particularly social interaction skills.

◆ Positive behavior support, including schoolwide, group, and individual strategies, has been shown to decrease problem behavior and improve opportunities for learning.

◆ Discrete trial teaching is one strategy derived from applied behavior analysis; it applies learning principles from operant psychology to provide an effective way of teaching skills to students with autism.

Including Students with Autism

◆ Relative to other students with disabilities, students with autism have one of the lowest rates of inclusion in general education classes.

Assessing Students' Progress

◆ Some systems and assessment packages, such as the Autism Screening Instrument for Educational Planning, provide teachers with organized ways to collect data on student progress, including progress in the general curriculum, across multiple domains.

◆ There are multiple means for collecting data on progress as a function of the implementation of positive behavior supports, most of which focus on collecting data on school referrals, types of problem behavior, and changes in absenteeism or tardiness.

◆ For students with autism, having a familiar person administer standardized tests may reduce test and schedule anxiety and improve their performance.

12

Understanding Students with Physical Disabilities and Other Health Impairments

◆ WHO IS RYAN FRISELLA?

Let's describe an all-American middle school student, shall we? Let's do it by referring to Ryan Frisella, an eighth grader at Pershing Middle School in San Diego, California, enrolled in the gifted and talented education program. With the help of sponsors whom he solicits for funds on behalf of his wheelchair sports team, he participates annually in a half-marathon by riding his hand-cycle, a three-wheeled bike that he propels with his hands instead of his feet. He also is on the junior varsity soccer team sponsored by San Diego's parks and recreation program for individuals with disabilities and travels to interstate competitions. He has endeared himself to his classmates and teachers. According to his mother, Mary, he's bright, witty, caring, and concerned about other students. According to his drama teacher, Terry Miller, he's got the courage of his convictions and a not-to-be-daunted work ethic. He has no fear of standing up for what he believes in: He has advocated for drama education by addressing the San Diego Unified City School District Board of Education. He acts, sings, and dances on stage. Terry says he is "an inspirational person because he is so commanding, in a soft way. His strong will gives him the power of presence."

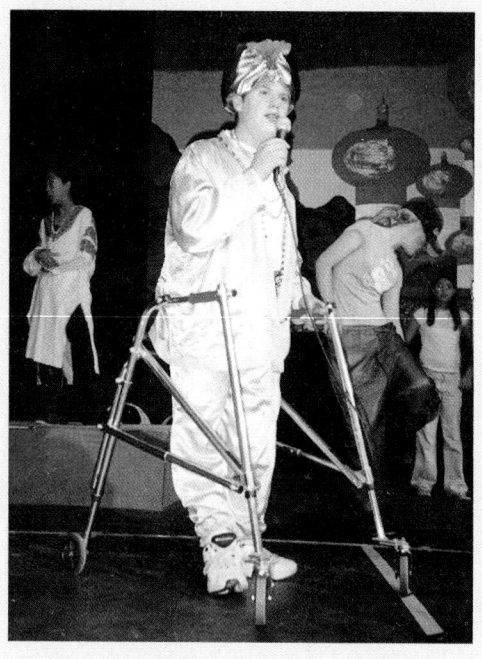

Do you have a good picture of Ryan? Now add this dimension: He has cerebral palsy; uses crutches, a walker, and a wheelchair; and has had two major surgeries on his legs and feet. When he was advocating before the school board, he hoisted himself out of his wheelchair, grasped a podium designed for standing-up adults, pulled himself to a standing position, and spoke his mind. His most recent surgery, in March 2005, did not prevent him from taking center stage in June as the sultan in his school's production of *Aladdin*. Nor does his disability keep him from dancing if that is what his role calls for, as it did in *The King and I*. He simply balances on his walker, fixes himself into place, and dances with his hands, his feet (holding fast to his walker), and, in Terry's words, "his whole being."

Dancing and taking a leading role, says Terry, is the extra dimension that theater—indeed, all of education—allows: the opportunity to innovate, to make drama or any form of education believable even though the actor or student has an obvious disability.

So Ryan follows his muse, the muse of the theater. Asked why, he says simply, "I like being on stage and pretending that I'm someone else." Not that he needs to pretend: In spite of the added dimension of his cerebral palsy, Ryan already is the all-American kid.

Why? Terry does not hesitate to answer: Mary, John, and his sister Nicole (a fifth grader) have always expected something unusual from Ryan, so Ryan expects that from himself and teaches his teachers to do likewise. The circle of great expectations began at home, but it has not been confined to that one site.

◆ WHO IS KWASHON DRAYTON?

Since the completion of the mapping of the human genome, it has become fashionable to believe that genes are destiny. In one sense, that is true of Kwashon Drayton, a 9-year-old fourth grader at Meadowfield Elementary School in Columbia, South Carolina. Like his great-grandmother, grandmother, and mother, Kwashon has asthma.

But the genes-as-destiny statement does not acknowledge the beneficial effects of medication for asthma. If it did, perhaps the saying would go something like "Genes are destiny, but medication mitigates them and changes a person's destiny." That's not quite as catchy a phrase, but it is far more accurate for Kwashon. The four medicines he takes daily to treat his asthma make it possible for him to participate fully in all of his school's activities except one, track, which takes a greater lung capacity than the basketball he now enjoys and the football that he plans to start in the fall of his fifth-grade year. And the one medicine he takes to counteract the effects of asthma attacks makes it possible for him to recover quickly, after lying down for a while, and return to his normal activities in the general academic curriculum, extracurricular activities, and other school activities.

CHAPTER OBJECTIVES

◆ You will learn about two types of physical disabilities, cerebral palsy and spina bifida, both of which cause mobility limitations. You also will learn about two types of other health impairments, epilepsy and asthma, both of which cause limitations in a student's strength, vitality, or alertness.

◆ You will learn that physical and neurological evaluations are useful to determine whether a student has a disability and, if so, how to design special education around the student's health conditions. You also will learn about an educational evaluation, the School Function Assessment, that complements the medical evaluations.

◆ You will learn that students' IEPs should refer to the students' comprehensive health plans, take into account assistive technologies (such as "switches") and electronic or digital text formats, and provide for adapted physical education for these students.

◆ You will learn about effective instructional strategies such as token economies, self-awareness instruction, and driver's education.

◆ You will learn that it is desirable to assess students' progress by using computer-based and curriculum-based measurements and mastery learning assessments, and that students often need accommodations such as extra time, a scribe, or computer administration of their assessment tests.

There is very little his mother, Michelle, and father, Vic, or his teachers have to do for him, but that "very little" makes a huge difference:

- Keep him away from peanuts and pets.
- Be sure he dusts his desk and around his home daily.
- Buy an expensive vacuum cleaner, one that has a filter on it, and use it every day.
- Keep the windows shut and, in the summer, the air conditioning on to filter out as much dust, pollen, and grass as possible.
- Encase his mattress and pillows so that their contents do not irritate his lungs.
- Above all, make sure that he takes his medicines daily and that he and his allergy specialist, school nurse, and parents communicate regularly about his health, usually by cell phone.

It's not asthma itself that requires Kwashon to have an IEP. Instead, it's the fact that he has some speech delays that result from his being born prematurely and from having contracted viral meningitis when he was only 3 months old. Two early surgeries partially corrected his hearing and speech: the insertion of tubes into his ears and the removal of his adenoids. But he has needed therapy ever since, though it is likely that he'll phase out of that next year in fifth grade.

So Kwashon has a health care plan for his asthma (under Section 504 of the Rehabilitation Act), an IEP for his speech challenges, nothing except kudos for being an honor roll student, and an insatiable case of "superfanitis" for the Miami Heat professional basketball team and the Atlanta Falcons professional football team. As his mother, Michelle, puts it, "He's all boy." So, too, are his younger brothers, Isiah, now 8 years old, and Joshua, now 1 year old. Yet they have defied the genes-as-destiny maxim: Neither has asthma or any other challenges.

When asked to compare her years in elementary, middle, and secondary school (before she graduated with her bachelor's degree from the University of South Carolina in 1995) with Kwashon's first 4 years in school, Michelle answered simply, "There's much more awareness and education now than before. And there are prescription medicines, not just the over-the-counter ones I used to use." Yes, genes are destiny, but they are not, by any means, a person's entire destiny.

IDENTIFYING STUDENTS WITH PHYSICAL DISABILITIES AND OTHER HEALTH IMPAIRMENTS

Unlike previous and subsequent chapters, this one discusses two categories of exceptionality: physical disabilities and other health impairments. We begin, as in the other chapters, by providing an overview of these categories. Because there are common educational issues involving students with physical disabilities and other health impairments, we address these issues in common throughout the chapter.

After reading this chapter, complete the Self-Assessment for Chapter 12 on MyEducationLab to gauge your initial understanding of chapter content.

PHYSICAL DISABILITIES

Defining Physical Disabilities

The regulations implementing IDEA refer to physical disabilities, such as Ryan's cerebral palsy, as orthopedic impairments and define the term as follows:

> "Orthopedic impairment" means a severe orthopedic impairment that adversely affects a child's educational performance. The term includes impairments caused by congenital anomaly, impairments caused by disease (e.g., poliomyelitis, bone tuberculosis, etc.), and impairments from other causes (e.g., cerebral palsy, amputations, and fractures or burns that cause contractures).

Although IDEA uses the term *orthopedic impairments,* educators typically use the term *physical disabilities* when referring to these same conditions. So there are two terms in use, the IDEA term and the educators' term. But special educators also sometimes refer to students with severe and multiple disabilities (see Chapter 10) or traumatic brain injury (see Chapter 13) as having physical disabilities. All of this different usage means that there is also an aggregate usage: the term *physical disabilities* typically refers to a large group of students who experience conditions that are quite different from each other, even though they may have the same condition. You may recall that Thomas Ellenson, from Chapter 1, also has cerebral palsy. Like Ryan, he has mobility challenges; unlike Ryan, however, he also has communication challenges. We focus in this chapter on cerebral palsy and spina bifida.

Because physical disabilities often occur in combination with other disabilities, it is hard to determine their prevalence. Nevertheless, data are available. In fall 2006, approximately 0.01 percent (61,329) of all students aged 6 through 21 in special education nationally were classified as having an orthopedic impairment (U.S. Department of Education, 2008).

Cerebral Palsy: Describing the Characteristics and Determining the Causes

What Is Cerebral Palsy?

Cerebral refers to the brain. *Palsy* describes the lack of muscle control that affects a student's ability to move and to maintain balance and posture. That is why Ryan uses crutches, a walker, and (like Thomas Ellenson) a wheelchair, choosing the assistance he needs according to the particular challenges of his environment or activities. **Cerebral palsy,** then, is a disorder of movement or posture. It occurs because a person's brain cannot control his or her muscles. The impairment occurs in the brain's development (usually by 6 years of age), and the brain damage is nonprogressive (Pellegrino, 2007). Cerebral palsy is a lifetime condition; but it is not a disease, so it is inappropriate to consider children and youth with cerebral palsy to be sick. The prevalence of cerebral palsy is 2 individuals with cerebral palsy per 1,000 individuals in the population, which represents a modest increase in prevalence over the last three decades (Winter, Autry, Boyle, & Yeargin-Allsopp, 2002).

There are multiple types of cerebral palsy; each refers to a person's specific movement patterns (Pellegrino, 2007):

- **Spastic** is characterized by tightness in one or more muscle groups and affects 70 percent to 80 percent of individuals with cerebral palsy. Ryan has this type.
- **Dyskinetic** involves impairments in muscle tone affecting the whole body and changing throughout the day and week.
- **Athetoid** involves abrupt, involuntary movements of the head, neck, face, and extremities, particularly the upper ones.
- **Ataxic** involves unsteadiness, lack of coordination and balance, and varying degrees of difficulty with standing and walking.
- **Mixed** combines two or more movement patterns when one type does not predominate over another.

Figure 12.1 ▷ Topographical classification system

Monoplegia: one limb
Paraplegia: legs only
Hemiplegia: one half of body
Triplegia: three limbs (usually two legs and one arm)
Quadriplegia: all four limbs
Diplegia: more affected in the legs than the arms
Double hemiplegia: arms more involved than the legs

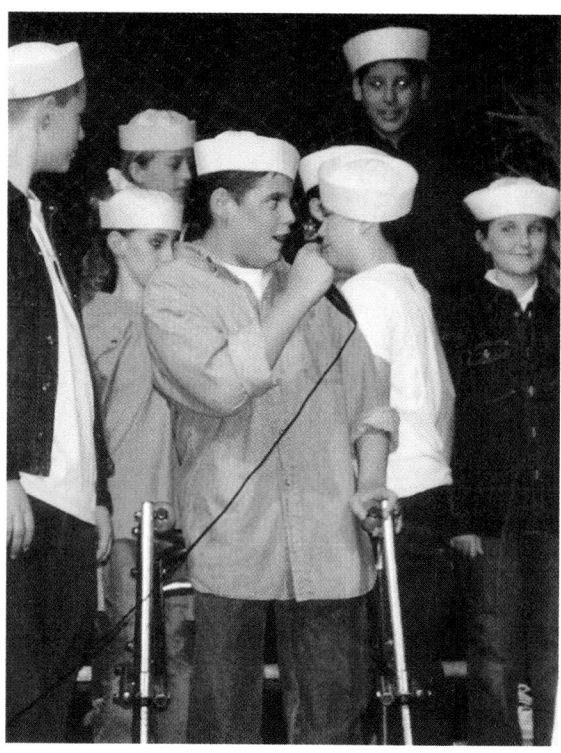

Despite his cerebral palsy, Ryan Frisella is a song-and-dance man. Students with disabilities can participate in general extracurricular activities with appropriate supports.

In addition to characterizing cerebral palsy by the nature of a person's movement, professionals also refer to the part of the person's body that is affected. In this **topographical classification system,** the specific body location of the movement impairment correlates with the location of the brain damage. Figure 12.1 describes the topographical classification system.

What Other Conditions Are Associated with Cerebral Palsy?

Many health and developmental problems may accompany cerebral palsy. Fifty percent to about 65 percent of people with cerebral palsy also have an intellectual disability (Pellegrino, 2007). It is important to remember, however, that some individuals with cerebral palsy, such as Ryan Frisella and Thomas Ellenson (Chapter 1), are intellectually quite capable.

Other conditions that are more common with children and youth with cerebral palsy include vision impairments, hearing/speech/language impairments, and seizures. In a study of adolescents and young adults with cerebral palsy who did not have significant learning problems, approximately 20 percent to 30 percent of the participants experienced restrictions in daily activities (for example, mobility and self-care) and social participation (for example, leisure activities and taking responsibility). Approximately one fourth of adolescents and adults with cerebral palsy experienced below-age-level functioning in daily activities and social participation (Donkervoort et al., 2007).

What Are the Causes of Cerebral Palsy?

Cerebral palsy is caused by **prenatal** (e.g., infection or brain malformation before birth), **perinatal** (e.g., lack of oxygen or infection during birth), or **postnatal** (e.g., brain injury or meningitis after birth) factors (Miller et al., 2006). The vast majority of children and youth with cerebral palsy have causes related to prenatal development and prematurity (Croen, Grether, Curry, & Nelson, 2001). That's the cause of Ryan's disability. He was born at $33\frac{1}{2}$ weeks, weighed 4 pounds, 5 ounces, and was on a respirator for his first 24 hours of life. Not until his mother, Mary, mentioned to his physicians when Ryan was 9 months old that his legs seemed stiff was he diagnosed as having cerebral palsy.

Spina Bifida: Describing the Characteristics and Determining the Causes

What Is Spina Bifida?

Spina bifida refers to a malformation of the spinal cord (Liptak, 2007). The spine is made up of separate bones called vertebrae, which normally cover and protect the

Figure 12.2 Types of spina bifida

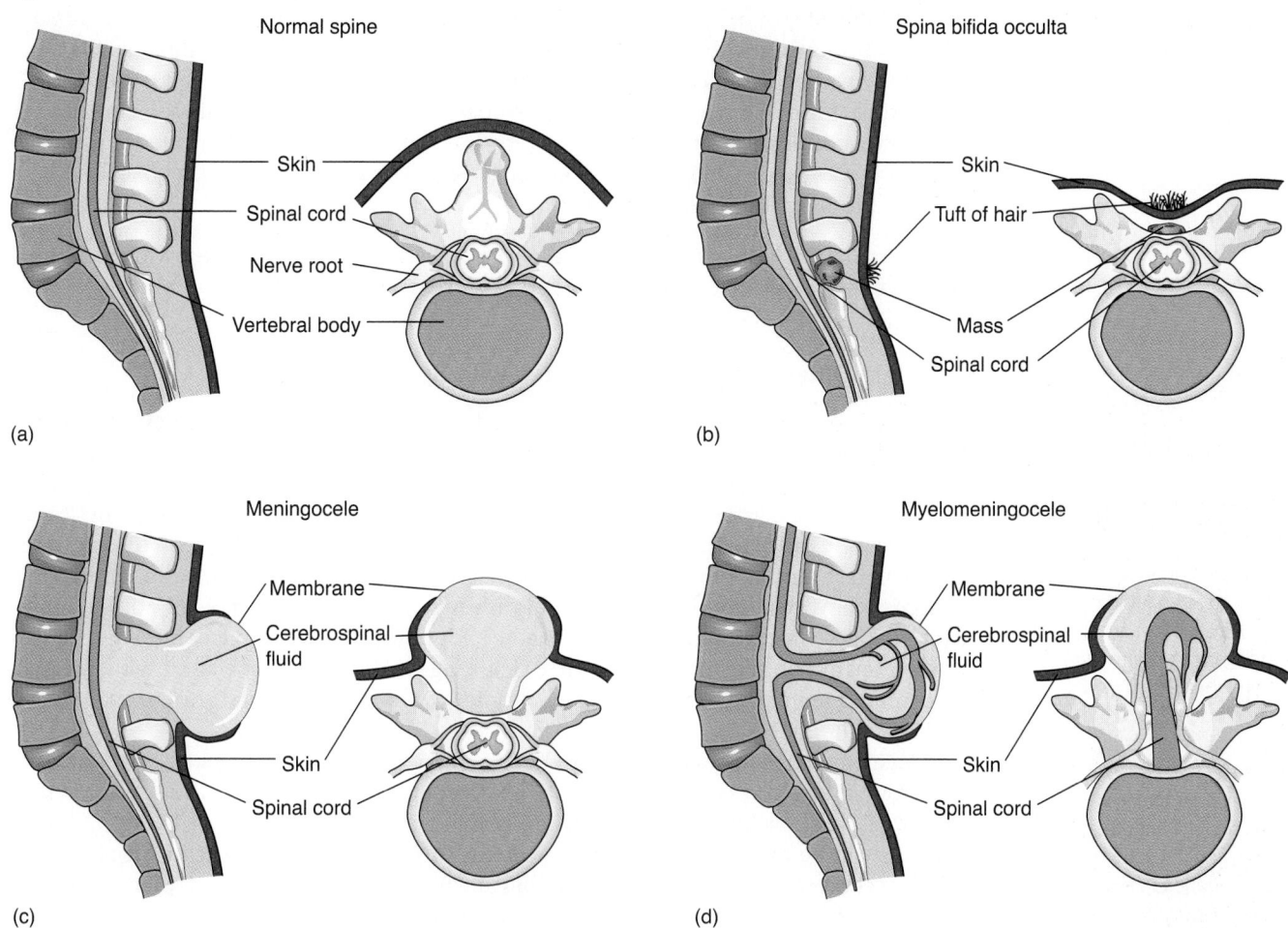

Source: From Umbreit, John. *Physical Disabilities and Health Impairments: An Introduction,* 1e. Published by Allyn and Bacon, Boston, MA. Copyright © 1983 by Pearson Education. Reprinted by permission of the publisher.

spinal cord. In a person with spina bifida, the spinal column does not close completely and cover the spinal cord, usually resulting in a protrusion of the spinal cord, its coverings, or both. A saclike bulge may occur in any part of the person's spine, from neck to buttocks. The higher on the spinal column the impairment appears, the more severe the person's loss of function. Typically, the impairment occurs in the lower region and causes loss of skin sensation and complete or partial paralysis of only the person's lower extremities. The prevalence of spina bifida is one individual out of 1,000 individuals, and this rate has been declining over the last several decades (Medway, 2006). Later in the chapter you will learn that one of the major contributors to this decrease in prevalence is attributable to daily vitamin supplements containing folic acid. Spina bifida is not a progressive condition and has three common forms (see Figure 12.2) (Liptak, 2007; Medway, 2006):

◆ **Spina bifida occulta.** An opening occurs in one or more bones of the spinal column, but there is no damage to the spinal cord. This is the mildest and most common form.

◆ **Meningocele.** The covering of the spinal cord, but not the cord itself, protrudes through the opening created by the defect in the spine. This more serious form can be repaired through surgery and usually does not cause a person to experience mobility impairments.

- ◆ **Myelomeningocele.** The protrusion or sac contains not only the spinal cord's covering but also a portion of the spinal cord or nerve roots. This is the most serious form and results in varying degrees of leg weakness, inability to control bowels or bladder, and a variety of physical problems such as dislocated hips or club feet (Shaer, Chescheir, & Schulkin, 2007). The term *spina bifida* typically is used to refer to myelomeningocele.

Spina bifida belongs to a larger group of malformations associated with the spinal cord, brain, and vertebra that are referred to as **neural tube defects.**

What Are Other Conditions Associated with Spina Bifida?

The extent of mobility and sensory loss in children and youth with myelomeningocele depends upon the location of the spinal impairment (Liptak, 2007). In a study of approximately 350 adolescents and young adults with myelomeningocele, 57 percent used wheelchairs, approximately one third used braces, and approximately one fourth used walking aids (Johnson, Dudgeon, Kuehn, & Walker, 2007). More extensive muscle weakness and mobility impairment occurs when the level of the myelomeningocele is higher; however, children and youth with myelomeningocele typically have significant mobility impairments. Approximately 75 percent have typical intelligence, although many of these students have learning challenges associated with abstract reasoning, memory, and executive functioning (Johnson, Dudgeon, Kuehn, & Walker, 2007; Liptak, 2007).

Myelomeningocele almost always occurs above the part of the spinal cord that controls the bladder and bowels (Liptak, 2007). Constipation, bladder paralysis, urinary tract infections, and resulting incontinence are common. Kidney failure can also result. Many students can be taught the technique of **clean intermittent catheterization** and effective bowel management (Best, Heller, & Bigge, 2005). Working with a school nurse trained in these techniques, teachers can monitor students' self-management abilities.

What Causes Spina Bifida?

Spina bifida occurs within 26 days of the human egg's fertilization (Copp, Fleming, & Greene, 1998). Environmental and genetic factors interact to lead to the spinal malformations associated with spina bifida (Kibar, Capra, & Gros, 2007; Shaer et al., 2007). Environmental contributors include maternal exposure to valproic acid, acne medication (Accutane), and hyperthermia (excessive use of saunas); maternal diabetes; and obesity (Hernández-Dìaz, Werler, Walker, & Mitchell, 2001; Liptak, 2007).

A woman who uses daily vitamin supplements containing folic acid reduces the risk that her baby will have spina bifida. Folic acid is a B vitamin that enables bodies to build healthy cells. Beginning in 1998, the federal Food and Drug Administration has required breads and enriched cereal grain products to be fortified with synthetic folic acid. Research in Canada evaluated rates of neural tube defects before and after folic acid fortification (De Wals, Tairou, Van Allen, & Uh, 2007). This study found a 46 percent reduction in the prevalence of neural tube defects after a large variety of cereal products had full fortification of folic acid.

OTHER HEALTH IMPAIRMENTS

Defining Other Health Impairments

The regulations implementing IDEA define students with other health impairments as those "having limited strength, vitality or alertness, including a heightened alertness to

IEP Tip

Students often can learn how to attend to their physical needs, such as by using clean intermittent catheterization (using a tube inserted into the urethra for urination), so the IEP team should provide for that kind of instruction, both to promote the students' dignity and to prepare them for a life of relatively independent living.

environmental stimuli, that results in limited alertness with respect to the educational environment, that:

1. is due to chronic or acute health problems such as asthma, attention deficit disorder or attention deficit hyperactivity disorder, diabetes, epilepsy, a heart condition, hemophilia, lead poisoning, leukemia, nephritis, rheumatic fever, and sickle cell anemia; and

2. adversely affects a child's educational performance."

The word *other* in the categorical name *other health impairments* distinguishes these from conditions such as multiple disabilities (Chapter 10), physical disabilities (this chapter), and traumatic brain injury (Chapter 13). To be served under the "other health impairments" category, the student's health condition must limit his strength, vitality, or alertness to such a degree that the student's educational progress is adversely affected. Kwashon Drayton does not qualify under IDEA; his educational progress is just fine, as evidenced by his receiving academic honors. But because his asthma requires accommodations in school (such as screening his food so he will not eat any peanuts or derivatives of them, authorizing his school nurse to administer medication in an emergency, and training his teachers to perform CPR), he qualifies under Section 504 of the Rehabilitation Act (which you learned about in Chapter 8).

As you also learned in Chapter 8, AD/HD falls into the category of other health impairments. In terms of the three criteria of limitations in strength, vitality, or alertness, students with AD/HD, including Kelsey, whom you met in Chapter 8, generally experience difficulty only with alertness.

Under the current IDEA definition, a student may have a chronic or an acute condition. A chronic condition develops slowly and has long-lasting symptoms. Students with diabetes, one chronic condition, experience lifelong medical needs. An acute condition typically develops quickly and has symptoms that last for a relatively short period of time. Students with pneumonia may need temporary homebound services; however, once they recover from this acute condition, they no longer are eligible for special education services.

In fall 2006, approximately 0.099 percent (595,073) of all students aged 6 through 21 in special education nationally were classified as having other health impairments (U.S. Department of Education, 2008). Ten percent to 30 percent of all students will experience a childhood chronic illness lasting 3 months or longer (Kliebenstein & Broome, 2000). More than 200 specific health impairments exist, and most are rare (Thies, 1999). For that reason, we focus on two relatively prevalent conditions: epilepsy and asthma.

Epilepsy: Describing the Characteristics and Determining the Causes

What Is Epilepsy?

Epilepsy is a condition characterized by **seizures,** which are temporary neurological abnormalities that result from unregulated electrical discharges in the brain, much like an electrical storm. If a person has seizures only once or temporarily, perhaps from a high fever or brain injury, he does not have epilepsy. To be classified as having epilepsy, an individual must have at least two seizures that are unprovoked on separate days and these must occur at least 24 hours apart (Berg, 2006). By 20 years of age, approximately 1 percent of the general population can be expected to develop epilepsy (Epilepsy Foundation, 2007). This figure increases to 3 percent of the population by 75 years of age. The prevalence is higher in racially diverse populations, especially for individuals with low income.

There are two types of seizures: partial seizures and generalized seizures (Barrett & Sachs, 2006). **Partial seizures** begin in one site of the cerebral hemisphere and typically involve only one motor or sensory system. Simple partial seizures typically involve motor symptoms such as uncontrollable bending and flailing. Complex partial seizures involve an alteration of consciousness involving mood, memory, typical behavior patterns, and/or personality traits. Children and youth with complex partial seizures are also more likely to have stereotypic, repetitive movements such as pursing or smacking their lips or moving in a repetitive way such as marching.

The second type of seizure is primary generalized seizures. As contrasted to partial seizures, primary generalized seizures involve both cerebral hemispheres. An alteration of consciousness is a primary characteristic, and the seizure affects both sides of the body (partial seizures typically affect only one side of the body, although they can affect the entire body as well). Primary generalized seizures can be further classified into tonic-clonic seizures and absence seizures Figure 12.3 describes first aid procedures for people having seizures.

Tonic-clonic seizures (once known as *grand mal*) cause the student to lose consciousness and go back and forth through rigid extensions of extremities (tonic phase) and rhythmic contractions of extremities (clonic phase) (Fisch & Olejniczak, 2006). Students may make unusual noises during tonic-clonic seizures, have a bluish hue,

Figure 12.3

First aid for seizures

Seizure Type	Characteristics	First Aid	Possibility of Injury
General seizures			
Tonic-clonic	Uncontrolled jerking Loss of consciousness Disorientation Violent reactions Cessation of breathing Vomiting Loss of continence	Lay the person on side. Move potentially dangerous or fragile objects. Place pillow under her head. Never attempt to restrain her or place anything in her mouth.	Fairly high; person often bumps into objects during seizure.
Tonic	Sudden stiffening of muscles Rigidity Falling to ground	Reassure the individual. Provide a place to lie down afterward. Stay calm.	Quite high; person may strike an object while falling
Atonic	Sudden loss of muscle tone resulting in a collapse on ground	Reassure the individual. Provide a place to rest.	High; person may fall into an object.
Absence	Very brief interruption in consciousness Appearance of momentary deja-vu	Reassure the individual following the event.	Fairly low
Partial seizures			
Simple partial	Twitching movements Sensation of deja-vu	Reassure the student.	Fairly low
Complex partial	Altered state of consciousness Psychomotor movements	Provide verbal reassurance during occurence.	Fairly low unless there is increased physical activity.

Seek medical attention immediately if . . .

- There is no previous history of seizures, especially if the student is experiencing a tonic-clonic seizure.
- Several tonic-clonic seizures follow one another in rapid succession.
- A tonic-clonic seizure lasts for more than 2 to 3 minutes.

Source: INTERVENTION IN SCHOOL AND CLINIC by Spiegel, G. L., Cutler, S. K., & Yetter, C. E. Copyright 1996 by Sage Publications Inc. Journals. Reproduced with permission of Sage Publications Inc. Journals in the formats Textbook and Other book via Copyright Clearance Center.

lose bladder control, require sleep or rest after the seizure, and typically have no memory of the seizure.

During **absence seizures** (formerly known as *petit mal*), the student also loses consciousness but only for a brief period lasting about 10 seconds (Benbadis & Berkovic, 2006). Frequently students also have motor movements such as blinking their eyes or changing the position of their head. The student, teachers, and peers might not realize a seizure has taken place. Absence seizures can occur up to hundreds of times a day and can severely affect learning.

What Other Conditions Are Associated with Epilepsy?

Students with epilepsy have lower intelligence and academic achievement than students without epilepsy (Taras & Potts-Datema, 2005b). Because the students experience absence seizures, they have difficulty paying attention to their teachers and their academic performance drops. Additionally, medication side effects can adversely affect their attention, energy, and other important school-related behaviors. Approximately 20 percent to 30 percent of students with epilepsy also have challenges related to emotional and behavioral considerations (Barrett & Sachs, 2006). Indeed, adolescents with epilepsy have a higher-than-average prevalence of depression than do adolescents without epilepsy (Dunn, Austin, & Huster, 1999). Youth who have negative attitudes about their epilepsy and who experience dissatisfaction with family relationships are more likely to experience depression.

What Are the Causes of Epilepsy?

Epilepsy is caused by a combination of genetic and environmental factors (Weinstein & Gaillard, 2007). Approximately 40 percent of individuals with epilepsy have a genetic contribution (Gardiner, 2000). Environmental causes include prenatal brain infections, birth trauma, poisoning, stress, fatigue, and sleep deprivation. In approximately three fourths of individuals with epilepsy, the precise cause of the brain insult that triggered the epilepsy is unknown (DePaepe, Garrison-Kane, & Doelling, 2002).

Asthma: Describing the Characteristics and Determining the Causes

What Is Asthma?

Asthma is a chronic lung condition characterized by airway obstruction, inflammation, and hyperirritability of the bronchial tubes (Adams, 2007). You probably have heard about asthma attacks, but you may never have been in the presence of someone who is experiencing an attack. Usually, asthma attacks are characterized by a shortness of breath with signs of struggles such as heaving of the chest and using neck muscles to breathe (Adams, 2007). Wheezing and coughing are often present, and individuals struggle so hard to breathe that they may not be able to talk or respond to questions. The symptoms and severity of asthma vary widely from person to person and are generally classified in the following ways (National Heart, Lung, and Blood Institute, 1997):

Kwashon Drayton is fully included in his school's academic program and earns academic honors.

◆ Mild intermittent (two or fewer episodes per week)

◆ Mild persistent (more than two per week)

Figure 12.4	▶ When to seek emergency care for asthma

- Symptoms worsen, even after the medication has had time to work (generally 5 to 10 minutes).
- The student cannot speak a sentence without pausing for breath, has difficulty walking, and/or stops playing and cannot start again.
- Chest and neck are pulled or sucked in with each breath.
- Peak flow rate lessens or does not improve after bronchodilator treatment or drops below 50 percent of the student's personal best.
- Lips and fingernails turn blue: emergency care is needed immediately!
- A second wave occurs after an episode subsides; the student is uncomfortable and having trouble breathing but does not wheeze.

◆ Moderate persistent (daily)

◆ Severe persistent (continual and interferes with physical activity, such as Kwashon's running track)

Asthma is the most common chronic disease among children in the United States. Approximately 7 percent to 10 percent of the general childhood population has a diagnosis of asthma (Bellenir, 2006). Approximately one half of children with asthma outgrow this condition as they reach their teenage years. The risk of asthma increases among students from diverse backgrounds. A study of the prevalence of asthma in children attending Head Start reported that the prevalence rate was two to five times higher than the rate that occurs in the general population of children (Ladebauche et al., 2001; Slezak, Persky, Kviz, Ramakrishnan, & Byars, 1998; Walders, McQuaid, & Dickstein, 2004). Researchers attribute this high level of asthma to the high-risk factors in low-income communities and, as in Kwashon's case, to genetic factors. If one of your students has an asthma attack, you may be reassured to know there are first aid and emergency aid measures you should take, as described in Figures 12.3 and 12.4.

IEP Tip

The IEP team of a student who has asthma should provide for supports and accommodations so the student can do homework assignments or learn the material missed when absent from school.

What Other Conditions Are Associated with Asthma?

Children and youth who have asthma often experience fatigue from waking during the night because of breathing difficulties, and they are frequently absent from school due to symptoms. A review of 66 research studies examining students with asthma concluded that, although students with asthma have a high rate of absenteeism, there are no measurable differences in their academic achievement when compared to that of students who do not have asthma (Taras & Potts-Datema, 2005a). Not surprisingly, students with asthma who adhered to a prescribed medical treatment plan had less school absenteeism. Equally unsurprisingly, students with asthma who experience lower achievement tended to have more severe and persistent symptoms and to have more sleep interruptions.

A study of children in urban environments found that 34 percent of children enrolled in special education experienced asthma as contrasted to 19 percent of children in general education (Stingone & Claudio, 2006). Children with asthma who received special education were significantly more likely to have been hospitalized in the previous 12 months and to be from families who had low income. It was found that asthma management devices were often not used by children in urban schools whose families had low incomes. In general, even though some students with asthma experience problems with their academic performance, it is important to remember that other students, such as Kwashon, earn academic honors.

Michelle and Kwashon Drayton are the poster-family for asthma prevention and treatment efforts in South Carolina.

What Are the Causes of Asthma?

Individuals with asthma have airways that are especially sensitive. Triggers of asthma attacks can include cigarette smoke, changes in air temperature, strong smells, air pollution, strong emotions, and medications (Bellenir, 2006). Kwashon's mother Michelle operates a program in Columbia, South Carolina, serving 77 families by educating them about the triggers that bring on asthma symptoms and the countermeasures that families should take to control dust, pollen, mold, and mites. In addition to environmental causes, approximately 10 genes have been found to have a significant impact on susceptibility to asthma (Adams, 2007).

EVALUATING STUDENTS WITH PHYSICAL DISABILITIES AND OTHER HEALTH IMPAIRMENTS

Determining the Presence of Physical Disabilities and Other Health Impairments

Figures 12.5 and 12.6 highlight the nondiscriminatory evaluation processes for determining the presence of physical disabilities and other health impairments, respectively. In both cases, a physical examination from a physician is often the first step in determining whether or not the student has a disability. Although medical exams are individualized according to the particular symptoms of each student, a neurological exam is frequently administered when there is any concern about the brain's involvement in a particular condition. **Neuroimaging** provides detailed pictures of various parts of the brain that are helpful in determining the presence of a disability. Neuroimaging is exceedingly helpful in determining the presence of cerebral palsy, spina bifida, and epilepsy (Pellegrino, 2007; Weinstein & Gaillard, 2007). Neuroimaging is not needed, however, for students who have symptoms associated only with asthma.

Prenatal screening is now used to detect spina bifida, and in the future it is likely to be used to detect many other conditions. The most frequently used prenatal test to detect spina bifida is **maternal serum alpha-fetoprotein** (Liptak, 2007). Alpha-fetoprotein is made by babies during their prenatal development. When a baby has spina bifida, its alpha-fetoprotein leaks from the open spine into the amniotic fluid and, in turn, into the mother's circulation. If a blood test of the mother at 16 weeks' gestation reveals a higher-than-normal level of alpha-fetoprotein, further testing can confirm or disconfirm the presence of spina bifida.

One way to prevent serious loss of neurological functioning due to spina bifida is to perform fetal surgery. Only a few medical centers have the capability to perform such surgery. Currently, the surgery does not restore neurological functioning that has already been lost but is designed to prevent further malformation before delivery. During the surgery, the neurosurgeon exposes the fetus, closes the lesions on the baby's back, and then closes the incision in the mother.

Although fetal surgery has many benefits, it also has risks. The risk for the fetus includes the greater likelihood of a premature delivery. The risk for the mother can include infection, gestational diabetes, and blood loss.

Determining the Nature of Specially Designed Instruction and Services

Physical therapists and occupational therapists test a student's functional competence. A test of functional competence developed by an educational therapist especially for elementary students with disabilities is the School Function Assessment (Coster, Mancini, & Ludlow, 1999). It has three parts:

◆ "Participation" evaluates students' level of participation in school activities and environments.

◆ "Task Supports" evaluates the extent to which students need supplementary aids and services to participate in school activities and environments.

◆ "Activity Performance" evaluates students' ability to complete functional activities requiring cognitive and physical skills.

Figure 12.5

Nondiscriminatory evaluation process for determining the presence of physical disabilities

Observation	***Parents or teacher observe:*** The student has difficulty with moving in an organized and efficient way; with fine-motor activities; with gross-motor activities; with activities of daily living, such as dressing; with postural control; and with speaking.
	Physician observes: The child is not passing developmental milestones. Movement is better on one side of the body than the other. Muscle tone is too floppy or stiff. The child has problems with balance or coordination or has neurological signs that suggest a physical disability.
Screening	***Assessment measures:***
	Developmental assessment: The child is not meeting developmental milestones or shows poor quality of movement on measures administered by a physician, physical therapist, occupational therapist, and psychologist.
	Functional assessment: Activities of daily living are affected.
Prereferral	Prereferral is typically not used with these students because of the need to quickly identify physical disabilities. Also, most children with physical disabilities will be identified by a physician before starting school.
Referral	Students with physical disabilities who are identified before starting school should receive early intervention services and a nondiscriminatory evaluation upon entering school. Because some physical disabilities may develop after a student enters school, teachers should refer any student who seems to have significant difficulty with motor-related activities.
Nondiscriminatory evaluation procedures and standards	***Assessment measures:***
	Individualized intelligence test: Standard administration guidelines may need to be adapted because the student's physical disability interferes with the ability to perform some tasks. Results may not be an accurate reflection of ability. The student may be average, above average, or below average in intelligence.
	Individualized achievement test: The student may be average, above average, or below average in specific areas of achievement. Standard administration guidelines may need to be adapted to accommodate student's response style. Results may not accurately reflect achievement.
	Motor functioning tests: The student's differences in range of motion, motor patterns, gaits, and postures may present learning problems. Also, length and circumference of limbs and degrees of muscle tone or muscle strength may affect his or her ability to learn specific skills.
	Tests of perceptual functioning: The student is unable or has difficulty in integrating visual/auditory input and motor output in skills such as cutting and carrying out verbal instructions in an organized manner.
	Adaptive behavior scales: The student may have difficulty in self-care, household, community, and communication skills because of the physical disability.
	Anecdotal records: Reports suggest that the student has functional deficits and requires extra time or assistance in mobility, self-care, household, community, and communication skills because of the physical disability.
	Curriculum-based assessment: The student's physical disability may limit accuracy of curriculum-based assessments.
	Direct observation: The student is unable to organize and complete work or has difficulty doing so.
Determination	The nondiscriminatory evaluation team determines that the student has a physical disability and needs special education and related services.

Figure 12.6

Nondiscriminatory evaluation process for determining the presence of other health impairments

Observation	***Parents or teacher observe:*** The student may seem sluggish or have other symptoms that suggest illness. The parent takes the student for a medical examination.
	Physician observes: During a routine physical or a physical resulting from symptoms, the physician determines why the student needs further medical assessment. Some health impairments are detemined before or shortly after birth.
Screening	***Assessment measures:***
	Battery of medical tests prescribed by physician and/or specialists: Results reveal that the student has a health impairment. A physician makes the diagnosis.
Prereferral	Prereferral may or may not be indicated, depending on the severity of the health impairment. Some students function well in the general classroom. A decision may be made to serve the student with a 504 plan if accommodations are needed solely to monitor medications and/or to make sure the faculty knows what to do if the student has a medical emergency.
Referral	Students with health impairments that adversely affect their learning or behavior need to be referred for educational assessment.
Nondiscriminatory evaluation procedures and standards	***Assessment measures:***
	Medical history: Completed jointly by parents and medical and school personnel, the history yields information needed to develop a health care plan.
	Individualized intelligence test: The student's condition or treatment may contribute to a decrease in IQ.
	Individualized achievement test: The student's medical condition and/or treatment regimen may affect achievement.
	Behavior rating scales: The student is not mastering the curriculum in one or more areas as a result of the condition, treatment, and/or resulting absences.
	Curriculum-based assessment: The student is not mastering the curriculum in one or more areas as a result of the condition, treatment, and/or resulting absences.
	Direct observation: The student may experience fatigue or other symptoms resulting from the condition or treatment, detrimentally affecting classroom progress.
Determination	The nondiscriminatory evaluation team determines that the student has an "other health impairment" and needs special education and related services.

The School Function Assessment is criterion-based. The items in each of its three parts represent increasing difficulty, from simpler to more complex tasks. Educators who are very familiar with the student in school settings are the respondents. They usually can complete the entire instrument in 5 to 10 minutes.

The reliability, validity, and psychometric characteristics of the School Function Assessment have been established at a respectable level (Coster et al., 1999; Coster, Deeney, Haltiwanger, & Haley, 1998). Validity studies have demonstrated that it differentiates among the profiles of students with and without disabilities and also distinguishes between groups of students with different disabilities, such as students with cerebral palsy and learning disabilities (Coster & Haltiwanger, 2004; Hwang, Davies, Taylor, & Gavin, 2002).

DESIGNING AN APPROPRIATE IEP

Partnering for Special Education and Related Services

Students are entitled to the benefits of IDEA and to an IEP if their health condition limits their strength, vitality, or alertness and adversely affects their educational performance. But, like Kwashon, not all students who have health impairments have an IEP because their impairments do not affect their educational performance. Instead, they usually need and have a Section 504 plan that covers their health services and other accommodations (Lee & Janik, 2006). Figure 12.7 describes the content of a health plan.

The health care plan for a student with asthma should identify triggers and a prevention protocol and should include a treatment plan developed by the student's asthma specialist, allergist, or pediatrician, describing the student's daily preventive medicines (Kwashon takes his regular meds at home), treatment for mild asthma attacks, and treatment regimens and procedures for more serious attacks (Kwashon receives emergency medication and post-attack rest at school) (Meadows, 2003). Similarly, health care plans for students with epilepsy should identify procedures to follow when seizure activity occurs, medicine for prevention and treatment, and emergency procedures. A student such as Kwashon who has a health care plan will be involved with many different professionals. A partnership among the professionals, family members, and student is essential to assure agreement and consistent treatment. Box 12.1 describes how Kwashon's health care plan can be regarded as an agreement among partners.

We have emphasized how important it is for you to work with a student's family and physicians. Perhaps Box 12.2, "My Voice," will give you insight into the life of parents of a young boy who has juvenile diabetes.

Determining Supplementary Aids and Services

You have already learned how important technology can be and about word processors that promote students' written perfor-

Asthma does not prevent Kwashon Drayton from playing basketball with his brother.

| *Figure 12.7* | ▶ | **Health care plans** |

A health care plan should include the following:
- Statements about who will know about the student's condition, how they will get this information, and how they will be trained in CPR, emergency, and standard first-aid procedures (Kleiberstein & Broome, 2000)
- Specified procedures and standards for taking naps, receiving medications, and making up work missed during absences
- Emergency-response plans, listing emergency-contact telephone numbers (DePaepe et al., 2002)
- Instructions on how to inventory and regularly check emergency medical kits (DePaepe et al., 2002)
- Written consents from the student's physicians and the student's parents or guardians
- Instructions on storage and administration of medication
- Descriptions of health goals and adaptations to school regimens
- Plans for transition from hospital to school (if the student has been hospitalized), especially to the general curriculum
- Descriptions of occupational, physical, respiratory, or other therapy the student will receive at school, or, if not at school, how the therapies will affect the student's education

Coordination Among Professionals and Family

There are, of course, general rules about partnerships. Some derive from IDEA, as we described in Chapter 2. Others derive from the best practices we described in Chapter 4. When students with other health impairments are the focus of a partnership, however, the general rules warrant some modifications. Here, for example, are modifications—described as partnership roles for various professionals—that could apply to Kwashon or other students with asthma.

None of these roles will produce any benefit for Kwashon unless all of the partners adhere to the seven principles of partnership: communicate, be professionally competent, respect each other, advocate for Kwashon and each other, treat each other as equally qualified to contribute to Kwashon, stay committed to him and each other, and build trust.

> *For Kwashon himself:* Know what asthma is, be aware of his symptoms, especially acute attacks, and know where to get help in school.

> *For Michelle; his mother:* Stay up to date on medications and other interventions, control the asthma triggers at home, and monitor Kwashon's health.

> *For Kwashon's regular physician (family or internal medicine):* Conduct regular physical examinations and alert Kwashon's asthma specialist whenever there are any alarming signs of change in his health.

> *For Kwashon's asthma specialist (pulmonologist):* Conduct regular lung evaluations, monitor and change as necessary any medications, and respond to and contact Kwashon's regular physician as needed.

> *For Kwashon's school nurse:* Secure authority from Kwashon's two physicians and his mother to administer emergency medication or other treatment, know what the medications and treatments are and when and why to use them, assist school administrators and especially the maintenance crews to eliminate as many asthma triggers as possible, and stay in regular contact with Kwashon and Michelle.

> *For Kwashon's teachers:* Be able to recognize symptoms of an asthma attack, know where the school nurse is at all times, know how to intervene if the nurse is not available, know what other emergency measures to take, and monitor Kwashon for any signs of asthma reactions or acute episodes.

Clearly, a health plan for a student such as Kwashon requires a partnership. But it also requires a "senior partner," so these professionals, Michelle, and Kwashon must designate one person to coordinate all of the information.

Putting These Tips to Work for Progress in the General Curriculum

1. Provide a rationale for including the student with a disability on the partnership team.

2. If you had a child with asthma in your classroom, how could partnering with the child's parents benefit you as a teacher?

3. Review websites that focus on asthma. What information and resources can you identify that could be helpful to you as a teacher?

---

mance, PDAs that help students with sequencing tasks, digital talking books and e-text formats, and adapted and augmentative communication devices. Students with physical disabilities, particularly students with cerebral palsy, will often benefit from the use of a variety of technologies, including AAC devices to help them overcome communication limitations.

Sometimes simple is better when it comes to technology; not every student needs high-end equipment. The only device that some students with physical disabilities may need as a supplementary aid is a simple switch to operate an educational tool such as a computer, mobility equipment such as an electric wheelchair, or a tape recorder that the student uses to record teachers' lessons (Cole & Swinth, 2004; Lancioni et al., 2002). Figure 12.8 describes various switches. Box 12.3 provides information about another technology that benefits students with physical disabilities and other health impairments: power wheelchairs.

● Diane Lorenzo

When our then 15-month-old child was diagnosed with juvenile diabetes (Type I) we thought, "Oh—we can handle this—he just can't have any sugar." After he was hospitalized for 1 week, we realized we were drastically wrong. We were told what this disease was and how hard it would be to maintain. We were trained on how to give insulin injections (three times a day), how to test his blood sugar by drawing blood from his finger with a needle (six times a day), how to count every gram of carbohydrate that enters his body, and how to monitor his exercise to keep him from dangerously low blood sugars that could lead to seizures and/or a coma. We also had to learn how to avoid high blood sugars that could lead to a coma and very serious long-term effects such as blindness, kidney failure, heart disease, and amputations. When we left the hospital, we felt completely alone and afraid to be unsupervised in taking care of our own son.

Austin is now five years old, and he has bravely faced more than 2,555 insulin injections and 7,665 blood tests since he was diagnosed. I have had people comment that they would never know from looking at Austin that there was anything wrong. In reality, diabetes is wearing down every organ in his body, and every day is a battle to keep his blood sugar level at the right level to avoid immediate danger.

As he gets older, he is becoming more aware of his special needs and that he is different from most kids. There are days where he embraces the fact that he is "special," as he calls it, and performs his own blood tests, and there are days that he screams "I hate diabetes!" when we try to give him his shots. We try to keep him focused on the things he likes—like Batman, and dinosaurs, and sugar-free chewing gum—and try to give him the most normal childhood he can possibly have facing these hourly medical responsibilities.

Being a parent of a child with Type I diabetes has its challenges. Every day I hope for a cure that will allow Austin the freedom to live without insulin injections, blood and urine testing, and having to eat regulated, scheduled meals. The freedom to play without interrupting him to test his blood because he might be low from too much activity. The freedom to eat when he is hungry and stop eating when he is full. The freedom to wake up each morning without being poked by needles. The freedom to sleep in when he is tired instead of woken up because he must follow the same daily schedule. Austin often wonders why he does not get to enjoy these normal freedoms of childhood. And we wonder if maintaining this rigid schedule will be enough to prevent him suffering from the devastating complications of diabetes such as blindness, amputations, and kidney and heart failure.

As a result of Austin's disease, we have become very involved with the Juvenile Diabetes Foundation (JDF). JDF was started in 1972 by parents of children with diabetes; their main goal is to find a cure through funding research. We were recently asked by JDF to travel to Capitol Hill and tell Congress what our son endures. As a result of many such efforts, Congress has for the first time formed a Diabetes Caucus, which currently has 250 representatives from across the country whose goal is to pass legislation for funding to help find a cure.

Planning for Universal Design for Learning

In Chapter 2, you learned that the 2004 amendments to IDEA included provisions for a national standard for electronic text materials, called the National Instructional Materials Accessibility Standard (NIMAS). NIMAS establishes technical standards for how electronic texts should be set up to ensure that they are accessible to students with sensory or learning disabilities. Technology standards assure the widest possible access to written text.

Figure 12.8 ▶ **Adaptive switches**

Switches vary according to how they are activated, how many functions they can operate, and what happens when you start them:

- Most single switches operate by pressure, which performs the switch-on, switch-off function (Johnston, 2003).
- Some pressure switches activate a timed sequence, instead of a simple on-off switch, thus allowing the device to begin operating and then to shut off at predetermined times.
- Other pressure switches perform only as long as they are depressed—for example, a motorized wheelchair activated by a joystick or similar switch.
- **Pneumatic, or puffing, switches** operate when the student, such as one who has no arm control, puffs air into a strawlike tube. If a student's lung capacity limits his ability to expel air, he can operate switches by sipping or inhaling air through the tube.
- Still other switches operate by detecting the user's movements, such as head movement, eyebrow twitching, or eye movement.
- Some switches can be activated by sounds.

TECHNOLOGY OUTCOMES

Box 12.3

Powered Mobility Equals Freedom! Electric Wheelchairs

Students with physical disabilities and other health impairments benefit considerably from technology such as the switches you learned about in Figure 12.8. Electronic wheelchairs are an advanced technology that create access to home, school, and community environments and the fellow students and adults in each of those places. Electric wheelchairs, often called power wheelchairs, can indeed mean freedom.

Electric wheelchairs involve a combination of technology applications. There's the motorized chair itself. Then there's the switch that operates the chair. Often people incorporate other technologies, like AAC devices, into the structure of the chair.

There are a number of issues that must be considered in supporting a student to purchase or use a power chair:

- *Transporting the chair.* Power chairs are heavy; transporting them requires the use of a modified van (modified to include a lift and internal equipment to stabilize the rider). If customized transportation is not available, perhaps a nonpowered chair is a better option or, alternatively, a smaller motorized vehicle, like a scooter. There are smaller, collapsible power chairs available that have two small motors and are for indoor use only, so perhaps having one of these at school would be better than a heavy power wheelchair.

- *Adjusting the size.* A power wheelchair's size limits the student's opportunity to navigate in school environments. Particularly for children, smaller is better.

- *Recharging the batteries.* Power chairs are battery operated, and their batteries need to be recharged. Teachers should place the student's chair near a power outlet.

- *Selecting navigation tools.* Many types of switches are available, and virtually any one can be used to operate a power chair, though joysticks are the most common type of navigation tool. These should be configured with regard to the student's physical capacities and personal preferences.

- *Assuring safety.* Power wheelchairs can be hazardous for the student and others. They are often hard to stop and navigate. Training is the first step in ensuring safe use, and teaching classmates about safety around the chair is also important. Power chairs can come with various configurations of braking mechanisms based on the student's needs, although most brake systems are not intended to stop a wheelchair but to keep it from rolling.

■ ■ ■

Just as DVDs are standardized, NIMAS sets a standard so that all e-text materials are identical in their accessibility.

E-text is created from a digital source file; the term *digital source file* refers to computer files or programs written in some digital format. Digital text can range from formats used for word processor to markup languages such as HTML or XML, to computer codes such as JAVA. Currently, XML (extensible markup language) and XSL (extensible stylesheet language) are the digital formats most commonly used to create electronic texts. The NIMAS standard is based on these digital formats. The electronic text is an output of the digital file.

The digital file can be read by commercially available media players that allow the information in the source file to be presented in multiple ways. Media players can convert digital source files into audio and video media, flexible text, or electronic Braille and can even create avatars (digitally created figures) that virtually present content in sign language. Think of these media players as similar to a web browser, which takes HTML (hypertext markup language) and converts it to output that includes text, pictures, graphics, audio, and so forth. Within a few years, most school textbooks will be available in a digital file format.

The NIMAS standard and media players are, however, mainly directions for the future. There are other ways of accessing e-text and digital documents today. For example, Tom Snyder Productions publishes a series of digital texts under its Thinking Reader series. Thinking Readers were designed by researchers at CAST and are digital talking book (DTB) formats of popular books, like *Tuck Everlasting*; *Bud, Not Buddy*; and *A Wrinkle in Time,* that are often taught in middle or junior high school. The DTB versions of these classics allow learners who are not reading at grade level to access the book through audio and video outputs and through supports programmed into the software and, as a result, improve reading skills. This approach can benefit students who have severe physical impairments that limit their ability to use print materials easily or to see print-based books. It also benefits students with more severe cognitive disabilities who otherwise could not read the book.

You can create many of your own electronic texts through simple programs like Microsoft Word or PowerPoint. Many of the materials that teachers use are not subject to copyright or have been developed by the teacher or the school district. Those can be converted to electronic versions. Also, there are copyright-free digital audio and video materials that can be incorporated into other materials to make them more accessible. Box 12.4 provides simple steps teachers can use to create electronic content materials. Sometimes even using simple e-text options can allow students with physical and other disabilities to have access to general education content and provide evidence of their knowledge and skills.

PEARSON
myeducationlab

Go to the Activities and Application section in Chapter 12 of MyEducationLab and complete Activity 2. As you watch the video and answer the accompanying questions, reflect on Ryan's needs and what his team does to enable him to participate fully in all areas of his social and academic life.

Planning for Other Educational Needs

One area in which both students with physical disabilities and students with other health impairments may need IEP goals to address other educational needs is the area of physical education. Like Ryan and Kwashon, students with these disabilities usually are limited with respect to the types, intensity, and duration of physical activities in which they can engage.

Accordingly, their IEP teams—Ryan's is one of them—need to consider adapted physical education (PE) goals and supports for the educational programs of these students. Adapted physical education is, quite simply, "physical education which has been adapted or modified so that it is appropriate for the person with a disability" (Cantu & Buswell, 2003, p. 58).

For people with disabilities, physical activities are undoubtedly important. The U.S. Department of Education's Rehabilitation Research and Training Center (RRTC) on Health and Wellness has documented the barriers that often limit access to physical activities for people with physical and other disabilities, as well as the importance of physical activities for this population (Krahn, 2003; Powers, 2003; Putnam et al., 2003).

Adapted physical education allows students with a disability to participate in typical sports or physical activities. Adapted PE specialists may suggest modifying the environment in which the sport or physical activity will occur or providing or modifying equip-

IEP Tip

The IEP team should consider the need for physical activity and exercise for students with physical disabilities and other health impairments. All students need exercise and physical activity of some sort, so IEP teams should consider accommodations and modifications to the curriculum that promote these activities.

Creating Electronic Text

It is a relatively simple process for teachers to create instructional materials that include the features embedded in Digital Talking Books and other universally designed materials. You can follow some simple steps to achieve these outcomes:

1. *Use word processing programs such as Microsoft Word to create content.* As you have learned, various programs allow electronic content generated through word processing software to be "read aloud," so any written content can be converted from text to speech. Also, the size and color of the letters and words can be changed to accommodate students who have visual impairments. Further, you can easily paste pictures into word processing documents as well as embed hyperlinks to access Internet content (see Step 3).

2. *Use presentation software such as Microsoft PowerPoint to create content.* Presentation software is a very powerful means to present nontext content, such as pictures and videos, and to provide content in, essentially, advance or graphic organizer formats. Like word processing software, it is simple to modify the text presentation by changing font size and color, and to embed Internet-based content through hyperlinks. You can also incorporate motion features when presenting text and pictures. Not only is it simple to cut and paste pictures into presentations, but it is quite simple to embed video and audio playback as well. Also, supporting students to create their own presentations is an excellent means to promote self-directed learning.

3. *Embed links to the Internet into content presentations.* Both word processing programs and presentation software readily support hyperlinks, so you can link to Internet-based content that expands on information you are presenting, defines key terms or ideas, presents content in video or audio format, or reinforces learned information. Web quests are frequently used to promote learning and generalization, and you can link to web quest sites quite easily. You can also use the hyperlink process to link to other content information on the computer's hard drive.

4. *Access existing electronic text.* It is important to remember that there are copyright restrictions on the types of content you can modify into electronic

versions. The above activities are primarily geared toward teacher-generated content. In addition to commercially available digital talking books, like the Thinking Reader software discussed in the text, there are several sources through which you can obtain electronic versions of texts that are in the public domain. Bookshare.org is a frequently used site from which you can download some public domain books in DTB, Digital Braille, Text, and HTML formats. Text and HTML formats could be played using a word processor, while DTB versions could be played using free media player software (see next step). Memberships to the Bookshare.org library are free to U.S. schools and students. Further, beginning in the 2008–2009 school year, Bookshare.org users can use a specially designed text-to-speech software program, Read:OutLoud, (manufactured by Don Johnston Incorporated) as a text reader (http://www.donjohnston.com/products/rol_bookshare/index.html). Also, the CAST web site has a library of electronic books that can be used by teachers (http://bookbuilder.cast.org/library.php).

5. *Download a Digital Talking Book Player.* There are a number of DTB players that are available for download and use for low or no cost. For example, the AMIS (Adaptive Multimedia Information System) software is an open source DTB player available for free download at http://www.amisproject.org/software/index.html. Once downloaded, you install the software on a Windows computer.

In addition, researchers and developers at CAST, a center that has led in the definition and application of universal design for learning, have provided numerous suggestions that assist teachers to create universally designed instructional materials. You can see sample UDL lesson plans and develop your own at the CAST UDL Lesson Builder web site (http://.lessonbuilder.cast.org/), as well as see examples of UDL books and prompts to create your own UDL book at the CAST UDL Book Builder web site (http://bookbuilder.cast.org/).

PEARSON
myeducationlab

Go to the Activities and Application section in Chapter 12 of MyEducationLab and complete Activity 3. As you examine this strategy, reflect on how it addresses universally designed learning.

ment to ensure the inclusion of students. For example, a student who is blind can participate in typical softball activities if the players use a beeping softball—an ordinary softball with an auditory sound that enables the person with the visual impairment to hear, and thus sense, the approaching ball.

In addition to developing these types of modifications and accommodations, however, adapted PE responds to students' unique or specific educational needs in areas such as sensory

Ryan's parents, Mary and John, and his sister, Nicole, have been important partners on Ryan's team. Their support and attitude have contributed to Ryan's confidence and independence.

awareness systems, reflexes, fine- and gross-motor skills, body image, locomotor skills, manipulation skills, muscular endurance, and agility or speed (Mears, 2004). Enabling students with physical disabilities or other health impairments to participate in sports and recreation activities may link that student to a source of lifelong enjoyment. Ryan's adapted physical education teacher concentrates first on building Ryan's strength and then on how he can participate in warm-ups and some sports.

USING EFFECTIVE INSTRUCTIONAL STRATEGIES

Early Childhood Students: Token Economy Systems

A number of instructional strategies you read about in this text are not specific to any disability category but are useful for students across disability categories and ages. Indeed, some are useful across age ranges for all students, with or without disabilities. One such strategy, the use of token economy systems, is useful in all classrooms.

As you learned in Chapter 10 when reading about discrete trial training, the basic laws governing the use of techniques from the field of applied behavior analysis involve the delivery of a discriminative stimulus intended to elicit a response, which is then followed by a reinforcing stimulus. In Chapter 8 you learned about errorless learning and about how using prompts is one way to modify the three-term contingency sequence (discriminative stimulus, response, and reinforcing stimulus) to ensure learning.

Another way to modify the three-term contingency is by changing aspects of the reinforcing stimulus, such as by altering the schedule on which a reinforcer is delivered (e.g., every time the student performs a behavior, every other time, infrequently) or modifying the type of reinforcer provided. In token economy systems, students are provided with tokens such as points, poker chips, or tickets to reinforce their behavior. You should remember from Chapter 10 that a reinforcer (or reinforcing stimulus) is anything that increases the probability that the desired response will be performed. How, then, can points, poker chips, or tickets serve that function? Well, think about the most common token economy system, one that you use every day. What is that? Money! The reason most people are willing to work hard to receive money is to use that money to buy items or activities—commodities—that they value.

Buying a valued commodity is the crux of token economy systems. Tokens take on a reinforcing value because students can trade them for a desired commodity. In some ways, token economy systems make it simpler to implement applied behavior analysis procedures. It is difficult and of questionable ethics to use primary reinforcers like food all of the time, and there are only so many other primary reinforcers available to teachers.

Smith (2004) and colleagues at the University of Minnesota's Early Childhood Behavior Project have identified the important elements of a token economy system for young children with disabilities. First, you need to make sure that the token keeps its value to the student by providing frequent enough opportunities to exchange the token and by setting the rate at which tokens can be earned on a frequent enough schedule. Requiring the accumulation of 1,000 points to get a candy bar but making it possible to acquire those points only over a period of, say, 6 months, creates a situation in which the tokens have no real value to the student. It is important to set up the token system early in the year so students can trade in their tokens once a day to get a desired reinforcer.

Second, determine with the students what the tokens can be used to buy. Again, students will only work for tokens if the tokens can be exchanged for something they want.

Students can buy a wide array of commodities, such as trading cards, inexpensive bracelets, time on the computer, a homework pass, extra recess, or extra free time.

Third, consider how you will fade out the token reinforcement system. You can do this by pairing the token reinforcers with other forms of reinforcement, such as verbal praise, and then slowly increasing the number of tokens needed to obtain reinforcers.

Smith (2004) and colleagues noted that token economy systems are particularly useful in early childhood settings because they can easily be used at both school and home. Parents frequently find that these systems are manageable and that using them provides helpful consistency between the two environments.

Elementary and Middle School Students: Self-Awareness

The middle school years are difficult for most students, with or without disabilities. Disabilities can adversely affect emerging adolescent milestones, one of which is the development of a student's self-awareness as distinct from the disability, health condition, or disorder. The term *self-awareness* refers to one's understanding of oneself as a unique individual and is often used in conjunction with the notions of self-understanding and self-knowledge. This includes the process referred to as *disability awareness,* which involves the capacity of an individual to appraise his own abilities as a function of a specific disabling condition.

Too frequently, the only time the issue of student self-awareness comes to the forefront in education is when people other than the student question the degree to which he has accepted his disability or, in less positive terms, accepts what he cannot do because of the disabling condition. Figure 12.9 describes some issues important to promoting health and disability awareness.

Students with disabilities and other health impairments can easily begin to think of themselves only in the context of their disability. Yet self-awareness is mediated by and tied to executive functioning capabilities, like decision making, problem solving, and self-regulation (you will learn more about executive functions in Chapter 13) (Turner & Levine, 2004). Box 12.5 provides strategies for promoting healthy self-awareness.

The most important theme is that, in all such efforts, the student must be the catalyst for change. Students need to be actively involved in identifying their interests, abilities, strengths, and unique learning needs, as well as in applying this knowledge to identify strategies and supports that can enable them to overcome limitations.

Secondary and Transition Students: Driver's Education

You can probably remember the day you passed your driver's test and received your license. It's a big day in any young person's life. Having a driver's license is like having a license to freedom. You can go places without your parents, and you can do more things you want to do. Many people assume that students with disabilities cannot drive, but many people with physical disabilities are quite capable drivers. In fact, given the lack of

---

Figure 12.9	▶ Issues in promoting self-awareness

- Do not regard a student's self-awareness as consisting only of acceptance of a limitation.
- Do not force the student to accept the disability and to do nothing more about the student's self-awareness.
- Recognize that, although disability awareness is an important part of self-awareness, understanding one's disability and its effects in typical situations should not be the goal of educational efforts to promote self-awareness.
- Instead, promote a student's self-acceptance through self-understanding and self-knowledge.
- Enable the student to use his unique skills and abilities to his greatest advantage.
(Wehmeyer, Sands, Knowlton, & Kozleski, 2002)

INTO PRACTICE   *Box 12.5*

Promoting Healthy Self-Awareness

As emphasized in Figure 12.8, self-awareness for students with disabilities must extend beyond disability awareness. The following steps and strategies can be used to promote healthy self-awareness for students with and without disabilities:

- ◆ Avoid overprotecting students with health impairments at any age but especially during early adolescence, when students want to fit in instead of standing out (Sullivan, Fulmer, & Zigmond, 2001).

- ◆ Begin instruction in self-awareness by identifying a student's basic physical and psychological needs, interests, and abilities.

- ◆ Help students distinguish between their physical and psychological needs, then teach them how to meet those needs.

- ◆ Encourage role-playing and brainstorming activities that explore students' interests and abilities.

- ◆ Ask students to discuss common emotions, such as self-worth; their own positive physical and psychological attributes and how these attributes make them feel; how other people's actions affect their feelings of self-worth, fear, love, hate, and sadness; how these feelings affect their and others' behavior; and how to cope with these emotions.

- ◆ Transition from emotional to basic physical awareness, teaching students about their physical selves and how their physical health and capacities affect their actions.

- ◆ Teach students that there are physical causes for the way they feel and that how they feel affects the way they behave.

- ◆ Import additional materials involving health, sexuality, and body systems.

- ◆ Help students explore others' perceptions of them, listing others' potential reactions and constructing a view of how others see them; discuss differences among people, including interests and abilities.

- ◆ Teach students how to give and accept praise and criticism appropriately and inappropriately, list the effects and purposes of praise and criticism, and offer strategies to give and receive both.

- ◆ Ask students to identify their own positive characteristics, how to express confidence in themselves, how to react to others' expressions of confidence, and how to appropriately make positive statements about themselves. (Wehmeyer et al., 2002)

myeducationlab

Go to the Activities and Application section in Chapter 12 of MyEducationLab and complete Activity 4. As you watch the videos and answer the accompanying questions, consider Ryan's self-awareness and how it appears to be developing.

accessible public transportation in many communities, a driver's license becomes the key to getting to a job and earning the money needed to live more independently.

Vogtle, Kern, and McCauley (2000) surveyed adolescents with and without disabilities on several issues pertaining to social inclusion and found that, although 88 percent of adolescents without disabilities had a driver's license, only 46 percent of students with disabilities (across all categories) had one. McGill and Vogtle (2001) interviewed adolescents with physical disabilities, particularly those with cerebral palsy and spina bifida, about their feelings about learning to drive. These students indicated that driving would give them the chance to be like everyone else, provide the usual benefits of being an adult, and minimize their isolation. They thought that their involvement in high school driver's education classes would contribute to their social inclusion as well.

How does one teach driving to young people with physical disabilities? Mainly, this involves direct instruction on using vehicle adaptations that enable a person with a physical disability to drive. For example, steering wheels can be outfitted with handles that allow students with limited motor control to grip and turn the wheel more easily. Vehicles can be reconfigured with a left-foot accelerator, additional mirrors, additional room for wheelchair storage and access, hand controls for accelerating and braking, and even a joystick modification to allow steering with feet instead of hands.

Not all students with physical disabilities will be able to obtain a driver's license, but if schools provide direct instruction with modified vehicles, perhaps more students will be able to do so. Just as important, students with physical disabilities will have the opportunity to undergo a rite of passage for adolescence—driver's education!

INCLUDING STUDENTS WITH PHYSICAL DISABILITIES AND OTHER HEALTH IMPAIRMENTS

Figures 12.10 and 12.11 display the percentage of students with physical disabilities and other health impairments, respectively, in inclusive placements.

As compared to students with other types of disabilities, students with other health impairments are more likely to receive services in home or hospital settings. Receiving an appropriate education while in the hospital or at home is important if students are to avoid

Figure 12.10 Educational placement of students with physical disabilities

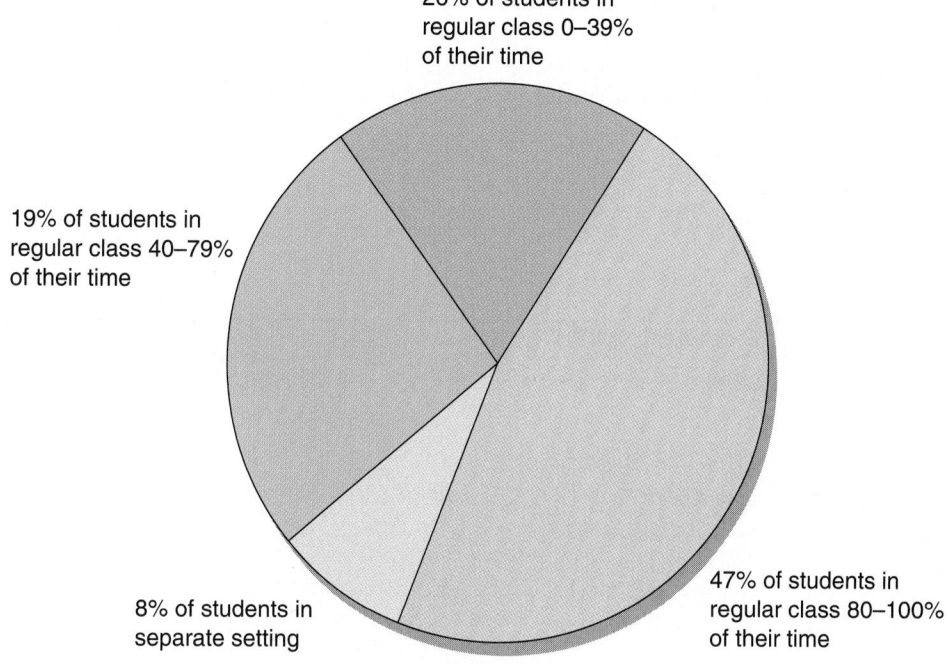

26% of students in regular class 0–39% of their time

19% of students in regular class 40–79% of their time

8% of students in separate setting

47% of students in regular class 80–100% of their time

Figure 12.11 Educational placement of students with other health impairments

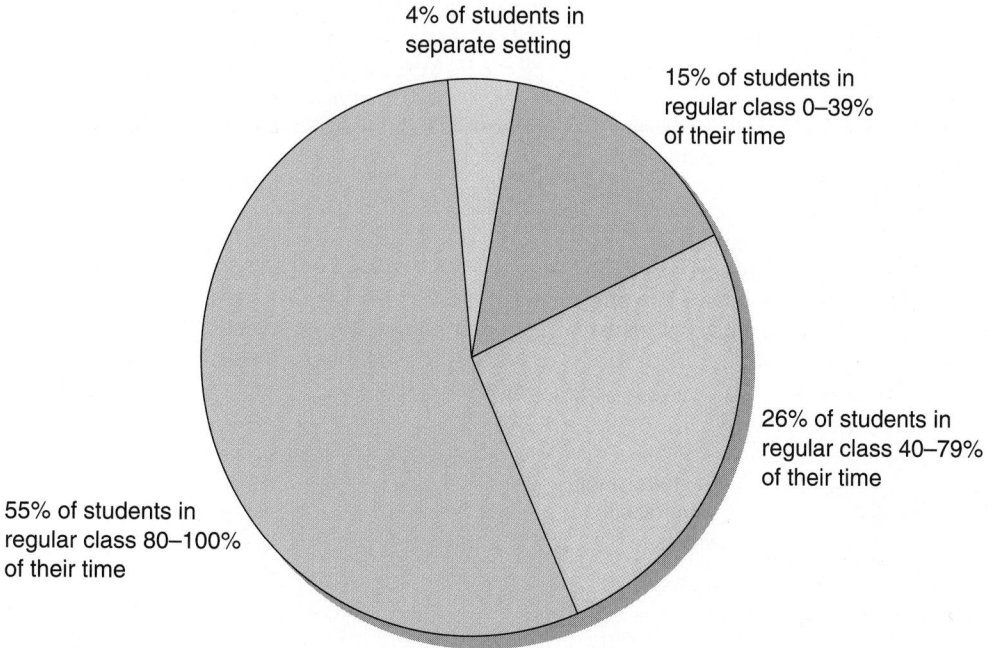

4% of students in separate setting

15% of students in regular class 0–39% of their time

26% of students in regular class 40–79% of their time

55% of students in regular class 80–100% of their time

grade retention, inappropriate special education placement, learned helplessness, or early dropout (Bessell, 2001b). In addition, students often feel isolated by homebound services (Bessell, 2001a). The Committee on School Health (2000) emphasizes that "homebound instruction is meant for acute or catastrophic health problems that confine a child or adolescent to home or hospital for a prolonged but defined period of time and is not intended to relieve the school or parent of the responsibility for providing education for the child in the least restrictive environment" (p. 1154).

Parents, school administrators, teachers, and the student's primary care physician need to partner with each other to consider how to address the curriculum standards and IEP goals that the student would achieve if still in school, what the specific duration of the homebound services will be, and how to return the student to school as quickly and smoothly as possible. Receiving dual enrollment in homebound and school-based instruction enables students to continue functioning as a classroom member (Bessell, 2001b). Box 12.6 offers suggestions for including students with other health impairments and physical disabilities in general education classrooms.

Box 12.6	**INCLUSION TIPS**			
	What You Might See	*What You Might Be Tempted to Do*	*Alternate Responses*	*Ways to Include Peers in the Process*
Behavior	The student becomes very anxious when he is not able to complete assignments at the same speed as his classmates.	Tell him to be realistic and face his own limitations.	Develop a 504 plan that incorporates the use of technology to enable the student to complete assignments more quickly.	Explore ways that all class members can benefit from assistive technology.
Social interactions	He may be self-conscious or embarrassed, so he withdraws from others.	Allow him to work alone, assuming he is merely low on energy or needs to be by himself.	Work with the school counselor to provide the student with self-awareness instruction.	Recognize that all students deal with self-esteem issues and involve the class in self-awareness instruction.
Educational performance	Lack of strength and use of a wheelchair hinder his capacity for full participation in physical education.	Excuse him from physical education and have him attend a study hall instead.	Use curriculum-based assessment to evaluate the student's strengths and needs related to adapted physical education.	Explore opportunities for him to participate in a wheelchair basketball league.
Classroom attitudes	He appears to be overwhelmed by class activities when feeling fatigued.	Tell the student that his only choice is to deal with it.	In a 504 plan, specify the appropriate length of work and rest periods for him.	Have classmates serve as scribes for him or offer other support as needed.

ASSESSING STUDENTS' PROGRESS

Measuring Students' Progress

Progress in the General Curriculum

Many means of assessing progress in the general curriculum involve paper/pencil examinations or other tests. But students with physical disabilities often have fine- and gross-motor limitations that reduce their capacity to demonstrate their abilities on these assessments; similarly, students with other health impairments may lack the stamina required to complete them on time.

An increasing number of alternatives to handwritten performance examinations make use of computer technology. For example, computer-based assessment augments curriculum-based measurement (Fuchs & Fuchs, 2001). As you learned in Chapter 5, curriculum-based measurement (CBM) involves frequent measurements of indicators that are tied to the curriculum, can be measured repeatedly, and provide indicators of student improvement. Using a computer for CBM purposes is an obvious accommodation for students with physical disabilities or other health impairments, but it also assists educators in assessing the progress of all of their students.

Progress in Addressing Other Educational Needs

As you have learned, physical activities have various important benefits for students with physical disabilities or other health impairments, and adapted physical education services can give these students the exercise they need. There is a variety of ways to track student progress in the area of physical education, including tracking students' correct performances of a physical task and measuring the frequency with which a student can engage in an activity. Haynes (2002) suggests that measurement in adapted physical education also include the following:

- Cardiovascular function, including resting and target heart rate (important for Kwashon, given his asthma)
- Body composition, mass, and weight
- Muscle strength and endurance (what Ryan works on when he does adaptive physical education)
- Muscle and joint flexibility
- Posture evaluation
- Mobility

Making Accommodations for Assessment

You have already learned that computer-based assessment can be an important strategy for measuring progress in the general curriculum for students with physical disabilities and other health impairments, and that it is also an important accommodation to enable students to participate in standardized testing. Students with other health impairments may require more frequent breaks or multiple test sessions in order to complete a test. If a computer-based assessment is not available, students with physical disabilities may need a scribe to record answers or extended time to complete the test. Because Ryan's disability affects his fine-motor coordination and his prematurity affected his eyesight, he has accommodations in taking his mathematics examinations and assessments.

You also have learned that there are many universal accommodations—those that benefit students with different disabilities. One particular accommodation that may be specific to students with physical disabilities, however, involves physical access to the testing environment. In many cases, concerns about ensuring security and minimizing the potential for cheating or disruption of the testing environment take priority over ensuring physical access. To make sure students with physical disabilities can participate in a test, test situations should consider mobility access, including the availability of an elevator, access to needed test materials, and environmental controls, such as the air conditioning that Kwashon needs to minimize pollen.

Recalling both Ryan and Kwashon, let's consider what values their teachers advance and what outcomes these students and their families reasonably can anticipate.

◆ Both students are plenty bright, and both have demonstrated they can be physically active, so it is not amiss to expect that they will attend postsecondary schools and remain active, perhaps with the help of personal trainers or community-based adaptive physical education specialists.

◆ Both will be able to contribute positively to their communities, working, perhaps acting in community theater (Ryan) or serving advocacy agencies (Kwashon might follow in his mother's footsteps as an advocate and community educator).

◆ Both have strengths—not the physical strengths that they would have if they did not have a disability, but the strengths to meet life head-on, recognize that their abilities outweigh their disabilities, and build on their abilities to offset their disabilities, both in school and at work.

◆ Both make choices—not to succumb (Ryan acts, Kwashon participates in sports), but to meet their academic responsibilities (with accommodations); both have learned not to depend on others, and both have chosen to be as independent as they can be.

◆ Both find no barriers to having friends—those with and those without disabilities; their impairments do not set them apart or create barriers to relationships.

◆ Both should expect to be full citizens of their communities; they can earn salaries, live relatively independently, and fully participate in the adult world just as they do at school.

WHAT DO YOU THINK?

1. Is it somewhat easier for students with physical disabilities to participate in the general curriculum than it is for students with other disabilities? Before answering, think about the effects of medication and absenteeism for these students and ask yourself whether there is any single portrait of students with physical or other health disabilities.

2. To what extent would you feel comfortable providing health care services to students with physical disabilities (such as suctioning a tube in a student's throat that allows him to breathe or performing CPR if he has an attack of acute asthma)? Would you first want to receive Red Cross and CPR training? Do any of your previous experiences make you more comfortable with these students (such as having been a volunteer in a hospital or nursing home or having learned emergency interventions in scouting programs or as part of life-guard training)?

3. Having (perhaps) seen photographs or met veterans injured in various combat operations and having observed how they use prosthetic devices, do you have a sense that, although physical disabilities are real, their effect is magnified when teachers single out these people as needing special education?

ADDRESSING THE STANDARDS: THE VALUES CONNECTION

The following CEC Knowledge and Skill Standards: Common Core and Values are addressed in this chapter through the content and concepts we discuss.

CEC Knowledge and Skill Standards: Common Core		Values/Standards Connection
CEC Knowledge and Skill Standard II. **Development and Characteristics of Learners**		Understanding the characteristics and needs of students with physical disabilities and other health impairments is an application of CEC Standard 2, Development and Characteristics of Learners.
CC2K1	Typical and atypical human growth and development.	
CC2K2	Educational implication of characteristics of various exceptionalities.	Cerebral palsy may impair a student in some ways, but it should not disguise a student's *strengths,* such as Ryan's literary and dramatic skills.
CC2K4	Family systems and the roles of families supporting development.	Because epilepsy and other disabilities can impair a person physically and emotionally, it is important for educators to instill *great expectations* in their students with disabilities,
CC2K5	Similarities and differences of individuals with and without exceptional learning needs.	sometimes by asking students to write a short biography about the success stories of relatively well-known people with a particular disbility.
CC2K6	Similarities and differences of individuals with exceptional learning needs.	
CEC Knowledge and Skill Standard III. **Individual Learning Differences**		Understanding the impact that asthma has on Kwashon's life is an application of CEC Standard 3, Individual Learning Differences.
CC3K1	Effects an exceptional condition(s) can have on an individual's life.	
CC3K2	Impact of learner's academic and social abilities, attitudes, interests, and values on instruction and career development.	
CEC Knowledge and Skill Standard IV. **Instructional Strategies**		Standard 4 emphasizes students' self-determination and *choice,* and builds on students' *strengths.*
CC4S1	Use strategies to facilitate integration into various settings.	
CC4S2	Teach individuals to use self-assessment, problem-solving, and other cognitive strategies to meet their needs.	
CC4S3	Select, adapt, and use instructional strategies and materials according to characteristics of the individual with exceptional learning needs.	
CC4S4	Use strategies to facilitate maintenance and generalization of skills across environments.	
CC4S5	Use procedures to increase the individual's self-awareness, self-management, self-control, self-reliance, and self-esteem.	
CC4S6	Use strategies that promote successful transitions for individuals with exceptional learning needs.	

continued

CEC Knowledge and Skill Standards: Common Core	Values/Standards Connection
CEC Knowledge and Skill Standard V. **Learning Environments and Social Interactions**	Assisting students with self-awareness and emotional health is an example of CEC Standard 5, Learning Environments and Social Interactions.
CC5S2 Identify realistic expectations for personal and social behavior in various settings.	
CC5S3 Identify supports needed for integration into various program placements.	Relationships among students with physical disabilities, such as Ryan, or other health impairments, such as Kwashon, can prosper when the students and their teachers are candid about the causes and treatment of a condition and about the prospects for students with the condition. Knowledge is power; it trumps ignorance every time.
CC5S4 Design learning environments that encourage active participation in individual and group settings.	
CC5S9 Create an environment that encourages self-advocacy and increased independence.	
CC5S12 Design and manage daily routines.	
CC5S15 Structure, direct, and support the activities of paraeducators, volunteers, and tutors.	
CEC Knowledge and Skill Standard VII. **Instructional Planning**	Even the use of simple technologies, like switches or a walker, can build on students' *strengths* and enable them to be more independent and *self-determined*. Relatively simple ideas can have a big impact!
CC7K5 Roles and responsibilities of the paraeducator related to instruction, intervention, and direct service.	
CC7S1 Identify and prioritize areas of the general curriculum and accommodations for individuals with exceptional learning needs.	Ensuring that students with disabilities have access to core content information through electronic and digital text materials ensures that they have *rights and opportunities* for learning.
CC7S3 Involve the individual and family in setting instructional goals and monitoring progress.	
CC7S6 Sequence, implement, and evaluate individualized learning objectives.	
CC7S7 Integrate affective, social, and life skills with academic curricula.	
CC7S9 Incorporate and implement instructional and assitive technology into the educational program.	

CEC Knowledge and Skill Standards: Common Core	Values/Standards Connection
CEC Knowledge and Skill Standard VIII. Assessment	Using technology to assist students with physical disabilities during assessments is an application of CEC Standard 8, Assessment. Technology augments students' *strengths*.
CC8K3 — Screening, prereferral, referral, and classification procedures.	
CC8S2 — Administer nonbiased formal and informal assessments.	
CC8S3 — Use technology to conduct assessments.	
CC8S6 — Use assessment information in making eligibility, program, and placement decisions for individuals with exceptional learning needs, including those from culturally and/or linguistically diverse backgrounds.	
CC8S8 — Evaluate instruction and monitor progress of individuals with exceptional learning needs.	
CEC Knowledge and Skill Standard X. Collaboration	Collaborating with families and others to address exceptional learning needs, such as in physical education, is an example of CEC Standard 10, Collaboration.
CC10S2 — Collaborate with families and others in assessment of individuals with exceptional learning needs.	Collaboration can lead to everyone, including the student, having *great expectations*.
CC10S3 — Foster respectful and beneficial relationships between families and professionals.	
CC10S4 — Assist individuals with exceptional learning needs and their families in becoming active participants in the educational team.	
CC10S5 — Plan and conduct collaborative conferences with individuals with exceptional learning needs and their families.	

Source: From CEC Knowledge and Skill Standards: Common Core and Values. Copyright by The Council for Exceptional Children. Reprinted with permission.

SUMMARY

Identifying Students with Physical Disabilities

◆ The term *physical disability* refers to a large group of students who, though quite different from each other, share the common challenge of mobility limitations.

◆ Cerebral palsy refers to a disorder of movement or posture occurring when the brain is in its early stages of development. The damage is not progressive or hereditary.

◆ Spina bifida is a malformation of the spinal cord. Its severity depends on both the extent of the malformation and its position on the spinal cord.

◆ Cerebral palsy is caused by prenatal, perinatal, or postnatal factors, whereas spina bifida is caused by an interaction of environmental and genetic factors.

Identifying Students with Other Health Impairments

◆ Other health impairments are chronic or acute health problems that result in limitations of strength, vitality, or alertness and adversely affect a student's educational performance.

◆ Epilepsy is a condition characterized by seizures that can be classified into two major types: partial seizures and generalized seizures.

◆ Asthma is a chronic lung condition characterized by airway obstruction, inflammation, and increased sensitivity. It is the most common chronic disease among children in the United States.

◆ Both epilepsy and asthma are caused by a combination of genetic and environmental factors.

◆ A physical examination from a physician is often the first step in determining whether or not a student has a physical disability or other health impairment.

Evaluating Students with Physical Disabilities and Other Health Impairments

◆ A physical examination, performed by a physician, is the standard method of evaluating a student with a physical disability or other health impairment.

◆ Sometimes a neurological examination is appropriate, and neuroimaging is a technique for that kind of examination.

◆ Prenatal screening assists in identifying some physical disabilities, including spina bifida; occasionally, prenatal surgery will be used to prevent further neurological loss.

◆ The School Function Assessment is a criterion-based measure of functional skills required of elementary students in school settings.

Designing an Appropriate IEP

◆ Students with physical disabilities and other health impairments will benefit from a comprehensive health plan that specifies the health supports and accommodations that will enable them to experience successful inclusion.

◆ IEP teams should consider the use of switches to provide greater access to the general curriculum for students with physical disabilities and other health impairments.

◆ Electronic or digital text formats enable educators to deliver core academic content in multiple ways.

◆ Physical exercise is important for *all* children. Adapted physical education provides students with opportunities for inclusion, exercise, and recreation.

Using Effective Instructional Strategies

◆ Token economy systems use tokens to reinforce positive behavior and academic outcomes. They can be incorporated into the educational programs of young children with disabilities to promote positive outcomes.

◆ Students with physical disabilities and other health impairments may have self-images that are derived more from their physical impairment or health status than from their many capacities and abilities. Teachers should include instruction on student self-awareness as part of the educational program.

◆ Driver's education is part of the transition to adulthood for most adolescents and should be for students with physical disabilities and other health impairments as well. Some students are able to learn to drive if they have instruction and are provided with vehicle modifications.

Assessing Students' Progress

◆ Students with physical disabilities and other health impairments may perform more effectively on curriculum-based measurement and mastery learning assessments if such measures are computer-based.

◆ There are multiple means to measure progress in physical education; teachers should focus on a wide array of health outcomes, including cardiovascular and others.

◆ Students with physical disabilities and other health impairments may need multiple accommodations for testing, such as extended time, a scribe, or computer administration. Physical access to the testing site is also important.

Now go to MyEducationLab at www.myeducationlab.com and take the Self-Assessment to gauge your initial comprehension of chapter content. Once you have taken the Self-Assessment, use your individualized Study Plan for Chapter 12 to enhance your understanding of the concepts discussed in the chapter.

13

Understanding Students with Traumatic Brain Injury

◆ WHO IS DYLAN OUTLAW?

Graduation.

One word.

One meaning: the awarding of an academic degree or diploma.

One connotation: Moving forward. Just as IDEA envisions for students with disabilities and NCLB envisions for all students.

For 12-year-old Dylan Outlaw of Atlantic Beach, North Carolina, graduation has occurred six times. Yes, six. Each time, it has consisted of far more than the awarding of degrees or diplomas. Think of graduation as moving from one stage to another. Then apply that meaning to Dylan.

In that sense, he graduated from the category of students who do not have disabilities into the class who do when a two-ton refrigerator truck plowed into his family's car and caused him to have traumatic brain injury. Dylan was only four years old.

Still thinking of graduation as moving from one stage to another, Dylan graduated again by defying the dire prognoses of physicians at Pitt County Hospital, in Greenville, North Carolina. They had warned Dylan's mother, Renee, and her family that he might not survive the injury. He had been evaluated as having the most  severe brain injury. Shards of bone from his eye sockets and temples were floating in his cerebral fluids, near his optic nerves. To prevent them from moving, doctors placed Dylan into an induced coma for five days. Seemingly miraculously—Renee attributes it to prayer—Dylan's body digested the shards; his many MRI evaluations revealed no bone residue. Still,

the brain injury has affected Dylan, as you will learn.

Dylan graduated from the hospital's critical care unit to its rehabilitation unit in a near-record time of six weeks, and from that unit to rehabilitation at home.

From there Dylan went to kindergarten. There and through fifth grade, he was classified as an IDEA student and had the requisite IEP.

When it came time for Dylan to enter sixth grade, however, Renee had attended a Partners in Policy Making training session sponsored by the state's council on developmental disabilities. There, she had learned about Section 504 of the Rehabilitation Act and its requirements of "reasonable accommodations." She told Dylan that having those accommodations was like another boy having a cast for a broken arm; it was no big deal to accept those benefits. Together, Renee and Dylan insisted that he receive Section 504 accommodations and that he graduate from his status as a student covered by IDEA. Instead of benefiting from the federal special education law, Dylan now benefited from the federal antidiscrimination law.

Count up the "graduations" in Dylan's life: from "nondisabled" to having a disability, from near death to life, from critical care to center-based rehabilitation, from that to home-based rehabilitation, from that to IDEA benefits, and from that to Section 504's protection.

No student graduates without first having been educated. Often, the student learns from professionals, sometimes from family, and sometimes from peers. Dylan's teachers—in the broadest sense—were from each of those groups.

His physicians saved his life. Occupational therapists, speech-language therapists, and physical therapists restored most of his functional abilities. His mother, Renee, resigned her job and stopped taking college courses to coordinate his care at home. His father, Bob, his aunt Laura, and his grandmother Ruby delivered the therapies they learned from his professionals. Dylan's older brother, also named Bob, was Dylan's model; no matter his circumstances, Dylan was determined to follow Bob into kindergarten and then through the grades ahead.

Dylan's classmates in special education also played a role, however accidentally. By having an IEP and being educated with them, Dylan learned that he could do a lot more for himself than his teachers allowed him to do. Having learned that much and armed with Renee's knowledge about Section 504, Dylan decided that he would abandon his IDEA rights, the special education pull-out programs, and (truth be told) the labeling that came with being in special education.

Dylan is bright enough to have understood something profound about himself: He wanted to be more typical than not. He's determined enough to have

CHAPTER OBJECTIVES

◆ You will learn why Dylan's characteristics are typical of students with traumatic brain injury and why the cause of his and other students' injuries almost always has the same implications for educators and their students.

◆ You will learn how medical and related services and educational evaluations arm teachers to appropriately educate students with traumatic brain injury.

◆ You will learn about "reasonable accommodations" under the federal antidiscrimination law that you read about in Chapter 1 and how they, as much as any IEP-based services, make it possible for students with traumatic brain injury to participate in and make progress through general education.

◆ You will learn how you can modify the curriculum for students with traumatic brain injury and help them take the "graduation" steps that Dylan has taken, moving from one stage in life to another, headed toward independence, full participation in all aspects of his life, and economic productivity.

persevered through physically challenging therapies and to have relabeled himself. And he's so value-driven that he, with his family wholly behind him and with support from his teachers (Patti Whipple and Kate Simsek at Tiller Middle School, a state-approved charter school in Morehead City, North Carolina), seeks inclusion and independence.

Yet he's limited enough that he still needs therapy and accommodations. Because he injured the right side of his brain, he has functional limitations on the left side of his body. Occupational therapists target his fine-motor skills. He receives accommodations in taking tests and doing homework because traumatic brain injury scrambles a person's executive functions—his or her ability to plan and to execute a plan.

Because he still has not fully recovered his strength, simply getting from one place to another in school exhausts him, often to the point that he physically cannot carry out his homework assignments as well as his classmates who do not have disabilities. Because academic demands—sparked by state and district assessments—increase from grade to grade, schoolwork becomes more and more difficult, despite the fact that Dylan is an excellent reader.

And because all of these circumstances together make him realize that he still has a disability, he is offended when students call him names, he prefers the company of compassionate peers (usually girls), and he cannot easily hide his frustration and sadness.

Tellingly, his teacher Patti Whipple cautions us all: "Don't judge before you deal with the student. TBI is not a death sentence. Indeed, I'd love to teach a classroom of a thousand Dylans."

myeducationlab

PEARSON

After reading this chapter, complete the Self-Assessment for Chapter 13 on MyEducationLab to gauge your initial understanding of chapter content.

IDENTIFYING STUDENTS WITH TRAUMATIC BRAIN INJURY

Defining Traumatic Brain Injury

IDEA defines **traumatic brain injury** (TBI) as

> an acquired injury to the brain caused by an external physical force, resulting in total or partial functional disability or psychosocial impairment, or both, that adversely affects a child's educational performance. Traumatic brain injury applies to open or closed head injuries resulting in impairments in one or more areas, such as cognition; language; memory; attention; reasoning; abstract thinking; judgment; problem-solving; sensory, perceptual, and motor abilities; psychosocial behavior; physical functions; information processing; and speech. Traumatic brain injury does not apply to brain injuries that are congenital or degenerative, or to brain injuries induced by birth trauma.

We call your attention to three aspects of this definition: First, TBI must be an **acquired injury** (occurring after a child is born). It is inappropriate to classify a student as having TBI if her brain injury was **congenital** (present at birth) or if it occurred at the time of delivery. Second, TBI must be caused by an external physical force. Thus, if a student had **encephalitis** (inflammation of the brain) and her brain was injured as a result of the inflammation, she would not be classified as having TBI. Finally, the term *TBI* applies to both open and closed head injuries (Stavinoha, 2005; Yeates, 2000). An **open head injury** penetrates the bones of the skull, allowing bacteria to have contact with the brain and potentially impairing specific functions, usually only those controlled by the injured part of the brain. Dylan Outlaw clearly meets all three criteria.

Figure 13.1 **Areas of the brain and related general functions**

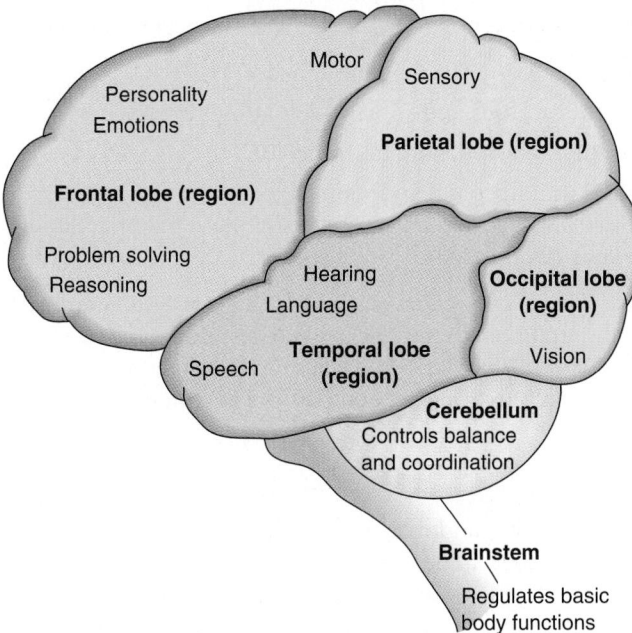

Source: From *Missouri Head Injury Guide for Survivors, Families, and Caregivers,* by Missouri Head Injury Foundation, 1991, Jefferson City, State of Missouri, Copyright 1991 by State of Missouri. Reprinted with permission.

Figure 13.1 illustrates the six areas of the brain (including the brain stem) and their related functions. A **closed head injury** does not involve penetration or fracture of the bones of the skull. It results from an external blow or from the brain being whipped back and forth rapidly, causing it to rub against and bounce off the rough, jagged interior of the skull. Figure 13.2 illustrates how a closed head injury can occur in an automobile accident.

Figure 13.2 **Closed head injury accident**

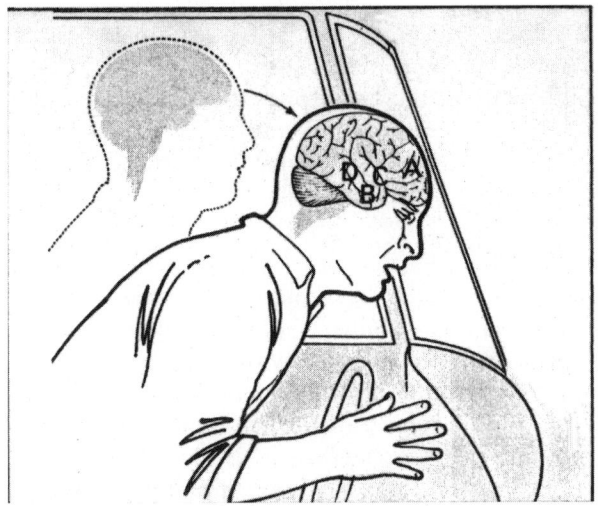

Source: From the U.S. Department of Health and Human Services. (1984). *Head injury: Hope through research.* Bethesda, MD: Author.

In fall 2006, approximately 0.04 percent (23,967) of all students aged 6 through 21 in special education nationally were classified as having a traumatic brain injury (U.S. Department of Education, 2008). Other data (Langlois, Rutland-Brown, & Thomas, 2004) reveal the following:

♦ Males are 1.5 times more likely to sustain TBI than are females.

♦ Students in the age groups of birth to four and 15 to 19 are at highest risk for TBI.

♦ African Americans experience the highest death rate from TBI.

♦ Of individuals who are admitted to a hospital, approximately 10 percent have a severe injury, another 10 percent have a moderate injury, and the remaining 80 percent have a mild injury (Kraus & Chu, 2005).

Overall, based on data in the United States alone, "an average of 1.4 million TBIs occur each year, including 1.1 million emergency department visits, 235,000 hospitalizations, and 50,000 deaths" (Langlois, Rutland-Brown, & Wald, 2006, p. 375). Dylan Outlaw certainly added to these data; emergency rooms and hospitalization have been part of his young life.

Describing the Characteristics

Students with TBI differ in onset, complexity, and recovery from students with other disabilities (Michaud et al., 2007; Stavinoha, 2005). Their injuries may affect them in many areas of their functioning; however, they often have the same or similar characteristics as students who have learning disabilities (Chapter 5), communication disorders (Chapter 6), emotional or behavioral disorders (Chapter 7), intellectual disability (Chapter 9), health impairments (Chapter 11), and physical disabilities (Chapter 12). Dylan's injury caused learning, communication, emotional, and physical challenges. Of those, the emotional challenges are the greatest, says his mother, Renee. Interestingly, his teacher Patti downplays those challenges: "When any student has any emotional problem, we deal with it right then. It doesn't take long. All kids have problems, especially during puberty. Then we move along in class." She knows that Dylan is not so unlike other students and that a short deviation from lesson plans, to address behaviors, makes teaching easier and learning more effective.

The number and magnitude of each student's post-TBI functional changes will vary according to the site and extent of injury, the length of time the student was in a **coma** (an unconscious state), and the student's maturational stage at the time of the injury (Gennarelli & Graham, 2005). The extent of functional changes and the course of recovery after the injury depend largely on whether it was mild, moderate, or severe. Twenty-nine percent of individuals with moderate to severe TBI die within 30 days of their accident, whereas only 0.2 percent of individuals with mild TBI die within the same period (Brown et al., 2004). Dylan was one of the lucky ones; he survived the dire prognosis, based on severity, and the bone shards that could have blinded him somehow left him.

Individuals with traumatic brain injury may benefit from physical rehabilitation, which can help address fatigue, poor coordination, and other temporary or permanent physical injuries as a result of an accident.

Physical Changes

The extent of students' physical changes can range from nonexistent to mild, moderate, or severe. "The site(s) of brain injury determines the type of motor dysfunction that follows. Spasticity, rigidity, and **ataxia**/tremor are the most common motor abnormalities" (Michaud et al., 2007, p. 465).

Coordination problems, physical weakness, and fatigue are common effects for students with TBI, as they are for Dylan. Students who were previously athletic find these changes to be especially frustrating. Fortunately, however, their coordination and physical strength usually improve as their brains heal and they undergo rehabilitation, especially occupational therapy to reacquire the fine-motor skills that help them function independently. Dylan's injury was on the right side of his brain, so his left side is impaired; his occupational therapy targeted his left-side fine-motor skills (holding eating utensils, for example). Students' fatigue often lingers, though, and if occupational therapy and other rehabilitation interventions are not brought to bear, their muscles may **atrophy**, resulting in lost or reduced muscle strength.

Typically, students also experience headaches (Buyer, 1999). Almost one third of students with TBI report headaches during the first year after the injury (Chapman, 1998). If your students have frequent headaches, you will need to make accommodations in their academic or other school schedules and assignments, give them opportunities to rest, and provide times and places for them to take medications.

Cognitive Changes

When a TBI injury is mild, students usually do not face significant academic challenges (Max, 2005), nor do they usually have long-term limitations on cognitive functioning; by contrast, students with severe TBI have significant cognitive impairments (Michaud et al., 2007). The impairments associated with severe TBI include a decline in IQ and memory and difficulties in academic areas such as word decoding, reading comprehension, spelling, and arithmetic; these impairments tend to persist (Semrud-Clikeman, 2001; Stavinoha, 2005). Almost half of children with severe TBI demonstrate significant attention problems and approximately one-fifth qualify for the diagnosis of AD/HD (Yeates et al., 2005). Impairments in attention include difficulty with dividing attention between two or more tasks relatively simultaneously, losing one's train of thought, becoming distracted, and following conversation. Despite the fact that Dylan has shed his IDEA/IEP program and taken on a 504 accommodations plan, he still has significant academic challenges in mathematics. But that's it—math is his only problem subject. And even it is not insurmountable. Dylan scored 2.8 (on a 4.0 scale) on his end-of-grade testing.

The child's age at the time of injury is a second factor significantly affecting cognitive functioning and rehabilitation prospects (Stavinoha, 2005). Infants or preschoolers, such as Dylan, tend to have a greater impairment of cognitive abilities than do children whose injury occurs at a later age. Moreover, very young children have greater brain vulnerability, and the impairment often becomes more evident over time, especially as cognitive demands increase (in part because of the statewide assessments administered under No Child Left Behind). Again, as with all aspects of TBI, specific changes are highly influenced by the area of the brain that is damaged. Children and youth with more severe TBI have a much higher likelihood of developing AD/HD within the first couple of years after their injury (Max et al., 2004).

A child's cognitive functioning often improves as a result of rehabilitation, especially when the child is over the age of 4 (Cheng, Khairi, & Ritter, 2006). Children (excluding infants) have a 55 percent chance for a good recovery as contrasted to a 21 percent chance for adults. Although many people believe that recovery of cognitive functioning happens only soon after the injury occurs, a 5-year longitudinal study found that 18 percent of injured teenagers and adults continued to improve from year 1 to year 5, approximately 75 percent stayed the same, and 7 percent increased their cognitive functioning (Hammond et al., 2004).

Undoubtedly, Dylan has improved cognitively. For a full month after his accident, he was unable to speak at all. He received speech-language therapy, but he seemed "locked into a shell," not just verbally impaired but emotionally closeted. His therapists elicited response by asking him to play video games. By using both his right and left hands to play the games, he began to reacquire coordination. By mastering one game and then another, he began to talk about himself and the games. The therapists used his favorite game, "Super Mario & Super Smash Brothers," as an incentive; whenever he completed one therapy successfully, he would earn the chance to play that game. They soon learned that Dylan was a competitive young boy. He was determined to succeed, as indeed he has.

IEP Tip

The student's IEP team should identify strategies to minimize challenges that cause a student to have headaches and to accommodate her when she does.

myeducationlab

Go to the Activities and Application section in Chapter 13 of MyEducationLab and complete Activity 1. As you read the case and answer the accompanying questions, reflect on the many issues the classroom teacher must keep in mind for a student with a traumatic brain injury.

Instructional tools such as computers can help students with disabilities write more easily.

His teacher Patti describes him as very bright, while acknowledging that math poses problems for him. She includes him in the general curriculum, allowing him extended time to complete tests and permitting him to mark the "bubbles" on test-score sheets but also to mark his textbook (an easier task than filling in the bubbles). The reasonable accommodation—marking both books and bubbles—serves two functions. By allowing Dylan to mark in the book, she lets him prove what he knows; by allowing him to mark the bubbles, she keeps him from being so different from his peers who do not have disabilities.

Emotional, Behavioral, and Social Changes

Emotional, behavioral, and social changes can be especially problematic for children and youth with TBI. Dylan "melts down" from time to time, his frustration getting the better of him when tasks he thinks he should be able to do elude him. One of Patti's reasonable accommodation is subtle; she allows him to leave the classroom, compose himself, give himself a pep talk, and return. Often he is out of the room for only a few minutes, so he does not lose much, if any, real instructional time and indeed he regains his ability to learn. Approximately one half to two thirds of children with severe TBI experience emotional and behavioral challenges approximately two years post-injury; however, this percentage drops to 10 percent to 21 percent for children with a mild to moderate injury (Max, 2005). Depending upon the extent and location of their injuries, students face a multitude of challenges (Max et al., 2004):

IEP Tip

To help students become more aware of the challenges facing them and of the capacities they still have, IEP teams should encourage students to attend IEP team meetings and participate in developing their IEPs, with support as appropriate. Recall that Dylan himself chose to remove himself from IDEA and IEP benefits and to receive a 504 plan instead.

◆ Significant increases in anxiety symptoms often occur; these include worry, obsessive-compulsive characteristics, separation anxiety, and phobias (Vasa et al., 2002). Anxiety characteristics are more likely in children who tended to be more anxious before the injury and in children who experienced TBI at a younger age.

◆ Post-traumatic stress disorder can occur in response to the stress of the accident, as well as to the stress associated with hospitalization and loss of a regular and predictable routine (Warden & Labbate, 2005). Approximately two thirds of children with TBI experienced post-traumatic stress syndrome in the first three months, but the percentage fell to about 10 percent two years post-injury (Max, 2005).

◆ Judgment can be impaired, and the injury can lead to impulsive, risky behavior (O'Shanich & O'Shanich, 2005). Often students are not aware that they have impaired judgment and that their behaviors are inappropriate.

◆ Irritability and aggressiveness often are experienced by individuals with TBI, especially in the acute phase just after the injury occurs. (Silver, Wudofsky, & Anderson, 2005)

Indeed, many students with TBI are not aware of their own impairments (Flashman, Amador, & McAllister, 2005). They may not know about specific deficits or difficulties facing them, they may experience emotional responses to recognizing that they do not function as they once did, and they may not comprehend the impact of the impairment in their daily lives. Dylan is one of the exceptions to this general rule; he is quite aware of his limitations and equally determined to overcome them.

Determining the Causes

There are four major causes of acquired TBI:

◆ *Falls* (accounting for 28 percent) are most frequent at each end of the life span—young children from birth to age 4 and adults aged 75 or older.

◆ *Automobile accidents* (accounting for 20 percent) occur most frequently among teenagers aged 15 to 19.

- *Events of being struck by/against* (accounting for 19 percent) typically occur in sports and recreation when a person collides with a moving or stationary object (sledding, skiing, snowboarding, diving, skateboarding, playing contact sports, or being hit by a ball). The majority of the 1.6 million to 3.8 million sports/recreation-related TBIs occurring annually are of a mild nature (Langlois et al., 2006).

- *Assaults* (accounting for 11 percent) frequently involve firearms, which are the leading cause of death related to TBI (CDC, 1999). Suicide accounts for approximately two thirds of the deaths from firearm-related TBI. Non-firearm assaults include child abuse that results in infant head injuries (National Institutes of Health, 1998).

Child abuse involving TBI accounts for approximately one fifth of hospital admissions in children younger than 6½ years old and approximately one third of admissions of children younger than 3 years old (Reece & Sege, 2000). **Shaken baby syndrome** refers to TBI that results when a caregiver has shaken a child violently, often in situations when the caregiver is frustrated because of the child's crying (Michaud et al., 2007). Thorough evaluation is required in order to confirm that child abuse has occurred and provide for clinical services to ensure child protection (Cobley & Sanders, 2006; Glick & Staley, 2007).

EVALUATING STUDENTS WITH TRAUMATIC BRAIN INJURY

The evaluation of students with TBI needs to be comprehensive (across the student's physical, cognitive, emotional-behavioral, and developmental faculties) and ongoing because children change, just as Dylan changed after his injuries (Russo, Dunn, Pace, & Codding, 2007; Turkstra et al., 2005). Figure 13.3 illustrates the evaluation process.

Determining the Presence of Traumatic Brain Injury

Immediately after a child experiences a head injury, the first action is resuscitation—stabilizing the child and, if necessary, performing surgery. The next step is to assess the extent of neurological impairment. The Glasgow Outcomes Scale is a standard scale for assessing the extent of neurological impairment. It classifies injuries into the following broad groups: "(1) death, (2) persistent vegetative state (i.e., no cerebral cortical function as judged behaviorally), (3) severe disability (conscious but dependent on 24-hour care), (4) moderate disability (disabled but capable of independent self-care), and (5) good recovery (mild impairment with persistent sequelae but able to participate in a normal social life)" (Kraus & Chu, 2005, p. 17). The scale focuses on the best response that an individual is able to make in terms of eye, verbal, and motor responses.

The Glasgow Outcomes Scale has a pediatric version that researchers believe has superior psychometric characteristics compared to other pediatric scales (Cheng, Khairi, & Ritter, 2006; Simpson, 2006). The items are as follows (Cheng, Khairi, & Ritter, 2006):

- Eyes open—spontaneously, to speech, to pain, none (graded from 4 to 1).

- Best verbal response—coos/babbles, irritable, cries to pain, moans, none (graded from 5 to 1).

- Best motor response—normal spontaneous movement, withdraws to touch, withdraws to pain, abnormal flexion, abnormal extension, none (graded from 6 to 1).

A severe injury would be a score of less than 9 points; a moderate head injury is indicated by a score of 9 to 12; and a mild injury is scored greater than 12. The maximum number of points would be 14, signifying the top score in each of the three areas.

Determining the Nature of Specially Designed Instruction and Services

Students with TBI need frequent evaluation and reevaluation because of the nature and trend of their recovery, especially in the first couple of years after the onset of injury. To evaluate frequently, teachers make classroom observations of the key neurological skills

Figure 13.3

Nondiscriminatory assessment process for determining the presence of traumatic brain injury

Observation	**Parents observe:** The student receives a head injury from an accident, fall, sports injury, act of violence, or other cause.
	Physicians observe: The student has an open or closed head injury caused by an external physical force.
	Teacher observes: In the case of a mild head injury that might not have been treated by a physician, the teacher observes changes—physical, cognitive, communication, social, behavioral, and/or personality.
Screening	**Assessment measures:**
	Scanning instruments: EEGs, CAT scans, MRIs, PETs, and other technology determine the extent of injury.
	Neurological exam: A neurologist examines the student for indications of brain injury.
	Coma scale: In instances of moderate to severe head injuries that induce comas, these scales provide some information about probable outcome.
Prereferral	Prereferral typically is not used with these students because the sudden onset and severity of the disability indicates a need for special education or related services.
Referral	Students with moderate to severe TBI should be referred to special education evaluation while still in rehabilitation. Teachers should refer students with mild head injuries if they notice any changes—physical, cognitive, communication, social, behavioral, and/or personality.
Nondiscriminatory evaluation procedures and standards	**Assessment measures:**
	Individualized intelligence test: The student tends to score higher on the verbal section than on the performance section.
	Individualized achievement tests: The student usually has peaks and valleys in scores. The student often retains skills in some areas, while other skills are affected adversely by the injury.
	Adaptive behavior scales: The student may have difficulty in social, self-care, household, and community skills as a result of the injury.
	Cognitive processing tests: The student may have difficulty in areas of attention, memory, concentration, motivation, and perceptual integration.
	Social, emotional, and behavioral changes: The student may demonstrate difficulty relating to others and behaving in socially appropriate ways. The student may have problem behavior and/or emotional disorders.
	Anecdotal records: The student's cognitive, communication, motor, and behavior skills appear to have changed from what was indicated in records before the accident.
	Curriculum-based assessment: The student may have difficulty in areas of curriculum that were not problematic before the injury.
	Direct observation: The student appears frustrated, has a limited attention span, fatigues easily, or lacks motivation to perform academic tasks. The student may have difficulty relating appropriately to others. Skills can improve rapidly, especially during the early post-injury stage.
Determination	The nondiscriminatory evaluation team determines that special education and related services are needed.

Functional Domain | **Examples of Problems**

Memory
- __ Cannot remember the previous day's lecture
- __ Difficulty finding the location of classrooms bathroom
- __ Cannot remember class schedule, locker combination
- __ Constantly losing books, assignments
- __ Struggles to learn new information

Attention and Concentration
- __ Loses track of conversations with peers
- __ Constantly repeats herself when talking to teacher/peers
- __ Difficulty listening to lectures, instructions
- __ Does not know homework assignments
- __ Does not complete tasks

Executive Functioning
- __ Gets easily confused with changes in daily routine
- __ Disorganized and cannot accomplish simple tasks
- __ Cannot give directions to others (e.g., how to get to her house).
- __ Difficulty starting and completing assignments

Self-Awareness
- __ Believes she already knows material to be presented
- __ Falsely assumes she has gotten an A on a failed test
- __ Does not give herself ample time to complete work

Language
- __ Knows what she wants to say but cannot find the right words to express herself
- __ Is teased by classmates because her speech sounds slurred
- __ No longer understands written language
- __ Cannot name familiar objects in the classroom (e.g., desk, pencil)
- __ May use inappropriate word or substitute a nonsense word for a real one

Source: TEACHING EXCEPTIONAL CHILDREN by Keyser-Marcus, L., Briel, L., Sherron-Targett, P., Yasuda, S., Johnson, S., & Wehmen, P. Copyright 2002 by Council for Exceptional Children (VA). Reproduced with permission of Council for Exceptional Children (VA) in the formats Textbook and Other book via Copyright Clearance Center.

affected by TBI. Figure 13.4 is a classroom observation checklist that includes the cognitive and academic domains frequently affected by TBI. Teachers can complete this checklist monthly during the first year after a head injury, and less frequently thereafter.

Sometimes, checklists are neither necessary nor desirable. There were only 16 students in Patti's class, and Dylan's academic abilities were quite strong (except in mathematics), so she did not use checklists, but she did observe closely and make accommodations for him as he needed them. Patti describes her approach in these words:

> We treated all the students equally, but each according to their individual needs. When one of them had a problem, we addressed it right then and there. That's what we did for Dylan, too. Yes, he wore his emotions on his sleeve. But all kids have issues; he was not unlike them. They were moving into their teenage years. Hormones were raging, in all of them. They were all very self-aware, so we just formed a circle and let them talk about themselves. We didn't single Dylan out. We didn't have to discipline him. He had no behavioral problems, he just withdrew a bit and we allowed him to do that. We were a charter school; we could set our own culture. It made a huge difference for every student—to be treated like every other but with acknowledgment of their differences.

IEP Tip

Monthly trends from the classroom observation checklist can be a helpful guide in formulating IEP goals and objectives.

DESIGNING AN APPROPRIATE IEP

Partnering for Special Education and Related Services

One of the most challenging times for students who have TBI occurs when they return to school after having been hospitalized or in a center-based rehabilitation program. Re-entry IEPs usually result from the collaboration of special and general education teachers and related school personnel, physicians, other health care providers, and rehabilitation professionals. Physicians and rehabilitation professionals play specialized roles in describing a student's brain functioning and prognosis and in designing and helping to implement the student's IEP. Many rehabilitation centers realize the particular importance of the student's re-entry to school and employ a hospital-school liaison (sometimes referred to as a school re-entry specialist).

Dylan was in preschool at the time he was injured, so he had an entry plan (not a re-entry plan) because he was moving from preschool to kindergarten. Thanks to intensive occupational, speech-language, and physical therapy at the hospital, in a rehabilitation center, and at home (where all the adult members of his family carried out therapy), Dylan "graduated" from preschool to kindergarten on time; he never missed a beat. In Box 13.1, you will find tips for creating partnerships for transitions such as Dylan's.

In many cases, teams formed for re-entry remain intact to support the student in school. Some schools have designated a core team to foster partnerships. The team usually consists of general and special education teachers, parents, a speech pathologist, a physical therapist, an occupational therapist, and the school district's director of curriculum. They all meet monthly to discuss how the student is developing and to consider how to respond to the student's academic, developmental, emotional-behavioral, and functional needs. Rather than responding to the needs in isolation, the team proposes solutions that its members can implement and evaluate as a team and with the cooperation of the student's parents. For example, if sign language is an effective augmentative communication for the student, the general education teacher may learn to sign or invite the district's deaf education teacher into the classroom to teach her and her students basic sign language. Dylan's team consisted of his teachers, including Patti Whipple; the school's director, Kate Simsek; a speech-language therapist; an occupational therapist; and a physical therapist. He had no IEP, but Kate coordinated these services, in cooperation with Renee, Dylan's mother.

Determining Supplementary Aids and Services

Many of the classroom modifications discussed in the chapter on students with autism (Chapter 11) also benefit students with TBI. There are also technology devices to support students with TBI, particularly to compensate for their impaired memory skills. O'Neil-Pirozzi, Kendrick, Goldstein, and Glenn (2004) conducted a study that identified the potential uses of memory aids:

- Following a routine schedule
- Keeping appointments that are not routine
- Taking medications
- Remembering to perform a new task
- Marking when to start or end a task (p. 183)

IEP teams should consider the role of technology in addressing these challenges, as illustrated in Box 13.2, which identifies electronic aids for memory support for students with TBI. Dylan does not use any assistive technologies. Like every other student at Tiller Middle School, he uses a three-ring spiral notebook in which he records his schedule and his responsibilities. Patti also uses it to commu-

Simple assistive technology devices can be invaluable tools for helping students with TBI complete their day-to-day tasks.

From Hospital-Based Rehabilitation to Successful School Reentry

Partnerships among various professionals and students with TBI and their families can make rehabilitation less traumatic for student and family. But collaboration is not always easy to achieve.

For one thing, physicians and other health care providers have a focus different from that of the other professionals. In some instances, they are intent on saving the student's life. If they are successful, they then focus on rehabilitation, itself a specialized field of medicine that involves not only physicians but also other professionals:

◆ Pulmonary therapists (to develop the student's lung and heart capacity)

◆ Physical therapists (to develop the student's muscle strength and stamina)

◆ Occupational therapists (to develop the student's ability to do the chores of daily living, such as brushing her teeth and tying her shoes)

◆ Psychologists or cognitive retrainers (to help the student learn how to think again)

◆ Speech-language therapists (to help the student regain the ability to communicate)

Whether these professionals work in a hospital or a rehabilitation center, they are trying to restore the student's ability to learn.

Educators, on the other hand, are teaching the student what she once knew, moving her to the next lesson, and always increasing her cognitive abilities. Educators are also helping students cope with behavioral and social challenges that typically arise in school.

Finally, the student's family members are experiencing their own grief and shock over the sudden onset of the TBI. Their goals may include all of the goals of the professionals, but they also have to learn to alter their family routines to address the emerging needs and challenges associated with the injury and rehabilitation and to re-integrate their child into their lives and family.

What Are Partnership Tips for Hospital-Based Rehabilitation?

◆ Keep the same long-term goal in mind.

◆ Identify the short-term goals and how they will help achieve the long-term goals.

◆ Show how one professional's techniques complement another's.

◆ Acknowledge that different professionals bring different but equally valuable strategies to partnership efforts, albeit at different times.

◆ Remember that the child and family are being launched into new territory and deserve the respect and support that will enable them to be as successful as possible.

What Are Partnership Tips for Hospital-to-School Transitions?

◆ Involve educators during the hospital stay.

◆ Keep school personnel updated on student medical progress.

◆ Make the period of homebound instruction as short as possible.

◆ Frequently monitor the student's progress after re-entry.

◆ Assign someone to be the point person for coordinating the transition (Ylvisaker et al., 2001, p. 83)

What Key Abilities Predict a Student's Successful Reentry?

◆ To attend to the instructor and instruction

◆ To understand and retain information

◆ To reason and express ideas

◆ To solve problems

◆ To plan and monitor his own performance (Semrud-Clikeman, 2001, p. 112)

---

nicate with Renee. For Dylan, low tech does the job. Indeed, given Dylan's immense curiosity and his unusually strong ability to remember how to spell words, Renee and Patti have found that it is best to keep a good dictionary at the ready for Dylan to use anytime he confronts a word whose precise meaning is unclear. Dylan is a "meaning maven," intent on mastering dictionary definitions.

Some teachers and students will want to combine technology with other strategies to help students remember what they need to know. Box 13.3 describes a mnemonic approach for solving problems.

Like most students with TBI, Dylan has short-term memory challenges. His daily planner—the three-ring spiral notebook—helps him stay on track. But so does Patti's approach. "When

IEP Tip

When considering technology to support students with TBI, IEP teams should remember that sometimes less is more. Not everything has to be high tech to be effective.

Electronic Aids for Memory Support

Throughout this text, you have learned how technology—from assistive technology to electronic and information technology, to educational technology—can promote student learning and greater independence. This is true for students with traumatic brain injury as well. In fact, there is a host of electronic aids available to support memory, organization, and scheduling activities. At the heart of all of these activities is memory support. Such electronic memory aids range from simple to complex technologies. In some cases, the student does not need anything as complex as a PDA and may do fine with only prompts to help her remember the time of an appointment, when to change classes, or when to take medication. In fact, when considering technology, the motto "simple is better" is worth keeping in mind. There is a tendency to want to get the latest and most fashionable technology support, but in most cases, a device's reliability, not its newness, is its most important feature. Quite simply, less-complex devices usually require less maintenance and are more reliable than more-complex devices.

You can support students with TBI to learn and function more effectively if you consider introducing some of these electronic memory aids:

Pagers: A pager (also called a beeper) is a small radio receiver that produces sounds (beeps, tones, buzzes) or visual stimuli (flashing lights, text messages) or vibrates when it receives a signal. The most common way to activate a pager is through a phone call, but any device that can send a radio signal can activate pagers. Pagers and digital beepers require a subscription service like a cellular phone or an Internet account.

Digital watches: Simple and inexpensive ($10 to $15) electronic watches can also be used to provide audio prompts (beeps). Most of those watches have different functions, including a timer, a stopwatch, and an alarm function. At least one watch also comes with a built-in pager. All of these can be used as memory aids. The downside with regard to use of off-the-shelf electronic watches is that they can often be very confusing to set up and use.

Medication reminder devices: Medication reminder devices provide prompts to remind people to take their medicine. Most are built into a pill tray or holder, into which the appropriate dosage can be inserted, and can be set to emit auditory sounds (beeps, chimes, rings) or to vibrate between 4 and 12 times per day.

Digital mobile phones: Sometimes, memory support can be both as complex and as simple as using a mobile phone! With the advent and wide adoption of text messaging, it is possible to provide prompts to students without the obtrusiveness of the ring of the phone.

PDA prompting systems: The Visual Assistant system you learned about in Chapter 10 is an example of a prompting system operating from a handheld computer. These systems can be very powerful, providing audio and video prompting supports. They are also more expensive. But if simpler prompting mechanisms don't work, they may be worth the investment.

Dylan can't remember something, I simply review what he needs to know, and review it again and again until it 'takes.' He has a folder of school work that he can refer to in order to trigger his memory. And his daily planner helps him with his executive skills, staying organized, and planning. When he does well, such as by being on time to class and completing his work, we put a 'stamp' into his book. Each teacher does that with every other student, so we don't treat Dylan specially. The more stamps a student gets, the more special field trips the student goes on. Dylan likes the challenge and loves the rewards."

Planning for Universal Design for Learning

A traumatic brain injury often makes it difficult for students to pay attention as teachers present a course's content; they also may have difficulty processing the information presented to them, particularly when it is presented in lecture format. Dylan faces that challenge. Indeed, he has traces of attention-deficit disorder and sometimes uses one kind of medication to regulate his hyperactivity and another to regulate his moods. Universal design for learning modifies how teachers present information. Almost every IEP team should consider the "how" challenge. Renee and Patti have learned that simply redirecting Dylan works most of the time. When he is especially fatigued and wanders off mentally, Patti

Mnemonics for Solving Problems

A good mnemonic must

- ◆ Solve a problem (i.e., make sense to people and their challenges); without this connection, students will not integrate the strategy into their learning
- ◆ Relate to the actual activity it is designed to address
- ◆ Have a sing-song quality, like a rhyme, that helps the student connect the word to the sound
- ◆ Imply activity and elicit a good mental image
- ◆ Be simple and easy to rehearse and recall

Often students with TBI have a great deal of difficulty solving a problem in a logical way. They benefit from a step-by-step method that can be applied in various situations. Using rhyming verse and word mnemonics, Parente and colleagues (2001) developed a mnemonic called SOLVE. Each letter of the word SOLVE reminds the person of some important aspect of a problem-solving process. Here is how SOLVE works:

- ◆ Specify the problem—define the problem
- ◆ Organize your solution—keep several options in mind
- ◆ Listen to advice—take others' advice
- ◆ Vary your thinking—ask, "What makes the problem worse?"
- ◆ Evaluate if your solution worked—read this verse again (p.18).

The next step is for students to decide which of the several possible options would be the solution. The DECIDE acronym teaches a rhyme that a student can follow to start thinking about a decision and to consider the decision from several possible viewpoints. DECIDE seeks the opinions of different people so

that the student will make more correct than incorrect decisions (Parente, Anderson-Parente, & Stapleton, 2001).

- ◆ Do not procrastinate—decide to begin
- ◆ Evaluate each option—choose those that are WIN-WIN
- ◆ Create new options when the others won't do
- ◆ Investigate existing policies—limit what you choose
- ◆ Discuss the decision with others and listen to them
- ◆ Evaluate your feelings—before acting think twice (p.18)

Putting These Strategies to Work for Progress in the General Curriculum

1. How might one of Dylan's teachers integrate the SOLVE and DECIDE strategies into his education?

2. Propose a plan for how Dylan might serve as a peer tutor using the SOLVE and DECIDE strategies in teaching problem solving to a younger student.

3. How can a partnership among the special and general education teacher and Dylan's family assist in implementing the use of mnemonics for solving problems? How could Renee and Bob incorporate mnemonics at home?

myeducationlab

Go to the Activities and Application section in Chapter 13 of MyEducationLab and complete Activity 2. As you interact with the simulation and answer the accompanying questions, think about how you could scaffold this problem-solving strategy for students who need extra support.

lets him lie down on the couch in her classroom. From there, he listens to her and his classmates so he does not wholly miss out on instruction. When he is physically able, he retakes his usual place in the classroom. These short times down help him greatly—his mind is engaged while his body refreshes itself. Patti adds, "Of course, I would do that for any student." How better to describe "universal"?

Teachers also can use the evidence-based practice of instructional pacing. This strategy involves delivering course content in smaller increments or packets of information, modifying the time periods between each delivery of new information, and allowing students to respond to smaller chunks of information (Ylvisaker et al., 2001). Hall (2002) identified instructional pacing as one evidence-based instructional strategy. There are others (Hall, 2002):

- ◆ *Appropriate instructional pacing:* Vary how fast you present information and how often you ask your students to respond, bearing in mind their differences in attention, information processing, and cognitive ability.

- ◆ *Frequent student responses:* Ask for frequent responses and require your students to respond through different formats so as to actively engage them in learning.

- ◆ *Adequate processing time:* Allow your students varying times to respond, taking into account their processing capacity and giving some students more "think" time than others.

- *Monitoring responses:* Monitor the quality and nature of your students' responses to determine if they are mastering the content of your course. If this monitoring suggests they are not, adjust your instruction soon; do not wait until the lesson is over.
- *Frequent feedback:* Provide supportive and specific feedback to your students on correct and incorrect responses and correct the latter immediately instead of waiting until after the lesson. (pp. 4–5)

Chapter 7 (emotional and behavioral disorders) discussed mastery assessment and mastery learning as a way to ensure ongoing progress. The strategies of appropriate pacing and explicit instruction incorporate a mastery learning approach, one in which teachers assess their students' knowledge frequently and pace their instruction accordingly.

IEP teams should simultaneously consider both instructional pacing strategies and technology to deliver content information. For example, watching a film may have the benefit of visual input, but in many cases information presented in video format is paced briskly. Students may have a difficult time paying attention throughout the entire film and processing the information it presents. Teachers can pause the videos to pace the video presentation, using that time to solicit student responses and determine student mastery. Alternatively, digital presentation of information in computer formats allows students to regulate the presentation of information and gives teachers the opportunity to probe their students' understanding.

Planning for Other Educational Needs

The long-term effects of frontal lobe injuries in children and adolescents require interventions to address present and anticipated future needs. As you know from reading about Dylan, students with TBI, particularly those in middle school and high school, need to develop or refine their self-management, learning, thinking, and problem-solving abilities. That is especially true when students are planning their transition from school to adulthood, including the transition to college.

It can be challenging and even frightening for a student with TBI to transition from high school to a college or university. In Box 13.4, you will read about Megan Kohnke and her experiences in rehabilitation. A gifted student and soccer player, she had plans to attend Pepperdine University on a full athletic scholarship. After her intensive rehabilitation, Megan entered Pepperdine a semester late. To prepare for her entry, Megan and her mother met with her rehabilitation team. Her neuropsychologist mapped out strategies and modifications that Megan would need to be successful.

Immediately after arriving at Pepperdine, Megan met with each professor, introduced herself, and explained her disability. To illustrate her injury, she brought pictures of herself immediately after the accident, showing significant damage to her skull and featuring a bald Megan with a scar reaching from ear to ear. She wasn't seeking sympathy; rather, she used the pictures to show the professors what had happened to her. Her hair had grown back and now covered the scar, but she wanted them to know that, even though she looked fine, she had significant challenges because of this injury. She also brought information about her high school grades and about the rehabilitation she had recently completed. Megan explains,

> I wasn't looking for a handout but, instead, I wanted my professors to know what I had been through. I let them know that I was going to try extra hard, but without accommodations I wouldn't succeed. This wasn't easy for me. I used to be a very social person; but like most people who suffer from a TBI, I had lost confidence in myself and was uncomfortable talking with people, especially about myself. However, I met with every professor and told them what my neurologist suggested and how I would need additional time to complete tests, I would need to tape every lecture, I would benefit from any type of handout that would further illustrate the lecture, and I would need the assistance of the writing center.

Megan's Story

Four days after graduation, my three friends Dan, Elizabeth, and Sundance and I went on a fishing trip for steelhead at CJ Strike Reservoir outside of Boise, Idaho. We were driving down a dirt road when our vehicle was in a head-on collision with another vehicle. Dan and Sundance suffered many external injuries and were flown by helicopter to a local air force base. Elizabeth was a lifesaver; she managed to get herself free and with a broken arm ran to the nearest house which was a few miles away. Guided only by a porch light she made a sling for her arm out of her shirt as she ran along the road. Covered in blood, Elizabeth arrived at the house and called for help. Within 25 minutes a Life Flight crew had arrived and transported me to Saint Alphonsus Hospital for immediate surgery.

I received multiple injuries but the one that was the most severe was to my head. At St. Alphonsus, I immediately underwent a craniotomy. Dr. Michael Henbest repaired my skull, correcting a posterior displacement of the cranial vault. My skull was basically destroyed, and it took titanium mesh and plates to piece my skull back together. During surgery, a priest administered last rites, figuring that it was unlikely I would live through the night. A day after the surgery, I was transported to the Elk's Rehabilitation Center, where I remained in a coma for a week. My prognosis was not good, and the chance of a full recovery was very slim.

After nearly two weeks in a coma, I awoke at the Elk's Rehabilitation Center, where my family and the Brain Injury Program's staff had already begun my rehabilitation. My parents, brothers, and friends were by my side twenty-four hours a day, assisting in shifts, talking to me, holding my hands, and letting me know what was happening. Although I didn't respond (nor do I remember this), the Elk's staff explained to me that this interaction served as the beginning of the slow road of recovery for me. After I came out of the coma, I began a more strenuous rahabilitation. Although I cried a lot and was often frustrated, I approached it as I had other athletic endeavors and simply figured I was preparing for next season. Each day I worked with a series of staff members, working my way through a series of physical and mental exercises designed to build my physical strength and mental acuity.

—Megan Kohnke

Megan's first semester at Pepperdine included a number of other hurdles. One of the first involved being independent and attending to her basic needs. Unfortunately, simple activities such as selecting food at the cafeteria proved to be a challenge. Her mother explains,

I went to Pepperdine with Megan and spent the first week with her. The first morning, we went over to the cafeteria, and I told Megan to get something to eat. I left to allow her the opportunity to make the appropriate selection. After a long time, she returned to the room not having eaten a thing. With all the choices, Megan didn't know how to make a selection. I quickly learned she needed direct instruction in how to select food items from the cafeteria if she was going to eat in this environment. So we went through the various lines and reviewed what a balanced meal would include and selected various items. This involved further demonstration and practice before Megan was comfortable and able to eat on her own.

When her classes began, Megan, armed with a tape recorder, recorded every lecture. At the end of the day, she returned home and transcribed these lectures by hand. Next, she reviewed her handwritten transcription and created another outline that would help her study. This was exceedingly time-consuming but necessary for Megan's learning needs. On test days, Megan was allowed to arrive early and begin the test 30 to 60 minutes ahead of the rest of her peers. As Megan explains, "I was the first person there and the last to leave for every one of my tests." Megan's hard work and postsecondary accommodations have paid off. She successfully completed her undergraduate degree.

In Chapter 5, we discussed the importance of teaching students with learning disabilities the self-advocacy skills they need to transition from high school to college. These skills are equally important for students with TBI, as Megan so clearly demonstrates. Students with TBI need to be equipped with the knowledge and skills required to succeed in postsecondary education, beginning with the IEP planning team's efforts to identify the assistance that students will need and the instructional and support strategies that will help them achieve a positive transition to the next level of education, including college.

As you may have detected, one of Dylan's skills is self-advocacy. He is a determined youngster, as evidenced by his many "graduations" and his decision to abandon his IDEA rights for Section 504 accommodations. His teacher Patti describes him as "very bright" (and certainly his end-of-year scores, 2.8 on a 4.0 scale, justify her judgment, considering that his math scores depressed his other scores). According to her, Dylan has no problem communicating, and anyone who listens carefully to him will sense his trust and openness. She also says he has good judgment. But, she says, he wears his emotions on his sleeve; perhaps his oversensitivity comes from having worn a helmet while he was in elementary school to protect him from any further injury. Although Dylan is not aggressive or especially irritable, Renee has noted that he gets into tussles with other students, often responding to them but never initiating any teasing or bullying. Both Patti and Renee acknowledge that, long term, Dylan will need to know how to mediate his emotions so as to avoid inappropriate confrontations with teachers, peers, and employers. And he will need to know how to manage the complexities of middle school, high school, and then either junior college or technical school and perhaps even a four-year college. Balancing his intelligence, emotions, self-image, and executive functions (planning ahead, for example) is not at all beyond Dylan, but he will need instruction and coaching.

PEARSON
myeducationlab

Go to the Activities and Application section in Chapter 13 of MyEducationLab and complete Activity 3. As you watch the video and answer the accompanying questions, identify how the members of his collaborative team work together to ensure his inclusion in the general education classroom.

USING EFFECTIVE INSTRUCTIONAL STRATEGIES

Early Childhood Students: Collaborative Teaming

When you think of instructional strategies, you probably think of methods a teacher uses when teaching students. But you have already learned about strategies that involve students teaching other students and students teaching themselves, so it is obvious that not all instructional strategies focus on the teacher-student interaction. Collaborative teaming is an important strategy to promote inclusive practices for all students with disabilities, from early childhood to high school. It focuses on the role of teachers and not specifically on teacher-student interactions. Quite simply, collaborative teaming involves two or more people working together to educate students with disabilities. Thousand, Villa, and Nevin (2007) identified a collaborative team as a group of people who:

- Partner to achieve a shared goal
- Believe that all team members have unique and needed expertise and skills, and value each person's contribution
- Distribute leadership throughout the team

Snell and Janney (2005) have identified five principal components of collaborative teaming. We describe them below.

Building Team Structure

This involves making sure that school policies support team teaching, defining the core team (those team members who are most directly responsible for the student's education) and the whole team (core team plus members who might occasionally teach the student), and creating time to plan for instruction.

Learning Teamwork Skills

To succeed, team members need to learn and practice teamwork skills such as active listening, negotiation and compromise skills, and role-release skills (turning over some of one's own responsibilities to other team members). Teams should discuss and agree on shared values and a shared goal related to a student's progress.

Taking Team Action

Teams begin by problem solving, creating an action plan, determining a schedule for program delivery, and identifying assessment and program evaluation components.

Teaching Collaboratively

After the groundwork has been laid, teaching collaboratively feels natural and is effective. Co-teachers learn one another's areas of instructional strength and how to best use those strengths to all students' benefit.

Improving Communication and Handling Conflict

Along with experience comes more open communication, stronger (and more effective) partnerships, and trust (as we pointed out in Chapter 4). In some circumstances, however, conflicts can arise, and it is important that team members treat one another with respect and practice effective conflict-resolution skills, especially when the student with a traumatic brain injury participates in team meetings.

Collaborative teaming is important across all age levels, including early childhood. Hunt and colleagues (2004) implemented collaborative teaming to support preschoolers with severe disabilities, including TBI. The core team consisted of the early childhood teacher, the special education teacher, an instructional assistant, the speech-language therapist, and a parent. The collaborative teaming strategies resulted in positive outcomes for the children, including reduced student nonengaged time, higher levels of social interactions with peers, and higher levels of child-initiated interactions with an adult in the classroom.

Elementary and Middle School Students: Cooperative Learning

One of the most important strategies to ensure progress in the general curriculum for students with disabilities, including students with TBI, involves the use of cooperative learning strategies. These strategies involve small groups of students who together focus on a common learning task or activity. Successfully implementing cooperative learning, however, involves much more than simply putting students together in small groups and giving them an assignment. A haphazard approach to group learning can result in the outcome of a few students doing most of the work and, indeed, most of the learning.

Early seminal work in cooperative learning by Johnson and Johnson (1991) identified the primary characteristics of cooperative learning groups, two of which are very important: positive interdependence and individual accountability.

Positive Interdependence

Positive interdependence refers to "linking students together so one cannot succeed unless all group members succeed" (Johnson, Johnson, & Holubec, 1998, p. 4). In essence, students are compelled to support and enable their fellow group members in order to succeed. Positive interdependence is created by assigning group members tasks that are critical to the overall goal and are individualized to the student's ability level. Students engage in different levels of learning and their tasks vary, as is the case in universally designed learning, but each task is essential to the overall success of the group.

PEARSON
myeducationlab

Go to the Building Teaching Skills section in Chapter 13 of MyEducationLab and complete the activities. As you watch the videos and answer the accompanying questions, reflect on the different types of cooperative groups you see depicted.

Cooperative learning can be a successful strategy when teachers allow the students to be both independent and accountable for their own and other's work.

Individual Accountability

In haphazardly created learning groups all students benefit or are punished equally by the group outcome, not necessarily by their individual contribution. One student may do all the work and that work may earn the group an *A,* but other students may not have individually deserved that grade. Similarly, one student may perform her portion of the task at a high-quality level, but the overall quality of the product may be dragged down by other students' performances; that one student is unfairly punished with a grade lower than she deserved.

By assigning students in cooperative learning groups discrete, identifiable tasks that contribute to the whole, teachers can individually assess their students on the quality of that one component task. However, more important to the implementation of cooperative learning is that students understand that each group member has a role and that the group as a whole will be accountable for the quality of the product.

Johnson and colleagues (1998) identified several ways to structure cooperative learning groups to ensure both individual and group success. One factor is group size; the smaller the group, the easier it is to fairly distribute tasks and to individualize those tasks to the unique needs of students. A second factor is detailing each student's individual task, providing examples of quality outcomes pertaining to that task, and making sure the student understands the contribution of her task to the group's task or goal. Instead of waiting until the group is finished, teachers should use frequent probes to determine what each group member is doing and learning. Additionally, peers can hold one another accountable. Researchers suggested that teachers assign one group member to be a "checker" and to question other group members to ensure that everyone understands (Johnson et al., 1998).

Secondary and Transition Students: Problem-Solving and Decision-Making Instruction

Even after a student has recuperated from a traumatic brain injury, she may still have difficulties in executive function areas. These are higher-level brain or intellectual functions that govern complex activities like making plans and decisions, solving problems, and setting goals. Impairments of executive function systems are not easily detected, at least not until the student is called upon to perform one of these tasks. So it is important to provide students with systematic instruction that will enable them to improve their executive functioning skills, including problem-solving or decision-making skills.

A problem is "a task, activity, or situation for which a solution is not immediately identified, known, or obtainable" (Agran & Wehmeyer, 2005, p. 256). Teaching problem-solving skills involves teaching students to identify a solution that solves the problem. Solving a problem, therefore, is the process of identifying a solution that resolves the initial perplexity or difficulty. The skills typically involved in problem solving are (1) problem identification, (2) problem explication or definition, and (3) solution generation.

Problem Identification

The first step in solving a problem is to recognize that a problem exists. Agran and Wehmeyer (in press) suggested that, as a part of this step, students should address the following questions: (1) Is the problem caused by me or someone else? and (2) How important is the problem? Students should also learn to estimate the time needed to solve a problem during this step.

Problem Explication or Definition

In many cases, students are too global in their definition of the problem. That is, they attribute the problem to broad factors ("That teacher is mean.") rather than the real problem at hand (failing a class, not meeting class deadlines, or arriving late). It is important to teach students to narrow the problem down to one that is solvable. This is accomplished by teaching the student to specify or define the problem.

Solution Generation

Once a student has defined the problem she must solve, she will need to learn how to generate potential solutions. Initially, it is important to allow students to generate as many solutions as feasible, even if they do not adequately address the problem. Discuss with students why a given solution does or does not solve the problem and whether the solution's implementation is feasible.

At this point students are ready to make a decision about the best option available, selecting from a pool of potential solutions the one that best fits their needs, circumstances, and capacity. This is, in essence, a decision-making action, the process for which is discussed next.

When teaching problem solving, teachers should use real-world situations. Adolescents face a myriad of problems, from relationship troubles to tobacco and alcohol use; using these problems as examples can enable students to learn problem-solving strategies and also can provide a means to address issues in adolescence.

As we have noted, the problem-solving process ends with making a decision about the best solution to the problem from among several possible solutions. Many people view problem solving and decision making as one and the same. This is not accurate, however. As you have learned, a problem-solving process requires students to identify potential solutions. The decision-making process involves coming to a judgment or conclusion, selecting the best potential solution.

Just as the typical problem-solving process ends with making a decision, the typical decision-making strategy begins with a problem-solving step. Teaching students to make decisions involves a number of steps:

Identify relevant alternatives or options. If students already know the alternatives from which to make a decision, then this step is straightforward: have them write down the solution. More often than not, students do not know all of the options or alternatives available to them, so the decision-making process begins by implementing a problem-solving process to identify relevant options.

Identify consequences of alternatives. One characteristic of many students with disabilities (indeed, many adolescents in general) is their tendency to act impulsively or without adequate thought about the consequences of their actions. In certain circumstances, like taking drugs, their impulsivity can be more than just exasperating; it can be life-threatening. Students need to be taught to think systematically through all the possible consequences of each alternative.

Identify the probability of each consequence. Teachers need to be clear about the consequences of a student's behavior. Consequences range from positive to neutral to negative. They also range from highly likely to occur to unlikely to occur. Students with TBI should learn to weigh the relative risk of the alternative against the relative likelihood that it will occur and against its potential benefits. The potential risks of some activities (cancer from smoking or AIDS from unprotected sex) are so negative that even the slightest possibility that they could occur should warrant discarding that option.

Determine the value placed on each option or alternative. Students should be supported to consider relevant issues as they consider risks, benefits, and consequences. Their values, preferences, and interests should come into play and often become the dominant factors in reaching a decision. Also, cultural, ethical, and religious factors can play a role in their decisions.

Integrate values and consequences to select a preferred option. The final step is to choose one option based on all the factors considered. As Ylvisaker and DeBonis (2000) noted, students with TBI (and AD/HD) are at increased risk for impairments in executive

IEP Tip

Problem solving and other executive function and self-regulation skills are critical to learners with TBI and should be a part of virtually all IEPs for this population.

Ready, Set, . . . Study! Teaching Study Skills

Teaching problem solving is but one strategy to use to teach the broader skill of effective study skills. Many students with TBI require more intensive instruction to learn how to study efficiently (Lambert & Nowacek, 2006). Like a lot of other complex tasks, learning to study involves learning the stages of studying: preparing to study, studying across content area, and following up after studying (Lambert & Nowacek, 2006).

Ready, Set . . .

Key steps in teaching skills related to preparing to study involve thinking through the when and where of the study process. Encourage students to:

◆ *Find a place to study that is free from distractions.*

◆ *Find a time to study that isn't too late.* As Lambert and Nowacek note, the most effective study times are during the day and not too late at night.

◆ *Establish a study routine.* Like most actions, when something is automated and routine, it is more likely to occur.

◆ *Gather all needed study materials together.* Stopping the study session to fetch a textbook or sharpen a pencil both disrupts the continuity of a study session and quickly becomes a strategy for avoiding studying.

◆ *Determine what to study.* Establish an agenda, use study guides, and prioritize study content based upon deadlines and assignments.

. . . Study!

◆ *Teach students to focus on discrete tasks for planned periods of time.* Lambert and Nowacek suggest that students should plan study times in one-hour blocks, with the last ten minutes of each hour set aside for a break.

◆ *Teach study strategies.* Teach students to use or develop advance organizers to identify big ideas in the reading.

◆ *Teach comprehension skills.* Teach students what to do when they reach content they have a difficult time understanding or remembering. Use mnemonic strategies such as those we discussed in Chapter 11 and the learning strategies you read about in Chapter 5 to provide means for students to tackle difficult content areas.

◆ *Teach students to summarize what they have learned.* This can be through written summaries, outlines, some form of graphic organizer, or just through questions that might be derived from the reading. It's clear that students with TBI can learn self-regulation skills that enable them to become more effective at studying, and it is time well spent by teachers working with these students.

PEARSON
myeducationlab

Go to the Activities and Application section in Chapter 13 of MyEducationLab and complete Activity 4. As you interact with the simulation, think about how using specific learning strategies and encouraging independent practice could enhance students' study skills.

function skills. Moreover, research has shown that students with TBI benefit from instruction in these areas.

An additional benefit of teaching problem solving and other executive function skills is that these skills can be applied to address some of the issues that limit the success of students with TBI in school, including study skills. Box 13.5 provides some steps to teaching students important study skills.

INCLUDING STUDENTS WITH TRAUMATIC BRAIN INJURY

Figure 13.5 indicates the educational placement of students with TBI, and Box 13.6 provides tips for increasing their success in general education classrooms.

ASSESSING STUDENTS' PROGRESS

Measuring Students' Progress

Progress in the General Curriculum

One strategy for determining progress in the general curriculum involves the use of analytic rubrics (Nolet & McLaughlin, 2000). A rubric is a scale developed by a teacher (or others) as a guide to scoring a student's performance. To create an analytic rubric, teachers identify specific outcomes linked to a standard, rank them from less to more positive,

Figure 13.5 Educational placement of students with traumatic brain injury (Fall, 2006)

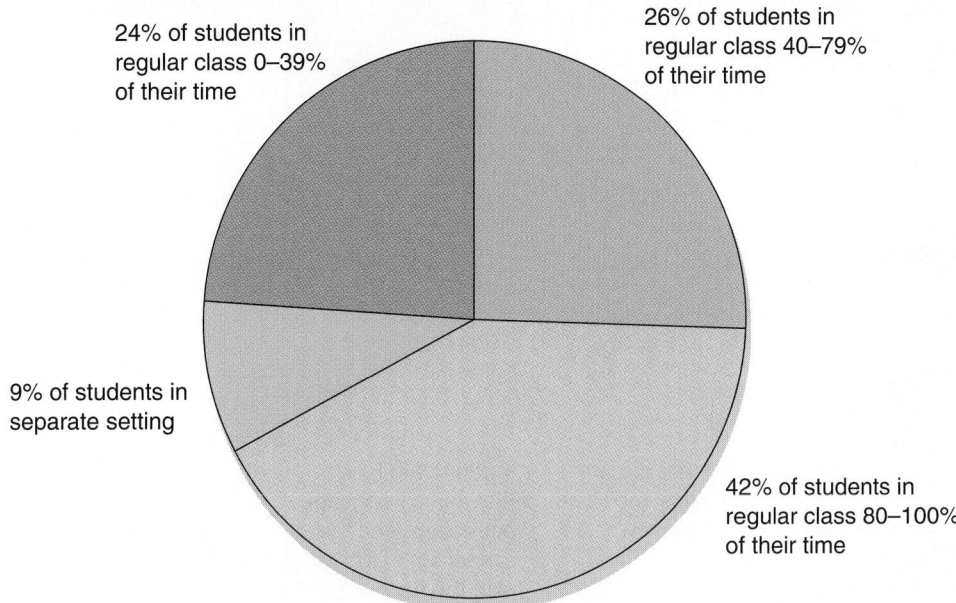

24% of students in regular class 0–39% of their time

26% of students in regular class 40–79% of their time

9% of students in separate setting

42% of students in regular class 80–100% of their time

and assign a score (typically from 0 or 1 to 4 or 5) to each outcome. For example, an analytic rubric for a first-grade writing standard might set the following outcomes:

1 = handwriting not legible; cannot be read by adult

2 = some words legible, but most are not

3 = most words legible; some cannot be read

4 = all words legible

When considering the development of rubrics to determine progress in the general curriculum, Nolet and McLaughlin (2000) suggest:

◆ The rubrics should link directly to specific content and student achievement standards.

◆ A rubric should focus on only one dimension of student performance (e.g., legibility versus content knowledge).

◆ There should be enough points in the scale to adequately judge performance but not so many as to confuse the issue. Nolet and McLaughlin recommend 3 to 7 points.

◆ The rubric should focus on specific outcomes rather than a process.

◆ Teachers should provide students with information about the rubrics and examples of high-quality performances that would meet the standard and be scored high.

Progress in Addressing Other Educational Needs

Traumatic brain injury can often result in perceptual and motor impairments that include difficulty with handwriting due to poor eye-hand coordination. You may recall that Dylan has fine-motor challenges and works with an occupational therapist to overcome them, learning, for example, how to hold a pen. Perceptual-motor skills are those skills that coordinate visual and sensory input with motor activities.

There are a number of widely used tests of perceptual-motor skills. For example, the Bender-Gestalt Visual Motor test provides a relatively quick way to measure children's visual-motor functioning, visual-perception skills, and the impact of brain injury on these functions. The test involves the administration of nine geometric designs, presented one at a time to the student, who is asked to reproduce them. Like many such standardized tests, the administration of the Bender-Gestalt test should be performed by a school psychologist.

Box 13.6

INCLUSION TIPS

	What You Might See	What You Might Be Tempted to Do	Alternate Responses	Ways to Include Peers in the Process
Behavior	The student shows behavior and personality changes, such as temper outbursts, anxiety, fatigue, or depression.	Respond with strong disapproval to her new behavior.	Teach problem solving using the SOLVE mnemonic to reduce frustration that is associated with problem behavior.	Give her time to work in natural settings with peers who will encourage appropriate behavior yet show acceptance during the relearning stage.
Social interactions	She has forgotten social skills and experiences social misunderstandings because of her new identity struggles.	Ignore her social difficulties and hope they go away.	Partner with both the speech-language pathologist and the school counselor to plan the best ways to teach successful language and social skills.	Allow friends with whom she feels secure to role-play social activities. Structure many opportunities for successful interactions. Use videotapes for self-evaluation.
Educational performance	Learning new information is difficult for her, or it takes her much longer to process information.	Require extra work in areas of difficulty.	Use cooperative learning groups to aid her in organization, memory, and cognitive processes.	Have her brainstorm and work with her peers/friends to practice skills as well as to plan future projects and educational aspirations.
Classroom attitudes	She is confused about exactly what is expected on assignments.	Excuse her from assignments.	Use rubrics as a way to delineate four months' worth of expectations for assignments.	Pair her with a partner and friend who can help her focus and participate meaningfully during instruction.

On a more applied level, teachers can assess student progress in specific perceptual-motor areas through collaborations among special and general educators and occupational or physical therapists. For example, evaluating students' handwriting is a common activity performed by occupational therapists. Working with special educators, occupational therapists can determine whether a student's handwriting difficulties are a function of visual impairments, perceptual difficulties, eye-hand coordination problems, motor tone problems, hand grasping or pinching difficulties, or general hand functioning. In turn, the teacher and occupational therapists can establish an instructional program to improve the student's handwriting or, if necessary, identify assistive writing devices, including adaptive word processors (such as those we discussed in Chapter 7).

Making Accommodations for Assessment

Students with TBI may experience difficulties concentrating and attending for long periods of time. Like students with AD/HD, they will benefit from the accommodations discussed in Chapter 8.

In addition, as you have learned in this chapter, problems with memory and retention are often barriers for students with TBI, so testing situations present special challenges to them. One accommodation involves the way in which test items are constructed. Students with TBI may perform better on exams that present multiple-choice or true-false options than on tests that rely on memory and recall, such as short answer or essay formats. While it is not usually a reasonable accommodation to reword items from one format to another, the use of a scribe (someone who writes the answer for the student) may benefit students with TBI. Having someone write the answer allows the student to focus or concentrate on recalling information, and students can most likely provide more information verbally than in writing, particularly if they have handwriting difficulties. You may remember that Patti gives Dylan extra time to take tests, permits him to mark the "bubbles" and his textbook, allows him to leave the room to compose himself, and lets him rest on the couch in her classroom if he is particularly tired. These simple accommodations do not give Dylan any special advantage relative to other students; they simply allow him to demonstrate what he knows.

VALUES AND OUTCOMES

VALUES — GREAT EXPECTATIONS — CHOICES — POSITIVE CONTRIBUTIONS — STRENGTHS — RELATIONSHIPS — FULL CITIZENSHIP

Asked what "great expectations" she has for Dylan, Renee answered immediately, "Everything." Does that mean higher education, such as at a community college and then perhaps a four-year college, and then work, perhaps with the computers he likes so much (remember the "Super Mario" game and how his therapists used it as an incentive for teaching fine-motor skills), Patti said, "Absolutely." She is a bit concerned about dormitory living, however; Dylan is easily influenced.

Renee regards Dylan's positive contributions as gifts, not traits he has developed. "He's an absolute riot, hilarious. He's blessed with a great sense of humor. He's the family clown." To add gaiety to others' lives is, indeed, to contribute mightily. And to be self-determined to boot is to combine joy of living with self-advocacy.

Taking a different perspective, Patti regards Dylan's empathy to be his greatest strength. "Yes, he's very smart, but he's also very sweet and empathetic. He's very open to other children; he's their 'listening ear.' He isn't judgmental. He listens to them. He'll be a great social worker or counselor."

There's no question that Dylan makes his own choices (with guidance, of course). Patti describes him as able to exercise good judgment, and Renee points to his decision to leave IDEA and his IEP behind for a Section 504 plan as evidence of his ability to choose the life he wants to live.

Not surprisingly, Dylan has good relationships with his classmates. Predictably, because he and they are in the years when (as Renee puts it) "the testosterone is kicking in," he has some confrontations. But they are minor and rare. As Patti has said, he's the empathetic student; his relationships are mature for a boy of his age.

Neither Renee nor Patti can define precisely what full citizenship means for Dylan, but both are confident he will exercise it. Higher education, work, voting, living in the community on his own but with support (especially around money management—that old math bug-a-boo will persist), and having friends, male and female, all await him.

WHAT DO YOU THINK?

1. If you were Dylan's parent or teacher, and if you knew as much about traumatic brain injury as you do now, would you have supported or opposed his exit from IDEA and his reliance on Section 504 reasonable accommodations? What if high school poses, as it is likely to do, academic challenges that may overwhelm Dylan? How far down the road should a teacher look when considering what is good, in "today's terms," for a student?

2. Is "good" defined only in academic terms? Think about what would be useful to Dylan and other students with TBI whose injuries cause emotional challenges.

3. Dylan has not used any assistive technologies for learning or managing his life. Given how much interest he has in video games, is it advisable for him to use some technologies, especially if they are off-the-shelf and therefore not stigmatizing?

ADDRESSING THE STANDARDS: THE VALUES CONNECTION

The following CEC Knowledge and Skill Standards: Common Core and Values are addressed in this chapter through the content and concepts we discuss.

CEC Knowledge and Skill Standards: Common Core		Values/Standards Connection
CEC Knowledge and Skill Standard II. **Development and Characteristics of Learners**		Learning about the characteristics of learners with TBI is an application of CEC Standard 2, Development and Characteristics of Learners.
CC2K1	Typical and atypical human growth and development.	
CC2K2	Educational implications of characteristics of various exceptionalities.	After a student experiences a head injury, it is especially important to maintain *great expectations* for the future. Additionally, because of the changes in cognitive functioning, you should offer *self-determination* training so your students can make and carry out good *choices* and decisions.
CC2K4	Family systems and the roles of families supporting development.	
CC2K5	Similarities and differences of individuals with and without exceptional learning needs.	
CC2K6	Similarities and differences of individuals with exceptional learning needs.	
CEC Knowledge and Skill Standard III. **Individual Learning Differences**		Standard 3 addresses students' needs and strengths.
CC3K1	Effects an exceptional condition(s) can have on an individual's life.	
CC3K2	Impact of learner's academic and social abilities, attitudes, interests, and values on instruction and career development.	

CEC Knowledge and Skill Standards: Common Core	Values/Standards Connection
CEC Knowledge and Skill Standard IV. Instructional Strategies CC4S1 Use strategies to facilitate integration into various settings. CC4S2 Teach individuals to use self-assessment, problem-solving, and other cognitive strategies to meet their needs. CC4S3 Select, adapt, and use instructional strategies and materials according to characteristics of the individual with exceptional learning needs. CC4S4 Use strategies to facilitate maintenance and generalization of skills across environments. CC4S5 Use procedures to increase the individual's self-awareness, self-management, self-control, self-reliance, and self-esteem. CC4S6 Use strategies that promote successful transitions for individuals with exceptional learning needs.	Selecting and adapting strategies to meet the needs of exceptional learners directly relates to CEC Standard 4, Instructional Strategies. Standard 4 emphasizes self-determination and *choice* even as its transition provision deals with students' *relationships*.
CEC Knowledge and Skill Standard V. Learning Environments and Social Interactions CC5S2 Identify realistic expectations for personal and social behavior in various settings. CC5S3 Identify supports needed for integration into various program placements. CC5S4 Design learning environments that encourage active participation in individual and group settings. CC5S9 Create an environment that encourages self-advocacy and increased independence. CC5S12 Design and manage daily routines. CC5S15 Structure, direct, and support the activities of paraeducators, volunteers, and tutors.	Standard 5's provisions call on teachers to have not only realistic but also *great expectations* for their students.

continued

CEC Knowledge and Skill Standards: Common Core	Values/Standards Connection
CEC Knowledge and Skill Standard VII. Instructional Planning	Providing technology to enable students to compensate for memory and other limitations enables them to be more independent and increases their *self-determination*.
CC7K5 Roles and responsibilities of the paraeducator related to instruction, intervention, and direct service.	
CC7S1 Identify and prioritize areas of the general curriculum and accommodations for individuals with exceptional learning needs.	
CC7S3 Involve the individual and family in setting instructional goals and monitoring progress.	
CC7S6 Sequence, implement, and evaluate individualized learning objectives.	
CC7S7 Intergrate affective, social, and life skills with academic curricula.	
CC7S9 Incorporate and implement instructional and assistive technology into the educational program.	
CEC Knowledge and Skill Standard VIII. Assessment	Identifying and using appropriate assessments reflects CEC Standard 8, Assessment.
CC8K3 Screening, prereferral, referral, and classification procedures.	Standard 8 asks teachers to consider their students' needs and *strengths*.
CC8S2 Administer nonbiased formal and informal assessments.	
CC8S6 Use assessment information in making eligibility, program, and placement decisions for individuals with exceptional learning needs, including those from culturally and/or linguistically diverse backgrounds.	
CC8S8 Evaluate instruction and monitor progress of individuals with exceptional learning needs.	
CEC Knowledge and Skill Standard X. Collaboration	Participating in collaborative teaming is an example of how you can address CEC Standard 10, Collaboration.
CC10S2 Collaborate with families and others in assessment of individuals with exceptional learning needs.	Partnering to ensure effective school reentry is necessary for the student's inclusion and peer *relationships*.
CC10S3 Foster respectful and beneficial relationships between families and professionals.	
CC10S4 Assist individuals with exceptional learning needs and their families in becoming active participants in the educational team.	
CC10S5 Plan and conduct collaborative conferences with individuals with exceptional learning needs and their families.	

Source: From CEC Knowledge and Skill Standards: Common Core and Values. Copyright by The Council for Exceptional Children. Reprinted with permission.

SUMMARY

Identifying Students with Traumatic Brain Injuries

- The IDEA definition of TBI includes acquired injuries to the brain caused by an external force but does not include brain injuries that are congenital, degenerative, or induced at birth.

- Closed head injuries and open head injuries are the two types of brain injuries included under the IDEA definition.

- Students with TBI often experience physical; cognitive; and emotional, behavioral, and social changes.

- Severity of the injury and age of onset are two critical factors in determining the severity of the disability and the prognosis for improvement.

- The four major causes of TBI are falls, automobile accidents, events associated with struck by/against, and assaults.

Evaluating Students with TBI

- The pediatric Glasgow Outcomes Scale is often used initially to measure the severity of injury.

- On an ongoing basis, teachers can use a classroom observation guide to pinpoint a student's precise cognitive functioning.

Designing an Appropriate IEP

- It is critical that educators partner with medical and other rehabilitation professionals to ensure success in the process of receiving hospital-based rehabilitation and transitioning back to school.

- Simple technologies, like pagers, alarms, and watches, can provide the support students need to be more independent and to minimize memory impairments.

- The rate at which teachers present content information affects student success when they have attention and processing difficulties related to TBI. Instructional pacing is important to consider.

- Many students with TBI can succeed in college if appropriate planning occurs and the student is prepared to provide ideas for accommodations.

Using Effective Instructional Strategies

- Collaborative teaming involves two or more educators working together to meet shared goals pertaining to student achievement.

- Cooperative learning groups are critical to the success of inclusive classrooms. Teachers need to be sure, however, that all students have a meaningful role in the process and contribute to the outcome.

- Problem-solving and decision-making skills are important for students with TBI, whose injuries often result in lifelong difficulties in these areas of executive function.

Including Students with Traumatic Brain Injury

- Approximately one third of students with TBI spend 80 percent or more of their time in general education classrooms.

Assessing Students' Progress

- Rubrics provide a means for teachers to quantify student progress in the general curriculum.

- A variety of neuropsychiatric assessments may help teachers who are working with students with TBI. Teachers should definitely focus on determining perceptual-motor skills because they directly impact handwriting.

- The use of a scribe and test item formats that minimize the use of essay exams are accommodations for students with TBI who have memory impairments.

Now go to MyEducationLab at www.myeducationlab.com and take the Self-Assessment to gauge your initial comprehension of chapter content. Once you have taken the Self-Assessment, use your individualized Study Plan for Chapter 13 to enhance your understanding of the concepts discussed in the chapter.

14

Understanding Students with Hearing Loss

by Sally L. Roberts, University of Kansas

◆ WHO ARE MARIAH, RICQUEL, AND SHYLAH THOMAS?

Who, indeed, are these three sisters? There are several ways we can describe them. Let's try a comparative approach, choosing the words *unusual* and *usual* as our criteria.

Mariah, Ricquel, and Shylah (ages 9, 7, and 3, respectively) are unusual in that they are the profoundly deaf daughters of Sharon and Sheddrick Thomas and the younger sisters of Bradley (age 11), who has no hearing loss at all. Three sisters with the same degree of hearing loss is an unusual constellation of disability. Unusual, yes, in one sense, but not in another. Like so many other students with disabilities and their families, the Thomas family is determined to move forward with their lives, undisturbed by the fact that Sharon is pregnant with their next child.

The sisters are also unusual in that, unlike many students with disabilities, they do not attend school in their home school district in Poway, California. Instead, they ride the school bus to schools operated by the San Diego Unified School District. Mariah and Ricquel attend the Lindbergh Schweitzer Elementary School, and Shylah attends the Lafayette Elementary School, schools on separate campuses but near each other. Sharon insisted on out-of-district busing so that all three would receive the most appropriate education available in the greater metropolitan San Diego area.

They are usual in that, like many students with disabilities, they are included in their school's general education curriculum, receive some of their education in a pullout program operated by a teacher of the deaf, and have friends with and

without disabilities. They are unusual in that they have the same disability, but they are usual in that two of them, Mariah and Ricquel, are auditory learners for whom the oral method comes easily, whereas Shylah is a visual learner who picks up sign language more readily than her sisters.

Enough of the comparisons! What is especially notable about Mariah, Ricquel, and Shylah is that the way they receive their education is deeply controversial. They receive it—and communicate with their parents, teachers, and peers, with and without disabilities—through a cochlear implant. This implant is an electronic device that compensates for the damaged or absent hair cells in a person's cochlea by stimulating the person's auditory nerve fibers. Unlike a hearing aid, the implant does not make sounds louder. Instead, it provides sound information by directly stimulating the functional auditory nerve fibers in the cochlea.

Why is a cochlear implant controversial? Isn't it like eyeglasses for a person with a visual impairment or a prosthesis for a person who has lost an arm or a leg? In part, the implant is comparable to eyeglasses or a prosthesis. It restores lost function. If we return to unusual and usual attributes, the implant seems quite usual. But it is also unusual because not all people with hearing loss can benefit from one.

Most of all, however, the cochlear implant is quite unusual because some individuals who are deaf or hard of hearing strongly object to it. They are opposed to any alteration of a deaf person's inherent deafness. They believe that deafness is only part of a person's being, so any mechanical alteration denies that person's essence and may diminish his or her worth. Further, they believe that deafness has allowed the formation of a subpopulation among Americans of people who have their own language, history, and culture: the Deaf community. To alter a person mechanically, then, could be tantamount to subverting a population proud of its distinctive culture.

Other people who are deaf or hard of hearing disagree. They hold that any intervention that helps a deaf person communicate with hearing people is worthwhile. Their position is not grounded on cultural identity but on pragmatics and efficacy: if an intervention benefits a person, they feel it should be used.

That's the position Sharon and Sheddrick took when they decided to transfer their children from the Poway School District to the one in San Diego. Individualized benefit governs their decision to brave a transfer and a loss of opportunity to be with neighborhood peers. But in this case, being brave does not mean acting alone.

Three professionals play special roles in supporting Sharon, Sheddrick, and their daughters. One is Vicki Maley, who is herself deaf and who taught Mariah and Ricquel until she retired a few years ago. Sharon describes Vicki as her "Deaf mentor,"

CHAPTER OBJECTIVES

◆ You will learn about the categories of hearing loss, including the profound loss experienced by Mariah, Ricquel, and Shylah.

◆ You will learn how people hear and about the anatomy of the ear, including the location of the area most likely related to the sisters' loss.

◆ You will learn how to design an IEP that conforms to the IDEA provision about students with hearing impairments learning with each other as well as from deaf adults.

◆ You will learn about the various modes of communication used by students with hearing impairment. Just as the three Thomas girls use different types of communication, oral and manual, so too do families have several options from which to choose.

◆ You will learn how to evaluate students for hearing loss and academic progress.

◆ You will learn about the Deaf community and Deaf culture, an important aspect of identity for a child with hearing loss. Sharon describes her Deaf mentor as an integral part of the family's early intervention team.

a person who introduced the concept of Deaf culture, recounted what it means to be a member of that culture, and shared with the Thomases how a deaf person can get along in the deaf and in the hearing worlds alike. Vicki gave Sharon hope for her daughters and entire family at a time when, in Sharon's words, "I felt that my life was over." Predictably, Sharon herself looks forward to the time when she, too, will be a mentor for another parent in a parent-to-parent relationship (see Chapter 4).

The second professional is Mary Maussang, the girls' deaf educator. She is, as Sharon puts it, "my lifeline." Mary is a member of a team of educators committed to Sharon's daughters. She team-teaches with a general educator in the kindergarten and third-grade classrooms. They teach in voice and sign language simultaneously, with the help of an interpreter and Mary's assistant teacher, both of whom sign the instruction. As these team members work collaboratively, they make it possible for the class of 2 deaf students and 17 hearing students to organize itself into smaller groups. Each group learns through both sign and oral communication, with the result that the deaf students have a support and communication network of their hearing peers.

Another significant benefit of team teaching is that each teacher works with small groups for guided reading, vocabulary, and other skill building once a day, so that every group receives two daily sessions of instruction. A third professional source of help is the girls' team of physicians, audiologists, and speech-language therapists at San Diego's Children's Hospital.

Let's return to the first question: who are Mariah, Ricquel, and Shylah? They are unusual and yet usual. They themselves are noncontroversial, yet they are in the middle of controversy. It's hard to pigeonhole them or any other students who are deaf or hard of hearing. The range of human variety is great. The Thomas family not only illustrates that fact but also is cause to celebrate it.

PEARSON
myeducationlab

After reading this chapter, complete the Self-Assessment for Chapter 14 on MyEducationLab to gauge your initial understanding of chapter content.

IDENTIFYING STUDENTS WITH HEARING LOSS

Defining Hearing Loss

Two terms, "deaf" and "hard of hearing," describe hearing loss. The term *deaf* is often overused to describe all individuals with hearing loss. The current regulations implementing IDEA define *deafness* as a hearing impairment that is so severe that the student is impaired in processing linguistic information through hearing (with or without amplification) and the student's educational performance is adversely affected. Two terms, **unilateral** and **bilateral,** describe whether the loss occurs in one or both ears.

The severity, or level, of a student's hearing loss determines whether the student will be classified as deaf or as hard of hearing. To be considered **deaf,** a person must have a hearing loss of 70 to 90 decibels (dB) or greater and be unable to use hearing, even with amplification, as the primary means for developing language. Figure 14.1 illustrates the degrees of hearing loss. By contrast, a person is considered to be **hard of hearing** if he has a hearing loss in the 20 to 70 dB range, benefits from amplification, and communicates primarily through speaking. **Congenital deafness** is a low-incidence disability affecting a small number of people. The majority of the people with whom this group interacts are hearing—including most of their family members.

Although some people use the term *hearing impaired* to describe a student with a hearing loss, special educators prefer to use person-first language ("student who is deaf") when referring to students with hearing loss. In addition, the **Deaf community** believes that the term *impaired* has negative connotations and prefers *deaf child.* Its members particularly resist the term *hearing impaired* because it implies a condition in need of correction or repair. Members of the Deaf community do not view themselves as needing to be fixed or cured but as a distinct cultural and linguistic group (Padden & Humphries, 2005).

Figure 14.1

Degrees of hearing loss

	125	250	500	1,000	2,000	4,000	8,000
0 10	(0–15 dB) *Normal*—There is no impact on communication.						
20	(16–25 dB) *Slight*—In noisy environments, faint speech is difficult to understand.						
30	(26–40 dB) *Mild*—Faint or distant speech is difficult to hear even in quiet environments. Classroom discussions are challenging to follow.						
40 50	(41–55 dB) *Moderate*—Conversational speech is heard only at a close distance. Group activities in a classroom present a challenge.						
60	(56–70 dB) *Moderate-severe*—Only loud, clear conversational speech can be heard, and group situations present great difficulty. Speech is intelligible, though noticeably impaired.						
70 80	(71–90 dB) *Severe*—Conversational speech cannot be heard unless it is loud; even then, many words cannot be recognized. Environment sounds can be detected, though not always identified. Speech is not always intelligible.						
90 100 110 120	(91+ dB) *Profound*—Conversational speech cannot be heard. Some loud environmental sounds may be heard. Speech is difficult to understand or may not be developed at all.						

Prevalence

Compared to other groups of students with disabilities, students with hearing loss are a relatively small group. The U.S. Department of Education Office of Special Education Programs (2006) reported that 71,589 students with hearing loss from ages 6 through 21 received some type of special education services in 2005–2006. Preschool programs (ages 3 to 5) served another 8,123 children, equivalent to about 1 percent of the total numbers of young children in preschools.

The Hearing Process

Before you can understand hearing loss, you must first understand what is involved in hearing sound. The hearing process is called **audition.** When we hear sounds, we are really interpreting patterns in the movement (vibration) of air molecules. Sounds are described in terms of their pitch or frequency (very low to very high) and intensity or loudness (very soft to very loud). Frequency is measured in **hertz (Hz),** named in honor of Heinrich Hertz, and loudness is measured in **decibels (dB),** named in honor of Alexander Graham Bell. Speech has a mix of high and low frequencies and soft and loud sounds.

Most of the sounds we hear every day occur in the 250 to 6,000 Hz range. Conversational speech is usually at about 45 dB to 50 dB of loudness. You have normal hearing if you can hear frequencies between 20 and 20,000 Hz and 0 and 120 dB. A whisper is about 20 dB, and a shout can be as loud as 70 dB. Vowel sounds like "o" have low frequencies; consonants like "f" and "sh" have higher frequencies. An individual who cannot hear high-frequency sounds will have a very hard time understanding speech. To help you understand what these speech ranges sound like, refer to Figure 14.2, which places familiar sounds within these ranges.

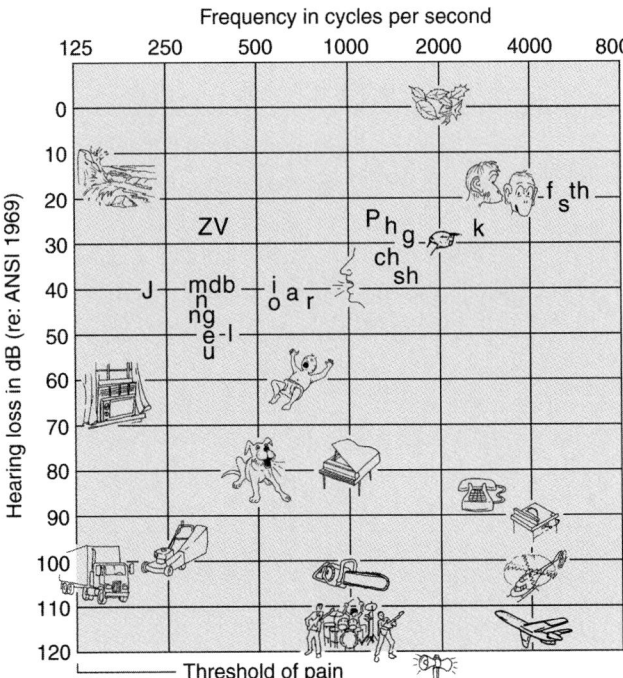

Figure 14.2 Frequency spectrum of familiar sounds plotted on a standard audiogram

Source: From *Hearing in Children* (5th ed.), by J. L. Northern and M. P. Downs, 2002, Philadelphia, Lippincott. Copyright 2002 by Lippincott Williams & Wilkins. Reprinted with permission.

The Hearing Mechanism

To understand what can go wrong with the hearing process, begin with the anatomy of the hearing mechanism, which consists of three parts: the outer, middle, and inner ears. Figure 14.3 illustrates the structure and anatomy of the ear. Look at it as you read the next few paragraphs.

The outer ear consists of the **auricle, or pinna,** and the **ear canal.** Its purpose is to collect the sound waves and funnel them to the tympanic membrane (or eardrum). The vibrating air molecules hit the eardrum and cause it to vibrate.

The middle ear is behind the eardrum and consists of three little bones, the **malleus, incus,** and **stapes.** Because of their shapes, you may know them as the hammer, anvil, and stirrup. We also call these bones the **ossicular chain.** The vibration of the eardrum transfers energy to the ossicular chain, causing the bones to vibrate and transmit the sound through the middle ear cavity.

Also found in the middle ear is the **eustachian tube.** It extends from the throat into the middle-ear cavity, and its primary purpose is to equalize the air pressure on the eardrum when we swallow or yawn. This is why our ears can feel plugged in the mountains or when an airplane is landing.

The inner ear contains the cochlea and the vestibular mechanism. The cochlea is just beyond the **oval window,** the membrane that separates the middle and the inner ear. The **cochlea** is a snail-shaped bony structure that houses the actual organ of hearing **(organ of Corti)** and the vestibular mechanism, the sensory organ of balance. The cochlea has multiple rows of delicate hair cells that are connected to the auditory nerve. These hair cells are actually sensory receptors for the auditory nerve. The cochlea is arranged **tonotopically,** meaning that the hair cells closest to the oval window respond to high-frequency sounds and those at the center (if the cochlea were unrolled) are more sensi-

Figure 14.3 Anatomical structure of the ear and a cross-section of the cochlea

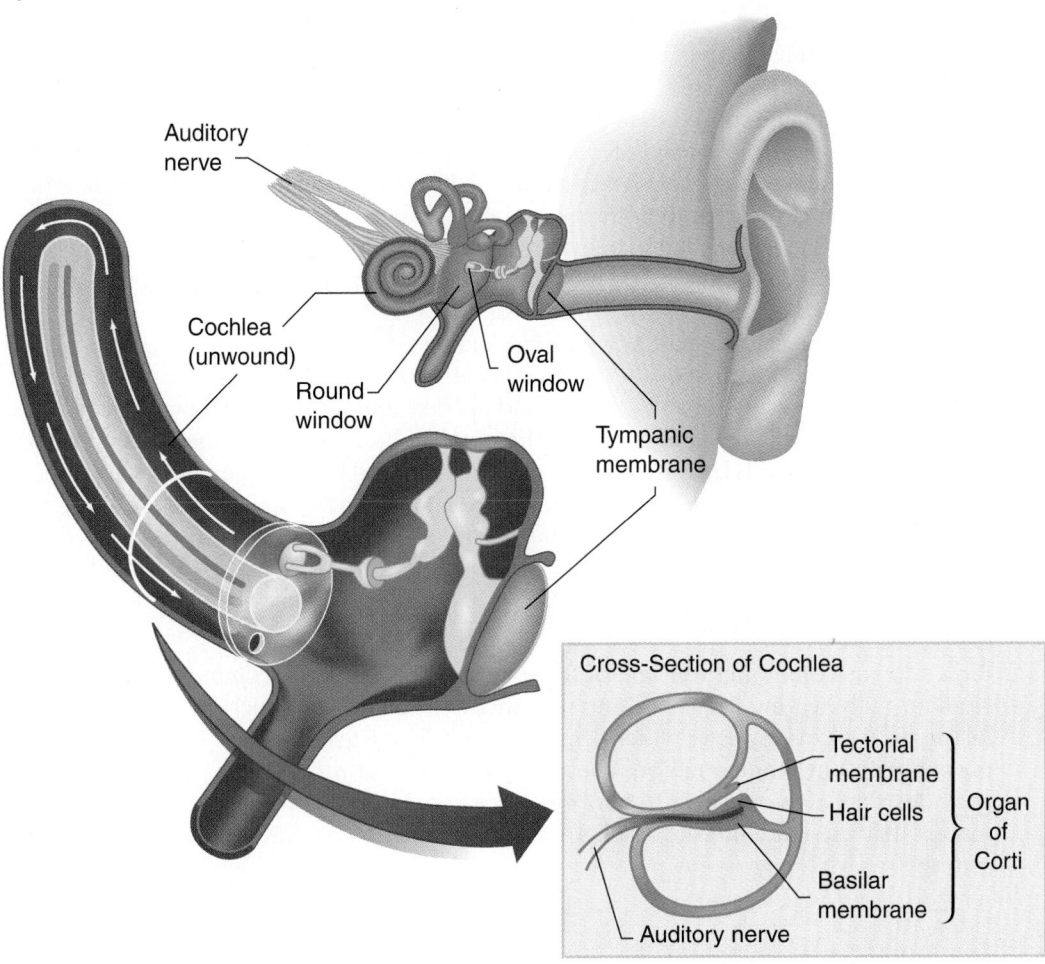

Auditory nerve

Cochlea (unwound)

Round window

Oval window

Tympanic membrane

Cross-Section of Cochlea

Tectorial membrane

Hair cells

Basilar membrane

Organ of Corti

Auditory nerve

tive to low-frequency sounds. The vibration of the middle-ear bones transfers the sound waves to the oval window, moving the fluid in the cochlea across the hair cells. This movement generates impulses to the auditory nerve.

The other structure in the inner ear, the **vestibular mechanism,** is a group of semicircular canals that controls balance. These canals are filled with the same fluid found in the cochlea. This fluid is sensitive to head movement, allowing the vestibular mechanism to help the body maintain its equilibrium. It is sensitive to both motion and gravity.

Sound moves from the inner ear to the temporal lobe of the brain by way of the auditory nerve. The route from the ear to the cochlea passes through at least four neural relay stations on its way to the brain. Think of this transfer of sound as a train trip that has stops at several stations along the route. Once sound reaches the auditory cortex, it can then be associated with other sensory information and memory, allowing us to perceive and integrate what we have heard (Gilbert, Knightly, & Steinberg, 2007).

Describing the Characteristics

Hearing loss impairs the development of spoken language, but the IQ range of students who are deaf or hard of hearing is much the same as it is in the general population (Moores, 2001; Nikolaraizi & Makri, 2004/2005). Most often, their academic problems are related to difficulties in speaking, reading, and writing, not to cognitive challenges.

Speech and English-Language Development

Children are born with an innate ability and desire to communicate. Normal language acquisition for hearing children follows a predetermined sequence that is similar across most languages and cultures. Children will usually become native speakers of at least one language just by being exposed to it. They usually do not need direct instruction.

The language development of children who are born deaf or hard of hearing will also follow this sequence; however, their language delays will range from mild to severe. These delays are a direct result of their inability to process auditory information or their lack of exposure to a visually encoded language. Their delays will vary, depending on the level of hearing loss and the amount of visual and auditory input they receive (Spencer, 2004; Blackorby & Knokey, 2006; Nicholas & Greers, 2006).

Even the speech of a student with a moderate loss may be affected. Although the student may be able to hear speech sounds, crucial information will elude him. By contrast, a child born deaf will be unable to hear most speech sounds, even with amplification. His receptive speech will be significantly impaired unless he is an exceptional **speech reader** (able to interpret words by watching the speaker's lips and facial movements without hearing the speaker's voice), and his expressive speech will most likely show problems with articulation, voice quality, and tone, making him difficult to understand.

IEP Tip

Under IDEA, a student's IEP team must consider the student's mode of communication.

Communication Options

Professionals commonly use one of three approaches to teach communication skills to students with hearing loss—oral/aural, manual, or total communication. There is a long history of controversy over which approach is the most appropriate. There is, however, probably no one single method that meets the needs of *all* students. That is why IDEA provides that a student's IEP team must consider the languages and communication modes that the student who is deaf or hard of hearing might use in the educational setting.

Oral/Aural Communication

This approach includes two primary teaching formats. The **oral/aural format** encourages early identification and subsequent amplification or cochlear implant. It emphasizes the amplification of sound and helping the child use what hearing remains (residual hearing). Auditory training enhances the student's listening skills and stresses using speech to communicate. This approach also emphasizes the use of amplified sound to develop oral language. In contrast to a strict auditory-verbal approach, however, this method allows for the use of visual input—speech reading—to augment auditory information. Unfortunately, this skill is extremely difficult to master because such a small amount of what is being said is visible on a speaker's lips.

Manual Communication

The **manual approach** to teaching communication stresses the use of some form of sign language. This approach makes use of the student's intact sight to receive information. Manual communication includes several different sign systems, each with its own proponents. **Sign language** uses combinations of hand, body, and facial movements to convey both words and concepts rather than individual letters. **Fingerspelling** uses a hand representation for each of the 26 letters of the alphabet. Figure 14.4 shows you the accepted forms of manual communication for the letters of the alphabet.

American Sign Language (ASL) is the most widely used sign language among deaf adults in North America. Although some individual ASL signs may have comparable English words, its signs are meant to represent concepts rather than single words. For example, the sign for "look" is made by pointing the index and middle fingers in the shape of

Figure 14.4 Chart of the manual alphabet

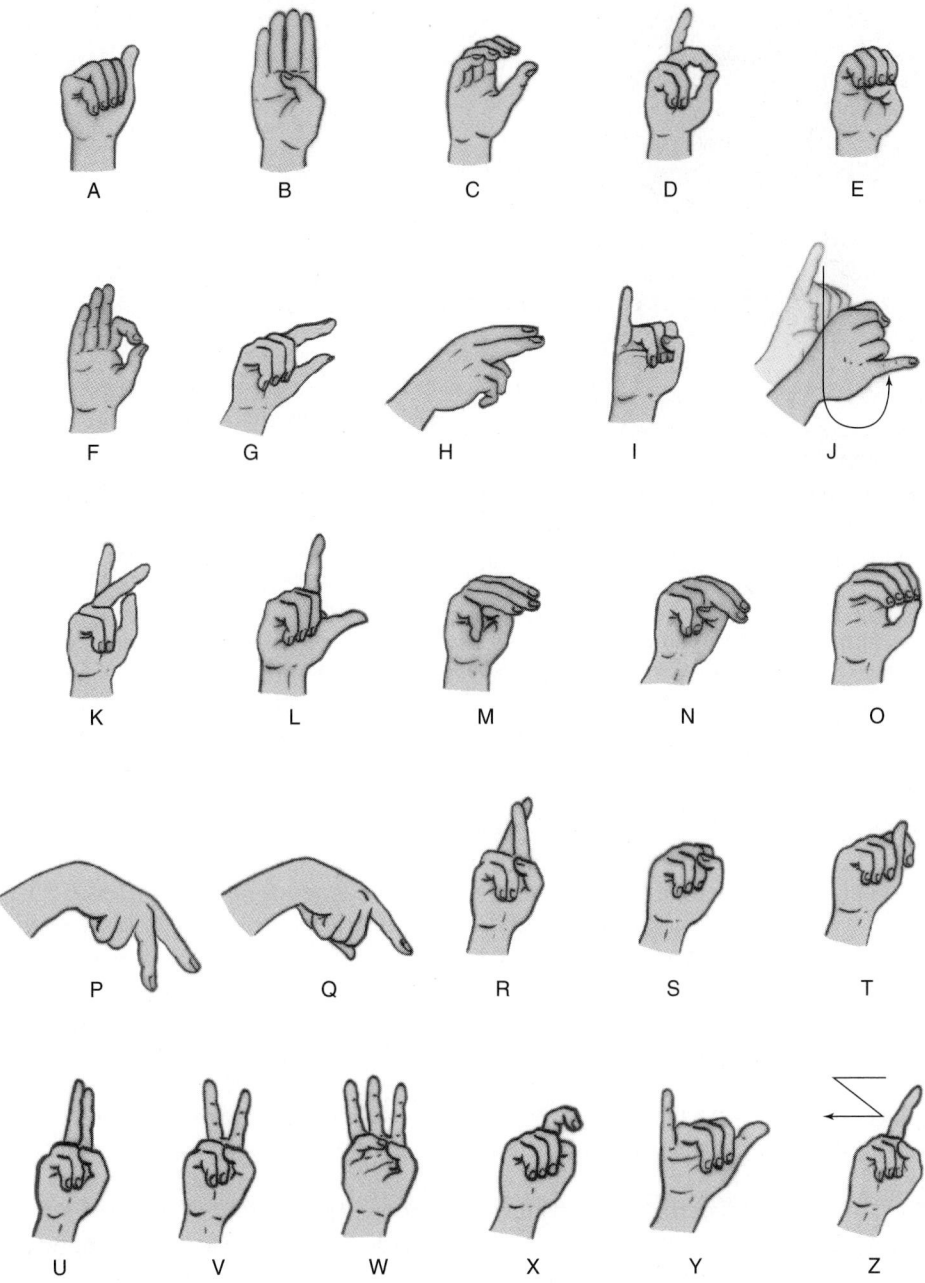

Source: From *The Signed English Starter,* by H. Bomstein and K. Saulnier, 1984, Washington, DC. Gallaudet University Press. Copyright 1984 by Gallaudet University Press. Reprinted with permission.

a *V* at the eyes and then turning to point forward. If the *V* moves from the eyes and then points upward, that small change indicates that the person is looking up.

Manually coded English sign language systems differ from ASL in that they are designed to be a visual representation of the English language. The primary sign systems used in the United States are **Pidgin Sign English (PSE); Seeing Essential English, Signing Exact English (SEE2);** and **Conceptually Accurate Signed English (CASE).**

An alternative to natural sign language and English sign systems is **cued speech.** Cued speech supplements spoken English and is intended to make its features fully visible

This teacher uses sign language to supplement the student's assistive technology hearing aid.

(LaSasso & Metzger, 1998; Torres, Moreno-Torres, & Santana, 2006). Because many sounds look the same on a speaker's lips when they are pronounced, cued speech uses 36 different cues to clarify the 44 different sounds in English. The placement of the cues on the face also indicates vowels and consonants. Unlike sign languages that provide information about meaning rather than about sound, cued speech communicates about sounds.

Total or Simultaneous Communication

This approach combines as many sources of information as possible, including simultaneous communication of both sign and spoken language and support for residual hearing. Amplification, speech reading, speech training, reading, and writing are all used in combination with signs.

The three Thomas girls are good examples of individuals who use a variety of communication options. All three learned sign language as their first language (before receiving their cochlear implants). Mariah and Ricquel now use a combination of oral and manual communication (total communication). They receive information auditorally and through sign, and they are able to express themselves by speaking and signing. Even with her cochlear implant, however, Shylah is more comfortable using sign language both receptively and expressively and has been slower to adapt to a strictly oral input.

Academic Achievement

The academic achievement of students with hearing loss depends on their individual characteristics as well as the characteristics of their parents, teachers, and school programs. Most of these children have specific educational challenges in the areas of reading and writing (Karchmer & Mitchell, 2003; Blackorby & Knokey, 2006). Because educational curricula are so language-based, communication and learning are strongly linked.

Two issues have confounded researchers who have attempted to identify the causes of the relatively low academic achievement of students who are deaf and hard of hearing. The first concerns the effects of inclusive education settings versus segregated ones. Much research has shown that students with hearing impairments who are in general education classrooms demonstrate higher academic achievement than do comparable students who are in self-contained classrooms or segregated settings (Kluwin, 1993; Hyde & Power, 2004). But research does not always prevail when placement decisions are being made. Sometimes families and students themselves want to be with other students who have hearing impairments, believing that their communication and learning will prosper when they are with others who have the same impairments.

IDEA recognizes the issue of integrated versus less integrated placements. It provides that when an IEP team is developing a student's IEP and making a placement decision for any child, not just a child who has a hearing impairment, the team must consider the child's communication needs. IDEA then provides that, if the child is deaf or hard of hearing, the team must consider the child's language and communication needs, opportunities for direct communications with peers and professionals in the child's language and communication mode, the child's academic level, and the child's full range of needs, including opportunities for direct instruction in the child's language and communication mode. If the IEP team strictly follows this provision, it may decide that the child's academic and other development will prosper more if the child is educated with others who have hearing impairments (because the child then would have opportunities for direct instruction in the child's language and communication mode) than in integrated general education programs.

PEARSON
myeducationlab

Go to the Activities and Application section in Chapter 14 of MyEducationLab and complete Activity 1. As you watch the video and answer the accompanying questions, consider the choices this student's IEP team has made in regard to her placement in the general education classroom.

Sheddrick and Sharon Thomas have chosen a general education (mainstream) setting for their three daughters, although they opted for an out-of-district program that would provide other peers with hearing loss, a deaf educator who could work closely with the regular educators, trained educational interpreters, and specialized individual support in reading, phonics, and speech. The choice seems to be a good one because all three are working at grade level and have both deaf and hearing friends.

The second issue involves the rising numbers of students with hearing loss who are from diverse racial, ethnic, and linguistic backgrounds. There has been a change in relative size among racial/ethnic groups of deaf children in the United States, beginning with the 1973–74 academic year. White deaf youth made up about 75 percent of the school-age population in 1974 but only 50.7 percent in 2004–2005. There is a critical need to meet the educational needs of deaf children and youth who are from other racial, ethnic, or cultural backgrounds (Andrews & Covell, 2007; Gallaudet Research Institute, 1973–1974 to 2004–2005).

Families and teachers struggle to find appropriate methods for improving language and literacy for students with hearing loss. For students with a hearing loss whose families do not use English as their primary language, educational opportunities and outcomes look even bleaker (Walker-Vann, 1998; Wolbers, 2002).

Academically, students who are hard of hearing are still among the least appropriately served groups. The issues and challenges of students with mild and moderate hearing losses are complex and have significant implications for their academic and social success. Their needs are often overlooked and misunderstood. Because these students can hear some sounds, they may not be immediately referred for services. Accumulated years of misunderstanding what they are hearing can result in grade retention and a gap between ability and academic achievement. They are also at risk socially because they may miss the small social nuances in schools' hallways, cafeterias, and gyms (Easterbrooks & Baker, 2002; Wake, Hughes, Poulakis, Collins, & Rickards, 2004).

Social and Emotional Development

The communication barriers that result from the difficulty of acquiring oral language, compounded by preconceived ideas of deafness held by the hearing world, significantly affect a student's psychosocial development. The average hearing person has difficulty communicating with a person with hearing loss, and deaf students soon become aware of these communication problems as they try to make their wants and needs known.

Four factors affect deaf students' social and emotional development. First, parent-child interaction plays a fundamental role in every child's development. Hearing parents may very early find it difficult to communicate with their child who is deaf or hard of hearing. This difficulty will affect their interactions as well as parent-child bonding.

Second, peers and teachers play a significant role in a student's social development. When communication is easy, students learn social norms, rules of conversation, appropriate ways of responding in various situations, and how to develop relationships. If, however, there is a communication barrier among a student, teachers, and peers, the resulting lack of interaction is likely to hamper the student's development of a positive self-concept as well as close friendships.

A third influence on a developing social presence involves awareness of social cues. These cues are most often spoken, and while a student with hearing loss may pick up on some visual cues to appropriate social behaviors, he may miss the auditory ones.

Finally, deaf children can feel an increasing sense of isolation and loneliness as they realize that others may not be comfortable interacting with them (Scheetz, 2004; Wauters & Knoors, 2007). They

Deaf and hearing students sign to each other and contribute to each others' social development.

IEP Tip

Social integration of deaf children in inclusive settings depends on the child's peer acceptance, social competence, and friendships. The student's IEP team should consider the child's social skills when developing the IEP.

PEARSON
myeducationlab

Go to the Activities and Application section in Chapter 14 of MyEducationLab and complete Activity 2. As you watch the videos and answer the accompanying questions reflect on the various causes of hearing loss.

may even begin to see themselves through the eyes of society and develop a feeling of being outsiders in a hearing world.

Determining the Causes

Determining the cause of hearing loss is often complicated by a delay in diagnosis, and many causes remain unknown. When a hearing loss is present at birth, the proper term is **congenital** loss, regardless of the cause. Losses that occur after birth are described as **acquired.** A number of factors can result in hearing loss. They include hereditary or genetic reasons, an event or injury during pregnancy (prenatal), or injury at or just following birth. Trauma, disease, and exposure to excessive noise can also cause hearing loss.

Genetic Causes

Hereditary loss occurs in approximately 1 in 2,000 children. Most hereditary hearing loss is a result of an inherited autosomal recessive gene (80 percent) and is not associated with any type of **syndrome.** There are more than 70 documented inherited syndromes associated with deafness; they can result in either a conductive, a sensorineural, or a mixed loss (Batshaw, Pellegrino, & Roizen, 2007).

Prenatal Causes

Exposure to viruses, bacteria, and other toxins before or after birth can result in a hearing loss. During delivery or in the newborn period, a number of complications, such as lack of oxygen **(hypoxia),** can damage the hearing mechanism, particularly the cochlea.

The major cause of congenital deafness is infection that occurs during pregnancy or soon after the baby is born. Before the development of a vaccine, **rubella** was one of the leading causes of deafness. The rubella epidemic in the United States in 1964–1965 resulted in a huge increase in the incidence of deafness. Due to the use of an anti-rubella vaccine, the incidence has decreased considerably.

Toxoplasmosis, herpes virus, syphilis, and **cytomegalovirus (CMV)** are prenatal infections that can cause hearing loss. The most prevalent of these infections is CMV, which has an incidence of 5 to 25 cases per 1,000 births (Batshaw et al., 2007). This viral infection is spread by close contact with an individual who is shedding the virus through body fluids. No vaccine is available for protection against CMV; people should wash their hands and avoid direct bodily contact with individuals who have the disease. Toxoplasmosis is characterized by **jaundice** and **anemia** and results in hearing loss in about 15 percent of infants born to mothers who have it. Pregnant women should avoid contact with cat feces and raw or undercooked meat, which may be contaminated with this virus. The herpes virus is transferred to the infant during the birth process as the infant passes through the birth canal. Mothers with genital herpes disease most often deliver babies by Caesarean section to avoid transferring the infection to their infants (National Center on Birth Defects and Developmental Disabilities, 2004).

Premature infants, particularly those weighing less than 1,500 grams (3⅓ pounds), have an increased susceptibility to hypoxia, **hyperbilirubinemia,** and **intracranial hemorrhage,** all of which have been associated with sensorineural hearing loss. Other factors associated with congenital sensorineural hearing loss are Rh incompatibility and the use of ototoxic drugs (Gilbert et al., 2007). **Maternal Rh incompatibility** used to be a much more common cause of hearing loss before the development of anti-Rh gamma globulin **(RhoGAM)** in 1968. The injection of RhoGAM in the first 72 hours following delivery of her first child will keep the mother from producing antibodies that could harm her later babies. Certain antibiotics are considered **ototoxic** and can destroy the outer row of hair cells in the cochlea. Physicians can monitor drug levels in the blood to prevent them from reaching toxic levels.

Postnatal Causes

Infections in infancy and childhood also can lead to a sensorineural hearing loss. For example, **bacterial meningitis** has a 10 percent risk of hearing loss from damage to the cochlea. The most common cause of hearing loss in young children is middle-ear disease or **acute otitis media** (ear infection). Fluid collects in the middle ear behind the eardrum. This disease can go undiagnosed, and, although it does not result in a permanent conductive hearing loss, it can cause hearing to fluctuate in young children during the time that they are acquiring speech and language in the first two years of life. In fact, 75 percent to 90 percent of all young children have at least one ear infection before they are 2 years old. As a teacher, you will want to be aware of the fluctuating conductive hearing loss that can occur in your students who have middle-ear infections; those students might be missing important information while they have an ear infection. You should be aware of any signs (such as inattention or cocking the head) that might indicate that the child is not hearing what you are saying.

Postlingual Causes

A blow to the skull can cause trauma to the cochlea and may lead to a sensorineural hearing loss. It can also damage the middle-ear bones, resulting in a conductive loss. Mild to moderate sensorineural hearing loss can occur as a result of being around excessive noise such as firecrackers and air guns. Transient or permanent sensorineural loss also may occur with exposure to very loud sound over time. Using headphones at high-intensity levels or attending rock concerts where noise levels can reach 100 to 110 dB may be damaging. In fact, any sustained exposure to sound levels of 90 dB or greater is potentially harmful to the cochlea and should be avoided (Batshaw et al., 2007).

EVALUATING STUDENTS WITH HEARING LOSS

Determining the Presence of Hearing Loss

Diagnostic Assessment

The earlier hearing loss is identified, the more quickly intervention can begin. Figure 14.5 illustrates a recommended infant hearing screening process. Most states now have an early hearing detection and intervention (EHDI) system that

1. Screens all newborns for hearing loss before 1 month of age, preferably before leaving the hospital
2. Refers all infants who screen positive for a diagnostic audiologic evaluation before 3 months of age
3. Provides all infants identified as having a hearing loss with appropriate early intervention services before 6 months of age

The diagnosis of a hearing loss is made by a combination of professionals, including the child's doctor, an **otologist** (a physician who specializes in diseases of the ear), and an **audiologist.** Audiologists have special training in testing and measuring hearing and are able to evaluate the hearing of any child at any age. Audiologists also have the skills to participate in the child's rehabilitation and treatment and to prescribe and evaluate the effectiveness of hearing aids and cochlear implants.

Hearing Aids

Audiologists provide assistance in selecting and using hearing aids. Hearing aids amplify sound but do not correct hearing; they make sound louder but not necessarily clearer.

The behind-the-ear aid is probably the most common type of hearing aid used by both children and adults. The case holding all of the components of the hearing aid is worn behind the ear, and the signal is delivered through a tube into the ear using an earmold. For

Figure 14.5 Infant hearing screening process

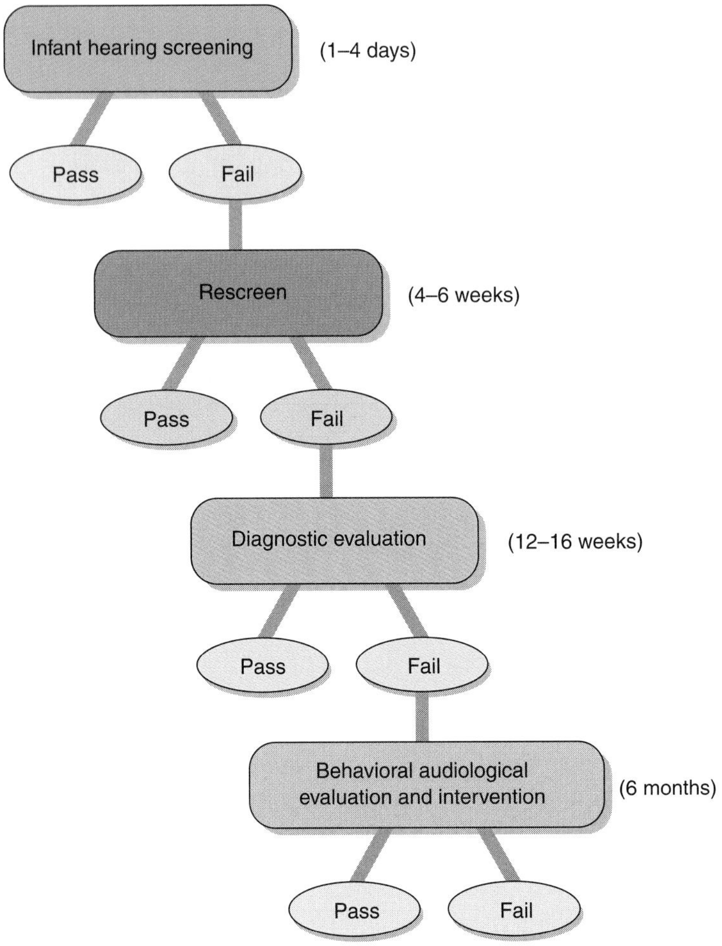

Infant hearing screening   (1–4 days)

Pass   Fail

Rescreen   (4–6 weeks)

Pass   Fail

Diagnostic evaluation   (12–16 weeks)

Pass   Fail

Behavioral audiological evaluation and intervention   (6 months)

Pass   Fail

Source: From "Universal Newborn Hearing Screening Using Transient Evoked Otoacoustic Emissions: Results of the Rhode Island Hearing Assessment Project," by K. R. White. B. R. Vohr, and T. R. Behrens, 1993. *Seminars in Hearing. 14*(1). pp. 18–29. Copyright 1993 by Thieme Medical Publishers. Reprinted with permission.

children, this type of aid has the advantage of durability. Behind-the-ear hearing aids are larger than the hearing aids worn inside the ear, making them easier to keep track of and better able to withstand the daily wear and tear that young children usually create.

In addition, behind-the-ear aids provide flexibility. As the child grows, the size of the ear also increases. When this happens, the earmold may no longer fit. With a behind-the-ear aid, accommodating growth means simply replacing the earmold rather than the entire hearing aid. Children can wear this type of aid behind one or both ears.

Cochlear Implants

A **cochlear implant,** which Mariah, Ricquel, and Shyla have, is an electronic device that is surgically implanted under the skin behind the ear and contains a magnet that couples to a magnet in a sound transmitter that is worn externally.

A surgeon inserts an electrode array into the cochlea to provide direct stimulation to the nerve fibers. A speech processor that can be worn on the body or behind the ear is connected to a headpiece by a cable. Sound is picked up by a microphone and sent to the speech processor, which then filters, analyzes, and digitizes the sound into coded electrical signals. These coded signals are sent through a coil across the skin to the internal implanted receiver/stimulator via an FM radio signal. The receiver delivers electrical stimulation to the appropriate implanted electrodes in the cochlea, and then this signal is carried to the brain through the auditory nerve.

The cochlear implant does not restore normal hearing or amplify sound. Rather, it provides a sense of sound to individuals who are profoundly deaf and cannot otherwise receive auditory signals. It "gets around" the blockage of damaged hair cells in the cochlea by bypassing them and directly stimulating the auditory nerve (National Institute on Deafness and Other Communication Disorders, 2007).

Determining the Nature of Specially Designed Instruction and Services

Educational Evaluation

As we pointed out in Chapter 2, nondiscriminatory evaluation has two purposes: to determine whether a student has a disability and, if so, to determine an appropriate program and placement for the student. The test for eligibility for special education services for students with hearing loss is usually their initial assessment, the hearing test. Figure 14.6 illustrates the evaluation process.

How Hearing Is Tested

Audiologists measure the type and severity of a hearing loss. The simplest test of hearing ability is pure tone audiometry. Audiologists use a machine called an **audiometer** to test hearing. It measures hearing threshold, the softest level at which sound can first be detected, at various sound frequencies.

Infants up to 6 months of age can be screened for hearing loss in two ways: evoked otoacoustic emissions (EOAE) and screening auditory brain stem response (SABR). EOAE is a fast and noninvasive test for a newborn that assesses how well the baby's cochlea is functioning and transmitting sound to the brain. The ear canal is sealed with a plastic probe, and clicks or tones of various frequencies are introduced into the ear canal. A computer records responses that are evoked from the cochlea.

The other newborn screening method, SABR, assesses more than the child's cochlea. It tests the child's auditory neural pathway as well. EEG sensors are placed in various places on the baby's scalp. Using an external or inserted earphone, tones or clicks are presented separately to each ear, stimulating neural activity along the path. The electrodes detect sound, and the computer averages the responses.

Finally, diagnostic ABR audiometry is a highly sensitive test for both hearing loss and problems in the neural pathway. The ABR generates waveforms composed of three distinct waves (I, II, and III); the absence of waveform at a given intensity suggests a hearing loss, whereas the complete absence of a particular wave suggests an abnormality at a particular location along the brain pathway (Batshaw et al., 2007).

According to Sharon, the diagnosis of hearing loss was very different for her three daughters. She began to suspect a problem when Mariah was 2 years old and was not yet speaking. An ABR exam showed that Mariah had a severe to profound loss. When Ricquel and Shylah were born, early hearing screening was provided in the hospital, resulting in a much earlier identification.

Behavioral audiological evaluations are appropriate for testing the hearing of older children. This test requires children to listen to a series of beeps called pure tones and indicate when they hear a sound.

The responses are recorded on an **audiogram,** a picture of what is heard. Figure 14.7 is Ricquel's audiogram, showing a severe to profound hearing loss, the type of loss all three Thomas sisters had at birth. It shows how much the hearing varies from normal if there is a loss (severity) and where the problem might be located in the auditory pathway (type). The vertical lines on an audiogram represent pitch or frequency (Hz), and the horizontal lines represent loudness or intensity (dB). The top of the audiogram on the left side shows 125 Hertz, a very low-pitched sound. As you look across, each line represents a higher and higher pitch. The critical pitches for speech are 500 to 3,000 Hz.

PEARSON
myeducationlab

Go to the Activities and Application section in Chapter 14 of MyEducationLab and complete Activity 3. As you watch the videos and answer the accompanying questions consider how this doctor might interact with the classroom teacher.

Figure 14.6
Nondiscriminatory evaluation process for determining the presence of a hearing loss

Observation	**Medical personnel observe:** The baby does not show a startle reflex to loud noises. As the child matures, speech and language are delayed.
	Teachers and parents observe: The child (1) does not respond to sound; (2) does not babble or engage in vocal play; and (3) experiences communication misunderstandings, speech difficulties, and inattention.
Screening	**Assessment measures:**
	Newborn screening: Most states require newborn screening for hearing loss.
	Auditory brain stem response: Results may show inadequate or slow response to sound.
	Transient evoked otoacoustic immittance: Results may show that measurement of sound in the ear is lower than normal.
	Behavioral audiological evaluation: Hearing thresholds are higher than 15 dB.
Prereferral	Prereferral is typically not used with these students because of the need to identify hearing loss quickly.
Referral	Children receive nondiscriminatory evaluation procedures as soon as they enter school. Intervention should occur as soon as the child is diagnosed. Students with mild hearing loss may be referred.
Nondiscriminatory evaluation procedures and and standards	**Assessment measures:**
	Audiological reassessment: Recent audiograms may indicate that the student's hearing loss has stabilized or is worsening. Testing for hearing aid function is a regular need.
	Speech and language evaluation: The student may have significant problems with receptive and expressive language. The student's speech is usually affected.
	Individualized intelligence test: The student's scores show a discrepancy between verbal and nonverbal measures. Nonverbal tests are considered the only reliable and valid measures of intelligence for this population.
	Individualized achievement test: The student may score significantly lower than peers.
	Adaptive behavior: The student may score below average in communication and possibly in other areas of adaptive behavior.
	Anecdotal records: The student's performance may indicate difficulty with reading, writing, or language arts.
	Curriculum-based assessment: The student may be performing below peers in one or more areas of the curriculum because of reading and/or language difficulties.
	Direct observation: The student may be difficult to understand and may misunderstand others.
Determination	The nondiscriminatory evaluation team determines that the student has a hearing loss and needs special education and related services. The student's IEP team proceeds to develop appropriate education options for the child.

When you read down the left side of the audiogram, you can see the increasing loudness of sound represented by decibels. The first number listed is minus 10 dB because there is never a complete absence of sound in our world. Moving downward, each number represents a louder and louder sound, as if the volume were being turned up on a stereo. Responses to sound are plotted on the graph in terms of how loud a sound must be at each frequency before it is heard. Every point on an audiogram represents a different sound.

Figure 14.7 Ricquel's audiogram, showing profound hearing loss in both ears

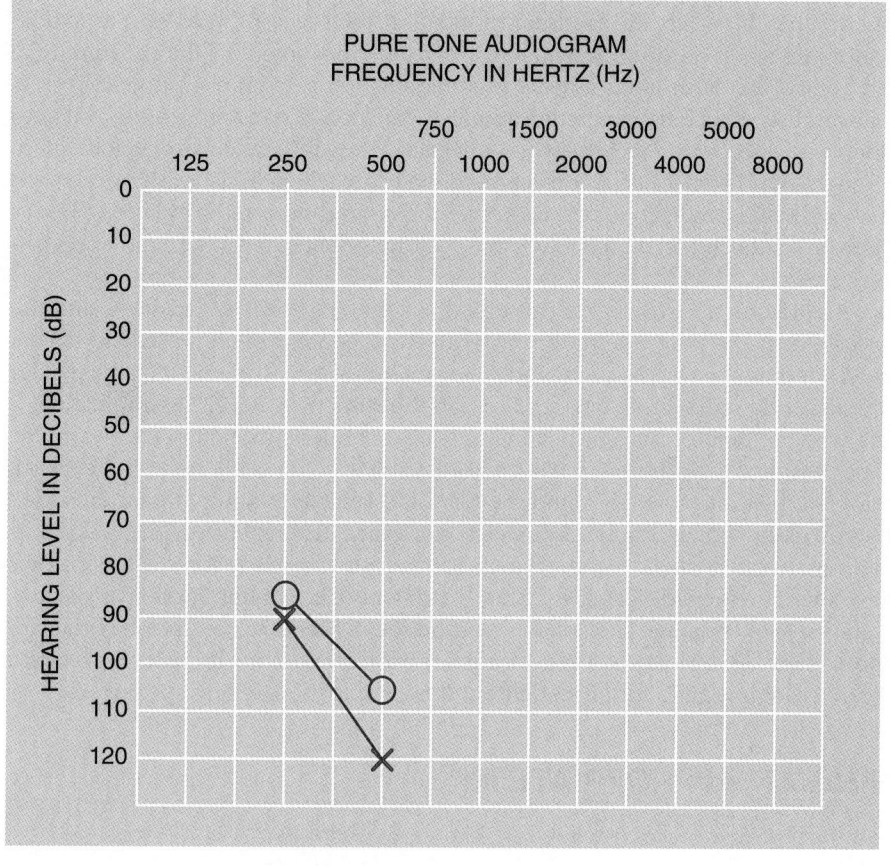

X = left ear   O = right ear

The audiologist tests the student's hearing by using air conduction (through earphones) and marks the hearing threshold on a graph with an *O* (for the right ear) and an *X* (for the left ear). The sound leaves the earphones, traveling through the air in the ear canal, through the middle ear, and to the cochlea in the inner ear.

The audiologist tests the sensitivity of the student's cochlea by using bone conduction through a small vibrator placed on the bone behind the ear. Sounds presented this way travel through the bones of the skull directly to the cochlea and auditory nerve, bypassing the outer and middle ear. When a bone-conduction vibrator is used to test for thresholds, a "<" symbol or a "[" symbol is used for the right ear and a ">" symbol or a "]" symbol is used for the left ear.

By comparing the headphone thresholds with the bone conduction thresholds at each pitch, the audiologist can determine whether a hearing loss is conductive, sensorineural, or mixed. If the air-conduction thresholds show a hearing loss but the bone-conduction thresholds are normal, then the individual has a conductive loss. If the hearing thresholds obtained by bone conduction are the same as by air conduction, there is no blockage of sound in the outer or middle ear and the hearing loss is caused by a loss of sensitivity in the cochlea or auditory nerve.

The audiologist usually will perform two additional tests, **tympanography** and speech **audiometry.** Tympanography is not a hearing test but a test of how well the middle ear is functioning and

Audiologists retest the hearing of children with suspected or known hearing loss four times a year until age 3, twice a year until age 6, and annually after 6 years of age.

how well the eardrum can move. To conduct this test, the audiologist places a small rubber tip in the ear and pumps a little air into the outer ear canal. If the middle ear is functioning properly, the air causes the eardrum to move. If there is a problem in the middle ear, it may show up as no eardrum movement. Very little movement of the eardrum may indicate fluid behind the eardrum as a result of a middle-ear infection (otitis media).

The ability to use speech for communication is a function of two things—the ability to detect the sounds of speech and the ability to understand speech. The pure tone audiogram shows how much sound someone can detect, but it does not tell us how clearly speech can be heard. We can make predictions based on the degree and type of hearing loss, but to measure a person's speech discrimination—how well he or she can understand speech—special tests are used.

For speech audiometry, words are presented at different levels of loudness and the student is asked to repeat them. A student with a sensorineural hearing loss may have a problem understanding the words, even when they are loud enough. Generally, the greater the student's sensorineural hearing loss, the poorer the student's speech discrimination.

Students who are deaf or hard of hearing may also require specific tests to determine the nature and extent of their disability. This is particularly true if a student has other problems in addition to hearing loss. IDEA and the No Child Left Behind Act require increased attention to curriculum content standards and accountability. Testing to provide feedback is important because teachers need to know whether their instruction is successful and parents want to know about their child's progress. The assessment of communication involves testing speech and/or sign language skills depending on the communication modality the student is using. Finally, assessment is used to guide instruction. It can be as complex as a state-mandated testing program for all students and as simple as a 10-item spelling test.

DESIGNING AN APPROPRIATE IEP

Partnering for Special Education and Related Services

Special and general educators, speech-language pathologists, audiologists, interpreters, paraprofessionals, family members, friends, and community members often become partners to contribute to a student's language, academic, and social development. In many school districts, an itinerant deaf educator—a professional who covers several schools in the same district—often becomes the key member and most informed advocate for the child. It is important to bear in mind that IDEA recognizes the contributions to the child's development that can be made by peers and professionals who can communicate directly with the child in the child's language and mode of communication. The law does so (as we pointed out earlier in this chapter) by requiring the IEP team to consider the child's language and communication needs, opportunities for direct communication (that is, not-interpreted communication) with peers and professionals in the child's language, and communication mode. Beyond peers and other professionals, the increased use of cochlear implants means that the professionals who implant and maintain the cochlear implant should be members of the child's IEP team as well. Their participation on the IEP team is particularly important because IDEA provides that a surgically implanted medical device, such as the cochlear implant, is not a related service; the school is not responsible to provide or maintain the device. That's the role for the implant team. Box 14.1 gives you tips on how partners educate a student who has a profound hearing loss.

Interpreter services, illustrated here and consisting of the translation of the spoken word into signs and signs into the spoken word, are now a related service under IDEA.

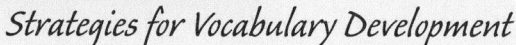
Strategies for Vocabulary Development

Partnerships among general and special educators, deaf educators, related service providers, interpreters, and students who are deaf or hard of hearing are indispensable if students are to make progress in the general curriculum. That much is obvious. But how to apply this proposition—that's another matter.

As you have already learned, regardless of how effectively a child with hearing loss can comprehend complex concepts presented from teacher to student, reading about these concepts requires that he be able to manipulate English sentence structure, which is an especially daunting task for children who are not proficient in English.

Because the vocabulary is difficult and the sentence structures complex, the social studies and science texts that Ben, age 10, must master for statewide assessment purposes are eluding him. The challenge is to provide Ben, who has a profound hearing loss, with the support he needs to continue being included in general instruction for these subject areas. The partners in this endeavor include Ben; Linda, his classroom teacher; Katie, his deaf educator; Todd, Ben's friend, who is hearing; John, his interpreter; and Ben's parents.

Linda has taught several reading strategies to her class of 28 children, knowing that Ben is not the only child in the class who can benefit from improved ability to read content-area material. Katie uses these same strategies with Ben and several other students during small-group time in the resource room.

Strategies

1. *Semantic mapping* is a strategy that builds on a student's prior knowledge. Semantic maps are diagrams that show visually the connections between different categories of a topic. You begin this strategy with a brainstorming session that encourages students to think about concepts they know and then to see graphically how these concepts relate to the new information they are trying to learn. Students can learn the meanings and uses of new words, see words they already know from a new perspective, and, ultimately, see how the words connect to each other.
    *   Write the new word to be learned in a circle in the middle of the white board.
    *   In the brainstorming session, have the students think of as many words as they can that relate to the new word.
    *   As the students give their words, write them on the board. Then have students categorize the different words by asking questions such as "What is it? What is it like?" Label the categories,

and then have students group their words into the categories.
    *   Remember to pace your instruction and pause for interpretation. John, Ben's interpreter, makes sure that Ben has opportunities to contribute to discussions by reminding Linda to pause between calling on children because the lag time between Linda's question and John's interpreting means that Ben is a few seconds behind the other children in "hearing" the question.

For example, Linda writes the new word, *journey,* on the board and draws a circle around it. The students suggest other words—*trip, vacation, travel, car, airplane, Disney World*—and the teacher categorizes these words into the categories of TYPES OF JOURNEYS, PLACES TO GO, HOW TO TRAVEL. Then the students come up with other words that fit into each category. Ben has been to Disney World and traveled by airplane to get there. He now understands that a "journey" can be a trip and to go on a journey, he must have some means of travel.

2. The K-W-L approach: *Know, what, learn*
    *   Before reading, ask the children to brainstorm what they know about the topic.
    *   Write all their ideas on the computer, project the display through an LCD projector, and then ask students to put their ideas into categories.
    *   After this group activity, ask them to create individual questions regarding what they want to learn about the topic.
    *   Assign the text material for homework.

Ben's parents make sure to set aside a few minutes every evening so that Ben can show them his vocabulary questions and the answers he finds. The next day, Linda asks her students to discuss what they have learned. She focuses their responses specifically on answering the questions they have written the previous day. She also draws their attention to similarities and differences between what they had previously known about the topic and what they have learned by reading the assignment.

3. *Thematic organization* is used to promote language development, critical thinking, independence, and collaboration among students. To be effective, thematic instruction must have meaning and purpose for students. It must also be relevant and interesting! The best way to achieve this is to have students participate in choosing the theme as well as the projects that will be part of a unit. Another important aspect of thematic organization is that it should build on the students' prior knowledge. This

continued

knowledge can be from their experiences, their families' cultures, and their understanding of themselves and others. There should be integrated opportunities for students to use language and literacy, collaborate with others, and help to guide all aspects of the process. Finally, use a multi-subject approach incorporating the theme across all academic areas—mathematics, social studies, science, reading, etc.

- Identify a theme. Linda's class chose "chocolate" as their theme.
- Have students create an outline or flow chart of major concepts and vocabulary they will encounter in completing the different activities around the theme.
- Develop a variety of lessons around the theme. Linda and Katie had the class read the book *Chocolate Touch*; write descriptive paragraphs using the five senses on paper shaped like Hershey's Kisses; learn about Hershey, Pennsylvania, find it on the map, and identify the state's capital; create 12 words out of the words "chocolate" and "Hershey"; and answer the question "If a candy bar snitcher took 12 of your 30 bars, how many would you have left? Now write this number as a fraction."
- Allow for additional supports as needed. Todd works as Ben's study buddy, and they share ideas about the lessons. Todd often helps explain a concept in a way that is understandable to Ben.

Ben has been able to keep up with his fourth-grade peers in comprehending the content material assigned as homework. His teachers and parents realize, however, that as text material becomes more difficult, Ben will be increasingly challenged to be independent in reading material written at grade level. In the future, Ben's teachers may wish to find supplementary material written at his reading level.

4. A *Venn diagram* strategy is another technique that can be used to compare and contrast things. It can be used with either expository or narrative text.
   - Write two target words (e.g., computer and brain) on the white board.
   - Have students list as many characteristics as they can under each word. Computer—out in the open, non-living, can talk, hard, dry, many forms, made of plastic, solves problems, remembers things, cannot do things without being programmed, can be damaged; Brain—is enclosed, living, soft, made of tissue, warm, one form, solves problems, remembers things, can talk, can be damaged. Ben works with a small group of his friends during this stage.
   - Draw two overlapping circles on the board (the Venn diagram). Ask students to determine which characteristics the two words have in common and write those in the overlapping part of the two circles; then have them write the unique characteristics for each word in the parts of the circles that don't overlap. Katie, Ben's deaf educator, helps him write a short paper comparing and contrasting the two.

PEARSON **myeducationlab**

Go to the Building Teaching Skills and Dispositions section in Chapter 14 of MyEducationLab and complete the activities. As you examine the process writing strategy, think about how you might incorporate it with the vocabulary development strategies discussed here.

PEARSON **myeducationlab**

Go to the Activities and Application section in Chapter 14 of MyEducationLab and complete Activity 4. As you watch the video and answer the accompanying questions reflect on the importance of this student's interpreter.

Using Interpreters in Educational Settings

Related services under Part B (ages 3 through 21) include interpreting services. Educational interpreters provide an essential service to both students and teachers. They translate the spoken word into signs for students with a hearing loss. Some perform additional duties within the school or classroom, such as tutoring, general classroom assistance, educational planning, and sign language instruction (Marschark, Sapare, Convertino, & Seewagen, 2005). The educational interpreter is often a student's communication bridge to the hearing world around him.

Determining Supplementary Aids and Services

Managing the Listening Environment/Acoustics

When a classroom is equipped with a **sound-field amplification system,** the teacher transmits his voice by using a lavaliere microphone and ceiling- or wall-mounted speakers. These in turn amplify his voice to 8 to 10 dB above the ambient room noise. Noisy environments, such as many classrooms, blunt the effects of hearing aids.

A student's hearing aid also allows access to **loop systems.** These involve closed-circuit wiring that sends FM signals from an audio system directly to an electronic coil in the student's hearing aid. The receiver picks up the signals much as a remote control sends infrared signals to a television. These systems allow students with residual hearing to participate in a variety of educational settings.

Assistive Technology

Just as a caption in a book is the text under a picture, **closed-captioned technology** translates dialogue from a spoken language to a printed form (captions) that is then inserted at the bottom of the television, movie, or videotape. Captioning increases deaf or hard-of-hearing students' ability to comprehend a speaker and understand the information presented (Block & Okrand, 1983). Box 14.2 provides you with tips on how real-time captioning in a classroom benefits students who are deaf or hard of hearing.

TECHNOLOGY OUTCOMES

Box 14.2

Real-Time Captioning in Classrooms

Undoubtedly, you have seen movies in which a court stenographer is recording what judges, lawyers, and witnesses say. The stenographer is making a record that participants in the trial can consult later. Now technology takes that service to a new level, making the words instantly available to students who are deaf or hard of hearing.

Communication Access Realtime Translation (CART) is a technology that instantly converts the spoken word into English text, using a stenotype machine, a notebook computer, and real-time software. An individual types the spoken word into the stenotype machine, and a software program converts the shorthand into text that then appears on a computer monitor. The real-time captionist is a related service provider, just like the student's educational interpreter. The regulations implementing the Americans with Disabilities Act recognize CART as an assistive technology that affords "effective communication access." Thus, communication access is what truly distinguishes CART from real-time reporting in a traditional courtroom sense. Real-time captioning in a classroom can give deaf and hard-of-hearing students instant access to a teacher's and peers' communications. Its power to advance students' inclusion is staggering.

Deaf students have had access to captioned movies and videos for many years, and captioning increases students' comprehension and their reading skills (Caldwell, 1973; Robson, 2004; Marschark et al., 2006). In fact, captions help both deaf and hearing students, particularly in classroom environments with poor acoustics (e.g., a large room or noisy conditions), where even hearing students have difficulties in hearing everything that is said.

What are the benefits of using real-time captioning in your classroom?

◆ *Independent learning*—With CART, the responsibility for your student's education rests with the student. He will have a verbatim record of the class discussion and can determine what is important. Using the highlighting or annotating features of the computer software, he can pick out exactly what he needs to study.

◆ *Full participation*—because CART provides information in real time, the student with hearing loss has the opportunity to participate in the class just like his classmates. Besides getting the text of the lecture, CART allows for the inclusion of classroom banter, discussion, and questions asked by other students. This gives him full access to the classroom experience, not just notes of the lesson's content provided after class.

How do you secure CART services for students with hearing loss? Just as with interpreters, there is a shortage of people skilled in this form of real-time captioning. Some companies, such as Caption First, provide CART services both locally and nationally through remote technology.

◆ When an IEP team has determined that a student will benefit from real-time captioning as a related service, the IEP should include the following specifics:
   a. Communication Access Realtime Translation (CART) will be provided by a court reporter who can write at a minimum speed of 225 words per minute.
   b. An electronic copy of the notes will be given to the student immediately after each class so the student can make his or her notes at home.
   c. Same-day substitutes will be provided when needed.
   d. The student will be allowed to follow the CART feed on a laptop computer on his or her desk.

The National Court Reporters Association (NCRA) has an online CART directory at http://www.cartinfo.org that you can use to find CART providers in your area.

■ ■ ■

Here, both the student and the teacher wear an assistive technology device (a transmitter and receiver), but neither relies on it alone to communicate.

Computers and the Internet

Personal computers provide students with hearing loss access to information in remarkably innovative ways. They can provide instructional support and can even assist students in learning sign language. A computer system (C-print) developed by the National Technical Institute for the Deaf (NTID) provides students who use software-equipped laptop computers with real-time translations of the spoken word. Students with hearing loss can attend a lecture, watch an interpreter without having to look down to take notes, and view the simultaneous written text of what is being said.

Planning for Universal Design for Learning

Children who are deaf or hard of hearing typically communicate in one of three ways: oral/aural, manual (ASL or English system), or simultaneous communication.

Communication Methods

Oral/aural methods include instruction in spoken English, a curriculum in speech and aural habilitation, and the expectation that students will use speech, speech reading, and auditory skills for communication. Not all students benefit from speech instruction; indeed, as students become older their motivation for speech intervention often declines.

Speech-language pathologists are responsible for carrying out instruction in speech and aural habilitation (teaching children to use their remaining hearing). Because many students with significant hearing loss do not hear speech or do not hear it without distortion, it is difficult for them to produce speech and to monitor their own speech without assistance. Their problems can include trouble with volume, pitch, and nasality. The speech-language pathologist helps them develop breath control, vocalization, voice patterns, and sound production.

The speech-language pathologist also usually educates students with hearing loss to use even their minimal residual hearing effectively. The pathologist teaches the student about awareness of sound, localization of sound, discrimination of sound differences, recognition of the sound, and, ultimately, comprehension of others' speech.

Total communication methods include instruction in simultaneous communication. Students are expected to use simultaneous communication for their academic and social discourse. Total communication methods also incorporate curricula in speech and aural habilitation, and they sometimes include a curriculum in ASL.

Total communication is somewhat out of favor. One reason is that it is unrealistic to expect a student to use every available communication technique and mode. Teachers typically emphasize speech and audition at the expense of sign language, or vice versa. And students often attend more to one mode than to the other.

A second reason for total communication's decreasing use is that it uses speech and sign language simultaneously. It is nearly impossible to speak and use ASL at the same time, so teachers use either manually coded English or Pidgin Sign English (Coryell & Holcomb, 1997; Woodward & Allen, 1993).

Many educators and members of the Deaf community are vociferous opponents of manually coded English sign systems because they believe that these systems are not languages at all but distortions of features of ASL. But researchers have found that most teachers using total communication methods actually use Pidgin Sign English, which is essentially an incomplete version of both ASL and English, providing none of the grammatical complexity of either language.

A Bilingual/Bicultural Model

One method of communication that interests both deaf and hearing parents of students with hearing loss is the bilingual/bicultural (bi-bi) program. This model is a bilingual/English-As-a-Second-Language model for deaf students acquiring and learning two languages—American Sign Language and English. The model takes theories and knowledge from ESL research and applies them to deaf education (Easterbrooks & Baker, 2002). The student learns ASL as a first language and English as a second language.

Lesson Planning for Speech and Language

Collaboration is critical when preparing instruction for students who are deaf or hard of hearing. To account for the gap between the child's language and the linguistic demands of the lesson, the lesson plan should include a section for language, a section for speech, and a section for auditory goals in addition to the concepts to be taught. The teacher may choose to focus initially on the concept to be taught and then follow up with practice on language, speech, and auditory goals. Instruction may involve a general education teacher, a teacher of the deaf, and a paraprofessional in collaboration with a speech-language pathologist. There should be four levels of planning: (1) concept planning, (2) language goals planning, (3) speech goals planning, and (4) auditory goals planning. Each participant should have input and responsibility for every aspect of planning and instruction. Box 14.3 provides an example of how you can plan a lesson considering all four levels.

Go to the Activities and Application section in Chapter 14 of MyEducationLab and complete Activity 5. As you watch the video and answer the accompanying questions think about how this student's auditory goals are being achieved.

PARTNERSHIP TIPS   *Box 14.3*

Planning for Concepts, Language, Speech, and Auditory Goals

Mrs. Burke's first-grade class is working on a unit on nutrition. Grace, a student in the class, has a profound hearing loss. She received a cochlear implant when she was 4 years old and has language, speech, and auditory IEP goals. Her language goals include using the infinitive verb form *to* (for example, *to eat*), the pronouns *we* and *they,* and the conjunctions *before* and *after.* Her speech goals include production of the /s/ sound at the end of words, the long /a/ vowel, and the long /e/ vowel. Grace also has an auditory goal that indicates she will be able to identify and understand these sounds when she hears them in a phrase by being able to repeat the phrase correctly. Mrs. Burke collaborates with Ms. Randle, the teacher of the deaf, and Mr. Gillespie, the speech-language pathologist. Together, they develop the following list of ways they will incorporate Grace's IEP goals into the nutrition unit:

- ◆ Concepts: What are the different food groups, where do different foods come from, what is the difference between fresh and cooked food, and how is food preserved?
- ◆ Language: Meat and vegetables can be cooked *to* eat. We have *to* put milk in the refrigerator *to* keep it fresh.

- ◆ Pronoun: *We* should eat foods from each of the food groups every day. Carrots and celery can be eaten raw. *They* are good for us.
- ◆ Conjunction: You can eat apples *after* you wash them.
- ◆ Speech: vegetable*s*, fruit*s*, rice (/*s*/ sound), food group*s*
- ◆ Auditory: *need, cheese, we* versus *steak, eggs, cake*

Together they decide who will be responsible for each aspect of teaching the unit and what activities will be included. Ms. Randle, the teacher of the deaf, will work on teaching about infinitives and how they are used. She will also develop some listening activities to help Grace hear the differences between the /e/ and /a/ sounds. Mr. Gillespie will work individually with Grace, teaching her to say the sounds. Mrs. Burke will focus on incorporating the language, speech, and auditory goals into the activities to reinforce what the others have worked on. For example, if Grace mispronounces the word *cheese*, Mrs. Burke will model the correct pronunciation and ask her to repeat the word. She will also provide auditory experiences by asking Grace to "get the eggs" or "stir the cake." She might also have a conversation with Grace about what she ate for breakfast that morning to help her practice her listening and speech skills.

Planning for Other Educational Needs

When the majority of students with hearing loss attended residential schools for the deaf, they were exposed to the culture of deafness as a normal part of their lives. The school played an integral part in the Deaf community. Deaf adults spent large amounts of time at the schools, attending sports events and social affairs, serving as role models for the students, and providing them with direct access to the critical elements of Deaf culture. This included information about Deaf history, the arts, and stories about their lives. The schools contained a treasure trove of photos, trophies, and artwork from the past.

Today most students with hearing loss attend public school programs, so "deaf immersion" is not an option (Stewart & Kluwin, 2001; Blackorby & Knokey, 2006). As a result, schools and communities must purposefully provide students with a study of their native language (ASL) and Deaf culture, and make sure that they have opportunities to socialize with deaf adults. Making Deaf studies an indispensable part of a student's educational program is essential to the growth and development of the student's identity, awareness of diversity, and self-esteem. The successful deaf adult is likely to function in both the hearing and the Deaf worlds, so deaf children need to be taught about both communities.

USING EFFECTIVE INSTRUCTIONAL STRATEGIES

Early Childhood Students: Facilitative Language Strategies

Early Intervention

Early intervention for children with hearing loss and their families is critical for developing the children's language, social, and academic skills. Programs should provide young children with similar peers, role models, appropriate developmental skills training, and support for acquiring communication and language. Early intervention programs also should help parents understand their child's needs, so they can make informed decisions about issues that will affect their child's and family's future (Joint Committee on Infant Hearing, 2007).

Early access to a language-rich environment is critical. This means better education for parents concerning strategies to enhance communication with their deaf or hard-of-hearing children, whether they use spoken or sign language. Getting and maintaining attention, labeling and commenting on objects, and explaining events are important components of a child's early language, social, and cognitive development. Hearing parents need to learn the effective visual communication techniques that are typically used by deaf parents (Marschark, Lang, & Albertini, 2002).

Shared Reading

The Shared Reading Project, another appropriate program for young children with hearing loss, was developed by teachers and researchers at the Clerc National Deaf Education Center at Gallaudet University (Schleper, 1997). It is based on how deaf adults read to deaf children and depends heavily on use of ASL, fluency in signing, and a knack for reading signs. Dramatization, connection of English sentences with the way they are signed in ASL, and engagement of children in the reading process are emphasized. This project was found to be of particular benefit to families who were not sharing books before their training and to those who spoke a language other than English. The Shared Reading Project is effective in helping parents learn to share books with traditionally underserved deaf and hard-of-hearing children (Swanwick & Watson, 2007).

Elementary and Middle School Students: Graphic Organizer Modifications

Because students with hearing loss suffer in the academic areas of reading and writing, teachers give high priority to instruction in these content areas. Students should be given hands-on experiences and taught the relationships among concepts and the multiple meanings of words. Visual aids can show links between words and their categories (e.g., animal–dog–golden retriever).

Use Authentic Experiences

Students acquire language and knowledge only when they are presented in ways that are meaningful to the students. Often traditional language programs for students who are deaf or hard of hearing are limited because these programs have no connection to the students' real-world or authentic experiences (Luckner, Sebald, Cooney, Young, & Muir, 2005).

A list of sentences in a book is relevant only if the student has had experiences related to what the sentences describe. Authentic experiences are particularly important for students with hearing loss because they may not have had the same experiences as their hearing peers, nor had them in the same way. For example, we explain to hearing children why they must put on mittens to go outside ("It's below freezing today, and your hands will turn blue!"). For a child with hearing loss who lacks the language for this explanation, parents may just put the mittens on without explanation. When the child later encounters a written sentence about freezing temperatures, he or she will have had no authentic experience with that situation.

Integrate Vocabulary Development

The integration of vocabulary occurs by showing that words are parts of related concepts, are presented in context, and are everywhere. Words occur in bunches and in context. The contexts help define the word and its meanings. "Spring" is a season of the year, a coiled piece of metal, a jump, a small body of water, and many other things. Words are everywhere. There is writing on toys, on clothing labels, and even on cereal boxes. In an integrated approach to vocabulary development, words appear on charts, bulletin boards, and objects in the room. As a teacher, you may find yourself using one of the standard models for increasing your students' language proficiency, the Cummins model, which Box 14.4 describes.

Create Opportunities for Self-Expression

Self-expression is a large part of a student's learning process. Teachers provide students with opportunities to practice their verbal skills and to define and refine ideas. They allow students to convert information into other forms and then express it. Self-expression shows how deeply and for what purposes a student has processed certain information.

Provide Deaf Role Models

Students with hearing loss should have the opportunity to meet and interact with deaf adults. A role model can be a positive example of adult behavior and show students what they can become. If the only adults in their world have hearing, it may be difficult for students with hearing loss to visualize their capabilities and to create future goals (Stewart & Kluwin, 2001).

Teach About Deaf Studies

Learning about deafness, the Deaf community, Deaf history, and famous deaf adults should be a part of the curriculum for students with hearing loss. Teachers can incorporate this information into social studies, health, and science content for all students, but for their deaf and hard-of-hearing students in particular. Just as teachers provide students with information about diverse ethnic and racial cultures, so they should provide them with information about deafness. The subject matter should include the basics for interacting with people with hearing loss, sensitivity activities, ASL as a language, Deaf social interaction norms, Deaf history and organizations, Deaf literature and arts, and Deaf values.

IEP Tip

Students with hearing loss should have knowledge of Deaf culture and the Deaf community. IEP team members should identify strategies for providing this information to the child.

Secondary and Transition Students: Augmented Input

In the early years of deaf education, schools for the deaf typically prepared their students to get a job. A few students went on to college, but the majority graduated expecting to join the workforce. Today advances in technology in America have changed the nature of jobs and employment. Obviously, a high school diploma no longer guarantees a well-paying job.

Using the Cummins Model of Language Proficiency

James Cummins (1980, 1992, 2003), a Canadian linguist, observed that language has two dimensions—conversational and academic. He used two terms to describe these dimensions: (1) BICS (basic interpersonal communicative skills) and (2) CALP (cognitive academic linguistic proficiency). For a student to be successful socially and academically, both dimensions must be developed: BICS + CALP = academic success. The Cummins Model can help team members to analyze tasks, write objectives, and plan appropriate mediated activities for students with hearing loss. Here's how it works:

The Cummins Model is a continuum along which a student's progress from conversation to dealing with challenging material is increased (from simple to complex and visual to language dependent). The model has four quadrants.

> Quadrant A: Activities and tasks that are very hands on and visual, such as art, music, and physical education
>
> Quadrant B: More-complex activities that are visual but tied to a context, such as math computation, science experiments, and social studies projects
>
> Quadrant C: Activities that are much more abstract and dependent on language, such as written instructions without examples; these activities demand a much higher cognitive level for comprehension to occur
>
> Quadrant D: Activities that require language competence and the ability to deal with abstract concepts

How can you use this model for students who are deaf and hard of hearing?

- ◆ Improve listening skills.
  a. Add context to listening skills by improving the room's acoustics, repeating directions two or three times, adding gestures, using a graphic support such as a picture or a drawing, or providing a word clue (e.g., "It rhymes with moon").
  b. Use the model to remind the team to be aware of one student's need to reduce some cognitive demands while recognizing that others may be ready for higher-level thinking skills.

- ◆ Add language comprehension skills.
  a. Include cognitively undemanding, context-embedded questions in Quadrant A: "What color is this table?" "Who is sitting by you?" "Which one is red?"
  b. Include cognitively undemanding, context-reduced questions in Quadrant B: "Where is your sister's classroom?" "What color is your house?" "What is your teacher's name?"
  c. Have more cognitively demanding questions in Quadrant C, but keep the context embedded: "What do you think this story is about?" "Why are shoes made of leather?" "How does electricity make a lamp go on?"
  d. The most cognitively demanding, context-reduced language level is in Quadrant D: "How is a state different from a country?" "What is similar about a horse and a cow?" "Is a mile longer than a kilometer?"

- ◆ Identify levels of student support.
  a. Quadrant A includes directly teaching the necessary subskills with mediation (e.g., define key words using terms "Joe" knows, provide a picture or diagram).
  b. Quadrant B involves directly teaching the substeps to the objective (e.g., have Joe paraphrase the main ideas of the instructions or construct a graphic organizer of the steps).
  c. Quadrant C activities are teacher-led rather than teacher-directed (e.g., assist Joe in verbalizing his thought process by using open-ended questions— "What does 'identify the subject' mean?").
  d. Quadrant D lists a skill that is difficult for the student (e.g., Joe will understand the written directions in his textbook).

PEARSON
myeducationlab)

Go to the Activities and Application section in Chapter 14 of MyEducationLab and complete Activity 6. As you watch the video and answer the accompanying questions, think about how you might use the Cummins Model in conjunction with the SmartBoard technology.

The result is that all schools must prepare their students with hearing loss for postsecondary education and training rather than for a specific job. This is particularly critical for deaf people because they experience higher unemployment and underemployment than do their hearing counterparts (Garay, 2003; Hanks & Luckner, 2003; Punch, Creed, & Hyde, 2006). Thus, transition planning is a key component of a deaf or hard of hearing student's education.

Transition Planning

To prepare students with hearing loss for the world after school, teachers must inform them about the employment, education, and living opportunities that will be available when they graduate. Beyond providing this information, teachers must actively engage their students in meaningful, goal-oriented activities that will prepare them for the future. This means that IEP teams must plan for an extensive evaluation of each student, coordinate a number of educational and employment experiences, and help students match them to their knowledge, experience, and preferences.

In the transition process, the student's reading level has implications for the future. Imagine a 16-year-old student who is reading at a fifth-grade level. His IEP has continually focused on increasing that level by one year. But this goal is inappropriate and probably unrealistic when planning for transition. Let's say that the student wants to enter a particular vocational program that requires a ninth-grade reading level. The questions to ask are, "Is this student a good candidate for this program?" "With sufficient support, such as help in learning the course's written materials and an interpreter to help with in-class communication, could this student succeed in this career?"

The Americans with Disabilities Act requires employers to offer reasonable accommodations for deaf employees, such as installing a telecommunications device for the deaf (TDD). This device consists of a keyboard, a display screen, and a modem. The user types into the machine, and the letters are converted into electrical signals that can travel over regular phone lines. When the signals reach another TDD, they are converted back into letters that appear on a display screen so that the individual with hearing loss can read them. Employees are also using pagers and interpreters for meetings and training.

Postsecondary Education

During the past few years, many colleges and universities have experienced a growth in the numbers of students who are deaf or hard of hearing. This increase has made the transition from high school to postsecondary education easier because students with hearing loss now may have a small community of supportive peers in attendance. In addition, most colleges and universities provide direct support through on-campus offices for students with disabilities. These offices often provide counselors, interpreters, tutoring, and training for professors who will have the students in their classes. They also make arrangements for note takers and even real-time captioning of lectures.

In Box 14.5, you will read about a teacher of the deaf, her two deaf children, and their journeys through school and college—their success stories in inclusive and separate programs alike, and their use of technology and implants.

INCLUDING STUDENTS WITH HEARING LOSS

Educational Quality

When the Commission on the Education of the Deaf (1988) assessed the quality of all educational services provided to students with hearing loss, it concluded that the present status of education for persons who are deaf in the United States was unsatisfactory. The commission recommended promoting English language development and recognizing the unique needs of students who are deaf. It requested that service providers take these needs into account when developing IEPs and urged the Department of Education to reconsider how the fourth principle of IDEA, placement in the least restrictive environment, should apply to deaf and hard-of-hearing students. It also requested that educators focus on the appropriateness of placement, taking into consideration the student's need to be taught by and be able to interact with others who use the same mode of communication (Commission on Education of the Deaf, 1988).

In direct response to the commission's report, the federal government issued new policy guidelines relative to the education of students who are deaf. The guidelines pointed out that "any setting, including a regular classroom, that prevents a child who is deaf from receiving an appropriate education that meets his or her needs, including communication needs, is not the LRE (least restrictive environment) for that child" (U.S. Department of Education, 1992, p. 49275). Educators have understood these guidelines to mean that the least restrictive environment for students who are deaf or hard of hearing may not be the

Great Expectations "Plus"

I wear two hats. I am a former teacher of the deaf and now am a university professor in deaf education. And I have two adopted daughters, Mary Pat and Marcy, who are deaf. Both were honors students in public school; both are honors students at Rochester Institute for Technology in New York, a university for the deaf and hearing-impaired. Both have helped me teach or do volunteer work in Japan, Taiwan, and Mexico, and one, Marcy, has volunteered in Africa and even returned to her place of birth, Bulgaria, and the orphanage she lived in until we adopted her at age four.

Except for the fact that they are adopted and deaf, these two daughters are not unlike other young women: public school and college/university education; athletic-team participation; music lessons; after-school work (albeit at a state school for the deaf); summer camp (yes, at a camp for the deaf); marriage (at age 19, Mary Pat married a young man who is deaf); age-appropriate use of at least two languages (spoken English and sign language); and post-college/aspirations career (Mary Pat as a teacher of the deaf and Marcy as a public policy specialist).

What made the difference for them? Undeniably, it helped that they grew up as daughters of a deaf-education specialist, me, and in a family (husband, wife, and other daughters) who learned how to use sign language and held them to high standards, for we had high expectations for them. Family makes a difference.

Being in separate school, after-school, and camp programs for the deaf and hearing impaired also was helpful. That's where they honed their signing skills, met other students with hearing challenges, and learned that they proudly belonged to a cultural minority in America, those who are deaf or have hearing impairments. Separation is not necessarily restrictive; it is different but beneficial.

But both also participated in the general curriculum with hearing students of their own age; benefited from a collaborating team of general and special educators, signing interpreters, and speech-language specialists; and had academic as well as extracurricular and social engagement with hearing peers. Inclusion had and continues to have huge academic and social benefits, not just for my daughters but for their hearing peers, too.

Both had hearing aids and both later had cochlear implants. Two types of technology—like two types of teaching (separate and included)—opened up the hearing world to them, just as two languages—spoken English and sign language—opened up two cultures (hearing and deaf) to them. My daughters are at home in any environment and any place. They have well-deserved self-confidence.

Sometimes teachers only see children for a year and never know what becomes of them as adults. I am thankful to all the people who helped to raise my children—it took a village. And I want others to know what can be done when great expectations combine with family, professional, and technological support.

—Barbara Luetke
Visiting Professor, Texas Women's College
Author, One Mother's Story *(Modern Sign Press, 1996);*
Contributor, Deaf Students Can Be Great Readers
(Modern Sign Press, 2003); Facebook-enrolled family

general education classroom. Accordingly, teachers balance appropriateness (i.e., the student's opportunity to benefit) against placement (i.e., inclusion) and place the priority on appropriateness when there is a conflict between it and an inclusive placement.

This approach seems defensible. When Congress reauthorized IDEA in 2004, it directed the IEP team for a student who is deaf or hard of hearing to consider the student's language and communication needs, opportunities for direct communications with peers in the student's language and mode of communication, and full range of needs, including opportunities for direct instruction in the student's language and mode of communication.

Box 14.6 provides you with tips for including deaf or hard-of-hearing students in your classrooms.

Box 14.6

INCLUSION TIPS

	What You Might See	What You Might Be Tempted to Do	Alternate Responses	Ways to Include Peers in the Process
Behavior	The student does not participate in cooperative learning activities.	Tell him in front of the rest of the class to participate appropriately.	Be sure he understands the activity and what is expected of him beforehand.	Use a buddy system to foster his greater participation.
Social interactions	Her speech is difficult to understand and the other students do not know how to sign, limiting his ability to interact during small-group discussions.	Randomly assign him to a group; assume the group will work out roles and participation.	Discuss the situation with the deaf educator and the educational interpreter. The deaf educator can work on making sure he is prepared for small-group discussions. The interpreter can encourage the other students to follow the teacher's rules for turn taking.	Arrange instruction for peers to learn more sign language. Use a student to facilitate a more structured approach that allows comments and input from everyone. Practice taking turns with everyone.
Educational performance	He misses some things other students say and appears not to understand.	Tell him to ask his interpreter.	Ensure that the other students face him when they are talking. Make sure the other students raise their hand before speaking so he can visually orient to the speaker. Have the interpreter move to the student who is talking so he can see both the interpreter and the student who is talking. If the vocabulary in the cooperative learning activity is unfamiliar, provide a study guide.	Check the notes taken by the student note taker to be sure they are adequate. Arrange for peer tutoring of unfamiliar vocabulary.
Classroom attitudes	He appears bored or inattentive due to not hearing all that is said or not watching the interpreter.	Discipline him for inattentiveness.	Be sure his hearing aid or cochlear implant is working and that his interpreting needs are being met during cooperative learning activities.	Group him with peers who are helpful and caring but do not "mother" him.

The IEP team should identify strategies to facilitate a student's success in the general education classroom, including appropriate interaction with an educational interpreter.

Educational Placement

Access to communication should drive decisions about educational placement for students with hearing loss, but access and placement for many students can be in the general curriculum. As Figure 14.8 shows, more and more students with hearing loss are educated in general education classrooms. They may be receiving special services, including classroom amplification, audiological evaluation, speech-language therapy, resource support from a trained deaf educator, instructional accommodations, and an educational **interpreter,** now an IDEA related service. Interpreting services include, but are not limited to, oral transliteration services, cued language services, and sign language interpreting.

Another placement option is a special classroom in the public school with other students who are deaf or hard of hearing. The teacher is usually a trained deaf educator, and the students may be included with their hearing peers for some academic subjects or for art, music, physical education, or other non-academic programs.

Yet another placement option is a segregated setting. Before the 1980s, most students with hearing loss (particularly those who were deaf) were educated in large residential schools for the deaf or in separate public or private day schools. They often entered those schools at age 5, learned to communicate from their peers and deaf adults who worked at the schools, made lifetime friendships, met their spouse, and settled in the area to live and work. In fact, this educational setting was the basis for the development and perpetuation of the Deaf community and Deaf culture.

IDEA has changed the nature and prevalence of these residential and day programs. Given the wider range of placement options in public schools, enrollment in residential schools has declined and many have closed, although members of the Deaf community and some professionals in the field of deafness continue to advocate for the right to choose this placement option (Moores, 2001). Figure 14.8 reveals the current placements.

Mariah and Ricquel are being educated using a unique educational model for students with hearing loss, an approach that is used in only a few school systems. Their school employs a team-teaching model that pairs a deaf educator with a regular educator. The girls are taught in voice and sign language simultaneously, using an educational interpreter and an assistant teacher who also signs. The teachers work collaboratively, allowing for small-group instruction within the larger classroom setting. As they work with small groups for

Figure 14.8 Educational placement of students with hearing impairment (Fall, 2006)

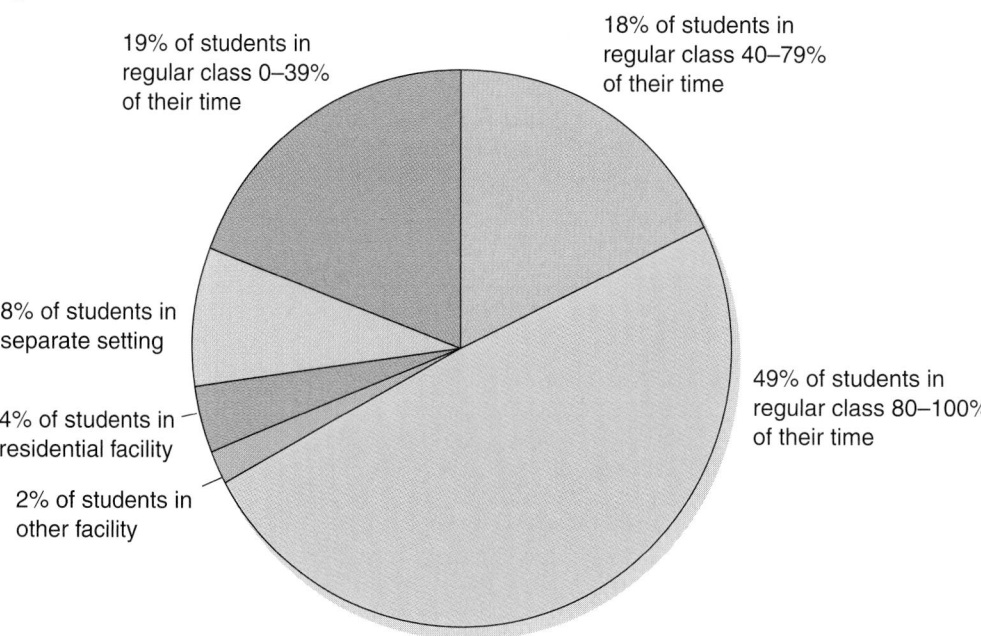

19% of students in regular class 0–39% of their time

18% of students in regular class 40–79% of their time

8% of students in separate setting

4% of students in residential facility

2% of students in other facility

49% of students in regular class 80–100% of their time

Source: U.S. Department of Education (2007).

subjects like guided reading and vocabulary, both the students with hearing loss and any other students in the class who might also need special support benefit. In this classroom, all of the children (both deaf and hearing) are exposed to sign language throughout the day, and the other students are learning to sign along with their deaf peers. This provides a great support for socialization for the girls because all of the students are learning to communicate directly with each other. Mariah and Ricquel are benefiting from inclusion, as are other students who are deaf and hard of hearing.

ASSESSING STUDENTS' PROGRESS

Measuring Students' Progress

Among some of the issues affecting deaf education under NCLB, IDEA, and state-mandated assessments of student progress are the goals of the state assessment system and challenges for including deaf students within that system. Educators of students with hearing loss typically test their hearing, communication, and school achievement. The assessment of communication depends on the particular mode used by the child. Students who are oral will be assessed for speech and hearing skills; students who are manual will be assessed on sign language skills. The problems educators face in assessing student progress include identifying and using necessary accommodations to make the tests more accessible for students with reading delays and impaired speech and/or language.

The general education classroom, with supports, offers many opportunities for academic and social success for students who are deaf or hard of hearing.

The assessment of academic achievement (or lack thereof) often focuses specifically on the child's reading and writing skills. There are two classic ways to assess reading: questions on comprehension following the reading of a short passage and use of the cloze procedure (Stewart & Kluwin, 2001).

A **cloze procedure** involves the modification of a text of at least 250 words by eliminating every fifth word and replacing it with a blank. The student then supplies the missing word without prompting. Cloze procedures emphasize prediction of content rather than comprehension and offer the teacher a quick and simple assessment of the match between reading materials and a student's abilities.

Teachers can assess a student's writing skills in three ways: surrogate skills, editing skills/grammar correction, and holistic or impressionistic scoring (Stewart & Kluwin, 2001; Albertini & Schley, 2003). Surrogate skills measure the components of writing with spelling or vocabulary tests. If a student can do well on tests of spelling or vocabulary, then he will probably be a good writer. Editing skill involves assessing the student's ability to correct his own grammar. For example, he might be asked to select the right grammatical form from among several options.

Researchers at the National Technical Institute for the Deaf and Gallaudet University developed the holistic or impressionistic measure of writing skills. This procedure provides the student with a writing prompt, such as a scenario or issue to be addressed, a likely audience for the writing, and some parameters for the writer to consider in his paper. For example, a student might be asked to write a letter to a child in a foreign country, asking to be a pen pal. Scoring protocols are rubrics for scoring the written document.

Making Accommodations for Assessment

Elliot, Kratochwill, and Schulte (1998) identified eight possible accommodations to state formats for students with disabilities. Using these categories, Stewart and Kluwin (2001) adapted the list and made the accommodations specific for deaf students. Their suggestions include providing assistance before testing to teach any new forms of test taking, providing

IEP Tip

As required by IDEA, the IEP team should consider what testing accommodations may be necessary so the student can participate in statewide testing.

a longer time period for the assessment, interpreting the directions, and even changing the format and content (rephrasing an item) if this can be done without altering the intent of the question. Accommodations allow for the greatest level of success for the students—the accurate measure of knowledge and performance on a level playing field (Cawthon, 2008).

VALUES AND OUTCOMES

VALUES	GREAT EXPECTATIONS	CHOICES	
	POSITIVE CONTRIBUTIONS		STRENGTHS
	RELATIONSHIPS		FULL CITIZENSHIP

The Thomas family has three daughters with profound hearing loss. They have made some strong and even controversial decisions, both medical and educational in nature.

♦ They expect their daughters to have a highly effective education; that's why they enrolled them in a school district other than their own.

♦ They and the girls' teachers recognize that the girls contribute to other students' education; when the girls learn sign language, so too do the students who don't have disabilities.

♦ They and the girls' teachers individualize each girl's education; one daughter is less able to sign than the others, but she has her own strengths.

♦ They have made their choice to use implants, no matter how controversial that decision may be in the Deaf community.

♦ They have made it possible for each daughter to have good relationships with other students by having all of them attend schools where there are other students with hearing impairments.

♦ They fully anticipate that their daughters will be full citizens; working, living on their own, and making their own choices in life will continue to depend on the technology and language the girls acquire. Equal opportunities may be technology-dependent, but that fact does not diminish at all the girls' citizenship—indeed, it advances it.

WHAT DO YOU THINK?

1. What are the implications of busing the Thomas daughters to a school so far from home? Is this contrary to the IDEA mandate? Why do you think Sharon and Sheddrick chose this placement for their daughters?

2. The choice of communication modality (oral or manual, type of sign language) is often fraught with strong opinions. Why do Sharon and Sheddrick allow their daughters to use a variety of modes? Do you agree?

3. Why did Sharon and Sheddrick decide to have each of the girls receive a cochlear implant? If you had the choice for your child, what would you decide?

4. Families of children with disabilities often feel very close to the professionals who serve them and their children. What do you believe is the basis of this trust and dependence? What should you do as a professional to make certain that families feel this way about you and your services?

5. What should you do to identify the learning styles and strengths of a child with hearing loss, and then take these characteristics into consideration in your instruction and interactions with the child?

ADDRESSING THE STANDARDS: THE VALUES CONNECTION

The following CEC Knowledge and Skill Standards: Common Core and Values are addressed in this chapter through the content and concepts we discuss.

CEC Knowledge and Skill Standards: Common Core		Values/Standards Connection
CEC Knowledge and Skill Standard II. **Development and Characteristics of Learners**		Understanding the hearing process conforms to CEC Standard 2, Development and Characteristics of Learners.
CC2K1	Typical and atypical human growth and development.	
CC2K2	Educational implications of characteristics of various exceptionalities.	
CC2K3	Characteristics and effects of the cultural and environmental milieu of the individual with exceptional learning needs and the family.	
CC2K4	Family systems and the roles of families supporting development.	
CC2K5	Similarities and differences of individuals with and without exceptional learning needs.	
CC2K6	Similarities and differences of individuals with exceptional learning needs.	
CEC Knowledge and Skill Standard IV. **Instructional Strategies**		Learning about appropriate methods and strategies to use with students with hearing loss is an application of CEC Standard 4, Instructional Strategies.
CC4S1	Use strategies to facilitate integration into various settings.	The debate about methods for teaching students who are deaf or hard of hearing should not obscure this simple fact: any effective means builds on the students' *strengths* and therefore is appropriate for the student.
CC4S3	Select, adapt, and use instructional strategies and materials according to characteristics of the individual with exceptional learning needs.	
CEC Knowledge and Skill Standard V. **Learning Environments and Social Interactions**		*Relationships* and attitudes interact with each other. So when teachers include students who are deaf or hard of hearing in the general curriculum, they create opportunities for hearing students to learn how their hearing-challenged peers contribute to everyone's education and how peer *relationships* can blunt discriminatory attitudes.
CC5S2	Identify realistic expectations for personal and social behavior in various settings.	
CC5S3	Identify supports needed for integration into various program placements.	Deaf and hard-of-hearing students can be *full citizens* in two different worlds—the one that their hearing peers occupy and the one that their non-hearing peers occupy.
CC5S4	Design learning environments that encourage active participation in individual and group settings.	
CC5S6	Use performance data and information from all stakeholders to make or suggest modifications in learning environments.	
CC5S8	Teach self-advocacy.	
CC5S9	Create an environment that encourages self-advocacy and increased independence.	

continued

CEC Knowledge and Skill Standards: Common Core	Values/Standards Connection
CEC Knowledge and Skill Standard VI. Language CC6K4 — Augmentative and assistive communication strategies. CC6S1 — Use strategies to support and enhance communication skills of individuals with exceptional learning needs.	Supporting and enhancing communication skills of individuals with hearing loss is an implementation of CEC Standard 6, Language. Communication—in all of its many forms for students who are deaf or hard of hearing—is the instrument by which students express their *self-determination*.
CEC Knowledge and Skill Standard VII. Instructional Planning CC7S1 — Identify and prioritize areas of the general curriculum and accommodations for individuals with exceptional learning needs. CC7S2 — Develop and implement comprehensive, longitudinal individualized programs in collaboration with team members. CC7S3 — Involve the individual and family in setting instructional goals and monitoring progress. CC7S6 — Sequence, implement, and evaluate individualized learning objectives. CC7S7 — Integrate affective, social, and life skills with academic curricula. CC7S9 — Incorporate and implement instructional and assistive technology into the educational program.	Standard 7 encourages teachers to develop their students' *self-determination*, including the *choice* of placements into the Deaf community.
CEC Knowledge and Skill Standard VIII. Assessment CC8K2 — Legal provisions and ethical principles regarding assessment of individuals. CC8K3 — Screening, prereferral, referral, and classification procedures. CC8K4 — Use and limitations of assessment instruments. CC8K5 — National, state or provincial, and local accommodations and modifications. CC8S2 — Administer nonbiased formal and informal assessments. CC8S6 — Use assessment information in making eligibility, program, and placement decisions for individuals with exceptional learning needs, including those from culturally and/or linguistically diverse backgrounds. CC8S7 — Report assessment results to all stakeholders using effective communication skills.	IDEA and NCLB provide that students with disabilities, including those who are deaf or hard of hearing, will participate in state and district assessments. These laws express the sense of *great expectations*, and the Stanford 9, as modified at Gallaudet Research Institute, accommodates deafness to that expectation and the law's commands.

CEC Knowledge and Skill Standards: Common Core		Values/Standards Connection
CEC Knowledge and Skill Standard X. Collaboration		Standard 9 suggests that the students themselves should collaborate in planning their education thereby building their *strengths* for self-determination and *choice*.
CC10S2	Collaborate with families and others in assessment of individuals with exceptional learning needs.	
CC10S3	Foster respectful and beneficial relationships between families and professionals.	
CC10S4	Assist individuals with exceptional learning needs and their families in becoming active participants in the educational team.	
CC10S5	Plan and conduct collaborative conferences with individuals with exceptional learning needs and their families.	
CC10S6	Collaborate with school personnel and community members in integrating individuals with exceptional learning needs into various settings.	
CC10S9	Communicate with school personnel about the characteristics and needs of individuals with exceptional learning needs.	

Source: From CEC Knowledge and Skill Standards: Common Core and Values. Copyright by The Council for Exceptional Children. Reprinted with permission.

SUMMARY

Identifying Students with Hearing Loss

◆ Children are typically classified as deaf or hard of hearing. Degree of hearing loss is categorized as mild, moderate, moderate-severe, severe, or profound.

◆ Conductive loss is caused by a problem in the outer and middle ear; sensorineural loss is caused by a problem in the inner ear or along the nerve pathway to the brain.

◆ Achievement levels, specifically in the areas of reading and writing, are primary concerns for students with hearing loss. They can be particularly problematic among children from diverse racial, ethnic, and linguistic backgrounds.

◆ Hearing loss in children is considered a low-incidence disability and is estimated at about 1.3 percent of the school-age population.

Evaluating Students with Hearing Loss

◆ An audiologist diagnoses hearing loss using an auditory brain stem response or otoacoustic immittance test with infants and young children and behavioral audiological evaluation with older children.

◆ Hearing aids make sound louder but do not restore normal hearing; there is always some distortion of sound.

◆ Cochlear implants provide sound information by directly stimulating the functioning auditory nerve fibers in the cochlea. Cochlear implants do not make sound louder.

◆ Assessment of language, speech, speech reading, signing, academic achievement, and socialization are essential for providing an appropriate education for students who are deaf or hard of hearing.

Designing an Appropriate IEP

◆ The increase in cochlear implants has resulted in increased input from the medical implant team.

◆ The educational interpreter is often the student's bridge to the hearing world around him.

◆ The various communication modes used by individuals with hearing loss include oral/aural, manual, and total communication.

◆ A bilingual/bicultural educational model combines the use of American Sign Language as the student's first language, English as his or her second language, and Deaf studies to teach the culture of deafness.

Using Effective Instructional Strategies

◆ Intervention for young children with hearing loss includes access to a language-rich environment.

◆ Shared reading emphasizes the importance of reading to young children as they connect the English sentences in the book to the way the sentences are signed in ASL.

◆ Real-world, or authentic, experiences are particularly important for students with hearing loss if they are to make a connection between what they know and what they read.

◆ Learning about deafness, the Deaf community, Deaf history, and famous deaf adults can be incorporated into social studies, health, and science curricula for all students.

Including Students with Hearing Loss

◆ Access to communication is critical when deciding on placement for students with hearing loss.

◆ IDEA now includes interpreting services as related services; oral transliteration, cued speech, and sign language interpreting are part of interpreting.

Assessing Students' Progress

◆ There may be problems in the assessment of a student with hearing loss if the student uses English as a second language (ASL being the first language), has unintelligible speech, or has difficulty with reading.

◆ Story retelling allows students to show that they understand what they have read, even though they may not have been able to sound out each individual word.

Now go to MyEducationLab at www.myeducationlab.com and take the Self-Assessment to gauge your initial comprehension of chapter content. Once you have taken the Self-Assessment, use your individualized Study Plan for Chapter 14 to enhance your understanding of the concepts discussed in the chapter.

15

Understanding Students with Visual Impairments

by Sandra Lewis, Florida State University

◆ WHO IS HALEY SUMNER?

As Mrs. Benson's second-grade class walks down the hallway of Robey Elementary School in Indianapolis, Indiana, one can't help but notice the petite, brown-haired girl with a big grin on her face who is leading the girls' line. She walks with a bounce in her step, moving her white cane in rhythm with her strides.

Haley Sumner's class is headed to the gymnasium for P.E. This week the class is working on bounce-passing balls and catching the ball after one bounce. Haley is prepared; she has practiced this activity for a few weeks with some of her friends during recess. Many of her friends have had to learn how to pass the ball correctly to Haley so that she can catch it more easily. She stands with her arms out in front of her, prepared to move her hands and arms quickly to embrace the ball after she hears it bounce.

Haley also enjoys attending music class, where the students are practicing for the upcoming second-grade concert. Art is another favorite subject. She proudly displays an art project she made in first grade that won an honorable mention in a national art competition. Pumping the swings is her chosen activity during recess, but when it is too cold to be outside, she plays Connect Four or Uno inside with her peers.

Every evening, Haley practices her spelling words, works on addition and subtraction facts, and reads to her grandparents from her reading book. On Thursdays, Haley attends Brownies with several of her classmates.

Haley seems to be a typical second grader, but she does have to do some things differently than her peers because she is visually impaired. Haley was born with

some ability to perceive light but is considered blind. At age 3, Haley and her family began to work in their home and a preschool classroom with Katie Culbertson, a teacher of students with visual impairments (TVI). Haley showed spunk and determination even then, telling adults, "I do it myself!" Since then, she has learned many new techniques and developed key blindness skills so that she can, indeed, do it herself.

Haley continues to work with Katie during and sometimes after school, in her general education classroom and a resource room, at home, and in the community. Haley and Katie focus on a wide variety of skills that are enabling Haley to be much more independent. Over summer break, they particularly emphasize independent living skills and other community-based activities.

Haley is reading fluently in braille at a third-grade level. She has learned how to write in braille using a Perkins braille writer and an electronic braille writer called the Mountbatten. She has also started to master the computer keyboard and loves typing letters to family members that can be read in print. Haley is anxiously awaiting the arrival of a new notetaker, a mini-braille computer device she will be able to use to complete assignments in braille and then print out one copy for herself in braille and another for her teacher in print.

In addition to using braille for reading, Haley has learned to read the Nemeth code, a special braille code for math and science. She uses this code daily in math. She is also continuing to develop skills in reading tactile graphs, tables, and charts for math and tactile maps and diagrams for science and social studies. Haley is also becoming quite proficient in using an abacus for solving addition and subtraction problems, although she and her classmates prefer to hear the talking calculator read the answer after she has entered a problem.

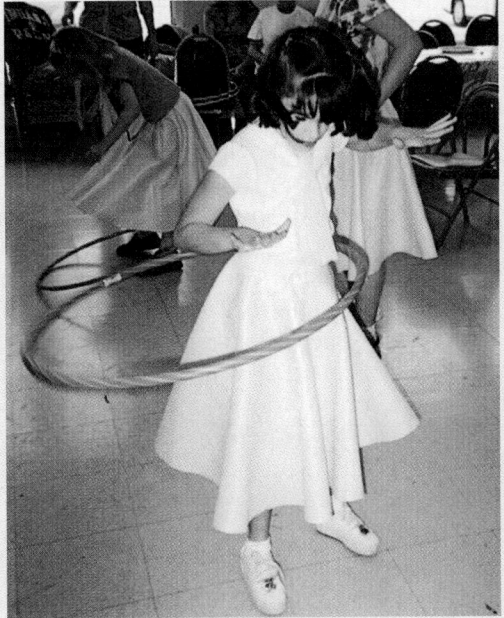

Katie is also a certified orientation and mobility specialist (COMS). Haley has received orientation and mobility (O&M) services at home and school since she was in preschool. She now displays confidence when traveling throughout school independently. She is even quite willing to give a tour to anyone unfamiliar with the building. "How did you know how to find the computer lab?" someone asked her one day. "I've known that since I was 4!" Haley answered. "I learned that from Miss Katie on a mobility lesson." Now that she is 7, Haley's O&M lessons have extended far beyond the walls of her school building. She has learned how to

CHAPTER OBJECTIVES

◆ You will learn about the two definitions of visual impairments, the three degrees of visual limitations, and the three types of limitations that students with visual impairments experience.

◆ You will learn the two causes of visual impairments (congenital and adventitious), how to evaluate a student's use of vision, who determines it, and how to use that knowledge to determine the appropriate reading medium for the student.

◆ You will learn about specially designed instruction, including the expanded core curriculum approach and orientation and mobility training, and you will learn how to design an appropriate IEP to address the student's reading instruction (including via Braille) and non-academic priorities.

◆ You will learn about supplementary aids and services, such as adapted materials, assistive technology, and universal design for learning, and how these make it possible for a student to be included in the general curriculum.

◆ You will learn that teaching and planning for daily living skills, training in orientation and mobility, developing a student's self-determination, and partnering with other professionals and the student are essential elements of a student's education.

◆ You will learn how to make accommodations as you assess a student's progress in school.

detect driveways and curbs with her cane, how to travel safely and independently around an unfamiliar block, and how to get clues from traffic noises around her. She has made numerous trips in the community to work on her cane technique and learn how to navigate using a sighted guide in busy stores and restaurants.

One of Haley's biggest struggles in the public school and community has been convincing others that she can do things on her own. "I don't like it when everyone asks me if they can do things for me all the time," Haley told her TVI one day. "But I try to be polite, and I just tell them, 'No, thank you; I can do it myself.'" But after working with her grandparents, her TVI, and her COMS in the community, Haley has begun to recognize that there are times when she might need someone's help, just as there are times when she can offer her assistance to others.

PEARSON
myeducationlab

After reading this chapter, complete the Self-Assessment for Chapter 15 on MyEducationLab to gauge your initial understanding of chapter content.

IDENTIFYING STUDENTS WITH VISUAL IMPAIRMENTS

Defining Visual Impairments

When you think about visual impairments and blindness, you might imagine someone such as Haley, who sees nothing at all and must use adaptive techniques for tasks that typically require vision, such as braille for reading or a cane to detect objects when traveling. It may surprise you to learn that most individuals with **legal blindness** have a great deal of useful vision and that most students who have visual impairments are print readers.

Two different definitions describe visual impairment. The legal definition of blindness is based on a clinical measurement of visual acuity. **Acuity** is determined by having an individual read the letters on a chart, each line of which is composed of letters written with a certain size of print. The ability to read the 20 line from a distance of 20 feet is typical, and a person who can read at that line is said to have 20/20 acuity. Individuals who from 20 feet can read only the top line, where the print size is 200 (the big E), when using both eyes and wearing their glasses, have 20/200 acuity; these people are legally blind. People are also legally blind if their **field of vision** (the area around them that they can visually detect when looking straight ahead) is less than 20 degrees (normal is 160 degrees), even if their visual acuity is normal. These individuals have **tunnel vision.** Figure 15.1 shows what people with various types of visual impairment might see.

The legal definition of blindness is established in federal law (Social Security Act, 2007). It is an arbitrary clinical measure that is used to determine eligibility for special government allowances; it does not provide reliable information about the way in which a person experiences and learns about the world (Flom, 2004).

How a person experiences and learns about the world is, however, at the core of the IDEA definition of visual impairments. The current regulations implementing IDEA define **visual disability (including blindness)** as "an impairment in vision that, even with correction, adversely affects a child's educational performance. The term includes both partial sight and blindness". Key to this definition is that the student has some kind of disorder of the visual system that interferes with learning. In fall 2006, approximately 0.04 percent (25,661) of all students ages 6 through 21 in special education nationally were classified as having visual impairments (U.S. Department of Education, 2008).

Because state and local educational agencies vary so widely in how they measure and report visual impairments, it is extremely difficult to count accurately the number of students with visual impairments who are served in schools (Kirchner & Diament, 1999). The best estimates indicate that approximately one to two students in 1,000 have a visual

Figure 15.1 Estimate of how a view appears for (a) individuals with 20/20 vision, (b) reduced visual acuity, and (c) and (d) restricted fields of vision.

(a)

(b)

(c)

(d)

disorder that interferes with learning; those children are eligible to receive special education services (Nelson & Dimitrova, 1993).

Students with visual impairments represent a wide range of visual abilities. Educators classify these students by their tendency or need to use visual or tactile means for learning (Lewis & Allman, 2000):

- **Low vision** describes individuals who read print, although they may depend on optical aids, such as magnifying lenses, to see better. A few read both braille and print; all rely primarily on vision for learning. Individuals with low vision may or may not be legally blind.

- **Functionally blind** describes individuals who typically use braille for efficient reading and writing. They may rely on their ability to use functional vision for other tasks, such as moving through the environment or sorting items by color. Thus, they use their limited vision to supplement a combination of tactile and auditory learning methods.

- **Totally blind** describes those individuals who do not receive meaningful input through the visual sense. These individuals use tactile and auditory means to learn about their environment, and they generally read Braille.

Every individual with visual impairment uses vision differently and in a way that is difficult to predict. When you teach these students, it is important to observe carefully how a student functions and then present instructional activities to maximize that student's learning.

Young children develop a "scheme" about tables through their experience with them. This incidental learning differs for a child who has always been visually impaired.

Describing the Characteristics

The population of students with visual impairments is surprisingly heterogeneous. The students differ from each other in how they learn and in their visual functioning, socioeconomic status, cultural background, age of onset of visual impairment, presence of other disabilities, and cognitive abilities. Some are gifted or have special talents. A large number also have multiple disabilities (Huebner, 2000; Pogrund, 2002; Silberman, 2000). Yet each possesses a characteristic in common: the limited ability to learn incidentally from the environment (Hatlen & Curry, 1987).

Almost from the moment they are born, children with good vision learn seemingly effortlessly through their visual sense. Their vision helps them organize, synthesize, and give meaning to their perceptions of the environment (Ferrell, 2000; Liefert, 2003; Lowenfeld, 1973). For example, a sighted baby spends hours looking at her hand before that hand becomes an efficient tool. A young child will drop a toy repeatedly, watching its path to the floor until she learns to understand "down." Through these recurring observations, the child is learning how to move her hands, the effects of her hands' movement (on herself, the toy, and her caretakers), and, as similar and diverse experiences occur with various objects, about the properties of nature (sound, gravity, weight, etc.). This learning occurs almost exclusively through the power of observation without direct instruction from others.

Think about the way in which a young child learns the concept of *table*. Even before she has a name for that object, she has observed a variety of tables in her environment: in the kitchen, in the living room, at the homes of relatives and friends, and at preschool. Tables are everywhere, and the sighted child begins to recognize that the things people call tables have certain features in common. Soon she perceives a relationship between the object and the word. Later, after more visual experiences, she will distinguish among desks, tables, counters, and other flat surfaces. Children learn this kind of conceptual information incidentally with little or no direct instruction.

Incidental learning is problematic for all visually impaired children (Ferrell, 2006; Hatlen & Curry, 1987; Liefert, 2003). The child with limited visual access to her environment may find it necessary for her family and teachers to provide her with opportunities to explore carefully and completely, either visually at a close distance or through tactile means, every part of a variety of tables before she can acquire, organize, and then synthesize information about "tableness."

Incidental learning also affects how children come to perform skills. For example, most children need little training when they make toast for the first time. They have few problems with any of the steps involved in this rather complex task because they have watched adults make toast hundreds of times. Without hands-on instruction, children with visual impairments may not even be aware that a special machine is used in this task. Even youngsters with low vision, who may not see clearly beyond a distance of 2 or 3 feet, usually need special instruction and practice time to perform this and other tasks.

Because of the important role played by incidental learning for most individuals, the presence of a visual impairment has the potential to influence motor, language, cognitive, and social skills development. Generally, however, these influences are not long-lasting if the student receives appropriate interventions (Ferrell, 2000). Visual impairment primarily affects how students learn skills but does not prevent the acquisition of skills when appropriate interventions are implemented. Interventions must be designed to reduce the limitations imposed on an individual by a significant visual impairment, including limitations in the range and variety of experiences, limitations in the ability to get around, and limitations in interactions with the environment.

Limitations in the Range and Variety of Experiences

Vision allows a person to experience the world meaningfully and safely from a distance. Touch is an ineffective substitute for vision: some objects are too big (skyscrapers, mountains), too small (ants, molecules), too fragile (snowflakes, moths), too dangerous (fire, boiling water), or too distant (the sun, the horizon) for their characteristics to be learned tactilely (Lowenfeld, 1973). The other senses do not fully compensate for what can be learned visually: the song of a bird or the smell of baking bread may provide evidence that those objects are nearby but do not provide useful information about many of their properties. Individuals with visual impairment often have not shared the experiences of their peers with typical vision, so their knowledge of the world may be different.

Students with visual impairments also experience different social interactions because they cannot share common experiences with sighted friends. The student who has not seen the latest movie, played the newest video game, or taken driver's training may be at a disadvantage within the school culture. The potential for inadequate development of social skills and the related negative impact on self-esteem are serious concerns that may have a lifelong impact (Lewis & Wolffe, 2006; Sacks, 2006; Wolffe, 2006).

Similarly, career development can be limited. While individuals with visual impairments are employed in a variety of occupations, many young adults struggle with determining an appropriate vocation because they are unaware of the jobs that people (with or without vision) perform (Wolffe, 2000).

Limitations in the Ability to Get Around

Individuals who are visually impaired are limited in their spontaneous ability to move safely in and through their environment. This restriction influences a child's early motor development and exploration of the world; in turn, the same restriction affects the child's knowledge base and social development. The ability to move through the environment spontaneously is one area over which probably only moderate control can be exercised and is a continuing source of frustration for many adults (Corn & Sacks, 1994) because it directly affects opportunities for experiences (Barraga & Erin, 2001). A child with impaired vision may not know what is interesting in the environment. Even if that child is aware of something to explore, he or she may not know how to get to the desired object. These children can become passive and in turn have fewer opportunities for intellectual and social stimulation (Anthony, Bleier, Fazzi, Kish, & Pogrund, 2002; Pogrund, 2002).

Limitations in Interactions with the Environment

Knowledge about and control over the environment often are areas of concern for individuals with visual impairments. In some cases, their limited vision reduces their level of readily acquired information about their environment and their ability to act on that information. For instance, they cannot determine at a glance the source of a loud crash or a burning smell, so

Young children with impaired vision need opportunities to explore a variety of environments to develop a healthy sense of competency.

they cannot quickly determine an appropriate reaction. Similarly, they cannot adequately inform themselves about the effects of their actions on the people and things around them.

In young children, reduced vision correlates with poor motivation to move through the environment, manipulate toys, and initiate interactions (Ferrell, 2000). Their tendency toward physical and social detachment (Wolffe, Sacks, & Thomas, 2000) and low motivation can have the long-lasting consequence of limiting their sense of competence and mastery. Individuals who have a poor sense of their ability to effect change in their lives are at risk for poor self-esteem, poor academic achievement, and reduced language and social skills (Harrell, 1992).

Determining the Causes

As you can tell from Figure 15.2, seeing involves both the eye and brain. Damage to or malfunction of any part of the visual system can impair how a student functions.

Figure 15.2 Anatomy of the eye

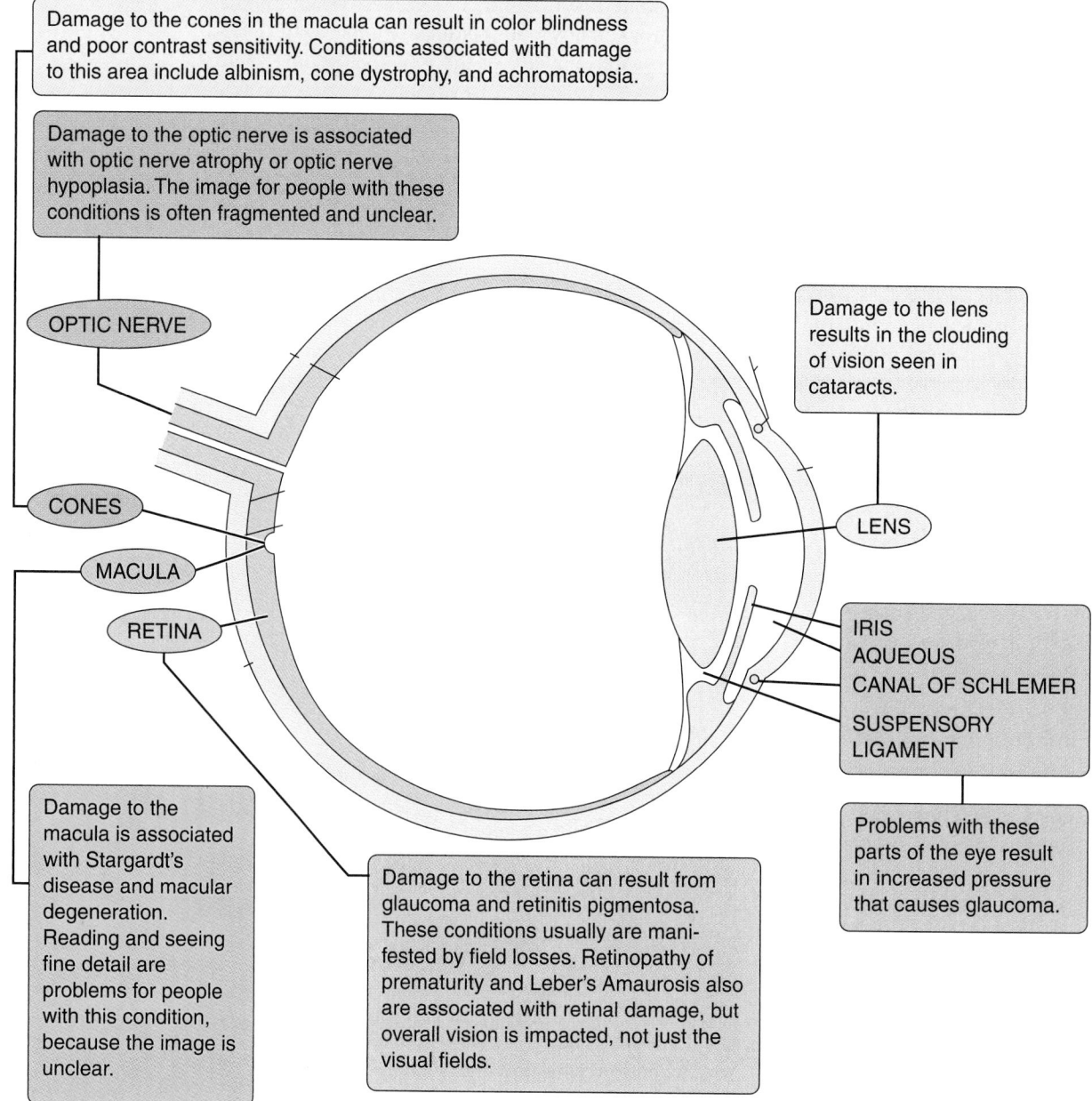

Damage to the cones in the macula can result in color blindness and poor contrast sensitivity. Conditions associated with damage to this area include albinism, cone dystrophy, and achromatopsia.

Damage to the optic nerve is associated with optic nerve atrophy or optic nerve hypoplasia. The image for people with these conditions is often fragmented and unclear.

Damage to the lens results in the clouding of vision seen in cataracts.

OPTIC NERVE

CONES

MACULA

RETINA

LENS

IRIS
AQUEOUS
CANAL OF SCHLEMER
SUSPENSORY
LIGAMENT

Damage to the macula is associated with Stargardt's disease and macular degeneration. Reading and seeing fine detail are problems for people with this condition, because the image is unclear.

Damage to the retina can result from glaucoma and retinitis pigmentosa. These conditions usually are manifested by field losses. Retinopathy of prematurity and Leber's Amaurosis also are associated with retinal damage, but overall vision is impacted, not just the visual fields.

Problems with these parts of the eye result in increased pressure that causes glaucoma.

Damage to the structures involved in the visual process can be the result of an event that happens during the development of the embryo, at or immediately after an infant's birth, or at any time during development. **Congenital** visual impairment occurs at birth or, in the case of blindness, before visual memories have been established. Haley has a congenital visual impairment. That type of impairment can affect any child's earliest access to information and experiences. Students who acquire a vision loss after having normal vision have an **adventitious** visual impairment. That is, their impairment results from an advent (e.g., loss of sight caused by a hereditary condition that has just manifested itself) or an event (e.g., loss of sight caused by trauma). Although the educational needs of students with adventitious and congenital visual impairments may be similar, even a short period of good vision can enrich the student's understanding of self, others, and the relationships among people, objects, and events in the environment (Scott, Jan, & Freeman, 1995).

EVALUATING STUDENTS WITH VISUAL IMPAIRMENTS

Determining the Presence of Visual Impairments

Like students with other disabilities, a student with visual impairment receives a nondiscriminatory evaluation (see Figure 15.3). Evaluations of students with visual impairments have several highly specialized aspects, however.

Medical specialists usually determine the presence of a disorder of a child's visual system. Physicians often detect a serious visual disorder when a child is very young or has just experienced a trauma. Their diagnosis generally is followed by a search for medical solutions to correct vision. When no such correction is possible, referrals to the schools occur.

It is important for educators to know the cause of a student's visual impairment. Although a diagnosis of the cause, or **etiology,** may not provide accurate information about how much a student sees, this information is invaluable as educators plan the student's program. An accurate diagnosis suggests typical characteristics associated with a particular eye condition, including probable lighting needs, a potential prognosis, and possible related medical disorders or learning problems.

When a school district receives a referral for services, the teacher of students with visual impairments first evaluates the referred student to determine how she uses any vision that is available and then whether the student learns best using the visual or tactile sense.

Determining How a Student Uses Vision

Even given an accurate diagnosis and standard visual acuity measurements, it is impossible to predict exactly how a student with impaired vision uses it to learn incidentally from the environment and to perform age-appropriate tasks. Teachers of students with visual impairments (TVIs) work with a student and her family to determine the effects of the disorder on the student's visual functioning when they conduct a **functional vision assessment (FVA)** (Anthony, 2000; Lueck, 2004). While the results of an examination by an eye specialist are reported in clinical terms (such as 20/120), the results of an FVA are reported in language that informs educators and others in more concrete ways. For example, an FVA report might read, "The student can see 3-inch-high printed letters at a distance of no more than 5 feet," or "The student can pick up a raisin on a white table when seen from 6 inches." Figure 15.4 shows part of an FVA designed for preschoolers.

Functional vision assessments describe how a student uses vision in a variety of natural environments, such as under the fluorescent lights in a grocery store, on the playground in the glare of the midday sun, or in a dimly lit corridor leading to the school library. Appropriate functional vision assessments also consider the different activities that occur in these environments. For example, a student at a grocery store may be able to see the products on the shelves but not able to read the aisle labels that hang directly below the bright lights or the value of paper money at the checkout counter. Obviously, this kind of information is extremely valuable to educators who work with the student because it helps them design relevant instructional strategies (Anthony, 2000).

Figure 15.3

Nondiscriminatory evaluation process for determining the presence of visual impairments

Observation	**Parents observe:** The child may not have any eye turn or may not respond to visual stimuli as expected. **Physicians observe:** The newborn or infant may have an identifiable visual disorder. **Teacher observes:** The student squints or seems to be bothered by light, the student's eyes water or are red, the student holds books too close, or the student bumps into objects.
Screening	**Assessment measures:** **Ophthalmological:** Medical procedures indicate the presence of a visual disorder or reduced visual functioning that cannot be improved to typical levels through surgery or medical intervention. **Functional vision evaluation:** A visual disorder interferes with the student's ability to incidentally learn from the environment and the student's use of vision for performance of tasks. **Low vision specialist:** A specialist evaluation indicates that visual functioning cannot be improved to typical levels through the use of lenses. **Vision screening in schools:** For students with low vision who have not been identified before entering school, screening indicates the need for further evaluation.
Prereferral	Prereferral typically is not used with these students because the severity of the disability indicates a need for special education or related services.
Referral	Students with visual impairments should be referred by medical personnel or parents for early intervention during the infancy/preschool years. Many states have child-find organizations to make sure these students receive services. Teachers should refer any students with possible vision impairments for immediate evaluation.
Nondiscriminatory evaluation procedures and standards	**Assessment measures:** **Individualized intelligence test:** Standardization may need to be violated because the student's visual impairment interferes with the ability to perform some tasks. Therefore, results may not be an accurate reflection of ability. Students may be average, above average or below average in intelligence. **Individualized achievement tests:** The student may not achieve in concept development and academic areas at levels of peers. Also, standardization of these tests, unless developed for students with visual impairments, may have to be violated because of the visual impairment. Results may not accurately reflect achievement. **Adaptive behavior scales:** The student may have difficulty in self-care, household, and community skills because of vision and mobility problems. **Orientation and mobility evaluation:** The student's ability to orient to the environment and to travel to desired locations may be limited. **Anecdotal records:** The student may not participate in age-appropriate self-help, social, and recreational activities in home, community, or school. **Curriculum-based assessment:** The student may not possess age-appropriate knowledge or skills in areas of communication, daily living, career awareness, sensory and fine motor abilities, social skills, and self-advocacy. **Direct observation–learning media assessment:** The student is unable to respond or has difficulty responding to print media without the use of magnification or alternative strategies, or the student cannot sustain reading in these texts for long periods of time.
Determination	The nondiscriminatory evaluation team determines that the student has a vision impairment or blindness and needs special education and related services.

Figure 15.4 ▷ Example of a functional vision assessment at the pre-kindergarten level

Distant Vision

- Mimics teacher's facial expressions at _____ feet.
- Locates the drinking fountain at _____ feet.
- Recognizes own name, shapes, numbers at _____ feet.
- Identifies classmates at _____ feet.
- Locates personal possessions (lunchbox, jacket, backpack) in closet at _____ feet.
- Locates own cubby at _____ feet.
- Locates _____ of four dropped coins on a _____ (color) floor: quarter at _____ feet; nickel at _____ feet; dime at _____ feet; penny at _____ feet.
- Tracks and locates a _____ (size) moving ball at _____ feet.
- Avoids obstacles when moving round P.E. apparatus. Yes _____ No _____
- Visually detects and smoothly navigates contour changes in surfaces such as ramps and steps. Yes _____ No _____

Near Vision

- Completes _____ (number of pieces) puzzle with head _____ inches from the board (describe how student performs task: e.g., trial and error, quickly, visually, tactually, etc.).
- Places pegs in pegboard at _____ inches from head _____ inches from pegs (describe now student performs task).

_____

Source: From *Functional Visual Evaluation,* by the Los Angeles Unified School District, 1990. Copyright 1990 by the Los Angeles Unified School District. Adapted with permission.

myeducationlab

Go to the Activities and Application section in Chapter 15 of MyEducationLab and complete Activity 1. As you watch the video and answer the accompanying questions, consider the many types of reading media presented in the clip.

Most youngsters with usable vision benefit from periodic evaluations by a **low vision specialist,** a person with special training who can prescribe optical and nonoptical devices appropriate to the individual's functioning (Lueck, 2004; Simons & Lapolice, 2000). Ideally, an FVA should occur before an examination by a low vision specialist, so the TVI can share information about the student's functioning. If optical aids are recommended, a follow-up FVA may be necessary to describe the student's improved functioning while using these devices.

Determining the Appropriate Learning Medium

For students such as Haley, it is easy for teachers to determine how educational materials should be presented. Because she cannot see, braille clearly is the appropriate learning medium for her. Remember, however, that most students who are visually impaired have some usable vision; determining the appropriate learning medium for them is more complex.

Learning medium is the term used to describe the options for accessing literacy materials; these may include braille, print, audiotapes, and access technology. Many children who can read print do so at such slow speeds or with such inefficiency that they also benefit from using braille. Teachers determine the appropriate reading media for students by conducting a **learning media assessment (LMA)** (Koenig & Holbrook, 1993). The LMA begins with a functional vision assessment but also includes additional considerations, such as the student's use of touch and vision in new situations or environments, the stability of the eye condition, visual stamina, and motivation.

Like an FVA, the LMA needs to be repeated at regular intervals to determine whether circumstances or the student's skills have changed and whether additional instruction in a different reading medium is necessary. Students who use both braille and print have the advantage of being able to choose the reading medium that works best for them under different conditions, such as when they are in a dimly lit restaurant or when reading assignments are long and eye fatigue is a problem.

IEP Tip

IDEA requires IEP teams to assume that the reading medium for all students with visual impairments is braille and that evidence must be presented to challenge this assumption, when appropriate.

Determining the Nature of Specially Designed Instruction and Services

The provision of special education and related services must be based on a student's specific needs as identified through a comprehensive assessment of the student's current level of functioning and knowledge in both the general education curriculum and what has been identified as the **expanded core curriculum** (Hatlen, 1996). The expanded core curriculum includes the following areas: compensatory and communication skills, social and interaction skills, **orientation and mobility (O&M)** skills, independent living skills, recreation and leisure skills, self determination skills, use of assistive technology, visual efficiency skills, and career/vocational skills (Brasher & Holbrook, 2006). Figure 15.5 describes the skills educators will evaluate in a complete assessment.

Figure 15.5 Skill areas within the domains of the expanded core curriculum

Compensatory Skills, Including Communication Modes
- Concept development
- Listening and speaking skills
- Study and organizational skills
- Use of reference skills
- Determination of reading modes
- Communication modes for students with additional disabilities (such as tactile symbols, a calendar system, sign language, and recorded materials)

Social Interaction Skills
- Socialization
- Affective education
- Knowledge of human sexuality
- Knowledge of visual impairment

O&M Skills
- Development of body image
- Understanding physical environment and space
- Orientation to different environments
- Ability to travel in school and community environments
- Opportunities for unrestricted, independent movement and play

Daily Living Skills
- Personal hygiene
- Dressing
- Housekeeping
- Clothing care
- Food preparation
- Eating
- Basic home repair
- Money management
- Telephone
- Time and calendar
- Shopping
- Use of community services

Recreation and Leisure Skills
- Competitive sports
- Noncompetitive sports
- Hobbies and games
- Choosing recreational activities

Career/Vocational Skills
- Relationships between work and play
- Understanding value of work
- Job and career awareness
- Job acquisition skills (want ads, résumés, applications, interviews)
- Typical job adaptations made by workers with visual impairments
- Prevocational skills (work habits, attitudes, motivation)
- Awareness of vocational interests
- Work experience

Assistive Technology
- Keyboarding skills
- Braille access devices
- Visual assistive software and devices
- Auditory assistive software and devices
- Choosing appropriate options
- Device maintenance and troubleshooting

Visual Efficiency Skills
- Use of nonoptical low vision devices
- Use of optical low vision devices
- Use of a combination of devices
- Use of environmental cues and modifications
- Recognizing when not to use vision

Self-Determination Skills
- Knowledge of laws protecting people with disabilities, particularly visual impairment
- Assertiveness skills
- Negotiation skills
- Public interaction skills
- Management of readers and drivers

Source: Reprinted from Lizbeth A. Barclay, Expanded Core Curriculum: Education, in *Collaborative Assessment: Working with Students Who Are Blind or Visually Impaired, Including Those with Additional Disabilities,* Stephen A. Goodman and Stuart H. Wittenstein, Editors, pp. 98–99. New York: AFB Press, 2003.

Assessment is best accomplished by a team of individuals with experience working with students with visual disabilities. In addition to those people who, under IDEA, must be members of the team, the team also should consist of an O&M specialist and a TVI. The outcome of a comprehensive assessment should be a description of the student's current level of functioning in all areas of the general and expanded core curriculum and the identification of skills to be addressed for that child to function optimally in current and future home, school, and community environments (Barclay, 2003b; Lewis & Russo, 1997; Pugh & Erin, 1999). Few teachers would consider it important to evaluate a straight-*A* high school student's ability to order a meal at a fast-food restaurant or to launder clothes, yet a student with a visual impairment who achieves at grade level may not function appropriately outside of the classroom. Many students with visual impairments lack these outside-school skills. Informal assessment techniques, including family and student interviews, the use of checklists, observation in natural environments, and authentic and performance assessments, are the most valuable methods for determining the level of functioning of students with visual impairments in the expanded core curriculum.

When assessing a student's needs, educators should evaluate the age-appropriateness of a task from two perspectives. First, what are the student's peers doing? If Haley's friends are at the stage of social development where participating in groups, such as Brownies, is common, an assessment of Haley's social skills should investigate this aspect of her functioning. Second, because sighted students are incidentally learning to perform some skills long before it is age-appropriate to expect mastery of them, educators should evaluate a student's involvement in these tasks earlier than they might for sighted students. For example, while some students are not expected to launder clothes independently until their late teens, an educator assessing Haley would want to assess her participation in this task's component parts, such as scooping soap, sorting clothes by color, or folding freshly laundered towels and socks, because these skills are within the range of her capability now and are being learned visually by her peers.

Teachers also should avoid making assumptions about a student's previously learned information. Because visual impairment often results in gaps in information, what seems like common knowledge must be assessed. One TVI was surprised to learn that her 18-year-old female student with low vision was unaware that men's sexual organs differ from her own. The TVI used the result of her assessment to work with the family to design an appropriate program to assure that the student graduated with this knowledge, so critical to her social functioning.

DESIGNING AN APPROPRIATE IEP

Partnering for Special Education and Related Services

Over 71 percent of students with visual impairments spend most of their school day in the general education classroom (U.S. Department of Education, 2007). Yet these students often learn differently from their peers. In order to include these students successfully in the general curriculum, close partnerships must be nurtured among the general educator, the TVI, the O&M specialist, the student's parents or guardians, and other professionals involved in the student's education. In particular, these individuals must collaborate when designing the IEP to make some important decisions about the following:

- ◆ Provision of instruction to support the child's success in the general education curriculum
- ◆ Nonacademic priorities on which the special educators will focus
- ◆ Location of special education and related services
- ◆ Ways in which partners will communicate to meet the student's needs

Providing Specialized Instruction

Because of the complex or highly visual nature of some academic areas, students with visual impairments may need specialized instruction to master the curriculum. For example, some students need specialized instruction to master writing braille with a **slate and stylus;** using the **abacus** for calculating; and developing listening, study, and organizational skills. For these purposes, special and general educators collaborate to provide appropriate learning experiences. As you read about how students who are blind learn braille, think about the level of interaction that must occur between the general and special educators.

Reading Instruction

Students who do not learn efficiently through their visual sense may access the academic curriculum through **braille,** a tactile method of reading. Like the print alphabet, braille is a code, a way of presenting spoken language in written form. As Figure 15.6 shows, there is one braille symbol for each of the 26 letters of the English alphabet. The early publishers of braille developed numerous shortcuts, called **braille contractions,** for writing common words or letter combinations. Because of the contractions, there is not a one-to-one correspondence between print and braille. In Figure 15.7, you can compare a print passage with its braille translation.

Figure 15.6 English braille symbols, including contractions

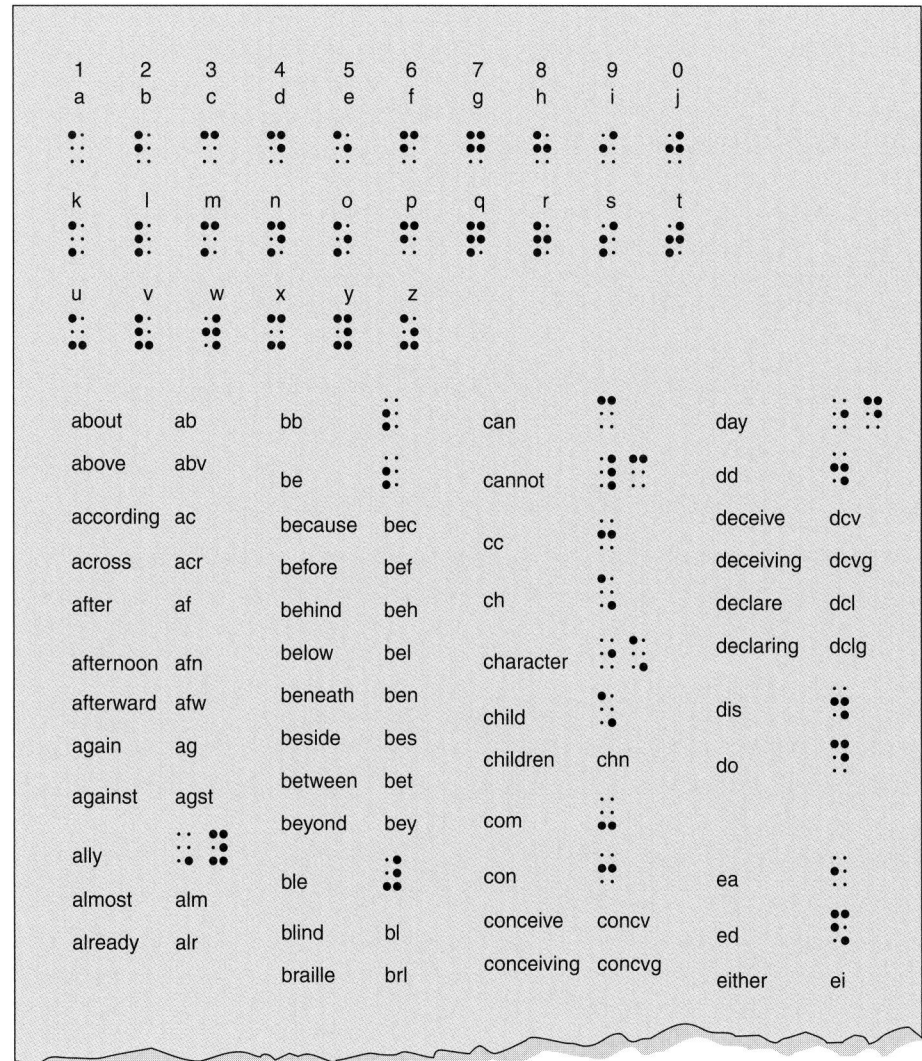

Figure 15.7 Comparison of "Old Mother Hubbard" in braille and print

Old Mother Hubbard

Old Mother Hubbard

Went to the cupboard

To get her poor doggie a bone,

When she got there

The cupboard was bare

So her poor little doggie had none.

The use of braille contractions requires that TVIs collaborate closely with general educators to introduce the 169 braille symbols in a way that allows the student to become competent in literacy skills. Because no single approach has been supported by scientific research, Haley's TVI, Katie, was faced with designing literacy instruction for Haley that supported the reading instruction that was occurring in Haley's general education class. In the past, TVIs have pulled a student like Haley out of the class for specialized instruction in reading in grades 1 through 3 and introduced reading words using their contracted form. Today, more TVIs are introducing early reading words in braille in their uncontracted form. Using this approach, when the general education teacher tells students to find the "a" in the word "sand," the braille reader can actually find an "a," not the "and" contraction. While teaching uncontracted braille facilitates inclusion, limited research exists to support this approach as best for teaching blind children to read. One problem with adopting this approach is that most textbooks and materials in braille are written in the contracted form. Children who are blind must learn contracted braille in order to access their math, social studies, and science books. In addition, statewide accountability assessments are usually available in contracted braille. At some point, the child who reads uncontracted braille must begin to learn the contractions and the 450 rules for using them.

You can imagine that the situation becomes even more complex for students who are second language learners. No curriculum exists for teaching literacy skills to students whose first language is not English (Conroy, 2005; Milian, 2000). Teachers of students with visual impairments, teachers of English as a second language, and general education teachers must collaborate to create appropriate materials that enhance acquisition of language, reading, and braille skills. Box 15.1 shows some strategies for teaching braille to these students.

Even before reading instruction begins, many students with visual impairments may not have had the same kind of exposure to literacy events as their sighted peers have had. Think of all of the opportunities that Haley's 3-year-old peers with typical vision had to see letters, long before they were expected to read. Letters are everywhere: they appear on cereal boxes, on toys, on the newspaper and envelopes delivered daily to the house, on billboards, on street signs, on television, and in books. Even if these children were not learning the letter names, they saw them and incidentally compared their outlines and shapes, setting the stage for future learning.

Collaborating teachers need to make certain that young students who have low vision have opportunities to be exposed to letters and words that can be seen clearly. For preschoolers who are blind, two essential components of an early literacy program include systematically introducing braille and flooding the environment with incidental opportunities to find braille, such as on labels, notes, books, schedules, and lunch menus.

Strategies for Teaching Braille to ESL Students

Educators of students with visual impairments who are not native English speakers and for whom braille has been determined to be the appropriate learning media must structure the learning environment so that students receive comprehensible language that capitalizes on the learning methods associated with the use of the tactile and auditory senses, including predictable routines, use of concrete objects, and contextualized language (Conroy, 2005). For these students, instruction in Braille and their second language really are inseparable.

General Strategies

General strategies for this process draw from the foundations of teaching children who are blind as well as the principles of second language learning.

- ◆ Collaborate with the ESL teacher, the O&M specialist, and others involved with the student's education to coordinate teachers' activities and address students' language and visual needs.
- ◆ Sequence language activities and structure lessons based on the school district's ESL curriculum.
- ◆ Use real objects instead of visual examples.
- ◆ Use thematic instruction whenever possible.

Strategies for the Early Production Stage of Developing English

During the first stage in second language acquisition, children develop receptive language skills. Typically learned through visual association of words to objects or pictures, this stage must provide children who are blind the opportunity to associate words presented both orally and in written form with real objects.

- ◆ Bring real objects that belong to a single category, such as fruits, to school. Make braille cards with words matching the objects. Assist the student in creating first oral and then written sentences using adjectives describing the objects (e.g., "The orange is bumpy").
- ◆ Create braille cards on which are written the names of classroom objects, such as *door, desk,* and *book.* Read each noun, give the card to the student, and ask the student to place the card on the correct classroom item.
- ◆ Provide the student with a braille copy of material presented orally, such as simple stories, poems, and rhymes that contain repeated phrases, and ask her to move her fingers, held in the correct reading position, over phrases.

Strategies for the Emergence-of-Speech Stage of Developing English

As the English language learner begins to use more complex forms of speech in English, it helps if learning continues to be scaffolded through the familiarity that is possible through repetition and contextualized activities, including opportunities to be exposed to the hand movement techniques used for accessing braille text.

- ◆ Ask the student to participate in an activity and then assist her in writing about the activity on the brailler.
- ◆ Give the student an audiotape and a braille version of an age-appropriate story. Encourage the student to read the braille while listening to the story and have her braille sentences or phrases about the story.
- ◆ Have the student participate in a daily living or an O&M activity, audiotape the sequence of activities, and then write keywords related to it on the brailler.

Strategies for the Intermediate Fluency Level

Integrating the use of the oral and written forms of the new language in a variety of contexts is important for the second language learner who is attaining mastery, whether the learning medium is print or braille. While less dependent on real situations and concrete objects, this learner still benefits from language activities that are grounded in experience.

- ◆ Have the student create a book about an experience and share it with classmates.
- ◆ Have the student keep a braille list of vocabulary words and a journal related to each of the content areas.
- ◆ Create meaningful activities that require the student to speak, listen, read, write, and interact with others.

For more information about teaching braille to second language learners, refer to M. Milian (1997). Teaching braille reading and writing to students who speak English as a second language. In D. P. Wormsley & F. M. D'Andrea (Eds.), *Instructional strategies for braille literacy* (pp. 189–230). New York: AFB Press.

myeducationlab

Go to the Activities and Application section in Chapter 15 of MyEducationLab and complete Activity 2. As you watch the video and answer the accompanying questions, consider how this situation would be different if one of these students was learning English as a second language.

Determining Nonacademic Priorities

As you reviewed Figure 15.5, you may have felt a bit overwhelmed at the list of areas in which a student with visual impairment may need specialized instruction. Once a child's performance in these areas is assessed and any needs for instruction identified, it becomes the task of the IEP team to prioritize those needs. Often, not all of the skills of the expanded core curriculum can be addressed every year. Nonetheless, it is critical that needed skills in these areas not be ignored in favor of the academic skills that are the focus of statewide achievement and accountability testing because all are skills needed for success in adult life. Ideally, the IEP team will identify some skills in each expanded core curriculum area for intensive instruction each year. The TVI must carefully monitor a student's acquisition and use of these skills, so that by the time the student is ready to transition from school to adult life, she has the skills necessary for success.

IEP Tip

Maintaining and annually reviewing a checklist of expanded core curriculum skills helps IEP teams to remember how needed skills were previously prioritized, resulting in the likelihood that a skill given a low priority one year is included as a targeted goal on the IEP during a subsequent year.

Determining the Location of Special Education and Related Services

Once decisions have been made about what is going to be taught, the IEP team must collaborate to determine where that instruction should take place. Sometimes it is more appropriate to provide initial instruction privately and then practice emerging skills within the general education classroom. To meet other needs, such as the acquisition of skills related to human sexuality, cooking, or shopping, instruction in specialized environments will be essential.

Communicating to Meet Students' Needs

For students who rely on adapted materials and who need increased opportunities for meaningful, hands-on activities, the level of communication necessary among all collaborators is extensive. General educators need to feel confident that their lessons will be accessible to their students with visual impairments. Because these adaptations, especially of math, science, and social studies materials, require significant time to create, the TVI must receive the materials well in advance of the date of their intended use.

Close communication to meet students' needs is also necessary when determining modifications to assigned work. Haley requires at least twice as much time as her peers do to complete a typical math assignment, in part because the braille math code is unfamiliar to her. Her teachers discussed the possibility of reducing the length of her assignments, but it was also obvious that, because of her lack of experience with numbers and math concepts, she needed additional opportunities in order to achieve at the level of her classmates. The IEP team had to deal with her competing needs for more time to complete the assigned work and more experiences to understand it thoroughly. They ultimately decided that her need for practice of these basic mathematical skills was critical to her long-term academic success, and, as a result, did not recommend this modification. Box 15.2 presents other strategies TVIs use to support the mathematics instruction of students with visual impairments.

Determining Supplementary Aids and Services

To participate in general education, many students who are blind or have low vision require curriculum modifications for accessing print, as well as access to appropriate assistive technology.

Providing Adapted Materials

A variety of adapted materials are available for use by students with visual impairments, including braille and large-print maps, measuring devices, graph paper, writing paper, calendars, flash cards, and geometric forms. A good source of adapted materials is the American Printing House for the Blind (http://www.aph.org/catalogs/).

Mathematics Instruction for Students with Visual Impairments

Students preparing to be teachers of children with visual impairments are often reminded that they are not supposed to be academic tutors. The example usually shared is that it is the job of the math teacher to teach math; the TVI only supports the math teacher's efforts. These roles, however, easily become clouded in practice because so much of mathematics is visual in nature. It is difficult to know if one is teaching a math concept or trying to overcome a basic lack of information related to the visual impairment.

The responsibilities of the TVI in math instruction include the following:

♦ Teaching students specialized computation methods, such as fingermath or use of an abacus

♦ Teaching students who are blind the Nemeth Code of Braille Mathematics

♦ Teaching students to use tactile charts, diagrams, and graphs

♦ Consulting with general education teachers on appropriate modifications for teaching mathematics to students with visual impairments

♦ Modifying materials used in mathematics instruction

Given that most math teachers have little background in visual impairment and limited understanding of how visual and spatial concepts can be presented to learners who don't learn visually, they must rely on TVIs for support. There are numerous practices that TVIs can use to support the general educator who is teaching mathematics to a class in which a student with visual impairments is enrolled.

Outside of the general education classroom, the TVI can:

♦ Get advance copies of transparencies and notes from the blackboard and make them available in the student's learning medium, so the student has access to them at the same time as peers.

♦ Preteach concepts or techniques before they are introduced in the general education class.

♦ Teach the student to be a self-advocate and to speak up when concepts or strategies are not understood.

♦ Provide opportunities to apply basic concepts and operations in real-life situations.

The TVI can help the math teacher make instruction more accessible to the student by:

♦ Encouraging the mathematics teacher to speak about mathematics consistently and unambiguously so that all students can understand.

♦ Teaching the math teacher to verbalize whatever is written on the blackboard or overhead projector transparencies.

♦ Bringing manipulatives, real objects, and appropriate three-dimensional models to be used for activities.

♦ Helping the math teacher to illustrate problems for students in a way that allows them to experience the principles being taught.

♦ Being present during math instruction to assist with students' understanding of the concepts.

PEARSON myeducationlab

Go to the Building Teaching Skills and Dispositions section in Chapter 15 of MyEducationLab and complete the activities. As you interact with the simulations, consider the general strategies presented here that you could adapt for teaching mathermatics to students with visual impairments.

TVI's often must adapt specific materials for assignments designed by general educators. Making these adaptations requires careful judgment by the special educator, who must determine what the essential and secondary purposes of the lesson are and what information can reasonably and meaningfully be represented in a tactile form. Adaptations can be simple, such as when a child is given real coins instead of pictures of coins to complete a math assignment. Occasionally, meaningful adaptations are impossible to create and alternative assignments that focus on the same skill must be prepared.

Students with low vision access print primarily through the use of optical devices such as glasses, telescopes, and magnifying lenses. In some instances, they may read large-print books, though some researchers suggest that this practice does not lead to faster reading rates or more comfortable reading distances (Lussenhop & Corn, 2002). One of the advantages of magnification devices is that they allow the student access to printed materials not only at school but also at home, at work, and in the community.

Accessing Appropriate Assistive Technology

As you have learned, students with visual impairments often require alternative methods to ensure progress in the general education curriculum. Today, several types of devices make access to the curriculum much easier for people with visual impairment. Box 15.3 describes some of these technologies.

Many students use these technologies in combination. For example, when she is older and is required to write an essay, Haley will probably access the library's online catalog with JAWS, which speaks the text on the monitor aloud to her. She may take notes about which books and articles to check out at the library on her braille note taker. Then, when she has the copies of the articles, she will scan them with her optical character reader, which will convert the print to an electronic form that she can either emboss in braille or read aloud using the computer's voice synthesizer. With braille translation software, Haley will be able to print her paper in braille to proofread before making the final print copy to turn in to her teacher.

These technologies create the opportunity for students with significant visual impairments to access and participate in the general education curriculum—as long as it remains print-based. There is a dark side to the technological revolution, however, particularly for students who are blind. As teachers supplement more and more of the general education

Go to the Activities and Application section in Chapter 15 of MyEducationLab and complete Activity 3. As you watch the videos and answer the accompanying questions, consider how beneficial these technologies are for students with visual impairments.

TECHNOLOGY OUTCOMES

Box 15.3

Assistive Technology for Students with Visual Impairments

Students with visual impairments often need to use a variety of technologies to access print materials and to create the products expected of all students engaged in the general curriculum. It helps to know the types of devices that your students might use to solve their access challenges.

◆ *When you have a student with low vision who needs to view a small object closely,* the student can use a handheld magnifier or a closed circuit television (CCTV). CCTVs come in either handheld or desktop models that enlarge the image to the desired size and project it on a television screen or computer monitor. The camera on some CCTVs can be adjusted to focus on a distant object, such as a demonstration or a whiteboard, thereby bringing the information to the computer screen directly in front of the student.

◆ *When you have a student who needs to scan a print document that is not available electronically,* the student can use an optical character reader (OCR) or scanner. Special software can be used with an off-the-shelf scanner to increase the accuracy with which material is scanned. Some OCRs are specifically designed for people who are visually impaired and can even scan information in columns accurately.

◆ *When you have a student with low vision who needs to read information displayed electronically on a computer screen,* the student can use a screen enlargement and navigation system. These systems increase the size of

the characters on the screen, the cursors, and the menu and dialogue boxes and provide features that allow easy access to displayed information.

◆ *When you have a student for whom electronic text on a computer screen is difficult to see,* the student can use a screen reader. Using synthesized speech, screen readers read the text that is displayed as the user moves the cursor (usually using keyboard strokes, not the mouse) or inputs from the keyboard.

◆ *When you have a student who needs to take notes in class,* the student can use a notetaking device. Several lightweight electronic notetaking devices (with either braille or qwerty keyboards) are available to take notes. The student can then download these notes to a computer for study or to be printed or embossed as braille. Most of these devices have audio output; some also create braille on an electronic display.

◆ *When you have a blind student who needs to create a personal braille copy of an assignment that has been created electronically,* the student can use a braille embosser, which, when connected to a computer and used in conjunction with braille translation software, will "print" a braille version of the text. Some braille embossers also print the ink-print translation on the same page.

curriculum with graphics-based sources, such as interactive software programs, they make it less likely that the curriculum will be accessible to students who cannot see the images on the screen. Already, vast areas of the Internet, because they are graphics-based, are not accessible to students with visual impairments. Even if these materials are presented with audio descriptions, they may be meaningless to the student who is blind simply because the student has limited or no experience with the object being described.

The challenge for classroom educators is to remain flexible in their use of curricular materials that are interesting and that can be meaningfully accessed by all students, including students with visual impairments. Through universally designed instruction, teachers can make a dark future bright.

Planning for Universal Design for Learning

The principles of universal design can be particularly beneficial for students with visual impairments. One recent initiative makes available electronic versions of print materials that can be easily accessed in a variety of ways by students who are blind or who have low vision. Similarly, when general and special educators partner to create learning experiences and assessments that are universally designed and use visual, auditory, and experiential activities, students with visual impairments benefit.

Often students with visual impairments have difficulty understanding some of the ideas that their teachers are presenting because they have not directly experienced these concepts. They may need many additional experiences to make up for their lack of incidental learning. Universally designed instruction provides these meaningful experiences and can benefit all students. For example, early reading books designed for sighted children rely heavily on pictures to convey the meaning of the story. In addition, the pictures reveal to young readers information about the world that they may not have directly experienced. Not all new readers have been for a walk in a forest or have gone for a ride in a rowboat, but from pictures they can discern what the words in the story convey (Koenig & Farrenkopf, 1997). General educators of students with visual impairments must provide more experiential activities in their classrooms to assure that all students understand the text.

Older students with visual impairments also benefit from instruction that incorporates real experiences that employ a tactile/kinesthetic approach to learning. Many concepts related to science, social studies, mathematics, art, and other subjects are especially appropriate for this kind of approach. For example, next year when Haley's science class studies germination, her teachers can arrange for students to use larger seeds so that Haley can feel them easily. Instead of having Haley plant her seed in the dirt in a yogurt container, as her classmates will, Haley will plant her seed in water. Then she and her classmates will check daily for changes in how the seed feels and smells. By using this method, she can learn about root growth (which will be accessible to her classmates through pictures in the science book) and also about seed germination and the growth of the leafy part of the plant.

As valuable as the principles of universal design are, educators should be cautious about how they apply them to curriculum and instruction for students with visual impairments. Educators tend to underestimate these students' abilities and provide too much support, leading to learned helplessness. In general, educators should expect students with visual impairments to master the same content and meet the same performance standards as students with vision, even though the students with visual impairments may use adapted methods to access the curriculum and demonstrate these standards. You can read about how teachers promote success in general education through high expectations and meaningful interaction with peers in Box 15.4.

Planning for Other Educational Needs

As you have read, students with visual impairments may have difficulty acquiring many of the functional and social skills that students with adequate vision learn by watching parents, siblings, other adults, and peers. Effective teachers recognize how a visual impairment impedes development of the skills of the expanded core curriculum.

Box 15.4

INCLUSION TIPS

	What You Might See	*What You Might Be Tempted to Do*	*Alternate Response*	*Ways to Include Peers in the Process*
Behavior	She is a loner on the playground, choosing to play or walk alone.	Allow her to stay in class and read or do homework.	Teach her board or card games.	Once she has mastered the games, set up a game table during recess where anyone who wants to play can do so.
Social interactions	She doesn't say hello to peers in hallways or acknowledge peers' presence when entering room.	Assume she is stuck up and unfriendly.	Have the entire class prepare autobiographies, including life history, special interests, and photos or objects, for her and others to study.	Teach peers to say both her name and their own in greeting because she may not be able to recognize them from their voices alone.
Educational performance	She is completing her arithmetic assignments more slowly than her peers are.	Immediately shorten the assignment for her.	Assess to determine if she understands the arithmetical concepts. Provide concrete objects and manipulatives, if necessary, for mastery. Shorten the assignment if concepts are mastered.	Have her act as a cross-age tutor to younger students who benefit from use of concrete materials in learning.
Classroom attitudes	She seems bored or uninterested during class demonstrations or teacher-directed activities.	Assume it is too difficult or simply ignore the inattention.	Make sure that she can "see" the teacher's materials by having copies of printed/brailled materials at her desk during the lesson.	Have her and peers help the teacher prepare a lesson by getting out materials and preparing overheads and hands-on materials for class use.

You might ask yourself how instruction in these areas affects the student's progress in the general education curriculum. When children with visual impairments have had the same experiences as their sighted peers and are encouraged to be autonomous and to make decisions for themselves, they are more interested and engaged in the content of the general curriculum and understand and appreciate it better. Mastery of these kinds of skills is critical to students' long-range educational and life outcomes. Students will need social, living, travel, and career skills to manage as competent adults and to apply the content and performance standards acquired in their general education programs. Typically, teachers need to focus on three areas in the curriculum of students with visual impairments: daily living skills, orientation and mobility, and self-determination.

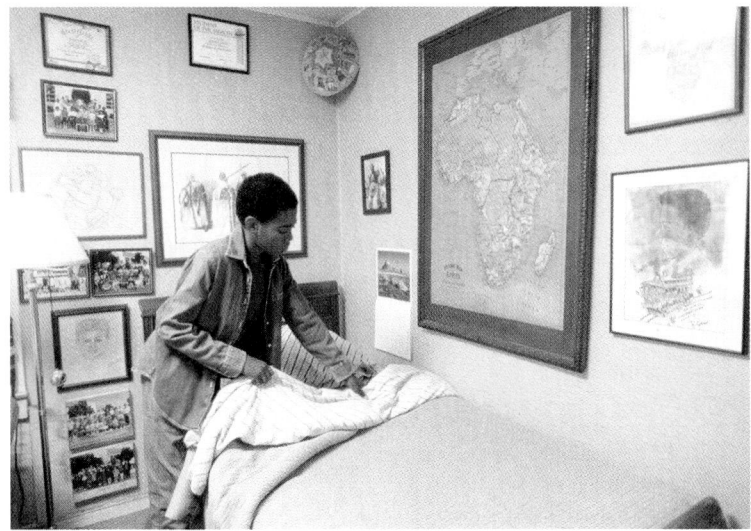

All students with visual impairments benefit from an education that focuses on such daily living skills as taking care of their own living space.

Daily Living Skills

Students with visual impairments require ongoing instruction in important skills of daily living, such as clothing management and kitchen skills. Generally, effective teaching strategies involve repeated visual or hand-over-hand kinesthetic demonstrations (or both), systematic instruction, gradual fading of assistance and prompts, and significant periods of practice (Koenig & Holbrook, 2000).

Often people do not think to include a child with visual impairment in simple activities of daily living. Involving the student in an activity and having high expectations that the skill can be acquired are critical factors in the acquisition of daily living skills. Because many adults think of people who are blind as helpless, they have low expectations for students with visual impairments. In addition, because adults may assume that students with low vision see more clearly than they do, the adults do not show them how to perform some of the activities that sighted children learn incidentally, such as buttoning a shirt, holding a spoon correctly, or making a bed. When students do not spontaneously develop these skills, teachers may mistakenly think that the students also have cognitive disabilities and may reduce their expectations even more.

Low and inaccurate expectations of their abilities are students' worst enemies. Skilled teachers know to be constantly alert to what students are not doing for themselves. These teachers are prepared to challenge students to promote independence and self-motivation.

Orientation and Mobility

O&M skills, an IDEA-related service, are those that people with visual impairment use to know where they are in their environment and how to move around that environment safely. Unlike sighted students, students with visual impairments must learn to listen to the flow of traffic; react to changes of street and road surfaces; and use their vision, other senses, and perhaps a cane or other mobility device to detect objects in the environment and to help them know where they are.

The development of O&M skills begins in infancy and continues until the student can reach a destination safely by using a variety of techniques. Young children concentrate on developing body image, mastering spatial and positional concepts, learning the layout of their homes and schools, and developing environmental awareness. Older students focus on crossing streets safely and negotiating travel in increasingly complex situations, such as a town's business district or a shopping mall.

Some blind adults learn how to travel with a guide dog. Primarily because of the responsibility associated with the care of these service animals, individuals under the age of 18 who still attend local schools rarely learn to use a guide dog, but children

These students work with an orientation and mobility specialist to learn how to move safely within their school neighborhood before tackling the challenge of a busy city street.

can be prepared to use guide dogs by learning to care for animals as pets (Young, 1997) and by becoming proficient at orientation skills, which are necessary for efficient traveling.

PEARSON
myeducationlab

Go to the Activities and Application section in Chapter 15 of MyEducationLab and complete Activity 4. As you watch the videos and answer the accompanying questions, consider the implications for classroom arrangements if you have a student that uses a cane.

Self-Determination

As adults, most people with visual impairments are required to explain their abilities and special needs to people they meet: bus drivers, prospective employers, landlords, restaurant workers, and flight attendants. Sometimes these explanations are simple, such as asking a bus driver to announce the name of every bus stop, but sometimes they require more detailed descriptions. For example, as a college student, Haley may need to ask each of her teachers for permission to record lectures, explain that it will be necessary to say aloud what they write on the board, and describe special accommodations that she needs (e.g., a reader or additional time during testing). Very likely, she will need to convince each of her professors that she can do the work for the class. In brief, she will have to be an effective self-advocate.

Haley has already begun developing self-advocacy skills. At first, she simply listened as Katie explained her needs to her teachers, but she is increasingly participating in this task, taking on the responsibility of explaining the special tools that she uses to her general education teacher. As an adult, Haley may need to advocate for her rights with landlords and, if she gets a guide dog, for access to public buildings. Her teachers will need to help her learn the laws (especially the Americans with Disabilities Act) and the communication techniques she can use to avoid confrontations (if possible) and to assert herself (as necessary). As part of Haley's lessons in self-determination, Katie is introducing her to successful adults who are blind.

Partnering Is Key

Meeting the academic, social, and functional life-skills needs of students with visual impairments frequently becomes a balancing act that demands considerable finesse, goal prioritization, and creative problem solving (Hatlen, 1996; Koenig & Holbrook, 2000; Pugh & Erin, 1999).

Creativity is the answer to many questions: creativity in scheduling, in instruction, in use of free time, and in collaboration among the many adults involved in each pupil's program. Critical to the success of this endeavor is that team members assume responsibility for the instruction and practice of newly learned skills whenever the natural opportunity to do so occurs. Each IEP team member also must believe that ultimate successful adult functioning depends on the student's attainment of skills in all of the curriculum areas—that no one area is more or less important than the others. It's a delicate balance.

In Box 15.5, you can read about the collaboration of general and special educators to meet the needs of a student who wanted to participate in his school's band.

USING EFFECTIVE INSTRUCTIONAL STRATEGIES

Early Childhood Students: Programming That Focuses on Real Experiences

Early intervention programs for young children with visual impairments generally are home-based, although many successful interventions, such as the BEGIN program at the Center for the Visually Impaired in Atlanta, also offer a center-based component where parents of infants go to observe preschool children with visual impairments and to meet the families of other youngsters who are blind or have low vision. The focus of early intervention is to help parents understand the effects of visual impairment on learning and to present effective methods that reduce the impact of these effects on development. These programs emphasize strategies that enhance children's acquisition of body image, language, self-help skills, sensorimotor skills, concepts, orientation, and early social interactions in home, school, and community environments where young children spend their time.

Making Beautiful Music Together

Adults who are not familiar with the techniques that individuals with visual impairments use to accomplish tasks often have difficulty imagining that the students can participate at all. Frequently, effective problem solving to change attitudes and create practical answers requires both local and distant collaborators.

One such partnership occurred when Ja'dine, a saxophone player in his school's orchestra, mentioned to his mother that he wanted to participate in the school's marching band. This situation would require extensive partnerships among many. Several steps led to his participation:

1. *Adults responded to a desired goal expressed by the student.* His mother's first thought was that Ja'dine was asking for too much—that, because of his blindness, he was going to be disappointed. She called Eloisa Ramirez, Ja'dine's TVI, and asked for her advice.

2. *The student's TVI arranged a meeting with the partners involved in making the student's goal possible.* Eloisa was pleased that Ja'dine was interested in becoming involved in this extracurricular activity and wanted to support him. She recognized, though, that others at the school might have doubts about the wisdom of the idea just as Ja'dine's mother did. She talked with the school principal, who, though not entirely supportive of the idea, was willing to meet with the individuals most likely to be involved in implementing the plan.

3. *The TVI and the student brainstormed potential benefits and obstacles to achieving the goal, which the student presented to the potential partners.* In preparation for this meeting, Eloisa and Ja'dine made two lists. The first set out the benefits he would experience as a member of the marching band. The second identified the adaptations that he might need. Before the meeting, Ja'dine practiced with Eloisa how he would present this information. Attending the meeting were the orientation and mobility specialist, the marching band director, the principal, Eloisa, and, of course, Ja'dine and his mother. Ja'dine persuasively presented his case for being involved in the marching band. Having decided that he was committed to the work that would be required to make his idea a

reality, the group then began examining how it might be accomplished.

4. *Possible strategies for overcoming identified obstacles were discussed and assigned to specific partners for further investigation.* The collaborators identified two issues that had to be resolved. First, the principal was concerned that the district would use insurance liability as an excuse to prevent Ja'dine from marching. Eloisa offered to contact a state advocacy group of blind adults to get information that he could use to counter any arguments that the school district's insurance expert presented. The advocacy group even sent a representative to meet with district representatives. The marching band director, who was uncertain how Ja'dine would be able stay in step, voiced the second concern. The O&M instructor suggested that there might be several ways in which Ja'dine could stay in formation with the rest of the band members. The band director wasn't too keen on this idea but agreed to allow the O&M specialist to attend band practice to work with him to identify the best solutions.

5. *The group worked as a team to resolve issues that arose; new partners were added as necessary.* During the summer, as the O&M specialist and the band director worked with Ja'dine and the other band members who were learning formations, other partners became involved. Eloisa had to contract with a faraway braillist who knew the braille music code and could emboss the needed braille sheet music. Ja'dine's peers in the band also became involved when his mother's work shift changed to early evenings and she was unable to get him to and from practice. Other band members had come to enjoy Ja'dine and his sense of humor as they practiced; they wanted to be with him and were willing to offer him rides.

6. *Successful collaboration and hard work resulted in the student reaching his goal.* At the first game of the season, Ja'dine proudly marched with the band. Watching from the stands were the partners who had helped to make this night possible. Farther away, but also smiling, were the advocate and the braillist. Indeed, success for students with visual impairments can involve both distant and local collaboration.

Preschool programs for children with visual impairments continue early intervention goals and provide many experiences that are the foundation for learning. Most of the activities are hands-on, meaningful, and related to real-life activities. Students make their own snacks, wash their dishes, and find opportunities to change their clothes often, thereby practicing daily living skills. They collect tangible memories of their day and include them in braille or print experience stories dictated to their teachers. TVIs facilitate students' movement, meaningful language, exploration, and control of the environment to reduce the impact of visual impairment on development.

Many students with visual impairments are in heterogeneously grouped preschools and in preschools for children without disabilities. With the proper supports, these programs can be valuable learning environments for some children. It is easy to forget, however, that sighted children acquire many of the benefits of these programs through incidental learning. Although students with visual impairments participate, there is a potential that they will fall behind others in the class unless they receive supplemental instruction.

Elementary and Middle School Students: Accommodations to Develop Basic Skills

Elementary school is a key time for sighted children to develop a positive self-image, lay a solid foundation in academic skills, and safely explore the world. For pupils with visual impairments, the focus of the educational program is the same as that for students with vision; however, the techniques for accomplishing these goals may be different, requiring TVIs to teach or reinforce concepts presented in class. In addition, and depending on the student's needs, the TVI emphasizes the development of career-awareness skills, social skills, knowledge of human sexuality, additional self-help skills, knowledge of one's visual impairment, and early advocacy skills. At the same time, the O&M specialist may be increasing the environments in which the youngster can travel safely.

A trip to the sculpture garden at the zoo provides a natural opportunity to encourage peer interactions.

TVIs spend much of their time adapting materials for students in elementary programs. As one TVI, Mary Gordon, from Lawrence, Kansas, explained, "When you can't see the chalkboard, and you can't see exactly where the rooms are, and you can't see this, and you can't see that, it takes twice as much energy to get through the day as it does for someone with sight. I provide instruction, materials, and support for students who may require many hours to master what a sighted child can learn through casual observation." TVIs who support inclusion of their students create braille sheet music for music class, provide maps with raised continents and tactilely different countries for social studies, and encourage peer-supported learning as students handle formaldehyde-soaked specimens in science.

Additionally, Mary noted, "Since so much of our social interaction is visual, blind children must learn behaviors of sighted persons in order to obtain acceptance from their peers. To accomplish this, my students and I spend many hours practicing social skills that other students learn by observing. Learning to face the person to whom they are speaking, standing or sitting with appropriate postures, and eliminating mannerisms that might detract from their appearance are all imperative" (personal communication, August, 1995).

Secondary and Transition Students: Preparing for Adult Life

For many students with visual impairments, the middle and high school years are a time to catch up, to learn skills that students with good vision have been learning incidentally but that are not used until the teen years. TVIs generally spend more time with students to meet needs related to the expanded core curriculum, while at the same time students are enrolled in general education classes to meet graduation requirements. Sometimes students choose to delay graduation in order to master all the skills needed for a successful transition to independent adult living.

PEARSON
myeducationlab

Go to the Activities and Application section in Chapter 15 of MyEducationLab and complete Activity 5. As you watch the videos and answer the accompanying questions, consider how students who do not have visual impairments would learn and master these activities.

Education includes training for job skills. Economic self-sufficiency is an obtainable goal for most people with visual impairments.

Mickey Damelio, an itinerant TVI from Tallahassee, Florida, works with his students on the transition skills they need. For example, his student Martin Vasquez could not make a sandwich or clean a sink when he entered high school. Because of his family's cultural attitude about the abilities of students labeled as blind, he had not been expected to help with general household tasks, and because of his visual impairment, he had not incidentally learned how to perform them. Mickey met several times with Martin's mother and gradually persuaded her that Martin needed to learn to do more for himself at home—and that his educational program needed to focus on both his academic and functional needs.

Today Martin and Mickey are making a list of the utility services that he will need to contact when he moves into an apartment. Martin practices his notetaking skills as he contacts directory assistance to request the telephone numbers of the different utility companies and keys them into his electronic notetaker. Later, he will retrieve the numbers and call to request information about having the utilities started.

On some days Martin also works with his O&M specialist. Recently they have been exploring apartment complexes close to the vocational school where Martin will enroll next year. He knows he must spend many hours learning to negotiate safely the routes to use around the school's campus and to the grocery store, the mall, and other community areas he will be using.

INCLUDING STUDENTS WITH VISUAL IMPAIRMENTS

As you have already read, blindness and low vision do not affect what a student can learn as much as they affect *how* a student learns. In 2006–2007, 57 percent of students spent 80 percent to 100 percent of their time in the general education classroom, like Haley, with another 15 percent receiving services from 40 percent to 79 percent of the school day in this setting (U.S. Department of Education, 2007). Since 1990, the percentage of students with visual impairments receiving most of their education in the general education class has risen by 7 percent. This change may reflect the increased access to the general education curriculum that has been made possible through new technologies. Figure 15.8 illustrates patterns of educational placement.

You've met Haley, who is included in Mrs. Benson's second-grade class and is expected to complete the same work that the other students are. When appropriate, Haley occasionally is pulled from class to work with Katie in another classroom or the community. Depending on the subject of instruction, however, there are times when Katie will provide support to Haley in Mrs. Benson's class. This flexible approach to placement benefits many students with visual impairments. There are, however, some students who are best served in the general education classroom all day and who are never pulled from that environment for special services. Still others receive educational benefit through placement at a school for the blind or in a special class.

The nature of visual impairment and the ways that youngsters with visual impairments learn about the world mitigate against successful inclusion in all cases. Inclusion is thought to be most successful when both the academic needs and the needs related to the expanded core curriculum are adequately addressed. For students with visual impairments, inclusion in adult society is considered the goal of special education; but inclusion in school is not always the means to that goal.

IEP Tip

Although IDEA requires that a student's needs be determined and prioritized before a placement decision is made, all too often the placement for students with visual impairments is determined by the limited options that are available in any district.

Figure 15.8 Educational placement of students with visual impairments (2006–2007)

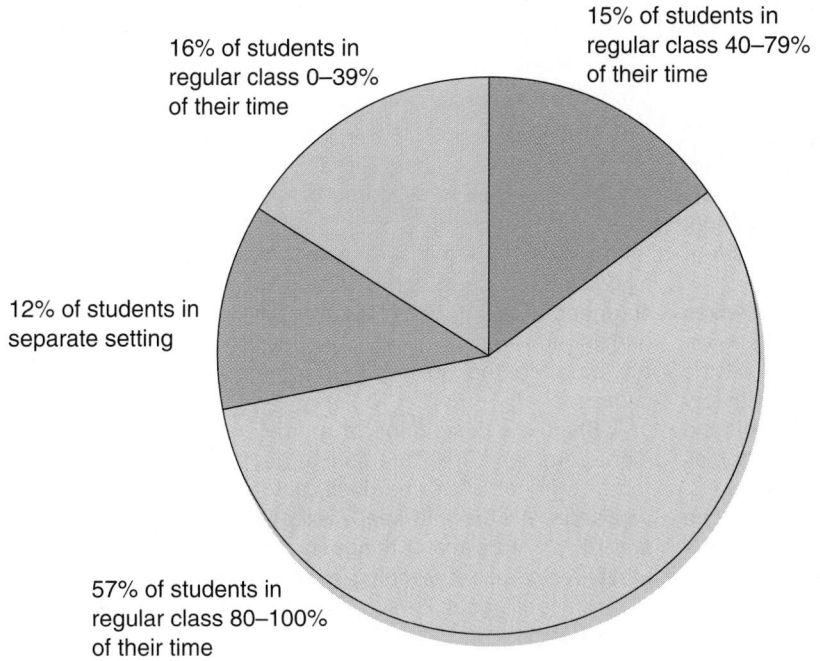

15% of students in regular class 40–79% of their time

16% of students in regular class 0–39% of their time

12% of students in separate setting

57% of students in regular class 80–100% of their time

In Box 15.6, you can read how Donna McNear, a TVI in Minnesota, describes her role in creating learning communities in which students with visual impairments have the opportunity to succeed.

ASSESSING STUDENTS' PROGRESS

Measuring Students' Progress

As is true for all other children, it is important to measure students' progress in school in order to make well-informed decisions about programming. The progress of students with visual impairments is measured in both the general and the expanded core curriculum.

Progress in the General Curriculum

Because most students with visual impairments are provided with educational services in the general education classroom, their progress is measured at the same time as their peers. They take the same math, social studies, language arts, and science tests as the other students in their class. Sometimes, of course, it is necessary for the TVI to transcribe print materials into braille or for the student to use a magnifier when reading the test, but these accommodations are not designed to modify the purpose or difficulty of the test in any way. When students prepare their answers in braille, the TVI writes in print above the braille exactly what is written in braille. After the general educator has graded the interlined work, the TVI prepares the general educator's comments in braille for the student.

It is not uncommon for students with visual impairments to take their tests in a separate classroom. Sometimes they must leave the general education classroom to use the assistive technology that is stored in another area; sometimes additional space is

● *Donna McNear*

"To teach is to learn twice" is a quotation I've placed in my home, my notebook, and my office (J. Joubert, 1754–1824). As a teacher of children with visual impairments, I am continually traveling a path of learning. My work day is immersed in learning to create caring school communities and learning opportunities where children can be successful.

As an itinerant teacher in seven rural school districts in east central Minnesota, I begin my day in my car, traveling to see children in their home school districts. At the first school, I observe Chad, a preschool student with low vision, and assist the school staff in providing materials and arranging the classroom so he can easily see and participate in all activities.

I also stop at the high school to teach Tracy, who reads and writes in braille. I bring the worksheets the teachers have given me to put into braille and quickly visit with teachers between classes to answer questions and problem-solve. Mr. Johnson, the science teacher, and I discuss the possibilities of providing tactual materials in a genetics unit. He comes up with a great idea and benefits from my support, approval, and encouragement. I meet with Tracy who wants help learning new Nemeth Code Braille signs in the beginning algebra math unit and wants to review the route to the new girls' locker room for gym.

After an hour of reviewing information with Tracy, I travel to the next town and have lunch with the adapted physical education teacher. This gives us the opportunity to plan the physical education activities for Shannon, an eighth-grade student who is blind and who is now working on swimming goals. After lunch I go to my office to make phone calls and have a meeting with the braillist, Connie. She wants to discuss the format for braille music.

On my way to the next town, I make a brief stop at Cory's house. He is 14 months old and has low vision. He just received glasses, and I spend a few minutes observing and assessing the difference his glasses make in how he uses his vision in daily activities at home. His parents also want to share new information from his ophthalmologist and ask a few questions.

My day ends with a mobility lesson with Annie, a high school student who is blind. I am dually certified as an orientation and mobility specialist, which allows children in rural areas to receive needed training. We review the route to the post office so Annie can pick up a package.

Sharing a description of my day with my family at dinner, I remember a statement attributed to Lewis Mumford, "It is not what one does, but in a manifold sense what one realizes that keeps existence from being vain and trivial." I do many things in a day for children, but what I realize about teaching and my students is what my work life is all about. I realize that I am a mirror, a window, and a doorway for my students: a mirror to reflect positively who they are and their capabilities, talents, and dreams; a window to show them their opportunities, possibilities, choices, and other ways of being; and, finally, a doorway for their future.

I have also realized my own mission in my work life. I see the meaning in my labor (beyond the reward of a paycheck); I see my abilities recognized and valued; I view myself as a craftsperson, creating something of beauty and value; I have a job that is large enough for my spirit; and I feel I am leaving the world better than I found it. Through my day-to-day teaching, I have learned love, fortitude, respectfulness, and humbleness. I have also learned to be delicate and to have passion for my time with children.

—*Donna McNear, Itinerant Teacher, Minnesota*

necessary to spread out their materials. Usually, though, these students require extra time to complete tests because of the slow reading rates often associated with having a visual impairment.

Progress in Addressing Other Educational Needs

Teachers of students with visual impairments are responsible for measuring students' progress in the expanded core curriculum. Generally, students' skill levels are determined through the use of informal measures, such as teacher observation, evaluation of needed prompt levels, and curriculum-based tests prepared by the TVI. For example, after Haley completed a unit of study on her eye condition, Katie prepared a test to determine Haley's level of retention and understanding of the information taught. To measure Haley's progress in learning to make a grilled cheese sandwich, however, Katie used a checklist of the steps needed to complete this task and noted on the list the level of prompting that Haley required. For assessing progress in keyboarding, a computer-based test can be utilized to measure Haley's speed and accuracy.

As with initial assessments to determine a child's level of functioning for the IEP, teachers of students with visual impairments must have knowledge of the kinds of skill development that are influenced by the presence of a visual impairment and the limitations in incidental learning that are related to it. They must devise progress measurements that measure changes in a variety of skill areas.

Making Accommodations for Assessment

Comprehensive assessments frequently include standardized and norm-referenced tests, which are often timed. An issue to consider about some tests is the additional time needed by students that is directly related to their visual impairment. Taking tests often requires complex use of vision, such as frequent eye movements between the test booklet and the answer sheet or scanning of multiple-choice answers and stimulus paragraphs. Similarly, readers who use braille, who tend to have reading rates significantly below their peers with sight and whose system of reading is not conducive to efficient scanning, have difficulty with tests (Bradley-Johnson, 1994). The amount of time needed should be determined individually (Allman, 2004).

Other accommodations used frequently by students with visual impairments when participating in formal assessments include a reader (for the nonreading sections of the test), a scribe, or a computer; placement in a quiet testing area; and frequent breaks. Of course, these accommodations must be listed on the IEP and must be the types of accommodations typically used by the student to complete assignments.

VALUES AND OUTCOMES

VALUES ▶ GREAT EXPECTATIONS · CHOICES · POSITIVE CONTRIBUTIONS · STRENGTHS · RELATIONSHIPS · FULL CITIZENSHIP

The outcomes envisioned for Haley are no different than the outcomes imagined for her schoolmates without disabilities. That is so because Haley, her parents, and her teachers have adopted values that underlie their expectations.

The adults in her life, both at home and at school, have great expectations for her success that Haley has adopted for herself. Everyone recognizes that hard work and specialized instruction and supports throughout school will be necessary to achieve the outcomes that they desire for Haley, and all are willing to do what they can to make these dreams for the future a reality.

They expect that Haley will overcome the limitations inherent in blindness through mastery of the expanded core curriculum skills that other students learn by watching others and that, by mastering those skills and putting to good use the other education she is receiving, she will work or volunteer in her community, making her own positive contributions to it.

Because she has many strengths that compensate for her visual impairments, they expect that she will travel, manage her daily routine, pay bills, shop, and participate as an equal in recreation activities in which she is interested.

They expect that through the collaboration of her TVIs and general educators, Haley will graduate from high school and pursue a career that she chooses for herself, based on her own understanding of her interests, strengths, and abilities.

They expect that Haley will continue to expand the number of people with whom she has meaningful relationships—as a friend, a neighbor, a partner, a parent, a mentor.

They expect that Haley will vote in elections, write letters to the editors of newspapers, volunteer to help others less fortunate than herself, and participate fully as an adult citizen.

WHAT DO YOU THINK?

1. Do you think that Katie's focus on the functional skills of the expanded core curriculum is appropriate, given that Haley's academic support needs are so extensive?

2. When do you think Haley should receive the specialized instruction in the expanded core curriculum, given that she also needs to master the general education curriculum expected of all students?

3. Do you think that Katie should be teaching Haley's peers braille? What would be the advantages and disadvantages to Haley if she and her peers could access one another's written work? What about her general education teachers? Should they be taught braille and required to use it with Haley?

4. At what age do you think Haley should be allowed to walk to her neighbor's house? Go to the mall alone? Go on a date? Besides instruction in safe travel skills, what would she need to be taught to be allowed to safely engage in these activities at the same time her peers are?

ADDRESSING THE STANDARDS: THE VALUES CONNECTION

The following CEC Knowledge and Skill Standards: Common Core and Values are addressed in this chapter through the content and concepts we discuss.

CEC Knowledge and Skill Standards: Common Core	Values/Standards Connection
CEC Knowledge and Skill Standard II. Development and Characteristics of Learners	By learning about the characteristics of students with visual impairments, you put into practice CEC Standard 2, Development and Characteristics of Learners.
CC2K1 Typical and atypical human growth and development.	Within the context of this chapter, this group of knowledge and skill standards encompasses many of the six values we discuss: great expectations, positive contributions, strengths, choices, relationships, and full citizenship. For instance, envisioning *great expectations* is the first of the values that you learned about in Chapter 1. By being aware of the nature, characteristics, and extent of visual impairments, teachers can more readily envision these great expectations for their students and plan for the interventions that can make them a reality.
CC2K2 Educational implications of characteristics of various exceptionalities.	
CC2K3 Characteristics and effects of the cultural and environmental milieu of the individual with exceptional learning needs and the family.	
CC2K4 Family systems and the roles of families supporting development.	
CC2K5 Similarities and differences of individuals with and without exceptional learning needs.	
CC2K6 Similarities and differences of individuals with exceptional learning needs.	

CEC Knowledge and Skill Standards: Common Core	Values/Standards Connection
CEC Knowledge and Skill Standard V. **Learning Environments and Social Interactions**	CEC Standard 5 relates to learning environments and social interactions. When you teach students with visual impairments appropriate social skills, expect them to use technology to independently complete assignments, and encourage self-determination, you are applying this standard.
CC5S2 Identify realistic expectations for personal and social behavior in various settings.	
CC5S3 Identify supports needed for integration into various program placements.	
CC5S4 Design learning environments that encourage active participation in individual and group settings.	When teachers carefully evaluate a student's functional vision and then use teaching strategies that emphasize those capabilities, they build on student *strengths,* an important value of special educators.
CC5S6 Use performance data and information from all stakeholders to make or suggest modifications in learning environments.	Teaching students to be their own advocates supports the value of enhancing *strengths, choices, and full citizenship.*
CC5S8 Teach self-advocacy.	
CC5S9 Create an environment that encourages self-advocacy and increased independence.	
CEC Knowledge and Skill Standard VII. **Instructional Planning**	Instruction in the skills of the expanded core curriculum reflects an application of CEC Standard 7, Instructional Planning.
CC7S1 Identify and prioritize areas of the general curriculum and accommodations for individuals with exceptional learning needs.	Meeting students' needs through individualized programming and placement decisions is one way to ensure that students with visual impairments are given the opportunities to develop the skills that lead to *full citizenship.*
CC7S2 Develop and implement comprehensive, longitudinal individualized programs in collaboration with team members.	
CC7S3 Involve the individual and family in setting instructional goals and monitoring progress.	
CC7S6 Sequence, implement, and evaluate individualized learning objectives.	
CC7S7 Integrate affective, social, and life skills with academic curricula.	
CC7S9 Incorporate and implement instructional and assistive technology into the educational program.	

continued

CEC Knowledge and Skill Standards: Common Core	Values/Standards Connection
CEC Knowledge and Skill Standard X. Collaboration	When educators partner with one another, they are applying the principles reflected in CEC Standard 10, Collaboration.
CC10S2 Collaborate with families and others in assessment of individuals with exceptional learning needs.	Thoughtful collaboration that includes families allows teams to better identify student *strengths,* create positive learning environments, and offer students meaningful *choices,* so that they can develop successful *relationships* and make *postitive contributions* within the general education class.
CC10S3 Foster respectful and beneficial relationships between families and professionals.	
CC10S4 Assist individuals with exceptional learning needs and their families in becoming active participants in the educational team.	
CC10S5 Plan and conduct collaborative conferences with individuals with exceptional learning needs and their families.	
CC10S6 Collaborate with school personnel and community members in integrating individuals with exceptional learning needs into various settings.	
CC10S8 Model techniques and coach others in the use of instructional methods and accommodations.	
CC10S9 Communicate with school personnel about the characteristics and needs of individuals with exceptional learning needs.	

Source: From CEC Knowledge and Skill Standards: Common Core and Values. Copyright by The Council for Exceptional Children. Reprinted with permission.

S U M M A R Y

Identifying Students with Visual Impairments

◆ Legal blindness is a measurement used primarily for eligibility for government or private-assistance programs.

◆ Within education, visual impairment, including blindness, is defined as an impairment in vision that adversely affects a student's educational performance.

◆ Students with visual impairments have a limited ability to learn incidentally from the environment and must be directly exposed to or taught much of what they need to know.

Evaluating Students with Visual Impairments

◆ Ophthalmologists determine the presence of a visual disorder, and optometrists and low vision specialists determine if a visual disorder can be corrected through lenses or optical devices.

◆ A functional low vision assessment determines how a student uses her vision in a variety of situations.

◆ A learning media assessment assists TVIs in determining the most efficient mode of reading and learning, such as braille, magnification, or large print.

◆ Educators determine the effects of visual impairment on students' development of skills in the expanded core curriculum, including compensatory skills, orientation and mobility, career education, independent living, technology, self-determination, recreation and leisure, visual efficiency, and social skills. They use observations, parent and student interviews, and other informal testing procedures.

Including Students with Visual Disabilities

◆ Most students with visual impairments who do not have other disabilities are educated for most of the school day in general education classrooms.

◆ Special education services are provided by a TVI who is assigned to that school either on a part-time or full-time basis.

Designing an Appropriate Individualized Education Program

◆ Students learn through meaningful involvement in activities from beginning to end. Often they take a hands-on approach that maximizes the use of all senses. Through practice, they have increased opportunities to develop new skills.

◆ Educators meet the academic needs of students through the principles of universally designed instruction.

◆ TVIs meet the functional and life-skill needs of students to facilitate their eventual integration and full participation in adult society.

◆ Instruction must focus on the skills acquired incidentally by sighted students and those skills that are specific to students who have visual impairments.

Using Effective Instructional Strategies

◆ In the early childhood years, TVIs emphasize teaching parents of young children with visual impairments to think like someone who can't see and teaching children to learn hands-on, real-life skills, such as changing clothes and making snacks.

◆ In the elementary years, the emphasis is on teaching through tactile methods (braille, raised maps, handling specimens), practicing social skills that facilitate inclusion, and developing orientation and mobility and self-advocacy skills.

◆ In the secondary and transition years, the focus is on transition from school to adulthood; from living at home with parents to living on one's own; on orientation and mobility training in the community; on choosing lifestyles, places of residence, and leisure-time activities; and on refining skills so that these choices can become realities.

Assessing Students' Progress

◆ Progress in the general curriculum is measured through materials selected by the general education teacher that are adapted appropriately by the TVI.

◆ Progress in the expanded core curriculum is measured by the TVI and O&M specialist using informal assessment techniques, including interviews, teacher-made tests, and rubrics.

◆ Options for the use of accommodations on statewide tests are determined by the IEP team and often include different presentation (braille or print), additional time, a quiet setting, and use of a reader or scribe.

PEARSON
myeducationlab

Now go to MyEducationLab at www.myeducationlab.com and take the Self-Assessment to gauge your initial comprhehension of chapter content. Once you have taken the Self-Assessment, use your individualized Study Plan for Chapter 15 to enhance your understanding of the concepts discussed in the chapter.

Understanding Students Who Are Gifted and Talented

◆ WHO IS BRIANA HOSKINS?

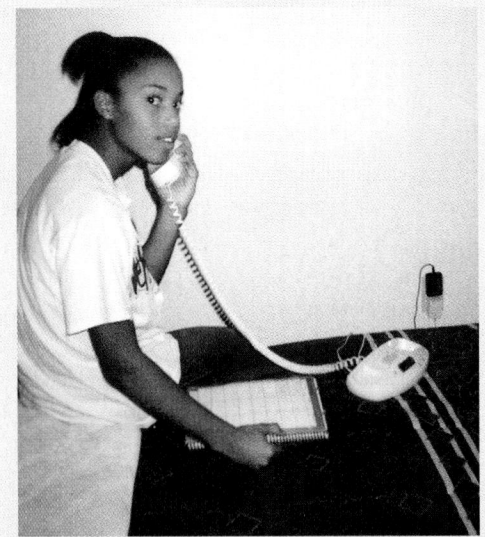

"Where are you taking me?" That is the question Forrester (played by Sean Connery) asked his gifted teenage neighbor Jamal (played by Rob Brown) in the 1996 movie *Finding Forrester* (Connery, Mark, Tollefson, & Van Sant, 2000). The movie depicts an unlikely friendship between a gifted 16-year-old African American student living in the Bronx (a borough of New York City) and a reclusive Pulitzer Prize–winning author, William Forrester. As the movie develops, Forrester teaches Jamal to make the most of one of his gifts: his writing.

There is a single, simple reason why Tyrone Hoskins encouraged his daughter Briana to watch this movie. It is because Jamal and Briana share several traits. Both excel in their academic and athletic pursuits, and both usually hide their gifts from their peers.

Briana's mother, Deborah, first noticed there was something unusual about her daughter when Briana was 3 years old. At that time, Briana's older sister Candice often baby-sat Briana. One day, Candice was reciting "And Still I Rise," a poem by Maya Angelou, while Briana sat quietly listening. Later that day, Briana surprised her family by reciting the entire poem from memory.

Deborah soon realized that Briana was able to read by herself many of the books that they read together at bedtime. By age 4, Briana was pronouncing challenging words.

Briana's kindergarten teacher was the first professional to talk with Deborah about

Briana's development and how advanced she was for her age. By first grade, Briana was being pulled out of her general education class 1 to 2 days a week to receive enrichment opportunities. Evaluations authenticated what Briana's family and teachers had been witnessing: Briana had an IQ of 154.

The results required Deborah to make some difficult choices. The pullout support was helping Briana, but the other 3 days a week were boring and frustrating her. Briana had exceptional abilities, but unfortunately the staff at her school were not fully prepared to meet her academic needs at such an early age.

They certainly would have allowed Briana to remain in her current setting. They recommended, however, that she and Deborah consider a more challenging environment. The closest and probably most appropriate school program for Briana meant an hour, round trip, in the car each day. Nevertheless, Deborah chose to enroll her daughter in this school because it offered an enrichment model that would challenge Briana academically and expand her educational opportunities.

Although the move to the new school offered academic benefits, it also created social challenges. At first, Briana's friends from her neighborhood asked her why she wasn't going to their school anymore. Like Jamal in *Finding Forrester,* Briana doesn't like to be regarded as smart. "Actually, she is often quite modest, which sets her apart from the norm," Deborah explains.

Not wanting to be seen as brainy, Briana began to remain inside the house more, preferring books to her old neighborhood friends. "It was a lot for a third grader to handle, being asked where she was and why she didn't go to school anymore," Deborah says.

Although Briana sometimes continues to prefer books to a social life, her social life is busy. Part of it consists of practicing and performing with her church dance and choir group. Recently, the group was invited to perform at the University of Missouri at Kansas City and to attend training under the instruction of the Alvin Ailey dance troupe from New York City. These days, dance practice and performances across the Kansas City metropolitan area keep Briana and her mother quite busy.

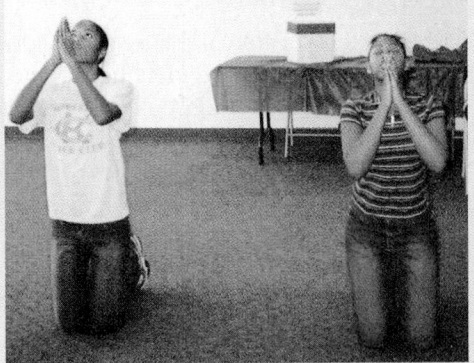

Briana also runs track. On most weekday afternoons, you'll find her running either for her middle school cross-country team or for her local Amateur Athletic Union track team. Briana started running during the summer after her fifth-grade year and is a "natural talent in the 400 and 200 meter," according to Deborah. "Every weekend we seem to be traveling to some

CHAPTER OBJECTIVES

◆ You will learn that "gifted" includes high performance capability in intellectual, creative, specific academic or leadership, or performing and visual arts domains, and that most state and local educational agencies recognize the intellectual domain if they recognize giftedness as a special education category.

◆ You will learn that students from diverse ethnic backgrounds and students from low-income families are under-represented in gifted education, and that the origins of giftedness are the combined environmental and biological factors in a child's life.

◆ You will learn that many educators regard giftedness as more than intellectual prowess and that they may use a performance-based, research-reliable assessment to identify giftedness in students, including those from diverse backgrounds.

◆ You will learn about differentiated instruction, co-teaching, accelerating and compacting, extended curricula, and autonomous learning as techniques to individualize a student's education.

◆ You will learn about the theory of multiple intelligences, schoolwide enrichment, and critical-thinking training.

◆ You will learn about "product and process" evaluations and learning contracts as techniques for assessing students' progress.

city or another. She just missed qualifying for nationals last year but did qualify for regionals in the 400 meter."

For Briana, running is serious business, as is the classroom. She is competitive and takes losing seriously. When she thinks she should have won, she often cries after a race. At the same time, she really cares for her other team members. According to her mother, "In cross-country events this year Briana was known to run beside a team member offering words of encouragement."

From all accounts, Briana is a well-rounded middle school student, but her teachers often find it demanding to create learning situations that challenge her and encourage her talents. Briana often exceeds her teachers' expectations and demands; she challenges them to think beyond the borders of typical curricula and related assignments. Currently, the school district's Program for Exceptional Gifted Students is addressing many of her intellectual needs as a seventh grader. However, Deborah wonders whether transitioning to high school and the ninth grade (skipping the eighth grade) might be an appropriate plan for next year. Although Deborah and Briana's teachers are considering the social consequences, Deborah says, "Briana is tall for her age and is often mistaken for being older than she actually is. She has always been able to interact well with older children and adults." So the questions facing Briana, her family, and her teachers are the same ones that Forrester put to Jamal: "Where are you taking me? Where are you headed?"

PEARSON
myeducationlab

After reading this chapter, complete the Self-Assessment for Chapter 16 on MyEducationLab to gauge your initial understanding of chapter content.

IEP Tip

Most states do not require educators to develop an IEP for students who are gifted and talented.

IDENTIFYING STUDENTS WHO ARE GIFTED AND TALENTED

Defining Gifted and Talented

Unlike the laws benefiting students with disabilities, such as IDEA, Section 504, and ADA, there is no federal legislation that requires state or local educational agencies to offer special education to students who are classified as specially gifted or talented. Although the federal Jacob Javits Gifted and Talented Students Education Act of 1988 provides limited funding for state and local educational agencies to offer special education to these students, it does not require them to do so (Zirkel, 2004). State and local laws or regulations, however, may apply to these students. The National Association for Gifted Children recently completed a survey focusing on the extent of state support for gifted education in the 2006–2007 school year (National Association for Gifted Children, 2007). Sadly, of the 28 states reporting they have a state mandate, only 6 indicated that they have full funding to implement it.

Unlike the disabilities you have read about in this book, giftedness is not well or easily defined. Most states adopt the definition the federal government promulgated in 1978 (Stephens & Karnes, 2000):

> [T]he term "gifted and talented children" means children and, whenever applicable, youth, who are identified at the preschool, elementary, or secondary level as possessing demonstrated or potential abilities that give evidence of high performance capability in areas such as intellectual, creative, specific academic, or leadership ability, or in the performing and visual arts, and who by reason thereof, require services or activities not ordinarily provided by the school (Gifted and Talented Children's Education Act, 1978)

This definition differs from earlier ones in two respects. First, it excludes psychomotor ability; second, it adds "preschool" and "youth" in place of "children," enlarging the age range (Stephens & Karnes, 2000).

Of the 42 states that responded to a survey asking how they define "gifted," 37 reported that they have a state-adopted definition of giftedness in state statutes or regulations. Furthermore, 27 states of 42 reported that they have a state requirement to identify and/or serve students who are gifted; however, not all states provide funding to meet this mandate. The 37 responding states that recognize particular attributes of giftedness report as follows:

- 35 address intellectually gifted.
- 22 address performing and visual arts.
- 19 address academically gifted.
- 19 address creatively gifted.
- 12 address leadership and specific academic areas.
- 7 address issues of cultural diversity.

Not only do the states' definitions and categories vary, but so do the terms that state agencies use to describe these exceptional children. Most use "gifted and talented"; 13 use only "gifted"; still others use "highly capable student" and "learner of high ability" (Stephens & Karnes, 2000).

Definitions of gifted and talented are multidimensional (span several domains). What, for example, are Briana's areas of giftedness and talent? Is she like those students who exhibit more than one area of giftedness, or is she like those who excel in one area only? Read on, and you will find an answer.

To account for the fact that giftedness spans more than one area of human development and achievement, Gardner (1983, 2006) has proposed a **multidimensional model of intelligence** that is broader and yet more specific than the federal definition. He described eight specific intelligences found across cultures and societies: musical, bodily-kinesthetic, linguistic, logical-mathematical, spatial, interpersonal, intrapersonal, and naturalistic. Figure 16.1 lists the typical characteristics and distinctive features common in gifted individuals in each of these eight areas. Gardner also (2006) described two predominant profiles of intelligences—searchlight and laser.

Searchlight profiles—especially characteristic of politicians and businessmen—involve a ready shifting among intelligences that are often of comparable strengths.

Laser profiles—especially characteristic of artists, scientists, and scholars—demonstrate one or two powerful intelligences used in great depth that overshadow the other intelligences (Gardner & Moran, 2006, pp. 228–229). Later in the chapter, you'll learn about how the multidimensional model of intelligence can be applied to education.

A recent definition of giftedness zeros in on the interpersonal dimension of Gardner's model and is referred to as emotional intelligence (Goleman, 1995). Goleman (1995) defined emotional intelligence as the capacity to know one's emotions, manage one's emotions, motivate oneself, recognize others' emotions, and effectively develop relationships with others. He described emotionally intelligent individuals as having specific characteristics associated with self-awareness, impulse control, persistence, self-motivation, empathy, hope, and optimism.

Goleman claimed that emotional intelligence shapes everything from personal to organizational success (Goleman, Boyatzis, & McKee, 2002). He also believes that success in top leadership positions relies much more on emotional intelligence than on IQ. Goleman pointed out that ". . . the relative contribution of EI [emotional intelligence] and IQ arose from a considerable body of previous research suggesting that IQ accounts for a relatively small amount of the variants in important life outcomes" (Cherniss, Extein, Goleman, & Weissberg, 2006, p. 242).

It is difficult to identify how many students are gifted and talented because state and local educational agencies use so many different definitions and criteria for classifying a student as gifted and talented. The National Association for Gifted Children (2007) estimates that there are three million students who are academically gifted and talented from pre-kindergarten through grade 12. Most agencies apply an IQ score of 125 to 130 as a baseline for identifying these students. On that measure alone, the top 2 or 3 percent of the general population is gifted.

PEARSON
myeducationlab

Go to the Activities and Application section in Chapter 16 of MyEducationLab and complete Activity 1. As you watch the video and answer the accompanying questions, reflect on the events that prompted Briana's parents and teachers to test her intelligence.

Figure 16.1

Potential areas of giftedness: An adaptation of Howard Gardner's eight areas of intelligence

Area	Gifted Person	Possible Characteristics of Giftedness	Early Indicators of Giftedness
Musical	Ella Fitzgerald Itzhak Perlman Ray Charles Carlos Santana Yo Yo Ma	Unusual awareness and sensitivity to pitch, rhythm, and timbre Ability may be apparent without musical training Uses music as a way of capturing feelings	Ability to sing or play instrument at an early age Ability to match and mimic segments of song Fascination with sounds
Bodily-kinesthetic	Michael Jordan Nadia Comanici Marla Runyon Jim Abbot	Ability can be seen before formal training Remarkable control of bodily movement Unusual poise	Skilled use of body Good sense of timing
Logical-mathematical	Albert Einsten Stephen Hawking John Nash	Loves dealing with abstraction Problem solving is remarkably rapid Solutions can be formulated before articulated: Aha! Ability to skillfully handle long chains of reasoning	Doesn't need hands-on methods to understand concepts Fascinated by and capable of making patterns Ability to figure things out without paper Loves to order and reorder objects
Linguistic	Virginia Woolf Maya Angelou Helen Keller Ralph Ellison Sandra Cisneros	Remarkable ability to use words Prolific in linguistic output, even at a young age	Unusual ability in mimicking adult speech style and register Rapidity and skill of language mastery Unusual kinds of words first uttered
Spatial	Pablo Picasso Frank Lloyd Wright I.M. Pei Maya Lin	Ability to conjure up mental imagery and then transform it Ability to recognize instances of the same element Ability to make transformations of one element into another	Intuitive knowledge of layout Able to see many perspectives Notices fine details, makes mental maps
Interpersonal	Martin Luther King, Jr. Madeleine Albright Rosa Parks Nelson Mandela	Great capacity to notice and make distinctions among people, contrasts in moods, temperaments, motivations, and intentions Ability to read intention and desire of others in social interactions; not dependent on language	Able to pretend or play-act different roles of adults Easily senses the moods of others; often able to motivate, encourage, and help others
Intrapersonal	Sigmund Freud Elizabeth Kubler-Ross	Extensive knowledge of the internal aspects of a person Increased access to one's own feelings and emotions Mature sense of self	Sensitivity to feeling (sometimes overly sensitive) Unusual maturity in understanding of self
Naturalist	Rachel Carson John James Audubon Jane Goodall Jacques Cousteau	Relates to the world around him or her In tune with the environment	Recognizes and differentiates among many types of an environmental item, such as different makes of cars Recognizes many different rocks, minerals, trees

Although it appears that females slightly outnumber males in gifted education placements (U.S. Department of Education, 2006), males and females appear to be equally represented in those programs (Council of State Directors of Programs for the Gifted and National Association for Gifted Children, 2003). Differences, however, occur in the academic interests of gifted males and females.

IEP Tip

As you work with the IEP team to develop each student's IEP, you might encourage strategies for both males and females to expand their interests and experiences in nontraditional ways.

◆ Girls tend to have more positive attitudes toward English, writing, and reading, while boys have more positive attitudes toward science and computers (Swiatek & Lupkowski-Shoplik, 2000).

◆ Boys are twice as likely as girls to receive a high score on mathematics tests (Olszewski-Kubilius & Turner, 2002).

◆ Girls tend to have a much higher interest in language arts and foreign language, two subjects that boys identify as least interesting (Olszewski-Kubilius & Turner, 2002).

There is a substantial and long-standing underrepresentation of students from racially diverse backgrounds in programs for gifted and talented students (Milner & Ford, 2007). (Remember, this was mentioned in Chapter 3.) The National Research Council (2002) reported that European American first and third graders were approximately three times more likely to score at the 75th percentile in reading and math than African American and Latino students. The Council attributed this difference to a higher rate of poverty among African American and Latino students than among European American students.

> In many ways, children of poverty are at a competitive disadvantage from the moment of conception onward. . . . Fewer of the marginalized children will develop to the full measure of their potential or acquire advanced intellectual competencies and academic skills that are clearly ahead of the norm for their age. In the ordinary course of events, they will be under-represented among academically gifted children. (Robinson, 2003, p. 257)

Describing the Characteristics

It is difficult to identify the characteristics of all people who are gifted and talented. Indeed, "no one profile exists of a gifted child or a gifted education program. Gifted children are a diverse group, and we need to move beyond a 'one-size-fits-all' conception both for identification and programming" (Rizza & Gentry, 2001, p. 175). Nevertheless, those who are gifted and talented typically have one or more of these characteristics: high general intellect; specific academic aptitude; creative, productive thinking; leadership ability; and visual or performing artistry. Paradoxically, high-ability students may have language, hearing, visual, physical, or learning disabilities. Thus, giftedness may co-occur with disability.

High General Intellect

From its earliest conceptions, giftedness has been associated primarily with students' high general intellectual ability (Nevo, 1994). That is still the case, as you have learned, with 37 states including intellectual giftedness in their state definition (National Association for Gifted Children, 2007). These students are able to grasp concepts, generalize, analyze, and synthesize new ideas or products far more easily than can other students their age (Bloom, 1956). They have understanding of exceedingly large quantities of information, broad and varied interests, a high level of verbal ability, flexible thinking skills, unusual intensity, and a heightened ability to generate original ideas and solutions (Clark, 2008). Their general intellect

Students of color are disproportionately underrepresented in gifted-talented programs.

is expressed through their application of these characteristics to various academic subjects and life problems.

Typically an IQ score of 125 to 130 is the baseline for identifying giftedness. Students who have an IQ range from about 130 to 144 are considered to be moderately gifted; those with an IQ range of 145 to 159 are considered to be highly gifted; and those with an IQ range over 160 are considered to be exceptionally gifted (Clark, 2008). Although IQ tests typically can record scores as high as 160, scores of 180 to 200 have been estimated by other methods. This means that the IQ of people in the gifted population ranges from 125 to 200 and that those at one end of the gifted spectrum may be very different from those at the other.

Exceptionally gifted individuals are sometimes referred to as prodigies. The term **prodigy** generally refers to a child who, before the age of 10, performs in an intellectually demanding way at the level of an adult professional. A child identified as a prodigy usually has a focus, a specialized domain of highly developed giftedness (Feldman, 2004).

MY VOICE

Box 16.1

Michael Kearney, Age 9, Describes His College Experience

Thinking back on my years of college, I can see that I've dealt with many issues, such as the difficulty of development discrepancies, problems of conformity, and the general lack of understanding and support from the majority of people. I am constantly trying to maintain my emotional balance as I confront disbelieving educators and students. At the same time I am trying to be myself—a child, who has the ability to learn and the desire to be educated.

Don't believe the myths about children like myself that we will not become an achieving and well-adjusted adult. On the contrary, research shows that acceleration is beneficial, both academically and socially. Given appropriate education and personal support, children like myself will make a major contribution to the future.

To understand what life is like for someone like me, I must go back to the day I received my IQ results. Being told that I am not just somewhat different, but dramatically different, was both thrilling and terrifying. The thrill was being told that I am extremely bright, but the terror was knowing that society could never learn to put a square peg in a round hole.

Growing up, I have dealt with teachers who have never knowingly met, much less taught, someone like me. I had to deal with principals who doubted my test results, who disliked the word *gifted,* who were reluctant to make special accommodations for my needs, and who, if encouraged by law or policy, did so at a snail's pace.

In addition to struggles around decision making about school, I faced a general lack of understanding and support when it came time to attend my first day in college. I remember going through the hallways, looking at the faces of these students, and listening to them refer to me as "Doogie Howser." I thought to myself, I don't look anything

like him, and I could never be a doctor. I hate the sight of blood and hospitals. Later, I came to realize that the general public is only aware of children like me through television. Well, any type of awareness is better than none.

Another issue that I had to deal with while attending college was the chatter of my classmates. They felt that my parents had pushed me. I beg to differ. My parents have done their best to see that I am a well-adjusted and a loving human being. For example, when I decided I wanted to go to college, they had to deal with the unexpected financial costs of early college attendance. They have been behind me 100 percent.

I started out at the age of six, as a child who thrived on learning and craved a stimulating educational system that would enhance my academic spirit. At the University of South Alabama, I was allowed the freedom to think, act independently, and pursue my educational excellence even though I was only eight. These educators believed that children like myself have the potential to excel in an appropriate education.

After I graduate, I plan to travel and then work on a graduate degree in biochemistry to gain whatever knowledge is out there for me to grasp. My life captures the essence of the pursuit of excellence as a personal journey to overcome creative barriers imposed by the necessities of everyday college life. To be passionately in love with my work in college provides meaning for my existence.

A life of quiet desperation awaits those who will not strive for excellence. My journey is not over, but I have come a long way. My life experiences are quite different from most, and the wisdom I can share at this moment is that individual differences do exist in society and we must learn to accept and encourage those with such differences.

Creativity

Educators have long regarded creativity as a defining trait of gifted and talented students (Torrance, 1964). Creativity has been defined as "the interplay between ability and process by which an individual or group produces an outcome or product that is both novel and useful as defined within some social context" (Plucker & Beghetto, 2004, p. 156). Creativity is often associated with the visual and performing arts, but students can express it in other ways, including divergent thinking ability (reasoning), openness to new ideas (sensing), high emotional energy (affective), and keen state of consciousness (intuitive) (Clark, 2008). Figure 16.2 illustrates these four areas of creativity.

Additionally, students can be creative in their approach to academic subjects. For example, mathematical creativity has been defined as "(a) the ability to produce original work that significantly extends the body of knowledge, and/or (b) the ability to open avenues of new questions for other mathematicians" (Sriraman, 2005, p. 23). Researchers agree that creativity correlates with higher-order cognitive thinking, intrinsic motivation, and a sheer love of creating (Piirto, 2004). It is nearly impossible to think of Einstein's

Figure 16.2 Four aspects of creativity

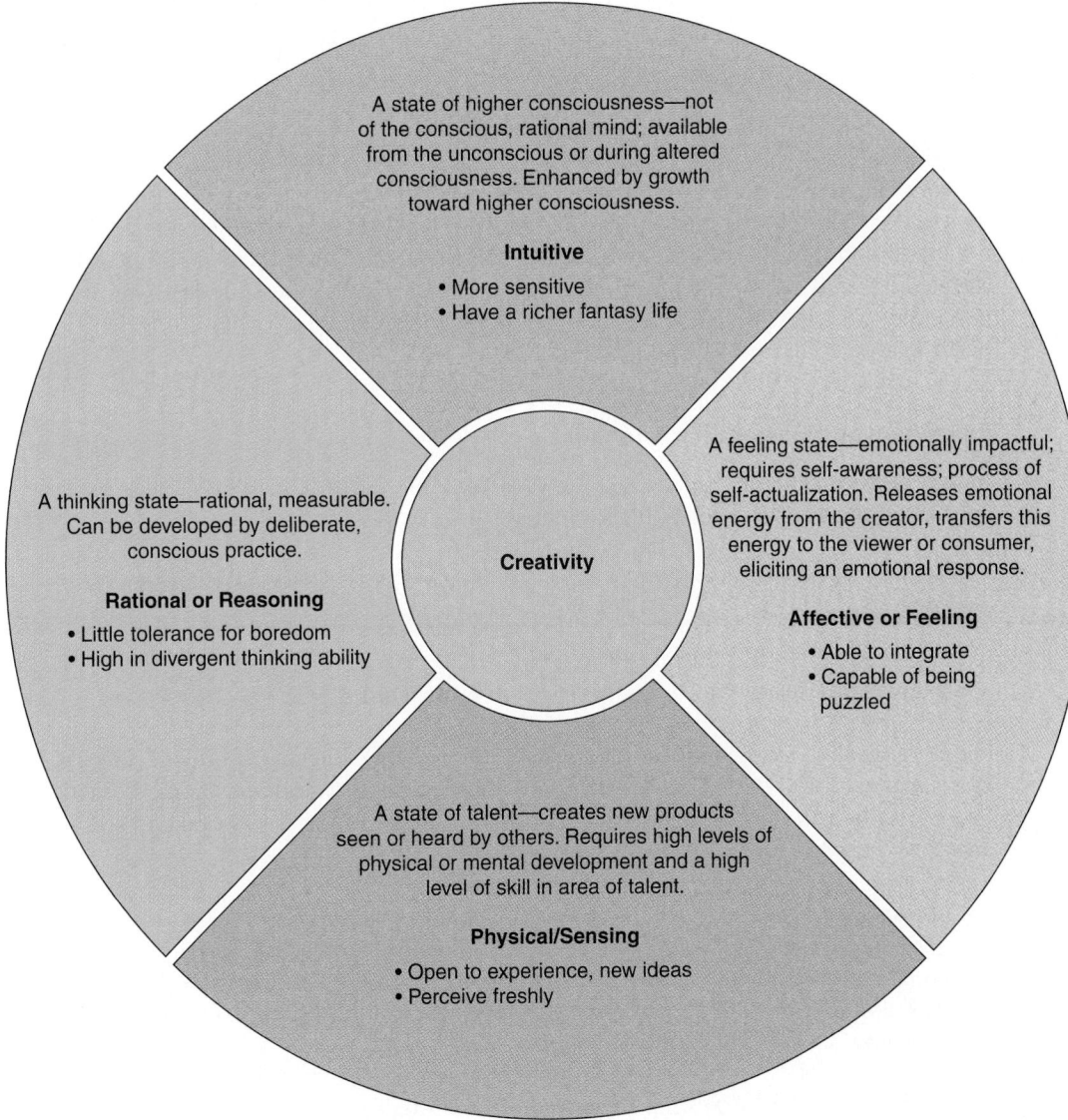

Source: Clark, B. (2008). *Growing up gifted* (7th ed.). Upper Saddle River, NJ: Merrill/Pearson, p. 159.

creation of the theory of relativity without seeing the characteristics of his creativity: independence, risk taking, originality, and intuition surely were all part of the process (Karolyi, Ramos-Ford, & Gardner, 2003).

Leadership Ability

IEP Tip

You can find an extensive annotated bibliography of books and websites with ideas for incorporating leadership activities into IEPs in "Leadership Education," an article by Bisland, Cobb, & Karnes, 2004.

Leaders are those who emerge in situations in which there is not a designated leader (Guastello, 2007). Two key characteristics associated with leadership include the ability to engender others' trust (Burke, Sims, Lazzara, & Salas, 2007) and "wisdom in spontaneity—the ability to assess situations quickly and step forward or backward in taking direction for the benefit of the group" (Roach et al., 1999, p. 17). The behaviors most attributed to emerging leaders are (1) keeping the group focused, (2) offering compromises that are accepted by the group, (3) being listened to and respected by group members, and (4) eliciting agreement from others (Jolly & Kettler, 2004).

Addressing issues related to values, ethics, and justice is a critically important type of leadership. Renzulli (2002) described characteristics of people who "mobilize their interpersonal, political, ethical, and moral lives in such ways that they place human concerns in the common good above materialism, ego enhancement, and self-indulgence" (p. 35). Their characteristics are optimism, courage, avid interest in a topic or discipline, sensitivity to human concerns, physical/mental energy, and vision/sense of destiny.

Talents in Visual and Performing Arts

The visual and performing arts are media in which students show many of the traits associated with creativity, general intellect, and specific academic aptitude, including rapid mastery of a subject matter. In addition, they may have highly developed nonverbal communication skills; physical coordination; exceptional awareness of where they are in relation to other things and people; or specific skills in music, dance, theater/acting and mime, storytelling, drawing, or painting. Clark (2008) suggests that the soundest way to determine giftedness in visual and performing arts is having a panel of experts judge a student's performance in his area of talent.

Emotional and Social Characteristics

In a review of research on the self-concept of adolescents who are gifted, Rinn (2006) concluded that the research is highly mixed.

- Some research shows that gifted students have higher social self-concepts (Bain & Bell, 2004).
- Other research finds that gifted students have lower self-concepts (Mayseless, 1993).
- Some studies show no differences (Hoge & Renzulli, 1993).

People typically view giftedness as an asset in terms of achieving academic success and even in terms of experiencing resilience (Neihart, 2002). Giftedness, however, has also been described as a burden, especially considering some of the behavioral and social ramifications (Peterson, 2006; Yoo & Moon, 2006).

> Comparative studies have found higher levels of anxiety (Tong & Yewchuk, 1996) and perfectionism (Schuler, 1997). Noncomparative studies have noted heightened sensitivity (Hébert, 2000), loneliness (Kaiser & Berndt, 1985), social isolation (Gross, 1993) . . . and depression in profoundly gifted youth (Jackson & Peterson, 2003). (Peterson, 2006, p. 46)

Peterson (2006) points out that slightly more than half of graduate programs in school counseling do not provide particular information about the unique strengths and needs of students who are gifted and neglect to teach counseling approaches that could help specially gifted students. Because many students who are gifted tend to have an orientation toward perfectionism, you can be helpful to students by encouraging them to have a balanced perspective toward their performance, allowing for a range of results from success to partial success and sometimes even to failure (Boland & Gross, 2007).

Determining the Causes

Does giftedness originate from nature or nurture? The answer has long been debated (Elkind, 1981; Rosenzweig, 1966; Siegel, 1999). Clark (2008) emphasizes the importance of both nature and nurture:

> High levels of intelligence or giftedness is [sic] the result of a dynamic, stimulating, interactive process that leads to quantitative and qualitative differences in performance. How giftedness is expressed depends both on the genetic patterns of the individual and on the experiences provided by that individual's environment. The opportunities to develop their abilities provided in the environment allow some individuals to enhance their abilities to the point of giftedness, whereas the lack of such opportunities inhibits others in their development, some even to the level of retardation. Children are not born gifted, but they are born with a unique and nearly unlimited potential. Clearly, there is an early and continuous need for talent development. (p. 50)

EVALUATING STUDENTS WHO ARE GIFTED AND TALENTED

As you will recall, students from culturally and linguistically diverse backgrounds are underrepresented in gifted programs (Brown et al., 2005; Milner & Ford, 2007; National Research Council, 2002). To identify students who are gifted and talented, educators often conduct a two-step diagnostic evaluation similar to the nondiscriminatory evaluation used to identify and evaluate students with disabilities.

Determining the Presence of Giftedness and Talents

To protect against discrimination, leaders in gifted education advocate using more than one means of evaluation (Gubbins, 2005). For example, educators can integrate a student's IQ test results with other documented evidence of their talents, such as creativity tests, behavior rating scales, samples of artwork or creative writing, photographs of a previously completed project, a videotape of an oral presentation, a leadership profile, or other material from parents or teachers.

One of the challenges in using more than one measure is deciding how to combine the scores and results to determine whether to classify a student as being gifted and talented. Gallagher (2002) recommends against "merely simple aggregation of the findings"; instead, he favors "creatively combining the results" (p. 104). Unhappily, guidelines for ensuring creative combinations are not explicit. Figure 16.3 shows the standard process for evaluating students for the presence of giftedness.

You learned about intelligence testing in Chapter 5; in this chapter we will focus on alternative assessments for identifying giftedness among students from diverse backgrounds. These assessments acknowledge the multiple domains of intelligence, the nearly exclusive reliance on IQ tests (Nevo, 1994), and the increasing concern about test bias (Baker, 1996; Sarouphim, 2001).

DISCOVER (Discovering Intellectual Strengths and Capabilities through Observation while allowing for Varied Ethnic Responses) is a performance-based, research-reliable, and research-validated assessment for identifying giftedness in students from diverse backgrounds (Maker, 2001; Sarouphim, 1999, 2001). It requires the student to undertake problem-solving

PEARSON
myeducationlab

Go to the Activities and Application section in Chapter 16 of MyEducationLab and complete Activity 2. As you watch the video and answer the accompanying questions, consider the importance of parents advocating for their children in gifted settings.

Figure 16.3
Evaluating whether or not a student is gifted, using an IDEA-like process

Observation	***Teacher and parents observe:*** The student may be bored with school or intensely interested in academic pursuits, has high vocabulary or specialized talents and interests, shows curiosity and frequently asks questions (especially *how* and *why*), is insightful, and has novel ideas and approaches to tasks.
Screening	***Assessment measures:*** **Classroom work products:** His work is consistently superior in one or more academic areas; or in the case of the underachieving gifted, products are inconsistent, with only work of special interest being superior. **Group intelligence tests:** Tests often indicate exceptional intelligence. **Group achievement tests:** The student usually performs above average in one or more areas of achievement. (Cutoff for screening purposes is an IQ of 115.)
Prereferral	Generally, prereferral is not used for students who may be evaluated as gifted.
Referral	Schools vary on their procedures for referral; in some cases, referral will be handled very similarly to the process of referring students who have disabilities.
Nondiscriminatory evaluation procedures and standards	***Assessment measures:*** **Individualized intelligence test:** The student scores in the upper 2% to 3% of the population. Because of cultural biases of standardized IQ tests, students from minority backgrounds are considered if their IQs do not meet the cutoff but other indicators suggest giftedness. **Individualized achievement test:** The student scores in the upper 2% to 3% in one or more areas of achievement. **Creativity assessment:** The student demonstrates unusual creativity in work products as judged by experts or performs exceptionally well on tests designed to assess creativity. The student does not have to be academically gifted to qualify. **Checklists of gifted characteristics:** These checklists are often completed by teachers, parents, peers, or others who know the student well. The student scores in the range that suggests giftedness as established by checklist developers. **Anecdotal records:** The student's records suggest high ability in one or more areas. **Curriculum-based assessment:** The student is performing at a level beyond peers in one or more areas of the curriculum used by the local school district. **Direct observation:** The student may be a model student or could have behavior problems as a result of being bored with classwork. If the student is a perfectionist, anxiety might be observed. Observations should occur in other settings besides the school. **Visual and performing arts assessment:** The studentís performance in visual or performing arts is judged by individuals with expertise in the specific area. The student does not have to be academically gifted to qualify. **Leadership assessment:** Peer nomination, parent nomination, and teacher nomination are generally used. However, self-nomination can also be a good predictor of leadership. Leadership in extracurricular activities is often an effective indicator. The student does not have to be academically gifted to qualify. **Case-study approach:** Determination of a student's giftedness is based on looking at all areas of assessment just described without adding special weight to one factor.
Determination	The nondiscriminatory evaluation team determines that the student is gifted and needs special education.

tasks in six of Gardner's domains of intelligence: spatial, logical-mathematical, linguistic, bodily-kinesthetic, interpersonal, and intrapersonal. The tasks increase in complexity and openness as the assessment progresses. Assessments are available at four grade levels: K–2, 3–5, 6–8, and 9–12. By using DISCOVER instead of other approaches, educators identify as gifted and talented a higher proportion of students from diverse ethnic, socioeconomic, and linguistic backgrounds (Sarouphim, 2002, 2004).

The instrument draws on Maker's (1993) definition of giftedness as "the ability to solve the most complex problems in the most efficient, effective, or economical ways" (p. 71). During the evaluation process, students work in small groups, while highly trained observers use standard observation sheets, pictures, and a video camera to note the students' problem-solving processes and products. Over a 2½-hour period, observers accept all products, give helpful clues when asked, adopt a nonjudgmental attitude, and rotate regularly to minimize bias.

Afterward, observers work as partners to rate the students' strengths on a scale of 1 to 5, from "no strength observed" to "definite strength observed." Students with a superior problem-solver rating are those with definite ratings in two or more activities.

Determining the Nature of Specially Designed Instruction and Services

In addition to measuring intellectual functioning, educators evaluate students' creativity. Because creativity is not a discrete personal trait but occurs through interaction with the sociocultural context (Nakamura & Csikszentmihalyi, 2001), it is difficult to find assessments that bring these interactions together. The Torrance Tests of Creative Thinking are the most frequently used tools for assessing creativity. They focus on the assessment of both words and pictures. *Thinking Creatively with Words* focuses on students' verbal or linguistic creativity from kindergarten through adulthood. Six exercises using words assess the mental characteristics of fluency, flexibility, and originality. *Thinking Creatively with Pictures* evaluates students' figural and spatial creativity from kindergarten through adulthood. Exercises using pictures assess the five mental characteristics of fluency, elaboration, originality, resistance to premature closure, and abstractness of titles. For both tests, a manual is provided for scoring that includes national norms with standard scores and national percentiles by grade and age.

DESIGNING AN APPROPRIATE EDUCATION

Partnering for Special Education and Related Services

Differentiated instruction is an effective strategy for teaching students who are gifted and talented, as well as many students with disabilities, in the general classroom. (See Chapter 9 for more information about differentiated instruction.) **Differentiated instruction** for students who are gifted focuses on implementing instructional approaches that match the strengths and needs of each gifted learner and offer opportunities for individualized responses. A leader in gifted education emphasizes just how important differentiated instruction is:

> Most schools' mission statements proclaim the intention of educating every child to the level of his or her potential, yet many times these words have no translation value for gifted students as they sit bored in classrooms where their instructional level exceeds by years their age-peers'. Thus, there is a real need to consider non-negotiable options for this population, regardless of age or grade considerations, as well as general program organizational approaches employed to effect sound service delivery. (VanTassel-Baska, 2005, p. 90).

Differentiated instruction requires partnerships not only among general education teachers and gifted education specialists, but also with students and families. In Chapter 9, you learned about self-determination instruction for students with intellectual disabilities. Fostering self-determination is also critically important for students who are gifted; it prepares them to advocate for appropriately differentiated instruction. Box 16.2 describes an action research program focused on preparing gifted students to be partners in ensuring differentiated instruction.

IEP Tip

Differentiated instruction is a foundational strategy to ensure high quality educational experiences for students with and without disabilities, not only for children who are gifted. IEP teams should ensure that opportunities exist to differentiate instruction across the curriculum and the school day.

Students as Partners in Differentiating Instruction

A partnership among teachers, students, and families resulted in the implementation of a year-long program to prepare 23 seventh-grade students in a gifted education program to advocate for instructional differentiation that would best match their individual needs. The program consisted of five introductory issue seminars facilitated by the gifted education coordinator. These one-class-period seminars focused on the nature of intelligence (for example, definitions, characteristics, and ways that people of high intelligence may differ from others) and future planning (ways that high intelligence and potential affect planning for high school, college, career, and beyond). Students had opportunities to learn their rights and responsibilities, explore a range of educational options, meet advocates, and explore effective ways to advocate for their own needs. Additionally, some students were in a book club focusing on the book *The Gifted Kids' Survival Guide: A Team Handbook* (Galbraith & Delisle, 1996) and had individual conferences with the seminar leader.

Students and parents were surveyed before and after the self-advocacy program. Students reported:

◆ Having a clearer understanding about their own learning strengths and needs.

◆ Having more knowledge of differentiated instructional options and more interest in participating in a variety of options.

◆ Communicating with their parents more about their special needs.

◆ Feeling more comfortable asking a teacher to modify instruction and talking to teachers about their needs.

Douglas (2004) suggest the following "lessons learned" from this experience:

◆ Remind students of their rights and responsibilities as they engage in problem solving about their instructional program on an ongoing basis.

◆ Using strategies such as casual hallway encounters and informal lunch discussions, remind students on an ongoing basis that the gifted education staff and counselors are available to support them.

◆ Provide information to parents about their advocacy role through newsletter and group meetings and inform classroom teachers about how parents are being encouraged to be advocates.

◆ Ensure that teachers and counselors are responsive when students use their self-advocacy skills to request instructional modifications.

◆ Work with students annually to assess their learning profiles and to compare and contrast results over time.

Source: Douglas, D. (2004). Self-advocacy: Encouraging students to become partners in differentiation. *Roeper Review, 26*(4).

PEARSON
myeducationlab

Go to the Activities and Application section in Chapter 16 of MyEducationLab and complete Activity 3. As you watch the video and answer the accompanying questions, think about how Briana's teachers are accommodating her needs.

Determining Supplementary Aids and Services

One of the most important decisions facing educators is how best to challenge a student in one or more content areas. Educators can achieve this goal through supplementary aids and services that modify the scope and sequence of the curriculum.

The first option is **acceleration**, which involves moving students "more rapidly through the standard sequence" of the curriculum (Gallagher, 2003, p. 17) by having the student move up a grade or skip a course in the normal sequence. That is what Graham does; he is an eighth-grade gifted student who goes to the high school each morning to take honors geometry at the ninth-grade level and then returns to his middle school for the remainder of his educational program. In his school district, many students who are gifted and talented have IEPs; by contrast, other school districts may not use the IEP method to assure an appropriate education for gifted and talented students. Graham's IEP team carefully considers the social effects of acceleration. Graham is mature and fits in fine at the high school, but if a student is physically, emotionally, or socially immature, it may not be in his best interest to be placed in classes with older students. Then the students' teachers need to consider other options.

One way to accelerate students without moving them up a grade or class sequence is to **compact the curriculum**. Compacting involves tests that reveal the aspects of the content that a student has already mastered; the teacher then provides instruction only on that content that the student has not yet mastered (Clark, 2002). Compacting often makes it possible for students to complete a couple of sequenced courses in a single semester (Stamps, 2004).

A variation on acceleration is the "most difficult first" strategy. Instead of doing all problems or activities on a task, the students complete the most difficult tasks (as identified in advance by the teacher). If they get all of the tasks correct, they move on to the next activity or task in the sequence. If they do not, then they complete the entire assignment. This variation allows for curriculum compacting on a day-to-day and lesson-to-lesson basis. Teachers often combine these modifications to the scope and sequence of the curriculum with universal design. Students' IEPs (as in Graham's school district) or their often individualized programs should identify both the modifications and the universal design features.

Planning for Universal Design for Learning

Two strategies that provide curriculum adaptations or augmentations are (1) the use of curriculum extension techniques and (2) the application of cognitive taxonomies to the design of activity, lesson, and unit plans.

Curriculum extension refers to efforts to expand the breadth and depth of coverage of a given topic. Students who are gifted learn content more quickly than their peers do and do not need as much repetition, so their curriculum extension activities should not simply repeat the same task but should challenge them at a higher level.

Teachers take their students to a higher level by using cognitive taxonomies. A taxonomy is an ordered list or classification of something. **Cognitive taxonomies** are ordered lists of cognitive skills or activities that can be used to differentiate expectations for students. The most familiar taxonomy is the one developed by Bloom and associates (1956). Bloom's taxonomy categorizes the cognitive skills that students use when achieving their learning goals. As students ascend Bloom's taxonomy, they face increasingly complex cognitive demands.

Teachers can differentiate what they expect from students by designing lesson and activity objectives that range from less to more complex levels of interaction with materials. They also can extend the curriculum for gifted students by having their students engage in activities that move up the taxonomy from "applying information and knowledge to solve novel problems" to "synthesizing information to create new patterns or structures." These activities will teach students the skills they need to be more creative and to develop effective thinking skills.

IEP Tip

Although a student's teacher will be the person who ultimately develops lesson plans using cognitive taxonomies, planning to use cognitive taxonomies to differentiate instruction begins with the IEP team or its equivalent. Teams can and should consider the design of teaching units and where multilevel lesson planning should be used.

Planning for Other Educational Needs

It is not always easy being gifted. If schools do not plan for and implement practices like differentiated instruction, acceleration, compaction, curriculum extension, and cognitive taxonomies, they can bore their gifted students.

But there is more. As Reis and Renzulli (2004) have noted, "Current press and popular television portray a rather skewed view of gifted and talented youth as the 'dorky' misfit" (p. 119). In fact, though, a study commissioned by the National Association for Gifted Children and the National Research Center on the Gifted and Talented concluded that "high ability students are generally at least as well adjusted as any other group" (Reis & Renzulli, 2004, p. 119).

Even if gifted students do not conform to media stereotypes, there are some aspects of the experience of being gifted that educators should address to ward off potential socioemotional problems. As we have noted, students who are gifted tend to be perfectionists and highly competitive.

Co-teaching typically involves a general and special education teacher working together for the benefit of students with special needs.

Autonomous Learning Model

Like problem-based learning, the autonomous learning model develops independent, self-directed learners who are not just exceptionally smart, but also are well-developed in social, emotional, and cognitive domains. The model features five areas in which students receive support and enrichment experiences:

1. *Orientation:* understanding giftedness, talent, intelligence, and creativity

2. *Individual development:* inter/intrapersonal skills, learning skills, technology, college and career involvement, organizational skills, productivity

3. *Enrichment:* explorations, investigations, cultural activities, service, adventure trips

4. *Seminars:* futuristic, problem-based, controversial, general interest, advanced knowledge

5. *In-depth study:* individual projects, group projects, mentorships, presentations, assessments

The strength of this program lies in its flexibility. As students and teachers work together, roles change and adapt to the experience. The teacher may become the student and the learner may become a facilitator of others' learning. By changing roles, all students develop and appreciate their own strengths and become independent learners.

PEARSON
myeducationlab)

Go to the Activities and Application section in Chapter 16 of MyEducationLab and complete Activity 4. As you watch this video and answer the accompanying questions, consider whether or not this lesson would fit into the autonomous learning model described here.

Their advanced cognitive abilities may make their age-appropriate socioemotional skills seem immature. They are more likely to be highly active, independent, nonconforming, persistent, curious, and self-critical (Clark, 2002).

One response to their needs is the **autonomous learning model** (Betts & Kercher, 1999), which assists students in dealing with the socioemotional issues that might accompany their giftedness. This model is effective for helping elementary through secondary school students explore the socioemotional aspects of being gifted and enabling them to become lifelong learners. Students involved with the autonomous learning model do the following (Clark, 2002):

- Explore what it means to be gifted
- Explore what intelligence and creativity mean
- Explore aspects of their personal/social development
- Consider their strengths and limitations
- Learn organizational skills
- Engage in self-directed study about topics in which they are interested
- Learn the importance of autonomous, lifelong learning

The activities in the autonomous learning model can benefit all students. Uresti, Goertz, and Bernal (2002) found that implementing the model with first-grade Latino children increased their independence and higher-order thinking skills and improved their scores on achievement tests. Box 16.3 outlines the five kinds of activities that comprise this model.

USING EFFECTIVE INSTRUCTIONAL STRATEGIES

Early Childhood Students: Multiple Intelligences

There are few gifted programs for very young children whose giftedness is in its most formative stage. Briana did not receive specialized support until the first grade. Unlike her, some gifted students may lose their capacity for reflection and creative thinking if schools fail to meet their educational needs (Hodge & Kemp, 2000).

Gardner defined intelligence as "the capacity to solve problems or to fashion products that are valued in one or more cultural settings" (Gardner & Hatch, 1989). Look at Figure 16.1, which describes Gardner's eight areas of potential giftedness and lists the typical characteristics and distinctive features common in gifted individuals.

The theory of multiple intelligences has the potential to fundamentally reshape schools. Learning activities can reflect student strengths across the eight areas of potential giftedness. Instead of just presenting information in words through texts or lectures, teachers use physical and social experiences, music, and engagement with the natural world. Sounds a lot like universal design, doesn't it? In fact, in schools incorporating multiple-intelligences theory, there is a "school-community broker," a person who searches for educational opportunities for students within the wider community. In one school in which the school day has been designed within this framework, students spend half of their day at school studying traditional subject areas through project-oriented learning activities and the other half in the community exploring the contexts in which they can apply what they have learned in school (Armstrong, 2006).

Educator Thomas Armstrong, who pioneered the application of Gardner's theory to education, explained it like this: "For whatever you wish to teach, link your instructional objective to words, numbers or logic, pictures, music, the body, social interaction and/or personal experience" (Armstrong, 1994, p. 26).

In Project Spectrum, Gardner and his colleagues applied his model to early childhood and early elementary education settings. Montgomery Knolls Elementary School in Silver Spring, Maryland, has based its early childhood gifted program on the Project Spectrum principles. There, teachers identify and serve different types of giftedness, ensuring that instruction and content correlate with their students' aptitudes, interests, and abilities. The teachers look for different types of giftedness, plan activities specific to these areas, and then provide options for each child. Twice a year, they fill out a strengths checklist for each child.

For instance, during a study of dinosaurs children with a strong spatial orientation wanted to know how big the dinosaurs were. To find out, they projected enlarged pictures onto the school wall to grasp the concept of size. By contrast, children with a linguistic orientation developed seven questions and then e-mailed them to a paleontologist who answered them. Children with artistic talents used papier-mâché to make life-sized features of the dinosaurs, and those with a musical ability wrote and sang songs about dinosaurs.

Elementary and Middle School Students: Schoolwide Enrichment

Because gifted students have unique cognitive and other characteristics and in order to address their students' challenges in motivation, attention, and behavior, good teachers match the content of their courses to students' aptitudes, sophistication, and interests. Often they use enrichment strategies to engage students.

The term *enrichment* refers to curricular and program delivery services (Schiever & Maker, 2003). Enrichment activities include the following (Clark, 2002, p. 264):

◆ Adding instruction on disciplines or learning domains not found within the typical curriculum

◆ Using more challenging or complex material to present content

◆ Using an expanded range of instructional strategies

◆ Teaching critical thinking and problem solving skills

Renzulli and colleagues developed and implemented an enrichment model known as the **schoolwide enrichment model** (Renzulli & Reis, 2003). Its major goal is to promote challenging, high-end learning across a range of school types, levels, and demographic differences by creating services that can be integrated across the general education curriculum to assist all students, not just those who are gifted. Box 16.4 provides more information about this model.

The Blue Valley School District, a suburban district located in Johnson County, Kansas, integrates features of the schoolwide enrichment model and the autonomous

Schoolwide Enrichment

You have already learned about the importance of school-wide application of high-quality educational practices in today's schools. Practices such as universal design for learning, positive behavior supports, response to intervention, and the schoolwide applications model discussed in Chapter 2 all feature a tiered approach to education in which the first tier or phase is the delivery of high quality, evidence-based practices to all students in the school. Similarly, providing support for students who are gifted should begin with schoolwide applications of high quality enrichment activities. That is the goal of the schoolwide enrichment model (Renzulli & Reis, 2003). Three are three types of enrichment approaches within the schoolwide enrichment program.

Type I enrichment exposes students to a wide variety of topics, disciplines, occupations, hobbies, people, places, and events that ordinarily would not be included in the general education curriculum. For example, Type I experiences may involve community speakers, demonstrations, performances, multimedia presentations, or other illustrative formats.

Type II enrichment focuses on resources that promote creative thinking, problem solving, and critical-thinking skills. This kind of enrichment consists of how-to-learn skills, including those for written, oral, and visual communication. Other Type II skills are specific to a students' particular talents and interests.

When a student becomes interested in pursuing a self-selected area of interest and commits the time necessary for this endeavor, Type III enrichment occurs. It consists of

1. Providing opportunities for applying interests
2. Acquiring advanced-level understanding of the content and process used within particular disciplines
3. Developing authentic products
4. Developing self-directed learning skills
5. Empowering the student to control learning through organization and feelings of accomplishment

myeducationlab

Go to the *Building Teaching Skills* section in Chapter 16 of *MyEducationLab*. As you complete the activities, consider how schoolwide enrichment could start on a small level and blossom into the schoolwide program discussed here.

learning model (discussed previously) for students in grades 1 through 6. For example, Lucie Medbery and her colleagues at Heartland Elementary School use this combined approach to address the specific needs of gifted students. Her instruction aims to expand the problem-based experiences that a student can complete individually or share with a group of learners.

A recent example of Lucie's efforts to facilitate group as well as problem-based learning involved simple household refrigerator magnets. "I brought in some refrigerator magnets one day and shared them with the group," she explains. "I asked them to investigate and problem-solve how these magnets are being used or what possible uses there are for magnets." Soon Lucie's highly engaged students were discussing magnetic resonance imaging. Next they researched the technology and its various applications. "It was fascinating to watch and listen to the students move from magnets to magnetic resonance imaging. One student quoted Einstein's statement about the power of observation and related this quote or idea to what they were doing as a group," Lucie notes (personal communication, August, 2002). To learn more, the group sought her help in identifying experts.

Lucie's group is also tracking the progress of a number of turtles with a local marine biologist. The biologist initially visited Lucie's class because he knew that one of her students was fascinated by turtles. That first visit led to others. Instead of simply marveling at the variety of turtles brought in for display, the students decided they wanted to track the turtles' growth and progress. During each visit,

The multiple intelligence theory encourages learning in real environments.

students collect data on the growth of each turtle, changes in its characteristics, and other information; they store that information in a Microsoft Excel document.

Lucie clearly regards herself as a facilitator, creating the appropriate environment for individual or group problem-based learning. She helps her students find research information and introduces technology applications that can help them learn. Lucie explains, "My role is to facilitate the learning experience, presenting problems for them to solve. I also feel it is my responsibility to help these students realize what it is to be gifted. That is why we like the autonomous learning model. It features problem-based learning but also stresses an understanding of what it is to be gifted, the characteristics one has as a gifted child, the issues that tend to come along with this exceptionality, as well as some of the skills one needs to fully develop, for example, time management" (personal communication, August, 2002).

Lucie also uses technology to benefit students, like Graham, who receive enrichment services. One innovative use of technology involves using the Internet to conduct WebQuests. Box 16.5 provides an overview of how to do this.

TECHNOLOGY OUTCOMES

Box 16.5

WebQuests

Today, most schools and many homes have Internet connections. In classrooms all across the United States, teachers and students are integrating the content of web pages into their daily instruction. Doing that is increasingly easy because web applications and resources seem to proliferate overnight. At the same time, educators often feel challenged by the amount of information available and wonder how to apply specific resources as they teach.

What Is the Technology?
A WebQuest is an inquiry-oriented activity in which most or all of the information that students use comes from the web. WebQuests are designed to use students' time well; to focus on using information rather than looking for it; and to support students' thinking at the levels of analysis, synthesis, and evaluation. WebQuests are appealing because they provide structure and guidance for both students and teachers. The ideal of engaging higher-level thinking skills by making good use of limited computer access resonates with many educators.

What Do We Do with It?
A WebQuest allows teachers and students to create activities around web-based resources. Instead of simply using a website, the teacher or student is directed through a quest in how to interact with the site(s), what activity to undertake, and how to evaluate success with the site(s). Follow these steps:

1. Most WebQuests begin with an introduction about the purpose of the quest. For example, students working on a WebQuest pertaining to space exploration might focus on issues such as looking for life on other planets, going on a mission to the moon or Mars, or mapping the course of Halley's comet.

2. Next the teacher assigns a task that focuses students on what they are going to do: specifically, the culminating performance or product that drives all the learning activities. Subsequently, an outline tells the student how he will accomplish the task. Continuing the space exploration theme, tasks might include preparing for a shuttle launch, leading an exploration team to discover which planet might be best for potential human settlement, or heading a design team to place a robot on Mars.

3. The next links in the WebQuest describe the process to be used and the resources available. Using scaffolding (the process of building one skill on top of another up through the skill levels), the student uses clear steps, resources, and tools for organizing information. Process information is provided step by step, so it is easy for students to follow.

4. Each WebQuest includes an evaluation component that enumerates the specific criteria students must meet to satisfy performance and content standards.

5. Finally, the WebQuest conclusion brings closure and encourages the student to reflect on his learning experience.

You can find more about WebQuests at *http://webquest.org/*. The website *http://webquest.sdsu.edu/adapting/* provides helpful suggestions for adapting existing WebQuests for your use. Like other materials, it's important to seek permission to use existing resources like WebQuests. ■■■

Secondary and Transition Students: Promoting Creativity and Critical-Thinking Skills

You have already learned that students who are gifted are highly original, independent, risk-taking, curious, motivated, and attracted to complexity. They are creative and effective critical thinkers. It would be wrong, however, for teachers to assume that students who are gifted are already highly skilled in creativity and critical thinking and do not need instruction in that area. Instead, teachers should focus on enhancing students' innate strengths by honing their creative talents and thinking abilities. According to Davis (2003, p. 319), a teacher can promote creativity by

- Fostering creative attitudes
- Improving student understanding of creativity
- Practicing and exercising creativity
- Teaching critical thinking and creative thinking skills
- Engaging students in creative activities

Developing critical thinking skills involves teaching students to develop more effective problem-solving skills, such as those assessed by the DISCOVER process; to think more productively; and to apply those skills to broader, meaningful problems.

Productive thinking refers to focusing on fluency, flexibility, originality, and elaboration in the thinking process (Feldhusen, 2003). Promoting fluency involves teaching students to consider a lot of ideas in addressing a problem. Flexible thinking refers to considering lots of types of ideas. Promoting originality means teaching students to come up with ideas that are their own. Teaching elaboration skills is teaching students to expand their ideas.

How does one teach these skills? Sometimes it's a matter of teaching students how to optimize their time and talents to achieve better results. Most people think more clearly and perform more effectively at certain times of the day, and teachers can help gifted students identify what tasks to undertake during the more productive times. Teaching strategies focused on developing creativity are less memory-based and have students do more thinking activities, focus their evaluation on big ideas and issues instead of on the microlevel of evaluation (such as handwriting or neatness), develop learning communities that support spontaneity and risk taking, pose provocative questions, and provide explicit models of the steps involved in solving problems and thinking through issues (Clark, 2002).

In many cases, the best way to teach these types of creative thinking is to involve students in some of the many competitions—such as those in math, science, or history. Examples of these competitions include MathCounts, Odyssey of the Mind, and Science Olympiad. These programs are appealing because students can compete with other students who are talented.

IEP Tip

Planning to ensure instruction to promote creativity and critical-thinking skills is just one more example of the need for IEP teams to ensure that instruction to promote self-regulation and executive functioning skills is a part of every student's educational program.

INCLUDING STUDENTS WHO ARE GIFTED AND TALENTED

Within the field of gifted education, there is an ongoing debate regarding student placement. On one hand, IDEA's principle of the least restrictive environment (access to the general curriculum and inclusion) has prompted state and local educational agencies to promote the inclusion of students who are gifted and talented in the normal general education curriculum (Robinson, 2003; Shaunessy, 2003). On the other hand, some leaders within the field of gifted education have expressed grave concern about the lack of curriculum breadth, depth, and specificity in general education classrooms (Pfeiffer, 2003). They have underscored the need to consider a broad range of options:

- **Cluster grouping:** assigning three to six students who are gifted and talented to the same general education classroom so that they can work together.
- **All-school enrichment programs:** addressing the top 20 percent of students in a school through special-interest groups, specialized instruction in small groups, and mentoring on individual projects (Renzulli & Reis, 2003).

◆ **Accelerative method:** starting kindergarten or college early, skipping one or more grades in order to experience higher levels of instruction, and/or attending a higher grade level program for part of the school day. (Schiever & Maker, 2003)

◆ **Magnet schools, charter schools, self-contained classes, special day schools, and residential schools:** drawing students together who are gifted and talented. (Gallagher, 2002; Robinson, 2003)

Box 16.6 provides tips that can be integrated with these practices to enhance success in the general education setting. As you read the tips, bear in mind that you must understand each student's needs in order to achieve the best match between those needs and the curriculum. And remember that inclusion means one thing for students who have disabilities and another for students who are gifted.

Throughout this book, we have driven home the point that special education overenrolls students from racially diverse backgrounds. The one great exception to this general rule relates to gifted education, where there is disproportionate underenrollment of students

Box 16.6	INCLUSION TIPS			
	What You Might See	*What You Might Be Tempted to Do*	*Alternate Responses*	*Ways to Include Peers in the Process*
Behavior	The student asks so many questions that there is time for nothing else.	Tell him to be quiet and pay attention to his work.	Begin a dialogue journal. Ask him to write down his questions. Then research and discuss some of the answers together.	Have an all-class "Challenge Box," where students can write questions they think are difficult. Then enable the students who are gifted to work on these in small groups with their peers.
Social interactions	He is unable to see another person's perspectives.	Avoid calling on him in class in order to avoid potential conflict.	Build on his leadership by giving him responsibility for leading a class discussion of major concepts.	Have him work with small groups, teaching the other students to be discussion facilitators.
Educational performance	He is very bored in class and is refusing to do homework.	Discipline him for inattentiveness or give additional work to reinforce the lesson.	Modify the scope and sequence of the student's curriculum through acceleration to create more challenge.	Explore the possibility of this student attending one or more classes in the next grade.
Classroom attitudes	He is achieving slightly below grade level, but he has unusual talents related to leadership and emotional intelligence.	Assume that he is being academically lazy and give him extra work to try to get him up to grade level.	Recognize his gifts and strengths and work with the school principal to find a school citizenship project for which he can provide leadership.	Identify other students with similar talents and get them involved in a cooperative citizenship project.

Effective Teaching in Gifted Education

In today's multicultural schools, there is no place for teachers who

♦ Expect little of their students from racially diverse backgrounds

♦ Do not understand how to teach them

♦ Treat them unfairly and unequally

♦ Condone racial prejudice among any of their students

There is always a place, however, for teachers who

♦ Expect high academic and behavioral accomplishments from all students, especially those from racially diverse backgrounds (teachers' "deficit perspectives" are the first barrier that gifted students from diverse backgrounds meet)

♦ Are especially motivated to teach students from diverse backgrounds (teachers' motivations shape their practices)

♦ Admit that they themselves may harbor prejudices (teachers' self-knowledge leads to self-reform)

♦ Refuse to judge the students' families as being not interested in their children's education (teachers who don't walk in others' shoes should refrain from evaluating others' worthiness as parents)

♦ Guard against misinterpreting their students' behavior (for example, the oral tradition encourages frank, direct, and honest communication and the use of puns, jokes, and innuendoes, but some teachers may misinterpret it as rudeness, lack of social skills, and lack of intelligence; likewise, verve and movement, also known as tactile and kinesthetic preferences, may be misinterpreted as hyperactivity; and an affective orientation, with easy expression of feelings, may be

misinterpreted as immaturity, irrationality, or low cognitive ability, meaning that teachers' own ignorance compounds teacher prejudice and thwarts their students' gifts and talents)

♦ Work with other committed teachers and administrators to identify gifted students from diverse backgrounds and educate them effectively (a loner tires soon, but a team can endure)

♦ Immediately squelch any forms of prejudice in their classrooms and throughout their schools (intolerance of intolerance can breed tolerance)

♦ Incorporate multicultural and diversity issues into their classes whenever possible, throughout the entire year, not just during special weeks or months that acknowledge different races, cultures, and ethnic heritages (giftedness and diversity are not occasional traits with their own birthdays and anniversaries)

♦ Invite members of racially diverse communities to lead classes, be mentors, and serve as role models (teaching by example is powerful)

♦ Adopt multicultural gifted curriculum materials, such as *Multicultural Gifted Education* by Ford & Harris (1999).

myeducationlab

Go to the Activities and Application section in Chapter 16 of MyEducationLab and complete Activity 5. As you answer the accompanying questions, think about the importance of constantly challenging your students in a culturally responsive manner.

Source: Adapted from Grantham, T. C. (2002). Underrepresentation in gifted education: How did we get here and what needs to change? *Roeper Review, 24*(2), 50–88; Morris, J. E. (2002). African-American students and gifted education: The politics of race and culture, *Roeper Review, 24*(2), 59–62; Harmon, D. (2002). They won't teach me: The voices of gifted African American inner-city students, *Roeper Review 24*(2), 68–80.

from racially diverse backgrounds. In Box 16.7, you will find tips on how teachers can ensure that they do not contribute to that shameful condition.

ASSESSING STUDENTS' PROGRESS

Measuring Students' Progress

Progress in the General Curriculum

After identifying a student as gifted, educators evaluate his progress by measuring performance on goals. In addition, they can place some of the evaluation responsibility on the student himself.

Product evaluation. Teachers commonly base academic assessment of students on written products of students' learning, often one or more tests. The test results help teachers track grades and learning, but they do not provide teachers or students with tools for understanding students' learning processes.

Moreover, some students have both gifts and obvious disabilities; product measures and process measures do not fully address such students' progress. These product and process approaches are appropriate for a student's gifted aspects, but other measures should be based on a student's IDEA-type disability.

Good teachers use product measures not just for grading but also for helping students who are gifted record their own progress and compete with themselves rather than with classmates. In addition, good teachers use product measures to assess the thoroughness of their teaching, looking for areas that need further or different instruction.

Process evaluation. Educators should also evaluate a student's learning process (Andrade, 2000). Process evaluation happens when a teacher attempts to observe and learn from a student's comments or work. Teachers formalize "kid watching" when they take notes on their students' strengths and weaknesses in solving problems and carrying out various learning activities. These notes are good resources during parent-teacher conferences. Likewise, reflective assessment or evaluation involves teaching students to become aware of and monitor the process of their own learning. Figure 16.4 shows how four areas of assessment work together on the student's behalf.

Progress in Addressing Other Educational Needs

One of the objectives of the autonomous learning model that you learned about earlier is to teach students who are gifted to become independent thinkers and autonomous learners. Using learning contracts can be a good way to support this and to help students evaluate their own progress toward their educational goals.

Learning contracts are agreements between a student and his teacher. They describe in detail the outcome of the student's learning, the product(s) that will provide evidence of that outcome, and, if necessary, the criteria for determining whether the products are of acceptable quality. The contracts also specify timelines, resources, and, importantly, reinforcement.

Learning contracts are effective with a wide range of students with disabilities and across many content areas. Their effectiveness derives in part from the fact that learning contracts are individualized and child-centered and promote independence and autonomy (Greenwood, 2003). These contracts are important components in high-quality gifted education programs, just as important as differentiated instruction, multiple intelligences, acceleration, and flexible grouping (Kapusnick & Hauslein, 2001).

Figure 16.4

Four areas of assessment

	Product	Process
Teacher uses	*Written Tests/Projects* • Teacher's grade book • Report card • How student compares	*Kid Watching: Teacher Portfolios* • Teacher's understanding of student • Teacher's instructional planning • Parent conferences
Student uses	*Written Tests/Projects* • Student understanding of what still needs to be learned • Review of material • How student compares to peers in the class	*Reflective Evaluation: Student Portfolios* • Active participation and responsibility in the assessment process • Development of self-monitoring strategies that use higher-order thinking skills

As you know from reading this chapter, students from ethnic and cultural minority populations are underrepresented in programs for gifted and talented students. That does not mean, however, that teachers should assume that general education programs do not offer opportunities for setting high standards for those students and offering them intense, frequently differentiated instruction. You may recall Mike Lamb, a teacher in Chicago's schools, who wrote, in Chapter 3, page 78, that he insists on high standards for his inner-city students, and that many excel beyond their own and their parents' expectations.

Making Accommodations for Assessment

Given that students who are gifted and talented have achieved at high levels and have unusual cognitive abilities, they usually do not need assessment accommodations. That is not true, however, if they also have a disability, such as a learning disability, attention disorder, or physical or sensory disability. Those students may need some of the same accommodations discussed in the chapters about those disabilities.

Although many students who are gifted do not need specific accommodations, they still warrant teachers' special attention. As you have learned, they tend to be very competitive and expect to perform very well. They may feel additional pressure to do well on

MY VOICE   *Box 16.8*

What It Means to Be Gifted

My name is Graham Wehmeyer, I'm in the 9th grade and I have been in the Gifted Education program since 2nd grade. Being in this program has really helped me challenge myself and it has opened me up to a lot of really good ideas and ways of thinking. I believe that every school should have some sort of a Gifted program.

For me personally, being gifted means that I need something more from school than what is taught in the general classroom. I need to be challenged mentally so I can learn. Being in Gifted Education means that I can push myself sometimes, but I can still have fun at the same time. And also, the program is fun, because we get to do a lot of neat projects, and the kids in the program usually have a lot of the same interests as me. I know that if I weren't in the Gifted program, school would be a lot more boring than it already is.

Because I am in the Gifted program, I get a lot of opportunities that other students don't. For example, in 6th grade, I got to test out of 6th grade math, and skip to 7th grade math, along with about twelve other kids. This kept me a lot more interested in the work, and from getting too bored in school. Additionally, I have had many opportunities to investigate careers that I might want to go into, so I am a lot more informed on that subject than most students are at my age. While I am in Gifted Education, I have an IEP, which sets year-long academic goals. These goals help me manage my time, and learn how to set reasonable goals. Another opportunity is that in 8th grade, I got the whole semester to investigate 5 colleges that I might want to got to. It helped me learn a lot more about the colleges I investigated, and about the entire higher education system.

Graham Wehmeyer displays the electronic circuit board he created in his 8th grade curriculum-enrichment program.

Personally, I really appreciate receiving Gifted Education services, because they have made my experience at school a lot better. Additionally, I think that the Gifted teachers, at least the teachers I have had, are really nice, fun, and well qualified for their position. So far, my experience in the program has been an immensely positive one, and I hope that the next 4 years will be too!

—*Graham Wehmeyer*

standardized tests and, as a result, may not perform as well as they could otherwise do. Teachers can help them keep the testing in perspective and reinforce that they should do as well as they can but not push too hard.

Among the standardized tests that gifted students will take are those used for college admission, typically the Scholastic Aptitude Test (SAT) or the American College Test (ACT). Students may feel extreme pressure to succeed on these examinations, particularly if they feel the need to qualify for exclusive colleges and/or scholarships. Whether a test is a state assessment or a college examination, students can learn skills like deep breathing to help them relax and perform well. Basic preparation skills, like pacing out study sessions (instead of cramming all at once) and being well rested before taking a test, are also important. Gifted students will not need as much of the rote practice that often accompanies test preparation in the schools, so teachers should adjust test preparation schedules accordingly (Moon, Brighton, & Callahan, 2003).

VALUES AND OUTCOMES

It is not at all difficult to have great expectations for Briana: admission to a highly selective college or honors program in public university, probably with scholarship aid as an inducement, based on her academic or artistic talents; perhaps admission to a conservatory for dance training. She will have many choices.

Nor is it difficult to identify her positive contributions—academic excellence and performance in dance or even athletics will enhance any college or university that accepts her.

Like many gifted students, Briana has more than one strength; as brightly as her academic strengths shine, they do not overshadow her artistic and athletic exceptionalities. In addition, Briana's modesty is a strength—she is no braggard and is inclined to hide her talents, making it easier for her to have friendships with students not quite as talented as her.

Briana will have many choices about her future—whether to dig deeply into academics or the performance arts, or to balance each against the other for some period of time, not hurrying her adulthood.

The meaning of "full citizenship" for Briana depends in large part on her choices—academics, arts, or both in balance; it is certain that whatever she chooses, she will be fully engaged in her school and community.

WHAT DO YOU THINK?

1. Have you regarded "giftedness" as an academic trait only? When you were in secondary school, were "gifted" students only those who were exceptionally academically superior? Did that seem right or not?

2. What talents do you bring to bear, or want to develop, to educate gifted and talented students? Are you willing to encounter the challenges they will pose? Will you be willing to offer differentiated instruction and various opportunities for them to face challenges peculiar to their special talents?

3. Recognizing that giftedness is a product of a student's natural talents and environment and remembering (from Chapters 1 and 3) that students from diverse ethnic, cultural, and linguistic backgrounds often are disproportionately underrepresented in disability-based special education, what are educators' responsibilities to the families of apparently gifted students who are from diverse backgrounds?

ADDRESSING THE STANDARDS: THE VALUES CONNECTION

The following CEC Knowledge and Skill Standards: Common Core and Values are addressed in this chapter through the content and concepts we discuss.

CEC Knowledge and Skill Standards: Common Core		Values/Standards Connection
CEC Knowledge and Skill Standard II. **Development and Characteristics of Learners**		When you learn about the characteristics of students who are gifted and address the similarities, differences, and varying needs of these students, you are applying CEC Standard 2, Development and Characteristics of Learners.
CC2K1	Typical and atypical human growth and development.	
CC2K2	Educational implications of characteristics of various exceptionalities.	
CC2K4	Family systems and the roles of families supporting development.	
CC2K5	Similarities and differences of individuals with and without exceptional learning needs.	
CC2K6	Similarities and differences of individuals with exceptional learning needs.	
CEC Knowledge and Skill Standard III. **Individual Learning Differences**		Standard 3 suggests differentiated instruction to develop a student's special gifts and *strengths* and create *great expectations*.
CC3K1	Effects that an exceptional condition(s) can have on an individual's life.	
CC3K2	Impact of learner's academic and social abilities, attitudes, interests, and values on instruction and career development.	
CEC Knowledge and Skill Standard IV. **Instructional Strategies**		Using differentiation strategies is one way to address CEC Standard 4, Instructional Strategies. By selecting and adapting strategies and materials, you are adapting for the individual and her *strengths*.
CC4S1	Use strategies to facilitate integration into various settings.	
CC4S2	Teach individuals to use self-assessment, problem-solving, and other cognitive strategies to meet their needs.	Because students who are gifted know what modifications work best for them, teachers should consider giving them a *choice* about how they would like to learn. When students choose how to learn, they often are more successful in their schoolwork.
CC4S3	Select, adapt, and use instructional strategies and materials according to characteristics of the individual with exceptional learning needs.	
CC4S5	Use procedures to increase the individual's self-awareness, self-management, self-control, self-reliance, and self-esteem.	Using the autonomous learning model discussed in this chapter—in regard to teaching self-assessment and problem-solving strategies—reflects CEC Standard 4, Instructional Strategies.

CEC Knowledge and Skill Standards: Common Core	Values/Standards Connection
CEC Knowledge and Skill Standard V. Learning Environments and Social Interactions	Promoting *self-determination* is one aspect of leadership development.
CC5K3 Effective management of teaching and learning.	Restructuring schools to reflect the multiple intelligence model is a concrete way to challenge students to meet and exceed their own, their teachers', and their parents' *great expectations* for them.
CC5K4 Teacher attitudes and behaviors that influence behavior of individuals with exceptional learning needs.	
CC5S4 Design learning environments that encourage active participation in individual and group settings.	
CC5S7 Establish and maintain rapport with individuals with and without exceptional learning needs.	
CC5S9 Create an environment that encourages self-advocacy and increased independence.	
CEC Knowledge and Skill Standard VII. Instructional Planning	Differentiated instruction builds on students' *strengths* by identifying how students learn best and then matching them with appropriate instructional settings and activities.
CC7K2 Scope and sequences of general and special curricula.	
CC7K4 Technology for planning and managing the teaching and learning environment.	
CC7S3 Involve the individual and family in setting instructional goals and monitoring progress.	
CC7S6 Sequence, implement, and evaluate individualized learning objectives.	
CC7S9 Incorporate and implement instructional and assistive technology into the educational program.	
CC7S13 Make responsive adjustments to instruction based on continued observations.	
CEC Knowledge and Skill Standard VIII. Assessment	Finding appropriate assessment instruments for children who are gifted is an application of CEC Standard 8, Assessment.
CC8S2 Administer nonbiased formal and informal assessments.	A non-discriminatory evaluation will identify a student's *strengths* in the several domains of giftedness.
CC8S6 Use assessment information in making eligibility, program, and placement decisions for individuals with exceptional learning needs, including those from culturally and/or linguistically diverse backgrounds.	
CC8S8 Evaluate instruction and monitor progress of individuals with exceptional learning needs.	

SUMMARY

Identifying Students Who Are Gifted and Talented

- Students who are gifted and talented demonstrate unusual capabilities in an intellectual, creative, academic, leadership, or performing and visual arts area. These students require special services not ordinarily provided by the public schools or covered under IDEA.

- Thirty-seven states have a definition of *gifted and talented,* and 27 states have a mandate to provide educational services and supports to students who are gifted and talented.

- The characteristic of gifted and talented students most recognized in schools is high intellectual ability.

- When IQ test scores are equated with giftedness, the top 2 percent to 3 percent of the general population is considered gifted.

- Students from ethnically diverse and poverty backgrounds are underrepresented in current gifted programs.

- Characteristics of students who are gifted include high general intellect, creativity, leadership ability, talents in visual or performing arts, and possible challenges related to behavioral and social characteristics.

- The origin of giftedness is an interaction of environmental and biological factors.

Evaluating Students Who Are Gifted and Talented

- Many gifted educators believe that it is appropriate to expand identification criteria beyond high intellectual ability to ensure cultural appropriateness for students from culturally and linguistically diverse backgrounds.

- DISCOVER is a performance-based, research-reliable, and research-validated assessment for identifying giftedness in students, including those from diverse backgrounds.

- The Torrance Tests of Creative Thinking are a valid and reliable way to assess the strengths and needs of students in the area of creativity.

Designing an Appropriate Education

- Differentiating instruction requires thoughtful planning and partnerships between regular education teachers and specialists in gifted education. Co-teaching is a model of partnerships, and IEP teams or their equivalents should consider what factors would support co-teaching and other needed partnerships.

- Modifications to the scope and sequence of a student's educational program through practices such as acceleration and compacting can ensure that students who are gifted have access to a challenging curriculum.

- Extending the curriculum through the use of cognitive taxonomies can ensure that unit, lesson, and activity objectives are appropriate for the needs of students who are gifted or talented.

- Addressing the socioemotional needs of students who are gifted through activities like the autonomous learning model is a critical feature of a student's IEP to which planning teams must attend.

Using Effective Instructional Strategies

- Gardner's multiple intelligences theory has a direct and significant impact on education. As with universal design, schools that focus on the multiple intelligences can ensure that a wider array of students will succeed, beginning with preschool children.

- The schoolwide enrichment model provides an effective way to implement important instructional strategies across a campus, thus ensuring that students who are gifted can be educated in the general education classroom.

- Even though students who are gifted are already ahead of their peers in many ways, they can still learn important skills related to creativity and critical thinking.

Including Students Who Are Gifted and Talented

- The majority of students who are gifted and talented spend most of their school day in general education classrooms.

- Leaders in gifted education disagree about the appropriateness of the general education classroom curriculum for students who are gifted and talented.

Assessing Students' Progress

- Product and process evaluations and learning contracts are ways in which students who are gifted can be involved in evaluating progress in their educational programs.

Now go to MyEducationLab at www.myeducationlab.com and take the Self-Assessment to gauge your initial comprehension of chapter content. Once you have taken the Self-Assessment, use your individualized Study Plan for Chapter 16 to enhance your understanding of the concepts discussed in the chapter.

Appendix

CEC Knowledge and Skill Standards Common Core

Standard I: Foundations

CC1K1: Models, theories, and philosophies that form the basis for special education practice.

CC1K2: Laws, policies, and ethical principles regarding behavior management, planning, and implementation.

CC1K3: Relationship of special education to the organization and function of educational agencies.

CC1K4: Rights and responsibilities of students, parents, teachers, and other professionals, and schools related to exceptional learning needs.

CC1K5: Issues in definition and identification of individuals with exceptional learning needs, including those from culturally and linguistically diverse backgrounds.

CC1K6: Issues, assurances, and due process rights related to assessment, eligibility, and placement within a continuum of services.

CC1K7: Family systems and the role of families in the educational process.

CC1K8: Historical points of view and contributions of culturally diverse groups.

CC1K9: Impact of the dominant culture on shaping schools and the individuals who study and work in them.

CC1K10: Potential impact of differences in values, languages, and customs that can exist between the home and school.

CC1S1: Articulate personal philosophy of special education.

Standard II: Development and Characteristics of Learners

CC2K1: Typical and atypical human growth and development.

CC2K2: Educational implications of characteristics of various exceptionalities.

CC2K3: Characteristics and effects of the cultural and environmental milieu of the individual with exceptional learning needs and the family.

CC2K4: Family systems and the role of families in supporting development.

CC2K5: Similarities and differences of individuals with and without exceptional learning needs.

CC2K6: Similarities and differences among individuals with exceptional learning needs.

CC2K7: Effects of various medications on individuals with exceptional learning needs.

Standard III: Individual Learning Differences

CC3K1: Effects an exceptional condition(s) can have on an individual's life.

CC3K2: Impact of learner's academic and social abilities, attitudes, interests, and values on instruction and career development.

CC3K3: Variations in beliefs, traditions, and values across and within cultures and their effects on relationships among individuals with exceptional learning needs, family, and schooling.

CC3K4: Cultural perspectives influencing the relationships among families, schools, and communities as related to instruction.

CC3K5: Differing ways of learning of individuals with exceptional learning needs including those from culturally diverse backgrounds and strategies for addressing these differences.

Standard IV: Instructional Strategies

CC4S1:   Use strategies to facilitate integration into various settings.
CC4S2:   Teach individuals to use self-assessment, problem-solving, and other cognitive strategies to meet their needs.
CC4S3:   Select, adapt, and use instructional strategies and materials according to characteristics of the individual with exceptional learning needs.
CC4S4:   Use strategies to facilitate maintenance and generalization of skills across environments.
CC4S5:   Use procedures to increase the individual's self-awareness, self-management, self-control, self-reliance, and self-esteem.
CC4S6:   Use strategies that promote successful transitions for individuals with exceptional learning needs.

Standard V: Learning Environments and Social Interactions

CC5K1:   Demands of learning environments.
CC5K2:   Basic classroom management theories and strategies for individuals with exceptional learning needs.
CC5K3:   Effective management of teaching and learning.
CC5K4:   Teacher attitudes and behaviors that influence behavior of individuals with exceptional learning needs.
CC5K5:   Social skills needed for educational and other environments.
CC5K6:   Strategies for crisis prevention and intervention.
CC5K7:   Strategies for preparing individuals to live harmoniously and productively in a culturally diverse world.
CC5K8:   Ways to create learning environments that allow individuals to retain and appreciate their own and each other's respective language and cultural heritage.
CC5K9:   Ways specific cultures are negatively stereotyped.
CC5K10:   Strategies used by diverse populations to cope with a legacy of former and continuing racism.
CC5S1:   Create a safe, equitable, positive, and supporting learning environment in which diversities are valued.
CC5S2:   Identify realistic expectations for personal and social behavior in various settings.
CC5S3:   Identify supports needed for integration into various program placements.
CC5S4:   Design learning environments that encourage active participation in individual and group settings.
CC5S5:   Modify the learning environment to manage behaviors.
CC5S6:   Use performance data and information from all stakeholders to make or suggest modifications in learning environments.
CC5S7:   Establish and maintain rapport with individuals with and without exceptional learning needs.
CC5S8:   Teach self-advocacy.
CC5S9:   Create an environment that encourages self-advocacy and increased independence.
CC5S10:   Use effective and varied behavior management strategies.
CC5S11:   Use the least intensive behavior management strategy consistent with the needs of the individual with exceptional learning needs.
CC5S12:   Design and manage daily routines.
CC5S13:   Organize, develop, and sustain learning environments that support positive intracultural and intercultural experiences.
CC5S14:   Mediate controversial intercultural issues among students within the learning environment in ways that enhance any culture, group, or person.
CC5S15:   Structure, direct, and support the activities of paraeducators, volunteers, and tutors.
CC5S16:   Use universal precautions.

Standard VI: Language

CC6K1: Effects of cultural and linguistic differences on growth and development.

CC6K2: Characteristics of one's own culture and use of language and the ways in which these can differ from other cultures and uses of languages.

CC6K3: Ways of behaving and communicating among cultures that can lead to misinterpretation and misunderstanding.

CC6K4: Augmentative and assistive communication strategies.

CC6S1: Use strategies to support and enhance communication skills of individuals with exceptional learning needs.

CC6S2: Use communication strategies and resources to facilitate understanding of subject matter for students whose primary language is not the dominant language.

Standard VII: Instructional Planning

CC7K1: Theories and research that form the basis of curriculum development and instructional practice.

CC7K2: Scope and sequences of general and special curricula.

CC7K3: National, state or provincial, and local curricula standards.

CC7K4: Technology for planning and managing the teaching and learning environment.

CC7K5: Roles and responsibilities of the paraeducator related to instruction, intervention, and direct service.

CC7S1: Identify and prioritize areas of the general curriculum and accommodations for individuals with exceptional learning needs.

CC7S2: Develop and implement comprehensive, longitudinal individualized programs in collaboration with team members.

CC7S3: Involve the individual and family in setting instructional goals and monitoring progress.

CC7S4: Use functional assessments to develop intervention plans.

CC7S5: Use task analysis.

CC7S6: Sequence, implement, and evaluate individualized learning objectives.

CC7S7: Integrate affective, social, and life skills with academic curricula.

CC7S8: Develop and select instructional content, resources, and strategies that respond to cultural, linguistic, and gender differences.

CC7S9: Incorporate and implement instructional and assistive technology into the educational program.

CC7S10: Prepare lesson plans.

CC7S11: Prepare and organize materials to implement daily lesson plans.

CC7S12: Use instructional time effectively.

CC7S13: Make responsive adjustments to instruction based on continued observations.

CC7S14: Prepare individuals to exhibit self-enhancing behavior in response to societal attitudes and actions.

Standard VIII: Assessment

CC8K1: Basic terminology used in assessment.

CC8K2: Legal provisions and ethical principles regarding assessment of individuals.

CC8K3: Screening, prereferral, referral, and classification procedures.

CC8K4: Use and limitations of assessment instruments.

CC8K5: National, state or provincial, and local accommodations and modifications.

CC8S1: Gather relevant background information.

CC8S2: Administer nonbiased formal and informal assessments.

CC8S3: Use technology to conduct assessments.

CC8S4: Develop or modify individualized assessment strategies.

CC8S5: Interpret information from formal and informal assessments.

CC8S6: Use assessment information in making eligibility, program, and placement decisions for individuals with exceptional learning needs, including those from culturally and/or linguistically diverse backgrounds.

CC8S7: Report assessment results to all stakeholders using effective communication skills.

CC8S8: Evaluate instruction and monitor progress of individuals with exceptional learning needs.

CC8S9: Develop or modify individualized assessment strategies.

CC8S10: Create and maintain records.

Standard IX: Professional and Ethical Practice

CC9K1:   Personal cultural biases and differences that affect one's teaching.
CC9K2:   Importance of the teacher serving as a model for individuals with exceptional learning needs.
CC9K3:   Continuum of lifelong professional development.
CC9K4:   Methods to remain current regarding research-validated practice.
CC9S1:   Practice within the CEC Code of Ethics and other standards of the profession.
CC9S2:   Uphold high standards of competence and integrity and exercise sound judgment in the practice of the professional.
CC9S3:   Act ethically in advocating for appropriate services.
CC9S4:   Conduct professional activities in compliance with applicable laws and policies.
CC9S5:   Demonstrate commitment to developing the highest education and quality-of-life potential of individuals with exceptional learning needs.
CC9S6:   Demonstrate sensitivity for the culture, language, religion, gender, disability, socioeconomic status, and sexual orientation of individuals.
CC9S7:   Practice within one's skill limit and obtain assistance as needed.
CC9S8:   Use verbal, nonverbal, and written language effectively.
CC9S9:   Conduct self-evaluation of instruction.
CC9S10: Access information on exceptionalities.
CC9S11: Reflect on one's practice to improve instruction and guide professional growth.
CC9S12: Engage in professional activities that benefit individuals with exceptional learning needs, their families, and one's colleagues.

Standard X: Collaboration

CC10K1:   Models and strategies of consultation and collaboration.
CC10K2:   Roles of individuals with exceptional learning needs, families, and school and community personnel in planning of an individualized program.
CC10K3:   Concerns of families of individuals with exceptional learning needs and strategies to help address these concerns.
CC10K4:   Culturally responsive factors that promote effective communication and collaboration with individuals with exceptional learning needs, families, school personnel, and community members.
CC10S1:   Maintain confidential communication about individuals with exceptional learning needs.
CC10S2:   Collaborate with families and others in assessment of individuals with exceptional learning needs.
CC10S3:   Foster respectful and beneficial relationships between families and professionals.
CC10S4:   Assist individuals with exceptional learning needs and their families in becoming active participants in the educational team.
CC10S5:   Plan and conduct collaborative conferences with individuals with exceptional learning needs and their families.
CC10S6:   Collaborate with school personnel and community members in integrating individuals with exceptional learning needs into various settings.
CC10S7:   Use group problem-solving skills to develop, implement, and evaluate collaborative activities.
CC10S8:   Model techniques and coach others in the use of instructional methods and accommodations.
CC10S9:   Communicate with school personnel about the characteristics and needs of individuals with exceptional learning needs.
CC10S10: Communicate effectively with families of individuals with exceptional learning needs from diverse backgrounds.
CC10S11: Observe, evaluate, and provide feedback to paraeducators.

Glossary

Abacus is a tool composed of beads on vertical rods that is used by students with visual impairments to help them with mathematical calculations. The abacus is not a calculator but is similar to solving a math problem with paper and pencil.

Absence seizures are a type of generalized seizure that cause the person to lose consciousness only briefly.

Academic content standards define the knowledge, skills, and understanding that students should attain in academic subjects.

Acceleration involves students' skipping one or more grades in order to experience higher levels of instruction and/or attending a higher-grade-level program for part of the school day.

Acquired refers to hearing losses that occur after birth.

Acquired disorder is a disorder that occurs well after birth.

Acquired injury means that the injury occurred after a child was born.

Activity task analysis identifies each step the student needs to master within ecological activities that are embedded in community-based instruction.

Acuity is a measure of the sharpness and clarity of vision. It is determined by having an individual stand at a specified distance to read a standard eye chart, each line of which is composed of symbols printed at a certain size.

Acute otitis media is an infection in the middle ear that can result in conductive hearing loss.

Adaptive behavior refers to the typical performance of individuals without disabilities in meeting the expectations of their various environments.

Additions occur when students place a vowel between two consonants.

Adventitious visual impairment means that the impairment results from an advent (e.g., loss of sight caused by a hereditary condition that has just manifested itself) or an event (e.g., loss of sight caused by trauma).

All-school enrichment programs address the top 20 percent of students in a school through special-interest groups, specialized instruction, small groups, and mentoring on individual projects.

Alternate achievement standards must align with the same academic content standards for all students so that these students will be able to make progress in the general curriculum.

Alternate assessment means evaluating performance for students for whom test accommodations are not sufficient to enable them to participate in the typical state- or district-wide assessment.

American Sign Language (ASL) is the most widely used sign language among deaf adults in North America.

Anemia is a disorder in which the blood has too few red blood cells or too little hemoglobin.

Anxiety disorder is characterized by overwhelming fear, worry, and/or uneasiness. The condition includes phobia, generalized anxiety disorder, panic disorder, obsessive-compulsive disorder, and post-traumatic stress disorder.

Apgar test is a method for determining the health of a newborn immediately in transition to life outside the womb. The screening occurs in the first minute after birth and again at the fifth minute after birth.

Applied behavior analysis uses the principles of operant psychology to develop techniques that reduce problem behavior and/or increase positive behavior.

Appropriate education is an IDEA principle that requires schools to provide an Individualized Educational Program for students with disabilities that is appropriate to their educational strengths and needs.

Apraxia is a motor speech disorder that affects the way in which a student plans to produce speech.

Aptitude-achievement discrepancy refers to a discrepancy between different abilities and areas of achievement.

Articulation is a speaker's production of individual or sequenced sounds.

Asperger syndrome describes the traits of individuals on the autism spectrum who have significant challenges in social and emotional functioning but without significant delays in language development or intellectual functioning.

Asthma is a chronic lung condition characterized by airway obstruction, inflammation, and increased sensitivity.

Ataxia refers to the inability to coordinate voluntary muscular movements.

Ataxic cerebral palsy involves unsteadiness, lack of coordination and balance, and varying degrees of difficulty with standing and walking.

Athetoid cerebral palsy involves abrupt, involuntary movements of the head, neck, face, and extremities, particularly the upper ones.

Atrophy refers to lost or reduced muscle strength.

Audiogram is a graphic representation of an individual's response to sound in terms of frequency (Hz) and loudness (dB).

Audiologist has special training in testing and measuring hearing.

Audiometer is a machine that measures hearing threshold, the softest level at which sound can first be detected at various sound frequencies.

Audiometry refers to a hearing test, using a device called an audiometer, which provides a graph showing hearing thresholds at various levels of pitch and loudness.

Audition is the hearing process.

Auditory-verbal format encourages early identification and subsequent amplification or cochlear implant. It emphasizes the amplification of sound and helping the child use what hearing remains (residual hearing).

Augmentative and alternative communication (AAC) refers to the devices, techniques, and strategies used by students who are unable to communicate fully through natural speech and/or writing.

Auricle or pinna is the top of the external ear; it channels sound into the ear canal.

Autism spectrum disorder refers to five types of pervasive developmental disorders, including autistic disorder, Rhett's disorder, childhood disintegrative disorder, Asperger syndrome, and pervasive developmental disorder not otherwise specified.

Autonomous learning model assists students in dealing with the socioemotional issues that might accompany their giftedness.

Autosomal chromosomes are all chromosomes other than the X or Y chromosomes that determine gender.

Bacterial meningitis is an infection of the meninges, the three membranes enveloping the brain and the spinal cord.

Behavioral audiological evaluations are hearing tests that require the child to respond to a series of beeps called pure tones to indicate that she hears a sound.

Bidialectal refers to someone who uses two variations of a language.

Bilateral is a hearing loss that occurs in both ears.

Bilingual refers to someone who uses two languages equally well.

Bipolar disorder refers to a condition in which a person experiences exaggerated mood swings—for example, sometimes feeling depressed and other times experiencing heightened activity, energy, and a sense of strength. (These latter experiences are sometimes referred to as *mania*.)

Braille is a method of writing that uses raised dots in specific configurations that can be read and interpreted by people who are blind (and who have received appropriate instruction) by running their fingers across the dots.

Braille contractions are shortcuts for writing letter combinations in braille. Intended to save space and reading time, these contractions may represent a whole word or part of a word. As a result, the braille version of printed material is usually composed of fewer symbols than the print version, even though both include the same words.

Catatonic behavior is behavior that lacks typical movement, activity, and/or expression.

Cerebral palsy refers to a lack of muscle control that affects a student's ability to move and to maintain balance and posture; it has a neurological basis.

Chromosomes direct each cell's activity and contain DNA and genes that determine a person's physical and mental condition.

Circle of friends refers to the individuals who surround a person with a disability with support that is consistent with the person's choices and that advances the person's self-determination, full citizenship, relationships, positive contributions, strengths, and choices.

Classroom-centered intervention refers to classroom-based strategies to intervene against poor academic achievement and aggressive or shy behavior.

Clean intermittent catheterization refers to the procedure whereby a person or an attendant (a trained health aide) inserts a tube into the person's urethra to induce urination. It is "clean" because the procedure is done under sterile conditions, and it is "intermittent" because it is done as needed or on a regular schedule; the tube is not permanently placed in the person's urethra.

Cleft palate or lip describes a condition in which a person has a split in the upper part of the oral cavity or the upper lip.

Closed-captioned technology translates dialogue from a spoken language to a printed form (captions) that is then inserted at the bottom of a television or movie screen.

Closed head injury results when the brain whips back and forth during an accident, causing it to bounce off the inside of the skull. It does not involve penetration or a fracture of the bone of the skull.

Cloze procedure involves the modification of a text of at least 250 words by eliminating every fifth word and replacing it with a blank.

Cluster grouping involves grouping three to six students who are gifted and talented in the same general education classroom so that they can work together.

Cochlea is a snail-shaped bony structure that houses the actual organ of hearing.

Cochlear implant is an electronic device that provides sound information by directly stimulating the functional auditory nerve fibers in the cochlea. The internal part is surgically implanted under the skin with electrodes inserted into the cochlea; the external part consists of a microphone, a speech processor, and a transmitting coil.

Cognitive-behavioral intervention focuses on problem solving and learning to resolve challenges in nonconflicting ways.

Cognitive behavioral therapy involves teaching the use of inner speech ("self-talk") to modify underlying cognitions that affect overt behavior.

Cognitive taxonomies are ordered lists of cognitive skills or activities that can be used to differentiate expectations for students.

Coma is a state of deep or prolonged unconsciousness usually caused by injury or illness.

Compacting the curriculum involves first testing students to identify the content they have already mastered and then teaching them only the concepts that they have not yet mastered.

Conceptually Accurate Signed English (CASE) is a sign system used in the United States that involves signing concepts rather than the literal English translation.

Conduct disorder consists of a persistent pattern of antisocial behavior that significantly interferes with others' rights or with schools and communities' behavioral expectations.

Congenital refers to an impairment that is present from birth or from the time very near birth; visual impairment occurs at birth or, in the case of blindness, before visual memories have been established.

Congenital deafness is a hearing loss that is present at birth.

Congenital disorder is a disorder that occurs at or before birth.

Cued speech is an alternative to natural sign language and English sign systems. Cued speech supplements spoken English and is intended to make its features fully visible.

Cultural deficit theory blames the failure of students from culturally and linguistically diverse backgrounds on the disadvantages that they experienced within their own cultures.

Cultural difference theories also called cultural mismatch theories, contend that failure of students from culturally and linguistically diverse backgrounds in school cannot be attributed solely to their lack of assimilation into European culture.

Cultural reproduction theory holds that "racial and class inequity are reproduced over time through institutional and individual actions and decisions that maintain the status quo at the expense of less privileged groups."

Curriculum-based measurement involves direct assessment of a student's skills in the content of the curriculum that is being taught.

Curriculum extension refers to efforts to expand the breadth and depth of the coverage of a given topic.

Cytomegalovirus (CMV) is a virus that may have very few symptoms in adults or might resemble mononucleosis. In a fetus, however, it can lead to severe malformations.

Deaf is a term used to describe a hearing loss greater than 70 to 90 dB that results in severe oral speech and language delay or that prevents a person from understanding spoken language through hearing.

Deaf community is a group of individuals who are deaf; share a culture, attitudes, and a set of beliefs; and use American Sign Language to communicate.

Decibel (dB) is the unit used to express how loud sound is.

Dialect is a regional variation of a language, as when someone speaks English using terms or pronunciations common only in that region.

Differentiated instruction involves using different strategies such as flexible student instructional grouping, learning stations and learning centers, and two educators in the same classroom.

Discrepancy analysis examines where and how the two **ecological inventories** differ and whether the points of difference can be the basis for instruction or can be addressed through other means, such as assistive technology.

Discrepancy model is the difference between a student's intellectual ability, as measured by an IQ test, and the student's achievement, as measured by a standardized achievement test.

Discrete trial teaching is based on the three-term contigency outlined by applied behavior analysis: the discriminative stimulus, the response, and the reinforcer or consequence.

Discriminative stimulus is a specific event or environmental condition that elicits a desired response. This stimulus "acquires control" over the desired response when the response is paired with a reinforcer.

Distortions are modifications of the production of a phoneme in a word.

Domains of family life include emotional well-being, parenting, family interaction, physical/material well-being, and disability-related support.

Dopamine is one of the brain's neurotransmitters, carrying signals between neurons.

Duration is the length of time any speech sound requires.

Dykinetic cerebral palsy involves impairments in muscle tone affecting the whole body and changing throughout the day and week.

Dyslexia refers to the condition of having severe difficulty in learning to read.

Ear canal is the channel through which sounds flow to the middle ear.

Echolalia is a form of communication in which a student echoes other people's language by constantly repeating a portion of what he or she hears. It is either immediate or delayed.

Ecological inventories identify the subenvironments in which students function, the activities involved in them, and the skills needed in them.

Encephalitis refers to inflammation of the brain.

Errorless learning refers to a procedure that presents the discriminative stimuli and arranges the delivery of prompts in a learning situation in such a way as to ensure that the student gives only correct responses.

Etiology describes the cause or origin of a medical condition.

Eugenics refers to procedures to improve the human race by encouraging the birth of children with allegedly "good" hereditary qualities and discouraging or preventing the birth of those with allegedly "undesirable" hereditary qualities.

Eustachian tube is the structure that extends from the throat into the middle ear cavity; its primary purpose is to equalize the air pressure on the eardrum when a person swallows or yawns.

Event recording involves an observer recording every occurrence of a behavior during an observation period instead of using the yes/no recording per interval that is characteristic of time sampling.

Exclusionary standard refers to embedding particular exemptions within a definition. For example, in the IDEA definition of learning disabilities, learning disabilities do not include learning problems that primarily result from visual impairment; hearing loss; mental retardation; emotional disturbance; or environmental, cultural, or economic disadvantages.

Expanded core curriculum describes the areas of instruction in which students with visual impairments need additional instruction because of the impact of their visual impairment on incidental learning. It includes compensatory skills, orientation and mobility, social interaction skills, independent living skills, recreation and leisure skills, career education, use of assistive technology, visual efficiency skills, and self-determination.

Expressive language disorder is characterized by difficulty in formulating ideas and information.

Externalizing behaviors are behavior disorders comprising aggressive, acting-out, and noncompliant behaviors.

Family means two or more people who regard themselves to be a family and who carry out the functions that families typically perform.

Family-professional partnerships are relationships in which families and professionals collaborate, capitalizing on each other's judgments and expertise in order to increase the benefits of education for students, families, and professionals.

Family quality of life refers to the extent to which the family's needs are met, family members enjoy their life together, and family members have the chance to do the things that are important to them.

Field observation involves observing and recording, in a longhand, anecdotal format, what a student is doing.

Field of vision (visual field) is the entire area of which an individual is visually aware when the person is directing his or her gaze straight ahead, typically 160 degrees.

Fingerspelling uses a hand representation for all 26 letters of the alphabet.

Fluency is the rate and rhythm of speaking.

Formative analysis means that analysis is conducted on an ongoing basis.

Functional behavioral assessment is a process used to determine a specific relationship between a student's behaviors and the circumstances that triggered those behaviors, especially those that impede a student's ability to learn.

Functional disorders are those with no identifiable organic or neurological cause.

Functionally blind describes individuals who can use their available vision to some limited degree but acquire information about the environment primarily through their auditory and tactile senses.

Functional visual assessment (FVA) is an evaluation of how an individual uses his or her vision to perform tasks. It results in a description of what an individual with a visual impairment does with his or her available vision, not an acuity measurement.

General education curriculum refers to the curriculum used by nondisabled students.

Generalization refers to the ability to transfer knowledge or behavior learned for doing one task to another task and to make that transfer across different settings or environments.

Generalized anxiety disorder consists of excessive, overwhelming worry not caused by any recent experience.

Genetic deficit theories typically support the notion that nonwhite people are genetically deficient when compared to white people.

Genome is the genetic material that constitutes the human body's DNA.

Goal attainment scaling is a process that enables teachers to compare goals and to quantify student goal attainment.

Hard of hearing is a term used for individuals who have hearing loss of 25 to 70 dB in the better ear, who benefit from amplification, and who communicate primarily through spoken language.

Herpes virus is a virus leading to symptoms that range from cold sores, to genital lesions, to encephalitis; it causes disabilities in early infancy.

Hertz (Hz) is the unit used to express the frequency of sound and is measured in terms of the number of cycles that vibrating sound molecules complete per second.

Hyperactivity refers to behaviors associated with frequent movement, difficulty concentrating, and talking excessively.

Hyperbilirubinemia results from an excess accumulation of bilirubin in the blood, which can result in jaundice: a yellowing of the complexion and the whites of the eyes.

Hypernasality is when air is allowed to pass through the nasal cavity on sounds other than /m/, /n/, and /ng/.

Hyponasality occurs because air cannot pass through the nose and comes through the mouth instead.

Hypoxia is the lack of oxygen.

Impulsivity refers to behaviors such as difficulty awaiting one's turn, interrupting or intruding on others, and blurting out answers before questions have been completed.

Incidental learning occurs when an individual learns about a process or concept primarily through observation and without others knowingly providing instruction.

Inclusionary standard refers to embedding certain criteria within a definition so as to clearly state the conditions that the definition covers. For example, in the IDEA definition of learning disabilities, perceptual disabilities, brain injury, minimal brain dysfunction, dyslexia, and developmental aphasia are included conditions.

Individualized Education Program (IEP) is a written plan for serving students with disabilities ages 3 through 21.

Individualized Family Services Plan (IFSP) is a written plan for providing services to infants and toddlers, ages zero to 3, and their families.

Intensity (loudness or softness) is based on the perception of the listener and is determined by the air pressure coming from the lungs through the vocal folds.

Internalizing behaviors are behavior disorders comprising social withdrawal, depression, anxiety, obsessions, and compulsions.

Interpreter is an individual who translates a spoken message into sign. Oral interpreters silently repeat with clear lip movements the message of the speaker. A transliterator provides word-for-word translation using signs in English word order.

Intra-achievement discrepancy refers to a discrepancy between different areas of academic achievement.

Intracognitive discrepancy refers to discrepancies between different abilities such as performance and verbal scores.

Intracranial hemorrhage is a neurological complication of extremely premature infants in which the immature blood vessels bleed into the brain.

Jaundice is a yellowing of the complexion and the whites of the eyes resulting from hyperbilirubinemia.

Keyword strategies teach students to link a keyword to a new word or concept to help them remember the new material.

Kinship care refers to the situation where children receive their basic care from some member of their family other than their parents.

Language is a structured, shared, rule-governed symbolic system for communicating.

Language disorder is difficulty in receiving, understanding, and formulating ideas and information.

Learning media assessment (LMA) is an evaluation of students who have visual impairments to determine the learning medium in which they function most efficiently as well as to identify those media in which additional instruction may be necessary.

Learning medium is the term used to describe the format(s) of reading and literacy materials available to individuals who have visual impairments and may include braille, print, large print, audiotapes, and access technology.

Learning strategies help students with learning disabilities to learn independently and to generalize, or transfer, their skills and behaviors to new situations.

Least restrictive environment (LRE) is an IDEA principle that requires that students with disabilities be educated to the maximum extent appropriate with students who do not have a disability and that they be removed from regular education settings only when the nature or severity of their disability cannot be addressed with the use of supplementary aids and services.

Legal blindness is a term that refers to individuals whose central visual acuity, when measured in both eyes and when they are wearing corrective lenses, is 20/200 or whose visual field is no more than 20 degrees.

Letter strategies employ acronyms or a string of letters to remember a list of words or concepts.

Life space analysis is a process in which teachers collect two kinds of data: first, baseline data about how well a student functions in certain community settings; next, information about the student's current environments and prospective environments for community-based instruction.

Long-term memory involves storing information permanently for later recall.

Loop systems involve closed-circuit wiring that sends FM signals from an audio system directly to an electronic coil in a student's hearing aid. The receiver picks up the signals, much as a remote-control device sends infrared signals to a television.

Low vision   is experienced by individuals with a visual impairment who can use their vision as a primary channel for learning.

Low vision specialist   is an individual, usually an optometrist, who has specialized in the measurement of the basic visual skills of individuals with low vision and who is knowledgeable about and prescribes glasses and other assistive devices that facilitate visual functioning in people whose vision is impaired.

Manifestation determination   is used when disciplining students who receive special education. The school must determine whether the student's behavior is a manifestation "caused by" his or her disability. This process must occur when the school proposes to change the student's placement for more than 10 days.

Manual approach   involves teaching the use of sign language for communication.

MAPs   is a process that customizes students' educational programs to their specific visions, strengths, and needs. It is especially effective in planning transitions from school to postschool activities.

Maternal Rh incompatibility   is a condition that occurs when a baby with Rh+ blood is born to a mother with Rh− blood. This leads to a breakdown of red blood cells in the baby.

Maternal serum alpha-fetoprotein   is a prenatal test to detect spina bifida.

Mean   refers to an average.

Meningocele   refers to the condition in which the covering of the spinal cord, but not the cord itself, protrudes through the opening created by the defect in the spine. This condition usually does not cause a person to experience mobility impairments.

Mixed cerebral palsy   combines spastic muscle tone and the involuntary movements of athetoid cerebral palsy.

Mnemonic   is a device such as a rhyme, formula, or acronym that is used to aid memory.

Mood disorder   involves an extreme deviation in either a depressed or an elevated direction or sometimes in both directions at different times.

Morpheme   is the smallest meaningful unit of speech.

Morphology   is the system that governs the structure of words.

Multidimensional model of intelligence   considers multiple domains of intelligence as contrasted to only intellectual ability or academic achievement.

Multimodal treatments   involves multiple interventions or treatments across modes or types of therapies.

Myelomeningocele   refers to a condition in which the protrusion or sac contains not only the spinal cord's covering but also a portion of the spinal cord or nerve roots. This condition results in varying degrees of leg weakness, inability to control bowels or bladder, and a variety of physical problems such as dislocated hips or club feet.

Neural tube defects   a large group of malformations associated with the spinal cord, brain, and vertebrae.

Neuroimaging   provides noninvasive detailed pictures of various parts of the brain that are helpful in determining the presence of a disability.

Neurotransmitters   are substances that transmit nerve impulses across synapses in the brain.

No cessation   is a term that refers to the discipline of students under IDEA and means that the school may not expel or suspend a student with a disability for more than 10 school days in any one school year, regardless of what the student does to violate a school code.

Nondiscriminatory evaluation   is an IDEA principle that requires schools to determine what each student's disability is and how it relates to the student's education. The evaluation must be carried out in a culturally responsive way.

Norm group   is a comparison group usually representing an average standard of achievement or development for a specific age group or grade level.

Norm-referenced   achievement test compares a student with his or her age- or grade-level peers in terms of performance.

Obsessions   are persistent thoughts, impulses, or images of a repetitive nature that create anxiety.

Obsessive-compulsive disorder   are obsessions manifesting as repetitive, persistent, and intrusive impulses, images, or thoughts (i.e., repetitive thoughts about death or illness) and/or compulsions manifesting as repetitive, stereotypical behaviors (i.e., handwashing or counting).

Omissions   occur when a child leaves a phoneme out of a word.

Open head injury   penetrates the bones of the skull, allowing bacteria to have contact with the brain and potentially impairing specific functions, usually only those controlled by the injured part of the brain.

Oppositional defiant disorder   causes a pattern of negativistic, hostile, disobedient, and defiant behaviors.

Oral/aural format   emphasizes the use of amplified sound to develop oral language.

Oral motor exam   is examination of the appearance, strength, and range of motion of the lips, tongue, palate, teeth, and jaw.

Organic disorders   are those caused by an identifiable problem in the neuromuscular mechanism of the person.

Organ of Corti   refers to the organ of hearing.

Orientation and mobility (O&M)   is a term used to describe the two components of travel: orientation (knowing where you are and where you want to go) and mobility (the safe, efficient, graceful movement between two locations). For students with visual impairments, instruction in O&M often is necessary.

Ossicular chain consists of the three small bones in the middle ear (**malleus, incus,** and **stapes**—hammer, anvil, and stirrup) that transmit the sound vibrations through the middle-ear cavity to the inner ear.

Otologist is a physician who specializes in diseases of the ear.

Ototoxic drugs affect the organs or nerves involved in hearing or balance.

Outer-directedness is a condition in which individuals distrust their own solutions and seek cues from others.

Oval window is the membrane that separates the middle from the inner ear.

Panic disorder involves overwhelming panic attacks resulting in rapid heartbeat, dizziness, and/or other physical symptoms.

Part B refers to the section of IDEA that addresses the social education of students who range from 3 through 21 years of age.

Part C represents the section of IDEA that addresses the needs of infants and toddlers ranging in age from birth through age 2.

Partial participation rejects an all-or-none approach under which students either function independently in a given environment or not at all. Instead, it asserts that students with severe and multiple disabilities can participate, even if only partially, and indeed can often learn and complete a task if it is adapted to their strengths.

Partial seizures cause the student to lose consciousness and often to fall to the ground and have sudden, involuntary contractions of groups of muscles.

Partnership is a relationship in which families and professionals collaborate with each other by capitalizing on each other's judgment and expertise in order to increase benefits for students, families, and professionals alike.

Peer tutoring involves pairing students one on one so that students who have already developed certain skills can help teach those and other skills to less advanced students and also help those students practice the skills they have already mastered.

Pegword strategy helps students remember numbered or ordered information by linking words that rhyme with numbers.

Perinatal means at birth.

Pervasive developmental disorders include five discrete disorders that are part of the autism spectrum, including autistic disorder, Rhett's disorder, childhood disintegrative disorder, and Asperger syndrome.

Phobia consists of the unrealistic, overwhelming fear of an object or situation.

Phonemes are individual speech sounds and how they are produced, depending on their placement in a syllable or word.

Phonological processing refers to the ability to process written and oral information by using the sound system of language.

Phonology is the use of sounds to make meaningful syllables and words.

Pidgin Sign English (PSE) is a sign system used in the United States and employs a basic ASL sign vocabulary in English word order.

Pitch is affected by the tension and size of the vocal folds, the health of the larynx, and the location of the larynx.

Pneumatic, or puffing, switches operate when the student, such as one who has no arm control, puffs air into a strawlike tube.

Portfolio-based assessment is a technique for assembling exemplars of a student's work, such as homework, in-class tests, artwork, journal writing, and other evidence of the student's strengths and needs.

Positive behavior support is a proactive, data-based approach to ensuring that students acquire needed skills and environmental supports.

Postnatal means after birth.

Post-traumatic stress disorder refers to flashbacks and other recurrent symptoms following exposure to an extremely distressing and dangerous event such as witnessing violence or a hurricane.

Pragmatics refers to the use of communication in context.

Prelinguistic milieu teaching is an effective language-acquisition instructional strategy based on the principle that children will learn if their instruction matches their interests and abilities.

Prenatal means before birth.

Prereferral occurs when a student's general education teacher asks others (educators and families) to help problem-solve in order to identify instructional strategies to adequately address learning and behavioral challenges.

Procedural due process is the principle of IDEA that seeks to make the schools and parents accountable to each other through a system of checks and balances.

Procedural problems in math refer to difficulty in sequencing the steps of complex problems.

Prodigy is a person who is gifted to the point of being unmistakably extraordinary.

Receptive language disorder is characterized by difficulty in receiving or understanding information.

Referral occurs when an educator or a parent submits a formal request for the student to be considered for a full and formal nondiscriminatory evaluation.

Reinforcing stimulus is an event or action that follows the response and increases the possibility that the response will be exhibited again.

Repetitive behavior involves obsessions, tics, and perseveration.

Resonance is determined by the way in which the tone coming from the vocal folds is modified by the spaces of the throat, mouth, and nose.

Response is the behavior a student performs when presented with a discriminative stimulus. The response is the behavior you are trying to teach the child.

Response-to-intervention model refers to procedures for providing generally effective instruction to students, monitoring their progress, and assessing the extent to which students make sufficient progress in response to their instruction.

Reverse-role tutoring refers to using students with disabilities as tutors for their peers without disabilities.

RhoGAM is a drug used for mothers who have Rh− blood to keep them from producing antibodies that could harm their future babies.

Risk ratios compare the proportion of a specific racial/ethnic group receiving special education services to the proportion among the total combined other racial/ethnic groups receiving special education.

Rubella is a viral infection, also called German measles, that causes a mild fever and skin rash. If a woman in the first 3 months of her pregnancy gets this disease, it can lead to severe birth defects in her child.

Savant syndrome is a condition in which individuals typically display extraordinary abilities in areas such as calendar calculating, musical ability, mathematical skills, memorization, and mechanical abilities.

Schizophrenia is characterized by psychotic periods resulting in hallucinations, delusions, inability to experience pleasure, and loss of contact with reality.

Schoolwide enrichment model promotes challenging, high-end learning across a range of school types, levels, and demographic differences by creating services that can be integrated across the general curriculum to assist all students, not just students who are gifted.

Schoolwide positive behavior support (SWPBS) is a systems-level and evidence-based method for improving valued social and learning outcomes for all students.

Screening is a routine test that helps school staff identify which students might need further testing to determine whether they qualify for special education.

Seeing Essential English, Signing Exact English (SEE2) is a sign system used in the United States that borrows sign from ASI and then adds signs that correspond to English morphemes.

Seizures are temporary neurological abnormalities that result from unregulated electrical discharges in the brain, much like an electrical storm.

Self-determination refers to the ability of individuals to live their lives as they choose, consistent with their own values, preferences, and abilities.

Self-instruction strategies involve teaching students to use their own verbal or other communication skills to direct their own learning.

Self-monitoring strategies enable students to learn to collect data on their progress toward educational goals. They can do this through various formats, such as by charting their progress on a sheet of graph paper or completing a checklist.

Semantic memory problems in math refer to difficulty in remembering math facts.

Semantics refers to the meaning of what is expressed.

Separation anxiety disorder is excessive and intense fear associated with separating from home, family, and others with whom a child has a close attachment.

Service learning is a method for students to develop newly acquired skills by active participation and structured reflection in organized opportunities to meet community needs.

Shaken baby syndrome refers to a brain injury resulting from a situation in which a caregiver has shaken a child violently, often because the caregiver is frustrated by the child's crying.

Short-term memory is the mental ability to recall information that has been stored for a few seconds to a few hours.

Sign language uses combinations of hand movements to convey words and concepts rather than individual letters.

Skilled dialogue is a strategy that involves **anchored understanding** (having a compassionate understanding of differences that comes from truly getting to know someone) and **third space** (a situation in which people creatively restate each other's diverse perspectives in order to reach a new perspective without abandoning individual points of view).

Slate and stylus is a tool used by people who are blind to write short notes to themselves. It consists of a slate, a hinged metal template, and a stylus (a small awl) that is used to punch the dots of a message in braille on a piece of paper inserted in the slate.

Social interaction theories emphasize that communication skills are learned through social interactions.

Social stories are written by educators, parents, or students and describe social situations, social cues, and appropriate responses to those cues.

Sound-field amplification system enables the teacher to transmit her voice by using a lavaliere microphone and ceiling- or wall-mounted speakers.

Spastic cerebral palsy involves tightness in one or more muscle groups.

Specially designed instruction refers to adaptations of the content, methodology, or delivery of instruction to address a student's unique needs and ensure that the student can participate and make progress in the general curriculum.

Specific language impairment describes a language disorder with no identifiable cause in a person with apparently normal development in all other areas.

Specific learning disability means a disorder in one or more of the basic psychological processes involved in understanding or using spoken or written language.

Speech is the oral expression of language. The disorder may manifest itself in an imperfect ability to listen, think, speak, read, write, spell, or do mathematical calculations.

Speech disorder refers to difficulty in producing sounds as well as disorders of voice quality (for example, a hoarse voice) or fluency of speech, often referred to as stuttering.

Speech reader is someone who is able to interpret words by watching the speaker's lips and facial movements without hearing the speaker's voice.

Spina bifida is a condition in which the person's vertebral arches (the connective tissue between one vertebra and another) are not completely closed; the person's spine is split—thus, spina (spine) bifida (split). Spina bifida is the most common form of neural tube defect.

Spina bifida occulta refers to a condition in which the spinal cord or its covering do not protrude and only a small portion of the vertebra, usually in the lower spine, is missing. This is the mildest and most common form of spina bifida.

Standard deviation is a way to determine how much a particular score differs from the mean (average).

Standards-based reform is a process that identifies the academic content (reading, mathematics) that students must master, the standards for the students' achievement of content proficiency, a general curriculum aligned with these standards, assessment of student progress in meeting the general curriculum and standards, and information from the assessments to improve teaching and learning and to demonstrate that the schools are indeed accountable to the students, their families, and the public.

Student achievement standards define the levels of achievement that students must meet to demonstrate their proficiency in the subjects.

Student-directed learning strategies teach students with and without disabilities to modify and regulate their own learning.

Substitutions occur when a person substitutes one sound for another, as when a child substitutes /d/ for the voiced /th/ ("doze" for "those"), /t/ for /k/ ("tat" for "cat"), or /w/ for /r/ ("wabbit" for "rabbit").

Summative evaluation is an evaluation that occurs after a product or project is completed.

Supplementary aids and services are aids, services, and other supports provided in general education classes or other education-related settings to enable children with disabilities to be educated with nondisabled children to the maximum extent appropriate.

Supports are the services, resources, and personal assistance that enable a person to develop, learn, and live effectively.

Syndrome is a collection of two or more features that result from a single cause.

Syntax provides rules for putting together a series of words to form sentences.

Syphilis is a sexually transmitted disease that can cause an intrauterine infection in a pregnant woman and result in severe birth defects in her child.

System for Augmenting Language (SAL) focuses on augmented input of language.

T-Charts are charts that are laid out in the form of a capital letter T; they allow teachers to track two aspects of a behavior together.

Temperament refers to behavioral tendencies that are biologically based.

Theory of mind is an explanation of the delayed social development that suggests that individuals with autism do not understand that their own beliefs, desires, and intentions may differ from those of others.

Time sampling involves an observer who is recording the occurrence or nonoccurrence of specific behaviors during short, predetermined intervals.

Tonic-clonic seizures affect a student's motor control area of the brain, as well as sensory, behavioral, and cognitive areas. Tonic-clonic seizures can either occur in only one region of the brain or spread to other brain hemispheres.

Tonotopically means that the hair cells closest to the ear's oval window respond to high-frequency sounds and those at the center (if the cochlea were unrolled) are more sensitive to low-frequency sounds.

Totally blind describes those individuals who do not receive meaningful input through the visual sense.

Toxoplasmosis is an infectious disease caused by a microorganism that can cause severe fetal malformations.

Transition services focus on planning educational services and supports for students who are moving from one level of education to another, such as from high school to postsecondary services.

Traumatic brain injury is caused by an external physical force, resulting in impaired functioning in one or more areas. Educational performance is adversely affected. The injury may be open or closed.

Tunnel vision occurs when an individual's visual field is reduced significantly so that only a small area of central visual acuity remains. The affected individual has the impression of looking through a tunnel or tube and is unaware of objects to the left, right, top, or bottom.

Tympanography is not a hearing test but a test of how well the middle ear is functioning and how well the eardrum can move.

Unilateral is hearing loss in one ear only.

Universal design for learning (UDL) is the application of principles to the design of curricular and instructional materials to provide students across a wide range of abilities and from a variety of backgrounds with access to academic content.

Vestibular mechanism (semicircular canals) controls balance, helps a body maintain its equilibrium, and is sensitive to both motion and gravity.

Visual disability (including blindness) is an impairment in vision that, even with correction, adversely affects a child's educational performance. The term includes both partial sight and blindness.

Visual-spatial problems in math refer to difficulties in reproducing numerals.

Working memory refers to how students process information in order to remember it.

Wraparound refers to a philosophy of care that includes a definable planning process involving the child and family that results in a unique set of community services and natural supports individualized for that child and family to achieve a positive set of outcomes.

Zero reject is an IDEA principle that requires schools to enroll all students who have disabilities.

References

Chapter 1

Bahr, M. W., Fuchs, D., & Fuchs, L. S. (1999). Mainstream assistance teams: A consultation-based approach to prereferral intervention. In S. Graham & K. Harris (Eds.), *Teachers working together: Enhancing the performance of students with special needs* (pp. 87–116). Cambridge, MA: Brookline.

Bahr, M. W., Whitten, E., Dieker, L., Kocarek, C. E., & Manson, D. (1999). A comparison of school-based teams: Implications for educational and legal reform. *Teaching Exceptional Children 66*(1), 67–83.

Boe, E. E., & Cook, L. H. (2006). The chronic and increasing shortage of fully certified teachers in special education and general education. *Exceptional Children, 72*(4), 443–460.

Brown v. Board of Education. 347 U.S. 483. (1954).

Bush, G. W. (2001a). *Foreword: No Child Left Behind.* Retrieved June 5, 2008, from http://www.whitehouse.gov/news/reports/no-child-left-behind.html

Bush, G. W. (2001b). *Overview: No Child Left Behind.* Retrieved June 5, 2008, from http://www.ed.gov/nclb/overview/intro/presidentplan/page_pg3.html

Carlson, E., Brauen, M., Klein, S., Schroll, K., & Willig, S. (2002). *Key findings for SPeNSE* (http://ferdig.coe.ufl.edu/spense).

Chambers, J. G., Shkolnik, J., & Pérez, M. (2003). *Total expenditures for students with disabilities, 1999–2000: Spending variation by disability.* Palo Alto, CA: Center for Special Education Finance/American Institutes for Research.

Donne, J. (1986). *Devotions upon emergent occasions.* In M. H. Abrams (Ed.), *The Norton Anthology of English Literature* (Mediation 17, pp. 1107–1108). New York: Norton. (Original work published 1624)

Goffman, E. (1963). *Behavior in public places: Notes on the social organization of gatherings.* Glencoe, IL: Free Press.

Huber, J., & Jones, G. (2003). Renovating to meet ADA standards. *School Planning and Management, 42*(2), 62–63.

Kemp, C. E., Hourcade, J. J., & Parette, H. P. (2000). Building an initial information base: Assistive technology funding resources for school-aged students with disabilities. *Journal of Special Education Technology, 15*(4), 15–24.

Lahm, E. A., Bausch, M. E., Hasselbring, T. S., & Blackhurst, A. E. (2001). National Assistive Technology Research Institute. *Journal of Special Education Technology, 16*(3), 19–26.

Lapadat, J. C. (1998). Implicit theories and stigmatizing labels. *Journal of College Reading and Learning, 29*(1), 73.

Mills v. Washington, DC, Board of Education. 348 F. Supp 866 (D.DC 1972); contempt proceedings, EHLR 551: 643 (D.DC 1980).

Moore-Brown, B. J., Montgomery, J. K., Bielinsky, J., & Shubin, J. (2005). Responsiveness to intervention: Teaching before testing helps avoid labeling. *Topics in Language Disorders, 25*(2), 148–168.

National Association for Gifted Children. (2007). State of the states in gifted education: 2006–2007. Washington, DC: Author.

National Council on Disability. (2000). *Federal policy barriers to assistive technology.* Washington, DC: Author.

National Organization on Disability. (2004). *N.O.D./Harris survey of Americans with disabilities.* (Study No. 20839). New York: Harris Interactive.

Parrish, T., Harr, J., Wolman, J., Anthony, J., Merickel, A., & Esra, P. (2004). *State special education finance systems, 1999–2000: Part 2: Special education revenues and expenditures.* Palo Alto, CA: Center for Special Education Finance/American Institutes for Research.

Pennsylvania Association for Retarded Children (PARC) v. Commonwealth of Pennsylvania. 334 F. Supp. 1257, 343 F. Supp. 279 (1971, 1972).

Perner, D. E. (2007). No Child Left Behind: Issues of assessing students with the most significant cognitive disabilities. *Education and Training in Developmental Disabilities, 43*(3), 243–251.

Rea, P. J., & Davis-Dorsey, J. (2004). ADA in the public school setting: Practitioners' reflections. *Journal of Disability Policy Studies, 15*(2), 66–69.

Schaffer v. Weast, 126 S. Ct. 528 (2005).

Smith, P. (1999). Drawing new maps: A radical cartography of developmental disabilities. *Review of Educational Research, 69*(2), 117–145.

Turnbull, H. R., Stowe, M. J., & Huerta, N. E. (2007). *Free appropriate public education* (7th ed., revised printing). Denver: Love.

Turnbull, A. P., Turnbull, H. R., Erwin, E., & Soodak, L. (2006). *Families, professionals, and exceptionality: Positive outcomes through partnerships and trust* (5th ed.). Upper Saddle River, NJ: Merrill/Pearson.

U.S. Department of Education. (2006a). *Office for Civil Rights, OCR elementary and secondary school survey: 2002.* Retrieved January 10, 2008, from http://nces.ed.gov/programs/digest/d06/tables/dt06_051.asp?referrer=list

U.S. Department of Education. (2006b). *The 26th annual report to Congress on the implementation of the Individuals with Disabilities Education Act, 2004,* Vol. 1. Washington, DC: Author.

U.S. Department of Education. (2007a). *State and local implementation of the No Child Left Behind Act, Vol. II: Teacher quality under NCLB: Interim report.* Retrieved January 18, 2008, from http://www.ed.gov/rschstat/eval/teaching/nclb/report07.pdf

U.S. Department of Education. (2007b). *The 26th annual report to Congress on the implementation of the Individuals with Disabilities Education Act, 2004,* Vol. 1. Washington, DC: Author.

U.S. Department of Education Office of Special Education Programs. (2008). *Individuals with Disabilities Education Act (IDEA) data.* Retrieved January 18, 2008, from https://www.IDEAdata.org/index.html

Wakeman, S. Y., Browder, D. M., Meier, I., & McColl, A. (2007). The implications of No Child Left Behind for students with developmental disabilities. *Mental Retardation and Development Disabilities Research Reviews, 13,* 143–150.

Wall, P. S., & Sarver, L. (2003). Disabled student access in an era of technology. *Internet and Higher Education, 6*(3), 277–284.

Yell, M. L., Drasgow, E., & Lowrey, K. A. (2005). No Child Left Behind and students with autism spectrum disorders. *Focus on Autism and Other Developmental Disabilities, 20*(3), 130–139.

Yell, M. L., Shriner, J. G., & Katsiyannis, A. (2006). Individuals with Disabilities Education Improvement Act of 2004 and IDEA regulations of 2006: Implications for educators, administrators, and teacher trainers. *Focus on Exceptional Children, 39*(1), 1–24.

Chapter 2

Agran, M., Alper, S., & Wehmeyer, M. (2002). Access to the general curriculum for students with significant disabilities: What it means to teachers. *Education and Training in Mental Retardation and Developmental Disabilities, 37*(2), 123–133.

Andrews, J. E., Carnine, D. W., Continho, M. J., Edgar, E. B., Forness, S. R., Fuchs, L. S., et al. (2000). Bridging the special education divide. *Remedial and Special Education, 21*(5), 258–260, 267.

Bambara, L. M., & Kern, L. (2005). *Individualized supports for students with problem behaviors: Designing positive behavior plans.* New York: Guilford Press.

Bolt, S. E., & Thurlow, M. (2004). Five of the most frequently allowed testing accommodations in state policy. *Remedial and Special Education, 25,* 141–152.

Browder, D. M., Spooner, F., Algrim-Delzell, L., Flowers, C., Algozzine, R., & Karvonen, M. (2004). A content analysis of the curricular philosophies reflected in states' alternate assessments. *Research and Practice for Persons with Severe Disabilities, 28,* 105–131.

Brown, L., Udvari-Solner, A., Frattura-Kampschroer, E., Davis, L., Ahlgren, C., Van Daventer, P., & Jorgensen, J. (1991). Integrated work: A rejection of segregated enclaves and mobile work crews. In L. H. Meyer, C. A. Peck, & L. Brown (Eds.), *Critical issues in the lives of people with severe disabilities* (pp. 219–228). Baltimore: Brookes.

Bruns, D. A., & Mogharreban, C. C. (2007). The gap between beliefs and practices. Early childhood practitioners' perceptions about inclusion. *Journal on Research in Childhood Education, 21*(3), 229–242.

Cole, C. M., Waldron, N., & Majd, M. (2004). Academic progress of students across inclusive and traditional settings. *Mental Retardation, 42*(2), 136–144.

Deshler, D. D., Mellard, D. F., Tollefson, J. M, & Byrd, S. E. (2005). Research topics in responsiveness to intervention: Introduction to the special series. *Journal of Learning Disabilities, 38*(6), 483–484.

Duhaney, L. M. G., & Salend, S. J. (2000). Parental perceptions of inclusive educational placements. *Remedial and Special Education, 21*(2), 121–128.

Erwin, E., Soodak, L., Winton, P., & Turnbull, A. (2001). "I wish it wouldn't all depend upon me": Research on families and early childhood inclusion. In M. J. Guralnick (Ed.), *Early childhood inclusion: Focus on change* (pp. 127–158). Baltimore: Brookes.

Fairbanks, S., Sugai, G., Guardino, D., & Lathrop, M. (2007). Response to intervention: Examining classroom behavior support in second grade. *Exceptional Children, 73*(3), 288–310.

Ford, A., Davern, L., & Schnorr, R. (2001). Learners with significant disabilities: Curricular relevance in an era of standards-based reform. *Remedial and Special Education, 22*(4), 214–222.

Frederickson, N., Dunsmuir, S., Lang, J., & Monsen, J. J. (2004). Mainstream–special school inclusion partnerships: Pupil, parent and teacher perspectives. *International Journal of Inclusive Education, 8*(1), 37–57.

Gartner, A., & Lipsky, D. K. (1987). Beyond special education: Toward a quality system for all students. *Harvard Educational Review, 57*(4), 367–395

Ghere, G., & York-Barr, J. (2007). Paraprofessional turnover and retention in inclusive programs: Hidden costs and promising practices. *Remedial and Special Education, 28*(1), 21–32.

Grosenick, J. K., & Reynolds, M. C. (1978). *Teacher education: Renegotiating roles for mainstreaming.* Minneapolis, MN: National Support Systems Project.

Grossen, B., Caros, J., Carnine, D., Davis, B., Deshler, D., Schumaker, J., et al. (2002). BIG ideas (plus a little effort) produce big results. *TEACHING Exceptional Children, 34*(4), 70–73.

Heinich, R., Molenda, M., Russel, J. D., & Smaldino, S. E. (1999). *Instructional media and technologies for learning.* Upper Saddle River, NJ: Prentice Hall.

Hunt, P., Hirose-Hatae, A., Doering, K., Karasoff, P., & Goetz, L. (2000). "Community" is what I think everyone is talking about. *Remedial and Special Education, 21*(5), 305–317.

Idol, L. (2006). Toward inclusion of special education students in general education. *Remedial and Special Education, 27*(2), 77–94.

Individuals with Disabilities Education Act regulations (IDEA), 20 U.S.C. § 1402 and 1412a (2004).

Janney, R., & Snell, M.E. (2008). *Behavioral support: Teachers' guides to inclusive practices.* Baltimore: Paul H. Brookes.

Kauffman, J. M. (1995). How we might achieve the radical reform of special education. In J. M. Kauffman & D. P. Hallahan (Eds.), *The illusion of full inclusion* (pp. 193–211). Austin, TX: Pro-Ed.

Kavale, K. A., & Forness, S. R. (1999). *Efficacy of special education and related services.* Washington, DC: American Association on Mental Retardation.

Kavale, K. A., & Forness, S. R. (2000). History, rhetoric, and reality: Analysis of the inclusion debate. *Remedial and Special Education, 21*(5), 279–296.

King-Sears, M. E. (2001). Three steps for gaining access to the general education curriculum for learners with disabilities. *Intervention in School and Clinic, 37*(2), 67–76.

Klingner, J. K., Vaughn, S., Schumm, J. S., Cohen, P., & Forgan, J. W. (1998). Inclusion or pull-out: Which do students prefer? *Journal of Learning Disabilities, 31*(2), 148–158.

Klotz, M. B, & Canter, A. (2007). *Response to intervention (RTI): A primer for parents.* Washington, DC: National Association of School Psychologists.

Kniveton, B. H. (2004). A study of perceptions that significant others hold of the inclusion of children with difficulties in mainstream classes. *Educational Studies, 30*(3), 331–343.

Knowlton, E. (2007). *Developing effective Individualized Education Programs: A case-based tutorial* (2nd ed.). Upper Saddle River, NJ: Pearson Education.

Laurents, A., & Sondheim, S. (1979). *West side story.* New York: Heinemann.

Leyser, Y., & Kirk, R. (2004). Evaluating inclusion: An examination of parent views and factors influencing their perspectives. *International Journal of Disability, Development and Education, 51*(3), 271–285.

Lohrmann, S., & Bambara, L. M. (2006). Elementary education teachers' beliefs about essential supports needed to successfully include students with developmental disabilities who engage in challenging behaviors. *Research and Practice for Persons with Severe Disabilities, 31*(2), 157–173.

MacMillan, D. L., Gresham, F. M., & Forness, S. R. (1996). Full inclusion: An empirical perspective. *Behavioral Disorders, 21*(2), 145–159.

McGregor, G., & Vogelsberg, R. T. (1998). *Inclusive schooling practices: Pedagogical and research foundations: A synthesis of the literature that informs best practices about inclusive schooling.* Pittsburgh, PA: Allegheny University of the Health Sciences.

McLaughlin, M. J., & Thurlow, M. (2003). Educational accountability and students with disabilities: Issues and challenges. *Educational Policy, 17,* 431–451.

McLeskey, J., Waldron, N. L., So, T. H., Swanson, K., & Loveland, T. (2001). Perspectives of teachers toward inclusive school programs. *Teacher Education and Special Education, 24*(2), 108–115.

National Association of State Directors of Special Education (NASDSE). 2005. *Response to intervention: Policy considerations and implementation.* Retrieved July 7, 2008, from www.nasdse.org

Nolet, V., & McLaughlin, M. (2000). *Accessing the general curriculum: Including students with disabilities in standards-based reform.* Thousand Oaks, CA: Corwin.

O'Neill, P. T. (2001). Special education and high stakes testing for high school graduation: An analysis of current law and policy. *Journal of Law and Education, 30*(2), 185–222.

Palmer, D. S., Fuller, K., Arora, T., & Nelson, M. (2001). Taking sides: Parents' views on inclusion for their children with severe disabilities. *Exceptional Children, 67*(4), 467–484.

Peck, C. A., Staub, D., Gallucci, C., & Schwartz, I. (2004). Parent perception of the impacts of inclusion on their nondisabled child. *Research and Practice for Persons with Severe Disabilities, 29*(2), 135–143.

Praisner, C. L. (2003). Attitudes of elementary school principals toward the inclusion of students with disabilities, *Exceptional Children, 69*, 135–145.

Pugach, M. C. (1995). On the failure of the imagination in inclusive schools. *Journal of Special Education, 29*, 212–223.

Pugach, M. C., and Johnson, L. J. (2002). *Collaborative practitioners, collaborative schools* (2nd ed.). Denver, CO: Love.

Pugach, M. C., & Warger, C. L. (2001). Curriculum matters: Raising expectations for students with disabilities. *Remedial and Special Education, 22*(4), 194–196, 213.

Reynolds, M. C., Wang, M. C., & Walberg, H. J. (1987). The necessary restructuring of special and general education. *Exceptional Children, 53*, 391–398.

Rose, D. H., & Meyer, A. (2006). *A practical reader in universal design for learning.* Cambridge, MA: Harvard Education Press.

Rose, D. H., Meyer, A., & Hitchcock, C. (2005). *The universally designed classroom: Accessible curriculum and digital technologies.* Cambridge, MA: Harvard Education Press.

Ryndak, D., & Fisher, D. (2003). *The foundations of inclusive education: A compendium of articles on effective strategies to achieve inclusive education.* Baltimore: TASH.

Sailor, W. (Ed.). (2002). *Building partnerships for learning, achievement, and accountability.* New York: Teachers College Press.

Sailor, W., & Roger, B. (2005). Rethinking inclusion: Schoolwide applications. *Phi Delta Kappan, 86*(7), 503–509.

Sailor, W., Stowe, M. J., Turnbull, H. R., & Kleinhammer-Tramill, P. J. (2007). A case for adding a social-behavioral standard to standards-based education with schoolwide positive behavior support as its basis. *Remedial and Special Education, 28*(6), 366–376.

Siperstein, G. N., Parker, R. C., Bardon, J. N., & Widaman, K. F. (2007). A national study of youth attitudes toward the inclusion of students with intellectual disabilities. *Exceptional Children, 73*(4), 435–455.

Soodak, L. C., Erwin, E. J., Winton, P., Brotherson, M. J., Turnbull, A. P., Hanson, M. J., et al. (2002). Implementing inclusive early childhood education: A call for professional empowerment. *Topics in Early Childhood Special Education, 22*(2), 91–102.

Soukup, J. H., Wehmeyer, M. L., Bashinski, S. M., & Bovaird, J. (2007). Classroom variables and access to the general education curriculum of students with intellectual and developmental disabilities. *Exceptional Children, 74*, 101–120.

Spooner, F., Baker, J. N., Harris, A. A., Ahlgrim-Delzell, L., & Browder, D. M. (2007). Effects of training in universal design for learning on lesson plan development. *Remedial and Special Education, 28*(2), 108–116.

Stahl, S. (2004). *The promise of accessible textbooks: Increased achievement for all students.* Wakefield, MA: National Center on Accessing the General Curriculum. Retrieved January 14, 2008, from http://www.cast.org/publications/ncac/ncacaccessible.html

Strangeman, N., Hitchcock, C., Hall, T., Meo, G., & Coyne, P. (2006). *Response-to-instruction and universal design for learning: How might they intersect in the general education classroom?* Washington, DC: The Access Center.

Study of Personnel Needs in Special Education (2002). *Key findings.* Washington, DC. U. S. Department of Education.

Taylor, S. (1988). Caught in the continuum: A critical analysis of the principle of least restrictive environment. *Journal of the Association for Persons with Severe Handicaps, 13*(1), 41–53.

Thompson, S., & Thurlow, M. (2003). *2003 state special education outcomes: Marching on.* Minneapolis: University of Minnesota, National Center on Educational Outcomes. Retrieved July 7, 2008, from http://education.umn.edu/NCEO/OnlinePubs/2003StateReport.htm

Thousand, J. S., Villa, R. A., & Nevin, A. I. (Eds.). (2002). *Creativity and collaborative learning* (2nd ed.). Baltimore: Brookes.

Thurlow, M. L. (2000). Standards-based reform and students with disabilities: Reflections on a decade of change. *Focus on Exceptional Children, 33*(3), 1–16.

Thurlow, M. L., House, A., Boys, C., Scott, D., & Ysseldyke, J. (2000). *State assessment policies on participation and accommodation for students with disabilities: 1999 update* (Synthesis Report 33). Minneapolis: University of Minnesota, National Center on Educational Outcomes.

Thurlow, M., Ysseldyke, J., Gutman, S., & Geenen, K. (1998). *An analysis of inclusion of students with disabilities in state standards documents* (Technical Report 19). Minneapolis: University of Minnesota, National Center on Educational Outcomes.

Turnbull, A. P., & Schultz, J. B. (1979). *Mainstreaming handicapped students: A guide for the classroom teacher.* Boston: Allyn & Bacon.

Turnbull, A. P., Turnbull, H. R., Erwin, E. J., & Soodak, L. C. (2007). *Families, professionals and exceptionality: Positive outcomes through partnership and trust* (5th ed.). Upper Saddle River, NJ: Merrill/Pearson.

Turnbull, H. R., Turnbull, A. P., Wehmeyer, M. L., & Park, J. (2003). A quality of life framework for special education outcomes. *Remedial and Special Education, 24*, 67–74.

U.S. Department of Education (2002). *2002 National Assessment of Educational Progress, Writing Assessment.* Retrieved January 16, 2008, from http://nces.ed.gov/nationsreportcard/nde/criteria.asp

U.S. Department of Education (2005a). Alternate achievement standards for students with the most significant cognitive disabilities: Non-regulatory guidance. Retrieved January 9, 2008, from http://www.ed.gov/policy/elsec/guid/altguidance.pdf

U.S. Department of Education (2005b). *2005 National Assessment of Educational Progress, Science Assessment.* Retrieved January 16, 2008, from http://nces.ed.gov/nationsreportcard/nde/criteria.asp

U.S. Department of Education (2007a). *2007 National Assessment of Educational Progress, Reading Assessment.* Retrieved January 16, 2008, from http://nces.ed.gov/nationsreportcard/nde/criteria.asp

U.S. Department of Education (2007b). *2007 National Assessment of Educational Progress, Mathematics Assessment.* Retrieved January 16, 2008, from http://nces.ed.gov/nationsreportcard/nde/criteria.asp

U.S. Department of Education (n.d.). IDEA Regulations: National Instructional Materials Accessibility Standard (NIMAS). Retrieved January 14, 2008, from http://idea.ed.gov/explore/view/p/%2Croot%2Cdynamic%2CTopicalBrief%2C12%2C

Van Reusen, A. K., Shoho, A. R., & Barker, K. S. (2000). High school teacher attitudes toward inclusion. *High School Journal, 84*(2), 7–20.

Vaughn, S., & Klingner, J. (1998). Students' perceptions of inclusion and resource room settings. *Journal of Special Education, 32*(2), 79–88.

Voltz, D. L., Brazil, N., & Ford, A. (2001). What matters most in inclusive education: A practical guide for moving forward. *Intervention in School and Clinic, 37*(1), 23–30.

Walther-Thomas, C., Korinek, L., & McLaughlin, V. L. (1999). Collaboration to support students' success. *Focus on Exceptional Children, 32*(3), 1–18.

Wehmeyer, M. L., Lattin, D., Lapp-Rincker, G., & Agran, M. (2003). Access to the general curriculum of middle-school students with mental retardation: An observational study. *Remedial and Special Education, 24,* 262–272.

Wehmeyer, M. L., Sands, D. J., Knowlton, H. E., & Kosleski, E. B. (2002). *Teaching students with mental retardation: Providing access to the general curriculum.* Baltimore: Brookes.

Wiener, J., & Tardif, C. Y. (2004). Social and emotional functioning of children with learning disabilities: Does special education placement make a difference? *Learning Disabilities Research and Practice, 19*(1), 20–32.

Will, M. C. (1986). Educating children with learning problems: A shared responsibility. *Exceptional Children, 52,* 411–416.

Zigmond, N., Jenkins, J., Fuchs, L. S., Deno, S., Fuchs, D., Baker, J. N., et al. (1995). Special education in restructured schools: Findings from three multi-year studies. *Phi Delta Kappan,* pp. 531–540.

Chapter 3

Aguilera, D., & LeCompte, M. D. (2007). Resiliency in native languages: The tale of three indigenous communities' experiences with language immersion. *Journal of American Indian Education, 46*(3), 11–36.

Artiles, A. J., Rueda, R., & Salazar, J. J. (2005). Within-group diversity in minority disproportionate representation: English language learners in urban school districts. *Exceptional Children, 71*(3), 283–300.

Banks, J. A. (2002). *An introduction to multicultural education.* Boston, MA: Allyn & Bacon.

Banks, J. A., & Banks, C. A. M. (2001). *Multicultural education: Issues and perspectives.* New York: Wiley.

Banks, J. A., & McGee-Banks, C. A. (1999). *Multicultural education: Issues and perspectives* (3rd ed., p. 15). Needham Heights, MA: Allyn & Bacon.

Barrera, M. (2006). Roles of definitional and assessment models in the identification of new or second language learners of English for special education. *Journal of Learning Disabilities, 39*(2), 142–156.

Berliner, D. C., & Biddle, B. J. (1995). *The manufactured crisis: Myths, frauds, and the attacks on America's public schools.* New York: Perseus Books.

Blanchett, W. J., Mumford, V., & Beachum, F. (2005). Urban school failure and disproportionality in a post-Brown era: Benign neglect of the constitutional rights of students of color. *Remedial and Special Education, 26*(2), 70–81.

Bowles, S., & Gintas, H. (1976). *Schooling in capitalist America.* New York: Basic Books.

Bronfenbrenner, U. (1979). *The ecology of human development: Experiments by*

nature and design. Cambridge, MA: Harvard University Press.

Brown v. Board of Education, 347 U.S. 483 (1954).

Cartledge, G., & Kourea, L. (2008). Culturally responsive classrooms for culturally diverse students with and at risk for disabilities. *Exceptional Children, 74*(3), 351–371.

Chalfant, J. C., & Pysh, M. V. (1989). Teacher assistance teams: Five descriptive studies on 96 teams. *Remedial and Special Education, 10*(6), 49–58.

Chamberlain, S. P. (2005). Recognizing and responding to cultural differences in the education of culturally and linguistically diverse learners. *Intervention in School and Clinic, 40*(4), 195–211.

DeForge, V., & Zehnder, S. (2001). Children's perceptions of homelessness. *Pediatric Nursing, 27*(4), 377–383.

Delgado, C. E. F., & Scott, K. G. (2006). Comparison of referral rates for preschool children at risk for disabilities using information obtained from birth certificate records. *The Journal of Special Education, 40*(1), 28–35.

Deschenes, S., Cubàn, L., & Tyack, D. (2001). Mismatch: Historical perspectives on schools and students who don't fit them. *Teachers College Record, 103,* 525–547.

de Valenzuela, J. S., Copeland, S. R., Qi, C. H., & Park, M. (2006). Examining educational equity: Revisiting the disproportionate representation of minority students in special education. *Exceptional Children, 72*(4), 425–441.

Diana v. State Board of Education, No. C-70–37 RFP (N. Cal. 1970).

Dunn, L. M. (1968). Special education for the mildly retarded: Is much of it justifiable? *Exceptional Children, 35*(1), 5–22.

Evans, R. (2005). Reframing the achievement gap. *Phi Delta Kappan, 86*(8), 582–589.

Ferri, B. A., & Connor, D. J. (2005). In the shadow of Brown: Special education and overrepresentation of students of color. *Remedial and Special Education, 26*(2), 93–100.

Fierros, E. G., & Conroy, J. W. (2002). Double jeopardy: An exploration of restrictiveness and race in special education. In D. J. Losen & G. Orfield (Eds.), *Racial inequity in special education* (pp. 39–70). Cambridge, MA: Harvard Education Press.

Fujiura, G. T., & Yamaki, K. (2000). Trends in demography of childhood poverty and disability. *Exceptional Children, 66*(2), 187–199.

Gargiulo, R. M. (2006). Homeless and disabled: Rights, responsibilities, and recommendations for serving young children with special needs. *Early Childhood Education Journal, 33*(5), 357–362.

Goff, C., Martin, J. E., & Thomas, M. K. (2007). The burden of acting white:

Implications for transition. *Career Development for Exceptional Individuals, 30*(3), 134–146.

Gravois, T. A., & Rosenfield, S. A. (2006). Impact of instructional consultation teams on the disproportionate referral and placement of minority students in special education. *Remedial and Special Education, 27*(1), 42–52.

Hanson, M. J. (2004). Families with Anglo-European roots. In E. W. Lynch & M. J. Hanson (Eds.), *Developing cross-cultural competence: A guide for working with children and their families* (3rd. ed.). Baltimore: Paul H. Brookes.

Harris-Murri, N., King, K., & Rostenberg, D. (2006). Reducing disproportionate minority representation in special education programs for students with emotional disturbances: Toward a culturally responsive response to intervention model. *Education and Treatment of Children, 29*(4), 779–799.

Harry, B., Kalyanpur, M., & Day, M. (1999). *Building cultural reciprocity with families.* Baltimore, MD: Paul H. Brookes.

Harry, B., & Klingner, J. (2006). *Why are so many minority students in special education?* New York: Teachers College Press.

Harry, B., & Klingner, J. (2007). Discarding the deficit model. *Educational Leadership, 64*(5), 16–21.

Harry, B., Klingner, J., & Hart, J. (2005). African American families under fire: Ethnographic views of family strengths. *Remedial and Special Education, 26*(2), 101–112.

Hermes, M. (2007). Moving toward the language: Reflections on teaching in an indigenous-immersion school. *Journal of American Indian Education, 46*(3), 54–71.

Herrstein, R. J., & Murray, C. (1994). *The bell curve: Intelligence and class structure in American life.* New York: Free Press.

Hoover, J. J., Klingner, J., Baca, L. M., & Patton, J. M. (2008). *Methods for teaching culturally and linguistically diverse exceptional leaders.* Upper Saddle River: Pearson Merrill/Prentice Hall.

Individuals with Disabilities Education Act (IDEA), 20 U.S.C. § 1400 (2004).

Jozefowicz-Simbeni, D. M. H., & Israel, N. (2006). Services to homeless students and families: The McKinney-Vento Act and its implications for school social work practice. *Children & Schools, 28*(1), 37–44.

Kalyanpur, M., & Harry, B. (1999). *Culture in special education: Building reciprocal family-professional relationships.* Baltimore, MD: Paul H. Brookes.

Kewal Ramani, A., Gilbertson, L., Fox, M. A., & Provasnik, S. (2007). *Status and trends in the education of racial and ethnic minorities.* Washington, DC: U.S. Department of Education.

Klingner, J. K., Artiles, A. J., & Méndez
Barletta, L. (2006). English language
learners who struggle with reading:
Language acquisition or learning disability?
Journal of Learning Disabilities, 39(2),
108–128.

Klingner, J., & Edwards, P. A. (2006). Cultural
considerations with response to
intervention models. *Reading Research
Quarterly, 41*(1), 108–117.

Klingner, J. K., & Harry, B. (2006). The
special education referral and decision-
making process for English language
learners: Child study team meetings and
placement conferences. *Teachers College
Record, 108*(11), 2247–2281.

Klingner, J. K., & Solano-Flores, G. (2007).
Cultural responsiveness in response-to-
intervention models. In C. C. Laitusis and
L. L. Cook (Eds.), *Large-scale assessment
and accommodations: What works?*
(pp. 229–241). Arlington, VA: Council for
Exceptional Children and Educational
Testing Service.

Kozol, J. (1991). *Savage inequalities: Children
in America's schools.* New York: Harper
Perennial.

Larry P. v. Riles, 343 F. Supp. 1306 (N.D. Cal.
1972), 502 F. 2d 963 (9th Cir. 1974), No.
C-71-2270 RFP (N.D. Cal., October 16,
1979), 793 F. 2d 969 (9th Cir. 1984).

Linan-Thompson, S., Cirino, P. T., & Vaughn,
S. (2007). Determining English language
learners' response to intervention:
Questions and some answers. *Learning
Disabilities Quarterly, 30*(3), 185–195.

Losen, D. J., & Orfield, G. (2002). *Racial
inequity in special education.* Cambridge,
MA: Harvard Education Press.

Lynch, E. W., & Hanson, M. J. (2004).
*Developing cross-cultural competence: A
guide for working with children and their
families* (3rd ed.). Baltimore: Paul H.
Brookes.

McCray, A. D., Webb-Johnson, G. C., & Neal,
L. I. (2003). The disproportionality of
African Americans in special education: An
enduring threat to equality and
opportunity. In C. C. Yeakey & R. D.
Henderson (Eds.), *Surmounting all odds:
Education, opportunity, and society in the
new millennium* (pp. 455–485).
Greenwich, CT: Information Age.

McMaster, K. L., Kung, S., Han, I., & Cao, M.
(2008). Peer-assisted learning strategies: A
"tier I" approach to promoting English
learners' response to intervention.
Exceptional Children, 74(2), 194–214.

Mehan, H. (1993). Beneath the skin and
between the ears: A case study in the
politics of representation. In S. Chaiklin &
J. Lave (Eds.), *Understanding perspectives
on activity and context.* Cambridge, MA:
Cambridge University Press.

Mercer, J. R. (1973). *Labeling the mentally
retarded.* Los Angeles: University of
California Press.

Merriam-Webster's collegiate dictionary
(11th ed.). (2003). Springfield, MA:
Merriam-Webster.

Mickelson, R. A. (2003). When are racial
disparities in education the result of racial
discrimination? A social science
perspective. *Teachers College Record, 105*,
1052–1086.

National Center for Educational Statistics.
(2001). *Characteristics of the 100
largest public elementary and secondary
school districts in the United States:
1999–2000.* Retrieved January 18, 2008,
from http://nces.ed.gov/pubs2001/
100_largest/discussion.asp

National Research Council. (2002).
*Minority students in special and gifted
education.* Washington, DC: National
Academy Press.

Oakes, J. (1982). The reproduction of
inequity: The content of secondary
school tracking. *Urban Review, 14*,
107–120.

O'Connor, C., & Fernandez, S. D.
(2006). Race, class, and
disproportionality: Reevaluating the
relationship between poverty and special
education placement. *Educational
Researcher, 35*(6), 6–11.

Ortiz, A. A., Wilkinson, C. Y., Robertson-
Courtney, P., & Kushner, M. I. (2006).
Considerations in implementing
intervention assistance teams to support
English language learners. *Remedial and
Special Education, 27*(1), 53–63.

Payne, R. K. (2001). A framework for
understanding poverty. Highlands, TX:
aha! Process.

Porterfield, S. L., & McBride, T. D. (2007).
The effect of poverty and caregiver
education on perceived need and access
to health services among children
with special health care needs.
American Journal of Public Health, 97(2),
323–329.

Reid, D. K., & Knight, M. G. (2006). Disability
justifies exclusion of minority students: A
critical history grounded in disability
studies. *Educational Researcher, 35*(6),
18–23.

Rueda, R., Klingner, J., Sager, N., & Velasco,
A. (2008). Reducing disproportionate
representation in special education:
Overview, explanations, and solutions. In
T. C. Jimenez, & V. L. Graff (Eds.),
*Education for all: Critical issues in the
education of children and youth with
disabilities* (pp. 131–166). San Francisco:
Jossey-Bass.

Rueda, R., & Windmueller, M. P. (2006).
English language learners, LD, and
overrepresentation: A multiple-level
analysis. *Journal of Learning Disabilities.
39*(2), 99–107.

Safford, P. L., & Safford, E. H. (1998). Visions
of the special class. *Remedial and Special
Education, 19*, 229–238.

Skiba, R. J., Bush, L. D., & Knesting, K. K.
(2002). Culturally competent assessment:
More than non-biased tests. *Journal of
Child and Family Studies, 11*, 61–78.

Skiba, R., Poloni-Staudinger, L., Gallini, S.,
Simmons, A., & Feggins-Azziz, L. R. (2006).
Disparate access: The disproportionality of
African American students with disabilities
across educational environments.
Exceptional Children, 72(4), 411–424.

Skiba, R., Poloni-Staudinger, L., Simmons, A.,
Feggins-Azziz, L. R., & Chung, C. (2005).
Unproven links: Can poverty explain
ethnic disproportionality in special
education? *The Journal of Special
Education, 39*(3), 130–144.

Skiba, R. J., Simmons, A. B., Ritter, S., Gibb,
A. C., Rausch, M. K., Cuadrado, J., et al.
(2008). Achieving equity in special
education: History, status, and current
challenges. *Exceptional Children, 74*(3),
264–288.

Skiba, R., Simmons, A., Ritter, A., Kohler, K.,
Henderson, M., & Wu, T. (2006). The
context of minority disproportionality:
Practitioner perspectives on special
education referral. *Teachers College
Record, 108*(7), 1424–1459.

Span, C. M. (2003). "Knowledge is light,
knowledge is power:" African American
education in antebellum America. In C. C.
Yeakey & R. D. Henderson (Eds.),
*Surmounting all odds: Education,
opportunity, and society in the new
millennium* (pp. 3–29). Greenwich, CT:
Information Age.

Sparks, S. (2008). Culturally and
linguistically diverse learners with
developmental disabilities. In H. P. Parette
& G. R. Peterson-Karlan (Eds.), *Research-
based practices in developmental
disabilities* (2nd ed., pp. 125–141). Austin,
TX: PRO-ED.

Turnbull, A. P., Turnbull, H. R., Erwin, E., &
Soodak, L. (2006). *Families,
professionals, and exceptionality: Positive
outcomes through partnerships and trust*
(5th ed.). Upper Saddle River, NJ:
Merrill/Pearson.

Turnbull, A. P., Turnbull, H. R., Summers, J. A.,
& Poston, D. (2008). Partnering with
families of children with developmental
disabilities to enhance family quality of
life. In H. P. Parette & G. R. Peterson-
Karlan (Eds.), *Research-based practices in
developmental disabilities.* Austin, TX:
PRO-ED.

Turnbull, H. R., Stowe, M. J., & Huerta, N. E.
(2007). *Free appropriate public education*
(7th ed., rev.). Denver: Love.

U.S Department of Education. (2001). *Survey
of the states' limited English proficient
students and available educational
programs and services.* Washington, DC:
Author.

U.S Department of Education. (2006). *Public
elementary and secondary students, staff,*

schools, and school districts: School year 2003–04.

U.S. Department of Education. (2007). *27th annual report to Congress on the implementation of the Individuals with Disabilities Education Act, 2005* (Vol. 1). Washington, DC: Author.

U.S. Department of Education. (2008). IDEAdata.org: Retrieved: February 2, 2008, from https://www.ideadata.org/tables30th/ar_1-9.xls

U.S Department of Education Office of Special Education Programs. (2005). *IDEA data* (http://www.ideadata.org).

van Garderen, D., & Whittaker, C. (2006). Planning differentiated, multicultural instruction for secondary inclusive classrooms. *TEACHING Exceptional Children, 38*(3), 12–20.

Vohs, J. (1993). On belonging: A place to stand, a gift to give. In A. P. Turnbull, J. M. Patterson, S. K. Behr, D. L. Murphy, J. G. Marquis, & M. J. Blue-Banning (Eds.), *Cognitive coping, families, & disability* (pp. 51–66). Baltimore: Paul Brookes.

Voltz, D. L., & Fore C, III. (2006). Urban special education in the context of standards-based reform. *Remedial and Special Education, 27*(6), 329–336.

Wagner, M., Marder, C., Blackorby, J., & Cardoso, D. (2002). *The children we serve: The demographic characteristics of elementary and middle school students with disabilities and their households.* Menlo Park: SRI International.

Wang, M., McCart, A., & Turnbull, A. P. (2007). Implementing positive behavior support with Chinese American families: Enhancing cultural competence. *Journal of Positive Behavior Interventions, 9*(1), 38–51.

Webb, D. A., Culhane, J., Metraux, S., Robbins, J. M., & Culhane, D. (2003). Prevalence of episodic homelessness among adult childbearing women in Philadelphia, PA. *American Journal of Public Health, 93,* 1895–1896.

Wilkinson, C. Y., Ortiz, A. A., Robertson, P. M., & Kushner, M. I. (2006). English language learners with reading related LD: Linking data from multiple sources to make eligibility determinants. *Journal of Learning Disabilities, 39*(2), 129–141.

Yazzie-Mintz, T. (2007). From a place deep inside: Culturally appropriate curriculum as the embodiment of Navajoness in classroom pedagogy. *Journal of American Indian Education, 46*(3), 72–93.

Chapter 4

Anguiano, R. P. V. (2003). Families and schools: The effect of parental involvement on high school completion. *Journal of Family Issues, 25*(1), 61–85.

Auerbach, S. (2004). Engaging Latino parents in supporting college pathways: Lessons from a college access program. *Journal of Hispanic Higher Education, 3*(2), 125–145.

Baier, A. C. (1986). Trust and antitrust. *Ethics, 96,* 231–260.

Bailey, D. B., & Winton, P. J. (1989). Friendship and acquaintance among families in a mainstreamed day care center. *Education and Training in Mental Retardation, 24,* 107–113.

Barnard, W. M. (2004). Parent involvement in elementary school and educational attainment. *Children & Youth Services Review, 26*(1), 39–62.

Barrera, I., & Corso, R. M. (2002). Cultural competency as skilled dialogue. *Topics in Early Childhood Special Education, 22*(2), 103–113.

Beach Center. (1999). [Transcripts of focus groups.] Unpublished research.

Beach Center. (2000). [Transcripts of focus groups.] Unpublished research.

Blue-Banning, M. J., Summers, J. A., Frankland, H. C., Nelson, L. L., & Beegle, G. (2004). Dimensions of family and professional partnerships: Constructive guidelines for collaboration. *Exceptional Children, 70*(2), 167–184.

Brantlinger, E. (1985). What low-income parents want from schools: A different view of aspirations. *Interchange, 16,* 14–28.

Brantlinger, E. (2001). Poverty, class, and disability: A historical, social, and political perspective. *Focus on Exceptional Children, 33*(7), 1–19.

Bryan, T., & Burstein, K. (2004). Improving homework completion and academic performance: Lessons from special education. *Theory into Practice, 43*(3), 213–217.

Dearing, E., Kreider, H., Simpkins, S., & Weiss, H. B. (2006). Family involvement in school and low-income children's literacy performance: Longitudinal association between and within families. *Journal of Educational Psychology, 98,* 653–664.

Dykens, E. M. (2005). Happiness, well-being, and character strengths: Outcomes for families and siblings of persons with mental retardation. *Mental Retardation, 43*(5), 360–364.

Epstein, M. H., Polloway, E. A., Foley, R. M., & Patton, J. R. (1993). Homework: A comparison of teachers' and parents' perceptions of the problems experienced by students identified as having behavioral disorders, learning disabilities. *Remedial and Special Education, 14*(5), 40–50.

Falvey, M. A., Forest, M. S., Pearpoint, J., & Rosenberg, R. L. (2002). Building connections. In J. S. Thousand, R. A. Villa & A. I. Nevin (Eds.), *Creativity and collaborative learning* (2nd ed., pp. 29–54). Baltimore: Brookes.

Fiedler, C. R. (2000). *Making a difference: Advocacy competencies for special education professionals.* Boston: Allyn & Bacon.

Frederickson, N., & Turner, J. (2003). Utilizing the classroom peer group to address children's social needs: An evaluation of the circle of friends intervention approach. *Journal of Special Education, 36*(4), 234–245.

Fujiura, G. T., & Yamaki, K. (2000). Trends in demography of childhood poverty and disability. *Exceptional Children, 66*(2), 187–200.

Gerdel, P. (1986). *Who are the researchers and why are they saying these horrible things about me?* Lawrence: University of Kansas, Beach Center.

Goddard, R. D., Tschannen-Moran, M., & Hoy, W. K. (2001). A multilevel examination of the distribution and effects of teacher trust in students and parents in urban elementary schools. *The Elementary School Journal, 102*(1), 3.

Guralnick, M. J., Conner, R. T., & Hammond, M. (1995). Parent perspectives of peer relationships and friendships in integrated and specialized settings. *American Journal on Mental Retardation, 99,* 457–476.

Harry, B., Klingner, J., & Hart, J. (2005). African American families under fire: Ethnographic views of family strengths. *Remedial and Special Education, 26*(2), 101–112.

Harvard Family Research Project. (2006, Spring). Family involvement in early childhood education. *Family Involvement Makes a Difference, 1,* 1–8.

Harvard Family Research Project. (2006/2007, Winter). Family involvement in elementary school children's education. *Family Involvement Makes a Difference, 2,* 1–11.

Harvard Family Research Project. (2007, Spring). Family involvement in middle and high school students' education. *Family Involvement Makes a Difference, 3,* 1–11.

Hoffman, L., Marquis, J. G., Poston, D. J., Summers, J. A., & Turnbull, A. P. (2006). Assessing family outcomes: Psychometric evaluation of the Beach Center Family Quality of Life Scale. *Journal of Marriage and Family, 68,* 1069–1083.

Hoover-Dempsey, K. V., Battiato, A. C., Walker, J. M. T., Reed, R. P., DeJong, J. M., & Jones, K. P. (2001). Parental involvement in homework. *Educational Psychologists, 36,* 195–209.

Hoy, W. K. (2002). Faculty trust: A key to student achievement. *Journal of Public School Relations, 23,* 88–103.

Hoy, W. K., & Tarter, C. J. (1997). *The road to open and healthy schools: A handbook for change (elementary and secondary school ed.).* Thousand Oaks, CA: Corwin.

Iceland, J. (2000). *The "family/couple/ household" unit of analysis in poverty measurement.* Retrieved September 27,

2001, from http://www.census.gov/hhes/poverty/povmeas/papers/famhh3.html#2

Jackson, C. W., & Turnbull, A. P. (2004). Impact of deafness on family life: A review of the literature. *Topics in Early Childhood Special Education, 24*, 15–29.

Jayanthi, M., Sawyer, V., Nelson, J. S., Bursuck, W. D., & Epstein, M. H. (1995). Recommendations for homework-communication problems. *Remedial and Special Education, 16*, 212–225.

Jeynes, W. H. (2005a). Effects of parent involvement and family structure on the academic achievement of adolescents. *Marriage and Family Review, 37*(3), 99–116.

Jeynes, W. H. (2005b). A meta-analysis of the relation of parent involvement to urban elementary school student academic achievement. *Urban Education, 40*(3), 237–269.

Johnson, J., Duffett, A., Farkas, S., & Wilson, L. (2002). *When it's your own child: A report on special education from the families who use it.* New York: Public Agenda.

Keirouz, K. S. (1990). Concerns of parents of gifted children: A research review. *Gifted Child Quarterly, 34*, 56–63.

Lake, J. E., & Billingsley, B. S. (2000). An analysis of factors that contribute to parent-school conflict in special education. *Remedial and Special Education, 21*(4), 240–251.

Lian, J. M., & Fontanez-Phelan, S. M. (2001). Perceptions of Latino parents regarding cultural and linguistic issues and advocacy for children with disabilities. *The Association for Persons with Severe Handicaps, 26*(3), 189–194.

Lord-Nelson, L. G., Summers, J. A., & Turnbull, A. P. (2004). Boundaries in family-professional relationships: Implications for special educators. *Remedial and Special Education, 25*(3), 153–165.

MacLeod, J. (1987). *Ain't no making it: Leveled aspirations in low-income neighborhoods.* Boulder, CO: Westview Press.

Mannan, H. (2005). *Examining family outcomes in early childhood services for families of children with disabilities.* Unpublished doctoral dissertation, University of Kansas, Lawrence.

Mantizicopoulos, P. (2003). Flunking kindergarten after Head Start: An inquiry into the contribution of contextual and individual variables. *Journal of Educational Psychology. 95*(2), 268–278.

Marcon, R. (1999). Positive relationships between parent school involvement and public school inner-city preschoolers' development and academic performance. *School Psychology Review, 28*(3), 395–412.

Marshall, M. (2006). Parent involvement and educational outcomes for Latino students.

Review of Policy Research, 23(5), 1052–1076.

McBride, B. A., Schoppe-Sullivan, S. J., & Moon-Ho, H. (2005). The mediating role of fathers' school involvement on student achievement. *Journal of Applied Developmental Psychology, 26*(2), 201–216.

McWayne, C., Hampton, V., Fantuzzo, J., Cohen, H. L., & Sekino, Y. (2004). A multivariate examination of parent involvement and the social and academic competencies of urban kindergarten. *Psychology in the Schools, 41*(3), 363–377.

Merriam-Webster's collegiate dictionary (10th ed.). (1996). Springfield, MA: Merriam-Webster.

Merriam-Webster's collegiate dictionary (11th ed.). (2003). Springfield, MA: Merriam-Webster.

Meyer, D. J., & Vadasy, P. F. (2008). Sibshops: Workshops for siblings of children with special needs (Rev. ed.). Baltimore: Brookes.

National Association for Gifted Children. (2007). *State of the states in gifted education: 2006–2007.* Washington, DC: Author.

National Forum on Education Statistics. (2004). *Forum guide to protecting the privacy of student information: State and local education agencies* (NCES 2004-330). Washington, DC: National Center for Education Statistics.

Newman, L. (2005). *Family involvement in the educational development of youth with disabilities: A special topic report of findings from the National Longitudinal Transition Study-2 (NLTS-2).* Menlo Park, CA: SRI International.

Orsmond, G. I., & Seltzer, M. M. (2007). Siblings of individuals with autism spectrum disorders across the life course. *Mental Retardation and Development Disabilities Research Reviews, 13*(4), 313–320.

Poston, D., Turnbull, A., Park, J., Mannan, H., Marquis, J., & Wang, M. (2003). Family quality of life: A qualitative inquiry. *Mental Retardation, 41*(5), 313–328.

Ruef, M., & Turnbull, A. P. (2001). Stakeholder opinions on accessible informational products helpful in building positive practical solutions to behavioral challenges of people with mental retardation and/or autism. *Education and Training in Mental Retardation and Developmental Disabilities, 36*(4), 441–456.

Ryan, R. M., Sheldon, K. M., Kasser, T., & Deci, E. L. (1996). *All goals are not created equal: An organismic perspective on the nature of goals and their regulation.* New York: Guildford Press.

Salembier, G., & Furney, K. S. (1997). Facilitating participation: Parents' perceptions of their involvement in the IEP/transition planning process. *Career*

Development for Exceptional Individuals, 20(1), 29–42.

Salend, S. J., Duhaney, D., Anderson, D. J., & Gottschalk, G. (2004). Using the Internet to improve homework communication and completion. *Teaching Exceptional Children, 36*(3), 34–73.

Satir, V. (1972). *Peoplemaking.* Palo Alto, CA: Science and Behavior Books.

Schaffer v. Weast, 126 S. Ct. 528 (2005).

Shapiro, J., Monzo, L. D., Rueda, R., Gomez, J. A., & Blacher, J. (2004). Alienated advocacy: Perspectives of Latina mothers of young adults with developmental disabilities on service systems. *Mental Retardation, 42*(1), 37–54.

Singer, G. (2006). Meta-analysis of comparative studies of depression in mothers of children with and without developmental disabilities. *American Journal on Mental Retardation, 111*, 155–169.

Starr, E., Foy, J. B., Cramer, K. M. & Singh H. (2006). How are schools doing? Parental perceptions of children with autism spectrum disorders, Down syndrome and learning disabilities: A comparative analysis. *Education and Training in Developmental Disabilities, 41*(4), 315–332.

Stephens, K. R. (1999). Parents of the gifted and talented: The forgotten partner. *Gifted Child Today, 22*(5), 38–43.

Stoneman, Z. (2005). Siblings of children with disabilities: Research themes. *Mental Retardation and Development Disabilities Research Reviews, 43*(5), 339–350.

Summers, J. A., Marquis, J. G., Mannan, H., Turnbull, A. P., Fleming, K., Poston, D. J., et al. (2007). Relationship of perceived adequacy of services, family-professional partnerships, and family quality of life in early childhood service programmes. *International Journal of Disability, Development and Education, 54*(3), 319–338.

Summers, J. A., Poston, D. J., Turnbull, A. P., Marquis, J. G., Hoffman, L., Mannan, H., et al. (2005). Conceptualizing and measuring family quality of life. *Journal of Intellectual Disability Research, 49*, 777–783.

Sweetland, S. R., & Hoy, W. K. (2000). School characteristics and educational outcomes: Toward an organizational model of student achievement in middle schools. *Educational Administration Quarterly, 36*(5), 703–729.

Tschannen-Moran, M., & Hoy, W. (2000). A multidisciplinary analysis of the nature, meaning, and measurement of trust. *Review of Educational Research, 70*(4), 547–593.

Turnbull, A. P., & Ruef, M. (1996). Family perspectives on problem behavior. *Mental Retardation, 34*, 280–293.

Turnbull, A. P., & Ruef, M. (1997). Family perspectives on inclusive lifestyle issues for individuals with problem behavior. *Exceptional Children, 63*(2), 211–227.

Turnbull, A. P., Summers, J. A., Lee, S. H., & Kyzar, K. (2007). Conceptualization and measurement of family outcomes associated with families of individuals with intellectual disabilities. *Mental Retardation and Developmental Disabilities Research Reviews, 13,* 346–356.

Turnbull, A. P., Turnbull, H. R., Erwin, E., & Soodak, L. (2006). *Families, professionals, and exceptionality: Positive outcomes through partnerships and trust* (5th ed.). Upper Saddle River, NJ: Merrill/Pearson.

Turnbull, A. P., Turnbull, H. R., Summers, J. A., & Poston, D. (2008). Partnering with families of children with developmental disabilities to enhance family quality of life. In G. Peterson-Karlan, R. Ringlaben, & P. Parette (Eds.), *Research-based and emerging practices in developmental disabilities.* Austin, TX: Pro-Ed.

Turnbull, A. P., Turnbull, H. R., & Wehmeyer, M. L. (2007). *Exceptional lives: Special education in today's schools* (5th ed.). Upper Saddle River, NJ: Merrill/Pearson.

Turnbull, H. R., Turnbull, A. P., & Wheat, M. (1982). Assumptions about parental participation: A legislative history. *Exceptional Education Quarterly, 3*(2), 1–8.

Turnbull, A. P., Zuna, N., Turnbull, R., Poston, D., & Summers, J. A. (2007). Families as partners in educational decision-making: Current implementation and future directions. In S. Odom, R. Horner, M. Snell, & J. Blacher (Eds.), *Handbook of developmental disabilities* (pp. 570–590). New York: Guilford.

Turnbull, K. (1997). Kate Turnbull, 18. In D. Meyer, (Ed.), *Views from our shoes: Growing up with a brother or sister with special needs* (pp. 90–94). Baltimore: Woodbine House.

U.S. Department of Education. (2002). *To assure the free appropriate public education of all children with disabilities: Twenty-fourth annual report to Congress on the implementation of the Individuals with Disabilities Education Act.* Washington, DC: Author.

U.S. Department of Education. (2003). *To assure the free appropriate public education of all children with disabilities: Twenty-fifth annual report to Congress on the implementation of the Individuals with Disabilities Education Act.* Washington, DC: Author.

U.S. Department of Education. (2006). *Issue Brief: School and parent interaction by household language and poverty status: 2002–03.* Retrieved January 18, 2008, from http://www.nces.ed.gov/pubs2006/2006086.pdf

U.S. Office of Special Education Programs (Ed.). (2005). *Parents' satisfaction with their children's schooling.* Washington, DC: U.S. Office of Special Education.

Wang, M., Mannan, H., Poston, D., Turnbull, A. P., Summers, J. A. (2004). Parents' perceptions of advocacy activities and their impact on family quality of life. *Research and Practice for Persons with Severe Disabilities, 29*(2), 144–155

Chapter 5

Ausubel, D. (1963). *The psychology of meaningful verbal learning: An introduction to school learning.* New York: Grune & Stratton.

Barbaresi, W. J., Katusic, S. K., Colligan, R. C., Weaver, A. L., & Jacobsen, S. J. (2005). Math learning disorder: Incidence in a population-based birth cohort. *Ambulatory Pediatrics, 5,* 281–289.

Bender, W. N., & Shores, C. (2007). *Response to Intervention: A practical guide for every teacher.* Thousand Oaks, CA: Corwin Press.

Berninger, V. W., & Amtmann, D. (2003). Preventing writing expression disabilities through early and continuing assessment and intervention for handwriting and/or spelling problems: Research into practice. In H. L. Swanson, K. R. Harris, & S. Graham (Eds.), *Handbook of learning disabilities* (pp. 345–363). New York: Guildford Press.

Blair, C., & Scott, K. G. (2002). Proportion of LD placements associated with low socioeconomic status: Evidence for a gradient? *Journal of special Education, 36*(1), 14–22.

Bradley, R., Danielson, L., & Doolittle, J. (2007). Responsiveness to intervention: 1997–2007. *TEACHING Exceptional Children, 39*(5), 8–12.

Bryan, T. (2005). Science-based advances in the social domain of learning disabilities. *Learning Disabilities Quarterly, 28*(2), 119–129.

Bryan, T., Burstein, K., & Ergul, C. (2004). The social-emotional side of learning disabilities: A science-based presentation of the state of the art. *Learning Disabilities Quarterly, 27*(1), 45–51.

Byrne, B., Olson, R. K., Samuelsson, S., Wadsworth, S., Corley, R., DeFries, J. C., et al. (2006). Genetic and environmental influences on early literacy. *Journal of Research in Reading, 29*(1), 33–49.

Calhoon, M. B., & Fuchs, L. (2003). The effects of peer-assisted learning strategies and curriculum-based measurement on the mathematics performance of secondary students with disabilities. *Remedial and Special Education, 24*(4), 235–245.

Calhoon, M. B., Fuchs, L., & Hamlett, C. (2000). Effects of computer-based test accommodations on mathematics performance assessments for secondary

students with learning disabilities. *Learning Disability Quarterly, 23,* 271–282.

Compton, D. L., Appleton, A. C., & Hosp, M. K. (2004). Exploring the relationship between text-leveling systems and reading accuracy and fluency in second-grade students who are average and poor decoders. *Learning Disabilities Research and Practice, 19*(3), 176–184.

Daugherty, S., Grisham-Brown, J., & Hemmeter, M.L. (2001). The effects of embedded skill instruction on the acquisition of target and nontarget skills in preschoolers with developmental delays. *Topics in Early Childhood Special Education, 21,* 213–221.

Deshler, D. D., & Schumaker, J. B. (2006). *High school students with disabilities: Strategies for accessing the curriculum.* New York: Corwin Press.

Eckert, T. L., Dunn, E. K., Codding, R. S., Begeny, J. C., & Kleinmann, A. E. (2006). Assessment of mathematics and reading performance: An examination of the correspondence between direct assessment of student performance and teacher report. *Psychology in the Schools, 43*(3), 247–265.

Espin, C. A., Busch, T. W., Shin, J., & Kruschwitz, R. (2001). Curriculum-based measurement in the content areas: Validity of vocabulary matching as an indicator of performance in social studies. *Learning Disabilities Research and Practice, 16*(3), 142–151.

Espin, C. A., Shin, J., & Busch, T. W. (2005). Curriculum-based measurement in the content areas: Vocabulary matching as an indicator of progress in social studies learning. *Journal of Learning Disabilities, 38*(4), 353–363.

Flanagan, D. P., Ortiz, S. O., Alfonso, V. C., & Dynda, A. M. (2006). Integration of response to intervention and norm-referenced tests in learning disability identification: Learning from the Tower of Babel. *Psychology in the Schools, 43*(7), 807–825.

Frankenberger, W., & Fronzaglio, K. (1991). A review of states' criteria and procedures for identifying children with learning disabilities. *Journal of Learning Disabilities, 24,* 495–500.

Friend, M., & Bursuck, W. D. (2002). *Including students with special needs: A practical guide for classroom teachers.* Boston: Allyn & Bacon.

Fuchs, L. S., Fuchs, D., Eaton, S. B., Hamlett, C. L., & Karns, K. M. (2000). Supplementing teacher judgments of mathematics test accommodations with objective data sources. *School Psychology Review, 29,* 65–85.

Fuchs, L., & Fuchs, D. (2002). Linking assessment to instructional interventions: An overview. *School Psychology Review, 15,* 318–324.

Fuchs & Fuchs (2007). A model for implementing responsiveness to intervention. *TEACHING Exceptional Children, 38*(5), 14–20.

Fuchs, D., & Young, C. L. (2006). On the irrelevance of intelligence in predicting responsiveness to reading instruction. *Exceptional Children, 73*(1), 8–30.

Fuchs, L. S., Fuchs, D., & Hollenbeck, K. N. (2007). Extending responsiveness to intervention to mathematics at first and third grades. *Learning Disabilities Research & Practice, 22*(1), 13–24.

Garrett, A. J., Mazzocco, M. M. M., & Baker, L. (2006). Development of metacognitive skills of prediction and evaluation in children with or without math disability. *Learning Disabilities Research & Practice, 21*(2), 77–88.

Geary, D. C. (2006). Learning disabilities in arithmetic: Problem-solving differences and cognitive deficits. In H. L. Swanson, K. R. Harris, & S. Graham (Eds.), *Handbook of learning disabilities.* New York: Guilford Press.

Haight, S. L. (2006). Review: Comprehensive test of phonological processing. *Assessment for effective intervention, 31*(2), 81–84.

Hale, J. B., Kaufman, A., Naglieri, J. A., & Kavale, K. A. (2006). Implementation of IDEA: Integrating response to intervention and cognitive assessment methods. *Psychology in the Schools, 43*(7), 753–770.

Horn, E., Leiber, J., & Li, S. (2000). Supporting young children's IEP goals in inclusive settings through embedded learning opportunities. *Topics in Early Childhood Special Education, 20,* 206–223.

Hosp, M. K., & Hosp, J. L. (2003). Curriculum-based measurement for reading, spelling, and math: How to do it and why. *Preventing School Failure, 48,* 10–17.

Individuals with Disabilities Education Act regulations (IDEA), 20 U.S.C. § 1400 (2004).

Isles, A. R., & Humby, T. (2006). Modes of imprinted gene action in learning disability. *Journal of Intellectual Disability Research, 50*(5), 318–325.

Izzo, M. V., Hertzfeld, J. E., & Aaron, J. H. (2001). Raising the bar: Student self-determination + good teaching = success. *Journal of Vocational Special Needs Education, 24,* 26–36.

Jacob, H. H. (2004). *Getting results with curriculum mapping.* Alexandria, VA: Association for Supervision and Curriculum Development.

Janney, R., & Snell, M. E. (2004). *Teachers' guides to inclusive practices: Modifying schoolwork* (2nd ed.). Baltimore: Brookes.

Jimerson, S. R., Burns, M. K., & VanDerHeyden, A. M. (2007). *Handbook of Response to Intervention: The science and practice of assessment and intervention.* New York: Springer.

Johnston, R. S., & Morrison, M. (2007). Toward a resolution of inconsistencies in the phonological deficit theory of reading disorders: Phonological reading difficulties are more severe in high-IQ poor readers. *Journal of Learning Disabilities, 40*(1), 66–79.

Jordan, N. C., Hanich, L. B., & Kaplan, D. (2003). Arithmetic fact mastery in young children: A longitudinal investigation. *Journal of Experimental Child Psychology, 85,* 103–119.

Kavale, K. A., & Forness, S. R. (1996). Social skill deficits and LD: A meta-analysis. *Journal of LD, 29,* 226–237.

Kavale, K. A., & Forness, S. R. (2000). What definitions of learning disability say and don't say: A critical analysis. *Journal of Learning Disabilities, 33,* 239–256.

Kavale, K. A., Holdnack, J. A., & Mostert, M. P. (2006). Responsiveness to intervention and the identification of specific learning disability: A critique and alternative proposal. *Learning Disabilities Quarterly, 29*(2), 113–127.

Lancaster, P. E., Schumaker, J. B., & Deshler, D. D. (2002). The development and validation of an interactive hypermedia program teaching a self-advocacy strategy to students with disabilities. *Learning Disability Quarterly, 25*(4), 277–302.

Lenz, B. K., Deshler, D. D., & Kissam, B. (2004). *Teaching content to all: Evidence-based practices for middle and high school settings.* New York: Allyn Bacon.

Lyon, G. R., Fletcher, J. M., & Barnes, M. C. (2003). Learning disabilities. In E. J. Mash & R. A. Barkley (Eds.), *Child psychopathology* (2nd ed., pp. 520–586). New York: Guilford Press.

Lyon, G. R., Fletcher, J. M., Shaywitz, S. E., Shaywitz, B. A., Torgesen, J. K., Wood, F. B., et al. (2001). Rethinking learning disabilities. In C. E. Finn, A. J. Rotherham, & C. R. Hokanson (Eds.), *Rethinking special education for a new century.* Washington, DC: Fordham Foundation.

Maller, S. J. (2005). *Wechsler Intelligence Scale for children* [review of the test]. Lincoln: University of Nebraska Press.

Martin, J. E., Marshall, L. H., Maxson, L. M., & Jerman, P. L. (1997). *The Self-Directed IEP.* Longmont, CO: Sopris West.

Martin, J. E., Marshall, L. H., & Sale, P. (2004). A 3-year study of middle, junior high, and high school IEP meetings. *Exceptional Children, 70,* 285–297.

Martin, J. E., Van Dycke, J., Christensen, W. R., Greene, B. A., Gardner, J. E., & Lovett, D. L. (2006). Increasing student participation in IEP meetings: Establishing the Self-Directed IEP as an evidence-based practice. *Exceptional Children, 72*(3), 299–316.

Mason, C., Field, S., & Sawilowsky, S. (2004). Implementation of self-determination activities and student participation in IEPs. *Exceptional Children, 70*(4), 441–451.

Mayes, S. D., & Calhoun, S. L. (2005). Test of the definition of learning disability based on the difference between IQ and achievement. *Psychological Reports, 97*(1), 109–116.

McBride-Chang, C., Cho, J.-R., Liu, H. Y., Wagner, R. K., Shu, H., Zhou, A., et al. (2005). Changing models across cultures: Associations of phonological awareness and morphological structure awareness with vocabulary and word recognition in second graders from Beijing, Hong Kong, Korea, and the United States. *Journal of Experimental Child Psychology, 92*(2), 140–160.

McNamara, B. E. (2007). *Learning disabilities: Bridging the gap between research and classroom practice.* Upper Saddle River, NJ: Merrill/Pearson.

Meltzer, L. (2007). *Executive function in education.* New York: Guilford Press.

Meltzer, L., & Krishnan, K. (2007). Executive function difficulties and learning disabilities: Understandings and misunderstandings. In L. Meltzer (Ed.), *Executive function in education* (pp. 77–105). New York: Guilford Press.

Mercer, C. D., & Pullen, P. C. (2005). *Students with learning disabilities.* Upper Saddle River, NJ: Merrill/Pearson.

Mody, M. (2003). Phonological basis in reading disability: A review and analysis of the evidence. *Reading and Writing, 16,* 21–39.

National Reading Panel. (2000). *Teaching children to read: An evidence-based assessment of the scientific research literature on reading and its implications for reading instruction.* Bethesda, MD: National Institute of Child Health and Human Development.

National Research Council. (2002). *Minority Students in Special and Gifted Education.* Washington, DC: National Academies Press.

Ofiesh, N. (2006). Response to intervention and the identification of specific learning disabilities: Why we need comprehensive evaluations as part of the process. *Psychology in the Schools, 43*(8), 883–888.

Petrill, S. A., Deater-Deckard, K., Schatschneider, C., & Davis, C. (2005). Measured environmental influences on early reading: Evidence from an adoption study. *Scientific Studies of Reading, 9*(3), 237–250.

Pickering, S. J. (2006). Working memory in dyslexia. In T. P. Alloway & S. E. Gathercole (Eds.), *Working memory and neurodevelopmental disorders* (pp. 2–39). New York: Psychology Press.

Pretti-Frontczak, K. L., Barr, D. M., Macy, M., & Carter, A. (2003). Research and resources related to activity-based intervention, embedded learning opportunities, and routines-based instruction: An annotated bibliography. *Topics in Early Childhood Special Education, 23*(1), 29–39.

Pretti-Frontczak, K. L., & Bricker, D. D. (2001). Use of the embedding strategy by early childhood education and early childhood special education teachers. *Infant and Toddler Intervention, 11*, 111–128.

Prifitera, A., Weiss, L. G., Saklofske, D. H., & Rolfhus, E. (2005). The WISC-IV in the clinical assessment context. In A. Prifitera, D. H. Saklofske, & L. G. Weiss (Eds.), *WISC-IV: Clinical use and interpretation* (pp. 3–32). Amsterdam: Elsevier Academic.

Pugh, K. R., Mend, W. E., Jenner, A. R., Katz, L., Frost, S. J., Lee, J. R., et al. (2000). Functional neuroimaging studies of reading and reading disability (developmental dyslexia). *Mental Retardation and Developmental Disabilities Research Reviews, 6*, 207–213.

Reis, S. M., McGuire, J. M., & Neu, T. W. (2000). Compensation strategies used by high-ability students with learning disabilities who succeed in college. *Gifted Child Quarterly, 44*, 123–134.

Robertshaw, B. A., & MacPherson, J. (2006). Scope for more genetic testing in learning disability: Case report of an inherited duplication on the X-chromosome. *British Journal of Psychiatry, 189*, 99–101.

Sandall, S., Schwartz, I., & Joseph, G. (2001). A building blocks model for effective instruction in inclusive early childhood settings. *Young Exceptional Children, 4*(3), 3–9.

Sawyer, D. J. (2006). Dyslexia: A generation of inquiry. *Topics in Language Disorders, 26*(2), 95–109.

Schatschneider, C., & Torgesen, J. K. (2004). Using our current understanding of dyslexia to support early identification and intervention. *Journal of Child Neurology, 19*(10), 759–765.

Schumaker, J., & Deshler, D. (2003). *The self-advocacy strategy*. Lawrence, KS: Edge Enterprises.

Shapiro, B. K., Church, R. P., & Lewis, M. E. B. (2002). Specific learning disabilities. In M. L. Batshaw (Ed.), *Children with disabilities* (5th ed., pp. 417–442). Baltimore: Brookes.

Shapiro, B., Church, R., & Lewis, M. E. B. (2007). Specific learning disabilities. In *Children with disabilities* (6th ed., pp. 367–385). Baltimore: Brookes.

Shaywitz, S. E., Escobar, M. D., Shaywitz, B. A., Fletcher, J. M., & Makuch, R. (1992). Evidence that dyslexia may represent the lower tail of a normal distribution of reading ability. *New England Journal of Medicine, 326*(3), 145–150.

Shaywitz, B. A., Shaywitz, S. E., Blachman, B. A., Pugh, K. R., Fulbright, R. K., Skudlarski, P., et al. (2004). Development of left occipitotemporal systems for skilled reading in children after a phonologically-based intervention. *Biological Psychiatry, 55*, 926–933.

Speece, D. L., & Hines, S. J. (2007). Learning disabilities. In E. J. Mash & R. A. Barkley (Eds.), *Assessment of childhood disorders* (4th ed., pp. 598–635). New York: Guilford Press.

Speece, D. L., & Shekitka, L. (2002). How should reading disabilities be operationalized? A survey of experts. *Learning Disabilities Research and Practice, 17*(2), 118–123.

Stecker, P. M. (2007). Tertiary intervention: Using progress monitoring with intensive services. *TEACHING Exceptional Children, 39*(5), 50–57.

Stecker, P. M., Fuchs, L. S., & Fuchs, D. (2005). Using curriculum-based measurement to improve student achievement: Review of research. *Psychology in the Schools, 42*(8), 795–819.

Stuebing, K. K., Fletcher, J. M., LeDoux, J. M., Lyon, G. R., Shaywitz, S. E., & Shaywitz, B. A. (2002). Validity of IQ-discrepancy classification of reading disabilities: A meta-analysis. *American Educational Research Journal, 39*(2), 469–518.

Swanson, H. L. (2001). Research on interventions for adolescents with learning disabilities: A meta-analysis of outcomes related to higher-order processing. *Elementary School Journal, 101*, 331–348.

Swanson, H. L., & Deshler, D. (2003). Instructing adolescents with learning disabilities: Converting a meta-analysis to practice. *Journal of Learning Disabilities, 36*(2), 124–135.

Swanson, H. L., & Jerman, O. (2006). Math disabilities: A selective meta-analysis of the literature. *Review of Educational Research, 76*(2), 249–279.

Swanson, H. L., & Jerman, O. (2007). The influence of working memory on reading growth in subgroups of children with reading disabilities. *Journal of Experimental Child Psychology, 96*(4), 249–283.

Swanson, H. L., & Saez, L. (2006). Memory difficulties in children and adults with learning disabilities. In H. L. Swanson, K. R. Harris, & S. Graham (Eds.), *Handbook of learning disabilities* (pp. 182–198). New York: Guilford Press.

Test, D. W., Mason, C., Hughes, C., Konrad, M., Neale, M., & Wood, W. M. (2004). Student involvement in Individualized Education Program meetings. *Exceptional Children, 70*(4), 391–412.

Test, D. W., & Neale, M. (2004). Using the Self-Advocacy Strategy to increase middle graders' IEP participation. *Journal of Behavioral Education, 13*(2), 135–145.

Thoma, C. A., & Wehmeyer, M. L. (2005). Self-determination and the transition to postsecondary education. In E. E. Getzel & P. Wehman (Eds.), *Going to college:* Expanding opportunities for people with disabilities (pp. 49–68). Baltimore: Brookes.

Tomlinson, C. A. (2001). *How to differentiate instruction in mixed abilities classrooms* (2nd ed.). Alexandria, VA: Association for Supervision and Curriculum Development.

Tomlinson, C. A. (2003). *Fulfilling the promise of differentiated classrooms: Strategies and tools for responsive teaching*. Alexandria, VA: Association for Supervision and Curriculum Development.

Torgesen, J. K. (2002). The prevention of reading difficulties. *Journal of School Psychology, 40*(1), 7–26.

Udelhofen, S. (2005). *Keys to curriculum mapping: Strategies and tools to make it work*. Thousand Oaks, CA: Corwin.

U.S. Department of Education. (2007). *27th annual report to Congress on the implementation of the Individuals with Disabilities Education Act, 2005* (Vol. 1). Washington, DC: Author.

U.S. Department of Education. (2008). IDEAdata.org. Retrieved February 2, 2008, from https://www.ideadata.org/tables30th/ar_1-9.xls

Van Dycke, J. L., Martin, J. E., & Lovett, D. L. (2006). Why is this cake on fire? Inviting students into the IEP process. *TEACHING Exceptional Children, 38*(3), 42–47.

Vaughn, S., & Roberts, G. (2007). Secondary interventions in reading: Providing additional instruction for students at risk. *TEACHING Exceptional Children, 39*(5), 40–46.

Warner, T. D., Dede, D. E., Garvan, C. W., & Conway, T. W. (2002). One size still does not fit all in specific learning disability assessment across ethnic groups. *Journal of Learning Disabilities, 35*(6), 500–508.

Weaver, S.M. (2000). The efficacy of extended time on tests for postsecondary students with learning disabilities. *Learning Disabilities: A Multidisciplinary Journal, 10*(2), 47–56.

Wehmeyer, M. L. (2002). Self-determined assessment: Critical components for transition planning. In C. Thoma & C. Sax (Eds.), *Transition assessment: Wise practices for quality lives* (pp. 25–38). Baltimore: Brookes.

Wehmeyer, M. L., Palmer, S., Agran, M., Mithaug, D., & Martin, J. (2000). Promoting causal agency: The self-determined learning model of instruction. *Exceptional Children, 66*, 439–453.

Wehmeyer, M. L., Sands, D. J., Knowlton, H. E., & Kozleski, E. B. (2002). *Teaching students with mental retardation: Providing access to the general curriculum*. Baltimore: Brookes.

Williams-Diehm, K., Wehmeyer, M. L., Palmer, S. B., Soukup, J. H., & Garner, N. W. (in press). Self-determination and student involvement in transition planning: A multivariate analysis. *Journal on Developmental Disabilities*.

Wolery, M., Anthony, L., Caldwell, N. K., Snyder, E. D., & Morgante, J. D. (2002). Embedding and distributing constant time delay in circle time and transitions. *Topics in Early Childhood Special Education, 22*(1), 14–25.

Woodcock, R. W. (1990). Theoretical foundations of the WJ-R measures of cognitive ability. *Journal of Psychoeducational Assessment, (8)*3, 231–258.

Young, A. R., & Beitchman, J. H. (2007). Learning disabilities. In G. O. Gabbard (Ed.), *Gabbard's treatments of psychiatric disorders* (4th ed., pp. 119–127). Washington, DC: American Psychiatric Publishing.

Chapter 6

Allington, R. L., & Cunningham, P. M. (2002). *Schools that work: Where all children read and write*. New York: HarperCollins.

American Speech-Language-Hearing Association (ASHA). (1984). *Clinical management of communicatively handicapped minority language populations*. Rockville, MD: Author.

American Speech-Language-Hearing Association (ASHA). (2000). *Guidelines for the roles and responsibilities of the school-based speech-language pathologist*. Rockville, MD: Author.

American Speech-Language-Hearing Association (ASHA). (2003). *A workload analysis approach for establishing speech-language caseload standards in the schools*. Rockville, MD: Author.

American Speech-Language-Hearing Association (ASHA). (2004). *Roles and responsibilities of speech-language pathologists with respect to augmentative and alternative communication: Technical report*. Retrieved July 7, 2008, from www.asha.org/policy

American Speech-Language-Hearing Association (ASHA). (2007a). *Accents and dialects*. Retrieved July 7, 2008, from http://www.asha.org/about/leadership-projects/multicultural/issues/ad.htm

American Speech-Language-Hearing Association (ASHA). (2007b). *Childhood apraxia of speech*. [Technical Report]. Retrieved July 7, 2008, from www.asha.org/policy

American Speech-Language-Hearing Association (ASHA). (2008a). *Communication facts: Incidence and prevalence of communication disorders and hearing loss in children—2008 edition*. Retrieved July 7, 2008, from http://www.asha.org/members/research/reports/children.htm

American Speech-Language-Hearing Association (ASHA). (2008b). *How does your child hear and talk?* Retrieved July 7, 2008, from http://www.asha.org./public/speech/development/01.htm

American Speech-Language-Hearing Association (ASHA). (2008c). *Stuttering: Causes and numbers*. Retrieved July 7, 2008, from http://www.asha.org/public/speech/disorders/StutteringCauses.htm

Apel, K., & Swank, L. K. (1999). Second chances: Improving decoding skills in the older student. *Language, Speech, and Hearing Services in Schools, 30*, 231–242.

Battle, D. (1998). *Communication disorders in multicultural populations* (2nd ed.). Boston: Butterworth-Heinemann.

Barry, L., & Burley, S. (2004). Using social stories to teach choice and play skills to children with autism. *Focus on Autism and Other Developmental Disabilities, 19*, 45–51.

Beukelman, D. R., & Mirenda, P. A. (2005). *Augmentative and alternative communication: Supporting children and adults with complex communication needs* (3rd ed.) Baltimore: Brookes.

Blackstone, S. (2006, September). The effects of modeling aided AAC. *Augmentative Communication News, 18*(3), 7–11.

Blackstone, S., Hunt-Berg, M., Nygard, J., & Schultz, J. (2004). *Social networks: A communication inventory for individuals with complex communication needs and their communication partners*. Verona, WI: Attainment.

Bloom, L., & Lahey, M. (1978). *Language development and language disorders*. New York: Wiley.

Boon, R., Burke, E., Fore, C., & Spencer, V. (2006, Winter). The impact of cognitive organizers and technology-based practices on student success in secondary social studies classrooms. *Journal of Special Education Technology. 21*(1), 5–16.

Bunce, B. (2003, August). *Using a language-focused curriculum in a preschool class-room: Language and literacy facilitation and intervention*. Workshop presented at the University of Virginia, Richmond.

Bunce, B. (2008). *Early literacy in action: The language-focused curriculum for preschool*. Baltimore: Brookes.

Bunce, B., & Watkins, R. (1995). Language intervention in a preschool classroom: Implementing a language-focused curriculum. In M. Rice & K. Wilcox (Eds.), *Building a language-focused curriculum for the preschool classroom: Vol. I. A foundation for lifelong communication*. Baltimore: Brookes.

Caruso A., & Strand, E. (1999). *Clinical management of motor speech disorders in children*. New York: Thieme.

Catts, H., & Kamhi, A. (1999). *Language and reading disabilities*. Needham, MA: Allyn & Bacon.

Chomsky, N. (1957). *Syntactic structures*. The Hague, the Netherlands: Mouton.

Cunningham, P. M., & Allington, R. L. (2007). *Classrooms that work: They can all read and write* (4th ed.). Boston: Pearson Education.

Downing, J. E. (2005). *Teaching communication skills to students with severe disabilities* (2nd ed.). Baltimore: Brookes.

Elder, P. S., & Goossens, C. (1994). *Engineering training environments for interactive augmentative communication: Strategies for adolescents and adults who are moderately severely developmentally delayed*. Birmingham, AL: Southeast Augmentative Communication Conference Publications.

Foley, B., & Staples, A. (2000, August). *Literature-based language intervention for students who use AAC*. Paper presented at the International Society for Augmentative and Alternative Communication Convention, Washington, DC.

Giangreco, M. (2000). Related services research for students with low-incidence disabilities: Implications for speech-language pathologists in inclusive classrooms. *Language, Speech, and Hearing Services in Schools, 31*(3), 230–239.

Gillon, G. T., (2007). Phonological awareness—Implications for children with expressive phonological impairment. In B. W. Hodson, *Evaluating and enhancing children's phonological systems—Research and theory to practice*. Greenville, SC: Thinking Publications.

Goossens, C., Crain, S., & Elder, P. (1992). *Engineering the preschool environment for interactive, symbolic communication*. Birmingham, AL: Southeast Augmentative Communication Conference Publications.

Gray, C. (2004). Social stories 10.0: The new defining criteria and guidelines. *Jenison Autism Journal, 14*(4), 2–21.

Hoff, E. (in press). *Language development* (4th ed) Belmont, CA: Wadsworth/Thompson Learning.

Howell, K. W., & Nolet, V. (2000). *Curriculum-based evaluation teaching and decision making* (3rd ed.). Belmont, CA: Wadsworth/Thompson Learning.

Hulit, H., & Howard, M. (2002). *Born to talk: An introduction to speech and language development* (3rd ed.). Boston: Allyn & Bacon.

Individuals with Disabilities Education Act regulations (IDEA) 34 C. F. R. 300.8 (2006).

Ivey, M., Heflin, J., & Alberto, P. (2004). The use of social stories to promote independent behaviors in novel events for children with PDD-NOS. *Focus on Autism and Other Developmental Disabilities, 19*, 164–176.

Kuder, J. S. (2008). *Teaching students with language and communication disabilities* (3rd ed.). Boston: Pearson Education.

Kumin, L. (2001). *Classroom language skills for children with Down syndrome: A guide for parents and teachers.* Bethesda, MD: Woodbine House.

Kuoch, H., & Mirenda, P. (2003). Social story interventions for young children with autism spectrum disorders. *Focus on Autism and Other Developmental Disabilities, 18,* 219–227.

Lombardino, L. J., Riccio, C. A., Hynd, G. W., & Pinheiro, S. B. (1997). Linguistic deficits in children with reading disabilities. *American Journal of Speech-Language Pathology, 6,* 71–78.

Losardo, A., & Notari-Syverson, A. (2001). *Alternative approaches to assessing young children.* Baltimore: Brookes.

McCormick, L. (2003). Introduction to language acquisition. In L. McCormick, D. Loeb, & D. Schiefelbusch (Eds.), *Supporting children with communication difficulties in inclusive settings: School-based language intervention* (2nd ed., pp. 1–42). Boston: Allyn & Bacon.

McCormick, L., & Loeb, D. (2003). Characteristics of students with language and communication difficulties. In L. McCormick, D. Loeb, & D. Schiefelbusch (Eds.), *Supporting children with communication difficulties in inclusive settings: School-based language intervention* (2nd ed., pp. 71–112). Boston: Allyn & Bacon.

Myles, B., & Simpson, R. (2003). *Asperger syndrome: A guide for educators and parents* (2nd ed.). Austin, TX: Pro-Ed.

Nelson, N., & Van Meter, A. (2004). *The writing lab approach to language instruction and intervention.* Baltimore: Brookes.

Owens, R. (2001). *Language development: An introduction* (5th ed.). Boston: Allyn & Bacon.

Owens, R. (2005). *Language development: An introduction* (6th ed.). Boston: Allyn & Bacon.

Pannbacker, M. (1999). Treatment of vocal nodules: Options and outcomes. *American Journal of Speech-Language Pathology, 8*(3), 209–217.

Rice, M. L. (1993). "Don't talk to him, He's weird": A social consequences account of language and social interactions. In A. P. Kaiser & D. B. Gray (Eds.), *Enhancing children's communication: Research foundations for intervention* (pp. 139–158). Baltimore: Brookes.

Rice, M., & Wilcox, K. (1995). *Building a language-focused curriculum for the preschool classroom: Vol. I. A foundation for lifelong communication.* Baltimore: Brookes.

Romski, M. A., & Sevcik, R. A. (1988). Augmentative communication system acquisition and use: A model for teaching and assessing progress. *National Student Speech Language Hearing Association Journal, 16,* 61–74.

Romski, M. A., & Sevcik, R. A. (1992). Developing augmented language in children with severe mental retardation. In S. F. Warren & J. Reichle (Eds.), *Communication and language intervention series: Vol. 1. Causes and effects in communication and language intervention* (pp. 113–130). Baltimore: Brookes.

Romski, M. A., & Sevcik, R. A. (1996). *Breaking the speech barrier: Language development through augmented means.* Baltimore: Brookes.

Romski, M. A., & Sevcik, R. A. (2003). Augmented input. In J. Light, D. Beukelman, & J. Reichle (Eds.), *Communicative competence for individuals who use AAC: From research to effective practice.* Baltimore: Brookes.

Romski, M. A., Sevcik, R. A., & Forrest, S. (2001). Assistive technology and augmentative communication in inclusive early childhood programs. In M. J. Guralnick (Ed.), *Early childhood inclusion: Focus on change* (pp. 465–479). Baltimore: Brookes.

Sandall, S., & Schwartz, I. (2002). *Building blocks for teaching preschoolers with special needs.* Baltimore: Brookes.

Stuart, S. (2002). Communication: Speech and language. In M. Batshaw (Ed.), *Children with disabilities* (5th ed., pp. 229–241). Baltimore: Brookes.

Sturm, J., & Rankin-Erickson, J. (2002). Effects of hand-drawn and computer-generated concept mapping on the expository writing of middle school students with learning disabilities. *Learning Disabilities Research and Practices, 17*(2), 124–139.

U.S. Department of Education. (2001). *To assure a free appropriate public education: Twenty-third annual report to Congress on the implementation of the Individuals with Disabilities Education Act.* Washington, DC: Author.

U.S. Department of Education. (2005). *To assure free appropriate public education: Twenty-seventh annual report to Congress on the implementation of the Individuals with Disabilities Education Act.* Washington, DC: Author.

Verdolini, K. (2000). Voice disorders. In J. Tomblin, H. Morris, & D. Spriestersbach (Eds.), *Diagnosis in speech-language pathology* (2nd ed., pp. 233–280). San Diego: Singular.

Vygotsky, L. S. (1978). *Thought and language.* Cambridge, MA: Harvard University Press.

Vygotsky, L. S. (1987). *The collected works of L. S. Vygotsky* (Vol. 1). New York: Plenum.

Wang, P. P., & Baron, M. A. (1997). Language and communication: Development and disorders. In M. L. Batshaw (Ed.), *Children with disabilities* (4th ed., pp. 275–292). Baltimore: Brookes.

Zebrowski, P. (2000). Stuttering. In J. Tomblin, H. Morris, & D. Spriestersbach (Eds.), *Diagnosis in speech-language pathology* (2nd ed., pp. 199–231). San Diego: Singular.

Chapter 7

Algozzine, R., Serna, L., & Patton, J. R. (2001). *Childhood behavior disorders: Applied research and educational practices* (2nd ed.). Austin, TX: Pro-Ed.

American Psychiatric Association. (2000). *Diagnostic and statistical manual of mental disorders* (4th ed., revised). Washington, DC: Author.

Billingsley, B. S., Fall, A. M., Williams, T. O., Jr., & Tech, V. (2006). Who is teaching students with emotional and behavioral disorders? A profile and comparison to other special educators. *Behavioral Disorders, 31*(3), 252–264.

Boos, H. B. M., Aleman, A., Cahn, W., Pol, H. H., & Kahn, R. S. (2007). Brain volumes in relatives of patients with schizophrenia: A meta-analysis. *Archives of General Psychiatry, 64*(3), 297–304.

Borgwardt, S. J., Riecher-Rossler, A., Dazzan, P., Chitnis, X., Aston, J., Drewe, M., et al. (2007). Regional gray matter volume abnormalities in the at risk mental state. *Biological Psychiatry, 61*(10), 1148–1156.

Breunlin, D. C., Cimmarusti, R. A., Bryant-Edwards, T. L., & Hetherington, J. S. (2002). Conflict resolution training as an alternative to suspension for violent behavior. *Journal of Educational Research, 95,* 349–357.

Bruns, E. J., Suter, J. C., Force, M. M., & Burchard, J. D. (2005). Adherence to wraparound principles and association with outcomes. *Journal of Child and Family Studies, 14,* 521–534.

Buckley, J. A., Ryser, G., Reid, R., & Epstein, M. H. (2006). Confirmatory factor analysis of the behavioral and emotional rating scale-2 (BERS-2) parent and youth rating scales. *Journal of Child and Family Studies, 15*(1), 27–38.

Bullis, M., Yovanoff, P., & Havel, E. (2004). The importance of getting started right: Further examination of the facility-to-community transition of formerly incarcerated youth. *The Journal of Special Education, 38*(2), 80–94.

Bullock, C., & Foegen, A. (2002). Constructive conflict resolution for students with behavioral disorders. *Behavioral Disorders, 27*(3), 289–295.

Burchard, J. D., Bruns, E. J., & Burchard, S. N. (2002). The wraparound approach. In B. J. Burns & K. Hoagwood (Eds.), *Community treatment for youth: Evidence-based interventions for severe emotional and behavioral disorders* (pp. 69–90). New York: Oxford University Press.

Cardno, A. G., & Gottesman, I. I. (2000). Twin studies of schizophrenia from bow-and-arrow concordances to star wars Mx and functional genomics. *American Journal of Medical Genetics, 97*(1), 12–17.

Centers for Disease Control (CDC). (2007). Suicide trends among youths and young adults aged 10–24 years—United States, 1990–2004. *Morbidity and Mortality Weekly Report, 56*(25), 905–908.

Children's Defense Fund. (2007). America's cradle to prison pipeline: A Children's Defense Fund report. Washington, DC: Author.

Christle, C. A., Jolivette, K., & Nelson, C. M. (2007). School characteristics related to high school dropout rates. *Remedial and Special Education, 28*(6), 325–339.

Cobb, B., Sample, P. L., Alwell, M., & Johns, N. R. (2006). Cognitive-behavioral interventions, dropout, and youth with disabilities: A systematic review. *Remedial and Special Education, 27*(5), 259–275.

Coles, R. (1989). *The call of stories.* Boston: Houghton Mifflin.

Consoli, A., Deniau, E., Huynh, C., Purper, D., & Cohen, D. (2007). Treatments in child and adolescent bipolar disorders. *European Child & Adolescent Psychiatry, 16*(3), 187–198.

Corbett, W. P., Sanders, R. L., Clark, H. B., & Blank, W. (2002). Employment and social outcomes associated with vocational programming for youths with emotional or behavioral disorders. *Behavioral Disorders, 27*, 358–370.

Coutinho, M. J., Oswald, D. P., Best, A. M., & Forness, S. R. (2002). Gender and socio-demographic factors and the disproportionate identification of minority students as emotionally disturbed. *Behavioral Disorders, 27*, 109–125.

Cox, K. F. (2006). Investigating the impact of strength-based assessment on youth with emotional or behavioral disorders. *Journal of Child and Family Studies, 15*(3), 287–301.

Cullinan, D. (2007). *Students with emotional and behavioral disorders: An introduction for teachers and other helping professionals.* Upper Saddle River, NJ: Merrill/Pearson.

Daunic, A. P., Smith, S. W., Robinson, T. W., Miller, M. D., & Landry, K. L. (2000). School-wide conflict resolution and peer mediation programs: Experiences in three middle schools. *Intervention in School and Clinic, 36*(2), 94–100.

D'Eon, M., Proctor, P., & Reeder, B. (2007). Comparing two cooperative small group formats used with physical therapy and medical students. *Innovations in Education and Teaching International, 44*(1), 31–44.

Dymond, S. K., Renzablia, A., & Chun, E. (2007). Elements of effective high school service learning programs that include students with and without disabilities. *Remedial and Special Education, 28*(4), 227–243.

Epstein, M. H. (1999). The development and validation of a scale to assess the emotional and behavioral strengths of children and adolescents. *Remedial and Special Education, 20*(5), 258–262.

Epstein, M. H. (2004). *Behavioral and Emotional Rating Scale (BERS-2): A strength-based approach to assessment* (2nd ed.). Austin, TX: Pro-Ed.

Epstein, M. H., Cullinan, D., Ryser, G., & Pearson, N. (2002). Development of a scale to assess emotional disturbance. *Behavioral Disorders, 28*(1), 5–22.

Epstein, M. H., Hertzog, M. A., & Reid, R. (2001). The behavioral and emotional rating scale: Long-term test-retest reliability. *Behavioral Disorders, 26*(4), 314–320.

Epstein, M. H., Nordness, P. D., Nelson, J. R., & Hertzog, M. (2002). Convergent validity of the behavioral and emotional rating scale with primary grade-level students. *Topics in Early Childhood Special Education, 22*(2), 114–121.

Epstein, M. H., & Sharma, J. (1998). *Behavioral and emotional rating scale: A strength-based approach to assessment.* Austin, TX: Pro-Ed.

Foley, R. M. (2001). Academic characteristics of incarcerated youth and correctional educational programs: A literature review. *Journal of Emotional and Behavioral Disorders, 9*(4), 248–259.

Frey, L. M. (2003). Abundent beautification: An effective service learning project for students with emotional or behavioral disorders. *Teaching Exceptional Children, 35*, 66–75.

Fujiki, M., Brinton, B., Morgan, M., & Hart, C. H. (1999). Withdrawn and sociable behavior of children with language impairment. *Language, Speech, and Hearing Services in Schools, 30*, 183–195.

Gagnon, J. C., & McLaughlin, M. J. (2004). Curriculum, assessment, and acountability in day treatment and residential schools. *Exceptional Children, 70*, 263–283.

Garber, J., & Carter, J. S. (2006). Major depression. In M. Hersen & J. C. Thomas (Eds.), *Comprehensive handbook of personality and psychopathology* (Vol. 3, pp. 165–216). Hoboken, NJ: John Wiley & Sons.

Geller, B., Tillman, R., Craney, J. L., & Bolhofner, K. (2004). Four-year prospective outcome and natural history of mania in children with a prepubertal and early adolescent bipolar disorder phenotype. *Archives of General Psychiatry, 61*, 459–467.

Gray, L., & Hannan, A. J. (2007). Dissecting cause and effect in the pathogenesis of psychiatric disorders: Genes, environment and behaviour. *Current Molecular Medicine, 7*(5), 470–478.

Greene, R. W. (2006). Oppositional defiant disorder. In M. Hersen & J. C. Thomas (Eds.), *Comprehensive handbook of personality and psychopathology* (Vol. 3, pp. 285–298). Hoboken, NJ: John Wiley & Sons.

Greene, R. W., & Ablon, J. S. (2005). *Training explosive kids: The collaborative problem solving approach.* New York: Guilford Press.

Gresham, F. M., & Elliott, S. N. (1990). *Social skills rating system.* Circle Pines, MN: American Guidance Service.

Gresham, F. M., Lane, K. L., MacMillan, D. L., & Bocian, K. M. (1999). Social and academic profiles of externalizing and internalizing groups: Risk factors for emotional and behavioral disorders. *Behavioral Disorders, 24*(3), 231–245.

Gunter, P. L., Denny, R. K., & Venn, M. (2000). Modification of instructional materials and procedures for curricular success of students with emotional and behavioral disorders. *Preventing School Failure, 44*, 116–122.

Haggerty, N. K., Black, R. S., & Smith, G. J. (2005). Increasing self-managed coping skills through social stories and apron storytelling. *TEACHING Exceptional Children, 37*(4), 40–47.

Hasselbring, T. S., & Glaser, C. H. W. (2000). Use of computer technology to help students with special needs. *Future of Children, 10*(2), 102–122.

Hinshaw, S. P., Owens, E. B., Wells, K. C., Kraemer, H. C., Abikoff, H. B., Arnold, L. E., et al. (2000). Family processes and treatment outcome in the MTA: Negative/ineffective parenting practices in relation to multimodal treatment. *Journal of Abnormal Child Psychology, 28*, 555–568.

Huang, L., Stroul, B., Friedman, R., Mrazek, P., Friesen, B., Pires, S., et al. (2005). Transforming mental health care for children and their families. *American Psychologist, 60*(6), 615–627.

Hunt, M. H., Meyers, J., Davies, G., Meyers, B., Grogg, K. R., & Neel, J. (2002). A comprehensive needs assessment to facilitate prevention of school dropout and violence. *Psychology in the Schools, 39*, 399–416.

Ialongo, N., Poduska, J., Werthamer, L., & Sheppard, K. (2001). The distal impact of two first-grade preventive interventions on conduct problem and disorder in early adolescence. *Journal of Emotional and Behavioral Disorders, 9*(3), 146–161.

Individuals with Disabilities Education Act regulations (IDEA), 34 C. F. R. § 300.8 (2006).

Johns, B. H., Crowley, E. P. & Guetzloe, E. (2005). The central role of teaching social skills. *Focus on Exceptional Children, 37*(8), 1–8.

Kamps, D., Kravits, T., Rauch, J., Kamps, J. L., & Chung, N. (2000). A prevention program for students with or at risk for ED: Moderating effects of variation in treatment and classroom structure. *Journal of Emotional and Behavioral Disorders, 8*, 141–152.

Kendall, P. C., Robin, J., Hedtke, K., Suveg, C., Flannery-Schroeder, E., & Gosch, E. (2005). Conducting CBT with anxious youth? Think exposures. *Journal of Cognitive-Behavior Practice, 12*, 136–149.

King-Sears, M., & Mooney, J. F. (2004). Teaching content in an academically diverse class. In B. K. Lenz, D. D. Deshler, & B. R. Kissam (Eds.), *Teaching content to all: Evidence-based inclusive practices in middle and secondary schools* (pp. 221–257). Boston: Allyn & Bacon.

Knopf, D., Park, M. J., & Mulye, T.P. (2008). *The mental health of adolescents: A national profile, 2008.* San Francisco: National Adolescent Health Information Center.

Kowatch, R. A., & Fristad, M. A. (2006). Bipolar disorders. In M. Hersen & J. C. Thomas (Eds.), *Comprehensive handbook of personality and psychopathology* (Vol. 3, pp. 217–232). Hoboken, NJ: John Wiley & Sons.

Laursen, E. K. (2000). Strength-based practice with children in trouble. *Reclaiming Children and Youth, 9*(2), 70–75.

Lee, D. L., Belfiore, P. J., & Toro-Zambrana, W. (2001). The effects of mastery training and explicit feedback on task design preference in a vocational setting. *Research in Developmental Disabilities, 22*, 333–351.

Lehman, A. F., Kreyenbuhl, J., Buchanan, R. W., Dickerson, F. B., Dixon, L. A., & Goldberg, R. E. A. (2004). The schizophrenia Patient Outcomes Research Team (PORT): Updated treatment recommendations 2003. *Schizophrenia Bulletin, 30*, 193–217.

Leone, P. E., Meisel, S. M., & Drakeford, W. (2002). Special education programs for youth with disabilities in juvenile corrections. *Journal of Correctional Education, 53*, 46–50.

Lochman, J. E., & Wells, K. C. (2004). The coping power program for preadolescent aggressive boys and their parents: Outcomes effects at the 1-year follow-up. *Journal of Consulting and Clinical Psychology, 72*, 571–578.

Mahoney, J. L. (2000). School extracurricular activity participation as moderator in the development of antisocial patterns. *Child Development, 71*, 502–516.

Martin, E. J., Tobin, T. J., Sugai, G. M. (2002). Current information on dropout prevention: Ideas from practitioners and the literature. *Preventing School Failure, 47*, 10–15.

McDonell, M. G., & McClellan, J. M. (2007). Early-onset schizophrenia. In E. J. Mash & R. A. Barkley (Eds.), *Assessment of childhood disorders* (4th ed., pp. 526–550). New York: Guilford Press.

McIntosh, K., Chard, D. J., Boland, J. B., & Horner, R. H. (2006). Demonstration of combined efforts in school-wide academic and behavioral systems and incidence of reading and behavior challenges in early elementary grades. *Journal of Positive Behavior Interventions, 8*(3), 146–154.

McMahon, R. J., & Frick, P. J. (2007). Conduct and oppositional disorders. In E. J. Mash & R. A. Barkley (Eds.), *Assessment of childhood disorders* (4th ed., pp. 132–183). New York: Guilford Press.

Miklowitz, D. J., & Goldstein, M. J. (1997). *Bipolar disorder. A family-focused treatment approach.* New York: Guilford Press.

Mitchem, K. J. (2001). CWPASM: A classwide peer-assisted self-management program for general education classrooms. *Education and Treatment of Children, 24*(2), 111–141.

Morris, A. S., Silk, J. S., Steinberg, L., Myers, S. S., & Robinson, L. R. (2007). The role of the family context in the development of emotion regulation. *Social Development, 16*(2), 361–387.

Muscott, H. (2001). Fostering learning, fun, and friendship among students with emotional and behavioral disorders and their peers: The SO Prepared for Citizenship program. *Beyond Behavior, 10*(3) 36–47.

Nelson, J. R., Benner, G. J., & Cheney, D. (2005). An investigation of the language skills of students with emotional disturbance served in public school settings. *The Journal of Special Education, 39*(2), 97–105.

Nelson, J. R., Benner, G. J., Neill, S., & Stage, S. A. (2006). Interrelationships among language skills, externalizing behavior, and academic fluency and their impact on the academic skills of students with ED. *Journal of Emotional and Behavioral Disorders, 14*(4), 209–216.

Nelson, J. R., Martella, R. M., & Marchand-Martella, N. (2002). Maximizing student learning: The effects of a comprehensive, school-based program for preventing problem behaviors. *Journal of Emotional and Behavioral Disorders, 10*(3), 136–148.

Nelson, J. R., Stage, S., Duppong-Hurley, K., Synhorst, L., & Epstein, M. H. (2007). Risk factors predictive of the problem behavior of children at risk for emotional and behavioral disorders. *Exceptional Children, 73*(3), 367–379.

Nelson-Gray, R. O., Keane, S. P., Hurst, R. M., Mitchell, J. T., Warburton, J. B., Chok, J. T., et al. (2006). A modified DBT skills training program for oppositional defiant adolescents: Promising preliminary findings. *Behaviour Research and Therapy, 44*(12), 1811–1820.

Quinn, K. P., & Lee, V. (2007). The wraparound approach for students with emotional and behavioral disorders: Opportunities for school psychologists. *Psychology in the Schools, 44*(1), 101–111.

Quinn, M. M., Rutherford, R. B., Leone, P. E., Osher, D. M., & Poirier, J. M. (2005). Youth with disabilities in juvenile corrections: A national survey. *Exceptional Children, 71*(3), 339–345.

Reschley, A. L., & Christenson, S. L. (2006). Prediction of dropout among students with mild disabilities. *Remedial and Special Education, 27*(5), 293–300.

Research Units on Pediatric Psychopharmacology Anxiety Study Group. (2001). Fluvoxamine for the treatment of anxiety disorders in children and adolescents. *New England Journal of Medicine, 344*, 1679–1685.

Robb, A., & Reber, M. (2007). Behavioral and psychiatric disorders in children with disabilities. In M. L. Batshaw, L. Pellegrino, & N. J. Roizen (Eds.), *Children with disabilities* (6th ed., pp. 297–311). Baltimore: Brookes.

Robin, J. A., Puliafico, A. C., Creed, T. A., Comer, J. S., Hofflich, S. A., Barmish, A. J., et al. (2006). Generalized anxiety disorder. In M. Hersen & J. C. Thomas (Eds.), *Comprehensive handbook of personality and psychopathology* (Vol. 3, pp. 117–134). Hoboken, NJ: John Wiley & Sons.

Rothbart, M. K., & Bates, J. E. (2006). Temperament. In W. Damon & R. M. Lerner (Eds.), *Handbook of child psychology* (6th ed., Vol. 6, pp. 99–166). Hoboken, NJ: John Wiley & Sons.

Rozenzweig, M. R., Breedlove, S. M., & Watson, N. V. (2005). *Biological psychology: An introduction to behavioral and cognitive neuroscience.* Sunderland, MA: Sinauer Associates.

Rubin, K., Chen, X., McDougall, P., Bowker, A., & McKinnon, J. (1995). The Waterloo Longitudinal Project: Predicting internalizing and externalizing problems in adolescence. *Development and Psychopathology, 7*, 751–764.

Rudolph, K. D., & Lambert, S. F. (2007). Child and adolescent depression. In E. J. Mash & R. A. Barkley (Eds.), *Assessment of childhood disorders* (4th ed., pp. 213–252). New York: Guilford Press.

Rutter, P. A., & Behrendt, A. E. (2004). Adolescent suicide risk: Four psychosocial factors. *Adolescence, 39*(154), 295–302.

Saarni, C., Campos, J. J., Camras, L., & Witherington, D. (2006). Emotional development: Action, communication, and understanding. In N. Eisenberg (Ed.), *Handbook of child psychology. Vol. 3:*

Social, emotional and personality development (6th ed.). New York: Wiley.

Sabornie, E. J., Cullinan, D., Osborne, S. S., & Brock, L. B. (2005). Intellectual, academic, and behavioral functioning of students with high-incidence disabilities: A cross-categorical meta-analysis. *Exceptional Children, 72*(1), 47–63.

Sabornie, E. J., Evans, C., & Cullinan, D. (2006). Comparing characteristics of high-incidence disability groups. *Remedial and Special Education, 27*(2), 95–104.

Scanlon, D., & Mellard, D. F. (2002). Academic and participation profiles of school-age dropouts with and without disabilities. *Exceptional Children, 68*, 239–259.

Severson, H. H., Walker, H. M., Hope-Doolittle, J., Kratochwill, T. R., & Gresham, F. M. (2007). Proactive, early screening to detect behaviorally at-risk students: Issues, approaches, emerging innovations, and professional practices. *Journal of School Psychology, 45*, 193–223.

Sickmund, M. (2002, March). *Juvenile offenders in residential placement: 1997–1999. OJJDP fact sheet.* Washington, DC: U.S. Department of Justice, Office of Juvenile Justice and Delinquency Prevention.

Silk, J. S., Shaw, D. S., Skuban, E. M., Oland, A. A., & Kovacs, M. (2006). Emotion regulation strategies in offspring of childhood-onset depressed mothers. *Journal of Child Psychology and Psychiatry, 47*, 69–78.

Sinclair, M. F., Christenson, S. L., & Thurlow, M. L. (2005). Promoting school completion of urban secondary youth with emotional or behavioral disabilities. *Exceptional Children, 71*(4), 465–482.

Sitlington, P. L., & Neubert, D. A. (2004). Preparing youths with emotional or behavioral disorders for transition to adult life: Can it be done within the standards-based reform movement? *Behavioral Disorders, 29*, 279–288.

Skoulos, V., & Tryon, G. S. (2007). Social skills of adolescents in special education who display symptoms of oppositional defiant disorder. *American Secondary Education, 35*(2), 103–115.

Southam-Gerow, M. A., & Chorpita, B. F. (2007). Anxiety in children and adolescents. In E. J. Mash & R. A. Barkley (Eds.), *Assessment of childhood disorders* (4th ed., pp. 347–397). New York: Guilford Press.

Thurlow, M. L., Lazarus, S., Thompson, S., & Robey, J. (2002). *2001 state policies on assessment participation and accommodations* (Synthesis Report 46). Minneapolis: University of Minnesota, National Center on Educational Outcomes. Retrieved July 7, 2008, http://education.umn.edu/NCEO/OnlinePubs/Synthesis46.html

Tournaki, N., & Criscitiello, E. (2003). Using peer tutoring as a successful part of behavior management. *Teaching Exceptional Children, 36*(2), 22–29.

Uhing, B. M., Mooney, P., & Ryser, G. R. (2005). Differences in strength assessment scores for youth with and without ED across the youth and parent rating scales of the BERS-2. *Journal of Emotional and Behavioral Disorders, 13*(3), 181–187.

U.S. Department of Education. (1998). *To assure the free appropriate public education of all children with disabilities: Twentieth annual report to Congress on the implementation of the Individuals with Disabilities Education Act.* Washington, DC: Author.

U.S. Department of Education. (2002). *To assure the free appropriate public education of all children with disabilities: Twenty-third annual report to Congress on the implementation of the Individuals with Disabilities Education Act.* Washington, DC: Author.

U.S. Department of Education, Office of Special Education Programs. (2008). Individuals with Disabilities Education Act (IDEA) data: Retrieved January 18, 2008 from http://www.IDEAdata.org/index.html

Wagner, M., Friend, M., Bursuck, W. D., Kutash, K., Duchnowski, A. J., Sumi, W. C., et al. (2006). Educating students with emotional disturbances: A national perspective on school programs and services. *Journal of Emotional and Behavioral Disorders, 14*(1), 12–30.

Wagner, M., Kutash, K., Duchnowski, A. J., Epstein, M. H., & Sumi, W. C. (2005). The children and youth we serve: A national picture of the characteristics of students with emotional disturbances receiving special education. *Journal of Emotional and Behavioral Disorders, 13*(2), 79–96.

Walker, J. S., & Schutte, K. M. (2004). Practice and process in wraparound teamwork. *Journal of Emotional and Behavioral Disorders, 12*, 182–192.

Waschbusch, D. A. (2002). A meta-analysis examination of comorbid hyperactive-impulsive-attention problems and conduct problems. *Psychological Bulletin, 128*, 118–150.

Whittinger, N. S., Langley, K., Fowler, T. A., Thomas, H. V., & Thapar, A. (2007). Clinical precursors of adolescent conduct disorder in children with attention-deficit/hyperactivity disorder. *Journal of the American Academy of Child and Adolescent Psychiatry, 46*(2), 179–187.

Wright, D., & Torrey, G. K. (2001). A comparison of two peer-referenced assessment techniques with parent and teacher ratings of social skills and problem behaviors. *Behavior Disorders, 26*, 273–282.

Yeh, M., Forness, S. R., Ho, J., McCabe, K., & Hough, R. L. (2004). Parental etiological explanations and disproportionate racial/ethnic representation in special education services for youths with emotional disturbance. *Behavioral Disorders, 29*(4), 348–358.

Youngstrom, E. (2007). Pediatric bipolar disorder. In E. J. Mash & R. A. Barkley (Eds.), *Assessment of childhood disorders* (4th ed., pp. 253–304). New York: Guilford Press.

Zhang, D., Katsiyannis, A., & Herbst, M. (2004). Disciplinary exclusions in special education: A 4-year analysis. *Behavioral Disorders, 29*(4), 337–347.

Chapter 8

Accardo, P. J. (Ed.), *Capute and Accardo's neurodevelopmental disabilities in infancy and childhood*, 3rd ed. Vol. II: The spectrum of developmental disabilities. Baltimore: Paul H. Brookes.

Alberto, P. A., & Troutman, A. C. (2003). *Applied behavior analysis for teachers* (6th ed.). Upper Saddle River, NJ: Merrill/Pearson.

American Psychiatric Association (APA). (2000). *Diagnostic and statistical manual of mental disorders* (4th ed., rev.). Washington, DC: Author.

Barkley, R. A. (2003). Attention-deficit/hyperactivity disorder. In E. J. Mash & R. A. Barkley (Eds.), *Child psychopathology* (2nd ed., pp. 75–143). New York: Guilford Press.

Barkley, R. A., Fischer, M., Smallish, L., & Fletcher, K. (2004). Young adult follow-up of hyperactive children: Antisocial activities and drug use. *Journal of Child Psychology and Psychiatry, 45*(2), 195–211.

Barkley, R. A., Fischer, M., Smallish, L., & Fletcher, K. (2006). Young adult outcome of hyperactive children: Adaptive functioning in major life activities. *Journal of the American Academy of Child and Adolescent Psychiatry, 45*(2), 192–202.

Barkley, R. A., Murphy, K. R., & Fischer, M. (2007). *ADHD in adults: Original research and clinical implications.* New York: Guilford Press.

Biederman, J. (2005). Attention-deficit/hyperactivity disorder: A selective overview. *Biological Psychiatry, 57*(11), 1215–1220.

Blazer, B. (1999). Developing 504 classroom accommodation plans: A collaborative, systematic parent-student-teacher approach. *Teaching Exceptional Children, 32*(2), 28–33.

Buggey, T. (2007). A picture is worth. . . : Video self-modeling applications at school and home. *Journal of Positive Behavior Interventions, 9*, 151–158.

Bussing, R., Lehninger, F., & Eyberg, S. (2006). Difficult child temperament and attention-deficit/hyperactivity disorder in preschool children. *Infants and Young Children, 19*(2), 123–131.

Carbone, E. (2001). Arranging the classroom with an eye (and ear) to students with ADHD. *Teaching Exceptional Children, 34*(2), 72–81.

Castellanos, F. X., Lee, P. P., Sharp, W., Jeffries, N. O., Greenstein, D. K., Clasen, L. S., et al. (2002). Developmental trajectories of brain volume abnormalities in children and adolescents with attention-deficit/hyperactivity disorder. *JAMA, 288*(14), 1740–1748.

Conners, C. K. (1997). *Conners' Rating Scales—Revised technical manual.* North Tonawanda, NY: Multi-Health Systems.

Cook, E. H. (1999). Genetics of attention-deficit hyperactivity disorder. *Mental Retardation and Developmental Disabilities Research Reviews, 5*(3), 191–198.

Cortese, S., Lecendreux, M., Mouren, M. C., & Konofal, E. (2006). ADHD and insomnia. *Journal of the American Academy of Child and Adolescent Psychiatry, 45*(4), 384–385.

Demaray, M. K., Elting, J., & Schaefer, K. (2003). Assessment of attention-deficit/hyperactivity disorder (AD/HD): A comparative evaluation of five commonly used, published rating scales. *Psychology in the Schools, 40*(4), 341–361.

Demaray, M. K., Schaefer, K., & Delong, L. K. (2003). Attention-deficit/hyperactivity disorder (ADHD): A national survey of training and current assessment practices in the schools. *Psychology in the Schools, 40*(6), 583–597.

dosReis, S., Owens, P. L., Puccia, K. B., & Leaf, P. J. (2004). Multimodal treatment for ADHD among youths in three Medicaid subgroups: Disabled, foster care, and low income. *Pychiatric Services, 55*, 1041–1048.

DuPaul, G. J., McGoey, K. E., Eckert, T. L., & VanBrakle, J. (2001). Preschool children with attention-deficit/hyperactivity disorder: Impairments in behavioral, social, and school functioning. *Journal of the American Academy of Child and Adolescent Psychiatry, 40*, 508–515.

Egger, H. L., Kondo, D., & Angold, A. (2006). The epidemiology and diagnostic issues in preschool attention-deficit/hyperactivity disorder: A review. *Infants & Young Children, 19*(2), 109–122.

Faraone, S. V., Perlis, R. H., Doyle, A. E., Smoller, J., Goralnick, J., Holmgren, M., et al. (2005). Molecular genetics of attention-deficit/hyperactivity disorder. *Biological Psychiatry, 57*, 1313–1323.

Flory, K., Molina, B. S. G., Pelham, W., Gnagy, B., & Smith, B. H. (2006). ADHD and risky behavior. *Journal of Clinical Child and Adolescent Psychology, 53*, 571–577.

Frazier, T. W., & Youngstrom, E. (2006). Evidence-based assessment of attention-deficit/hyperactivity disorder: Using

multiple sources of information. *Journal of the American Academy of Child and Adolescent Psychiatry, 45*(5), 614–620.

Glanzman, M., & Blum, N. J. (2007). Genetics, imaging, and neurochemistry in attention-deficit/hyperactivity disorder (ADHD). In P. J. Accardo (Ed.), *Capute and Accardo's neurodevelopmental disabilities in infancy and childhood: Vol. 2: The spectrum of developmental disabilities* (3rd ed.). Baltimore: Brookes.

Glanzman, M. M., & Blum, N. J. (2007). Attention deficits and hyperactivity. In M. L. Batshaw, L. Pellegrino, & N. J. Roizen (Eds.), *Children with disabilities* (6th ed., pp. 345–365). Baltimore: Brookes.

Haile Mariam, A., Bradley-Johnson, S., & Johnson, C. M. (2002). Pediatricians' preferences for ADHD information from schools. *School Psychology Review, 31*, 94–105.

Harman, P. L., & Barkley, R. (2000). One-on-one with Russell Barkley. *Attention! 6*(4), 12–14.

Hitchcock, C. H., Dowrick, P. W., & Prater, M. A. (2003). Video self-modeling intervention in school-based settings: A review. *Remedial and Special Education, 24*, 36–45.

Individuals with Disabilities Education Act regulations (IDEA), 34 C. F. R. § 300.8 (2006).

Kaplan, B. J., Crawford, S. G., Dewey, D. M., & Fisher, G. C. (2000). The IQs of children with ADHD are normally distributed. *Journal of Learning Disabilities, 33*(5), 425–432.

Kern, L., DuPaul, G. J., Volpe, R. J., Sokol, N. G., Lutz, J. G, Arbolino, L. A. et al. (2007). Multisetting assessment-based intervention for young children at risk for attention deficit hyperactivity disorder: Initial effects on academic and behavioral functioning. *The School Psychology Review, 36*, 237–255.

Kiersuk, T. J., Smith, A., & Cardillo, A. (1994). *Goal attainment scaling: Applications and measurement.* Hillsdale, NJ: Erlbaum.

Klassen, A. F., Miller, A., & Fine, S. (2004). Health-related quality of life in children and adolescents who have a diagnosis of attention-deficit/hyperactivity disorder. *Pediatrics, 114*(5), 1322–1323.

Larsson, J. O., Larsson, H., & Lichtenstein, P. (2004). Genetic and environmental contributions to stability and change of ADHD symptoms between 8 and 13 years of age: A longitudinal twin study. *American Academy for Child and Adolescent Psychiatry, 43*(10), 1267–1275.

Locke, E. A., & Latham, G. P. (2002). Building a practically useful theory of goal setting and task motivation: A 35-year odyssey. *American Psychologist, 57*(9), 705–717.

McGoey, K. E., Eckert, T. L., & DuPaul, G. J. (2002). Early intervention for preschool-age children with ADHD: A literature

review. *Journal of Emotional and Behavioral Disorders, 10*, 14–28.

Mechling, L. (2005). The effect of instructor-created video programs to teach students with disabilities: A literature review. *Journal of Special Education Technology, 20*(2), 25–36.

Miranda, A., & Presentacion, M. J. (2000). Efficacy of cognitive-behavioral therapy in the treatment of children with ADHD, with and without aggressiveness. *Psychology in the Schools, 37*, 169–182.

Palmer, S. B., Wehmeyer, M. L., Gibson, K., & Agran, M. (2004). Promoting access to the general curriculum by teaching self-determination skills. *Exceptional Children, 70*, 427–439.

Parker, H. C. (1992). ADAPT accommodation plan. *ADD Warehouse.* Retrieved July 7, 2008, from http://www.addwarehouse.com

Pfiffner, L. J., McBurnett, K., Lahey, B. B., Loeber, R., Green, S., Frick, P. J., et al. (1999). Association of parental psychopathology to the comorbid disorders of boys with attention-deficit hyperactivity disorder. *Journal of Consulting and Clinical Psychology, 67*, 881–893.

Prigge, D. J. (2002). 20 ways to promote brain-based teaching and learning. *Intervention in School and Clinic, 37*(4), 237–241.

Roach, A. T., & Elliott, S. N. (2005). Goal attainment scaling: An efficient and effective approach to monitoring student progress. *Teaching Exceptional Children, 37*(4), 8–17.

Sands, D., & Doll, B. (2005). Teaching goal setting and decision making to students with developmental disabilities. In M. Wehmeyer & M. Agran (Eds.), *Mental retardation and intellectual disabilities: Teaching students using innovative and research-based strategies* (pp. 273–296). Upper Saddle River, NJ: Pearson.

Schnoes, C., Reid, R., Wagner, M., & Marder, C. (2006). ADHD among students receiving special education services: A national survey. *Council for Exceptional Children, 72*(4), 483–496.

Smith, S. (2002). *Applying cognitive behavioral strategies to social skills instruction.* Arlington, VA: ERIC/OSEP Digest.

Smith, B. H., Barkley, R. A., & Shapiro, C. J. (2007). Attention-deficit/hyperactivity disorder. In E. J. Mash & R. A. Barkley (Eds.), *Assessment of childhood disorders* (4th ed., pp. 53–122). New York: Guilford Press.

Snider, V. E., Busch, T., & Arrowood, L. (2003). Teacher knowledge of stimulant medication and ADHD. *Remedial and Special Education, 24*(1), 1–16.

Stanford, P., & Reeves, S. (2005). Assessment that drives instruction. *Teaching Exceptional Children, 37*(4), 18–23.

Stevens, J., & Ward-Estes, J. (2006). Attention-deficit/hyperactivity disorder. *Comprehensive Handbook of Personality and Psychopathology, 3*, 316–329.

Tannock, R., & Martinussen, R. (2001) Reconceptualizing ADHD. *Educational Leadership, 59*(3), 20–25.

Walker, B. (2004). *The girls' guide to AD/HD.* Bethesda, MD: Woodbine House.

Weyandt, L. L. (2005). Executive function in children, adolescents, and adults with attention-deficit/hyperactivity disorder: An introduction to the special issue. *Developmental Neuropsychology, 27*, 1–10.

Wilens, T. E., Hahesey, A. L., Biederman, J., Bredin, E., Tanguay, S., Kwon, A., et al. (2005). Influence of parental SUD and ADHD on ADD in their offspring: Preliminary results from a pilot-controlled family study. *American Journal of Addictions, 14*, 179–187.

Zentall, S. S. (2006). *ADHD and education: Foundations, characteristics, methods, and collaboration.* Upper Saddle River, NJ: Pearson Education.

Chapter 9

Abbeduto, L. (2003). Language and communication in mental retardation. *International Review of Research in Mental Retardation* (Vol. 27). New York: Academic Press.

Agran, M., Blanchard, C., &Wehmeyer, M. L. (2000). Promoting transition goals and self-determination through student-directed learning: The self-determined learning model of instruction. *Education and Training in Mental Retardation and Developmental Disabilities, 35*, 351–364.

Agran, M., King-Sears, M., Wehmeyer, M. L., & Copeland, S. R. (2003). *Teachers' guides to inclusive practices: Student-directed learning strategies.* Baltimore: Brookes.

Agran, M., Snow, K., & Swaner, J. (1999). A survey of secondary level teachers' opinions on community-based instruction and inclusive education. *Journal of the Association for Persons with Severe Handicaps, 24*(1), 58–62.

American Psychiatric Association (APA). (2000). *Diagnostic and statistical manual of mental disorders* (4th ed., rev.). Washington, DC: Author.

Avchen, R. N., Bhasin, T. K., Braun, K. V., & Yeargin-Allsopp, M. (2007). Public health impact: Metropolitan Atlanta developmental disabilities surveillance program. *International Review of Research in Mental Retardation, 33*, 149–190.

Bambara, L. M., Wilson, B. A., & McKenzie, M. (2007). Transition and quality of life. In S. L. Odom, R. H. Horner, M. E. Snell, & J. Blacher (Eds.), *Handbook of developmental disabilities* (pp. 371–389). New York: Guilford Press.

Bates, P. E., Quvo, T., Miner, C. A., & Korabek, C. A. (2001). Simulated and community-based instruction involving persons with mild and moderate mental retardation. *Research and Developmental Disabilities, 22*, 95–115.

Batshaw, M. L., Shapiro, B., & Farber, M. L. Z. (2007). Developmental delay and intellectual disability. In M. L. Batshaw, L. Pellegrino, & N. J. Roizen (Eds.), *Children with disabilities* (6th ed., pp. 245–261). Baltimore: Brookes.

Bebko, J. M., & McPherson, M. J. (1997). *Teaching mnemonic strategies as a functional skill to cognitively impaired students.* North York, Ontario, Canada: York University.

Blank, R. M. (2001). An overview of trends in social and economic well-being, by race. In N. J. Smelser, W. J. Wilson, & F. Mitchell (Eds.), *America becoming: Racial trends and their consequences* (Vol. 1, pp. 21–39). Washington, DC: National Academy Press.

Blaylock, G. (1996). Community transition teams as the foundation for transition services for youth with learning disabilities. *Journal of Learning Disabilities, 29*, 148–159.

Borkowski, J. G., Noria, C. W., Lefever, J. B., Keogh, D. A., Whitman, T. L., Lounds, J. J. et al. (2004). Precursors of mild mental retardation in children with adolescent mothers. *International Review of Research in Mental Retardation, 29*, 197–228.

Borthwick-Duffy, S. A. (2007). Adaptive behavior. In J. W. Jacobson, J. A. Mulick, & J. Rojahn (Eds.), *Handbook of intellectual disabilities* (pp. 279–293). New York: Springer Science + Business Media.

Brady, N. C., & Warren, S. F. (2003). Language interventions for children with mental retardation. In L. Masters-Glidden & L. Abbeduto (Eds.), *Language and communication in mental retardation* (pp. 231–250). Boston: Academic Press.

Bray, N. W., Fletcher, K. L., & Turner, L. A. (1997). Cognitive competencies and strategy use in individuals with mental retardation. In W. E. MacLean, Jr. (Ed.), *Ellis' handbook of mental deficiency, psychological theory, and research* (3rd ed., pp. 197–217). Mahwah, NJ: Erlbaum.

Browder, D., & Spooner, F. (2005). *Teaching reading, math, and science to students with significant cognitive disabilities.* Baltimore: Brookes.

Brown, L., Branston-McClean, M. B., Baumgart, D., Vincent, L., Falvey, M., & Schroeder, J. (1979). Using the characteristics of current and subsequent least restrictive environments in the development of curricular content for severely handicapped students. *AAESPH Review, 4*, 407–424.

Brown, L., Nisbet, J., Ford, A., Sweet, M., Shiraga, B., York, J., et al. (1983). The critical need for nonschool instruction in educational programs for severely handicapped students. *Journal of the Association for Persons with Severe Disabilities, 8*, 71–77.

Bryant, B. R., Bryant, D. P., & Chamberlain, S. (1999). Examination of gender and race factors in the assessment of adaptive behavior. In R. L. Schalock (Ed.), *Adaptive behavior and its measurement: Implications for the field of mental retardation* (pp. 141–160). Washington, DC: American Association on Mental Retardation.

Burbacher, T. M., & Grant, K. S. (2006). Neurodevelopmental effects of alcohol. In P. W. Davidson, G. J. Myers, & B. Weiss (Eds.), *International review of research in mental retardation: Neurotoxicity and developmental disabilities* (Vol. 30, pp. 1–45). San Diego, CA: Elsevier.

Causton-Theoharis, J. N., Giangreco, M. F., Doyle, M. B., & Vadasy, P. F. (2007). Paraprofessionals: The "sous-chefs" of literacy instruction. *TEACHING Exceptional Children, 40*(1), 56–62.

Clark, G. M. (2007). *Assessment for transitions planning* (2nd ed.). Austin, TX: Pro-Ed.

Clark, G. M., & Patton, J. R. (2006). *Transition planning inventory: Updated version.* Austin, TX: Pro-Ed.

Dixon, D. R. (2007). Adaptive behavior scales. In J. L. Matson (Ed.), *International review of research in mental retardation: Vol. 34. Handbook of assessment in persons wtih intellectual disability* (pp. 99–140). San Diego, CA: Elsevier.

Ellis, N. R. (1970). Memory processes in retardates and normals. In N. R. Ellis (Ed.), *International review of research in mental retardation* (Vol. 4, pp. 1–32). New York: Academic Press.

Emerson, E. (2007). Poverty and people with intellectual disabilities. *Mental Retardation and Development Disabilities Research Reviews, 13*, 107–113.

Emerson, E., Graham, H., & Hatton, C. (2006). Household income and health status in children and adolescents: Cross sectional study. *European Journal of Public Health, 16*, 354–360.

Farlow, L., & Snell, M. (2005). Making the most of student performance data. In M. Wehmeyer & M. Argan (Eds.), *Mental retardation and intellectual disabilities: Teaching students using innovative and research-based strategies* (pp. 27–77). Upper Saddle River, NJ: Merrill/Pearson.

Ferguson, D. L. (1995). The real challenge of inclusion: Confessions of a "rabid inclusionist." *Phi Delta Kappan, 77*, 281–287.

Fey, M. E., Warren, S. F., Brady, N., Finestack, L. H., Bredin-Oja, S. L., Fairchild, M., et al. (2006). Early effects of responsivity education/prelinguistic milieu teaching for children with developmental delays and their parents. *Journal of Speech, Language, and Hearing Research, 49*, 526–547.

Fletcher, K. L., Huffman, L. F., & Bray, N. W. (2003). Effects of verbal and physical prompts on external strategy use in children with and without mild mental retardation. *American Journal on Mental Retardation, 108*(4), 245–256.

Fujiura, G. T., & Parish, S. L. (2007). Emerging policy challenges in intellectual disabilities. *Mental Retardation and Developmental Disabilities Research Reviews, 13*(2), 188–194.

Getzel, E. E., & Wehman, P. (2005). *Going to college: Expanding opportunities for people with disabilities.* Baltimore: Brookes.

Giangreco, M. F., & Broer, S. M. (2007). School-based screening to determine overreliance on paraprofessionals. *Focus on Autism and Other Developmental Disabilities, 22*(3), 149–158.

Glynn, L. M., & Sandman, C. A. (2006). The influence of prenatal stress and adverse birth outcome on human cognitive and neurological development. In L. M. Glidden (Ed.), *International review of research in mental retardation* (Vol. 32, pp. 109–129). San Diego, CA: Elsevier.

Harris, J. C. (2006). *Intellectual disability: Understanding its development, causes, classification, evaluation, and treatment.* Oxford, England: Oxford University Press.

Hasazi, S., Johnson, D., Thurlow, M., Cobb, B., Trach, J., Stodden, B., et al. (2005). Transitions from home and school to the roles and supports of adulthood. In K. C. Lakin & A. Turnbull (Eds.), *National goals and research for people with intellectual and developmental disabilities* (pp. 65–92). Washington, DC: American Association on Mental Retardation.

Hessl, D., Rivera, S. M., & Reiss, A. L. (2004). The neuroanatomy and neuroendocrinology of Fragile X syndrome. *Mental Retardation and Developmental Disabilities Research Reviews, 10*, 17–24.

Horner, R. H., Dunlap, G., & Koegel, R. L. (Eds.). (1988). *Generalization and maintenance: Life-style changes in applied settings.* Baltimore: Brookes.

Individuals with Disabilities Education Act regulations (IDEA), 34 C.F.R. § 300.8 (2006).

Jarrold, C., Purser, H. R. M., & Brock, J. (2006). Short-term memory in Down syndrome. In T. P. Alloway & S. E. Gathercole (Eds.), *Working memory and neurodevelopmental conditions* (pp. 239–266). Hove, East Sussex, England: Psychology Press.

Kaiser, A. P., & Grim, J. C. (2006). Teaching functional communication skills. In M. E. Snell & F. Brown (Eds.), *Instruction of students with severe disabilities* (6th ed., pp. 447–488). Upper Saddle River, NJ: Merrill/Pearson.

Katsiyannis, A., Zhang, D., & Archwamety, T. (2002). Placement and exit patterns for students with mental retardation: An analysis of national trends. *Education and Training in Mental Retardation and Developmental Disabilities, 37*(2), 134–145.

Keller, C. L., Bucholz, J., & Brady, M. P. (2007). Yes I can! Empowering paraprofessionals to teach learning strategies. *TEACHING Exceptional Children, 39*(3), 18–23.

Kluth, P. (2000). Community-referenced learning and the inclusive classroom [Electronic version]. *Remedial and Special Education, 21*(1), 19–26.

Lambert, N., Nihira, K., & Leland, H. (1993). *AAMR adaptive behavior scale—school* (2nd ed.). Austin, TX: Pro-Ed.

Lane, K. L., Fletcher, T., Carter, E., Dejud, C., & Delorenzo, J. (2007). Paraprofessional-led phonological awareness training with youngsters at risk for reading and behavioral concerns. *Remedial and Special Education, 28*(5), 266–276.

Langone, J., Langone, C. A., & McLaughlin, P. J. (2000). Analyzing special educators' views on community-based instruction for students with mental retardation and developmental disabilities: Implications for teacher education. *Journal of Developmental and Physical Disabilities, 12*(1), 17–34.

Lovering, J. S., & Percy, M. (2007). Down syndrome. In I. Brown & M. Percy (Eds.), *A comprehensive guide to intellectual and developmental disabilities* (pp. 149–172). Baltimore: Brookes.

Luckasson, R., Borthwick-Duffy, S., Buntinx, W. H. E., Coulter, D. L., Craig, E. M., Reeve A. I., et al. (2002). *Mental retardation: Definition, classification, and systems of supports.* Washington, DC: American Association on Mental Retardation.

Luckasson, R., Coulter, D. L., Polloway, E. A., Reiss, S., Schalock, R. L., Snell, M. E., et al. (1992). *Mental retardation: Definition, classification, and systems of supports.* Washington, DC: American Association on Mental Retardation.

Lytle, R., Lieberman, L., & Aiello, R. (2007). Motivating paraeducators to be actively involved in physical education programs. *The Journal of Physical Education, Recreation & Dance, 78*(4), 26–30.

Martin, J., Jorgensen, C. M., & Klein, J. (1998). The promise of friendship for students with disabilities. In C. M. Jorgensen (Ed.), *Restructuring high schools for all students: Taking inclusion to the next level* (pp. 145–181). Baltimore: Brookes.

Mechling, L. C., Gast, D. L., & Langone, J. (2002). Computer-based video instruction to teach persons with moderate intellectual disabilities to read grocery aisle signs and locate items. *Journal of Special Education 35*(4), 224–240.

Mechling, L. C., & Ortega-Hurndon, F. (2007). Computer-based video instruction to teach young adults with moderate intellectual disabilities to perform multiple step job tasks in a generalized setting. *Education and Training in Developmental Disabilities, 42*(1), 24–37.

Murphy, C. C., Boyle, C., Schendel, D., Decouflé, P., & Yeargin-Allsopp, M. (1998). Epidemiology of mental retardation in children. *Mental Retardation and Developmental Disabilities Research Reviews, 4*, 6–13.

National Research Council. (2002). *Minority students in special and gifted education.* Washington, DC: National Academy Press.

Noonan, P. M., Morningstar, M. E., & Erikson, A. G. (in press). Improving inter-agency collaboration: Effective strategies used by high performing local districts and communities. *Career Development for Exceptional Individuals.*

Palmer, S. B., Wehmeyer, M. L., Gibson, K., & Agran, M. (2004). Promoting access to the general curriculum by teaching self-determination skills. *Exceptional Children, 70*, 427–439.

Palmer, S., & Wehmeyer, M. L. (1998). Students' expectations of the future: Hopelessness as a barrier to self-determination. *Mental Retardation, 36*, 128–136.

Percy, M. (2007). Factors that cause or contribute to intellectual and developmental disabilities. In I. Brown & M. Percy (Eds.), *A comprehensive guide to intellectual & developmental disabilities* (pp. 125–148). Baltimore: Brookes.

Quilty, K. M. (2007). Teaching paraprofessionals how to write and implement social stories for students with autism spectrum disorders. *Remedial and Special Education, 28*(3), 182–191.

Riggs, C. G., & Mueller, P. H. (2001). Employment and utilization of paraeducators in inclusive settings. *Journal of Special Education, 35*(1), 54–62.

Schalock, R., Luckasson, R., Shogren, K., Bradley, V., Borthwick-Duffy, S., Buntix, W., et al. (2007). The renaming of mental retardation: Understanding the change to the term intellectual disability. *Intellectual and Developmental Disabilities, 45*, 116–124.

Shogren, K. A., Lopez, S. J., Wehmeyer, M. L., Little, T. D., & Pressgrove, C. L. (2006). The role of positive psychology constructs in predicting life satisfaction in adolescents with and without cognitive disabilities: An exploratory study. *Journal of Positive Psychology, 1*, 37–52.

Snell, M., & Brown, F. (2001). *Instruction of students with severe disabilities* (5th ed.). Upper Saddle River, NJ: Merrill/Pearson.

Stevens, S. L. (2006). An investigation of the content validity, stability, and internal consistency of the Spanish version of the

Transition Planning Inventory Home Form. Unpublished doctoral dissertation, University of Kansas, Lawrence, KS.

Stinnett, T. A., Fuqua, D. R., & Coombs, W. T. (1999). Construct validity of the AAMR adaptive behavior scale—school: 2. *School Psychology Review, 28*(1), 31–43.

Stodden, R. A., Brown, S. E., Galloway, L. M., Mrazek, S., & Noy, L. (2005). *Essential tools: Interagency transition team development and facilitation.* Minneapolis, MN: University of Minnesota, Institute on Community Integration, National Center on Secondary Education and Transition.

Stokes, T. F., & Baer, D. M. (1977). An implicit technology of generalization. *Journal of Applied Behavior Analysis, 10,* 349–367.

Switzky, H. (2006). *International review of research in mental retardation: Vol. 31. Mental retardation, personality, and motivational systems.* San Diego, CA: Academic Press.

Tassé, M. J., & Havercamp, S. M. (2006). The role of motivation and psychopathology in understanding the IQ-adaptive behavior discrepancy. In L. M. Glidden (Series Ed.) & H. Switzky (Vol. Ed.), *International review of research in mental retardation: Vol. 31. Mental retardation, personality and motivational systems* (pp. 231–260). San Diego, CA: Academic Press.

Taylor, R. L., Richards, S. B., & Brady, M. P. (2005). *Mental retardation: Historical perspectives, current practices, and future directions.* Boston: Pearson.

Test, D., & Spooner, F. (2005). Community-based instructional support. In M. Wehmeyer & M. Agran (Eds.), *Mental retardation and intellectual disabilities: Teaching students using innovative and research-based strategies* (pp. 79–100). Boston, MA: Merrill/Pearson.

Thurlow, M., & Bolt, S. (2001). *Empirical support for accommodations most often allowed in state policy* (Synthesis Report 41). Minneapolis: University of Minnesota, National Center on Educational Outcomes.

Tylenda, B., Beckett, J., & Barrett, R. P. (2007). Assessing mental retardation using standardized intelligence tests. In J. L. Matson (Ed.), *International review of research in mental retardation: Vol. 34. Handbook of assessment in persons with intellectual disability* (pp. 27–97). San Diego, CA: Elsevier.

U.S. Department of Education. (1999). *To assure the free appropriate public education of all children with disabilities: Twenty-first annual report to Congress on the implementation of the Individuals with Disabilities Education Act.* Washington, DC: Author.

U.S. Department of Education, Office of Special Education Programs. (2008). Individuals with Disabilities Education Act (IDEA) data. Retrieved January 18, 2008, from https://www.IDEAdata.org/index.html

Vadasy, P. F., Sanders, E. A., & Peyton, J. A. (2006a). Code-oriented instruction for kindergarten students at risk for reading difficulties: A randomized field trial with paraeducator implementers. *Journal of Educational Psychology, 98,* 508–528.

Vadasy, P. F., Sanders, E. A., & Peyton, J. A. (2006b). Paraeducator-supplemented instruction in structural analysis with text reading practice for second and third graders at risk for reading problems. *Remedial and Special Education, 27*(6), 365–378.

Wagner, M., Newman, L., Cameto, R., Levine, P., & Garza, N. (2006). *An overview of findings from wave 2 of the National Longitudinal Transition Study-2 (NLTS2).* Menlo Park, CA: SRI International. Retrieved july 7, 2008, from http://www.nlts2.org/reports/2006_08/nlts2_report_2006_08_complete.pdf

Wehmeyer, M. L., Abery, B., Mithaug, D. E., & Stancliffe, R. J. (2003). *Theory in self-determination: Foundations for educational practice.* Springfield, IL: Thomas.

Wehmeyer, M. L., Agran, M., Hughes, C., Martin, J., Mithaug, D. E., & Palmer, S. (2007). *Promoting self-determination in students with intellectual and developmental disabilities.* New York: Guilford Press.

Wehmeyer, M. L., Agran, M., Palmer, S. B., & Mithaug, D. (1999). A teacher' guide to implementing the self-determined learning model of instruction (adolescent version). Lawrence: University of Kansas, Beach Center.

Wehmeyer, M. L., Garner, N., Lawrence, M., Yeager, D., & Davis, A. K. (2006). Infusing self-determination into 18–21 services for students with intellectual or developmental disabilities: A multi-stage, multiple component model. *Education and Training in Developmental Disabilities, 41,* 3–13.

Wehmeyer, M. L., & Mithaug, D. (2006). Self-determination, causal agency, and mental retardation. In L. M. Glidden (Series Ed.) & H. Switzky (Vol. Ed.), *International review of research in mental retardation: Vol. 31. Mental retardation, personality, and motivational systems.* (pp. 31–71). San Diego, CA: Academic Press.

Wehmeyer, M. L., & Sailor, W. (2004). High school. In C. Kennedy & E. Horn (Eds.), *Including students with severe disabilities* (pp. 259–281). Boston: Allyn & Bacon.

Wehmeyer, M. L., Sands, D. J., Knowlton, H. E., & Kozleski, E. B. (2002). *Teaching students with mental retardation: Providing access to the general curriculum.* Baltimore: Brookes.

Winter-Messiers, M. A. (2007). From tarantulas to toilet brushes: Understanding the special interest areas of children and youth with Asperger syndrome. *Remedial and Special Education, 28*(3), 140–152.

World Health Organization. (2001). *International classification of functioning, disability, and health—ICF.* Geneva: Author.

Yeargin-Allsopp, M., Murphy, C. C., Cordero, J. F., Decouflé, P., & Hollowell, J. G. (1997). Reported biomedical causes and associated medical conditions for mental retardation among 10-year-old children, metropolitan Atlanta, 1985 to 1987. *Developmental Medicine and Child Neurology, 39*(3), 142–149.

Yoder, P. J., & Warren, S. F. (2001). Relative treatment effects of two prelinguistic communication interventions on language development in toddlers with developmental delays vary by maternal characteristics. *Journal of Speech, Language, and Hearing Research, 44,* 224–237.

Zigler, E. (2001). Looking back 40 years and still seeing the person with mental retardation as a whole person. In H. Switzky (Ed.), *Personality and motivational differences in persons with mental retardation* (pp. 3–56). Mahwah, NJ: Erlbaum.

Chapter 10

Agran, M., King-Sears, M., Wehmeyer, M. L., & Copeland, S. R. (2003). *Teachers' guide to inclusive practices: Student-directed learning strategies.* Baltimore: Brookes.

Bambara, L. M., Browder, D. M., & Koger, F. (2006). Home and community. In M. Snell & F. Brown (Eds.), *Instruction of students with severe disabilities* (6th ed., pp. 526–528). Upper Saddle River, NJ: Merrill/Pearson.

Batshaw, M. L., Shapiro, B., & Farber, M. L. Z. (2007). Developmental delay and intellectual disability. In M. L. Batshaw, L. Pellegrino, & N. J. Roizen (Eds.), *Children with disabilities* (6th ed., pp. 245–261). Baltimore: Brookes.

Baumgart, D., Brown, L., Pumpian, I., Nisbet, J., Ford, A., Sweet, M., et al. (1982). Principle of partial participation and individualized adaptations in educational programs for severely handicapped students. *Journal of the Association for Persons with Severe Disabilities, 7,* 17–27.

Bigge, J. L., Best, S. J., & Heller, K. W. (2001). *Teaching individuals with physical, health, or multiple disabilities* (4th ed.). Upper Saddle River, NJ: Merrill/Pearson.

Blackstone, S. W., Williams, M. B., & Wilkins, D. P. (2007). Key principles underlying research and practice in AAC. *Augmentative and Alternative Communication, 23*(3), 191–203.

Browder, D., & Spooner, F. (2006). *Teaching language arts, math, and science to students with significant cognitive disabilities*. Baltimore: Brookes.

Browder, D. M., Ahlgrim-Delzell, L., Courtade-Little, G., & Snell, M. (2006). General curriculum access. In M. Snell & F. Brown (Eds.), *Instruction of students with severe disabilities* (6th ed., pp. 489–525). Upper Saddle River, NJ: Merrill/Pearson.

Browder, D. M., Spooner, F., Algozzine, R., Ahlgrim-Delzell, L., Flowers, C., & Karvonen, M. (2003). What we know and need to know about alternate assessment. *Exceptional Children, 70*(1), 45–61.

Brown, F., & Snell, M. E. (2006). Measurement, assessment, and evaluation. In M. Snell & F. Brown (Eds.), *Instruction of students with severe disabilities* (6th ed., pp. 170–205). Upper Saddle River, NJ: Merrill/Pearson.

Brown, F., Snell, M. E., & Lehr, D. (2006). Meaningful assessment. In M. Snell & F. Brown (Eds.), *Instruction of students with severe disabilities* (6th ed., pp. 67–110). Upper Saddle River, NJ: Merrill/Pearson.

Brown, I., Galambos, D., Poston, D. J., & Turnbull, A. P. (2007). Person-centered and family-centered support. In I. Brown & M. Percy (Eds.), *A comprehensive guide to intellectual & developmental disabilities* (pp. 351–361). Baltimore: Brookes.

Bui, Y. N., & Turnbull, A. (2003). East meets west: Analysis of person-centered planning in the context of Asian American values. *Education and Training in Mental Retardation and Developmental Disabilities, 28*(1), 18–31.

Calhoon, M. B. (2005). Effects of a peer-mediated phonological skill and reading comprehension program on reading skill acquisition for middle school students with reading disabilities. *Journal of Learning Disabilities, 38*(5), 424–433.

Campbell, P. H. (2006). Addressing motor disabilities. In M. E. Snell & F. Brown (Eds.), *Instruction of students with severe disabilities* (6th ed., pp. 291–327). Upper Saddle River, NJ: Merrill/Pearson.

Carter, E. W., & Hughes, C. (2005). Increasing social interaction among adolescents with intellectual disabilities and their general education peers: Effective interventions. *Research and Practice for Persons with Severe Disabilities, 30*(4), 179–193.

Chambers, C., & Childres, A. (2005). Fostering family-professional collaboration through person-centered IEP meetings: The "true directions" model. *Young Exceptional Children, 8*(3), 20–28.

Collins, B. C., Hendricks, T. B., Fetko, K., & Land, L. A. (2002). Student-2-student learning in inclusive classrooms. *Teaching Exceptional Children, 34*(4), 56–61.

Copeland, S. R., Hughes, C., Carter, E. W., Guth, C., Presley, J. A., Williams, C. R., et al. (2004). Increasing access to general education: Perspectives of participants in a high school peer support program. *Remedial and Special Education, 25*(6), 342–352.

Copeland, S. R., & Keefe, E. B. (2007). *Effective literacy instruction for students with moderate or severe disabilities.* Baltimore: Brookes.

Copeland, S. R., McCall, J., Williams, C. R., Guth, C., Carter, E. W., Fowler, S. E., et al. (2002). High school peer buddies: A win-win situation. *TEACHING Exceptional Children, 35*(1), 16–21.

Davies, D. M., Stock, S., & Wehmeyer, M. L. (2002a). Enhancing independent task performance for individuals with mental retardation through use of a handheld self-directed visual and audio prompting system. *Education and Training in Mental Retardation and Developmental Disabilities, 37*, 209–218.

Davies, D. M., Stock, S., & Wehmeyer, M. L. (2002b). Enhancing independent time management and personal scheduling for individuals with mental retardation through use of a palmtop visual and audio prompting system. *Mental Retardation, 40*, 358–365.

Downing, J. E. (2002). *Including students with severe and multiple disabilities in typical classrooms* (2nd ed.). Baltimore: Brookes.

Downing, J. E. (2005). *Teaching literacy to students with significant disabilities.* Thousand Oaks, CA: Corwin Press.

Downing, J. E. (2008). *Including students with severe and multiple disabilities in typical classrooms* (3rd ed.). Baltimore: Brookes.

Engleman, M. D., Griffin, H. C., Griffin, L. W., & Maddox, J. I. (1999). A teacher's guide to communicating with students with deaf-blindness. *Teaching Exceptional Children, 31*(5), 64–70.

Eshilian, L., Falvey, M. A., Bove, C., Hibbard, M. J., Laiblin, J., Miller, C., et al. (2000). Restructuring to create a high school community of learners. In R. A. Villa & J. S. Thousand (Eds.), *Restructuring for caring and effective education* (pp. 402–427). Baltimore: Brookes.

Falvey, M. A., Eshilian, L., & Hibbard, J. (2000, April). Collaboration at Whittier High School. *TASH Newsletter, 26*, 8–9.

Falvey, M. A., Forest, M. S., Pearpoint, J., & Rosenberg, R. L. (2002). Building connections. In J. S. Thousand, R. A. Villa, & A. I. Nevin (Eds.), *Creativity and collaborative learning* (2nd ed., pp. 29–54). Baltimore: Brookes.

Farlow, L. J., & Snell, M. E. (2006). Teaching self-care skills. In M. E. Snell & F. Brown (Eds.), *Instruction of students with severe disabilities* (6th ed., pp. 328–374). Upper Saddle River, NJ: Merrill/Pearson.

Ferguson, D. L., & Baumgart, D. (1991). Partial participation revisited. *Journal of the Association for Persons with Severe Disabilities, 16*, 218–227.

Fossett, B., & Mirenda, P. (2007). Augmentative and alternative communication. In S. L. Odom, R. H. Horner, M. E. Snell, & J. Blacher (Eds.), *Handbook of developmental disabilities* (pp. 330–348). New York: Guilford Press.

Frey, G. C. (2007). Physical activity and youth with developmental disabilities. In S. L. Odom, R. H. Horner, M. E. Snell, & J. Blacher (Eds.), *Handbook of developmental disabilities* (pp. 349–365). New York: Guilford Press.

Giangreco, M. F. (2006). Foundational concepts and practices for educating students with severe disabilities. In M. E. Snell & F. Brown (Eds.), *Instruction of students with severe disabilities* (6th ed., pp. 1–27). Upper Saddle River, NJ: Merrill/Pearson.

Gilberts, G. H., Agran, M., Hughes, C., & Wehmeyer, M. (2001). The effects of peer delivered self-monitoring strategies on the participation of students with severe disabilities in general education classrooms. *Journal of the Association for Persons with Severe Handicaps, 26*(1), 25–36.

Heller, K. W. (2000). *Meeting physical and health needs of children with disabilities: Teaching student participation and management.* Pacific Grove, CA: Brooks/Cole.

Holburn, S., Gordon, A., & Vietze, P. M. (2007). *Person-centered planning made easy: The picture method.* Baltimore: Brookes.

Horn, E., Thompson, B., Palmer, S., Jensen, R., & Turbiville, V. (2004). Preschool. In C. H. Kennedy & E. M. Horn (Eds.), *Inclusion of students with severe disabilities* (pp. 207–221). Boston: Allyn and Bacon.

Hughes, C., Carter, E. W., Hughes, T., Bradford, E., & Copeland, S. R. (2002). Effects of instructional versus non-instructional roles on the social interactions of high school students. *Education and Training in Mental Retardation and Developmental Disabilities, 37*(2), 146–162.

Hughes, C., Copeland, S. R., Guth, C., Rung, L. L., Hwang, B., Kleeb, G., et al. (2001). General education students' perspectives on their involvement in a high school peer buddy program. *Education and Training in Developmental Disabilities, 36*(4), 343–356.

Hughes, C., Rung, L. L., Wehmeyer, M. L., Agran, M., Copeland, S. R., & Hwang, B. (2000). Self-prompted communication book use to increase social interaction among high school students. *Journal of the Association for Persons with Severe Disabilities, 25*, 153–166.

Individuals with Disabilities Education Act regulations (IDEA), 34 C. F. R. § 300.8 (2006).

Kaiser, A. P., & Grim, J. C. (2006). Teaching functional communication skills. In M. E. Snell & F. Brown (Eds.) *Instruction of students with severe disabilities* (6th ed., pp. 447–488). Upper Saddle River, NJ: Merrill/Pearson.

Kearnes, J. F., Burdge, M. D., & Kleinert, H. L. (2005). Alternate assessment and standards-based instruction: Practical strategies for teachers. In M. L. Wehmeyer & M. Agran (Eds.), *Empirically-validated practices for teaching students with mental retardation and intellectual disabilities.* Upper Saddle River, NJ: Merrill/Pearson.

Keller, C. L. (2002). A new twist on spelling instruction for elementary school teachers. *Instruction in School and Clinic, 38*(1), 3–7.

Kim, K. H., & Turnbull, A. (2004). Transition to adulthood for students with severe intellectual disabilities: Shifting toward person-family interdependent planning. *Research and Practice for Persons with Severe Disabilities, 29,* 53–57.

Kleinert, H. L., & Kearns, J. F. (2001). *Alternate assessment: Measuring outcomes and supports for students with disabilities.* Baltimore: Brookes.

Lancioni, G. E., O'Reilly, M. F., Singh, N. N., Sigafoos, J., Didden, R., Oliva, D., et al. (2006). A microswitch-based program to enable students with multiple disabilities to choose among environmental stimuli. *Journal of Visual Impairment & Blindness, 100*(8), 488–493.

Leiber, J., Horn, E., Palmer, S., & Fleming, K. (2008). *Access to the general education curriculum for preschoolers with disabilities: Children's school success.* Manuscript submitted for publication.

Mandal, R. L., Smiroldo, B., & Haynes-Powell, J. (2007). Self-care skills. In J. L. Matson (Ed.), *International review of research in mental retardation: Vol. 34. Handbook of assessment in persons wtih intellectual disability* (pp. 365–386). San Diego, CA: Elsevier.

Martin, J., Marshall, L., Maxson, L., & Jerman, M. (1993). *Self-directed IEP: Teacher's manual.* Colorado Springs: University of Colorado, Center for Educational Research.

Mazzocco, M. M. M., & Holden, J. J. A. (2007). Fragile X syndrome. In I. Brown & M. Percy (Eds.), *A comprehensive guide to intellectual & developmental disabilities* (pp. 173–187). Baltimore: Brookes.

McDonnell, J. M., Mathot-Buckner, C., Thorson, N., & Fister, S. (2001). Supporting the inclusion of students with moderate and severe disabilities in junior high school general education classes: The effects of classwide peer tutoring, multi-element curriculum, and accommodations. *Education and Treatment of Children, 24*(2), 141–160.

Moser, H. W. (2004). Genetic causes of mental retardation. *Annals of the New York Academy of Sciences, 1038,* 44–48.

Mount, B., & O'Brien, C. L. (2002). *Exploring new worlds for students with disabilities in transition from high school to adult life.* New York: Job Path.

National Institutes of Health. (n.d.). Fact sheet: Human Genome Project. Retrieved October 8, 2007, from http://www.nih.gov/about/researchresultsforthepublic/HumanGenomeProject.pdf

Odom, S., Butera, G., Schneider, R., Lieber, J., Sharpatwari, S., Horn, E., et al. (2007, April). *Children's School Success (CSS): Child outcomes from three years of research.* Paper presented at the meeting of the Council for Exceptional Children, Louisville, Kentucky.

Orelove, F. P., Sobsey, D., & Silberman, R. K. (2004). *Educating children with multiple disabilities: A collaborative approach* (4th ed.). Baltimore: Brookes.

Palmer, D. S., Fuller, K., Arora, T., & Nelson, M. (2001). Taking sides: Parent views on inclusion for their children with severe disabilities. *Council for Exceptional Children, 67*(4), 467–484.

Percy, M. (2007). Factors that cause or contribute to intellectual and developmental disabilities. In I. Brown & M. Percy (Eds.), *A comprehensive guide to intellectual & developmental disabilities* (pp. 125–148). Baltimore: Brookes.

Percy, M., Cheetham, T., Gitta, M., Morrison, B., Machalek, K., Bega, S., et al. (2007). Other syndromes and disorders associated with intellectual and developmental disabilities. In I. Brown, & M. Percy (Eds.), *A comprehensive guide to intellectual & developmental disabilities* (pp. 229–267). Baltimore: Brookes.

Quenemoen, R., Thompson, S., & Thurlow, M. (2003). *Measuring academic achievement of students with significant cognitive disabilities: Building understanding of alternate assessment scoring criteria* (Synthesis Report 50). Minneapolis: University of Minnesota, National Center on Educational Outcomes. Retrieved july 7, 2008, from http://education.umn.edu/NCEO/OnlinePubs/Synthesis50.html.

Riffel, L. A., Wehmeyer, M. L., Turnbull, A. P., Lattimore, J., Davies, D., Stock, S., et al. (2005). Promoting independent performance of transition-related tasks using a palmtop PC-based self-directed visual and auditory prompting system. *Journal of Special Education Technology, 20*(2), 5–14.

Rowland, C., & Schweigert, P. (2003). Cognitive skills and AAC. In D. R. Beukelman & J. Reichle (Series Eds.), J. C. Light, D. R. Beukelman, & J. Reichle (Vol. Eds.), *Augmentative and alternative communication series: Communicative competence for individuals who use AAC: From research to effective practice* (pp. 241–275). Baltimore: Brookes.

Ryndak, D. L., & Fisher, D. (Eds.). (2003). *The foundations of inclusive education: A compendium of articles on effective strategies to achieve inclusive education* (2nd ed.). Baltimore: TASH.

Sailor, W. (2002). Devolution, school/community/family partnerships, and inclusive education. In W. Sailor (Ed.), *Whole-school success and inclusive education: Building partnerships for learning, achievement, and accountability* (pp. 7–25). New York: Teachers College Press.

Schlosser, R. W. (2003). *The efficacy of augmentative and alternative communication: Toward evidence-based practice.* San Diego, CA: Academic Press.

Schlosser, R. W., Sigafoos, J., Rothschild, N., Burke, M., & Palace, L. M. (2007). Speech and language disorders. In I. Brown & M. Percy (Eds.), *A comprehensive guide to intellectual & developmental disabilities* (pp. 383–401). Baltimore: Brookes.

Scott, V. G. (2006). Incorporating service learning into your special education classroom. *Intervention in School and Clinic, 42*(1), 25–29.

Silberman, R. K., Bruce, S. M., & Nelson, C. (2004). Children with sensory impairments. In F. P. Orelove, D. Sobsey, & R. K. Silberman (Eds.), *Educating children with multiple disabilities: A collaborative approach* (4th ed., pp. 425–527). Baltimore: Brookes.

Skuse, D. H. (2005). X-linked genes and mental functioning. *Human Molecular Genetics, 14*(Spec. No. 1), R27–R32.

Smith, M. G. (2000). Secondary teachers' perceptions toward inclusion of students with severe disabilities. *NASSP Bulletin, 84*(613), 54–60.

Snell, M. E., & Brown, F. (2006). Designing and implementing instructional programs. In M. Snell & F. Brown (Eds.), *Instruction of students with severe disabilities* (6th ed., pp. 111–169). Upper Saddle River, NJ: Merrill/Pearson.

Soodak, L. C., Erwin, E. J., Winton, P., Brotherson, M. J., Turnbull, A. P., Hanson, M. J., et al. (2002). Implementing inclusive early childhood education: A call for professional empowerment. *Topics in Early Childhood Special Education, 22*(2), 91–102.

Stowe, M. J., Turnbull, H. R., Schrandt, S., & Rack, J. (2007). Looking to the future: Intellectual and developmental disabilities in the genetics era. *Journal of Developmental Disabilities, 13*(2), 1–64.

Szczepanski, M. (2004). Physical management in the classroom: Handling and positioning. In F. P. Orelove, D. Sobsey, & R. K. Silberman (Eds.), *Educating children with multiple disabilities: A collaborative approach* (4th ed., pp. 249–309). Baltimore: Brookes.

Tartaglia, N. R., Hansen, R. L., & Hagerman, R. J. (2007). Advances in genetics. In S. L. Odom, R. H. Horner, M. E. Snell, & J. Blacher (Eds.), *Handbook of developmental disabilities* (pp. 98–128). New York: Guilford Press.

Thousand, J. S., Villa, R. A., & Nevin, A. I. (2002). *Creativity and collaborative learning: The practical guide to empowering students, teachers, and families* (2nd ed.). Baltimore: Brookes.

Trainor, A. A. (2007). Person-centered planning in two culturally distinct communities: Responding to divergent needs and preferences. *Career Development for Exceptional Individuals, 30*(2), 92–103.

Turnbull, A. P., Turnbull, H. R., Erwin, E., & Soodak, L. (2006). *Families, professionals, and exceptionality: Positive outcomes through partnerships and trust* (5th ed.). Upper Saddle River, NJ: Merrill/Pearson.

U.S. Department of Education, Office of Special Education Programs. (2008). Individuals with Disabilities Education Act (IDEA) data: Retrieved January 18, 2008, from https://www.IDEAdata.org/index.html

Ward, L. P., & McCune, S. K. (2002). The first weeks of life. In M. L. Batshaw (Ed.), *Children with disabilities* (5th ed., pp. 69–83). Baltimore: Brookes.

Will, M. C. (1993). The question of personal autonomy. *Journal of Vocational Rehabilitation, 3*(2), 9–10.

Wolfe, P., & Hall, T. E. (2003). Making inclusion a reality for students with severe disabilities. *Teaching Exceptional Children, 35*(4), 56–60.

Wood, W. M., Fowler, C. H., Uphold, N., & Test, D. W. (2005). A review of self-determination interventions with individuals with severe disabilities. *Research and Practice for Persons with Severe Disabilities, 30*(3), 121–146.

Zabala, J. S. (2002). *SETTing the stage for success: Building success through effective selection and use of assistive technology systems*. Retrieved October 18, 2007, from http://sweb.uky.edu/~jszaba0/SETT2.html

Chapter 11

Afzal, M. A., Ozoemena, L. C., O'Hare, A., Kidger, K. A., Bentley, M. L., & Minor, P. D. (2006). Absence of detectable measles virus genome sequence in blood of autistic children who have had their MMR vaccination during the routine childhood immunization schedule of the UK. *Journal of Medical Virology, 78,* 623–630.

Agosta, E., Graetz, J. E., Matropieri, M. A., & Scruggs, T. E. (2004). Teacher-researcher partnerships to improve social behavior through social stories. *Intervention in School and Clinic, 39*(5), 276–287.

American Psychiatric Association. (2000). *Diagnostic and statistical manual of mental disorders* (4th ed., rev.). Washington, DC: Author.

Arick, J. R., Young, H. F., Falco, R. A., Loos, L. M., Krug, D. A., Gense, M. H., et al. (2003). Designing an outcome study to monitor the progress of students with autism spectrum disorders. *Focus on Autism and Other Developmental Disabilities, 18,* 75–87.

Avchen, R. N., Bhasin, T. K., Braun, K. V., & Yeargin-Allsopp, M. (2007). Public health impact: Metropolitan Atlanta developmental disabilities surveillance program. *International Review of Research in Mental Retardation, 33,* 149–191.

Baer, D. M., Wolf, M. M., & Risley, T. R. (1968). Some current dimensions of applied behavior analysis. *Journal of Applied Behavior Analysis, 1,* 91–97.

Ballaban-Gil, K., Rapin, I., Tuchman, R. F., & Shinnar, S. (1996). Longitudinal examination of the behavioral, language, and social changes in a population of adolescents and young adults with autistic disorder. *Pediatric Neurology, 15,* 217–223.

Bambara, L. M., & Kern, L. (2005). *Individualized supports for students with problem behaviors: Designing positive behavior plans.* New York: Guilford Press.

Baron-Cohen, S. (2001). Theory of mind and autism: A review. *International Review of Research in Mental Retardation, 23,* 169–184.

Baron-Cohen, S., Golan, O., Wheelwright, S., & Hill, J. J. (2004). *Mind reading: The interactive guide to emotions.* London: Jessica Kingsley Limited.

Baron-Cohen, S., & Wheelwright, S. (2004). The empathy quotient: An investigation of adults with Asperger syndrome or high functioning autism, and normal sex differences. *Journal of Autism and Developmental Disorders, 34*(2), 163–175.

Baron-Cohen, S., Wheelwright, S., Lawson, J., Griffin, R., & Hill, J. (2002). The exact mind: Empathizing and systemizing in autism spectrum conditions. In U. Goswami (Ed.), *Blackwell handbook of childhood cognitive development* (pp. 491–508). Oxford, England: Blackwell.

Bellini, S., Peters, J. K., Benner, L., & Hopf, A. (2007). A meta-analysis of school-based social skills interventions for children with autism spectrum disorders. *Remedial and Special Education, 28*(3), 153–162.

Blacher, J. (2007). Unlocking the mystery of social deficits in autism: Theory of mind as key. *Exceptional Parent, 37*(8), 96–97.

Boutot, E. A. (2007). Fitting in: Tips for promoting acceptance and friendships for students with autism spectrum disorders in inclusive classrooms. *Intervention in School and Clinic, 42*(3), 158–161.

Cardon, T. A. (2007). *Initiations and Interactions: Early intervention techniques for parents of children with autism spectrum disorders.* Shawnee Mission, KS: Autism Asperger Publishing.

Carr, E. G. (2007). The expanding vision of positive behavior support. *Journal of Positive Behavior Interventions, 9*(1), 3–14.

Carr, E. G., Dunlap, G., Horner, R. H., Koegel, R. L., Turnbull, A. P., Sailor, W., et al. (2002). Positive behavior support: Evolution of an applied science. *Journal of Positive Behavior Interventions, 4*(1), 4–16.

Carr, E. G., Horner, R. H., Turnbull, A. P., Marquis, J. G., Magito-McLaughlin, D., McAtee, M. L., et al. (1999). *Positive behavior support as an approach for dealing with problem behavior in people with developmental disabilities: A research synthesis.* Washington, DC: AAMR.

Carr, E. G., Levin, L., McConnachie, G., Carlson, J. I., Kemp, D. C., & Smith, C. E. (1994). *Communication-based intervention for problem behavior: A user's guide to producing positive change.* Baltimore: Brookes.

Chakrabarti, S., & Fombonne, E. (2001). Pervasive developmental disorders in preschool children. *Journal of the American Medical Association, 285*(24), 3093–3099.

Cheatham, S. K., Smith, J. D., Rucker, H. N., Polloway, E. A., & Lewis, G. W. (1995, September). Savant syndrome: Case studies, hypotheses, and implications for special education. *Education and Training in Mental Retardation,* pp. 243–253.

Cohen, R., Kincaid, D., & Childs, K. E. (2007). Measuring school-wide positive behavior support implementation: Development and validation of the Benchmarks of Quality. *Journal of Positive Behavior Interventions, 9*(4), 203–213.

Crone, D. A., Hawken, L. S., & Bergstrom, M. K. (2007). A demonstration of training, implementing, and using functional behavioral asessment in 10 elementary and middle school settings. *Journal of Positive Behavior Interventions, 9*(1), 15–29.

Crone, D. A., & Horner, R. H. (2003). *Building positive behavior support systems in schools.* New York: Guilford.

Dawson, G., & Watling, R. (2000). Interventions to facilitate auditory, visual, and motor integration in autism: A review of the evidence. *Journal of Autism and Developmental Disorders, 30*(5), 415–421.

DeBoer, S. R. (2007). *How to do discrete trial training.* Austin, TX: Pro-Ed.

Delano, M., & Snell, M. E. (2006). The effects of social stories on the social engagement of children with autism. *Journal of Positive Behavior Interventions* 8(1), 29–42.

Demicheli, V., Jefferson, T., Rivetti, A., & Price, D. (2005). Vaccines for measles, mumps, and rubella in children. *Cochrane Database of Systematic Reviews*, CD004407.

Dib, N., & Sturmey, P. (2007). Reducing student stereotypy by improving teachers' implementation of discrete-trial teaching. *Journal of Applied Behavior Analysis, 40*(3), 339–343.

Donnellan, A. M. (1999). Invented knowledge and autism: Highlighting our strengths and expanding the conversation. *Journal of the Association for Persons with Severe Handicaps, 24*(3), 230–236.

Farrugia, S., & Hudson, J. (2006). Anxiety in adolescents with Asperger syndrome: Negative thoughts, behavorial problems, and life interference. *Focus on Autism and Other Developmental Disabilities, 21*(1), 25–35.

Fombonne, E. (2003). Epidemiological surveys of autism and other pervasive developmental disorders: An update. *Journal of Autism and Developmental Disorders, 33*(4), 365–382.

Freeman, R., Eber, L., Anderson, C., Irvin, L., Horner, R., Bounds, M, et al. (2006). Building inclusive school cultures using school-wide positive behavior support: Designing effective individual support systems for students with significant disabilities. *Research and Practice for Persons with Severe Disabilities, 31*(1), 4–17.

Fuchs, D., & Fuchs, L. S. (1986). Test procedure bias: A meta-analysis of examiner familiarity effects. *Review of Educational Research, 56.* 243–262.

Golan, O., & Baron-Cohen, S. (2006). *Teaching children with Asperger syndrome and high functioning autism to recognize emotions using interactive multimedia.* Cambridge, England: University of Cambridge, Autism Research Centre.

Goldstein, H. (2003). Communication intervention for children with autism: A review of treatment efficacy. *Journal of Autism and Developmental Disorders, 32,* 373–396.

Grandin, T. (1988). Teaching tips from a recovered autistic. *Focus on Autistic Behavior, 3*(1), 1–8.

Gray, C. A. (1998). Social stories and comic strip conversations with students with Asperger syndrome and high-functioning autism. In E. Schopler, G. B. Mesibov, & L. J. Kunce (Eds.), *Asperger syndrome or high-functioning autism?* (pp. 167–198). New York: Plenum.

Gray, C., & White, A. L. (2002). *My social stories book.* Florence, KY: Taylor & Francis.

Green, V. A., Sigafoos, J., Pituch, K. A., Itchon, J., O'Reilly, M., & Lancioni, G. E. (2006). Assessing behavioral flexibility in individuals with developmental disabilities. *Focus on Autism and Other Developmental Disabilities, 21*(4), 230–236.

Griffin, H. C., Griffin, L. W., Fitch, C. W., Albera, V., & Gingras, H. (2006). Educational interventions for individuals with Asperger syndrome. *Intervention in School and Clinic, 41*(3), 150–155.

Hastings, R. P., & Noone, S. J. (2005). Self-injurious behavior and functional analysis: Ethics and evidence: *Education and Training in Developmental Disabilities, 40*(4), 335–342.

Horner, R. H., Albin, R. W., Todd, A. W., & Sprague, J. (2006). Positive behavior support for individuals with disabilities. In M. E. Snell & F. Brown (Eds.), *Instruction of students with severe disabilities* (6th ed., pp. 206–250). Baltimore: Brookes.

Horner, R. H., Carr, E. G., Strain, P. S., Todd, A. W., & Reed, H. K. (2002). Problem behavior interventions for young children with autism: A research synthesis. *Journal of Autism and Developmental Disorders, 32,* 423–446.

Horner, R. H., Salentine, S. P., & Albin, R. (2003). *Self-assessment of contextual fit in schools.* Eugene: University of Oregon.

Horner, R. H., Todd, A. W., Lewis-Palmer, T., Irvin, L. K., Sugai, G., & Boland, J. (2006). The School-Wide Evaluation Tool (SET): A research instrument for assessing school-wide positive behavior support. *Journal of Positive Behavior Interventions, 6*(1), 3–12.

Hyman, S. L., & Towbin, K. E. (2007). Autism spectrum disorders. In M. L. Batshaw, L. Pellegrino, & N. J. Roizen (Eds.), *Children with disabilities* (6th ed., pp. 325–343). Baltimore: Paul H. Brookes.

Individuals with Disabilities Act regulations (IDEA), 34 C. F. R. § 300.8 (2006).

Ivey, J. K. (2007). Outcomes for students with autism spectrum disorders: What is important and likely according to teachers? *Education and Training in Developmental Disabilities, 42*(1), 3–13.

Janney, R., & Snell, M. (2006). *Social relationships and peer support: Teachers' guides to inclusive practices* (2nd ed.). Baltimore: Paul H. Brookes.

Janney, R., & Snell, M. E. (2008). *Behavioral support: Teachers guides to inclusive practices.* Baltimore: Paul H. Brookes.

Kadesjo, B., Gillberg, C., & Nagberg, B. (1999). Autism and Asperger syndrome in seven-year-old children: A total population study. *Journal of Autism and Developmental Disorders, 29,* 327–332.

Kau, A. (2006). Autism centers of excellence (R01). *Environmental Health Perspectives, 114*(5), 309.

Kemner, C., & van Engeland, H. (2005). ERPS and eye movements reflect atypical visual perception in pervasive development disorder. *Journal of Autism and Developmental Disorders, 36*(1), 45–54.

Kincaid, D., Childs, K., & George, H. (2005). *School-wide benchmarks of quality.* Tampa, FL: University of South Florida.

Kluth, P. (2003). *You're going to love this child: Teaching students with autism in the inclusive classroom.* Baltimore: Paul H. Brookes.

Koegel, L. (2000). Interventions to facilitate communication in autism. *Journal of Autism and Developmental Disorders, 30,* 383–391.

Koegel, L. K., Koegel, R. L., & Smith, A. (1997). Variables related to differences in standardized test outcomes for children with autism. *Journal of Autism and Developmental Disorders, 27,* 233–243.

Koegel, R. L. (2007). Social development in individuals with high functioning autism and Asperger disorder. *Research and Practice for Persons with Severe Disabilities, 32*(2), 140–141.

Koegel, R. L., & Koegel, L. K. (2006). *Pivotal response treatments for autism: Communication, social, & academic development.* Baltimore: Paul H. Brookes.

Krug, D. A., Arick, J. R., & Almond, P.(1993). *Autism screening instrument for educational planning—2.* Austin, TX: Pro-Ed.

LaCava, P. G., Golan, O., Baron-Cohen, S., & Myles, B. S. (2007). Using assistive technology to teach emotion recognition to students with Asperger syndrome: A pilot study. *Remedial and Special Education, 28*(3), 174–181.

Landa, R. (2007). Early communication development and intervention for children with autism. *Mental Retardation and Development Disabilities Research Reviews, 13,* 16–25.

Lane, K. L., Barton-Arwood, S. M., Spencer, J. L., & Kalberg, J. R. (2007). Teaching elementary school educators to design, implement, and evaluate functional assessment-based interventions: Successes and challenges. *Preventing School Failure, 41*(4), 35–46.

Leary, M. R., & Hill, D. A. (1996). Moving on: Autism and movement disturbance. *Mental Retardation, 34*(1), 39–53.

Lee, H. J., & Park, H. R. (2007). An integrated literature review on the adaptive behavior of individuals with Asperger syndrome. *Remedial and Special Education, 28*(3), 132–139.

Lee, S. H., Amos, B. A., Gragoudas, S., Lee, Y., Shogren, K. A., Theoharis, R., & Wehmeyer, M. L. (2004). *Curriculum augmentation and adaptation strategies to promote access to the general curriculum for students with intellectual and developmental disabilities.* Unpublished paper.

Lord, C., & Luyster, R. (2006). Early diagnosis of children with autism spectrum disorders. *Clinical Neuroscience Research,* 6(3–4), 189–194.

Lorimer, P. A., Simpson, R. L., Myles, B. S., & Ganz, J. B. (2002). The use of social stories as a preventative behavioral intervention in a home setting with a child with autism. *Journal of Positive Behavior Interventions, 4,* 53–60.

Mace, F. C., & Mauk, J. E. (1999). Biobehavioral diagnosis and treatment of self-injury. In A. Repp & R. H. Horner (Eds.), *Functional analysis of problem behavior: From effective assessment to effective support* (pp. 78–96). Belmont, CA: Wadsworth.

Marks, S. U., Shaw-Hegwer, J., Schrader, C., Longaker, T., Peters, I., Powers, F., et al. (2003). Instructional management tips for teachers of students with autism spectrum disorders. *Teaching Exceptional Children,* 35(4), 50–55.

Mattila, M. L., Kielinen, M., Jussila, K., Linna, S. L., Bloigu, R., Ebeling, H., et al. (2007). An epidemiological and diagnostic study of Asperger syndrome according to four sets of diagnostic criteria. *Journal of the American Academy of Child and Adolescent Psychiatry,* 46(5), 636–646.

May, S., Ard, W., Todd, A. W., Horner, R., Sugai, G., Glasgow, A., et al. (2003). *School-wide information system.* Eugene: University of Oregon.

Mayes, S. D., & Calhoun, S. L. (2003). Analysis of WISC-III, Stanford-Binet: IV, and academic achievement test scores in children with autism. *Journal of Autism and Developmental Disorders.* 33(3), 329–341.

McConnell, S. R. (2002). Interventions to facilitate social interaction for young children with autism: Review of available research and recommendations for educational intervention and future research. *Journal of Autism and Developmental Disorders, 32,* 351–372.

McGee, G. G., Morrier, M. J., & Daly, T. (1999). An incidental teaching approach to early intervention for toddlers with autism. *Journal of the Association for Persons with Severe Handicaps,* 24(3), 133–146.

Miller, L. K. (2005). What the savant syndrome can tell us about the nature and nurture of talent. *Journal for the Education of the Gifted,* 28(3/4), 361–373.

Mottron, L., Lemmens, K., Gagnon, L., & Seron, X. (2006). Non-algorithmic access to calendar information in a calendar calculator with autism. *Journal of Autism and Developmental Disorders,* 36(2), 239–247.

Myles, B. S., Huggins, A., Rome-Lake, M., Hagiwara, T., Barnhill, G. P., & Griswold, D. E. (2003). Written language profile of children and youth with Asperger syndrome: From research to practice.

Education and Training in Developmental Disabilities, 38(4), 362–369.

National Research Council. (2001). *Educating children with autism.* Washington, DC: National Academy Press.

Nettelbeck, T., & Young, R. (1996). Intelligence and savant syndrome: Is the whole greater than the sum of the fragments? *Intelligence, 22,* 49–68.

O'Riordan, M., & Passetti, F. (2006). Discrimination in autism within different sensory modalities. *Journal of Autism and Developmental Disorders, 36,* 665–675.

Orsmond, G. I., Krauss, M. W., & Seltzer, M. M. (2004). Peer relationships and social and recreational activities among adolescents and adults with autism. *Journal of Autism and Developmental Disorders, 34,* 245–256.

Ozonoff, S., Dawson, G., & McPartland, J. (2002). *A parent's guide to Asperger syndrome and high-functioning autism: How to meet the challenges and help your child thrive.* New York: Guilford.

Parker, S. K., Schwartz, B., Todd, J., & Pickering, L. K. (2005). Thimersol-containing vaccines and autism spectrum disorder: A critical review of published original data. *Evidence Based Mental Health,* 8(23).

Pickles, A., Starr, E., Kazak, S., Bolton, P., Papanikolaou, K., & Bailey, A., et al. (2000). Variable expression of the autism broader phenotype: Findings from extended pedigrees. *Journal of Child Psychology Psychiatry, 41,* 491–502.

Prizant, B. M. (1983). Language acquisition and communicative behavior in autism: Toward an understanding of the "whole" of it. *Journal of Speech and Hearing Disorders, 48,* 296–307.

Rapin, I., & Dunn, M. (2003). Update on the language disorders of individuals on the autistic spectrum. *Brain & Development,* 25(3), 166–172.

Redcay, E., & Courchesne, E. (2005). When is the brain enlarged in autism? A meta-analysis of all brain size reports. *Biological Psychiatry, 58,* 1–9.

Reese, R. M., Richman, D. M., Belmont, J. M., & Morse, P. (2005). Functional characteristics of disruptive behavior in developmentally disabled children with and without autism. *Journal of Autism and Developmental Disorders,* 35(4), 419–428.

Richler, J., Bishop, S. L., Kleinke, J. R., & Lord, C. (2007). Restricted and repetitive behaviors in young children with autism spectrum disorders. *Journal of Autism and Developmental Disorders,* 37(1), 73–85.

Risi, S., Lord, C., Gotham, K., Corsello, C., Chrysler, C., Szatmari, P., et al. (2006). Combining information from multiple sources in the diagnosis of autism spectrum disorders. *Journal of the*

American Academy of Child and Adolescent Psychiatry, 45(9), 1094–1103.

Robertson, K., Chamberlain, B., & Kasari, C. (2003). General education teachers' relationships with included students with autism. *Journal of Autism and Developmental Disorders,* 33(2), 123–130.

Rogers, S. J., Hepburn, S., & Wehner, E. (2003). Parent reports of sensory symptoms in toddlers with autism and those with other developmental disorders. *Journal of Autism and Developmental Disorders,* 33(6), 631–642.

Rutter, M. (2005). Incidence of autism spectrum disorders: Changes over time and their meaning. *Acta Paediatrica,* 94(1), 2–15.

Sansosti, F. J., & Powell-Smith, K. A. (2006). Using social stories to improve the social behavior of children with Asperger syndrome. *Journal of Positive Behavior Interventions,* 8(1), 43–57.

Sansosti, F. J., Powell-Smith, K. A., & Kincaid, D. (2004). A research synthesis of social story interventions for children with autism spectrum disorders. *Focus on Autism and Other Developmental Disabilities, 19,* 194–204.

Scott, F. J., Baron-Cohen, S., Bolton, P., & Brayne, C. (2002). Brief report: Prevalence of autism spectrum conditions in children aged 5–11 years in Cambridgeshire, UK. *Autism, 6,* 231–237.

Scott, M. M., & Deneris, E. S. (2005). Making and breaking serotonin neurons and autism. *International Journal of Developmental Neuroscience, 23,* 277–285.

Shattuck, P. T., & Grosse, S. D. (2007). Issues related to the diagnosis and treatment of autism specturm disorders. *Mental Retardation and Development Disabilities Research Reviews, 13,* 129–135.

Simpson, R., & Myles, B. (2008). *Educating children and youth with autism: Strategies for effective practice* (2nd ed.). Austin, TX: Pro-Ed.

Simpson, R. L. (2005). Evidence-based practices and students with autism spectrum disorders. *Focus on Autism and Other Developmental Disabilities,* 20(3), 140–149.

Sugai, G., Horner, R. H., Dunlap, G., Hieneman, M., Lewis, T. J., Nelson, C. M., et al. (2000). Applying positive behavior support and functional behavioral assessment in schools. *Journal of Positive Behavior Interventions,* 2(3), 131–143.

Szarko, J. (2000). Familiar versus unfamiliar examiners: The effects on testing performance and behaviors of children with autism and related developmental disabilities. *Dissertation Abstracts International,* 61(4-B), 2247.

Tadevosyan-Leyfer, O., Dowd, M., Mankoski, R., Winklosky, B., Putnam, S., McGrath, L., Tager-Flusberg, H., & Folstein, S. E. (2003).

A principal components analysis of the autism diagnostic interview—Revised. *Journal of the American Academy of Child and Adolescent Psychiatry, 42*(7), 864–872.

Theimann, K. S., & Goldstein, H. (2004). Effects of peer training and written text cueing on social communication of school-age children with pervasive developmental disorder. *Jornal of Speech, Language, and Hearing Research, 47*, 126–144.

Thompson, T. (2007). *Making sense of autism.* Baltimore: Paul H. Brookes.

Thompson, T. (2008). *Dr. Thompson's straight talk an autism.* Baltimore: Paul H. Brookes.

Uberti, H. Z., Scruggs. T. E., & Mastropiere, M. A. (2003). Keywords make the difference! Mnemonic instruction in inclusive classrooms. *Teaching Exceptional Children 35*(3), 56–61.

Volkmar, F. R., Cicchetti, D. V., Dykens, E., Sparrow, S. S., Leckman, J. F., & Cohen, D. J. (1988). An evaluation of the autism behavior checklist. *Journal of Autism and Developmental Disorders, 18*, 81–97.

Wadden, N. P., Bryson, S. E., & Rodger, R. S. (1991). A closer look at the autism behavior checklist: Discriminant validity and factor structure. *Journal of Autism and Developmental Disorders. 21*, 529–541.

Williams, J. H., Waiter, G. D., Gilchrist, A., Perrett, D., Murray, A., & Whiten, A. (2005). Neural mechanisms of imitation and "mirror neuron" functioning in autistic spectrum disorder. *Neuropsychologia.*

Yeargin-Allsopp, M., Rice, C., Karapurkar, T., Doernberg, N., Boyle, C., & Murphy, C. (2003). Prevalence of autism in a US metropolitan area. *Journal of the American Medical Association, 289*(1), 49–55.

Chapter 12

Adams, F. V. (2007), *The asthma sourcebook.* New York: McGraw-Hill.

Barrett, R. P., & Sachs, H. T. (2006). Epilepsy and seizures. In L. Phelps (Ed.), *Chronic health-related disorders in children* (pp. 91–110). Washington, DC: American Psychological Association.

Bellenir, K. (2006). *Asthma sourcebook* (2nd ed.). Detroit, MI: Omnigraphics.

Benbadis, S. R., & Berkovic, S. F. (2006). Absense seizures. In E. Wyllie (Ed.), *The treatment of epilepsy: Principles and practice* (4th ed., pp. 305–315). Philadelphia: Lippincott, Williams & Wilkins.

Berg, A. T. (2006). Epidemiologic aspects of epilepsy. In E. Wyllie (Ed.), *The treatment of epilepsy: Principles and practice* (4th ed., pp. 109–116). Philadelphia: Lippincott, Williams & Wilkins.

Bessell, A. G. (2001a). Children surviving cancer: Psychosocial adjustment, quality of life, and school experiences. *Exceptional Children, 67*(3), 345–359.

Bessell, A. G. (2001b, September). Educating children with chronic illness. *Exceptional Parent Magazine, 31*(9), 44.

Best, S. J., Heller, K. W., & Bigge, J. L. (2005). *Teaching individuals with physical or multiple disabilities* (5th ed.). Upper Saddle River, NJ: Merrill/Pearson.

Cantu, C., & Buswell, D. J. (2003). Adapted PE: A vital contribution to health and well-being. *Exceptional Parent, 33*(10), 58–61.

Cole, J., & Swinth, Y. (2004). Comparison of the TouchFree switch to a physical switch: Children's abilities and preferences: A pilot study. *Journal of Special Education Technology, 19*(2), 19–30.

Committee on School Health. (2000). Home, hospital, and other non-school-based instruction for children and adolescents who are medically unable to attend school [Electronic version]. *Pediatrics, 106*(5), 1154–1155.

Copp, A. J., Fleming, A., & Greene, N. D. E. (1998). Embryonic mechanisms underlying the prevention of neural tube defects. *Mental Retardation and Developmental Disabilities Research Reviews, 4*, 264–268.

Coster, W. J., Deeney, T. A., Haltiwanger, J. T., & Haley, S. M. (1998). *School function assessment.* San Antonio, TX: Psychological Corporation/Therapy Skill Builders.

Coster, W. J., & Haltiwanger, J. T. (2004). Social-behavioral skills of elementary students with physical disabilities included in general education classrooms. *Remedial and Special Education, 25*(2), 95–103.

Coster, W. J., Mancini, M. C., & Ludlow, L. (1999). Factor structure of the school function assessment. *Educational and Psychological Measurement, 59*(4), 665–677.

Croen, L. A., Grether, J. K., Curry, C. J., & Nelson, K. B. (2001). Congenital abnormalities among children with cerebral palsy: More evidence of prenatal antecedents. *Journal of Pediatrics, 138*, 804–810.

DePaepe, P., Garrison-Kane, L., & Doelling, J. (2002). Supporting students with health needs in schools: An overview of selected health conditions. *Focus on Exceptional Children, 35*(1), 1–24.

De Wals, P., Tairou, F., Van Allen, M. I., & Uh, S. H. (2007). Reduction in neural-tube defects after folic acid fortification in Canada. *New England Journal of Medicine, 357*(2), 135–142.

Donkervoort, M., Roebroeck, M., Wiegerink, D., Van Der Heijden-Maessen, H., & Stam, H. (2007). Determinants of functioning of adolescents and young adults with cerebral palsy. *Disability & Rehabilitation, 29*(6), 453–463.

Dunn, D. W., Austin, J. K., & Huster, G. A. (1999). Symptoms of depression in adolescents with epilepsy. *Journal of the American Academy of Child and Adolescent Psychiatry, 38*(9), 1132–1138.

Epilepsy Foundation. (2007). Epilepsy and seizure statistics. Retrieved December 29, 2007, from http://www.epilepsyfoundation.org/about/statistics.cfm

Fisch, B. J., & Olejniczak, P. W. (2006). Generalized tonic-clonic seizures. In E. Wyllie (Ed.), *The treatment of epilepsy: Principles and practice* (4th ed., pp. 281–304). Philadelphia: Lippincott, Williams & Wilkins.

Fuchs, L., & Fuchs, D. (2001). Computer applications to curriculum-based measurement. *Special Services in the Schools, 17*, 1–14.

Gardiner, R. M. (2000). Impact of our understanding of the genetic aetiology of epilepsy. *Journal of Neurology, 247*, 327–334.

Haynes, J. (2002). *California community colleges adapted physical education handbook.* Sacramento: California Community College System.

Hernandez-Diaz, S., Werler, M. M., Walker, M. W., & Mitchell, A. A. (2001). Neural tube defects in relation to use of folic acid antagonists during pregnancy. *American Journal of Epidemiology, 153*(10), 961–968.

Hwang, J. L., Davies, P. L., Taylor, M. P., & Gavin, W. J. (2002). Validation of school function assessment with elementary school children. *OTJR, 22*(2), 48–58.

Individuals with Disabilities Education Act regulations (IDEA), 34 C. F. R. § 300.8 (2006).

Johnson, K. L., Dudgeon, B., Kuehn, C., & Walker, W. (2007). Assistive technology use among adolescents and young adults with spina bifida. *American Journal of Public Health, 97*(8), 330–336.

Kibar, Z., Capra, V., & Gros, P. (2007). Toward understanding the genetic basis of neural tube defects. *Clinical Genetics, 71*(4), 295–310.

Kliebenstein, M. A., & Broome, M. E. (2000). School re-entry for the child with chronic illness: Parent and school personnel perceptions. *Pediatric Nursing, 26*(6), 579–583.

Krahn, G. L. (2003). Survey of physician wellness practices with persons with disabilities. In RRTC Health and Wellness Consortium (Eds.), *Changing concepts of health and disability: State of the science conference and policy forum 2003* (pp. 47–51). Portland: Oregon Health and Sciences University.

Ladebauche, P., Nicholsi, R., Reece, S., Saucedo, K., Volicer, B., & Richards, T. (2001). Asthma in Head Start children: Prevalence, risk factors, and health care utilization. *Pediatric Nursing, 27*, 396–399.

Lancioni, G. E., Singh, N. N., O'Reilly, M. F., Oliva, D., Baccani, S., & Canevaro, A. (2002). Using simple hand-movement responses with optic microswitches with two persons with multiple disabilities.

Research and Practice in Severe Disabilities, 27, 276–279.

Lee, S. W., & Janik, M. (2006). Provision of psychoeducational services in the schools: IDEA, section 504, and NCLB. In L. Phelps (Ed.), Chronic health-related disorders in children (pp. 25–40). Washington, DC: American Psychological Association.

Liptak, G. S. (2007). Neural tube defects. In Children with disabilities (6th ed., pp. 419–438). Baltimore: Paul H. Brookes.

McGill, T., & Vogtle, L. K. (2001). Driver's education for students with physical disabilities. Exceptional Children, 67, 455–466.

Meadows, M. (2003). Breathing better: Action plans keep asthma in check. FDA Consumer, 37(2), 20–27.

Mears, B. (2004). Adapted physical education and therapeutic recreation in schools. Intervention in School and Clinic, 39(4), 223–232.

Medway, F. J. (2006). Neurological and central nervous system impairments. In L. Phelps (Ed.), Chronic health-related disorders in children (pp. 175–192). Washington, DC: American Psychological Association.

Miller, F., Bachrach, S. J., Boos, M. L., Dabney, K., Duffy, L., Meyers, R. C., et al. (2006). Cerebral palsy: A complete guide for caregiving (2nd ed.). Baltimore: Johns Hopkins University Press.

National Heart, Lung, and Blood Institute. (1997). National asthma education and prevention program expert panel report 2: Guidelines for the diagnosis and management of asthma. Rockville, MD: National Institutes of Health.

Pellegrino, L. (2007). Cerebral palsy. In Children with disabilities (6th ed., pp. 387–408). Baltimore: Paul H. Brookes.

Powers, L. (2003). Health and wellness among persons with disability. In RRTC Health and Wellness Consortium (Eds.), Changing concepts of health and disability: State of the science conference and policy forum 2003 (pp. 73–77). Portland: Oregon Health and Sciences University.

Putnam, M., Geenen, S., Powers, L. E., Saxton, M., Finney, S., & Dautel, P. (2003). Health and wellness: People with disabilities discuss barriers and facilitators to well being. Journal of Rehabilitation, 69(1), 37–45.

Shaer, C. M., Chescheir, N., & Schulkin, J. (2007). Myelomeningocele: A review of the epidemiology, genetics, risk factors for conception, prenatal diagnosis, and prognosis for affected individuals. Obstetrical & Gynecological Survey, 62(7), 471–479.

Slezak, J. A., Persky, V. W., Kviz, F. J., Ramakrishnan, V., & Byers, C. (1998). Asthma prevalence and risk factors in selected Head Start sites in Chicago. Asthma, 35, 203–212.

Smith, K. (2004). Token economies: A proactive intervention for the classroom. Minneapolis: University of Minnesota, Institute for Community Integration.

Spiegel, G. L., Cutler, S. K., & Yetter, C. E. (1996). What every teacher should know about epilepsy. Intervention in School and Clinic, 32(1), 35–37.

Stingone, J. A., & Claudio, L. (2006). Asthma and enrollment in special education among urban schoolchildren. American Journal of Public Health, 96(9), 1593–1598.

Sullivan, N. A., Fulmer, D. L., & Zigmond, N. (2001). School: The normalizing factor for children with childhood leukemia. Preventing School Failure, 46(1), 4–14.

Taras, H., & Potts-Datema, W. (2005a). Childhood asthma and student performance at school. Journal of School Health, 75(8), 296–312.

Taras, H., & Potts-Datema, W. (2005b). Chronic health conditions and student performance at school. Journal of School Health, 75(7), 255–266.

Thies, K. (1999). Identifying the educational implications of chronic illness in school children. Journal of School Health, 69(10), 392–398.

Turner, G. R., & Levine, B. (2004). Disorders of executive functioning and self-awareness. In J. Ponsford (Ed.), Cognitive and behavioral rehabilitation: From neurobiology to clinical practice (pp. 224–268). New York: Guilford.

Umbreit, J. (Ed.). (1983). Physical disabilities and health impairments: An introduction. Upper Saddle River, NJ: Merrill/Pearson.

U.S. Department of Education. (2008). IDEAdata.org: Retrieved: February 2, 2008, from https://www.ideadata.org/tables30th/ar_1-9.xls

Vogtle, L. K., Kern, D., & McCauley, A. (2000). Differences in the perception of social function between adolescents with and without disabilities. Developmental Medicine and Child Neurology, 83, 16–17.

Walders, N., McQuaid, E., & Dickstein, S. (2004). Asthma knowledge, awareness, and training: Among Head Start and early Head Start staff. Journal of School Health, 74(1), 32–34.

Wehmeyer, M. L., Sands, D. J., Knowlton, H. E., & Kozleski, E. B. (2002). Teaching students with mental retardation: Providing access to the general curriculum. Baltimore: Paul H. Brookes.

Weinstein, S. L., & Gaillard, W. D. (2007). Epilepsy. In Children with Disablties (6th ed., pp. 439–460). Baltimore: Paul H. Brookes.

Winter, S., Autry, A., Boyle, C., & Yeargin-Allsopp, M. (2002). Trends in the prevalence of cerebral palsy in a population-based study. Pediatrics, 110(6), 1220–1225.

Chapter 13

Agran, M., & Wehmeyer, M. (2005). Teaching problem solving to students with mental retardation. In M. Wehmeyer & M. Agran (Eds.), Mental retardation and intellectual disabilities: Teaching students using innovative and research-based strategies (pp. 255–272). Boston, MA: Merrill/Pearson.

Agran, M., & Wehmeyer, M. (in press). Teaching problem solving to students with mental retardation. In M. Wehmeyer & M. Agran (Eds.), Evidence-based practices for teaching students with mental retardation and intellectual disabilities. Upper Saddle River, NJ: Merrill/Prentice Hall.

Brown, A. W., Leibson, C. L., Malec, J. F., Perkins, P. K., Diehl, N. N., & Larson, D. R. (2004). Long-term survival after traumatic brain injury: A population-based analysis. Neuro Rehabilitation, 19, 37–43.

Buyer, D. M. (1999). Neuropsychological assessment and schools. Brain Injury Source, 3(3), 18–20.

Chapman, S. B. (1998). Bridging the gap between research and education reintegration: Direct instruction on processing connected discourse. Aphasiology, 12, 1081–1088.

Cheng, M. L., Khairi, S., & Ritter, A. M. (2006). Pediatric head injury. In P. L. Reilly & R. Bullock (Eds.), Head injury: Pathophysiology and management (pp. 356–367). London: Hodder Arnold.

Cobley, C., & Sanders, T. (2006). Non-accidental head injury in young children: Medical, legal and social responses. London: Jessica Kingsley.

Flashman, L. A., Amador, X., & McAllister, T. W. (2005). Awareness of deficits. In J. S. Silver, T. W. McAllister, & S. C. Yudofsky (Eds.), Textbook of traumatic brain injury (pp. 353–367). Washington, DC: American Psychiatric.

Gennarelli, T. A., & Graham, D. I. (2005). Neuropathology. In J. M. Silver, T. W. McAllister, & S. C. Yudofsky (Eds.), Textbook of traumatic brain injury (pp. 27–50). Washington, DC: American Psychiatric.

Glick, J. C., & Staley, K. (2007). Inflicted traumatic brain injury: Advances in evaluation and collaborative diagnosis. Pediatric Neurosurgery, 43(5), 436–441.

Hall, T. (2002). Explicit instruction: Effective classroom practices report. Boston: National Center on Accessing the Curriculum.

Hammond, F. M., Grattan, K. D., Sasser, H., Corrigan, J. D. Rosenthal, M., Bushnik, T., et al. (2004). Five years after traumatic brain injury: A study of individual outcomes and predictors of change in function. Neuro Rehabilitation, 19, 25–35.

Hunt, P., Soto, G., Maier, J., Liboiron, N., & Bae, S. (2004). Collaborative teaming to support preschoolers with severe disabilities who are placed in general education early childhood programs. *Topics in Early Childhood Special Education, 24*, 123–142.

Individuals with Disabilities Education Act regulations (IDEA), 34 C. F. R. § 300.8 (2006).

Johnson, D. W., & Johnson, R. T. (1991). *Cooperation and competition: Theory and research*. Edina, MN: Interaction.

Johnson, D., Johnson, R., & Holubec, E. (1998). *Cooperation in the classroom*. Boston: Allyn & Bacon.

Keyser-Marcus, L., Briel, L., Sherron-Targett, P., Yasuda, S., Johnson, S., & Wehmen, P. (2002). Enhancing the schooling of students with traumatic brain injury. *Teaching Exceptional Children 38*(4), 62–67.

Kraus, J. F., & Chu, L. D. (2005). Epidemiology. In J. M. Silver, T. W. McAllister, & S. C. Yudofsky (Eds.), *Textbook of traumatic brain injury* (pp. 3–26). Washington, DC: American Psychiatric.

Lambert, M. A., & Nowacek, J. (2006). 20 ways to help high school students improve their study skills. *Intervention in School and Clinic, 41*(4), 241–243.

Langlois, J. A., Rutland-Brown, W., & Thomas, K. E. (2004). *Traumatic brain injury in the United States: Emergency department visits, hospitalizations, and deaths*. Atlanta: Centers for Disease Control and Prevention, National Center for Injury Prevention and Control.

Langlois, J. A., Rutland-Brown, W., & Wald, M. (2006). The epidemiology and impact of traumatic brain injury: A brief overview. *Journal of Head Trauma Rehabilitation, 21*(5), 375–378.

Max, J. E. (2005). Children and adolescents. In J. M. Silver, T. W. McAllister, & S. C. Yudofsky (Eds.), *Textbook of traumatic brain injury* (pp. 477–494). Washington, DC: American Psychiatric.

Max, J. E., Lansing, A. E., Koele, S. L., Castillo, C. S., Bokura, H., & Schachar, R. (2004). Attention deficit hyperactivity disorder in children and adolescents following traumatic brain injury. *Developmental Neuropsychology 25*, 159–177.

McCullagh, S., & Feinstein, A. (2005). Cognitive changes. In J. M. Silver, T. W. McAllister, & S. C. Yudofsky (Eds.), *Textbook of traumatic brain injury* (pp. 321–335). Washington, DC: American Psychiatric Publishing.

Michaud, L. J., Duhaime, A. C., Wade, S. L., Rabin, J. P., Jones, D. O., & Lazar, M. F. (2007). Traumatic brain injury. In M. L. Batshaw, L. Pellegrino, & N. J. Roizen (Eds.), *Children with disabilities* (pp. 461–476). Baltimore: Paul H. Brookes.

Missouri Head Injury Foundation. (1991). *Missouri head injury guide for survivors, families, and caregivers*. Jefferson City: State of Missouri.

National Institutes of Health. (1998). Rehabilitation of persons with traumatic brain injury. *National Institutes of Health consensus statement, 16*(1), 1–41.

Nolet, V., & McLaughlin, M. (2000). *Accessing the general curriculum*. Thousand Oaks, CA: Corwin.

O'Neil-Pirozzi, T. M., Kendrick, H., Goldstein, R., & Glenn, M. (2004). Clinician influences on use of portable electronic memory devices in traumatic brain injury rehabilitation. *Brain Injury, 18*, 179–189.

O'Shanich, G. J., & O'Shanich, A. M. (2005). Personality disorders. In J. M. Silver, T. W. McAllister, & S. C. Yudofsky (Eds.), *Textbook of traumatic brain injury* (pp. 245–258). Washington, DC: American Psychiatric.

Parente, R., Anderson-Parente, J., & Stapleton, M. (2001). The use of rhymes and mnemonics for teaching cognitive skills to persons with acquired brain injury. *Brain Injury Source, 5*(1), 16–19.

Reece, R. M., & Sege, R. (2000). Childhood head injuries: Accidental or inflicted? *Archives of Pediatric and Adolescent Medicine, 154*, 11–15.

Russo, D. C., Dunn, E., Pace, G., & Codding, R. S. (2007). Pediatric brain injury. In J. W. Jacobson, J. A. Mulick, & J. Rojahn (Eds.), *Handbook of intellectual and developmental disabilities* (pp. 97–114). New York: Springer.

Semrud-Clikeman, M. (2001). *Traumatic brain injury in children and adolescents: Assessment and intervention*. New York: Guilford.

Silver, J. M., Yudofsky, S. C., & Anderson, K. E. (2005). Aggressive disorders. In J. M. Silver, T. W. McAllister, & S. C. Yudofsky (Eds.), *Textbook of traumatic brain injury* (pp. 259–277). Washington, DC: American Psychiatric.

Simpson, D. A. (2006). Clinical examination and grading. In P. L. Reilly & R. Bullock (Eds.), *Head injury: Pathophysiology and management* (pp. 143–163). London: Hodder Arnold.

Snell, M., & Janney, R. (2005). *Teachers' guides to inclusive practices: Collaborative teaming* (2nd ed.). Baltimore: Paul H. Brookes.

Stavinoha, P. L. (2005). Integration of neuropsychology in educational planning following traumatic brain injury. *Preventing School Failure, 49*(4), 11–16.

Teasdale, G., & Jennett, B. (1974). Assessment of coma and impaired consciousness: A practical scale. *Lancet, 2*, 81–84.

Thousand, J., Villa, R., & Nevin, A. (2007). *Differentiating instruction: Collaborative planning and teaching for universally designed learning*. Thousand Oaks, CA: Corwin Press, Inc.

Turkstra, L., Ylvisaker, M., Coelho, C., Kennedy, M., Sohlberg, M. M., Avery, J., et al. (2005). Practice guidelines for standardized assessment for persons with traumatic brain injury. *Journal of Medical Speech-Language Pathology, 13*(2), x–xxxvi.

U.S. Department of Education. (2008). IDEAdata.org. Retrieved February 2, 2008, from https://www.ideadata.org/tables30th/ar_1-9.xls

U.S. Department of Health and Human Services. (1984). *Head injury: Hope through research*. Bethesda, MD: Author.

Vasa, R. A., Gerring, J. P., Grados, M., Slomine, B., Christensen, J. R., Rising, W., et al. (2002). Anxiety after severe pediatric closed head injury. *Journal of the American Academy of Child and Adolescent Psychiatry, 41*(2), 148–156.

Warden, D. L., & Labbate, L. A. (2005). Posttraumatic stress disorder and other anxiety disorders. In J. S. Silver, T. W. McAllister, & S. C. Yudofsky (Eds.), *Textbook of traumatic brain injury*. (pp. 231–242). Washington, DC: American Psychiatric.

Yeates, K. O. (2000). Closed head injury. In K. O. Yeates, M. D. Ris, & H. G. Taylor (Eds.), *Pediatric neuropsychology: Research, theory, and practice* (pp. 92–116). New York: Guilford Press.

Yeates, K. O., Armstrong, K., Janusz, J., Taylor, H. G., Wade, S., Stancin, T., et al. (2005). Long-term attention problems in children with traumatic brain injury. *Journal of the American Academy of Child and Adolescent Psychiatry, 44*(6), 574–584.

Ylvisaker, M., & DeBonis, D. (2000). Executive function impairment in adolescence: TBI and ADHD. *Topics in Language Disorders, 20*(2), 29–57.

Ylvisaker, M., Todia, B., Glang, A., Urbanczyk, B., Franklin, C., DePompei, R., et al. (2001). Educating students with TBI: Themes and recommendations. *Journal of Head Trauma Rehabilitation, 16*(1), 76.

Chapter 14

Albertini, J., & Schley, S. (2003). Writing: Characteristics, instruction, and assessment. In M. Marschark & P. Spencer (Eds.), *Oxford handbook of deaf studies, language, and education* (pp. 123–135). New York: Oxford University Press.

Andrews, J. F., & Covell, J. A. (2007). Preparing future teachers and doctoral level leaders in deaf education: Meeting the challenge. *American Annals of the Deaf, 151*(5), 464–475.

Batshaw, M. L., Pellegrino, L., & Roizen, N. (Eds.). (2007). *Children with disabilities* (6th ed.). Baltimore: Paul H. Brookes.

Blackorby, J., & Knokey, A. (2006). *A national profile of students with hearing impairments in elementary and middle* school: A special topic report of the special education elementary longitudinal study. (Special Education Elementary Longitudinal Study [SEELS], U.S. Department of Education, Office of Special Education Programs [OSEP]). Retrieved from http://www.seels.net/grindex.html

Block, M. H., & Okrand, M. (1983). Real-time closed-captioned television as an educational tool. *American Annals of the Deaf, 128*(5), 636–641.

Bomstein, H., & Saulnier, K. (1984). *The signed English starter*. Washington, DC: Gallaudet University Press.

Caldwell, D. C. (1973). Use of graded captions with instructional television for deaf learners. *American Annals of the Deaf, 118*(4), 500–507.

Cawthon, S. W. (2008). Accommodations use for statewide standardized assessments: Prevalence and recommendations for students who are deaf or hard of hearing. *Journal of Deaf Studies and Deaf Education, 13*(1), 55–76.

Commission on Education of the Deaf (1988). *Toward equality: Education of the deaf*. Washington, DC: U.S. Government Printing Office.

Coryell, J., & Holcomb, T. K. (1997). The use of sign language and sign systems in facilitating language acquisition and communication of deaf students. *Language, Speech, and Hearing Services in Schools, 28*, 384–394.

Cummins, J. (1980). The entry and exit fallacy in bilingual education. *National Association for Bilingual Education, 4*, 25–60.

Cummins, J. (1992). Language proficiency, bilingualism, and academic achievement. In P. A. Richard-Amato & M. A. Snow (Eds.), *The multicultural classroom: Readings for content-area teachers* (pp. 16–26). Reading, MA: Addison-Wesley.

Cummins, J. (2003). BICS and CALP: Origins and rationale for the distinction. In C. B. Paulston & G. R. Tucker (Eds.). *Sociolinguistics: The essential readings* (pp. 322–328). London: Blackwell.

Easterbrooks, S. R., & Baker, S. (2002). *Language learning in children who are deaf and hard of hearing: Multiple pathways*. Boston, MA: Allyn & Bacon.

Elliot, S. N., Kratochwill, T. R., & Schulte, A. G. (1998). The assessment accommodation checklist: Who, what, where, when, why, and how? *Teaching Exceptional Children, 3*(2), 10–14.

Gallaudet Research Institute (1973–1974 to 2004–2005). *Annual survey of deaf and hard of hearing children and youth*. Washington, DC: Gallaudet University.

Garay, S. (2003). Listening to the voices of deaf students: Essential transition issues. *Teaching Exceptional Children, 35*(4), 44–48.

Gilbert, R. H., Knightly, C. A., & Steinberg, A. G. (2007). Hearing: Sounds and silences. In M. Batshaw, L. Pellegrino, & N. Rozen (Eds.), *Children with disabilities* (pp. 157–184). Baltimore: Paul H. Brookes.

Hanks, J., & Luckner, J. (2003). Job satisfaction: Perceptions of a national sample of teachers of students who are deaf or hard of hearing. *American Annals of the Deaf, 148*(1), 5–17.

Hyde, M., & Power, D. (2004). Inclusion of deaf students: An examination of definitions of inclusion in relation to findings of a recent Australian study of deaf students in regular classes. *Deafness and Education International, 6*, 82–99.

Joint Committee on Infant Hearing (2007). Year 2007 position statement: Principles and guidelines for early hearing detection and intervention programs. *Pediatrics, 120*(4), 898–921.

Karchmer, M., & Mitchell, R. (2003). Demographic and achievement characteristics of deaf and hard-of-hearing students. In M. Marschark & P. Spencer (Eds.), *Oxford handbook of deaf studies, language, and education* (pp. 21–37). New York: Oxford University Press.

Kluwin, T. (1993). The cumulative effects of mainstreaming on the achievement of hearing impaired adolescents. *Exceptional Children, 60*(1), 73–81.

LaSasso, C. J., & Metzger, M. A. (1998). An alternative route for preparing deaf children for BiBi programs: The home language as L1 and cued speech for conveying traditionally-spoken languages. *Journal of Deaf Studies and Deaf Education, 3*, 265–289.

Luckner, J., Sebald, A. M., Cooney, J., Young, J., & Muir, S. G. (2005). An examination of the evidence-based literacy research in deaf education. *American Annals of the Deaf, 150*(5), 443–456.

Marschark, M., Lang, H. G., & Albertini, J. A. (2002). *Educating deaf students: From research to practice*. New York: Oxford University Press.

Marschark, M., Leigh, G., Sapere, P., Burnham, D., Convertino, C., Stinson, M., et al. (2006). Benefits of sign language interpreting and text alternatives for deaf students' classroom learning. *Journal of Deaf Studies and Deaf Education, 11*(4), 421–437.

Marschark, M., Sapare, P., Convertino, C., & Seewagen, R. (2005). Educational interpreting: Access and outcomes. In M. Marshark, R. Peterson, & E. Winston (Eds.), *Sign language interpreting and interpreter education* (pp. 57–83). New York: Oxford University Press.

Moores, D. F. (2001). *Educating the deaf: Psychology, principles and practices* (5th ed.). Boston: Houghton Mifflin.

National Center on Birth Defects and Developmental Disabilities. (2004).

Hearing loss [Electronic version]. Atlanta, GA: Author. Retrieved from http://www.cdc.gov/ncbddd/

National Institute on Deafness and Other Communication Disorders. (2007). *Cochlear implants. Improving the lives of people who have communication disorders* [Electronic version]. Retrieved from http://www.nidc.nih.gov/health/hearing/coch.asp

Nicholas, J., & Greers, A. (2006). Effects of early auditory experience on the spoken language of deaf children at 3 years of age. *Ear & Hearing, 27*(3), 286–298.

Nikolaraizi, M., & Makri, M. (2004/2005). Deaf and hearing individuals' beliefs about the capabilities of deaf people. *American Annals of the Deaf, 149*, 404–414.

Northern, J. L., & Downs, M. P. (2002) *Hearing in children* (5th ed.). Philadelphia: Lippincott.

Padden, C., & Humphries, T. (2005). *Inside deaf culture*. Cambridge, MA: Harvard University Press.

Punch, R., Creed, P. A., & Hyde, M. B. (2006). Career barriers perceived by hard-of-hearing adolescents: Implications for practice from a mixed-methods study. *Journal of Deaf Studies and Deaf Education, 11*(2), 225–237.

Robson, G. (2004). *The closed captioning handbook*. Burlington, MA: Focal Press.

Scheetz, N. A. (2004). *Psychosocial aspects of deafness*. Boston: Pearson.

Schleper, D. (1997). *Reading to deaf children: Learning from deaf adults* (pp. 3–4). Washington, DC: Pre-College National Mission Programs.

Spencer, P. (2004). Individual differences in language performance after cochlear implantation at 1 to 3 years of age: Child, family, and linguistic factors. *Journal of Deaf Studies and Deaf Education, 9*, 395–412.

Stewart, D. A., & Kluwin, T. N. (2001). *Teaching deaf and hard of hearing students: Content, strategies, and curriculum*. Needham Heights, MA: Allyn & Bacon.

Swanwick, R., & Watson, L. (2007). Parents sharing books with young deaf children in spoken English and in BSL: The common and diverse features of different language settings. *Journal of Deaf Studies and Deaf Education, 12*(3), 385–405.

Torres, S., Moreno-Torres, I., & Santana, R. (2006). Quantitative and qualitative evaluation of linguistic input support to a prelingually deaf child with cued speech: A case study. *Journal of Deaf Studies and Deaf Education, 11*(4), 438–448.

U.S. Department of Education (1992). Deaf students education services: Policy guidance. *Federal Register, 57*(211). (Friday, October 30, 1992): 49274–49276.

U.S. Department of Education. (2007). *27th annual report to Congress on the implementation of the Individuals with Disabilities Education Act, 2005* (Vol. 1). Washington, DC: U.S. Department of Education.

U.S. Department of Education, Office of Special Education Programs. (2006). Individuals with Disabilities Education Act (IDEA) data. [Electronic version]. Retrieved http://www.ideadata.org/

Wake, M., Hughes, E., Poulakis, Z., Collins, C., & Rickards, W. (2004). Outcomes of mild-profound hearing impairment at age 7–8 years: A population study. *Ear Hear, 25*, 1–8.

Walker-Vann, C., (1998). Profiling Hispanic Deaf Students. *American Annals of the Deaf, 143*, 46–54.

Wauters, L. N., & Knoors, H. (2007). Social integration of deaf children in inclusive settings. *Journal of Deaf Studies and Deaf Education, 13*(1), 21–36.

White, K. R., Vohr, B. R., & Behrens, T. R. (1993). Universal newborn hearing screening using transient evoked otoacoustic emissions: Results of the Rhode Island Hearing Assessment Project. *Seminars in Hearing, 14*(1), 18–29.

Wolbers, K. A. (2002). Cultural factors and the achievement of black and Hispanic deaf students. *Multicultural Education, 10*, 43–52.

Woodward, J., & Allen, T. E. (1993). Sociolinguistic differences: U.S. teachers in residential schools and nonresidential schools. *Sign Language Studies, 81*, 361–374.

Chapter 15

Allman, C. B. (2004). *Position paper. Use of extended time.* Louisville, KY: American Printing House for the Blind.

Anthony, T. L. (2000). Performing a functional low vision assessment. In F. M. D'Andrea & C. Farrenkopf (Eds.), *Looking to learn: Promoting literacy for students with low vision* (pp. 32–83). New York: AFB Press.

Anthony, T. L., Bleier, H., Fazzi, D. L., Kish, D., & Pogrund, R. L. (2002). Mobility focus: Developing early skills for orientation and mobility. In R. L. Pogrund & D. L. Fazzi (Eds.), *Early focus: Working with young children who are blind or visually impaired and their families* (2nd ed., pp. 326–404). New York: AFB Press.

Barclay, E. (2003a). Expanded core curriculum: Education. In S. A. Goodman & S. H. Wittenstein (Eds.), *Collaborative assessment: Working with students who are blind or visually impaired, including those with additional disabilities.* (pp. 98–99). New York: AFB Press.

Barclay, L. A. (2003b). Preparation for assessment. In S. A. Goodman & S. H. Wittenstein (Eds.), *Collaborative assessment: Working with students who are blind or visually impaired, including those with additional disabilities* (pp. 37–70). New York: AFB Press.

Barraga, N. C., & Erin, J. N. (2001). *Visual impairments and learning* (4th ed.). Austin, TX: Pro-Ed.

Bradley-Johnson, S. (1994). *Psychoeducational assessment of students who are visually impaired or blind.* Austin, TX: Pro-Ed.

Brasher, B., & Holbrook, M. C. (2006). Early intervention and special education. In M. C. Holbrook (Ed.), *Children with visual impairments: A parent's guide* (2nd ed., pp. 201–237). Bethesda, MD: Woodbine House.

Conroy, P. W. (2005). English language learners with visual impairments: Strategies to enhance learning. *RE:view, 37*(3), 101–108.

Corn, A. L., & Sacks, S. Z. (1994). The impact of non-driving on adults with visual impairments. *Journal of Visual Impairment and Blindness, 88*(1), 53–68.

Ferrell, K. A. (2000). Growth and development of young children. In M. C. Holbrook & A. J. Koenig (Eds.), *Foundations of education* (2nd ed.), *Volume 1. History and theory of teaching children and youths with visual impairments* (pp. 111–134). New York: AFB Press.

Ferrell, K. A. (2006). Your child's development. In M. C. Holbrook (Ed.), *Children with visual impairments: A parent's guide* (2nd ed., pp. 73–96). Bethesda, MD: Woodbine House.

Flom, R. (2004). Visual functions as components of functional vision. In A. H. Lueck (Ed.), *Functional vision: A practitioner's guide to evaluation and intervention* (pp. 25–60). New York: AFB Press.

Harrell, L. (1992). *Children's vision concerns: Looks beyond the eyes!* Placerville, CA: L. Harrell Productions.

Hatlen, P. H. (1996). The core curriculum for blind and visually impaired students, including those with additional disabilities. *RE:view, 28*(1), 25–32.

Hatlen, P. H., & Curry, S. A. (1987). In support of specialized programs for blind and visually impaired children: The impact of vision loss on learning. *Journal of Visual Impairment and Blindness, 81*(1), 7–13.

Huebner, K. M. (2000). Visual impairment. In M. C. Holbrook & A. J. Koenig (Eds.), *Foundations of education* (2nd ed.), *Volume I. History and theory of teaching children and youths with visual impairments* (pp. 55–76). New York: AFB Press.

Individuals with Disabilities Education Act regulations, (IDEA), 34 C.F.R. § 300.8 (2006).

Kirchner, C., & Diament, S. (1999). Estimates of the number of visually impaired students, their teachers, and orientation and mobility specialists. *Journal of Visual Impairment and Blindness, 93*(9), 600–606.

Koenig, A. J., & Farrenkopf, C. (1997). Essential experiences to undergird the early development of literacy. *Journal of Visual Impairment and Blindness, 91*(1), 14–24.

Koenig, A. J., & Holbrook, M. C. (1993). *Learning media assessment of students with visual impairments: A resource guide for teachers.* Austin, TX: Texas School for the Blind and Visually Impaired.

Koenig, A. J., & Holbrook, M. C. (2000). Planning instruction in unique skills. In A. J. Koenig & M. C. Holbrook (Eds.), *Foundations of education* (2nd ed.), *Volume II. Instructional strategies for teaching children and youths with visual impairments* (pp. 196–221). New York: AFB Press.

Lewis, S., & Allman, C. B. (2000). Educational programming. In M. C. Holbrook & A. J. Koenig (Eds.), *Foundations of education* (2nd ed.), *Volume I. History and theory of teaching children and youths with visual impairments* (pp. 218–259). New York: AFB Press.

Lewis, S., & Russo, R. (1997). Educational assessment for students who have visual impairments with other disabilities. In S. Z. Sacks & R. K. Silberman (Eds.), *Educating students who have visual impairments with other disabilities* (pp. 39–71). Baltimore: Paul H. Brookes.

Lewis, S., & Wolffe, K. E. (2006). Promoting and nurturing self-esteem. In S. Z. Sacks and K. E. Wolffe (Eds.). *Teaching social skills to students with visual impairments: From theory to practice* (pp. 122–162). New York: AFB Press.

Liefert, F. (2003). Introduction to visual impairment. In S. A. Goodman & S. H. Wittenstein (Eds.), *Collaborative assessment: Working with students who are blind or visually impaired, including those with additional disabilities* (pp. 1–22). New York: AFB Press.

Los Angeles Unified School District. (1990). *Functional visual evaluation.* Los Angeles: Author.

Lowenfeld, B. (1973). Psychological considerations. In B. Lowenfeld (Ed.), *The visually handicapped child in school* (pp. 27–60). New York: Day.

Lueck, A. H. (2004). Comprehensive low vision care. In A. H. Lueck (Ed.), *Functional vision: A practitioner's guide to evaluation and intervention* (pp. 3–24). Alexandria, VA: Association for Education and Rehabilitation of the Blind and Visually Impaired.

Lussenhop, K., & Corn, A. L. (2002). Comparative studies of the reading performance of students with low vision. *RE:view, 34*(2), 57–69.

Milian, M. (1997). Teaching braille reading and writing to students who speak English as a second language. In D. P. Wormsley & F. M. D'Andrea (Eds.), *Instructional strategies for braille literacy* (pp. 189–230). New York: AFB Press.

Milian, M. (2000). Multicultural issues. In M. C. Holbrook & A. J. Koenig (Eds.), *Foundations of education* (2nd ed.), *Volume I. History and theory of teaching children and youths with visual impairments* (pp. 197–217). New York: AFB Press.

Nelson, K. A., & Dimitrova, E. (1993). Severe visual impairment in the United States and in each state. *Journal of Visual Impairment and Blindness, 87*(3), 80–85.

Pogrund, R. L. (2002). Refocus: Setting the stage for working with young children who are blind or visually impaired. In R. L. Pogrund & D. L. Fazzi (Eds.), *Early focus: Working with young children who are blind or visually impaired and their families* (2nd ed., pp. 1–15). New York: AFB Press.

Pugh, G. S., & Erin, J. (Eds.). (1999). *Blind and visually impaired students: Educational service guidelines.* Watertown, MA: Perkins School for the Blind.

Sacks, S. Z. (2006). Theoretical perspectives on the early years of social development. In S. Z. Sacks and K. E. Wolffe (Eds.), *Teaching social skills to students with visual impairments: From theory to practice* (pp. 51–80). New York: AFB Press.

Scott, E. P., Jan, J. E., & Freeman, R. D. (1995). *Can't your child see? A guide for parents of visually impaired children* (3rd ed.). Austin, TX: Pro-Ed.

Silberman, R. K. (2000). Children and youth with visual impairments and other exceptionalities. In M. C. Holbrook & A. J. Koening (Eds.), *Foundations of education* (2nd ed.), *Volume I. History and theory of teaching children and youths with visual impairments* (pp. 173–196). New York: AFB Press.

Simons, B., & Lapolice, D. J. (2000). Working effectively with a low vision clinic. In F. M. D'Andrea & C. Farrenkopf (Eds.), *Looking to learn: Promoting literacy for students with low vision* (pp. 84–116). New York: AFB Press.

Social Security Act, 42 U.S.C. 1382c § 1614 (2007).

U.S. Department of Education. (2007). *Twenty-seventh annual report to Congress on the implementation of the Individuals with Disabilities Education Act, 2005.* Washington, DC: Author.

U.S. Department of Education. (2008). IDEA data.org. Retrieved February 2, 2008, from https://www.ideadata.org/tables30th/ar_1-9.xls

Wolffe, K. (2000). Career education. In A. J. Koenig & M. C. Holbrook (Eds.), *Foundations of education* (2nd ed.), *Volume II. Instructional strategies for teaching children and youths with visual impairments* (pp. 679–719). New York: AFB Press.

Wolffe, K. E. (2006). Theoretical perspectives on the development of social skills in adolescence. In S. Z. Sacks and K. E. Wolffe (Eds.), *Teaching social skills to students with visual impairments: From theory to practice* (pp. 81–116). New York: AFB Press.

Wolffe, K. E., Sacks, S. Z., & Thomas, K. L. (2000). *Focused on: Importance and need for social skills.* New York: AFB Press.

Young, L. (1997). Adding positive experiences with dogs to the curriculum. *RE:view, 29*(2), 55–61.

Chapter 16

Andrade, H. G. (2000). Using rubrics to promote thinking and learning. *Educational Leadership, 57*(5), 13–18.

Armstrong, T. (1994) *Multiple intelligences in the classroom.* Alexandria, VA: Association for Supervision and Curriculum Development.

Armstrong, T. (2006). *The best schools: How human development research should inform educational practice.* Alexandria, VA: Association for Supervision and Curriculum Development.

Bain, S. K., & Bell, S. M. (2004). Social self-concept, social attributions, and peer relationships in fourth, fifth, and sixth graders who are gifted compared to high achievers. *Gifted Child Quarterly, 48*(3), 167–178.

Baker, E. L. (1996). Introduction to theme issue in educational assessment. *Journal of Educational Research, 89*, 194–196.

Betts, G., & Kercher, J. (1999). *Autonomous learner model: Optimizing ability.* Greeley, CO: ALPS.

Bisland, A., Cobb, Y. B., & Karnes, F. A. (2004). Leadership education: Resources and web sites for teachers of gifted students. *Gifted Child Today, 27*(1).

Bloom, B. S. (Ed.). (1956). *Handbook I: Cognitive domain.* New York: McKay.

Boland, C. M., & Gross, M. U. M. (2007). Counseling highly gifted children and adolescents. In *Models of counseling gifted children, adolescents and young adults* (pp. 153–198). Waco, TX: Prufrock Press.

Brown, S. W., Renzulli, J. S., Gubbins, E. J., Seiegle, D., Zhang, W., & Chen, C. H. (2005). Assumptions underlying the identification of gifted and talented students. *Gifted Child Quarterly, 49*(1), 68–80.

Burke, C. S., Sims, D. E., Lazzara, E. H., & Salas, E. (2007). Trust in leadership: A multi-level review and integration. *The Leadership Quarterly, 18*(6), 606–632.

Cherniss, C., Extein, M., Goleman, D., & Weissberg, R. P. (2006). Emotional intelligence: What does the research really indicate? *Educational Psychologists, 41*(4), 239–245.

Clark, B. (2002). *Growing up gifted: Developing the potential of children at home and at school.* Upper Saddle River, NJ: Merrill/Pearson.

Clark, B. (2008). *Growing up gifted: Developing the potential of children at home and school* (7th ed.). Upper Saddle River, NJ: Merrill/Pearson.

Connery, S. Mark, L., & Tollefson, R. (Producers), & Van Sant, G. (Director). (2000). *Finding Forrester* [Motion picture.] United States: Columbia Pictures.

Council of State Directors of Programs for the Gifted and National Association for Gifted Children. (2003). *State of the states: Gifted and talented education report 2001–2002.* Washington, DC: Author.

Davis, G. A. (2003). Identifying creative students, teaching for creative growth. In N. Colangelo & G. A. Davis (Eds.), *Handbook of gifted education* (3rd ed.). Boston: Allyn & Bacon.

Douglas, D. (2004). Self-advocacy: Encouraging students to become partners in differentiation. *Roeper Review, 26*(4), 223–228.

Elkind, D. (1981). *The hurried child: Growing up too fast, too soon.* Reading, MA: Addison-Wesley.

Feldhusen, J. F. (2003). Prococity and acceleration. *Gifted Education International, 17*, 55–58.

Feldman, D. H. (2004). Child prodigies: A distinctive form of giftedness. In R. J. Sternberg (Ed.), *Definitions and conceptions of giftedness. Essential reading in gifted education* (pp. 133–144). Thousand Oaks, CA: Corwin Press.

Ford, D. Y., & Harris, J. J., III. (1999). *Multicultural gifted education.* New York: Teachers College Press.

Galbraith, J., & Delisle, J. (1996). *The gifted kids' survival guide.* Minneapolis: Free Spirit.

Gallagher, J. J. (2002). Gifted education in the 21st century. *Gifted Education International, 16*, 100–110.

Gardner, H. (1983). *Frames of mind: The theory of multiple intelligences.* New York: Basic Books.

Gardner, H. (2006). *Multiple intelligences: New horizons.* New York: Basic Books.

Gardner, H., & Hatch, T. (1989). Multiple intelligences go to school: Educational implications of the theory of multiple intelligences. *Educational Researcher, 18*(8), 4–9.

Gardner, H., & Moran, S. (2006). The science of multiple intelligences theory: A response to Lynn Waterhouse. *Educational Psychologists, 41*(4), 227–232.

Gifted and Talented Children's Education Act, 20 U. S. C. § 3312 (1978).

Goleman, D. (1995). *Emotional intelligence.* New York: McGraw-Hill.

Goleman, D., Boyatzis, R., & McKee, A. (2002). *Primal leadership: Realizing the power of emotional intelligence.* Boston, MA: Harvard Business School Press.

Grantham, T. C. (2002). Underrepresentation in gifted education: How did we get here and what needs to change? *Roeper Review, 24*(2), 50–88.

Grantham, T. C. (2003). Increasing black student enrollment in gifted programs: An exploration of the Pulaski County special school district's advocacy efforts. *Gifted Child Quarterly, 47*(1), 46–65.

Greenwood, S. D. (2003). Contracting revisited: Lessons learned in literacy differentiation. *Journal of Adolescent and Adult Literacy, 46*, 338–350.

Gross, M. U. M. (1993). *Exceptionally gifted children.* London: Routledge.

Guastello, S. J. (2007). Non-linear dynamics and leadership emergence. *The Leadership Quarterly, 18*(4), 357–369.

Gubbins, J. E. (2005). Constructing identification procedures. In J. H. Purcell & R. D. Eckert (Eds.), *Designing services and programs for high-ability learners: A guidebook for gifted education* (pp. 49–61). Thousand Oaks, CA: Corwin Press.

Harmon, D. (2002). They won't teach me: The voices of gifted African American inner-city students, *Roeper Review 24*(2), 68–80.

Hébert, T. P. (2000). Helping high ability students overcome math anxiety through bibliotherapy. *Journal of Secondary Gifted Education, 8*, 164–178.

Hodge, K. A., & Kemp, C. R. (2000). Exploring the nature of giftedness in preschool children. *Journal for the Education of the Gifted, 24*, 46–73.

Hoge, R. D., & Renzulli, J. S. (1993). Exploring the link between giftedness and self-concept. *Review of Educational Research, 63*, 449–465.

Jackson, S. M., & Peterson, J. S. (2003). Depressive disorder in highly gifted adolescents. *Journal of Secondary Gifted Education, 14*, 175–186.

Jolly, J., & Kettler, T. (2004). Authentic assessment of leadership in problem-solving groups. *Gifted Child Today, 27*(1), 32–39.

Kaiser, C. F., & Berndt, D. J. (1985). Predictors of loneliness in the gifted adolescent. *Gifted Child Quarterly, 29*, 74–77.

Kapusnick, R. A., & Hauslein, C. M. (2001). The "silver cup" of differentiated instruction. *Kappa Delta Pi Record, 37*, 156–159.

Karolyi, C. V., Ramos-Ford, V., & Gardner, H. (2003). Multiple intelligences: A perspective on giftedness. In N. Colangelo & G. A. Davis (Eds.), *Handbook of gifted education* (3rd ed., pp. 100–112). Boston: Allyn & Bacon.

Maker, C. J. (1993). Creativity, intelligence and problem solving: A definition and design for cross-cultural research and measurement related to giftedness. *Gifted Education International, 9*, 68–77.

Maker, C. J. (2001). DISCOVER: Assessing and developing problem solving. *Gifted Education International, 15*, 232–251.

Mayseless, O. (1993). Gifted adolescents and intimacy in close same-sex friendships. *Journal of Youth and Adolescence, 22*, 135–146.

Mendaglio, S., & Peterson, J. S. (Eds.). (2007). *Models of counseling gifted children, adolescents, and young adults.* Waco, TX: Prufrock Press.

Milner, H. R., & Ford, D. Y. (2007). Cultural considerations in the underrepresentation of culturally diverse elementary students in gifted education. *Roeper Review, 29*(3), 166–173.

Moon, T. R., Brighton, C. M., & Callahan, C. M. (2003). State standardized testing programs: Friend or foe of gifted education? *Roeper Review, 25*(2), 49–60.

Morris, J. E. (2002). African-American students and gifted education: The politics of race and culture. *Roeper Review, 24*(2), 59–62.

Nakamura, J., & Csikszentmihalyi, M. (2001). Catalytic creativity: The case of Linus Pauling. *American Psychologist, 56*, 337–341.

National Association for Gifted Children. (2007). *State of the sates in gifted education: 2006–2007.* Washington, DC: Author.

National Research Council, Division of Behavior and Social Sciences and Education. (2002). *Minority Students in special and gifted education.* Washington, DC: National Academy Press.

Neihart, M. (2002). Risk and resilience in gifted children: A conceptual framework. In M. Neihart, S. M. Reis, N. M. Robinson & S. M. Moon (Eds.), *The social and emotional developmental of gifted children: What do we know?* (pp. 113–122). Waco, TX: Prufrock Press.

Nevo, B. (1994). Definitions, ideologies, and hypotheses in gifted education. *Gifted Child Quarterly, 38*(4), 184–186.

Olszewski-Kubilius, P., & Turner, D. (2002). Gender differences among elementary school-aged gifted students in achievement, perceptions of ability, and subject preference. *Journal for the Education of the Gifted, 25*(3), 233–268.

Peterson, J. S. (2006). Addressing counseling needs of gifted students. *Professional School Counseling, 10*(1), 43–51.

Pfeiffer, S. I. (2003). Challenges and opportunities for students who are gifted: What the experts say. *Gifted Child Quarterly, 47*(2), 161–169.

Piirto, J. (2004). *Understanding creativity.* Scottsdale, AZ: Great Potential Press.

Plucker, J., & Beghetto, R. A. (2004). Why creativity is domain general, why it looks domain specific, and why the distinction does not matter. In R. J. Sternberg, E. L. Grigorenko, & J. L. Singer (Eds.), *Creativity: From potential to realization* (pp. 153–168.). Washington, DC: American Psychological Association.

Reis, S. M., & Renzulli, J. S. (2004). Current research on the social and emotional development of gifted and talented students: Good news and future possibilities. *Psychology in the Schools, 41*(1), 119.

Renzulli, J. S. (2002). Expanding the conception of giftedness to include co-cognitive traits to promote social capital. *Phi Delta Kappan, 84*(1), 33–58.

Renzulli, J. S., & Reis, S. M. (2003). The schoolwide enrichment model: Developing creative and productive giftedness. In N. Colangelo & G. A. Davis (Eds.), *Handbook of gifted education* (3rd ed., pp. 184–203). Boston: Allyn & Bacon.

Rinn, A. N. (2006). Effects of a summer program on the social self-concepts of gifted adolescents. *Journal of Secondary Gifted Education, 17*(2), 65–76.

Rizza, M. G., & Gentry, M. (2001). A legacy of promise: Reflections, suggestions, and directions from contemporary leaders in the field of gifted education. *Teacher Education, 36*(3), 167–184.

Roach, A. A., Wyman, L. T., Brookes, H., Chavez, C., Heath, S. B., & Valdes, G. (1999). Leadership giftedness: Models revisited. *Gifted Child Quarterly, 43*(1), 13–24.

Robinson, N. M. (2003). Two wrongs do not make a right: Sacrificing the needs of gifted students does not solve society's unsolved problems. *Journal for the Education of the Gifted, 26*(4), 251–273.

Rosenzweig, M. (1966). Environmental complexity, cerebral change and behavior. *American Psychologist, 21*, 321–332.

Sarouphim, K. M. (1999). Discovering multiple intelligences through a performance-based assessment: Consistency with independent ratings. *Exceptional Children, 65*(2), 151–161.

Sarouphim, K. M. (2001). DISCOVER: Concurrent validity, gender differences, and identification of minority students. *Gifted Child Quarterly, 45*(2), 130–138.

Sarouphim, K. M. (2002). DISCOVER in high school: Identifying gifted Hispanic and Native American students. *Journal of Secondary Gifted Education, 14*(1), 30–38.

Sarouphim, K. M. (2004). DISCOVER in middle school: Identifying gifted minority students. *Journal of Secondary Gifted Education, 15*(2), 61–69.

Schiever, S., & Maker, C. J. (2003). In N. Colangelo & G. A. Davis (Eds.), *Handbook of gifted education* (3rd ed., pp. 444–452). Boston: Allyn & Bacon.

Schuler, P. (1997). Characteristics and perceptions of perfectionism in gifted adolescents in a rural school environment. Unpublished doctoral dissertation, University of Connecticut, Storrs.

Shaunessy, E. (2003). State policies regarding gifted education. *Gifted Child Today, 26*(3), 16–21.

Siegel, D. J. (1999). *The developing mind.* New York: Guilford.

Sriraman, B. (2005). Are giftedness and creativity synonyms in mathematics? *Journal of Secondary Gifted Education, 17*(1), 20–36.

Stamps, L. S. (2004). The effectiveness of curriculum compacting in first grade classrooms. *Roeper Review, 27*(1), 31–41.

Stephens, K. R., & Karnes, F. (2000). State definitions for the gifted and talented revisited. *Exceptional Children, 66*(2), 219–238.

Swiatek, M. A., & Lupkowski-Shoplik, A. (2000). Gender differences in academic attitudes among gifted elementary school students. *Journal for the Education of the Gifted, 23,* 360–377.

Tong, J., & Yewchuck, C. (1996). Self-concept and sex-role orientation in gifted high school students. *Gifted Child Quarterly, 40,* 15–23.

Torrance, E. P. (1964). *Rewarding creative behavior.* Upper Saddle River, NJ: Merrill/Pearson.

Uresti, R., Goertz, J., & Bernal, E. M. (2002). Maximizing achievement for potentially gifted and talented and regular minority students in a primary classroom. *Roeper Review, 25,* 27–31.

U.S. Department of Education. (2006). *Public elementary and secondary students, staff, schools, and school districts: School year 2003–04.*

Van Tassel-Baska, J. (2005). Gifted programs and services: What are the nonnegotiables? *Theory into Practice, 44*(2), 90–99.

White, B. Y., & Fredericksen, J. R. (1998). Inquiry, modeling, and metacognition: Making science accessible to all students. *Cognition and Instruction, 16*(1), 3–118.

Yoo, J. E., & Moon, S. M. (2006). Counseling needs of gifted students: An analysis of intake forms at a university-based counseling center. *Gifted Child Quarterly, 50,* 52–61.

Zirkel, P. A. (2004). The case law on gifted education: A new look. *The Gifted Child Quarterly, 48*(4), 309–314.

Name Index

McBride, B. A., 103
McBride, T. D., 82
McBride-Chang, C., 136
McCabe, K., 191
McCart, A., 88, 89
McCauley, A., 354
McClellan, J. M., 188
McConnell, S. R., 303, 317
McCormick, L., 158, 161
McCray, A. D., 69
McCullagh, S., 369
McCune, Kreg, 270, 271, 272, 274, 275, 290, 295
McCune, S. K., 276
McDonell, M. G., 188
McDonnell, J. M., 279
McDougall, P., 189
McElmurray, Mary (Bo), 166
McGee, De'ja, 64–66, 67, 69, 71, 73, 74, 76–77, 80, 82, 86, 92–94
McGee, G. G., 318
McGee, Sharilyn, 64–66, 67, 69, 71, 77, 81, 82, 86, 92–93
McGill, T., 354
McGoey, K. E., 214
McGregor, G., 45, 47, 49
McGuire, J. M., 142
McIntosh, K., 199
McKee, A., 463
McKenzie, M., 251
McKinnon, J., 189
McLaughlin, M., 35, 384, 385
McLaughlin, M. J., 35, 205
McLaughlin, P. J., 255
McLaughlin, V. L., 46
McLeskey, J., 48
McMahon, R. J., 187
McMahon, Sheri, 194
McMaster, K. L., 92
McNamara, B. E., 127
McNear, Donna, 453, 454
McPartland, J., 315
McPherson, M. J., 244
McQuaid, E., 342
McWayne, C., 103
Meadows, M., 346
Mears, B., 352
Mechling, L., 229
Mechling, L. C., 244
Medbery, Lucie, 476–477
Medway, F. J., 337
Mehan, H., 69
Meier, L., 21
Meisel, S. M., 203
Mellard, D. F., 58, 197
Meltzer, L., 129
Mencl, W. E., 130
Méndez Barletta, L., 79
Mercer, C. D., 134
Mercer, J. R., 70
Merickel, A., 19
Merrier, M. J., 318
Metraux, S., 82
Metzger, M. A., 400
Meyer, A., 41
Meyer, D. J., 110
Meyers, Geraldine, 301, 313, 323
Michaud, L. J., 368, 369, 371
Mickelson, R. A., 70
Miklowitz, D. J., 186
Milian, M., 441, 442
Miller, A., 214
Miller, F., 336
Miller, L. K., 306
Miller, M. D., 201
Miller, Terry, 332, 333
Milner, H. R., 465, 469

Miner, C. A., 255
Miranda, A., 228
Mirenda, P., 169, 275
Mirenda, P. A., 167
Missouri Head Injury Foundation, 367
Mitchell, A. A., 338
Mitchell, Jim, 98, 99, 100
Mitchell, R., 400
Mitchell, Rochella, 301, 313, 323
Mitchem, K. J., 194
Mithaug, D., 139
Mithaug, D. E., 244, 258
Mody, M., 127
Mogharreban, C. C., 48
Molenda, M., 55
Molina, B. S. G., 217
Monsen, J. J., 48
Montgomery, J. K., 7
Monzo, L. D., 115
Moon, S. M., 468
Moon, T. R., 483
Mooney, J. F., 203, 204
Mooney, P., 192
Moon-Ho, H., 103
Moore, Florence, 125, 126, 141
Moore, Jeff, 125
Moore-Brown, B. J., 7
Moores, D. F., 397, 420
Moran, S., 463
Moreno-Torres, I., 400
Morgan, M., 189
Morgante, J. D., 142
Morningstar, M. E., 252
Morris, A. S., 191
Morris, J. E., 480
Morrison, M., 127, 136
Morse, P., 306
Moser, H. W., 275
Moss, Jerry, 259
Mostert, M. P., 135
Mottron, L., 306
Mount, B., 279
Mouren, M. C., 214
Mrazek, S., 251
Mueller, P. H., 253
Muir, S. G., 415
Muller, Margaret, 246, 247
Mulye, T. P., 186
Mumford, Lewis, 454
Mumford, V., 70
Mundweiler, Chery, 51
Murphy, C. C., 246
Murphy, K. R., 217
Murray, C., 69
Murray, Deb, 51
Muscott, H., 200
Myers, S. S., 191
Myles, B., 170, 318, 319
Myles, B. S., 302, 317, 318, 319

Nagberg, B., 302
Naglieri, J. A., 135
Nakamura, J., 471
National Assessment of Educational Progress, 36, 38
National Association for Gifted Children, 6, 103, 462, 463, 465, 473
National Association of State Directors of Special Education (NASDSE), 58, 59
National Center for Educational Statistics, 85
National Center on Birth Defects and Developmental Disabilities, 402
National Council on Disability, 26
National Forum on Education Statistics, 120
National Heart, Lung, and Blood Institute, 341

National Institute on Deafness and Other Communication Disorders, 405
National Institutes of Health, 276, 308, 371
National Organization on Disability, 26
National Reading Panel, 127
National Research Center on the Gifted and Talented, 473
National Research Council, 70, 74, 82, 127, 247, 302, 303, 306, 465, 469
National Society for Autistic Children, 308
National Wraparound Initiative Advisory Group, 194
Neal, L. I., 69
Neale, M., 139
Neihart, M., 468
Neill, S., 189
Neil-Pirozzi, T. M., 374
Nelson, C., 274
Nelson, C. M., 197
Nelson, J. R., 188, 189, 191, 192, 201
Nelson, J. S., 109
Nelson, K. A., 431
Nelson, K. B., 336
Nelson, L. L., 114, 116
Nelson, M., 48, 291
Nelson, N., 170
Nelson-Gray, R. O., 187, 191
Nettelbeck, T., 306
Neu, T. W., 142
Neubert, D. A., 196–197
Nevin, A., 380
Nevin, A. I., 45, 48, 289
Nevo, B., 465, 469
Newman, L., 104, 108, 250
Nicholas, J., 398
Nihira, K., 248
Nikolaraizi, M., 397
Nolet, V., 35, 165, 176, 384, 385
Noonan, P. M., 252
Noone, S. J., 306
Nordness, P. D., 192
Northern, J. L., 396
Notari-Syverson, A., 165, 176
Nowacek, J., 384
Noy, L., 251
Nygard, J., 173

Oakes, J., 69
O'Brien, C. L., 279
O'Connor, C., 74, 82
Odom, S., 286
Ofiesh, N., 135
O'Halloran, Casey, 256
Okrand, M., 411
Olejniczak, P. W., 340
Olszewski-Kubilius, P., 465
O'Neill, P. T., 38
Orelove, F. P., 289
Orfield, G., 69
O'Riordan, M., 306
Orsmond, G. I., 109, 316
Ortega-Hurndon, F., 244
Ortiz, A. A., 79, 90
Ortiz, S. O., 135
Osborne, S. S., 188
O'Shanich, A. M., 370
O'Shanich, G. J., 370
Osher, D. M., 187
Oswald, D. P., 184, 308
Outlaw, Bob, 365
Outlaw, Dylan, 364–366, 368, 369–370, 373, 374–377, 380, 385, 387, 388
Outlaw, Renee, 364, 365, 368, 374, 375, 376, 380, 387
Owens, P. L., 226

Owens, R., 157, 158
Ozonoff, S., 315

Pace, G., 371
Padden, C., 394
Palace, L. M., 275
Palmer, D. S., 48, 291
Palmer, S., 139, 245, 285, 286
Palmer, S. B., 138, 258, 259
Pannbacker, M., 160
Parente, R., 377
Parette, H. P., 23
Parish, S. L., 247
Park, H. R., 304, 306
Park, J., 51
Park, M., 73, 80
Park, M. J., 186
Parker, H. C., 223
Parker, R. C., 49
Parker, S. K., 302
Parrish, T., 19
Parsons, Karen, 99
Passetti, F., 306
Patton, J. M., 77
Patton, J. R., 108, 205, 250
Payne, R. K., 83
Pearpoint, J., 106, 279
Pearson, N., 192
Peck, C. A., 48
Pelham, W., 217
Pellegrino, L., 335, 336, 343, 402
Percy, M., 246, 275, 276
Pérez, M., 19
Perner, D. E., 21
Persky, V. W., 342
Peters, J. K., 305
Peterson, J. S., 468
Petrill, S. A., 131
Peyton, J. A., 253
Pfeiffer, S. I., 478
Pfiffner, L. J., 214
Pickering, L. K., 302
Pickering, S. J., 128
Pickles, A., 308
Piirto, J., 267
Pinheiro, S. B., 161
Plucker, J., 267
Poduska, J., 198
Pogrund, R. L., 432, 433
Poirier, J. M., 187
Pol, H. H., 189
Polloway, E. A., 108, 242, 306
Poloni-Staudinger, L., 73, 74
Porterfield, S. L., 82
Poston, D., 83, 100, 105, 113
Poston, D. J., 104, 279
Potts-Datema, W., 341, 342
Poulakis, Z., 401
Powell-Smith, K. A., 319
Power, D., 400
Powers, L., 350
Praisner, C. L., 48
Prater, M. A., 229
Presentacion, M. J., 228
Pressgrove, C. L., 245
Pretti-Frontczak, K. L., 142
Priest, Lauren, 32, 33, 44, 51, 60
Prifitera, A., 133
Prigge, D. J., 228, 229
Prizant, B. M., 303
Proctor, R., 202
Provasnik, S., 76
Puccia, K. B., 226
Pugach, M. C., 35, 45
Pugh, G. S., 439, 449
Pugh, K. R., 130
Pullen, P. C., 134
Punch, R., 416

Biomedical factors. *See also* Genetic factors
  autism, 308
  emotional or behavioral disorders, 189–190
  intellectual disability, 246, 247
Bipolar disorder, 186
Blacks. *See* African Americans
Blindness, 430. *See also* Visual impairments
Bloom's taxonomy, 57, 473
Bodily-kinesthetic intelligence, 464
Bookshare.org, 351
Boys. *See* Gender
Braille, 440–442
Braille contractions, 440–441
Braille embossers, 445
Brain-based learning, 228, 229
Brain differences, 217
Brain injury. *See* Traumatic brain injury
Brothers, 109–110. *See also* Families
Brown v. Board of Education (1954), 8, 70, 71

California
  nondiscriminatory evaluation, 71
  students learning English, 79–80
CALP (cognitive academic linguistic proficiency), 416
Captioning, 411
Car accidents, 370
CART (Communication Access Realtime Translation), 411
CAS (Childhood Apraxia of Speech), 160
CASE (Conceptually Accurate Signed English), 399
Case studies
  attention-deficit/hyperactivity disorder, 210–212, 216, 233
  autism, 300–301, 307, 314, 326–327
  cerebral palsy, 2–4, 25, 27–28, 332–333
  communication disorders, 152–154, 177–178
  emotional or behavioral disorders, 182–184, 205–206
  family-professional partnerships, 98–100
  gifted and talented students, 460–462, 466, 482, 483
  hearing loss, 392–394, 418, 422
  intellectual disability, 238–240, 247, 266
  learning disabilities, 54, 124–126, 147–148
  multicultural considerations, 64–66, 92–94
  multiple disabilities, 270–272, 295
  physical disabilities and other health impairments, 332–334, 348, 358
  speech impairment, 32–34
  traumatic brain injury, 364–366, 378–379, 387–388
  visual impairments, 428–430, 450, 455–456
Catatonic behavior, 188
Catheterization, clean intermittent, 338
CBM. *See* Curriculum-based measurement
CCTVs (closed circuit televisions), 445
CEC Knowledge and Skill Standards
  attention-deficit/hyperactivity disorder, 233–235
  autism, 327–329
  communication disorders, 178–180
  emotional or behavioral disorders, 206–208

family-professional partnerships, 121–122
general education curriculum, 60–62
gifted and talented students, 484–485
hearing loss, 422–425
intellectual disability, 266–268
learning disabilities, 148–150
multicultural considerations, 94–96
multiple disabilities, 295–298
physical disabilities and other health impairments, 358–361
special education overview, 28–29
traumatic brain injury, 388–390
visual impairments, 456–458
Cerebral palsy, 2–4, 25, 27–28, 332–333, 335–336
Certification, 7, 8
Charter schools, 479
"Check and connect" strategy, 198
Checklists, 232
Child abuse, 371
Childhood Apraxia of Speech (CAS), 160
Children's School Success (CSS) model, 285–286
Child study teams, 90, 92
Chromosomes, 246
Chronic conditions, 339
Circle of friends, 106, 107
Classroom-centered intervention, 198–199
Classwide, peer-assisted self-management, 194, 196
Clean intermittent catheterization, 338
Cleft palate/lip, 155, 160
Closed-captioned technology, 411
Closed circuit televisions (CCTVs), 445
Closed head injury, 367
Cloze procedure, 421
Cluster grouping, 478
CMV (cytomegalovirus), 402
Cochlea, 396, 397
Cochlear implants, 393, 404–405, 408
Cognitive/academic characteristics
  attention-deficit/hyperactivity disorder, 215, 223
  autism, 306
  emotional or behavioral disorders, 189
  gifted and talented students, 465–466
  hearing loss, 400–401
  intellectual disability, 243–245, 248
  learning disabilities, 127–128
  multiple disabilities, 273
  traumatic brain injury, 369–370
Cognitive academic linguistic proficiency (CALP), 416
Cognitive behavioral therapies, 185–186, 187, 227–229
Cognitive distortions, 228
Cognitive retrainers, 375
Cognitive taxonomies, 57, 473
Collaborative teaming, 380–381
Coma, 368
Combined type of AD/HD, 214
Commitment, 117–118
Communication
  augmentative and alternative, 166–167, 172–174, 275, 282, 284–285
  autism and, 303, 306
  bilingual/bicultural communication model, 413
  development of, 156–158
  in family-professional partnerships, 114–116

hearing loss and, 398–400, 412–413
importance of, 154
manual, 398–400, 412
multicultural considerations, 155
multiple disabilities and, 275
oral/aural, 398, 412
total (simultaneous), 173, 400, 412
visual impairments and, 443
Communication Access Realtime Translation (CART), 411
Communication boards, 284, 285
Communication disorders, 152–181. *See also specific disorders*
  assessing student progress, 175–177
  case study, 152–154, 177–178
  causes, 162
  CEC Knowledge and Skill Standards, 178–180
  characteristics, 156–162
  defined, 154–155
  evaluating students with, 162–165
  identifying students with, 154–162
  IEP design, 165–169
  including students with, 174–175
  instructional strategies, 169–174
  language impairments, 161–162
  multicultural considerations, 155, 164–165
  prevalence, 156
  speech disorders, 159–161
Community-based instruction, 255, 256, 259–260, 261–262
Compacted curriculum, 472
Complementary teaching, 168
Complex partial seizures, 339–340
Comprehensive Test of Phonological Processing, 136, 138
Computers, handheld, 282
Concept diagrams, 145, 169–172, 414–415
Conceptually Accurate Signed English (CASE), 399
Conduct disorders, 187–188, 198–199, 215
Conferences, 17
Confidentiality, 120
Conflict resolution, 201, 202
Congenital brain injury, 366
Congenital communication disorders, 162
Congenital deafness, 394
Congenital hearing loss, 402
Congenital visual impairments, 435
Conners' Rating Scales–Revised, 218
Constant time delay, 142
Consultation, 168
Content integration, 90
Continuum of services, 18, 46–47
Contractions, braille, 440–441
Contracts, learning, 481
Contrast, focused, 170
Cooperative Controversy strategy, 202
Cooperative learning, 202, 204, 381–382
Correction programs, juvenile, 187–188, 203
Council for Exceptional Children. *See* CEC Knowledge and Skill Standards
Counseling services, 11
Creativity, 467–468, 478
Critical-thinking skills, 478
CSS (Children's School Success) model, 285–286
Cued speech, 399–400
Cues, social, 401
Cultural deficit theory, 69
Cultural difference theory, 69
Cultural reciprocity, 88–89
Cultural reproduction theory, 69

Cultural responsiveness, 68, 87–92, 93
Culture, 66–68. *See also* Multicultural considerations
Cummins model of language proficiency, 415, 416
Curriculum
  compacted, 472
  expanded core, 438, 443
  general education, 34–36, 38, 60–62
Curriculum augmentation. *See* Supplementary aids and services; Universal design for learning
Curriculum-based measurement (CBM)
  attention-deficit/hyperactivity disorder, 231
  communication disorders, 165
  learning disabilities, 145, 147
  physical disabilities and other health impairments, 357
Curriculum extension, 473
Curriculum mapping, 139–140
Cytomegalovirus (CMV), 402

DABS (Diagnostic Adaptive Behavior Scale), 248
Daily living skills. *See* Adaptive skills
Dandy Walker syndrome, 152, 162
Data-based assessment, 294
Data-based instructional decisions, 264
Deaf, 394. *See also* Hearing loss
Deaf-blindness, 274–275. *See also* Multiple disabilities
Deaf children, as term, 394. *See also* Hearing loss
Deaf community/culture, 394, 412, 414, 415, 420
Deaf studies, 414, 415
Decibels (dB), 395
DECIDE mnemonic strategy, 377
Decision-making instruction, 383–384
Demographics, family, 101–102
Depression, 186–187
Diabetes, 348
Diagnosis. *See* Evaluation
Diagnostic Adaptive Behavior Scale (DABS), 248
Diagnostic and Statistical Manual of Mental Disorders (DSM-IV-TR)
  attention-deficit/hyperactivity disorder, 212–213
  conduct disorders, 187
  emotional or behavioral disorders, 185, 187, 188
  intellectual disability, 243
  oppositional defiant disorder, 187
  pervasive developmental disorders, 302
  schizophrenia, 188
Diagnostic auditory brainstem response, 405
Dialects, 155
Diana v. State Board of Education (1970), 71
"Did-next-ask" strategy, 289
"Did-next-now" strategy, 289
Differentiated instruction, 124–125, 143, 471–472
Digital mobile phones, 376
Digital Talking Books, 350, 351
Digital watches, 376
Diplegia, 336
Disability
  prevalence, 4
  as term, 7
Disability awareness, 353
Discipline, 12–13
DISCOVER assessment, 469, 471, 478
Discrepancy analysis, 265

Generalization, 244
Generalized anxiety disorder, 185
General seizures, 340–341
Genetic deficit theories, 68–69
Genetic factors
    attention-deficit/hyperactivity
        disorder, 217
    autism, 308
    epilepsy, 341
    hearing loss, 402
    learning disabilities, 130
    multiple disabilities, 275–276
Genomes, 276
Gifted and Talented Children's
    Education Act (1978), 462
Gifted and talented students, 460–487
    assessing student progress, 480–483
    case studies, 460–462, 466, 482, 483
    causes, 469
    CEC Knowledge and Skill
        Standards, 484–485
    characteristics, 465–469
    defined, 462–463
    disproportionate representation,
        73–74
    evaluating, 469–471
    identifying, 462–469
    IEP design, 471–474
    including, 478–480
    instructional strategies, 474–478
    prevalence, 5–6, 463, 465
Girls. See Gender
Girls' Guide to AD/HD, The (Walker),
    229, 231
Glasgow Outcomes Scale, 371
Goal attainment scaling, 232
Goals, annual, 54–56
Goal-setting, 224–225
Good-behavior game, 198–199
Grade-appropriate placements, 46
Graduation rates, 26
Grammar correction, 421
Graphic organizers, 145, 169–172,
    414–415
Group behavior support, 320
Group problem solving, 202
Guide dogs, 448–449

Haitian American family relationships,
    101
Handheld computers, 282
Handicap, as term, 7
Handwriting, 128
HapMap, 276
Hard of hearing, 394. See also Hearing
    loss
Headaches, 369
Health care plans, 346
Health services, 11
Hearing aids, 403–404, 410–411
Hearing impaired, as term, 394. See
    also Hearing loss
Hearing loss, 392–427
    acquired, 402
    assessing student progress, 421–422
    bilateral, 394
    case studies, 392–394, 418, 422
    causes, 402–403
    CEC Knowledge and Skill
        Standards, 422–425
    characteristics, 397–402
    congenital, 402
    defined, 394
    evaluating students with, 403–408
    identifying students with, 394–403
    IEP design, 401, 408–414
    including students with, 400–401,
        417–421
    instructional strategies, 414–417

postlingual, 403
prevalence, 395
unilateral, 394
Hearing mechanism, 396–397
Hearing process, 395–396
Hemiplegia, 336
Heredity. See Genetic factors
Herpes virus, 402
Hertz (Hz), 395
HGP (Human Genome Project), 276
High school instructional strategies. See
    Secondary/transition instructional
    strategies
Hispanic Americans
    attention-deficit/hyperactivity
        disorder, 213
    discrimination against, 70–71
    disproportionate representation, 72,
        73–74, 79–80
    emotional or behavioral disorders,
        191
    family-professional partnerships,
        111–112
    gifted and talented students, 73–74,
        465
    risk ratios, 72
    students learning English, 79–80
HIV, 23
Holistic scoring, 421
Homeless students, 82
Home-school placement, 45–46
Homework assistance, 108, 109
Hospital placements, 43–44
Human Genome Project (HGP), 276
Hyperactivity. See Attention-
    deficit/hyperactivity disorder
Hyperbilirubinemia, 402
Hypermedia, 140
Hypernasality, 160
Hyponasality, 160
Hypoxia, 402

IDEA. See Individuals with Disabilities
    Education Act
IEP. See Individualized Education
    Program; Individualized Education
    Program design
IFSP (Individualized Family Services
    Plan), 16, 17, 51, 120
Impressionistic scoring, 421
Impulsivity, 214, 223
Inattention, 223
Incidental learning, 432
Inclusion
    attention-deficit/hyperactivity
        disorder, 229–231
    autism, 322–324
    characteristics, 45–46
    communication disorders, 174–175
    controversies regarding, 46–47
    defined, 44–45
    emotional or behavioral disorders,
        201, 203, 204
    gifted and talented students,
        478–480
    hearing loss, 400–401, 417–421
    intellectual disability, 260, 263
    learning disabilities, 145, 146
    least restrictive environment and,
        17–18
    multiple disabilities, 289–292
    outcomes associated with, 47, 49
    perspectives on, 47, 48–49
    phases, 45
    physical disabilities and other
        health impairments, 355–356
    progress, facilitation of, 49–51
    through accommodations, 45
    through restructuring, 45

traumatic brain injury, 384, 385, 386
visual impairments, 447, 452–453,
    454
Inclusionary standard, for specific
    learning disability, 126
Inclusion Tips
    attention-deficit/hyperactivity
        disorder, 230
    autism, 324
    communication disorders, 175
    emotional or behavioral disorders,
        204
    general, 50
    gifted and talented students, 479
    hearing loss, 419
    intellectual disability, 263
    learning disabilities, 146
    multicultural considerations, 81
    multiple disabilities, 290
    physical disabilities and other
        health impairments, 356
    traumatic brain injury, 386
    visual impairments, 447
Incus, 396
Independent living, 26
Indicators, 36
Individual behavior support, 320
Individualized Education Program
    (IEP), 51–56
    assessment accommodations, 56
    components, 52–55
    conferences, 17
    confidentiality and, 120
    content, 16
    goals, annual, 54–56
    IDEA and, 51–52, 54
    participants, 15, 16, 51–52
    related services, 56
    self-directed, 139
    special factors, 52
    specially designed instruction, 56
    student involvement in planning,
        138–139
    supplementary aids and services, 55
    timelines, 16
Individualized Education Program (IEP)
    design
    attention-deficit/hyperactivity
        disorder, 220–226
    autism, 313–318
    communication disorders, 165–169
    emotional or behavioral disorders,
        194–198
    gifted and talented students,
        471–474
    hearing loss, 401, 408–414
    intellectual disability, 250–255
    learning disabilities, 138–142
    multiple disabilities, 279–285
    physical disabilities and other
        health impairments, 346–352
    traumatic brain injury, 374–380
    visual impairments, 439–449
Individualized Family Services Plan
    (IFSP), 16, 17, 51, 120
Individuals with Disabilities Education
    Act (IDEA), 9–21
    age groups covered by, 9–10
    alternate assessment, 36
    appropriate education, 12, 15–17
    attention-deficit/hyperactivity
        disorder, 212, 213, 220–221
    authorizations, 24
    communication disorders, 155, 162
    confidentiality, 120
    connecting curriculum to standards,
        35–36
    deaf-blindness, 274
    discipline, 12–13

educational placement, 10
eligibility based on need, 10
emotional disturbance, 184, 192
entitlements, 23
federal funding, 19–21
gifted and talented students, 478
hearing loss, 394, 398, 400, 408,
    418, 420
homeless students, 82
inclusion, 44–45
Individualized Education Program,
    51–52, 54
intellectual disability, 240
learning disabilities, 126, 131,
    134–135
least restrictive environment, 12,
    17–18
multicultural considerations, 67,
    68–71
multiple disabilities, 272–273
nondiscriminatory evaluation, 12,
    13–15
orthopedic impairments, 335
other health impairments, 338–339
outcomes, 24, 26–27
parent-student participation
    principle, 12, 19
Part B, 9–10
Part C, 10
positive behavior support, 305, 320
principles, 11–19, 20
procedural due process, 12, 18–19
related services, 10–11
special education components,
    10–11
supplementary aids and services, 39
transition planning, 138
traumatic brain injury, 366
visual impairments, 430
zero-reject principle, 12–13
Injury, 13
Instructional consultation teams, 90, 92
Instructional strategies
    attention-deficit/hyperactivity
        disorder, 226–229
    autism, 318–322
    communication disorders, 169–174
    emotional or behavioral disorders,
        198–201
    gifted and talented students,
        474–478
    hearing loss, 414–417
    intellectual disability, 255–260,
        261–262
    learning disabilities, 142–145
    multiple disabilities, 285–289
    physical disabilities and other
        health impairments, 352–354
    schoolwide, 58
    traumatic brain injury, 380–384
    visual impairments, 449–452
Integration rule. See Inclusion
Intellectual characteristics. See
    Cognitive/academic characteristics
Intellectual disability, 238–269
    assessing student progress, 264–266
    attention-deficit/hyperactivity
        disorder and, 215
    case studies, 238–240, 247, 266
    causes, 245–248
    CEC Knowledge and Skill
        Standards, 266–268
    cerebral palsy and, 336
    characteristics, 243–245
    defined, 240–242
    evaluating students with, 248–250
    identifying students with, 240–248
    IEP design, 250–255
    including students with, 260, 263

UDL. *See* Universal design for learning
Understanding, anchored, 119
Unilateral hearing loss, 394
Units of study, designing, 57
Universal behavior support, 320
Universal design for learning (UDL)
    attention-deficit/hyperactivity
      disorder, 224–225
    autism, 315–316, 317–318
    communication disorders, 167–168
    emotional or behavioral disorders,
      196, 197
    gifted and talented students, 473
    hearing loss, 412–413
    intellectual disability, 253, 254
    learning disabilities, 141
    multiple disabilities, 282, 283
    physical disabilities and other
      health impairments, 348, 350
    progress, facilitation of, 41–42
    supplementary aids and services, 39
    training on, 57

    traumatic brain injury, 376–378
    visual impairments, 446
Universally Designed Picture Book, 254

Vaccines, 302, 308
Values, 5, 84–85, 93
Velcroed effect, 253
Venn diagrams, 410
Verbal prompts, 226–227, 244
Vestibular mechanism, 397
Video self-modeling (VSM), 229
Vignettes. *See* Case studies
Vision services, 11
Visual Assistant, 282, 283, 288, 376
Visual impairments, 428–459
    assessing student progress, 453–455
    case studies, 428–430, 450, 455–456
    causes, 434–435
    CEC Knowledge and Skill
      Standards, 456–458
    cerebral palsy and, 336
    characteristics, 432–434

    defined, 430–431
    evaluating students with, 435–439
    identifying students with, 430–435
    IEP design, 439–449
    including students with, 447,
      452–453, 454
    instructional strategies, 449–452
    prevalence, 430–431
Visual/performing arts, 468
Visual prompts, 227, 288
Visual-spatial math problems, 128
Vocabulary development, 409–410,
    415, 416
Voice disorders, 160, 164
VSM (video self-modeling), 229

Watches, digital, 376
Weapons, 13
WebQuests, 351, 477
Webs, 145, 169–172, 414–415
Wechsler Individualized Achievement
    Test–Second Edition (WIAT-II), 133

Wechsler Intelligence Scale for
    Children–IV Integrated (WISC-IV),
    131–133, 243, 248
"What-where" strategy, 289
Wheelchairs, 349
Whites. *See* European Americans
WIAT-II (Wechsler Individualized
    Achievement Test–Second Edition),
    133
WISC-IV (Wechsler Intelligence Scale
    for Children–IV Integrated),
    131–133, 243, 248
Word processing, 196, 197, 350, 351
Working memory, 128
Wraparound process, 194, 195
Writing, 421
Written language, 127–128

Zero-reject principle, 12–13